Curve

THE BEST-SELLING LESBIAN MAGAZINE

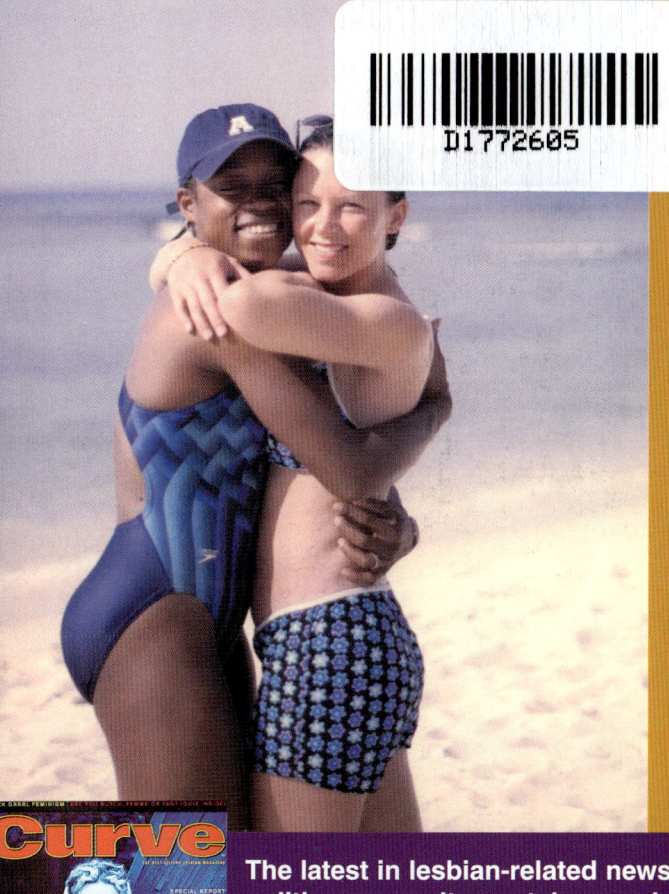

The latest in lesbian-related news, politics, pop culture, style, people, social issues, and entertainment. On the web at www.curvemag.com

FOR YOUR FREE TRIAL ISSUE CALL (800) 705-0070
www.curvemag.com

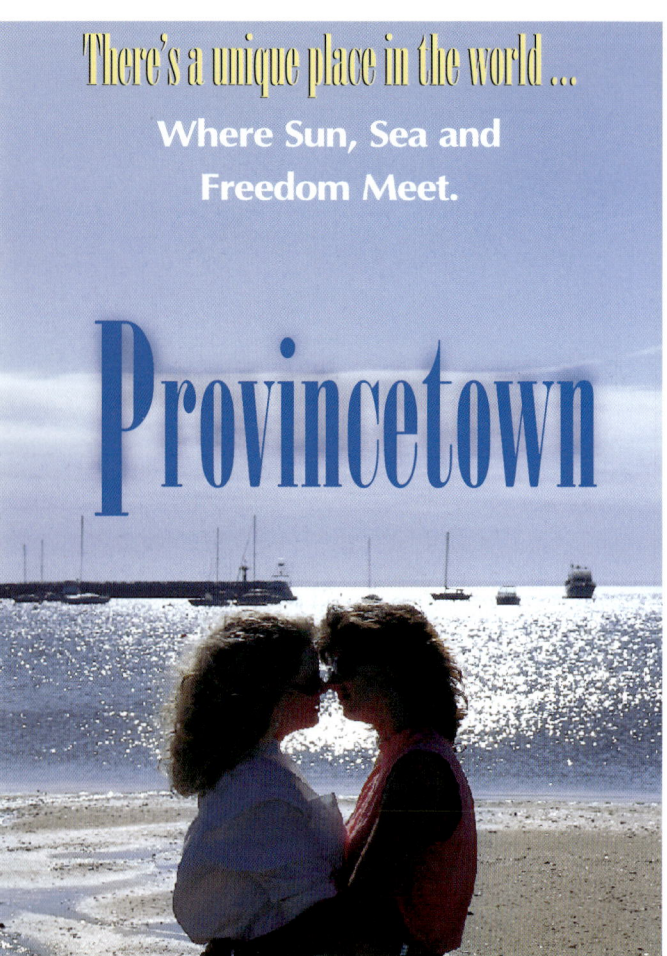

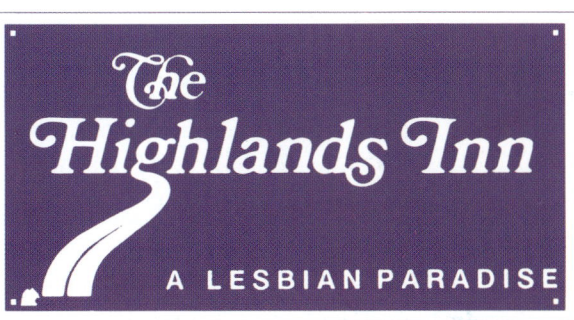

The Highlands Inn
A LESBIAN PARADISE

Secluded, romantic mountain hideaway on 100 scenic acres, centrally located between Boston, Montreal & the Maine coast. Close to Provincetown.

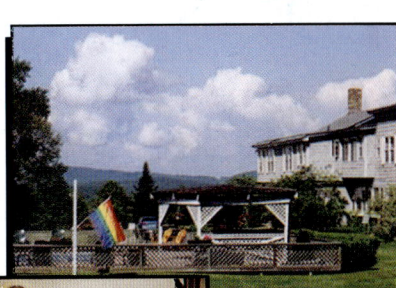

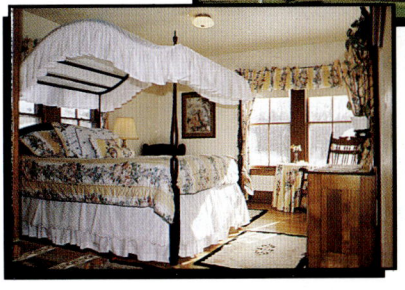

Experience the warm hospitality of a New England country inn YOUR way... a lesbian paradise!

PO BOX 118WT
VALLEY VIEW LANE
BETHLEHEM, NEW HAMPSHIRE 03574
603 • 869 • 3978
1-877-LES-B-INN (537-2466)
vacation@highlandsinn-nh.com
www.highlandsinn-nh.com

See Our Listing Under New Hampshire

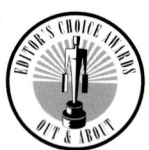

RSVP

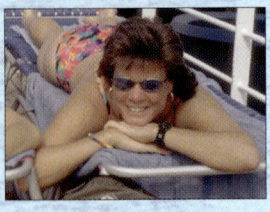

The first and the leading lesbian & gay vacation events. RSVP charters the whole ship and resort to create a lesbian & gay paradise. And at a better value than other vacations.

2002 RSVP Cruises

LA - Mexico Cruise

Carnival Ecstasy®
10-day cruise
Feb. 15-25, 2002

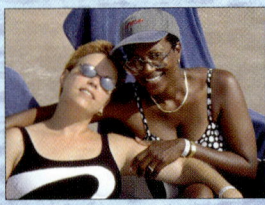

Barbados - Aruba

Renaissance R-6®
7-day cruise
March 1-8, 2002

Mediterranean

Royal Clipper®
7 & 14 day cruises
France, Italy, Greece & Turkey
July & August, 2002

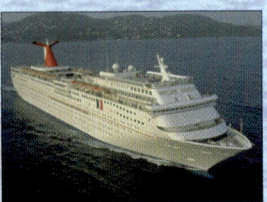

© Carnival Cruises 2001

2002 Club RSVP

See our web site or your travel agent

800-328-RSVP (7787)

Ship registry: Ecstasy, Panama; R-6, Liberia; Royal Clipper, Luxemburg.
CST #2020963-50
Information subject to change.

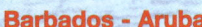

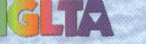

American Airlines®

RSVPVACATIONS.COM

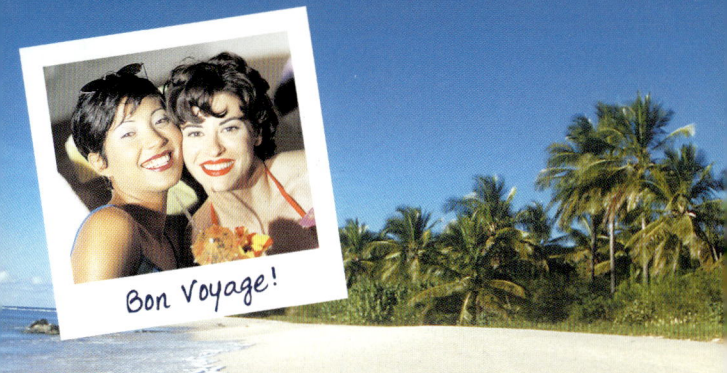

Bon Voyage!

2002
VACATIONS

- Australia/New Zealand Land Tours...*February*
- Tahiti South Pacific Cruise...*March*
- Bahamas Club Med Resort...*April*
- Greece/Turkey Cruise...*June*
- Scandinavia/Northern Europe Cruise...*August*
- Mexican Club Med Resort...*November*

2003
VACATIONS

- Friends and Family Resort...*July*
  Ixtapa Club Med
  Children of all ages welcome!

Olivia
CRUISES & RESORTS
Vacations for Lesbians

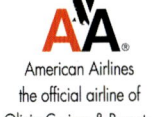
American Airlines
the official airline of
Olivia Cruises & Resorts.

4400 Market Street, Oakland, CA 94608
Phone: 510.655.0364   Fax: 510.655.4334
Email: info@olivia.com

CST#1009281-40   **Visit our web site at www.olivia.com**   DAM2002

Call for our FREE catalog
800-631-6277

SAN FRANCISCO INTERNATIONAL

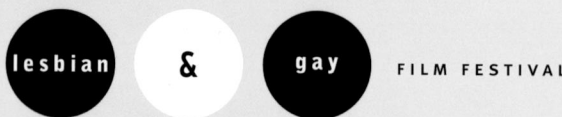 FILM FESTIVAL

26TH

ANNIVERSARY

JUNE 20-30, 2002

FRAMELINE

Get out of the city. Get into the country.
Wine Country, that is.

Sonoma County Itinerary: 2 nights, 3 days

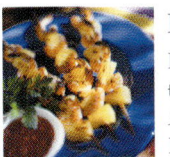

Day 1
Drive over the Golden Gate Bridge. Explore the vineyards by back roads or bicycle. Antiques and lunch on the Plaza in Healdsburg. More wine tasting in quaint Geyserville and Cloverdale. Try a bistro meal before retiring to a hidden B&B.

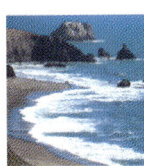

Day 2
Gather a picnic from area farms and shops. Hike around Lake Sonoma, then to the coast at spectacular Sea Ranch. Afternoon golf! Watch sea otters play during a fresh-catch seafood dinner. Fall asleep in your vacation rental to the sounds of the ocean.

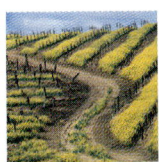

Day 3
Russian River resort area. Wonderful food, wineries, shopping, and art to explore in Duncans Mills, Cazadero and Guerneville. Kayak the river or hike through the redwoods at Armstrong Grove. Al fresco dinner, then slumber in your serene, woodsy cottage.

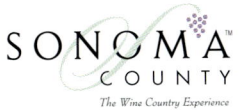

Stay in Sonoma County and experience more
of what the Wine Country can offer.

For more itineraries visit **www.sonomacounty.com**.
Call 1-800-576-6662 to request a free Visitor's Guide.

Club Skirts and Girlbar

Join thousands of women from all over the world for the nation's largest weekend event for women!

4 colossal dance parties
2 mega-pool parties with live bands
Comedy with the nation's top comics

Stay at our host hotels and be in the heart of the action!

The Riviera Resort
1600 Indian Canyon way
800-444-8311

The Foral Resort
67-967 Vista Chino
888-386-4677

When booking your room, you must mention the Dinah Shore Weekend

Three night VIP packages available. Call the hotline for information.

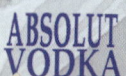 **Miller Light**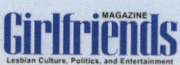

Dinah Shore Weekend 2002

March 28-31

For more information and to view photos from last year's event, visit:
www.clubskirts.com or www.girlbar.com

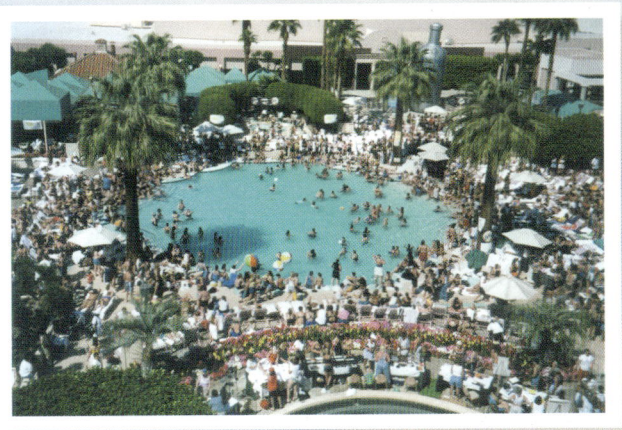

For a brochure, call:
Brochures available after 12/1/02

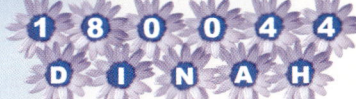

1 800 44 DINAH

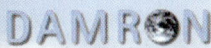

DAMRON

Lesbian Nation

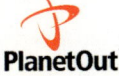

PlanetOut

American Airlines
American Eagle

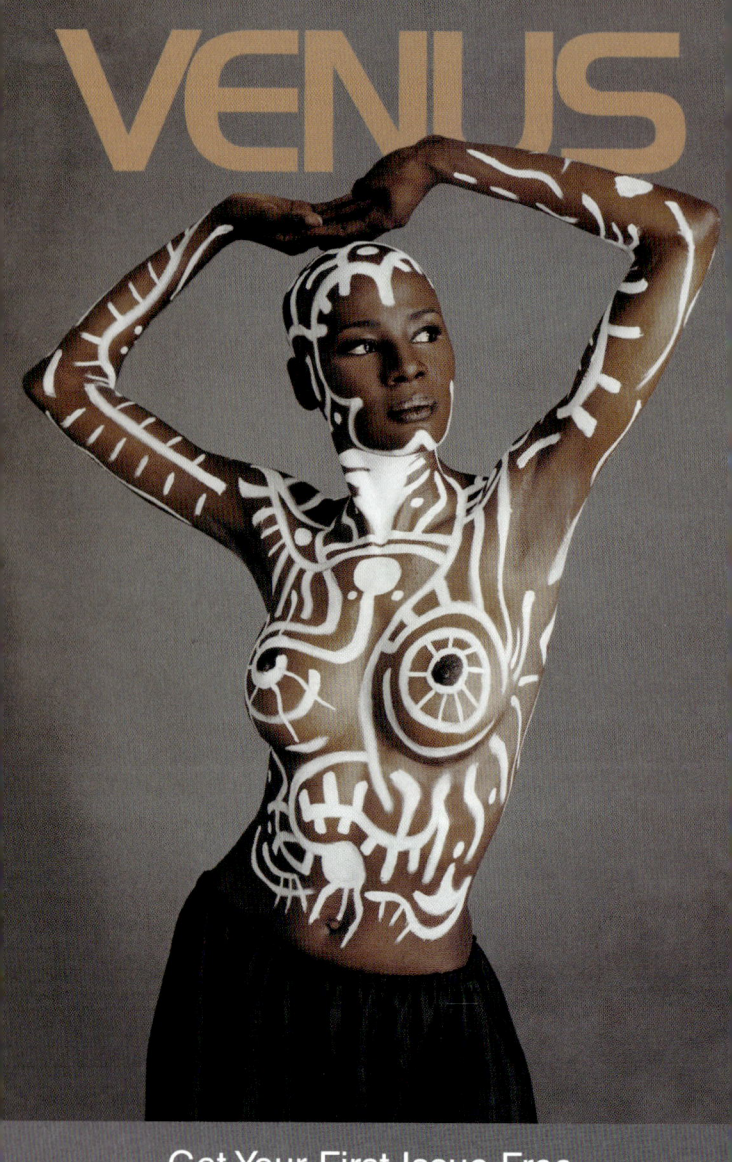

Subscribe Today!

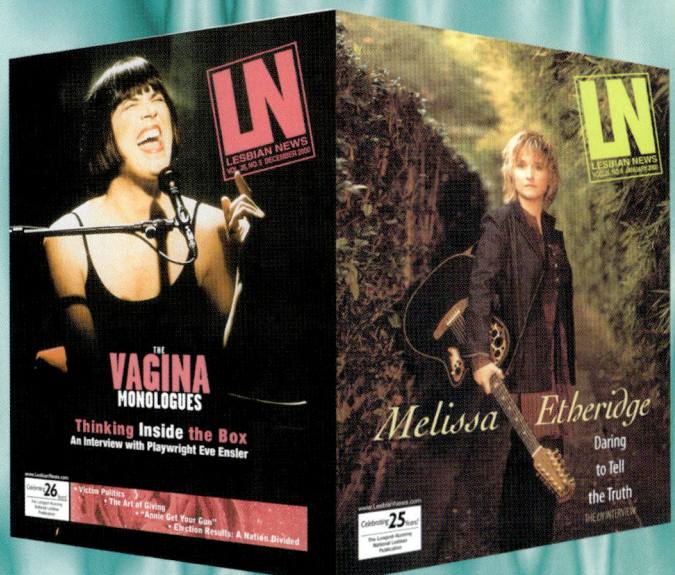

The Lesbian News
The Longest-Running National Lesbian Publication

Subscriptions or Advertising **800. 458. 9888**

E-mail: The LN@earthlink.net • P.O. Box 55 Torrance, CA 90507
Visit us at: www.LesbianNews.com

pjur

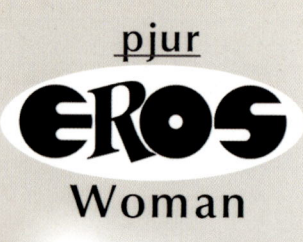

Woman

MOISTURIZING LUBRICANT

Travel with the best.

www.erosusa.com

For more information contact: A.S.I. • 65 Bank Street • Suite #9
New York, NY 10014
Tel. (212) 337-3767   Fax (212) 367-9389
e-mail: eroslube@aol.com

Made in Germany

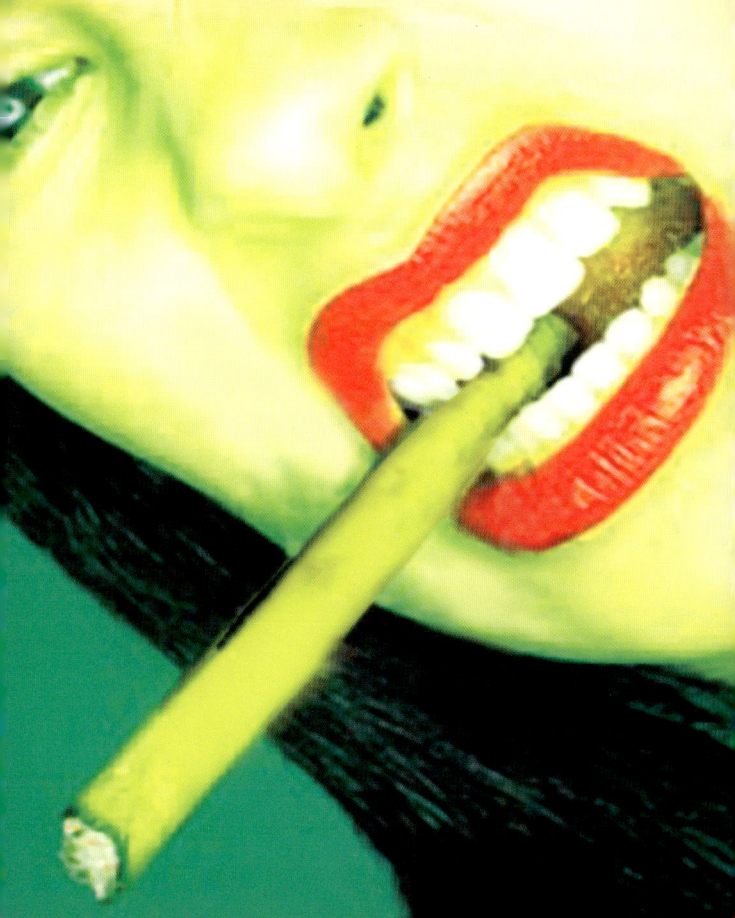

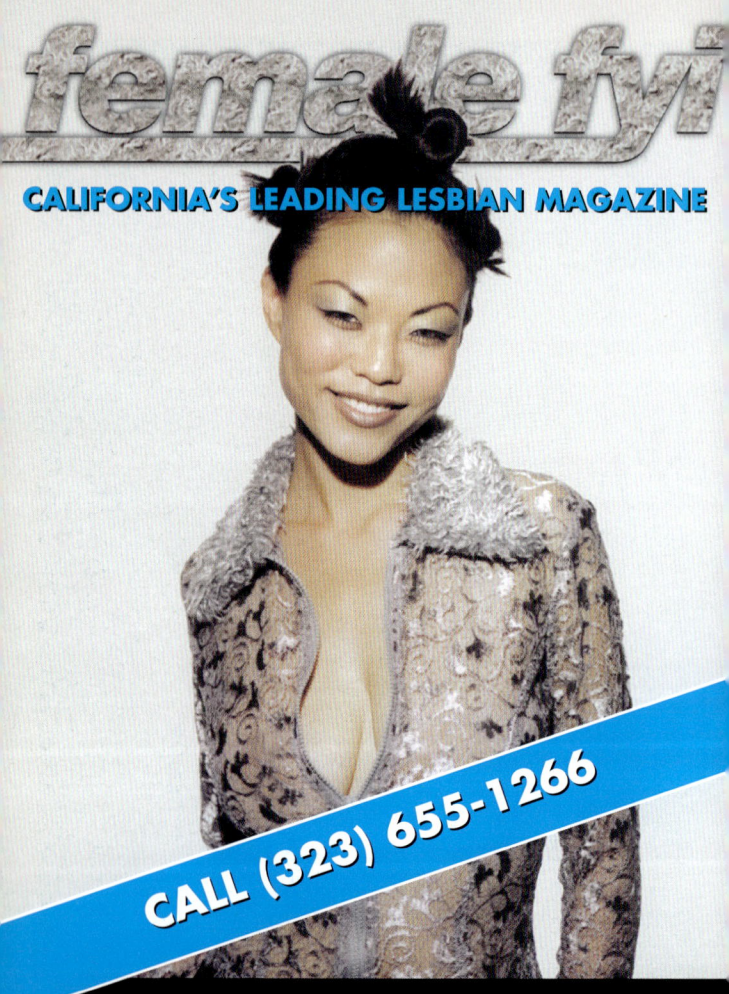

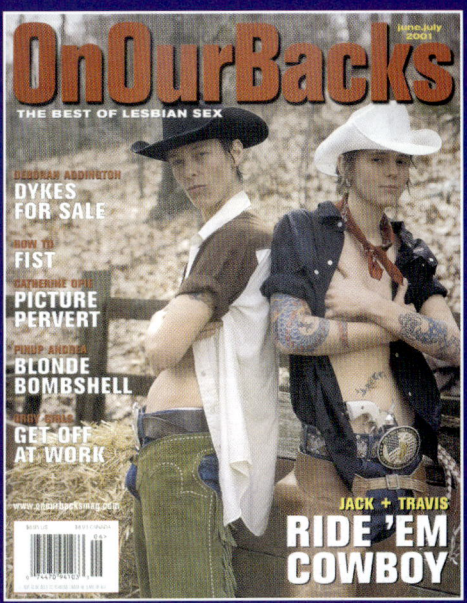

subscribe online.
www.onourbacksmag.com

OnOurBacks
THE BEST OF LESBIAN SEX

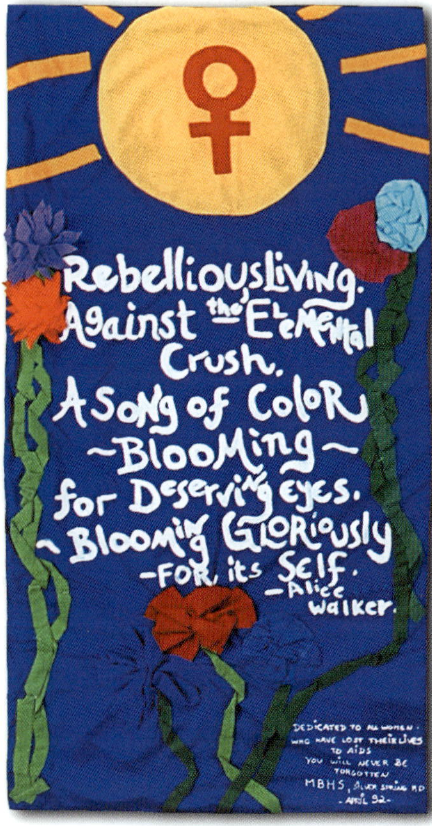

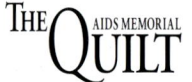

THE AIDS MEMORIAL QUILT

the Damron Women's Traveller®

Publisher	Damron Company
President & Editor-in-Chief	Gina M. Gatta
Managing Editor	Ian Philips
Deputy Editor	Erika O'Connor
Design & Layout	Rebecca Davenport
Assistant Editors	Chane Binderup
	Christina Woolner
Art Director	Kathleen Pratt
Asst Production Mgr	Jim Buchanan
Cover Photo	Erica Mainshine
Cover Design	Rick Avila

Board of Directors
Mikal Shively, Gina M. Gatta, Edward Gatta, Jr., Louise Mock

How to Contact Us

Mail:	PO Box 422458, San Francisco, CA 94142-2458
Email:	damron@damron.com
Web:	www.damron.com
Fax:	(415) 703-9049
Phone:	(415) 255-0404

Damron Company reserves the right to make its own independent judgment as to the acceptability of advertising copy and illustrations in advertisements. Advertiser and advertising agency assume liability for all content (including text, representation, photographs, and illustrations) of advertisements printed and also assume responsibility for any claims arising therefrom against the publisher. Offers to sell products that appear in the *Damron Women's Traveller* are subject to all laws and regulations and are void where so prohibited.

Copyright ©2001 Damron Company Inc. • Printed in Hong Kong

All rights reserved. Reproduction of the *Damron Women's Traveller* in whole or in part without written permission from the Damron Company is prohibited.

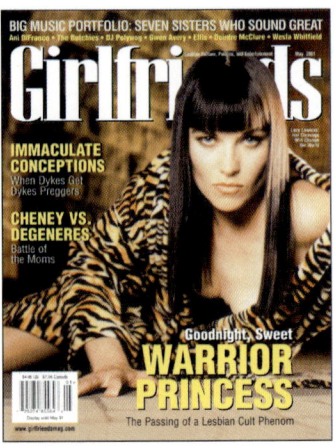

Girlfriends

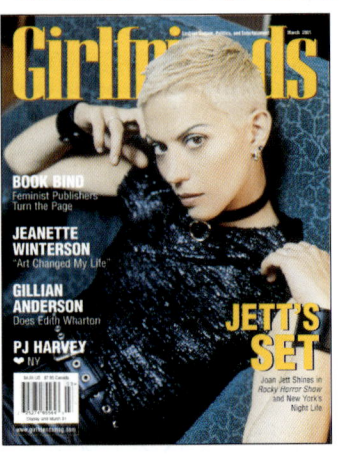

CULTURE, POLITICS, & ENTERTAINMENT
FROM A LESBIAN PERSPECTIVE

Subscribe online **www.girlfriendsmag.com**
or call **800.GRL.FRND (800.475.3763)**

Damron Road Atlas

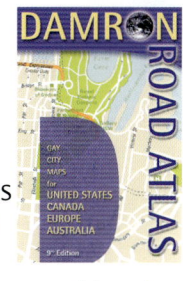

The perfect travelling companion to the **Women's Traveller**! Features **more than** 135 maps (fully revised yearly) with color-coded dots that pinpoint LGBT bars, accommodations, and bookstores in over 70 cities and resorts worldwide (including Sydney!) — tons more maps and listings than any other gay map guide! Full-color pages. 9th Edition: only **$21.95.**

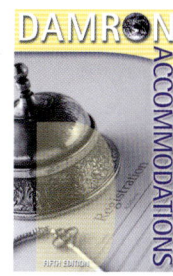

Damron Accommodations

Now you'll always have a home away from home! It's the only full-color guide to gay-friendly B&Bs, inns, hotels, and other accommodations around the world — with **hundreds of color photographs** and in-depth descriptions. 5th Edition: only **$22.95.**

To order, call (800) 462-6654

Ask for your **FREE** Damron Book List of international LGBT travel guides!

Traveller Codes

Most of the codes used in this book are self-explanatory. Here are the few, however, which aren't.

▲—This symbol marks an advertiser. Please look for their display ad near this listing, and be sure to tell them you saw their ad in the *Damron Women's Traveller*.

Popular—So we've heard from the business and/or a reader.

Mostly Women—80-90% lesbian crowd.

Mostly Gay Men—Women welcome.

Lesbians/Gay Men—60%(L)/40%(G) to a 40%(L)/60%(G) mix.

LGBT—Lesbian, Gay, Bisexual, and Transgendered.

Gay/Straight—A little bit of everything.

Gay-Friendly—LGBT folk are definitely welcome but are rarely the ones hosting the party.

Neighborhood Bar—Regulars and a local flavor, often has a pool table.

Dancing/DJ—Usually has a DJ at least Fri and Sat nights.

Transgender-Friendly—Transsexuals, cross-dressers, and other transgendered people welcome.

Live Shows—From a piano bar to drag queens and dancers.

MultiRacial—A good mix of women of color and their friends.

Beer/Wine—Beer and/or wine. No hard liquor.

Smokefree—No smoking anywhere inside premises.

Private Club—Found mainly in the US South where it's the only way to keep a liquor license. Call the bar before you go out and tell them you're visiting. They will advise you of their policy regarding membership. Usually have set-ups so you can BYOB.

Wheelchair Access—Includes restrooms.

National Resources

LGBT INFOLINES
Gay/Lesbian National Hotline — [888] 843-4564

AIDS/HIV
National AIDS/HIV Hotlines — [800] 342-2437
TTY: [800] 243-7889
en español: [800] 344-7432

Sexual Health Information Line (Canada) — [613] 563-2437

HATE CRIMES
Lambda Gay/Lesbian Hate Crimes Hotline — [800] 616-4283

LEGAL RIGHTS
Lambda Legal Defense Fund (New York City, NY) — [212] 809-8585

National Gay/Lesbian Task Force (Washington, DC) — [202] 332-6483
TTY: [202] 332-6219

YOUTH SERVICES
Hetrick-Martin Institute (New York City, NY) — *voice:* [212] 674-2400

LYRIC – Lavender Youth Recreation/Information Center (San Francisco, CA) — [800] 246-7743 / [415] 863-3636

CHEMICAL DEPENDENCY
Alternatives — [800] 342-5429
Pride Institute — [800] 547-7433

GAY TRAVEL
Damron Website & Database — www.damron.com
International Gay/Lesbian Travel Association (IGLTA) — [800] 448-8550

National Association of Lesbian/Gay Community Centers (New York City, NY) — [212] 620-7310

TAG (Travel Alternatives Group) — [800] 464-2987

Table of Contents

United States

Alabama	24
Alaska	26
Arizona	29
Arkansas	38
California	42
Colorado	128
Connecticut	136
Delaware	141
District of Columbia	144
Florida	151
Georgia	187
Hawaii	197
Idaho	210
Illinois	211
Indiana	225
Iowa	229
Kansas	232
Kentucky	235
Louisiana	239
Maine	249
Maryland	256
Massachusetts	260
Michigan	290
Minnesota	299
Mississippi	304
Missouri	305
Montana	313
Nebraska	315
Nevada	316
New Hampshire	320
New Jersey	322
New Mexico	326
New York	334
North Carolina	357
North Dakota	369
Ohio	369

Table of Contents

Oklahoma	380
Oregon	385
Pennsylvania	393
Rhode Island	404
South Carolina	406
South Dakota	409
Tennessee	410
Texas	415
Utah	434
Vermont	437
Virginia	441
Washington	447
West Virginia	457
Wisconsin	459
Wyoming	467

International

Canada	468
Caribbean	504
Mexico	512
Costa Rica	523
Austria • Vienna	526
England • London	528
France • Paris	535
Germany • Berlin	545
Italy • Rome	551
The Netherlands • Amsterdam	553
Spain • Barcelona, Madrid, Sitges	559

Calendar of Tours & Events

Camping & RV Spots	570
2002 Tours & Tour Operators	577
2002 Calendar of Events	587
Mail Order	612
Update Form	616

Alabama • USA

ALABAMA
Statewide
INFO LINES & SERVICES
Alabama Bureau of Tourism & Travel 334/242-4169, 800/252-2262

PUBLICATIONS
Alabama Forum 205/328-9228 • lgbt newspaper

▲ **Southern Voice** 404/876-1819 • weekly lgbt newspaper for AL, FL (panhandle), GA, LA, MS, TN w/ resource listings

Atmore
ACCOMMODATIONS
Royal Oaks B&B 5415 Hwy 21 N 334/368-8722 • gay/ straight • full brkfst • kids ok • swimming • $65-75

Birmingham
INFO LINES & SERVICES
Birmingham Gay & Lesbian Info Line 205/326-8600 • 7pm-10pm Mon-Fri

ACCOMMODATIONS
The Tutwiler 2021 Park Pl N (at 21st St N) 205/322-2100 • gay-friendly • also restaurant & lounge • wheelchair access • $99-178

BARS
Club 729 2830 7th Ave S (at 29th St) 205/324-0997 • 3pm-close • mostly women • dancing/ DJ • live shows Sat • karaoke Sun • wheelchair access

Kings Knight 2627 7th Ave S (btwn 26th & 27th) 205/326-3637 • 24 hrs • mostly gay men • dancing/DJ • country/ western • drag shows • 2 outdoor patios

Misconceptions Tavern 600 32nd St S (at 6th Ave S) 205/322-1210 • noon-3am • lesbians/ gay men • videos • patio • wheelchair access

The Tool Box 5120 5th Ave S (at 51st) 205/595-5120 • 2pm-close, till 2am Sat • mostly gay men • more women Wed-Th for country/ western • neighborhood bar • dancing/DJ • patio • wheelchair access

NIGHTCLUBS
22nd Street Jazz Cafe 710 22nd St S (at 7th Ave S) 205/252-0407 • 5pm-close, clsd Sun-Tue • gay-friendly • multiracial • live music • dancing/DJ • food served

Club 21 117-1/2 21st St N (btwn 1st & 2nd Ave N) 205/322-0469 • 10pm-close Th-Sat • popular • gay-friendly • dancing/DJ • mostly African-American • live shows

---

Birmingham

LGBT PRIDE: June.

ANNUAL EVENTS: April/May - Festival of the Arts.
June - City Stages.
June - Shakespeare Renaissance Fair 334/271-5353 or 800/841-4273.

CITY INFO: 205/458-8000, web: www.birminghamal.org.

ATTRACTIONS: Alabama Jazz Hall of Fame 205/254-2731.
Birmingham Zoo & Botanical Gardens 205/879-0408.
Civil Rights Museum 205/328-9696.
Vulcan Statue at 20th St S & Valley Ave atop Red Mountain.

BEST VIEW: Overlook Park.

WEATHER: Hot and humid in the 80's and 90's during the summer, mild in the 50's to low 40's during the winter.

TRANSIT: ABC Taxi 205/833-6974.
Birmingham Transit Authority 205/521-0101.

Mobile • Alabama

The Club Latroy 316 20th St S (btwn 3rd & 4th Aves S) **205/322-8338** • 11pm-close Fri-Sat, noon-9pm Sun • lesbians/gay men • dancing/DJ • multiracial • live shows • 19+ • wheelchair access • cover charge (none Sun)

The Quest Club 416 24th St S (at 5th Ave S) **205/251-4313** • 24hrs • mostly gay men • dancing/DJ • 19+ Wed-Sun (nights only) • live shows • private club • patio • wheelchair access

The Station 2025 Morris Ave (at 21st) **205/254-3750, 888/453-3299** • 10pm-6am Fri-Sat • popular • gay-friendly • dancing/DJ • patio • wheelchair access • cover charge

Restaurants

Anthony's 2131 7th Ave S (at 20th) **205/324-1215** • dinner, Sun brunch, clsd Mon • lesbians/gay men • cont'l/Italian • some veggie • full bar • wheelchair access • $6-15

Bottega Cafe & Restaurant 2240 Highland Ave (btwn 22nd & 23rd) **205/939-1000** • lunch & dinner, clsd Sun • some veggie • full bar • wheelchair access • $17-21

Crestwood Grill 5500 Crestwood Blvd **205/595-1995** • lunch & dinner • full bar • wheelchair access

Highlands Bar & Grill 2011 11th Ave S (at 20th St) **205/939-1400** • 6pm-10pm, bar from 4pm, clsd Sun-Mon • wheelchair access

John's 112 21st St N (btwn 1st & 2nd Ave N) **205/322-6014** • 11am-10pm, clsd Sun • seafood & steak • full bar • wheelchair access

PT's Sports Grill 350 Hollywood Blvd (at Hwy 280 S) **205/879-8519** • 11am-close • burgers & seafood • wheelchair access

Silvertron Cafe 3813 Clairmont Ave S (at 39th St S) **205/591-3707** • 11am-10pm, till 9pm Sun • also full bar • more gay Mon

Entertainment & Recreation

Terrific New Theater 2821 2nd Ave S (in Dr Pepper Design Complex) **205/328-0868**

Bookstores

Lodestar Books 2827 Highland Ave (at 29th St S) **205/328-0144** • 10am-8pm, till 5pm Sun • feminist bookstore w/ lgbt section • also vegetarian cafe • wheelchair access • woman-owned/run

Retail Shops

The Bad Seed 2030 11th Ave S (btwn 20th & 21st) **205/933-7333** • noon-8pm, clsd Sun • music, videos & gifts • gay-owned/run

Spiritual Groups

Covenant MCC 5117 1st Ave N **205/599-3363** • 11am & 7pm Sun, lecture series 7pm Wed

Decatur

Accommodations

Days Inn 810 6th Ave NE (Hwy 31 N at Church) **256/355-3520, 800/DAYS-INN** • gay-friendly • swimming • La Cabana Mex restaurant • wheelchair access • discount w/ Damron mention • $40

Dothan

Nightclubs

The Vault 111 E Main St (at N Foster) **334/794-0230** • 7pm-close, clsd Sun • lesbians/gay men • dancing/DJ • live shows • 19+ • wheelchair access

Geneva

Accommodations

Spring Creek Campground 163 Campground Rd (at Hwy 52 & Country Rd 4) **334/684-3891** • mostly gay men • cabins • also tent & RV sites • swimming • nudity permitted • some theme wknds w/ DJ • gay-owned/run • $15-60

Huntsville

Bars

Vieux Carre 1204 Posey (at Larkin) **256/534-5970** • 7pm-2am • lesbians/gay men • neighborhood bar • DJ Th-Sun • live shows Sun • patio • wheelchair access

Nightclubs

Upscale 2021 Golf Rd **256/881-8820** • 7pm-2am Fri, 8pm-2am Sat • lesbians/gay men • dancing/DJ • live shows • 'Alabama's largest alternative entertainment complex' • also cafe • wheelchair access

Spiritual Groups

MCC 3015 Sparkman Dr NW (at Pulaski Pike) **256/851-6914** • 11am & 6:30pm Sun

Mobile

see also Pensacola, Florida

Info Lines & Services

Pink Triangle AA Group at Cornerstone MCC **334/438-1679 (AA#)** • 7pm Th & Sat

Bars

B-Bob's 6157 Airport Blvd #201 **334/341-0102** • 5pm-close, from 8pm Sat, from 6pm Sun • lesbians/gay men • country/western dancing Th • DJ Th-Sun • live shows Wed, Fri & Sun • young crowd • private club • also lgbt giftshop • wheelchair access

Alabama/ Alaska • USA

Gabriel's Downtown 55 S Joachim St (at Government) 334/432-4900 • 4:30pm-close, from 7pm Sat, from 3pm Sun • lesbians/ gay men • videos • karaoke • private club

Society Lounge 51 S Conception (at Conti) 334/433-9141 • noon-close • popular • lesbians/ gay men • dancing • live shows • private club • wheelchair access

NIGHTCLUBS

On The Roxx 20 S Conception 334/432-9056 • 4pm-close, clsd Mon-Tue • lesbians/ gay men • dancing/DJ • live shows • women-owned/ run

Troopers 215 Conti St (nr Joachim) 334/433-7436 • 8pm-close • lesbians/ gay men • dancing/DJ • live shows Th • private club • patio • wheelchair access • open since 1965!

CAFES

Big E's Delicatessen 263 St. Francis St (at N Jackson St) 334/694-0585 • lunch Mon-Fri • private parties & catering services available • wheelchair access

SPIRITUAL GROUPS

Cornerstone MCC 2201 Government St (at Mohawk) 334/476-4621 • 11am & 7pm Sun

Montgomery

NIGHTCLUBS

The Bar 62 Dexter Ave (at Court St) 334/263-0550 • 8pm-close, clsd Mon-Tue • lesbians/ gay men • dancing/DJ • live shows Sun • 19+ Fri • two-stepping Tue • cabaret Wed

SPIRITUAL GROUPS

New Hope MCC 566 Oliver Rd 334/213-0490 • 5:30pm Sun

Tuscaloosa

BARS

Michael's 2201 6th St (at 22nd Ave) 205/758-9223 • 5pm-close, clsd Mon-Tue & Sun • lesbians/ gay men • women's night Th • dancing/DJ • live shows

SPIRITUAL GROUPS

MCC Living Waters 1053 MLK Dr, Northport 205/391-0077 • 11am & 7pm Sun • wheelchair access

ALASKA

Statewide

INFO LINES & SERVICES

Alaska Travel Industry Association 907/929-2200 • ask for vacation planner

Anchorage

INFO LINES & SERVICES

AA Gay/ Lesbian 3201 Turnagain St (at Unitarian Universalist Church) 907/272-2312 • 7pm Mon

Gay/ Lesbian Helpline 907/258-4777, 888/901-9876 • 6pm-11pm, ask about women's events; traditionally something every Sat except summers when everyone's outdoors

Women Over 50 907/248-2662, 907/694-5450 • social support group • wheelchair access

Women's Coffeehouse 907/258-4777 (HELPLINE #), 907/243-7805 • 2nd Sat (winters)

Women's Resource Center 111 W 9th St (at A St) 907/276-0528 • 8:30am-5pm, clsd wknds • one-on-one counseling & referrals • wheelchair access

ACCOMMODATIONS

Alaska Bear Company B&B 535 E 6th Ave (at Fairbanks) 907/277-BEAR • gay/ straight • in downtown Anchorage

Aurora Winds B&B Resort 7501 Upper O'Malley 907/346-2533 • gay/ straight • on a hillside above Anchorage • full brkfst • hot tub • swimming • kids/ pets ok • wheelchair access • gay-owned/ run • $55-225

Bed & Breakfast at Orca Park 907/274-2262 • gay/ straight • smokefree • gay-owned/ run • wheelchair access • $90-200

Cheney Lake B&B 6333 Colgate Dr (at Baxter) 907/337-4391, 888/337-4391 • gay-friendly • smokefree • lesbian-owned/ run • $65-95

Gallery B&B 1229 'G' St (at 12th) 907/274-2567 • gay/ straight • kids/ pets ok • wheelchair access • lesbian-owned/ run • $35-95

'Off The Tracks' Women's Guesthouse 342 W 11th Ave 907/272-6537 • women only • 'a safe place for women' • kids welcome (boys under 12 only) • shared baths • $50-75

Anchorage • Alaska

Bars

Mad Myrna's 530 E 5th Ave (at Fairbanks) **907/276-9762** • 3pm-3am, noon-close Sun • lesbians/gay men • neighborhood bar • dancing/DJ • food served • live shows

Raven 708 E 4th St **907/276-9672** • 1pm-3am • lesbians/gay men • neighborhood bar • wheelchair access

Restaurants

At Last a Deli 701 W 36th Ave (at Arctic Blvd) **907/563-3354** • 7:30am-6pm, 11am-4pm Sat, clsd Sun

China Lights 12110 Business Blvd, Eagle River **907/694-8080** • 11:30am-10pm

Garcia's 1901 Business Blvd (next to Safeway), Eagle River **907/694-8600** • 11:30am-10:30pm, noon-midnight wknds • Mexican • $9-15

Kodiak Kafe & Dinner House 225 E 5th Ave (btwn Cordova & Barrow) **907/258-5233** • brkfst, lunch & dinner

O'Brady's Burgers & Brew 6901 E Tudor Rd (in Chugach Sq) **907/338-1080** • 11am-midnight, noon-10pm Sun • gay-friendly • some veggie • also at 800 E Dimond (in Dimond Center), 907/344-8033

Simon & Seafort's 420 'L' St (btwn 4th & 5th) **907/274-3502** • lunch weekdays, dinner nightly • seafood & prime rib • full bar

Anchorage

LGBT Pride: June. web: www.anchoragepride.com.

Annual Events: March - Iditarod Sled Dog Race 907/376-5155.
Int'l Ice Carving Competition 907/276-5015.
June - Midnight Sun Marathon 907/343-4474.
August - Alaska State Fair 907/754-4827.
October - Quyana Alaska (native dance celebration) 907/274-3611.

City Info: 907/276-4118 or 800/478-1255, web: www.anchorage.net.

Attractions: Alaska Museum of Natural History, 907/694-0819, web: www.alaskamuseum.org.
Alaska Native Heritage Center 907/330-8000, web: www.alaskanative.net.
Big Game Drive-Thru Wildlife Park (in Portage) 907/783-2025, web: www.biggamealaska.com.
Portage Glacier.
Wolf Song of Alaska Museum 907/274-9653, web: www.wolfsongalaska.org.

Best View: The 11-mile-long paved Tony Knowles Coastal Trail along Cook Inlet offers spectacular views of several mountains, including Denali (Mt McKinley).

Weather: Anchorage's climate is milder than one might think, due to its coastal location. It is cold in the winter (but rarely below 0°F), and it does warm up considerably in June, July, and August. Winter sets in around October. Expect more rain in late summer/early fall.

Transit: Ride Line (bus) 907/343-6543.

Alaska • USA

BOOKSTORES

Cyrano's Bookstore & Cafe 413 'D' St (btwn 1st & 5th) **907/274-2599** • 11am-10pm, from 10am summer, clsd Mon • open later on wknds • live shows • food served • beer/ wine • wheelchair access

RETAIL SHOPS

The Sports Shop 570 E Benson Blvd **907/272-7755** • women's outdoor clothing • adventure gear & equipment

Stonewall'd 528 E 5th Ave (btwn Eagle & Fairbanks St) **907/276-1992** • 11am-7pm, clsd Mon • cards • gifts • T-shirts • books

PUBLICATIONS

Anchorage Press 907/561-7737 • alternative paper • arts & entertainment listings

Identity Northview 907/258-4777 • lgbt • also sponsors 4th Fri potluck, helpline & June Pride events

Klondyke Kontact 907/345-3818 • newsmagazine published every other month

SPIRITUAL GROUPS

Lamb of God MCC 2311 Pembroke (at Immanuel Presbytarian Church) **907/258-5266** • 2pm Sun

Unitarian Universalist Fellowship 3201 Turnagain St (at 32nd) **907/248-3737, 907/248-0715** • 9am & 10:45am Sun • wheelchair access

EROTICA

Ace's 305 W Dimond Blvd **907/522-1987** • 6am-2am

Swingers Books & Gifts 710 W Northern Lights Blvd (at Arctic) **907/561-5039** • 6am-2am

Clam Gulch

ACCOMMODATIONS

Alaska Sea Arch Retreats 15181 Razor Clam Cir **907/260-1942** • gay-friendly • unique accommodations on Kenai Peninsula • seasonal

Fairbanks

INFO LINES & SERVICES

Gay/ Lesbian Info Line 907/458-8288 • 8pm-10pm Tue & Th

ACCOMMODATIONS

Ah, Rose Marie Downtown B&B 302 Cowles St (at 3rd Ave) **907/456-2040** • gay/ straight • full brkfst • some shared baths • kids ok • gay-owned • $60-90

Billie's Backpackers Hostel 2895 Mack Rd **907/457-2034** • gay-friendly • hostel & campsites • kids ok • food served • women-owned/ run • $18

Crabtree Guest House 724 College Rd **907/451-6501** • mostly gay men • shared baths • kitchens • kids ok • $40-60

Fairbanks Hotel 517 3rd Ave (btwn Cushman & Lacey) **907/456-6411, 888/329-4685** • gay-friendly • recently restored to art deco style • kids ok • lesbian-owned/ run • $40-109

BARS

Palace Saloon 3175 College Rd (at Alaskaland) **907/456-5960, 907/456-5964** • 10pm-3am Fri-Sat (seasonal), gay after 11pm Fri-Sat only • gay-friendly • dancing/DJ • live shows

NIGHTCLUBS

Club Galaxy 150 Farmers Extension Loop Rd **907/451-7625** • 8pm-3:30am Fri-Sat • gay-friendly • dancing/DJ • alternative • eclectic club • live shows • wheelchair access

BOOKSTORES

Into the Woods Bookshop 3560 College Rd **907/479-7701** • noon-midnight, from 6pm Mon-Tue • new/ used titles • also cafe • live music • wheelchair access

SPIRITUAL GROUPS

Unitarian Universalist Fellowship 4448 Pikes Landing Rd (across from the 'Princess Hotel') **907/451-8838** • 11am Sun

Homer

ACCOMMODATIONS

Island Watch B&B 4241 Claudia St (at W Hill Rd) **907/235-2265** • gay-friendly • also cabins • full brkfst • kitchens • smokefree • kids/ pets ok • wheelchair access • women-owned/ run • $90-140/ double

The Shorebird Guest House 4774 Kachemak Dr **907/235-2107** • gay/ straight • popular • cottage rental • beach access • wheelchair access

Skyline B&B 63540 Skyline Dr **907/235-3823** • gay-friendly • full brkfst • hot tub • lesbian-owned/ run • $80-115

Cottonwood • Arizona

ENTERTAINMENT & RECREATION

Alaska Fantastic Fishing Charters 800/478-7777 • deluxe cabin cruiser for big-game fishing (halibut) • $159 (per person)

Juneau

INFO LINES & SERVICES

SEAGLA (Southeast Alaska Gay & Lesbian Alliance) PO Box 21542 99802 907/586-4297 • also publishes newsletter

ACCOMMODATIONS

Alaskan Suites Juneau 2141-5 Crowhill Dr 907/789-3772, 888/658-6328 • gay-friendly • extended stay suites • smokefree • kids/ pets ok • $65-195

Pearson's Pond Luxury Inn 4541 Sawa Circle 907/789-3772, 888/658-6328 • gay-friendly • b&b resort & spa • hot tub • smokefree • $99-269

RESTAURANTS

Inn at the Waterfront 455 S Franklin St 907/586-2050 • 5pm-9pm • full bar • $15-38

ENTERTAINMENT & RECREATION

Women's Prerogative KTO 104.3 & 103.1 FM 907/586-1670 • 9pm Wed • women's music

Ketchikan

ACCOMMODATIONS

Millar Street House 1430 Millar St 907/225-1258, 800/287-1607 • gay-friendly • also kayak tours • $85

Kodiak

SPIRITUAL GROUPS

St James the Fisherman Episcopal Church 421 Thorsheim 907/486-5276 • 7:30am & 10am Sun

Seward

ACCOMMODATIONS

Sauerdough Lodging 907/224-8946, 877/224-8946 • gay-friendly • some shared baths • smokefree • wheelchair access • $89-225

Sitka

ACCOMMODATIONS

A Crescent Harbor Hideaway 709 Lincoln St 907/747-4900 • gay-friendly • restored historic waterfront home • hosts also offer educational wildlife & marine tours • $110-145

CAFES

Backdoor Cafe 104 Barracks (behind 'Old Harbor Books' on Lincoln St) 907/747-8856 • 7am-5pm, 9am-3pm Sun • gay-friendly • pleasant & funky hangout

RETAIL SHOPS

Otter Place Gifts 336 Lincoln St 907/747-3217 • 9am-6pm, local gifts & souvenirs • gay-owned

ARIZONA

Statewide

PUBLICATIONS

Women's Community Connection 480/946-5570 • monthly newspaper w/ events listings, articles, personals & lesbian resources

Apache Junction

ACCOMMODATIONS

Susa's Serendipity Ranch 4375 E Superstition Blvd 480/288-9333 • women only • guesthouses • 2 RV hookups • great views! • hot tub • smokefree • pets ok • lesbian-owned/ run • $40+

Bisbee

ACCOMMODATIONS

102—A Premier B&B 102 Tombstone Canyon 520/432-5424 • gay/ straight • full-service B&B in heart of historic district • full brkfst • mtn views • gay-owned/ run • $115

BARS

St Elmo's 36 Brewery Gulch Ave 520/432-5578 • 10am-1am • gay-friendly • live bands Fri-Sat

Bullhead City

includes Laughlin, Nevada

BARS

The Lariat Saloon 1161 Hancock Rd (at 95) 520/758-8479 • 10am-1am • lesbians/ gay men • neighborhood bar • multiracial • DJ wknds • wheelchair access • woman-owned/ run

Cottonwood

RETAIL SHOPS

Seasons Party Shoppe 895 S Main St (on Rte 89-A, N of 260) 520/649-1747 • 10am-5pm, clsd Sun • pride items • party supplies • costumes • gay-owned

Arizona • USA

Flagstaff

Info Lines & Services

Northern Arizona Rainbow Community Center 1300 S Milton Rd **520/774-6416** • serving northern AZ, call for hours

Accommodations

Chalet in the Pines PO Box 25640, Munds Park 86017 **520/286-2417** • mostly gay men • full brkfst • $75-125

Hotel Monte Vista 100 N San Francisco St **520/779-6971, 800/545-3068** • gay-friendly • historic lodging circa 1927 • some shared baths • full bar • $50-130

Piñon Country Cottage 5339 Parsons Ranch Rd **520/526-4797** • mostly women • cabin • $65

Bars

Charlie's 23 N Leroux (at Aspen) **520/779-1919** • 11am-1am • gay-friendly • food served • some veggie • patio • wheelchair access • $7-14

Monte Vista Lounge 100 N San Francisco St (at Aspen) **520/774-2403** • noon-1am, from 11am Fri-Sun • gay-friendly • live bands

Restaurants

Cafe Olé 119 S San Francisco (at Butler) **520/774-8272** • lunch & dinner, clsd wknds • plenty veggie • beer/wine • wheelchair access

Pasto 19 E Aspen (at San Francisco) **520/779-1937** • 5pm-9pm, till 10pm Fri-Sat • Italian • beer/wine • wheelchair access • $7-15

Bookstores

Aradia Books 116 W Cottage (at Beaver) **520/779-3817** • 10:30am-5:30pm, clsd Sun • lesbian/feminist • wheelchair access • women-owned/run • also mail order

Spiritual Groups

Episcopal Church of the Epiphany 423 N Beaver St **520/774-2911** • 6pm Sat, 8am, 9am & 10am Sun • child care provided at Sun services • wheelchair access

Flagstaff MCC 1300 S Milton Rd, Ste 221 (at Community Ctr) **520/526-5419** • 11am • wheelchair access

Golden Valley

Erotica

Pleasure Palace Adult Bookstore 3583 US Hwy 68 #7 **520/565-5600**

Jerome

Accommodations

The Cottage Inn Jerome **520/634-0701** • gay-friendly • full brkfst • kids/pets ok • $70

Kingman

Accommodations

Kings Inn Best Western 2930 E Andy Devine **520/753-6101, 800/750-6101** • gay-friendly • swimming • non-smoking rooms available • food served • bakery on premises • kids/pets ok • wheelchair access • $58-78

Lake Powell

Accommodations

Dreamkatchers of Lake Powell B&B PO Box 5114, Page 86040 **435/675-5828, 888/479-9419** • gay/straight • 8-person spa on deck • $65-95

Mesa

Erotica

Castle Megastore 8315 E Apache Tr **480/986-6114** • 24hrs

Mohave Valley

Erotica

Eros Adult Emporium 10185 Harbor Ave **520/768-6300**

Phoenix

see also Scottsdale & Tempe

Info Lines & Services

AA Lambda Club 2622 N 16th St **602/264-1341** • 6pm & 8pm • call for more times & info

Arizona Office of Tourism 2702 N 3rd St #4015 **602/230-7733, 800/842-8257** • 8am-5pm Mon-Fri

Lesbian Social Network 4400 N Central Ave (at the Community Church of Hope) **480/946-5570** • 7:30pm-10pm Fri • popular informal social evenings of games, videos, and discussions

Valley of the Sun LGBT Center & Arizona AIDS info line **602/265-7283, 602/234-2752 (also TDD)** • 10am-10pm (volunteers permitting) • switchboard • info • meetings • library

Phoenix • Arizona

Valley One In Ten 4400 N Central Ave (at Community Church of Hope) **602/264-5437, 602/265-7283** • 7pm Wed • youth group • HIV peer education

Accommodations

Arrowzona 'Private' Casitas 623/561-1200 • lesbians/ gay men • condos • hot tub • $69-199

Larry's B&B 502 W Claremont Ave (btwn Maryland & Bethany Home) **602/249-2974** • European-style B&B • lesbians/ gay men • full brkfst • swimming • hot tub • nudity • smokefree • wheelchair access • $50-70

Yum Yum Tree Guest House 90 W Virginia Ave #1 (at 3rd Ave) **602/265-2590** • gay/ straight • suites in historic neighborhood • courtyard • swimming • gay-owned/ run • $99-129

Bars

307 on Central **602/252-0001** • 10am-4am • lesbians/ gay men • neighborhood bar • live shows • transgender-friendly • dancing/DJ • also restaurant • wheelchair access

Ain't Nobody's Bizness 3031 E Indian School #7 (at 32nd St) **602/224-9977** • 4pm-1am, from 2pm wknds • mostly women • dancing/DJ • multiracial • live music • karaoke Mon • wheelchair access

Amsterdam 718 N Central Ave (btwn Roosevelt & Fillmore) **602/258-6122** • 4pm-1am • lesbians/ gay men • upscale bar • live music Sun-Mon

Apollo's 5749 N 7th St (S of Bethany Home) **602/277-9373** • 10am-1am, from 10am Sun • mostly gay men • neighborhood bar • karaoke

Cash Inn Country 2140 E McDowell Rd (at 22nd St) **602/244-9943** • 4pm-1am, clsd Mon • mostly women • dancing/DJ • country/western • wheelchair access

The Crowbar 702 N Central (N of Van Buren) **602/258-8343** • 9pm-3am Fri-Sun • lesbians/ gay men • women's night Tue • dancing/DJ • live shows

Harley's 155 155 W Camelback Rd (btwn 3rd & Central Aves) **602/274-8505** • noon-1am • mostly gay men • dancing/DJ

Phoenix

WHERE THE GIRLS ARE: Everywhere. Phoenix doesn't have one section of town where lesbians hang out, but the area between 5th Ave & 32nd St, and Camelback & Thomas Streets does contain most of the women's bars.

LGBT PRIDE: April. 602/279-1771, web: www.azpride.org.

ANNUAL EVENTS: October - AIDS Walk 602/253-2437.

CITY INFO: 602/254-6500. Arizona Office of Tourism 602/230-7733 or 800/842-8257, web: www.phxcenter.org; www.phoenixcenter.org.

ATTRACTIONS: Castles & Coasters Park on Black Canyon Fwy & Peoria 602/997-7577. Heard Museum 602/252-8840. Phoenix Zoo & Desert Botanical Garden in Papago Park.

BEST VIEW: South Mountain Park at sunset, watching the city lights come on.

WEATHER: Beautifully mild and comfortable (60°s-80°s) October through March or April. Hot (90°s-100°s) in summer. August brings the rainy season (severe monsoon storms) with flash flooding.

TRANSIT: Yellow Cab 602/252-5252. Super Shuttle 602/244-9000. Phoenix Transit 602/253-5000.

Arizona • USA

Reply **Forward** **Delete**

Date: Tue, Dec 4, 2001 11:51:33
From: Girl-on-the-Go
To: Editor@Damron.com
Subject: Phoenix

> Can't stand another cloudy day? Sick of spending your summers in a fog bank and your winters in a snowdrift? Try Phoenix, a sun worshiper's paradise. Here the winters are warm and the summers sizzle. And each day ends with a dramatic desert sunset.

> The people of Phoenix have perfected many ways to soak up the incredible sunshine. Some do it as they hike or ride horseback on the many trails along Squaw Peak (off Lincoln Drive) or Camelback Mountain. Some do it by the pool or on the golf course or tennis court. Some do it as they hover over the valley in a hot air balloon.

> Some do it between galleries as they enjoy the popular Thursday night Art Walk along Main Street, Marshall Way, and 5th Avenue in Scottsdale. Others do it dashing from the car to the Scottsdale Galleria or Fashion Square. Still others get sun on the half-hour trip north to Rawhide (800/527-1880), Arizona's real live Old West town and Native American village, complete with gunfights and hayrides.*

> What do lesbians do in Phoenix? Pretty much the same things, but usually in couples. Whether travelling with your honey or on your own, you'll probably enjoy one of the many women's bars in town: **Ain't Nobody's Bizness (The Biz), Misty's, Cash Inn,** or **Nasty's Sports Bar.** Phoenix also has a large sober women's community and its own AA club house. And many lesbians just like to get away from it all on camping, fishing, or hiking trips. Call the **Lesbian Social Network** to find out what social events will be on while you're in town.

> *Driving in the Arizona desert during the summer can be dangerous. Always carry a few gallons of water in your vehicle, and check all fluids in your car both before you leave and frequently during your trip.

Incognito Lounge 2424 E Thomas Rd (at 24th St) **602/955-9805** • 3pm-1am, till 3am Fri-Sat, clsd Mon • lesbians/ gay men • dancing/DJ • hip hop wknds • live shows • wheelchair access

JC's Fun One 5542 N 43rd Ave (at Missouri), Glendale **623/939-0528** • noon-1am, from 11am wknds • mostly gay men • dancing/DJ • live shows • wheelchair access

Phoenix • Arizona

Marlys' 15615 N Cave Creek Rd (btwn Greenway Pkwy & Greenway Rd) **602/867-2463** • 3pm-1am • lesbians/ gay men • neighborhood bar

Misty's 4301 N 7th Ave (at Indian School Rd) **602/265-3233** • 4pm-close, 11am-1am wknds • mostly women • dancing/DJ • multiracial • karaoke • live shows • wheelchair access • women-owned/ run

Nasty's Sports Bar 3108 E McDowell Rd (at 32nd St) **602/231-9427** • noon-1am • mostly women • karaoke

Pookie's Cafe 4540 N 7th St (at Camelback) **602/277-2121** • 11am-midnight, kitchen till 11pm, Sun brunch • lesbians/ gay men • live shows • videos • wheelchair access

Roscoe's on 7th 4531 N 7th St (at Minnezona) **602/285-0833** • 3pm-1am, from 11am Sun • mostly gay men • appetizers • sports bar

The Waterhole 8830 N 43rd Ave (at Dunlap) **623/937-3139** • 3pm-1am • lesbians/ gay men • neighborhood bar • karaoke

Winks 5707 N 7th St (btwn Bethany Home & Missouri) **602/265-9002** • 10am-1am • popular • mostly gay men • drag shows • lunch & Sun brunch served • $5-10

NIGHTCLUBS

Boom 1724 E McDowell (at 16th St) **602/254-0231** • 4pm-1am, till 3am Fri, till 4am Sat • mostly gay men • dancing/DJ • circuit crowd Sat • young crowd • wheelchair access

RESTAURANTS

Alexi's 3550 N Central (in 'Valley Bank Bldg' at Osborn) **602/279-0982** • lunch & dinner • full bar • patio • wheelchair access • $8-23

Katz's Deli 5144 N Central (at Camelback) **602/277-8814** • 6:30am-3pm, till 7pm Tue-Fri, from 8am Sun • kosher-style deli

Los Dos Molinos 8646 S Central Ave **602/243-9113** • 11am-9pm, clsd Sun-Mon • robust homecooking

Pookie's Cafe 4540 N 7th St (at Camelback) **602/277-2121** • 11am-midnight, kitchen till 11pm, Sun brunch • lesbians/ gay men • live shows • videos • also full bar • wheelchair access

Vincent Guerithault on Camelback 3930 E Camelback Rd (at 40th St) **602/224-0225** • lunch Mon-Fri • dinner nightly • Southwestern • some veggie • wheelchair access • $20 à la carte

ENTERTAINMENT & RECREATION

Friends of Ellen Brunch 16th St & Camelback (at Einstein's Bagels) **602/307-9931** • 10:30am 1st & 3rd Sun

Lather, Rinse, Repeat KZZP 104.7FM **602/279-5577** • lgbt radio show 7pm-11pm Sun

BOOKSTORES

Obelisk the Bookstore 24 W Camelback #A (at Central) **602/266-2665** • 10am-10pm, noon-9pm Sun • lgbt • wheelchair access

RETAIL SHOPS

Unique on Central 4700 N Central Ave #105 (at Highland) **602/279-9691, 800/269-4840 (MAIL ORDER)** • 10am-9pm, till 6pm Sun • cards & gifts • wheelchair access

PUBLICATIONS

Echo Magazine **602/266-0550** • bi-weekly lgbt newsmagazine

HeatStroke **602/264-3646** • bi-weekly lgbt newspaper

Women's Community Connection **480/946-5570** • monthly newspaper w/ events listings, articles, personals & lesbian resources

SPIRITUAL GROUPS

Augustana Lutheran Church 2604 N 14th St (at Virginia) **602/265-8400** • 10:30am Sun

Casa de Cristo Evangelical Church 1029 E Turney (at Indian School) **602/265-2831** • 10am & 6:30pm Sun, 6:30pm Wed

Community Church of Hope 4400 N Central (at Turney) **602/234-2180** • 9am & 11am Sun • independent Christian church & counseling center

Dignity/ Integrity Phoenix 2604 N 14th St (at Virginia), Tempe **602/222-8664** • 6:30pm Sat, weekly services in Phoenix & Tempe • call for info

Gentle Shepherd MCC 2604 N 14th (at Augustana Lutheran) **602/864-6404** • 9am Sun

EROTICA

Adult Shoppe 111 S 24th St (at Jefferson) **602/306-1130** • also 5021 W Indian School Rd (at 51st Ave), 623/245-3008

Castle Megastore 300 E Camelback (at Central) **602/266-3348**

International Bookstore 3640 E Thomas Rd (at 36th St) **602/955-2000**

Tuff Stuff 1716 E McDowell Rd (at 17th St) **602/254-9651** • clsd Sun-Mon • custom leather shop

Arizona • USA

Prescott

INFO LINES & SERVICES

Prescott Pride Center 520/445-8800 • 1:30pm-5:50pm Tue, Th & Sat, call for special activities • wheelchair access

ACCOMMODATIONS

Briar Wreath Inn B&B 232 S Arizona Ave (at Gurley) 520/778-6048 • gay/ straight • Craftsman bungalow • full brkfst • hot tub • gay-owned/ run • $100-125

Edge of the Sky Tipi&B HC 31, Box 398 86303 520/899-8733 • mostly women • rustic mtn lodge in nat'l forest • full brkfst • hot tub • sweat lodge • also tipi & campsites • lesbian-owned/ run • $10 (camping) • call for lodge pkgs

Scottsdale

ACCOMMODATIONS

Southwest Inn at Eagle Mountain 9800 N Summer Hill Blvd, Fountain Hills 480/816-3000, 800/992-8083 • gay-friendly • on 18-hole championship golf course • 1/4 mile from Scottsdale • smokefree • $99-295

BARS

BS West 7125 E 5th Ave (in pedestrian mall) 480/945-9028 • 1pm-1am • lesbians/ gay men • dancing/DJ • videos • Sun bbq • wheelchair access

CAFES

Espresso Country 1422 N Scottsdale Rd (at McDowell) 480/994-5110 • 6am-7pm, 7am-6pm Sun • bagels & sandwiches

RESTAURANTS

AZ-88 7553 E Scottsdale Mall 480/994-5576 • 11am-1am, from 5pm wknds • upscale American • some veggie • full bar • $8-15

Malee's 7131 E Main 480/947-6042 • lunch & dinner • Thai • plenty veggie • full bar • $12-20

EROTICA

Zorba's Adult Book Shop 2924 N Scottsdale Rd (N of Thomas) 480/941-9891 • video rentals & arcade

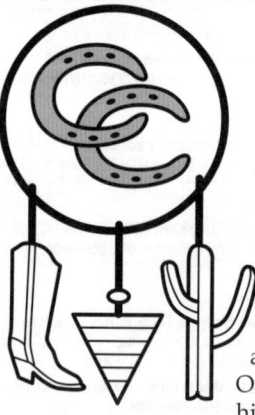

Cactus Cowgirls

PO Box 3173, Sedona, AZ 86340
(928) 203-4818
email: ccowgirls@sedona.net

Country comfort in the heart of the red rocks can be found at Cactus Cowgirls. This lovely smoke-free, furnished B&B is on a quiet road, walking distance to Oak Creek's fishing, swimming and hiking. Our cozy accommodations include queen-size bed, private bath, color cable TV & VCR, air conditioning, heater, kitchenette with continental breakfast and offers a scenic view of Cathedral Rock from the private entrance and patio.

Tucson • Arizona

Sedona

ACCOMMODATIONS

Apple Orchard Inn 656 Jordan Rd **928/282-5328, 800/663-6968** • gay-friendly • full brkfst • hot tub • swimming • hiking • scenic views • smokefree • wheel|chair access • $135-230

▲ **Cactus Cowgirls 928/203-4818** • mostly women • kitchenette • nr outdoor recreation • lesbian-owned/run • $85-100

Iris Garden Inn 390 Jordan Rd **928/282-2552, 800/321-8988** • gay-friendly • motel • jacuzzi • smokefree • wheelchair access • $74-125

Marti's Place PO Box 510, Cornville 86325 **928/634-4842** • lesbians/gay men • rustic cottages along Oak Creek on working ranch nr Sedona

Paradise by the Creek B&B 215 Disney Ln **928/282-7107** • mostly women • private suite • Red Rock views • nr hiking • $85+ • 2-night minimum stay

Southwest Inn at Sedona 3250 W Hwy 89-A **928/282-3344, 800/483-7422** • gay-friendly • smokefree • $115-225

Two Angels Guesthouse 928/204-2083 • lesbians/gay men • smokefree • lesbian-owned/run • $100

RESTAURANTS

Judi's 40 Soldier Pass Rd **928/282-4449** • 11:30am-9pm • some veggie • full bar • $11-21

Shugrue's West 2250 W Hwy 89-A **928/282-2943** • 11:30am-3pm & 5pm-8:30pm • some veggie • also bar • wheelchair access

Surprise

ENTERTAINMENT & RECREATION

RVing Women Inc PO Box 1960 85378-1960 **888/557-8464 (55R-VING), 623/975-2250** • nonprofit RV club for women only

Tempe

NIGHTCLUBS

The Windmill 3300 S Price Rd (at Mill Steakhouse & Saloon) **480/756-2445** • 7pm-1am Wed-Th, till 4am Fri-Sat • lesbians/gay men • dancing/DJ • live bands wknds • also restaurant

RESTAURANTS

Restaurant Mexico 120 E University Dr **480/967-3280** • 11am-9pm, till 10pm Fri-Sat, clsd Sun

ENTERTAINMENT & RECREATION

Tuesday Night Lesbian Scrabble League at the Muse, 1032 S Terrace **480/946-5570** • 6pm Tue

BOOKSTORES

Changing Hands 6428 S McClintock Dr **480/730-0205** • 10am-9pm, till 10pm Fri-Sat, from 9am wknds • new & used • lgbt section

EROTICA

Modern World 1812 E Apache (at McClintock Dr) **480/967-9052** • 24hrs

Tucson

INFO LINES & SERVICES

AA Gay/Lesbian 520/624-4183 • many mtgs • call for schedule

Wingspan Community Center 300 E 6th St (at 5th Ave) **520/624-1779, 520/624-0348** • 11am-7pm Mon-Sat • lgbt & youth info • lgbt AA • library • call for events

ACCOMMODATIONS

Adobe Desert Vacation Rentals **520/578-3998** • gay-friendly • hot tub • swimming • smokefree • kids ok • patio • $550-1400/week

Adobe Rose Inn B&B 940 N Olsen Ave **520/318-4644, 800/328-4122** • gay-friendly • full brkfst, always veggie option • swimming • hot tub • woman-owned/run • $60-135

Adobeland Campground 12150 W Calle Seneca **520/883-6471** • women only • tents & cabins available • solar shower • fragrance-free • lesbian-owned/run • $3/night

Armory Park Guesthouse 219 S 5th Ave **520/206-9252** • gay-friendly • renovated 1896 residence w/ 2 detached guest units • $60-110

Casa Alegre B&B Inn 316 E Speedway Blvd **520/628-1800, 800/628-5654** • gay-friendly • 1915 Craftsman-style bungalow • full brkfst • hot tub • swimming • smokefree • kids ok by arrangement • patio • $70-135

Catalina Park Inn 309 E 1st St **520/792-4541, 800/792-4885** • gay-friendly • full brkfst • smokefree • kids 10+ ok • gay-owned/run • $75-124

Desert Trails B&B 12851 E Speedway Blvd **520/885-7295** • gay-friendly • adobe hacienda on 3 acres bordering Saguaro Nat'l Park • far from the maddening crowd • swimming • smoking outside only • $85-115

Arizona • USA

Elysian Grove Market B&B 400 W Simpson **520/628-1522** • gay-friendly • renovated historic adobe building w/ garden • full brkfst • smokefree • kitchen in suite • woman-owned/ run • $85

Gateway Villas B&B 228 N 4th Ave (at 9th St) **520/740-0767, 888/239-8125** • gay/ straight • jacuzzi • swimming • some kitchens • smokefree • gay-owned/ run • $69-99

Hacienda del Sol Guest Ranch Resort 5601 N Hacienda del Sol Rd **520/299-1501, 800/728-6514** • gay-friendly • food served • swimming • wheelchair access • $140-425

Hills of Gold B&B 3650 W Hills of Gold **520/743-4229** • women only • private suite on 4 acres • swimming • hot tub • $80

Hotel Congress 311 E Congress **520/622-8848, 800/722-8848** • gay-friendly • $29-70 • also 'Cup Cafe' • plenty veggie • also full bar

Milagras B&B 11185 W Calle Pima **520/578-8577** • mostly women • natural adobe guesthouse • suites • garden courtyard • private patio • hot tub • smokefree • lesbian-owned/ run • wheelchair access • $75+

Montecito House **520/795-7592** • gay-friendly • smokefree • kids ok by arrangement • lesbian-owned/ run • $40-45/ night, $250-280/ week

Natural B&B **520/881-4582** • lesbians/ gay men • full brkfst • smokefree • non-toxic/ allergenic • some shared baths • kids ok • massage available • stay 2+ days & get free 1/2-hr massage • gay-owned/ run • $65-75

Royal Elizabeth B&B Inn 204 S Scott Ave (at Broadway) **520/670-9022, 877/670-9022** • gay-friendly • historic 1878 downtown mansion • full brkfst • swimming • hot tub • kids ok • smokefree • $90-180 • gay-owned/ run

BARS

Ain't Nobody's Bizness 2900 E Broadway #118 (at Tucson) **520/318-4838** • 2pm-1am • mostly women • dancing/DJ • wheelchair access

Congress Tap Room 311 E Congress (at Hotel Congress) **520/622-8848** • noon-1am • gay-friendly • neighborhood bar • dance club from 9pm • alternative • live bands • theme nights

Tucson

LGBT Pride: June.

Annual Events: February - La Fiesta de los Vaqueros (rodeo & parade) 520/741-2233, web: www.tucsonrodeo.com.
August - Norteño Music Festival 520/622-2801.
October - Lesbian/ Gay Film Festival 520/624-1779 (Wingspan #), web: members.aol.com/tucsonfilmfest/.

City Info: 520/624-1817, web: www.visittucson.org.

Attractions: Arizona-Sonora Desert Museum 520/883-2702, web: www.desert.net/museum.
Arizona State Museum 520/621-6302, web: www.statemuseum.arizona.edu.
Biosphere 2 800/828-2462, web: www.bio2.edu.
Catalina State Park.
Colossal Cave.
Mission San Xavier del Bac, 520/294-2624.
Old Tucson.
Saguaro National Park.

Best View: From a ski lift heading up to the top of Mount Lemmon.

Weather: 350 days of sunshine a year. Need we say more?

Tucson • Arizona

[Reply] [Forward] **[Delete]**

```
Date: Mon, Dec 3, 2001 14:06:59
From: Girl-on-the-Go
To: Editor@Damron.com
Subject: Tucson
```

> Mention Tucson's torrid weather, and you're likely to hear, "Yeah, but it's dry heat!" Whether you believe that or know better, you can make the most of Tucson's sunshine. Leave your overcoat at home, pack your SPF 160 sun lotion and a good pair of shades, and prepare for a great time.

> You'll see the rainbow everywhere, but mainly around shops on 4th Avenue, the downtown Arts District, and residences in the Armory Park Historic neighborhood.

> Downtown is where you'll find such gay-friendly establishments as **Rainbow Planet Coffee House,** the **Grill on Congress, Cafe Quebec,** and **Hydra,** purveyor of fine BDSM gear. At night, grab a beer at the **Congress Tap Room** or **IBT's** or pay a visit to the women's bar, **Ain't Nobody's Bizness.**

> Just a few blocks northeast is 4th Avenue, where you'll find queer businesses standing strong between sports bars. In addition to gay-owned hair and skin care salons, real estate offices, restaurants, and retail stores, you'll find **Wingspan,** the LGBT community center, which hosts various women's groups and events, as well as **Antigone Books,** one of the best women's bookstores in the Southwest.

> If you're traveling with your laptop, check out the **Tucson Lesbian Community** home page — http://www.flash.net/~cbozarth/ — for the latest in what's going on about town.

> West of Tucson, near the famed Desert Museum (520/883-1380), is a women's community called **Adobeland** that offers weary travellers camping and has cabins available as well.

> LGBT spirituality and healing groups abound, as do Latina, discussion, writers, and readers groups. For films, try the Loft or Catalina Theater, or The Screening Room. Tucson also hosts three film festivals, including the Lesbian & Gay Film Festival in October.

> When you're done with the entertainment, and the temperature at midnight has dropped its usual 30 or 40 degrees, settle in at one of the many gay-owned or gay-friendly B&Bs in town, like women-only **Hills of Gold B&B.**

Arizona/ Arkansas • USA

IBT's (It's About Time) 616 N 4th Ave (at University) **520/882-3053** • 9am-1am, from 11am Sun • lesbians/gay men • dancing/DJ • live shows • wheelchair access

Woody's 3710 N Oracle **520/292-6702** • noon-1am, from 11am wknds • mostly gay men • video/ sports bar • wheelchair accessible

The Yard Dog Saloon 2449 N Stone **520/624-3858** • 6am-1am, from 10am Sun • mixed crowd • transgender-friendly • patio • wheelchair access

CAFES

Cafe Quebec 121 E Broadway (at Arizona Ave) **520/798-3552** • 8am-midnight • mostly veggie • wheelchair access

The Cottage Bakery Cafe 3022 E Broadway (at Country Club) **520/325-5549** • 7am-5:30pm, 8am-4:30pm Sat, clsd Sun • lowfat baked goods • gourmet lunch menu

Rainbow Planet Coffee House 606 N 4th Ave **520/620-1770** • 7:00am-11pm, 8am-midnight wknds • lesbians/gay men • plenty veggie

RESTAURANTS

Blue Willow 2616 N Campbell (at Grant) **520/327-7577** • 7am-9pm, 8am-10pm wknds • brkfst served all day • $5-8

Cafe Terra Cotta 3500 E Sunrise **520/577-8100** • 11:00am-9:30 pm • full bar • wheelchair access • $6-20

The Grill on Congress 100 E Congress (at Scott) **520/623-7621** • 24 hrs • plenty veggie • beer/ wine

ENTERTAINMENT & RECREATION

Old Pueblo Tours **520/795-7448** • May-Sept • see the sights in Tucson • lesbian-owned/ run

BOOKSTORES

Antigone Books 411 N 4th Ave (at 7th St) **520/792-3715** • 10am-6pm, till 9pm Fri-Sat, noon-5pm Sun • lgbt/ feminist • gifts • wheelchair access

RETAIL SHOPS

Desert Pride 300 E 6th St (at 5th Ave) **520/388-9829** • noon-6pm Mon-Fri, till 5pm wknds • pride gifts • T-shirts • videos • posters • CDs • wheelchair access • gay-owned/ run

PUBLICATIONS

The Observer **520/622-7176**

SPIRITUAL GROUPS

Cornerstone Fellowship 2902 N Geronimo (at Glen) **520/622-4626** • 10:30am Sun • 6pm Wed Bible study

Water of Life MCC 3269 N Mountain Ave (N of Fort Lowell) **520/292-9151** • 9:15am & 11:15am Sun

EROTICA

The Bookstore Southwest 5754 E Speedway Blvd **520/790-1550**

Caesar's Bookstore 2540 N Oracle Rd (btwn Glen & Grant) **520/622-9479**

Hydra 145 E Congress (at 6th) **520/791-3711** • vinyl • leather • toys • shoes • lingerie

ARKANSAS

Statewide

INFO LINES & SERVICES

Arkansas Department of Tourism **800/628-8725**

Crossett

CAFES

Pig Trail Cafe Rte 16 (E of Elkins) **501/643-3307** • 6am-9pm • popular • American/ Mexican • under $5

Eureka Springs

INFO LINES & SERVICES

White Wing Services 45 1/2 Spring St (at Main) **501/253-5445** • commitment ceremonies • lesbian-owned/ run

ACCOMMODATIONS

11 Singleton House B&B 11 Singleton **501/253-9111, 800/833-3394** • gay-friendly • 1890s Victorian • full brkfst • jacuzzi • smokefree • also private cottage • women-owned/ run • $75-125

A Cliff Cottage Inn—Luxury B&B Suites & Cottages 42 Armstrong St **501/253-7409, 800/799-7409** • gay-friendly • full brkfst • special meals • dinner cruises • smokefree • women-owned/ run • $149-195

Arbour Glen Victorian Inn B&B 7 Lema **501/253-9010, 800/515-4536** • gay-friendly • historic Victorian home • full brkfst • jacuzzis • fireplaces • $85-135

Basin Park Hotel 12 Spring St **501/253-7837, 800/643-4972** • gay/ straight • $55-195

Eureka Springs • Arkansas

Brass Bed 501/253-5291 • women only • suite w/ kitchen • wheelchair access • women-owned/ run • $50-60

Comfort Inn of Eureka Springs Hwy 62 E (at Jct 23 S) 501/253-5241, 800/828-0109 • gay-friendly • 3-story Victorian hotel • swimming • wheelchair access • woman-owned/ run • $39-84

Enchanted Cottages 18 Nut St 501/253-6790, 800/862-2788 • gay-friendly • nr downtown • hot tub • $89-165

Greenwood Hollow Ridge B&B 501/253-5283 • exclusively lgbt • on 5 quiet acres • nr outdoor recreation • some shared baths • kitchens • pets ok • RV hookups • wheelchair access • gay-owned/run • $75

Heart of the Hills Inn 5 Summit 501/253-7468, 800/253-7468 • gay/ straight • historic inn nr downtown • private decks • gay-owned/ run • $119-139

Home Suite Home 888/281-5488 • gay-friendly • suites or cottage available • jacuzzi • kids ok • gay-owned/ run • $130-280

▲ **Mark E Cook Historic Guest House** 27 Paxos (at Edgewood Manor) 501/253-6555, 800/210-5683 • gay/ straight • Victorian suites & cottages • jacuzzis • fireplaces • $99-139

Morningstar Retreat on the Kings River Hwy 221 S & Kings River 501/253-5995, 800/298-5995 • gay-friendly • cottages • jacuzzi • kids ok • smokefree • $95-175/ double • $10/ each add'l person

Palace Hotel & Bath House 135 Spring St 501/253-7474 • gay-friendly • historic bath house open to all • $136-156

Pond Mountain Lodge & Resort 501/253-5877, 800/583-8043 • gay/ straight • mountaintop inn on 159 acres • cabins • full brkfst • swimming • smokefree • jacuzzi • wheelchair access • lesbian-owned/ run • $110-140

Rock Cottage Gardens 10 Eugenia St 501/253-8659, 800/624-6646 • lesbians/ gay men • cottages • full brkfst • jacuzzis in room • fireplaces • gay-owned/ run • $115-125

The Woods Resort 50 Wall St (off Hwy 62) 501/253-8281 • lesbians/ gay men • cottages • some treehouse cottages • treehouse hot tub • jacuzzis • kitchens • smokefree • gay-owned/ run • $120-150

★ Eureka Springs

"Ozarks Best Kept Secret"
Mark E. Cook
Historic Lodging
in EUREKA SPRINGS, ARKANSAS
1-800-210-5683

the Peabody • the Edgewood
Sweet Seasons

- Elegant Victorian suites, Eurekan-style townhouses, private bungalows
- Jacuzzis for 2, fireplaces, kitchens, privacy
- Open Year Round with Weekday, extended stay & off season rates

edgewood@ipa.net
www.cookslodging.com
www.eureka-springs-usa.com

Arkansas • USA

Bars

Center Street Bar & Grille 10 Center St **501/253-8102** • 5pm-2am, till 10pm Sun • popular • gay-friendly • live shows • food till 10pm Th-Mon • Mexican • plenty veggie

Chelsea's Corner Cafe 10 Mountain St **501/253-6723** • 11am-2am, clsd Sun • gay-friendly • patio • also restaurant • plenty veggie • women-owned/run • $5-8

Restaurants

Autumn Breeze Hwy 23 S **501/253-7734** • 5pm-9pm, clsd Sun • cont'l • $9-18

Cottage Inn Hwy 62 W **501/253-5282** • seasonal • dinner Tue-Sat • Mediterranean • full bar • $8-19

Ermilio's 26 White **501/253-8806** • 5pm-9pm, clsd Th • Italian • plenty veggie • full bar • $8-17

Gaskins Cabin Restaurant 2883 Hwy 23 N (Hwy 187) **501/253-5466** • 5pm-9pm Tue-Sat • steak • seafood • some vegetarian

Jim & Brent's Bistro 173 S Main **501/253-7457** • 5pm-10pm, clsd Wed-Th

The Plaza 55 S Main **501/253-8866** • lunch & dinner • French • full bar • $9-19

Sonny's Pizzeria 119 N Main St (at Mountain) **501/253-2329** • 3pm-9pm, from 11am Wed, till 10pm Fri-Sat, clsd Tue • pizza & pasta • also 'Olives' piano bar

Retail Shops

The Emerald Rainbow 45-1/2 Spring St **501/253-5445** • metaphysical & pride store • visitor info for lesbians & gay men

Spiritual Groups

MCC of the Living Spring 17 Elk St (at Unitarian Church) **501/253-9337** • 7pm Sun

Fayetteville

Info Lines & Services

AA Gay/Lesbian 568 W Sycamore **501/443-6366 (AA#)** • meetings 5:30pm daily, call for info

Bars

Radar's 9 S School St **501/251-1742** • 6pm-2am Th-Sat

Ron's Place 523 W Poplar **501/442-3052** • 9pm-2am Th-Sun • mostly gay men • neighborhood bar • live shows Sun

Sycamore Pub 716 W Sycamore #2 (at Gregg Ave) **501/571-1300** • 6pm-2am, clsd Tue • lesbians/gay men • neighborhood bar • dancing/DJ Fri-Sat • videos • private club • gay-owned/run

Cafes

The Common Grounds 412 W Dickson **501/442-3515** • 7am-2am, from 9am wknds • soup • salads • sandwiches • pastries

Bookstores

Hastings Bookstore 3009 N College Ave (Fiesta Sq Shopping Ctr) **501/521-0244** • 9am-11pm

Passages 2332 N College Ave **501/442-5845** • 10am-6pm, till 8pm Fri, from noon Sun • new age/metaphysical • classes

Fort Smith

Bars

Kinkead's 1004 1/2 Garrison Ave (at Towson) **501/783-9988** • 6pm-1am, till midnight Sat, clsd Sun • popular • gay/straight • neighborhood bar • dancing/DJ • live shows • 18+

Nightclubs

Burnzee's on the Hill 1217 South 'W' **501/494-7300** • 8pm-2am, from 4pm Sun, clsd Mon • popular • lesbians/gay men • dancing/DJ • live shows • private club

Helena

Accommodations

Foxglove B&B 229 Beech **870/338-9391, 800/863-1926** • gay-friendly • 100-yr-old mansion • full brkfst • jacuzzi • $85-165

Hot Springs

Accommodations

The Cottage 108 Tom Ellworth Dr (at Park Ave) **501/318-1098** • gay-friendly • restored cottage in historic district • kids ok • $135 (2-night minimum stay)

Nightclubs

Our House Lounge & Restaurant 660 E Grand Ave **501/624-6868** • 7pm-3am, till 2am Sat, clsd Sun • popular • lesbians/gay men • dancing/DJ • shows monthly • wheelchair access

Huntsville

see also Eureka Springs & Fayetteville

Accommodations

Cabin at Ribbon Ridge RR 5 Box 2025 **501/665-4151** • lesbians/gay men • deluxe 2-rm cabin • 5-person jacuzzi • horseback riding available • smokefree • wheelchair access • lesbian-owned/run • $90

Little Rock

Info Lines & Services

AA Gay/ Lesbian 501/224-6769 (PRIVATE HOME) • 8pm Wed & 6pm Sun • call for more info

PALS (People of Alternative Lifestyles) 210 S Pulaski St 501/374-3605 • for teenagers & young adults up to 24

Bars

Backstreet 1021 Jessie Rd #Q (btwn Cantrell & Riverfront) 501/664-2744 • 9pm-5am • lesbians/ gay men • dancing/DJ • country/ western • live shows • private club • wheelchair access

The Factory 412 S Louisiana St (btwn 4th & Center) 501/372-3070 • 5pm-2am, 7pm-1am Sat, clsd Sun • mostly gay men • neighborhood bar • dancing/DJ • food served • live shows • karaoke • wheelchair access • gay-owned/ run

Nightclubs

Discovery: The Experience 1021 Jessie Rd (btwn Cantrell & Riverfront) 501/664-4784 • 9pm-5am Sat • popular • gay/ straight • dancing/DJ • transgender-friendly • live shows • live music • private club • wheelchair access

Cafes

Beyond the Edge Cafe 1009 W 7th St 501/372-0660 • 10am-2pm & 5pm-10pm, clsd Sun-Mon

Restaurants

Vino's Pizza 923 W 7th St (at Chester) 501/375-8466 • 11am-midnight, till 10pm Tue-Wed • beer/ wine • inquire about monthly women's coffeehouse

Entertainment & Recreation

The Weekend Theatre W 7th St (at Chester) 501/374-3761 • beer & wine • plays & musicals on wknds • gay-owned

Bookstores

Women's Project 2224 Main St (at 23rd) 501/372-5113, 501/372-6853 (TDD) • 10am-5pm Mon-Fri • feminist resource • call for info

Little Rock

Where the Girls Are: Scattered. Popular hangouts are the Women's Project, local bookstores, and Vino's Pizza - women's coffeehouse.

LGBT Pride: June.

Annual Events: October - State Fair.

City Info: Arkansas Dept of Tourism 800/628-8725. What's Going on in Little Rock 502/244-8463, web: www.littlerock.com.

Attractions: Check out Bill & Hillary's old digs at 18th & Center Sts. Decorative Arts Museum 501/372-4000.

Best View: Quapaw Quarter (in the heart of the city).

Weather: When it comes to natural precipitation, Arkansas is far from being a dry state. Be prepared for the occasional severe thunderstorm or ice storm. Summers are hot and humid (mid 90°s). Winters can be cold (30°s) with some snow and ice. Spring and fall are the best times to come and be awed by the colorful beauty of Mother Nature.

Transit: Black & White Cab 501/374-0333. Central Arkansas Transit 501/375-1163.

Arkansas/ California • USA

Retail Shops

A Twisted Gift Shop 1007 W 7th St (at Chester) **501/376-7723** • 11am-10pm, clsd Tue • gift shop • also 7201 Asher Ave, 501/568-4262

Wild Card 400 N Bowman (at Maralynn) **501/223-9071** • 10am-8pm, noon-5pm Sun • novelties & gifts

Spiritual Groups

MCC of the Rock 2017 Chandler, North Little Rock **501/753-7075** • 11am Sun, 7pm Wed

Unitarian Universalist Church 1818 Reservoir Rd **501/225-1503** • 10:30am Sun • wheelchair access

CALIFORNIA

Arcata

Restaurants

Wildflower Bakery and Cafe 1604 G St **707/822-0360** • 8am-8pm, 9am-1pm Sun • vegetarian

Bookstores

Northtown Books 957 H St **707/822-2834** • 10am-7pm, till 9pm Fri, till 6pm Sat, noon-5pm Sun • lgbt section • carries 'The L Word' paper

Arnold

Accommodations

Dorrington Inn at Big Trees 3450 Hwy 4, Dorrington 95223 **209/795-2164, 888/874-2164** • gay/ straight • cottages & suites • 3 hours from San Francisco, 18 miles from Bear Valley • gay-owned/ run

Atascadero

Erotica

Diamond Adult World 5915 El Camino Real (at Traffic Wy) **805/462-0404** • books • toys • videos

Bakersfield

Info Lines & Services

Friends **661/323-7311** • 7pm-11:30pm • info • support groups & community outreach

Accommodations

Rio Bravo Resort 11200 Lake Ming Rd **661/872-5000, 888/517-5500** • gay-friendly • swimming • wheelchair access • $68-108

Bars

Casablanca Club 1825 'N' St **661/324-0661** • 7pm-2am, 4pm-midnight Sun, clsd Mon • mostly gay men • dancing/DJ • shows

The Mint 1207 19th St (btwn 'M' & 'L') **661/325-4048** • 6pm-2am • gay-friendly • neighborhood bar • wheelchair access

Padre Bar 1813 'H' St (at 18th, on lower level of Padre Hotel) **661/324-2594** • 10am-2am • gay-friendly • piano bar

Nightclubs

Rainbow Club Wilson & Real Rds (in the Kmart shopping ctr) **661/832-7711** • 7pm-2am, clsd Mon • lesbians/ gay men • dancing/DJ

Spiritual Groups

MCC of the Harvest 2421 Alta Vista Dr **661/327-3724** • 7pm Sun

Erotica

Deja Vu 1524 Golden State Hwy (at Chester Ave) **661/322-7300**

Wildcat Books 2620 Chester Ave (at 21st) **661/324-4243**

Bell Gardens

Erotica

Le Sex Shoppe 6816 Eastern Ave (at Florence) **323/560-9473** • 24hrs

Benicia

see Vallejo

Berkeley

see East Bay

Big Bear Lake

Accommodations

Alpine Retreats 433 Edgemoor (at Big Bear Blvd) **818/535-9272** • gay/ straight • indoor spas • fireplaces • private entrances • gay-owned/ run

Eagles' Nest B&B 41675 Big Bear Blvd **909/866-6465, 888/866-6465** • gay-friendly • 5 cottages • full brkfst • spa • $85-150

Grey Squirrel Resort **909/866-4335, 800/381-5569** • gay-friendly • 19 private rental homes • swimming • wheelchair access • lesbian-owned • $75-600

Columbia • California

Hillcrest Lodge 40241 Big Bear Blvd **909/866-6040, 800/843-4449** • gay/ straight • motel • cabins • jacuzzi suites • kitchens • fireplaces • smokefree rooms available • kids ok • wheelchair access • $39-200

Knickerbocker Mansion Country Inn 869 Knickerbocker Rd **909/878-9190, 800/388-4179** • gay/ straight • log mansion on lake w/ rooms & suites • full brkfst • jacuzzi • hiking • smokefree • wheelchair access • gay-owned/ run • $110-225

Majestic Moose Lodge 39328 Big Bear Blvd (at Cienga) **909/866-2435** • gay-friendly • cabins • jacuzzi • swimming • pets ok • $79-259

Bishop

Accommodations

Starlite Motel 192 Short St (at hwy 395) **760/873-4912** • gay-friendly • swimming • $45

Buena Park

Bars

Ozz Supper Club 6231 Manchester Blvd **714/522-1542** • 6pm-10pm Th-Fri, till 10:30 Sat, 5pm-9pm Sun • popular • lesbians/ gay men • dancing/DJ • live shows • cabaret • call for events • also restaurant • some veggie • $9-25

Carmel

see also Monterey

Accommodations

Happy Landing Inn **831/624-7917** • gay-friendly • Hansel & Gretel 1925 inn • full brkfst • smokefree • kids 13+ ok • wheelchair access • $90-180

Chico

Info Lines & Services

Stonewall Alliance Center 341 Broadway # 416 **530/893-3336, 530/893-3338** • hotline • meetings • call for times

Accommodations

Inn at Shallow Creek Farm 4712 Road DD, Orland **530/865-4093, 800/865-4093** • gay-friendly • smokefree • some shared baths • $60-85

Chula Vista

Erotica

F St Bookstore 1141 3rd Ave (at Naples) **619/585-3314** • 24hrs • wheelchair access

Clear Lake

Accommodations

Blue Fish Cove Resort 10573 E Hwy 20, Clearlake Oaks **707/998-1769** • gay-friendly • lakeside resort cottages • fishing • kitchens • kids ok • pets ok by arrangement • boat launch facilities & rentals • $45-110

Edgewater Resort 6420 Soda Bay Rd (at Hohape Rd), Kelseyville **707/279-0208, 800/396-6224** • 'gay-owned, straight-friendly' • cabin • camping & RV hookups • lake access & pool • theme wknds • boat facilities • smoking outside • pets ok • $25-250

Lake Vacation Rentals 1855 S Main St, Lakeport **707/263-7188** • gay-friendly • rental homes on the lake • $185-400

Sea Breeze Resort 9595 Harbor Dr, Glenhaven **707/998-3327** • gay/ straight • cottages • swimming • 2 night minimum • smokefree • wheelchair access • gay-owned/ run • $70-100

Restaurants

The Brentwood 6278 E Hwy 20, Lucerne **707/274-2301** • dinner only, clsd Tue-Wed, brkfst, lunch & dinner wknds • $7-14

Kathy's Inn 14677 Lake Shore Dr, Clearlake **707/994-9933** • lunch Wed-Fri, open from 4pm wknds, clsd Mon-Tue • full bar • wheelchair access

Cloverdale

see also Healdsburg

Accommodations

Asti Ranch 25750 River Rd **707/894-5960** • women only • cottage nr lake & river in wine country • tennis court • wheelchair access • $500-750 weekly, $250-350 wknds

Vintage Towers B&B 302 N Main St (at 3rd) **707/894-4535, 888/886-9377** • gay-friendly • Queen Anne mansion • full brkfst • smokefree • kids 10+ ok • $95-180

Columbia

Entertainment & Recreation

Ahwahnee Whitewater near Yosemite & Lake Tahoe **209/533-1401, 800/359-9790** • women-only, co-ed & charter rafting

California • USA

Concord

Info Lines & Services

Rainbow Community Center 2118 Willow Pass Rd #500 (at Diablo) **925/692-0090** • 10am-5pm, clsd Sun • support groups • library • social events • referral line

Erotica

Pleasant Hill Adult Books & Videos 2294 Monument Blvd (at Buskirk) **925/676-2962**

Costa Mesa

Bars

Tin Lizzie Saloon 752 St Clair (at Bristol) **714/966-2029** • 11am-2am • mostly gay men • neighborhood bar • wheelchair access

Nightclubs

Lion's Den 719 W 19th St (at Pomona) **949/645-3830** • 9pm-2am • lesbians/gay men • dancing/DJ • karaoke • live shows • young crowd

Cupertino

Bars

Dar's Hideaway 10095 Saich Wy (at Stevens Creek Blvd) **408/255-7474** • 4pm-2am • lesbians/gay men • neighborhood bar • live shows • wheelchair access

Davis

see also Sacramento

Info Lines & Services

DavisDykes 530/752-2452 (CENTER#) • social group • call for events

LGBT Resource Center University Annex **530/752-2452** • info • referrals • mtgs • call for hours • wheelchair access

Cafes

Cafe Roma 231 'E' St (btwn 2nd & 3rd) **530/756-1615** • 6am-10pm, from 6:30am wknds • popular • coffee & pastries • student hangout

East Bay

includes Berkeley & Oakland, see also Concord, Fremont, Lafayette, Hayward, Pleasant Hill, San Lorenzo, Walnut Creek

Info Lines & Services

La Peña 3105 Shattuck Ave, Berkeley **510/849-2568, 510/849-2572** • 10am-5pm Mon-Fri • also cafe 5:30pm- 9:30pm Wed-Sun • multicultural center • hosts meetings, dances, events

Lesbians of Color Group 2712 Telegraph Ave (at Derby, in the Pacific Center), Berkeley **510/548-8283** • 7pm Th • workshops • activities

Pacific Center 2712 Telegraph Ave (at Derby), Berkeley **510/548-8283** • 10am-10pm, noon-3pm & 7pm-10pm Sat, 6pm-9pm Sun

SMAAC (Sexual Minority Alliance of Alameda County) 1738 Telegraph (nr 17th), Oakland **510/834-9578** • 2pm-10pm, clsd Sun • center for youth questioning their sexuality

What's Up! Events Hotline for Sistahs **510/835-6126** • for lesbians of African descent

Accommodations

Bates House B&B 399 Bellevue Ave (at Van Buren), Oakland **510/893-3881** • gay/straight • gay-owned/run • $85-130

Elmwood House **510/540-5123** • gay/straight • guesthouse • smokefree • gay-owned/run • $75-100

Washington Inn 495 10th St (at Broadway), Oakland **510/452-1776** • gay/straight • historic boutique hotel • full brkfst • smokefree • wheelchair access • gay-owned/run • $79-198

Bars

Bench & Bar 120 11th St (btwn Madison & Oak), Oakland **510/444-2266** • 4pm-2am • popular • mostly gay men • women's night Th • dancing/DJ • professional crowd • Latino/a clientele • live shows • wheelchair access

Cabel's Reef 2272 Telegraph Ave (at Grand), Oakland **510/451-3777** • 2pm-2am • lesbians/gay men • women's night Wed • dancing/DJ • multiracial • karaoke • live shows

White Horse 6551 Telegraph Ave (at 66th), Oakland **510/652-3820** • 1pm-2am, from 3pm Mon-Tue • popular wknds • lesbians/gay men • dancing/DJ • wheelchair access

Cafes

Cafe Sorrento 2510 Channing (at Telegraph), Berkeley **510/548-8220** • 11am-7pm • Italian • vegetarian • $5-10

Cafe Strada 2300 College Ave (at Bancroft), Berkeley **510/843-5282** • 6:30am-midnight • popular • students • great patio & bianca (white chocolate) mochas • wheelchair access

Mimosa Cafe 462 Santa Clara (at Grand), Oakland **510/465-2948** • 11am-9pm, from 9am wknds, till 2pm Sun, clsd Mon • natural & healthy • plenty veggie • beer/wine • $7-12

Restaurants

Betty's To Go 1807 4th St (at Hearst), Berkeley **510/548-9494** • 6:30am-5pm, from 8am wknds • sandwiches • some veggie • $5

Bison Brewery 2598 Telegraph (at Parker), Berkeley **510/841-7734** • 11am-1am • live music • sandwiches • some veggie • beer/wine • wheelchair access • $5-10

Chez Panisse 1517 Shattuck Ave (at Cedar), Berkeley **510/548-5525** • clsd Sun • nouvelle Californian • beer/wine • $38-68

La Mediterranée 2936 College Ave (at Ashby), Berkeley **510/540-7773** • 10am-10pm, till 11pm wknds • beer/wine • $12-17

Mama's Royale 4012 Broadway (at 40th), Oakland **510/547-7600** • 7am-3pm, from 8am wknds • popular • mostly lesbians • come early for excellent wknd brunch • beer/wine • wheelchair access • $5-10

East Bay

WHERE THE GIRLS ARE: Though there's no lesbian ghetto, you'll find more of us in North Oakland (Rockridge) and North Berkeley, Lake Merritt, around Grand Lake & Piedmont, the Solano/Albany area, or at a cafe along 4th St in Berkeley.

LGBT PRIDE: June. 510/663-3980. September - Mardi Gras East Bay Pride 510/663-3980.

ANNUAL EVENTS: June - Gay Prom/Project Eden (for lgbt youth) 510/247-8200.
October/November - Halloween Spiral Dance 510/444-7724. Annual rite celebrating the crone.

CITY INFO: Oakland Convention & Visitors Bureau 510/839-9000, web: www.oaklandcvb.com.

ATTRACTIONS: The Claremont Hotel & Restaurant, Berkeley 510/843-3000.
Emeryville Marina Public Market.
Jack London Square, Oakland.
Oakland Museum of California 510/238-2200, web: www.museumca.org.
The Paramount Theater, Oakland 510/465-6400.
UC Berkeley.

BEST VIEW: Claremont Hotel, Tilden Park, various locations in the Berkeley and Oakland Hills. Or from the top of Sather Tower on the UC Berkeley campus.

WEATHER: While San Francisco is fogged in during the summers, the East Bay remains sunny and warm. Some areas even get hot (90°s-100°s). As for the winter, the temperature drops along with rain (upper 30°s-40°s in the winter). Spring is the time to come – the usually brown hills explode with the colors of green grass and wildflowers.

TRANSIT: Yellow Cab (Berkeley) 510/527-8294.
Veteran's Cab (Oakland) 510/533-1900.
Bayporter Express 510/864-4000.
AC Transit 510/817-1717.
BART (subway) 510/465-2278.
Ferry 510/522-3300.

California • USA

[Reply] [Forward] **[Delete]**

```
Date: Thu, Dec 13, 2001 12:03:47
From: Girl-on-the-Go
To: Editor@Damron.com
Subject: East Bay
```

> So what exactly is the East Bay? To most Northern Californians, it's simply the string of cities and counties across the Bay Bridge from San Francisco—with weather that's consistently sunnier and 10 to 20 degrees warmer than Fog City. For the *Damron Women's Traveller*, it is the more lesbian-friendly cities of Berkeley and Oakland.

> Berkeley—both the campus of the University of California and the city where it's located—was immortalized in the '60s as a hotbed of student/counterculture activism. Today, most of the people taking to the streets, especially Telegraph and College Avenues, are tourists or kids from the suburbs in search of consumer thrills such as a good book, exotic cuisine, and funky jewelry and crafts sold by street vendors.

> Locals and visitors alike will enjoy people-watching on Telegraph or University Avenue. Or you can just take to the hills—vast Tilden Park offers incredible views and trails to hike and bike.

> As for Oakland, Gertrude Stein once said, "There is no there there." Well, Gertrude, a lot has happened since you were in Oakland!

> Today Oakland is a city with an incredible diversity of races, cultures, and classes. The birthplace of the Black Panthers, this city has been especially influential in urban African-American music, fashion, and politics. Lately Oakland has also become a vital artists' enclave, as Bay Area artists flee high rent in San Francisco for spacious lofts downtown or in West Oakland.

> And where are all the women? Well, many are in couples or covens or both, which can make them hard to find. But if you want to start a couple or a coven of your own, stop by **Mama Bears** (in Oakland) or one of the other women's bookstores—they're also great informal resource centers, and often host popular performances and author signings. And speaking of "hot mamas," try the popular weekend brunch at **Mama's Royale** (in Oakland). The Emeryville Marina Public

East Bay • California

[Reply] [Forward]　　　　　　　　　　　　　　　　[Delete]

Market off I-80 is popular with gastronomically inclined lesbians.

> For info on groups and events, cruise by the **Pacific Center** in Berkeley. The center hosts meetings for lesbian moms & kids, bisexuals, transgendered women, separatists, and more. Those interested in women's spirituality should drop by **Ancient Ways** (in Oakland), the pagan emporium extraordinaire.

> If you're the outdoors type, consider an adventure in Northern California with **Mariah Wilderness Expeditions** (510/233-2303). Or make a day of it at one of the nearby state parks: Point Reyes is a beautiful destination with a hostel, and Point Isabel is rumored to be a good meeting place for dykes with dogs.

> If you'd rather exercise indoors, make some moves on the dance floor of the **White Horse** (in Oakland). For plays, performances, and events, grab a copy of the **Bay Times** and check out the calendar section. Or pick up some entertainment of your own at the East Bay **Good Vibrations** (in Berkeley) or **Passion Flower** (in Oakland)—both are women-friendly, clean sex toy stores.

> There are also lots of resources for women of color in the East Bay. Start with **La Peña Cultural Center** (in Berkeley), an active center with many events for Latina-Americans and African-Americans. There's also **What's Up!**, an events hotline for lesbian sistahs of African descent.

California • USA

BOOKSTORES

Boadecia's Books 398 Colusa Ave (1/2 mile from Solano), North Berkeley **510/559-9184** • noon-8pm, from 11am wknds • lgbt • readings • wheelchair access • lesbian-owned/ run • special events

Cody's 2454 Telegraph Ave (at Haste), Berkeley **510/845-7852** • 10am-10pm • general • lgbt section • frequent readings & lectures • wheelchair access

Easy Going 1385 Shattuck (at Rose), Berkeley **510/843-3533, 510/843-6725** • 10am-7pm, till 6pm Sat, noon-6pm Sun • travel books & accessories • also 1617 Locust, Walnut Creek 510/947-6660

Mama Bears Women's Bookstore 6536 Telegraph Ave (btwn Alcatraz & Ashby), Oakland **510/428-9684, 800/643-8629** • 10:30am-8pm • women's books • readings & performances • cafe • lesbian-owned/ run

Shambhala Booksellers 2482 Telegraph Ave (at Dwight), Berkeley **510/848-8443** • 11am-8pm • metaphysical feminist/ goddess section • wheelchair access

RETAIL SHOPS

Ancient Ways 4075 Telegraph Ave (at 41st), Oakland **510/653-3244** • 11am-7pm • extensive occult supplies • classes • readings • woman-owned/ run

PUBLICATIONS

San Francisco Bay Times 415/626-0260 • popular • a 'must read' for Bay Area resources & personals

SPIRITUAL GROUPS

Albany United Methodist Church 980 Stannage Ave (at Marin), Albany 510/526-7346 • 10am Sun

Mamaroots Afracentrik Temple of AfraKamaati 6025 Shattuck Ave, Oakland 510/658-7123 • 10am-noon most Sats • women-only • call for details & special events

MCC New Life 1823 9th St (at Hearst), Berkeley 510/843-9355 • 12:30pm Sun • transgender friendly • wheelchair access

Moon Sistahs 510/547-8386 • drumming circles & classes open to 'womyn on all spiritual paths'

EROTICA

▲ **Good Vibrations** 2504 San Pablo (at Dwight), Berkeley 510/841-8987 • 11am-7pm, till 8pm Fri-Sat • clean, well-lighted sex toy store • workshops and events • also mail order • wheelchair access • (see ad in San Francisco section)

Hollywood Adult Books 5686 Telegraph Ave (at 57th), Oakland **510/654-1169**

L'Amour Shoppe 1905 San Pablo Ave, Oakland **510/465-4216**

Passion Flower 4 Yosemite Ave (at Piedmont), Oakland **510/601-7750** • 2pm-7pm, clsd Mon-Wed • toys • lingerie • leather

El Cajon

EROTICA

F St Bookstore 158 E Main (at Magnolia) **619/447-0381** • 24hrs • wheelchair access

Escondido

EROTICA

Video Specialties 2322 S Escondido Blvd **760/745-6697** • wheelchair access

Eureka

INFO LINES & SERVICES

The Center: Northcoast Lesbian, Gay, Bisexual & Transgender Alliance 707/445-9760, 707/444-1061 • hours vary, call first • referrals • support groups • social events • wheelchair access

ACCOMMODATIONS

A Weaver's Inn 1440 'B' St 707/443-8119, 800/992-8119 • gay-friendly • stately Queen Anne w/ beautiful gardens • full brkfst • $80-140

Abigail's Elegant Victorian Mansion Historic B&B Inn 1406 'C' St 707/444-3144 • gay-friendly • 1878 Nat'l Historic landmark • full brkfst • sauna • smokefree • $95-185

Carter House Victorians 301 'L' St 707/444-8062, 800/404-1390 • gay-friendly • enclave of 4 unique inns • full brkfst • smokefree • kids ok • wheelchair access • $99-497

BARS

Lost Coast Brewery Pub 617 4th St (btwn 'G' & 'H') 707/445-4480 • 11am-midnight • gay-friendly • food served • beer/ wine • wheelchair access • women-owned/ run

The Shanty 213 3rd St (at C) 707/444-2053 • noon-2am • lesbians/ gay men • neighborhood bar • lesbian-owned

NIGHTCLUBS

Club Triangle (Club West) 535 5th St (at 'G' St) 707/444-2582 • 9pm-2am • gay-friendly • gay Sun • dancing/DJ • alternative • country/ western • 18+ • also restaurant • wheelchair access

Fresno • California

RESTAURANTS

Folie Deuce 1551 'G' St, Arcata **707/822–1042** • dinner from 5:30pm, clsd Sun-Mon • bistro • beer/ wine • wheelchair access • $8-20

Seafood Grotto 605 Broadway (at 6th) **707/443-2075** • low prices • informal setting

BOOKSTORES

Booklegger 402 2nd St (at 'E' St) **707/445-1344** • 10am-5:30pm, 11am-4pm Sun • mostly used • some lesbian titles • wheelchair access • women-owned/ run

PUBLICATIONS

The 'L' Word PO Box 272, Bayside 95524 • lesbian newsletter for Humboldt County • available at 'Booklegger' and 'North Town Books' in Arcata

EROTICA

Good Relations 308 2nd St **707/441-9570** • lingerie • toys • books • videos • wheelchair access • bisexual-owned/ run

Fairfield

see Vacaville

Ferndale

ACCOMMODATIONS

The Gingerbread Mansion Inn 400 Berding St, PO Box 40 **707/786-4000, 800/952-4136** • gay-friendly • a grand lady w/ beautifully restored interior • full brkfst • afternoon tea • nr outdoor recreation • smokefree • kids ok • $150-385

Fontana

EROTICA

Le Sex Shoppe 14589 Valley Blvd (at Cherry) **909/350-4717** • 24hrs

Fort Bragg

ACCOMMODATIONS

Annie's Jug Handle Beach B&B 32980 Gibney Ln **707/964-1415, 800/964-9957** • gay-friendly • full Cajun brkfst • smoking outside only • kids ok • $89-229

Aslan House 24600 N Hwy 1 **707/964-2788, 800/400-2189 (IN N CA)** • gay-friendly • beach house • ideal place for romance & privacy on the Mendocino Coast • partial ocean view • hot tub • kids 10+ ok • $165 +

Cleone Garden Inn 24600 N Hwy 1 **707/964-2788, 800/400-2189 (CA ONLY)** • gay-friendly • rooms & cottage suite • country garden retreat on 9 1/2 acres • hot tub • $85-165

RESTAURANTS

Purple Rose Mill Creek Dr **707/964-6507** • 5pm-9pm, clsd Mon-Tue • Mexican

BOOKSTORES

Windsong Books & Records 324 N Main (at Redwood Ave) **707/964-2050** • 10am-5:30pm, till 4pm Sun • mostly used • large selection of women's/ lesbian titles

Fremont

EROTICA

L'Amour Shoppe 40555 Grimmer Blvd (at Fremont) **510/659-8161**

Fresno

INFO LINES & SERVICES

Community Link **559/266-5465** • info • lgbt support • also publishes 'Pink Pages'

GUS (Gay United Service) 404 W McKinley (at Fruit) **559/268-3541** • 8am-5pm Mon-Fri • counseling & referrals

Serenity Fellowship AA 900 N Fulton #D (btwn Olive & Belmont) **559/221-6907** • various mtg times • women's mtg 7pm Mon at Alano Club (1350 N 11th St)

BARS

Bam Bam's Cafe 2915 N Maroa (at Michigan) **559/244-4844** • 7pm-2am, DJ Wed-Sun • mostly gay men • dancing/DJ Wed-Sun • 18+ • food served • patio

The Cave 4538 E Belmont Ave (btwn Barton & Maple) **559/251-5972** • 5pm-2am • mostly gay men • neighborhood bar • leather • transgender-friendly • ladies night Th • beer/wine • patio • wheelchair access

El Sombrero 3848 E Belmont Ave (btwn 8th & 9th) **559/442-1818** • 9pm-1am Wed, 6pm-1am Fri-Sun • lesbians/ gay men • multiracial • live shows

The Express 3075 N Maroa (at Shields) **559/224-1024** • 10pm-2am • lesbians/ gay men • dancing/DJ • piano bar • also restaurant • live entertainment • videos • popular patio • wheelchair access

North Tower Circle 2777 N Maroa **559/229-4188** • 8pm-2am, from 5pm Th-Sun • lesbians/ gay men • dancing/DJ Wed-Sun • patio

California • USA

Red Lantern 4618 E Belmont Ave (at Maple) **559/251-5898** • 2pm-2am • mostly gay men • neighborhood bar • country/ western • wheelchair access

RESTAURANTS

Cabaret 21 3075 N Maroa (at Shields) **559/224-1024** • 5pm-midnight, brunch 10am-3pm Sun, clsd Mon • lesbians/ gay men • fine dining • piano bar • wheelchair access • $12-30

SPIRITUAL GROUPS

Wesley United Methodist Church 1343 E Barstow Ave (at 4th) **559/224-1947** • 8:30am & 11am Sun, summer hrs vary • reconciling congregation

EROTICA

Only For You 1460 N Van Ness Ave (at McKinley) **559/498-0284** • 11am-8:30pm • lgbt

Wildcat Book Store 1535 Fresno St (at 'G' St) **559/237-4525** • video arcade • books • adult novelties

Garberville

ACCOMMODATIONS

Giant Redwoods RV & Camp **707/943-3198** • gay-friendly • campsites • RV • located off the Avenue of the Giants on the Eel River • shared baths • kids/ pets ok • $19(tent)-27

Garden Grove

INFO LINES & SERVICES

Gay/ Lesbian Community Services Center 12832 Garden Grove Blvd #A (at Harbor) **714/534-0862** • 9am-9pm, clsd wknds

BARS

Frat House 8112 Garden Grove Blvd **714/897-3431** • 9am-2am • popular • lesbians/ gay men • dancing/DJ • multiracial • theme nights • live shows • piano bar • young crowd • wheelchair access

Happy Hour 12081 Garden Grove Blvd (at Harbor) **714/537-9079** • 2pm-2am, from noon wknds • mostly women • dancing/DJ • wheelchair access • lesbian-owned/ run for over 30 years!

EROTICA

A-Z Bookstore 8192 Garden Grove Blvd (Beach) **714/534-9349** • 24hrs wknds

Hip Pocket 12686 Garden Grove Blvd (at Harbor) **714/638-8595**

Party House 8743 Garden Grove Blvd (at Magnolia) **714/534-9996**

Glendale

SPIRITUAL GROUPS

MCC Divine Redeemer 346 Riverdale Dr **818/500-7124** • 6pm Sun

Grass Valley

see also Nevada City

RESTAURANTS

Friar Tucks 111 N Pine St (at Commercial), Nevada City **530/265-9093** • dinner from 5pm • American/ fondue • full bar • wheelchair access • $15-20

Gualala

ACCOMMODATIONS

Breakers Inn 39300 S Hwy 1 **707/884-3200, 800/BREAKER** • gay/ straight • women-owned/ run • $105-235

Half Moon Bay

ACCOMMODATIONS

Mill Rose Inn 615 Mill St **650/726-8750, 800/900-7673** • gay-friendly • classic European elegance by the sea • full brkfst • hot tub • smokefree • kids 10+ ok • $180-310

RESTAURANTS

Moss Beach Distillery 140 Beach Way (Ocean) **650/728-5595** • lunch & dinner • some veggie • $9-40

Pasta Moon 315 Main St (Mill) **650/726-5125** • lunch & dinner, 11am-3pm brunch Sun • full bar • wheelchair access

San Benito House 356 Main St **650/726-3425** • dinner Th-Sun • Mediterranean • full bar • wheelchair access • $12-18

Hayward

BARS

Rainbow Room 21859 Mission Blvd (at Sunset) **510/582-8078** • noon-2am, from 10am wknds • lesbians/ gay men • dancing/DJ • drag shows weekly • women-owned/ run

Rumors Cocktail Lounge 22554 Main St (btwn 'A' & 'B') **510/733-2334** • noon-2am, 10am-2am wknds • mostly gay men • neighborhood bar • dancing/DJ • karaoke Th • free buffet Fri • wheelchair access

Turf Club 22519 Main St (at 'A') **510/881-9877** • 10am-2am • lesbians/ gay men • dancing/DJ • live shows • patio

Laguna Beach • California

EROTICA

L'Amour Shoppe 22553 Main St (btwn 'A' & 'B') **510/886-7777**

Healdsburg

see also Russian River

ACCOMMODATIONS

Camellia Inn 211 North St **707/433-8182, 800/727-8182** • gay-friendly • Italianate Victorian • smokefree • $99-199

Madrona Manor 707/433-4231, 800/258-4003 • gay-friendly • elegant Victorian country inn • full brkfst • swimming • smokefree • some rooms ok for kids • wheelchair access • $215-380

Twin Towers River Ranch Rentals 615 Bailhache (at Redwood Hwy) **707/433-4443** • gay-friendly • 1864 Victorian farmhouse located on 5 rolling acres • also vacation house • kids & pets by arrangement • $125

RESTAURANTS

Chateau Souverain 400 Souverain Rd, Geyserville **707/433-8281** • lunch daily, dinner Fri-Sun only • fine dining

Hemet

NIGHTCLUBS

Club Don't You Know 133 N Harvard St (at Florida) **909/658-5939** • 3pm-midnight, till 2am Fri-Sat • lesbians/ gay men • dancing/DJ • transgender-friendly • food served • karaoke • wheelchair access • gay-owned/ run

Hermosa Beach

EROTICA

Tender Box 809 Pacific Coast Hwy (7th) **310/318-2882** • videos

Huntington Beach

EROTICA

Paradise Specialties 7344 Center (at Gothard) **714/898-0400**

Idyllwild

ACCOMMODATIONS

The Rainbow Inn 909/659-0111 • gay/ straight • full brkfst • smokefree • patio • fireplaces • also conference ctr • gay-owned/ run • $90-120+ tax

Imperial Beach

EROTICA

Palm Avenue Books 1177 Palm Ave (Florida) **619/575-5081** • 24hrs

Joshua Tree Nat'l Park

ACCOMMODATIONS

Mojave Rock Ranch Lodge 64976 Starlight **760/366-8455** • gay/ straight • private 100-acre ranch • funky & unique • $275-325/ cabin

Klamath

ACCOMMODATIONS

Rhodes' End B&B 115 Trobitz Rd **707/482-1654** • gay-friendly • full brkfst • smokefree • $80-95

Laguna Beach

INFO LINES & SERVICES

AA Gay/ Lesbian 31872 Coast Hwy (at South Coast Medical Hospital) **949/499-7150** • call for mtg times

Laguna Outreach 949/497-4237 • educational/ social group for Orange County

ACCOMMODATIONS

By The Sea Inn 475 N Coast Hwy **949/497-6645, 800/297-0007** • gay-friendly • hot tub • swimming • kids ok • wheelchair access • $139-199

Casa Laguna B&B Inn 2510 S Coast Hwy **949/494-2996, 800/233-0449** • gay-friendly • inn & cottages overlooking the Pacific • swimming • kids/ pets ok • smokefree • $85-295

Holiday Inn Laguna Beach 696 S Coast Hwy **949/494-1001, 800/228-5691** • gay-friendly • swimming • kids ok • food served • wheelchair access • $99-279

Laguna Brisas Spa Hotel 1600 S Coast Hwy (at Bluebird) **949/497-7272, 877/503-1461** • gay-friendly • resort hotel • free brkfst • swimming • 2-person whirlpool spa in every room • wheelchair access • $99-259

BARS

Main St 1460 S Coast Hwy **949/494-0056** • 2pm-2am • mostly gay men • more lesbians on Wed-Th & Sat • piano bar

Woody's at the Beach 1305 S Coast Hwy (at Cress) **949/376-8809** • 4pm-2am, from noon Sun • mostly gay men • also restaurant • patio

California • USA

Nightclubs

Boom Boom Room 1401 S Coast Hwy (at the Coast Inn) **949/494-7588** • 10am-2am • popular • mostly gay men • dancing/DJ • live shows • videos • young crowd • wheelchair access

Cafes

Cafe Zinc 350 Ocean Ave (at Broadway) **949/494-6302** • 7am-4:30pm, till 5pm Sun • vegetarian • beer/wine • patio • also market • wheelchair access • $5-10

The Koffee Klatch 1440 S Coast Hwy (btwn Mountain & Pacific Coast Hwy) **949/376-6867** • 7am-11pm, till midnight Fri-Sat• brkfst, lunch & dinner • desserts

Restaurants

Cafe Zoolu 860 Glenneyre **949/494-6825** • dinner only • Californian • some veggie • wheelchair access • $10-20

The Cottage 308 N Coast Hwy (at Aster) **949/494-3023** • lunch & dinner • homestyle cooking • some veggie

Dizz's As Is 2794 S Coast Hwy **949/494-5250** • open 5:30pm, seating at 6pm, clsd Mon • cont'l • full bar • patio • $17-29

Drew's Caribbean Cafe 31732 Pacific Coast Hwy (at 3rd), South Laguna Beach **949/499-6311** • 5pm-9pm, till 10pm Fri-Sat, clsd Mon-Tue • beer/wine • gay-owned/run

Madison Square & Garden Restaurant 3320 N Coast Hwy **949/494-0137** • 8am-3am, from 7am wknds

Mark's Restaurant 858 S Coast Hwy (at Thalia) **949/494-6711** • dinner Mon-Sat • also full bar

Entertainment & Recreation

West Street Beach

Bookstores

Different Drummer Books 1294-C S Coast Hwy **949/497-6699** • 10am-8pm, till 9pm Sat • lgbt bookstore • wheelchair access • gay-owned/run

Retail Shops

GayMartUSA 168 Mountain Rd **949/497-9108** • 10am-midnight, till 1am Fri-Sat

▲ **Jewelry by Poncé** 1417 S Coast Hwy **949/497-4154, 800/969-RING** • 11am-7pm Wed-Sun, by appt Mon-Tue • lesbigay commitment rings & other jewelry • (see ad in mail order section)

Publications

Orange County/ Long Beach Blade **949/494-4898**

Spiritual Groups

Christ Chapel of Laguna 286 St Anne's Dr (at Glenneyre) **949/376-2099** • 10am Sun

Unitarian Universalist Fellowship 429 Cypress Dr (S of Myrtle) **949/497-4568, 714/645-8597** • 10:30am Sun

Erotica

Video Horizons 31678 Coast Hwy (at 3rd Ave) **949/499-4519** • 11am-9pm, till 10pm Fri-Sat, noon-9pm Sun

Lake Tahoe

see also Lake Tahoe, Nevada

Accommodations

Black Bear Inn **530/544-4411, 800/431-4411** • gay/straight • full brkfst • hot tub • fireplaces • smokefree • gay-owned/run • $175-450

Drake's 126 Tiger Tail Rd, Olympic Valley **530/581-3722** • lesbians/gay men • some shared baths • lesbian-owned/run • $50-150

▲ **Holly's Place** **530/544-7040, 800/745-7041** • women only • guesthouse • cabins • fireplaces • kitchens • hot tub • smokefree • kids/dogs ok • group facilities • lesbian-owned/run • $91-295

Ridgewood Inn 1341 Emerald Bay Rd **530/541-8589** • gay-friendly • hot tub • quiet wooded setting • $40-185

Sierrawood Guest House South Lake Tahoe **530/577-6073, 800/700-3802** • lesbians/gay men • cozy, romantic chalet • kids ok • hot tub • gay-owned/run • $90-150 (includes brkfst & dinner)

Silver Shadows Lodge 1251 Emerald Bay Rd, South Lake Tahoe **530/541-3575** • gay-friendly • motel • swimming • kids/pets ok • $35+

Spruce Grove Cabins & Suites **530/544-0549, 800/777-0914** • gay/straight • private cabins & cottages • nr Heavenly ski resort & lake • $150-225

Tahoe Bungalow 1031 Herbert Ave (at Hwy 50), South Lake Tahoe **530/544-8642, 888/321-5984** • lesbians/gay men • guest cabin • sleeps 4 • hot tub • kitchen • smokefree • pets ok • gay-owned/run • $85-159

Nightclubs

Faces 270 Kingsbury Grade, Stateline, NV **775/588-2333** • 5pm-2am, till 4am Fri-Sat • lesbians/gay men • dancing/DJ

Lake Tahoe • California

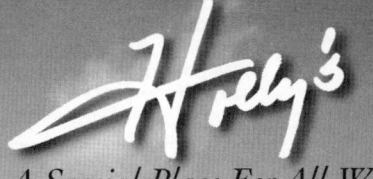

A Special Place For All Women

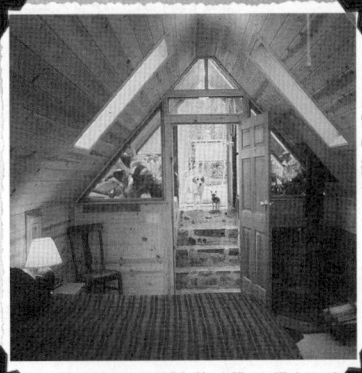

Private Cozy Cabins BBQ's Fireplaces

Year-Round Fun

Children Welcome

Dog Friendly!

More than 2 acres completely fenced

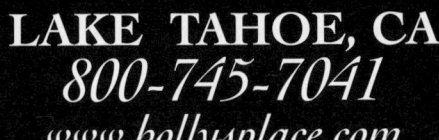

LAKE TAHOE, CA
800-745-7041
www.hollysplace.com

California • USA

Cafes

Syd's Bagelry 550 North Lake Blvd, Tahoe City **530/583-2666** • 6am-7pm daily • bagel sandwiches • plenty veggie

Restaurants

Driftwood Cafe 4119 Laurel Ave (at Poplar) **530/544-6545** • 7am-2pm • homecooking • some veggie • wheelchair access • $4-8

Passaretti's 1181 Emerald Bay Rd/ Hwy 50 **530/541-3433** • 9am-9:30pm • Italian • $10-15

Lancaster

Nightclubs

Back Door 1255 W Ave 'I' (at 13th St W) **661/945-2566** • 2pm-2am • lesbians/ gay men • dancing/DJ • karaoke

Spiritual Groups

Sunrise MCC of the High Desert 39149 8th St E (btwn P & Q at Unity Church) **661/265-6156** • 1pm Sun

Leucadia

Accommodations

Ocean Inn 1444 N Hwy 101 **760/436-1988, 800/546-1598** • gay-friendly • mission decor in quiet neighborhood setting • $79-139

Long Beach

Info Lines & Services

AA Gay/ Lesbian (Atlantic Alano Club) 441 E 1st St **562/432-7476** • hours vary

South Bay Lesbian/ Gay Community Organization 2009 Artesia Blvd #A, Redondo Beach **310/379-2850** • support/ education for Manhattan, Hermosa & Redondo Beaches, Torrance, Palos Verdes, El Segundo

The Gay & Lesbian Community Center of Greater Long Beach 2017 E 4th St (at Cherry) **562/434-4455** • 9am-10pm Mon-Fri, 9am-6pm Sat, 5pm-9pm Sun • also newsletter

---

[Reply] [Forward] [Delete]

Date: Fri, Dec 7, 2001 12:16:35
From: Girl-on-the-Go
To: Editor@Damron.com
Subject: Long Beach

> Though it's often overshadowed by its neighbor Los Angeles, Long Beach is a large harbor city with plenty of bars and shopping of its own...and, of course, lesbians.

> According to local rumor, Long Beach is second only to San Francisco in lesbian/gay population, at approximately 45,000— though many of these gay residents are 'married', making Long Beach a bedroom community of professional couples.

> The city itself is melded from overlapping suburbs and industrial areas. The cleaner air, mild weather, and reasonable traffic make it an obvious choice for those looking for a livable refuge away from LA. Of course the nightlife is milder as well, but nobody's complaining about the women's bar—**Club Broadway**, perfect for casual hanging out. Or the **Executive Suite**, whose dancefloor welcomes women seven nights a week. For other events, check with the **Lesbian/Gay Center**.

Long Beach • California

BARS

The Brit 1744 E Broadway (at Cherry) 562/432-9742 • 10am-2am • mostly gay men • neighborhood bar

The Broadway 1100 E Broadway (at Cerritos) 562/432-3646 • 10am-2am • lesbians/ gay men • neighborhood bar • karaoke • wheelchair access

Club 5211 5211 N Atlantic St (at 52nd) 562/428-5545 • noon-10pm, 11am-3am wknds • lesbians/ gay men • neighborhood bar • wheelchair access

Club Broadway 3348 E Broadway (at Redondo) 562/438-7700 • 11am-2am • mostly women • neighborhood bar • videos • wheelchair access • women-owned/ run

The Crest 5935 Cherry Ave (at South) 562/423-6650 • 2pm-2am • mostly gay men • leather

Fire Island 3325 E Anaheim St (at Redondo) 562/597-0014 • 3pm-2am, from noon wknds • mostly gay men • dancing/ DJ • patio • wheelchair access

Pistons 2020 E Artesia (at Cherry) 562/422-1928 • 6pm-2am, till 4am Fri-Sat, from 3pm Sun • mostly gay men • bears • leather • patio

Que Será 1923 E 7th St (at Cherry) 562/599-6170, 562/918-0529 • 5pm-2am, from noon Sun • gay/ straight • dancing/DJ • alternative • live music

Ripples 5101 E Ocean (at Granada) 562/433-0357 • noon-2am • popular • mostly gay men • dancing/DJ • multiracial clientele • food served • karaoke • videos • patio

Silver Fox 411 Redondo (at 4th) 562/439-6343 • 4pm-2am, from noon wknds • popular happy hour • mostly gay men • karaoke Wed & Sun • videos • wheelchair access

Long Beach

WHERE THE GIRLS ARE: Schmoozing with the boys on Broadway between Atlantic and Cherry Avenues, or elsewhere between Pacific Coast Hwy and the beach. Or at home snuggling.

LGBT PRIDE: 3rd wknd in May. 562/987-9191, web: www.longbeachpride.com.

ANNUAL EVENTS: April - AIDS Walk. September - Pride Picnic. November - The Gatsby Show at the Sheraton, benefitting the Center.

CITY INFO: 562/436-3645, web: www.golongbeach.org.

ATTRACTIONS: Belmont Shores area on 2nd St, south of Pacific Coast Highway — lots of restaurants & shopping, only blocks from the beach.
Long Beach Downtown Marketplace, 10am-4pm Fri.
The Queen Mary 562/435-3511.

BEST VIEW: On the deck of the Queen Mary, docked overlooking most of Long Beach. Or Signal Hill, off 405. Take the Cherry exit.

WEATHER: Quite temperate: highs in the mid-80°s July through September, and cooling down at night. In the winter, January to March, highs are in the upper 60°s, and lows in the upper 40°s.

TRANSIT: Long Beach Taxi Co-op 562/435-6111.
Long Beach Transit & Runabout (free downtown shuttle) 562/591-8753.

California • USA

Sweetwater Saloon 1201 E Broadway (at Orange) **562/432-7044** • 6am-2am • popular days • mostly gay men • neighborhood bar • wheelchair access

Nightclubs

Executive Suite 3428 E Pacific Coast Hwy (at Redondo) **562/597-3884** • 4pm-close, from 5pm wknds • popular • mostly women • dancing/DJ • Latin night Th • live music Fri

Pussycat Lounge **562/901-3040** • mostly women • dancing/ DJ • monthly dance party • call for location and times

Cafes

Cafe Haven 1708 E Broadway (at Gaviota) **562/437-3785** • 6am-midnight, till 1am Tue, till 3am Fri-Sat

Restaurants

Cha Cha Cha 762 8th (at Pacific Ave) **562/436-3900** • lunch & dinner • Caribbean • plenty veggie • wheelchair access

Egg Heaven 4358 E 4th St **562/433-9277** • 7am-2pm, till 3pm wknds • some veggie

Hamburger Mary's 740 E Broadway (at Alamitos) **562/983-7001** • 7am-2am • lesbians/ gay men • full menu • Sun champagne brunch

House of Madame JoJo 2941 E Broadway (btwn Temple & Redondo) **562/439-3672** • 5:30pm-10pm • popular • lesbians/ gay men • Mediterranean • some veggie • beer/ wine • wheelchair access • $12-20

Omelette Inn 108 W 3rd St (at Pine) **562/437-5625** • 7am-2:30pm

Original Park Pantry 2104 E Broadway (at Junipero) **562/434-0451** • lunch & dinner • lesbians/ gay men • int'l • some veggie • wheelchair access • $8-12

Porch Cafe 2708 E 4th St (at Ohio Ave) **562/433-0118** • 7am-2pm, till 3pm wknds • lesbians/ gay men • garden patio • lesbian-owned

Retail Shops

Hot Stuff 2121 E Broadway (at Cherry) **562/433-0692** • 11am-7pm, 10am-6pm wknds • cards • gifts • novelties

Toto's Revenge 2947 E Broadway Ave (at Orizaba) **562/434-2777, 877/688-8686** • 10am-9pm • unique cards & gifts • dog-friendly • also mail-order • gay-owned/ run

Publications

Center Post **562/983-1220**

Spiritual Groups

Christ Chapel 3935 E 10th St **562/438-5303** • 10am Sun, 7pm Wed • non-denominational • wheelchair access

First United Methodist Church 507 Pacific Ave (at 5th) **562/437-1289** • 10am Sun • wheelchair access

Lesbian & Gay Havurah 3801 E Willow St (at Jewish Comm Ctr) **562/426-7601 x31**

Trinity Lutheran Church 759 Linden Ave (btwn 7th & 8th) **562/437-4002** • 10:30am Sun, 7pm Wed • wheelchair access

Erotica

The Crypt on Broadway 1712 E Broadway (btwn Cherry & Falcon) **562/983-6560** • leather • toys

The Rubber Tree 5018 E 2nd St (at Granada) **562/434-0027** • 11am-9pm, till 10pm Fri-Sat, noon-7pm Sun • women-owned

LOS ANGELES

Los Angeles is divided into 7 geographical areas:
LA—Overview
LA—West Hollywood
LA—Hollywood
LA—West LA & Santa Monica
LA—Silverlake
LA—Midtown
LA—Valley

LA—Overview

Info Lines & Services

Alcoholics Together Center 1773 Griffith Park Blvd (at Hyperion) **323/663-8882, 323/936-4343 (AA#)** • 12-step groups

BWX (Black Women's Xchange) 160 S La Brea **310/419-1969** • 7pm Mon • social/ support group for African-American women who love women • wheelchair access

COOL (Coalition of Older Lesbians) at The Village', 1125 N McCadden Pl **323/913-3722** • social/ support group • rap 1pm 3rd Sun • wheelchair access

GLLU (Gay/ Lesbian Latinos Unidos) **213/243-9443** • social/ support group

La Casa 5301 E Beverly Blvd (at La Casa/ Bienestar Ctr) **323/727-7897** • social/ support group for lesbian/bi Latinas & Chicanas 21+

LAAPIS (Los Angeles Asian Pacific Islander Sisters) 323/969-4084 (REFERRALS ONLY) • referrals for LA-area API women

LA—Overview • California

Los Angeles Gay/ Lesbian Community Center 1625 N Shrader **323/993-7400** • 9am-9pm, 9am-1pm Sat, clsd Sun • wide variety of services

ONE Institute & Archives 909 W Adams Blvd (nr USC campus) **213/741-0094** • int'l lgbt archives/ research ctr • call for appt

South Bay Lesbian/ Gay Community Organization 2009 Artesia Blvd #A, Redondo Beach **310/379-2850** • support/ education for Manhattan, Hermosa & Redondo Beaches, Torrance, Palos Verdes, El Segundo

ULOAH (United Lesbians of African Heritage) 323/960-5051 • empowerment group 'for all lesbian descendants of the African Diaspora'

Los Angeles

WHERE THE GIRLS ARE: Hip dykes hang out in West Hollywood, with the boys along Santa Monica Blvd, or cruising funky Venice Beach and Santa Monica. The S&M ('Stand & Model') glamourdykes pose in chichi clubs and posh eateries in West LA and Beverly Hills. There's a scattered community of women in Silverlake. And more suburban lesbians frequent the gay bars in Studio City and North Hollywood. If you're used to makeup-free lesbians, you may be surprised that coiffed and lipsticked lesbian style is the norm in LA.

ENTERTAINMENT: Gay Men's Chorus 323/650-0756, web: www.gmcla.org.

LGBT PRIDE: June. 323/969-8302.

ANNUAL EVENTS: May/June - California AIDS Ride 323/874-7474 or 800/825-1000. AIDS benefit bike ride from San Francisco to LA.
July - Outfest 323/960-9200. LA's lgbt film & video festival.
August - Sunset Junction Fair 323/661-7771. Carnival, arts & information fair on Sunset Blvd in Silverlake benefits Sunset Junction Youth Center.
October - AIDS Walk-a-thon 213/201-9255.
Gay Night at Disneyland gayland@aol.com.

CITY INFO: 800/228-2452, web: www.lacvb.com.

ATTRACTIONS: 3rd St. outdoor mall in Santa Monica.
Chinatown, near downtown.
City Walk in Universal Studios.
Graveline Tours — tours of (in)famous deaths, violence & the supernatural 323/469-4149.
Mann's Chinese Theater on Hollywood Blvd 323/464-8111.
Melrose Ave.
Theme Parks: Disneyland, Knotts Berry Farm & Magic Mountain.
Watts Towers, not far from LAX 213/847-4646.
Westwood Village premiere movie theaters & restaurants.
Venice Beach.

BEST VIEW: Drive up Mulholland Drive, in the hills between Hollywood and the Valley, for a panoramic view of the city, and the Hollywood sign.

WEATHER: Summers are hot, dry, and smoggy, with temperatures in the 80°s-90°s. LA's weather is at its finest — sunny, blue skies and moderate temperatures (mid 70°s) — during the months of March, April and May.

TRANSIT: United Taxi 323/870-4664.LA Express 800/427-7483. Super Shuttle 310/782-6600.Metro Transit Authority 213/626-4455.

California • USA

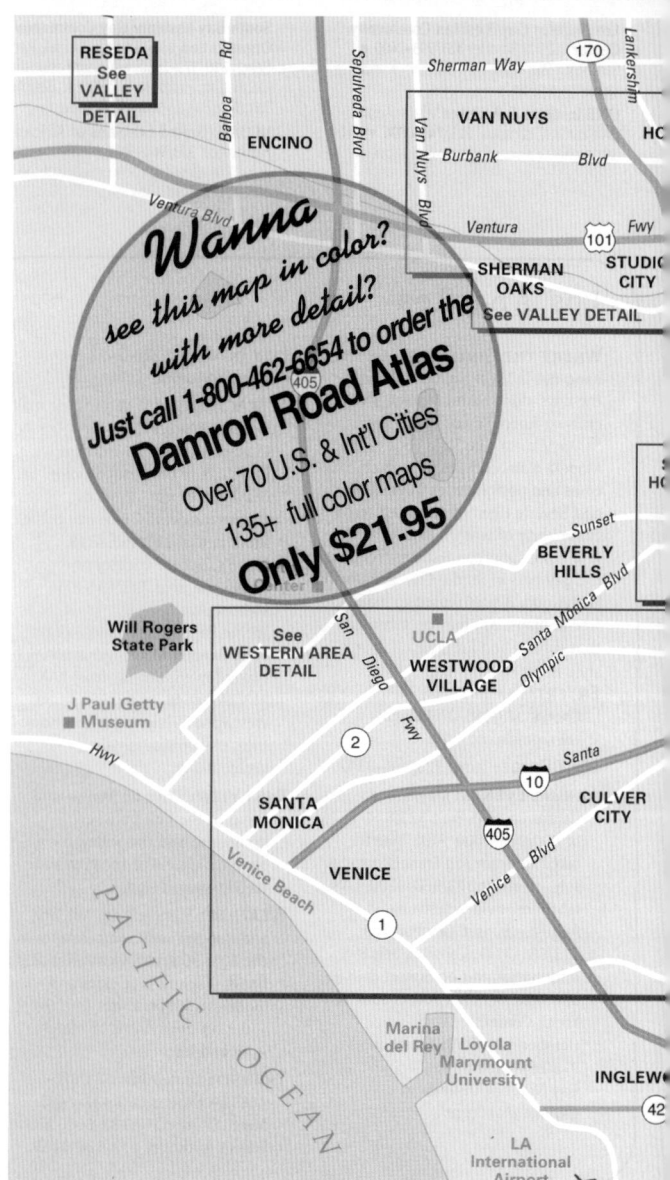

LA—Overview • California

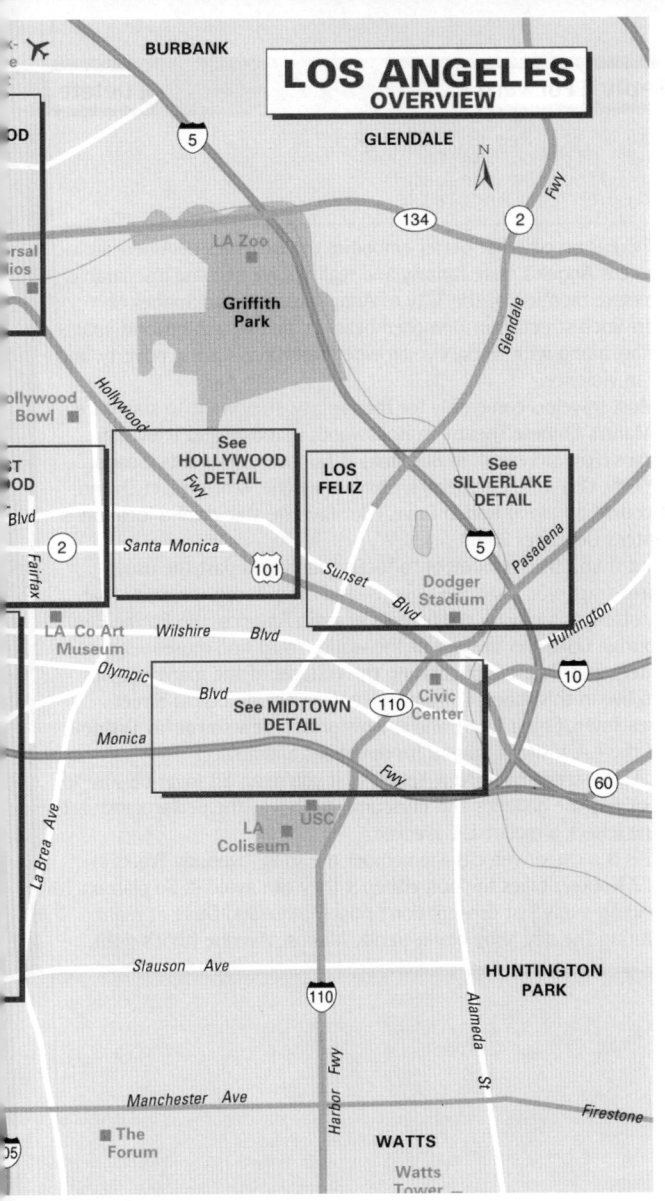

California • USA

Reply **Forward** **Delete**

Date: Sat, Dec 8, 2001 12:22:10
From: Girl-on-the-Go
To: Editor@Damron.com
Subject: Los Angeles

> There is no city that better embodies the extremes of American life than Los Angeles. Here fantasy and reality have become inseparable. The mere mention of the 'City of Angels' conjures up images of palm-lined streets, sun-drenched beaches, and wealth beyond imagination, along with smog, overcrowded freeways, searing poverty, and urban violence.

> Most travelers come only for the fantasy. They want to star-gaze at Mann's Chinese Theatre in Hollywood; at movie and television studios (Fox, Universal) in Burbank; at famous restaurants (Spago, The City, Chasen's, Citrus, Ivy's, Chaya Brasserie, Morton's, etc.); and, of course, all along Rodeo Drive. (Our favorite star-gazing location is Canter's Deli after 2am.)

> But if you take a moment to focus your sights past the usual tourist traps, you'll see the unique—and often tense—diversity that L.A. offers as a city on the borders of Latin America, the Pacific Rim, Suburbia USA, and the rest of the world. You'll find museums, centers, and theaters celebrating the cultures of the many peoples who live in this valley. Cultural epicenters include Olvera Street, Korea Town, China Town, and the historically Jewish Fairfax District. Call the L.A. Visitor's Bureau for directions and advice.

> LA's art scene rivals New York's, so if you're an art lover be sure to check out the galleries and museums, as well as the performance art scene (check a recent *L.A. Weekly*).

> This is a car-driven city—remember the song, "Nobody Walks in L.A."? Nobody takes the bus, either, if they can avoid it. So plan on spending a day just driving; don't miss Mulholland Drive at night.

> During the day, shop along trendy Melrose Avenue (that's right,

[**Reply**] [**Forward**]　　　　　　　　　　　　　　[**Delete**]

Avenue not Place). Or check out Los Feliz (pronounced anglo-style: *Lahss Feel-iss*), the funky neighborhood to cruise between Silverlake and Hollywood. Los Feliz is home to many hip restaurants & shops. For coffee and girls with British accents, stop by **Van Go's Ear** in Venice.

> As for lesbian nightlife in L.A., there are several full-time women's bars (some of them in the Valley), and many women's nights. L.A. is where the one-nighter women's dance bar revolution began, so make sure to double-check the papers before you go out (**Female FYI**, the more topical **Lesbian News, Next LA,** or **Odyssey**). On Fridays, don't miss **Girl Bar** at the Factory.

> For serious girl-watching, cruise by **Michele's XXX** at 7969 on Tuesdays. Any night of the week, you can visit that perennially popular lesbian night spot, **The Palms**.

California • USA

The Village (Gay/ Lesbian Center Extension) 1125 N McCadden Pl (at Santa Monica) **323/860-7302** • cafe • theaters • call for events & hours

Entertainment & Recreation

The Celebration Theatre 7051–B Santa Monica Blvd (at La Brea) **323/957-1884** • lgbt theater • call for more info

The Getty Center 1200 Getty Center Dr, Brentwood **310/440-7300** • clsd Mon • LA's shining city on a hill & world-class museum • of course, it's still in LA so you'll need to make reservations for parking (!)

Highways 1651 18th St, Santa Monica **310/315-1459 (RESERVATION LINE), 310/453-1755 (ADMIN LINE)** • 'full-service performance center'

IMRU Gay Radio KPFK LA 90.7 FM **818/985-2711** • 7pm Mon

▲ **Outfest** **323/960-9200** • lgbt media arts foundation that sponsors the annual lgbt film festival each July (see Film Festival Calendar in back Events section)

Sunwolf Farms **661/245-9653** • private ranch w/ customized day trips • lesbian-owned/ run

Publications

Community Yellow Pages **323/848-3033** • annual survial guide to lgbt southern CA

Female FYI **323/655-1266** • monthly coverage of LA & southern CA lesbian club scene

▲ **GBF (Gay Black Female)** **323/376-2157** • nat'l newsmagazine w/ some listings for LA

▲ **Lesbian News (LN)** **310/787-8658, 800/458-9888** • nat'l w/ strong coverage of southern CA • see ad front color section

Nightlife **323/462-5400** • club listings

Odyssey Magazine **323/874-8788** • all the dish on LA's club scene

The Women's Yellow Pages **818/995-6646**

Spiritual Groups

Beth Chayim Chadashim (BCC) 6000 W Pico Blvd (at Crescent Hts) **323/931-7023** • 8pm Fri

Christ Chapel of the Valley 11050 Hartsook St (S of Magnolia), North Hollywood **818/985-8977** • 10am Sun • full gospel fellowship

Congregation Kol Ami 7350 Sunset Blvd (at Martel) **310/248-6320** • 8pm Fri

Dignity LA 126 S Ave 64 **323/344-8064** • 5:30pm Sun • Spanish Mass 3rd Sat

Holy Trinity Community Church 4209 Santa Monica Blvd (at Delmar) **323/662-9118** • 10am Sun

MCC in the Valley 5730 Cahuenga Blvd (2 blks N of Burbank Blvd), North Hollywood **818/762-1133** • 10:30am Sun

MCC LA 8714 Santa Monica Blvd (at Westbourne) **310/854-9110** • 9am, 10:45am, 1pm (en español) & 6pm gospel service Sun • wheelchair access

St Andrew's Episcopal Church 1432 Engracia Ave (at Cabrillo), Torrance **310/328-3781** • 8am & 10am Sun

Unity Fellowship Church 5148 W Jefferson Blvd **323/938-8322, 323/936-4948** • 11:30am Sun • mostly African-American congregation • wheelchair access

West Hollywood Presbyterian Church 7350 Sunset Blvd (at Martel) **323/874-6646** • 11am Sun • wheelchair access

LA—West Hollywood

Accommodations

The Grafton on Sunset 8462 W Sunset Blvd (at La Cienega) **323/654-4600, 800/821-3660** • gay-friendly • swimming • sundeck • panoramic views • located in heart of Sunset Strip • wheelchair access • $250-375

The Grove Guesthouse 1325 N Orange Grove Ave (at Sunset) **323/876-8887, 888/524-7683** • lesbians/ gay men • 1-bdrm villa • hot tub • swimming • kitchens • pets ok by arrangement • gay-owned/ run • $179+

Holloway Motel 8465 Santa Monica Blvd (at La Cienega), West Hollywood **323/654-2454, 888/654-6400** • gay/ straight • kitchens • centrally located • $80-90

Hyatt West Hollywood 8401 Sunset Blvd (at Kings Rd) **323/656-1234, 800/233-1234** • gay-friendly • on the Sunset Strip • swimming • $150-250

Just Right Reservations, Inc **978/934-9931** • covers hotels & B&Bs • also Palm Springs & Boston, MA

▲ **Le Montrose Suite Hotel** 900 Hammond St (at Sunset) **310/855-1115, 800/776-0666** • popular • gay-friendly • hot tub • swimming • kitchens • fireplaces • smokefree • kids/ pets ok • gym • also full restaurant • rooftop patio • wheelchair access • $195-560

Le Rêve Hotel 8822 Cynthia St (at Larrabee), West Hollywood **310/854-1114, 800/835-7997** • gay-friendly • all-suite hotel • hot tub • swimming • kids ok • wheelchair access • $139-265

GBF MEDIA

www.gayblackfemale.com

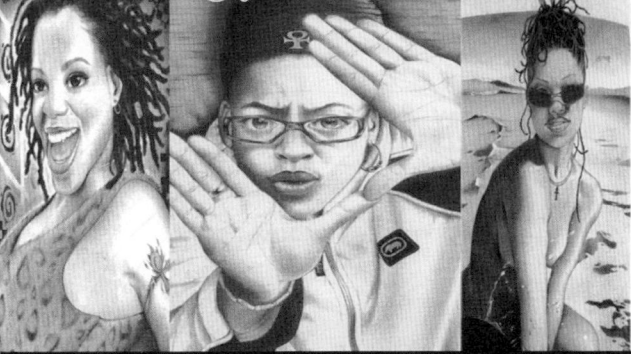

Also available is the GBF Compilation of short films. GBF short stories brought to life!
Never Say Never, Train Station, Gay Black Female, Rashida X, If She Only Knew, & O.P.P.
All six for $24.95 includes shipping. *Use info below to purchase*

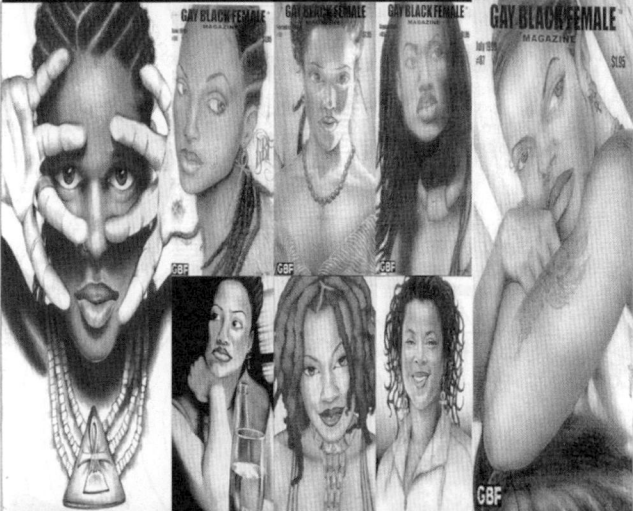

Subscriptions $15 for 10 issues w/t-shirt $25
Make checks payable to: GBF PO BOX 57087
Los Angeles, CA 90057
phone/fax (877) 850-1017

since 1990

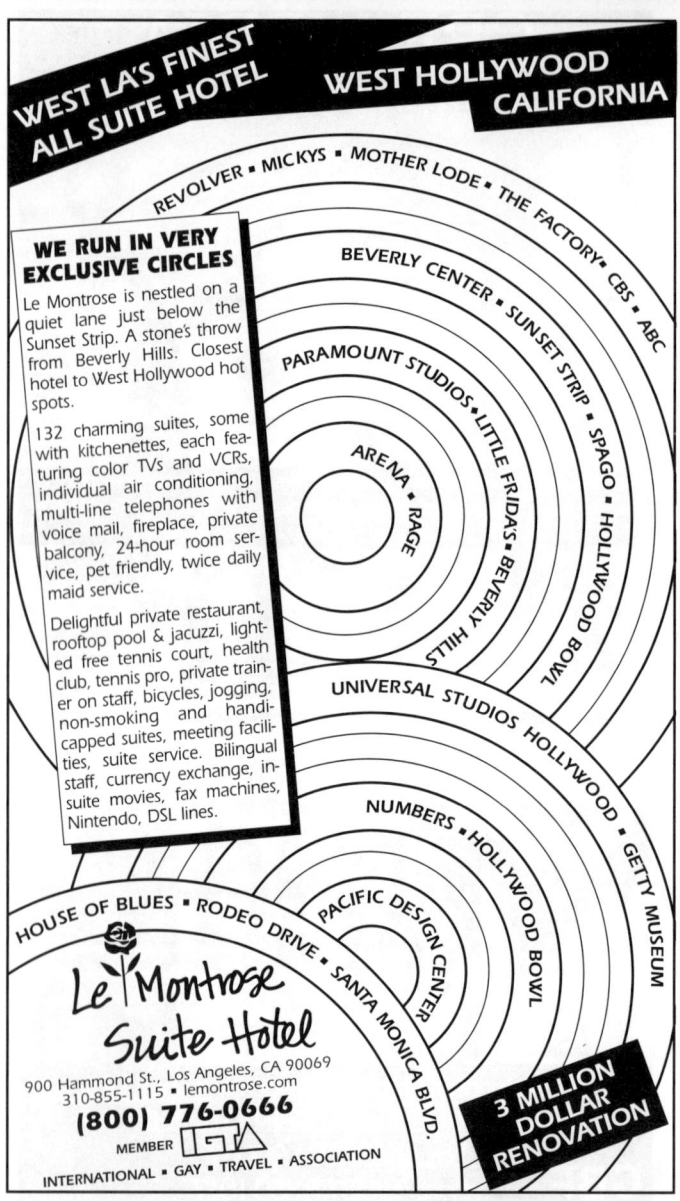

LA—West Hollywood • California

Ramada West Hollywood 8585 Santa Monica Blvd (at La Cienega) 310/652-6400, 800/845-8585 • gay-friendly • modern art deco hotel & suites • swimming • kids ok • wheelchair access • $105-275

San Vicente Inn Resort 845 N San Vicente Blvd (at Santa Monica), West Hollywood 310/854-6915 • mostly gay men • swimming • hot tub • nudity • gay-owned/ run • $59-199

Summerfield Suites by Wyndham 1000 Westmount Dr (nr Holloway), West Hollywood 310/657-7400, 800/833-4353 • gay/ straight • swimming • $259-319

West Hollywood Suites 310/652-9600 • mostly gay men • full service hotel • hot tub • swimming • kids/ pets ok • wheelchair access • gay-owned/ run • $140-249

BARS

7702 SM Club 7702 Santa Monica Blvd (at Spaulding) 323/654-3336 • noon-2am • lesbians/ gay men • neighborhood bar • dancing/DJ

Comedy Store 8433 Sunset Blvd (at La Cienega) 323/650-6268 • 8pm-2am • gay-friendly • stand-up club

Improvisation 8162 Melrose Ave (at Crescent Heights) 323/651-2583 • gay-friendly • stand-up comedy • also restaurant

The Normandie Room 8737 Santa Monica Blvd (at Westbourne) 310/659-6204 • 5pm-2am • gay/ straight • neighborhood bar • wheelchair access

The Palms 8572 Santa Monica Blvd (at La Cienega) 310/652-6188 • 4pm-2am, from 2pm wknds • popular • mostly women • multiracial • neighborhood bar • dancing/DJ • theme nights • bbq Sun • karaoke • patio • wheelchair access

Rage 8911 Santa Monica Blvd (at San Vicente) 310/652-7055, 877/648-RAGE • 11am-2am • popular • mostly gay men • dancing/DJ • live shows • videos • young crowd • lunch & dinner daily • wheelchair access

Revolver 8851 Santa Monica Blvd (at San Vicente) 310/659-8851 • 4pm-2am, from 2pm wknds • popular • mostly gay men • alternative • videos

Tempest 7323 Santa Monica Blvd (E of Fuller Ave) 323/850-5115 • 8:30pm-close • popular • gay/ straight • dancing/DJ • live shows • theme nights • also restaurant (dinner only) • French/Italian • some veggie • patio

Tiki Bar at Tahiti 7910 W 3rd St (W of Fairfax) 323/651-1213 • 5pm-close • more gay Wed • also restaurant

Viper Room 8852 Sunset Blvd (btwn San Vicente & Larabie) 310/358-1880 • 9pm-2am • gay-friendly • dancing/DJ • live shows • cover charge

NIGHTCLUBS

7969 7969 Santa Monica Blvd (at Fairfax) 323/654-0280 • 9pm-2am • gay/ straight • dancing/DJ • transgender-friendly • also 'Michelle's XXX Review' 9pm Tue • strip show/ dance club for women

The Factory 652 N La Peer Dr (at Santa Monica) 310/659-4551 • 9pm-2am Wed-Sun • mostly gay men • women's night Fri for 'Girl Bar' • dancing/DJ • live shows • videos • young crowd

▲ **Girl Bar** 652 N La Peer (at Santa Monica, at The Factory) 877/447-5252 • popular • 9pm-3am Fri only • women only • dancing/DJ • call hotline for events

CAFES

Eat-Well 8252 Santa Monica Blvd (at La Jolla) 323/656-1383 • 7am-3pm & 5:30pm-10pm, 8am-3pm wknds • popular

Mani's Bakery 519 S Fairfax Ave (at Maryland Dr) 323/938-8800 • 6:30am-midnight • coffee & dessert bar • wheelchair access

Stonewall Gourmet Coffee Company 8717 Santa Monica Blvd (nr La Cienega) 818/769-4517 • 7am-midnight, till 1am Fri-Sat, from 8am Sun • popular • lesbians/ gay men • live entertainment • wheelchair access • also location at 12135 Victory Blvd in North Hollywood (818) 506-4736

WeHo Lounge 8861 Santa Monica Blvd (at San Vicente) 310/659-6180 • 2pm-2am • desserts & light lunch fare

Who's On Third Cafe 8369 W 3rd St (at Orlando) 323/651-2928 • 7:30am-3pm wkdays, from 8am wknds

RESTAURANTS

The Abbey 692 N Robertson (at Santa Monica) 310/289-8410 • 7am-3am • lesbians/ gay men • popular • American/ cont'l • full bar • patio • wheelchair access

African Restaurant Row Fairfax btwn Olympic & Pico • many Ethiopian, Nigerian & other African restaurants to choose from on this block

Alto Palato 755 N La Cienega Blvd (at Waring) 310/657-9271 • 5pm-10:30pm • bargain pasta & comfortable chairs • full bar • $12-17

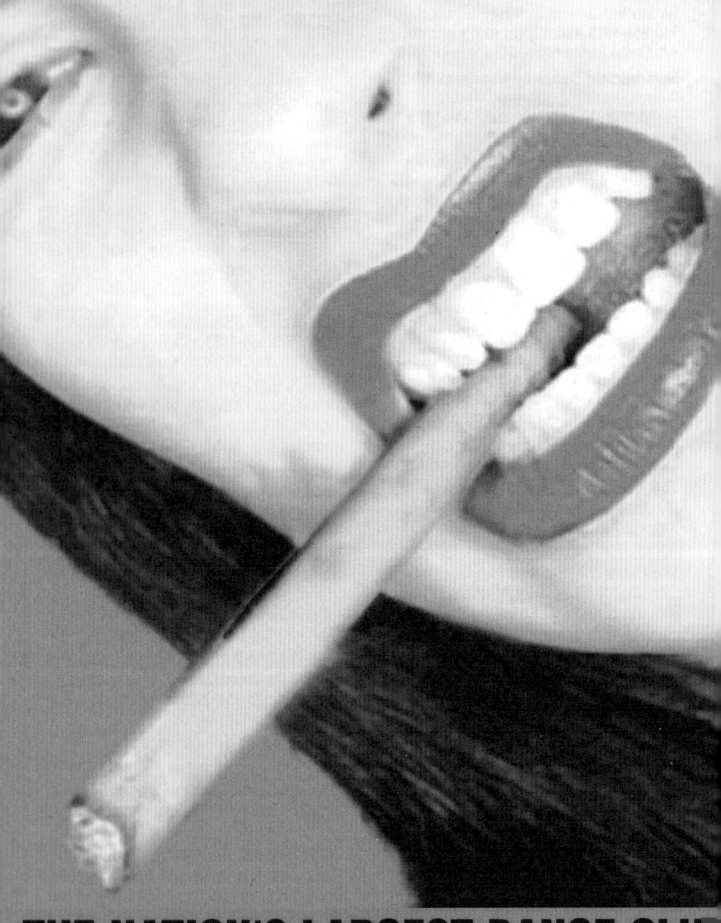

LA—West Hollywood • California

Baja Bud's 8575 Santa Monica Blvd (at La Cienega) **310/659–1911** • 7am-10pm, till 11pm Fri-Sat • healthy Mexican • patio • wheelchair access

Benvenuto Cafe 8512 Santa Monica Blvd (at La Cienega) **310/659-8635** • lunch Tue-Fri, dinner nightly • Italian • full bar • wheelchair access

Bossa Nova 685 N Robertson Blvd (at Santa Monica) **310/657-5070** • 11am-11pm • Brazilian • beer/ wine • patio • wheelchair access

Caffe Luna 7463 Melrose Ave (btwn Vista & Gardner) **323/655-9177** • 10:30am-midnight, till 4am wknds • popular after-hours • country Italian • some veggie • wheelchair access

Canter's Deli 419 N Fairfax (btwn Melrose & Beverly) **323/651-2030** • 24hrs • hip after-hours • Jewish/ American • some veggie • wheelchair access

The Cobalt Cantina 616 N Robertson Blvd (at Melrose) **310/659-8691** • noon-11pm, 10am-10pm Sun, bar open till 2am wknds • lesbians/ gay men • Cal-Mex • some veggie • patio • wheelchair access

Il Pastaio 400 N Cannon Dr (at Brighton Wy), Beverly Hills **310/205-5444** • lunch & dinner • homemade pasta & great colorful risotto • $8-12

Il Piccolino Trattoria 350 N Robertson Blvd (btwn Melrose & Beverly) **310/659-2220** • lunch & dinner, clsd Sun • full bar • patio • wheelchair access

Itana Bahia 8711 Santa Monica Blvd (at Westbourne) **310/657-6306** • lunch & dinner Tue-Sat • reservations required for dinner • great Brazilian food • full bar • live music Wed-Fri • wheelchair access

Koo Koo Roo 8520 Santa Monica Blvd (at La Cienega Blvd) **310/657-3300** • 11am-11pm • lots of healthy chicken dishes • plenty veggie • beer/ wine • wheelchair access

L'Orangerie 903 N La Cienega Blvd (btwn Melrose & Santa Monica) **310/652-9770** • dinner only, clsd Mon • haute French • patio • $28-38

Louise's Trattoria 7505 Melrose Ave (at Gardner) **323/651-3880** • 11am-11pm, till midnight Fri-Sat • Italian • great foccacia bread • beer/ wine

Lucques 8474 Melrose Ave (at La Cienega) **323/655-6277** • lunch & dinner, clsd Mon • French • full bar • patio • wheelchair access

Luna Park 665 N Robertson (btwn Melrose & Santa Monica) **310/652-0611** • dinner, clsd Mon • progressive American • some veggie • 3 bars • cabaret • patio • wheelchair access • $10-15

Marco's Trattoria 8136 Santa Monica (at Crescent Hts) **323/650-2771** • 11am-10pm, from 3pm Sun • wheelchair access

Marix Tex Mex 1108 N Flores (btwn La Cienega & Fairfax) **323/656-8800** • 11:30am-11pm• lesbians/ gay men • some veggie • great margaritas • wheelchair access • $10-15

Mark's Restaurant 861 N La Cienega Blvd (at Santa Monica) **310/652-5252** • 6pm-10pm, till 11:30pm Fri-Sat, Sun brunch • full bar

North 8029 W Sunset (at Laurel Canyon, enter rear) **323/654-1313** • 6pm-2am, from 8pm Mon • popular • full bar • 70s ski lodge decor

Real Food Daily 414 N La Cienega (btwn Beverly & Melrose) **310/289-9910** • 11:30am-11pm • organic vegetarian • beer/ wine • wheelchair access • $8-12

Sante Libre 345 N La Brea (btwn Melrose & Beverly) **323/857-0412** • 10am-10pm • pastas, salads & wraps • plenty veggie & vegan • cheap • also 13016 San Vicente (at 26th) in Venice, 310/451-1813

Sapori Cucina 8945 Santa Monica Blvd (at Robertson) **310/275-9518** • Italian • some veggie • wheelchair access

Skewers 8939 Santa Monica Blvd (at Robertson) **310/271-0555** • 11am-10pm • Middle Eastern • grill, salads, dips • beer/ wine • under $10

Tacos Tacos 8948 Santa Monica Blvd (at N Robertson) **310/657-4832** • 11am-11pm, till 1am wknds • yummy • fresh • inexpensive Mexican • plenty veggie • wheelchair access

Tango Grill 8807 Santa Monica Blvd (at San Vicente) **310/659-3663** • 11:30am-11:30pm • lesbians/ gay men • Argentinian • some veggie • beer/ wine • wheelchair access • $6-12

Tommy Tang's 7313 Melrose Ave (at Poinsettia) **323/937-5733** • noon-10pm, till 11pm wknds • popular drag night Tue • beer/ wine

Trocadero 8280 Sunset Blvd (at Sweetzer) **323/656-7161** • 6pm-2am, clsd Sun-Mon • pastas & salads • full bar • patio • wheelchair access

California • USA

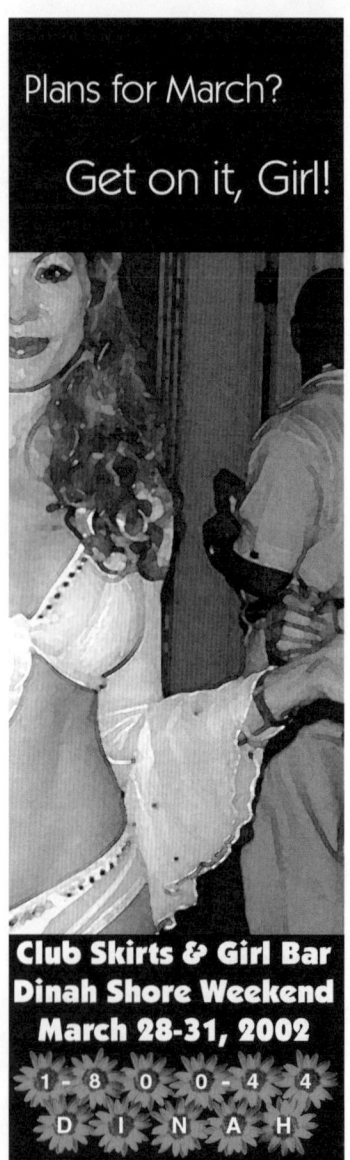

Yukon Mining Co 7328 Santa Monica Blvd (at Fuller) **323/851-8833** • 24hrs • popular • champagne brunch wknds • beer/wine • wheelchair access

Entertainment & Recreation

Stonewall Dollar Bingo 8717 Santa Monica Blvd (nr La Cienega) **818/769-4517** • 8pm Th • celebrity guest stars

Bookstores

A Different Light 8853 Santa Monica Blvd (btwn San Vicente & Larrabee) **310/854-6601** • 10am-10pm, till 11pm Fri-Sat • popular • lgbt

Book Soup 8818 W Sunset Blvd (at Larrabee) **310/659-3110** • 9am-midnight • lgbt section

Retail Shops

Dorothy's Surrender 7985 Santa Monica Blvd #111 (at Laurel) **323/650-4111** • 10am-11:30pm • cards • magazines • gifts

GayMartUSA 8214 Santa Monica Blvd (at N LaJolla Ave) **323/656-7732** • 10am-10pm • clothes & gifts

Raving Rainbow 8515 Santa Monica Blvd **310/358-1935** • 11am-7:30pm, clsd Sun • pride gear

Syren 7225 Beverly Blvd **323/936-6693, 800/667-9736** • clsd Sun-Mon • leather & latex

Gyms & Health Clubs

Easton's Gym 8053 Beverly Blvd (at Crescent Hts) **323/651-3636** • gay-friendly

Erotica

Circus of Books 8230 Santa Monica Blvd (at La Jolla) **323/656-6533**

Drake's 8932 Santa Monica Blvd (at San Vicente) **310/289-8932** • also 7566 Melrose Ave, 323/651-5600

Hustler Hollywood 8920 Sunset Blvd (at San Vicente) **310/860-9009** • chic erotic department store • also cafe

Pleasure Chest 7733 Santa Monica Blvd (at Genesee) **323/650-1022** • 10am-midnight, till 1am Fri-Sat

Unicorn Bookstore 8940 Santa Monica (at Robertson) **310/652-6253** • 10am-2:30am • wheelchair access

LA—Hollywood

ACCOMMODATIONS

Holiday Inn Hollywood 2005 N Highland (at Franklin) 323/850-5811 • gay-friendly • also restaurant & lounge • swimming • exercise room • wheelchair access • $109-149

Hollywood Celebrity Hotel 1775 Orchid Ave (btwn Hollywood & Franklin) 323/850-6464, 800/222-7017 • gay-friendly • 1930s art deco hotel • kids/pets ok • non-smoking rooms available • $59-115

Hollywood Metropolitan Hotel 5825 Sunset Blvd (btwn Bronson & Van Ness) 323/962-5800, 800/962-5800 • gay-friendly • kids ok • also restaurant • $79-145

Ramada Hotel Hollywood 1160 N Vermont Ave (at Santa Monica) 323/660-1788, 800/272-6232 • gay-friendly • swimming • wheelchair access • $79-139

BARS

Blacklite 1159 N Western (at Santa Monica) 323/469-0211 • 6am-2am • lesbians/ gay men • neighborhood bar • transgender-friendly

Faultline 4216 Melrose Ave (at Normandie) 323/660-0889 • 4pm-2am, 2pm-4am Fri-Sat, clsd Mon • popular • mostly gay men • dancing/DJ • occasional women's events • leather • videos • patio

Spit 4216 Melrose Ave (at 'Faultline') 323/969-2530 • 9pm-3am 3rd Sat • popular • mostly gay men • dancing/DJ • leather • alternative

NIGHTCLUBS

Beige at 360° Restaurant & Lounge 6290 Sunset Blvd (at Vine) 323/871-2995 • Tue only • lesbians/ gay men • popular • dancing/ DJ • food served

Tempo 5520 Santa Monica Blvd (at Western) 323/466-1094 • 9pm-2pm, till 3am Th-Sat, from 2pm Sun • mostly gay men • dancing/DJ • mostly Latino/a • live shows

RESTAURANTS

360° Restaurant & Lounge 6290 Sunset Blvd (at Vine) 323/871-2995 • dinner • more gay Tue • popular • modern day supper club • dancing/ DJ • amazing views • live jazz wknds • wheelchair access • gay-owned/ run

Hollywood Canteen 1006 N Seward St (at Santa Monica) 323/465-0961 • 11:30am-midnight, till 1am Fri-Sat, dinner only Sat, clsd Sun • popular • classic • full bar

La Poubelle 5907 Franklin Ave (at Bronson) 323/465-0807 • noon-2am, from 6pm Mon • French/ Italian • some veggie • wheelchair access • $20-25

Lucy's Cafe El Adobe 5536 Melrose Ave (nr Gower St) 323/462-9421 • lunch & dinner, clsd Sun • Mexican • live shows • patio • $10-15

Musso & Frank Grill 6667 Hollywood Blvd (nr Las Palmas) 323/467-7788 • 11am-11pm, clsd Sun-Mon • the grand-dame diner/ steakhouse of Hollywood • great pancakes, potpie & martinis!

Off Vine 6263 Leland Wy (at Vine) 323/962-1900 • lunch & dinner, Sun brunch • beer/wine

Prado 244 N Larchmont Blvd (at Beverly) 323/467-3871 • lunch & dinner, dinner only Sun • Caribbean • some veggie • wheelchair access • $20-30

Quality 8030 W 3rd St (at Laurel) 323/658-5959 • 8am-3pm • homestyle brkfst • some veggie • wheelchair access • $8-12

Rosco's House of Chicken & Waffles 1514 N Gower (at Sunset) 323/466-7453 • 8:30am-midnight

RETAIL SHOPS

Archaic Idiot/ Mondo Video-A-Go-Go 1718 N Vermont (at Hollywood) 323/953-8896 • noon-10pm • vintage clothes • cult & lgbt videos

Videoactive 2522 Hyperion Ave (at Griffith Park Blvd) 323/669-8544 • 10am-11pm, till midnight wknds • lgbt section • adult videos • wheelchair access

GYMS & HEALTH CLUBS

Gold's Gym 1016 N Cole Ave (nr Santa Monica & Vine) 323/462-7012 • gay-friendly

EROTICA

Le Sex Shoppe 6315–1/2 Hollywood Blvd (at Vine) 323/464-9435

LA—West LA & Santa Monica

ACCOMMODATIONS

The Georgian Hotel 1415 Ocean Ave (btwn Santa Monica & Broadway), Santa Monica 310/395-9945, 800/538-8147 • gay-friendly • food served • wheelchair access • $210-475

The Inn at Venice Beach 327 Washington Blvd (at Via Dolce), Marina Del Rey 310/821-2557, 800/828-0688 • gay-friendly • 43-room European-style inn • kids ok • wheelchair access • $99-155

California • USA

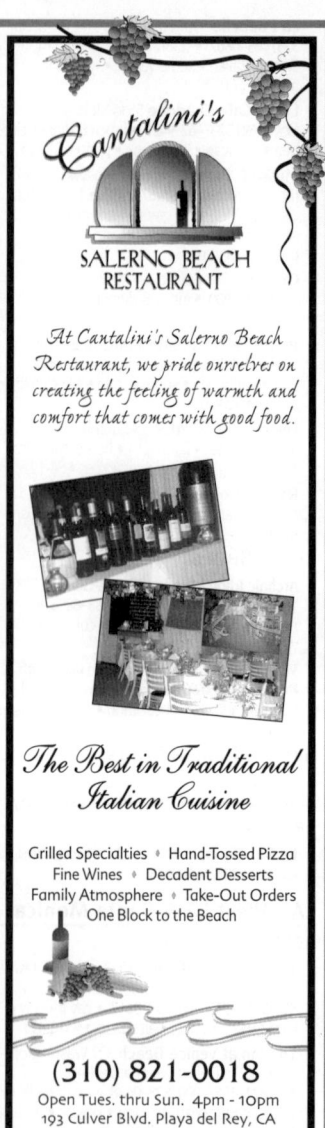

W Hotel Los Angeles 930 Hilgard Ave (at Le Conte) **310/208-8765, 800/421-2317** • gay-friendly • suites • also restaurant • gym • day spa • swimming • $219-379

Bars

Annex 835 S La Brea (at Arbor Vitae), Inglewood **310/671-7323** • 2pm-2am • mostly gay men • ladies night Sun • neighborhood bar • dancing/DJ • African-American clientele • karaoke • wheelchair access

Cafe Club Fais Do-do 5257 W Adams Blvd (btwn Fairfax & LaBrea) **323/954-8080** • 8pm Th only • mostly women for 'Milk' • rock 'n' roll dykes • dancing/DJ • also restaurant

Dolphin 1995 Artesia Blvd (at Aviation Blvd), Redondo Beach **310/318-3339** • noon-2am • lesbians/gay men • neighborhood bar • karaoke • patio • wheelchair access

Maverick's 2692 S La Cienega (at Washington Blvd) **310/837-7443** • 11am-2am • mostly gay men • neighborhood bar • food served • karaoke • live shows • wheelchair access

Cafes

Anastasia's Asylum 1028 Wilshire Blvd (at 11th St), Santa Monica **310/394-7113** • 8am-1am • plenty veggie • live music evenings

Van Go's Ear 796 Main St (at Brooks), Venice **310/396-1987** • 24hrs • plenty veggie • cheap

Restaurants

12 Washington 12 Washington Blvd (at Pacific), Venice **310/822-5566** • dinner from 6pm • cont'l • $10-30

Baja Cantina 311 Washington Blvd (at Sanborn), Venice **310/821-2252** • lunch & dinner Mon-Fri, also brunch wknds

Border Grill 1445 Fourth St, Santa Monica **310/451-1655** • lunch & dinner

▲ **Cantalini's Salerno Beach Restaurant** 193 Culver Blvd (at Vista del Mar), Playa del Rey **310/821-0018** • 4pm-10:30pm, clsd Mon • Italian • beer/wine • live music • lesbian-owned/run

Cheesecake Factory 4142 Via Marina (at Washington), Venice **310/306-3344** • 11:30am-11:30pm, 11am-midnight Fri-Sat, 10am-11pm Sun • full menu • $5-20

Drago 2628 Wilshire Blvd (btwn 26th & Princeton), Santa Monica **310/828-1585** • lunch Mon-Fri, dinner nightly • Sicilian Italian • wheelchair access

Golden Bull 170 W Channel Rd (at Pacific Coast Hwy), Santa Monica **310/230-0402** • dinner only, Sun brunch (summers) • American • full bar

LA—Midtown • California

Joe's 1023 Abbot Kinney Blvd, Venice **310/399-5811** • lunch Tue-Fri, dinner Th-Sun, clsd Mon • French/ Californian

The Local Yolk 3414 Highlands Ave (at Rosecranz), Manhattan Beach **310/546-4407** • 6:30am-2:30pm

Real Food Daily 514 Santa Monica Blvd (btwn 5th & 6th) **310/451-7544** • 11:30am-10pm • organic vegetarian • beer/ wine • wheelchair access • $8-12

Wolfgang Puck Cafe 1323 Montana Ave (at 14th St), Santa Monica **310/393-0290** • lunch & dinner, colorful entrees à la Puck (fast-food versions) • $10-13

SPIRITUAL GROUPS

MCC in the South Bay 2600 Nelson Ave (Felton), Redondo Beach **310/535-7100** • 6pm Sun

EROTICA

The Love Boutique 2924 Wilshire Blvd (W of Bundy), Santa Monica **310/453-3459** • toys • books

LA—Silverlake

ACCOMMODATIONS

Sanborn GuestHouse 1005 1/2 Sanborn Ave (nr Sunset) **323/666-3947, 800/663-7262** • gay/ straight • private unit w/ kitchen • gay-owned/ run • $49-59

NIGHTCLUBS

Dragstrip 66 2500 Riverside Dr (at 'Rudolpho's') **323/969-2596** • 9pm-4am 2nd Sat • popular • trashy pansexual rock 'n' roll club • dancing/DJ • live shows • cover charge

Rudolpho's 2500 Riverside Dr (at Fletcher) **323/669-1226** • 8pm-2am • lesbians/ gay men • more gay Sat • theme nights • salsa music & dancing lessons • patio

CAFES

The Coffee Table 2930 Rowena Ave **323/644-8111** • 7am-11pm, till midnight wknds • patio • fab mosaic magic

RESTAURANTS

Casita Del Campo 1920 Hyperion Ave **323/662-4255** • 11am-10pm, till 11:30pm Fri-Sat • popular • Mexican • patio • also The Plush Life' cabaret Sat • call 323/969-2596 for details

Cha Cha Cha 656 N Virgil (at Melrose) **323/664-7723** • 8am-10pm, till 11pm Fri-Sat • lesbians/ gay men • Caribbean • plenty veggie • wheelchair access

The Cobalt Cantina 4326 Sunset Blvd (at Fountain) **323/953-9991** • lunch & dinner • popular • lesbians/ gay men • Cal-Mex • some veggie • full bar • patio • wheelchair access • $10-15

The Crest Restaurant 3725 Sunset Blvd (at Lucille) **323/660-3645** • 6am-10pm • diner/ Greek • $5-10

Da Giannino 2630 Hyperion Ave (at Griffith Park Blvd) **323/664-7979** • dinner Tue-Sun, clsd Mon • beer/ wine • patio

El Conquistador 3701 W Sunset Blvd (at Lucille) **323/666-5136** • dinner from 4pm, lunch & dinner wknds • Mexican • beer/ wine • patio • $5-10

Lunch to Latenite Kitchen 4348 Fountain Ave (at Sunset Blvd) **323/664-3663** • noon-1am, 10am-3am Fri-Sat • neighborhood eatery • from veggie entrees to chicken & dumplings • gay-owned/ run

Vida 1930 Hillhurst Ave (at Franklin, in Los Feliz) **323/660-4446** • hip with Asian accent • $12-17

Zen Restaurant 2609 Hyperion Ave (at Griffith Park) **323/665-2929, 323/665-2930** • open late • Japanese • some veggie • full bar • karaoke Wed-Sat • $9-12

GYMS & HEALTH CLUBS

Body Builders 2516 Hyperion Ave (at Griffith Park Blvd) **323/668-0802** • gay-friendly

EROTICA

Circus of Books 4001 Sunset Blvd (at Sanborn) **323/666-1304** • 24hrs Fri-Sat

LA—Midtown

BARS

The Redhead Bar (Redz) 2218 E 1st St (btwn Soto & Chicago, Boyle Hts) **323/263-2995** • 2pm-midnight, till 2am wknds • mostly women • neighborhood bar • mostly Latina

Score 107 W 4th St (at Main) **213/625-7382** • 2pm-2am Mon-Th, from 11:30am Fri-Sun • 'Sweatbox' Fri • lesbians/ gay men • neighborhood bar • dancing/DJ • mostly Latina/o • live shows

NIGHTCLUBS

Jewel's Catch One Disco 4067 W Pico Blvd (at Crenshaw) **323/734-8849** • noon-2am, till 5am Fri-Sat, clsd Mon-Tue • popular • lesbians/ gay men • dancing/DJ • alternative • mostly African-American • women dancers Th & Sat • karaoke • wheelchair access

California • USA

Restaurants

Atlas 3760 Wilshire Blvd (at Western) **213/380-8400** • 11am-2am, clsd Sun • global cuisine • plenty veggie • full bar • dancing/DJ • live shows • wheelchair access • $8-19

Cassell's 3266 W 6th St (at Vermont) **213/480-8668** • 10:30am-4pm, clsd Sun • great burgers

Du-Par's 6333 W 3rd St (at the Farmer's Market) **323/933-8446** • 6am-10pm • plush diner schmoozing

LA—Valley

includes San Fernando & San Gabriel Valleys

Bars

Apache Territory 11608 Ventura Blvd (at Laurel Canyon), Studio City **818/506-0404** • 3pm-2am, from noon wknds • popular • mostly gay men • dancing/DJ • karaoke • wheelchair access

Bananas 7026 Reseda Blvd (at Hart), Reseda **818/996-2976** • 3pm-2am • popular • mostly gay men • Latin Wed • neighborhood bar • dancing/DJ • karaoke • live shows • patio • wheelchair access

Escapades 10437 Burbank Blvd (at Cahuenga), North Hollywood **818/508-7008** • 1pm-2am • popular • lesbians/gay men • neighborhood bar • dancing/DJ • karaoke • live shows • wheelchair access

Gold 9 13625 Moorpark St (at Woodman), Sherman Oaks **818/986-0285** • 11am-2am • mostly gay men • neighborhood bar • karaoke • wheelchair access

Oasis 11916 Ventura Blvd (btwn Laurel Canyon & Colfax), Studio City **818/980-4811** • 2pm-2am • lesbians/gay men • neighborhood bar • piano bar • patio

Oxwood Inn 13713 Oxnard (at Woodman), Van Nuys **818/997-9666 (PAY PHONE)** • 3pm-2am, from 2pm wknds • mostly women • neighborhood bar • dancing/DJ • karaoke • one of the oldest lesbian bars in the country • women-owned/run

Rawhide & Shooterz 10937 Burbank Blvd (nr Vineland), North Hollywood **818/760-9798** • 1pm-1am, till 2am Fri-Sat, 2pm-2am Sun • popular • mostly gay men • dancing/DJ • country/western • Latin music wknds • karaoke • live shows • wheelchair access

Rumours 10622 Magnolia Blvd (at Cahuenga), North Hollywood **818/506-9651** • 6pm-2am, from 3pm Fri • mostly women • neighborhood bar • dancing/DJ • karaoke • women-owned/run

Silver Rail 11518 Burbank Blvd (btwn Colfax & Lankershim) **818/980-8310** • 4pm-2am, from noon wknds • lesbians/gay men • neighborhood bar

Sugar Shack 4101 Arden Dr (at Valley Blvd), El Monte **626/448-6579** • 5pm-close, clsd Mon • lesbians/gay men • neighborhood bar • DJ Fri-Sat • wheelchair access

Nightclubs

La Victoria 19655 Sherman Way (at Corbin Ave), Reseda **818/998-8464** • 9pm-2am • gay/straight • more gay Wed-Th • dancing/DJ • mostly Latino/a clientele • dinner served 7:30pm-11pm • live shows

Queen Mary 12449 Ventura Blvd (at Whitsett), Studio City **818/506-5619** • 7pm-2am, from 5pm Fri-Sun, clsd Mon • popular • gay-friendly • dancing/DJ • karaoke • shows wknds

Cafes

Coffee Junction 19221 Ventura Blvd, Tarzana **818/342-3405** • 7am-7pm, till 11pm Fri-Sat, 9am-5pm Sun • live music Th-Sat • women-owned/run

Restaurants

Du-Par's 12036 Ventura Blvd (Laurel Canon), Studio City **818/766-4437** • 6am-1am, till 4am Fri-Sat • plush diner schmoozing • also 75 W Thousand Oaks Blvd, Thousand Oaks, 805/373-8785 • 6am-10:30pm, till 11:30pm wknds

Venture Inn 11938 Ventura Blvd (at Laurel Canyon), Studio City **818/769-5400** • lunch & dinner, champagne brunch wknds • popular • lesbians/gay men • full bar • wheelchair access • $10-15

Gyms & Health Clubs

Gold's Gym 6233 N Laurel Canyon Blvd (at Oxnard), North Hollywood **818/506-4600**

Erotica

Le Sex Shoppe 12323 Ventura Blvd (at Laurel Canyon), Studio City **818/760-9352** • 24hrs

Le Sex Shoppe 21625 Sherman Wy (at Nelson), Canoga Park **818/992-9801**

Le Sex Shoppe 4539 Van Nuys Blvd (at Ventura), Sherman Oaks **818/501-9609** • 24hrs

Le Sex Shoppe 4877 Lankershim Blvd (at Houston), North Hollywood **818/760-9529** • 24hrs

Stan's Video 7505 Foothill Blvd (at Fernglen Blvd), Tujunga **818/352-8735**

Manhattan Beach

see also LA—West LA & Santa Monica

ACCOMMODATIONS

▲ **Sea View Inn at the Beach** 3400 Highland Ave **310/545-1504** • gay-friendly • ocean views • pool • courtyard • $95-225

Marin County

includes Corte Madera, Mill Valley, San Rafael, Sausalito, Tiburon

INFO LINES & SERVICES

Spectrum Center for LGBT Concerns 1000 Sir Francis Drake Blvd Ste 10, San Anselmo **415/457–1115** • referrals noon-9pm Mon-Th • social/ support groups • wheelchair access

ACCOMMODATIONS

▲ **Acqua Hotel** 555 Redwood Hwy, Mill Valley **415/380–0400, 888/662–9555** • gay-friendly • smokefree • kids ok • wheelchair access • $150-175

Design Hotels 323 Pine St #B, Sausalito **415/332–4885, 800/337–4685** • reservation service

Marin Suites Hotel 45 Tamal Vista Blvd (at Lucky Dr), Corte Madera **415/924–3608** • gay-friendly • all-suite hotel w/ full kitchens • $99-199

Tiburon Lodge 1651 Tiburon Blvd, Tiburon **415/435–3133, 800/762–7770** • gay-friendly • hotel • swimming • $159-339

Waters Edge 25 Main St, Tiburon **415/789–5999, 877/789–5999** • gay/ straight • smokefree • wheelchair access • $195-350

RETAIL SHOPS

Cowgirl Creamery 80 4th St, Pt Reyes Station **415/663–9335** • 10am-6pm Wed-Sun • handmade cheeses • picnic lunches to go • women-owned/ run

PUBLICATIONS

The Slant 415/492–1500 • monthly lgbt newspaper

SPIRITUAL GROUPS

Faith Community Church 1473 S Novato Blvd (at United Methodist Church), Novato **415/491–9695** • 5pm Sat

Unitarian Universalist Congregation of Marin 240 Channing Wy, San Rafael **415/ 479–4131** • Sun 9:30am & 11am • childcare

RELAX.

(OR NOT)

Swim in our Pool.

Run on the Beach.

Surf.

Ride our free Bikes.

Walk to the Pier.

Shop.

Play Volleyball.

Rollerblade.

Sea View Inn
at the beach

3400 Highland Avenue
Manhattan Beach, CA 90266
310.545.1504 310.545.4052 fax
www.seaview-inn.com

California • USA

Marina del Rey

ACCOMMODATIONS

The Inn at Venice Beach 327 Washington Blvd, Venice **310/821-2557, 800/828-0688** • gay-friendly • 43-room European-style inn • kids ok • wheelchair access • $89-145

Mendocino

ACCOMMODATIONS

Agate Cove Inn 11201 N Lansing **707/937-0551, 800/527-3111** • gay-friendly • full brkfst • fireplaces • smokefree • $99-250

Bellflower Box 867 95460 **707/937-0783** • lesbians only • secluded cabin w/ kitchen • nr outdoor recreation • hot tub • fireplaces • smokefree • kids/ pets ok • lesbian-owned/ run • $65

Blair House & Cottage 45110 Little Lake St (at Ford St) **707/937-1800, 1-800/699-9269** • gay-friendly • smokefree • pets ok in 'Blair Cottage' at $10/ day • $80-210

Glendeven Inn 8205 N Hwy 1, Little River **707/937-0083** • gay-friendly • charming farmhouse on the coast • full brkfst • smokefree • wheelchair access • $100-240

Inn at Schoolhouse Creek 7051 N Hwy 1, Little River **707/937-5525, 800/731-5525** • gay/ straight • B&B w/ cottages • full brkfst • hot tub • smokefree • $95-225

MacCallum House Inn 45020 Albion St (at Lansing) **707/937-0289, 800/609-0492** • gay/ straight • smokefree • wheelchair access • kids ok • restaurant with full bar • $100-190

McElroy's Inn 998 Main St **707/937-1734, 888/262-3576 (CA ONLY)** • gay-friendly • located in the village • smokefree • kids ok • $70-115

Mendocino Coastal Reservations **800/262-7801, 707/937-5033** • 9am-6pm • gay-friendly • call for available rentals

Mendocino Hotel & Garden Suites 45080 Main St **800/548-0513** • gay-friendly • Victorian w/ garden cottages • $85-275

Sallie & Eileen's Place 44594 Albion St **707/937-2028** • women only • cabins • hot tub • kitchens • fireplaces • kids/ pets ok • 2-night minimum stay • $73-90 • $15/ additional person

Seagull Inn 44594 Albion St **707/937-5204** • gay-friendly • 9 units in the heart of historic Mendocino • smokefree • kids ok • wheelchair access • woman-owned/ run • $45-155

Stanford Inn by the Sea—A Country Inn Coast Hwy 1 & Comptche-Ukiah Rd **707/937-5615, 800/331-8884** • gay-friendly • full brkfst • hot tub • swimming • organic vegetarian restaurant • smokefree • kids/ pets ok • wheelchair access • $215-275

Wildflower Ridge **925/735-2079** • women only • secluded cabin in Medocino • kids ok (no male children over 8) • pets ok ($5/ night for dogs) • lesbian-owned/ run • $55

RESTAURANTS

Cafe Beaujolais 961 Ukiah **707/937-5614** • dinner from 5:45pm, reservations required • California country food • some veggie • garden • wheelchair access • $20-30

Menlo Park

see Palo Alto

Mill Valley

see Marin County

Modesto

see also Stockton

BARS

Brave Bull 701 S 9th **209/529-6712** • 7pm-2am, from 4pm Sun • lesbians/ gay men • dancing • levi/ leather

CAFES

Espresso Caffe 3025 McHenry Ave (at Rumble) **209/571-3337** • 8am-9pm, till 11pm Fri, 10am-11pm Sat, 4pm-10pm Sun • $4-7

EROTICA

Liberty Adult Book Store 1030 Kansas Ave **209/524-7603**

Monterey

INFO LINES & SERVICES

AA Gay/ Lesbian **831/373-3713 (AA#)** • call for times & locations

ACCOMMODATIONS

Gosby House Inn 643 Lighthouse Ave (at 18th), Pacific Grove **831/375-1287, 800/527-8828** • gay-friendly • full brkfst • smokefree • kids ok • wheelchair access • $90-170

Monterey Fireside Lodge 1131 10th St **831/373-4172, 800/722-2624** • gay-friendly • hot tub • fireplaces • non-smoking rooms available • kids ok • $79-350

Oxnard • California

Bars

Eddie's 2200 N Fremont (at De La Vina) **831/375-6116** • gay-friendly • neighborhood bar • dancing/DJ • bbq

Lighthouse Bar & Grill 281 Lighthouse Ave (at Dickman), New Monterey **831/373-4488** • 11:30am-2am, from 5pm Mon-Tue • lesbians/gay men

Nightclubs

Franco's/ Norma Jean 10639 Merritt, Castroville **831/633-2090** • 8pm Fri only • mostly gay men • dancing/DJ • Latino/a clientele • also 'Franco's' restaurant next door • 11am-9pm Fri-Sun

Restaurants

Cafe Abrego 565 Abrego St **831/375-3750** • lunch & dinner, lunch only Mon, Sun brunch • fine dining • some veggie • patio • full bar • wheelchair access • $10-22

Fisherman's Grotto 39 Fisherman's Wharf #1 **831/375-4604** • 11am-9pm • $20-40

Tarpy's Roadhouse 2999 Hwy 68 (at Canyon Dr) **831/647-1444** • lunch & dinner

Mountain View

Accommodations

Hotel Avante 860 El Camino Real **650/940-1000, 800/538-1600** • gay/ straight • swimming • jacuzzi

Bars

Daybreak 1711 W El Camino Real (at El Monte) **650/940-9778** • 5pm-2am • lesbians/gay men • dancing/DJ • karaoke Th & Sun • wheelchair access

Napa Valley

Accommodations

Beazley House B&B Inn 1910 First St, Napa **707/257-1649, 800/559-1649** • gay-friendly • full brkfst • smokefree • wheelchair access • $125-275

Bed & Breakfast Inns of Napa Valley Napa **707/944-4444** • gay-friendly • reservation service

La Belle Epoque B&B Inns 1386 Calistoga Ave, Napa **707/257-2161, 800/238-8070** • in Napa's historic Old Town • nr outdoor recreation • garden • in-room fireplaces • full gourmet breakfast • $160-295

Chateau de Vie 3250 Hwy 128, Calistoga **707/942-6446** • gay/ straight • full brkfst • gay-owned/ run • $169-249

The Ink House B&B 1575 St Helena Hwy, St Helena **707/963-3890** • gay-friendly • 1884 Italianate Victorian among the vineyards • full brkfst • smokefree • kids ok • $105-210 + tax

Tara Guest House 707/967-9347 • lesbians/gay men • 1-bdrm cabin • kitchen • wood stove • lesbian-owned/ run • $200

White Sulphur Springs Resort & Spa 3100 White Sulphur Springs Rd, St Helena **707/963-8588, 800/593-8873 (IN CA & NV ONLY)** • gay-friendly • secluded Napa Valley retreat • swimming • natural sulphur pool • $85-185

Restaurants

Travigne 1050 Charter Oak Ave (Hwy 29), St Helena **707/963-4444** • 11:30am-10pm • Northern Italian • $15

Nevada City

Cafes

Java John's 306 Broad St **530/265-3653** • 6:30am-5pm

Nice

Accommodations

Gingerbread Cottages B&B 4057 E Hwy 20 **707/274-0200** • gay/ straight • lakefront w/ private beach • antiques & art • swimming • $195-195

Oceanside

Bars

Greystokes 1903 S Coast Hwy (btwn Kelly & Vista Wy) **760/757-2955** • 9am-2am • lesbians/ gay men • live shows • also restaurant

Ted's Capri Lounge 207 N Tremont (at Mission) **760/722-7284** • 6pm-10pm Mon, 2pm-2am Wed-Fri, from 10am wknds, clsd Tue • mostly gay men • neighborhood bar • wheelchair access

Orange County

see Anaheim, Costa Mesa, Garden Grove, Huntington Beach, Laguna Beach, Newport Beach

Oxnard

Erotica

Oxnard Books 2320 N Vineyard (at St Mary's Dr) **805/981-4611**

Bee Charmer Inn

A Private Hotel for Women
In the Quiet Paradise of Palm Springs

- Pool and Private Courtyard
- Outdoor Misting System
- Air Conditioning
- Expanded Continental Breakfast

For Reservations or Brochure Call:
760.778.5883 or Toll Free 888.321.5699

1600 East Palm Canyon Dr. • Palm Springs, CA 92264
BeeCharmPS@aol.com   www.beecharmer.com

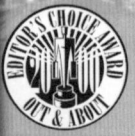

OUT & ABOUT Editor's Choice Award for 1999 & 2000, recognizing "outstanding achievement" in gay travel.

IGLTA

Palm Springs • California

Palm Springs

INFO LINES & SERVICES

AA Gay/ Lesbian 760/324-4880 **(AA#)** • call for mtg schedule

Gay Associated Youth 35-325 Date Palm Dr, Cathedral City **760/202-7510** • drop-in ctr for sexual minority youth & allies • mtgs 7pm Fri • dinner and a movie Sat

ACCOMMODATIONS

Ballantine's 1420 N Indian Canyon Dr (at Vista Chino) **760/320-1178** • gay-friendly • '50s chic • swimming • kids ok • $129-149

▲ **Bee Charmer Inn** 1600 E Palm Canyon Dr (btwn Calle Marcus & Sunrise) **760/778-5883, 888/321-5699** • women only • swimming • smokefree • lesbian-owned/ run • $105-130

▲ **Casitas Laquita** 450 E Palm Canyon Dr (nr Camino Real) **760/416-9999, 877/203-3410** • women-only resort • swimming • smokefree • pets welcome • wheelchair access • gay-owned/ run • $115-300

Desert Palms Inn 67–580 E Palm Canyon Dr (at Gene Autry Tr), Cathedral City **760/324-3000, 800/801-8696** • mostly gay men • hot tub • swimming • courtyard • also restaurant • some veggie • full bar • wheelchair access • gay-owned/ run • $69-109

Escape 2 Palm Springs Condo Rentals **760/323-4848** • gay/ straight • swimming • kids/ pets ok • $500/ week

Estrella Inn & Villas 415 S Belardo Rd (at Ramon) **760/320-4117, 800/237-3687** • gay-friendly • swimming • jacuzzi • kids/ dogs ok • $135-385

Palm Springs

WHERE THE GIRLS ARE: Vacationers will be staying on E Palm Canyon near Sunrise Way. Women do hang out at the boys' bars too. Try the bar at The Desert Palms Inn, or just about anywhere on Perez Rd.

LGBT PRIDE: November.

ANNUAL EVENTS: Spring - Nabisco Dinah Shore Golf Tournament 760/324-4546 & 888/443-4624, one of the biggest gatherings of lesbians on the continent. December - Out on Film 760/778-4100, lgbt film & cultural festival.

CITY INFO: Palm Springs Visitors Bureau 760/778-8418, web: www.palm-springs.org. Desert Gay Tourism Guild 888/200-4469.

ATTRACTIONS: Palm Springs Aerial Tramway to the top of Mt San Jacinto, on Tramway Rd.

BEST VIEW: Top of Mt San Jacinto. Driving through the surrounding desert, you can see great views of the mountains. Be careful in the summer-always carry water in your vehicle, and be sure to check all fluids in your car before you leave and frequently during your trip.

WEATHER: Palm Springs is sunny and warm in the winter, with temperatures in the 70°s. Summers are scorching (100°+).

TRANSIT: Airport Taxi 760/321-4470.
Rainbow Cab 760/325-2868.
Desert Valley Shuttle 760/329-3334 or 800/413-3999.
Sun Line Transit Agency 760/343-3451.

California • USA

Reply **Forward** **Delete**

```
Date: Wed, Dec 5, 2001 12:26:42
From: Girl-on-the-Go
To: Editor@Damron.com
Subject: Palm Springs
```

> Each and every spring, since 1972, the LPGA has converged upon the city of Palm Springs to present the premier event of its tournament schedule. Many women plan their vacations around the **Nabisco Golf Championship** (previously known as Dinah Shore!) and calendars are blocked out as soon as the tournament dates for the following year are released. Visitors pour into the valley to admire the beauty of springtime and to engage in the myriad events that occur between March and May.

> But did you know Palm Springs is open for business during the other nine months of the year as well? This has been a well-kept secret, but we are willing to divulge this information to expose the different faces and personalities of a truly year-round resort destination for women.

> Year-round businesses that welcome women are abundant. All you have to do is stroll along Arenas Road to find food, merchandise, and entertainment. Friendly faces welcome you at the door of **Ground Zero** and **Oscar's,** and you can pick up sex supplies and pride items at **GayMart**.

> There is plenty of outdoor entertainment, as well. Take a day trip to the spectacular Joshua Tree National Park, or for a little danger and an amazing view, catch a ride on the Aerial Tram that goes from the desert floor to the top of Mount San Jacinto. When you come back to earth, it's time to lay back and treat yourself to some sun and outdoor fun.

> Of course, you are going to need a place to rest, rejuvenate, and recharge for the next day's activities. Three women-only establishments — the **Bee Charmer Inn, Casitas Laquita**, and the **Queen of Hearts Resort** — provide travelers with comfortable and friendly accommodations. As you bask in the sun, soak up the warm desert air, and drift into a peaceful state of tranquillity, you'll ask yourself why you didn't visit paradise sooner.

Palm Springs • California

Ingleside Inn 200 W Ramon Rd (at Palm Canyon Dr) **760/325-0046, 800/772-6655** • gay-friendly • jacuzzi • swimming • smokefree • also restaurant • con't'l • wheelchair access • $95-395

Just Right Reservations, Inc 978/934-9931 • covers hotels & B&Bs • also W Hollywood & Boston, MA

Mountain View Villa 305/294-1525 (FL#) • vacation rental • jacuzzi • swimming • kids ok • smokefree • $129-169

The Pine Cove Inn 23481 Hwy 243, Idyllwild **909/659-5033, 888/659-5033** • gay/straight • full brkfst • smokefree • gay-owned/run • $80-110

Pink Coyote Resort 370 W Arenas Rd **760/318-0519, 877/845-5200** • mostly gay men • 180° view of mtns • swimming • spa

Queen of Hearts Resort 435 E Avenida Olancha **760/322-5793, 888/275-9903** • women only • swimming • full kitchens • lesbian-owned/run • $95-125

Villa Mykonos 67-590 Jones Rd (at Cree), Cathedral City **760/321-2898, 800/471-4753** • lesbians/gay men • swimming • $180-245

The Villa Palm Springs 67-670 Carey Rd (at Cree), Cathedral City **760/328-7211, 800/845-5265** • popular • gay/straight • bungalows • swimming • 2 restaurants & bars • $79-225

Viola's Resort 1200 S Palm Canyon Dr **760/318-8400, 800/843-6908** • 'for gays & lesbians, their families & their friends' • hotel w/ B&B feel • swimming • smokefree • gay-owned/run • $140-165

BARS

Ground Zero 36-737 Cathedral Canyon Dr (at Commercial), Cathedral City **760/321-0031** • 2pm-2am • lesbians/gay men • dancing/DJ • country/western Sat • karaoke

Hunter's 302 E Arenas Rd (at Calle Encilia) **760/323-0700** • 10am-2am • popular • mostly gay men • dancing/DJ • video bar

Oscar's 440 El Cielo Rd (off Ramon) **760/325-7072** • 11am-midnight (grill till 10pm) • lesbians/gay men • neighborhood bar

Sweetwater Saloon 2420 N Palm Canyon (at Racquet Club Dr) **760/320-8878** • 11am-2am • lesbians/gay men • neighborhood bar • food served

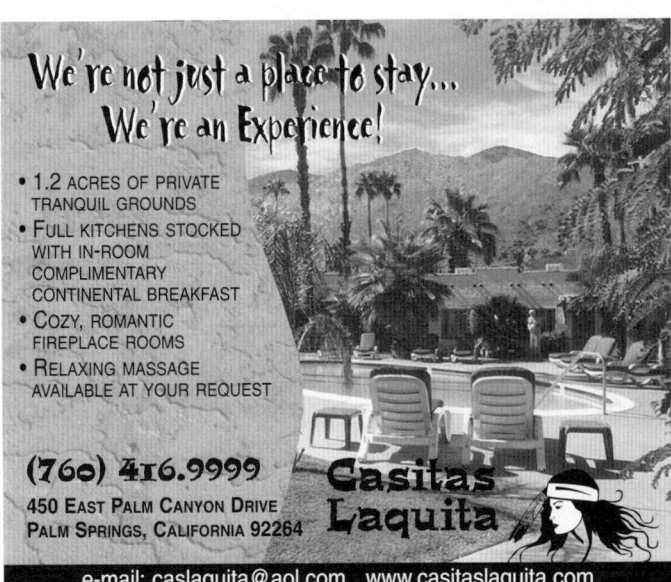

We're not just a place to stay... We're an Experience!

- 1.2 ACRES OF PRIVATE TRANQUIL GROUNDS
- FULL KITCHENS STOCKED WITH IN-ROOM COMPLIMENTARY CONTINENTAL BREAKFAST
- COZY, ROMANTIC FIREPLACE ROOMS
- RELAXING MASSAGE AVAILABLE AT YOUR REQUEST

(760) 416.9999
450 EAST PALM CANYON DRIVE
PALM SPRINGS, CALIFORNIA 92264

Casitas Laquita

e-mail: caslaquita@aol.com   www.casitaslaquita.com

California • USA

RESTAURANTS

Billy Reed's 1800 N Palm Canyon Rd (at Vista Chino) **760/325-1946** • some veggie • full bar • also bakery • $7-13

Coffee Dot Com 241 Tahquitz Canyon Wy **760/322-5280** • 7am-9pm • popular • also Internet access • full bar

El Gallito Mexican Restaurant 68820 Grove St (at Palm Canyon), Cathedral City **760/328-7794** • beer/ wine • $3-8

Las Casuelas 368 N Palm Canyon Dr (btwn Amado & Alejo) **760/325-3213** • 10am-11pm • Mexican • some veggie

Le Peep 2665 E Palm Canyon Dr **760/416-1444** • brkfst & lunch only

The Left Bank 150 E Vista Chino (at Indian Canyon) **760/320-6116** • dinner only • French • full bar • $12-20

Maria's Italian Cuisine 67-778 Hwy 111 (at Perez), Cathedral City **760/328-4378** • 5:30pm-9:30pm, clsd Mon • plenty veggie • beer/ wine • $8-15

Muriel's Supper Club 210 S Palm Canyon Dr **760/325-8839** • clsd Mon-Tue • super swanky ($$$) & fun

Rainbow Cactus Cafe 212 S Indian Canyon (at Arenas) **760/325-3868** • lunch & dinner, Sun brunch only • Mexican • also piano bar

Red Tomato 68-784 E Palm Canyon (btwn Date Palm & Cathedral Canyon), Cathedral City **760/328-7518** • 5pm-10pm • Italian • beer/ wine • wheelchair access • $10-15

Shame on the Moon 69-950 Frank Sinatra Dr (at Hwy 111), Rancho Mirage **760/324-5515** • 6pm-10:30pm • cont'l • plenty veggie • full bar • patio • wheelchair access • $14-21

Simba's 190 N Sunrise **760/778-7630** • lunch & dinner, clsd Mon-Tue • ribs

SweetHeat Palm Springs 448 S Indian Canyon Dr (at Ramon) **760/323-5691** • dinner only, clsd Mon • beer/ wine • gay-owned/ run

Tomboyz Cafe 214 E Arenas Rd (at Indian) **760/322-9915** • 7am-11pm

Triangles 68-805 Hwy 111, Cathedral City **760/321-9555** • 5pm-10pm, till midnight Fri-Sat

The Wilde Goose 67-938 Hwy 111 (at Perez), Cathedral City **760/328-5775** • 5pm-close • cont'l/ wild game • plenty veggie • full bar • live shows • $20-40

ENTERTAINMENT & RECREATION

Ruddy's 1930s General Store Museum 221 S Palm Canyon Dr **760/327-2156** • 10am-4pm Th-Sun • 'the most you can spend is 50c'

RETAIL SHOPS

Blink 319 E Arenas Rd (at Indian Canyon) **760/323-1667** • noon-10pm • books • queer gifts & clothing

GayMartUSA 305 E Arenas Rd (at Indian Canyon) **760/416-6436**

PUBLICATIONS

The Bottom Line **760/323-0552** • lgbt bar guide & classifieds

Desert Daily Guide **760/320-3237** • lgbt weekly

Gay/ Lesbian Times **760/320-5676** • lgbt newsmagazine

SPIRITUAL GROUPS

Unity Church of Palm Springs 815 S Camino Real (at Riverside S) **760/325-7377** • 11am Sun, 7:30pm Tue • also bookstore & classes

GYMS & HEALTH CLUBS

Gold's Gym 40-70 Airport Center Dr (at Ramon) **760/322-4653** • gay-friendly

EROTICA

Black Moon Leather 531 Industrial Pl **760/322-5924** • noon-9pm, till 2am Fri-Sat, clsd Mon-Tue

Palo Alto

INFO LINES & SERVICES

Peninsula Women's Group 605 Cambridge Ave (at 'Lavender Dragon'), Menlo Park **650/323-4778** • 7pm-8:30pm Wed

BOOKSTORES

Books Inc 157 Stanford Shopping Center **650/321-0600** • 9:30am-9pm, 10am-8pm Sat, till 7pm Sun • general • lgbt section

Lavender Dragon 605 Cambridge Ave (at El Camino Rd), Menlo Park **650/323-4778** • 11am-9pm, 10am-5pm Sat, from noon Sun, clsd Mon • women's • also cafe • wheelchair access • women-owned/ run

Pasadena

BARS

Boulevard 3199 E Foothill Blvd (at Sierra Madre Villa) **626/356-9304** • 3pm-2am • mostly gay men • neighborhood bar • karaoke

Redding • California

Encounters 203 N Sierra Madre Blvd (at Foothill) **626/792-3735** • 4pm-2am, 3pm-2am wknds • lesbians/ gay men • neighborhood bar • dancing/DJ • patio

Nightclubs

Copa Pasadena Nightclub 162 N Sierra Madre Blvd (at Foothill) **626/395-9535** • 3pm-2am • lesbians/ gay men • dancing/DJ • karaoke Mon • disco bingo Tue • salsa Wed • Latin Th • T-dance Sun

Restaurants

Twin Palms 101 W Green St (at De Lacey Ave) **626/577-2567** • lunch & dinner • chic decor • reasonable prices • huge menu w/ unusual combinations • $7-15

Spiritual Groups

First Congregational United Church of Christ 464 E Walnut (at Las Robles) **626/795-0696** • 10am Sun

Erotica

Le Sex Shoppe 45 E Colorado (Raymond) **626/683-9468** • 24 hrs

Paso Robles

Accommodations

Sapaque Valley Ranch Inn 48491 Sapaque Valley Rd, Bradley **805/472-2750** • gay-friendly • B&B • rustic rental • nr Big Sur & San Simeon • group facilities available

Pescadero

Accommodations

Costanoa 2001 Rossi Rd **650/879-1100, 800/738-7477** • gay/ straight • also tent bungalows & cabins • 1 hr south of San Francisco • $70-205

Estancia del Mar **650/879-1500** • gay-friendly • cottage rentals w/ ocean views • smokefree • kids/ pets ok • $100

Petaluma

Restaurants

Twisted Vines 16 Kentucky St (in Lanmart Bldg) **707/766-8162** • lunch & dinner, clsd Sun-Mon • popular • also wine store

Bookstores

Copperfield's Books 140 Kentucky St (btwn Western & Washington, downtown) **707/762-0563** • 9am-9pm, till 10pm Fri-Sat, till 6pm Sun • new & used books • also great little cafe

Pismo Beach

Accommodations

The Palomar Inn 1601 Shell Beach Rd, Shell Beach **805/773-4204** • gay/ straight • nr nude beach • gay-owned/ run • $32-73

Placerville

Accommodations

Rancho Cicada Retreat **209/245-4841** • mostly gay men • secluded riverside retreat in the Sierra foothills w/ two-person tents & cabin • swimming • nudity • gay-owned/ run • $100-200 (lower during week)

Pomona

Bars

Alibi East 225 S San Antonio Ave (at 2nd) **909/623-9422** • 10am-2am, till 4am Fri-Sat • mostly gay men • dancing/DJ • strip shows Sat

Mary's Restaurant & Lounge 1047 E 2nd St (at Pico) **909/622-1971** • 5pm-2am, 3pm-2am Sun • lesbians/ gay men • dancing/DJ • food served • wheelchair access

Nightclubs

Robbie's 390 E 2nd St (at College Plaza) **909/620-4371** • 6pm-2am, clsd Mon-Th • lesbians/ gay men • ladies' night Th • dancing/DJ • live shows • call for events

Cafes

Café Con Libros 252-c S Main St **909/623-4492** • 11am-6pm, clsd Sun

Erotica

Mustang Books 961 N Central, Upland **909/981-0227**

Redding

Bars

Rainbow Lounge & Grille 2151 Market St (at Gold St off Pine) **530/247-1691** • 6pm-2am, from 4pm Sun • lesbians/ gay men • neighborhood bar • dancing/DJ • karaoke • food served Fri-Sat • wheelchair access • gay-owned/ run

Nightclubs

Club 501 1244 California St (at Center & Division, enter rear) **530/243-7869** • 6pm-2am, from 4pm Sun • lesbians/ gay men • dancing/DJ • food served • young crowd

California • USA

Redondo Beach

see also Los Angeles—West LA & Santa Monica

Info Lines & Services

South Bay Lesbian, Gay & Bi Community Organization 2009 Artesia Blvd #A **310/379-2850** • support/ education for Manhattan, Hermosa & Redondo Beaches, Torrance, Palos Verdes, El Segundo

Accommodations

Palos Verdes Inn 1700 S Pacific Coast Hwy **310/316-4211** • gay-friendly • jacuzzi • swimming • food served • kids ok • wheelchair access • $110-125

Redwood City

Erotica

Golden Gate Books 739 El Camino Real (at Brewster) **650/364-6913** • 24hrs

Riverside

see also San Bernardino

Accommodations

Inland Empire Retreat House 22780 Downing St, Moreno Valley **909/654-4188** • mostly women • elegant, modern home • jacuzzi • wheelchair access • pets ok • lesbian-owned/ run • $165-205

Nightclubs

Menagerie 3581 University Ave (at Orange) **909/788-8000** • 4pm-2am • mostly gay men • dancing/DJ • karaoke • wheelchair access

VIP Club 3673 Merrill Ave (at Magnolia) **909/784-2370** • 4pm-2am, clsd Mon-Tue • lesbians/ gay men • dancing/DJ • karaoke • shows • food served • wheelchair access

Spiritual Groups

St Bride's 3645 Locust St **909/369-0992** • 11am Sun • gay-friendly • Celtic Catholic service

Erotica

Riverside Bookstore 3945 Market St (at University) **909/788-5194** • 24hrs

Russian River

includes Cazadero, Forestville, Guerneville & Monte Rio

Info Lines & Services

Russian River Concierge 707/869-0914, 800/767-1759 • reservation service

Russian River Tourist Bureau 800/253-8800

Accommodations

Applewood 13555 Hwy 116 (at Mays Canyon), Guerneville **707/869-9093, 800/555-8509** • gay-friendly • 21+ • full brkfst • swimming • smokefree • food served • wheelchair access • $155-295

Avalon Inn 16484 4th St (at Brookside Ln), Guerneville **707/869-9566** • gay-friendly • swimming • $50-175

Eagle's Peak 11644 Our Peak Rd (at McPeak Rd), Forestville **707/887-9218** • mostly gay men • vacation house w/ deck & spa on 26 acres • gay-owned/ run • $195

Faerie Ring Campground 16747 Armstrong Woods Rd, Guerneville **707/869-2746** • gay-friendly • on 14 acres • RV spaces • nr outdoor recreation • pets ok • lesbian-owned/ run • $20-25

▲ **Fern Falls** **707/632-6108** • popular • lesbians/ gay men • main house w/ deck overlooking creek • also cabin • hot tub • waterfall • kids/ pets ok • smokefree • gay-owned/ run • $175

Fern Grove Cottages 16650 River Rd, Guerneville **707/869-8105** • gay-friendly • California craftsman cottages circa 1926 • swimming • kids/ pets ok • $69-169

Fife's Resort 16467 River Rd (at Brookside Ln), Guerneville **707/869-9500, 800/734-3371** • lesbians/ gay men • cabins • campsites • swimming • also restaurant • some veggie • full bar • gym • wheelchair access • $50-215

▲ **Highlands Resort** 14000 Woodland Dr, Guerneville **707/869-0333** • lesbians/ gay men • country retreat on 4 wooded acres • hot tub • swimming • nudity • pets ok • $45-130

Huckleberry Springs Country Inn & Spa 8105 Old Beedle, Monte Rio **707/865-2683, 800/822-2683** • gay-friendly • private cottages • full brkfst • swimming • Japanese spa • massage therapy • smokefree • videos • women-owned/ run • $165-180

Jacques' Cottage at Russian River 6471 Old Trenton Rd, Forestville **707/575-1033** • lesbians/ gay men • hot tub • swimming • nudity • pets ok • $100-125

Russian River

WHERE THE GIRLS ARE: Guerneville is a small town, so you won't miss the scantily-clad, vacationing women walking toward the bars downtown or the beach.

ANNUAL EVENTS: May & September - Women's Weekend 707/869-9000.
September - Jazz Festival.

CITY INFO: Russian River Visitors Info 800/253-8800.

ATTRACTIONS: Armstrong Redwood State Park.
Bodega Bay.
Mudbaths of Calistoga.
Wineries of Napa and Sonoma Counties.

BEST VIEW: Anywhere in Armstrong Woods, the Napa Wine Country and on the ride along the coast on Highway 1.

WEATHER: Summer days are sunny and warm (80°s-90°s) but usually begin with a dense fog. Winter days have the same pattern but are a lot cooler and wetter. Winter nights can be very damp and chilly (low 40°s).

TRANSIT: Bill's Taxi Service 707/869-2177.
The area is easiest to reach by car.

Cabins with fireplaces
Rooms, Camping and Day use.
Swimming Pool and Hot Tub.
Nude Sunbathing

Located a short walk from town on 3 acres of redwood trees and beautiful gardens.

Open all year!

HIGHLANDS RESORT

P.O. Box 346/14000 Woodland Dr.
Guerneville, CA 95446
www.highlandsresort.com
(707) 869-0333 Fax (707) 869-0370

California • USA

Fern Falls

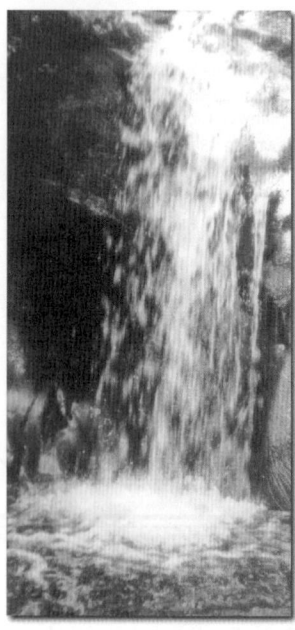

Romance & Redwoods!
- natural waterfall
- swimming hole
- creek & gardens
- cabins & suites
- fireplaces
- spa & nudity
- pets ok

Close to Guerneville

Phone: (707) 632-6108
PO Box 228
Cazadero, CA 95421
www.fernfalls.com

Redwood Properties 707/869-7368 • gay/straight • rental homes • smokefree • some w/pools & hot tubs • $150-350

Retreat Resort & Spa 14711 Armstrong Woods Rd, Guerneville **707/869-2706, 866/737-3529** • gay/straight • newly renovated resort w/ full-service spa • kids/pets ok • swimming • smokefree • jacuzzi • $175-275

Rio Villa Beach Resort 20292 Hwy 116 (at Bohemian Hwy), Monte Rio **707/865-1143** • gay-friendly • on the river • cabins • kids ok • $69-189

River Village Resort & Spa 14880 River Rd, Guerneville **707/869-8139, 800/529-3376** • gay/straight • cottages • swimming • hot tub • kids/pets ok • $75-195

Russian River Resort/ Triple 'R' Resort 16390 4th St (at Mill), Guerneville **707/869-0691, 800/417-3767** • lesbians/gay men • hot tub • swimming • nudity permitted • also restaurant • some veggie • full bar • videos • wheelchair access • $70-175

Russian River View Retreat **707/869-3040** • gay-friendly • vacation home • hot tub • kids/pets ok • smokefree • deck • 2 bikes provided • private dock & boat • $300-500/wknd, $650-1,150/ week

Schoolhouse Canyon Park 12600 River Rd (at Oddfellows Park Rd), Guerneville **707/869-2311** • gay-friendly • open May-Sept • campsites • RV • private beach • kids/pets ok • $25

Tim & Tony's Treehouse **707/887-9531, 888/887-9531** • gay/straight • studio cottage • swimming • hot tub • sauna • nudity permitted • smokefree • gay-owned/ run • $95-125

Wildwood Resort Retreat Old Cazadero Rd (off River Rd), Guerneville **707/632-5321** • gay-friendly • facilities are for groups of 20 or more • swimming • smokefree • $80-100 (meals included)

The Willows 15905 River Rd (at Hwy 116), Guerneville **707/869-2824, 800/953-2828** • lesbians/ gay men • old-fashioned country lodge & campground • smokefree • $79-139

BARS

Mc T's Bullpen 16246 1st St (at Church), Guerneville **707/869-3377** • 8am-2am • gay/straight • sports bar • patio • wheelchair access

Rainbow Cattle Co 16220 Main St (at Armstrong Woods Rd), Guerneville **707/869-0206** • 6am-2am • mostly gay men • neighborhood bar

Russian River • California

The Russian River Eagle 16225 Main St (at Armstrong Woods Rd), Guerneville **707/869-3400** • noon-2am • lesbians/gay men • neighborhood bar • leather • alternative • theme nights • wheelchair access

Nightclubs

Club Fab 16135 River Rd (at Armstrong Woods Rd), Guerneville **707/869-5708** • 9pm-2am, 4pm-close Sun, clsd Mon-Wed • popular • mostly gay men • dancing/DJ • 4 levels

Cafes

Coffee Bazaar 14045 Armstrong Woods Rd (at River Rd), Guerneville **707/869-9706** • 6am-8pm • cafe • soups • salads • pastries

Restaurants

Big Bertha's Burgers 16357 Main St, Guerneville **707/869-2239** • 11am-9pm • beer/wine

Burdon's 15405 River Rd (at Orchard Rd), Guerneville **707/869-2615** • dinner Wed-Sat • lesbians/gay men • cont'l/pasta • plenty veggie • full bar • wheelchair access • $10-15

Cape Fear Cafe 25191 Main St, Duncans Mills **707/865-9246** • 9am-9pm, clsd 3pm-5pm

Cat's Place at George's Hideaway 18100 Hwy 116 (at Old Cazadero Rd) **707/869-3634** • 4pm-9pm, till 10pm wknds, clsd Mon-Tue • homecooking • full bar

---

```
Date: Fri, Dec 14, 2001  13:29:53
From: Girl-on-the-Go
To: Editor@Damron.com
Subject: Russian River
```

> The Russian River resort area is hidden away in the redwood forests of Northern California, an hour and a half north of the San Francisco Bay Area. The warm summer days and cool starlit nights have made it a favorite secret getaway for many of San Francisco's lesbians and gays—especially when they can't stand another foggy, cold day in the City.

> Life at 'The River', as it's fondly called, is laid back. You can take a canoe ride, hike under the redwoods, or just lie back on the riverbank and soak up the sun. There's plenty of camping and RV parking, including The Willows (camping) and Fife's Resort (camping & RV). If you're in the mood for other soothing and sensual delights, you're in luck. The River is in the heart of the famous California Wine Country. Plan a tour to the many wineries, and don't forget to designate a sober driver, so you can taste the world-class wines as you go. Or see some of the world's most beautiful coastline as you cruise along the Pacific Coast Highway—only fifteen minutes away!

> The River becomes a lesbian garden of earthly delights several times a year. Women's Weekend happens in May and late September, and women pack the tiny town as they enjoy the many entertainers, dances, and barbecues.

California • USA

Flavors Unlimited 16450 Main St/ River Rd, Guerneville **707/869-0425** • hours vary • custom-blended ice cream

Mill St Grill 16390 4th St (at 'Triple 'R' Resort'), Guerneville **707/869-0691** • lesbians/ gay men • some veggie • full bar • patio • wheelchair access • $5-10

River Inn Restaurant 16141 Main St, Guerneville **707/869-0481** • seasonal • local favorite • wheelchair access • $10-15

Sweet's River Grill 16251 Main St (at Armstrong Woods Rd), Guerneville **707/869-3383** • 11am-9pm • popular • full bar

BOOKSTORES

River Reader 16355 Main St (at Mill), Guerneville **707/869-2240** • 10am-6pm (extended hours during summer) • wheelchair access

RETAIL SHOPS

Up the River 16212 Main St (at Armstrong Woods Rd), Guerneville **707/869-3167** • cards • gifts • T-shirts

SPIRITUAL GROUPS

MCC of the Redwood Empire 16219 First Street (at The Redwood Lodge, Odd Fellows Hall), Guerneville **707/869-0552** • 10am Sun

Sacramento

INFO LINES & SERVICES

Lambda Community Center 1927 'L' St **916/442-0185** • 10am-6pm • youth groups • discussion groups • referrals • library

Northall Gay AA 2015 'J' St #32 **916/454-1100** • 8pm Mon, noon & 8pm Wed

ACCOMMODATIONS

Capitol Park B&B 1300 'T' St (at 13th) **916/414-1300, 877/753-9982** • gay-friendly • gay-owned/ run • $129-195

Hartley House B&B Inn 700 22nd St (at 'G' St) **916/447-7829, 800/831-5806** • gay-friendly • turn-of-the-century mansion • full brkfst • smokefree • older kids ok • gay-owned/ run • $124-190

Verona Village River Resort 6985 Garden Hwy, Nicolaus **530/656-1320** • lesbians/ gay men • RV space $15 • trailers for rent • full bar • restaurant • store • marina

BARS

The Depot 2001 'K' St **916/441-6823** • 4pm-2am, till 4am Fri-Sat, from 2pm wknds • popular • mostly gay men • neighborhood bar • transgender-friendly • videos • wheelchair access

The Townhouse 1517 21st St (at 'P' St) **916/441-5122** • 3pm-2am • lesbians/ gay men • neighborhood bar • also restaurant • wheelchair access

NIGHTCLUBS

Faces 2000 'K' St (at 20th St) **916/448-7798** • 3pm-2am • popular • lesbians/ gay men • dancing/DJ • country/ western • transgender-friendly • live shows • karaoke • videos • patio • wheelchair access

Club 21 1119 21st St (at 'L' St) **916/443-1537** • 9pm-2am Th-Sun • mostly women • dancing/DJ • multiracial clientele • videos • lesbian-owned

RESTAURANTS

Ernesto's 1901 16th St (at 'S' St) **916/441-5850** • 11am-10pm, till 11pm Fri-Sat • Mexican • full bar

Hamburger Mary's 1630 'J' St (at 17th) **916/441-4340** • 11am-10pm, till 11pm Fri-Sat • full bar

Jack's 20th & Capitol **916/444-0307** • lunch Mon-Fri, dinner nightly

Kip's Kabobs 1000 'J' St #100 (at 10th) **916/498-9171** • 7am-4pm Mon-Fri

Rick's Dessert Diner 2322 'K' St (at 23rd) **916/444-0969** • 10am-11pm Sun-Mon, till midnight Tue-Th, till 1am Fri-Sat • coffee & dessert

Thai Palace 3262 'J' St (33rd St) **916/447-5353** • lunch & dinner • Thai • $10-20

BOOKSTORES

The Open Book 910 21st St (btwn 'I' & 'J' Sts) **916/498-1004** • 10am-11pm, till midnight Fri-Sat • lgbt • also coffeehouse • wheelchair access

PUBLICATIONS

MGW (Mom Guess What) **916/441-6397** • lgbt newspaper • women-owned/ run

Outword **916/329-9280** • lgbt newspaper

SPIRITUAL GROUPS

Integrity Northern California **916/394-1715, 916/446-2513** • 3pm 2nd Sun • lgbt Episcopalians • call for location

EROTICA

Goldie's I 201 N 12th St (at North 'B' St) **916/447-5860** • 24hrs • also 2138 Del Paso Blvd location, 916/922-0103

Goldie's Outlet 1800 Del Paso Blvd (at Oxford Blvd) **916/920-8659**

Kiss-N-Tell 4201 Sunrise Blvd (at Fair Oaks) **916/966-5477**

San Diego • California

L'Amour Shoppe 2531 Broadway (at 26th) 916/736-3467

Salinas

SPIRITUAL GROUPS

St Paul's Episcopal Church 1071 Pajaro St (at San Miguel Ave) **831/424-7331** • 8am & 10am Sun

EROTICA

L'Amour Shoppe 325 E Alisal St **831/758-9600**

San Bernardino

see also Riverside

INFO LINES & SERVICES

AA Gay/ Lesbian 909/825-4700 • numerous mtgs for Inland Empire • call for times

Gay/ Lesbian Community Center Hotline 2286 N LeRoy **909/882-4488** • 6:30pm-10pm

ACCOMMODATIONS

Rainbow View Lodge 2726 View Dr (at Hilltop), Running Springs **909/867-1810, 888/868-1810** • gay/ straight • kids ok • smokefree • $79-149

NIGHTCLUBS

The Lark 917 Inland Center Dr **909/884-8770** • noon-2am • lesbians/ gay men • DJ Fri-Sat • live shows • karaoke • videos • huge patio • wheelchair access

San Diego

INFO LINES & SERVICES

AA Gay/ Lesbian 1730 Monroe Ave #B **619/298-8008** • 10:30am-10pm, from 8:30am wknds • 'Live & Let Live Alano' • also contact for 'Sober Sisters'

Lesbian/ Gay Men's Community Center 3909 Centre St (at University) **619/692-2077** • 9am-10pm, till 7pm Sat, 9am-5pm Sun

SAGE Center of California 3138 Fifth Ave **619/298-9900** • 11am-5pm Mon-Fri • seniors' social group

▲ **Turn Key Real Estate 619/299-DEAN**

ACCOMMODATIONS

Balboa Park Inn 3402 Park Blvd (at Upas) **619/298-0823, 800/938-8181** • gay-friendly • charming guest house in the heart of San Diego • $89-199

San Diego

WHERE THE GIRLS ARE: Lesbians tend to live near Normal Heights, in the northwest part of the city. But for partying, women go to the bars near I-5, or to Hillcrest to hang out with the boys.

LGBT PRIDE: July. 619/297-7683, web: www.sdpride.org.

CITY INFO: San Diego Visitors Bureau 619/232-3101, web: www.sandiego.com.

ATTRACTIONS: Globe Theatre 619/231-1941.
San Diego Wild Animal Park 760/747-8702.
San Diego Zoo 619/234-3153.
Sea World 619/226-3915.

BEST VIEW: Cabrillo National Monument on Point Loma or from a harbor cruise.

WEATHER: San Diego is sunny and warm (upper 60°s-70°s) year-round, with higher humidity in the summer.

TRANSIT: Orange Cab 619/234-6161.
San Diego Cab 619/232-6566.
Silver Cab/Co-op 619/280-5555.
Cloud Nine Shuttle 800/974-8885.
San Diego Transit System 619/233-3004.
San Diego Trolley (through downtown or to Tijuana).

California • USA

SOUTHERN CALIFORNIA'S HOST TO THE GAY & LESBIAN COMMUNITY

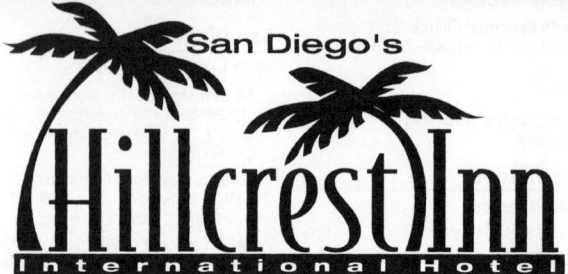

San Diego's **Hillcrest Inn** International Hotel

Near Everywhere You Want To Be!

1-800-258-2280
San Diego, CA
(619) 293-7078 • fax (619) 293-3861

RESIDENTIAL AND INVESTMENT SALES

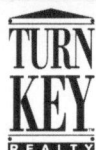

TURN KEY REALTY

PURCHASE AND REFINANCE LOANS

PERSONAL ATTENTION
it's what you deserve

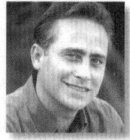

Dean M. Burrows, MBA, Broker, CRS
619-299-DEAN (3326)
www.deanburrows.com

San Diego • California

Beach Area B&B/ Elsbree House 5054 Narragansett Ave (at Sunset Cliffs Blvd) **619/226-4133** • gay-friendly • nr beach • smokefree • $110-125 • $1,250-1,400/week (condo)

The Beach Place 2158 Sunset Cliffs Blvd (at Muir) **619/225-0746** • lesbians/gay men • hot tub • nudity • kids ok • pets by arrangement • 4 blks from beach • $59-69/night, $350-400/week

The Blom House B&B on Kensington 1372 Minden Dr (nr Friars & Ulric) **858/467-0890, 800/797-2566** • gay-friendly • charming 1948 cottage-style home • full brkfst • magnificent view • smokefree • kids ok • women-owned/run • $85-135

Dmitri's Guesthouse 931 21st St (at Broadway) **619/238-5547** • lesbians/gay men • swimming • hot tub • nudity permitted • smokefree • overlooks downtown • wheelchair access • $75-110

The Gallery B&B 1404 Meade Ave (at Maryland St) **619/692-0041, 888/355-6439** • mostly lesbians • 1907 home • queen suite w/ fireplace • spa • lesbian-owned/run • $65-90

▲ **Hillcrest Inn Hotel** 3754 5th Ave (btwn Robinson & Pennsylvania) **619/293-7078, 800/258-2280** • lesbians/gay men • int'l hotel in the heart of Hillcrest • hot tub • wheelchair access • $55-79

[Reply] [Forward]   [Delete]

```
Date: Thu, Dec 6, 2001 13:01:44
From: Girl-on-the-Go
To: Editor@Damron.com
Subject: San Diego
```

> San Diego is a West Coast paradise. This city sprawls from the bays and beaches of the Pacific to the foothills of the desert mountains. The days are always warm, and the nights can be refreshingly cool.

> Stay at one of the city's quaint lesbian-friendly inns, like the lesbian-owned **Gallery B&B.** During the days, follow the tourist circuit which includes the world-famous San Diego Zoo and Sea World. Call the Visitor's Center for a brochure on all the sites.

> Once the sun sets, you're ready to tour the lesbian circuit. Where to begin? Check out **Club Bombay** and **The Flame**, San Diego's two lesbian dance bars. If you're a country/western gal, **Kickers** is a popular place to two-step.

> In mid-August, check out the Hillcrest Street Fair, popular with the many lesbian and gay residents of the happening Hillcrest district. (Be warned though: Because of its location between super-freeways and construction, rush-hour traffic has been known to crawl through Hillcrest.)

> If you're feeling adventurous, cruise by the **Crypt** for some sex toys or a piercing, and pick up your safer sex supplies at **Condoms Plus**. If you just want to network, stop in at the **Community Center** or pick up one of the LGBT papers at **Obelisk the Bookstore** for all the latest information about San Diego's lesbian community.

California • USA

Inn Suites Hotel 2223 El Cajon Blvd (btwn Louisiana & Mississippi) **619/296-2101** • gay-friendly • swimming • kids ok • also restaurant • wheelchair access • $89-200

Keating House 2331 2nd Ave (at Juniper) **619/239-8585, 800/995-8644** • gay-friendly • graceful Victorian on Bankers Hill • full brkfst • smokefree • kids ok • gay-owned/ run • $85-135

Park Manor Suites 525 Spruce St (btwn 5th & 6th) **619/291-0999, 800/874-2649** • gay-friendly • 1926 hotel • kids ok • $79-199

Villa Serena B&B 2164 Rosecrans St (btwn Udall & Voltaire) **619/224-1451, 888/416-7415** • gay-friendly • Italian villa in residential neighborhood • full brkfst • swimming • hot tub • $95-300

BARS

The Brass Rail 3796 5th Ave (at Robinson) **619/298-2233** • noon-2am • lesbians/ gay men • dancing/DJ • wheelchair access

Club Bombay 3175 India St (enter on Spruce St) **619/296-6789** • 4pm-2am, from 2pm wknds • popular • mostly women • dancing/DJ • live shows • Sun bbq • patio • wheelchair access • women-owned/ run

The Flame 3780 Park Blvd (at University) **619/295-4163** • 5pm-2am, from 4pm Fri • popular • mostly women • dancing/DJ • theme nights • women-owned/ run

Kickers 308 University Ave (at 3rd Ave) **619/491-0400** • 7pm-2am • popular • mostly gay men • dancing/DJ • country/ western • lessons at 7pm Wed-Sat • T-dance Sun • wheelchair access

No 1 Fifth Ave (no sign) 3845 5th Ave (at University) **619/299-1911** • noon-2am • mostly gay men • professional crowd • videos • patio

Redwing Bar & Grill 4012 30th St (at Lincoln) **619/281-8700** • 10am-midnight, till 2am Fri-Sat • mostly gay men • cocktail lounge • patio

Shooterz/ Club Odyssey 3815 30th St (at University) **619/574-0744** • noon-2am, mostly gay men • sports bar • dancing/DJ

Zone 3040 North Park Wy (at 30th) **619/295-8072** • 4pm-2am, from 2pm wknds • mostly gay men • neighborhood bar • wheelchair access

NIGHTCLUBS

Club Montage 2028 Hancock St (at Washington Ave) **619/294-9590** • 8pm-2am, till 4am Fri-Sat • popular • mostly gay men • dancing/DJ • live shows • videos • also restaurant • wheelchair access

CAFES

The Big Kitchen 3003 Grape St (at 30th) **619/234-5789** • 8am-2pm, 7am-3pm wknds • some veggie • wheelchair access • women-owned/ run • $5-10

Cafe Roma UCSD Price Center #76 (at Voight), La Jolla **858/450-2141** • 7am-midnight

David's Place 3766 5th Ave (at Robinson) **619/296-4173** • 7am-midnight, till 1am wknds • lesbians/ gay men • coffeehouse for positive people & their friends • patio • wheelchair access

Extraordinary Desserts 2929 5th Ave **619/294-7001** • 8:30am-11pm, till midnight Fri-Sat • the name says it all

RESTAURANTS

Adams Avenue Grill 2201 Adams Ave (at Mississippi) **619/298-8440** • lunch, dinner & Sun brunch • bistro • plenty veggie • beer/ wine • wheelchair access • gay-owned/ run

Bayou Bar & Grill 329 Market St (btwn 3rd & 4th) **619/696-8747** • lunch & dinner, Sun champagne brunch • Creole/ Cajun • wheelchair access • $12-18

Cafe Eleven 1440 University Ave (at Normal) **619/260-8023** • dinner, clsd Mon • country French • some veggie • wheelchair access • $15-20

California Cuisine 1027 University Ave (at 10th Ave) **619/543-0790** • 11am-10pm, clsd Mon • French/ Italian • some veggie • also bar • wheelchair access • women-owned/ run • $15-20

City Deli 535 University Ave (at 6th Ave) **619/295-2747** • 7am-midnight, till 2am Fri-Sat • NY deli • plenty veggie • beer/ wine

The Cottage 7702 Fay (at Klein), La Jolla **858/454-8409** • 7:30am-3pm • fresh-baked items

Crest Cafe 425 Robinson (btwn 4th & 5th) **619/295-2510** • 7am-midnight • some veggie • wheelchair access • $5-10

Hamburger Mary's 308 University Ave (at 3rd) **619/491-0400** • 9am-11pm, till midnight wknds • some veggie • full bar • patio • wheelchair access • $5-10

San Diego • California

Your complete guide to Southern California news, entertainment & happenings!

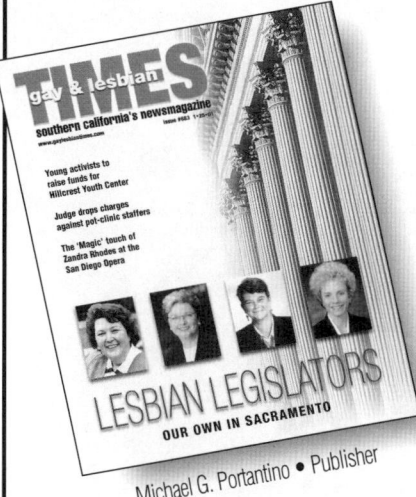

More Copies, More Often, To More Locations Throughout All Of Southern California Than Any Other Gay & Lesbian Publication, Period!

Michael G. Portantino • Publisher

San Diego/SoCal Edition
619.299.6397
3911 Normal St. San Diego, CA 92103

1.800.438.8786

Desert Edition
760.320.5676
1039 South Palm Canyon Dr. Palm Springs, CA 92264

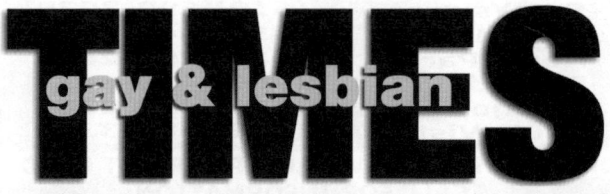

www.gaylesbiantimes.com

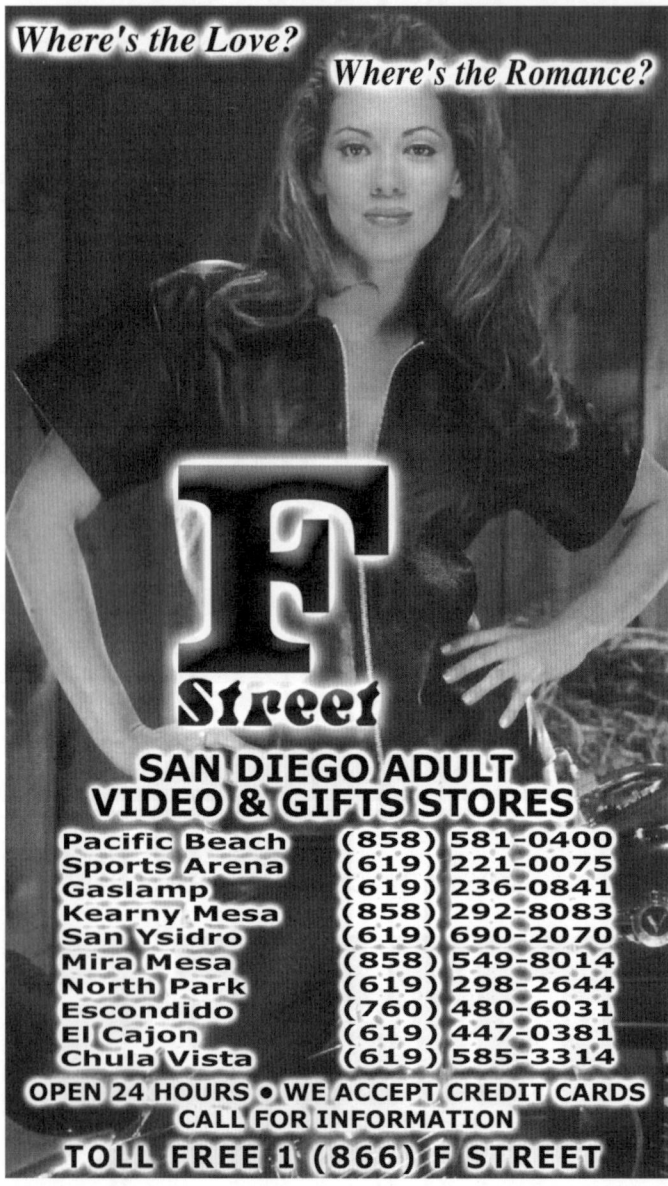

San Diego • California

Liaison 2202 4th Ave (at Ivy) **619/234–5540** • dinner only, clsd Mon • French country • wheelchair access • $18-24 (prix fixe)

Lips 2770 5th Ave (at Olive) **619/295–7900** • clsd Mon • 'the ultimate in drag dining' • 'Bitchy Bingo' Wed • DJ wknds

The Mission 3795 Mission Blvd (at San Jose), Mission Beach **858/488–9060** • mostly lesbians/gay men • brkfst & lunch • gay-owned

Mixx 3671 5th Ave **619/299–6499** • mostly lesbians/gay men • dinner only • live shows • gay-owned

Vegetarian Zone 2949 5th Ave (at Quince) **619/298–7302** • 10am-9pm • deli & restaurant

ENTERTAINMENT & RECREATION

Aztec Bowl 4356 30th St, North Park **619/283–3135** • gay Th night

Diversionary Theatre 4545 Park Blvd #101 (at Madison) **619/220–6830, 619/220–0097 (BOX OFFICE #)** • lgbt theater

BOOKSTORES

Groundworks Books UCSD Student Center 0323 (at Gilman Dr), La Jolla **858/452–9625** • 9am-7pm, 10am-6pm Fri-Sat, clsd Sun • alternative • lgbt section • wheelchair access

▲ **Obelisk the Bookstore** 1029 University Ave (at 10th) **619/297–4171** • 10am-11pm, till 9pm Sun • lgbt • wheelchair access

RETAIL SHOPS

Auntie Helen's 4028 30th St (at Lincoln) **619/584–8438** • 10am-5pm, clsd Sun-Mon • thrift shop benefits PWAs • wheelchair access

Flesh Skin Grafix 1155 Palm Ave, Imperial Beach **619/424–8983** • tattoos • piercing

GayMartUSA 550 University Ave (at 6th Ave) **619/543–1221** • 10am-10pm

Mastodon 4638 Mission Blvd (at Emerald), Pacific Beach **858/272–1188, 800/743–8743** • body piercing

Rainbow Road 141 University Ave (at 3rd) **619/296–8222** • 10am-10pm • gay gifts

PUBLICATIONS

▲ **Gay/Lesbian Times** 3911 Normal St **619/299–6397, 800/438–8786** • lgbt newsmagazine

Update 619/299–4104

SPIRITUAL GROUPS

Dignity 4190 Front St (at First Unitarian Universalist Church in Hillcrest) **619/645–8240** • 6pm Sun, potlucks 3rd Sun after Mass

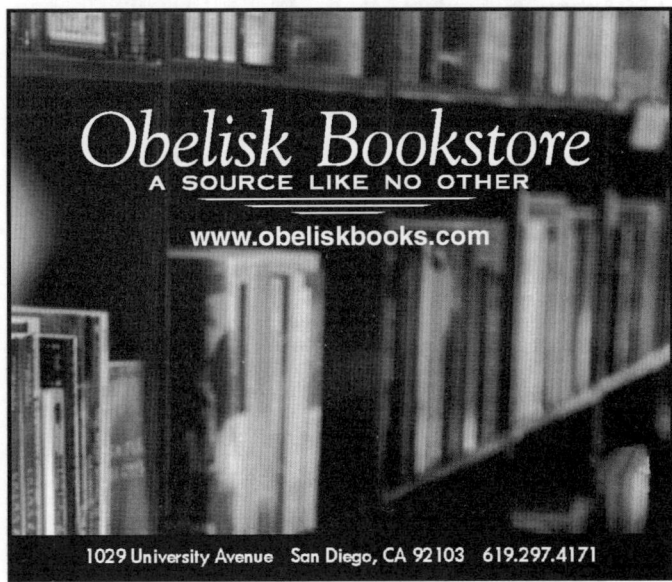

Obelisk Bookstore
A SOURCE LIKE NO OTHER
www.obeliskbooks.com
1029 University Avenue San Diego, CA 92103 619.297.4171

California • USA

First Unitarian Universalist Church 4190 Front St (Arbor) **619/298-9978** • 10am (July-Aug) • 9am & 11am (Sept-June)

MCC 4333 30th St (at El Cajon Blvd) **619/280-4333** • 9am, 11am, 1:30pm (in Spanish)

Gyms & Health Clubs

Frog's Athletic Club 901 Hotel Circle S (at Washington), Mission Valley **619/291-3500**

Erotica

Condoms Plus 1220 University Ave (at Vermont) **619/291-7400** • 11am-midnight, till 2am Fri-Sat, 1pm-9pm Sun • safer sex gifts for women & men • wheelchair access

The Crypt 3841 Park Blvd (at University) **619/692-9499** • also 30th St location, 619/284-4724

▲ **F St Bookstore** 2004 University Ave (at Florida) **619/298-2644** • 24hrs

▲ **F St Bookstore** 3112 Midway Dr (at Rosecrans) **619/221-0075** • 24hrs

▲ **F St Bookstore** 4626 Albuquerque **858/581-0400** • 24hrs

▲ **F St Bookstore** 751 4th Ave (at 'F' St) **619/236-0841** • 24hrs

▲ **F St Bookstore** 7865 Balboa Ave (at Mercury), Kearny Mesa **858/292-8083** • 24hrs

▲ **F St Bookstore** 7998 Miramar Rd (at Dowdy) **858/549-8014** • 24hrs

▲ **F St Bookstore** 4650 Border Village (at San Ysidro Blvd), San Ysidro **619/690-2070**

Midnight Books 1407 University Ave (at Richmond) **619/299-7186** • 24hrs

Midnight Books 3606 Midway Dr (at Kemper) **619/222-9973** • 24hrs

Midnight Videos 4790 El Cajon Blvd (at 48th) **619/582-1997** • 24hrs

Pleasureland 836 5th Ave (btwn E & F Sts) **619/237-9056** • 24hrs

Trademark **619/296-1700** • pro & amateur videos • skin care • by appt only

San Francisco

San Francisco is divided into 7 geographical areas:
SF—Overview
SF—Castro & Noe Valley
SF—South of Market
SF—Polk Street Area
SF—Downtown & North Beach
SF—Mission District
SF—Haight, Fillmore, Hayes Valley

SF—Overview

Info Lines & Services

AA Gay/ Lesbian **415/621-1326** • call for meeting times

Bay Area American Indian Two Spirits (BAAITS) PO Box 31177 94131-0177 **415/561-9756** • call for recorded info, mtg times & locations

The Exiles 3543 18th St (btwn Guerrero & Valencia, in the 'Women's Bldg') **415/835-4739** • mtgs 7:30pm 3rd Fri • social/ educational group for all women over 18 interested in S/M btwn women

FTM International **415/553-5987** • 2pm-5pm 2nd Sun • info & support for female-to-male transgendered people • newsletter • resource guide

Gay/ Lesbian Outreach to Elders 1853 Market St **415/255-2937**

Gay/ Lesbian Sierrans **415/281-5666** • outdoor group

The LGBT Community Center Project of SF 1800 Market St. (at Octavia) **415/437-2257**

LGBT Hotline of San Francisco **415/355-0099** • 5pm-9pm Mon-Fri • peer-counseling, information, resources

LYRIC (Lavender Youth Recreation/ Information Cntr) 127 Collingwood (between 18th & 19th) **415/703-6150, 800/246-7743 (outside Bay Area)** • support & social groups • also crisis counseling for lgbt youth under 24 at 415/863-3636 (hotline #)

New Leaf 1853 Market **415/626-7000** • 9am-9pm, till 8pm Fri, till 1pm Sat, clsd Sun • variety of services including lgbt AA mtgs at 15th & Market • mental heath services • HIV/ AIDS prevention and couseling

New Village 495 Clementina St **415/674-0900** • transgender support group

Pacific Center 510/548-8283 • 10am-10pm Mon-Fri • info • referrals • rap line • peer support • social activities

TARC (Tenderloin AIDS Resource Center) 187 Golden Gate Ave (at Leavenworth) 415/431-7476 • 9am-noon (drop-in) & 1pm-4pm (appt only)

Transgender Support Group 187 Golden Gate Ave (at TARC) 415/241-2530 • 4pm-6pm Mon-Fri

Transgender Support Groups 50 Lech Walesa (at Tom Waddell Clinic, btwn Polk & Van Ness and Grove & Hayes Sts) 415/554-2940 • 5pm-8:30pm Tue • support groups & counseling for MTF & FTM transsexuals • low-cost TG health clinic

What's Up! Events Hotline for Sistahs East Bay 510/835-6126 • for lesbians of African descent

San Francisco

WHERE THE GIRLS ARE: Younger, radical dykes call the Mission or the lower Haight home, while upwardly mobile couples stake out Bernal Heights and Noe Valley. Hip, moneyed dykes live in the Castro. The East Bay is home to lots of lesbian feminists, older lesbians, and lesbian moms (see East Bay listings).

LGBT PRIDE: June. 415/864-3733.

ANNUAL EVENTS: June - San Francisco Int'l Lesbian/Gay Film Festival 415/703-8650.
September - Folsom Street Fair 415/861-3247. Huge SM/leather street fair, topping a week of kinky events.
Mad Cat Women's Int'l Film Fest 415/436-9523.
October - Castro Street Fair 415/467-3354. Arts and community groups street fair.

CITY INFO: San Francisco Convention & Visitors Bureau 415/391-2000, web: www.sfvisitor.org.

ATTRACTIONS: Alcatraz.
Chinatown.
Coit Tower.
De Young Museum 415/750-3600.
Exploratorium 415/561-0360.
Fisherman's Wharf.
Golden Gate Park.
Haight & Ashbury Sts.
Japantown.
North Beach.
Mission San Francisco de Assisi.
SF Museum of Modern Art 415/357-4035.
Twin Peaks.

BEST VIEW: After a great Italian meal in North Beach, go to the top floor of the North Beach parking garage on Vallejo near Stockton, next to the police station. If you're in the Castro or the Mission, head for Dolores Park, at Dolores and 20th St.

WEATHER: A beautiful summer comes at the end of September and lasts through October. Much of the city is cold and fogged-in June through September, though the Castro and Mission are usually sunny. The cold in winter is damp, so bring lots of layers. When there isn't a drought, it also rains in the winter months of November through February.

TRANSIT: Yellow Cab 415/626-2345.
Luxor Cab 415/282-4141.
Quake City Shuttle 415/255-4899.
MUNI 415/673-6864.
Bay Area Rapid Transit (BART) 650/992-2278, subway.

California • USA

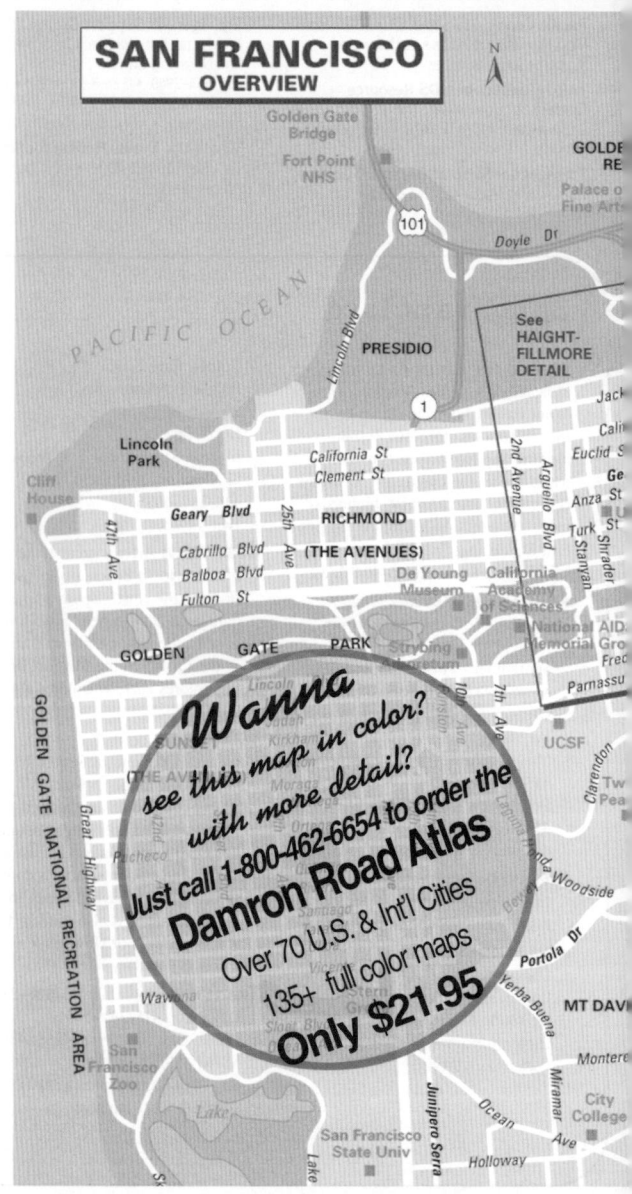

SF–Overview • California

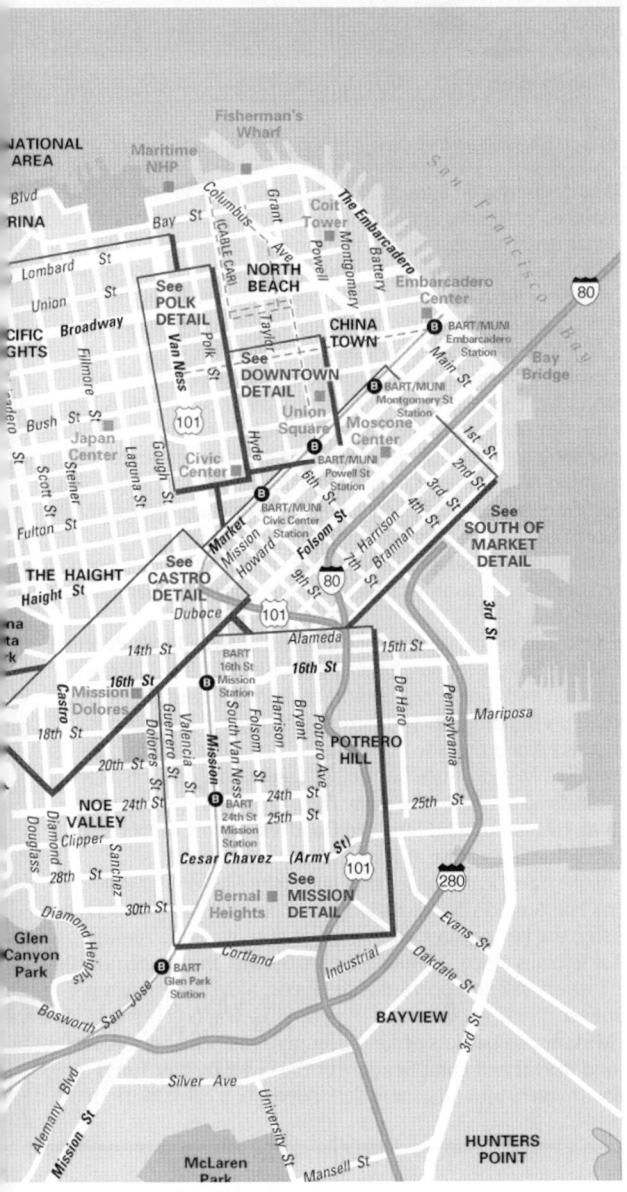

California • USA

Reply **Forward** **Delete**

Date: Wed, Dec 12, 2001 12:26:42
From: Girl-on-the-Go
To: Editor@Damron.com
Subject: San Francisco

> San Francisco may be a top tourist destination because of its cable cars, beatniks, Victorians, and the Haight-Ashbury district, but we know what really makes it shine: its legendary lesbian and gay community. So unless standing in long lines for a little kitsch is your thing, skip Fisherman's Wharf and the cable cars, and head for San Francisco's queerest and quirkiest neighborhoods: the Mission, the Castro, Noe Valley, and South of Market (SoMa).

> Any lesbian walking along Valencia between Market Street and 24th Street can't miss all the hot women of all sizes and colors that live in this neighborhood. Valencia Street borders the upscale, predominantly gay Castro area, and the Mission, San Francisco's largest Latino neighborhood. This intersection of cultures results in a truly San Franciscan mix of punk dykes, dykes of color, lesbian-feminists, working class straights, and a shrinking number of funky artists. Many upscale eateries have sprung up, and more fancy cars line the streets, but the original flavor of this spicy neighborhood is still pungent.

> Your first stop in the Mission should be either **Red Dora's Bearded Lady Cafe & Gallery** (be sure to check out **Black & Blue Tattoo** next door) on 14th Street or the more traditional resource center, the **Women's Building**, on 18th Street. (You can't miss their stunning murals.) Along the way from 14th to 18th, pick up a famous 'San Francisco Mission-Style Burrito' (as they're advertised in New York these days) at one of the many cheap and delicious taquerias. After that, rush up to 23rd Street to **Good Vibrations** women's sex toy store before they close at 7pm.

> You might have heard the legends about the Mission's one-time women's bar, Amelia's. Sadly, it's long gone. Instead, head for its hip little sister, the **Lexington Club**, a popular dyke hangout. Another must for lesbians along Valencia Street is **Osento**, the women's bathhouse. Just off Valencia on 16th is the **Roxie**, a dyke-friendly repertory cinema.

> The Mission also has lots of fun queer performance at places like **Build** and **Brava!** and **Luna Sea**—check the biweekly **Bay Times** calendar. If you're into artsy or radical video, get a calendar from

Artists' Television Access (415/824-3890).

> You'll also find lots of lesbians in nearby Noe Valley, though this area tends to be a couples haven for professional women and lesbian moms. You'll enjoy an afternoon in one or all of the many quirky shops and cafes along upper 24th Street.

> If you cruise the Castro, you'll be surprised how many sisters—ranging from executives to queer chicks—you'll see walking the streets of what was the 'Boys' Town' of the 1970s. Drop in at **A Different Light**, the LGBT bookstore, or **The Cafe** for a game of pool or girl-watching from the balcony. The Castro also boasts three great 24-hour diners—**Bagdad Cafe**, **Sparky's**, and **Orphan Andy's**. For LGBT-themed films, don't miss an evening at the **Castro Theater**.

> SoMa (South of Market) is home to many of the city's dance clubs and live music venues. **The Stud** hosts several popular women's nights.

> While you're south of Market, you might also want to check out the women's S/M scene in this kinky city: **Stormy Leather** is a women-owned/run fetish store. And if you're inspired to get that piercing you've been thinking about, visit one of the queer-friendly piercing parlors in town—we like **Body Manipulations**, right between the Mission and the Castro on 16th Street at Guerrero.

> You still have energy? Wanna dance? Single (or not) on a Saturday night? Then boogie on down to the ever-popular **G-Spot**. But don't stop there. Be sure to check out the listings in **Frontiers,** or the 'Jet Girl' section of **Odyssey**, to see if tonight's the night for one of those legendary one-night clubs like **Sushi Sundays,** or monthly parties like **Club Q** and **Backstreet**.

> Finally, if you're a fan of Diane Di Prima, Anne Waldman, the late Allen Ginsberg, or other beatniks, **City Lights Bookstore** in North Beach is a required pilgrimage. Afterward, have a drink or an espresso at beatnik hangout Café Vesuvius, just across Jack Kerouac Alley from City Lights.

> Sound like a lot? They don't call it Mecca for nothing.

California • USA

Women's Building 3543 18th St (btwn Valencia & Guerrero) 415/431-1180 • 9am-5pm Mon-Fri • space for many women's organizations • social/ support groups • housing & job listings • beautiful murals

ACCOMMODATIONS

Dockside Boat & Bed 510/444-5858, 800/436-2574 • gay-friendly • private yachts • also Oakland location • smokefree • kids ok • $115-300

Mi Casa Su Casa 510/531-4511, 800/215-2272 • lesbians/ gay men • int'l home exchange network

ENTERTAINMENT & RECREATION

Beach Blanket Babylon 678 Green St (at Powell, in 'Club Fugazi') 415/421-4222 • the USA's longest running musical revue & wigs that must be seen to be believed • very popular • also restaurant & full bar

Brava! 2781 24th St (btwn York & Hampshire) 415/641-7657 • culturally diverse performances by women • wheelchair access

Castro Theatre 429 Castro (at Market) 415/621-6120 • art house cinema • many lgbt & cult classics • live organ evenings

Cruisin' the Castro 415/550-8110 • 5-star walking tour of the Castro • brunch included

▲ **Frameline** 415/703-8650, 800/869-1996 (OUTSIDE CA) • lgbt media arts foundation • sponsors annual SF Int'l Lesbian/ Gay Film Festival in June (see Film Festival Calendar in back Events section)

Hanarchy Now Productions 415/550-1902 • queer & alternative events in and around San Francisco

Luna Sea 2940 16th St Rm 216–C (btwn Capp & S Van Ness) 415/863-2989 • lesbian performance space

The Marsh 1062 Valencia (at 22nd St) 415/641-0235 • queer-positive theater

▲ **National AIDS Memorial Grove** Golden Gate Park 415/750-8345, 888/294-7683 • located in a lush, historic dell • guided tours available • wheelchair access

SF GayTours.com 415/648-7758, 877/734-2986 • SF Queer history tour • Tales of the City tour • commitment ceremonies

Sistah Boom 510/595-4693 • women's percussion ensemble

Theatre Rhinoceros 2926 16th St (at S Van Ness) 415/861-5079 • lgbt theater

Victorian Home Walks 415/252-9485 • custom-tailored walking tours w/ San Francisco resident • gay-owned/ run

PUBLICATIONS

BAR (Bay Area Reporter) 415/861-5019 • the weekly lgbt newspaper

Odyssey Magazine 415/621-6514 • all the dish on SF's club scene

Q San Francisco 800/999-9718 (SUBSCRIPTIONS) • glossy w/ extensive arts, clubs & restaurant listings for the City

San Francisco Bay Times 415/626-0260 • popular • a 'must read' for Bay Area resources & personals

San Francisco Frontiers 415/487-6000 • lgbt newsmagazine

SPIRITUAL GROUPS

Bay Area Pagan Assemblies 408/559-4242 • open rituals 6pm-9pm last Sun of month, call for info

Dignity San Francisco 1329 7th Ave (at Presbyterian church, btwn Irving & Judah) 415/681-2491 • 5:30pm Sun • lgbt Roman Catholic services

Hartford Street Zen Center 57 Hartford St (btwn 17th & 18th Sts) 415/863-2507 • 6am & 6pm daily sittings

Q-Spirit 415/281-9377 • queer spirituality events & discussions

Reclaiming PO Box 14404 94110 • pagan infoline & network • classes • newsletter

SF—Castro & Noe Valley

ACCOMMODATIONS

18th Inn Castro 415/252-7192 • lesbians/ gay men • Victorian guesthouse in the Castro • $95-185

24 Henry & Village House 24 Henry St & 4080 18th St (btwn Sanchez & Noe) 415/864-5686, 800/900-5686 • mostly gay men • smokefree • one-bdrm apt also available • $65-139

Albion House Inn 135 Gough St (at Fell) 415/621-0896, 800/625-2466 • gay-friendly • full brkfst • smokefree • kids ok • woman-owned/ run • $115-185

Beck's Motor Lodge 2222 Market St (at Sanchez) 415/621-8212 • gay-friendly • in the heart of the Castro • $95-114

▲ **Belvedere House** 598 Belvedere St (at 17th) 415/731-6654, 877/226-3273 • popular • lesbians/ gay men • wall-to-wall books, art & style • just up the hill from the heart of the Castro • French & German spoken • $55-75

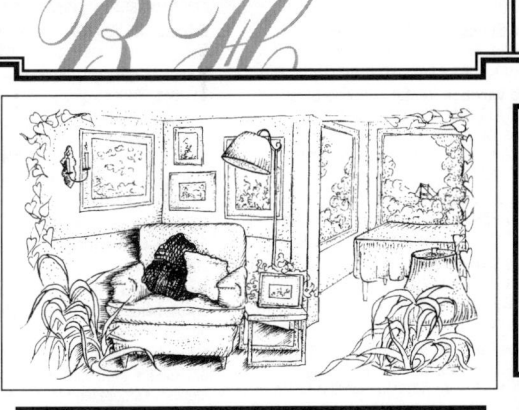

BELVEDERE HOUSE
A place to be and let be.

10% DISCOUNT
for bookings made 4 weeks in advance*

toll free 1.877.B and B SF
phone 415.731.6654
fax 415.681.0719
email BelvedereHouse@mindspring.com
www.GayBedandBreakfast.net

598 Belvedere Street
(corner of 17th Street, right above the Castro)

Your popular gay stay in The City
Walk to the bars, restaurants, shops and all the fun
Continental breakfast
Rooms with mini bar, computer/modem line and TV*
Laundry service available

Rooms from $105.00
Private bath, private half-bath, shared bath available

*some restrictions apply

California • USA

Casa Buena Vista near Market & Castro **916/974-7409** • gay-friendly • rental apt • $175-250

Castro Suites 927 14th St (at Noe) **415/437-1783** • mostly gay men • furnished apts • smokefree • gay-owned/run • $180-195

Castro Vacation Rental 72 Eureka St (at Market) **415/626-7126, 888/626-7126** • lesbians/gay men • apt 3 blks from the Castro • kids ok • smokefree • gay-owned/run • $1,000/week

Castro Victorian Vacation Rental 415/621-3580 • gay/straight • furnished apts in the Castro • gay-owned/run • $80-150

Church Street B&B 325 Church St (at 15th) **415/621-7600** • gay/straight • restored 1905 Edwardian in the Castro • smokefree • woman-owned/run • $85-110

Dolores Park Inn 3641 17th St (btwn Church & Dolores) **415/621-0482** • gay-friendly • Italianate Victorian mansion • hot tub • some shared baths • kitchens • fireplaces • smokefree • kids ok • $99-239

▲ **Edwardian San Francisco** 1668 Market St (btwn Franklin & Gough) **415/864-1271, 888/864-8070** • gay-friendly • some shared baths • smokefree • $59-149

Ethel's Garden in the Castro 415/864-6171 • women only • hot tub • kitchenette • private entrance • nr everything • $90

Friends 415/826-5972 • lesbians/gay men • B&B in private home • gay-owned/run • $50-65

House O' Chicks Guesthouse 415/861-9849 • women only • $75-125

Inn on Castro 321 Castro St (btwn 16th & 17th) **415/861-0321** • lesbians/gay men • B&B known for its hospitality & friendly atmosphere • full brkfst • smokefree • gay-owned/run • $100-250

Le Grenier 347 Noe St (at 16th St) **415/864-4748** • lesbians/gay men • suite • $60-90

Nancy's Bed 415/239-5692 • women only • private home • kitchen • smokefree • kids ok • $25+

Noe's Nest B&B 3973 23rd St (at Noe) **415/821-0751** • gay-friendly • full brkfst • hot tub • fireplace • smokefree • kids ok • $135-205

▲ **The Parker House Guest House** 520 Church St (at 17th) **415/621-3222, 888/520-7275** • popular • mostly gay men • Edwardian guesthouse w/ gardens • steam spa • smokefree • gay-owned/run • $119-199

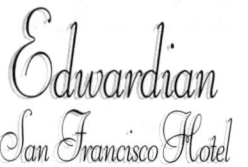

A small boutique hotel that possesses character with a distinctly European flavor

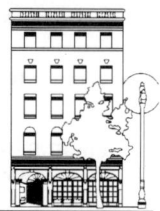

Recipient of the *New York Times' Budget Choice.*

☆ Centrally located six blocks east of Castro Street
☆ On San Francisco's main corridor of public transportation
☆ City tours available ☆ Hotel recently renovated
☆ Charming rooms ☆ Jacuzzi available in selected rooms
☆ Visa, Mastercard & American Express welcome

We are pleased to offer accommodations at reasonable rates featuring rooms with direct dial phone, cable TV, coffee and fresh flowers.

**1668 MARKET STREET • SAN FRANCISCO, CA 94102
TEL (415) 864-1271 • 1-888-864-8070 • FAX (415) 861-8116
www.edwardiansfhotel.com**

SF—Castro & Noe Valley • California

Ruth's House 415/641-8898 • women only • shared bath • smokefree • small kids ok • lesbian-owned/run • $40-50

SF Noe Valley Tourist Apt 225 28th St (at Church) 415/695-9782 • gay/straight • cozy upstairs apt • kids ok • gay-owned/run • $100

Terrace Place 415/241-0425 • lesbians/gay men • guest suite • $125-200

Travelodge Central 1707 Market St (at Valencia) 415/621-6775, 800/578-7878 • gay-friendly • smokefree rooms available • $99-169

The Willows Inn 710 14th St (at Church) 415/431-4770 • lesbians/gay men • smokefree • gay-owned/run • $85-125

BARS

The Bar on Castro 456 Castro St 415/626-7220 • 3pm-2am, from noon wknds • popular • mostly gay men • neighborhood bar • a little bit of NYC's Chelsea District swank in SF • wheelchair access

The Cafe 2367 Market St 415/861-3846 • 2pm-2am • popular • lesbians/gay men • dancing/DJ • young crowd • deck overlooking Castro & Market

Cafe du Nord 2170 Market St (at Sanchez) 415/861-5016 • 4pm-2am • gay-friendly • alternative • theme nights • live music • food served 6:30pm-11pm Wed-Sun • some veggie • $5-10

Daddy's 440 Castro St 415/621-8732 • 9am-2am, from 8am wknds • popular • mostly gay men • neighborhood bar • leather • women genuinely welcome

Harvey's 500 Castro St 415/431-4278 • 11am-2am, from 9am wknds • popular • lesbians/gay men • neighborhood bar • live shows • also restaurant • wheelchair access

Martuni's 4 Valencia St (at Market) 415/241-0205 • 4pm-2am • popular • gay/straight • piano bar & lounge • great martinis

The Metro 3600 16th St (at Noe) 415/703-9750 • 4pm-2am, from 1pm wknds • mostly gay men • karaoke Tue • deck overlooking Market St • also Chinese restaurant

The Mint 1942 Market St (at Buchanan) 415/626-4726 • 11am-2am • lesbians/gay men • popular karaoke bar nights • videos • also restaurant • food served till 11pm (till midnight wknds)

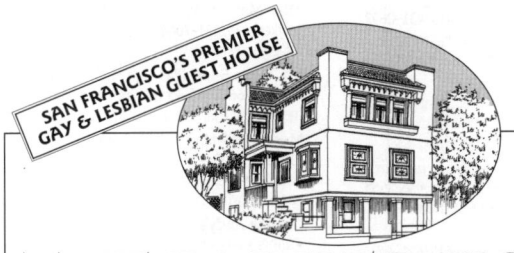

SAN FRANCISCO'S PREMIER GAY & LESBIAN GUEST HOUSE

IGLTA

THE PARKER HOUSE
"Historic Guest House and Gardens"

"Highest Rating" –DAMRON, FODOR'S *and* OUT & ABOUT

- Perfect Castro location
- Well appointed public rooms, gardens & steam spa
- Complete business and leisure traveler amenities

VISIT OUR WEBSITE AT: **www.parkerguesthouse.com** ◆ OR CALL US TOLL FREE: **888-520-7275**

520 CHURCH STREET, SAN FRANCISCO, CA 94114

California • USA

Moby Dick's 4049 18th St • mostly gay men • neighborhood bar • videos

Pilsner Inn 225 Church St (at Market) **415/621–7058** • 9am-2am • popular • mostly gay men • neighborhood bar • young crowd • great patio

Uncle Bert's Place 4086 18th St **415/431–8616** • 9am-2am, from 6am wknds • mostly gay men • neighborhood bar • heated patio • wknd bbq

CAFES

Cafe Flore 2298 Market St **415/621–8579** • 7am-11pm • popular • lesbians/gay men • some veggie • beer/wine • great patio

Jumpin' Java 139 Noe St (at 14th St) **415/431–5282** • 6am-10pm, from 7am wknds

Just Desserts 248 Church St **415/626–5774** • 7am-11pm • lesbians/gay men • cafe • delicious cakes • quiet patio

Orbit Room Cafe 1900 Market St (at Laguna) **415/252–9525** • 8am-1am, till 2am Fri-Sat, till midnight Sun • food served • great view of Market St • also bar

Sweet Inspiration 2239 Market St **415/621–8664** • 7am-11pm • popular wknd nights • fabulous desserts

RESTAURANTS

2223 Market 2223 Market St **415/431–0692** • dinner, brunch Sun • popular • contemporary American • full bar • wheelchair access • $13-16

Alfred Schilling 1695 Market St (at Valencia) **415/431–8447** • lunch & dinner • gourmet fare • also outdoor cafe & chocolatier

Anchor Oyster Bar 579 Castro St (at 19th) **415/431–3990** • lesbians/gay men • seafood • some veggie • beer/wine • women-owned/run • $10-20

Bagdad Cafe 2295 Market St **415/621–4434** • 24hrs • lesbians/gay men • diner • some veggie • $5-10

Blue 2337 Market St (btwn Castro & Noe) **415/863–2583** • 11:30am-11pm, wknd brunch • popular • homecooking served w/ style • some veggie • beer/wine • $7-15

Cafe Cuvee 2073 Market St (at 14th St) **415/621–7488** • dinner Tue-Sat, brunch wknds, clsd Mon • lesbian-owned/run

Caffe Luna Piena 558 Castro St **415/621–2566** • lunch & dinner, clsd Mon • lesbians/gay men • Californian • patio

Carta 1760 Market St (nr Gough) **415/863–3516** • lunch & dinner, Sun brunch • theme menus • gay-owned/run

China Court 599 Castro **415/626–5358** • lunch Mon-Fri, dinner nightly • Chinese • some veggie • beer/wine • $5-10

Chloe's 1399 Church St, Noe Valley (at 26th St) **415/648–4116** • 8am-3pm • popular • come early for the excellent wknd brunch

Chow 215 Church St **415/552–2469** • 11am-11pm, till midnight Th-Sat • popular • eclectic & affordable

Cove Cafe 434 Castro St **415/626–0462** • 7am-10pm • lesbians/gay men • some veggie • wheelchair access • $8-12

Delfina 3621 18th St (at Dolores) **415/552–4055** • 5:30pm-10pm • excellent Tuscan cuisine • $25-30

Eric's Chinese Restaurant 1500 Church St, Noe Valley (at 27th St) **415/282–0919** • 11am-9pm • popular • some veggie • $7-12

Hot 'N Hunky 4039 18th St **415/621–6365** • 11am-midnight • lesbians/gay men • hamburgers • some veggie • $5-10

It's Tops 1801 Market St (at Octavia) **415/431–6395** • 8am-3pm, till 3am Wed-Sat • classic diner • great hotcakes

Johnfrank 2100 Market St (at Church) **415/503–0333** • mostly gay men • dinner • upscale American

M&L Market (May's) 691 14th St (at Market) **415/431–7044** • clsd Sun • great huge sandwiches

Ma Tante Sumi 4243 18th St (at Diamond) **415/552–6663** • 5:30pm-10pm • lesbians/gay men • cont'l/ Japanese

Mecca 2029 Market St (at Dolores) **415/621–7000** • dinner from 5:30pm • popular • Mediterranean • swanky bar • valet parking • wheelchair access • $13-19

Orphan Andy's 3991 17th St **415/864–9795** • 24hrs • diner • gay-owned/ run

Pasta Pomodoro 2304 Market St **415/558–8123** • open till midnight • popular • lesbians/gay men • inexpensive Italian • also 24th & Noe location

Patio Cafe 531 Castro St **415/621–4640** • lesbians/gay men • California cuisine • enclosed patio • popular brunch • $10-20

Piaf's 1686 Market St (at Gough) **415/864–3700** • 5pm-close • oyster & seafood bar • also cabaret • 'Queer Comedy' 8pm Mon

Red Grill 4063 18th St **415/255–2733** • steak and seafood • also 'Whiskey Lounge' upstairs

… SF—Castro & Noe Valley • California

The Sausage Factory 517 Castro St **415/626-1250** • noon-1am • lesbians/ gay men • pizza & pasta • some veggie • beer/ wine • $8-15

Sparky's 242 Church St **415/626-8666** • 24hrs • diner • some veggie • popular late night • $8-12

Tin-Pan Asian Bistro 2251 Market St **415/565-0733** • 11am-11pm, wknd brunch • popular • sake cocktails

Tita's Hale'aina 3870 17th St (btwn Sanchez & Noe) **415/626-2477** • 11am-10pm, from 9am Sat, till 3pm Sun • popular • traditional Hawaiian • plenty veggie • wheelchair access • lesbian-owned/ run • $6-10

Welcome Home 464 Castro St **415/626-3600** • 8am-11pm • popular • lesbians/ gay men • homestyle • some veggie • beer/ wine • $7-12

Zuni Cafe 1658 Market St (at Haight) **415/552-2522** • clsd Mon • popular • upscale cont'l/ Mediterranean • full bar • $30-40

Entertainment & Recreation

Castro Country Club 4058 18th St **415/552-6102** • 2pm-11pm, 10am-11pm Sat, noon-8pm Sun, clsd Mon-Tue • lesbians/ gay men • alcohol & drug-free club

Bookstores

A Different Light 489 Castro St **415/431-0891** • 10am-10pm • popular • lgbt bookstore & queer info clearinghouse • readings

Aardvark Books 227 Church St **415/552-6733** • 10:30am-10:30pm • mostly used • good lgbt section • say hello to Ace, the bookstore cat par excellence

Books, Inc 2275 Market St **415/864-6777** • 10am-11pm • lgbt section • readings • wheelchair access

Get Lost 1825 Market St (at Guerrero) **415/437-0529** • 10am-7pm, till 6pm Sat, 11am-5pm Sun • travel books • lgbt section

Retail Shops

A Taste of Leather 2370 Market (near Castro) **415/552-4500, 800/367-0786** • noon-8pm, 10am-10pm wknds

Does Your Father Know? 548 Castro St **415/241-9865** • 9:30am-10pm, till 11pm Fri-Sat, 10am-9pm Sun • lgbt gifts & videos

Does Your Mother Know? 4079 18th St **415/864-3160** • 9:30am-10pm • cards • T-shirts

---

See Jane Run. sports
ATHLETIC GEAR FOR WOMEN

Largest selection of women's fitness apparel and footwear in the Bay Area

See Jane Run
3870 24th Street
San Francisco
www.SeeJaneRunSports.com

FREE Personal shopper Fitness Consultant! Call for appointment

415.401.8338

We Carry Plus Sizes

Running   Cycling   Swimming   Hiking   Yoga   Soccer

California • USA

Don't Panic 541 Castro St **415/553-8989** • 10am-10pm, 11am-9pm Sun • campy T-shirts • gifts

Image Leather 2199 Market St (at Sanchez) **415/621-7551** • 9am-10pm, 11am-7pm Sun • custom leather clothing • accessories • toys

Just for Fun 3982 24th St (at Noe) **415/285-4068** • 9am-9pm, till 8pm Sat, 10am-6pm Sun • gift shop • wheelchair access

La Sirena Botanica 1509 Church St (at 27th St) **415/285-0612** • noon-6pm • Afro-Caribbean religious articles

Leather Zone of San Francisco 2352 Market St **415/255-8585** • 11am-7pm, noon-6pm Sun, open later in summer • new & used fetishwear

Rolo 2351 Market St **415/431-4545** • 10am-8pm, till 7pm Sun • designer labels • also 450 Castro location, 415/626-7171

▲ **See Jane Run Sports** 3870 24th St (at Sanchez) **415/401-8338** • 11am-7pm, 10am-6pm Sat, till 5pm Sun

Stormy Leather 582C Castro (upstairs) **415/671-1295** • noon-7pm, till 8pm Fri • leather • latex • toys • magazines • women-owned/ run

Uncle Mame 2241 Market St (btwn Sanchez & Noe) **415/626-1953** • noon-7pm, till 5pm Sun • kitsch lover's wonderland

Under One Roof 549 Castro **415/252-9430** • 11am-7pm • 100% donated to AIDS relief • wheelchair access

Spiritual Groups

Congregation Sha'ar Zahav 290 Dolores (at 16th) **415/861-6932** • call for services

MCC of San Francisco 150 Eureka St (btwn 18th & 19th Sts) **415/863-4434** • 9am, 11am & 7pm Sun, 7pm Wed

Most Holy Redeemer Church 100 Diamond St (at 18th St) **415/863-6259** • 8am & 10am Sun, 5pm Sat (vigil mass) • mostly lesbian/gay Roman Catholic parish

Gyms & Health Clubs

Gold's Gym Castro 2301 Market St **415/626-4488** • popular • lesbians/ gay men • day passes available

Erotica

Jaguar 4057 18th St **415/863-4777**

Le Salon 4126 18th St **415/552-4213**

The MMO (Mercury Mail Order) 4084 18th St **415/621-1188** • leather • toys

Romantasy Exquisite Corsetry **415/585-0760** • call for appt • corsets & fetish clothing • woman-owned/ run

SF—South of Market

Accommodations

Ramada Market St 1231 Market St (btwn 8th & 9th) **415/626-8000, 800/227-4747** • gay-friendly • wheelchair access

Victorian Hotel 54 4th St (btwn Market & Mission) **415/986-4400, 800/227-3804** • gay-friendly • 1913 landmark hotel • some shared baths • also restaurant • SF cuisine • full bar • $69-209

Bars

The Eagle Tavern 398 12th St (at Harrison) **415/626-0880** • noon-2am • mostly gay men • popular • leather • occasional women's leather events • live music • patio

Hole in the Wall Saloon 289 8th St (at Folsom) **415/431-4695** • noon-2am, from 6am Fri-Mon • mostly gay men • neighborhood bar • leather

Rawhide II 280 7th St (btwn Howard & Folsom) **415/621-1197** • 8pm-2am, clsd Mon • mostly gay men • dancing/DJ • country/ western nights

Nightclubs

1015 Folsom 1015 Folsom St (at 6th) **415/431-1200** • 10pm-4:30am • gay/ straight • popular • dancing/DJ • call for events • cover charge

Asia SF 201 9th St (at Howard) **415/255-2742** • 10:30pm-close Wed-Sat • popular • gay/ straight • dancing/DJ • multiracial-Asian • theme nights • go-go boys • cover charge • also Cal-Asian restaurant w/ en-drag service 5pm-10pm

Azucar 201 9th St (at 'Asia SF') **415/255-2742** • 10pm-3am 1st Sat • popular • mostly gay men • dancing/DJ • mostly Latino• go-go boys & girls

Club Asia 174 King St (in 'King St Garage') **415/285-2742** • 10pm-close 2nd & 4th Fri • popular • mostly gay men • dancing/DJ • mostly Asian- American • live shows • cover charge

▲ **Club Q** 177 Townsend (btwn 2nd & 3rd Sts) **415/647-8258 (HIT 2#)** • 9pm-3am 1st Fri • mostly women • popular dance party • cover charge

Club Red 399 9th St (at 'The Stud') **415/339-8310** • 10pm-3am 3rd Fri • women only • dancing/DJ • multiracial • go-go dancers • wheelchair access

SF—South of Market • California

Club Universe 177 Townsend (at 3rd St) **415/974-6020, 415/289-6650** • 9:30pm-7am Sat • popular • mostly gay men • dancing/DJ • cover charge

Endup 401 6th St (at Harrison) **415/357-0827** • clsd Tue • mostly gay men • dancing/DJ • multiracial • theme nights • popular Sun mornings

Futura 174 King St (in 'King St Garage') **415/665-6715** • 10pm-3am 2nd & 4th Sat • popular • mostly gay men • dancing/DJ • mostly Latino/a • live shows • cover charge

G-Spot 401 6th St (at the 'Endup') **415/337-4962 (ENDUP#)** • 9pm-close Sat only • popular • mostly women • dancing/DJ • go-go dancers

Pleasuredome 177 Townsend (at 3rd St) **415/289-6699, 415/974-6020** • 9pm-3am Sun • mostly gay men • dancing/DJ • cover charge

Shaft 399 9th St (at 'The Stud') **415/252-7883 (STUD #)** • 9am-2am Mon • popular • mostly gay men • dancing/DJ • mostly African-American • young crowd

The Stud 399 9th St (at Harrison) **415/252-7883 (INFO LINE), 415/863-6623** • 5pm-2am • popular • lesbians/gay men • dancing/DJ • theme nights • outrageous 'Trannyshack' Tue • more women Fri (multiracial clientele) • young crowd

Sugar 399 9th St (at 'The Stud') **415/252-7883 (STUD #)** • 9pm-5am Sat • popular • mostly gay men • dancing/DJ • great music & wall-to-wall alternababes • young crowd

Trannyshack 399 9th St (at the Stud) **415/863-6623** • 10pm-3am Tue • popular • mostly gay men • dancing/DJ • weekly party for trannies & their friends & admirers

Cafes

Brain Wash 1122 Folsom St (at 7th St) **415/861-3663, 415/431-9274** • 7am-11pm • popular • cafe & laundromat • beer/wine

Restaurants

Ananda Fuara 1298 Market St (at 9th) **415/621-1994** • 8am-8pm, till 3pm Wed, clsd Sun • vegetarian

Boulevard 1 Mission St (at Steuart) **415/543-6084** • lunch Mon-Fri & dinner daily • one of SF's finest

Butter 354 11th St **415/863-5964** • 5pm-2am Tue-Sat • 'white trash bistro' • full bar • theme nights

Fringale 570 4th St (btwn Bryant & Brannan) **415/543-0573** • lunch & dinner, clsd Sun • French bistro • wheelchair access • $11-16

Harvey's SoMa 1582 Folsom St (at 12th St) **415/626-1985** • 11:30am-10:30pm, till 2am Fri-Sat • some veggie • wheelchair access

Hawthorne Lane 22 Hawthorne St (btwn 2nd & 3rd off Howard) **415/777-9779** • dinner nightly, lunch Mon-Fri

Le Charm 315 5th St (at Folsom) **415/546-6128** • lunch Mon-Fri, dinner Mon-Sat, clsd Sun

Lulu 816 Folsom St (at 4th St) **415/495-5775** • lunch & dinner • popular • upscale Mediterrranean • some veggie • full bar • wheelchair access • $12-20

Manora's Thai Cuisine 1600 Folsom (at 12th) **415/861-6224** • lunch & dinner • some veggie

Tu Lan 8 6th St (at Market) **415/626-0927** • lunch & dinner • Vietnamese • some veggie • dicey neighborhood but delicious (& cheap) food

Woodward's Garden 1700 Mission St (at Duboce) **415/621-7122** • dinner seatings at 6pm & 8pm, clsd Mon • wheelchair access

Retail Shops

A Taste of Leather 1339 Folsom (btwn 9th & 10th) **415/252-9166, 800/367-0786** • noon-8pm, till midnight Fri-Sat

Dandelion 55 Potrero Ave (at Alameda St) **415/436-9500, 888/548-1968** • 10am-6pm, clsd Sun-Mon • gifts, books erotica & more • gay-owned/ run

Leather Etc 1201 Folsom St (at 8th St) **415/864-7558** • 10:30am-7pm, 11am-6pm Sat, noon-5pm Sun

Mr S Leather 310 7th St (at Folsom) **415/863-7764** • 11am-7pm, noon-6pm Sun • erotic goods • custom leather • latex

Stompers 323 10th St (at Folsom) **415/255-6422** • noon-8pm, till 6pm Sun • boots • cigars • gloves

Stormy Leather 1158 Howard St (btwn 7th & 8th) **415/626-1672** • noon-7pm • leather • latex • toys • magazines • women-owned/ run

Gyms & Health Clubs

Gold's Gym San Francisco 9th & Brannan **415/552-4653** • popular • gay/ straight • day passes available

Sex Clubs

Power Exchange Substation I 86 Otis St (btwn S Van Ness & Gough) **415/487-9944** • call for hours • playspace for female, transgendered, bi & straight couples

California • USA

SF—Polk Street Area

ACCOMMODATIONS

Atherton Hotel 685 Ellis St (at Larkin) **415/474-5720, 800/474-5720** • gay-friendly • food served • full bar • $99-159

▲ **Essex Hotel** 684 Ellis St **415/474-4664, 800/443-7739 (IN CA)** • gay-friendly • smokefree • $79-99

The Monarch Hotel 1015 Geary St (at Polk) **415/673-5232, 800/777-3210** • gay-friendly • kids ok • non-smoking rooms available • up to $139

▲ **The Phoenix Hotel** 601 Eddy St (at Larkin) **415/776-1380, 800/248-9466** • gay-friendly • 1950s-style motor lodge • popular • swimming • kids ok • fabulous 'Back Flip' bar • $119-225

BARS

▲ **Back Flip** 601 Eddy St (at The Phoenix Hotel) **415/771-3547** • 7pm-2am, clsd Sun-Mon • popular • gay-friendly • dancing/DJ • cocktails w/ class • dinner nightly

The Cinch 1723 Polk St (at Clay) **415/776-4162** • 6am-2am • mostly gay men • neighborhood bar • patio • lots of pool tables & no attitude • wheelchair access

Gangway 841 Larkin St (btwn Geary & O'Farrell) **415/776-6828** • 10am-2am • mostly gay men • neighborhood bar

Jezebel's Joint 510 Larkin (at Turk) **415/345-9832** • 6pm-2am Th-Sun • gay/straight • cocktail lounge • 'Devil's Den' downstairs • transgender-friendly • live shows

Kimo's 1351 Polk St (at Pine) **415/885-4535** • 8am-2am • mostly gay men • neighborhood bar • live bands upstairs

Lush Lounge 1092 Post (at Polk) **415/771-2022** • 4pm-2am, from 3pm Fri-Sat • gay/straight • martini bar & piano lounge • wheelchair access

Mother Lode/ Divas 1081 Post St (at Larkin) **415/928-6006, 415/474-DIVA** • 6am-2am • mostly gay men • neighborhood bar • dancing/DJ • multiracial • transsexuals, transvestites & their admirers • live shows

NIGHTCLUBS

dBar 1550 California St, 2nd flr (at Tango Tango) **415/775-0442** • 9pm-2am 4th Sat only • popular • mostly women • dancing/DJ • mostly Asian-American

Tango Tango 1550 California, 2nd flr (at Polk) **415/775-0442** • 5pm-2am • gay/straight • dancing/DJ • karaoke • theme nights • popular drag shows Fri-Sat

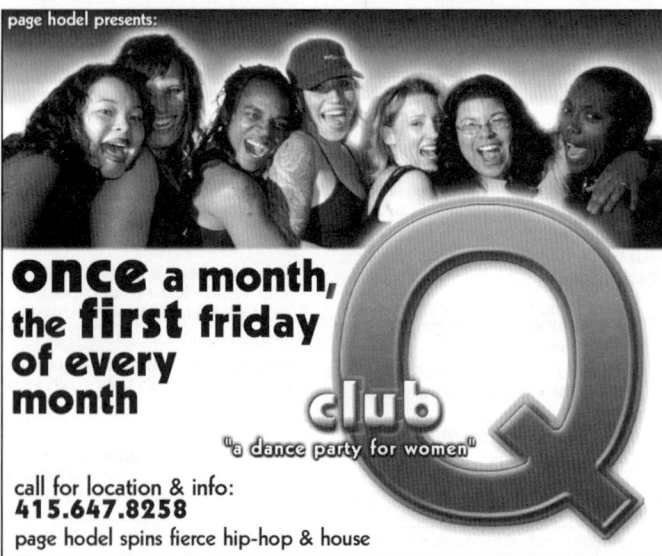

SF—Polk Street Area • California

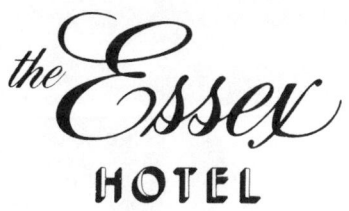

the Essex HOTEL

With a European charm and tradition, the Essex is only one block from Polk Street. Close to shopping, bars, restaurants, theatres, and the City's gay life!

415-474-4664

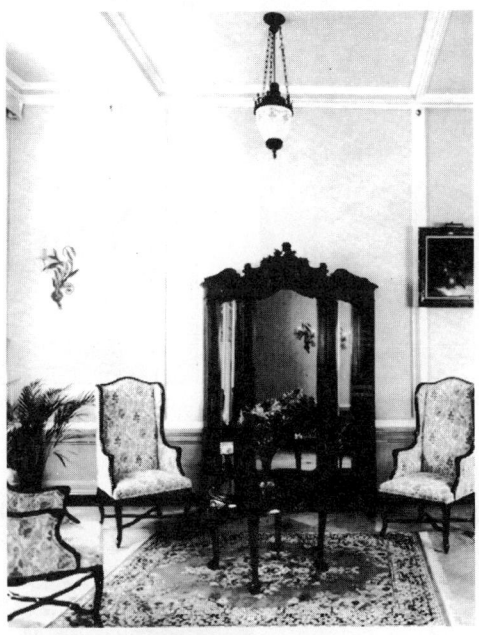

- Toll free for reservation -
1-800-453-7739 USA • 1-800-443-7739 CA
684 Ellis Street · S.F., CA · 94109

The San Francisco Bay Area's Unique Collection of Boutique Hotels and Escapes

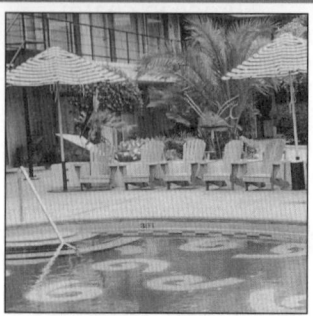

Phoenix Hotel • Civic Center
800.248.9466

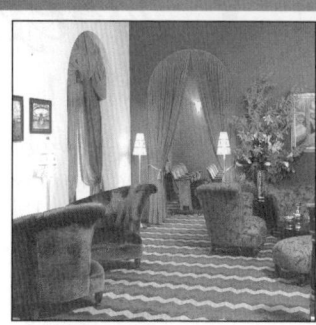

Hotel Bijou • Union Square
800.771.1022

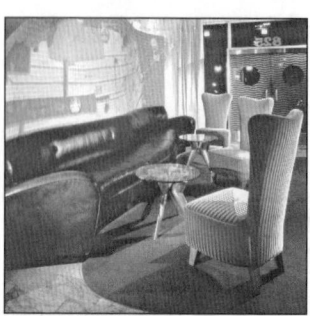

Commodore Hotel • Union Square
800.338.6848

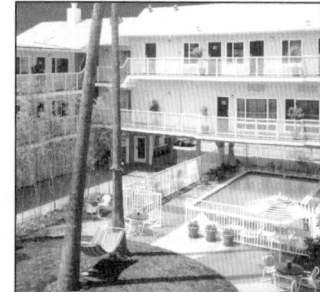

Hotel Del Sol • Marina District
877.433.5765

Central Reservations for all Joie de Vivre Hotels
800.738.7477

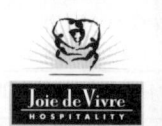

These hotels are all distinctive Joie de Vivre properties.

www.jdvhospitality.com
Access Code: JV

escape, explore, experience

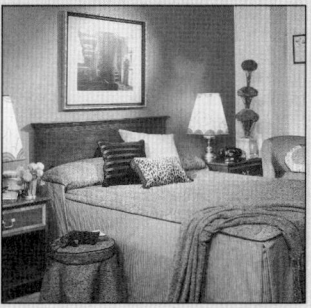

Maxwell Hotel • Union Square
888.734.6299

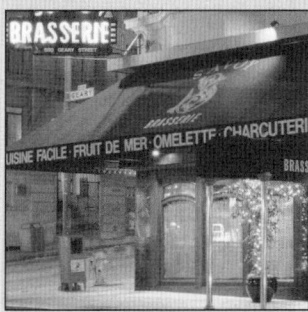

Savoy Hotel • Union Square
800.227.4223

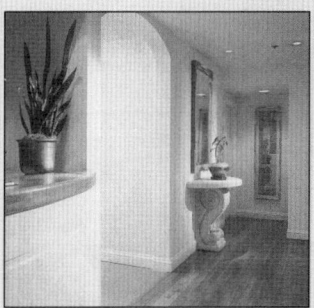

Nob Hill Lambourne • Nob Hill
800.274.8466

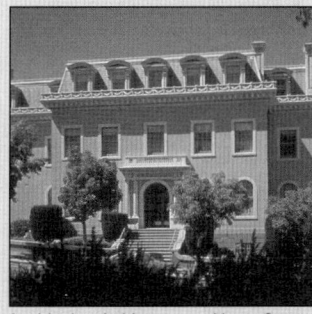

Archbishop's Mansion • Alamo Square
800.543.5820

Visit our web site for our new Silicon Valley Properties

www.jdvhospitality.com

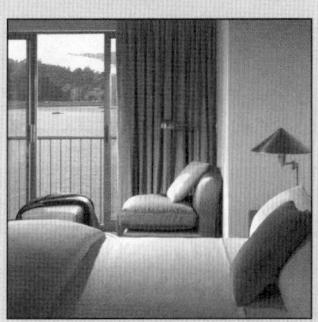

Acqua Hotel • Mill Valley
888.662.9555

Photo Credit: Cesar Rubio, Nathaneal Bennett, Russell Abrahams, Chris Opel

California • USA

CAFES

Quetzal 1234 Polk St (at Sutter) **415/673–4181** • 6am-11pm • food served • beer/ wine • live shows • videos • Internet access

RESTAURANTS

Antica Trattoria 2400 Polk St (at Union) **415/928-5797** • dinner Tue-Sun • Italian

Bistro Zare 1507 Polk St **415/775–4304** • dinner, clsd Sun-Mon • Mediterranean

California Culinary Academy 625 Polk St (at Polk) • lunch & dinner • popular • cooking school where future top chefs serve up what they've learned

Edinburgh Castle 950 Geary St (at Polk) **415/885–4074** • 5pm-2am • mostly straight but rockin' Scottish pub w/ single malts, beer, darts & authentic fish & chips • live bands • occassional hangout for alternadykes

El Super Burrito 1200 Polk St (at Sutter) **415/771–9700** • 9am-11pm

Grubstake II 1525 Pine St (at Polk) **415/673–8268** • 5pm-4am, from 10am wknds • lesbians/ gay men • diner • beer/ wine

Johnny Wok 1237 Polk St (at Bush) **415/928–6888** • lunch & dinner, clsd Sun • Chinese

Tai Chi 2031 Polk St (at Pacific) **415/441–6758** • lunch Mon-Fri, dinner nightly • popular • Chinese

BOOKSTORES

A Clean Well Lighted Place For Books 601 Van Ness Ave (at Turk) **415/441–6670** • 10am-11pm, till 9pm Sun • independent • lgbt section • many readings

Aaben Books 1546 California St (btwn Polk & Larkin) **415/563–3525** • 10am-10pm, till 11pm Fri-Sat • independent • new & used

SF—Downtown & North Beach

ACCOMMODATIONS

Allison Hotel 417 Stockton St (at Sutter) **415/986-8737, 800/628-6456** • gay-friendly • some shared baths • $59-179

Amsterdam Hotel 749 Taylor St (at Sutter) **415/673–3277, 800/637–3444** • gay-friendly • charming European-style hotel • $99-149

Andrews 624 Post St (at Taylor) **415/563-6877, 800/926–3739** • gay-friendly • Victorian hotel • also restaurant • Italian • $99-175

Canterbury Hotel 750 Sutter St (at Taylor) **415/474–6464, 800/227–4788** • gay-friendly • also 'Murray's Glasshouse' restaurant & bar • $107-275

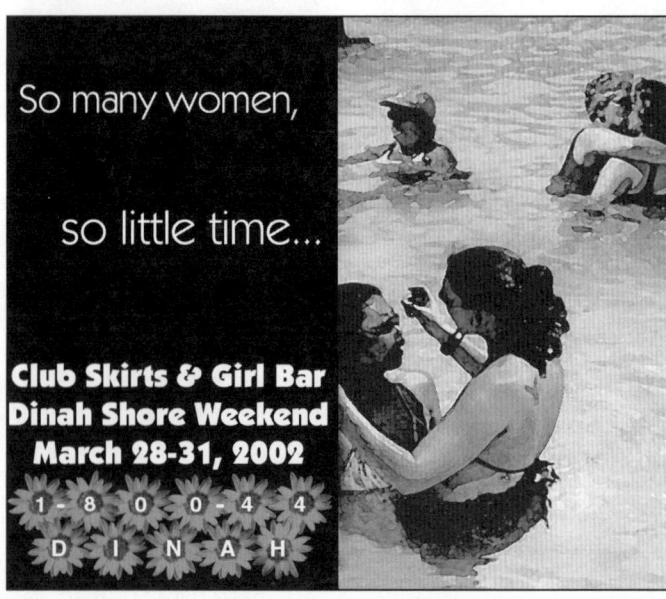

SF—Downtown & North Beach • California

Cartwright Hotel 524 Sutter St (at Powell) **415/421-2865, 800/794-7661** • gay-friendly • free gym passes • afternoon tea • wine hour • $89-279

▲ **The Commodore International Hotel** 825 Sutter St (at Jones) **415/923-6800, 800/338-6848** • gay-friendly • also popular 'Red Room' lounge • kids ok • $129-159

Dakota Hotel 606 Post St (at Taylor) **415/931-7475** • gay-friendly • nr Union Square • kids ok • $79-119

Galleria Park Hotel 191 Sutter St (at Kearny) **415/781-3060, 800/792-9639** • gay-friendly • live jazz Wed-Sun • $99+

Grand Hyatt San Francisco 345 Stockton St (at Sutter) **415/398-1234, 800/233-1234** • gay-friendly • restaurant & lounge • $165-345

Harbor Court Hotel 165 Steuart St (btwn Howard & Mission) **415/882-1300, 800/346-0555** • gay-friendly • in the heart of the Financial District • gym • $210-375

▲ **Hotel Bijou** 111 Mason St (at Eddy) **415/771-1200, 800/771-1022** • gay/ straight • smokefree • wheelchair access • kids ok • $119-189

Hotel Diva 440 Geary (at Mason) **415/885-0200, 800/553-1900** • gay-friendly • also Italian restaurant • gym • $139-249

Hotel Griffon 155 Steuart St (at Mission) **415/495-2100, 800/321-2201** • gay-friendly • also restaurant • bistro/ cont'l • wheelchair access • $230-495

Hotel Monaco 501 Geary St (at Taylor) **415/292-8132, 888/882-3551** • gay-friendly • full bar • pets ok • $269+

Hotel Nikko San Francisco 222 Mason St **415/394-1111, 800/645-5687** • gay/ straight • swimming • health club & spa • also restaurant • wheelchair access • $215-395

▲ **The Hotel Rex** 562 Sutter St (at Powell) **415/433-4434, 800/433-4434** • gay-friendly • full bar • wheelchair access • $175+

Hotel Triton 342 Grant Ave (at Bush) **415/394-0500, 800/800-1299** • gay-friendly • designer theme rooms • wheelchair access • $239-389

Hotel Vintage Court 650 Bush St (at Powell) **415/392-4666, 800/654-1100** • gay-friendly • fireplaces • smokefree • also world-famous 5-star 'Masa's' restaurant • French • $75 prix fixe • wheelchair access • $149-239

Hyatt Regency San Francisco 5 Embarcadero Center (at California) **415/788-1234, 800/233-1234** • gay-friendly • luxury waterfront hotel

Juliana Hotel 590 Bush St (at Stockton) **415/392-2540, 800/328-3880** • gay-friendly • featured on 'Lifestyles of the Rich & Famous' as one of SF's finest hotels • $189-429

King George Hotel 334 Mason St (at O'Farrell) **415/781-5050, 800/288-6005** • gay-friendly • also The Bread & Honey Tearoom' • wheelchair access • $140-175

▲ **Maxwell Hotel** 386 Geary St (at Mason) **415/986-2000, 888/734-6299** • gay-friendly • newly-restored 1908 art deco masterpiece • wheelchair access • $160-235

Nob Hill Hotel 835 Hyde St (btwn Bush & Sutter) **415/885-2987, 877/662-4455** • gay-friendly • European-style hotel • smokefree • kids ok • also restaurant • $99-179

▲ **Nob Hill Lambourne** 725 Pine St (at Powell) **415/433-2287, 800/274-8466** • gay-friendly • luxurious 'business accommodation' • kitchens • kids ok • $210-350

Pensione International Hotel 875 Post St (at Hyde) **415/775-3344, 800/358-8123** • gay/ straight • Victorian-styled hotel built in early 1900s • some shared baths • smokefree • $70-110

Ramada Union Square 345 Taylor St (at Ellis) **415/673-2332, 800/228-2828** • gay-friendly • also restaurant & full bar • wheelchair access • $125-255

Renoir Hotel 45 McAllister St (at Market St) **415/626-5200, 800/576-3388** • gay/ straight • bar & restaurant • wheelchair access • $119-250

Savoy Hotel 580 Geary St (at Jones) **415/441-2700, 800/227-4223** • gay-friendly • also popular restaurant & bar • $149-279

Suites at Fisherman's Wharf **415/771-2000, 800/227-3608** • gay-friendly • Mediterranean-inspired 1- & 2-bdrm suites • sundeck • kitchens • $279+

The York Hotel 940 Sutter St (at Leavenworth) **415/885-6800, 800/808-9675** • gay-friendly • boutique hotel • also cabaret • $99-210

BARS

Aunt Charlie's Lounge 133 Turk St (at Taylor) **415/441-2922** • 6am-2am • mostly gay men • neighborhood bar • drag shows Sat • 'Skid Marx' 2nd Fri • DJ • alternative

CAFES

Caffe Trieste 601 Vallejo St **415/392-6739** • popular • get a taste of the real North Beach (past & present) and a great cappuccino

California • USA

Restaurants

Cafe Claude 7 Claude (nr Bush & Kearny) 415/392-3505 • 11:30am-close, clsd Sun • live jazz Th-Sat • as close to Paris as you can get in SF • beer/ wine

Dottie's True Blue Cafe 522 Jones St (at Geary) 415/885-2767 • 7:30am-3pm, clsd Wed • plenty veggie • great brkfst • gay-owned/ run

Mario's Bohemian Cigar Store Cafe 566 Columbus Ave (at Union) 415/362-0536 • great foccacia sandwiches • some veggie • beer/ wine

Masa's 650 Bush St (at 'Hotel Vintage Court') 415/989-7154 • world-famous 5-star French restaurant • wheelchair access

Max's on the Square 398 Geary St (at Mason) 415/646-8600 • lunch & dinner • popular • seafood • full bar

Millennium 246 McAllister St (at Hyde, at the Abigail Hotel) 415/487-9800 • dinner only • Euro-Mediterranean • upscale vegetarian

Moose's 1652 Stockton (btwn Filbert & Union) 415/989-7800 • popular • upscale bistro menu

Original Joe's 144 Taylor (btwn Turk & Eddy) 415/775-4877 • lunch & dinner • Italian • since 1937 • also art deco cocktail lounge

Bookstores

City Lights Bookstore 261 Columbus Ave, North Beach (at Pacific) 415/362-8193 • 10am-midnight • historic beatnik bookstore • many progressive titles • whole flr for poetry

Retail Shops

Billy Blue 54 Geary (at Grant) 415/781-2111, 800/772-BLUE • 10am-6pm, clsd Sun • men's clothing tailored for women

SF—Mission District

Accommodations

▲ **Andora Inn** 2438 Mission (btwn 20th & 21st) 415/282-0337, 800/967-9219 • lesbians/ gay men • guesthouse • nr Castro & public transportation • smokefree • also restaurant • full bar • $79-249

Clebia's Place 415/648-0135 • gay/ straight • apartment w/ great view • lesbian-owned/ run • $195

Elaine's Hidden Haven 4005 Folsom St 415/647-2726, 800/446-9050 • gay/ straight • private garden apt • lesbian-owned/ run • $59-139

Andora Inn... The Jewel of the Mission in the Heart of San Francisco

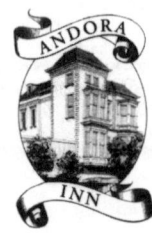

The Andora Inn is a 12 room fully restored 1875 Victorian Manor located in the heart of San Francisco's oldest and most colorful district, the Mission Dolores — fast becoming one of the hippest neighborhoods in the city, with wonderful art galleries, murals, bookstore/cafés and exciting new restaurants.

All rooms are equipped with:
- 5 Star Serta Mattresses -
- color T.V.'s with built-in V.C.R. and remote control -
- telephones • AM/FM clock radios -

Guests also enjoy a complimentary Continental Breakfast served daily in our beautiful Dining Room.

European Shared Bath *$79 to 119   Deluxe Rooms & Suites *$119 to $269

Discounted Rates for extended stays!

IGLTA   2438 Mission Street, San Francisco, CA 94110
Ph: 415-282-0337 **800-967-9219** Fax: 415-282-2608
Email: andorasf@aol.com Web: www.andorainn.com

SF—Mission District • California

▲ **The Inn San Francisco** 943 S Van Ness Ave (btwn 20th & 21st) **415/641-0188, 800/359-0913** • gay-friendly • Victorian mansion • full brkfst • hot tub • some shared baths • kitchens • fireplaces • patio • smokefree • $95-265

Bars

El Rio 3158–A Mission St (at Cesar Chavez) **415/282-3325** • 3pm-2am, till midnight Mon • gay/ straight • neighborhood bar • Latino/a clientele • live shows • patio

Joy 2925 16th St (btwn Mission & S Van Ness, at 'Liquid') **415/431-8889** • 9pm-2am Mon • popular • gay/ straight • neighborhood bar • dancing/DJ • eclectic mix of young & hip

▲ **Lexington Club** 3464 19th St (at Lexington) **415/863-2052** • 3pm-2am • popular • mostly women • neighborhood bar • hip young crowd • lesbian-owned/ run

Phone Booth 1398 S Van Ness Ave (at 25th) **415/648-4683** • 11am-2am • lesbians/ gay men • neighborhood bar • piano bar wknds

Sadie's Flying Elephant 491 Potrero (at Mariposa) **415/551-7988** • 3pm-2am • gay/straight • neighborhood bar • 9pm 1st Sun 'K'vetsh' queer open mike

Wild Side West 424 Cortland, Bernal Heights (at Bennington) **415/647-3099** • 1pm-2am • gay/ straight • neighborhood bar • patio • magic garden • wheelchair access

Nightclubs

26 Mix 3024 Mission St (btwn 26th & Cesar Chavez) **415/826-7378, 415/248-1319** • 5pm-2am • gay/ straight • intimate dance club • younger crowd • some women's events

Backstreet 550 Barneveld (2 blks off Bayshore) **415/339-8310** • 10pm-3am 2nd Sat • women only • popular • dancing/DJ • multiracial • go-go dancers • cover charge

Esta Noche 3079 16th St (at Mission) **415/861-5757** • 1pm-2am • mostly gay men • dancing/DJ • mostly Latino/a • transgender-friendly • live shows • salsa & disco in a classic Tijuana dive

Mango 3158 Mission St (at 'El Rio') **415/339-8310** • 3pm-7:30pm 4th Sat April-Nov • women only • dancing/DJ • multiracial • food served

Sushi Sundays 3024 Mission St (at 26th, at '26 Mix') **415/820-9661** • 7pm-midnight Sun only • popular • mostly women • dancing/ DJ

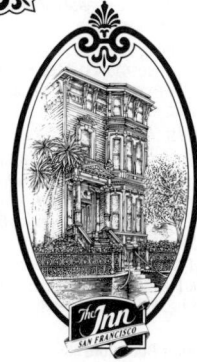

The Inn San Francisco

Distinct San Franciscan hospitality.
Gracious 1872 Victorian Mansion.
Historic residential neighborhood.
Antiques, fresh flowers, beverages.
Spa tubs, hot tubs, fireplaces.
Sundeck, lovely English Garden.
Full Buffet Breakfast.

943 SOUTH VAN NESS AVENUE, SAN FRANCISCO, CA 94110
(415)641-0188 • (800)359-0913 • FAX: (415)641-1701
E-MAIL: innkeeper@innsf.com
www.innsf.com

California • USA

Cafes

Cafe Commons 3161 Mission St (btwn Cesar Chavez & Valencia) **415/282-2928** • 7am-9pm, 8am-10pm wknds • sandwiches • plenty veggie • patio • wheelchair access • women-owned/ run • $4-7

Farleys 1315 18th St (at Texas St, Potrero Hill) **415/648-1545** • 7am-10pm, from 8am wknds • coffeehouse

Red Dora's Bearded Lady 485 14th St (at Guerrero) **415/626-2805** • 7am-7pm, from 9am wknds • popular • mostly women • transgender- friendly • funky brunch & sandwiches • plenty veggie • also gallery • special events • patio • lesbian-owned/ run • $4-7

Restaurants

42 Degrees 499 Illinois St, China Basin (nr 16th St) **415/777-5558** • Wed-Sun only • jazz supper club • full bar

The Barking Basset Cafe 803 Cortland Ave (at Ellsworth) **415/648-2146** • 8am-3pm, clsd Tue, dinner 5pm-9pm Th-Sat only

Cafe Istanbul 525 Valencia St **415/863-8854** • noon-11pm, till midnight Fri-Sat, Mediterranean • some veggie • authentic Turkish coffee • bellydancers Sat • wheelchair access

Charanga 2351 Mission St (at 20th St) **415/282-1813** • popular • 5:30pm-10pm, till 11pm Th-Sat, clsd Sun-Mon • tapas • beer/ wine/ sangria • plenty veggie • wheelchair access • women-owned/ run

El Farolito 2777 Mission St (at 24th) **415/824-7877** • popular • 11am-1am, till 3am Fri-Sat • delicious, cheap burritos & more

Firecracker 1007 1/2 Valencia St (at 21st) **415/642-3470** • popular • Chinese • some veggie

Herbivore 983 Valencia (nr 21st St) **415/826-5657** • 11am-10pm, till 11pm wknds • moderately priced vegan food in upscale setting • beer/ wine

Just For You 1453 18th St, Potrero Hill (btwn Missouri & Connecticut) **415/647-3033** • 7am-2pm, 8:30am-3pm wknds • popular • lesbians/ gay men • Southern brkfst • some veggie • women-owned/ run • $4-7

Klein's Delicatessen 501 Connecticut St (at 20th St, Potrero Hill) **415/821-9149** • 7am-7pm, 8am-5pm Sun • patio • sandwiches & salads • some veggie • beer/ wine • women-owned/ run • $4-10

Pancho Villa 3071 16th St (btwn Mission & Valencia) **415/864-8840** • 10am-midnight • also 'El Toro' at 18th & Valencia • some veggie • beer/ wine • wheelchair access • $4-8

Pauline's Pizza Pie 260 Valencia St (btwn 14th & Duboce) **415/552-2050** • 5pm-10pm, clsd Sun-Mon • popular • lesbians/ gay men • gourmet pizza • beer/ wine

Picaro 3120 16th St (at Valencia) **415/431-4089** • dinner only • Spanish tapas bar • beer/ wine • wheelchair access

The Slanted Door 584 Valencia St (at 17th) **415/861-8032** • popular • Vietnamese • reservations advised

Slow Club 2501 Mariposa (at Hampshire) **415/241-9390** • 11:30am-2:30 Mon-Fri, dinner 6:30pm-10pm Tue-Sat, wknd brunch • full bar • wheelchair access

Ti-Couz 3108 16th St **415/252-7373** • 11am-11pm, from 10am wknds • Breton dinner & dessert crepes • plenty veggie • beer/ wine • wheelchair access • $5-10

Yamo Thai Kitchen 3406 18th St (at Mission) **415/553-8911** • 11am-9:30pm, clsd Sun • small, no frills outfit w/ great cheap food

Entertainment & Recreation

Brendita's Latin Tour **415/921-0625** • walking tours of the Mission

Metronome Ballroom 1830 17th St (at De Haro) **415/252-9000** • gay/ straight • dance lessons • salsa to swing • dance parties wknds • call for events • cover charge

Women's Building 3543 18th St (btwn Valencia & Guerrero) **415/431-1180** • check out some of the most beautiful murals in the Mission District

Bookstores

Bernal Books 401 Cortland Ave, Bernal Hts (at Bennington) **415/550-0293** • 10am-7pm, till 5pm Sat, till 4pm Sun, clsd Mon • community bookstore for Bernal Heights & beyond • lgbt section

Dog Eared Books 900 Valencia St (at 20th) **415/282-1901** • 10am-10pm, till 8pm Sun • new & used • good lgbt section • wheelchair access

Modern Times Bookstore 888 Valencia St **415/282-9246** • 10am-9pm, till 10pm Fri-Sat, 11am-6pm Sun • progressive • lgbt section • readings • wheelchair access

Retail Shops

Body Manipulations 3234 16th St (btwn Guerrero & Dolores) **415/621-0408** • noon-7pm • piercing (walk-in basis) • jewelry

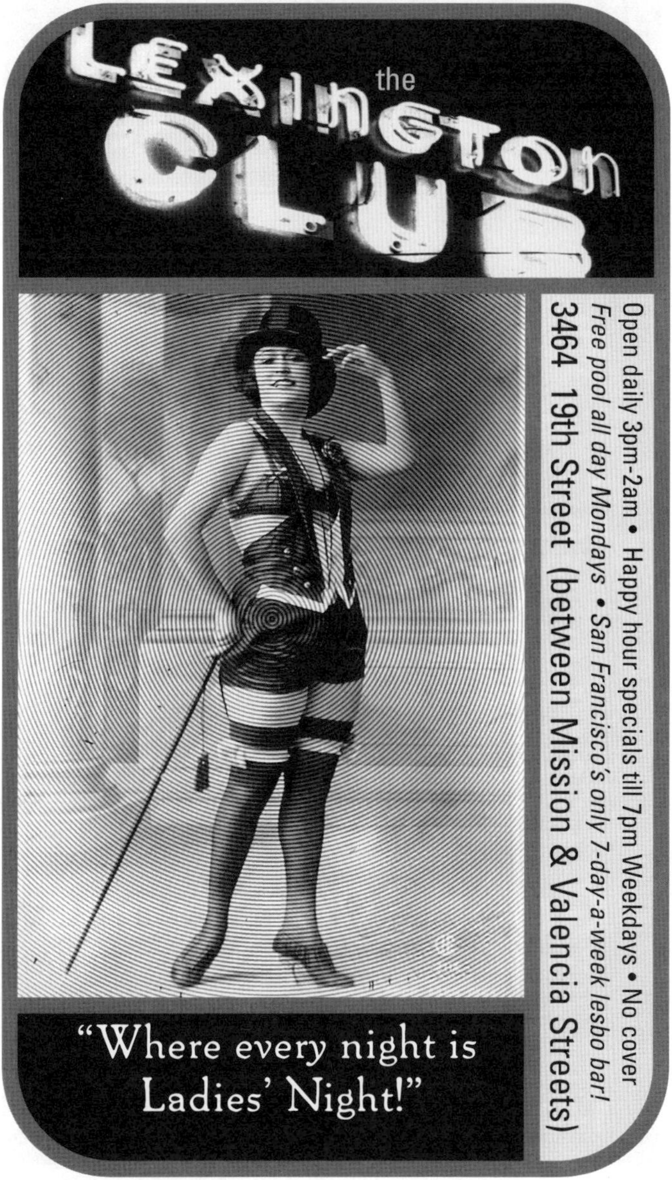

SF—Mission District • California

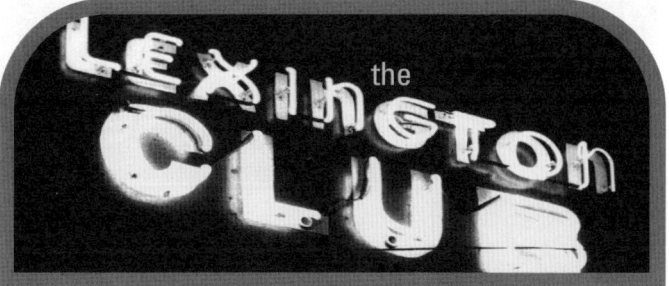

the LEXINGTON CLUB

Open daily 3pm-2am • Happy hour specials till 7pm Weekdays • No cover • Free pool all day Mondays • San Francisco's only 7-day-a-week lesbo bar!

3464 19th Street (between Mission & Valencia Streets)

"Where every night is Ladies' Night!"

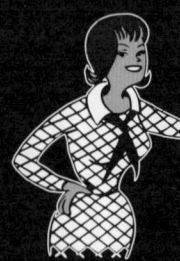

SF—Haight, Fillmore, Hayes Valley • California

Spiritual Groups

The Episcopal Church of St John the Evangelist 1661 15th St (btwn Mission & Valencia, enter on Julian Ave) **415/861-1436** • 11am Sun & 6pm most Weds • Oasis congregation • wheelchair access

Gyms & Health Clubs

Osento 955 Valencia St **415/282-6333** • 1pm-midnight • women only • baths • hot tub • massage

Erotica

▲ **Good Vibrations** 1210 Valencia St (at 23rd) **415/550-7399** • 11am-7pm, till 8pm Fri-Sat • clean, well-lighted sex toy store • also mail order

SF—Haight, Fillmore, Hayes Valley

Accommodations

Alamo Square Inn 719 Scott St (at Grove) **415/922-2055, 800/345-9888** • gay-friendly • 1895 Queen Anne & 1896 Tudor Revival Victorian mansions • full brkfst • smokefree • kids ok • $85-295

▲ **The Archbishop's Mansion** 1000 Fulton St (at Steiner) **415/563-7872, 800/543-5820** • gay-friendly • smokefree • one of SF's grandest homes • gay-owned/ run • $195-425

Baby Bear's House 1424 Page St (btwn Central & Masonic) **415/255-9777** • gay/ straight • 1892 Victorian • close to the Castro • gay families especially welcome • smokefree • gay-owned/ run • $50-175

Bock's B&B 1448 Willard St (at Parnassus) **415/664-6842** • gay-friendly • restored 1906 Edwardian residence • some shared baths • smokefree • lesbian-owned/ run • $50-90

Casa Loma Hotel 610 Fillmore St (at Fell) **415/552-7100** • gay-friendly • shared bath • kids ok • $40

The Chateau Tivoli 1057 Steiner St (at Golden Gate) **415/776-5462, 800/228-1647** • gay-friendly • historic San Francisco B&B • smokefree • $99-250

Hayes Valley Inn 417 Gough St (at Hayes) **415/431-9131, 800/930-7999** • gay/ straight • European-style pension • $58-99

▲ **Hotel Del Sol** 3100 Webster St (at Greenwich) **415/921-5520, 877/433-5765** • popular • gay/ straight • swimming • smokefree • $109-350

Hotel Majestic 1500 Sutter St (at Gough) **415/441-1100, 800/869-8966** • gay-friendly • one of SF's earliest grand hotels • also restaurant • full bar • wheelchair access • $159-450

Inn 1890 1890 Page St (nr Stanyan) **415/386-0486, 888/INN-1890** • gay/ straight • Victorian nr Golden Gate Park • kitchens • fireplaces • kids/ pets ok • smokefree • apt available • gay-owned/ run • $89-159

Inn at the Opera 333 Fulton St (at Franklin) **415/863-8400, 800/325-2708** • gay-friendly • also French restaurant • $155-350

Jackson Court 2198 Jackson St (at Buchanan) **415/929-7670** • gay-friendly • 19th-c brownstone mansion • smokefree • $160-215

Lombard Plaza Motel 2026 Lombard St (at Webster) **415/921-2444** • gay-friendly • $59-99

Metro Hotel 319 Divisadero St (at Haight) **415/861-5364** • gay-friendly • food served • $59-109

The Queen Anne Hotel 1590 Sutter St (at Octavia) **415/441-2828, 800/227-3970** • gay-friendly • popular • 1890 landmark • fireplaces • kids ok • wheelchair access • gay-owned/ run • $139-315

Radisson Miyako Hotel 1625 Post St (at Laguna) **415/922-3200, 800/533-4567** • gay-friendly • in the heart of Japantown • wheelchair access • $179-299

Shannon-Kavanaugh Guest House 722 Steiner St (at Hayes) **415/563-2727** • gay-friendly • 1-bdrm garden apt • wheelchair access • gay-owned/ ruin • $175-250

Stanyan Park Hotel 750 Stanyan St (at Waller) **415/751-1000** • gay-friendly • restored Victorian hotel listed on the Nat'l Register of Historic Places • kids ok • wheelchair access • $125-325

Bars

An Bodhran 668 Haight St **415/431-4724** • 4pm-2am, from 6pm Sat • gay-friendly • traditional Irish pub w/ live bands Wed & Sun

Hayes & Vine 377 Hayes St (at Gough) **415/626-5301** • 5pm-midnight, till 1am wknds, 4pm-10pm Sun • gay/ straight • wine bar

The Lion Pub 2062 Divisadero St (at Sacramento) **415/567-6565** • 3pm-2am • mostly gay men • professional crowd

Marlena's 488 Hayes St (at Octavia) **415/864-6672** • noon-2am, from 10am wknds • mostly gay men • neighborhood bar • drag shows wknds • also piano bar • wheelchair access

California • USA

National AIDS Memorial

Golden Gate Park, San Francisco

www.aidsmemorial.org • 888-29-GROVE

San Jose • California

Noc Noc 557 Haight St (at Fillmore) 415/861-5811 • 5pm-2am • gay-friendly • beer/ wine

Traxx 1437 Haight St (at Masonic) 415/864-4213 • noon-2am • mostly gay men • neighborhood bar

Nightclubs

The Top 424 Haight St (at Webster) 415/864-7386 • gay-friendly • dancing/DJ • alternative • theme nights • call for events

Cafes

Fillmore Grind 711 Fillmore (at Hayes) 415/775-5680 • 6:30am-7pm

Restaurants

Alamo Square Seafood 803 Fillmore (at Grove) 415/440-2828 • dinner only

Blue Muse 409 Gough St (at Fell) 415/626-7505 • 8am-10pm, wknd brunch • some veggie • full bar • wheelchair access • $10-15

Cafe Delle Stelle 395 Hayes (at Gough) 415/252-1110 • popular • Italian • beer/ wine

Cha Cha Cha 1801 Haight St (at Shrader) 415/386-7670 • open till 11pm • Cuban/ Cajun • excellent sangria • worth the wait!

Doidge's 2217 Union St (at Fillmore) 415/921-2149 • 8am-1:45pm, till 2:45pm wknds • great brkfst • wheelchair access

Eliza's 2877 California (at Broderick) 415/621-4819 • dinner • excellent Chinese food & stylish decor

Ella's 500 Presidio Ave (at California) 415/441-5669 • brkfst, lunch (Mon-Fri) & dinner, popular wknd brunch

Garibaldi's 347 Presidio (at Sacramento) 415/563-8841 • lunch & dinner • Mediterranean • full bar • wheelchair access • gay-owned/ run

Greens Fort Mason, Bldg 'A' (nr Van Ness & Bay) 415/771-6222 • lunch Tue-Sun, dinner nightly, Sun brunch • gourmet vegetarian • $20-40

Jardinière 300 Grove St 415/861-5555 • 5pm-midnight, till 10:30pm Sun-Mon • popular • oh-so-chic Californian-French cuisine • full bar

Joubert's 4115 Judah St (at 46th Ave) 415/753-5448 • 6pm-10pm, 5pm-9pm Sun, clsd Mon-Tue (reservations a must Sat) • popular • excellent South African vegetarian • beer/ wine • gay-owned/ run

Kan Zaman 1793 Haight (at Shrader) 415/751-9656 • 5pm-midnight, noon-2am wknds • Mediterranean • some veggie • beer/ wine • hookahs & tobacco available

Suppenküche 525 Laguna St (at Fell) 415/252-9289 • German cuisine served at communal tables • gay-owned/ run

Thep-Phanom 400 Waller St (at Fillmore) 415/431-2526 • 5:30pm-10pm • popular • excellent Thai food (worth the wait!) • beer/ wine

Retail Shops

La Riga 1391 Haight St (at Masonic) 415/552-1525 • 11am-7pm • leather

Mainline Gifts 1928 Fillmore St (at Bush) 415/563-4438 • hours vary

Nomad 575 Haight (at Steiner) 415/563-7771 • noon-7pm, clsd Wed • piercing (walk-in) • jewelry

San Jose

Info Lines & Services

AA Gay/ Lesbian 408/374-8511 • 24 hour helpline

Billy DeFrank Lesbian/ Gay Community Center 938 The Alameda 408/293-2429, 408/293-3040 • noon-10pm, noon-6pm wknds • wheelchair access

Pro-Latino/ Pro-Latina 938 The Alameda (at Billy DeFrank Ctr) 408/293-2429, 408/293-3040 • men's & women's support groups • meet 7pm alternate Mon • wheelchair access

Rainbow Gender Association 408/984-4044 • transgender group • recorded info

South Bay Queer & Asian 938 The Alameda (at Billy DeFrank Ctr) 408/345-1268 (VOICEMAIL) • 7pm 2nd & 4th Tue • social/ support group for lgbt Asians & Pacific Islanders • wheelchair access

Accommodations

Hensley House B&B 456 N 3rd St 408/298-3537, 800/498-3537 • lesbians/ gay men • located in a historic landmark • full brkfst • hot tub • kids ok • gay-owned/ run • $200-300

Hotel De Anza 233 W Santa Clara 408/286-1000, 800/843-3700 • gay-friendly • art deco gem • smokefree • Italian restaurant • $125-329

California • USA

Bars

The Foxtail 551 W Julian (at N Montgomery) **408/286-4388** • 5pm-2am, from noon wknds • lesbians/gay men • dancing/DJ • multiracial • transgender-friendly • live shows • patio

Mac's Club 39 Post (btwn 1st & Market) **408/288-8221** • noon-2am • lesbians/gay men • neighborhood bar • dancing/DJ

Cafes

Espresso Garden & Cafe 814 S Bascom Ave (at Moorpark) **408/298-0808** • 8am-9pm, till 11pm Th-Sat, clsd Sun • women's open mic 3pm-5pm 2nd Sat • food served • wheelchair access

Restaurants

Eulipia Restaurant & Bar 374 S 1st St (at San Carlos) **408/280-6161** • dinner only, clsd Mon • eclectic new American • full bar

Entertainment & Recreation

Tech Museum of Innovation 201 S Market St (at Park Ave) **408/294-8324** • 10am-5pm, clsd Mon • IMAX Dome Theater • a must-see for digital junkies

Bookstores

Sisterspirit 938 The Alameda **408/293-9372** • 6:30pm-9pm, 5pm-8pm Wed, noon-6pm Sat, 1pm-4pm Sun • women's • occasional coffeehouse

Publications

Entre Nous **408/281-4321** • lesbian newsmagazine & calendar for South Bay

Out Now Newsmagazine 1020 The Alameda **408/293-1598** • lgbt newspaper

Spiritual Groups

MCC of San Jose 65 S 7th St (at Santa Clara) **408/279-2711** • 10:30am Sun

Erotica

Leather Masters 969 Park Ave **408/293-7660** • leather & fetish • clothes • toys • publications

Pleasures from the Heart 1427 The Alameda (at Hamilton & Winchester) **408/292-4040** • also 1575-C S Winchester Blvd, Campbell, 408/871-1826 • woman-owned

San Lorenzo

Spiritual Groups

MCC of Greater Hayward 100 Hacienda (at Christ Lutheran Church) **510/481-9720** • 12:30pm Sun

San Luis Obispo

Info Lines & Services

Wayne McCaughan Community Pride Center 11573 Los Osos Valley Rd **805/541-4252** • 5pm-8pm, clsd wknds

Women's Community Center 1009 Morro St #201 (at Monterey) **805/544-9313** • counseling • support • referrals

Accommodations

Adobe Inn 1473 Monterey St **805/549-0321, 800/676-1588** • gay-friendly • cozy, comfortable & congenial inn • full brkfst • kitchens • smokefree • kids ok • $59-125

Casa De Amigas B&B 1202 8th St, Los Osos **805/528-1964** • lesbians/gay men • suite • smokefree • women-owned/run • $75 (2-night minimum)

The J Patrick House B&B 2990 Burton Dr (1/2 mile off Hwy 1), Cambria **805/927-3812, 800/341-5258** • gay-friendly • full brkfst • authentic log cabin • fireplaces • smokefree • $135-200

The Madonna Inn 1000 Madonna Rd **805/543-3000, 800/543-9666** • gay-friendly • theme rooms • $137-300

Palomar Inn 1601 Shell Beach Rd, Shell Beach **805/773-4204** • gay/straight • close to nude beach • gay-owned/run • $32-73

Cafes

Linnea's Cafe 1110 Garden (at Marsh) **805/541-5888** • 7am-midnight, till 7pm Sun • plenty veggie • $5

Restaurants

Big Sky Cafe 1121 Broad (at Marsh) **805/545-5401** • 7am-10pm, 8am-9pm Sun

Bookstores

Coalesce Bookstore & Garden Wedding Chapel 845 Main St, Morro Bay **805/772-2880** • 10am-5:30pm, 11am-4pm Sun • lgbt section • women-owned/run

Volumes of Pleasure 1016 Los Osos Valley Rd, Los Osos **805/528-5565** • 10am-6pm, noon-5pm Sun • general • lgbt section • wheelchair access • lesbian-owned/run

Retail Shops

Twisted Orbits 1022 Morro St (Higuera) **805/782-0278** • 11am-7pm, clsd Sun • clothing • cards • lgbt gifts

Publications

GALA News & Reviews **805/541-4252** • news & events for Central California coast

Santa Cruz • California

SPIRITUAL GROUPS

Integrity 805/467-3042, 805/534-0332 • 5:30pm 3rd Sun • call for location

San Rafael

see Marin County

Santa Ana

SPIRITUAL GROUPS

Christ Chapel MCC 720 N Spurgeon (at 8th & Main) 714/835-0722 • 10am Sun

Santa Barbara

INFO LINES & SERVICES

Pacific Pride Foundation 126 E Haley St #A-11 805/963-3636, 805/965-2925 (CRISIS HOTLINE ONLY) • 10am-5pm Mon-Fri • social/ educational & support services • youth groups • newsletter

ACCOMMODATIONS

The Bayberry Inn 111 W Valerio St (at Chapala Ave) 805/569-3398 • gay-friendly • in historic 1894 house • full brkfst • kids ok • smokefree • $129-200

Blue Dolphin Inn 420 W Montecito St 805/965-2333, 877/722-3657 • gay/ straight • 1900s Queen Anne Victorian • full brkfst • smokefree • wheelchair access • gay-owned/ run • $125-225

Glenborough Inn 1327 Bath St (at Sola) 805/966-0589, 888/966-0589 • gay/ straight • 6 different homes w/ 6 different personalities • full brkfst • fireplaces • jacuzzis/ hot tubs • smokefree • kids ok • $110-300

Ivanhoe Inn 1406 Castillo St 805/963-8832 • gay-friendly • lovely old Victorian house • private/shared baths • kitchens • smokefree • kids/ pets ok • $95-195

Old Yacht Club Inn 431 Corona Del Mar Dr 805/962-1277, 800/676-1676 • gay-friendly • full brkfst • only B&B on beach • $110-190

NIGHTCLUBS

Gold Coast 30 W Cota (at State) 805/965-6701 • 4pm-2am • lesbians/ gay men • neighborhood bar • dancing/DJ • wheelchair access

CAFES

Hot Spot Espresso Bar & Reservation Service 36 State St 805/564-1637 • 24hrs

RESTAURANTS

Mousse Odile 18 E Cota St 805/962-5393 • brkfst, lunch & dinner • clsd Sun • French • patio

Sojourner Cafe 134 E Canon Perdido (at Santa Barbara) 805/965-7922 • 11am-11pm, till 10pm Sun • plenty veggie • beer/ wine • wheelchair access

Zelo's 630 State (at Ortega) 805/966-5792 • lunch & dinner, 11am-2am, clsd Mon • full bar • also nightclub • from 10pm nightly • popular • dancing/DJ • live music

BOOKSTORES

Chaucer's Books 3321 State St (at Las Positas) 805/682-6787 • 9am-9pm, till 10pm Fri-Sat, till 6pm Sun • general • lgbt section

EROTICA

The Riviera Adult Superstore 4135 State St 805/967-8282 • pride items

Santa Clara

NIGHTCLUBS

Club Savoy 3546 Flora Vista 408/247-7109 • 5pm-2am • popular • mostly women • dancing/ DJ • country/ western • live shows • karaoke • wheelchair access • women-owned/ run

Tinker's Damn (TD's) 46 N Saratoga (at Stevens Creek) 408/243-4595 • 3pm-2am, 1pm-2am wknds • mostly gay men • dancing/DJ

EROTICA

Borderline 36 N Saratoga Ave (at Stevens Creek) 408/241-2177 • toys • videos

Santa Cruz

INFO LINES & SERVICES

AA Gay/ Lesbian 831/475-5782 • call for mtgs

The Diversity Center 1328 Commerce Ln 831/425-5422 • call for events & hours

ACCOMMODATIONS

Chateau Victorian B&B Inn 118 First St 831/458-9458 • lesbians/ gay men • 1885 Victorian inn w/ warm friendly atmosphere • fireplaces • smokefree • woman-owned/ run • $115-145

Compassion Flower Inn 216 Laurel St 831/466-0420 • gay/ straight • medical marijuana-friendly • clothing optional jacuzzi & spa • wheelchair access • women-owned/ run • $125-175

California • USA

The Grove: A Women's Country Retreat by the Sea 40 Lily Wy, La Selva Beach **831/724-3459** • women only • 2 cottages • kitchens • fireplaces • hot tub • on a mini-farm nr the beach

NIGHTCLUBS

Blue Lagoon 923 Pacific Ave **831/423-7117** • 4pm-2am, from 2pm Sun • gay-friendly • dancing/DJ • alternative • transgender-friendly • videos • wheelchair access

Dakota 1209 Pacific Ave (at Soquel) **831/454-9030** • noon-2am • lesbians/gay men • dancing/DJ • salsa Mon • women's night Wed • men's night Th • wheelchair access

RESTAURANTS

Costa Brava Taco Stand 505 Seabright **831/423-8190** • 8am-11pm, till 10pm Sun-Mon • Mexican • some veggie • $4-8

Crêpe Place 1134 Soquel Ave (at Seabright) **831/429-6994** • 11am-midnight, 10am-1am Fri-Sat • plenty veggie • full bar • garden patio • wheelchair access • $5-11

Saturn Cafe 145 Laurel (at Pacific) **831/429-8505** • 11am-2:30am, till 3:30am Fri-Sat • light fare • plenty veggie • lesbian-owned/run • $4-7

BOOKSTORES

Book Loft 1207 Soquel Ave (at Seabright) **831/429-1812** • 10am-10pm, noon-6pm Sun, 10am-6pm Mon • mostly used books

Bookshop Santa Cruz 1520 Pacific Garden Mall **831/423-0900** • 9am-11pm • general • lgbt section • cafe • wheelchair access

Herland: The WanderGround 1014 Cedar St (at Locust) **831/429-6636** • 10am-6pm, from noon Sun • wheelchair access

PUBLICATIONS

Manifesto **831/761-3176** • monthly

SPIRITUAL GROUPS

Lavender Road MCC Sanctuary of Trinity Presbyterian Church, 420 Melrose Ave **831/459-8442** • 5pm Sun • also 10am at LGBT Center

GYMS & HEALTH CLUBS

Heartwood Spa Hot Tub & Sauna Garden 3150-A Mission Dr (off Soquel, behind hospital) **831/462-2192** • noon-11pm • gay-friendly • women-only 6:30pm-11pm Sun

Kiva Retreat House Spa 702 Water St (at Ocean) **831/429-1142** • noon-11pm, till midnight Fri-Sat • women-only 9am-1:30pm Sun

Santa Maria

INFO LINES & SERVICES

'Pacific Pride' Gay/ Lesbian Resource Center 819 W Church St (at Depot) **805/349-9947** • 9am-5pm Mon-Fri

CAFES

Cafe Monet 1555 S Broadway (at Battles) **805/928-1912** • 5:45am-9pm, 6:30am-5pm Sat, 7:30am-3pm Sun • wheelchair access

EROTICA

Diamond Adult World 938 W Main St (at Western) **805/922-2828** • large lgbt video section

Santa Rosa

INFO LINES & SERVICES

Santa Rosa AA **707/544-1300 (AA#)** • call for meeting times

CAFES

Aroma Roasters 95 5th St (Railroad Sq) **707/576-7765** • 6am-11pm, till midnight Fri-Sat, 7:30am-10:30pm Sun • lesbians/gay men • live music Fri • wheelchair access • lesbian-owned/run

RESTAURANTS

Syrah 205 5th St **707/568-4002** • 11:30am-2:30pm & 5:30pm-9pm, till 10pm Fri-Sat, clsd Sun-Mon • creative California/French bistro fare • eclectic wine list • moderate prices

BOOKSTORES

North Light Books 550 E Cotati Rd, Cotati **707/792-4300** • 9am-9pm, till 10pm Fri-Sat, 10am-8pm Sun • anti-establishment • strong lgbt emphasis • also coffeehouse • lesbian-owned/run

Sawyer's News 733 4th St (btwn 'D' & 'E') **707/542-1311** • 7am-9pm, till 10pm Fri-Sat • general news & bookstand

PUBLICATIONS

We the People **707/581-1809**

SPIRITUAL GROUPS

1st Congregational United Church of Christ 2000 Humboldt St (at Silva) **707/546-0998** • 10:30am Sun

New Hope MCC 855 7th St **707/526-4673** • 10am & 6pm Sun

EROTICA

Santa Rosa Adult Books 3301 Santa Rosa Ave **707/542-8248**

Van Nuys • California

Sausalito
see Marin County

Sebastopol
CAFES
Coffee Catz 6761 Sebastopol Ave (at Hwy 116) **707/829-6600** • 7am-6pm, till 10pm Th-Sat • live entertainment • wheelchair access

RETAIL SHOPS
Milk & Honey 123 N Main St **707/824-1155** • 10am-6pm, from 11am Mon, Wed & Sun • goddess- & woman-oriented crafts

EROTICA
The Sensuality Shoppe 2371-A Gravenstein Hwy S **707/829-3999** • open daily • toys • books • videos • jewelry • woman-owned/ run

Sequoia Nat'l Park
ACCOMMODATIONS
Organic Gardens B&B 44095 Dinely Dr, Three Rivers **559/561-0916** • gay-friendly • 5 miles from entrance to Sequoia Nat'l Park • hot tub • smokefree • lesbian-owned/ run • $115-130

Sonoma
ACCOMMODATIONS
Gaige House Inn 13540 Arnold Dr, Glen Ellen **707/935-0237, 800/935-0237** • gay-friendly • swimming • full brkfst • $150-450

Springville
ACCOMMODATIONS
Great Energy 559/539-2382 • gay-friendly • retreat in foothills of Sierra Nevada mtns • swimming • hiking • kids ok • lesbian-owned/ run • $70-125

Statewide
ACCOMMODATIONS
Bed & Breakfast California 800/872-4500 • gay-friendly • reservation service

Stockton
see also Modesto
NIGHTCLUBS
Paradise 10100 N Lower Sacramento Rd **209/477-4724** • 6pm-2am, from 3pm Sun • lesbians/ gay men • dancing/DJ • live shows • live bands • young crowd

Tiburon
see Marin County

Ukiah
ACCOMMODATIONS
Orr Hot Springs 13201 Orr Springs Rd **707/462-6277** • gay-friendly • mineral hot springs • hostel-style cabins, private cottages & campsites • clothing optional • kids ok • guests must bring all own food • $40-168/ person

BARS
Perkins St Grill 228 E Perkins St **707/462-0327** • lunch & dinner, clsd Mon • gay-friendly • dancing/DJ • also restaurant • Californian • $10-15

Upland
EROTICA
Mustang Books 961 N Central (at Foothill) **909/981-0227** • 24hrs
The Toy Box 1999 W Arrow Rte (at Central) **909/920-1135** • 24hrs

Vacaville
INFO LINES & SERVICES
Solano County Gay/ Lesbian Infoline 707/448-1010

SPIRITUAL GROUPS
St Paul's United Methodist Church 101 West St (at Monte Vista) **707/448-5154** • 10:30am Sun

Vallejo
NIGHTCLUBS
Nobody's Place 437 Virginia St (at Sonoma Blvd) **707/645-7298** • noon-2am • lesbians/ gay men • dancing/DJ • patio • wheelchair access

BOOKSTORES
Black Spring Books 503 Georgia St **707/556-9766** • 10:30am-8pm, clsd Sun • specializing in ethnic studies titles • lgbt section

Van Nuys
PUBLICATIONS
After Dark 818/285-2580

EROTICA
Diamond Adult World 6406 Van Nuys Blvd (at Victory) **818/997-3665** • 24hrs • books • toys • videos

California • USA

Venice

Accommodations

Comfort Zone 530 Grand Blvd (at Venice Blvd) **310/306-4556** • gay-friendly • apt w/ kitchen • 3 blks from Venice Beach • smokefree • $75-120

Ventura

Info Lines & Services

AA Gay/ Lesbian 739 E Main **805/389-1444** • women's mtg 7pm Wed at G/L Comm Center

Gay/ Lesbian Community Center 3503 Arundell Cir **805/339-6340** • 9am-9pm, clsd wknds

SCWU **800/798-7298** • social/ support group

Bars

Paddy McDermott's 2 W Main St (at Ventura) **805/652-1071** • 2pm-2am • lesbians/ gay men • dancing/DJ • karaoke • live shows

Erotica

Three Star Books 359 E Main St **805/653-9068** • 24hrs

Victorville

Bars

West Side 15 16868 Stoddard Wells Rd (off I-15) **760/243-9600** • 3pm-2am, from 2pm Sun • lesbians/ gay men • neighborhood bar • ladies night Th

Walnut Creek

Info Lines & Services

AA Gay/ Lesbian 193 Mayhew Wy (at St Paul's Church) **925/939-4155** • 8:30pm Fri & 5:30pm Sat

Nightclubs

Club 1220 1220 Pine St (at Civic Dr) **925/938-4550** • 4pm-2am • lesbians/ gay men • women's night Fri • dancing/DJ • wheelchair access

Spiritual Groups

MCC of the New Vision 1543 Sunnyvale (at United Methodist Church) **925/941-4146** • noon Sun

Whittier

Info Lines & Services

Together in Pride AA 11931 Washington Blvd (at the church) **562/696-6213 (church #)** • 7:30pm Th

Accommodations

Whittier House 12133 S Colima Blvd **562/941-7222** • women only • full brkfst • hot tub • smokefree • kids/ pets ok

Spiritual Groups

Good Samaritan MCC 11931 E Washington Blvd **562/696-6213** • 10am Sun, 6pm Sat

Willits

Restaurants

Purple Thistle 50 S Main St **707/459-4750** • 4pm-8pm • Japanese • $8-13

Entertainment & Recreation

Skunk Train California Western 299 E Commercial St **707/459-5248** • scenic train trips

Bookstores

Leaves of Grass 630 S Main St **707/459-3744** • 10am-5:30pm, noon-5pm Sun • alternative

Yosemite Nat'l Park

Accommodations

The Ahwahnee Hotel Yosemite Valley Floor **559/252-4848** • gay-friendly • incredibly dramatic & expensive grand fortress • swimming • also restaurant

▲ **The Homestead** 41110 Rd 600, Ahwahnee **559/683-0495** • gay-friendly • cottages • kitchens • fireplaces • smokefree • $125-225

The Lakehouse B&B at Bass Lake 39131 Lake Drive (at Hill), Bass Lake **559/683-8220, 877/656-1022** • gay-friendly • full brkfst • hot tub • smokefree • kids/ pets ok • $135-235

Yosemite Nat'l Park • California

THE HOMESTEAD... Near the southern entrance to **YOSEMITE NATIONAL PARK** lies 160 wooded acres that now embrace luxury cottages of adobe and stone. Experience a hideaway that flows in tune with nature's quiet rhythm.

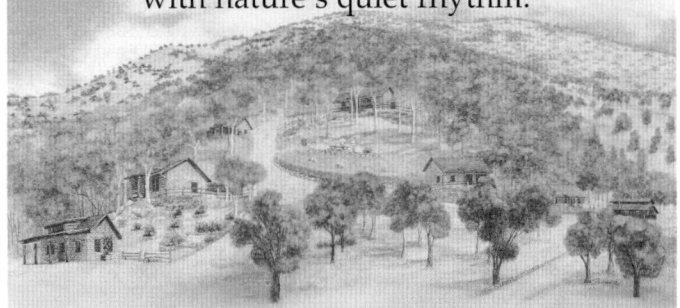

Each cottage features romantic & comfortable:

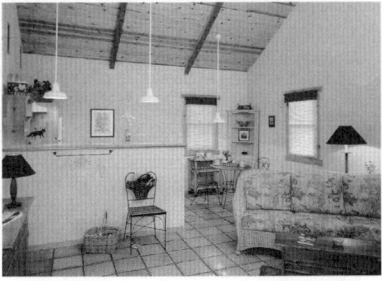

- Country Kitchen
- Living Room
- Fireplace
- Bedroom
- Bathroom

The Homestead is a great place to be together alone or take advantage of nearby golfing, hiking, horseback riding, restaurants & shops.

CALL *proprietors Cindy & Larry for assistance in planning your well deserved getaway.*

(559) 683-0495

See us at http://www.homesteadcottages.com

Colorado • USA

COLORADO

Statewide

INFO LINES & SERVICES

Colorado Travel and Tourism Authority 800/265-6723

PUBLICATIONS

▲ **Out Front Colorado** 303/778-7900 • statewide lgbt newspaper

Rainbow List 303/443-7768 • extensive statewide resources

Weird Sisters 970/482-4393 • statewide calendar w/ political, social & arts coverage

Alamosa

ACCOMMODATIONS

Cottonwood Inn 123 San Juan Ave 719/589-3882, 800/955-2623 • gay-friendly • full brkfst • art gallery • nr sand dunes • smokefree • $57-125

Aspen

INFO LINES & SERVICES

Aspen Gay/ Lesbian Community 970/925-9249 • 8pm-midnight (live) • recorded local info & events

ACCOMMODATIONS

Aspen Mountain Lodge 311 W Main St 970/925-7650, 800/362-7736 • gay-friendly • full brkfst • après-ski wine & cheese • hot tub • swimming • $89-349

Hotel Aspen 110 W Main St 970/925-3441, 800/527-7369 • gay-friendly • mountain brkfst • hot tub • swimming • smokefree • kids/ pets ok • $89-549

Hotel Lenado 200 S Aspen St 970/925-6246, 800/321-3457 • gay-friendly • full brkfst • hot tub • full bar • $245-495

Sardy House 128 E Main St 970/920-2525, 800/321-3457 • gay-friendly • hot tub • swimming • also restaurant • $249-700

Snow Queen Victorian B&B/ Cooper St Lofts 124 E Cooper 970/925-8455 • gay-friendly • 1880s Victorian & studios • nr town & skiing • hot tub • $95-175

BARS

Double Diamond 450 S Galena 970/920-6905 • seasonal, 9pm-2am • gay-friendly • live shows

RESTAURANTS

Jimmy's 205 S Mill St (at Hopkins) 970/925-6020 • 5:30pm-11pm • also bar

Syzygy 520 E Hyman 970/925-3700 • seasonal • 6pm-10pm, bar till 2am • some veggie • live jazz & pianist • wheelchair access

BOOKSTORES

Explore Booksellers & Bistro 221 E Main (at Aspen) 970/925-5336 • 10am-8pm • also gourmet vegetarian restaurant • wheelchair access

Boulder

ACCOMMODATIONS

Boulder Victoria Historic B&B 1305 Pine St (at 13th) 303/938-1300 • gay-friendly • patio • $109-189

The Briar Rose B&B 2151 Arapahoe Ave (at 22nd St) 303/442-3007 • gay-friendly • full brkfst • smokefree • $100-190

BARS

The Foundry 1109 Walnut 303/447-1803 • 11am-1:30am • also cafe from 6am • gay-friendly • dancing/DJ • live shows • wheelchair access

NIGHTCLUBS

The Yard 2690 28th St #C (at Bluff) 303/443-1987 • 4pm-2am, from 2pm wknds • lesbians/ gay men • dancing/DJ • wheelchair access • women-owned/ run

CAFES

Walnut Cafe 3073 Walnut (at 30th) 303/447-2315 • 7am-4pm • popular • plenty veggie • patio • wheelchair access • women-owned/ run • $5-9

BOOKSTORES

Left Hand Books 1200 Pearl St lower level (E of Broadway) 303/443-8252 • 10am-9pm, noon-6pm Sun • progressive literature

Word Is Out 1731 15th St (btwn Canyon & Arapahoe) 303/449-1415 • 10am-7pm, noon-5pm Sun • women's bookstore w/ lgbt sections • wheelchair access

RETAIL SHOPS

Aria 2043 Broadway (at Spruce) 303/442-5694 • 10am-6pm, noon-5pm Sun • cards • T-shirts • gifts • wheelchair access

EROTICA

The News Stand 1720 15th St (at Grove) 303/442-9515

Denver • Colorado

Breckenridge

ACCOMMODATIONS

Allaire Timbers Inn 9511 Hwy 9, S Main St **970/453-7530, 800/624-4904** • gay-friendly • full brkfst • hot tub • wheelchair access • $140-450

Mountain House 970/453-6475 • gay-friendly • rental home • sleeps 8 • sauna • gay-owned/ run

Colorado Springs

(includes Manitou Springs)

INFO LINES & SERVICES

Pikes Peak Gay/ Lesbian Community Center Helpline 719/471-4429 • 8am-4pm Mon-Fri • call for events

ACCOMMODATIONS

Authentic Inns of the Pikes Peak Region 888/892-2237

Blue Skies Inn B&B 402 Manitou Ave (at Mayfair), Manitou Springs **719/685-3899, 800/398-7949** • gay/ straight • Gothic Revival built by artist/ innkeeper • full brkfst • gazebo hot tub • smokefree • $125-195

Chalice House 1116 N Wahsatch Ave (at Uintah) **888/475-7505, 719/475-7505** • gay/ straight • full brkfst • nr outdoor recreation • hot tub • fireplaces • women-owned/ run • $68-148

Old Town Guest House B&B 115 S 26th St **719/632-9194, 888/375-4210** • gay-friendly • full brkfst • hot tub • wheelchair access • $95-175

Pikes Peak Paradise Woodland Park **719/687-6656, 800/728-8282** • gay-friendly • mansion w/ view of Pikes Peak • full brkfst • hot tub • fireplaces • smokefree • kids 12+ ok • $110-230

Quality Inn—Garden of the Gods 555 W Garden of the Gods **719/593-9119** • gay-friendly • swimming • mtn views • $59-119

Rockledge Country Inn 328 El Paso Blvd, Manitou Springs **719/685-4515, 888/685-4515** • gay-friendly • Tudor country home on historic estate • full brkfst • $170-295

NIGHTCLUBS

Hide & Seek Complex 512 W Colorado (at Walnut) **719/634-9303** • 10:30am-2am, till 5am Fri-Sat • popular • lesbians/ gay men • dancing/DJ • country/ western • live shows • young crowd • also restaurant • some veggie • wheelchair access • $5-12

RESTAURANTS

Dale Street Cafe 115 E Dale (at Nevada) **719/578-9898** • 11am-9pm, clsd Sun • some veggie • full bar • $6-11

SPIRITUAL GROUPS

Pikes Peak MCC 1102 S 21st St (at Broadway) **719/634-3771** • 10:30am Sun

EROTICA

First Amendment Adult Bookstore 220 E Fillmore (at Nevada) **719/630-7676**

Denver

INFO LINES & SERVICES

AA Gay/ Lesbian 303/322-4440 • many mtgs

Gender Identity Center of Colorado (GIC) 303/202-6466 • transgender resources & support

Lesbian/ Gay/ Bisexual Community Services Center of Colorado 234 Broadway (at 2nd Ave) **303/733-7743, 303/837-1598 (TDD)** • 10am-6pm Mon-Fri • extensive resources & support groups • wheelchair access

Rainbow Alley 919 E 14th Ave **303/832-2260** • drop-in center for lgbt youth, social/ support groups • also medical clinic

ACCOMMODATIONS

Elyria's Western Guest House 1655 E 47th Ave (nr I-70 & Brighton) **303/291-0915** • lesbians/ gay men • Western ambiance in historic Denver neighborhood • hot tub • shared baths • smokefree • $40-50

The Gregory Inn, LoDo 2500 Arapahoe St (at 25th St) **303/295-6570, 800/925-6570** • gay-friendly • full brkfst • jacuzzis • fireplaces • gay-owned/ run • $74-199

Hotel Monaco 1717 Champa St (at 17th) **303/296-1717, 800/397-5380** • gay-friendly • gym • spa • also Italian restaurant • pets ok • $175-915

Lumber Baron Inn 2555 W 37th Ave (at Bryant) **303/477-8205** • gay-friendly • Victorian mansion furnished w/ antiques • full brkfst • hot tub • $125-235

Radisson Hotel Denver Stapleton Plaza 3333 Quebec St (at 35th) **303/321-3500, 800/333-3333** • gay-friendly • swimming • gym • also restaurant • wheelchair access • $79-149

Victoria Oaks Inn 1575 Race St (at 16th) **303/355-1818** • gay/ straight • fireplaces • gay-owned/ run • $60-95

Colorado • USA

Bars

BJ's Carousel 1380 S Broadway (at Arkansas) **303/777-9880** • noon-2am, from 10am wknds • popular • gay/straight • neighborhood bar • live shows • karaoke • transgender-friendly • also restaurant • wheelchair access • gay-owned/run

Brick's 1600 E 17th Ave (at Franklin) **303/377-5400** • 10am-2am • lunch Mon-Fri, brunch wknds • mostly gay men • neighborhood bar • wheelchair access

C's 7900 E Colfax Ave (at Trenton) **303/322-4436** • 5pm-midnight, till 2am Fri-Sat • mostly women • dancing/DJ

Cafe Cero 1446 S Broadway (btwn Arkansas & Florida) **303/282-1446** • 4pm-1:30am Tue-Sat • gay/straight • neighborhood bar • also restaurant

The Compound 145 Broadway (at 2nd Ave) **303/722-7977** • 7am-2am, from 8am Sun • mostly gay men • neighborhood bar • dancing/DJ • alternative

The Den 5110 W Colfax Ave (at Sheridan) **303/623-7998** • 11am-2am, from 10am wknds • lesbians/gay men • neighborhood bar • also restaurant • dinner nightly • brunch Sun • wheelchair access

Denver Detour 551 E Colfax Ave (at Pearl, use back entrance) **303/861-1497** • 11am-2am • popular • lesbians/gay men • live shows • lunch & dinner daily • some veggie • wheelchair access

Down Under 266 S Downing (at Alameda, enter on alley) **303/777-4377** • 3pm-2am, from 11am wknds • piano bar Th • live jazz wknds

Fox Hole 2936 Fox St (at 20th St) **303/298-7391** • 9pm-2am, from 1pm Sun, clsd Mon-Tue • lesbians/gay men

The Grand 538 E 17th Ave (at Pearl) **303/839-5390** • 3pm-2am, from 6pm wknds • mostly gay men • upscale piano bar • patio • wheelchair access

Denver

Where the Girls Are: Many lesbians reside in the Capitol Hill area, near the gay and mixed bars, but hang out in cafes and women's bars scattered around the city.

Entertainment: Denver Women's Chorus 303/274-4177.

LGBT Pride: June. 303/733-7743 ext 23.

Annual Events: February - Mtn States Gay & Lesbian Film Festival. October - Annual Halloween Cheshire Ball.

City Info: 303/892-1112, web: www.denverco.org.

Attractions: 16th Street Mall. Black American West Museum 303/292-2566. Denver Art Museum 720/865-5000. Elitch Gardens 303/595-4386. LoDo (Lower Downtown). Molly Brown House 303/832-4092.

Best View: Lookout Mountain (at night especially) or the top of the Capitol rotunda.

Weather: Summer temperatures average in the 90°s and winter ones in the 40°s. The sun shines an average of 300 days a year with humidity in the single digits.

Transit: Yellow Cab 303/777-7777. Metro Taxi 303/333-3333. Super Shuttle 303/370-1300. RTD 303/628-9000 or 303/299-6000 (infoline).

Celebrating *25 years* of serving Colorado's gay and lesbian community.

We are Colorado's largest, oldest and most widely distributed Gay & Lesbian publication.

Since 1976 *Out Front Colorado* has been the premiere resource for news, entertainment and information in our vibrant community.

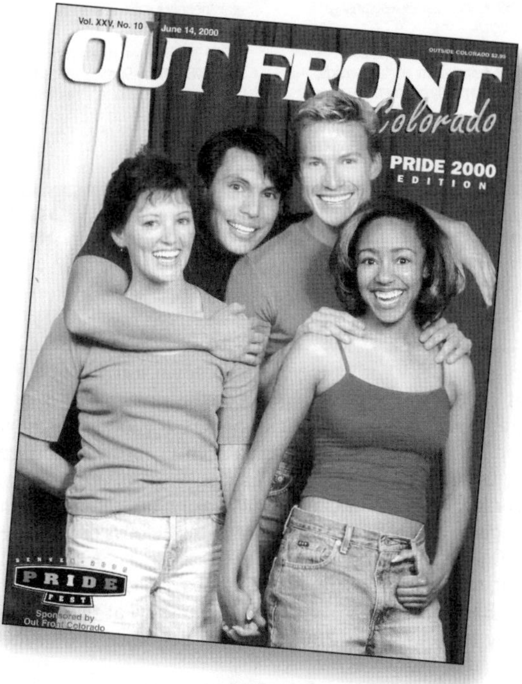

Advertise wisely! Reach 1000's of dedicated readers every issue. Please phone to receive a media kit and complimentary issue:

303-778-7900

Single issue purchases and subscriptions available.

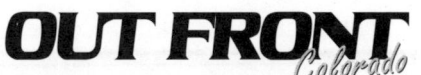

244 WASHINGTON STREET   DENVER COLORADO 80203

Colorado • USA

Highland Bar 2532 15th St (at Boulder)
303/455-9978 • 2pm-2am • mostly women • neighborhood bar • wheelchair access

The Longhorn 3014 E Colfax Ave (at St Paul)
303/321-6627 • 7am-2am • lesbians/ gay men • neighborhood bar • strippers • live shows • wheelchair access

R&R Denver 4958 E Colfax Ave (at Elm)
303/320-9337 • 1pm-2am, from 11am wknds • lesbians/ gay men • neighborhood bar

Safari Bar 500 Denargo St (at 31st)
303/298-7959 • noon-2am • lesbians/ gay men • dancing/DJ

The Triangle 2036 Broadway (at 20th Ave)
303/293-9009 • 3pm-2am, till 4am wknds, from 11am Sun • mostly gay men • leather

The Zu 60 S Broadway (at Bayaud)
303/777-0193 • 2pm-2am • lesbians/ gay men • women's night Wed • dancing/DJ • karaoke • drag king/ queen shows • wheelchair access • women-owned/ run

Nightclubs

Amsterdam 2901 Walnut (at 29th)
303/405-4458 • popular • gay/ straight • after hours Fri-Sat • dancing/DJ

La Rumba 99 W 9th Ave (at Broadway)
303/572-8006 • 9pm-2am, clsd Mon-Wed • gay-friendly • salsa dance club/ lessons • live shows

Pure 2637 Welton (btwn 26th & 27th)
303/298-7873 • 9pm-close, clsd Mon-Tue • gay/ straight • dancing/DJ • theme nights

---

[Reply] [Forward]   [Delete]

```
Date: Sat, Dec 1, 2001 14:11:59
From: Girl-on-the-Go
To: Editor@Damron.com
Subject: Denver
```

> Denver is a big city with a friendly small town feel. To get the most out of your stay, start with a visit to the women's **Book Garden,** and pick up a copy of **Weird Sisters,** the local lesbian paper. Next, drop by the **Lesbian/Gay/Bisexual Center** for the inside scoop on where to go and what to do in Denver.

> Look for local lesbians in Capitol Hill, soaking up sun in Cheesman Park, or sipping coffee at **Java Creek** or with the boys on 9th Avenue between Ogden and Marion.

> At night, taste the local cuisine at **Basil,** have a cocktail at the **Highland Bar,** check out a popular drag king show at the **Zu** on Wednesday, head to **Tracks 2000** Friday, or get down at **C's** dance bar any night of the week.

> Be sure to take advantage of the Rocky Mountain snows with a ski trip to one of the many nearby resorts: Aspen, Telluride, or Rocky Mountain National Park.

Denver • Colorado

Rock Island 1614 15th St (at Wazee) **303/572-7625** • 9pm-2am • gay-friendly • dancing/DJ • alternative • young crowd • call for events • wheelchair access

Tracks 2000 2975 Fox St (btwn 20th & Chestnut) **303/292-6600** • 8pm-2am, from 5:30pm Fri, clsd Sun-Tue • popular • mostly gay men • women's night Fri • dancing/DJ • 18+ Th • wheelchair access

The Wave Nightclub 2101 Champa St (at 21st) **303/299-9283** • 8pm-close Wed-Sat • lesbians/ gay men • dancing/ DJ • live shows • women-owned/ run

CAFES

Bump & Grind Cafe 439 E 17th Ave (at Pennsylvania) **303/861-4841** • 7am-5:30pm, wknd brunch, clsd Mon • food served

Diedrich Coffee 1201 E 9th (at Downing) **303/837-1275** • popular

Java Creek 287 Columbine St (at 3rd Ave) **303/377-8902** • 7am-6pm, 9am-4pm Sun • wheelchair access

RESTAURANTS

The Avenue Grill 630 E 17th Ave (at Washington) **303/861-2820**

Basil Ristorante 846 Broadway (at Bayaud) **303/832-8009** • lunch Mon-Fri, dinner nightly • popular • nouvelle Italian • plenty veggie • beer/ wine • wheelchair access • women-owned/ run • $6-16

Benny's 301 E 7th Ave (at Grand St) **303/894-0788** • 8am-11pm • Mexican

Dazzle 930 Lincoln St (at 9th) **303/839-5100** • lunch & dinner, clsd Mon • also lounge

Janleone 1509 Marion (at Colfax) **303/863-8433** • dinner, also Sun brunch, clsd Mon • live shows • patio • wheelchair access • $11-19

Las Margaritas 1066 Old S Gaylord St **303/777-0194** • 11am-close, bar till 2am • popular • Mexican • some veggie • wheelchair access

McCole 1469 S Pearl (btwn Florida & Arkansas) **303/744-1940** • 6pm-10pm, from 5pm Fri-Sat, clsd Sun-Mon • some veggie • full bar

Painted Bench 400 E 20th Ave (at Logan) **303/863-7473** • lunch & dinner, clsd Sun

Paris on the Platte 1553 Platte (at 15th) **303/455-2451** • 7am-1am, till 3am wknds • popular after hrs

Racine's 850 Bannock St (btwn 8th & 9th) **303/595-0418** • brkfst, lunch, dinner & Sun brunch • plenty veggie • full bar

Wazee Supper Club 1600 15th St (at Wazee) **303/623-9518** • 11am-2am, noon-midnight Sun • beer/ wine

Zaidy's Deli 121 Adams (at First) **303/333-5336** • 7am-4pm Mon-Tue, till 8pm Wed-Fri, 8am-4pm wknds

ENTERTAINMENT & RECREATION

Denver Women's Chorus 303/274-4177

BOOKSTORES

The Book Garden 2625 E 12th Ave (at Elizabeth) **303/399-2004, 800/279-2426** • 10am-6pm, till 8pm Th • feminist • gifts • toys • wheelchair access • lesbian-owned/ run

Isis Bookstore 5701 E Colfax Ave (at Ivanhoe) **303/321-0867** • 10am-7pm, till 6pm Fri-Sat, noon-5pm Sun • new age • metaphysical • wheelchair access

Tattered Cover Book Store 2955 E 1st Ave (at Milwaukee) **303/322-7727, 800/833-9327** • 9am-11pm, 10am-6pm Sun • also 1536 Wynkoop St • 4 flrs • wheelchair access

Vicious Rumors 630 E 6th Ave (at Washington) **303/777-6060** • 7am-10pm, till 3pm Sun • popular • wheelchair access

RETAIL SHOPS

Arco Iris Design 19 E Bayaud **303/765-5116** • pride jewelry & design

Bound By Design 1336 E Colfax (at Humboldt) **303/830-7272, 303/832-TAT2** • 11am-11pm, noon-10pm Sun • piercing & tattoos • lesbian-owned/ run

Unique of Denver 2626 E 12th (btwn Elizabeth & Clayton) **303/355-0689** • 10am-6pm, till 7pm summers • lgbt gift shop • wheelchair access

PUBLICATIONS

H Ink 303/722-5965

▲ **Out Front Colorado** 303/778-7900 • statewide lgbt newspaper

Pride Magazine 773/769-6328 • also publish Denver Pink Pages

SPIRITUAL GROUPS

Dignity Denver 1100 Fillmore (at Capitol Hts Presb Church) **303/322-8485** • 5pm Sun

MCC of the Rockies 980 Clarkson St (at 10th) **303/860-1819** • 9am & 11am Sun • wheelchair access

St Paul's United Methodist Church 1615 Ogden (at 16th Ave) **303/832-4929** • 10:30am Sun • reconciling congregation • also Buddhist-Christian contemplative prayer • 5pm Sun

Colorado • USA

Gyms & Health Clubs

Broadway Bodyworks 160 S Broadway (at Maple) **303/722-4342** • lesbians/gay men • wheelchair access

Erotica

Adult Book & Video 4810 Pontiac St **303/288-9529**

The Crypt 131 Broadway (btwn 1st & 2nd) **303/733-3112** • leather & more

Las Vegas Adult Palace 550 W Mississippi Ave (at Santa Fe) **303/698-9119**

Pandora's Toy Box 528 S Broadway **303/778-8828**

Durango

Accommodations

Leland House 721 E 2nd Ave **970/385-1920, 800/664-1920** • popular • gay-friendly • rooms & suites w/ kitchens • full brkfst • wheelchair access • $139-320

Rochester Hotel 721 E 2nd Ave **970/385-1920, 800/664-1920** • gay-friendly • popular • newly renovated 1892 house decorated in Old West motif • full brkfst • smokefree • kids/pets ok • wheelchair access • $109-209

Florissant

Entertainment & Recreation

McNamara Ranch 4620 County Rd 100 **719/748-3466** • horseback tours & more

Fort Collins

Accommodations

Never Summer Nordic **970/482-9411** • lesbians/gay men • camping in yurts (portable Mongolian round houses) in Colorado Rockies • sleep 5-9 • mtn biking & skiing • $55-105

Bars

Choice City Shots 124 LaPorte Ave (at College) **970/221-4333** • 3pm-midnight, 4pm-2am Th-Sat • lesbians/gay men • neighborhood bar • dancing/DJ Fri-Sat • live shows wknds • wheelchair access • lesbian/gay-owned

Nightclubs

Tornado Club 1437 E Mulberry St (at Link Ln) **970/493-0251** • 4pm-2am, clsd Sun-Mon • popular • lesbians/gay men • dancing/DJ • theme nights • patio • wheelchair access

Grand Junction

Bars

Quincy's 609 Main St (btwn 7th & Main) **970/242-9633** • 7am-2am • gay after 8pm • neighbor-hood bar • theater crowd • wheelchair access

Greeley

Info Lines & Services

In & Out U of Northern Colorado **970/351-1484** • hours vary • call for events • leave message for referrals

Green Mountain Falls

Accommodations

▲ **Columbine Inn** 10755 Ute Pass Ave **888/684-9576** • lesbians/gay men • also restaurant • $95-175

Mancos

Accommodations

Old Mancos Inn 200 W Grand Ave **970/533-9019** • gay/straight • some shared baths • gay-owned/run • $25-50

Pueblo

Info Lines & Services

Pueblo After 2 **719/564-4004** • social/educational network • monthly mtgs

Bars

Pirate's Cove 105 Central Plaza (off 1st & Union) **719/542-9624** • 2pm-2am, clsd Mon • lesbians/gay men • wheelchair access

Spiritual Groups

MCC Pueblo 1003 Liberty Ln (at United Church of Christ), Belmont **719/543-6460** • 5pm Sun

Steamboat Springs

Accommodations

Elk River Estates **970/879-7556** • gay-friendly • suburban townhouse B&B nr hiking, skiing & natural hot springs • full brkfst • $35-40

Trinidad

Accommodations

High Desert Decadence PO Box 44, Aguilar 81020 **719/680-0418** • lesbians/gay men • B&B • camping & 2 RV hookups • on 400 acres • hot tub • kids/pets ok • lesbian-owned/run • $45-100

COLUMBINE INN
nestled in the shadows of majestic Pikes Peak, tucked away in beautiful Green Mountain Falls

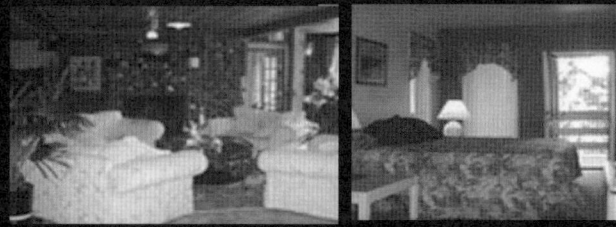

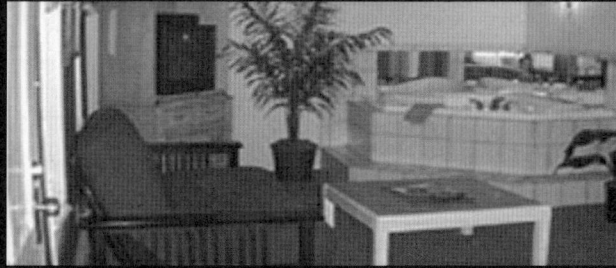

In-room jacuzzi for two*

each non-smoking room features:*
private deck
fridge/microwave   complimentary
color tv/vcr/phone   in-room coffee

Romantic get-a-way packages,
Close drive to theatres, galleries, antique
& specialty shops, hiking, biking, fishing,
boating, golfing, 4 wheel drive tours,
horseback rides, swimming and gambling

13 mi. from downtown Colorado Springs
For reservations call 888-684-9576
Visit our web site: www.gmfresorts.com

Colorado/ Connecticut • USA

Vail

Accommodations

Antlers at Vail 680 W Lionshead Pl **970/476-2471, 800/843-8245** • gay-friendly • apts • hot tub • swimming • fireplace • balcony • kids ok • $130-1,200

Restaurants

Larkspur Restaurant & Market 458 Vail Valley Dr (in the Golden Peak Lodge) **970/479-8050** • lunch & dinner • fine dining • also bar • patio • ski-in/out • wheelchair access

Sweet Basil 193 E Gore Creek Dr **970/476-0125** • lunch & dinner • some veggie • full bar • wheelchair access

Winter Park

Accommodations

The Bear Paw Inn 871 Bear Paw Dr **970/887-1351** • gay-friendly • massive log lodge on top of mtn w/ spectacular views of Rocky Mtn Nat'l Park • full brkfst • $170-215

Silverado II 490 Kings Crossing Rd **970/726-5753** • gay-friendly • condo ski resort • swimming • $65-330

Entertainment & Recreation

Black Dog Mountaineering 78902 US Hwy 40 **970/726-4412** • ski & snowboard rentals • also raft trips (summers)

Connecticut

Statewide

Info Lines & Services

Gay/ Lesbian Guide Line Hartford **203/366-3734** • 8pm-10pm Mon-Wed • statewide info

Publications

Lesbian Position PO Box 9205, New Haven 06533 • lesbian newsletter for all CT w/ columns & many entertainment & events listings • monthly

Metroline 860/233-8334 • regional newspaper & entertainment guide, covers CT, RI & MA

Bethel

Restaurants

Bethel Pizza House 206 Greenwood Ave **203/748-1427** • 11am-11pm

Emerald City Cafe 269 Greenwood Ave **203/778-4100** • dinner & Sun brunch, clsd Mon • cont'l

Bridgeport

Restaurants

Bloodroot Restaurant 85 Ferris St **203/576-9168** • lunch Tue & Th-Sat, dinner Tue-Sat, Sun brunch, clsd Mon • vegetarian • call for events • patio • wheelchair access • women-owned/ run • $8-12

Bookstores

Bloodroot 85 Ferris St **203/576-9168** • clsd Mon, call for hours • feminist • wheelchair access

Danbury

Bars

Triangles Cafe 66 Sugar Hollow Rd, Rte 7 **203/798-6996** • 5pm-1am, till 2am Fri-Sat • popular • lesbians/ gay men • dancing/DJ • live shows • patio

Restaurants

Goulash Place 42 Highland Ave **203/744-1971** • lunch & dinner, clsd Mon • Hungarian • beer/ wine

Enfield

Erotica

Bookends 44 Enfield St/ Rte 5 **860/745-3988**

Groton

Accommodations

Flagship Inn & Suites 470 Gold Star Hwy (Rte 184, off I-95) **860/445-7458, 888/800-0770** • gay-friendly • full brkfst • gym passes • in-room movies • kids ok • wheelchair access • gay-owned/ run

Hartford

Info Lines & Services

Lesbian Rap Group 135 Broad St (at YWCA) **860/525-1163** • 7:30pm Tue

Project 100/ The Community Center 1841 Broad St (at New Britain) **860/724-5542** • hours vary • meetings & activities • wheelchair access

Accommodations

Butternut Farm 1654 Main St, Glastonbury **860/633-7197** • gay/ straight • 18th-century house furnished with antiques • full brkfst • $79-99

Holiday Inn East Hartford 363 Roberts St, East Hartford **860/528-9611** • gay-friendly • swimming • also restaurant pets ok • wheelchair access

Hartford • Connecticut

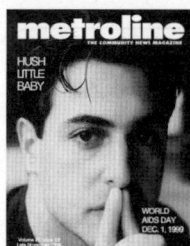 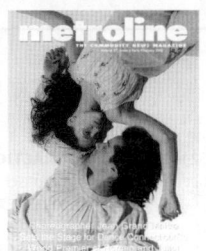 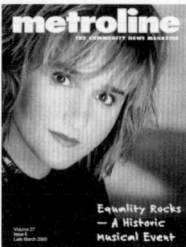

metroline

27 Years Strong

When traveling in southern New England, ask for the number one rated news resource and area guide for the gay community since 1974.

1.888.233.8334 / www.metroline-online.com

MetroStore

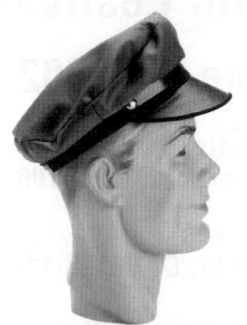 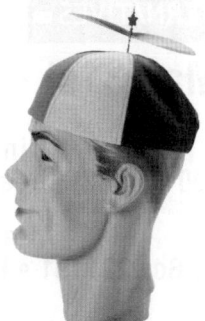

for all things gay and fabulous

When in Hartford, stop by MetroStore for a selection of magazines, videos, gift items, jewelry, dance music, cards, novelties and much, much more...
"100% gay owned and operated." 495 Farmington Avenue • 860.231.8845

Connecticut • USA

Hartford

LGBT Pride: June. 860/524-8114, email: et_pride@hotmail.com.

Annual Events: June - Lesbian/Gay Film Festival.

City Info: Greater Hartford Tourism District 800/793-4480.

Attractions: Bushnell Park Carousel.
Harriet Beecher Stowe House.
Mark Twain House 860/247-0998.
Real Art Ways 860/232-1006.
Wadsworth Atheneum 860/278-2670.

Transit: Yellow Cab 860/666-6666.
Airport Connection 860/627-3400 (downtown hotels only).
Connecticut Transit 860/525-9181.

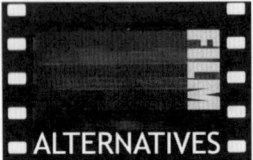

15th Connecticut Gay & Lesbian Film Festival

May 31st - June 8th 2002

Cinestudio
300 Summit Street • Hartford, CT 06106

Alternatives
P.O. Box 231191 • Hartford, CT 06123-1191

TEL: 860.586.1136 • www.ctglff.org

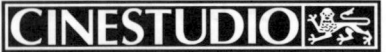

New Haven • Connecticut

BARS

Bar One 1306 Main St, East Hartford **860/282-6106** • Sun only • mostly women • dancing/ DJ

Chez Est 458 Wethersfield Ave (at Main St) **860/525-3243** • 3pm-1am, till 2am wknds • popular • lesbians/ gay men • dancing/DJ • live shows • 'Bushfire' women's night 2nd Sat

The Polo Club 678 Maple Ave (btwn Preston & Mapleton) **860/278-3333** • 7pm-1am Th-Sat, till 2am wknds • lesbians/ gay men • live shows

Women After Hours 363 Roberts St (at the Holiday Inn), East Hartford **860/895-1934** • women only • dance party 4th Sat • older crowd

NIGHTCLUBS

Nick's Cafe 1943 Broad St (at Mapleton) **860/956-1573** • 4pm-1am, till 2am wknds, clsd Mon-Tue • lesbians/ gay men • women's night 2nd Fri • dancing/DJ • Latin night Sat • live shows

Velvet 50 Union Pl **860/278-6333** • clsd Mon-Wed • gay/ straight • gay night Sun • dancing/DJ • live shows

Webster Theatre 31 Webster St (at Whitmore) **860/246-8001** • 9pm-2am • gay/ straight • dancing/ DJ • goth/ fetish party 1st Sat • 'Club Lucy' for women 3rd Sat • live music

RESTAURANTS

Arugula 953 Farmington Ave, West Hartford **860/561-4888** • lunch & dinner, clsd Sun-Mon • Mediterranean

Peppercorn's 357 Main St **860/547-1714** • lunch & dinner • Italian

Pond House Cafe 155 Asylum Rd, West Hartford **860/231-8823** • 11am-2:30pm & 5pm-9pm, Sun brunch, clsd Mon • patio

The Union 2935 Main St, Glastonbury **860/633-0880** • lunch, dinner & Sun brunch • full bar till 1am, till 2am wknds • patio

BOOKSTORES

Reader's Feast Bookstore Cafe 529 Farmington Ave (at Sisson Ave) **860/232-3710** • 11am-6pm, 10am-2pm Sun • lgbt bookstore

RETAIL SHOPS

▲ **MetroStore** 493 Farmington Ave (at Sisson Ave) **860/231-8845** • 8:30am-8pm, till 5:30pm Tue, Wed & Sat, clsd Sun • magazines • travel guides • leather & more

PUBLICATIONS

▲ **Metroline** **860/233-8334** • regional newspaper & entertainment guide, covers CT, RI & MA

SPIRITUAL GROUPS

Congregation Am Segulah **800/734-8524** (IN CT ONLY) • call for service times & location

MCC 1841 Broad St (at Hartford Community Center) **860/724-4605** • 10:30am Sun

EROTICA

Very Intimate Pleasures 100 Brainard Ave (exit 27 off I-91) **860/246-1875**

Manchester

BARS

Hartford Road Cafe 378 Hartford Rd (at Fairfield) **860/647-0489** • 4pm-2am, clsd Mon (clsd Sun-Tue winters) • gay/ straight • neighborhood bar • DJ Fri-Sat • food served • karaoke Fri

CAFES

Cafe on Main 1071 Main St **860/647-7444** • 7am-2pm, clsd Tue

Meriden

EROTICA

The D/ S Toy Chest 975 Broad St (at rear) **203/639-0622** • 10am-8pm Mon-Th, till 9:30 Fri-Sat, clsd Sun • mostly women

Middletown

INFO LINES & SERVICES

Wesleyan Women's Resource Center 287 High St **860/685-3297** • library

New Haven

INFO LINES & SERVICES

New Haven Gay/ Lesbian Community Center 50 Fitch St **203/387-2252** • Mon, Wed-Fri 6pm-9pm • meetings • resources • library • weekly movies

Yale Women's Center 198 Elm St **203/432-0388** • 10am-10pm, till 5pm Fri, noon-5pm Sat, clsd Sun • resources • support groups • library • wheelchair access

ACCOMMODATIONS

The Inn at Oyster Point 104 Howard Ave (at 6th St) **203/773-3334** • gay/ straight • full brkfst • gay-owned/ run • $105-269

Connecticut • USA

Bars

The Bar 254 Crown St **203/495-8924** • 4pm-1am • gay/straight • more gay Tue • dancing/DJ • wheelchair access

Partners 365 Crown St (at Park St) **203/776-1014** • 5pm-1am, till 2am Fri-Sat • lesbians/gay men • neighborhood bar • dancing/DJ • occasional women's night

Nightclubs

Gotham Citi Cafe 130 Crown St (at Church) **203/498-2484** • from 10pm Wed-Sat • gay/straight • dancing/DJ • more gay Sat • drag shows

Cafes

Chapel Sweet Shoppe 1042 Chapel St **203/624-2411** • 10am-8pm, noon-6pm Sun • full ice cream fountain • seasonal outside cafe

Restaurants

168 York St Cafe 168 York St **203/789-1915** • 3pm-1am • lesbians/gay men • some veggie • full bar • patio • gay-owned/run • $4-7

Beach Head Cafe 3 Cosey Beach Ave • dinner only, clsd Mon

Cafe Tibwin Grill 220 College St (at Crown) **203/624-1883** • lunch Wed-Fri, dinner nightly, clsd Sun-Mon • smokefree • also full bar

Claire's Corner 1000 Chapel St **203/562-3888** • 8am-9pm, till 10pm Fri-Sat • vegetarian Mexican cafe • great soup • wheelchair access

Spiritual Groups

MCC 34 Harrison St (at United Church) **203/752-2456** • 9:30am Sun

New London

Info Lines & Services

New London People's Forum Affirming Lesbian/Gay Identity 76 Federal (at St James Church) **860/443-8855** • 6:30pm Wed • social & educational support group

Bars

Frank's Place 9 Tilley St **860/443-8883** • 4pm-1am, till 2am Fri-Sat • lesbians/gay men • dancing/DJ • live shows • patio • wheelchair access

Heroes 33 Golden St **860/442-4376** • 4pm-1am, till 2am wknds, 3pm-1am Sun • lesbians/gay men • neighborhood bar • dancing/DJ

Bookstores

Greene's Books & Beans 140 Bank St (at Golden) **860/443-3312** • call for hours • also cafe • wheelchair access

Norfolk

Accommodations

Manor House B&B 69 Maple Ave **860/542-5690** • gay-friendly • elegant & romantic 1898 Victorian Tudor estate • full brkfst • fireplaces • whirlpool • smokefree • $125-250

Norwalk

Info Lines & Services

Triangle Community Center 16 River St **203/853-0600** • 7:30pm-9:30pm Mon-Fri • activities • newsletter • call for info

Accommodations

Silk Orchid **203/847-2561** • women only • 1 suite • swimming • whirlpool • fireplace • lesbian-owned/run • $95

Norwich

Bookstores

Magazines & More 77 Salem Tpke #105 **860/886-1855** • 10am-6pm, till 8pm Th-Fri, till 5pm Sat, clsd Sun • lgbt

Ridgefield

Restaurants

Gail's Station House 378 Main St **203/438-9775** • brkfst & lunch, dinner Fri-Sun • great cheddar corn pancakes

South Windsor

Accommodations

The Watson House 1876 Main St (at Sullivan Ave) **860/282-8888** • gay/straight • kids ok • gay-owned/run • $99-129

Stratford

Nightclubs

Stephanie's Living Room **203/377-2119** • popular • women only • 'quality social events for women' • dances • multiracial • all ages • wheelchair access • discounts for physically challenged

Washington Depot

Restaurants

GW Tavern 20 Bee Brook Rd (Rte 47) **860/868-6633** • 11:30am-1am, more gay late & 10pm 3rd Tue • nouvelle Yankee food

Rehoboth Beach • Delaware

Waterbury

BARS

The Brownstone 29 Leavenworth St (at Grande) **203/597-1838** • 5pm-1am, till 2am Fri-Sat • lesbians/ gay men • more women Th-Fri • live shows • wheelchair access

SPIRITUAL GROUPS

Integrity/ Waterbury Area 16 Church St (at St John's) **203/754-3116** • meet 2nd Sun • call for time

Westport

BARS

Cedar Brook Cafe 919 Post Rd E **203/221-7429** • 8pm-1am Mon, 6pm-1am Tue-Th, till 2am Fri-Sat, 4pm-11pm Sun • mostly gay men • dancing/DJ • live shows • patio • wheelchair access

ENTERTAINMENT & RECREATION

Sherwood Island State Park Beach left to gay area

Willimantic

CAFES

Cafe Earth 1244 Storrs **860/429-5304** • 7am-10pm • some veggie

RESTAURANTS

Paradise Eatery 713 Main St **860/423-7682** • 11:30am-10pm, clsd Wed • wheelchair access

DELAWARE

Statewide

INFO LINES & SERVICES

Delaware Tourism Office 800/441-8846 (OUTSIDE DE), 800/282-8667 (IN-STATE ONLY)

Gay & Lesbian AA 302/856-6452

Bethany Beach

BARS

Nomad Village Rte 1 (3 miles N of Bethany Beach, in Tower Shores) **302/644-2717** • 10am-1am (seasonal) • lesbians/ gay men • neighborhood bar • dancing/DJ • also motel & shops

Rehoboth Beach

INFO LINES & SERVICES

▲ **Camp Rehoboth** 39–B Baltimore Ave **302/227-5620** • 10am-5pm, clsd wknds • info service for lgbt businesses • newsletter w/ extensive listings

ACCOMMODATIONS

An Inn by the Bay 205 Savannah Rd, Lewes **302/644-8878, 866/833-2565** • gay/ straight • smokefree • gay-owned/ run • $55-75

At Melissa's B&B 36 Delaware Ave (btwn 1st & 2nd) **302/227-7504, 800/396-8090** • gay-friendly • open year round • 1 blk from beach • women-owned/ run • $75-225

Rehoboth Beach

ANNUAL EVENTS: November - Rehoboth Beach Independent Film Festival 302/645-9095, web: www.rehobothfilm.com.
July - Fireworks 302/227-2772.

CITY INFO: Rehoboth Beach-Dewey Beach Chamber of Commerce 302/227-2233 & 800/441-1329. Rehoboth Convention Center 800/282-8667 (in-state) and 800/441-8846 (out-of-state).

ATTRACTIONS: Main Street 302/227-2772.
North Shores beach.

TRANSIT: Seaport Taxi 302/645-6800.
Jolly Trolley 302/227-1197 (seasonal tour & shuttle).

Delaware • USA

Beach House B&B 302/227-7074, 800/283-4667 • lesbians/ gay men • swimming • nr boardwalk & beach • wheelchair access • $39-166

Cabana Gardens B&B 20 Lake Ave (at 3rd St) 302/227-5429 • lesbians/ gay men • lake & ocean views • deck • swimming • smokefree • $65-235

Chesapeake Landing B&B 101 Chesapeake St (at King Charles) 302/227-2973 • gay-friendly • full brkfst • swimming • smokefree • lakefront • nr Poodle Beach • gay-owned/ run • $125-275

The Delaware Inn B&B 55 Delaware Ave 302/227-6031, 800/246-5244 • gay-friendly • country inn atmosphere • nr beach • swimming • gay-owned/ run • $50-190

The Hidden Treasure B&B 302/945-9456 • gay/ straight • full brkfst • hot tub • 8 miles out of town in private setting • teens ok • $55-150

The Lighthouse Inn B&B 20 Delaware Ave 302/226-0407, 800/600-9092 • seasonal • gay/ straight • B&B •also apt w/full kitchen & private deck (weekly rental) • 1 blk from beach • $85-180

Lord Hamilton Seaside B&B Inn 20 Brooklyn Ave (at 1st) 302/227-6960, 877/227-6960 • lesbians/gay men • Victorian home • 1/2 blk to beach & boardwalk • gay-owned/ run • $95-225

The Pelican Loft 45 Baltimore Ave 302/226-5080, 800/550-9551 • mostly women • nr beach & boardwalk • some shared baths • teens ok • smokefree • lesbian-owned/ run • $75-150

Rehoboth Guest House 40 Maryland Ave (at King Charles) 302/227-4117, 800/564-0493 • seasonal • lesbians/ gay men • Victorian beach house • deck • nr boardwalk & beach • $40-165

Renegade Restaurant & Lounge/ Motel 4274 Hwy 1 (nr Rehoboth Ave) 302/227-4713, 302/227-1222 • lesbians/ gay men • popular • 10-acre resort • swimming • full bar • dancing/DJ • karaoke • also restaurant (dinner only) • some veggie • wheelchair access • $35-175

Shore Inn at Rehoboth 703 Rehoboth Ave (nr Church) 302/227-8487, 800/597-8899 • mostly gay men • hot tub • swimming • gay-owned/ run • $95-160

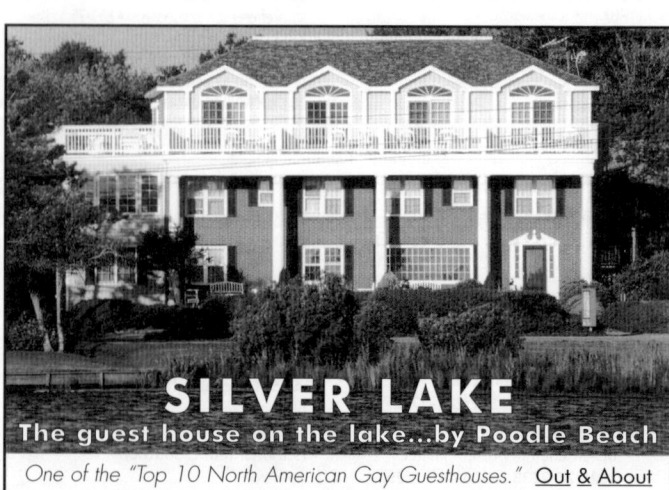

SILVER LAKE
The guest house on the lake...by Poodle Beach

One of the "Top 10 North American Gay Guesthouses." **Out & About**
"The best of the bunch." **Fodor's Gay Guide**

133 Silver Lake Drive • Rehoboth Beach, DE 19971
www.silverlakeguesthouse.com • 800/842-2115

Rehoboth Beach • Delaware

▲ **Silver Lake Guest House** 133 Silver Lake Dr **302/226-2115, 800/842-2115** • lesbians/ gay men • nr Poodle Beach • pets ok • $80-350

Summer Place Hotel 30 Olive Ave (at 1st) **302/226-0766, 800/815-3925** • gay/ straight • also apts • nr beach • $39-200

The Sussex House B&B 601 Bayard Ave (at New Castle Ave) **302/227-7860, 877/787-7392** • gay/ straight • 2 blks to beach • some shared baths • smokefree • gay-owned/ run • $45-175

BARS

The Blue Moon 35 Baltimore Ave (btwn 1st & 2nd) **302/227-6515** • 4pm-2am, clsd Jan • lesbians/ gay men • popular happy hour • T-dance • also restaurant • Sun brunch • plenty veggie • $18-30

Double L Bar 622 Rehoboth Ave **302/227-0818** • 3pm-2am, clsd Sun • open year round • mostly gay men • leather

Frogg Pond 3 S 1st St (at Rehoboth Ave) **302/227-2234** • 10am-1am • gay-friendly • popular w/ women in summer • neighborhood bar • food served • popular happy hour

The Renegade at Renegade Motel **302/227-4713** • lesbians/ gay men • popular • full bar & restaurant • karaoke • swimming • hosts very popular women's T-dance major summer holiday wknds • wheelchair access

NIGHTCLUBS

The Beach House Restaurant & Bar 316 Rehoboth Ave **302/227-4227** • mostly women • seasonal • dinner & dance club • live entertainment • wheelchair access

Purple Parrot Grill 247 Rehoboth Ave **302/226-1139** • call for hrs • gay/ straight • dancing/DJ • also restaurant • wheelchair access • $8-22

CAFES

Java Beach 167 Rehoboth Ave **302/227-8418** • 7am-6pm, open later in summer • cafe • patio

Lori's 39 Baltimore Ave (at 1st) **302/226-3066** • seasonal, call for hrs • also sandwiches • woman-owned/ run

RESTAURANTS

Back Porch Cafe 59 Rehoboth Ave **302/227-3674** • lunch & dinner • Sun brunch • some veggie • full bar • wheelchair access • $9-29

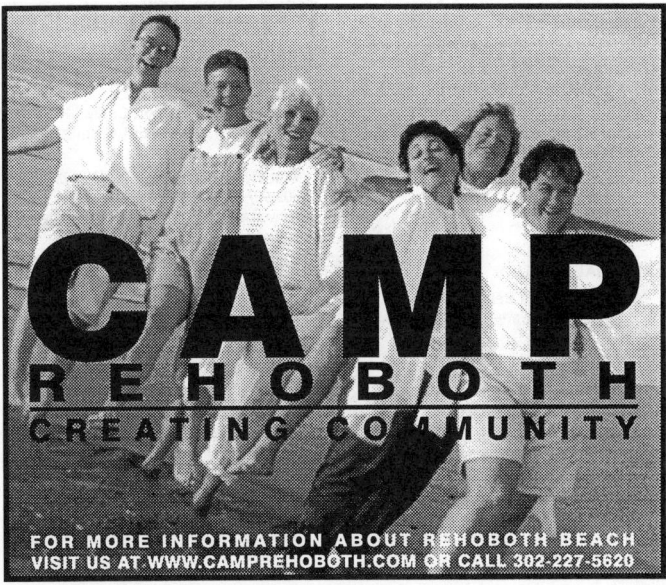

Delaware/ District of Columbia • USA

Celsius 50–C Wilmington Ave **302/227–5767** • dinner only Th-Sun • French-Mediterranean • some veggie • wheelchair access • $15-25

Cloud Nine 234 Rehoboth Ave (at 2nd) **302/226-1999** • 4pm-2am • popular • fusion bistro • full bar • dancing/DJ wknds • wheelchair access • $10-22

The Cultured Pearl 19 Wilmington Ave A (off 1st St) **302/227–8493** • 5pm-10pm Th-Sat • sushi bar • cocktail lounge • $16-24

Dream Cafe 26 Baltimore Ave **302/226–2233** • 7am-5pm • some veggie • $3-7

La La Land 22 Wilmington Ave **302/227–3887** • 6pm-1am (seasonal) • seafood & more • full bar • patio • $19-28

Sydney's Side Street Restaurant & Blues Place 25 Christian St (at 2nd St) **302/227–1339** • 4pm-1am (seasonal) • healthy entrees • full bar • live shows • patio • $12-20

Tijuana Taxi 207 Rehoboth Ave (at 2nd St) **302/227–1986** • 5pm-10pm, from noon wknds • full bar • wheelchair access • $6-13

Yum-Yum Pan Asian Bistro 37 Wilmington Ave **302/226–0400** • popular • name says it all • patio • T-dance Sun

ENTERTAINMENT & RECREATION

North Shores S end of Cape Henlopen State Park (at jetty S of watch tower) • popular women's beach • 20 min walk from boardwalk • by car follow the shoreline road to State Park entrance

BOOKSTORES

Lambda Rising 39 Baltimore Ave (btwn 1st & 2nd) **302/227–6969** • 10am-midnight, till 8pm in winter • lgbt • wheelchair access

PUBLICATIONS

▲ **Letters from Camp Rehoboth** **302/227–5620** • newsmagazine w/ events & entertainment listings

SPIRITUAL GROUPS

MCC of Rehoboth Beach 521 Glade Rd/ Rd 271 (at Ocean Wave Hall) **302/645–4945** • 9am & 11am Sun

GYMS & HEALTH CLUBS

Body Shop 401 N Boardwalk (at Virginia) **302/226–0920** • lesbians/ gay men

The Firm Fitness Center 6 Camelot Shopping Ctr/ Rte 1 **302/227–8363** • 7am-9pm

Wilmington

BARS

814 Club 814 Shipley St (btwn 8th & 9th) **302/657–5730** • 5pm-1am • lesbians/ gay men • dancing/DJ • transgender-friendly • also restaurant • $5-15

Roam at 'Anthony's on Shipley' (upstairs) **302/658–7626** • 6pm-2am • popular • lesbians/ gay men • dancing/DJ • multiracial • men's night Th • piano bar Fri 5pm • dancing/DJ wknds

RESTAURANTS

Anthony's on Shipley 913 Shipley St (at 10th) **302/652–7797** • lunch & dinner • fine dining • full bar • live shows upstairs • gay-owned/ run • $17-24

Mrs Robino's 520 N Union (at Pennsylvania) **302/652–9223** • 11am-9pm Mon-Fri, till 10pm wknds • family-style Italian • bar • wheelchair access

Queen Bean Cafe 205 W 7th St **302/429–0700** • lunch Tue-Fri, dinner Tue-Sat, clsd Sun-Mon • hours vary • veggie

SPIRITUAL GROUPS

More Light Hanover Presb Church (at 18th & Baynard Blvd) **302/658–5114** • 11am Sun

DISTRICT OF COLUMBIA

Washington

INFO LINES & SERVICES

Black Lesbian Support Group 1407 'S' St NW (at 14th) **202/797–3593** • 3pm 2nd & 4th Sat

Bon Vivant Foundation **202/234–2824, 301/907–7073** • professional women's networking group • sponsors monthly dance parties • also publishes newsletter

Gay/ Lesbian Hotline (at Whitman-Walker Clinic) **202/833–3234** • 7pm-11pm • resources • crisis counseling

HIV+ Coffeehouse 2111 Florida Ave NW (Friends Meeting House, enter on Decatur Pl) **202/483–3310** • 7:30pm-10pm 1st & 3rd Sat • HIV+ & friends

The HOPE Foundation 2120 'L' St NW #210 **202/466–5783** • monthly socials for positive people • seminars • call for info

LLEGO (Latino/a Lesbian/ Gay Organization) 1420 'K' St NW #200 **202/466–8240** • center open 9am-6pm Mon-Fri • also publishes newsletter 'Noticias de LLEGO'

Washington • District of Columbia

Transgender Education Association 301/949-3822 • social/ support group for transgendered people & their partners

Triangle Club 2030 'P' St NW 202/659-8641 • site for various 12-step groups • call for times

Women in the Life 1611 Connecticut Ave NW #2B 202/483-9818, 202/483-9818 • party 1st Fri • sports teams • open mics • racially diverse

ACCOMMODATIONS

1836 California 1836 California St NW (btwn 18th & 19th) 202/462-6502 • gay/ straight • 1900s house w/ period furnishings & sundeck • some shared baths • kids ok • $80-110

Bull Moose B&B on Capitol Hill 101 5th St NE (at 'A' St) 202/547-1050, 800/261-2768 • gay/ straight • Victorian row house in historic Capitol Hill district • smokefree • $89-199

Washington

WHERE THE GIRLS ARE: Strolling around DuPont Circle or cruising a bar in the lgbt bar ghetto southeast of The Mall.

ENTERTAINMENT: Gay Men's Chorus 202/338-7464.

LGBT PRIDE: June. 202/986-1119.

ANNUAL EVENTS: October - Reel Affirmations Film Festival 202/986-1119.
March - Women's History Month at various Smithsonian Museums 202/357-2700.

CITY INFO: DC Visitors Assoc. 202/789-7000, web: www.washington.org.

ATTRACTIONS: Ford's Theatre 202/347-4833.
Jefferson Memorial.
JFK Center for the Performing Arts.
Lincoln Memorial.
National Gallery 202/737-4215.
National Museum of Women in the Arts 202/783-5000.
National Zoo 202/673-4717.
Smithsonian 202/357-1300.
Vietnam Veteran's Memorial.

BEST VIEW: From the top of the Washington Monument.

WEATHER: Summers are hot (90°s) and MUGGY (the city was built on marshes). In the winter, temperatures drop to the 30°s and 40°s with rain. Spring is the time of cherry blossoms.

TRANSIT: Yellow Cab 202/544-1212.
Washington Flier 703/661-8230 & 703/685-1400 (from Dulles or National).
Super Shuttle 800/809-7080.
Metro Transit Authority 202/637-7000.

District of Columbia • USA

The Carlyle Suites Hotel 1731 New Hampshire Ave NW (btwn 'R' & 'S' Sts) **202/234-3200, 800/964-5377** • gay/ straight • art deco hotel • gym • also restaurant & bar • popular gay Sun brunch • wheelchair access • $69-149

Creekside B&B **301/261-9438** • mostly women • private home on the shore of the Chesapeake • 40 minutes from DC • swimming • full brkfst • lesbian-owned/ run • $75

The Embassy Inn 1627 16th St NW **202/234-7800, 800/423-9111** • gay-friendly • small hotel w/ B&B atmosphere • $79-129

Embassy Suites Alexandria 1900 Diagonal Rd, Alexandria, VA **703/684-5900** • gay/ straight • full brkfst • kids ok • swimming • $119-240

Embassy Suites—Chevy Chase Pavilion 4300 Military Rd NW **202/362-9300, 800/362-2779** • gay-friendly • swimming • gym • pets ok • wheelchair access

▲ **Kalorama Guest House at Kalorama Park** 1854 Mintwood Pl NW (at Columbia Rd) **202/667-6369** • gay/ straight • Victorian townhouse nr Dupont Circle • $50-120

▲ **Kalorama Guest House at Woodley Park** 2700 Cathedral Ave NW (off Connecticut Ave) **202/328-0860** • gay/ straight • nr Nat'l Zoo & Washington Cathedral • smokefree • $45-100

Morrison-Clark Historic Inn & Restaurant Massachusetts Ave NW (at 11th St NW) **202/898-1200** • gay-friendly • $155-265

One Washington Circle Hotel One Washington Cir NW **202/872-1680, 800/424-9671** • gay-friendly • suites w/ kitchens • swimming • also restaurant & piano bar • kids ok • $129-259

Radisson Barcelo Hotel Washington 2121 'P' St NW (at 21st St) **202/293-3100, 800/333-3333** • gay-friendly • pool • restaurant • $99-285

The River Inn 924 25th St NW (at 'K' St) **202/337-7600, 800/424-2741** • gay-friendly • suites w/ kitchen • gym • also 'Foggy Bottom Cafe' • wheelchair access • $89-165

Savoy Suites Hotel 2505 Wisconsin Ave NW (at Calvert, in Georgetown) **202/337-9700, 800/944-5377** • gay-friendly • also restaurant • Italian • wheelchair access • $99-199

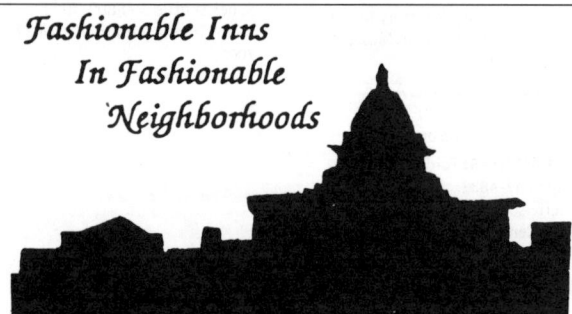

Fashionable Inns In Fashionable Neighborhoods

o Walk to Dupont Circle, fashionable clubs and restuarants, and the subway (Metro)
o Enjoy breakfast and evening aperitif

THE KALORAMA GUEST HOUSES
Kalorama Park (202) 667-6369
Woodley Park (202) 328-0860

Washington • District of Columbia

Reply **Forward** **Delete**

```
Date: Mon, Nov 12, 2001 14:19:37
From: Girl-on-the-Go
To: Editor@Damron.com
Subject: Washington, DC
```

> Even though Washington, DC is known worldwide as a showcase of American culture and a command center of global politics, many people overlook this international 'hot spot' when traveling in the United States. But DC is not all boring museums and stuffy bureaucrats.

> For instance, begin your stay in DC at one of the gay-friendly hotels or guesthouses in and around the city. **Creekside B&B** in Maryland has a strong lesbian following.

> Of course, you could tour the usual sites—starting with the heart of DC—the 'Mall'—a two-mile-long grass strip bordered by many museums and monuments: the Smithsonian, the National Air and Space Museum, the National Gallery of Art, the Museum of Natural History, the Museum of American History, the Washington Monument, the Lincoln Memorial, and the Vietnam Veterans Memorial.

> For a truly interesting change of pace, check out these less touristy attractions: the outstanding National Museum of Women in the Arts, the hip shops and exotic eateries along Massachusetts Avenue, and of course, DuPont Circle, the pulsing heart of LGBT DC. The Circle is also home to the oldest modern art museum in the country, the Phillips Collection, as well as the LGBT bookstore **Lambda Rising,** and the kinky **Pleasure Place.**

> For nightlife, don't miss **Hung Jury**, a popular club for women. **Phase One** is a more casual bar for lesbians, and there are several women's nights at the mixed bars. For the latest events for women in DC and its environs, pick up a copy of **Woman's Monthly** or **Women in the Life**.

> Still can't find your crowd? Drop by **Sisterspace & Books,** specializing in books by and about African-American women; call the **Black Lesbian Support Group**; or stop in at Stompin' Grounds, a cafe popular with local women. If you're plugged in, check out **www.grrlscout.com/dcgrrl/** for the latest events and news.

District of Columbia • USA

Swann House Historic B&B 1808 New Hampshire Ave NW (at Swann St) **202/265-4414** • gay/ straight • 1883 Victorian mansion in Dupont Circle • swimming • roof deck • fireplaces • tenns ok • $140-295

Washington Plaza 10 Thomas Cir NW (at 14th & Massachusetts) **202/842-1300, 800/424-1140** • gay-friendly • full-service hotel • also restaurant • $99-200

The Windsor Inn 1842 16th St NW **202/667-0300, 800/423-9111** • gay-friendly • small hotel w/ B&B atmosphere • $79-159

BARS

Club Chaos 1603 17th St NW (at 'Q' St) **202/232-4141** • 5pm-2am, brunch 11am Sun • lesbians/ gay men • dancing/DJ • multiracial • drag king/ queen shows • women's night Wed • Latin Th • also restaurant • some veggie • wheelchair access

DC Eagle 639 New York Ave NW (btwn 6th & 7th) **202/347-6025** • 4pm-2am Sun-Th, till 3am Fri-Sat • popular • mostly gay men • leather • wheelchair access

The Fireplace 2161 'P' St NW (at 22nd St) **202/293-1293** • 1pm-2am, wknds till 3am • mostly gay men • neighborhood bar • multiracial clientele • videos • wheelchair access

JR's Bar 1519 17th St NW (at Church) **202/328-0090** • 11:30am-2am, till 3am Fri-Sat • popular • mostly gay men • neighborhood bar • videos • young crowd

Larry's Lounge 1840 18th St NW (at 'T' St) **202/483-1483** • 5pm-2am, till 3am Fri-Sat • lesbians/ gay men • neighborhood bar • food served • wheelchair access

The Lillies 1731 New Hampshire (at 18th & 'R' Sts, in the 'Carlyle Suites') **202/518-5011** • 5pm-2am • mostly gay men • also restaurant, 7am-10:30pm • wheelchair access

Mr Henry's Capitol Hill 601 Pennsylvania Ave SE (at 6th) **202/546-8412** • 11:30am-midnight, till 1am wknds • popular • gay-friendly • multiracial • live jazz • also restaurant

Nob Hill 1101 Kenyon NW (at 11th St) **202/797-1101** • 6pm-2am, till 3am wknds, clsd Mon-Tue • lesbians/ gay men • neighborhood bar • dancing/DJ • mostly African-American • live shows

Phase One 525 8th St SE (btwn 'E' & 'G' Sts) **202/544-6831** • 7pm-2am, till 3am Fri-Sat (clsd Mon-Tue winter) • mostly women • neighborhood bar • dancing/DJ • multiracial • live shows • last Fri leather night • wheelchair access

Remington's 639 Pennsylvania Ave SE (btwn 6th & 7th) **202/543-3113** • 4pm-2am, till 3am Fri-Sat • popular • mostly gay men • dancing/DJ • country/ western • dance lessons Mon, Wed-Th • karaoke Wed • drag show Sun

NIGHTCLUBS

Atlas 1520 14th St NW (at 'The Saint') **202/331-4422** • dance parties • mostly gay men • locations vary • call for info

Bachelors Mill 1104 8th St SE (downstairs at 'Back Door Pub') **202/544-1931** • 10pm-close, clsd Mon • lesbians/ gay men • more women Wed • popular • dancing/DJ • mostly African-American • live shows • wheelchair access

Chief Ike's Mambo Room 1725 Columbia Rd NW (at Ontario) **202/332-2211** • 6pm-2am, 4pm-3am wknds • gay-friendly • dancing/DJ • also restaurant • Cajun • wheelchair access

Club Diversité 1526 14th St NW (btwn 'P' & 'Q' Sts) **202/234-5740** • 11:30am-2am, till 3am wknds • restaurant till 10pm • mostly gay men • dancing/DJ • live shows • Latin music Fri-Sat • mostly African-American Sun

Club One 1129 Pennsylvania Ave SE (at 12th) **202/544-6406** • open Th-Sat • lesbians/ gay men • dancing/ DJ • multiracial clientele • live shows • women's night Th • Latin Fri-Sat • piano bar • open mic • special events

The Edge 56 'L' St SE (at Half St) **202/488-1200** • 10pm-close, 11pm-5am Fri-Sat, clsd Sun • mostly gay men • women's night Wed • multiracial • women's party last Sat 3pm-7pm • dancing/DJ • videos • 18+ • wheelchair access

Hung Jury 1819 'H' St NW (at 18th St) **202/785-8181** • 10pm-3am Fri, 9pm-4am Sat • popular • mostly women • dancing/DJ • food served • live shows • call for events • wheelchair access

Lizard Lounge 1520 14th St NW (at 'The Saint') **202/331-4422** • 8pm-2am Sun • popular • mostly gay men • dance parties • call for info • also restaurant

Velvet corner of S Capitol & 'K' Sts SE (at 'Nation') **202/554-1500** • 10pm Sat • popular • mostly gay men • dancing/DJ • live shows • young crowd • cover charge

Ziegfield's 1345 Half St SE (at 'O' St) **202/554-5141** • 8pm-3am, till 2am Th & Sun, clsd Mon-Wed • lesbians/ gay men • dancing/DJ • alternative • multiracial • live shows • wheelchair access

Washington • District of Columbia

Cafes

Cafe Luna 1633 'P' St NW (at 17th) **202/387-4005** • 8am-11pm, from 10am wknds, till 1:30am Fri-Sat • popular • lesbians/ gay men • healthy • plenty veggie

Franklyn's Coffee House 2000 18th St NW (at 'U' St) **202/319-1800** • 8am-8pm • popular • beer/ wine • patio

Jolt n' Bolt 1918 18th St NW (at Florida) **202/232-0077** • 6am-12:30am, till 1:30am wknds • popular • food served • patio

Soho Tea & Coffee 2150 'P' St NW **202/463-7646** • 6am-4am, till 5am Fri-Sat • cybercafe & more • patio • wheelchair access

Stompin' Grounds 666 Pennsylvania Ave SE (at 7th) **202/546-5228** • 7am-8pm • lesbian hangout • patio • outdoor music wknds • also poetry readings & events • lesbian-owned/ run • wheelchair access

Xando 1647 20th St **202/332-6364** • 6:30am-midnight, till 2am wknds • full bar from 4pm • popular • make your own s'mores

Restaurants

17th Street Bar & Grill 1516 Rhode Island Ave NW (at 17th) **202/872-1126** • brkfst, lunch & dinner • popular Sun brunch • patio

Annie's Paramount Steak House 1609 17th St NW (at Corcoran) **202/232-0395** • 11am-4am, 24hrs Fri-Sat • popular • full bar

Armand's Chicago Pizza 4231 Wisconsin Ave NW (at Veazey) **202/686-9450** • 11:30am-10pm • full bar • also 226 Massachusetts Ave NE, Capitol Hill, 202/547-6600

Banana Cafe & Piano Bar 500 8th St SE (at 'E' St) **202/543-5906** • lunch & dinner • Puerto Rican/ Cuban food • some veggie • famous margaritas • gay-owned/ run

Cafe Berlin 322 Massachusetts Ave NE (btwn 3rd & 4th) **202/543-7656** • lunch & dinner, dinner only Sun • German • some veggie • wheelchair access • $14-17

Cafe Japoné 2032 'P' St NW (at 21st) **202/223-1573** • 6pm-2am • mostly Asian-American • popular • Japanese food • full bar • live jazz Wed-Th • karaoke • $10-15

Dupont Italian Kitchen & Bar 1637 17th St NW (at 'R' St) **202/328-3222, 202/328-0100** • 11am-midnight, bar from 4pm • some veggie

Fio's 3636 16th St NW (at the 'Woodner') **202/667-3040** • clsd Mon • dinner • Italian • $6-16

Food For Thought 1831 14th St NW (at the 'Black Cat') **202/797-1095** • 7pm-11pm Mon-Sat • gay-friendly • plenty veggie • also live music • indie/ punk • young crowd

Gabriel 2121 'P' St NW (at 21st) **202/956-6690** • 10:30am-10pm • Mediterranean/ Latin • full bar • wheelchair access • $17-27

Guapo's 4515 Wisconsin Ave NW (at Albemale) **202/686-3588** • lunch & dinner • Mexican • some veggie • full bar • wheelchair access • $5-14

Il Radicchio 1509 17th St NW (btwn 'P' & 'Q') **202/986-2627** • lunch & dinner • popular • Italian

Jaleo 480 7th St NW (at 'E' St) **202/628-7949** • lunch & dinner • tapas • full bar • wheelchair access • $8-16

Lauriol Plaza 1835 18th St NW (at 'S') **202/387-0035** • lunch & dinner • Latin American

Mediterranean Blue 1910 18th St NW (at 'T') **202/483-2583** • dinner, wknd brunch • lesbians/ gay men • upscale Middle Eastern • $7-15

Mercury Grill 1602 17th St NW **202/667-5937** • dinner • Sun brunch • full bar • patio • gay-owned/ run

Occidental Grill 1475 Pennsylvania Ave NW (btwn 14th & 15th) **202/783-1475** • lunch & dinner • political player hangout • $8-22

Pearl 2228 18th St NW (at Kalorama) **202/328-0846** • dinner only • upstairs lounge open wknds • lesbian-owned

Pepper's 1527 17th St NW (btwn 'P' & 'Q') **202/ 328-8193** • 11:30am-2am • popular • global American • full bar • patio • great people watching • wheelchair access • $8-12

Perry's 1811 Columbia Rd NW (at 18th) **202/234-6218** • 5:30pm-11:30pm, popular drag Sun brunch • fusion • full bar • roof deck

Red Sea 2463 18th St NW **202/483-5000** • lunch & dinner • Ethiopian • plenty veggie • $7-11

Rocklands 2418 Wisconsin Ave NW (at Calvert) **202/333-2558** • lunch & dinner • bbq & take-out

Roxanne 2319 18th St NW (at Belmont) **202/462-8330** • lunch wknds, dinner nightly • Tex/ Mex • full bar • also 'Peyote Cafe' • $7-15

Sala Thai 2016 'P' St NW (at 21st) **202/872-1144** • lunch & dinner • some veggie • $6-13

District of Columbia • USA

Sheridan's 713 8th St SE **202/546-6955** • dinner only, clsd Mon-Tue • lesbians/gay men • steakhouse • saloon • dancing/DJ • country/western • professional crowd • live shows • gay-owned/run

Skewers 1633 'P' St NW (at 17th) **202/387-7400** • 11:30am-11pm • popular • Middle-Eastern • full bar • $7-17

Soul Vegetarian 2606 Georgia Ave NW **202/328-7685** • 11am-9pm, till 3pm Sun (brunch) • all-vegan menu

Trio 1537 17th St NW **202/232-6305** • 7:30am-midnight • American • some veggie • full bar • $6-16

Trocadero Cafe 1914 Connecticut Ave (in 'Hotel Sofitel') **202/797-2000** • lunch & dinner • French • intimate setting • wheelchair access • $25-35

Two Quail 320 Massachusetts Ave NE **202/543-8030** • lunch Mon-Fri, dinner nightly, Sun brunch • popular • New American • some veggie • full bar • gay-owned/run • $10-18

Entertainment & Recreation

Anecdotal History Tours 301/294-9514 • variety of guided tours

Phillips Collection 1612 21st St NW (at 'Q' St) **202/387-0961** • clsd Mon • America's oldest museum of modern art • nr Dupont Circle

Bookstores

ADC Map & Travel Center 1636 'I' St NW (at 17th St) **202/628-2608, 800/544-2659** • 9am-5:30pm, till 6:30pm Wed-Th, 10am-4pm Sat, clsd Sun • many maps & travel guides

Kramer Books & Afterwords 1517 Connecticut Ave NW (at 'Q') **202/387-1400** • 7:30am-1am, 24hrs wknds • general • also cafe • wheelchair access

Lambda Rising 1625 Connecticut Ave NW (btwn 'Q' & 'R' Sts) **202/462-6969** • 9am-10pm Mon-Th, till midnight Fri-Sun • lgbt • wheelchair access

Sisterspace & Books 1515 'U' St NW (at 15th St) **202/332-3433** • 10am-7pm, clsd Sun • specialize in books by & about African-American women • workshops & seminars • women-owned/run

Retail Shops

Universal Gear 1601 17th St NW (at 'Q') **202/319-1157** • 11am-10pm Sun-Th, till midnight Fri-Sat • casual, club, athletic & designer clothing

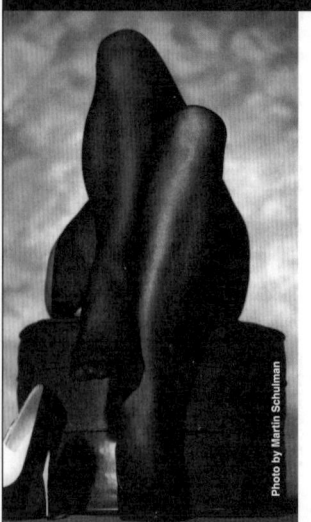

The Pleasure Place

Washington's Premier Erotic Boutique
Since 1979

*An Upscale Toy Store for the Sophisticated Women
Featuring intimate apparel, high heels, DVDs, videos, silicone products, harnesses, erotic literature, toys galore, & more...!*

• For Mail Orders: 1-800-386-2386
• Visit our online catalogue at: www.pleasureplace.com
• Email: pleasure@pleasureplace.com

• Open 7 Days A Week •

Georgetown: 1063 Wisconsin Ave, NW
(202) 333-8570

Dupont Circle: 1710 Connecticut Ave, NW
(202) 483-3297

Photo by Martin Schulman

PUBLICATIONS

MW (Metro Arts & Entertainment) 202/638-6830 • extensive club listings

Washington Blade 202/797-7000 • huge lgbt newspaper • extensive resource listings

Woman's Monthly 202/965-5399 • articles • calendar of community/ arts events for greater DC/ Baltimore area

Women in the Life 1623 Connecticut Ave NW, Rear Carriage House 20009 202/483-9818

SPIRITUAL GROUPS

Bet Mishpachah 16th & Q Sts NW (at the DCJCC) 202/833-1638 • lgbt synagogue

Dignity Washington 1820 Connecticut Ave NW (at St Margaret's Church) 202/546-2235 • call for service times

Faith Temple (Evangelical) 1313 New York Ave NW 202/232-4911 • 1pm Sun

Friends (Quaker) 2111 Florida Ave NW (enter on Decatur Pl) 202/483-3310 • 10am Sun, 7pm Wed

MCC Washington 474 Ridge St NW (btwn M & N) 202/638-7373 • 9am, 11am & 7pm Sun, 6:30pm Wed

More Light Presbyterians 400 'I' St SW (at Westminster Church) 202/484-7700 • 11am Sun

GYMS & HEALTH CLUBS

Results—The Gym 1612 'U' St NW (at 17th St) 202/518-0001 • gay-friendly • also women-only fitness area • also 'Aurora Basics Health Cafe,' 9am-10pm, 202/234-6822

Washington Sports Club 1835 Connecticut Ave NW (at Columbia & Florida) 202/332-0100 • gay-friendly • clsd Sun

EROTICA

Leather Rack 1723 Connecticut Ave NW (btwn 'R' & 'S' Sts) 202/797-7401

▲ **Pleasure Place** 1710 Connecticut Ave NW (btwn 'R' & 'S' Sts) 202/483-3297 • 10am-midnight, till 10pm Mon-Tue, noon-7pm Sun • leather • latex • shoes & more • wheelchair access

▲ **Pleasure Place** 1063 Wisconsin Ave NW, Georgetown (at 'M' St) 202/333-8570 • 10am-midnight, till 10pm Mon-Tue, noon-7pm Sun • leather • latex • shoes & more • wheelchair access

FLORIDA

Alligator Point

ACCOMMODATIONS

Simple Addition/ Simple Interest PO Box 10543, Tallahassee 800/533-1973, 850/539-5965 • mostly women • 2 elegant & private waterfront vacation homes on the Gulf of Mexico • $750/ week

Amelia Island

ACCOMMODATIONS

The Amelia Island Williams House B&B 103 S 9th St 904/277-2328, 800/414-9257 • gay-friendly • magnificent 1856 antebellum mansion • jacuzzi • fireplace • wheelchair access • gay-owned/ run • $145-235

RESTAURANTS

Beech Street Grill 810 Beech St (at 8th St), Fernandina Beach 904/277-3662 • dinner only

Bretts 1 Front St 904/261-2660 • lunch & dinner

Boynton Beach

SPIRITUAL GROUPS

Church of our Savior MCC 2011 S Federal Hwy 561/733-4000 • 9am & 11am Sun

Bradenton

RESTAURANTS

Greasy Spoon 5604 15th St E/ Old 301 941/739-9810 • 4am-4pm • gay-friendly • diner • beer/ wine

Bradenton Beach

ACCOMMODATIONS

Bungalow Beach Resort 2000 Gulf Dr N 941/778-3600, 800/779-3601 • gay-friendly • swimming • hot tub • kitchens • non-smoking rooms available • wheelchair access • $90-329

Brandon

NIGHTCLUBS

City Limits 902 E Brandon Blvd 813/643-1244 • noon-3am • lesbians/ gay men • dancing/DJ • also restaurant • karaoke • live shows • gay-owned / run

Florida • USA

Clearwater

see also Dunedin, New Port Richey, Port Richey & St Petersburg

Accommodations

Americana Gulf Resort 325 S Gulfview Blvd 727/461-7695, 800/462-1213 • gay-friendly • rooms, suites & efficiencies • on the beach • kids ok • $95-150

Bars

Lost & Found 5858 Roosevelt Blvd/ State Rd 686 727/539-8903 • 4pm-2am • mostly gay men • live shows • karaoke • patio • wheelchair access

Pro Shop Pub 840 Cleveland St (at Prospect) 727/447-4259 • 11:30am-2am, from 1pm Sun • popular • mostly gay men • neighborhood bar

Cocoa Beach

Nightclubs

Mixers Nightclub 610 Forrest Ave (at US 1), Cocoa 321/639-0103 • 4pm-2am • lesbians/ gay men • dancing/DJ • patio • wheelchair access

Restaurants

Flaminias 3210 S Atlantic Ave 321/783-9908 • dinner only • Italian • beer/ wine

Lobster Shanty 2200 S Orlando Ave 321/783-1350 • lunch & dinner • full bar • wheelchair access

Mango Tree 118 N Atlantic Ave 321/799-0513 • 6pm-close, clsd Mon • fine dining • single malt Scotch bar • wheelchair access • $12-17

Dade City

Accommodations

Sawmill Camping Resort 352/583-0664 • popular • mostly gay men • theme wknds w/ entertainment • RV hookups • cabins • tent spots • swimming • nudity • gay-owned/ run

Daytona Beach

Info Lines & Services

Lambda Center 320 Harvey Ave (at Hollywood) 904/255-0280 • support groups • youth services • 12-step mtgs

Accommodations

Acapulco Hotel & Resort 2505 S Atlantic Blvd (at Int'l Speedway Blvd) 904/761-2210 • gay-friendly • hot tub • kids ok • wheelchair access • $69-159

Best Western Mayan Inn Beachfront 103 S Ocean Ave 904/252-2378, 800/443-5323 • gay-friendly • some rms w/ ocean views • swimming • kids ok • wheelchair access • $59-205

Coquina Inn B&B 544 S Palmetto Ave 904/254-4969, 800/805-7533 • gay-friendly • full brkfst • fireplaces • hot tub • smokefree • $90-110

The Villa B&B 801 N Peninsula Dr 904/248-2020 • gay-friendly • historic Spanish mansion • hot tub • swimming • nudity • smokefree • gay-owned/ run • $65-185

Restaurants

Anna's Trattoria 304 Seabreeze Blvd 904/239-9624 • dinner only, clsd Sun-Mon • Italian • beer/ wine

Frappes North 123 W Granada Blvd 904/615-4888 • lunch & dinner, clsd Sun • some veggie • patio

Madison's 116 Madison Ave 904/323-0607 • dinner nightly, drag brunch from noon Sun • lesbians/ gay men • live shows • also video bar • wheelchair access

Sapporo 501 Seabreeze Ave 904/257-4477 • lunch Mon-Fri only, dinner 7 days • Japanese • full bar

Sweetwater's 3633 Halifax Dr, Port Orange 904/761-6724 • lunch & dinner • seafood & steaks • wheelchair access

Spiritual Groups

Hope MCC 500 S Ridgewood Ave 904/254-0993 • 11am Sun

Delray Beach

Bars

Lulu's Place 640 E Atlantic Ave Bay 6 (at E Federal Hwy) 561/278-4004 • 4pm-1am, clsd Mon • lesbians/ gay men • piano bar

Restaurants

Masquerade Cafe 640 E Atlantic Ave (at E Federal Hwy) 561/279-0229 • dinner Tue-Sun • wheelchair access

Spiritual Groups

New Hope First Community Church 400 S Swinton Ave 561/540-8065 • 11am Sun

Fort Lauderdale • Florida

Dunedin

see also St Petersburg

BARS

1470 West 325 Main St (at Douglass) **727/736-5483** • 4pm-2am, from 1pm Sun • lesbians/ gay men • dancing/DJ • live shows • patio • wheelchair access

Fort Lauderdale

INFO LINES & SERVICES

Gay/ Lesbian Community Center 1717 N Andrews Ave **954/563-9500** • 9am-10pm, till 5pm wknds • library • wellness center • wheelchair access

Lambda South 1231 E Las Olas Blvd **954/761-9072** • mtg-space for lgbt in recovery • wheelchair access

ACCOMMODATIONS

Bahama Hotel 401 N Atlantic Blvd (at Bayshore) **954/467-7315, 800/622-9995** • gay-friendly • swimming • full gym • also 'The Deck' restaurant & bar • wheelchair access • $70-179

▲ **California Dream Inn** 300–315 Walnut St, Hollywood **954/923-2100** • gay-friendly • located directly on oceanfront • very lesbian-friendly • gay-owned/ run • $79-149

Comfort Suites Fort Lauderdale 1800 S Federal Hwy (at 17th St) **954/767-8700, 800/760-0000** • gay/ straight • swimming • $69-209

Deauville Inn 2916 N Ocean Blvd (Oakland Park Blvd & A-1-A) **954/568-5000** • gay/ straight • in heart of Fort Lauderdale Beach • swimming • kids/ pets ok • wheelchair access • lesbian-owned • $45-95

Eighteenth Street Inn 712 SE 18th St **954/467-7841, 888/828-4466** • gay/ straight • swimming • small pets ok • gay-owned/ run

Embassy Suites Hotel 1100 SE 17th St **954/527-2700, 800/362-2779** • gay-friendly • full brkfst • hot tub • tropical outdoor pool • kids ok • wheelchair access • $134-239

Flamingo Resort 2727 Terramar St (nr Birch) **954/561-4658, 800/283-4786** • mostly gay men • art deco rooms & suites • swimming • gay-owned/ run • $69-159

Gigi's Resort by the Beach 3005 Alhambra St (at Birch) **954/463-4827, 800/910-2357** • mostly gay men • guesthouse on the beach • hot tub • nudity • gay-owned/ run • $49-169

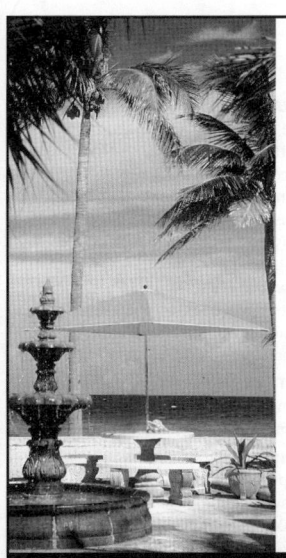

Oceanfront

"...Tucked away...right on the beach. The California Dream Inn reminds us of some other time, some other place, somewhere redolent of our dreams..."

–SOUTH FLORIDA MAGAZINE

California DREAM INN

Warning: Not Cruisy!
B.Y.O.F (Bring your own friend)

300-315 Walnut Street
Hollywood, FL 33019
(954) 923-2100

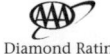

Diamond Rating

Superior Small Lodging Award Of Excellence

www.californiadreaminn.com

Florida • USA

▲ **JP's Beach Villas** 4621 N Ocean Dr (btwn Commercial & A1A), Lauderdale-by-the-Sea **954/772-3672, 888/992-3224** • mostly gay men • all-suite hotel • full kitchen • swimming • 1/2 blk to ocean • kids/ small pets ok • gay-owned/ run • $125-250

King Henry Arms Motel 543 Breakers Ave (nr Bayshore) **954/561-0039, 800/205-5464** • mostly gay men • just steps from the ocean • swimming • gay-owned/ run • $76-135

Liberty Apartment & Garden Suites 1501 SW 2nd Ave (at Sheridan), Dania Beach **954/927-0090, 877/927-0090** • lesbians/ gay men • furnished apts • swimming • nr beach • smokefree available • pets ok • wheelchair access • gay-owned/ run • $275-795/ week

Palm Plaza Resort 2801 Rio Mar St (at Birch) **954/260-6568, 800/962-5517 x11** • gay/ straight • tropical gardens • steps to beach • hot tub • swimming • gay-owned/ run • $35-135

The Royal Palms Resort 2901 Terramar St (at Birch) **954/564-6444, 800/237-7256** • popular • mostly gay men • swimming • jacuzzi • gay-owned/ run • $139-269

Villa Venice Resort 2900 Terramar St (at Orton) **954/564-7855, 877/284-5522** • mostly gay men • 2 blks to beach • swimming • kitchens • gay-owned/ run • $69-165

BARS

Bill's Filling Station 1243 NE 11th Ave (at 13th St) **954/525-9403** • 11am-2am, till 3am wknds, from noon Sun • mostly gay men • neighborhood bar • patio • wheelchair access

The Bushes 3038 N Federal Hwy (at Oakland Park Blvd) **954/561-1724** • 9am-2am, till 3am wknds • popular • mostly gay men • neighborhood bar • wheelchair access

Cathode Ray Club 1307 E Las Olas Blvd (at 13th Ave) **954/462-8611** • 2pm-2am, till 3am wknds • popular • mostly gay men • sports & piano bars • dancing/DJ • live shows • videos • also 'Bar Amici' restaurant next door

Chaps at the Corral 1727 N Andrews Wy (at 16th St) **954/767-0027** • 2pm-2am, till 3am wknds • mostly gay men • leather/ levi • wheelchair access

Eagle 1951 Powerline Rd/ NW 9th Ave (at NW 19th St) **954/462-7224** • 3pm-2am, till 3am wknds • popular • mostly gay men • leather • wheelchair access

Fort Lauderdale

WHERE THE GIRLS ARE: On the beach near the lesbigay accommodations, just south of Birch State Recreation Area. Or at one of the cafes or bars in Wilton Manors or Oakland Park.

LGBT PRIDE: February. 954/561-2020, web: www.pridesouthflorida.org.

ANNUAL EVENTS: June - Film Fest. December - AIDS Walk 954/563-9500.

CITY INFO: 954/765-4466 or 800/227-8669, web: www.sunny.org.

ATTRACTIONS: Broward Center for the Performing Arts 954/522-5334. Butterfly World 954/977-4400. Everglades.
Flamingo Gardens 954/473-2955.
Museum of Art 954/525-5500.
Museum of Discovery & Science 954/467-6637.
Sawgrass Mills, world's largest outlet mall 954/846-2350.
Six Flags Atlantis: The Water Kingdom.

WEATHER: The average year-round temperature in this sub-tropical climate is 75-90°.

TRANSIT: Yellow Cab 954/565-5400. Super Shuttle 954/764-1700. Broward County Transit 954/357-8400.

JP's Beach Villas

Fort Lauderdale

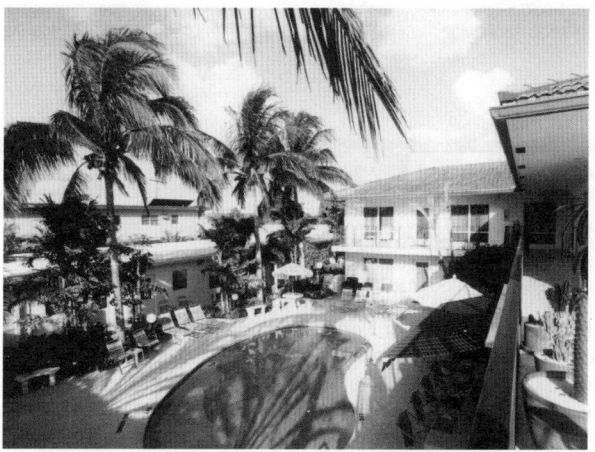

**An All-Suites Hotel featuring Luxurious
1 and 2 Bedroom Apartments
only a 1/2 Block from the Beach**

Lush Tropical Landscaping ■ Heated Pool
Tennis ■ Near Shopping, Clubs, and Restaurants
Outdoor Barbeque ■ Fully Equipped Kitchens
Cable TV and Telephone ■ Daily Maid Service

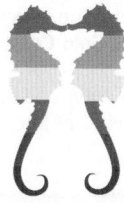

**For more information
call 954/772-3672
or 888/99-BEACH
www.jpsbeachvillas.com**

Florida • USA

Everglades 1931 S Federal Hwy (at 19th St) **954/462-9165** • 1pm-2am, till 3am wknds • mostly gay men • dancing/DJ • leather • wheelchair access

Georgie's Alibi 2266 Wilton Dr (at NE 6th Ave) **954/565-2526** • 11am-2am, till 3am Sat • popular • lesbians/ gay men • food served • videos • wheelchair access

J's Bar 2780 W Davie Blvd (at SW 28th Ave) **954/581-8400** • 3pm-2am, till 3am wknds • popular • mostly women • dancing/DJ • packed Wed & Fri

Kicks Sports Bar 2008 Wilton Dr (at NE 20th St), Wilton Manors **954/564-8480** • 4pm-2am, from noon wknds • lesbians/ gay men • neighborhood bar

Mona's 502 E Sunrise Blvd (at 6th Ave) **954/525-6662** • noon-2am, till 3am wknds • mostly gay men • neighborhood bar

Ramrod 1508 NE 4th Ave (at 16th St) **954/763-8219** • 3pm-2am, till 3am wknds • popular • mostly gay men • dancing/DJ • leather/levi cruise bar • bbq Sun • patio • also 'Dungeon Bear Leather' store

---

[Reply] [Forward]   [Delete]

Date: Sun, Nov 18, 2001 14:31:09
From: Girl-on-the-Go
To: Editor@Damron.com
Subject: Fort Lauderdale

> Fort Lauderdale, one of Florida's most popular cities and resort areas, has everything that makes the whole state a natural paradise—sunny skies, balmy nights, hot sands, and a clear blue sea.

> Honeycombed by the Intercoastal Waterway of rivers, bays, canals, and inlets, Fort Lauderdale is known as the American Venice. If you'd rather keep your feet on solid ground, you can tour the Seminole Indian Reservation, shop at Sawgrass Mills outlet mega-mall, or take in a jai alai game.

> For more breathtaking attractions, however, check out Fort Lauderdale's growing lesbian community. You'll find a number of lesbian-friendly accommodations, including the lesbian-owned **Deauville Inn.**

> **Victoria Park** is a popular spot for dinner, and afterward you can check out **J's Bar,** the **Saint** (where more women head on weekends), the **Sea Monster** (especially Saturdays), or the **Copa,** a complete bar complex, where women mix it up with the gay boys. Or you can head to nearby Hollywood (Florida, that is) and pay a visit to **Zachary's** and **Partners** women's bars. For retro fun, check out Fort Lauderdale's Gay Skate Night on Tuesdays at **Gold Coast Roller Rink.**

> But, if you want to get the latest scoop when you arrive and have it served up with style, your best bet is to pick up a copy of **She** magazine, Florida's monthly lesbian magazine.

Fort Lauderdale • Florida

Nightclubs

Copa 2800 S Federal Hwy (N of airport) **954/463-1507** • 10pm-6am • popular • mostly gay men • dancing/DJ • multiracial • live shows • food served • young crowd • inside & outside bars

The Saint 1000 State Rd 84 (at I-95) **954/525-7883** • 9pm-2am, till 3am wknds, clsd Mon • lesbians/ gay men • more women wknds • theme nights • dancing/DJ

The Sea Monster 2 S New River Dr W (under the Andrews Drawbridge, across from Las Olas shopping ctr) **954/463-4641** • 8pm-2am, till 3am Fri-Sat, from 6pm Sun, clsd Mon-Tue • lesbians/ gay men • more women Sat • dancing/ DJ • transgender-friendly • wheelchair access • gay-owned/ run

Cafes

The Storks 2505 NE 15th Ave (at NE 26th St) **954/567-3220** • 7am-midnight • patio • wheelchair access

Restaurants

Baraka Restaurant/ Hamsa Cafe 3025 N Ocean Blvd (S of Oakland Park Blvd) **954/567-2515** • 10am-2am, clsd 4pm Fri • Middle Eastern • plenty veggie

Chardee's 2209 Wilton Dr (at NE 6th Ave) **954/563-1800** • dinner from 6pm, also bar, open 4:30pm-2am • lesbians/ gay men • dancing/DJ • professional crowd • live entertainment • wheelchair access • some veggie • $12-30

Costello's 2345 Wilton Dr, Wilton Manors **954/563-7752** • dinner nightly • also bar

The Deck 401 N Atlantic Blvd (at the 'Bahama Hotel') **954/467-7315** • also bar • wheelchair access

Grandma's French Cafe 3354 N Ocean Blvd (N of Oakland Park Blvd) **954/564-3671** • lunch & dinner • also ice cream parlor

Hi-Life Cafe 3000 N Federal Hwy #12 (at Oakland Park Blvd, in the 'Plaza 3000') **954/563-1395** • dinner Tue-Sun • bistro • some veggie • $10-18

Lester's Diner 250 State Rd 84 **954/525-5641** • 24hrs • popular • more gay late nights • $5-10

Mustards Bar & Grill 2256 Wilton Dr (btwn 4th & 6th) **954/564-5116** • 5pm-10pm, till 11pm Fri-Sat • Mediterranean/ California cuisine • wheelchair access • gay-owned/ run • $10-20

Simply Delish Cafe 2287 Wilton Dr, Wilton Manors **954/565-8646** • 7am-3pm daily, 5pm-9pm Tue-Sun

Sukothai 1930 E Sunrise Blvd **954/764-0148** • lunch Mon-Fri, dinner nightly • popular • Thai • some veggie

Tropics Cabaret & Restaurant 2004 Wilton Dr (at 20th) **954/537-6000** • dinner from 6pm • new American • also piano bar 4pm-2am, till 3am Sat • lesbians/ gay men • live shows • wheelchair access

Victoria Park 900 NE 20th Ave **954/764-6868** • dinner only • popular • beer/ wine • some veggie • call for reservations

Entertainment & Recreation

Gold Coast Roller Rink 2604 S Federal Hwy **954/523-6783** • 8pm-midnight Tue • gay skate

John U Lloyd State Park-Dania Beach Dania • popular gay beach • first parking lot over the bridge, off Dania Beach Blvd • walk right

Bookstores

Pride Factory & CyberCafe 845 N Federal Hwy (at Sunrise) **954/463-6600** • 9am-11pm Mon-Sat, 11am-7pm Sun • books • pride gifts • coffee • also cybercafe

Retail Shops

Catalog X Retail & Clothing Outlet 850 NE 13th St **954/524-5050** • 9am-10pm, 10am-9pm Sat, 11am-7pm Sun

GayMartUSA 2240 Wilton Dr (at NE 6th Ave) **954/630-0360** • 10am-10pm • clothes & gifts

The Girl Next Door 231 S Federal Hwy (S of Atlantic Blvd) **954/786-8077** • clubwear, accessories & more

Pridestuff 1735 N Andrews Ave Extn **954/764-0394, 877/442-9383** • noon-midnight, till 2am wknds

Publications

Express Gay News 954/568-1880

Hot Spots 954/928-1862, 800/522-8775 • Florida's weekly bar guide

She 954/474-0183 • Florida's hippest & hottest lesbian magazine • monthly

Spiritual Groups

Congregation Etz Chaim 3970 NW 21st Ave (btwn Commercial & Oakland Park) **954/564-9232** • 8:30pm Fri • lgbt synagogue • social, educational & community services

Florida • USA

Dignity Fort Lauderdale 1400 N Federal Hwy (The Sanctuary, 2nd Presbyterian Church) **954/463-4528** • 7pm Sun • Roman Catholic liturgy

Sunshine Cathedral MCC 330 SW 27th St **954/462-2004** • 9:15am, 11am & 6pm Sun • wheelchair access

Gyms & Health Clubs

Firm Fitness 928 N Federal Hwy (at Sunrise) **954/767-6277** • 5am-11pm, 8am-8pm wknds

Erotica

Fetish Factory 821 N Federal Hwy (at Sunrise) **954/462-0032**

Romantix 3520 N Federal Hwy (at Oakland) **954/568-1220**

Tropixxx Video 1514 NE 4th Ave (at 16th St), Wilton Manors **954/522-5988**

Wicked Leather 2422 Wilton Dr, Wilton Manors **954/564-7529** • clsd Mon

Fort Myers

Accommodations

Golf View Motel 3523 Cleveland Ave **941/936-1858** • gay-friendly • swimming • wheelchair access

Marthas' Retreat 941/693-8709 • women only • country cottage on 3 wooded acres • swimming • kids/ pets ok • lesbian-owned

▲ **The Resort on Carefree Blvd** 3000 Carefree Blvd (at Del Prado) **941/731-3000, 800/326-0364** • mostly lesbian • women's community for vacation rentals & retirement • swimming • nature trails • tennis • gym • kids/ pets ok • wheelchair access • $49-139

Bars

Office Pub 3704 Cleveland Ave **941/936-3212** • noon-2am • mostly gay men • neighborhood bar • beer/ wine • leather Fri

Nightclubs

The Bottom Line (TBL) 3090 Evans Ave **941/337-7292** • 2pm-2am • lesbians/ gay men • more women wknds • dancing/DJ • live shows • videos • wheelchair access

Restaurants

Oasis 2222 McGregor Blvd **941/334-1566** • brkfst & lunch only • beer/ wine • wheelchair access • women-owned/ run • $4-6

Spiritual Groups

St John the Apostle MCC 3049 McGregor Blvd **941/341-0012** • 9:30am Sun & 7pm Wed • wheelchair access

---

• NAPLES • SANIBEL • CAPTIVA •
CAPE CORAL — THE BEACHES
FORT MYERS — MARCO ISLAND

Mark Griffin
REALTOR

Representing Our Community In Southwest Florida

(800) 726-1489

E-mail: sellingguy@aol.com

Fort Myers • Florida

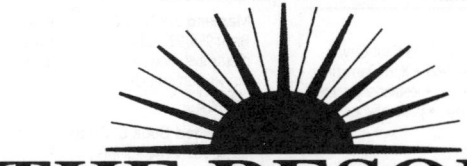

THE RESORT
on Carefree Boulevard

A Place Where You Can Be You

Located on 50 secluded acres of beautiful pineland on Florida's magnificent Gulf Coast, The Resort on Carefree Boulevard offers the amenities & facilities you would expect in a first class resort complex, in a beautiful wooded setting. Gather in the plush, private, 10,000 square foot clubhouse overlooking Lake Phyllis.
Featuring • large pool & spa • tennis court • putting green • shuffleboard court • a main gathering room for parties, dances & receptions • billiard room • library • arts & crafts room • exercise room and a big screen TV room.
Make The Resort on Carefree Boulevard, located in tropical Fort Myers, Florida, your next vacation destination

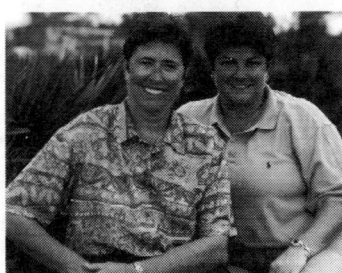

"Wish You Were Here"
Cathy Groene & Gina Razete
Developers of
The Resort on
Carefree Boulevard

"We know that you will return again & again"
For more information regarding seasonal rates & availability call New Concept Realty, Inc. today.
3000 Carefree Boulevard, Fort Myers, Florida 33917-7135
1-800-326-0364 (941) 731-3000
www.resortoncb.com • e mail- cg@resortoncb.com

Florida • USA

Fort Walton Beach

Nightclubs

Frankly Scarlett 223 Hwy 98 E (at City Parking Lot) **850/664-2966** • 8pm-2am, till 4am wknds, clsd Tue-Wed • lesbians/gay men • dancing/DJ • live shows • patio • wheelchair access

Gainesville

Info Lines & Services

Gay Switchboard **352/332-0700** • live 6pm-11pm • 24hr touchtone service • extensive info on Gainesville area • AA info

Bars

Spikes 4130 NW 6th St **352/376-3772** • 4pm-2am • popular • lesbians/gay men • country/western

The University Club 18 E University Ave (enter rear) **352/378-6814** • 5pm-2am, till 11pm Sun • lesbians/gay men • more women Fri • young crowd • dancing/DJ • live shows • patio • wheelchair access

Wild Angels 4130 NW 6th St **352/376-3772** • 9pm-2am Th-Sat • mostly women • dancing/DJ • live shows • also Pandora's gift shop

Bookstores

Wild Iris Books 802 W University Ave (at 8th St) **352/375-7477** • 10am-6pm, till 7pm Fri, 11am-5pm Sun • feminist/lgbt bookstore • wheelchair access

Spiritual Groups

Trinity MCC 11604 SW Archer Rd **352/495-3378** • 10:15am Sun • wheelchair access

Hollywood

see also Miami

Accommodations

Ocean Mist Motel 1500 N Ocean Dr **954/922-1744, 888/322-1744** • gay-friendly • deck • kids ok • $225-625/week

Bars

Partners 625 Dania Beach Blvd (at Federal Hwy), Dania **954/921-9893** • noon-3am • mostly women • neighborhood bar • dancing/DJ • live music • gay-owned/run

Zachary's 2217 N Federal Hwy **954/920-5479** • 4pm-2am • mostly women • neighborhood bar • beer/wine • wheelchair access

Nightclubs

Mankind 219 N 21st Ave (nr Hollywood Blvd) **954/922-1144** • till 4am • mostly gay men • live shows • also restaurant • lunch & dinner, Sun brunch

Erotica

Hollywood Book & Video 1235 S State Rd 7 **954/981-2164** • 24hrs

Jacksonville

Bars

616 616 Park St (at I-95) **904/358-6969** • 4pm-2am, from 6pm Sat • mostly gay men • women's night Tue • neighborhood bar • karaoke • patio • movies Wed

AJ's Bar & Grill 10244 Atlantic Blvd (in Regency Walk Shopping Center) **904/805-9060** • noon-2am • mostly women • dancing/DJ • food • live bands • karaoke Tue • live shows • wheelchair access • women-owned/run

Boot Rack Saloon 4751 Lenox Ave (at Cassat Ave) **904/384-7090** • 4pm-2am • mostly gay men • country/western • cruise bar • beer/wine • patio • wheelchair access

HMS 1702 E 8th St (at Buckman) **904/353-9200** • 2pm-2am • mostly gay men • neighborhood bar • beer/wine • patio

The Metro 2929 Plum St **904/388-8719, 904/388-7192** • 4pm-2am, 6pm-midnight Sun-Mon • popular • lesbians/gay men • dancing/DJ • karaoke • also piano bar • 18+ • wheelchair access

The Norm 2952 Roosevelt Blvd (at College) **904/388-9503** • 4pm-2am • mostly women • dancing/DJ • live shows • wheelchair access

Park Place Lounge 931 King St **904/389-6616** • noon-2am • lesbians/gay men • neighborhood bar • dancing/DJ • wheelchair access

Third Dimension 711 Edison Ave (btwn Riverside & Park) **904/353-6316** • 3pm-2am, from 6pm Sat, from 5pm Sun • mostly gay men • 5 bars • dancing/DJ • alternative • multiracial • karaoke • live shows • wheelchair access

Cafes

Fuel Coffee House 1037 Park St **904/425-FUEL** • 9am-3am, till 10pm Sun, till midnight Mon-Tue • also sandwiches, soups & salads

Restaurants

European Street Cafe 2753 Park St **904/384-9999** • 10am-10pm • deli • salads • large beer selection • gay-owned/run

Key West • Florida

Retail Shops

Rainbows & Stars 1046 Park St (in historic '5-Points') **904/356-7702** • 11am-7pm, till 9pm Fri-Sat, noon-4pm Sun • pride giftstore • T-shirts • rainbow items • jewelry • also community bulletin board

Spiritual Groups

St Luke's MCC 1140 S McDuff Ave (at Remington) **904/389-7726** • 8:30am, 10:15pm & 6:30pm Sun

Jacksonville Beach

Bars

Bo's Coral Reef 201 5th Ave N **904/246-9874** • 2pm-2am • lesbians/ gay men • dancing/DJ • live shows

Key Largo

Accommodations

Grandma Jean's 234 Palm Drive **305/453-0242** • gay-friendly • $65

Key West

Info Lines & Services

Commitment Ceremonies by Capt Linda Schuh **305/745-8886** • on the sea or shore • certificate • woman-owned/ run

Gay/ Lesbian AA **305/296-8654**

Gay/Lesbian Community Center 1075 Duval St **305/292-3223** • many mtgs & groups • call for info

KISS (Keep It Simple, Sweetie) 1215 Petronia St (at MCC) **305/294-8912** • variety of AA meetings • call Center for a schedule

Accommodations

Alexander Palms Court 715 South St (at Vernon) **305/296-6413, 800/858-1943** • gay-friendly • swimming • hot tub • private patios • pets ok • $110-415

Alexander's Guest House 1118 Fleming St (at Frances) **305/294-9919, 800/654-9919** • lesbians/ gay men • hot tub • swimming • nudity • sundeck • wheelchair access • gay-owned/ run • $80-300

Ambrosia House Tropical Lodging 615 & 618-622 Fleming St (at Simonton) **305/296-9838, 800/535-9838** • gay-friendly • swimming • hot tub • sea captain's house • $110-210

Andrew's Inn Zero Whalton Ln (at Duval) **305/294-7730, 888/263-7393** • gay-friendly • swimming • kids ok • smokefree • wheelchair access • $115-399

The Artist House 534 Eaton St (at Duval) **305/296-3977, 800/582-7882** • gay-friendly • Victorian guesthouse • swimming • jacuzzi • patio • smokefree • $129-299

▲ **Atlantic Shores Resort** 510 South St (at Duval) **305/296-2491, 877/778-7711** • popular • gay/ lesbian resort • home of WomenFest • swimming • nudity • sundeck • 2 bars • T-dance Sun • also restaurant • wheelchair access • $75-280

Author's Key West 725 White St (entrance on Petronia) **305/294-7381, 800/898-6909** • gay/ straight • swimming • fine arts gallery • gay-owned/ run

Avalon B&B 1317 Duval St (at United) **305/294-8233, 800/848-1317** • gay-friendly • restored Victorian • sundeck • spa • pets ok • $79-209

Bananas Foster B&B 537 Caroline St (at Simonton St) **305/294-9061, 800/653-4888** • gay-friendly • hot tub • spa • gay-owned/ run • $110-320

Beach Bungalow & Beach Guest Suite Box 165 **305/294-1525** • gay/ straight • hot tub • vacation rental • 3-day minimum stay • gay-owned/ run • $119-169

Big Ruby's Guesthouse 409 Appelrouth Ln (at Duval & Whitehead) **305/296-2323, 800/477-7829** • mostly gay men • full brkfst • swimming • nudity • evening wine • sundeck • wheelchair access • gay-owned/ run • $85-245

Blue Parrot Inn 916 Elizabeth St (at Olivia) **305/296-0033, 800/231-2473** • gay-friendly • historic Bahamian home • swimming • nudity • sundeck • wheelchair access • gay-owned/ run • $79-189

Chelsea House 707 Truman Ave (at Elizabeth) **305/296-2211, 800/845-8859** • lesbians/ gay men • swimming • nudity • wheelchair access • gay-owned/ run • $79-305

The Courtyard of Key West 910 Simonton St (at Truman) **305/296-1148, 800/296-1148** • gay-friendly • apt suites • hot tub • $79-355

Cuban Club Suites 1102-1108 Duval St (at Virginia) **305/296-0465, 800/432-4849** • gay-friendly • award-winning historic hotel • suites w/ kitchens • kids/ dogs ok • $159-399

Cypress House 601 Caroline (at Simonton) **305/294-6969, 800/525-2488** • gay-friendly • swimming • sundeck • guesthouse • $99-325

Deja Vu Resort 611 Truman Ave (at Simonton) **305/292-9339, 800/724-5351** • gay/ straight • hot tub • swimming • nudity

Florida • USA

Reply **Forward** **Delete**

Date: Wed, Nov 21, 2001 14:45:02
From: Girl-on-the-Go
To: Editor@Damron.com
Subject: Key West

> This tiny Caribbean island at the very tip of Florida, closer to Havana than to Miami, has had more crashing busts and facelifting booms than most Hollywood celebrities have had cosmetic surgeries. During its earliest boom days, it was home to pirates and those who salvaged the ships they and the reefs would wreck. Later came robber barons who made a killing in the cigar-rolling and sponge-harvesting businesses. With another boom came Harry Truman and his Little White House and Ernest Hemingway and his cats. And since the '80s, gays and lesbians have helped create the tropical boom town visited today by tourists from around the world.

> The famous Old Town area is dotted with Victorian homes and mansions. Many of them are now fully renovated as accommodations, such as the women-only guesthouse **Pearl's Rainbow.**

> As soon as you arrive, you realize Key West is a way of life, not just an exotic resort. Locals have perfected a laissez-faire attitude and you'll quickly fall into the relaxed rhythm. You'll be thoroughly entertained spending your days lounging poolside with warm tropical breezes in your hair and a cool drink in your hand.

> Or get out of that lounge chair and sail the emerald waters around Key West. This ocean is home to the hemisphere's largest living coral reef, accessible by snorkeling, which can be arranged for you by the **Mangrove Mistress** (in addition to commitment ceremonies) or by the lesbian owned and run **Venus Charters** (along with dolphin watching and light tackle fishing). For an inexpensive and fun way to get around the island, rent a bicycle or moped from one of the many bike rental shops.

> Don't miss **Womenfest** in September, the annual women's week in Key West—the ideal time and place to experience women entertainers, sailing, boating, snorkeling, a street fair, dances, and more. **Fantasy Fest** in October is seven days of Halloween in a tropical heaven: costumes, contests, parades, and parties galore. For information on other fun events, pick up a **Southern Exposure** paper, or call the **Gay/Lesbian Community Center.**

Key West's Hottest Oceanfront Resort

- 72 Deco-Caribbean Style Rooms
- Clothing Optional Pool & Pier
- Famous Sunday Night Tea Dance
- Nightly Sunset Happy Hour
- Thursday Night Outdoor Cinema

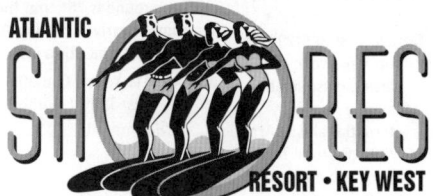

ATLANTIC SHORES RESORT • KEY WEST

www.atlanticshoresresort.com
U.S. Toll Free 877-293-9662
510 South St, Key West, FL 33040

Florida • USA

Duval House 815 Duval St (at Petronia) 305/292-9491, 800/223-8825 • gay-friendly • Victorians w/ gardens • swimming • sundeck • gay-owned/ run • $110-325

Eaton Lodge 511 Eaton St (at Duval) 305/292-2170, 800/294-2170 • gay-friendly • 1886 mansion & conch house w/ gardens • hot tub • swimming • $95-475

Fleur de Key Guesthouse 412 Frances St (at Eaton) 305/296-4719, 800/932-9119 • popular • mostly gay men • luxury guesthouse • full brkfst • swimming • nudity • hot tub • wheelchair access • gay-owned/ run • $95-315

▲ **Heartbreak Hotel** 716 Duval St (at Petronia) 305/296-5558 • lesbians/ gay men • kitchens • gay-owned/ run • $99-139

Heron House 512 Simonton St (at Fleming) 305/294-9227, 888/861-9066 • gay-friendly • swimming • hot tub • evening wine • wheelchair access • $119-349

Key West Harbor Inn B&B 219 Elizabeth St (at Greene) 305/296-2978, 800/608-6569 • lesbians/ gay men • swimming • hot tub • smokefree • wheelchair assecible • $100-400

Knowles House B&B 1004 Eaton St (at Grinnell) 305/296-8132, 800/352-4414 • gay/ straight • restored 1880s conch house • swimming • nudity • smokefree • gay-owned/ run • $109-175

La Casa de Luces 422 Amelia St (at Whitehead) 305/296-3993, 800/432-4849 • gay-friendly • early 1900s conch house • jacuzzi • wheelchair access • $79-249

La Te Da 1125 Duval St (at Catherine) 305/296-6706, 877/528-3320 • popular • lesbians/gay men • tropical setting • swimming • nudity • restaurant & 3 bars • live shows • Sun T-dance • wheelchair access • gay-owned/ run • $115-275

Key West

WHERE THE GIRLS ARE: You can't miss 'em during WomenFest in September, but other times they're just off Duval St., somewhere between Eaton and South Streets. Or on the beach. Or in the water.

LGBT PRIDE: June. 305/293-9348, web: keywestpridealliance.org

ANNUAL EVENTS: February - Kelly McGillis Classic Women's & Girls' Flag Football Tournament 305/293-9315, web: www.iwffa.com.
September - WomenFest 800/535-7797, web: www.womenfest.net.
October - Fantasy Fest 305/296-1817. Week-long Halloween celebration with parties, masquerade balls & parades.
December - International Gay Arts Fest 800/535-7797. Cultural festival of film, theatre, art, concerts, seminars, parties & a parade.

CITY INFO: Key West Business Guild 305/294-4603.

ATTRACTIONS: Audubon House and Gardens 305/294-2116.
Dolphin Research Center.
Glass-bottom boats.
Hemingway House 305/294-1575.
Mallory Market.
Red Barn Theatre 305/296-9911.
Southernmost Point USA.

BEST VIEW: Old Town Trolley Tour (1/2 hour).

WEATHER: The average temperature year-round is 78°, and the sun shines nearly every day. Any time is the right time for a visit.

TRANSIT: Yellow Cab 305/294-2227.
Key West Transit Authority 305/292-8161.

Key West • Florida

Lightbourn Inn 907 Truman Ave (at Packer) **305/296-5152, 800/352-6011** • gay-friendly • Conch mansion • swimming • sundeck • full brkfst • largest private teddy bear collection in Key West • smokefree • wheelchair access • gay-owned/ run • $158-228

Marquesa Hotel 600 Fleming St (at Simonton) **305/292-1919, 800/869-4631** • gay-friendly • swimming • also restaurant ($17-31) • some veggie • full bar • wheelchair access • $155-380

Marrero's Guest Mansion 410 Fleming St (btwn Duval & Whitehead) **305/294-6977, 800/459-6212** • gay-friendly • 1890 Victorian mansion • swimming • hot tub • smokefree • $90-220

Merlinn Inn 811 Simonton St (at Petronia) **305/296-3336, 800/642-4753** • gay-friendly • full brkfst • swimming • smokefree • wheelchair access • $89-235

The Mermaid and the Alligator 729 Truman Ave (at Elizabeth) **305/294-1894, 800/773-1894** • gay/ straight • full brkfst • swimming • smokefree • gay-owned/ run • $108-228

Nassau House 1016 Fleming St (at Grinnell) **305/296-8513, 800/296-8513** • gay-friendly • swimming • smokefree • sundeck • hot tub • wheelchair access • $115-215

▲ **Pearl's Rainbow** 525 United St (at Duval) **305/292-1450, 800/749-6696** • popular • women only • swimming • hot tub • sundeck • nudity • smokefree • also bar • wheelchair access • lesbian-owned/ run • $69-249 • (see page 167 and inside front cover)

Pier House Resort & Caribbean Spa 1 Duval St (at Front) **305/296-4600, 800/327-8340** • gay-friendly • private beach • hot tub • swimming • restaurants • live music • bars • spa • fitness center • kids ok • smokefree • wheelchair access • $200-460

Pilot House Guest House 414 Simonton St (at Eaton) **305/293-6600, 800/648-3780** • gay-friendly • Victorian mansion in Old Town • hot tub • swimming • nudity • non-smoking available • wheelchair access • $100-300

Red Rooster Inn 709 Truman Ave (at Elizabeth) **305/296-6558, 800/845-0825** • gay-friendly • 19th-century, 3-story inn • swimming • nudity • pets ok • smokefree • $69-189

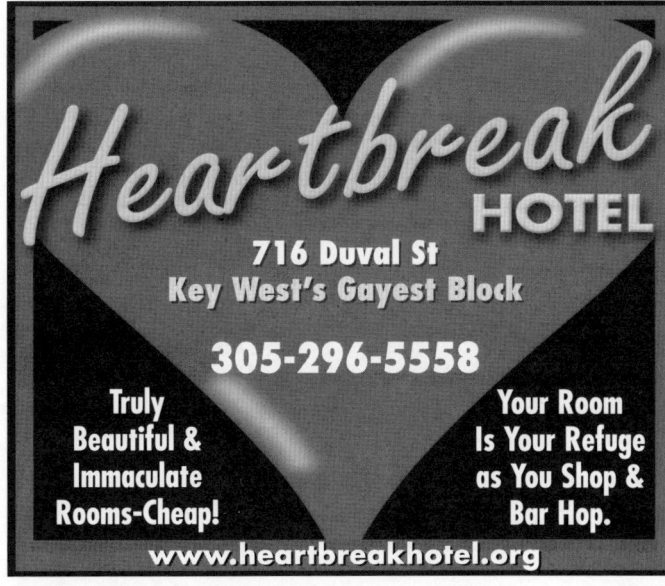

Florida • USA

Sea Isle Resort 915 Windsor Ln (at Olivia) 305/294-5188, 800/995-4786 • popular • mostly gay men • hot tub • swimming • nudity • private courtyard • gym • sundeck • wheelchair access • gay-owned/ run • $75-175

Seascape Tropical Inn 420 Olivia St (at Duval) 305/296-7776, 800/765-6438 • gay-friendly • also cottages • swimming • hot tub • sundeck • smokefree • $79-199

Sheraton Suites—Key West 2001 S Roosevelt Blvd 305/292-9800, 800/452-3224 • gay-friendly • swimming • hot tub • also restaurant • wheelchair access • $199-375

Simonton Court Historic Inn & Cottages 320 Simonton St (at Caroline) 305/294-6386, 800/944-2687 • gay-friendly • built in 1880s • hot tub • 4 pools • $150-540

Travelers Palm 905–907 White St (at Truman) 305/295-9599, 800/294-9560 • gay-friendly • swimming • $85-265

Tropical Inn 812 Duval St (at Petronia) 305/294-9977, 888/611-6510 • gay-friendly • rooms & cottages • swimming • sundeck • $100-275

Watson House 525 Simonton St (btwn Fleming & Southard) 305/294-6712, 800/621-9405 • gay/ straight • swimming • $105-380

William Anthony House 613 Caroline St (at Simonton) 305/294-2887, 800/613-2276 • gay/ straight • 1895 inn • kitchenettes • social hour • smokefree • wheelchair access • gay-owned/ run • $89-199

Bars

801 801 Duval St (at Petronia) 305/294-4737 • 11am-4am • lesbians/ gay men • neighborhood bar • dancing/ DJ • popular drag shows • also 'Red Light Bar' • mostly gay men • leather

Bourbon Street Pub 724 Duval St (at Angela) 305/296-1992 • noon-4am • mostly gay men • popular • live shows • videos • wheelchair access

Diva's 711 Duval St (at Angela) 305/292-8500 • noon-4am • popular • lesbians/ gay men • dancing/DJ • live shows • also 'Shag' next door from 4pm • more straight

Donnie's 900 Simonton St (at Olivia) 305/294-2655 • noon-4am • lesbians/ gay men • neighborhood bar • wheelchair access

Epoch 623 Duval St (at Southard) 305/296-8521 • hrs vary (pls call), clsd Mon • gay-friendly • popular • dancing/DJ

La Te Da 1125 Duval St (at Virginia) 305/296-6706 • 5pm-9pm Sun • popular • mostly gay men • dancing/DJ • also piano bar

Pearl's Patio 525 United St (at Duval, at Pearl's Rainbow) 305/292-1450 • open during cocktail hour, till 10pm Sat • women only

Cafes

Croissants de France 816 Duval St (at Petronia) 305/294-2624 • 7:30am-7pm • lesbians/ gay men • French pastries • some veggie • beer/ wine • patio • $5-7

Restaurants

Alice's at 'La Te Da' accommodations 305/296-6706 x39 • clsd Mon • popular • fusion • home of award-winning chef Alice Weingarten • $7-28

Antonia's 615 Duval St (at Southard) 305/294-6565 • 6pm-11pm • popular • northern Italian • full bar • some veggie • $16-22

Bo's Fish Wagon 801 Caroline (at Williams) 305/294-9272 • lunch, dinner in-season only, clsd Sun • popular • 'seafood & eat it' • $4-12

Cafe des Artistes 1007 Simonton St (at Truman) 305/294-7100 • 6pm-11pm • tropical French • full bar • $22-30

Camille's 703 1/2 Duval St (at Angela) 305/296-4811 • 8am-3pm, 6pm-10pm, no dinner Sun-Mon • bistro • hearty brkfst • $10-18

Kelly's Caribbean Bar Grill & Brewery 301 Whitehead St (at Caroline) 305/293-8484 • lunch & dinner • beer/ wine • owned by actress Kelly McGillis • $7-22

La Trattoria Venezia 524 Duval St (at Fleming) 305/296-1075 • 5:30pm-11pm • lesbians/ gay men • Italian • full bar • $10-22

Lobos 611 1/2 Duval St 305/296-5303 • 11am-6pm • sandwiches • plenty veggie • beer/ wine • $4-7

Louie's Backyard 700 Waddell Ave (at Vernon) 305/294-1061 • lunch & dinner, bar 11:30am-2am • popular • fine cont'l dining • $22-30

Mangia Mangia 900 Southard St 305/294-2469 • dinner only • fresh pasta • beer/ wine • patio • $9-16

Mangoes 700 Duval St (at Angela) 305/292-4606 • 11am-11pm • 'Floribbean' cuisine • plenty veggie • full bar • patio • wheelchair access • $6-23

The Quay 12 Duval St (at Front) 305/294-4446 • lunch & dinner • gourmet • some veggie • live entertainment • $6-30

Rooftop Cafe 310 Front St (at Duval) 305/294-2042 • best Key Lime pie • some veggie • $15+

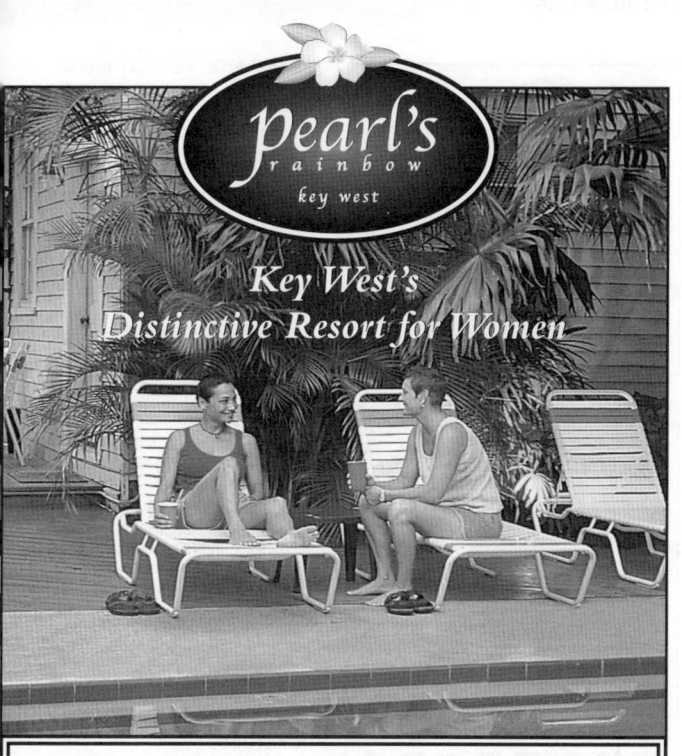

*I*DEALLY LOCATED in Key West, our intimate and historic complex features amenities you might only expect in a larger resort — swimming pools, hot tubs, concierge services, a poolside bar and grill, deluxe toiletries, private baths, expanded continental breakfast. From our "Love Shack" to our Deluxe Suite, we've got accommodations to suit a wide variety of tastes and budgets. And best of all, our friendly staff, like Pearl herself, is dedicated to making your vacation unforgettable. Make your reservation now to be pampered at Pearl's.

pearl's rainbow

800.749.6696 • 305.292.1450 • www.pearlsrainbow.com
525 United Street, Key West, FL 33040

**Call 800.749.6696 for a free brochure,
or visit us online at www.pearlsrainbow.com.**

Florida • USA

Seven Fish 632 Olivia St (at Elizabeth) **305/296-2777** • 6pm-10pm, clsd Tue • popular • $12-15

Square One 1075 Duval St (at Truman) **305/296-4300** • 6pm-10:30pm • full bar • wheelchair access • $15-21

Entertainment & Recreation

Bahia Honda State Park & Beach 35 miles N of Key West • Viking Beach is best

Brigadoon 201 William St, Dock E **305/923-7245** • all-gay sails • sunset & snorkel cruises • $35-70

Fort Zachary Taylor Beach • more gay to the right

Mangrove Mistress **305/745-8886, 305/304-0806** • nature exploring & snorkeling • ceremonies • woman-owned/run

Moped Hospital 601 Truman **305/296-3344** • forget the car—mopeds are a must for touring the island

Rude Awakening 92.5 FM WEOW **305/292-9403** • 6am-10am Mon-Fri • a morning zoo show with a lesbian twist • music • comedy • contests • news

▲ **Venus Charters** **305/292-9403, 305/744-8241** • snorkeling • light tackle fishing • dolphin watching • personalized excursions • lesbian-owned/run

Water Sport People 1430 Thompson **305/296-4546** • scuba-diving instruction & group charters

Bookstores

Blue Heron Books 1018 Truman Ave (at Grinnell) **305/296-3508** • 10am-8pm • general • lgbt section

Flaming Maggie's 830 Fleming St (at Margaret) **305/294-3931** • 10am-6pm • lgbt bookstore • also coffeehouse

Key West Island Books 513 Fleming St (at Duval) **305/294-2904** • 10am-9pm • new & used rare books • lgbt section

Retail Shops

Fast Buck Freddie's 500 Duval St (at Fleming) **305/294-2007** • 10am-6pm, till 10pm Sat • clothing • gifts • wheelchair access

In Touch 715 Duval St (at Angela) **305/292-7293** • 9:30am-11pm • gay gifts

Key West Aloe 524 Front St (at Duval) **305/294-5592, 800/445-2563 (MAIL ORDER)** • 8:30am-8pm • mail order available

Lido 532 Duval St (at Fleming) **305/294-5300** • 10am-10pm, 11am-7pm Sun • clothing • gifts • gay-owned/run

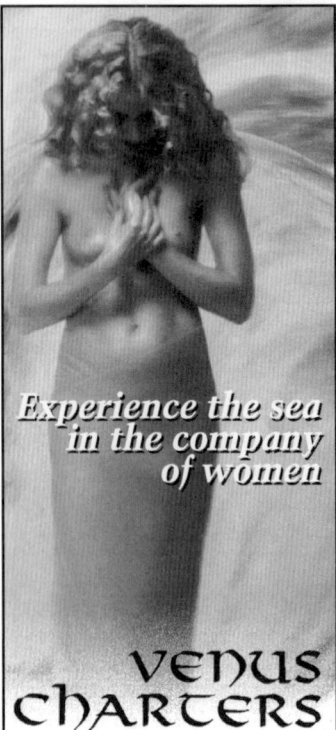

Experience the sea in the company of women

VENUS CHARTERS

Snorkeling
Light Tackle Fishing
Back Country Tours
Dolphin Watching
Personalized Excursions

Captain Karen Luknis

305-292-9403

Cell: 305-744-8241
E-mail: venuschtrs@aol.com

Lesbian Owned & Operated

P.O Box 4394 • Key West, FL 33041

Melbourne • Florida

PUBLICATIONS

Southern Exposure 305/294-6303

SPIRITUAL GROUPS

MCC Key West 1215 Petronia St
305/294-8912 • 10am Sun • wheelchair access

St Paul's Episcopal Church 401 Duval (at Eden) 305/296-5142 • 7:30am, 9am & 11am Sun, 5:30pm Tue, 9am Wed • wheelchair access

GYMS & HEALTH CLUBS

Bodies on South 2740 N Roosevelt Blvd
305/292-2930

Club Body Tech 1075 Duval St (at Virginia)
305/292-9683 • lesbians/ gay men • full gym • steam room • massage therapy available

EROTICA

Leather Master 418–A Appelrouth Ln (btwn Duval & Whitehead) 305/292-5051 • custom leather & more • also 'Annex' next door

Lake Worth

BARS

The 502 502 Lucerne Ave 561/540-8881 • 5:30pm-1am, till midnight Sun, clsd Mon • lesbians/ gay men • more women Sun • dancing/DJ • karaoke • live music • also restaurant • some veggie • wheelchair access

K & E's 29 S Dixie Hwy 561/533-6020 • 4pm-2am, clsd Tue • lesbians/ gay men • food served

The Mad Hatter Bar & Grill 1532 N Dixie Hwy (16th Ave) 561/547-8860 • 10am-2am • lesbians/ gay men • neighborhood bar • food served

Lakeland

INFO LINES & SERVICES

PGLA (Polk Gay/ Lesbian Alliance)
863/299-8126

ACCOMMODATIONS

Sunset Motel 2301 New Tampa Hwy
863/683-6464 • gay-friendly • motels, apts & private home on 3 acres • swimming • wheelchair access • gay-owned/ run • $41-99

BARS

Dockside 3770 Hwy 92 E 863/665-2590 • 4pm-2am, till midnight Sun • popular • lesbians/ gay men • dancing/DJ • food served • live shows • patio • truck parking • wheelchair access • gay-owned/ run

Green Parrot 1030 E Main St 863/683-6021 • 4pm-2am, till midnight Sun • mostly gay men • dancing/DJ • live shows • beer/ wine • wheelchair access

Largo

BARS

Sports Page Pub 13344 66th St N (at Ulmerton Rd) 727/538-2430 • 4pm-2am, from 1pm Sun • mostly women • live bands • wheelchair access

Leesburg

NIGHTCLUBS

Attitudes 1850 E Main St/ Hwy 441
352/728-1968 • 6pm-2am Tue-Sat • lesbians/ gay men • dancing/ DJ • live shows

Madeira Beach

see St Petersburg

Melbourne

INFO LINES & SERVICES

Brevard Together 321/729-0669 x2082 • lgbt community group • monthly newsletter • special events

ACCOMMODATIONS

Crane Creek Inn B&B 907 E Melbourne Ave 321/768-6416 • gay/ straight • full brkfst • swimming • hot tub • tropical waterfront setting • gay-owned/ run • $75-150

BARS

Cold Keg 4060 W New Haven Ave (E of I-95) 321/724-1510 • 2pm-2am • popular • lesbians/ gay men • dancing/DJ • live shows • wheelchair access

Florida • USA

MIAMI

Miami is divided into 2 geographical areas:
Miami—Greater Miami
Miami—Miami Beach/ South Beach

Miami—Greater Miami

INFO LINES & SERVICES

Lambda Dade AA 317 NE 24th St (off Biscayne) **305/573-9608** • call for mtg times • wheelchair access

Switchboard of Miami 305/358-4357 • 24hrs • gay-friendly info & referrals for Dade County

ACCOMMODATIONS

Miami River Inn 118 SW S River Dr **305/325-0045, 800/468-3589** • gay-friendly • B&B located in Miami's Little Havana district • swimming • jacuzzi • kids ok • woman-owned/run • $89-149

BARS

Power T Dance 3701 NE 2nd Ave (near Biscayne Blvd) **305/576-1336** • 4pm-9pm Sun only • mostly women • dancing/ DJ

Sugar's 17060 W Dixie (at 172nd), North Miami Beach **305/940-9887** • 3pm-6am • mostly gay men • more women Fri • neighborhood bar • dancing/DJ • videos • wheelchair access

Miami

WHERE THE GIRLS ARE: In Miami proper, Coral Gables and the University district, as well as Biscayne Blvd. along the coast, are the lesbian hangouts of choice. You'll see women everywhere in South Beach, but especially along Ocean Dr., Washington, Collins and Lincoln Roads.

LGBT PRIDE: Spring. 305/358-8245, email: pridemiami@aol.com.

ANNUAL EVENTS: March - Winter Party 305/572-1841. AIDS benefit dance on the beach.
April/May - Gay & Lesbian Film Festival 305/534-9924, web: www.miamigaylesbianfilm.com.
November - White Party Vizcaya 305/667-9296. AIDS benefit.

CITY INFO: Greater Miami Convention and Visitors Bureau, 701 Brickell Ave. 305/539-3000.

ATTRACTIONS: Art Deco Welcome Center 305/672-2014.
Bayside Market Place 305/577-3344.
Miami Museum of Science & Space Transit Planetarium 305/854-4247.
Orchid Jungle.
Parrot Jungle and Gardens 305/666-7834.
Sanford L. Ziff Jewish Museum of Florida 305/672-5044.

BEST VIEW: If you've got money to burn, a helicopter flight over Miami Beach is a great way to see the city. Otherwise, hit the beach.

WEATHER: Warm all year. Temperatures stay in the 90°s during the summer and drop into the mid-60°s in the winter. Be prepared for sunshine!

TRANSIT: Yellow Cab 305/444-4444.
Metro Taxi 305/888-8888.
Super Shuttle 305/871-2000.
Metro Bus 305/770-3131.

Miami—Miami Beach/ South Beach • Florida

NIGHTCLUBS

Oz Miami 3470 SW 8th St (nr SW 35th Ave) 305/444-0369 • 5pm-5am Wed-Sun • mostly gay men • women's night Fri • dancing/ DJ • multiracial clientele

RESTAURANTS

Something Special 7762 NW 14th Ct (private home) 305/696-8826 • 6pm-10pm Wed-Sun • women only • vegetarian • also rental 1-bdrm apt on Miami Beach • also tent space

BOOKSTORES

Lambda Passages Bookstore 7545 Biscayne Blvd (at 76th) 305/754-6900 • 11am-9pm, noon-6pm Sun • lgbt/ feminist

Miami—Miami Beach/ South Beach

ACCOMMODATIONS

Abbey Hotel 300 21st St (at Collins) 305/531-0031, 888/612-2239 • gay/ straight • chic restored art deco • full brkfst • gym • rooftop lounge

Aqua Hotel & Lounge 1530 Collins Ave, Miami Beach 305/538-4361 • gay/ straight • swimming • $75-345

The Astor 956 Washington Ave (at 10th St) 305/531-8081, 800/270-4981 • popular • gay-friendly • food served • swimming • wheelchair access • $150-900

The Bayliss 504 14th St 305/538-5620, 888/305-4683 • lesbians/ gay men • tropical art deco hotel • nr beach • $55-115

The Beachcomber 1340 Collins Ave (at 13th St) 305/531-3755, 888/305-4683 • gay-friendly • intimate art deco hotel • bar & bistro • nr beach • $70-145

The Blue Moon Hotel 944 Collins Ave 305/673-2262, 800/724-1623 • gay-friendly • restaurant & lounge • $121+

Brigham Gardens 1411 Collins Ave (at 14th) 305/531-1331 • gay/ straight • art deco guesthouse • also apts w/ kitchens • kids/ pets ok • women-owned/ run • $70-145

The Cardozo Hotel 1300 Ocean Dr 305/535-6500, 800/782-6500 • gay-friendly • food served (Chin Chin from LA) • Gloria Estefan's plush hotel • kids ok • wheelchair access • $170-620

Cavalier 1320 Ocean Dr 305/604-5000, 800/688-7678 • gay/ straight • restored art deco on the ocean • bistro & bar • wheelchair access • $170-395

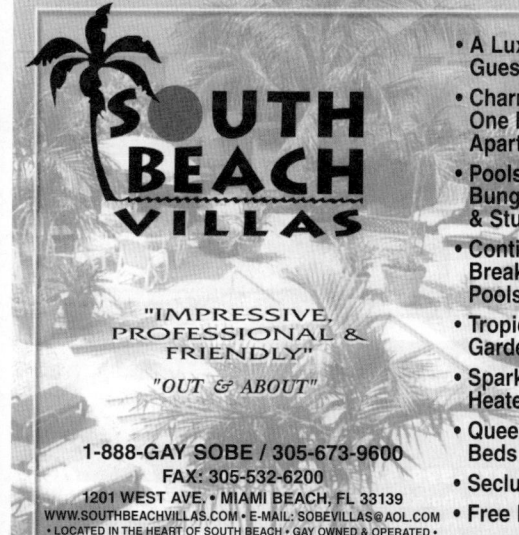

SOUTH BEACH VILLAS

"IMPRESSIVE, PROFESSIONAL & FRIENDLY"

"OUT & ABOUT"

1-888-GAY SOBE / 305-673-9600
FAX: 305-532-6200
1201 WEST AVE. • MIAMI BEACH, FL 33139
WWW.SOUTHBEACHVILLAS.COM • E-MAIL: SOBEVILLAS@AOL.COM
• LOCATED IN THE HEART OF SOUTH BEACH • GAY OWNED & OPERATED •

- A Luxury Guesthouse
- Charming One Bedroom Apartment Suites
- Poolside Bungalows & Studios
- Continental Breakfast Poolside
- Tropical Garden Setting
- Sparkling Heated Pool
- Queen-Sized Beds
- Secluded Jacuzzi
- Free Local Calls

Florida • USA

The Century 140 Ocean Dr **305/674-8855, 888/982-3688** • gay-friendly • restored art deco • also Joia restaurant • celebrity hangout • $119-250

Chesterfield Hotel 855 Collins Ave **305/531-5831, 800/244-6023** • gay/straight • animal-print decor • $129

Collins Plaza 318 20th St **305/532-0849** • gay-friendly • no frills • 1 blk from ocean • restaurant • $49-89

The Colony Hotel 736 Ocean Dr (at 7th St) **305/673-0088, 800/226-5669** • gay-friendly • newly renovated art deco • bistro • oceanfront • wheelchair access • $89-240

Deco Walk Hotel 928 Ocean Dr **305/531-5511, 888/505-5027** • gay/straight • restored art deco • also Ice Cream Cafe • $65-150

Delano Hotel 1685 Collins Ave **305/672-2000, 800/555-5001** • gay-friendly • food served • great bar scene (see & be seen) • swimming • $240+

Destinations International—Mantell 255 W 24th St **305/532-9341, 800/277-4825** • lesbians/gay men • hotel reservation service for several art deco hotels & apts • swimming • gay-owned/run • $69-169

Fairfax Hotel 1776 Collins Ave **305/538-3837** • gay-friendly • newly renovated art deco • scenic view

Florida Hotel Network **305/538-3616, 800/538-3616** • popular • gay-friendly • hotel reservations • vacation rentals • gay-owned/run

Florida Sunbreak **305/532-1516, 800/786-2732** • reservation service for condos & rentals

Fountainbleu Hilton Resort & Spa 4441 Collins Ave **305/538-2000, 800/445-8667** • gay-friendly • restaurants • swimming • on beach • wheelchair access

The Governor Hotel 435 21st St **305/532-2100, 800/542-0444** • gay-friendly • tropical courtyard • nr ocean • swimming • $69-95

the hotel 801 Collins Ave **305/531-2222, 877/843-4683** • gay-friendly • interior design by Todd Oldham • restaurant • also bar • swimming • $215-405

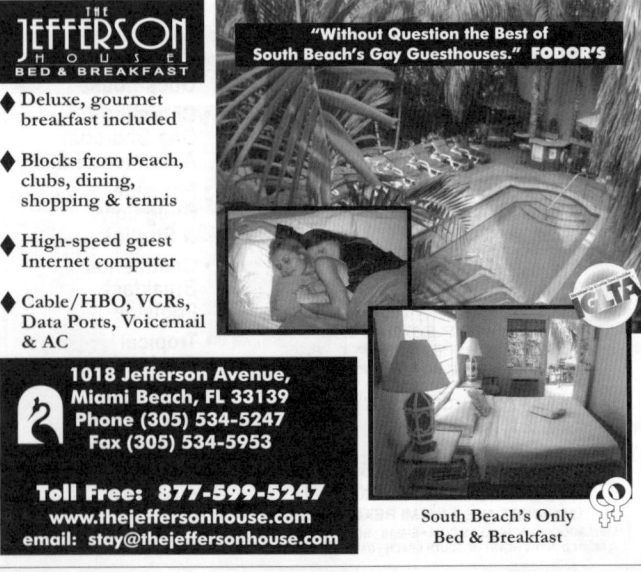

THE JEFFERSON HOUSE BED & BREAKFAST

"Without Question the Best of South Beach's Gay Guesthouses." **FODOR'S**

◆ Deluxe, gourmet breakfast included

◆ Blocks from beach, clubs, dining, shopping & tennis

◆ High-speed guest Internet computer

◆ Cable/HBO, VCRs, Data Ports, Voicemail & AC

1018 Jefferson Avenue, Miami Beach, FL 33139
Phone (305) 534-5247
Fax (305) 534-5953

Toll Free: 877-599-5247
www.thejeffersonhouse.com
email: stay@thejeffersonhouse.com

South Beach's Only Bed & Breakfast

Miami—Miami Beach/ South Beach • Florida

Reply **Forward** **Delete**

Date: Mon, Nov 19, 2001 14:48:13
From: Girl-on-the-Go
To: Editor@Damron.com
Subject: Miami Beach/South Beach

> As a key center of business and politics in the Americas, Miami has an incredibly multicultural look and feel. You'll discover a diversity of people, from a growing population of transplanted seniors to large communities of Cubans, Latin Americans, and African Americans.

> Miami is also a tourist's winter wonderland of sun, sand, and sea. Make the most of it with trips to Seaquarium, Key Biscayne, or the nearby Everglades. For a relaxing evening with the girls, try the Women's Film Series on the fourth Friday at the New Alliance Theater (600 Lincoln Road #219 at Penn Avenue).

> Or make reservations to dine at **Something Special,** a women-only restaurant in a private home. Get the latest on local nightlife from **TWN** or **Wire**, available at **Lambda Passages,** the LGBT bookstore.

> But if you're really hungry for loads of LGBT culture, head directly for South Beach (SoBe). This section of Miami Beach has been given an incredible makeover by gays and lesbians, and has fast become one of *the* hottest spots on the East Coast. Much of the SoBe scene is gay boys, drag queens, and straight couples in little more than sunscreen and a thong, but svelte, hot-blooded, women-loving-women can be found. During the day, start your search and deepen your tan at the 12th Street gay beach. Or, go window-shopping along Lincoln Road.

> If you manage to look beyond the endless parade of bodies beautiful, you'll discover South Beach's historic Art Deco architecture. To make the most of the Art Deco District, take the walking tour that leaves from the Miami Welcome Center at 1224 Ocean Drive for under $10.

> Try the **Palace Grill** for a queer mid-afternoon munch and great people-watching. **News Cafe** on Ocean Drive (open 24 hrs) is always an option for late night snacks.

> While there are no full-time women's bars in Miami or Miami Beach, there are several women's nights. **Score** is the place to be on Thursdays. On Friday you have two choices: **Oz Miami** or **Sugar's.** On Saturday, dance into the wee hours with the gorgeous boys at **Salvation.** And, on Sunday, groove with the girls at the **Power T Dance.**

> There are also plenty of local lesbian promoters, so be sure to check out the hip **She** magazine for roaming women's parties.

Florida • USA

Hotel Impala 1228 Collins Ave **305/673-2021, 800/646-7252** • gay-friendly • luxury hotel nr beach • wheelchair access • also Italian restaurant • $225-400

Hotel Leon 841 Collins Ave (at 8th St) **305/673-3767** • gay-friendly • stylish decor • bar & restaurants • nr ocean • kids/ pets ok • wheelchair access • $145-395

Hotel Nash 1120 Collins Ave **305/674-7800** • gay-friendly • sleek & modern new boutique hotel • spa • swimming • gardens • $130-1,300

Hotel Ocean 1230-38 Ocean Dr **305/672-2579, 800/783-1725** • popular • gay-friendly • great location • pets ok • wheelchair access • $215-575

Hotel Shelley 844 Collins Ave **305/531-3341, 800/414-0612** • gay/ straight • 1930s art deco hotel • kids ok • wheelchair access • $89-249

The Indian Creek Hotel 2727 Indian Creek Dr **305/531-2727, 800/491-2772** • gay-friendly • food served • swimming • simple & away from the action • nr ocean • kids ok • wheelchair access • gay-owned/ run • $90-150

▲ **Jefferson House B&B** 1018 Jefferson Ave **305/534-5247, 877/599-5247** • lesbians/ gay men • private tropical garden • swimming • full brkfst • quiet neighborhood • nr beach • gay-owned/ run • $139-255

Kenmore Hotel 1050 Washington Ave **305/674-1930, 888/333-6719** • gay/ straight • 4 small art deco hotels • swimming • wheelchair access • $75-209

The Kent 1131 Collins Ave (at 11th St) **305/531-6771, 800/688-7678** • gay/ straight • on the beach • cafe • wheelchair access • $100-275

The Leslie 1244 Ocean Ave **305/531-8800, 800/688-7678** • gay/ straight • art deco gem featured in 'The Birdcage' • outdoor cafe • $130-375

Lily Guesthouse 835 Collins Ave **305/535-9900, 888/742-6600** • lesbians/ gay men • studios • suites • sundeck • kids/ pets ok • wheelchair access • woman-run • $109-269

The Loft Hotel 952 Collins Ave **305/534-2244** • gay/ straight • upscale boutique hotel • 1 blk to beach • kids/ small pets ok • $125-169

Marlin Hotel 1200 Collins Ave **305/531-8800, 800/688-7678** • gay/ straight • fabulous studios • full kitchens • stereo & WebTV • bar • wheelchair access • $150-450

The Nassau Suite Hotel 1414 Collins Ave **305/532-0043, 888/305-4683** • gay-friendly • renovated art deco • nr beach • $115-190

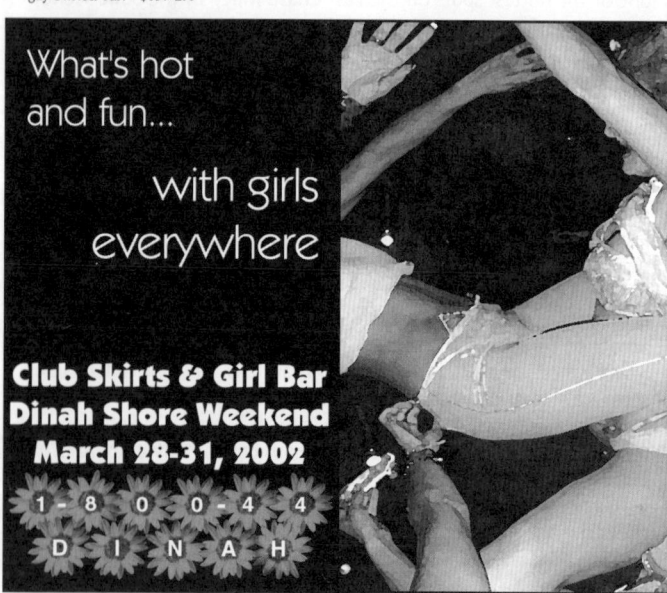

Miami—Miami Beach/ South Beach • Florida

The National Hotel 1677 Collins Ave **305/532-2311, 800/327-8370** • gay/ straight • swimming • kids okay • restaurant & lounge • wheelchair access • $255-450

Ocean Surf Hotel 7436 Ocean Terr (nr 75th St & Collins Ave) **305/866-1648, 800/555-0411** • gay-friendly • beautiful restored art deco • in quiet North Beach • kids ok • wheelchair access • $69-134

The Park Central 640 Ocean Dr **305/538-1611, 800/727-5236** • gay-friendly • ocean views • food served • swimming • $115+

Park Washington Resort 1020 Washington **305/532-1930, 888/424-1930** • gay/ straight • swimming • tiki bar • $69-109

The Pelican 826 Ocean Dr (btwn 8th & 9th Sts) **305/673-3373, 800/773-5422** • popular • gay/ straight • designer theme rooms • restaurant w/ live DJ • on beach • $135-400

Penguin Hotel & Bar 1418 Ocean Dr **305/534-9334, 800/235-3296** • lesbians/ gay men • renovated art deco • full restaurant • kids ok • wheelchair access • $115-250

The Raleigh Hotel 1775 Collins Ave **305/534-6300, 800/848-1775** • gay/ straight • swimming • outdoor gym • restaurant & bars • $199-749

Richmond Hotel 1757 Collins Ave **305/538-2331, 800/327-3163** • gay-friendly • full brkfst • hot tub • swimming • food served • private beach access • kids ok • 145-400

The Shelborne Beach Resort 1801 Collins Ave (at 18th) **305/531-1271, 800/327-8757** • gay-friendly • full brkfst • swimming • restaurant & bars • wheelchair access • $189-1,500

▲ **South Beach Villas** 1201 West Ave (at 12th St) **305/673-9600, 888/429-7623** • lesbians/ gay men • swimming • smokefree • gay-owned/ run • $99-195 • see ad page 171

South Seas 1751 Collins Ave **305/538-1411, 800/345-2678** • gay-friendly • clean & basic • beach access • brkfst included • swimming • $105-195

The Tides 1220 Ocean Dr **305/604-5000, 800/688-7678** • gay/ straight • food served • swimming • showcase Island Outpost hotel • $350-525

The Tropics Hotel & Hostel 1550 Collins Ave (btwn 15th & 16th Sts) **305/531-0361** • gay/ straight • modern hotel rooms & hostel • swimming • nr beach & attractions • $15-80

Villa Paradiso Guesthouse 1415 Collins Ave **305/532-0616** • lesbians/ gay men • studios w/ full kitchens • courtyard • kids/ pets ok • $75-150

The Wave Hotel 350 Ocean Dr **305/673-0401, 800/501-0401** • gay-friendly • tropical style • newly renovated • restaurant & bar • $155-175

The Winterhaven 1400 Ocean Dr **305/531-5571, 800/395-2322** • gay/ straight • ocean views • also restaurant & bar • $129+

BARS

Laundry Bar 721 N Lincoln Ln **305/531-7700** • 7am-5am • lesbians/ gay men • neighbhooroood bar • cafe • live shows Wed & Fri • video games • Internet access • also laundromat

NIGHTCLUBS

Crobar 1445 Washington Ave (at the Cameo Theater) **305/531-5027** • 10pm-5am • popular • gay-friendly • gay only Sun for 'Anthem' • dancing/DJ • wheelchair access

Level/ Federation 1235 Washington Ave **305/532-1525, 305/695-1834** • 10pm-5am Fri only • popular • mostly gay men • dancing/ DJ • live shows • dancers • cover charge

Pump 841 Washington Ave (btwn 8th & 9th) **305/538-7867** • 4am-close Fri-Sat • popular • mostly gay men • dancing • world-famous DJs • circuit crowd • wheelchair access

Salvation 1771 West Ave (at Alton Rd & 18th St) **305/673-6508** • Fri-Mon • popular • mostly gay men • dancing/DJ • alternative • cover charge

Score 727 Lincoln Rd (at Meridian) **305/535-1111** • lounge opens 1pm, dance club 10pm-5am • popular • lesbians/ gay men • women's night Th • live shows • videos

Twist 1057 Washington Ave (at 11th) **305/538-9478** • 1pm-5am • popular • mostly gay men • neighborhood bar • dancing/DJ • wheelchair access

CAFES

News Cafe 800 Ocean Dr **305/538-6397** • 24hrs • popular • healthy sandwiches • some veggie • $4-6

RESTAURANTS

11th Street Diner 11th & Washington **305/534-6373** • 24hrs • full bar

A Fish Called Avalon 700 Ocean Dr **305/532-1727** • 6pm-11pm • popular • some veggie • patio • full bar • wheelchair access • $12-22

Florida • USA

Balans 1022 Lincoln Rd **305/534-9191** • 8am-2am • int'l • some veggie

El Rancho Grande 1626 Pennsylvania Ave **305/673-0480** • 11:30am-11pm • Mexican

The Front Porch 1420 Ocean Dr **305/531-8300** • 8am-10:30pm • healthy homecooking • some veggie • full bar • $6-10

Jeffrey's 1629 Michigan Ave (at Lincoln Rd) **305/673-0690** • 6pm-11pm, from 5pm Sun, clsd Mon • popular • romantic bistro

Joe's Stone Crab 11 Washington Ave **305/673-0365** • lunch & dinner

Larios on the Beach 820 Ocean Dr **305/532-9577** • 11:30am-11:30pm, till 2am Fri-Sat • Cuban

Nemos 100 Collins Ave (at 1st St) **305/532-4550** • lunch & dinner, Sun brunch • Pacific Rim & South American cuisine • chic decor • $22

Nexxt Cafe 700 Lincoln Rd **305/532-6643** • 9am-11pm • popular • $6-14

Ortanique on the Mile 278 Miracle Mile **305/446-7710** • lunch Mon-Fri, dinner 7 days • popular • Caribbean • full bar • $11-19

Pacific Time 915 Lincoln Rd (btwn Jefferson & Michigan) **305/534-5979** • lunch & dinner Mon-Fri • pan-Pacific • some veggie • beer/ wine • $10-30

Palace Bar & Grill 1200 Ocean Dr (at 12th) **305/531-9077** • 8am-midnight, till 1am wknds • salads & sandwiches • full bar • $10-15

Spiga 1228 Collins Ave (at 12th St) **305/534-0079** • lunch & dinner • tasty homemade pastas

Sushi Rock Cafe 1351 Collins Ave (at 14th) **305/532-2133** • popular • full bar

Wolfie's Jewish Deli 2038 Collins Ave (at 21st St) **305/538-6626** • 24hrs • popular • $6-8

Yuca 501 Lincoln Rd (at Drexel Ave) **305/532-9822** • New Cuban cuisine • great afternoon tapas & cocktails • live shows Fri-Sat

ENTERTAINMENT & RECREATION

Beach Scooter Rentals 1461 Collins Ave **305/532-0977**

Fritz's Skate & Bike 726 Lincoln Rd (at Euclid & Meridian) **305/532-1954** • rentals • in pedestrian mall

Lincoln Rd Lincoln Rd (btwn West & Collins Aves) • pedestrian mall that embodies the rebirth of South Beach—fabulous restaurants, stores, galleries, museums, theaters, people at every step

BOOKSTORES

The 9th Chakra 811 Lincoln Rd (at Meridian) **305/538-0671** • metaphysical books • supplies • gifts

RETAIL SHOPS

GayMartUSA 1200 Ocean Dr #2 (at 12th) **305/535-1545** • 10am-7pm

Whittall & Shon 1319 Washington (at 13th) **305/538-2606** • 11am-9:30pm, till midnight Fri-Sat • funky clothes & clubwear for boys

PUBLICATIONS

She **954/474-0183** • Florida's hippest & hottest lesbian magazine • monthly

TWN (The Weekly News) **305/757-6333** • lgbt newspaper for South Florida

Wire **305/538-3111**

GYMS & HEALTH CLUBS

David Barton Gym 1685 Collins Ave (in the 'Delano Hotel') **305/674-5757** • gay-friendly • $20 day pass

EROTICA

Pleasure Emporium 1019 5th St **305/673-3311**

Romantix Adult Emporium 8831 SW 40th St **305/226-8332**

Romantix Emporium 19800 S Dixie Hwy **305/255-2190**

Naples

INFO LINES & SERVICES

Lesbian/ Gay AA 2740 Bayshore Dr (at New Attitudes Club) **941/262-6535** • 8pm Th

BARS

The Galley 509 3rd St S **941/262-2808** • 4pm-2am, from 2pm wknds, till midnight Sun • lesbians/ gay men • more women Fri • neighborhood bar • karaoke • live shows • gay-owned/ run

CAFES

Cafe Flamingo 536 9th St N **941/262-8181** • 7:30am-2pm • some veggie • women-owned/ run • $3-7

Ocala

BARS

The Connection 3331 S Pine Ave/ US 441 **352/620-2511** • 2pm-2am • lesbians/ gay men • neighborhood bar • dancing/DJ • live shows • wheelchair access

Orlando • Florida

BOOKSTORES

Barnes & Noble 3500 SW College Rd (at Hwy 200) **352/854-3999** • 9am-10pm, till 11pm wknds • lgbt section

EROTICA

Secrets of Ocala 815 N Magnolia Ave **352/622-3858**

Orlando

INFO LINES & SERVICES

Gay, Lesbian & Bisexual Community Center of Central Florida 946 N Mills Ave **407/228-8272** • 11am-9pm Mon-Thurs, noon-5pm Fri-Sun • extensive referrals

LCN (Loving Committed Network) 407/332-2311 • lesbian community social/ support group • monthly events • 'LCN Express' newsletter

ACCOMMODATIONS

EO Inn & Spa 227 N Eola Dr (at Robinson) **407/481-8485, 888/481-8488** • gay/straight • smokefree • sundeck • hot tub • cafe onsite • $129-219

Leora's B&B 407/649-0009 • women only • lesbian-owned/run • $55-75

Parliament House Motor Inn 410 N Orange Blossom Tr **407/425-7571** • lesbians/ gay men • swimming • restaurant • wheelchair access • $59-99+tax • also 5 bars • multiracial • live shows • dancing/DJ • young crowd

Rick's B&B **407/396-7751, 407/414-7751** • mostly gay men • full brkfst • swimming • nudity • patio • nr Walt Disney World • gay-owned/run • $85-120

Things Worth Remembering 2603 Coventry Ln **407/291-2127, 800/484-3585** (CODE: 6908) • gay/straight • swimming • smokefree • owners are former theme park employees w/ many behind-the-scenes stories • gay-owned/run • $65-125

The Veranda B&B 115 N Summerlin Ave **407/849-0321, 800/420-6822** • gay-friendly • swimming • hot tub • smokefree • wheelchair access • $99-199

Westside Inn & Suites 3200 W Colonial Dr (at John Young Pkwy) **407/295-5270, 800/828-5270** • gay-friendly • swimming • wheelchair access • $69+

BARS

The Cactus Club 1300 N Mills Ave **407/894-3041** • 3pm-2am • mostly gay men • more women wknds • professional crowd • patio

Copper Rocket 106 Lake Ave (at 17-92), Maitland **407/645-0069** • 11:30am-2am, 4pm-midnight Sun • gay-friendly • also restaurant • microbrews • wheelchair access

Faces 4910 Edgewater Dr **407/291-7571** • 4pm-2am • mostly women • popular • neighborhood bar • dancing/DJ wknds • live shows • wheelchair access

Orlando

WHERE THE GIRLS ARE: Women who live here hang out at Will's Pub or Faces bar. Tourists are—where else?—at the tourist attractions, including Disney World.

ENTERTAINMENT: Orlando Gay Chorus 407/841-7464.

LGBT PRIDE: June.

ANNUAL EVENTS: June (1st Sat) - Gay Day at Disney World 407/896-8431, web: gaydays.com.

CITY INFO: 407/363-5871. 8723 International Dr, 8am-8pm.

ATTRACTIONS: Sea World 407/351-3600.
Universal Studios 407/363-8000.
Walt Disney World 407/824-4321.
Wet & Wild Waterpark 407/351-3200.

WEATHER: Mild winters, hot summers.

TRANSIT: Yellow Cab 407/699-9999.
Gray Line 407/422-0744.
Lynx 407/841-8240.

Florida • USA

Reply **Forward** **Delete**

Date: Sat, Nov 17, 2001 14:50:48
From: Girl-on-the-Go
To: Editor@Damron.com
Subject: Orlando

> For most vacationers, Orlando means one thing: Disney World. If you're a fan of the Mouse, show your appreciation during the first weekend of June at Disney's (unofficial) Gay Days. 'Family' traditionally wear red T-shirts, while protesters wear white. (Queer Christians go for red-and-white stripes!) Check out **www.gaydays.com** for details and other events.

> Save some time for the enormous Epcot Center and MGM Studios, too. You'll need at least three days to traverse the 27,000 acres of this entertainment mecca. And if you still crave infotainment, visit Universal Studios, Wet 'n' Wild, Sea World, the Tupperware Museum (yes, Tupperware), Busch Gardens, or Cypress Gardens—a natural wonderland of lagoons, moss-draped trees, and exotic plants from around the world.

> Call the **Gay, Lesbian & Bisexual Community Center** to find out when the next Gay Day in the Busch (Gardens, that is) will be. If you like food on a stick, be sure to stop by the Central Florida Fair in February for Gay/Lesbian Day. After a long day of theme park-ing, settle in at one of the local lesbian-friendly B&Bs, like women-only **Leora's B&B,** or stay at the gay resort complex the **Parliament House.**

> **Faces** is the neighborhood lesbian bar, while **Southern Nights** and **The Club** (aka Firestone) are the places to dance, especially on Saturdays when women show up in throngs. For more local info, stop by **Out & About Books, Rainbow City,** or the Center, and pick up a copy of the LGBT paper **Watermark.**

> The lesbian social group **LCN** sponsors plenty of other events, including picnics at Wekiva Falls in the spring and around Halloween, and a dance in mid-January.

Full Moon Saloon 500 N Orange Blossom Tr **407/648-8725** • noon-2am • popular Sun afternoon • mostly gay men • leather • country/western • patio

Hank's 5026 Edgewater Dr **407/291-2399** • noon-2am • mostly gay men • neighborhood bar • beer/wine • patio • wheelchair access

Orlando • Florida

Little Orphan Andy's 5700 N Orange Blossom Tr (in Rosemont Plaza) 407/299-7717 • 3pm-2am • lesbians/gay men • neighborhood bar • live shows wknds • wheelchair access

Stable 410 N Orange Blossom Tr (at 'Parliament House') 407/425-7571 • 8pm-2am • mostly gay men • country/western • levi/leather

Will's Pub 1820-50 N Mills Ave 407/898-5070 • 4pm-2am • gay-friendly • neighborhood bar • food served • beer/wine • wheelchair access • also 'Loch Haven Motor Inn,' 407/896-3611

NIGHTCLUBS

Chaos 745 Ridgewood Ave (at US 1 & 8th St), Holly Hill 904/257-1967 • 3pm-2am, till 6am Fri-Sat • gay/straight • dancing/DJ • live shows • 18+ • wheelchair access • gay-owned/run

The Club 578 N Orange Ave 407/872-0066 • 9pm-3am • popular • gay/straight • more gay Sat • dancing/DJ • 18+ • live shows • videos

Club Quest 745 Bennett Rd 407/228-8226 • 10pm-3am Th-Sat only • gay/straight • dancing/DJ • multiracial • live shows • 18+

Empire 4315 N Orange Blossom Trail (at Lee) 407/522-0411 • gay Sat night & at Sun T-dance only

Parliament House Motor Inn 410 N Orange Blossom Tr 407/425-7571 • lesbians/gay men • 5 bars (open at 8pm) • dancing/DJ • multiracial • live shows • young crowd • also restaurant • wheelchair access

Southern Nights 375 S Bumby Ave 407/898-0424 • 4pm-2am • popular • lesbians/gay men • Latin Mon • more women Wed & Sat • dancing/DJ • multiracial • live shows • wheelchair access

CAFES

Shaffer Coffeehouse 535 W New England Ave, Winter Park 407/740-7782 • 8am-10pm (clsd 5pm-7:30pm), 9am-4pm Sun • wheelchair access

White Wolf Cafe & Antique Shop 1829 N Orange Ave (at Princeton) 407/895-5590 • 10am-10pm, till 11pm wknds, clsd Sun • salads • sandwiches • beer/wine • wheelchair access

RESTAURANTS

Brian's 1409 N Orange Ave (at Virginia) 407/896-9912 • 6am-4pm • popular Sun

Captain Mary's 1881 W Fairbanks Ave 407/599-9269 • 11:30am-3pm & 6pm-10pm, clsd Sun • full bar • gay-owned/run

Harvey's Bistro 390 N Orange Ave (in Nations Bank Tower) 407/246-6560 • popular cocktail hour

Hemingway's at the Hyatt 1 Grand Cypress Blvd, Lake Buena Vista 407/239-1234 • lunch & dinner • popular • cont'l • $20-25

La Sontanella 900 E Washington 407/425-0033 • 11am-10pm • seafood/Italian • some veggie • beer/wine • patio • wheelchair access • $9-17

Le Provence 50 E. Pine St 407/843-1320 • lunch & dinner, clsd Sun • French bistro • some veggie • full bar till 2am • live jazz wknds • $18-34

Nicole St Pierre 1300 S Orlando Ave, Maitland 407/647-7575 • lunch & dinner, clsd Sun • full bar • wheelchair access • $17-28

The Rainbow Cafe at 'Parliament House' 407/425-7571x711 • 24hrs Fri-Sat, till 11pm Sun-Th • lesbians/gay men

Taqueria Quetzalcoatl 350 W Fairbanks Ave, Winter Park 407/629-4123 • 11am-11pm, from noon Sun • some veggie • beer/wine

ENTERTAINMENT & RECREATION

The Enzian Theater 1300 S Orlando Ave (at Magnolia), Maitland 407/629-0054 • Central FL's only art house cinema • cafe • beer/wine

Family Values WPRK 91.5 FM • 3pm Fri • lgbt radio

Universal Studios Florida 1000 Universal Studios Pl 407/363-8000, 800/232-7827

Walt Disney World Resort 407/824-4321 • don't even pretend you came to Orlando for any other reason

BOOKSTORES

Out & About Books 930 N Mills Ave (at E Marks St) 407/896-0204 • 10am-8pm, till 9pm Fri-Sat, noon-7pm Sun • lgbt

RETAIL SHOPS

Harmony Designs 496 N Orange Blossom Tr 407/481-9850 • 1:30pm-11pm • pride store • wheelchair access

Rainbow City 936 N Mills Ave 407/898-6096 • 10am-9pm, noon-6pm Sun • lgbt gift shop • wheelchair access

Twisted Palms 1321 N Mills Ave 407/999-0111 • 11am-5pm, clsd Sun • new & gently worn clothing for men • also 'Twisted Palms Annex' 498-B N Orange Blossom Tr, 407/835-8998

PUBLICATIONS

Watermark 407/481-2243 • bi-weekly lgbt newspaper

Florida • USA

Spiritual Groups

Joy MCC 2351 S Ferncreek Ave **407/894-1081**
• 9am, 11am & 7pm Sun • wheelchair access

Erotica

Fairvilla Video 1740 N Orange Blossom Tr **407/425-5352**

Palm Beach

Accommodations

Heart of Palm Beach 160 Royal Palm Wy **561/655-5600** • gay-friendly • charming European-style hotel • swimming • kids ok • also restaurant • full bar • $79-299

Restaurants

Ta-Boo 221 Worth Ave **561/835-3500** • 11:30am-10:30pm • cont'l • live shows • wheelchair access • $12-25

Panama City

Bars

La Royale Lounge & Liquor Store 100 Harrison (at Beach Dr) **850/763-1755, 850/784-9311 (PAYPHONE)** • 3pm-3am • lesbians/ gay men • neighborhood bar • courtyard • wheelchair access

Nightclubs

The Construction Zone 5101 W Hwy 98 **850/747-8455** • 8pm-4am • popular • lesbians/ gay men • dancing/DJ • drag shows • male strippers Wed & Fri-Sun • 18+ • young crowd • wheelchair access

Fiesta Room 110 Harrison Ave (at Beach Dr) **850/763-1755, 850/784-9311 (PAYPHONE)** • 8pm-4am, till 4am wknds • popular • lesbians/ gay men • dancing/DJ • live shows • wheelchair access

Pensacola

Info Lines & Services

AA Gay/ Lesbian 415 N Alcaniz **850/433-8528** • 7:30pm Mon & Fri

Accommodations

Mill House Inn 9603 Lillian Hwy **850/455-3400, 888/999-4575** • mostly gay men • B&B on Perdido Bay • hot springs spa • smokefree • gay-owned/ run • $74-95

Bars

Red Carpet 937 N New Warrington Rd **850/453-9918** • 3pm-3am • mostly women • dancing/DJ • live shows Sat • patio • wheelchair access

Round-Up 706 E Gregory St (nr 9th Ave) **850/433-8482** • 2pm-3am • popular • mostly gay men • neighborhood bar • patio • wheelchair access

Nightclubs

Emerald City 406 E Wright St (at Alcaniz) **850/433-9491** • 5pm-3am • popular • lesbians/ gay men • dancing/DJ • live shows • 18+ • patio • wheelchair access

Retail Shops

Gulf Coast Pride 675 W Garden (at 'A' St) **850/433-1443** • 11am-7pm, clsd Sun • gifts • toys • magazines • wheelchair access

Spiritual Groups

Holy Cross MCC 415 N Alcaniz **850/433-8528** • 9am & 11am Sun, 7pm Wed

Unitarian Universalist Fellowship 9888 Pensacola Blvd **850/475-9077** • 10:30am Sun

Port Charlotte

Retail Shops

The Realm 2721 Tamiami Tr **941/766-1933** • 10am-9pm • fetishwear • gifts • books

Port Richey

Bars

BT's 7737 Grand Blvd (2 blks off US 19) **727/841-7900** • 6pm-2am • lesbians/ gay men • more women Tue • dancing/DJ • karaoke • live shows • wheelchair access

Spiritual Groups

Spirit of Life MCC 4133 Thys Rd (off State Rd 54), New Port Richey **727/849-6962** • 10:30am Sun, 6:30pm Wed • wheelchair access

Port St Lucie

Nightclubs

Club Babylon 8283 S Federal Hwy (Fiesta Sq) **561/340-7777** • 3pm-2am, 1pm-midnight Sun • gay/ straight • dancing/DJ • drag shows • karaoke • ladies' night Wed

Sarasota

Info Lines & Services

ALSO **941/252-2576 (PAGER)** • lgbt youth • confidential weekly mtgs

Friends Group (Gay AA) 1844 17th St, Bldg C (enter off Osprey) **941/951-6810** • 8pm Mon

Gay Info Line **941/923-4636** • 24hrs • recorded info

South Beach • Florida

Accommodations

The Cypress 621 Gulfstream Ave S **941/955-4683** • gay-friendly • B&B inn • overlooking Sarasota Bay • full gourmet brkfst • smokefree • $150-225

Normandy Inn 400 N Tamiami Tr (at 4th St) **941/366-0000** • gay-friendly • courtyard • $50-120

Siesta Holidays 1017 Seaside Dr & 1011 Crescent St, Siesta Key **941/312-9882, 800/720-6885** • gay-friendly • smokefree • 2 locations • apts nr Crescent Beach • $450-1,375/week

Bars

Rowdy's 1330 Martin Luther King Jr Wy **941/953-5945** • 1pm-2am • popular • mostly gay men • dancing/DJ • live shows • videos • patio • wheelchair access

Twisted Sisters 2941 N Tamiami Tr **941/355-7210** • 8pm-2am Fri-Sat, 5pm-midnight Sun • mostly women • neighborhood bar • live bands

Publications

MainStream 941/330-0888, 877/363-6246

Spiritual Groups

Church of the Trinity MCC 7225 N Lockwood Ridge Rd **941/355-0847** • 9:15am & 11am Sun • wheelchair access

Erotica

Romantix Adult Emporium 1038 N Washington Blvd **941/953-4545**

Romantix Adult Emporium 7338 S Tamiami Tr **941/923-7626**

Satellite Beach

Erotica

Space Age Books & Temptations 63 Ocean Blvd **321/773-7660**

Seagrove Beach

Accommodations

▲ **For Your Pleasure Rentals** 800/854-9266 • 2 cozy cabins

South Beach

see Miami Beach/ South Beach

Play on the sugarsand beach at **...Seagrove Beach, FL.**
~2 cozy cottages~Viewing Tower~
A short walk to Seaside (near Destin, FL.)
Many wonderful restaurants, galleries & shops

~~~

Relax in the mountains of **Franklin, North Carolina**
Secluded chalet in the foothills of Franklin
Stone fireplace and skylights
Deck with a great view

~~~

FOR YOUR PLEASURE
RENTAL PROPERTIES

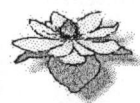

Milo (800) 854-9266
e-mail: smilogirl@digitalexp.com

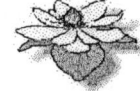

~Pets can come too~

Florida • USA

St Augustine

ACCOMMODATIONS

Pagoda by the Sea 2854 Coastal Hwy **904/824-2970** • women only • 2 apts • guesthouse • nr beach • swimming • wheelchair access • women-owned/run • $50-75

The Saragossa Inn 34 Saragossa St (at Sevilla) **904/808-7384** • gay/straight • B&B • full brkfst • gay-owned/run • $89-175

St Petersburg

see also Tampa

INFO LINES & SERVICES

Gay Information Line (The Line) **727/586-4297** • volunteers 7pm-11pm • touchtone 24hrs

WEB (Women's Energy Bank) PO Box 15548 **727/823-5353** • many services & activities for lesbians

ACCOMMODATIONS

Bay Gables B&B 340 Rowland Ct **727/822-8855, 800/822-8803** • gay-friendly • 3-story Key West-style inn • smokefree • kids ok • $85-135

Boca Ciega 727/381-2755 • women only • B&B in private home • swimming • lesbian-owned/run • $40-50

Changing Tides Cottages 225 Boca Ciega Dr, Madeira Beach **727/397-7706** • women-only • fully furnished rental cottages on harbor • women-owned/run • $115-225

Dicken's House B&B 335 8th Ave NE **727/822-8622, 800/381-2022** • gay/straight • swimming • newly restored 1900s home • nr beach • jacuzzi • massage • $95-210

Pass-A-Grille Beach Co-op 709 Gulf Way, St Petersburg Beach **727/367-4726** • gay-friendly • swimming • kids ok • $60-95

Sea Oats by the Gulf 12625 Sunshine Ln, Treasure Island 33706 **727/367-7568** • gay-friendly • motel & apts • on the Gulf of Mexico • kids/pets ok • wheelchair access • $350-795/week

Suncoast Resort 3000 34th St S/ Hwy 19 S (at 32nd Ave S) **727/867-1111** • lesbians/gay men • popular • dancing/DJ • live shows • swimming • 5 bars • 2 restaurants • outdoor recreation • gay shopping mall • wheelchair access • gay-owned/run • $59-89

BARS

The Back Room Bar @ Surf & Sand Bar 14601 Gulf Blvd, Madeira Beach **727/391-2680** • noon-2am, from 1pm Sun • mostly gay men • neighborhood bar • karaoke • beach access • patio • wheelchair access

Common Ground 5571 4th St N (at 'Elsie's' restaurant) **727/522-7413** • 1pm-2am • lesbians/gay men • dancing/DJ • live shows • beer/wine • also German restaurant till 9pm • wheelchair access

DT's 2612 Central Ave (at 26th) **727/327-8204** • 6pm-2am • mostly gay men • neighborhood bar • male dancers Th-Sun • patio • wheelchair access

---

St Petersburg

LGBT PRIDE: June. 727/586-4297.

ANNUAL EVENTS: October - Film Festival & Gay Men's Chorus 800/729-2787, web: flagg.net/filmfestival/intro.htm.

CITY INFO: Chamber of Commerce 727/821-6164. 8am-5pm Mon-Fri.

ATTRACTIONS: Great Explorations interactive kids museum 727/821-8992.
Salvador Dalí Museum 727/823-3767.

BEST VIEW: Pass-A-Grille Beach in Tampa.

WEATHER: Some say it's the Garden of Eden—winter temperatures occasionally dip into the 40°s but for the rest of the year temperatures stay in the 70°-80°s.

TRANSIT: Yellow Cab 727/821-7777.

St Petersburg • Florida

[Reply] [Forward] **[Delete]**

Date: Thu, Nov 22, 2001 14:52:29
From: Girl-on-the-Go
To: Editor@Damron.com
Subject: Tampa & St. Petersburg

> The Sunshine State draws a fair number of lesbians to its shores, and the Tampa/St. Petersburg area seems to be particularly attractive. And no wonder—gorgeous Gulf-side beaches, sunny days, and a tolerant, laid-back attitude are certainly ideal qualities.

> You'll find plenty of resources and activities here, and plenty of friendly women. When you arrive, call the **Women's Energy Bank (WEB).**

> Before you arrive, of course, you should reserve a place to stay. If you are interested in women-only accommodations, you have two choices: **Changing Tides Cottages** or the **Boca Ciega** B&B, both of which are in St. Pete.

> Despite the popular image of relaxed afternoons and sunset strolls on the beach, there is another side to Tampa and St. Pete: a great nightlife! There are not one, not two, but three (!) women's bars in the area: the diverse **Klub Trendz** (in Tampa), the **Hideaway** (in St. Pete) and the **Sahara** (in Tampa). If you prefer a more mixed venue, head over to **Sharp A's** for drinks and dancing with the girls and boys there. On weekends, you'll find the girls dancing the night away at **La Femme Buvette** (in Tampa).

> If partying is not your thang, don't fret! There are lots of other activities to keep you occupied while you're in town.... For some good old-fashioned/retro fun, don your pink satin jacket and knee socks and strut your stuff on the waxed floor of the **United Skates of America,** at Tuesday's LGBT skate night.

> Those in search of headier pursuits should pay a visit to **Affinity** LGBT bookstore or **Brigit Books,** a women's bookstore. Look for a copy of the latest edition of **Watermark**—the local bi-weekly LGBT paper—for other ideas.

Florida • USA

The Hideaway 8302 4th St N (at 83rd) **727/570-9025** • 2pm-2am • mostly women • neighborhood bar • live shows • karaoke • wheelchair access

Sharp A's 4918 Gulfport Blvd S (at 49th), Gulfport **727/327-4897** • 4pm-2am • popular • lesbians/ gay men • dancing/DJ • karaoke • wheelchair access

VIP Lounge & Mexican Food Grill 10625 Gulf Blvd **727/360-5062** • 9am-2am • food served 11am-10pm • gay-friendly • wheelchair access

West Side Lounge 4900 Central Ave (at 49th) **727/328-2636** • 1pm-2am • lesbians/ gay men • neighborhood bar • patio

NIGHTCLUBS

The New Connection 3100 3rd Ave N (at 31st St N) **727/321-2112** • 1pm-2am • mostly gay men • 3 bars • neighborhood bar • dancing/DJ • live shows • videos • wheelchair access • gay-owned/ run

CAFES

Beaux Arts 2635 Central Ave **727/328-0702** • noon-5pm • lesbians/ gay men • historic gallery w/ coffeehouse • 8pm Sat open mic

RESTAURANTS

Anna's Ravioli & Pasta Company 5625 4th St N **727/522-6627** • 9am-5pm deli, 5pm-10pm dinner • gay-owned/ run

BOOKSTORES

Affinity Books 2435 9th St N (at 25th Ave) **727/823-3662, 800/355-3662** • 10am-6pm, till 5pm Sat, noon-5pm Sun • lgbt • gifts • wheelchair access

Brigit Books 406 11th Ave N **727/502-5642, 800/566-2333** • 10am-6pm, till 8pm Tue & Th, 1pm-5pm Sun • women's/ feminist

RETAIL SHOPS

The MC Film Festival Video & Music Store 3000 34th St S #30 (in Suncoast Resort) **727/866-0904** • noon-7pm • nonerotic lgbt videos • CDs & pride gifts • also business ctr

PUBLICATIONS

The Gazette **813/689-7566** • the Suncoast's monthly gay/ lesbian newsmagazine

MainStream **941/330-0888, 877/363-6246**

SPIRITUAL GROUPS

King of Peace MCC 3150 5th Ave N **727/323-5857** • 10:30am & 7pm Sun • wheelchair access

Tallahassee

BARS

Brothers 926 W Tharpe St (near Old Bainbridge) **850/386-2399** • 4pm-2am • lesbians/ gay men • dancing/DJ • multiracial • live shows • videos • 18+ • wheelchair access

NIGHTCLUBS

Club Park Ave 115 E Park Ave **850/681-6880** • 10pm-2am Wed-Sun, clsd Mon-Tue • popular • gay-friendly (gay Sat & Sun only) • dancing/DJ • multiracial • drag shows • young crowd

RESTAURANTS

The Village Inn 2690 N Monroe St **850/385-2903** • 6am-3am, 24hrs wknds • popular

Tampa

see also St Petersburg

INFO LINES & SERVICES

Gay Information Line (The Line) **727/586-4297** • volunteers 7pm-11pm • touchtone service 24hrs

Women's Center **813/677-8136** • women's helpline • resources

ACCOMMODATIONS

Gram's Place B&B & Artist Retreat 3109 N Ola Ave **813/221-0596** • gay/ straight • nudity • hot tub • BYOB • $50-100

Ruskin House B&B **813/645-3842** • lesbians/ gay men • 1910 Victorian home • 30 minutes south of Tampa & 30 minutes north of Sarasota • full brkfst • $75

BARS

2606 2606 Armenia Ave (at St Conrad) **813/875-6993** • 8pm-3am, from 6am Sun • popular • mostly gay men • levi/ leather • strippers wknds • also leather shop from 9pm • wheelchair access • gay-owned/ run

City Side 3810 Neptune St (at Dale Mabry) **813/254-6466** • noon-3am • mostly gay men • neighborhood bar • professional crowd • patio

Jungle 3703 Henderson Blvd (at Dale Mabry) **813/877-3290** • 3pm-3am • popular • lesbians/ gay men • neighborhood bar • patio

Klub Trendz 2408 W Kennedy Blvd (at Armenia) **813/254-4188** • 5pm-3am, from 6pm Tue-Wed, clsd Sun-Mon • mostly women • multiracial • dancing/DJ • karaoke • live shows • wheelchair access • patio

Tampa • Florida

Metropolis 3447 W Kennedy Blvd (at Himes) 813/871-2410 • noon-3am, from 1pm Sun • lesbians/ gay men • neighborhood bar • live shows Fri-Sat • wheelchair access

The Sahara 4643 W Kennedy Blvd (at W Shore) 813/282-0183 • noon-3am, from 1pm Sun • mostly women • dancing/DJ wknds • karaoke • neighborhood bar • Wed Latin night • wheelchair access

The Tampa Brigg 9002 N Florida Ave (at Busch) 813/931-3396 • 3pm-3am • mostly gay men • neighborhood bar • strippers wknds • gay-owned/ run

Nightclubs

Chrome 901 N Franklin St (at Cass) 813/226-2476 • 10pm-3am Sat only • lesbians/ gay men • dancing/DJ

Club Matrix 105 W Martin Luther King Blvd (at Tampa St) 813/237-8883 • 4pm-3am • popular • lesbians/gay men • dancing/DJ • live shows • theme nights • call for details • also restaurant, clsd Sun-Mon • gay-owned/ run

The Garage 802 E Whiting St (at Jefferson) 813/221-2582 • 9:30pm-3am Fri & Sun only • popular • mostly gay men • dancing/DJ • strippers • 18+

La Femme Buvette 1328 E 9th Ave (at Republica de Cuba), Ybor City 813/247-9966 • 9pm-3am Fri-Sun only • mostly women • dancing/DJ • live shows • call for events

Pleasuredome 1430 E 7th Ave (at 15th) 813/247-2711 • 9pm-3am Tue & Fri-Sat only • gay/ straight • more gay Tue • dancing/DJ • drag shows • videos • wheelchair access

Cafes

Sacred Grounds 4819 E Busch Blvd 813/983-0837 • 6:30pm-1am, till 2am Fri-Sat, till midnight Sun • lesbians/ gay men • live music & poetry slams

Restaurants

Ho Ho Chinese 533 S Howard 813/254-9557 • 11:30am-10pm • full bar • wheelchair access • gay-owned/ run

Taqueria Quetzalcoatl 402 S Howard Ave 813/259-9982 • 11am-11pm, from noon Sun • Mexican • some veggie • beer/ wine

Tropics Cabaret & Restaurant 2801 S MacDill 813/837-1836 • 5:30pm-close • lesbians/ gay men • bar open from 4pm • live entertainment nightly

Entertainment & Recreation

Sail More Life 5000 13th Ave S (at 49th St S), Gulfport 727/328-2907 • sailboat charter • seasonal • gay-owned/ run

United Skates of America 5121 N Armenia 813/876-5826 • lgbt skate 9pm-11:30pm Tue • seasonal

The Women's Show WMNF 88.5 FM 813/238-8001 • 10am-noon Sat

Tampa

Entertainment: Tampa Bay Gay Men's Chorus 727/865-9004, web: www.tampabayarts.com. Crescendo, Tampa Bay Womyn's Chorus 813/930-9055. web: www.crescendochorus.com.

LGBT Pride: July. 813/854-8160 or 800/825-1000.

City Info: Greater Tampa Chamber of Commerce 813/228-7777, web: www.tampachamber.com. Tampa/Hillsborough Convention & Visitors Bureau 727/223-1111.

Attractions: Busch Gardens 813/987-5082. Florida Aquarium 813/273-4000. Harbour Island. Museum of Science & Industry 813/987-6100. Ybor Square.

Transit: The Limo 727/572-1111. Yellow Cab 813/253-0121. Hartline Transit (bus) 813/254-4278.

Florida • USA

BOOKSTORES

Tomes & Treasures 406-408 S Howard Ave (at Swann) **813/251-9368** • 11am-8pm, 1pm-6pm Sun • lgbt • also coffeehouse till midnight, till 10pm Sun • live music • gallery

PUBLICATIONS

The Gazette 813/689-7566 • Florida's gay/lesbian newsmagazine

Watermark 407/481-2243 • bi-weekly lgbt newspaper

SPIRITUAL GROUPS

Dignity Tampa Bay 3010 Perry Ave (at Franciscan Center) **813/238-2868** • 7pm Sun

MCC 408 E Cayuga St (at Central Ave) **813/239-1951** • 10:30am Sun & 7pm Wed

GYMS & HEALTH CLUBS

Metro Flex Fitness 2511 Swann Ave (at Armenia) **813/876-3539**

Venice

RESTAURANTS

Maggie May's 1550 US 41 Bypass S **941/497-1077** • 8am-3pm • homecooking • some veggie • beer/wine • wheelchair access • women-owned/run

SPIRITUAL GROUPS

Suncoast Cathedral MCC 3276 E Venice Ave **941/484-7068** • 11am Sun

West Palm Beach

INFO LINES & SERVICES

Compass Community Center 7600 S Dixie Hwy **561/533-9699** • 10am-9pm, till 5:30pm Fri, 6pm-8pm Sun, clsd Sat • wheelchair access

The Whimsy 561/686-1354 • resources & archives • political clearinghouse • also camping/RV space & apt • wheelchair access

ACCOMMODATIONS

Hibiscus House B&B 501 30th St **561/863-5633, 800/203-4927** • gay/straight • full brkfst • swimming • smokefree • gay-owned/run • $65-250

Tropical Gardens B&B 419 32nd St, Old Northwood **561/848-4064, 800/736-4064** • mostly gay men • guesthouse • swimming • gay-owned/run • $55-125

BARS

5101 Bar 5101 S Dixie Hwy **561/585-2379** • 7am-3am, till 4am Fri-Sat, from noon Sun • mostly gay men • neighborhood bar • karaoke Th • wheelchair access

HG Rooster's 823 Belvedere Rd (btwn Parker & Lake) **561/832-9119** • 3pm-3am, till 4am Fri-Sat • popular • mostly gay men • neighborhood bar • wheelchair access

Kozlow's 6205 Georgia Ave (at Colonial) **561/533-5355** • noon-3am, till 4am wknds • popular • mostly gay men • neighborhood bar • dancing/DJ wknds • patio • wheelchair access

NIGHTCLUBS

Respectable Street Cafe 518 Clematis St **561/832-9999** • 9pm-3am, clsd Sun-Tue • gay-friendly • dancing/DJ • alternative • retro & new wave nights • Goth night Fri • live shows

RESTAURANTS

Antonio's South 3001 S Congress Ave, Palm Springs **561/965-0707** • dinner only, clsd Mon • popular • southern Italian • beer/wine • $9-18

Rhythm Cafe 3800-A S Dixie Hwy **561/833-3406** • 6pm-10pm, clsd Sun-Mon • some veggie • beer/wine • $12-19

BOOKSTORES

Changing Times Bookstore 911 Village Blvd #806 (at Palm Beach Lakes) **561/640-0496** • 10am-7pm, noon-5pm Sun • spiritual • lgbt section • community bulletin board • wheelchair access

RETAIL SHOPS

Eurotique 3109 45th St #300 **561/684-2302** • 11am-7pm, noon-6pm Sat, clsd Sun • leather • books • videos

Studio 205 600 Lake Ave (at North 'L' St), Lake Worth **561/533-5272** • hrs vary • gay pride items • books & home accessories

SPIRITUAL GROUPS

MCC of the Palm Beaches 4857 Northlake Blvd, Palm Beach Gardens **561/775-5900** • 11am Sun

Wilton Manors

see Fort Lauderdale

Winter Park

BARS

New Phoenix 7124 Aloma Ave (at Forsythe) **407/678-9070** • 4pm-2am • lesbians/gay men • neighborhood bar • dancing/DJ • live shows

Atlanta • Georgia

GEORGIA

Statewide

PUBLICATIONS

▲ **ETC Magazine** 404/888-0063 • weekly entertainment guide & news resource for lgbt Atlanta & Southeast

▲ **Southern Voice** 404/876-1819 • weekly lgbt newspaper for AL, FL (panhandle), GA, LA, MS, TN w/ resource listings

Athens

INFO LINES & SERVICES

Lesbian Support Group 706/546-4611

ACCOMMODATIONS

The River's Edge 2311 Pulliam Mill Rd, Dewy Rose 706/213-8081 • mostly gay men • cabins • camping • RV • live entertainment • swimming • nudity • smokefree • wheelchair access • $12-47

BARS

Georgia Bar 159 W Clayton (at Lumpkin) 706/546-9884 • 3pm-2am, clsd Sun • gay-friendly • more gay wknights • neighborhood bar • wheelchair access

The Globe 199 N Lumpkin (at Clayton) 706/353-4721 • 4pm-2am, till 1am Mon-Tue, clsd Sun • gay-friendly • 55 single-malt scotches

NIGHTCLUBS

Boneshakers 433 E Hancock Ave 706/543-1555 • 8pm-3am, from 9:30pm Fri, till 4am Sat, clsd Sun • lesbians/ gay men • dancing/DJ • live shows • 18+ • wheelchair access

Forty Watt Club 285 W Washington St (at Pulaski) 706/549-7871 • 9pm-2am, clsd Sun • gay-friendly • alternative • live music • wheelchair access

CAFES

Espresso Royale Cafe 297 E Broad St (at Jackson) 706/613-7449 • 7am-midnight, from 8am wknds • best coffee in Athens • gallery • wheelchair access

RESTAURANTS

The Bluebird 493 E Clayton 706/549-3663 • 8am-3pm • popular brunch wknds • plenty veggie • $5-10

The Grit 199 Prince Ave 706/543-6592 • 11am-10pm (clsd 3pm-5pm Sat-Sun) • ethnic vegetarian • great wknd brunch • wheelchair access • $5-10

BOOKSTORES

Barnett's Newsstand 147 College Ave (at Clayton) 706/353-0530 • 7:30am-10pm, 8am-11pm Fri-Sat, from 8am Sun

Atlanta

INFO LINES & SERVICES

Atlanta Gay/ Lesbian Center 159 Ralph McGill Blvd, #600 (at Piedmont Ave) 404/523-7500 • 5:30pm-9:30pm Mon-Fri • social services center • clinic

Galano Club 585 Dutch Valley Rd 404/881-9188 • lgbt recovery club, call for meeting times

Gay Helpline 404/525-4357 • 24hrs • live 6pm-11pm • info & counseling

ACCOMMODATIONS

Abbett Inn 1746 Virginia Ave 404/767-3708 • gay/ straight • 1880s Victorian • smokefree • kids 10+ ok • gay-owned/ run • $79-149

▲ **Ansley Inn B&B** 253 15th St 404/872-9000, 800/446-5416 • gay/ straight • full brkfst • smokefree • gay-owned/ run • $99-189

Hello B&B 1865 Windemere Dr 404/892-8111 • lesbians/ gay men • B&B in private home • hot tub • smokefree • $69-135

Midtown Manor 811 Piedmont Ave NE 404/872-5846, 800/680-9236 • gay/ straight • charming Victorian guesthouse • gay-owned/ run • $45-85

Rendezvous for Two 770/933-8951, 877/790-8673 • gay-friendly • romantic accommodations • $275+

Sheraton Atlanta Hotel 165 Courtland St (at International Blvd) 404/659-6500, 800/325-3535 • gay-friendly • swimming • 3 restaurants • bar • wheelchair access • $95-235

BARS

Atlanta Eagle 306 Ponce de Leon Ave NE (at Argonne) 404/873-2453 • 8pm-3am, from 5pm Sun • popular • mostly gay men • dancing/DJ • leather • also leather store • gay-owned/ run

Blake's (on the Park) 227 10th St (at Piedmont) 404/892-5786, 888/441-8984 • 3pm-2am • lesbians/ gay men • neighborhood bar • upscale • drag shows • videos

Buddies 2345 Cheshire Bridge Rd (at La Vista) 404/634-5895 • 1:30pm-4am, till 3am Sat • mostly gay men • neighborhood bar • country/ western

Georgia • USA

Buddies Midtown 239 Ponce de Leon (at Penn) 404/872-2655 • 3pm-4am, from noon wknds • lesbians/ gay men • sports bar • food served • wheelchair access

Burkhart's Pub 1492–F Piedmont Ave (at Monroe, in Ansley Mall) 404/872-4403 • 4pm-4am, 2pm-3am wknds • lesbians/ gay men • neighborhood bar • food served • karaoke • live shows • patio • wheelchair access

Eddie's Attic 515–B N McDonough St (at Trinity Place), Decatur 404/377-4976 • 4pm-close • gay/ straight • occasional lesbian hangout • rooftop deck • live music • gay comedy 4th Tue • also restaurant

Hoedowns 931 Monroe Dr #B (at Midtown Promenade) 404/876-0001 • 3pm-3am, clsd Mon • popular • mostly gay men • more women Th • dancing/DJ • country/ western • live shows • wheelchair access

Kaya 1068 Peachtree St NE (at 12th) 404/874-4460 • call for hrs • gay/ straight • more gay wknds • T-dance Sun • dancing/DJ • mostly African-American • live shows • also restaurant • some veggie • $6-12

Le Buzz 585 Franklin Rd A-10 (at S Marietta Pkwy, in Longhorn Plaza), Marietta 770/424-1337 • 7pm-3am, from 6pm Sat, clsd Sun • lesbians/ gay men • neighborhood bar • dancing/DJ Fri-Sat • also restaurant • karaoke Tue & Th • drag shows Wed • patio • wheelchair access

Mary's 1287 Glenwood Ave (at Flat Shoals) 404/624-4411 • 5pm-2am, till 3am Sat, 4pm-midnight Sun • lesbians/ gay men • friendly neighborhood cocktail bar • videos

Midtown Saloon & Grill 738 Ponce de Leon Ave NE (at Ponce de Leon Plaza) 404/874-1655 • 2pm-4am, food served 5pm-10pm • mostly gay men • popular • neighborhood bar & grill • patio

The Moreland Tavern 1196 Moreland Ave SE (at Confederate) 404/622-4650 • noon-2am • lesbians/ gay men • neighborhood bar • food served • patio • wheelchair access

My Sister's Room 222 E Howard Ave (at E Trinity Pl), Decatur 404/370-1990 • 6pm-2am Tue-Th, till 3am Fri-Sat, 4pm-midnight Sun, clsd Mon • popular • mostly women • DJ wknds • live music • karaoke • also restaurant • younger crowd • patio

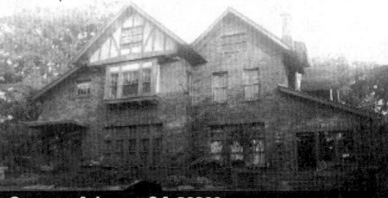

Experience Atlanta

from the INN-Side
ANSLEY INN
Atlanta's finest bed & breakfast

22 rooms w/private bath, jaccuzzi, cable TV, wet bar, coffee maker

scrumptious full breakfast, afternoon snacks

open all year round

an elegant english tudor located in the heart of midtown Atlanta's historic district

253 Fifteenth Street • Atlanta, GA 30309
404-872-9000 • 800-446-5416 • FAX 404-892-2318
e-mail: reservations@ansleyinn.com • web site: www.ansleyinn.com

Atlanta • Georgia

[Reply] [Forward] **[Delete]**

Date: Thu, Nov 15, 2001 10:51:37
From: Girl-on-the-Go
To: Editor@Damron.com
Subject: Atlanta

> If you watched the 1996 Olympic Games, you saw how proud the residents of Atlanta are of their city. Today's Southerners have worked hard to move beyond stereotypes of the Old South. Of course, Atlanta's large population of lesbians and gay men is an integral part of that work.

> Atlanta houses the must-see Martin Luther King, Jr. Center and the Carter Presidential Center—tributes to icons of peace and positive change—and hosts the nationally known Black Arts Festival (404/730-7315).

> Lesbian culture in Atlanta is spread out between **Charis** women's bookstore in L'il Five Points (cruise their readings), the **Atlanta Gay/Lesbian Center** in posh Midtown, and in between, along Piedmont and Cheshire Bridge roads. Midway between the gay Ansley Square area (Piedmont at Monroe) and downtown, stop by **Outwrite,** Atlanta's LGBT bookstore and cafe. Pick up a copy of **Southern Voice,** the LGBT newspaper, or **ETC** to get the dish on the bar scene. For more shopping, **Brushstrokes** is Atlanta's LGBT goodies store.

> Unless you're a serious mall-crawler, skip the overly commercial (but much hyped) Underground Atlanta, and head for Lenox Mall instead, where you'll see more stylish queers. And, just a couple miles south on Highland, you'll run smack into funky shopping, dining, and live music in the alternative capital of Atlanta: **L'il Five Points** (not to be confused with 'Five Points' downtown).

> **Tower 2** is the local neighborhood dyke bar, and the country/ western flavored **Hoedowns** has a women's night on Thursdays. African-American women won't want to miss the weekly **Ladies of the Night** party. And don't miss nearby Decatur, home to two popular lesbian hangouts—**My Sister's Room** and **Eddie's Attic,** featuring live music (and rumored to be a sometime hangout of the Indigo Girls).

> If you're looking for women's accommodations, head an hour north to one of the women's guesthouses in lush, wooded Dahlonega, such as **Above the Clouds** or **Swiftwaters.**

> If you're a fan of R.E.M. or the B-52s, head northeast on Highway 306 or 78 about an hour-and-a-half to the university town of Athens, Georgia. (Be forewarned that on weekends during football season, traffic is hellish.) Pick up a Flagpole magazine to find out what's going on, and stop by **Boneshakers,** Athens's LGBT dance bar.

Georgia • USA

Opus I 1086 Alco St NE (at Cheshire Bridge) **404/634-6478** • 9am-4am, from 12:30pm Sun • mostly gay men • neighborhood bar • older crowd • wheelchair access

The Palace 91 Broad St **404/522-3000** • 5pm-close • mostly gay men • dancing/DJ • mostly African-American • 3 levels

Pin Up's 2788 E Ponce de Leon Ave, Decatur **404/373-9477** • 11am-3am, from 1pm Sat, from 6pm Sun • gay-friendly • strip club • food served • 18+ • wheelchair access

Rico's View on Ponce 736 Ponce de Leon, NE (at Ponce de Leon Pl) **404/873-3220** • 9am-4am, till 3am Sat, 12:30pm-midnight Sun • mostly gay men • neighborhood sports & video bar • karaoke • rooftop patio

Scandals 1510-G Piedmont Ave NE (in Ansley Mall) **404/875-5957** • 11:30am-4am, till 3am Sat, from 12:30pm Sun • popular • mostly gay men • neighborhood bar • karaoke • wheelchair access

Atlanta

WHERE THE GIRLS ARE: Many lesbians live in DeKalb county, in the northeast part of the city of Decatur. For fun, women head for Midtown or Buckhead if they're professionals, Virginia-Highlands if they're funky or 30ish, and Little Five Points if they're young and wild.

ENTERTAINMENT: Atlanta Feminist Women's Chorus 770/438-5823. Lefont Screening Room 404/231-1924, gay film.

LGBT PRIDE: June. 404/876-3700, web: atlantapride.org.

ANNUAL EVENTS: May - Armory Sports Classic 404/881-9280 (Armory Bar). Softball & many other sports competitions. Midtown Music Festival 404/577-8686.
August - Hotlanta 404/874-3796. Weekend of river rafting, pageants & parties for boys.
December - Women's Christmas Ball/Good Friends for Good Causes 770/938-1194.

CITY INFO: 404/521-6600 or 800/285-2682 (in GA), web: www.atlanta.com

ATTRACTIONS: Atlanta Botanical Garden 404/876-5859. CNN Center 404/827-1700. Coca-Cola Museum. Margaret Mitchell House 404/249-7015. Martin Luther King Jr. Memorial Center. Piedmont Park. Underground Atlanta 404/523-2311.

BEST VIEW: 70th floor of the Peachtree Plaza, in the Sun Dial restaurant. Also from the top of Stone Mountain.

WEATHER: Summers are warm and humid (upper 80°s to low 90°s) with occasional thunderstorms. Winters are icy with occasional snow. Temperatures can drop into the low 30°s. Spring and fall are temperate – spring brings blossoming dogwoods and magnolias, while fall festoons the trees with Northeast Georgia's awesome fall foliage.

TRANSIT: Yellow Cab 404/521-0200. Atlanta Airport Shuttle 404/524-3400. Marta 404/848-5000.

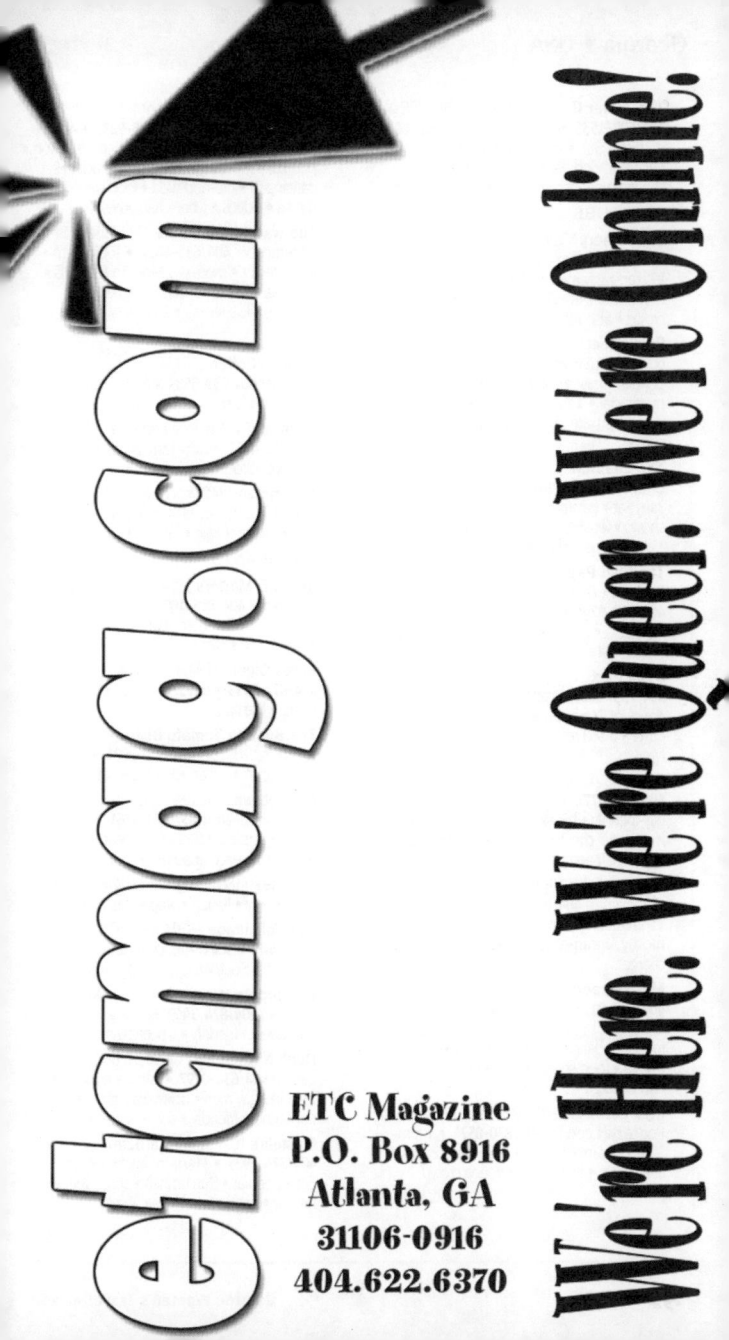

Georgia • USA

The Tower II 735 Ralph McGill Blvd NE **404/523-1535** • 5pm-2am, till 3am Fri-Sat, till midnight Sun • mostly women • neighborhood bar • dancing/ DJ Fri • live shows • younger crowd • wheelchair access

Nightclubs

The Armory 836 Juniper St NE (at 7th) **404/881-9280** • 4pm-3am, till 4am Fri • popular • lesbians/ gay men • 4 bars • dancing/DJ • multiracial • live shows • videos • young crowd • also restaurant • wheelchair access

Backstreet 845 Peachtree St NE (btwn 5th & 6th, enter rear) **404/873-1986** • 24hrs • popular • gay/ straight • dancing/DJ • multiracial • 3 flrs • live shows • videos • young crowd • private club • also gift shop • cover charge

The Chamber 2115 Faulkner Dr (at Cheshire Bridge) **404/248-1612** • 10pm-4am Th-Fri, till 3am Sat • gay-friendly • dancing/DJ • live shows • fetish crowd • 18+ Th • also 'Glitterdome' 3rd Fri • queer glamrock club

The Chili Pepper 208 Pharr Rd (btwn Piedmont & Peachtree in Buckhead) **404/812-9266** • 9pm-4am, till 3am Sat, clsd Sun-Mon • gay-friendly • dancing/ DJ • live music • wheelchair access

Deux Plex 1789 Cheshire Bridge Rd **404/733-5900** • call for hours • gay/ straight • dancing/ DJ • multiracial • live shows • $10 cover • also French bistro • 5pm-2:30am, clsd Mon

ESSO 489 Courtland St (at Pine) **404/872-3776** • 10pm-3am, clsd Sun-Wed • gay-friendly • hip hop/ R&B dancing/DJ • multiracial clientele • 3 flrs • rooftop deck • wheelchair access

Ladies of the Night 1231 W Peachtree (at Club Jaguar) **404/874-5673, 800/970-5833** • 11pm-4am Fri • mostly women • dancing/DJ • mostly African-American • food served • cover charge

Masquerade 695 North Ave NE **404/577-8178, 404/577-2002** • 10pm-4am Wed-Fri, till 3am Sat, 7pm-midnight Sun • gay-friendly • dancing/DJ • live shows • call for events • food served • 18+ • private club • cover charge

MJQ Concourse 736 Ponce de Leon Ave (at Ponce de Leon Pl) **404/870-0575** • 10pm-3am • gay-friendly • popular • dancing/DJ • alternative • live shows • young crowd

The Rarity 1924 Piedmont Rd NE (at Cheshire Bridge Rd) **404/875-5238** • 4pm-4am, till 3am Sat, till midnight Sun, clsd Mon • popular • mostly gay men • multiracial • dancing/DJ • hip-hop Wed • food served • live shows • videos • wheelchair access

The Warehouse/ Traxx 339 Marietta St NW (at Simpson) **404/681-4422** • 10pm-3am • gay/ straight • more gay Mon, Th & wknds • dancing/ DJ • mostly African-American clientele • live shows • 18+

Cafes

Caribou Coffee 1551 Piedmont Ave (at Monroe) **404/733-5539** • 6am-11pm, 7am-midnight wknds

Innovox 499 Ponce de Leon Ave NE **404/872-4482** • 7am-1am, 24hrs wknds • Internet coffeehouse

Intermezzo 1845 Peachtree Rd NE **404/355-0411** • 11am-3am, till 4am Fri-Sat • classy cafe • plenty veggie • full bar • great desserts

Restaurants

Agnes & Muriel's 1514 Monroe Dr (nr Piedmont) **404/885-1000** • 11am-11pm, till midnight Fri-Sat, from 10am wknds • popular • beer/ wine • patio

Apres Diem 931 Monroe Dr #C-103 **404/872-3333** • lunch & dinner • French bistro • live jazz

The Big Red Tomato Bistro 980 Piedmont Rd NE (at 10th St) **404/870-9881** • dinner & Sun brunch • Italian • full bar • patio • $8-18

Bridgetown Grill 689 Peachtree (across from Fox Theater) **404/873-5361** • 11am-11pm • popular • funky Caribbean • some veggie • wheelchair access • $5-15

Camille's 1186 N Highland **404/872-7203** • dinner only • Italian • wheelchair access

The Colonnade 1879 Cheshire Bridge Rd NE **404/874-5642** • lunch & dinner • traditional Southern

Cowtippers 1600 Piedmont Ave NE (at Monroe) **404/873-3469** • 11:30am-11pm • transgender-friendly • wheelchair access

Dunk N' Dine 2277 Cheshire Bridge Rd (at Lenox) **404/636-0197** • 24hrs • popular • lesbians/ gay men • downscale diner • transgender-friendly • some veggie • $4-10

Einstein's 1077 Juniper (at 12th) **404/876-7925** • 11am-midnight, till 1am Fri-Sat • popular • Sun brunch • some veggie • full bar • patio • wheelchair access

Atlanta • Georgia

The Flying Biscuit Cafe 1655 McLendon Ave (at Clifton) **404/687-8888** • 9am-10pm, clsd Mon • popular • healthy brkfst all day • plenty veggie • beer/wine • wheelchair access • lesbian-owned/run • $6-12

Majestic Diner 1031 Ponce de Leon (at Clayton Terrace) **404/875-0276** • 24hrs • popular diner right from the '50s w/ cantankerous waitresses included • at your own risk • some veggie • $3-8

Murphy's 997 Virginia Ave (at N Highland Ave) **404/872-0904** • 11am-10pm, till midnight Fri, from 8am wknds • popular • plenty veggie • best brunch in town • wheelchair access

North Park Square 23 N Park Sq (at Church St), Marietta **770/919-2693** • lunch Mon-Sat & dinner Tue-Th, lunch & dinner Fri-Sat, brunch 8am-4pm Sun • upscale wine bar & bistro • eclectic cuisine • $16-25

R Thomas 1812 Peachtree Rd NE **404/872-2942** • 24hrs • popular • beer/wine • healthy Californian/juice bar • plenty veggie • wheelchair access • $5-10

Swan Coach House 3130 Slaton Dr NW, Buckhead **404/261-0636** • lunch & dinner

Veni Vidi Vici 41 14th St **404/875-8424** • lunch Mon-Fri, dinner 5pm-11pm nightly • upscale Italian • some veggie • $14-25

Watershed 406 W Ponce de Leon, Decatur **404/378-4900** • 11am-10pm, clsd Sun • wine bar • also gift shop • owned by Emily Saliers of the Indigo Girls

ENTERTAINMENT & RECREATION

Alternative Talk WRFG 89.3FM **404/523-8989 (STATION #), 404/523-3471 (OFFICE #)** • 5pm-5:30pm Fri • radio program for Atlanta's African-American lgbt community

Atlanta Feminist Women's Chorus 770/438-5823

Funny That Way Theater Company 404/893-3344, 404/627-6672 • lgbt theater company • seasonal musicals • call for schedule

Lambda Radio WRFG 89.3 FM **404/523-8989** • 6pm Tue • lgbt radio program

Little 5 Points, Moreland & Euclid Ave S of Ponce de Leon Ave • hip & funky area w/ too many restaurants & shops to list

Martin Luther King, Jr. Center for Non-Violent Social Change 449 Auburn Ave NE **404/524-1956** • 9am-5pm daily • includes King's birth home, the church where he preached in the 60s & his gravesite

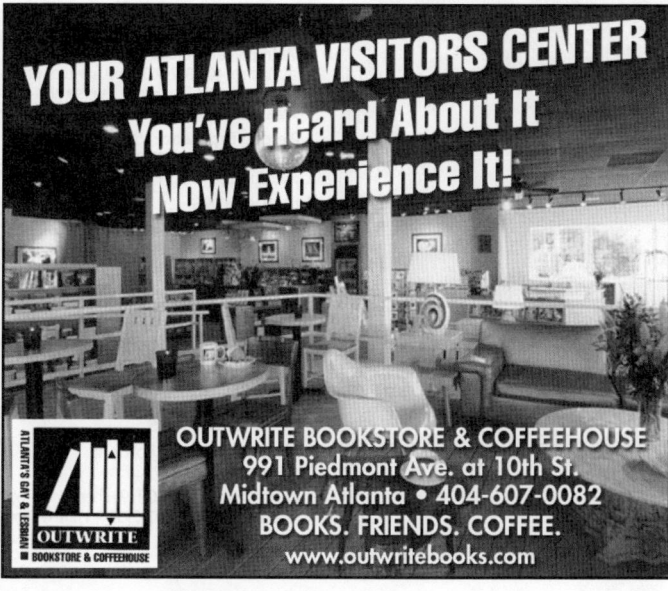

Georgia • USA

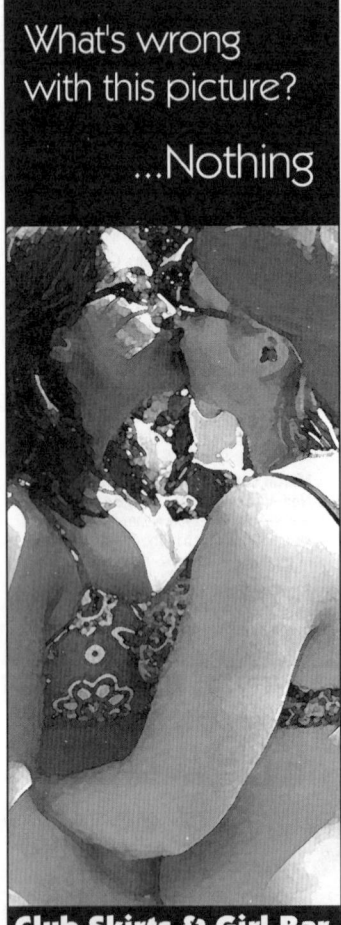

Club Skirts & Girl Bar Dinah Shore Weekend
March 28-31, 2002

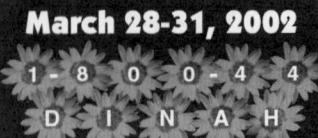

Bookstores

Brushstrokes 1510-J Piedmont Ave NE (nr Monroe) **404/876-6567** • 10am-10pm, till 11pm Fri-Sat • lgbt variety store

Charis Books & More 1189 Euclid Ave NE (at Moreland) **404/524-0304** • 10:30am-6:30pm, till 8pm Wed-Sat, noon-6pm Sun • feminist • wheelchair access

▲ **Outwrite Bookstore & Coffeehouse** 991 Piedmont Ave NE (at 10th) **404/607-0082** • 8am-11pm, till midnight Fri-Sat • lgbt • music • videos • gifts • cafe • wheelchair access

Retail Shops

The Boy Next Door 1447 Piedmont Ave NE (btwn 14th & Monroe) **404/873-2664** • 11am-7pm, noon-6pm Sun • clothing

Dress To Thrill 1544 Piedmont Ave Ste 310 (Ansley Mall) **404/872-6575** • club wear

The House of Warlords 2111 Faulkner Rd **404/315-9000, 877/993-7377 (ORDER LINE)** • 11am-7pm, till 9pm Sat, clsd Sun-Mon • custom leather

In the Moment 626 N Highland Ave (at North Ave) **404/817-7005** • noon-7pm, till 8pm Fri-Sat, till 6pm Sun • art • furnishings • gifts • gay-owned/ run

The Junkman's Daughter 464 Moreland Ave (at Euclid) **404/577-3188** • 11am-7pm, till 8pm Sat • hip stuff

Metropolitan Deluxe 1034 N Highland NE (at Virginia) **404/892-9337** • 10am-10pm, till 11pm Fri-Sat, till 7pm Sun • flowers • gifts • wheelchair access

Piercing Experience 1654 McLendon Ave NE (at Clifton) **404/378-9100** • noon-9pm, till 5pm Sun, clsd Mon

Publications

Clikque Magazine **404/817-3898** • glossy newsmagazine for lgbt African-Americans • some nat'l club listings

▲ **ETC Magazine** **404/888-0063** • weekly entertainment guide & news resource for lgbt Atlanta & Southeast

▲ **Southern Voice** **404/876-1819** • weekly lgbt newspaper for AL, FL (panhandle), GA, LA, MS, TN w/ resource listings

Spiritual Groups

All Saints MCC 2352 Bolton Rd **404/296-9822** • 11am Sun

Christ Covenant MCC 109 Hibernia Ave (off Adair), Decatur **404/373-2933** • 11am & 7pm Sun

Marietta • Georgia

Congregation Bet Haverim 701 W Howard Ave, Decatur **404/607-0054** • 8pm Fri • lgbt synagogue

First MCC of Atlanta 1379 Tullie Rd NE (at I-85 & N Druid Hills Rd) **404/325-4143** • 11am Sun, 7:30pm Wed • wheelchair access

Integrity Atlanta 2089 Ponce de Leon **770/642-3183** • call for schedule • lgbt Episcopalians

GYMS & HEALTH CLUBS

Boot Camp 1544 Piedmont Ave NE #105 (in Ansley Mall) **404/876-8686** • gay-friendly • full gym

The Fitness Factory 500 N Amsterdam (in 'Amsterdam Outlets') **404/815-7900** • popular • gay-friendly • full gym

Mid-City Fitness Center 2201 Faulkner Dr NE (at Cheshire Bridge) **404/321-6507** • lesbians/ gay men

SEX CLUBS

The Sanctuary 1417 Dutch Valley Pl **404/874-4838** • women's night last Fri only 7pm-1am • cover charge

EROTICA

Heaven 2628 Piedmont (at Sidney Marcus Blvd) **404/262-9113**

Inserection 505 Peachtree St NE **404/888-0878** • call for other locations

The Poster Hut/ Scream Boutique 2175 Cheshire Bridge Rd **404/633-7491** • clothing • toys

Southern Nights Videos 2205 Cheshire Br Rd (at Lenox Rd) **404/728-0701** • 24hrs

Starship 2275 Cheshire Bridge Rd **404/320-9101** • leather • novelties • 7 locations in Atlanta

Augusta

see also Aiken, South Carolina

NIGHTCLUBS

The Coliseum 1632 Walton Wy **706/733-2603** • 7pm-3am, clsd Sun • lesbians/ gay men • dancing/DJ • live shows

SPIRITUAL GROUPS

MCC Augusta 924 Green St **706/722-6454** • 11am & 7pm Sun

Columbus

SPIRITUAL GROUPS

Family of God MCC 1442 Double Churches Rd (at Unitarian Church) **706/321-9202** • 6:30pm Sun

Dahlonega

ACCOMMODATIONS

Above the Clouds **706/864-5211** • women only • mountainside B&B • full brkfst • hot tub • wheelchair access • lesbian-owned/ run • $95

Black Mountain Lodge 330 Black Mountain Lodge Dr **706/864-5542, 800/923-5530** • gay/ straight • resort • nature trails • swimming • hot tub • tennis • brkfst & dinner included • 1 hr from Atlanta • smokefree • $99-250

Swiftwaters Womanspace **706/864-3229, 888/808-5021** • women only • on scenic river • full brkfst • hot tub • seasonal • smokefree • deck • dogs ok • women-owned/ run • $69-95 (B&B)/ $10 (camping)

RESTAURANTS

Renee's Cafe 135 N Chestatee (at Hawkins) **706/864-6829** • dinner only • clsd Sun-Mon • gourmet • wine bar

Smith House 84 S Chestatee St **706/864-3566** • lunch & dinner • clsd Mon • family-style Southern

Dalton

RESTAURANTS

Dalton Depot 110 Depot St **706/226-3160** • 11am-10pm, clsd Sun

Decatur

see Atlanta

Lake Lanier

ENTERTAINMENT & RECREATION

Mile Marker 21 ('Cocktail Cove') • a rainbow rendezvous for the pleasure-boating crowd—look for the pink triangle

Macon

NIGHTCLUBS

Reactions 425 Cherry St (at MLK, Jr Blvd) **478/755-9383** • 8pm-2am, till 3am Fri & 4am Sat, clsd Sun-Tue • lesbians/ gay men • 4 bars • dancing/DJ • live shows • wheelchair access

Marietta

see Atlanta

Georgia • USA

Mountain City

ACCOMMODATIONS

The York House 416 York House Rd **706/746-2068, 800/231-9675** • gay-friendly • 1896 historic country inn • located btwn towns of Clayton & Dillard • full brkfst • smokefree • also mtg facilities • wheelchair access • $69-129

Norcross

INFO LINES & SERVICES

N85GLC Gay & Lesbian Connection 770/931-3860 • social events for singles & couples (in & around Gwinett County)

Savannah

INFO LINES & SERVICES

First City Network 307 E Harris St **912/236-CITY** • complete info & events line • social group • also newsletter

ACCOMMODATIONS

912 Barnard Victorian B&B 912 Barnard St **912/234-9121** • lesbians/ gay men • shared baths • fireplaces • period furnishings • smokefree • garden • sundeck • $99

Catherine Ward House Inn 118 E Waldburg St (at Abercorn) **912/234-8564, 800/327-4270** • gay/ straight • Victorian Italianate b&b • full brkfst • jacuzzi • gay-owned/ run • $139-300

Fox House Inn 536 E Harris St (btwn Price & E Broad) **912/644-7444** • gay/ straight • full brkfst • smokefree • gay-owned/ run • $135-175

Green Palm Inn 546 E President St (at Houston) **912/447-8901, 888/606-9510** • gay/ straight • full brkfst • smokefree • gay-owned/ run • $99-169

Paradise Inn 512 Tattnall St (at Gaston) **912/443-0200, 888/846-5093** • gay-friendly • newly renovated 1866 townhouse • afternoon cocktails • swimming • gay-owned/ run • $99-145

Park Avenue Manor 107–109 W Park Ave **912/233-0352** • lesbians/ gay men • 1889 Victorian B&B • full brkfst • smokefree • $95-150

BARS

Faces II 17 Lincoln St (at Bryan) **912/233-3520** • noon-3am • mostly gay men • neighborhood bar • also restaurant • patio • $8-10

The Loading Dock 641 Indian St **912/232-0068, 912/232-0130** • 5pm-3am, clsd Sun • mostly gay men • dancing/DJ • karaoke Th • women's night 6pm-9pm Fri • wheelchair access

Teasers 416 W Liberty St **912/238-4788** • noon-3am, till 2am Sun • lesbians/ gay men • restaurant • wheelchair accessible

NIGHTCLUBS

Club One 1 Jefferson St (at Bay) **912/232-0200** • 5pm-3am, till 2am Sun • lesbians/ gay men • dancing/DJ • food served • live shows Th-Sun • videos

Club Tru Colores 425 W Hwy 80, Garden City **912/966-1855** • 9pm-3am Th-Sat • mostly women • dancing • DJ Fri-Sat • drag shows Sat

RESTAURANTS

Barbary Coast Burritos 103 W Congress St (at Whitaker St) **912/447-1099** • 11am-9pm, till 4am Fri-Sat • gay-owned/ run • wheelchair access

Clary's Cafe 404 Abercorn (at Jones) **912/233-0402** • 7am-4pm, from 8am wknds • country cookin'

Good Eats 606 Abercorn **912/447-5444** • lunch Tue-Fri, dinner Fri-Sat, brunch wknds • eclectic cuisine • also Southern folk art gallery

ENTERTAINMENT & RECREATION

Savannah Walks, Inc **912/238-9255** • gay-friendly • variety of walking tours of downtown Savannah, from 'Historic Homes' to a 'Ye Old Pub Walk'

BOOKSTORES

Hannah Banana Books 4515 Habersham St (at 61st) **912/353-7447** • 9:30am-7pm, 1pm-5pm Sun • general w/ lgbt section • wheelchair access

Moon Dance 306 W St Julian St **912/236-9003** • 10am-6pm, till 7pm Fri-Sat, 11am-5pm Sun • lgbt books • metaphysical supplies • gifts

PUBLICATIONS

Network News PO Box 2442 31402 **912/236-2489** • monthly newsletter for Savannah & surrounding regions

Valdosta

RESTAURANTS

Warren's Blue Bayou 500 N Ashley St (at Central Ave) **229/253-0555** • 11am-close, clsd Sun-Mon • Cajun/ bbq • also bar • live blues/ jazz • gay-owned/ run

Hawaii (Big Island) • Hawaii

HAWAII

Please note that cities are grouped by islands:
Hawaii (Big Island)
Kauai
Maui
Molokai
Oahu (includes Honolulu)

STATEWIDE

ACCOMMODATIONS

Bed & Breakfast Honolulu (Statewide) 3242 Kaohinani Dr (at Pelekane), Oahu **808/595-7533, 800/288-4666** • clientele & ownership vary • represents 414 locations on all islands • $55-200

Pacific Ocean Holidays Oahu **808/923-2400, 800/735-6600** • Hawaii vacation packages

HAWAII (BIG ISLAND)

INFO LINES & SERVICES

Lezbrunch Brunch 808/328-2441 • 2nd Sun, also publish newsletter

PUBLICATIONS

Island Lesbian Connection 808/573-3077 • newsletter • covers all islands

Captain Cook

ACCOMMODATIONS

Affordable Hawaii at Pomaika'i (Lucky) Farm B&B 83-5465 Mamalahoa Hwy **808/328-2112, 800/325-6427** • gay/ straight • working, century-old Kona farm • full brkfst • smokefree • $55-65

Areca Palms Estate B&B 808/323-2276 • gay-friendly • full brkfst • gardens • jacuzzi • smokefree • $80-125

Hale Aloha Guest Ranch 84-4780 Mamalahoa Hwy **808/328-8955, 800/897-3188** • lesbians/ gay men • full brkfst • nudity • smokefree • kids ok • gay-owned/ run • $70-140

Horizon Guesthouse 808/328-2540, 888/328-8301 • gay/ straight • full brkfst • swimming • smokefree • wheelchair access • gay-owned/ run • $175-250

Kealakekua Bay B&B 808/328-8150, 800/328-8150 • gay/ straight • Mediterranean-style villa • smokefree • kids ok • also 2-bdrm guesthouse • $95-300

Rainbow Plantation B&B 808/323-2393, 800/494-2829 • gay-friendly • on coffee & macadamia nut plantation • kayak rentals • smokefree • $50-95

Hamakua Coast

ACCOMMODATIONS

Hawaiian Vacation Home 808/963-6789, 808/599-7763 • gay/ straight • 2 units in 1 guesthouse on 11 acres • smokefree • hot tub • ocean views • gay-owned/ run • $700-1000/ week

Hilo

ACCOMMODATIONS

Aloha Hawaii Healing Retreat 400 Hualani #325 (at Monono) **808/969-9622, 888/967-8622** • mostly women • 3-14 day all-inclusive holistic healing retreats • tennis • swimming • guided tours • gourmet meals • kids ok • wheelchair access • women-owned/ run • $200-300

The Butterfly Inn for Women 808/966-7936, 800/546-2442 • women only • hot tub • kitchens • smokefree • women-owned/ run • $55-65

Oceanfront B&B 1923 Kalanianaole St (3 miles from intersection of Hwys 11 & 19) **808/934-9004, 800/363-9524** • gay-friendly • 2 units • ocean views • hot tub • kids/ pets ok • wheelchair access • $110-140

Our Place Papaikou's B&B 3 Mamalahoa Hwy, Papaikou, Hilo **808/964-5250** • gay/ straight • 3-rm tropical healing retreat • 4 miles north of Hilo • organic meals avail • lesbian-owned/ run • $60-90

CAFES

Kope-Kope 1261 Kilauea Ave, Ste 220 (in Hilo Shopping Ctr) **808/933-1221** • espresso bar

RESTAURANTS

Cafe Pesto 308 Kamehameha Ave **808/969-6640** • lunch & dinner • Hawaiian/ Californian style bistro w/ pizzas, salads, pastas • on the waterfront • also at Kawaihae Shopping Center, 808/882-1071

ENTERTAINMENT & RECREATION

Richardson's Beach at end of Kalanianaole Ave (Keaukaha)

Hawaii • USA

BOOKSTORES

Borders 301 Maka'ala St (at Kanoelehua Hwy) **808/933-1410** • 9am-9pm, till 10pm Fri-Sat • lgbt section

PUBLICATIONS

Lesbian Brunch Bulletin 808/328-2441 • info on 2nd Sun brunch as well as calendar of events

Honaunau-Kona

ACCOMMODATIONS

Dragonfly Ranch Healing Arts Retreat 1 1/2 miles down City of Refuge Rd **808/328-2159, 800/487-2159** • gay/ straight • nr ancient sanctuary w/ friendly dolphins • hot tub • smokefree • $85-200

Honokaa

ACCOMMODATIONS

Paauhau Plantation Inn 808/775-7222, 800/789-7614 • gay-friendly • B&B • cottages built on ocean point • tennis • $100-200

Kailua-Kona

ACCOMMODATIONS

1st Class B&B Kona Hawaii 77–6504 Kilohana St **808/329-8778, 888/769-1110** • gay-friendly • private luxury suites • ocean views • full gourmet brkfst • smokefree • $115-130

▲ **Hale Kipa 'O Pele 808/329-8676, 800/528-2456** • lesbians/ gay men • plantation-style B&B • also bungalow w/ kitchen • hot tub • gay-owned/ run • $85-115

Pu'ukala Lodge 72-3998 E Mamalahoa Hwy (at Pu'ukala Rd) **808/325-1729, 888/325-1729** • lesbians/ gay men • on the slopes of Mt Hualalai • full brkfst • smokefree • gay-owned/ run • $70-140

Royal Kona Resort 75–5852 Ali'i Dr **808/329-3111, 800/222-5642** • gay-friendly • set atop dramatic lava outcroppings overlooking Kailua Bay • swimming • private beach • bar • live entertainment • wheelchair access • $99-250

Plantation-style home on a gated tropical estate

Expansive covered decks, ceilings fans & jacuzzi

Interior atrium with lava rock falls & koi pond

Only 5 miles to the beach and all activities

Large bungalow & kitchen

HALE KIPA 'O PELE

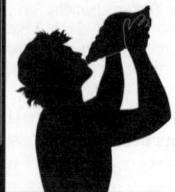

A distinctive Bed & Breakfast on the Big Island

PO Box 5252 Kailua-Kona, Hawaii 96745

1-800-LAVAGLO

www.gaystayhawaii.com

This secret little hideaway will offer you a quiet and memorable reminder that "Mother nature bats last."

You truly have reached...

The RAINBOW'S INN & ADVENTURES

B&B Hideaway or Vacation Rentals

Out & About's Editor's Choice Award 1998

Located on the Big Island of Hawaii.

Five Secluded Acres of Tropical Jungle with Hot Tub, Large Lanai for Breakfast or Lounging, Hawaiian Library, Video Library and Locally Handmade Gifts available to our Guests.

We are located just minutes from the ocean, volcanically heated baths and steam vents, black sand beach (clothing optional) and old style Pahoa Village (20 miles south of Hilo) with many fabulous restaurants.

Accommodations include 3 one-bedroom suites with private entrance, private bath, kitchenettes, and private parking. Also ask about our alternative accommodations, or transitional housing or extended stays, of rental homes & cottages in the area.

PO Box 983 • Pahoa, HI 96778
Phone: 808-965-9011
Email: yikesdykes@alohafun.com
www.alohafun.com

Also featuring:
- full service activities desk
- lei making & lauhala weaving
- discounted rental cars
- discounted inter-island airfare travel
- women's only work exchange program

Lesbian guided Rainbow Adventures

Custom made remote land & sea excursions include:
— the jungle with ancient Hawaiian ruins
— black sands beaches (clothing optional)
— remote snorkeling ponds w/coral gardens
— warm volcanically heated baths & steam vents
— kayak tours with the dolphins

Hawaii • USA

Bars

Mask Bar & Grill 75–5660 Kopiko St (at Cathedral Plaza) **808/329-8558** • 9am-2am • popular • lesbians/gay men • neighborhood bar • dancing/DJ • live shows • food served • karaoke • only lesbian/gay bar on the island

Restaurants

Cassandra's Greek Taverna 75-5719 Alii Dr **808/334-1066** • 11:30am-10pm, from 4:30pm wknds

Edward's at Kanaloa 78–261 Manukai St (at Kamehameha III) **808/322-1003** • 8am-2pm & 5pm-9pm • Mediterranean • full bar from 8am-9pm • gay-owned/run

Huggo's 75-5828 Kahakai Rd (on Kailua Bay) **808/329-1493** • lunch & dinner, from 5:30pm wknds • seafood & steak • karaoke • patio

Entertainment & Recreation

Eco-Adventures 75-5660 Palani Rd (in King Kamehameha's Kona Beach Hotel) **808/329-0076, 800/949-3483** • complete Hawaiian vacations (scuba, snorkeling, hiking)—any island, any adventure • gay-owned/run

Publications

Lesbian Brunch Bulletin **808/328-2441** • info on 2nd Sun brunch as well as calendar of events

Kamuela

Accommodations

Aaah, the Views! B&B Inn 66–1773 Alaneo (at Kawaihae Rd [Rte 19]) **808/885-3455** • gay-friendly • 15 min to world's best beaches • wheelchair access • women-owned/run • $65-110

Ho'onanea PO Box 6450 96743 **808/882-1177** • women only • private B&B • hot tub • swimming • kids ok • smokefree • wheelchair access • lesbian-owned/run • $80-90

Naalehu

Accommodations

Earthsong **808/929-8043** • mostly women • retreat center w/cottages on 3 acres • Hawaiian massage • Goddess temple • substance-free • lesbian-owned/run

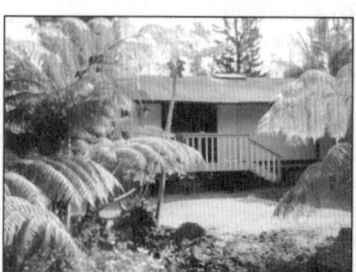
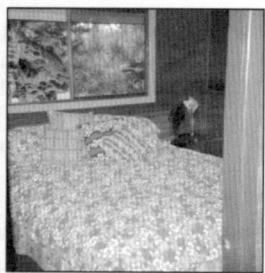

LEILANI HOUSE
Paradise with some personality!

Secluded 2 bedroom vacation rental on the eastside of the Big Island of Hawaii.
$450 week **$75**/night. **Call 415.370.2067** or e-mail **catdraper@earthlink.net**

www.leilanihouse.com

Ocean View

RESTAURANTS

Cafe Ohia 525 Lotus Blossom Ln #3 (nr South Point, about 1 hr S of Kailua-Kona) **808/929-8086** • 11am-8pm, from 8am wknds, till 4pm Sun, clsd Mon • Mexican • espresso drinks • lesbian-owned/ run

Pahoa

ACCOMMODATIONS

Kalani Oceanside Eco-Resort & Adventures 808/965-7828, 800/800-6886 • gay/ straight • coastal retreat & spa • on 113 acres • full brkfst • swimming • food served • wheelchair access • gay-owned/ run • $60-240 • $20-25 camping

▲ **Leilani House** 13-3458 Makamae St **415/452-8543, 415/370-2067** • gay/ straight • 2-bdrm house on secluded, tropical acre • kids ok • $75/ night, $425/ week

Pamalu—Hawaiian Country House **808/965-0830** • gay/ straight • country retreat on 5 secluded acres • swimming • nr hiking • snorkeling • warm ponds • kids ok • gay-owned/ run • $60-100

Rainbow Dreams Cottage 13-6412 Kalapana Beach Rd, Pahoa **808/936-9883, 808/969-9268** • gay/ straight • oceanfront cottage • kitchen • smokefree • kids ok • gay-owned/ run • $85

▲ **Rainbow's Inn & Adventures** **808/965-9011** • gay/ straight • B&B hideaway by the sea • swimming • hot tub • kids/ pets ok • smokefree • offers activity desk to plan your Hawaii experience • see also 'Rainbow Adventures' • lesbian-owned/ run • $75-95

RESTAURANTS

The Godmother 15269 Gov't Main Rd **808/965-0055** • 7am-9pm • Italian • patio • full bar • lesbian-owned/ run

ENTERTAINMENT & RECREATION

Kehena Beach off Hwy 137 (trailhead at 19-mile marker phone booth) • lava rock trail to clothing-optional black sand beach

Rainbow Adventures 808/965-9011 • custom-made remote land & sea excursions • lesbian-owned/ run

BOOKSTORES

Huna Ohana Main St **808/965-9661** • 8am-6pm, till 3pm Sun • metaphysical books • vegetarian cafe

Volcano Village

ACCOMMODATIONS

The Chalet Kilauea Collection 60 Keawe St **808/967-7786, 800/937-7786** • gay-friendly • full brkfst • hot tub • smokefree • $49-399

Hale Ohia Cottages 808/967-7986, 800/455-3803 • gay/ straight • hot tub • wheelchair access • gay-owned/ run • $85-150

KAUAI

INFO LINES & SERVICES

Black Bamboo Guest Services **808/328-9607, 800/527-7789** • lesbians/ gay men • free reservation service

Lambda Aloha 808/823-6248

Anahola

ACCOMMODATIONS

Mahina Kai Ocean Villa 4933 Aliomanu Rd **808/822-9451, 800/337-1134** • popular • gay/ straight • Japanese style farmhouse B&B overlooking Anahola Bay • swimming • hot tub • nudity • smokefree • gay-owned/ run • $135-225

Hanalei

NIGHTCLUBS

Tahiti Nui 5-5134 Kuhio Hwy (nr Hanalei Ctr) **808/826-6277** • 9pm-2am • gay-friendly • live music most nights • also restaurant from 7am-3pm, then 5pm-10pm • Thai, Vietnamese & Chinese • luaus Wed • karaoke • wheelchair access

Kapaa

ACCOMMODATIONS

Aloha Dude Vacation Rentals 4442 Mahaka Rd **808/822-8886** • gay/ straight • guesthouse & apt • pets ok • smokefree • gay-owned/ run • $75-150

Aloha Kauai B&B 156 Lihau St **808/822-6966, 800/262-4652** • lesbians/ gay men • full brkfst • swimming • smokefree • wheelchair access • gay-owned/ run • $65-90

Kauai Coconut Beach Resort 484 Kuhio Hwy **808/822-3455, 800/222-5642** • gay-friendly • newly redecorated oceanfront resort • swimming • tennis • nightly torchlighting ceremony & luau • kids ok • wheelchair access • $165-500

Hawaii • USA

Kauai Kualapa Cottage 1471 Kualapa Pl **808/822-1626** • gay-friendly • private cottage overlooking hidden valley • 10 minutes to beaches • kitchen • $85–95

Kauai Waterfall B&B 5783 Haaheo St **808/823-9533, 800/996-9533** • lesbians/gay men • swimming • hot tub • overlooking Wailua River State Park Waterfall • gay-owned/run • $90-100

Mahina's Guest House 4433 Panihi Rd **808/823-9364** • women-only beach house • private & hostel-style accommodations • lesbian-owned • $30-50 per person

Mohala Ke Ola B&B Retreat 5663 Ohelo Rd (at Kuamoo Rd/ Hwy 580) **808/823-6398, 888/465-2824** • gay-friendly • swimming • jacuzzi • gay-owned/run • $75-105

Royal Drive Cottages 147 Royal Dr **808/822-2321** • gay/ straight • private garden cottages w/ kitchenettes • nr beach • smokefree • wheelchair access • gay-owned/run • $80-130

Villa Aloha **808/823-9606, 800/830-3403 x39** • gay/ straight • modern 2-story house • lush tropical garden, waterfalls & water garden • $150

Restaurants

A Pacific Cafe 4831 Kuhio Hwy #200 **808/822-0013** • dinner only • gourmet • reservations req'd

Bull Shed 796 Kuhio Hwy **808/822-3791** • 5:30pm-10pm • steak & seafood • full bar

Eggbert's 4–484 Kuhio Hwy (in Coconut Plantation Marketplace) **808/822-3787** • 7am-3pm & 5pm-9pm • popular for brkfast • gay-owned/ run

Me Ma's Thai 4361 Kuhio Hwy (in shopping ctr) **808/823-0899** • lunch Mon-Fri, dinner nightly

Kilauea

Accommodations

Kai Mana **808/828-1280, 800/837-1782** • gay-friendly • Shakti Gawain's paradise home set on a cliff surrounded by ocean & mountains • cottages • hot tub • kitchens • smokefree • $75-150

Kalihiwai Jungle Home **808/828-1626** • gay/ straight • clifftop hideaway overlooking jungle & waterfalls • nr beaches • snorkeling equipment & boogie boards • fireplace • nudity • smokefree • kids ok • gay-owned/ run • $135-150

Ku'oko'a at Plumeria Moon **808/828-0228, 888/8-KUOKOA** • lesbians/ gay men • upscale 3-acre Hawaiian hideaway overlooking ocean • private path to secluded beach • swimming • jacuzzi • smokefree • lesbian-owned/ run

Cafes

Mango Mama's Fruitstand Cafe 4640 Hookui Rd (at Kuhio Hwy) **808/828-1020** • 7:30am-6pm • natural foods, fruit smoothies & more

Lihue

Bookstores

Borders Bookstore & Cafe 4303 Nawiliwili Rd **808/246-0862** • 8:30am-10pm, till 11pm Fri-Sat, till 8pm Sun • large lgbt section

Poipu Beach

Accommodations

Poipu Plantation Resort 1792 Pe'e Rd, Koloa **808/742-6757, 800/634-0263** • gay/ straight • rooms & cottages • full brkfst • hot tub • nr beach • kids ok • $85-165

Puunene

Restaurants

Roy's Bar & Grill 2360 Kiahuna Plantation Dr **808/742-5000** • 5:30pm-9:30pm

Wailua

Cafes

Caffe Coco 4–369 Kuhio Hwy **808/822-7990** • 9am-9pm, clsd Mon • gay friendly • art gallery • live music nightly • patio

Maui

Info Lines & Services

Both Sides Now 808/244-4566 • recorded events info

▲ **Forever Maui Productions** 866/879-1357 • lesbians/ gay men • activities, accommodations & commitment ceremonies

Maui Dreamtime Weddings 888/424-5550 • religious or non-religious commitment ceremonies in secluded Maui locations

Royal Hawaiian Weddings 800/659-1866 • specializes in scenic gay weddings • women-owned/ run

Women's Information Line 808/573-3077 • covers entire island

Maui • Hawaii

Get Lei'd On Maui!
Aloha

Welcome to Forever Maui Productions, a gay-owned & operated company specializing in Maui's finest:

Accommodations
Activities
Commitment Ceremonies

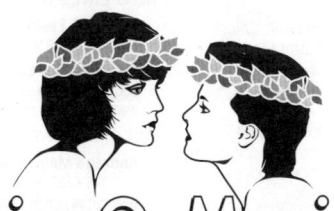

LesbianOnMaui.com™

FOREVER MAUI PRODUCTIONS, LLC
Toll Free: 1-866-866-1357
Phone: 808-875-4483
Fax: 808-879-2913
Email: aloha@forevermaui.com

Hawaii • USA

ACCOMMODATIONS

Eva Villa 815 Kumulani Dr, Kihei, Maui **808/874-6407, 800/884-1845** • gay-friendly • B&B • close to Wailea beaches • hot tub • swimming • kids over 12yrs ok • wheelchair access • $120-130

PUBLICATIONS

Island Lesbian Connection 808/573-3077 • newsletter • covers all islands

Out In Maui 808/244-4566 (24HR INFO) • monthly LGBT newspaper • free at locations throughout HI

SPIRITUAL GROUPS

Dignity Maui 808/874-3950 • contact Ron

Haiku

ACCOMMODATIONS

Golden Bamboo Ranch 422 Kaupakalua Rd (at Holokai) **808/572-7824, 800/344-1238** • gay/straight • cottages & suites on 7-acre estate • panoramic ocean views • smokefree • wheelchair access • $77-105

Hale Huelo B&B Door of Faith Church Rd, Huelo (at Hana Hwy) **808/572-8669** • gay/straight • panoramic ocean views

Halfway to Hana House 101 W Waipio Rd **808/572-1176** • gay-friendly • private guest studio w/ sunrise ocean view • smokefree • nr waterfall & natural pool • woman-owned/run • $70-85

Huelo Point Flower Farm Huelo Church Rd **808/572-1850** • gay/straight • vacation rentals • oceanfront estate & organic farm • swimming • 3 hot tubs • gay-owned/run • $145-425

Kailua Maui Gardens 808/572-9726, 800/258-8588 • gay/straight • also cottages • hot tub • swimming • nudity • kids ok • gay-owned/run • $70-200

Hana

ACCOMMODATIONS

Hana Accommodations PO Box 564 96713 **808/248-7868, 800/228-4262** • gay/straight • studios & tropical cottages • kids ok • gay-owned/run • $72-150

Hana Alii Holidays 808/248-7742, 800/548-0478 • reservations service

Heavenly Flora 70 Maia Rd 96713 **808/248-8680** • gay-friendly • B&B on 5-acre tropical flower farm • panoramic ocean views • swimming • gay-owned/run • $95-175

Na Pualani 'Ohana 808/248-8935 & 248-7092, 800/628-7092 • gay/straight • 2 full units • ocean & mtn views • non-smoking rooms available • kids/pets ok • lanai • wheelchair access • gay-owned/run

Huelo

ACCOMMODATIONS

Cliff's Edge 808/572-4530 • gay-friendly • seasonal • $100-115

Triple Lei B&B/ Huelo Point Lookout **808/573-0914** • gay-friendly • private cottages • full kitchens • swimming • hot tub • $145-450

Kaanapali

ACCOMMODATIONS

The Royal Lahaina Resort 2780 Kekaa Dr **808/661-3611, 800/222-5642** • gay-friendly • full service resort • restaurants • swimming • wheelchair access • $215-1,500

Kahului

INFO LINES & SERVICES

AA Gay & Lesbian 101 W Kam Ave (at Kahului Union Church) **808/874-3589** • 6:30pm Wed

Kihei

INFO LINES & SERVICES

AA Gay & Lesbian Kalama Park South Pavilion **808/874-3589** • 7:30am Sun

Gay Hawaiian Excursions 808/891-8603, 800/311-4460 • extensive activities • tours & travel arrangements • commitment ceremonies

ACCOMMODATIONS

Andrea's Maui Condos 800/289-1522, 877/445-5885 • gay/straight • 1 & 2-bdrm beachfront condos • swimming • nr outdoor recreation • smokefree • wheelchair access • lesbian-owned/run • $79-300

▲ **Anfora's Dreams** 323/467-2991, 800/788-5046 • gay/straight • rental condo nr ocean • hot tub • swimming • gay-owned/run • $79-135

Hale Kumulani 808/891-0425 • gay-friendly • private cottage w/ gardens • nr beaches • smokefree • $125

Hale Makaleka Women's B&B 539 Kupulau Drive **808/879-2971** • women only • full brkfst • smokefree • lesbian-owned/run • $65

Maui • Hawaii

Jack & Tom's Maui Condos/ Maui Suncoast Realty 808/874-1048, 800/800-8608 • gay/ straight • fully equipped condos & apts • non-smoking rooms available • gay-owned/ run • $50-190

Ko'a Kai Rentals 1993 S Kihei Rd #401 808/879-6058, 800/399-6058 x33 • gay/ straight • swimming • smokefree • gay-owned/ run • $45/ night, $275/ week

Koa Lagoon 800 S Kihei Rd 808/879-3002, 800/367-8030 • gay-friendly • oceanfront suites • swimming • wheelchair access • $90-140

Two Mermaids on the Sunnyside of Maui B&B 2840 Umalu Pl (at Ohina), Kihei 808/874-8687, 800/598-9550 • gay/ straight • jacuzzi • swimming • nr beach • women-owned/ run • $85-125

Wailana Inn 14 Wailana Pl 808/874-3131, 800/399-3885 • gay/ straight • studios w/ kitchens • rooftop hot tub • nr beach • gay-owned/ run • $75-100

NIGHTCLUBS

Aloha Lounge 1345 Pillani Hwy (at Lipoa) 808/879-0515 • 9pm-2am Th only • lesbians/ gay men • dancing/DJ

Odyssey Nights at Hapa's Brew Haus 41 E Lipoa St (in Lipoa Ctr) 808/879-9001 • 10pm-2am • lesbians/ gay men • dancing/DJ Tue

Rainbow Nights at Cafe Navaca 1945 S Kihei Rd 808/879-0717 • 10pm-2am Fri • lesbians/ gay men • dancing/DJ

CAFES

Stella Blues 1215 S Kihei Rd 808/874-3779 • 8am-9pm • deli

EROTICA

The Love Shack 1794 S Kihei Rd (across from Tony Roma's) 808/875-0303 • 9am-9pm • lingerie & gifts

Kula

ACCOMMODATIONS

Camp Kula Maui B&B 808/876-0000 • popular • lesbians/ gay men • on the slopes of Mt Haleakala • HIV+ welcome • wheelchair access • $35-78

Anfora's Dreams
MAUI CONDOS

Affordable, completely furnished deluxe units from singles to large homes with your total comfort in mind...
• Pool • Jacuzzi • Beach Access •
Starting from $79.00 a day

The Best Deal On Maui!
(800) 788-5046 or **(323) 467-2991**

PO Box 74030, Los Angeles, CA 90004
mauicondo@earthlink.net
www.home.earthlink.net/~mauicondo

Hawaii • USA

Lahaina

Restaurants

Lahaina Coolers 180 Dickenson St **808/661–7082** • 8am-2am • international • patio • women-owned/ run

Retail Shops

Skin Deep Tattoo 626 Front St (across from the Banyan Tree) **808/661–8531** • 10am-10pm

Makawao

Accommodations

Hale Ho'okipa Inn B&B 32 Pakani Pl **808/572–6698** • gay-friendly • restored Hawaiian plantation home • smokefree • wheelchair access • woman-owned • $75+

I Ke Kala 3675 Brewer, Makawao **808/572–0664, 877/787–4440** • mostly women • also holistic healing & tour services • wheelchair access • lesbian-owned/ run • $55-65

Restaurants

Cassanova Restaurant & Deli 1188 Makawao Ave **808/572–0220** • lunch & dinner • Italian • full bar till 2am • gay-friendly • live music & shows Wed-Sat

Makena

Entertainment & Recreation

Little Beach at Makena • lesbians/ gay men • Pilani Hwy south to Wailea • right at Wailea Ike Dr • left on Wailea Alanui Dr to public beach • take trail up hill at end of beach

Pukalani

Accommodations

Heavenly Gate Vacation Rental 276 Hiwalani Loop (at Iolani St) **808/572–0321** • gay/ straight • bungalow home • tropical gardens • kids ok • smokefree • gay-owned/ run • $100

Wailea

Accommodations

The Palms at Wailea 3200 Wailea Alanui Drive Unit #2203 **808/572–4530** • condo • nr beach • swimming • smokefree • $175

Cafes

Maui Rainbow Factory nr Little Beach at Makena (1 mi S of Maui Prince Hotel) • shave ice • fresh fruit smoothies • vegetarian food • gay-owned/ run

Wailuku

Info Lines & Services

"Bridges" Youth Group **808/242–6821, 808/665–5990** • lgbt youth group, meets Wed

Spiritual Groups

Aloha MCC 2371 Vineyard St (at Iao Congregational Church) **808/879–1953** • 11:30 1st & 3rd Sun

Erotica

Paradise Spice 1325 Lower Main Suite 202 **808/249–2449** • toys, magazines, dvds

MOLOKAI

Kaunakakai

Accommodations

Molokai Beachfront Escapes PO Box 564, Hana 96713 **808/248–7868, 800/228–4262** • gay-friendly • beachfront units on the serene island of Molokai • swimming • gay-owned/ run • $89-109

OAHU

Info Lines & Services

Global Aloha Weddings **808/922–5176, 800/982–5176** • lgbt commitment ceremonies

Lesbian Info Line **808/531–4140** • recording of upcoming events

Publications

Island Lesbian Connection **808/573–3077** • newsletter • covers all islands

Odyssey Magazine Hawaii **808/955–5959** • everything you need to know about gay Hawaii

Pocket Guide to Hawaii PO Box 88245 96830-8245 **808/923–2400** • distributed free in the islands or $5 by mail order

Erotica

Velvet Video 2155 Lau'ula St, Waikiki, 2nd floor (above In Between) **808/924–0868** • 10am -5pm • videos for sale & rent • preview booths • toys

Aiea

Erotica

C 'n' N Liquor Aiea Shopping Ctr **808/487–2944**

Honolulu

INFO LINES & SERVICES

Always Yours by The Wedding Connection 808/923-9734 • lgbt commitment ceremonies

The Center 2424 S Beretania (btwn Isenberg & University) **808/951-7000** • 10am-7pm, clsd Sun • lesbian support group 7:30pm Wed • lgbt resource center • library • church • home of Marriage Project Hawaii

Gay/ Lesbian AA 277 Ohua (at Waikiki Health Ctr) **808/946-1438** • 8pm daily

Hawaii Transgendered Outreach 808/923-4270 • social/ support mtgs every other Fri 6:30pm

Hawaii Visitors Bureau 2270 Kalakaua Ave #801 **808/923-1811, 1-800/464-2924**

Leis of Hawaii 888/534-7644 • personalized Hawaiian greeting service complete w/ fresh flower leis

ACCOMMODATIONS

Astin Waikiki Beach Hotel 2570 Kalakaua Ave (at Paoakalani Ave) **808/922-2511, 800/877-7666** • gay-friendly • ocean views • restaurant • live entertainment • swimming • wheelchair access • $99-559

Breakers Hotel 250 Beachwalk **808/923-3181, 800/426-0494** • gay-friendly • swimming • also bar & grill • $88-146

The Cabana at Waikiki 2551 Cartwright Rd (off Kapahulu Ave) **808/926-5555, 877/902-2121** • popular • mostly gay men • 1-bdrm suites w/ kitchens & lanais • hot tub • gay-owned/ run • $99-175

The Coconut Plaza Hotel 450 Lewers St, Waikiki (at Ala Wai) **808/923-8828** • gay-friendly • swimming • kitchenettes • nr beach • wheelchair access • $70-175

Hale Plumeria 3044 Hollinger St **808/732-7719** • apt • 4 blks to Waikiki Beach • $45

Jerry's Vacation Condo Waikiki **808/737-1281, 888/261-7092** • gay/ straight • 1/2 blk from gay beach • $500+/ week

Outrigger Hotels & Resorts 808/921-6600, 800/688-7444 • gay-friendly

Queen's Surf Vacation Rentals 134 Kapahulu (at Lemon Rd, in Waikiki Grand Hotel) **808/732-4368, 888/336-4368** • gay/ straight • swimming • ocean views • gay-owned/ run • $75-145

Waikiki GLBT Vacation Rentals 1580 Makaloa St, Ste 770 **808/922-1659, 800/543-5663** • gay-friendly • reservation service • ask for Walt Flood • smokefree • $55-200

Waikiki Joy Hotel 320 Lewers St **808/923-2300, 800/733-5569** • gay-friendly • boutique hotel • swimming • jacuzzis • nr beach • cafe • also bar • karaoke • $125-285

Honolulu

WHERE THE GIRLS ARE: Where else? On the beach. Or cruising Kuhio Ave.

LGBT PRIDE: June. 808/951-7000 (GLCC).

ANNUAL EVENTS: April - Merrie Monarch Festival.
May - Golden Week, celebration of Japanese culture.
September - Aloha Week.

CITY INFO: 808/923-1811, web: www.gohawaii.com.

ATTRACTIONS: Bishop Museum 808/848-4174.
Foster Botanical Gardens.
Hanauma Bay.
Honolulu Academy of Arts 808/532-8741.
Polynesian Cultural Center.
Waimea Falls Park.

BEST VIEW: Helicopter tour.

WEATHER: Usually paradise perfect, but humid. It rarely gets hotter than the upper 80°s.

TRANSIT: Charley's 808/955-2211.
The Bus 808/848-5555.

Hawaii • USA

Waikiki Parkside Hotel 1850 Ala Moana Blvd (at Kalai & Ena) **808/955-1567, 800/237-9666** • gay-friendly • swimming • kids ok • smokefree • wheelchair access • $125-275

Waikiki Vacation Studio Condo 134 Kapahulu Ave #722 **808/737-1281, 888/261-7092** • gay/ straight • self-catering condo • nr beach • swimming • smokefree • gay-owned/ run • 3-night minimum stay • $85-100/ night, $500-750/ week

Bars

Angles 2256 Kuhio Ave, 2nd flr, Waikiki (at Seaside) **808/926-9766, 808/923-1130 (INFOLINE)** • 10am-2am • lesbians/ gay men • neighborhood bar • dancing/DJ Wed-Sun • more women Sun • live shows • videos • theme nights • free Internet access

Hula's Bar & Lei Stand 134 Kapahulu Ave (2nd flr of Waikiki Grand Hotel) **808/923-0669** • 10am-2am • popular • lesbians/ gay men • dancing/DJ • theme nights • transgender-friendly • food served • live shows

In Between 2155 Lau'ula St, Waikiki (off Lewers, across from 'Planet Hollywood') **808/926-7060** • 2pm-2am • gay/ straight • neighborhood bar • karaoke

Nightclubs

Fusion Waikiki 2260 Kuhio Ave, upstairs (at Seaside) **808/924-2422** • 9pm-4am, from 8pm Fri-Sat, from 10pm Sun • popular • mostly gay men • dancing/DJ • alternative • transgender-friendly • live shows • karaoke

Cafes

Caffe Giovannini 1888 Kalakaua Ave, Waikiki (across from the 'Wave') **808/979-2299** • 8am-midnight • great coffee • sandwiches & desserts • patio • gay-owned/ run

Mocha Java Cafe 1200 Ala Moana Blvd (in Ward Ctr) **808/591-9023** • 8am-9pm, till 5pm Sun • plenty veggie

Restaurants

A Pacific Cafe 1200 Ala Moana Blvd (in Ward Ctr) **808/593-0035** • dinner nightly • Pacific Rim & Mediterranean • reservations req'd • wheelchair access

Café Che Pasta 1001 Bishop St (enter off Alakea St) **808/524-0004, 808/531-4140 (INFO LINE)** • 11am-8pm, from 5pm Sat, clsd Sun • full bar • 'Black Garter Cafe' for women 9pm-2am Fri • daning/ DJ • karaoke 7pm-2am Wed

Cafe Sistina 1314 S King St **808/596-0061** • lunch Mon-Fri, dinner nightly • northern Italian • some veggie • full bar • wheelchair access • $9-16

Eggs n' Things 1911-B Kalakaua Ave **808/949-0820** • 11pm-2pm • diner • popular after-hours

Indigo 1121 Nu'uanu Ave **808/521-2900** • lunch Tue-Fri, dinner Tue-Sat • Eurasian • live jazz Fri-Sat

Keo's Thai 2028 Kuhio Ave **808/951-9355** • 7:30pm-11pm • popular • reservations advised

La Cucaracha 102 Nahua Rd (at Kuhio Ave) **808/922-2288** • 2pm-2am • Mexican • full bar

Lewers St. Steak & Seafood 412 Lewers St (at the Marc Suites) **808/926-1881** • brkst & dinner • full bar • wheelchair access

Singha Thai 1910 Ala Moana Blvd **808/941-2898** • 4pm-11pm • live shows

Sunset Terrace 2335 Kalakaua Ave (on 2nd Fl of Outrigger Waikiki on the Beach Hotel) **808/971-3595** • 7am-9:30pm • Asian-Pacific seafood & American • live entertainment

Entertainment & Recreation

Honolulu Gay/ Lesbian Cultural Foundation 1877 Kalakaua Ave **808/941-0424 x18** • annual film festival Memorial Day wknd • art exhibits • concerts • plays • call for events

LikeHike **808/455-8193** • gay hiking tours every other Sun • also gay kayaking trips • call for info & locations

Rainbow Charters PO Box 75422, Honolulu 96836 **808/943-2628** • whale watching • snorkeling • sunset cocktails • commitment ceremonies • lesbian-owned/ run

Taking the Plunge **808/922-2600, 888/922-3483** • various diving trips • free hotel pickup

Retail Shops

Eighty Percent Straight 1917 Kalakaua Ave, Waikiki (at Ala Moana) **808/923-9996** • 10am-10pm, till 11pm Fri-Sat • lgbt clothing • books • videos • cards • toys • also 2139 Kuhio Ave, 808/923-4222

Publications

DaKine Magazine **808/923-7378** • lgbt newsmagazine for all islands • club & nightlife listings • monthly

Odyssey Magazine Hawaii **808/955-5959** • everything you need to know about gay Hawaii

Pocket Guide to Hawaii **808/923-2400** • distributed free in the islands or $5 by mail order

Spiritual Groups

Dignity Honolulu 539 Kapahulu Ave (at St Mark's Church) **808/536-5536** • 7:30pm Sun

Oahu • Hawaii

Reply **Forward** **Delete**

```
Date: Mon, Dec 10, 2001 11:11:59
From: Girl-on-the-Go
To: Editor@Damron.com
Subject: Honolulu
```

> The city of Honolulu suffers from a bad case of mistaken identity. The highrise tourist hotels of Waikiki, six miles away, overshadow the downtown area of Honolulu, the center of the state government that teems with a vibrant culture all its own. Chinatown, a designated National Historic Landmark, offers a living history of Asian immigration to Hawaii, with street vendors, grocers, herbalists, and acupuncture clinics. Authentic Chinese, Vietnamese, and Filipino restaurants cram the area north of downtown, off of North King Street.

> On the other side of downtown, on South King Street, sits 'Iolani Palace, the heart and soul of modern Hawaiian history. The graceful structure served as a prison for Queen Lili'uokalani, Hawaii's last reigning monarch, when she was placed under house arrest by armed US forces intent on her signing over the nation's sovereignty. Don't miss the Hawaii Maritime Center next door for a glance back at the history of the islands. If you're staying in Waikiki, you can catch a trolley downtown from any of the main streets, saving yourself a mountain of parking headaches.

> Waikiki sits on the southwest corner of Oahu and offers a mind-boggling number of hotels, restaurants, and shops that are just waiting to consume your tourist dollars. Campy though it is, enjoy the postcard pleasure of a mai tai on the patio of the magnificently restored Sheraton Moana Surfrider while the sun sets over the Pacific. **Hula's**, a neighborhood bar with a homey feel, is the most welcoming of the local bars. On Sundays, **Angles** puts on a women's night. If you want to shake it with the boys, you can dance the night away at **Fusion.** Call the **Lesbian Info Line** for the latest women's events.

> **Odyssey Magazine** gives boys the dirt on the club scene. Occasionally, they have something for women. And **Island Lesbian Connection** lists events of interest to lesbians throughout the island chain. You can pick either of these up, along with a good book to read on the beach, at the LGBT shop **Eighty Percent Straight.**

> If you'd like to see the Big Island from offshore, give lesbian-owned **Rainbow Charters** a call. They offer whale watching cruises, snorkeling, and commitment ceremonies.

Hawaii/ Idaho • USA

Interweave 808/623-4726 • Unitarian Universalists • call for mtg times

Ke Anuenue O Ke Aloha MCC 277 Ohua St (at Waikiki Health Ctr) **808/924-3060** • 7pm Sun

Our Family Christian Church 1666 Mott–Smith Dr (at Makiki, in RLDS Church) **808/951-6670** • 5:30pm Sun

Unity Church of Hawaii 3608 Diamond Head Cir (at Montserrat) **808/735-4436** • 7:30am, 9am & 11am Sun • wheelchair access

Erotica

Diamond Head Video 870 Kapahulu Ave (near 'Genki Sushi') **808/735-6066**

Kailua

Accommodations

Hale Pueo 1142 Koohoo Pl (at A'alapapa) **808/262-2820, 888/712-5698** • gay/ straight • 3 units w/ kitchens • ocean views • kids ok • smokefree • lesbian-owned/ run • $100-200

Tropic Paradise 43 Laiki Pl **808/381-4503, 888/362-4488** • gay/ straight • B&B inn, also suites and home for rent • serene & beautiful • swimming • jacuzzi • kids ok • gay-owned/ run

Windward Coast

Accommodations

Ali'i Bluffs Windward B&B 46–251 Ikiiki St, Kane'ohe **808/235-1124, 800/235-1151** • gay/ straight • swimming • gay-owned/ run • $60–75

IDAHO

Statewide

Publications

Diversity Newsmagazine 208/336-3870 #2 • statewide lgbt newspaper • monthly

Boise

Info Lines & Services

AA Gay/ Lesbian 23rd & Woodlawn (at First Congregational Church) **208/344-6611** • 8pm Sun & Tue

The Community Center 919–A N 27th St (at Jordan) **208/336-3870, 208/939-1629** • 6:30pm-9pm Tue, 6pm-9pm Wed, 10am-2pm wknds, Youth Alliance 7pm Fri • 24hr touchtone info line

Women's Night 208/344-4295, 208/336-8471 • events by women for women • dances • camp-outs • music • comedy • theater

Bars

The Locker Room 1108 Front St (at 11th) **208/333-0074** • 4pm-close, 3pm-2am wknds, fetish night 1st Fri • mostly gay men • neighborhood bar • patio

Nightclubs

The Balcony Club 180 N 8th St #224 (at Idaho) **208/336-1313** • 2pm-2am • gay/ straight • popular • dancing/DJ • theme parties • wheelchair access • gay-owned/ run

Emerald City Club 415 S 9th (at Myrtle) **208/342-5446** • 10am-2am • lesbians/ gay men • dancing/DJ from 10pm • live shows • women-owned/ run

Cafes

Flying M Coffeehouse 500 W Idaho (at 5th St) **208/345-4320** • 6:30am-10pm, till 11pm Fri-Sat, 7:30am-6pm Sun • food served • some veggie & vegan • live shows wknds

Restaurants

The Klatsch 409 S 8th (across from 8th St Marketplace) **208/345-0452** • brkfst, lunch & dinner, till 3pm Sun-Mon • organic & plenty veggie • live music eves & wknds • beer/ wine • also full juice & coffee/ espresso bar

Entertainment & Recreation

The Boise Gay Couples Supper Club 208/853-1110 • 6pm on 3rd Sat • call for info

Flicks & Rick's Cafe American 646 Fulton St **208/342-4288** • opens 4pm, from noon wknds • 4 movie theaters • multiracial • live shows • food served • beer/ wine • patio • wheelchair access

Idaho Pride Center 6023 Clinton **208/440-0325, 800/677-2437** • 5pm-9:30pm, till midnight Fri-Sat, noon-6pm Sun • many social and educational activities • call for info

Treasure Valley Singles Supper Club 208/571-9096 • call for info

Triangle Connection 208/336-3870 • 24hr activities hotline • meet at the Flicks 7pm 2nd Th

Bookstores

Crone's Cupboard 3601 Overland Rd **208/333-0831** • 10am-7pm, 11am-5pm Sun • feminist/ lesbian books & art

Alton • Illinois

RETAIL SHOPS

The Edge 1101 W Idaho St (at 11th)
208/344-5383 • 6:30am-10pm, 9am-7pm Sun
• gifts • lgbt magazines • also cafe

Form 113 N 11th St (btwn W Idaho & Main)
208/336-5034 • 11am-7pm, till 6pm Sat, noon-5pm Sun • sassy stuff • wheelchair access

SPIRITUAL GROUPS

Treasure Valley MCC 408 N Garden St (at Morris Hill) 208/342-6764 • 4:45pm Sun

EROTICA

Pleasure Boutique 424 N Orchard
208/433-1161 • toys, video rental and sales

Coeur D'Alene

see also Spokane, Washington

ACCOMMODATIONS

The Clark House on Hayden Lake 5250 E Hayden Lake Rd, Hayden Lake 208/772-3470, 800/765-4593 • popular • gay-friendly • mansion on a wooded 12-acre estate • full brkfst • also fine dining • hot tub • smokefree • $100-225

BARS

Mik-N-Mak's 406 N 4th (at Wallace)
208/667-4858 • noon-2am, 2pm-2am Mon-Wed • lesbians/ gay men • neighborhood bar • dancing/DJ • karaoke • live shows

Ketchum

RETAIL SHOPS

Davis 320 Leadville Ave N (at 4th Ave)
208/725-0180 • 11am-6pm

Lava Hot Springs

see also Pocatello

ACCOMMODATIONS

Lava Hot Springs Inn 208/776-5830 • gay-friendly • full brkfst • mineral pools • kids/ pets ok • smokefree • wheelchair access • $69-195

BOOKSTORES

Aura Soma Lava 97 N 2nd St E (at Portneuf River Rd) 208/776-5800, 800/757-1233 • seasonal • 11am-5pm • metaphysical & lgbt books

Moscow

INFO LINES & SERVICES

University of Idaho Queer Students Association 208/885-2691 • seasonal • 7pm Tue at Women's Center

Women's Center (Univ of Idaho) corner of Idaho & Line Sts 208/885-6616 • library & resources • support • limited outreach • call first

BOOKSTORES

Bookpeople 521 S Main (btwn 5th & 6th)
208/882-7957 • 9am-8pm • general

Pocatello

NIGHTCLUBS

Charleys 331 E Center 208/232-9606 • 5pm-2am, 8pm-midnight Sun, clsd Mon • lesbians/ gay men • dancing/DJ • live shows • wheelchair access

CAFES

Main St Coffee & News 234 N Main (btwn Lander & Clark) 208/234-9834 • 7am-8pm, till 4pm Sat, 9am-4pm Sun

EROTICA

The Silver Fox 143 S 2nd St (at Center)
208/234-2477

Stanley

ACCOMMODATIONS

Las Tejanas B&B Hwy 75, Lower Stanley
208 /376-6077, 208/774-3301 • May-Sept • gay-friendly • full brkfst • natural hot tub • in the Sawtooth Mtns • nr outdoor recreation • women-owned/ run • $60-75

ILLINOIS

Statewide

INFO LINES & SERVICES

Illinois Bureau of Tourism 310 S Michigan #108, Chicago 800/226-6632

PUBLICATIONS

Prairie Flame 217/753-2887 • lgbt newspaper for downstate IL

Alton

see also St Louis, Missouri

ACCOMMODATIONS

MotherSource Travels 187 W 19th St
618/462-4051, 314/973-1890 • mostly women • B&B network • St Louis & Alton locations • lesbian-owned/ run

Illinois • USA

NIGHTCLUBS

Mabel's Budget Beauty Shop & Chainsaw Repair 602 Belle (at 6th) **618/465-8687** • 5pm-2am, till 3am wknds • mostly gay men • dancing/DJ • live shows • wheelchair access

Arlington Heights

see Chicago

Aurora

see also Chicago

EROTICA

Denmark Book Store 1300 US Hwy 30 (2 miles S of Rte 34) **630/898-9838** • 24hrs

Bloomington

INFO LINES & SERVICES

Connections Community Center 313 N Main St (at Monroe St) **309/827-2437** • 24hr recorded info • staffed 7:00pm–10:00 pm Mon–Sat • Fri pm invite only

BARS

Bistro 316 N Main St (at Jefferson) **309/829-2278** • 4pm-1am, till 2am Fri-Sat, from 8pm wknds • lesbians/gay men • dancing/DJ Wed-Sat • wheelchair access

EROTICA

Risque's 1506 N Main (at Division) **309/827-9279** • 24hrs

Bloominton

SPIRITUAL GROUPS

Unitarian Church of Bloomington 1613 E Emerson, Bloomington **309/828-0235** • 9:30am & 11:15am Sun

Blue Island

NIGHTCLUBS

The Edge 13126 S Western (at Grove) **708/597-8379** • 8pm-3am, 6pm-2am Sun • lesbians/gay men • neighborhood bar • dancing/DJ • transgender-friendly • live shows • wheelchair access

Calumet City

see also Chicago & Hammond, Indiana

BARS

Are You Crazy 48 154th Pl (at Forsythe) **708/862-4605** • 4pm-2am, till 3am Wed, Fri-Sat • mostly gay men • neighborhood bar

John L's Place 335 154th Pl **708/862-2386** • 7pm-close • lesbians/gay men • neighborhood bar • wheelchair access

The Patch 201 155th St (at Wentworth) **708/891-9854** • 4pm-2am, from noon Th, from 6pm Sun, clsd Mon • mostly women • neighborhood bar • dancing/DJ • live shows • women-owned/run

NIGHTCLUBS

Pour House 103 155th Pl (at Forsythe) **708/891-3980** • 9:30pm-2am, till 3am Wed, Fri-Sat, clsd Th • mostly gay men • dancing/DJ

Carbondale

INFO LINES & SERVICES

AA Lesbian/Gay 618/549-4633

The Saluki Rainbow Network (Southern Illinois University) 618/453-5151

Women's Services 618/453-3655 • 8am-4:30pm

NIGHTCLUBS

Club Traz 213 E Main St **618/549-4270** • 7pm-2am, clsd Mon-Tue • lesbians/gay men • dancing/DJ • alternative • live shows • wheelchair access

Champaign/Urbana

INFO LINES & SERVICES

Safe Zone at University of Illinois, Urbana **217/333-1187** • 5:30pm Tue • student group

ACCOMMODATIONS

The Little House on the Prairie RR 2, Patterson Rd (by Country Club Rd), Sullivan **217/728-4727** • gay/straight • 'Home of the Stars' • Queen Anne Victorian • full brkfst • swimming • hot tub • gay-owned/run • $65-145

BARS

Ruby's 207 W Clark (at State), Champaign **217/359-8644** • 5pm-1am • lesbians/gay men • dancing/DJ • wheelchair access

NIGHTCLUBS

Chester Street 63 Chester St (at Water St), Champaign **217/356-5607** • 5pm-1am • lesbians/gay men • dancing/DJ • gay-owned/run • wheelchair access

CAFES

Espresso Royale 602 E Daniel, Champaign **217/328-1112** • 7am-midnight, from 8am wknds

Restaurants

Fiesta Cafe 216 S 1st St (at White, nr U of IL campus), Champaign **217/352-5902** • 11am-1am • Mexican • gay-owned

Bookstores

Jane Addams Book Shop 208 N Neil (at University) **217/356-2555** • 10am-5pm from 1pm Sun • full service antiquarian bookstore w/ children's room • lgbt & women's sections

Chicago

Chicago is divided into 5 geographical areas:
Chicago—Overview
Chicago—North Side
Chicago—New Town
Chicago—Near North
Chicago—South Side

Chicago

Where the Girls Are: In the Belmont area—on Halsted or Clark streets—with the boys, or hanging out elsewhere in New Town. Upwardly-mobile lesbians live in Lincoln Park or Wrigleyville, while their working-class sisters live in Andersonville (way north).

LGBT Pride: June. 773/348-8243, web: www.chicagopridecalendar.org.

Annual Events: March - Women's Film Festival 773/907-0610.
June - Lambda Literary Awards 202/682-0952. The Oscars of lgbt writing & publishing.
Chicago Blues Festival 312/744-3315.
August - Halsted Street Fair 773/868-3010 ext. 27.
November - Chicago Lesbian & Gay Film Festival 773/293-1447.

City Info: Chicago Office of Tourism 312/744-2400. web: www.chicago.il.org.

Attractions: 900 North Michigan Shops.
The Art Institute of Chicago 312/443-3600.
Historic Water Tower.
Museum of Science and Industry 773/684-1414.
Sears Tower Skydeck Observatory 312/875-9696.
Second City & the Improv Comedy Clubs.

Best View: Skydeck of the 110-story Sears Tower.

Weather: 'The Windy City' earned its name. Winter temperatures have been known to be as low as -46°. Summers are humid, normally in the 80°s.

Transit: Yellow & Checker Cabs 312/829-4222.
Chicago Airport Shuttle Service 773/247-7678.
Chicago Transit Authority 312/836-7000.
Amtrak 312/655-2385.

Illinois • USA

Chicago—Overview

Info Lines & Services

AA Gay/ Lesbian New Town Al-Anon Club 909 W Belmont St, 2nd flr (btwn Clark & Sheffield) 773/529-0321 • 5pm-11pm Mon-Fri, from 8:30am wknds • wheelchair access

Affinity 5650 S Woodlawn 773/324-0377 • South Side's African-American women's center

Amigas Latinas 312/409-5697 • support group & social events for Latina lesbians & bisexuals

Chicago 35 929 Belmont (at Clark, at 'Ann Sather's' restaurant) 773/271-5909 • 3:30pm-6pm 3rd Sun • group for women over 35

The Chicago Area Gay/ Lesbian Chamber of Commerce 3356 N Halstead, 2nd flr 773/871-4190 • drop in or call for maps, member lists & more

Chicago Black Lesbians/ Gays 312/409-4917 (HOTLINE#) • citywide group for lgbt activism & visibility • 24hr touchtone events line

Chicagoland Bisexual Network 312/458-0983 • variety of political, social & support resources, newsletter

Gay/ Lesbian Visitors Center 3713 N Halsted 773/871-6240 • drop in or call for maps

Gerber/ Hart Library & Archives 1127 W Granville Ave (at Broadway) 773/381-8030 • 6pm-9pm Wed-Th, noon-4pm Fri-Sun • lgbt resource center • wheelchair access

Horizons Community Services 961 W Montana (at Fullerton & Sheffield) 773/472-6469 • 9am-10pm, till 5pm Fri, 11am-3pm Sat, clsd Sun

Khuli Zaban 312/409-2753 • organization for South Asian & Middle Eastern lesbians, bisexual, and transgendered women • meets 3rd Fri

Lesbian/ Gay Helpline 773/929-4357 • 6pm-10pm

SANGAT (Gay/ Lesbian South Asians) 773/506-8810

Entertainment & Recreation

Artemis Singers 773/764-4465 • lesbian feminist chorus

Bailiwick Arts Center 1229 W Belmont 773/883-1090 • Bailiwick Repertory presents many lgbt-themed productions w/ popular Pride Series

---

COMING TO THE WINDY CITY?

LAMBDA PUBLICATIONS

... we've got the community covered

The voice of the gay, lesbian, bi & trans community, serving the Chicago & suburban communities since 1985.

WINDY CITY TIMES   BLACKLINES   En La Vida
Nightlines   OUT! Resources Guide
www.wctimes.com   e-mail outlines@suba.com
(773) 871-7610   FAX (773) 871-7609
1115 West Belmont, 2-D, Chicago, Il 60657

Chicago—Overview • Illinois

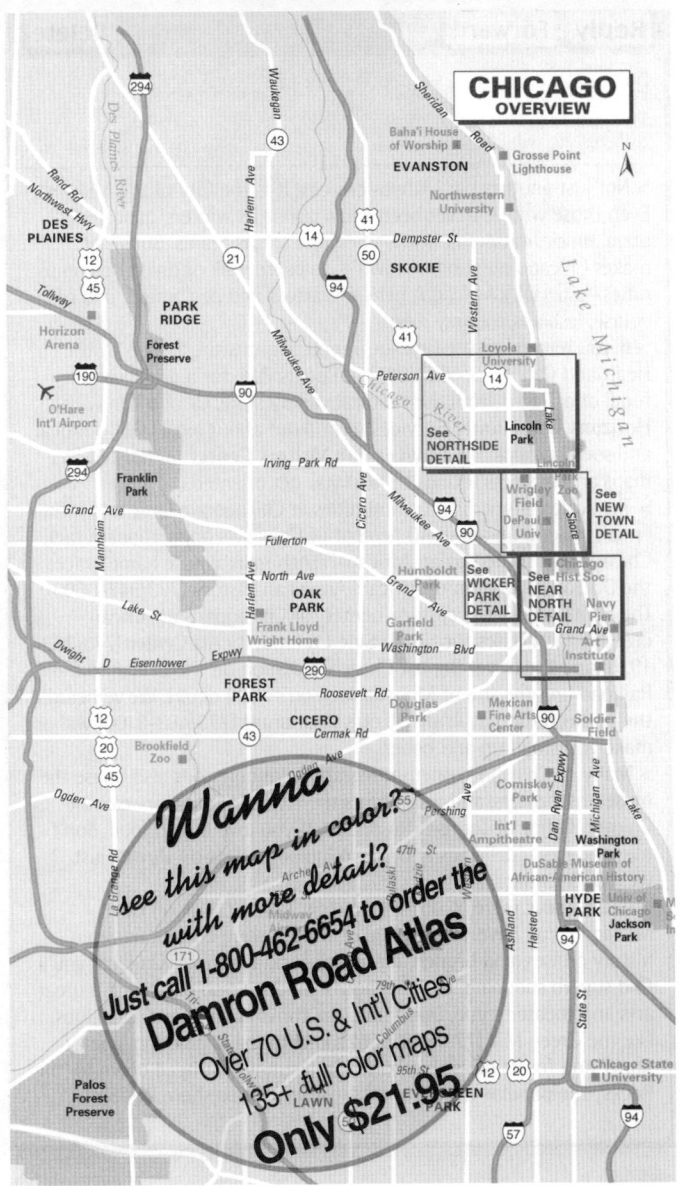

Illinois • USA

Reply **Forward** **Delete**

Date: Wed, Dec 26, 2001 11:16:32
From: Girl-on-the-Go
To: Editor@Damron.com
Subject: Chicago

> Not just another big Midwestern city, it is The City of the Midwest. Even those who've never been know about its winters, gangsters, pizza, music, museums, universities, and sports teams. But what makes Chicago our kind of town is its patchwork of diverse communities—especially African Americans, artists and performers, and of course, lesbians and gay men.

> If you remember the Chicago 7, you might want to stop by the Heartland Cafe (773/465-8005) in Rogers Park for a drink, some food, or a T-shirt from their radical variety store. Or check in with **Horizons Community Services** to find out about local LGBT political and social groups. The **Gay/Lesbian Visitors Center** on Halsted has maps and business listings to help you get oriented.

> The African-American communities in Chicago are large and influential, making up about 40 percent of Chicago's population. In fact, Chicago was settled by an African-French man, whose name graces the Du Sable Museum of African-American History (773/947-0600). The South Side is the cultural center for Chicagoans of African descent and houses the South Side Community Art Center (773/373-1026) and the Olivet Baptist Church, a station on the Underground Railroad and the site of Mahalia Jackson's 1928 debut. We've heard the homecooking at Army & Lou's Restaurant (773/483-3100) will make you stand up and holler.

> Many of Chicago's other immigrant neighborhoods also house the museums, centers, and restaurants the city is famous for—call the Chicago Office of Tourism for details. If you love Indian food, don't miss the many delicious and cheap Indian buffets on Devon, just west of Sheridan.

> What else is there to do? For starters, take a cruise on Lake Michigan. You have your choice of wine-tasting cruises, narrated history cruises, and brunch, dinner, or cocktail cruises. On land, you'll find superb shopping, real Chicago-style deep dish pizza, and a great arts and theater scene. Don't miss the thriving blues and jazz clubs, like the Green Mill (773/878-5552), known for originating 'poetry slams' and for its house big band. On a sunny day, head down to 'the Rocks', the popular waterfront hang-out off Lakeshore Drive, at

Chicago—North Side • Illinois

[Reply] [Forward]   [Delete]

Belmont Harbor.

And you'll never have a dull moment in Chicago's women's scene. A lot of it happens in Chicago's North Side. Here, you'll find **Women & Children First** bookstore where you can check out the books while the women check out you. Be sure to pick up a copy of **Outlines** for the dish on what's hot. Grab a bite to eat at lesbian-owned **Tomboy**, then check out one of the North Side's two women's bars: **Lost & Found** and **Star Gaze**. At night, you can rest your head at **A Sister's Place**, a women-only guesthouse.

And while New Town may be known as 'Boys' Town', sisters can be found getting down with their gay brothers at **Berlin** or the **Closet**. Or, better yet, help your sisters do it for themselves at **Girlbar.**

Chicago Neighborhood Tours 78 E Washington St (at the Chicago Cultural Ctr) **312/742-1190** • gay-friendly • the best way to make the Windy City your kind of town

The Hancock Observatory 875 N Michigan Ave (in John Hancock Center) **888/875-8439** • renovated 94th-flr observatory w/ outside 'Skywalk'

Leather Archives & Museum 6418 N Greenview **773/761-9200** • by appt

Sears Tower Skydeck 233 S Wacker Dr (enter at Jackson Blvd) **312/875-9696** • see the City from one of the world's tallest buildings

PUBLICATIONS

The Alternative Phone Book **773/472-6319** • directory of local businesses

BLACKlines 773/871-7610 • monthly news & features for Black lgbts

Chicago Free Press 773/325-0005 • lgbt newspaper

En La Vida 773/871-7610 • monthly news & features for Latino/a lgbts

Gab 773/248-4542 • has got the dirt on Chicago's club scene

Gay Chicago 773/327-7271 • weekly • extensive resource listings

Hotspots Magazine 847/475-7966 • free monthly lgbt guide to bars, clubs & the scene

Pride Magazine 773/769-6328 • also publish Chicago Pink Pages

▲ **Windy City Times/ Outlines 773/871-7610** • weekly lgbt newspaper & weekly calendar guide

SPIRITUAL GROUPS

Congregation Or Chadash 656 W Barry (at 2nd Unitarian Church) **773/248-9456** • call for Shabbat services & monthly activities

Dignity Chicago 3344 N Broadway (at Broadway United Methodist Church, in Lakeview) **773/296-0780** • mass & social hour 5pm Sun

MCC Good Shepherd 1700 W Farragut (1 blk W of Ashland) **773/262-0099, 773/275-7776** • 11am & 7pm Sun

Chicago—North Side

ACCOMMODATIONS

A Sister's Place 773/275-1319 • women only • guestrooms in artist's flat • women-owned/ run • pls reserve 2 wks ahead • lesbian-owned/ run • $45

Illinois • USA

Gregory House—A Chicago B&B 1718 W Gregory St (btwn Clark & Foster) 773/878-3019 • gay/ straight • 1925 bungalow in charming Andersonville • some shared baths • gay-owned/ run • $99-175

Bars

Big Chicks 5024 N Sheridan (btwn Foster & Argyle) 773/728-5511 • 4pm-2am, from 2pm wknds • lesbians/ gay men • neighborhood bar • dancing/DJ • videos • patio • Sun bbq • wheelchair access

Chicago Eagle 5015 N Clark St (at Argyle) 773/728-0050 • 8pm-4am, till 5am Sat • lesbians/ gay men • leather • wheelchair access

Clark's on Clark 5001 N Clark St (at Argyle) 773/728-2373 • 4pm-4am, till 5am Sat, from 8pm Sun • popular • mostly gay men • neighborhood bar

Different Strokes 4923 N Clark St (at Argyle) 773/989-1958 • noon-2am, till 3am Sat • mostly gay men • neighborhood bar • multiracial clientele • dancers Sat 5pm

Jackhammer 6406 N Clark St (at Devon) 773/743-5772 • 4pm-4am, till 5am Sat • lesbians/ gay men • neighborhood bar • dancing/DJ • leather • shows • videos • patio

Lost & Found 3058 W Irving Park Rd (at Albany) 773/463-7599 • 7pm-2am, from 3pm Sat, clsd Mon • mostly women • neighborhood bar

Madrigal's 5316 N Clark St (at Balmoral) 773/334-3033 • 5pm-2am, till 3am Sat • lesbians/ gay men • Latino/a clientele • strippers Th-Sun

Scot's 1829 W Montrose (at Damen) 773/528-3253 • 3pm-2am, from 11am wknds • lesbians/ gay men • neighborhood bar

Star Gaze 5419 N Clark St (at Foster) 773/561-7363 • 5pm-2am, 3pm-3am Sat, from noon Sun • mostly women • neighborhood bar • theme nights • food served • live shows

Touché 6412 N Clark St (at Devon) 773/465-7400 • 5pm-4am, from 3pm wknds • popular • mostly gay men • leather

Cafes

Mountain Moving Coffeehouse 1700 W Farragut (in basement of Summerdale church) 312/409-0276 • 7:30pm some Sats, check gay paper for dates • women & girls only • non-alcoholic beverages • live shows • collectively run

Restaurants

Chicago Diner 3411 N Halsted St 773/935-6696 • 11am-10pm, from 10am wknds • hip & vegetarian • beer/ wine

Fireside 5739 N Ravenswood (at Rosehill) 773/878-5942 • 11am-4am, from 10am Sat • Cajun & pizza • patio • full bar

Julie Mai's 5025 N Clark (at Winnemac) 773/784-6000 • 4pm-10pm, till 11pm Fri-Sat • French/Vietnamese • full bar

Lolita's Cafe 4400 N Clark St (at Montrose) 773/561-3356 • 5pm-2am, clsd Mon • lesbians/ gay men • mostly Latina/o clientele • transgender-friendly • authentic Mexican food • full bar • also club from 11pm Fri-Sat • dancing/DJ • live shows

Tendino's 5335 N Sheridan (at Broadway) 773/275-8100 • 11am-11pm, till midnight wknds • pizzeria • full bar • wheelchair access

Tomboy 5402 N Clark (at Balmoral) 773/907-0636 • 5pm-10pm, till 11pm wknds, clsd Mon • popular • BYOB • wheelchair access • lesbian-owned

Entertainment & Recreation

Hollywood Beach at Hollywood & Sheridan Sts • popular • 'the' gay beach

Bookstores

KOPI: A Traveler's Cafe 5317 N Clark St (at Summerdale) 773/989-5674 • 8am-11pm, till midnight Fri, from 9am Sat, from 10am Sun • live shows • also boutique & gallery • mostly veggie • soup, sandwiches, pastries

Women & Children First 5233 N Clark St (at Foster) 773/769-9299, 888/923-7323 • 11am-7pm, till 9pm Wed-Fri, from 10am Sat, till 6pm Sun • wheelchair access • women-owned/ run

Retail Shops

Gay Mart 3457 N Halsted St (at Cornelius) 773/929-4272

Specialty Video Films 5307 N Clark St (at Foster) 773/878-3434 • 10am-10pm, till 11pm Fri-Sat • foreign, cult, art house, lgbt & erotic videos • gay-owned/ run

Gyms & Health Clubs

Cheetah Gym 5248 N Clark St (at Foster) 773/728-7777

Chicago—New Town

ACCOMMODATIONS

Best Western Hawthorne Terrace 3434 N Broadway (at Hawthorne Pl) 773/244-3434, 888/675-2378 • gay-friendly • located in the heart of Chicago's gay community • wheelchair access • $129-189

City Suites Hotel 933 W Belmont (btwn Clark & Sheffield) 773/404-3400, 800/248-9108 • gay-friendly • accommodations w/ touch of European style • $99-200

Majestic Hotel 528 W Brompton Pl (at Addison) 773/404-3499, 800/727-5108 • gay-friendly • romantic 19th-century atmosphere • $99-200

Villa Toscana B&B 3447 N Halsted St 773/404-2643, 800/404-2643 • lesbians/ gay men • 1890s coach house • gay-owned/ run • $99-159

The Willows 555 W Surf St (at Broadway) 773/528-8400, 800/787-3108 • gay-friendly • hotel w/ 19th century French flare in Lincoln Park • $99-200

BARS

Annex 3 3160 N Clark St (at Belmont) 773/327-5969 • noon-2am, till 3am Sat • lesbians/ gay men • neighborhood bar • videos • sports bar • wheelchair access

Beat Kitchen 2100 W Belmont (btwn Hoyne & Damen) 773/281-4444 • noon-2am • gay-friendly • live music • also grill • some veggie • wheelchair access

Berlin 954 W Belmont (at Sheffield) 773/348-4975 • 5pm-4am, till 5am Sat, from 8pm Mon • popular • lesbians/ gay men • transgender-friendly • dancing/DJ • women's night Wed • live shows • wheelchair access

Blues 2519 N Halsted 773/528-1012, 773/549-9436 • 8pm-2am, till 3am Sat • gay-friendly • popular • classic Chicago blues spot • live shows

Bobby Love's 3729 N Halsted St (at Waveland) 773/525-1200 • 3pm-2am, from noon wknds, till 3am Sat • lesbians/ gay men • neighborhood bar • piano bar • wheelchair access

Buck's Saloon 3439 N Halsted St (btwn Cornelia & Newport) 773/525-1125 • 10am-2am • mostly gay men • neighborhood bar • patio

Buddies 3301 N Clark St (at Aldine) 773/477-4066 • 3pm-2am, from 9pm wknds, till 3am Sat • lesbians/ gay men • popular • country/ western • also restaurant from 11am

Cell Block 3702 N Halsted (at Waveland) 773/665-8064 • 4pm-2am, from 2pm Sun • mostly gay men • dancing/DJ • leather • also 'Holding Cell' from 10pm Th-Sun • strict leather/ latex/ uniform code • also 'Leather Cell' store • wheelchair access

Charlie's Chicago 3726 N Broadway (btwn Waveland & Grace) 773/871-8887 • 3pm-4am, till 5am Sat • mostly gay men • dancing/DJ • country/ western

Circuit/ Rehab 3641 N Halsted St (at Addison) 773/325-2233 • 9pm-4am, till 5am Sat, clsd Mon-Tue • gay/ straight • dancing/DJ • multiracial clientele • karaoke Tue • live shows • also 'Club Rehab' from 4pm • Latin Wed-Th

The Closet 3325 N Broadway St (at Buckingham) 773/477-8533 • 2pm-4am, till 5am Sat, from noon wknds • popular • lesbians/ gay men • neighborhood bar • videos

Cocktail 3359 Halsted St (at Roscoe) 773/477-1420 • 4pm-2am, from 2pm wknds, till 3am Sat • lesbians/ gay men • more women Mon • neighborhood bar • dancing/DJ • wheelchair access

Gentry on Halsted 3320 N Halsted (at Aldine) 773/348-1053 • 4pm-2am, till 3am Sat, from 3pm Sun • mostly gay men • upscale piano bar

Girlbar 2625 N Halsted St (btwn Fullerton & Diversey) 773/871-4210 • 7pm-2am, from 4pm Sun, till 3am Sat, clsd Mon • mostly women • dancing/DJ • live shows • salsa 2nd Th • 'Boybar' Wed • 2 levels • patio • wheelchair access

Little Jim's 3501 N Halsted St (at Cornelia) 773/871-6116 • 11am-4am, till 5am Sat • popular • mostly gay men • neighborhood bar

Lucky Horseshoe 3169 N Halsted St (at Briar) 773/404-3169, 800/443-3169 • 2pm-2am, from noon wknds • mostly gay men • neighborhood bar • live shows • patio

The North End 3733 N Halsted St (at Grace) 773/477-7999 • 3pm-2am, till 3am Sat, from 11am wknds • mostly gay men • neighborhood sports bar • wheelchair access

Roscoe's 3354-56 N Halsted St (at W Roscoe) 773/281-3355 • 2pm-2am, noon-3am Sat • popular • lesbians/ gay men • neighborhood bar • dancing/DJ • live shows • 6 bars • patio cafe in summer

Illinois • USA

Spin 800 W Belmont (enter on Halsted) **773/327-7711** • 4pm-2am, till 3am Sat, from noon wknds • gay/ straight • dancing/DJ • live shows • theme nights • 3 bars • lounge • 80s Th

Nightclubs

Manhole 3458 N Halsted St (at Cornelia) **773/975-9244** • 9pm-4am, till 5am Sat • popular • mostly gay men • dancing/DJ • leather

Smart Bar 3730 N Clark St (downstairs at the 'Metro') **773/549-4140** • 10pm-4am, till 5am Sat • gay-friendly • dancing/DJ • popular • goth Tue • punk Wed

Cafes

Mike's Broadway Cafe 3805 N Broadway (btwn Grace & Halsted) **773/404-2205** • 7am-10pm, 24hrs Fri-Sat • lesbians/ gay men • popular brunch • American • some veggie • wheelchair access • $5-12

Pick Me Up Cafe & All Nite Express Lounge 3408 N Clark **773/248-6613** • 5pm-3am, 24hrs Fri-Sat • brkfst all day

Restaurants

Angelina Ristorante 3561 N Broadway (at Addison) **773/935-5933** • 5:30pm-11pm, Sun brunch • Italian • full bar • wheelchair access • $10-20

Ann Sather's 929 W Belmont Ave (at Sheffield) **773/348-2378** • 7am-10pm • popular • Swedish diner & New Town fixture

Buddies Restaurant & Bar 3301 N Clark St (at Aldine) **773/477-4066** • 11am-11pm, from 9am wknds • popular • lesbians/ gay men • full bar • some veggie • wheelchair access • $9-13

Cornelia's 750 W Cornelia Ave (at Halsted) **773/248-8333** • dinner, clsd Mon • some veggie • upscale Italian • full bar • wheelchair access • $14-20

The Pepper Lounge 3441 N Sheffield (btwn Newport & Clark) **773/665-7377** • 6pm-1:30am, till midnight Sun, clsd Mon • lesbians/ gay men • supper club • gourmet Italian • plenty veggie • full bar • $15-24

The Raw Bar & Grill 3720 N Clark St (at Waveland) **773/348-7291** • 5pm-2am • seafood • lounge • live entertainment • wheelchair access • $10-13

Technicolor Kitchen 3210 N Lincoln Ave (at Belmont & Ashland) **773/665-2111** • dinner, clsd Mon • kitschy decor • eclectic fusion menu • some veggie • wheelchair access • $14-24

Zoom Kitchen 620 W Belmont (at Broadway) **773/325-1400** • 11am-10pm, from 9am-9pm Sun • American • plenty veggie • $4-8

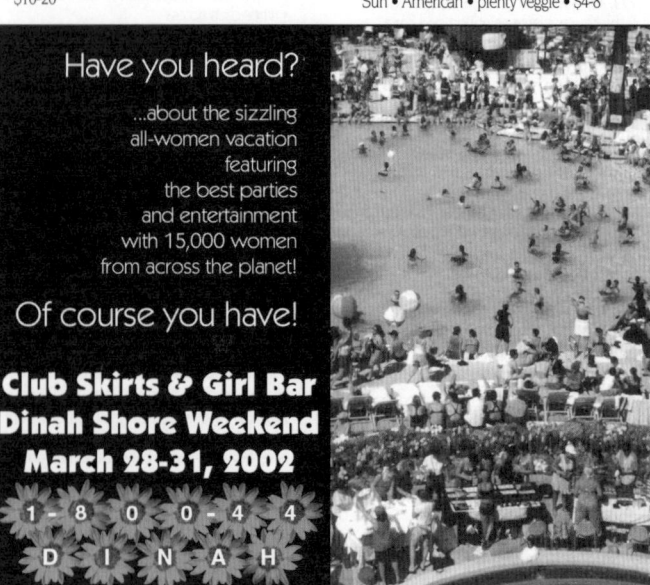

Have you heard?
...about the sizzling all-women vacation featuring the best parties and entertainment with 15,000 women from across the planet!

Of course you have!

Club Skirts & Girl Bar Dinah Shore Weekend March 28-31, 2002

1-800-44 DINAH

Chicago—Near North • Illinois

Bookstores

Unabridged Books 3251 N Broadway St (at Aldine) **773/883-9119** • 10am-10pm

Retail Shops

Specialty Video Films 3221 N Broadway St (at Belmont) **773/248-3434** • 10am-10pm, till 11pm Fri-Sat • foreign, cult, art house, lgbt & erotic videos • gay-owned/ run

Universal Gear 3153 N Broadway (at Belmont) **773/296-1090** • 11am-10pm, till 11pm Fri-Sat • casual, club, athletic & designer clothing

We're Everywhere 3434 N Halsted St (at Newport) **773/404-0590, 800/772-6411** • noon-9pm, 11am-8pm wknds • also mail order catalog • lesbian-owned/ run

Gyms & Health Clubs

Chicago Sweat Shop 3215 N Broadway (at Belmont) **773/871-2789** • gay-friendly

Erotica

Batteries Not Included 3420 N Halsted (btwn Roscoe & Addison) **773/935-9900** • 50% of all profits donated to charity

Male Hide Leathers 2816 N Lincoln Ave (at Diversey) **773/929-0069** • noon-8pm, 1pm-5pm Sun, clsd Mon • custom leather

The Pleasure Chest 3155 N Broadway (at Belmont Ave) **773/525-7152**

Chicago—Near North

Accommodations

Allegro 171 W Randolph (at LaSalle) **312/236-0123, 800/643-1500** • gay-friendly • upscale lounge & restaurant • live entertainment • wheelchair access • $139-399

Best Western Inn of Chicago 162 E Ohio St (at Michigan Ave) **312/787-3100, 800/557-2378** • gay-friendly • food service • wheelchair access • $129-189

Comfort Inn & Suites Downtown 15 E Ohio St **888/775-4111** • gay-friendly • $139-249

Days Inn Gold Coast 1816 N Clark St (at Lincoln) **312/664-3040, 800/329-7466** • gay-friendly • also restaurant & lounge • wheelchair access • $129-189

Flemish House of Chicago 68 E Cedar St (btwn Rush & Lake Shore Dr) **312/664-9981** • gay/ straight • B&B, studios & apts in grey-stone row house • gay-owned/ run • $155-195

Gold Coast Guesthouse 113 W Elm St 60610 **312/337-0361** • gay-friendly • 1873 townhouse • smokefree • women-owned/ run • $129-229 • also 2 studios available

Hotel Monaco 225 N Wabash (at S Water & Wacker Pl) **312/960-8500, 800/397-7661** • upscale • gay-friendly • gym • restaurant • $250+

Hyatt Regency Chicago 151 E Wacker Dr (at Michigan Ave) **312/565-1234, 800/233-1234** • gay-friendly • restaurant • cafe • bar

Knickerbocker Hotel 163 E Walton Pl (Michigan Ave) **312/751-8100, 800/621-8140** • gay/ straight • restaurant • martini bar • gym • right off Magnificent Mile • wheelchair access • $129-269

Old Town B&B **312/440-9268** • gay/ straight • roof deck • gym • $139-169

Bars

Artful Dodger 1734 W Wabansia (at Hermitage, in Wicker Park) **773/227-6859** • 5pm-2am, 8pm-3am Sat • gay-friendly • dancing/DJ

Club Foot 1824 W Augusta (in Wicker Park) **773/489-0379** • 8pm-2am, till 3am Sat • gay-friendly • neighborhood bar • dancing/ DJ • kitschy • alternative

Gentry on State 440 N State (at Illinois) **312/664-1033** • 4pm-2am, till 3am Sat • popular • mostly gay men • live shows • professional crowd

Nightclubs

Baton Show Lounge 436 N Clark St (btwn Illinois & Hubbard) **312/644-5269** • 8pm-4am, clsd Mon-Tue • lesbians/ gay men • drag shows • wheelchair access

Boom Boom Room at Red Dog 1958 W North Ave (enter in alley behind 'Border Line Tap') **773/278-1009** • 10:30pm-4am Mon, also 'Resurrection' Sat • popular • gay-friendly • dancing/DJ • live shows • cover charge

Club Intimus 312 W Randolph St (at 'Cafe Bacetti') **773/901-1703** • 9pm-3am Sat only • mostly women • dancing/DJ • mostly African-American • live shows • wheelchair access

Condo Club 1931 N Milwaukee (at Western, in Wicker Park) **773/235-5875** • 9pm-2am, till 3am Sat, after hrs Fri, clsd Mon-Tue • lesbians/ gay men • dancing/ DJ • live shows • multiracial clientele • 18+ Fri • also restaurant

The Crobar 1543 N Kingsbury (at Sheffield) **312/243-4800** • 10pm-4am, clsd Mon-Tue • popular • gay-friendly • more gay Sun for 'Glee Club' • dancing/DJ

The Rails 1675 N Elston Ave (at North Ave, at 'Prop House' in Wicker Park) **708/802-1705, 312/486-2086** • 11pm-4am Fri only • mostly gay men • dancing/DJ • live shows • African-American clientele • cover charge

Illinois • USA

Second City 1608 N Wells St (at North) **312/337-3992, 877/337-4707** • gay-friendly • legendary comedy club • call for reservations

Cafes

Earwax Records 1564 N Milwaukee Ave (in Wicker Park) **773/772-4019** • 11am-midnight, till 1am Fri-Sat, from 10am wknds, plenty veggie

Local Grind 1585 N Milwaukee Ave (in Wicker Park) **773/489-3490** • 6am-1am, till 3am Fri-Sat, 7am-midnight Sun • popular brunch • plenty veggie

Restaurants

The Berghoff 17 W Adams St (at State) **312/427-3170** • 11am-9pm, till 10pm Sat, clsd Sun • German • great mashed potatoes

Fireplace Inn 1448 N Wells St (at North Ave) **312/664-5264** • 4pm-10pm, till 11pm Fri-Sat, from 11am Sun • bbq/ American • full bar • $13-25

Iggy's 700 N Milwaukee, River North (at Chicago) **312/829-4449** • dinner nightly, till 4am Th-Sat, till 2am Sun • int'l • full bar • patio

Kiki's Bistro 900 N Franklin St (at Locust) **312/335-5454** • French • full bar • $11-20

Manny's 1141 S Jefferson St (at Roosevelt) **312/939-2855** • 5am-4pm, clsd Sun • killer corned beef

The Mashed Potato Club 316 W Erie St (at Orleans) **312/255-8579** • dinner nightly, till midnight wkdays, till 2am Fri-Sat • over 100 potato toppings • full bar • wheelchair access

Shaw's Crab House 21 W Hubbard (at State St) **312/527-2722** • lunch & dinner • full bar • wheelchair access

Bookstores

Barbara's Bookstore 1350 N Wells St (at Schiller, in Old Town) **312/642-5044** • 9am-10pm, 10am-9pm Sun • women's/ lgbt section • wheelchair access • other locations: 700 E Grand Ave at Navy Pier, 312/222-0890 • Oak Park, 708/848-9140

Quimby's Queer Store 1854 W North Ave (at Wolcott, in Wicker Park) **773/342-0910** • noon-8pm, till 10pm Fri-Sat, till 6pm Sun • alternative literature & comics • wheelchair access

Gyms & Health Clubs

Thousand Waves Spa 1212 W Belmont Ave (at Racine) **773/549-0700** • noon-9pm, 10am-7pm wknds, clsd Mon • women only • health spa only • women-owned/ run

Chicago—South Side

Bars

Club Escape 1530 E 75th St (at Stoney Island) **773/667-6454** • 4pm-2am, till 3am Sat • lesbians/ gay men • dancing/DJ • mostly African-American • food served • women's night Tue & Th

Inn Exile 5758 W 65th St (at Menard, nr Midway Airport) **773/582-3510** • 8pm-2am, till 3am Sat • mostly gay men • dancing/DJ • wheelchair access

Jeffery Pub 7041 S Jeffery (at 71st) **773/363-8555** • 4pm-4am, from 11am Fri-Sun • popular • lesbians/ gay men • dancing/DJ • mostly African-American • live shows • wheelchair access

Nightclubs

Escapades 6301 S Harlem **773/229-0886** • 10pm-4am, till 5am Sat • mostly gay men • dancing/DJ

Bookstores

57th St Books 1301 E 57th St, Hyde Park (at Kimbark St) **773/684-1300** • 10am-10pm, till 8pm Sun • lgbt section

Spiritual Groups

Resurrection MCC 5757 S University, Hyde Park (at Woodlawn) **773/288-1535** • 10:30am Sun

Decatur

Info Lines & Services

Gay/ Lesbian Assocation of Decatur (GLAD) **217/422-3277** • youth group, monthly socials • free newsletter

Bars

The Flashback Lounge 2239 E Wood St (at 22nd) **217/422-3530** • 9am-2am • lesbians/ gay men • neighborhood bar • karaoke Fri • drag shows every other Sat

Du Quoin

Accommodations

The Pit 7403 Persimmon Rd **618/542-9470** • lesbians/ gay men • primitive camping • 18+ • nudity permitted • swimming • wheelchair access • gay-owned/ run • free except $5 on holiday wknds

Peoria • Illinois

Effingham

BOOKSTORES

Langes News & Books 129 E Jefferson **217/342-6066** • 6am-8pm, till 6pm Sat, till 5pm Sun

Elgin

see also Chicago

NIGHTCLUBS

The Mission 209 E Chicago **847/488-0320** • 10pm-4am Fri-Sat only • lesbians/ gay men • dancing/DJ

Elk Grove Village

see also Chicago

NIGHTCLUBS

Hunters 1932 E Higgins (at Busse) **847/439-8840** • 4pm-4am • popular • mostly gay men • dancing/DJ • patio

Evanston

INFO LINES & SERVICES

Kindred Heart Women's Center 2214 Ridge Ave **847/604-0913** • call for events

Forest Park

see also Chicago

NIGHTCLUBS

Club 7301 7301 W Roosevelt Rd (at Marengo) **708/771-4459** • 3pm-2am, till 3am Fri-Sat • mostly gay men • dancing/DJ • live shows

Nut Bush 7201 Franklin (at Harlem) **708/366-5117** • 3pm-2am, till 3am Fri-Sat, from 1pm wknds • mostly gay men • dancing/DJ • live shows

Franklin Park

NIGHTCLUBS

Temptations 10235 W Grand Ave (at Mannheim) **847/455-0008** • 6pm-4am, till 5am Fri-Sat • popular • mostly women • dancing/DJ • transgender-friendly • wheelchair access

Galesburg

ACCOMMODATIONS

The Fahnestock House 591 N Prairie St (at Losey) **309/344-0270** • gay/ straight • full brkfst • Queen Anne Victorian • gay-owned/ run • $125

Granite City

see also St Louis, Missouri

NIGHTCLUBS

Inside Out 3145 W Chain of Rocks Rd **618/797-0700** • 8pm-2am, till 3am Sat, from 2pm Sun, clsd Mon-Wed • popular • lesbians/ gay men • food served • entertainment • live shows • outdoor complex

Hinsdale

SPIRITUAL GROUPS

MCC Holy Covenant Unitarian Church, 17 W Maple (at Washington) **630/325-8488** • 6pm Sun • wheelchair access

Joliet

NIGHTCLUBS

Maneuvers 118 E Jefferson (at Chicago) **815/727-7069** • 8pm-2am, till 3am Fri-Sat • lesbians/ gay men • dancing/DJ • patio

Oak Park

SPIRITUAL GROUPS

MCC of the Incarnation 460 Lake St (at Ridgeland, in the chapel) **708/383-3033** • 11am Sun, 10am summers

Ottawa

EROTICA

Brown Bag Video 3042 N Rte 71 (at I-80) **815/434-0820** • 24hrs

Peoria

BARS

David's 807 SW Adams (at Oak) **309/676-3987** • 1pm-2am, till 1am Sun-Wed • lesbians/ gay men • neighborhood bar

NIGHTCLUBS

The Club 815 SW Adams, upper level (at Elm) **309/672-0933** • 8pm-2am Th-Sat • lesbians/ gay men • dancing/DJ • drag shows Th • karaoke every other Fri • gay-owned/ run

Red Fox Den 800 N Knoxville Ave (at Glendale) **309/674-8013** • 9pm-4am • lesbians/ gay men • dancing/DJ • live shows

PUBLICATIONS

The Alternative Times **309/688-1930**

Prairie Flame **217/753-2887** • lgbt newspaper for downstate IL

Illinois • USA

Erotica
Brown Bag Video 801 SW Adams (at Oak) 309/676-3003

Quincy

Nightclubs
Irene's Cabaret 124 N 5th St (at Washington Park) 217/222-6292 • 9pm-2:30am, from 7pm Fri-Sat, till 3:30am Sat, clsd Sun-Mon • lesbians/ gay men • dancing/DJ • karaoke • live shows • wheelchair access

Rock Island

see also Davenport, Iowa

Bars
Augie's 313 20th St (at 3rd) 309/788-7389 • 11am-3am • lesbians/ gay men • neighborhood bar

Nightclubs
JR's 325 20th St (at 4th Ave) 309/786-9411 • 3pm-3am, from noon Sun • lesbians/ gay men • dancing/DJ • karaoke • live shows • also restaurant • under $10 • wheelchair access

Bookstores
All Kinds of People 1806 2nd Ave (at 18th St) 309/788-2567 • 10am-10pm, till midnight Fri-Sat • alternative • also cafe • plenty veggie • wheelchair access

Rockford

Info Lines & Services
Diversity of Rockford 117 S 3rd St #A 815/964-2639 • many activities including teen groups & some referrals

Bars
Oh Zone 1014 Charles St (at E State) 815/964-9663 • 5pm-2am, noon-midnight Sun • lesbians/ gay men • dancing /DJ • live entertainment • karaoke • shows

Nightclubs
Office 513 E State St (btwn 2nd & 3rd) 815/965-0344 • 5pm-2am, noon-midnight Sun • popular • lesbians/ gay men • dancing/DJ • food served • live shows

Restaurants
Lucernes 845 N Church St (at Whitman) 815/968-2665 • 5pm-11pm, clsd Mon • fondue • full bar • wheelchair access

Maria's 828 Cunningham St (at Corbin) 815/968-6781 • 4:30pm-9pm, clsd Sun-Mon • Italian • full bar • $7-20

Springfield

Info Lines & Services
The Phoenix-Rainbow Youth Center 122 E Laurel 217/528-5253 • youth groups, 4pm-10pm Mon, 7pm-10pm Th, 4pm-11pm Fri, noon-11pm Sat, '20 something' group Th, youth group Fri

Springfield Area Lesbian Outreach (SALO) 217/528-7256

Accommodations
The Henry Mischler House 802 E Edwards St (btwn 8th & 9th Sts) 217/525-2660 • gay-friendly • full brkfst • smokefree • gay-owned/ run • $75-95

Bars
Jimmez & Co 2143 N 11th St 217/525-6717 • 6pm-1am • lesbians/ gay men • dancing/DJ • karaoke • live shows • young crowd • wheelchair access

The Station House 304–306 E Washington (btwn 3rd & 4th Sts) 217/525-0438 • 9am-1am, till 3am Fri-Sat, from noon Sun • lesbians/ gay men • neighborhood bar • dancing/DJ Wed & Sat • wheelchair access

Nightclubs
Smokey's Den 411 E Washington (btwn 4th & 5th) 217/522-0301 • 6pm-1am, till 3am Fri-Sat • lesbians/ gay men • dancing/DJ • wheelchair access

Zoo Babies 3036 Peoria Rd (nr State Fairgrounds) 217/528-0535, 217/787-0559 • 10pm-3am, clsd Sun-Mon • lesbians/ gay men • dancing/DJ • food served • live shows

Entertainment & Recreation
Triangle Camping Club 217/753-2887 • Central IL, seasonal, call for info

Bookstores
Sundance 1428 E Sangamon Ave (at Peoria Rd) 217/788-5243 • 10am-6pm, clsd Sun • new age books & gifts • lgbt titles

Publications
Prairie Flame 217/753-2887 • lgbt newspaper for downstate IL

Spiritual Groups
Faith Eternal MCC 304 W Allen (at College) 217/525-9597 • 10am & 6pm Sun

Erotica
Expo I Books 302 N 5th St (at Madison) 217/544-5145

Indiana

Bloomington

Info Lines & Services

Indiana University LGBT Student Services 705 E 7th St **812/855-4252** • drop-in 9am-noon Mon-Fri, also by appt 1-5pm • also library & video collection

Indiana Youth Group 800/347-8336 • 7pm-10pm Fri-Sat • lgbt youth hotline

Office for Women's Affairs Memorial Hall E #123 **812/855-3849** • 8am-noon & 1pm-5pm, clsd wknds • support/ discussion groups • call for info

Accommodations

Holiday Inn Bloomington 1710 Kinser Pike **812/334-3252, 800/465-4329** • gay-friendly • $69-99

Bars

The Other Bar 414 S Walnut (btwn 2nd & 4th) **812/332-0033** • 5pm-3am, clsd Sun • lesbians/ gay men • neighborhood bar • patio • wheelchair access

Uncle Elizabeth's 502 N Morton (at 9th) **812/331-0060** • 4pm-3am, clsd Sun • lesbians/ gay men • neighborhood bar • patio

Nightclubs

Bullwinkle's 201 S College St (at 4th St) **812/334-3232** • 8pm-3am, clsd Sun • lesbians/ gay men • dancing/DJ • karaoke • live shows

Restaurants

Village Deli 409 E Kirkwood **812/336-2303** • 7am-10pm, till 4pm wknds • lesbians/ gay men • some veggie

Retail Shops

Athena Gallery 108 E Kirkwood Ave (at Walnut) **812/339-0734** • 10:30am-6pm, till 7pm Wed-Th, till 8pm Fri-Sat, noon-5pm Sun • wheelchair access

Fourth Street Emporium 212 W 4th St **812/334-3567** • 10am-6pm, noon-5pm Sun, clsd Mon • antiques mall • gay-owned/ run

Spiritual Groups

Integrity Bloomington 400 E Kirkwood Ave (at Trinity Episcopal Church) **812/336-4466** • 7:30pm 2nd Wed • co-op dinner • wheelchair access

Unity of Bloomington 1101 N Dunn (at 14th) **812/333-2484** • 9am & 11am Sun • wheelchair access

Elkhart

see also South Bend

Info Lines & Services

Info Helpline 219/293-8671 • 24hrs

Spiritual Groups

Unitarian Universalist Fellowship 1732 Garden (at Johnson) **219/264-6525** • 10:30am Sun • wheelchair access

Evansville

Info Lines & Services

Tri-State Alliance 812/474-4853 • info • monthly social group • newsletter

Nightclubs

Someplace Else 930 Main St (at Sycamore) **812/424-3202** • 4pm-3am, clsd Sun • lesbians/ gay men • dancing/DJ Wed-Sat • live shows Th-Sat • karaoke Wed • patio • also 'Down Under' pride gift shop • 10pm-3am Fri-Sat

Bookstores

AA Michael Books 1541 S Green River Rd (at Covert) **812/479-8979** • 10am-6pm, till 8pm Fri, 10am-5pm Sat, noon-5pm Sun • spiritual • wheelchair access

Fort Wayne

Info Lines & Services

Gay/ Lesbian AA at 'Up the Stairs Community Center' **219/744-1199** • 7:30pm Tue & Sat, 4:30pm Sun

Up the Stairs Community Center 3426 Broadway **219/744-1199, 219/744-5430** • helpline 7pm-10pm, till midnight Fri-Sat, 8pm-9pm Sun • space for various groups

Bars

Hide-n-Seeks Pub & Eatery 1008 N Wells St **219/423-2202** • 5pm-3am, till 12:30am Sun • mostly gay men • neighborhood bar • dancing/DJ • food served

Out On Main 2809 W Main St (at W Jefferson Blvd) **219/436-4166** • 6pm-1am, 3am Sat, till midnight Sun • mostly gay men • neighborhood bar • food served • wheelchair access

Up the Street 2322 S Calhoun (at Creighton) **219/456-7166** • 6pm-3am, 5pm-midnight Sun • mostly women • dancing/DJ Fri-Sat • food served • live shows Th-Fri • wheelchair access

Nightclubs

After Dark 231 Pearl St (at Maiden Ln) **219/424-6130** • noon-3am, from 5pm Sun• lesbians/ gay men • dancing/DJ • live shows • wheelchair access

Indiana • USA

RETAIL SHOPS
Subterranean 301 W Washington (at Webster) **219/424-8417** • 11am-9pm, noon-4pm Sun • gifts • sex toys • leather

SPIRITUAL GROUPS
Open Door Chapel at Up the Stairs Community Center **219/744-1199** • 7pm Sun

Hammond

RESTAURANTS
Phil Smidt & Son 1205 N Calumet Ave (at Indianapolis Blvd) **219/659-0025** • lunch & dinner, clsd Mon • seafood • full bar

Indianapolis

INFO LINES & SERVICES
AA Gay/ Lesbian 317/632-7864 • call for mtg times & locations • lesbian mtg 7pm Mon

Chris Gonzales Memorial Gay/ Lesbian Archives 723 Massachusetts Ave **317/639-4297** • 6pm-9pm Wed & 1pm-5pm wknds • library of printed, visual & audio materials about central Indiana lgbt community

The Switchboard 317/251-7955 • 7pm-11pm • resources • crisis counseling

ACCOMMODATIONS
Renaissance Tower Historic Inn 230 E 9th St (btwn Delaware & Alabama) **317/262-8648, 800/676-7786** • gay-friendly • studio suites • full kitchens • downtown location • $95-225

BARS
501 Eagle 608 E Market (at College) **317/632-2100** • 5pm-3am, clsd Sun • popular • mostly gay men • dancing/DJ Fri-Sat • leather • also 'Options' safer-sex info center

Brothers Bar & Grill 822 N Illinois St (at St Clair) **317/636-1020** • 4pm-midnight, till 10pm Sun • restaurant till 10pm • lesbians/gay men • wheelchair access

Illusions 1446 E Washington (at Arsenal) **317/266-0535** • 7am-3am, noon-12:30am Sun • lesbians/gay men • dancing/DJ • karaoke • live shows

The Metro 707 Massachusetts Ave (at College) **317/639-6022** • 4pm-3am, noon-12:30am Sun • lesbians/ gay men • dancing/DJ • live shows • also restaurant • some veggie • patio • wheelchair access • also 'Colors' shop

Varsity Lounge 1517 N Pennsylvania St (S of 16th) **317/635-9998** • 10am-3am, noon-midnight Sun • mostly gay men • neighborhood bar • food served

Indianapolis

ENTERTAINMENT: Women's Chorus 317/931-9464.
Men's Chorus at the Crossroads Performing Arts 317/931-9464.

LGBT PRIDE: June.

ANNUAL EVENTS: Memorial Day Weekend - Indy 500 auto race. June - National Women's Music Festival (in Muncie, IN) 317/927-9355.

CITY INFO: Indianapolis Visitor's Bureau 317/639-4282, 800/323-4639, web: www.indy.org.

ATTRACTIONS: Indianapolis Museum of Art 317/923-1331. Speedway 500 317/481-8500. Zoo 317/630-2001.

WEATHER: The spring weather is moderate (50°s-60°s) with occasional storms. The summers are typically midwestern: hot (mid-90°s) and humid. The autumns are mild and colorful in southeastern Indiana. As for winter, it's the wind chill that'll get to you.

TRANSIT: Yellow Cab 317/487-7777. Metro Transit 317/635-3344.

Indianapolis • Indiana

Nightclubs

The Ten 1218 N Pennsylvania St (at 12th, enter rear) 317/638-5802 • 6pm-3am, clsd Sun • popular • mostly women • dancing/DJ • live shows • wheelchair access

Utopia 924 N Pennsylvania St (at St Joseph's) 317/638-0215 • 6pm-1am, till 3am Fri-Sat, clsd Mon • popular • lesbians/ gay men • dancing/DJ • also restaurant

Cafes

Cath's Coffeehouse 5401 N College (at 54th) 317/251-2677 • 7am-7pm, 8am-3pm Sun • live shows

The MT Cup 314 Massachusetts Ave (at New Jersey) 317/639-1099 • 7am-7pm, 8am-1am Sat • sandwiches • baked goods

Restaurants

Aesop's Tables 600 N Massachusetts Ave (at East) 317/631-0055 • 11am-9pm, till 10pm Fri-Sat • authentic Mediterranean • some veggie • beer/ wine • wheelchair access • $8-15

English Ivy's 944 N Alabama (N of 9th St) 317/822-5070 • till 3am Mon-Sat, 11am-12:30am Sun • also full bar

Peter's 8505 Keystone Crossing Blvd 317/465-1155, 800/479-0909 • dinner only, clsd Sun • upscale dining • full bar

Entertainment & Recreation

Women's Chorus 317/931-9464

Bookstores

Borders 5612 Castleton Corner Ln (at 86th St) 317/849-8660 • 9am-10pm, 10am-8pm Sun • some lgbt titles

Out Word Bound 625 N East St (at Massachusetts Ave) 317/951-9100 • 11:30am-9pm, till 10pm Fri-Sat, noon-6pm Sun • lgbt books & gifts • special events

Retail Shops

Colors Pride & Leather Shop 707 Massachusetts Ave (upstairs at 'Metro') 317/686-0984 • hrs vary

---

[Reply] [Forward]   [Delete]

```
Date: Mon, Dec 24, 2001 11:26:57
From: Girl-on-the-Go
To: Editor@Damron.com
Subject: Indianapolis
```

> Indianapolis, the capital of the Hoosier state, may look like your typical Midwestern industrial city, but you'll find a few surprises under the surface.

> You probably won't find lesbians dancing in the streets (unless it's Pride Day), but they're there. Check out some of the fun boutiques and restaurants in the Broad Ripple district. Later fuel up on caffeine at the **MT Cup** and dance with the girls at **Utopia** or **The Ten.** For the latest one-nighters and other events, check the latest issue of **OUTlines** or the **Word,** which you can pick up at the LGBT bookstore **Out Word Bound.**

> If you're into women's music, plan to be in Indiana during the first weekend in June for the **National Women's Music Festival** in Muncie.

> If fast cars are more your style, be sure to be in Indianapolis for the Indy 500 on Memorial Day weekend.

Indiana • USA

Contours/ Torso 719 Massachusetts (at College) 317/916-9054 • 2pm-11pm, till midnight Fri-Sat, 1pm-5pm Sun • clothing • gifts

Dawghouse Cards & Gifts 222 E Market St (at Delaware) 317/822-1757 • 8am-6pm, clsd Sun • wheelchair access

Gaia Wines 608 Massachusetts Ave (at North) 317/634-9463 • 11am-8pm, noon-6pm Sun • gay-owned/ run

Indy News 20 E Maryland (at Meridian) 317/632-7680 • 6am-7pm, till 6pm wknds

Southside News 8063 Madison Ave 317/887-1020 • 6am-9pm, till 7pm Sun

PUBLICATIONS

OUTlines—The Indiana Gay/Lesbian Newspaper 317/923-8550 • lgbt newsmagazine w/ extensive resources

The Word 317/725-8840 • lgbt newspaper

SPIRITUAL GROUPS

Jesus MCC Unitarian Church, 5805 E 56th (at Channing) 317/894-5110 • 6pm Sun & 7:30pm Wed

Kokomo

BARS

Club Millennium 1400 W Markland Ave (at Park) 765/452-1611 • 5pm-3am, clsd Sun • lesbians/ gay men • dancing/DJ • live shows wknds • food served

Lafayette

BARS

The Sportsman 644 Main St (at Columbia) 765/742-6321 • 1pm-3:30am, from 5pm Sat, clsd Sun • lesbians/ gay men • neighborhood bar • dancing/DJ Fri-Sat

EROTICA

Fantasy East 2311 Concord Rd (at Teal) 765/474-2417 • books & videos

Madison

ACCOMMODATIONS

Lanham House B&B Inn 703 W Main (at Mill) 812/273-3198 • gay/ straight • smokefree • gay-owned/ run • $115-135

Merrillville

see Gary & Hammond

Michigan City

NIGHTCLUBS

Helen's 4960 W US 20 (at 520) 219/874-1100 • 5pm-2am, till 3am Th-Sat, 2pm-12:30am Sun • lesbians/ gay men • dancing/DJ • transgender-friendly • live shows • patio (in-season) • also restaurant • wheelchair access

Mishawaka

see South Bend

Muncie

BARS

Mark III Tap Room 107 E Main St (at Walnut) 765/282-8273 • 11am-3am, 6pm-1am Sun • lesbians/ gay men • dancing/DJ • live shows

Richmond

BARS

Coachman 911 E Main St (at N 9th St) 765/966-2835 • 7pm-3am • lesbians/ gay men • more women Sat • dancing/DJ Fri-Sat • wheelchair access

South Bend

INFO LINES & SERVICES

Community Resource Center Helpline 219/232-2522 • 9am-5pm Mon-Fri • limited lgbt info • also 24hr crisis hotline 219/232-3344

ACCOMMODATIONS

The Gray Goose Inn B&B 350 Indian Boundary Rd (at I-95), Chesterton 219/926-5781, 800/521-5127 • gay/ straight • full brkfst • $80-175

BARS

Jeannie's Tavern 621 S Bendix (at Ford St) 219/288-2962 • 10am-3am • gay-friendly • transgender-friendly • gay-owned/ run

Vickies Inc 112 W Monroe (at Michigan Ave) 219/232-4090 • 11am-3am, clsd Sun • gay-friendly • neighborhood bar • food served • karaoke • football party every Sat in season • gay-owned/ run

NIGHTCLUBS

Sea Horse II Cabaret 1902 Western Ave (at Brookfield) 219/237-9139 • 8pm-3am, 9pm-midnight Mon, 7pm-midnight Sun • lesbians/ gay men • dancing/DJ • live shows Wed-Sat • wheelchair access

Truman's 100 N Center St, Mishawaka **219/259-2282** • 8pm-3am, till 12:30am Sun • popular • lesbians/ gay men • dancing/DJ • live shows • also 'John's Grille' • also gift shop • pride items • clothing

Terre Haute

NIGHTCLUBS

The Velvet Lady 684 Lafayette Ave (at 3rd Ave) **812/232-9119** • 8pm-3am, clsd Sun-Mon • lesbians/ gay men • dancing/DJ • drag shows Fri-Sat

IOWA

Statewide

INFO LINES & SERVICES

Iowa Division of Tourism **800/345-4692**

PUBLICATIONS

Access Line **319/232-6805** • lgbt newspaper

Ames

INFO LINES & SERVICES

Help Central **515/232-0000** • 8:30am-4:30pm Mon-Fri • community info service • some lgbt referrals

LGBT Alliance **515/294-2104** • 11am-5pm • also LGBT Student Services at 515/294-5433

Margaret Sloss Women's Center Sloss House, ISU **515/294-4154** • 8am-5pm, clsd wknds • call for programs

BARS

Studio Cafe 604 E Lincoln Wy **515/663-0929** • 5pm-1am, till 2am Fri-Sat, clsd Sun • lesbians/ gay men • food served • live shows • wheelchair access

RESTAURANTS

Lucallen's 400 Main St (at Kellogg) **515/232-8484** • 11am-9pm, till 10pm Fri-Sat • Italian • some veggie • full bar • $6-12

Pizza Kitchen 120 Hayward (btwn Chamberlain & Lincoln) **515/292-1710** • lunch & dinner • lesbians/ gay men • beer/ wine

Burlington

ACCOMMODATIONS

Arrowhead Motel 2520 Mt Pleasant St **319/752-6353** • gay-friendly • kids ok • wheelchair access • $42-72

BARS

Steve's Place 852 Washington (at Central Ave) **319/752-9109** • 10am-2am • gay-friendly • neighborhood bar • restaurant • wheelchair access

Cedar Falls

see also Waterloo

BOOKSTORES

Gateways 109 E 2nd St (at Main) **319/277-3973** • noon-5:30pm, 9:30am-4pm Sat, clsd Sun • gay section

Cedar Rapids

INFO LINES & SERVICES

Gay/ Lesbian Resource Center 305 2nd St SE #324 **319/366-2055** • noon-3pm Mon, Wed & Fri • 24hr recorded info • support groups • library

NIGHTCLUBS

Club Basix 3916 1st Ave NE (btwn 39th & 40th) **319/363-3194** • 5pm-2am • lesbians/ gay men • transgender-friendly • dancing/DJ • drag shows • Leather Party last wknd of every month • gay/ lesbian-owned/ run

CAFES

Flavorable Reviews 500 1st St SE (in Cedar Rapids Public Library) **319/981-2880** • 9am-5pm, from 10am Sat, clsd Sun • espresso • sandwiches • desserts

RESTAURANTS

The Happy Chef 1906 Blairs Ferry Rd NE **319/395-7793** • 24hrs • American • salad bar

ENTERTAINMENT & RECREATION

CSPS Arts Center 1103 3rd St SE **319/369-1580** • galleries • concerts • plays • many lgbt events

SPIRITUAL GROUPS

Faith United Methodist Church 1000 30th St NE **319/363-8454, 319/895-6678** • 10:30am Sun

Council Bluffs

see Omaha, Nebraska

Iowa • USA

Davenport

see also Rock Island, Illinois

Bars

Mary's on 2nd 832 W 2nd St **319/884-8014** • 4pm-2am, from noon Sun • lesbians/ gay men • neighborhood bar • dancing/DJ • patio • wheelchair access

Nightclubs

Liquid 822 W 2nd St (at Centennial Bridge) **319/324-9675** • 2pm-2am • mostly gay men • dancing/DJ • drag shows • male & female strippers • huge patio bar • volleyball • theme parties • wheelchair access • gay-owned/ run

Spiritual Groups

MCC Quad Cities 3011 N Harrison **319/324-8281** • 11am Sun & 7pm Wed

Des Moines

Info Lines & Services

Corn Haulers Leather & Levi Club PO Box 632 50303 • lesbians/ gay men • social/ support group

GLRC (Gay/ Lesbian Resource Center) of Central Iowa **515/277-7884** • 24hr recorded info • library • youth groups • many other mtgs • also publish newsletter

Out-Reach **515/830-1777** • lesbians/ gay men • social/ support group

Women's Cultural Collective **515/830-1775** • 24hr hotline • weekly meetings • monthly events

Young Women's Resource Center 1909 Ingersoll Ave (at 19th) **515/244-4901** • 8am-5pm, clsd wknds • also social group for youth

Accommodations

The Cottage B&B 1094 28th St (at Cottage Grove) **515/274-7559** • gay-friendly • gay-owned/ run • $75-89

The Hotel Savery 401 Locust St (at 4th) **515/244-2151, 800/798-2151** • gay-friendly • historic luxury hotel & spa • restaurant • $89-239

Kingman House 2920 Kingman Blvd **515/279-7312, 515/996-2829** • lesbians/ gay men • turn-of-the-century B&B • full brkfst • wheelchair access • $40

Quality Inn & Suites Des Moines 4995 N Merle Hay Rd **515/278-2381** • gay-friendly • kids/ pets ok • swimming • hot tub • $65-99

Racoon River Resort **515/279-7312, 515/996-2829** • lesbians/ gay men • rustic lodge 20 minutes from Des Moines • camping & RV hook ups • full brkfst • food served • hot tub • nudity ok • available for groups • wheelchair access • $15-50

Bars

The Blazing Saddle 416 E 5th St (btwn Grand & Locust) **515/246-1299** • 2pm-2am, from noon wknds • popular • mostly gay men • dancing/DJ • leather • shows • wheelchair access

Dally's Pub & Emporium 430 E Locust (1 blk S of Grand, btwn E 4th & 5th) **515/243-9760** • 2pm-2am • popular • lesbians/ gay men • dancing/DJ • country western Th • pizza served • karaoke • live shows • wheelchair access

Faces 416 E Walnut (at 4th St) **515/280-5463** • 9am-2am • lesbians/ gay men • dancing/DJ wknds • live shows • wheelchair access

Nightclubs

The Garden 112 SE 4th St **515/243-3965** • 8pm-2am, clsd Mon-Tue • lesbians/ gay men • dancing/DJ • live shows • karaoke • patio • young crowd • wheelchair access

Cafes

Chat Noir Cafe 644 18th St (at Woodland) **515/244-1353** • 10am-11pm, till midnight Fri-Sat, clsd Sun-Mon • some veggie • beer/ wine • wheelchair access • $6-12

Java Joe's 214 4th St (at Court Ave) **515/288-5282** • 7:30am-11:30pm, till 1am Fri-Sat, 9am-11pm Sun • live shows • community artist gallery next door

Zanzibar's Coffee Adventure 2723 Ingersoll **515/244-7694** • 6:30am-9pm, till 11pm Fri-Sat, till 6pm Sun

Restaurants

Paradise Pizza 2025 Grand, West Des Moines **515/222-9959** • 11am-9pm, till 10pm Fri-Sat

Bookstores

Borders 4100 University, suite #115 (at 42nd), West Des Moines **515/223-1620** • 9am-11pm, till 9pm Sun • lgbt section • wheelchair access

Publications

GLRC Newsletter **515/277-7884** • monthly newsletter of the GLRC of Central Iowa

Spiritual Groups

Church of the Holy Spirit MCC 1165 25th St (at Gay/ Lesbian Resource Center) **515/287-9787** • 10am

Sioux City • Iowa

EROTICA

Gallery Book Store 1000 Cherry (at 10th) **515/244-2916** • 24hrs

Dubuque

INFO LINES & SERVICES

Triangle Coalition of the Tri-State Area **319/588-9220** • lgbt social/ support group • weekly meetings 8pm Th • ask for Dennis

BARS

One Flight Up 44-48 Main St **319/582-8357** • 5pm-2am • lesbians/ gay men • food served wknds • live shows

Fort Dodge

EROTICA

Mini Cinema 15 N 5th St (on the square) **515/955-9756**

Grinnell

INFO LINES & SERVICES

Stonewall Resource Center Grinnell College **515/269-3327** • also quarterly newsletter

Iowa City

INFO LINES & SERVICES

AA Gay/ Lesbian **319/338-9111** (AA#)

LGBT People's Union **319/335-3251** • call for hrs • info

Women's Resource/ Action Center 130 N Madison (at Market) **319/335-1486** • 10am-5pm, clsd wknds • community center • lesbian support group • coming out group • wheelchair access

BARS

The Alley Cat 13 S Linn St (in the alley btwn Linn & Dubuque Sts) **319/887-1305** • 4pm-2am, from 8pm Sat, clsd Sun • lesbians/ gay men • dancing/DJ

Deadwood 6 S Dubuque St **319/351-9417** • 10am-2am • popular • mostly straight • neighborhood bar • college crowd

BOOKSTORES

Prairie Lights Bookstore 15 S Dubuque St (at Washington) **319/337-2681** • 9am-10pm, till 6pm Sun • also cafe • wheelchair access

RETAIL SHOPS

Alternatives 323 E Market St (at Gilbert) **319/337-4124** • noon-6pm, from 10am Sat, clsd Sun • pride gifts • wheelchair access

New Pioneer Co-op & Bakehouse 22 S Van Buren **319/338-9441, 319/358-5513** • 8am-10pm, health food store & deli • also Coralville location at 1101 2nd St (at 12th Ave) • 7am-10pm

Vortex 211 E Washington **319/337-3434** • 10am-9pm • unique gifts, some pride items

SPIRITUAL GROUPS

Faith United Church of Christ 1600 Deforest St (off Sycamore St, nr Hwy 6) **319/338-5238** • 9:30am Sun • wheelchair access

Lansing

ACCOMMODATIONS

Suzanne's B&B 120 N 3rd St (30 miles S of La Crosse, WI) **319/538-3040** • gay-friendly • clsd Jan • full brkfst • shared bath • sauna • fireplace • $60-80

Marshalltown

EROTICA

Adult Odyssey 907 Iowa Ave E **515/752-6550** • videos • toys • leather

Mason City

INFO LINES & SERVICES

GLNCI (Gays/ Lesbians of North Central Iowa) Box 43 50402 • social/ support group • monthly events • newsletter

Newton

ACCOMMODATIONS

La Corsette Maison Inn 629 1st Ave E **641/792-6833** • gay-friendly • 3-course brkfst • antique jacuzzi • 4-star restaurant • kids/ pets ok • $70-185

Pella

ACCOMMODATIONS

Comfort Inn & Suites Pella 910 W 16th, Hwy 163 **641/621-1421** • gay-friendly • kids/ pets ok • swimming • hot tub • wheelchair access • $69-99

Sioux City

BARS

3 Cheers 414 20th St **712/255-8005** • open Wed-Sat • lesbians/ gay men • neighborhood bar • dancing/DJ • live shows • wheelchair access

Iowa/ Kansas • USA

Spencer

Info Lines & Services

Gay & Lesbian Support/ Social Group 201 E 11th St **712/262-2922, 800/242-5101** • 7:30pm 4th Mon

Waterloo

Info Lines & Services

Access 319/232-6805 • info & support

KANSAS

Statewide

Info Lines & Services

Kansas Travel & Tourism Department 800/252-6727

Publications

▲ **The Liberty Press**· 316/652-7737, 785/842-7714 (in Lawrence) • statewide lgbt newspaper

Abilene

Retail Shops

Triangle Artworks 1605 NW 3rd St (at Buckeye) **785/263-7849** • clsd Sun • gallery & gifts • custom orders • ask about gay discount • gay-owned

Emporia

Bookstores

Town Crier 716 Commercial St **316/343-9649** • 9am-8pm, till 6pm Sat, 10am-5pm Sun • woman-owned/ run

Humboldt

Accommodations

Bailey Hotel B&B 822 Bridge St (at 9th St) **316/473-3322** • gay-friendly • restored historic hotel in Civil War era town • full brkfst • smokefree • also restaurant • jacuzzi • $55-99

Kansas City

see Kansas City, Missouri

Lawrence

Info Lines & Services

KU Queers & Allies 785/864-3091 • student group

Bars

Teller's Restaurant & Bar 746 Massachusetts St (at 8th) **785/843-4111** • 11am-2am • gay-friendly • more gay Tue pm • also restaurant • southern Italian/ pizza • some veggie • $12-21 • wheelchair access

Nightclubs

Jazzhaus 926-1/2 Massachusetts St **785/749-3320, 785/749-1387** • 4pm-2am • gay-friendly • live music

Cafes

Henry's 11 E 8th St (at Henry St) **785/331-3511** • 7am-2am • espresso & sandwiches • plenty veggie

Java Break 17 E 7th St (btwn Mass and New Hampshire) **785/749-5282** • 24hrs • sandwiches • desserts • gay-owned/ run

Entertainment & Recreation

Queer Radio KJHK 90.7 FM **785/864-4746** • 4pm-6pm Mon

Bookstores

The Dusty Bookshelf 708 Massachusetts St **785/749-4643** • 10am-8pm, till 10pm Fri-Sat, noon-5pm Sun • used books, feminist & lgbt section • gay-owned/ run

Retail Shops

Naughty But Nice 1741 Mass St (btwn 17th & 18th) **785/832-1000** • 10am-1am, 10pm-3am Fri-Sat, noon-10pm Sun • pride items • erotica

Liberal

Bookstores

Second Street Bookstore 11 W 2nd St **316/624-8105** • 9:30am-8pm, from 11am Sun • large gay magazine selection

Manhattan

Bookstores

The Dusty Bookshelf 700 N Manhattan **785/539-2839** • 10am-8pm, 1pm-5pm Sun, used books • feminist & lgbt section • gay-owned/ run

Matfield Green

Accommodations

Homestead Ranch Guest Programs/ Prairie Women Adventures 316/753-3465 • gay-friendly • bunkhouse for 4 • hot tub • also Youth Adventures for 10-14 yrs old • $150 for four ($15 each additional)

Wichita • Kansas

Spearville

Restaurants

Straw Bales Saloon & Grill 223 N Main St **316/385-2769** • lunch & dinner • gay-owned/run

Topeka

Info Lines & Services

LIFT (Lesbians in Fellowship Together) 2425 SE Indiana (at MCC) **785/232-6196** • 6pm 3rd Th • call for details

Bars

Club U.B.U 110 SE 8th Ave **785/232-7531** • 4pm-2am, till midnight Tue, clsd Mon • gay/straight • dancing • karaoke • monthly shows

Lyz 921 S Kansas **785/234-0482** • 2pm-2am, from 1pm wknds • mostly gay men • neighborhood bar

Bookstores

Barnes & Noble 6130 SW 17th St #101 **785/273-9600** • 9am-11pm, till 9pm Sun • lgbt section

Retail Shops

The Enchanted Willow Alchemy Shoppe 418 SW 6th Ave **785/235-3776** • 10am-6pm Sat-Mon, 4pm-6pm Tue-Fri (may vary) • pride items • pagan, occult & metaphysical supplies • herbs • aromatherapy • books • workshops • gay-owned/run

Spiritual Groups

MCC Topeka 2425 SE Indiana Ave **785/232-6196** • 10am & 6pm Sun

Pagan Earth Circle PO Box 3886 66604-6884 **785/235-3981** • call for info

Wichita

Info Lines & Services

Land of Awes Info Line **316/269-0913** • touchtone info

One Day at a Time Gay AA 2821 S Hydraulic **316/522-7411** • 8pm Mon-Fri, 9pm Sat, 12:30pm Sun

Transitions **316/687-3524** • mtgs for lgbt youth 18-24 at 1054 N Waco

Accommodations

Hawthorn Suites 2405 N Ridge Rd **316/729-5700** • gay-friendly • kids/small pets ok • brkfst buffet • wheelchair access • $50-150

Bars

Dreamers II 4000 S Broadway (at MacArthur) **316/522-2028** • 4pm-2am • mostly women • dancing/DJ • food served • wheelchair access • women-owned/run

J Lounge 513 E Central (at Emporia) **316/262-1363** • 4pm-2am • lesbians/gay men • cabaret • live entertainment • karaoke • wheelchair access

Kirby's Beer Store 3227 E 17th (at Holyoke) **316/685-7013** • 2pm-2am • gay-friendly • live bands • food served

Ralph's 3210 E Osie (at George Washington) **316/682-4461** • 3pm-2am • lesbians/gay men • neighborhood bar • karaoke

---

Wichita

LGBT Pride: June.

City Info: Kansas Travel & Tourism Dept 800/252-6727, web: www.kansascommerce.com.

Attractions: Old Cowtown Museum 316/264-6398.
Pyradomes.
Wichita Art Museum 316/268-4921.

Transit: American Cab Co. 316/262-7511.
Metropolitan Transit Authority 316/265-7221.

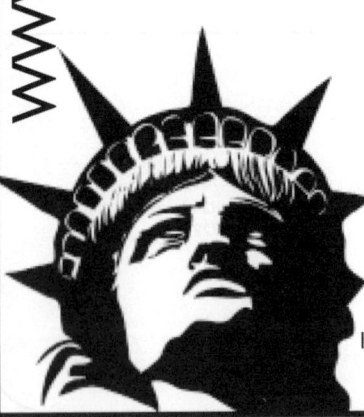

Covington • Kentucky

Side Street Saloon 1106 S Pattie (nr Lincoln & Hydraulic) **316/267-0324** • 2pm-2am • mostly gay men • neighborhood bar • wheelchair access

The T-Room 1507 E Pawnee (at K-15) **316/262-9327** • 3pm-2am • mostly gay men • neighborhood bar • wheelchair access

Nightclubs

Club Vixon 223 S St Francis (at Waterman) **316/618-1756** • 9pm-2am, till 3am wknds, clsd Tue • lesbians/ gay men • dancing/DJ • karaoke

Fantasy Complex 3201 S Hillside (at 31st) **316/682-5494** • 8pm-2am, clsd Mon-Tue • lesbians/ gay men • dancing/DJ • live shows • also 'South Forty' (country/ western bar) open from 3pm Tue-Sun • wheelchair access

Metro 458 N Waco (at Central) **316/262-8130** • 9pm-2am Th-Sun • mostly gay men • dancing/DJ • professional crowd • 18+ Fri & Sun • live shows • also restaurant

Cafes

Riverside Perk 1144 Bidding (at 11th) **316/264-6464** • 7am-10pm, till midnight Fri-Sat, from 10am Sun

Restaurants

Lexie D's 430 E Douglas **316/264-8280** • 11am-11pm wknds • some veggie

Moe's Sub Shop 2815 S Hydraulic (at Wassall) **316/524-5511** • 11am-8pm, clsd Sun

Old Mill Tasty Shop 604 E Douglas (at St Francis) **316/264-6500** • 11am-3pm, 8am-5pm Sat, clsd Sun • old-fashioned soda fountain • lunch menu • some veggie

Tanya's Soup Kitchen 725 E Douglas (behind Black Canyon Grill) **316/267-5349** • lunch Mon-Sat, dinner Wed-Sat, clsd Sun • eclectic cuisine • some veggie

The Upper Crust 7038 E Lincoln **316/683-8088** • lunch only, clsd wknds • homestyle • some veggie • $4-7

Vientiane 3141 S Hillside **316/618-6470** • 11am-8pm • Thai & Laotian food

Entertainment & Recreation

Cabaret Oldtown Theatre 412 1/2 E Douglas (at Topeka) **316/265-4400** • edgy, kitschy productions

Bookshops

The Dusty Bookshelf 922 E Douglas (at Washington) **316/262-7415** • 10am-8pm, 1pm-5pm Sun • used • lgbt books in gender section • gay-owned/ run

Retail Shops

Holier Than Thou Body Piercing 1111 E Douglas Ave (at Washington) **316/266-4100** • noon-8pm, till 6pm Sun

Mother's 3100 E 31st St S (at Hillside) **316/686-8116** • hrs vary • lgbt gifts

Spiritual Groups

College Hill United Methodist Church 2930 E 1st St **316/683-4643** • 8:30am, 9:40 & 11am Sun

First Metropolitan Community Church 156 S Kansas Ave **316/267-1852** • 10:30am

First Unitarian Universalist Church 1501 Fairmount (nr 13th St) **316/684-3481** • 11am Sun

Erotica

Priscilla's 6143 W Kellogg (at Dugan) **316/942-1244**

Kentucky

Statewide

Publications

The Letter 502/636-0935 **(news)**, 502/772-7570 **(advertising)** • statewide lgbt newspaper

Bowling Green

Accommodations

Maple Grove Farm 2841 Hwy 185 **502/843-7433** • gay/ straight • large 1916 bungalow on 8 acres • full brkfst • hot tub • gay-owned/ run • $40-60

Covington

see also Cincinnati, Ohio

Accommodations

First Farm Inn 2510 Stevens Rd, Petersburg **859/586-0199, 800/277-9527** • gay-friendly • 1800s farmhouse B&B • nr Cincinnati • full brkfst • horseback riding • massage • $50-109

Licking Riverside 516 Garrard St **859/291-0191, 800/483-7822** • gay-friendly • 1870 Greek Revival B&B • jacuzzi • private sundeck • nr Cincinnati • woman-owned/ run • $115-169

Bars

Rosie's Tavern 643 Bakewell St **859/291-9707** • 3pm-2:30am • gay/ straight • neighborhood bar • lesbian-owned

Kentucky • USA

Elizabethtown

Spiritual Groups

Elizabethtown MCC 119 Brook St (at Mulberry) **888/340-6223** • 11am Sun

Harned

Accommodations

Kentucky Holler House Rte 1 Box 51BB **270/547-4507** • B&B on 48 acres • lesbians/ gay men • private decks • smokefree • also antique shop • lesbian-owned/ run • $75-95

Lexington

Info Lines & Services

Gay/ Lesbian AA 859/245-7471 **(private home),** 859/276-2917 **(AA#)** • 8pm Mon & Wed, 7:30pm Fri

Pride Center of the Bluegrass 389 Waller Ave #100 **859/253-3233**

Sistahs in the Life 859/233-3751 • 7pm 4th Wed • meetings for lesbians of African descent • ask for Letonia

Bars

The Bar Complex 224 E Main St **859/255-1551** • 4pm-1am, till 3:30am Sat, clsd Sun • popular • lesbians/ gay men • dancing/DJ • live shows • wheelchair access

Nightclubs

Club 141 141 W Vine St (at Limestone) **859/233-4262** • 8:30pm-1am, till 3am Sat, clsd Sun-Mon • popular • lesbians/ gay men • dancing/DJ • alternative • live shows • wheelchair access

Restaurants

Alfalfa 557 S Limestone **859/253-0014** • lunch & dinner • healthy multi-ethnic • plenty veggie • folk music nightly • $6-12

Bookstores

Joseph-Beth 161 Lexington Green Circle **859/273-2911, 800/248-6849** • 9am-10pm, till 11pm Fri-Sat, 11am-9pm Sun • also cafe & travel agency • wheelchair access

Publications

GLSO (Gay/ Lesbian) News • local news & calendar

The Letter 502/636-0935 **(news),** 502/772-7570 **(advertising)** • statewide lgbt newspaper

Spiritual Groups

Faith MCC 145 Burt Rd Suite 7 **859/539-3622** • 10:30am Sun • wheelchair access

Pagan Forum 859/268-1640 • call for info on 10+ area pagan groups

Louisville

Info Lines & Services

LGBT Hotline 502/454-7613 • counseling 6pm-10pm • 24hr hotline • AA referrals

Louisville Youth Group 502/894-9787, **800/347-8336** • 8:30pm 1st & 3rd Fri • call for location

The Williams-Nichols Institute 2301 S 3rd St (at University of Louisville Ekstrom Library) **502/852-6752** • 4pm-9pm, till 8pm Th, clsd wknds • lgbt archives • library • referrals

Accommodations

Columbine Inn 1707 S 3rd St (nr Leet St) **502/635-5000, 800/635-5010** • gay-friendly • 1896 Greek revivial mansion • full brkfst • smokefree • $75-140

Holiday Inn Southwest 4110 Dixie Hwy (at I-264) **502/448-2020** • gay-friendly • swimming • restaurant • lounge • wheelchair access

Inn at the Park 1332 S 4th St (at Park Ave) **502/637-6930, 800/700-7275** • gay-friendly • restored mansion • $89-169

Bars

Gypsies 319 E Market (at Floyd) **502/561-0752** • 4pm-close, clsd Mon • gay/ straight • dancing/ DJ wknds • food served • drag shows • karaoke • wheelchair access • women-owned/ run

Magnolia Bar 1398 S 2nd St (at Magnolia) **502/637-9052** • noon-4am • gay-friendly • neighborhood bar • young crowd

Teddy Bears Bar & Grill 1148 Garvin Pl (at St Catherine) **502/589-2619** • 11am-4am, from 1pm Sun • mostly gay men • neighborhood bar • wheelchair access

Tryangles 209 S Preston St (at Market) **502/583-6395** • 4pm-4am • mostly gay men • country/ western • live shows • wheelchair access

Nightclubs

The Connection Complex 120 S Floyd St (at Market) **502/585-5752** • 5pm-4am • popular • lesbians/ gay men • dancing/DJ • piano bar & cabaret • video bar • gift shop • also restaurant • some veggie • wheelchair access • $5-15

Cafes

Days Coffeehouse 1420 Bardstown Rd (at Edenside) **502/456-1170** • 8am-10pm, till 11pm wknds • lesbian-owned/ run

Louisville • Kentucky

Restaurants

Cafe Mimosa 1216 Bardstown Rd **502/458-2233** • lunch & dinner • Vietnamese, Chinese & sushi

El Mundo 2345 Frankfort Ave **502/899-9930** • 11:30am-10pm, clsd Sun • popular • Mexican

Lynn's Paradise Cafe 984 Barret Ave (at Baxter) **502/583-3447** • 7am-10pm, clsd Mon • lesbians/gay men • also bar • lesbian-owned/ run

Queenie's Pizza & Such 2622 S 4th St **502/636-3708** • 11am-10pm, till 11pm Fri-Sat, 4pm-8pm Sun, clsd Mon • gay-owned/ run

Rudyard Kipling 422 W Oak St **502/636-1311** • lunch Mon-Fri, dinner from 5:30pm Mon-Sat • also English pub & theater • live music

Entertainment & Recreation

Community Chorus 502/327-4099

Bookstores

Carmichael's 1295 Bardstown Rd (at Longest Ave) **502/456-6950** • 8am-10pm, till 11pm Fri-Sat, from 10am Sun • large lgbt section • also 2866 Frankfort Ave, 502/895-6950

Hawley Cooke Books 3024 Bardstown Rd (in Gardiner Lane Shopping Ctr) **502/456-6660** • 9am-9pm, 10am-6pm Sun • also 27 Shelbyville Rd Plaza, 502/893-0133 • also 2400 Lime Kiln Ln, 502/425-9100

Retail Shops

MT Closets 120 S Floyd (in the Connection Complex) **502/587-1060, 800/606-4524** • 4pm-1am, 7pm-3am Fri-Sat, 7pm-1am Sun, clsd Mon-Tue • clubwear • pride gifts

---

[Reply] [Forward] **[Delete]**

Date: Sun, Dec 23, 2001 12:22:05
From: Girl-on-the-Go
To: Editor@Damron.com
Subject: Louisville

> Beautiful Louisville sits on the banks of the Ohio River and is home to the world-famous Kentucky Derby. This spectacular race occurs during the first week of May at Churchill Downs.
> Louisville is also home to many whiskey distilleries. If neither watching horses run in circles, nor swilling homegrown booze excites you, check out the Louisville Slugger Museum (502/588-7228). Then there's the Belle of Louisville (502/574-2355), one of the last authentic sternwheelers in the country as well as the oldest operating steamboat on the Mississippi River.
> Whatever you do, you're certain to enjoy this city's slower pace of life and Southern charm—Louisville is, after all, known as the 'northern border for southern hospitality'. The best way to get a feel for this Louisville is to walk among the elegant homes of St. James Court.
> Before you leave, sample the whiskey and the hospitality at **Gypsies** or at the popular **Connection Complex**. Or enjoy a meal at lesbian-owned **Lynn's Paradise Cafe.**
> Only a few hours to the east, make sure to rest a spell in the beautiful bluegrass country of Lexington, Kentucky. Then you can get up and dance at the **Bar Complex** or **Club 141.**

Kentucky • USA

Publications

The Letter 502/636-0935 **(news)**, 502/772-7570 **(advertising)** • statewide lgbt newspaper

The Rainbow Pages 502/899-3551 • lgbt resource guide

Spiritual Groups

B'nai Shalom 502/896-0475 • lgbt Jewish group

Central Presbyterian Church 502/587-6935 • 11am Sun • 'More Light' congregation

Dignity 1864 Frankfurt Ave (at Third Lutheran Church) **502/473-1458** • 7pm 2nd Sun

MCC Louisville 1432 Highland Ave **502/587-6225** • 11am & 6pm Sun, 7:45pm Wed • wheelchair access

Newport

Bars

The Crazy Fox Saloon 901 Washington Ave **859/261-2143** • 4pm-2:30am • gay/ straight • friendly neighborhood bar

Paducah

Nightclubs

The Pride Factory 2118 Bridge St **270/575-1995** • 9pm-3am, clsd Mon • lesbians/ gay men • neighborhood bar • dancing/DJ • live shows • wheelchair access

Spiritual Groups

MCC of Paducah 626B Broadway ((behind Curtis & Mays)) **270/443-3339** • 11am Sun & 7pm Wed • wheelchair access

Somerset

Info Lines & Services

Lesbigay Info 606/678-5814 • ask for Linda

Versailles

Accommodations

Rose Hill Inn 233 Rose Hill **800/307-0460** • gay-friendly • 1823 Victorian mansion • full brkfst • nr Lexington • women-owned/ run • $85-139

Louisville

Where the Girls Are: On Main or Market Streets near 1st, and generally in the north-central part of town, just west of I-65.

Entertainment: Community Chorus 502/327-4099.

LGBT Pride: June.

Annual Events: May - Kentucky Derby.
June - Kentucky Shakespeare Festival 502/583-8738.
October - Halloween Cruise on the Ohio River.

City Info: Louisville Visitor Center 800/792-5595.

Attractions: Belle Of Louisville Steamboat 502/574-2992.
Churchill Downs 502/636-4400.
Farmington.
Hadley Pottery 502/584-2171.
Kentucky Derby 502/584-6383.
Locust Grove.
St. James Court.
The Waterfront.
West Main Street Historic District.

Best View: The Spire Restaurant and Cocktail Lounge on the 19th floor of the Hyatt Regency Louisville.

Weather: Mild winters and long, hot summers!

Transit: Yellow Taxi 502/636-5511.
TARC Bus System 502/585-1234.
Toonerville II Trolley or Louisville Horse Trams 502/581-0100.

Lake Charles • Louisiana

LOUISIANA

Statewide

INFO LINES & SERVICES

Louisiana Office of Tourism 800/334-8626

PUBLICATIONS

Ambush Mag 504/522-8049 • lgbt newspaper

▲ **Southern Voice** 404/876-1819 • weekly lgbt newspaper for AL, FL (panhandle), GA, LA, MS, TN w/ resource listings

Alexandria

NIGHTCLUBS

Unique Bar & Lounge 1919 N MacArthur Dr **318/448-0555** • 9pm-2am, till 3am wknds, clsd Mon-Tue • popular • lesbians/ gay men • dancing/DJ • transgender-friendly • live shows • patio • wheelchair access

Baton Rouge

INFO LINES & SERVICES

Freedom of Choice/ Gay AA 333 E Chimes St (at United Campus Ministries, upstairs) **225/924-0030 (AA#)** • 8pm Th & 9pm Sat

BARS

George's Place 860 St Louis **225/387-9798** • 3pm-2am, from 5pm Sat, clsd Sun • popular • lesbians/ gay men • neighborhood bar • karaoke • live shows • wheelchair access

Hide-A-Way 7367 Exchange Pl **225/923-3632** • 8pm-2am, clsd Sun-Tue • mostly women • neighborhood bar • dancing/DJ • wheelchair access • women-owned/ run

NIGHTCLUBS

Icon 2183 Highland Rd **225/242-9491** • 9pm-2am, clsd Sun-Tue • mostly gay men • dancing/DJ • live shows • alternative • 18+ • wheelchair access

RESTAURANTS

Chalet Brant 7655 Old Hammond Hwy (nr Jefferson) **225/927-6040** • 6pm-10pm, lunch Wed-Fri only, clsd Sun • cont'l • $15-30

Drusilla Seafood 3482 Drusilla Ln (at Jefferson Hwy) **225/923-0896** • dinner till 10pm • $15-20

Ralph & Kacoo's 6110 Bluebonnet Blvd (off I-10 & Perkins) **225/766-2113** • lunch & dinner • Cajun • $8-20

BOOKSTORES

Hibiscus Bookstore 635 Main St (btwn 6th & 7th) **225/387-4264** • 11am-6pm • lgbt

SPIRITUAL GROUPS

Joie de Vivre MCC 333 E Chimes St **225/383-0450** • 11am Sun

EROTICA

Cyber Video & Novelties 2160 Highland Rd (at W Polk) **225/338-9000** • 24hrs • also Cyber Cafe

Folsom

ACCOMMODATIONS

Woods Hole Inn 78253 Woods Hole Ln (at Thompson Rd) **504/796-9077** • gay-friendly • secluded getaway • 40 mins from New Orleans • suites & cabin • fireplaces • smokefree • $85-120

Houma

NIGHTCLUBS

Kixx 112 N Hollywood **504/876-9587** • 6pm-2am, clsd Sun-Mon • lesbians/ gay men • dancing/DJ • live shows • wheelchair access

Lafayette

INFO LINES & SERVICES

AA Gay/ Lesbian 1119-C Johnson St **337/991-0830 (AA)** • 8pm Wed

ACCOMMODATIONS

The Estorge House B&B 417 N Market St (at Bloch), Opelousas **337/942-8151, 888/655-9539** • lesbians/ gay men • antique-filled 1827 house • full brkfst • swimming • smokefree • lesbian-owned • $125

BARS

Jules' Tavern 533 Jefferson **337/264-8000** • 8pm-2am • lesbians/ gay men • dancing/DJ • karaoke • live shows • wheelchair access

Mojo Monkey's 116 Spring St **337/261-9020** • 7pm-2am, 4pm-midnight Sun, clsd Mon-Tue • mostly women • dancing/DJ • live entertainment • wheelchair access

NIGHTCLUBS

Sound Factory 209 Jefferson St (at Cypress) **337/269-6011** • 6pm-2am, noon-midnight Sun • mostly gay men • young crowd • dancing/DJ • drag shows

Lake Charles

ACCOMMODATIONS

Aunt Ruby's 504 Pujo St (at Hodges) **337/430-0603** • gay/ straight • B&B • full brkfst • complimentary cocktails in evening • gay-owned/ run • $75-125

Louisiana • USA

NIGHTCLUBS

Crystal's 112 W Broad St **337/433–5457** • 8pm-2am, from 9pm Fri-Sat, till 4am Fri, clsd Sun • lesbians/gay men • dancing/DJ • country/western • live shows • wheelchair access

RESTAURANTS

Pujo St Café 901 Ryan St (at Pujo) **337/439–2054** • 11am-9pm, till 10pm wknds • gay-owned/run

Monroe

BARS

The Corner Bar 512 N 3rd St (at Pine) **318/329–0046** • 5pm-2am, clsd Sun • lesbians/gay men • neighborhood bar • multiracial • live shows • karaoke • 18+ • gay-owned/run

New Orleans

INFO LINES & SERVICES

Lesbian/Gay Community Center of New Orleans 2114 Decatur St **504/945–1103** • 2pm-8pm, 11am-6pm Sat, 10am-6pm Sun • call first • wheelchair access

ACCOMMODATIONS

1227 Easton House 1227 N Rendon St (btwn Esplanade & Grand Rte St John) **504/488–5543, 877/311–1023** • gay/straight • b&b • full brkfst • nr City Park • some shared baths • smokefree • gay-owned/run • $85-210

A Creole House Hotel 1013 St Ann (btwn Burgundy & Rampart) **504/524–8076, 800/535–7858** • gay/straight • 1830s building furnished in period style • smokefree • kids ok • $59-250

▲ **Alternative Accommodations/ French Quarter Accommodation Service** 1001 Marigny St **504/949–5815, 800/209–9408** • 4 gay-friendly guesthouses

Andrew Jackson Hotel 919 Royal St (btwn St Philip & Dumaine) **504/561–5881, 800/654–0224** • gay-friendly • historic inn • tropical courtyard • $80-169

Annunciation Place 1235 Annunciation St **504/522–8834** • lesbians/gay men • 2-rm suite w/ private balcony • full kitchen • smokefree • kids ok • gay-owned/run • $100-175

B&W Courtyards B&B 2425 Chartres St (btwn Mandeville & Spain) **504/945–9418, 800/585–5731** • gay/straight • hot tub • gay-owned/run • $115-165

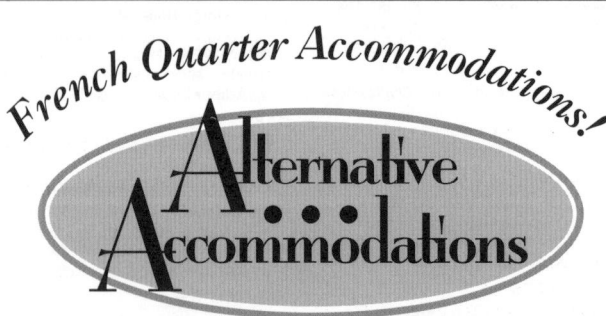

French Quarter Accommodations!

Alternative Accommodations

Property Listings:
www.fqaccommodations.com
800-209-9408

"The unique New Orleans experience"

1001 Marigny Street, New Orleans, LA 70117

New Orleans • Louisiana

Reply **Forward** **Delete**

Date: Fri, Nov 23, 2001 11:23:19
From: Girl-on-the-Go
To: Editor@Damron.com
Subject: New Orleans

> If you haven't been to New Orleans for Mardi Gras, you've missed the party of the year. But there's still time to plan next year's visit to the French Quarter's blowout of a block party—complete with its elaborate balls, parades, and dancing in the streets. It all starts the day before Ash Wednesday (usually in February).

> Of course, there's more to 'The Big Easy' than Mardi Gras, especially if you like life hot, humid, and spiced with steamy jazz and hot pepper. Park your bags in one of the MANY lesbian/gay inns in the area. Then venture into the French Quarter, where you'll find the infamous Bourbon Street with people strolling—or occasionally staggering—from jazz club to jazz club, bar to bar, restaurants to shops, twenty-four hours a day. Kitsch-lovers won't want to miss Pat O'Brien's, home of the Hurricane and the #1 bar in the country for alcohol volume sold—even if you don't drink, a campy photo in front of the fountain is a must. Jazz lovers, make a pilgrimage to Preservation Hall.

> If you love to shop, check out the French Market, the Jackson Brewery, and Riverwalk. Antique hunting is best on Rue Royal or Decatur Street. And you can't leave New Orleans without a trip through the Garden District to see the incredible antebellum and revival homes—a trip best made on the St. Charles Trolley.

> Gourmands must try real Cajun & Creole food in its natural environment—though if you're vegetarian, the **Old Dog New Trick Cafe** is your best bet. For melt-in-your-mouth, hot, sugar-powdered beignets, run, don't walk to Café du Monde.

> The morbidly inclined among us are bound to see shadows of vampires and other creatures of the night in this town of mysticism and the occult. With residents like Anne Rice, Poppy Z. Brite, and (the late) Marie LaVeau stirring up the spirits, perhaps a protective amulet from Marie LaVeau's House of Voodoo (739 Bourbon St, 504/581-3751) would be a good idea. For a peek at traditional voodoo—the Afro-Caribbean religion, not the B-movie schlock—visit the Voodoo Museum (504/523-7685). Or sate that urge for blood with a body piercing at **Rings of Desire** or some fresh fetish wear from **Second Skin Leather.**

Louisiana • USA

Bed & Beverage Guest Apts 612 St Philip St **504/588–1483, 800/809–7815** • gay/ straight • furnished studios in the French Quarter • swimming • kids/ pets ok • wheelchair access • $85-165

Big D's B&B 704 Franklin Ave (at Royal) **504/945–8049** • lesbians/ gay men • lesbian-owned/ run • $65-95

Big Easy/ French Quarter Lodging 233 Cottonwood Dr, Gretna **504/433–2563, 800/368–4876** • gay/ straight • free reservation service • gay-owned/ run

The Big Easy Guest House 2633 Dauphine St (at Franklin) **504/943–3717, 800/679–0640** • gay/ straight • 1830s private home • 8 blks from French Quarter • $65

New Orleans

WHERE THE GIRLS ARE: Wandering the Quarter, or in the small artsy area known as Mid-City, north of the Quarter up Esplanade St.

LGBT PRIDE: September. 504/522-0907.

ANNUAL EVENTS: February - Mardi Gras 504/566-5011. North America's rowdiest block party.
April - Gay Easter Parade 504/581-4173.
Gulf Coast Womyn's Festival at Camp SisterSpirit (in Ovett, MS) 601/344-1411.
April/May - New Orleans Jazz & Heritage Festival.
Labor Day - Southern Decadence 504/522-8047. Gay mini-Mardi Gras.

CITY INFO: 504/566-5011, web: www.neworleanscvb.com. Louisiana Office of Tourism 800/334-8626.

ATTRACTIONS: Bourbon Street in the French Quarter.
Cafe du Monde for beignets 504/587-0835.
Garden District.
Moon Walk.
New Orleans Museum of Art 504/488-2631.
Pat O'Brien's for a hurricane 504/525-4823.
Preservation Hall 504/522-2841.
Top of the Market.

BEST VIEW: Top of the Mart Lounge (504/522-9795) on the 33rd floor of the World Trade Center of New Orleans.

WEATHER: Summer temperatures hover in the 90°s with subtropical humidity. Winters can be rainy and chilly. The average temperature in February (Mardi Gras month) is 58° while the average precipitation is 5.23".

TRANSIT: United Cab 504/522-9771. Airport Shuttle 504/522-3500. Regional Transit Authority 504/248-3900.

New Orleans • Louisiana

The Biscuit Palace 730 Dumaine (btwn Royal & Bourbon) **504/525–9949** • gay-friendly • 1820s Creole mansion • B&B & apts • in the French Quarter • kids ok • wheelchair access • $85-150

Block-Keller House 3620 Canal St (at Telemachus) **504/483–3033, 877/588–3033** • gay/straight • smokefree • kids ok • gay-owned/run • $110-135

Bon Maison Guest House 835 Bourbon St (btwn Lafittes & Bourbon Pub) **504/561–8498** • popular • gay-friendly •1833 townhouse • $85-165

Bourbon Orleans Hotel 717 Orleans (at Bourbon St) **504/523–2222, 800/521–5338** • popular • gay-friendly • swimming • restaurant & lounge

Bourgoyne Guest House 839 Bourbon St (at Dumaine St) **504/524–3621, 504/525–3983** • popular • lesbians/gay men • 1830s Creole mansion • courtyard • $80-170

Bywater B&B 1026 Clouet St **504/944–8438** • gay-friendly • Victorian cottage • kitchen • fireplace • smokefree • kids/pets ok • women-owned/run • $65-85

Casa de Marigny Creole Guest Cottages 818 Frenchmen St (at Dauphine) **504/948–3875** • gay/straight • private cottages • tropical garden • patio • swimming • $75-225

The Chimes B&B Constantinople at Coliseum (in Garden District) **504/488-4640, 800/729-4640** • gay-friendly • 1876 home • smokefree • kids/pets ok • $85-130

Dauzat House 1000 Conti St (at Burgundy) **504/524-2075** • gay-friendly • jacuzzis • fireplaces

Empress Hotel 1317 Ursulines Ave (btwn Treme & Marais) **504/529–4100, 888/524–9200** • gay-friendly • 2 blks to French Quarter • kids/pets ok • $25-50

Fourteen Twelve Thalia—A B&B 1412 Thalia (btwn Prytania & Coliseum) **504/522-0453** • gay/straight • 1-bdrm apt in the Lower Garden District • pets ok • patio • gay-owned/run • $85-250

French Quarter B&B 1132 Ursulines (btwn N Rampart & St Claude Ave) **504/525-3390** • lesbians/gay men • apt • swimming • kids ok • smokefree • gay-owned/run • $75-175

▲ **French Quarter Reservation Service** **504/523-1246, 800/523-9091** • kids ok • some w/ swimming • some w/ wheelchair access

French Quarter Accommodations

Make Your Plans NOW!

French Quarter Reservation Service

N'AWLINS OLDEST & LARGEST GAY RESERVATION SERVICE

1-800-523-9091

504-523-1246 • FAX 504-527-6327
1000 Bourbon St., PMB #263, New Orleans, LA 70116
e-mail: fqrsinc@bellsouth.net   www.neworleansgay.com

member IGLTA

Louisiana • USA

French Quarter Suites 1119 N Rampart (at Ursulines) 504/524-7725, 800/457-2253 • gay-friendly • apt & suites • hot tub • swimming • kitchens • kids/pets ok • wheelchair access • gay-owned/run • $70+

The Frenchmen Hotel 417 Frenchmen St (where Esplanade, Decatur & Frenchmen intersect) 504/948-2166, 888/365-2775 • popular • gay/straight • 1860s Creole townhouses • spa • swimming • smokefree • kids ok • wheelchair access • $59-180

Glimmer Inn B&B 1631 7th St (at St Charles) 504/897-1895 • gay-friendly • 1891 Victorian & cottage • kids/pets ok • some shared baths • women-owned/run • $60-85

Green House Inn 1212 Magazine St (at Erato) 504/525-1333, 800/966-1303 • lesbians/gay men • 1840s guesthouse • gym • hot tub • swimming • non-smoking rooms available • pets ok • gay-owned/run • $69-149

HH Whitney House on Esplanade 1923 Esplanade Ave (at N Prieur St) 504/948-9448, 877/944-9448 • gay/straight • 1865 B&B • hot tub • some shared baths • kids ok • smokefree • gay-owned/run • $95-250

Hotel de la Monnaie 405 Esplanade Ave (btwn Decatur & N Peters) 504/947-0009 • gay-friendly • all-suite hotel • hot tub • swimming • courtyard • wheelchair access • $125+

House of David 735 Touro St (at Dauphine) 504/948-3438 • lesbians/gay men • newly remodeled 1820s Creole cottage • jacuzzi • private courtyard • gay-owned/run • $79-100

Ingram Haus 1012 Elysian Fields Ave (btwn N Rampart & St Claude) 504/949-3110 • gay/straight • apts • courtyard • gay-owned/run • $75-150

Inn The Quarter 888/523-5235 • gay-friendly • 1840s townhouse • private courtyard • smokefree • $79-185

La Dauphine, Residence des Artistes 2316 Dauphine St (btwn Elysian Fields & Marigny) 504/948-2217 • gay/straight • smokefree • free airport pickup (call for details) • gay-owned/run • $65-125 (3-night minimum)

La Maison Marigny B&B on Bourbon 1421 Bourbon St (at Esplanade) 504/948-3638, 800/570-2014 • gay-friendly • on the quiet end of Bourbon St • smokefree • gay-owned • $99-199

La Residence Esplanade & Marais Sts 504/832-4131, 800/826-9718 x11 • gay/straight • 1840s Creole cottage • 1 & 2-bdrm apts • kitchens • tropical courtyard • $75-175

Lafitte Guest House 1003 Bourbon St (at St Philip) 504/581-2678, 800/331-7971 • popular • gay/straight • elegant French manor house • smokefree • kids ok • full bar • gay-owned/run • $129-219

Lamothe House Hotel 621 Esplanade Ave (btwn Royal & Chartres) 504/947-1161, 800/367-5858 • gay/straight • 1800s Victorian guesthouse • courtyard • jacuzzi • swimming • smokefree • kids ok • gay-owned/run • $70-250

Lanata House 1220 Chartres St #5 (at Gov Nicholls) 504/522-0374 • gay/straight • furnished residential accommodations • swimming • gay-owned/run • $145-250

▲ **Macarty Park Guesthouse** 3820 Burgundy St 504/943-4994, 800/521-2790 • gay/straight • swimming • hot tub • also cottages & condos • gay-owned/run • $59-190

Maison Burgundy 1860 Burgundy St (on corner of Pauger, btwn Pauger & Burgundy) 504/948-2355, 800/863-8813 • gay/straight • full brkfst • swimming • private entrances • gay-owned/run • $125-250

Marigny Guest House 621 Esplanade (btwn Royal & Chartres) 504/944-9700, 800/367-5858 • gay-friendly • quaint Creole cottage • swimming • smokefree • $59-175

Mazant Guest House 906 Mazant (at Burgundy) 504/944-2662 • gay-friendly • 1880s Greek revival B&B • inexpensive

The McKendrick-Breaux House 1474 Magazine St (at Euterpe) 504/586-1700, 888/570-1700 • gay-friendly • 1860s restored Greek Revival • hot tub • $110-175

Mentone B&B 1437 Pauger St (at Kerlerec) 504/943-3019 • gay-friendly • suite in Victorian in the Faubourg Marigny district • smokefree • women-owned/run • $100-150

New Orleans Guest House 1118 Ursulines Ave (at N Rampart) 504/566-1177, 800/562-1177 • gay-friendly • Creole cottage dated back to 1848 • courtyard • parking • $79-99

Olde Town Inn 1001 Marigny St 504/949-5815, 800/209-9408 • gay/straight • historic guesthouse • tropical courtyard • walk-ins welcome • kids/pets ok • $49-129

Parkview Marigny B&B 726 Frenchmen (at Dauphine) 504/945-7875, 877/645-8617 • gay/straight • 1870s Creole townhouse • smokefree • patio • gay-owned/run • $105-175

Pauger Guest Suites 1722 Pauger St 504/944-2601 • gay/straight • nr French Quarter • swimming • kids ok • gay-owned/run • $55+

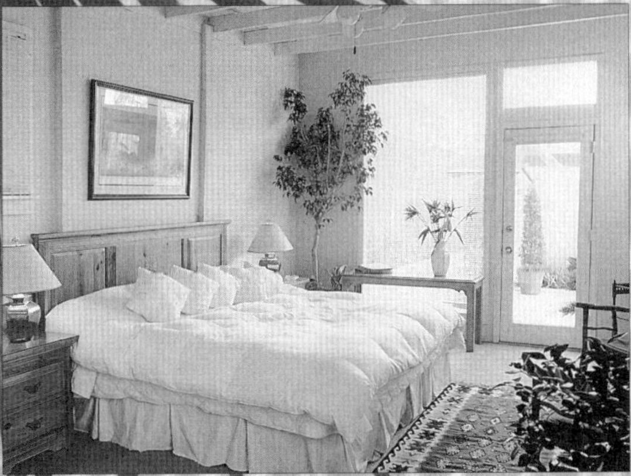

Go for a splash in our refreshing heated pool and hot tub. Enjoy beautiful cottages and rooms with color cable TV, phone, private baths and continental breakfast. Great romantic getaway.

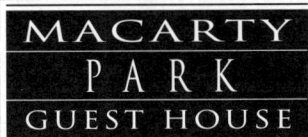

MACARTY PARK GUEST HOUSE

3820 Burgundy Street • New Orleans, LA 70117
(504) 943-4994 • (800) 521-2790
faxmehard@aol.com • www.macartypark.com

Louisiana • USA

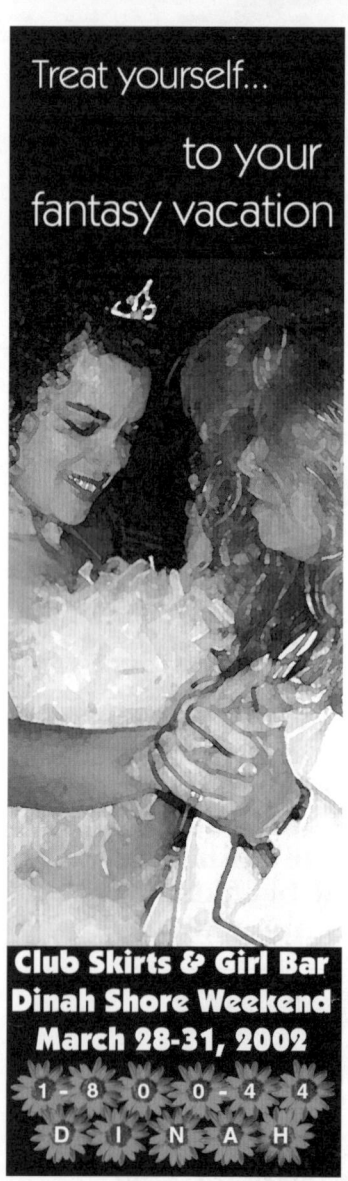

Radisson Hotel New Orleans 1500 Canal St (at LaSalle St) **504/522-4500** • gay-friendly • food served • swimming

Rober House Condos 822 Ursulines Ave (at Dauphine) **504/529-4663, 800/523-9091** • gay/straight • apt • swimming • non-smoking room available • kids/pets ok • courtyard • wheelchair access • gay-owned/run • $89-150

Royal Barracks Guest House 717 Barracks St (at Bourbon) **504/529-7269, 888/255-7269** • lesbians/gay men • hot tub • private patios • gay-owned/run • $85-150

Royal St Courtyard 2438 Royal St (at Spain) **504/943-6818, 888/846-4004** • lesbians/gay men • suites • hot tub • kitchens • pets ok • gay-owned/run • $55-135

Rue Royal Inn 1006 Royal St (at St Philip) **504/524-3900, 800/776-3901** • gay/straight • historic 1830s Creole townhouse in the heart of the French Quarter • wheelchair access • $85-165

Ruffino's Guest House 631 St Philip (btwn Chartres & Royal) **504/588-9004, 888/687-3900** • gay-friendly • in the French Quarter • kids/pets ok • smokefree • woman-owned/run • $85-135

Southern Comforts 323/850-5623 (IN CA), 800/889-7359 • gay-friendly • French Quarter rentals • hot tub • swimming • pets ok • smokefree • wheelchair access • gay-owned/run • $125-325

St Charles Guest House 1748 Prytania St (at Felicity) **504/523-6556** • gay-friendly • pensione-style guest house • some shared baths • swimming • patio • $45-125

St Peter Guest House 1005 St Peter St (at Burgundy) **504/524-9232, 888/604-6300** • gay-friendly • antique-furnished early-1800s building • historic location • $60-250

Sun & Moon B&B 1037 N Rampart St (at Ursulines) **504/529-4652, 800/638-9169** • gay/straight • Creole cottage • courtyard • women-owned/run • $85-110

Sun Oak Museum & Guesthouse 2020 Burgundy St **504/945-0322** • gay/straight • Greek Revival Creole cottage circa 1836 • gardens • gay-owned • $100-200

Sweet Olive B&B 2460 N Rampart (at Spain) **504/947-4332, 877/470-5323** • gay-friendly • $99-150

Ursuline Guest House 708 Ursulines Ave (btwn Royal & Bourbon) **504/525-8509, 800/654-2351** • popular • gay/straight • hot tub • evening socials • gay-owned/run • $85-125

New Orleans • Louisiana

Vieux Carré Rentals 841 Bourbon St **504/525-3983** • gay-friendly • 1 & 2-bdrm apts

Bars

Angles 2301 N Causeway Blvd (at 34th), Metairie **504/834-7979** • 6pm-2am, till 4am Th-Sat, 4pm-midnight Sun • lesbians/ gay men • neighborhood bar • dancing/DJ • karaoke Th • live shows • 18+ • wheelchair access

Big Daddy's 2513 Royal (at Franklin) **504/948-6288** • 24hrs • lesbians/ gay men • neighborhood bar • food served • live entertainment Sun • wheelchair access

Cafe Lafitte in Exile/ The Balcony Bar 901 Bourbon St (at Dumaine) **504/522-8397** • 24hrs • popular • mostly gay men • dancing/DJ • live shows • videos • 'Balcony Bar' upstairs features area's first cyber bar

Club Park Avenue 3515 Hessmer (btwn Veterans Blvd & 18th St), Metairie **504/454-1120** • 6pm-close, clsd Sun-Mon • mostly women • dancing/DJ • live shows

Country Club 634 Louisa St (at Chartres) **504/945-0742** • 11am-1am, from 4pm wkdays in winter • lesbians/ gay men • neighborhood bar • food served • live shows • hot tub • swimming

Double D's Half Moon Saloon 706 Franklin Ave (at Royal) **504/948-2300** • 24hrs • mostly gay men • neighborhood bar • dancing/DJ • wheelchair access

The Double Play 439 Dauphine (at St Louis) **504/523-4517** • 24hrs • mostly gay men • neighborhood bar

The Four Seasons 3229 N Causeway Blvd (at 18th), Metairie **504/832-0659** • 3pm-4am • popular • lesbians/ gay men • neighborhood bar • food served • live shows • karaoke • 18+ • patio • also the 'Outback Bar' • gay-owned/ run

The Friendly Bar 2301 Chartres St (at Marigny) **504/943-8929** • 11am-3am • popular • lesbians/ gay men • neighborhood bar • food served • wheelchair access • women-owned/ run

Golden Lantern 1239 Royal St (at Barracks) **504/529-2860** • 24hrs • mostly gay men • neighborhood bar

Good Friends Bar 740 Dauphine (at St Ann) **504/566-7191** • 24hrs • popular • mostly gay men • neighborhood bar • professional crowd • wheelchair access • also 'Queens Head Pub' Th-Sun • piano singalong

Hi-Ho Lounge 2239 St Claude Ave (at Elysian Fields) **504/947-9344** • eves • gay-friendly • casual cocktail lounge • alternative • live music some wknds • younger crowd • women-owned/ run

Le Roundup 819 St Louis (at Dauphine) **504/561-8340** • 24hrs • mostly gay men • neighborhood bar • country/ western • transgender-friendly

The Mint 940 Elysian Fields Ave (at N Rampart) **504/944-4888** • 2pm-close • lesbians/ gay men • neighborhood bar • dancing/DJ • live shows • karaoke

Ninth Circle 700 N Rampart (at St Peter) **504/524-7654** • 24hrs • mostly gay men • neighborhood bar • transgender-friendly • cabaret • shows on wknds

Phoenix 941 Elysian Fields Ave (at N Rampart) **504/945-9264** • 24hrs • popular • mostly gay men • neighborhood bar • leather • also Eagle's Nest • 9pm-5am • dancing/DJ • videos • leather store • gay-owned/ run

Rawhide 2010 740 Burgundy (at St Ann) **504/525-8106** • 24hrs • popular • mostly gay men • neighborhood bar • alternative, underground sound • leather/ fetish • videos

Nightclubs

735 Nightclub 735 Bourbon St (at Orleans) **504/581-6740** • 24hrs • mostly gay men • dancing/DJ • live shows

Oz 800 Bourbon St (at St Ann) **504/593-9491** • 24hrs • popular • mostly gay men • dancing/DJ • live shows • videos • young crowd • wheelchair access

Rainbows 3536 18th St (btwn Edenborn & N Arnoult), Metairie **504/454-3200** • 6pm-close, from 3pm Sun, clsd Mon • lesbians/ gay men • dancing/DJ • gay-owned

Cafes

PJ's 634 Frenchmen St **504/949-2292** • 7am-11pm, till midnight Fri-Sat • popular

Red Bike Bakery & Cafe 746 Tchoupitoulas (off Julia) **504/529-2453** • lunch daily, dinner Tue-Sat • outdoor dining • plenty veggie

Restaurants

Cafe Sbisa 1011 Decatur **504/522-5565** • dinner & Sun brunch • French Creole • patio

Casamento's 4330 Magazine (at Napoleon Ave) **504/895-9761** • 5:30pm-9pm, clsd Jun-Aug • best oyster loaf in city

Clover Grill 900 Bourbon St (at Dumaine) **504/523-0904** • 24hrs • popular • diner fare • $5-10

Louisiana • USA

Commander's Palace 1403 Washington Ave (in Garden District) **504/899-8221** • lunch & dinner • upscale Creole • Sun jazz brunch • $30-50

Eve's Market 4601 Freret (at Cadiz) **504/891-4015** • 10am-7pm, clsd Sun • natural foods store & healthy deli • plenty veggie • women-owned/ run

Feelings Cafe 2600 Chartres St (at Franklin Ave) **504/945-2222** • dinner nightly, lunch Fri, Sun brunch • Creole • piano bar wknds • courtyard • $10-20

Fiorella's Cafe 45 French Market Pl (at Gov Nicholls & Ursulines) **504/528-9566** • 7am-5pm, clsd Sun • homecooking

La Peniche 1940 Dauphine St (at Touro St) **504/943-1460** • 24hrs • diner • some veggie • $5-20

Lucky Cheng's 720 St Louis (btwn Bourbon & Royal) **504/529-2045** • lunch & dinner, Sun brunch • Asian Creole • full bar • drag-queen waitresses • cabaret

Mama Rosa 616 N Rampart (at Toulouse & St Louis) **504/523-5546** • 11am-9pm, till 11pm wknds • Italian • $6-11

Mona Lisa 1212 Royal St (at Barracks) **504/522-6746** • 11am-10:30pm, till midnight wknds • Italian • some veggie • beer/ wine • $10-15

Nola 534 St Louis (btwn Chartres & Decatur) **504/522-6652** • lunch (except Sun) & dinner • fusion • Creole • wheelchair access

Old Dog New Trick Cafe 307 Exchange Alley (btwn Royal & Chartres off Conti) **504/522-4569** • 11:30am-9pm • vegetarian • outdoor dining • wheelchair access • $7-10

Olivier's 204 Decatur St **504/525-7734** • lunch & dinner • Creole • wheelchair access • $10-15

Petunia's 817 St Louis (at Bourbon) **504/522-6440** • 8am-11pm • popular • Cajun/ Creole • crepes • full bar • $10-20

Pontchartrain Cafe 2031 St Charles Ave (in 'Grand Heritage Hotel') **504/524-0581** • 7am-2:30pm & 5pm-9pm • Creole • $8-15

Poppy's Grill 717 St Peter (at Royal & Bourbon) **504/524-3287** • 24hrs • diner • wheelchair access

Praline Connection 542 Frenchmen St (at Chartres) **504/943-3934** • 10:30am-9pm • soul food • Sun gospel jazz brunch

Quarter Scene 900 Dumaine St (at Dauphine) **504/522-6533** • 8am-midnight, dinner only Tue • homecooking • some veggie • $4-15

Quartermaster 1100 Bourbon St **504/529-1416** • 24hrs • sandwiches & more

Sammy's Seafood 627 Bourbon St (across from Pat O' Brien's) **504/525-8442** • 11am-midnight • Creole/ Cajun • $9-28

Secret Garden 538 St Philip St (at Decatur) **504/524-2041** • 5:30pm-10pm, Sun brunch • Creole +

Vaqueros 4938 Prytania (at Robert) **504/891-6441** • lunch & dinner • Southwestern/ Mexican • good margaritas • $9-17

Vera Cruz 7537 Maple (at Hillard) **504/866-1736** • 5pm-11pm, clsd Sun • Mexican • wheelchair access

Entertainment & Recreation

Café du Monde 1039 Decatur St (Old Jackson Square) **504/587-0835, 800/772-2927** • till you've a had a beignet—fried dough, powdered w/ sugar, that melts in your mouth—you haven't been to New Orleans & this is 'the' place to have them 24hrs a day

Gay Heritage Tour 909 Bourbon St **504/945-6789** • call for details • departs from 'Alternatives' bookstore

Haunted History Tour **888/644-6787** • guided 2-1/2-hr tours of New Orleans' most famous haunts, including Anne Rice's home

Pat O'Brien's 718 St Peter St (btwn Bourbon & Royal) **800/597-4823** • gay-friendly • more than just a bar—come for the Hurricane, stay for the kitsch

St Charles Streetcar Canal St (btwn Bourbon & Royal Sts) **504/248-3900 (RTA #)** • it's not named Desire, but you should still ride it if you want to see the Garden District, Blanche

Bookstores

Alternatives 907 Bourbon St (at Dumaine) **504/524-5222** • 11am-7pm, till 9pm Fri-Sat, clsd Tue • lgbt

Bookstar 414 N Peters (in Jax Brewery Complex) **504/523-6411** • 9am-midnight • wheelchair access

Faubourg Marigny Bookstore 600 Frenchmen St (at Chartres) **504/943-9875** • 10am-8pm, till 6pm wknds • lgbt • wheelchair access

Sidney's News Stand 917 Decatur St (btwn St Philip & Dumaine) **504/524-6872** • 8am-9pm, till 10pm Sat • some lgbt titles

Retail Shops

Hit Parade 741 Bourbon St **504/524-7700** • 11am-midnight, till 2am Fri-Sat • popular • lgbt books • designer circuit clothing & more

Bangor • Maine

Postmark New Orleans 631 Toulouse St (btwn Chartres & Royal) **504/529–2052, 800/285–4247** • 10am-6pm, from noon Sun • gay gifts • furniture • art • postcards

Rings of Desire 1128 Decatur St, 2nd flr **504/524–6147** • piercing studio

Second Skin Leather 521 St Philip St (btwn Decatur & Chartres) **504/561–8167** • noon-10pm, till 6pm Sun

Something Different 5300 Tchoupitoulas (in Riverside Market) **504/891–9056** • 10am-9pm, till 7pm Sat, noon-6pm Sun • gay-owned/ run

PUBLICATIONS

Ambush Mag **504/522–8049** • lgbt newspaper

▲ **Southern Voice** **404/876–1819** • weekly lgbt newspaper for AL, FL (panhandle), GA, LA, MS, TN w/ resource listings

SPIRITUAL GROUPS

MCC of Greater New Orleans 1128 St Roch **504/945–5390** • 12:15pm Sun

EROTICA

Gargoyles 1201 Decatur St (at Gov Nicholls) **504/529–4386** • leather/ fetish/ goth store

Panda Bear 415 Bourbon St (at St Louis) **504/529–3593** • leather • toys • wheelchair access

Paradise 41 W 24th St (at Crestview), Kenner **504/461–0000** • wheelchair access

Shreveport

BARS

Korner Lounge 800 Louisiana (nr Cotton) **318/222–9796** • 5pm-close, sometimes clsd Sun • mostly gay men • neighborhood bar

NIGHTCLUBS

Central Station 1025 Marshall (btwn Fairfield & Creswell) **318/222–2216** • 3pm-6am • popular • lesbians/ gay men • dancing/DJ • country/ western • transgender-friendly • live shows • wheelchair access

EROTICA

Fun Shop 1601 Marshall (at Creswell) **318/226–1308** • clsd Sun

Slidell

BARS

Billy's 2600 Hwy 190 W **504/847–1921** • 6pm-2am, clsd Mon • lesbians/ gay men • neighborhood bar • food served • karaoke

MAINE

Statewide

INFO LINES & SERVICES

Maine Tourism Line **800/533–9595**

PUBLICATIONS

In Newsweekly **617/426–8264** • New England's lgbt newspaper

Augusta

ACCOMMODATIONS

Maple Hill Farm B&B Inn **207/622–2708, 800/622–2708** • gay/ straight • Victorian farmhouse on 130 acres • full brkfst • whirlpools • swimming pond • smokefree • wheelchair access • gay-owned/ run • $55-180

NIGHTCLUBS

PJ's 80 Water St (btwn Laurel & Bridge) **207/623–4041** • 7pm-1am Wed-Sat • popular • lesbians/ gay men • dancing/DJ • food served • piano bar • patio

SPIRITUAL GROUPS

Northern Lights MCC 1040 Riverside Dr **207/621–2658** • 4pm Sun

Bangor

INFO LINES & SERVICES

Outright Bangor 80 Exchange St, 4th floor Fleet Bank Center (at State) **207/990–2095, 800/429–1481** • 6pm-8pm 1st & 3rd Mon • social/ support group for lgbt youth ages 22 & under

Wilde-Stein Club Shibels Hall Rm #202, Univ of Maine, Orono **207/581–1596** • Sept-May only • 7pm Th

ACCOMMODATIONS

Maine Wilderness Lake Island 26 5th St **207/990–5839** • lesbians/ gay men • summer only • weekly rental cabins in the forest • $300

NIGHTCLUBS

The Spectrum 190 Harlow St (next to Federal Bldg) **207/942–3000** • 8pm-1:30am, clsd Mon-Tue • lesbians/ gay men • dancing/DJ • karaoke Th • live shows • wheelchair access

BOOKSTORES

Pro Libris Bookshop 10 3rd St (at Union) **207/942–3019** • 10am-6pm, noon-4pm Sun • new & used

Maine • USA

Bar Harbor

Info Lines & Services

Out on MDI 207/664-0328 • lgbt social group for rural Mount Desert Island area • potlucks

Accommodations

Manor House Inn 106 West St (nr Bridge St) **207/288-3759, 800/437-0086** • open May-Nov • gay-friendly • 1880s Victorian mansion • full brkfst • $65-225

Restaurants

Mama DiMatteo's 34 Kennebec Pl (at Rodick St) **207/288-3666** • 5pm-9pm, clsd Sun-Mon • upscale casual dining • seafood, steak, pasta • full bar • gay-owned/run

Bath

Accommodations

The Galen C Moses House 1009 Washington St **207/442-8771, 888/442-8771** • gay/ straight • 1874 Victorian • full brkfst • smokefree • gay-owned/run • $99-139

The Inn at Bath 969 Washington St **207/443-4294** • gay/ straight • 1810 B&B • full brkfst • jacuzzi • kids/ pets ok • smokefree • wheelchair access • gay-owned/ run • $85-350

Booth Bay Harbor

Restaurants

The Vault 4 Townsend Ave **207/633-7226** • lunch & dinner • bistro

Boothbay

Accommodations

Hodgdon Island Inn Barter's Island Rd (at Sawyer's Island Rd) **207/633-7474** • gay/ straight • 1810 sea captain's home • full brkfst • swimming • smokefree • gay-owned/ run • $105-135

Brunswick

Info Lines & Services

Bowdoin College Women's Resource Center **207/725-3620** • 7pm-11pm Sun-Th Sept-May

Maine TransSupport PO Box 4075, 04101 **207/774-7029** • peer support group for transgendered people & friends • newsletter

Restaurants

Star Fish Grill 100 Pleasant St/ Rte 1 (at Mill St) **207/725-7828** • dinner only • seasonal • fresh seafood & natural meats • full bar • lesbian-owned

Bookstores

Gulf of Maine Books 134 Maine St (at Pleasant) **207/729-5083** • 9:30am-5:30pm, clsd Sun • alternative

Caribou

Info Lines & Services

Gay/ Lesbian Phoneline 398 S Main St **207/498-2088, 800/468-2088 (ME only)** • 7pm-9pm Mon-Fri • social & networking group for northern ME & NW New Brunswick, Canada

Corea

Accommodations

The Black Duck Inn on Corea Harbor Crowley Island Rd (Rte 195), Corea Harbor **207/963-2689, 877/963-2689** • gay/ straight • restored farmhouse • also cottages • full brkfst • gay-owned/ run • $95-155

Restaurants

Fisherman's Inn 7 Newman St, Winter Harbor **207/963-5585** • 4:30pm-9pm • seasonal

Deer Isle

Restaurants

Fisherman's Friend School St, Stonington **207/367-2442** • 11am-8pm • April-Oct

Dexter

Accommodations

Brewster Inn 37 Zions Hill **207/924-3130** • gay-friendly • historic mansion • full brkfst • tennis • kids ok • wheelchair access • $49-95

Farmington

Cafes

Wizbe Cafe (aka Java Joe's) 42 Main St **207/779-1000** • 7am-5pm, till 4pm Sat, till 3pm Sun • fresh baked goods • sandwiches • soup

Bookstores

Devany, Doak & Garrett Booksellers 193 Broadway **207/778-3454** • hours vary • lgbt section

Freeport

ACCOMMODATIONS

The Bagley House 1290 Royalsborough Rd, Durham 207/865-6566, 800/765-1772 • gay/straight • full brkfst • smokefree • kids ok • conference room for 20 • lesbian-owned/run • $75-150

Country at Heart B&B 37 Bow St 207/865-0512 • gay-friendly • 1870s country home • full brkfst • located in Maine's outlet shopping mecca • $65-150

RESTAURANTS

Harraseeket Lunch & Lobster Co 207/865-3535 • lunch & dinner • open May-Oct

Hallowell

RESTAURANTS

Slate's 167 Water St (Franklin) 207/622-9575 • lunch & dinner, till 2pm Sun • live shows Mon

Hancock

RESTAURANTS

Le Domaine Restaurant & Inn 207/422-3395 • 6pm-9pm, clsd Sun-Mon • open June-Oct

Kennebunkport

ACCOMMODATIONS

Arundel Meadows Inn 1024 Portland Rd (at Walker Ln), Arundel 207/985-3770 • gay-friendly • full brkfst • hot tub • swimming • smokefree • $85-145

The Colony Hotel 140 Ocean Ave (at Kings Hwy) 207/967-3331, 800/552-2363 • seasonal • gay-friendly • 1914 grand oceanfront property • private beach • swimming • smokefree • wheelchair access • $120-425

White Barn Inn 37 Beach St 207/967-2321 • gay-friendly • restaurant • $230-575

RESTAURANTS

Bartley's Dockside by the bridge 207/967-5050 • lunch & dinner May-Dec, lunch only Jan-April • 11am-10pm • seafood • some veggie • full bar • wheelchair access

Kittery

see also Portsmouth, New Hampshire

RESTAURANTS

Chauncey Creek Lobster Pier Chauncey Creek Rd (off 103), Kittery Point 207/439-1030 • 11am-8pm • open May-Oct • BYOB

Lewiston

ACCOMMODATIONS

Ware Street Inn B&B 52 Ware St (at College St) 207/783-8171, 877/783-8171 • gay-friendly • elegant 1940s Colonial • well-behaved kids ok • $65-145

BARS

The Sportsman's Club 2 Bates St (at Main) 207/784-2251 • 8pm-1am • popular • lesbians/gay men • neighborhood bar • dancing/DJ • karaoke Th • live shows • 'oldest gay bah in Maine'

EROTICA

Paris Book Store 297 Lisbon St (at Chestnut) 207/783-6677

Newcastle

ACCOMMODATIONS

The Tipsy Butler B&B 11 High St, Newcastle 207/563-3394 • B&B on the Damariscotta River • full brkfst • woman-owned • $130-220

Ogunquit

ACCOMMODATIONS

Admiral's Inn Resort Hotel 87 Main St (at Agamenticus) 207/646-7093, 888/263-6318 • mostly gay men • restaurant & lounge • swimming • hot tub • nudity • gay-owned/run • $110-130

Beach Haven Ogunquit 69 Cottage St 207/646-5639 • gay-friendly • seasonal guesthouse • 5 mins to beach • kids ok • gay-owned/run • $95-105

Beauport Inn & Suites on Clay Hill 381 Agamenticus Rd (at Clay Hill Rd) 800/646-8681 • gay/straight • full brkfst • jacuzzi • wheelchair access • $135-155

Black Boar Inn 47 Main St 207/646-2112 • gay/straight • B&B built in 1674 • full gourmet brkfst • afternoon tea • gay-owned/run • $115-185

The Clipper Ship B&B 207/646-9735, 407/951-1977 • gay-friendly • smokefree • pets ok • open May-Oct • $59-99

Distant Sands B&B 207/646-8686 • gay/straight • 18th-century farmhouse • full brkfst • smokefree • overlooks Ogunquit River • also cottage • $125-175

Maine • USA

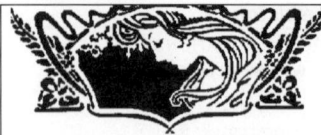

THE HERITAGE OF OGUNQUIT
IN OGUNQUIT, MAINE

"Beautiful-Place by-the-Sea"

Efficiency Rentals ▼ *B&B*

Walk to Beach, Cove, Town

NON-SMOKING

All Private Baths & TV's

Hot Tub & deck

Quiet, Private Area

P.O. BOX 1788
OGUNQUIT, ME 03907
(207)646-7787

www.heritageogunquit.com

heritage@maine.rr.com

Advance reservations only

*Efficiency Rentals
"In Season"*

▲ **The Heritage of Ogunquit** PO Box 1788, 03907 **207/646-7787** • lesbians/gay men • efficiencies & B&B • full baths • hot tub • deck • smokefree • kids ok • lesbian-owned/ run • $60-95

The Inn at Two Village Square 2 Village Square Ln, Box 864 **207/646-5779, 941/643-4874 (WINTER #)** • open May-Oct • mostly gay men • oceanside Victorian • swimming • smokefree • gay-owned/ run • $50-135

Leisure Inn 73 School St **207/646-2737** • gay/ straight • B&B & apts • seasonal • gay-owned/ run • $70-149

Moon Over Maine B&B Berwick Rd **207/646-6666, 800/851-6837** • lesbians/gay men • hot tub • gay-owned/ run • $69-129

Ogunquit Beach Inn & Vacation Apartments 67 School St **207/646-1112, 888/976-2463** • lesbians/gay men • guesthouse B&B • 5 mins to beach • some shared baths • gay-owned/ run • $69-125 • also house & apt rentals

The Ogunquit House 3 Glen Ave **207/646-2967** • clsd Jan-Feb • popular • lesbians/gay men • Victorian B&B • also cottages • gay-owned/ run • $59-145

Ogunquit Innkeepers 252 US Rte 1 N **207/646-2167** • gay/straight • suites & cottage • patio • wheelchair access • women-owned/ run • $129-175

Ogunquit Weekly Rentals **207/646-0482** • cottage, apt & house rentals

OgunquitCottages.com 60 Highland Rd (Berwick Rd & Rte 1) **207/646-3840, 978/664-5813** • lesbians/gay men • wknd rentals • nr bars & beach • smokefree • pets/kids (12+) ok • gay-owned/ run • $100-200

Old Village Inn 30 Main St **207/646-7088** • gay-friendly • 1880s B&B • ocean views • kids/pets ok • also restaurant • seafood • upscale • $60-95

Rockmere Lodge B&B 150 Stearns Rd **207/646-2985** • gay/ straight • Maine shingle cottage • nr beach • smokefree • gay-owned/ run • $100-200

Sea ME Rentals of Ogunquit **207/641-2637** • lesbians/gay men • rental units w/ kitchens • pets ok • gay-owned/ run

Shore House 7 Shore Rd **207/646-0627** • gay/ straight • seasonal guesthouse • also cottages w/ kitchenettes • gay-owned/ run • $75-125

Portland • Maine

Yellow Monkey Guest Houses/ Hotel 44 Main St 207/646-9056 • gay/ straight • seasonal • roofdeck • jacuzzi • fitness room • kids/ pets ok • gay-owned/ run • $90-125

BARS

Front Porch Cafe Ogunquit Sq 207/646-3976, 207/646-4005 • 4pm-1am, from 11:30am wknds (seasonal) • gay/ straight • piano bar • full menu • $6-16

NIGHTCLUBS

The Club 237 Main St 207/646-6655 • 9pm-close Fri-Sun • seasonal • popular • mostly gay men • dancing/DJ • food served • live shows • videos • T-dance Sat-Sun • also The Rooftop Cafe' martini bar from 4pm wknds

Maine Street 131 Main St/ US Rte 1 207/646-5101 • 3pm-1am Th-Sun • popular • lesbians/ gay men • dancing/DJ • cabaret • videos • T-dance 4pm-8pm wknds • food served • gay-owned/ run

CAFES

Fancy That Cafe Village Square (corner of Beach St & Rte 1) 207/646-4118 • seasonal • 6:30am-11pm • pastries • coffee • sandwiches • soup • right next door to Village Food Market

RESTAURANTS

Arrows Berrick Rd (18 miles W of Center) 207/361-1100 • 6pm-9pm, clsd Mon • open April-Sept • popular • cont'l • some veggie • $20-27

The Cape Neddick Inn 1233 Rte 1, York 207/363-2899 • 5:30pm-9pm • also brewery • wheelchair access

Clay Hill Farm Agamenticus Rd (2 miles W of Rte 1) 207/646-2272 • dinner, clsd Tue • seafood • some veggie • piano bar • $13-24

Five-0 50 Shore Rd 207/646-6365 • full bar

Grey Gull Inn 475 Webhannet Dr, Wells 207/646-7501 • dinner • New England fine dining • $14-28 • also oceanview rooms • $79-139

Johnathan's 2 Bourne Ln 207/646-4777 • 5pm-8:30pm, till 10pm wknds • veggie/ seafood • full bar • wheelchair access • $13-25

La Pizzeria 25 Main St (at Rte 1) 207/646-1143 • lunch & dinner • open April-Dec • some veggie • gay-owned/ run • $5-15

Poor Richard's Tavern 125 Shore Rd (at Pine Hill) 207/646-4722 • 5:30pm-9pm, clsd Sun (Sun brunch off-season) • New England fare • some veggie • full bar • $11-22

BOOKSTORES

Ogunquit Round Table 24 Shore Rd (at School St) 207/646-2332 • 10am-5pm • lgbt section • woman-owned/ run

PUBLICATIONS

In Newsweekly 617/426-8246 • New England's lgbt newspaper

Portland

INFO LINES & SERVICES

Alliance for Sexual Diversity 207/874-6596 • Mon-Fri • call for info

Gays in Sobriety 32 Thomas St (at United Church of Christ) 207/774-4060 • 6pm Sun

ACCOMMODATIONS

Andrews-on-Auburn B&B 417 Auburn St 207/797-9157 • gay-friendly • 1780s farmhouse • full brkfst • kitchen • smokefree • pets ok • patio • $89-175

Auberge by the Sea 103 East Grand Ave, Old Orchard Beach 207/934-2355 • gay/ straight • private pathway to beach • $79-139

The Danforth 163 Danforth St 207/879-8755, 800/991-6557 • gay-friendly • 1821 mansion • conference/ reception facilities • smokefree • kids/ pets ok • woman-owned • $129-329

▲ **The Inn at St John** 939 Congress St 207/773-6481, 800/636-9127 • gay/ straight • unique historic inn • kids/ pets ok • gay-owned/ run • $65-175

The Inn by the Sea 40 Bowery Beach Rd, Cape Elizabeth 207/799-3134, 800/888-4287 • gay-friendly • condo-style suites w/ ocean views • women-owned • $129-449

The Parkside Parrot Inn 273 State St 207/775-0224 • gay/ straight • B&B • conveniently located in downtown Portland • hot tub • lesbian-owned/ run • $55-90

The Pomegranate Inn 49 Neal St 207/772-1006, 800/356-0408 • gay-friendly • upscale B&B • full brkfst • private garden • smokefree • $95-205

Sea View Motel 65 W Grand Ave (at Atlantic Ave), Old Orchard Beach 207/934-4180, 800/541-8439 • gay-friendly • on the beach • swimming • patio • kids/ pets ok • gift shop • $50-240

West End Inn 146 Pine St 207/772-1377, 800/338-1377 • gay-friendly • 1870 townhouse • full brkfst • smokefree • women-owned/ run • $99-199

Damron Women's Traveller 2002

Maine • USA

Portland

LGBT Pride: June. 207/774-7800.

Annual Events: August - Portland Chamber Music Festival 800/320-0257, web: www.lsiweb.com/festival/.

City Info: 207/772-5800, web: www.visitportland.com.

Attractions: Old Port. Portland Head Light 207/799-2661. Portland Museum of Art 207/775-6148, web: www.portlandmuseum.org. Wadsworth-Longfellow House 207/774-1822.

Weather: Portland has a mild marine climate. Winter temperatures are in the 20°s-40°s, and summers are breezy and mild, with temperatures in the 60°s-80°s.

Transit: Airport Limo/Taxi 800-517-9442. Metro (bus) 207/774-0351.

European Charm...

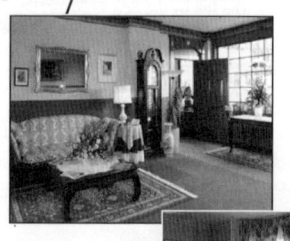

...in the heart of Portland
- Continental breakfast
- Non-smoking rooms available
- Walking distance to historic Old Port/Arts District
  Free Cable/HBO
  Local Calls
  Airport pick-up
  Parking

(207) 773-6481
(800) 636-9127

The Victorian
Inn at St. John

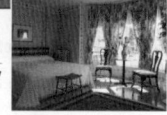

939 Congress Street, Portland, Maine 04102
info@innatstjohn.com • www.innatstjohn.com

Sebago Lake • Maine

Bars

Blackstones 6 Pine St (off Longfellow Sq) 207/775-2885 • 4pm-1am, from 3pm Sun • mostly gay men • neighborhood bar • wheelchair access

Sisters 45 Danforth St (at Maple) 207/774-1505 • 5pm-close, noon-8pm Sun, clsd Mon-Tue • mostly women • dancing/DJ wknds • country/ western Tue • live shows • karaoke

Somewhere 117 Spring St (at High) 207/871-9169 • 4pm-1am • lesbians/ gay men • neighborhood bar • dancing/ DJ • multiracial clientele • piano bar • Sun buffet • karaoke • 18+ • wheelchair access

Nightclubs

The Underground 3 Spring St 207/773-3315 • 4pm-1am, from 8pm Mon-Tue • popular • lesbians/gay men • dancing/DJ Th-Sun • live shows • karaoke

Restaurants

Blue Mango Cafe 129 Spring St 207/772-1374 • 5pm-10pm, clsd Mon, (lunch & brunch served Sept-May) • Maine coastal menu w/ Asian/ Caribbean influences • full bar • wheelchair access • $7-15

Cafe UFFA 190 State St (at Congress) 207/775-3380 • 5pm-10pm Wed-Sat, 8am-noon Sat, 9am-noon Sun, clsd Mon-Tue

Katahdin 106 High St (at Spring) 207/774-1740 • 5pm-9:30pm, clsd Sun-Mon • American menu • full bar

Siam City Cafe 339 Fore St (at Pearl) 207/773-8389 • 11am-2pm Tue-Fri & 4pm-9pm Tue-Sun • Thai • beer/ wine • wheelchair access • gay-owned/ run

Street & Co 33 Wharf St (btwn Dana & Union) 207/775-0887 • 5:30pm-9:30pm, till 10pm Fri-Sat • popular • seafood • beer/ wine • wheelchair access • $12-18

Walter's Cafe 15 Exchange St 207/871-9258 • 11am-3pm & 5pm-9pm (open later Fri-Sat), dinner only Sun • some veggie • $11-16

Bookstores

Longfellow Books 1 Monument Wy 207/772-4045 • 9am-7pm • lgbt section

Retail Shops

Communiques 3 Moulton St (at Commercial) 207/773-5181 • 9am-5:30pm, till 9pm summers • cards • gifts • clothing

Condom Sense 424 Fore St (at Union) 207/871-0356 • hours vary

Drop Me A Line 611 Congress St (at High) 207/773-5547 • 10am-6pm, till 4pm Sun • card & gift shop • pride items • gay-owned/ run

Publications

Casco Bay Weekly 207/775-6601, 800/286-6601 • weekly alternative newspaper

Spiritual Groups

Am Chofshi 207/833-6004 • lgbt Jews

Congregation Bet Ha'am 81 Westbrook St, South Portland 207/879-0028 • 7:30pm Fri • gay-friendly synagogue

Dignity Maine 143 State St (at St Luke's, side chapel) 207/646-2820 • 6pm Sun

Richmond

Entertainment & Recreation

Province Mountain Outfitters 13 Church St 207/737-4695 • gay-friendly • fishing, sightseeing, biking & boat tours • April-Sept • women-owned/ run • mention 'Damron' for 10% discount

Rockport

Accommodations

The Old Granite Inn 546 Main St, Rockland 207/594-9036, 800/386-9036 • gay-friendly • stately 1880s stone guesthouse • full brkfst • harbor views • wheelchair access • $90-140

Restaurants

Chez Michel Rte 1, Lincolnville Beach 207/789-5600 • dinner, Sun brunch, clsd Mon • full bar

Lobster Pound Rte 1, Lincolnville Beach 207/789-5550 • 11:30am-8pm • May-Sept • full bar

Saco

Info Lines & Services

SisterSpace 207/878-2152, EXT. 3 • lesbian social group • monthly potlucks

Sebago Lake

Accommodations

Bear Mountain Village 207/583-6980 (SUMMER), 207/782-2275 (WINTER) • gay/ straight • on lake • hiking • boat rentals • cabins • $50+ • campsites • $10-25 • women's camping area

Lambs Mill Inn 207/693-6253 • gay/ straight • 1890s farmhouse on 20 acres • full brkfst • hot tub • swimming • lesbian-owned/ run • $70-120

Maryland • USA

Restaurants

The Olde House Rte 85, off 302, Raymond **207/655-7841** • dinner & Sun brunch, clsd Mon-Tue, wknds only in off-season • cont'l

Sydney's Rte 302, Naples **207/693-3333** • open April-Jan • 4pm-9pm, till 10pm Sat • full bar

Tenants Harbor

Accommodations

Blueberry Cove Camp Harts Neck Road **207/372-6353, 617/876-2897** • gay-friendly • cabins • private campsites • nr Penobscot Bay

Eastwind Inn **207/372-6366** • clsd Dec-April • gay-friendly • rooms & apts • full brkfst • pets ok • $90–275 • also restaurant • old-fashioned New England fare

York Harbor

Accommodations

Canterbury House Box 881, 432 York St **207/363-3505, 888/385-3505** • gay-friendly • spacious Victorian home • gay-owned/ run • $65-115

Restaurants

York Harbor Inn Rte 1A **207/363-5119** • lunch Mon-Fri, dinner Th-Sat, Sun brunch • also the 'Cellar Pub' • also lodging

MARYLAND

Statewide

Info Lines & Services

Maryland Office of Tourism 800/543-1036

Annapolis

Info Lines & Services

AA Gay/ Lesbian 199 Duke of Gloucester St (at St Anne's Parish) **410/268-5441** • 8pm Tue

Accommodations

Two-O-One B&B 201 Prince George St (at Maryland Ave) **410/268-8053** • gay/ straight • English country house • full brkfst • smokefree • gay-owned/ run

William Page Inn 8 Martin St **410/626-1506, 800/364-4160** • gay/ straight • elegantly renovated 1908 home • full brkfst • smokefree • teens ok • gay-owned/ run • $115-225

Baltimore

Info Lines & Services

AA Gay/ Lesbian **410/663-1922** • call for times & locations

BWMT/ PACT—Baltimore **410/366-9565** • Black & White Men Together/ People of All Colors Together

FIST (Females Investigating Sexual Terrain) PO Box 41032, 21203-6032 • leather-S/M group

Gay/ Lesbian Community Center 241 W Chase St (at Read) **410/837-5445** • 10am-4pm, clsd wknds • many groups & services

Gay/ Lesbian Switchboard **410/837-8888** • live 7pm-10pm

Transgender Support Group at G/L Community Center **410/837-5445** • 8pm 4th Sat

Accommodations

Abacrombie Badger B&B 58 W Biddle St (at Cathedral) **410/244-7227, 888/922-3437** • gay/ straight • 1880s townhouse • smokefree • also restaurant • gay-owned/ run • $85-155

Biltmore Suites 205 W Madison St (at Park) **410/728-6550, 800/868-5064** • gay-friendly • kids/ pets ok • $89-169

Clarion Hotel—Mt Vernon Square 612 Cathedral St (at W Monument) **410/727-7101, 800/292-5500** • gay-friendly • restaurant • lounge • gym • jacuzzis • wheelchair access • $90-350

Harbor Inn Pier 5 711 Eastern Ave (at President) **410/539-2000** • gay/ straight • boutique hotel on waterfront • full brkfst • restaurant • wheelchair access

Mr Mole B&B 1601 Bolton St (at McMechen) **410/728-1179** • popular • gay/ straight • splendid suites on historic Bolton Hill • gay-owned/ run • $115-175

Bars

The Allegro 1101 Cathedral St (at Chase) **410/837-3906** • 6pm-2am • mostly gay men • dancing/DJ • live shows • videos

Baltimore Eagle 2022 N Charles St (enter on 21st) **410/823-2453** • 3pm-2am, from 2pm wknds • popular • mostly gay men • leather store • patio • wheelchair access

Central Station 1001 N Charles St (at Eager) **410/752-7133** • 3pm-2am • popular • lesbians/ gay men • 2 bars • videos • karaoke Mon • drag shows Tue • also sidewalk cafe • some veggie • $7-15

Baltimore • Maryland

Club Bunns 608 W Lexington St (at Greene St) **410/234–2866** • 5pm-2am • lesbians/gay men • dancing/DJ • mostly African-American • live shows • female strippers Sat

Club Mardi Gras 228 Park Ave (at Saratoga) **410/783–9873** • 4pm-2am • mostly gay men • neighborhood bar • mostly African-American • live shows • wheelchair access

Coconuts Cafe 311 W Madison (at Eutaw) **410/383–6064** • 4pm-2am, from 6pm Mon, from 11am Fri • call for summer hours • popular • mostly women • dancing/DJ • food served • wheelchair access • lesbian-owned/run

The Gallery Bar & Studio Restaurant 1735 Maryland Ave (at Lafayette) **410/539–6965** • 2pm-1:30am • lesbians/gay men • wheelchair access • dinner nightly • $10-15

Harmon's Pub 3230 E Fairmont Ave (at N East Ave) **410/563–9417** • 2pm-1am • lesbians/gay men • neighborhood bar • unconfirmed

Hippo 1 W Eager St (at Charles) **410/547–0069, 410/576–0018** • 4pm-2am • popular • lesbians/gay men • more women 1st wknd • dancing/DJ • transgender-friendly • karaoke • videos • piano bar • wheelchair access

Port in a Storm 4330 E Lombard St (at Kresson) **410/732–5608** • 10am-2am • mostly women • neighborhood bar • dancing/DJ • food served • wheelchair access • lesbian-owned/run

---

[Reply] [Forward] **[Delete]**

Date: Wed, Nov 14, 2001 19:28:01
From: Girl-on-the-Go
To: Editor@Damron.com
Subject: Baltimore

> Baltimore, one of the 'hub' cities of the Chesapeake Bay, is a quaint, working-class city by the sea, with a friendly and diverse population. It's not far from Washington, DC and, like the nation's capital, is packed with museums and history.

> To many, Baltimore is best known as the nation's capital of kitsch, home and movie-set for the fabulously filthy queer filmmaker John Waters. You too can follow in the immortal footsteps of Divine, the biggest drag queen movie star we know of. Baltimore is also the site of Edgar Allen Poe's home and grave.

> After visiting the Aquarium, dining on soft-shell crabs, and shopping, stop into **Lambda Rising**, Baltimore's LGBT bookstore, and pick up a copy of the **Baltimore Alternative** or **Gay Life** to find out the latest goings on about town.

> At night, visit one of Baltimore's two women's bars: **Coconuts** and **Port in a Storm**. Women of color and their friends should check out Saturdays at **Club Bunns**, and **Hippo** is always a popular spot to mix it up with the boys, especially on the first weekend of each month.

Maryland • USA

Stagecoach 1003 N Charles St (at Eager) **410/547-0107** • 4pm-2am • lesbians/ gay men • dancing/DJ • country/ western • piano bar • free dance lessons • karaoke • live shows • also restaurant • Tex/ Mex • some veggie • wheelchair access • $5-18

NIGHTCLUBS

Club 1722 1722 N Charles St (at Lafayette) **410/727-7431** • 1:45am-5am, clsd Mon-Wed • mostly gay men • dancing/DJ

Orpheus 1001 E Pratt St (at Exeter) **410/276-5599** • gay-friendly • dancing/DJ • alternative • leather • goth Th • fetish party Sat • 18+

Paloma's 15 W Eager St (at Cathedral) **410/783-9004** • 8pm-4am, till 11pm Sun • gay/ straight • dancing/DJ • food served • live entertainment

The Paradox 1310 Russell St (at 13th) **410/837-9110** • 10pm-4am, midnight-6am Fri-Sat • popular • lesbians/ gay men • dancing/DJ • mostly African-American • food served • live shows • videos • wheelchair access

CAFES

Donna's Coffee Bar 2 W Madison (at Charles) **410/385-0180** • 7:30am-11pm, 9am-midnight wknds • beer/ wine

Louie's the Bookstore Cafe 518 N Charles (at Franklin) **410/230-2998** • 11am-midnight, till 2am wknds • live shows • plenty veggie • full bar • wheelchair access • $4-18

RESTAURANTS

Alonso's 415 W Cold Spring Lake (at Keswick Rd) **410/235-3433** • 11am-midnight, till 1am Fri-Sat • Italian • wheelchair access

Cafe Hon 1002 W 36th St (at Roland) **410/243-1230** • 7am-9pm, 9am-10pm wknds • some veggie • wheelchair access • $6-11

Gampy's 904 N Charles St (at Read) **410/837-9797** • 11:30am-1am, till 2am Wed-Th, till 3am wknds • lesbians/ gay men • wheelchair access

Loco Hombre 413 E Cold Spring Ln (at Roland) **410/889-2233** • 11am-10pm

The Millrace 5201 Franklintown Rd (at Security) **410/448-3663** • 10am-midnight, till 2am Th-Sat, clsd Sun • seafood • $5-20

Mount Vernon Stable & Saloon 909 N Charles St (btwn Eager & Read) **410/685-7427** • lunch & dinner • some veggie • also bar 11:30am-2am • $8-12

Spike & Charlie's Restaurant/ Wine Bar 1225 Cathedral St (at Preston) **410/752-8144** • 5:30pm-11:30pm, clsd Mon • $9-23

Baltimore

WHERE THE GIRLS ARE: The women's bars are in southeast Baltimore, near the intersection of Haven and Lombard. Of course, the boys' playground, downtown around Chase St. and Park Ave., is also a popular hangout.

LGBT PRIDE: June. 410/837-5445 (GLCC #).

CITY INFO: Baltimore Tourism Office 410/659-7300 or 800/543-1036.

ATTRACTIONS: Baltimore Museum of Art 410/396-7100.
Fort McHenry 410/962-4299.
Harborplace.
National Aquarium 410/576-3800.
Poe House & Museum 410/396-7932.

BEST VIEW: Top of the World Trade Center at the Inner Harbor.

WEATHER: Unpredictable rains and heavy winds. In summer, the weather can be hot (90°s) and sticky.

TRANSIT: Yellow Cab 410/685-1212.
MBA Transit 410/539-5000.

Towson • Maryland

BOOKSTORES

Lambda Rising 241 W Chase St (at Read) 410/234-0069 • 10am-10pm • lgbt • wheelchair access

PUBLICATIONS

The Baltimore Alternative 410/235-3401 • lgbt newspaper

Gay Life 410/837-7748 • lgbt newspaper

Woman's Monthly 202/965-5399 • articles • calendar of community/ arts events for greater DC/ Baltimore area

SPIRITUAL GROUPS

Beit Tikvah 5802 Roland Ave (at Lake in First Christian Church) 410/560-2062 • welcoming Jewish Reconstructionist congregation • call for services & times

Dignity Baltimore 740 N Calvert St (at Madison in St Ignatius Church) 410/325-1519 • call for meeting times

Grace & St Peter's Episcopal Church 707 Park Ave (at Monument) 410/539-1395 • 8am & 10am Sun

MCC 1000 Cathedral St (at Waxter Ctr) 410/234-1676 • 10am Sun

St Mark's Lutheran Church 1900 St Paul St (at 20th) 410/752-5804 • 11am Sun & 6:30pm Th

Unity Fellowship Church 241 W Chase St, Rm 201 410/659-7222 • 3pm Sun • uplifting service in the African-American tradition • at G/L Community Center

Cockeysville

RESTAURANTS

The York Inn 10010 York Rd 410/666-0006 • 11am-10pm, till 11pm wknds, clsd Mon • full bar • live jazz Sat • plenty veggie

College Park

BOOKSTORES

Vertigo Books 7346 Baltimore Ave 301/301-9300 • 10am-7pm, noon-5pm Sun • African-American emphasis

Columbia

SPIRITUAL GROUPS

MCC Oakland Mills Interfaith Ctr (Robert Oliver Place) 410/234-1676 • 6:30pm Sun

Cumberland

ACCOMMODATIONS

Red Lamp Post B&B 849 Braddock Rd 301/777-7476 • lesbians/ gay men • theme rooms • some shared baths • full brkfst • dinner available • hot tub • sundeck • gym • smokefree • $65-75

RESTAURANTS

Acropolis 47 E Main St, Frostburg 301/689-8277 • 4pm-10pm, clsd Sun-Mon • Greek & American • full bar

Au Petite Paris 86 E Main St 301/689-8946 • 6pm-9:30pm, clsd Sun-Mon • French • wheelchair access • $12-20

Frederick

CAFES

The Frederick Coffee Co & Cafe 100 East St (at Church) 301/698-0039 • 7am-7pm, till 10pm Sat, 8am-6pm Sun • live shows • wheelchair access • women-owned/ run

Havre de Grace

ACCOMMODATIONS

La Clé D'Or 226 N Union Ave (at Chesapeake Bay) 410/939-6562, 888/484-4837 • gay/ straight • 1868 home of the Johns Hopkins family • full brkfst • hot tub • teens ok • gay-owned/ run • $110-135

Rock Hall

ACCOMMODATIONS

Tallulah's on Main 5750 Main St (at Sharp St) 410/639-2596 • gay/ straight • small suite hotel • kids ok • wheelchair access • gay-owned/ run • $115-150

Rockville

SPIRITUAL GROUPS

Open Door MCC 15817 Barnesville Rd 301/601-9112 • 10am Sun

Towson

SPIRITUAL GROUPS

Towson Unitarian Universalist Church 1710 Dulaney Valley Rd, Lutherville 410/825-6045 • 9am & 11am Sun

Massachusetts

Statewide

Info Lines & Services
Massachusetts Office of Travel & Tourism 800/447-6277

Publications
In Newsweekly 617/426-8246 • New England's lgbt newspaper

Spiritual Groups
RI & SE Mass Gay Jewish Group Boston 508/992-7927 (PRIVATE HOME) • call for info

Acton

Restaurants
Acton Jazz Cafe 452 Great Rd/ Rte 2-A 978/263-6161 • noon-2:30pm Tue-Fri, 5:30pm-10pm, clsd Mon • some veggie • full bar • live shows • smokefree • cover charge

Amherst

Info Lines & Services
Everywoman's Center Wilder Hall, UMass 413/545-0883, 413/545-0800 (CRISIS LINE) • call for office hours

Accommodations
Ivy House B&B 1 Sunset Ct 413/549-7554 • gay/ straight • restored Colonial Cape • full brkfst • gay-owned/ run • $60-90

Restaurants
Amber Waves 63 Main St 413/253-9200 • 11:30am-9pm, till 10pm Th-Sat, from 12:30pm Sun • inexpensive Thai • plenty veggie • wheelchair access

Bookstores
Food For Thought 106 N Pleasant St (at Main) 413/253-5432 • 9:30am-6pm, till 8pm Wed-Fri, noon-5pm Sun • progressive bookstore • wheelchair access • collectively run

Barre

Accommodations
Jenkins Inn & Restaurant 978/355-6444, 800/378-7373 • gay-friendly • full brkfst • restaurant • full bar • smokefree • English garden • gay-owned/ run • $140-185

Winterwood 19 N Main St, Petersham 978/724-8885 • gay-friendly • Greek Revival mansion • fireplaces • smokefree • $89-109

Restaurants
Barre Mill 90 Main St, South Barre 978/355-2987, 978/355-6417 • 5pm-9pm, noon-8pm Sun, clsd Mon-Tue • Italian • $9-17

Bedford

Info Lines & Services
The Pinkham Center The Great Rd 781/275-9071, 781/746-5426 • lgbt therapy & resource center

Berkshires

Info Lines & Services
GLBT Support Group 413/243-8484 • adult meetings 6:30pm 1st Tue, youth meetings 6:30pm 3rd Tue • call for location

Accommodations
The B&B at Howden Farm Rannapo Rd, Sheffield 413/229-8481 • lesbians/ gay men • 250 acre working farm • nr river & outdoor recreation • full brkfst • smokefree • some shared baths • gay-owned/ run • $79-149

Summer Hill Farm 950 East St, Lenox 413/442-2057, 800/442-2059 • gay-friendly • colonial guesthouse & cottage • full brkfst • smokefree • kids ok • wheelchair access • $85-250

Walker House 64 Walker St, Lenox 413/637-1271, 800/235-3098 • gay-friendly • 1804 guesthouse • smokefree • kids 12+/ pets ok • wheelchair access • $70-210

Windflower Inn 684 S Egremont Rd, Great Barrington 413/528-2720, 800/992-1993 • gay-friendly • gracious country inn • full brkfst • smokefree • kids ok • $100-200

Restaurants
Cafe Lucia 80 Church St, Lenox 413/637-2640 • dinner only, clsd Sun-Mon • $14-32

Church Street Cafe 65 Church St, Lenox 413/637-2745 • lunch & dinner • some veggie • $13-22

Gateways 51 Walker St, Lenox 413/637-2532 • dinner, clsd Sun-Mon • plenty veggie • wheelchair access • $13-35

Boston • Massachusetts

Boston

INFO LINES & SERVICES

BAGLY (Boston Alliance of LGBT Youth) 617/227-4313, 800/422-2459 • talkline 10am-7pm • mtgs 6pm-9pm Wed • ask about other services

Bisexual Resource Center 29 Stanhope St, 4th flr **617/424-9595** • publishes bi resource guide • also Boston Bisexual Women's Network • wheelchair access

Cambridge Women's Center 46 Pleasant St, Cambridge **617/354-8807** • 10am-10pm, till 8pm Fri, 11am-4pm Sat, clsd Sun

Daughters of Bilitis 1151 Massachusetts Ave (in the Old Cambridge Baptist Church, in Harvard Sq), Cambridge **617/661-3633** • women's social & support networks • call for schedule

Entre Nous, Inc 617/265-4586 • gay men's & women's leather group • annual Provincetown wknd in Oct

Gay/ Lesbian Helpline 617/267-9001 • 6pm-11pm, 5pm-10pm wknds

International Foundation for Gender Education 781/899-2212 • transgender info & support

Lesbian Al-Anon at the Women's Center **617/354-8807** • 6:30pm Wed

Tiffany Club of New England 781/891-9325 • trans support group • also trans AA info

Boston

WHERE THE GIRLS ARE: Sipping coffee and reading somewhere in Cambridge or Harvard Square, strolling the South End near Columbus & Mass. Avenues, or hanging out in the Fenway or Jamaica Plain.

ENTERTAINMENT: Gay Men's Chorus 617/424-8900.
The Theatre Offensive 617/542-4214.
Tool Box Productions 617/497-9215.

LGBT PRIDE: June. 617/522-7890.

ANNUAL EVENTS: May - Gay & Lesbian Film/Video Festival 617/369-3300 (MFA #).
June - AIDS Walk www.aidswalk.net.

CITY INFO: Boston Visitor's Bureau 800/447-6277.

ATTRACTIONS: Beacon Hill.
Black Heritage Trail.
Boston Common.
Faneuil Hall.
Freedom Trail.
Harvard University.
Isabella Stewart Gardner Museum 617/566-1401.
Museum of Afro-American History 617/725-0022.
Museum of Fine Arts 617/267-9300.
Museum of Science 617/723-2500.
New England Aquarium 617/973-5281.
Old North Church 617/523-6676.
Walden Pond.

WEATHER: Extreme—from freezing winters to boiling summers with a beautiful spring and fall.

TRANSIT: Boston Cab 617/536-5010.
Instyle Transportation limo service 617/ 641-2400 or 877/ 64-STYLE.
MBTA (the 'T') 800/392-6100.

Massachusetts • USA

ACCOMMODATIONS

463 Beacon St Guest House 463 Beacon St **617/536-1302** • gay-friendly • minutes from Boston's heart • $69-129

82 Chandler B&B 82 Chandler St **617/482-0408, 888/482-0408** • gay/straight • historic townhouse in South End • great views • smokefree • $150-175

't Amsterdammertje 617/471-8454, 800/484-6401 x1676 • lesbians/gay men • Euro-American B&B • full brkfst • smokefree • nr Boston • $69-99

Carolyn's B&B 102 Holworthy St, Cambridge **617/864-7042** • gay-friendly • full brkfst • nr Harvard Square • smokefree • women-owned/run • $90-99

▲ **Chandler Inn** 26 Chandler St **617/482-3450, 800/842-3450** • gay-friendly • centrally located • $105-155

Clarendon Square B&B 198 W Brookline St (at Tremont/Boylston) **617/536-2229** • lesbians/gay men • restored Victorian townhouse • fireplaces • $129-279

Encore B&B 16 W Newton St (at Tremont St) **617/247-3425** • gay/straight • 19th-century townhouse in Boston's historic South End • gay-owned • $140-170

Just Right Reservations, Inc 978/934-9931 • covers hotels & B&Bs in MA • also West Hollywood & Palm Springs, CA

▲ **Oasis Guest House** 22 Edgerly Rd **617/267-2262** • popular • gay/straight • Back Bay location • some shared baths • wheelchair access • gay-owned/run • $85-135

Rutland Square House B&B 56 Rutland Sq **617/247-0018, 800/786-6567** • gay/straight • Victorian townhouse • smokefree • gay-owned/run • $85-150

Taylor House B&B 50 Burroughs St **617/983-9334, 888/228-2956** • gay/straight • Italianate Victorian • smokefree • gay-owned/run • $100-175

Victorian B&B 617/536-3285 • women only • full brkfst • smokefree • lesbian-owned/run • $65-90 (1-3 guests)

BARS

Boston Ramrod 1254-56 Boylston St (at Ipswich, 1 blk from Fenway Park) **617/266-2986** • noon-2am • popular • mostly gay men • leather • dancing/DJ • game room • wheelchair access • also 'Rubberworks' fetish store • 3rd Fri pansexual fetish night

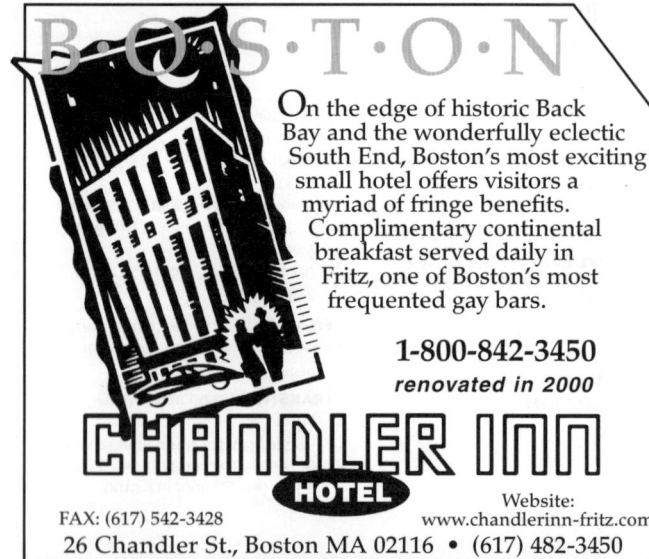

B·O·S·T·O·N

On the edge of historic Back Bay and the wonderfully eclectic South End, Boston's most exciting small hotel offers visitors a myriad of fringe benefits. Complimentary continental breakfast served daily in Fritz, one of Boston's most frequented gay bars.

1-800-842-3450
renovated in 2000

CHANDLER INN
HOTEL

FAX: (617) 542-3428

Website: www.chandlerinn-fritz.com

26 Chandler St., Boston MA 02116 • (617) 482-3450

Boston • Massachusetts

Chaps/ Vapor 100 Warrenton St (at Stuart) **617/695-9500** • noon-2am • popular • mostly gay men • dancing/DJ • piano bar Mon • Latin night Wed • T-dance Sun • dancers

Club Cafe 209 Columbus (at Berkeley) **617/536-0966** • 11:30am-2am, from 2pm Sat • popular • lesbians/ gay men • 3 bars • upscale • piano bar • live shows • also restaurant • some veggie • wheelchair access • $10-20

Jacque's 79 Broadway (at Stuart) **617/426-8902** • 11am-midnight • mostly gay men • popular • drag cabaret • live music Fri-Sat

Lava Bar 575 Commonwealth, top flr (in Kenmore Sq) **617/267-7707** • 10pm-2am, clsd Mon-Wed • gay/ straight • women's night Sat • dancing/DJ

Luxor 69 Church St (btwn Stuart & Arlington, in Theater District) **617/423-6969** • 4pm-1am • mostly gay men • popular • videos • also '69 Church St' lounge & 'Mario's' Italian restaurant downstairs • $9-13

Midway Cafe 3496 Washington St, Jamaica Plain **617/524-9038** • 9pm-2am Th • mostly women • neighborhood bar • dancing/DJ • live entertainment • younger crowd • wheelchair access

Milky Way Lounge & Lanes 403 Centre St, Jamaica Plain **617/524-3740** • 6pm-1am • gay/ straight • food served • live music • women's poetry readings

Upstairs at the Hideaway 20 Concord Ln, Cambridge **617/661-8828** • 6pm-2am Th & Sun only • mostly women • neighborhood bar

Nightclubs

Avalon 15 Lansdowne St **617/262-2424** • 9pm-2am Th-Sun • popular • mostly gay men • dancing/DJ • more gay Sun • young crowd • $10 cover charge

Buzz 67 Stuart St **617/267-8969** • 10pm-2am Sat • popular • mostly gay men • dancing/DJ • $8 cover charge

Manray 21 Brookline St (off Mass Ave, in Central Sq), Cambridge **617/864-0400** • 9pm-2am, clsd Sun-Tue • gay/ straight • more gay Th at 'Campus' (men, 19+) & Sat at 'Liquid' • more women Sun • dancing/DJ • alternative • goth Wed • fetish Fri • young crowd

The Middle East 472 Massachusetts Ave (in Central Sq), Cambridge **617/497-0576** • 11am-1am, till 2am wknds • gay-friendly • alternative • live music • also restaurant

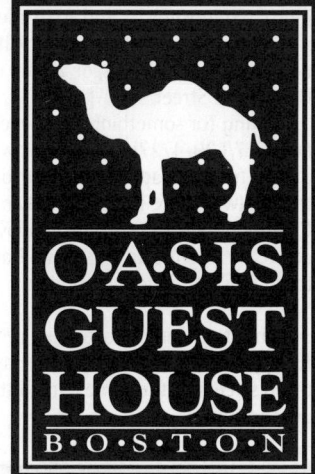

BOSTON

Two townhouses in the heart of Boston ♥ Telephones ♥ Color TV's ♥ Central Air ♥ Outdoor Decks ♥ Private & Shared Baths ♥ Continental Breakfast & Evening Snacks ♥ Close To All Major Sights & Nightlife
♥ Reasonable Rates
♥ MC, VISA & AMEX

22 Edgerly Road
Boston, MA 02115
Phone: 617-267-2262
Fax: 617-267-1920
Web: www.oasisgh.com
Email: oasisgh@tiac.net

O·A·S·I·S GUEST HOUSE
B·O·S·T·O·N

Massachusetts • USA

Reply **Forward** **Delete**

Date: Sun, Nov 4, 2001 16:49:36
From: Girl-on-the-Go
To: Editor@Damron.com
Subject: Boston

> Home to 65 colleges and universities, Boston has been an intellectual center for the continent for over three centuries. Since that famed tea party, it's also been home to some of New England's most rebellious radicals. The result is a city whose character is both traditional and free-thinking, high-brow and free-wheeling*, stuffy and energetic.

> Not only is this city complex, it's cluttered...with plenty of historic and mind-sparking sites to visit. Check out the high/low culture in Harvard Square and the shopping along Newbury Street in the Back Bay, as well as the touristy vendors in Faneuil Hall. Don't miss the North End's fabulous Italian food.

> Boston's women's community is, not surprisingly, strong and politically diverse. And it's decentralized: while you will find some women in the 'gay ghetto' of the South End, local lesbians tend to gravitate toward Cambridge, Jamaica Plain, and Somerville. To find out what the latest hotspots are, pick up a copy of **Bay Windows** or **IN Newsweekly** at the well-stocked women's bookstore, **New Words Books** (in Cambridge). While you're there, check out the many national lesbian magazines published in Boston, from feminist newsjournal **Sojourner** to **Bad Attitude,** an erotic 'zine for S/M dykes.

> Hungry? Grab a bite to eat at **City Girl Caffe,** just a few doors down from New Words, or at one of the great restaurants on nearby Cambridge Street.

> Looking for something more exciting? Call **Hanarchy Now**'s info line (617/629-4727) to see what wild event this local promoter has on tap for alternadykes. On Thursday nights, dance with the girls at the **Midway Cafe** in Jamaica Plain. Cruise by the **Hideaway** (in Cambridge) on Thursday or Sunday for a game of pool. If you like to dance the night away, try **Lava Bar** on Saturday or **Ryles** or **Manray** (both in Cambridge) on Sunday.

> * About driving in Boston: its drivers are notoriously the most freeform in the country. The streets of Boston can be confusing— often streets of the same name intersect, and six-way intersections are the rule.

Boston • Massachusetts

Someplace Else at Ryles 212 Hampshire St (at Cambridge St, in Inman Sq), Cambridge **617/876-9330** • 5pm-2am Sun • mostly women • dancing/DJ • food served

Static 13 Lansdowne (at Axis) **617/262-2437** • 10pm-2am Mon • lesbians/gay men • dancing/DJ • drag shows • 18+

CAFES

1369 Cafe 757 Massachusetts Ave (in Central Sq), Cambridge **617/576-4600** • coffee & baked goods • also 1369 Cambridge St location, 617/576-1369

Designs for Living 52 Queensberry St (at Jersey St) **617/536-6150** • 7am-6:30pm, till noon Wed, from 8am Sat, from 9am Sun • cybercafe & bookstore

Diesel Cafe 257 Elm St (in Davis Sq), Somerville **617/629-8717** • 7am-midnight, till 1am Fri-Sat, from 8am wknds • sandwiches • plenty veggie • pool tables • lesbian-owned/run

Francesca's 564 Tremont St (at Clarendon) **617/482-9026** • 8am-11pm, till midnight wknds • popular • lesbians/gay men • excellent pastries • wheelchair access

Geoffrey's Cafe 578 Tremont St (at Dartmouth) **617/266-1122** • 9am-10pm, till 11pm wknds • great desserts • beer/wine • gay-owned/run

RESTAURANTS

Biba 272 Boylston St (at Arlington) **617/426-7878** • popular • lunch & dinner • upscale dining • eclectic California cuisine • wheelchair access • $14-39

Blackstone's on the Square 1525 Washington St **617/247-4455** • lunch Mon-Fri, brunch Sun, dinner nightly • popular • gay/ straight • bistro fare • martini bar • wheelchair access • $12-15

Brandy Pete's 267 Franklin St (at Congress) **617/439-4165** • lunch & dinner Mon-Fri only

Buddha's Delight 3 Beach St, 2nd flr **617/451-2395** • 11am-9:30pm • Chinese • vegetarian

Casa Romero 30 Gloucester St **617/536-4341** • 5pm-10pm, till 11pm wknds • Mexican

City Girl Caffe 204 Hampshire St (at Prospect), Cambridge **617/864-2809** • 11am-9pm, from 10am wknds, clsd Mon • Italian • great sandwiches • plenty veggie • wknd brunch • lesbian-owned/run

Club Cafe 209 Columbus (at Berkeley) **617/536-0966** • dinner & wknd brunch • popular • lesbians/gay men • some veggie • also 3 bars • videos • wheelchair access • $10-20

Icarus 3 Appleton St (off Tremont) **617/426-1790** • dinner only • New American • $30-40

Johnny D's 17 Holland St (in Davis Sq), Somerville **617/776-2004** • dinner Tue-Sat & wknd brunch • Southern • plenty veggie • women's hangout • dancing • live music

Laurel 142 Berkeley St (at Columbus) **617/424-6711, 617/424-6664** • lunch & dinner, Sun brunch

New Blue Diner 150 Kneeland St (at South St) **617/695-0087** • 7am-4pm, 24hrs Th-Sun • lesbians/gay men • Southern bbq • plenty veggie • wheelchair access

Rabia's 73 Salem St (at Cross St) **617/227-6637** • lunch & dinner • fine Italian • some veggie • wheelchair access • $10-25

Ristorante Lucia 415 Hanover St **617/367-2353** • lunch Fri-Sun, dinner nightly • great North End pasta • some veggie • $8-15

Trattoria Pulcinella 147 Huron Ave (at Concord), Cambridge **617/491-6336** • dinner • fine Italian • cash only

ENTERTAINMENT & RECREATION

Freedom Trail • start at the Visitor Information Center in Boston Common (at Tremont & West Sts), the most famous cow pasture & oldest public park in the US, and follow the red line to some of Boston's most famous sites

Isabella Stewart Gardner Museum 280 The Fenway **617/566-1401** • Venetian palazzo filled w/ Old Masters to Impressionists • gorgeous courtyard • clsd Mon

John Hancock Observatory 200 Clarendon St, 60th flr (at St James St) **617/247-1977**

Museum of Afro-American History/ Black Heritage Trail 46 Joy St (at Smith Ct, on Beacon Hill) **617/425-0022** • exhibits in the African Meeting House, the oldest standing African-American church in the US

Theater Offensive **617/542-4214** • 'New England's foremost presenter of lgbt theater' • 'Out on the Edge' festival in Sept

Tool Box Productions 60 Bishop Allen Dr #4, Cambridge 02139 **617/497-9215** • multi-media cabaret & events • women of all colors

BOOKSTORES

Calamus Bookstore 92-B South St **617/338-1931, 888/800-7300** • 9am-7pm, noon-6pm • lgbt • also cards • music • jewelry • videos • magazines

Massachusetts • USA

▲ **New Words Bookstore** 186 Hampshire St (at Prospect), Cambridge **617/876-5310, 800/928-4788** • noon-8pm, from 10am Sat, till 6pm wknds, clsd Mon • feminist • wheelchair access

Trident Booksellers & Cafe 338 Newbury St (off Mass Ave) **617/267-8688** • 9am-midnight • good magazine browsing • beer/wine • wheelchair access

Unicorn Books 1210 Massachusetts Ave (at Appleton), Arlington Hts **781/646-3680** • 10am-9pm, till 5pm wknds, from noon Sun • spiritual titles

We Think The World of You 540 Tremont St (btwn Berkeley & Clarendon) **617/574-5000** • 10am-7pm, till 6:30pm Sat, 11:30am-5:50pm Sun • popular • lgbt

Wordsworth 30 Brattle St (at Mt Auburn, in Harvard Sq), Cambridge **617/354-5201** • 9am-11pm, 10am-10pm Sun • general • some lgbt titles

Publications

Bay Windows **617/266-6670** • lgbt newspaper

In Newsweekly **617/426-8246** • New England's lgbt newspaper

Sojourner—The Women's Forum **617/524-0415** • monthly progressive paper

Spiritual Groups

Am Tikva 50 Sewall Ave, Brookline **617/883-0893** • 8pm 1st & 3rd Fri • lgbt Jewish services

Dignity 35 Bowdoin St (at St John the Evangelist Church, Beacon Hill) **617/421-1915** • 5:30pm Sun

MCC 131 Cambridge St (at Old West Church) **617/325-8204** • 6pm Sun

Gyms & Health Clubs

Metropolitan Fitness 209 Columbus **617/536-3006** • gay-friendly

Mike's Gym II 560 Harrison Ave (at Waltham St) **617/338-6210, 617/338-6677** • popular • gay-owned/run

Erotica

Eros Boutique 581-A Tremont St, 2nd flr **617/425-0345** • fetish wear • toys

Grand Opening! 318 Harvard St, 2nd flr (at Beacon, in Arcade Bldg), Brookline **617/731-2626** • women's sex toy store

Hubba Hubba 534 Massachusetts Ave (at Brookline, in Central Sq), Cambridge **617/492-9082** • noon-8pm • fetish gear

---

Don't leave Boston without visiting...

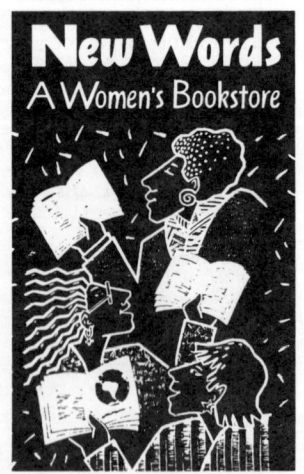

New Words
A Women's Bookstore

A FABULOUS COLLECTION OF LESBIAN & WOMEN'S TITLES

PLUS:
T-shirts • Cards • CDs • Tapes
Jewelry & Other Gift Items

186 Hampshire Street
Cambridge, MA 02139 ♿
617-876-5310 • 800-928-4788
newwords@world.std.com
www.newwordsbooks.com

Tue-Fri: noon-8, Sat: 10-6, Sun: noon-6, clsd Mon
Full Mail Order Service Available

Marquis de Sade 73 Berkeley St (at Chandler) **617/426-2120**

Brookline

see Boston

Cambridge

see Boston

Cape Cod

see also Provincetown listings

INFO LINES & SERVICES

Gay/ Lesbian AA Cape Cod Hospital (at Whitcomb Pavilion), Hyannis **508/775-7060** • 6pm Sun

ACCOMMODATIONS

15 Park Square 15 Park Square (at Main St), Hyannis **508/771-4760** • mostly gay men • guesthouse • shared baths • smokefree • gay-owned/ run • $50-130

Blue Heron B&B 464 Pleasant Lake Ave, Harwich **508/430-0219** • mostly women • swimming • private beach • lesbian-owned/ run • $65-85

Gull Cottage 10 Old Church St, Yarmouth Port **508/362-8747** • mostly gay men • nr beach • shared baths • wheelchair access • $150/ week

Holbrook House 223 Main St (at Whit's Ln), Wellfleet **508/349-6706** • gay/ straight • restored 1820s Capt's home • full brkfst • smokefree • lesbian-owned/ run • $100-125

The Marlborough B&B Inn 320 Woods Hole Rd, Woods Hole **508/548-6218, 800/320-2322** • gay-friendly • guesthouse & cottage • full brkfst • swimming • tennis • smokefree • $85-165

Private Cape Cod Cottage 35 Rolling Ln (at Herring Brook Rd), Eastham **631/689-9456** • mostly women • 2-bdrm cottage • 2 miles to beach • 20 mins to Provincetown • seasonal • smokefree • lesbian-owned/ run • $800/ week

Woods Hole Passage 186 Woods Hole Rd, Falmouth **508/548-9575, 800/790-8976** • gay-friendly • full brkfst • nr beaches • $100-165

NIGHTCLUBS

Club 477 477 Yarmouth Rd, Hyannis **508/775-9835, 800/393-6161** • 6pm-1am • popular • lesbians/ gay men • Cape Cod's largest gay complex • dancing/DJ • wheelchair access

Gloucester

BOOKSTORES

The Bookstore 61 Main St **978/281-1548** • 9am-6pm • lgbt section

Greenfield

ACCOMMODATIONS

Brandt House 29 Highland Ave **413/774-3329, 800/235-3329** • gay-friendly • full brkfst • kids ok • woman-owned/ run • $95-205

The Charlemont Inn Rte 2, Mohawk Trail, Charlemont **413/339-5796** • gay-friendly • $35-65 • restaurant • some veggie • full bar • live music wknds • $10-20 • lesbian-owned/ run

BOOKSTORES

World Eye Bookshop 156 Main St **413/772-2186** • 9am-7pm, till 8pm Fri, till 6pm Sat, noon-5pm Sun • general • lgbt section • community bulletin board • women-owned/ run

Haverhill

BARS

Friend's Landing 85 Water St **978/374-9400** • 6pm-1am, till 2am Fri, from 4pm wknds • popular • lesbians/ gay men • dancing/DJ • karaoke • 6 bars • 2 dance floors • cabaret • waterfront deck • wheelchair access

Lincoln

ACCOMMODATIONS

Thoreau's Walden B&B 2 Concord Rd **781/259-1899** • gay-friendly • nr historic Walden Pond • full brkfst • kids ok • $75

Lynn

BARS

Fran's Place 776 Washington (at Sagamore) **781/598-5618** • 4pm-2am • lesbians/ gay men • dancing/DJ • men's night Mon • karaoke Tue • college night and drag show Th • Latin night Sun • wheelchair access

Joseph's 191 Oxford St (off Market St) **781/599-9483** • 5pm-2am • lesbians/ gay men • dancing/DJ • videos • wheelchair access

The Pub at 47 Central 47 Central Ave **781/586-0551** • 2pm-2am • mostly gay men • neighborhood bar • dancing/DJ wknds • karaoke Th • live shows Fri-Sat • food served • gay-owned/ run

Massachusetts • USA

Martha's Vineyard

ACCOMMODATIONS

Captain Dexter House of Edgartown
508/627-7289 • gay-friendly • country inn circa 1840 • $95-300

Captain Dexter House of Vineyard Haven 508/693-6564 • gay-friendly • 1840s sea captain's home • $105-275

Four Gables 41 New York Ave, Oak Bluffs 508/696-8384 • gay/ straight • turn-of-the-century inn • nr beach • private sundecks • kids/ pets ok • smokefree • $100-185

Martha's Place B&B 508/693-0253 • lesbians/ gay men • harbor views • fireplaces • smokefree • kids ok • gay-owned/ run • $175-395

The Shiverick Inn 5 Pease's Pt Wy, Edgartown (at Pent Ln) 508/627-3797, 800/723-4292 • gay/ straight • restored 1840 mansion • antique filled • gay-owned/ run • $145-360

RESTAURANTS

The Black Dog Tavern Beach St Extension #21 508/693-9223 • 7am-9pm • wheelchair access • $13-25

Le Grenier 96 Main St, Vineyard Haven 508/693-4906 • 5:30pm-close • French • $13-25

Louis' Cafe 350 State Rd, Vineyard Haven 508/693-3255 • Italian • plenty veggie • gay-owned/ run • $6-17

BOOKSTORES

Bunch of Grapes 44 Main St, Vineyard Haven 508/693-2291 • 9am-6pm • general • some lgbt titles & magazines

Nantucket

ACCOMMODATIONS

The Chestnut House 3 Chestnut St 508/228-0049 • gay-friendly • smokefree • also cottage • $130-300

New Bedford

BARS

Puzzles 428 N Front St (at Philips Ave) 508/997-0466 • 2:30pm-2am, from 11am Sun • lesbians/ gay men • dancing/DJ Fri-Sat • strippers Fri & Mon • karaoke Wed • Sun brunch • wheelchair access

Newburyport

ACCOMMODATIONS

46 High Road B&B 46 High Rd, Newbury 978/462-4664 • gay-friendly • old family homestead • full brkfst • smokefree • kids/ pets ok • $85-95

RESTAURANTS

Glenns Restaurant 44 Merrimac St 978/465-3811 • 5:30pm-10pm, from 4pm wknds, clsd Mon • full bar till midnight • live music • wheelchair access • $19-27

Newton

see Boston

North Adams

RESTAURANTS

Fifty-Five Main 55 Main St (at Rte 8) 423/664-8558 • lunch & dinner, clsd Sun • full bar • hosts 'Red Party' on Halloween & other theme parties • gay-owned/ run

Northampton

INFO LINES & SERVICES

East Coast FTM Group 413/584-7616 • support group for FTM TG/TS, their partners & friends

Sexual Minorities Archives 413/584-7616 • lgbt & SM collection • by appt

ACCOMMODATIONS

Clark Tavern Inn B&B 98 Bay Rd, Hadley 413/586-1900 • gay-friendly • full brkfst • smokefree • teens ok • $115-145

Corner Porches 82 Baptist Corner Rd, Ashfield 413/628-4592 • gay/ straight • 1880s farmhouse • 30 mins from Northampton • shared bath • full brkfst • kids ok • smokefree • woman-owned/ run • $60-75

The Hotel Northampton 36 King St 413/584-3100, 800/547-3529 • gay-friendly • in the heart of downtown • gym • cafe & historic tavern • wheelchair access • $99-325

The Inn at Northampton 1 Atwood Dr 413/586-1211, 800/582-2929 • gay-friendly • swimming • tennis • also restaurant & bar • wheelchair access • $109-169

The McKinley House 3 McKinley Ave (at Rte 10), Easthampton 413/527-5116 • lesbians/ gay men • full brkfst • some shared baths • 4 miles south of Northampton • gay-owned/ run • $95-145

Northampton • Massachusetts

Old Red Schoolhouse 67 Park St 413/584-1228 • apts • studios • also 'Lesbian Towers' in East Hampton • pets ok • gay-owned/run • $75-200

Tin Roof B&B 413/586-8665 • mostly women • 1909 farmhouse w/ spectacular view of the Berkshires • shared baths • kids ok • lesbian-owned/run • $60-65

Bars

The Grotto 25 West St 413/586-6900 • 5pm-1am, till 2am Wed, Fri & Sat, clsd Mon • lesbians/gay men • dancing/DJ • drag shows Wed • 18+ Wed & Fri • patio

Nightclubs

Club Metro 492 Pleasant St 413/582-9898 • clsd Mon • gay-friendly • gay night Th • T-dance Sat • dancing/DJ •

Date: Mon, Nov 5, 2001 14:41:56
From: Girl-on-the-Go
To: Editor@Damron.com
Subject: Northampton

> With all the hype a while back about Northampton being the lesbian capital of the world, visitors are often surprised by the low-key atmosphere of this quaint and quiet New England town. It's the sort of place where the people are nice, the streets are safe, and most groups come in multiples of two.

> Sure, you'll be free to smooch with your honey just about everywhere, but don't expect to see the throngs of Sapphic sisters you've heard about in the *National Enquirer* or on *20/20* milling around the streets. They're there all right, but they're probably home with the kids, cuddling with their other half, or studying for that big exam at one of the five colleges in the area.

> Still, there's plenty for a visiting lesbian to enjoy in Northampton. For lesbian-friendly accommodations, check out the **Tin Roof** in Hadley. The **Green Street Cafe** and vegetarian, lesbian-owned **Bela** are popular with the local girls. At night, head to the **Grotto** or **Club Metro** for dancing and drinks. For something different, make an appointment to view the **Sexual Minorities Archives,** or take a tour of Emily Dickinson's House in nearby Amherst.

> With two women's colleges, Smith and Mount Holyoke, progressive Hampshire College, Amherst College, and the University of Massachusetts all in the area, there's something fun to do every night of the week, from readings to performance art. Check out the **Lesbian Calendar,** a comprehensive monthly listing of events. It's available at **Pride & Joy** LGBT bookstore. While you're there, pick up a copy of the Lesbian/Gay Business Guild's listing of 'family' businesses in the area.

Massachusetts • USA

The Iron Horse 20 Center St **413/584-0610** • 7:30pm-close • gay-friendly • live music • all ages • smokefree • food served • some veggie • $5-15

Pearl Street 10 Pearl St **413/584-0610** • 7:30pm-1am • gay/ straight • dancing/DJ • live music • young crowd • women-owned/ run

Cafes

Bart's Homemade 235 Main St **413/584-0721** • 7:30am-11pm, till midnight Fri-Sat • cafe menu & ice cream (!)

Haymarket Cafe 15 Amber Ln **413/586-9969** • 10am-11pm • popular

Restaurants

Bela 68 Masonic St **413/586-8011** • noon-8:45pm, clsd Sun-Mon • vegetarian • wheelchair access • lesbian-owned/ run • $5-10

Cha Cha Cha 134 Main St **413/586-7311** • 11:30am-10pm, till 11pm Fri-Sat, noon-9pm Sun • Mexican

Green Street Cafe 64 Green St (at Main) **413/586-5650** • lunch & dinner • plenty veggie • beer/ wine • gay-owned/ run • $11-17

La Cazuela 7 Old South St **413/586-0400** • 5pm-9pm • Southwestern • full bar

Paul & Elizabeth's 150 Main St (in Thorne's Marketplace) **413/586-4832** • lunch & dinner • seafood • plenty veggie • beer/ wine • wheelchair access • $7-12

Retail Shops

Piercings by the Bearded Lady 222 State St **413/586-0829** • 1pm-7pm, clsd Sun • lesbian-owned/ run

Northampton

WHERE THE GIRLS ARE: Just off Main St., browsing in the small shops, strolling down an avenue, or sipping a beverage at one of the cafes.

LGBT PRIDE: May. 413/586-5602, web: www.northamptonpride.org.

ANNUAL EVENTS: October - Paradise City Arts Festival 413/527-8994, web: www.paradise-city.com. October/November - Northampton Film Festival (includes an LGBT segment) 413/586-3471, web: www.nohofilm.org.

CITY INFO: 415/584-1900 or 800/238-6869, web: www.northamptonuncommon.com

ATTRACTIONS: Academy of Music 413/584-9023.
The Berkshires.
Emily Dickinson Homestead, Amherst 413/542-8161.
Historic Northampton 413/584-6011, web: www.historic-northampton.org.
Northampton Center for the Arts 413/584-7327, web: www.nohoarts.org.

BEST VIEW: At the top of Skinner Mountain, up Route 47 by bus, car, or bike.

WEATHER: Late summer/early fall is the best season, with warm, sunny days. Mid-summer gets to the low 90°s, while winter brings snow from November to March, with temperatures in the 20°s and 30°s.

TRANSIT: Florence/Paradise Taxi 413/584-0055.
Peter Pan Shuttle 413/586-1030.
Pioneer Valley Transit Authority (PVTA) 413/781-7882, web: www.pvta.com.

Provincetown • Massachusetts

Pride & Joy 20 Crafts Ave **413/585-0683** • open 7 days • lgbt books & gifts • wheelchair access

PUBLICATIONS

In Newsweekly **617/426-8246** • New England's lgbt newspaper

Lesbian Calendar **413/586-5514** • monthly newsletter for the Pioneer Valley women's community

Metroline **860/233-8334** • regional newspaper & entertainment guide, covers CT, RI & MA

EROTICA

Intimacies 28 Center St **413/582-0709** • 11am-8pm, till 6pm Tue-Wed, noon-5pm Sun • lesbian-owned/run

Plymouth

ACCOMMODATIONS

Symphony Hollow B&B 127 Brook St, Plympton **781/585-7823, 888/655-1200** • gay-friendly • on 7 acres • gardens • fireplaces • nr outdoor recreation • gay-owned/run • $105-135

Provincetown

INFO LINES & SERVICES

▲ **In Town Reservations, Real Estate & Travel** 4 Standish St **508/487-1883, 800/67P-TOWN (677-8696)** • gay-owned/run

Provincetown Business Guild **508/487-2313, 800/637-8696**

▲ **Provincetown Reservations System** 293 Commercial St **508/487-2400, 800/648-0364** • shows • rooms • rentals

ACCOMMODATIONS

1807 House 54 Commercial St (btwn W Vine & Point St) **508/487-2173, 888/522-1807** • lesbians/gay men • wheelchair access • $70-175

Admiral's Landing Guest House 158 Bradford St (btwn Conwell & Pearl) **508/487-9665, 800/934-0925** • mostly gay men • 1840s Greek Revival home & studio efficiencies • gay-owned/run • $65-135

▲ **Aerie House & Beach Club** 184 Bradford St (at Miller Hill) **508/487-1197, 800/487-1197** • lesbians/gay men • intimate guest house on the tip of Cape Cod • hot tub • sundeck • gay-owned/run • $85-210

www.intownreservations.com

- ▼ Condo and House Rentals
- ▼ B&B and Motel Bookings
- ▼ Show Tickets ▼ Local Tours
- ▼ Real Estate Sales
- ▼ Full Service Travel Agency
- ▼ Computer Rental Stations
- ▼ Limo Service

1-800-67P-TOWN
508-487-1883
4 Standish Street

IN TOWN RESERVATIONS
▼ PROVINCETOWN ▼

Massachusetts • USA

▲ **Anchor Inn Beach House** 175 Commercial St **508/487-0432, 800/858-2657** • popular • gay/ straight • smokefree • central location • private beach • harbor view • wheelchair access • gay-owned/ run • $95-375

Bayberry Accommodations 16 Winthrop St **508/487-4605, 800/422-4605** • lesbians/ gay men • award-winning home • hot tub • smokefree • gay-owned/ run • $75-215

Bayshore 493 Commercial St (at Howland) **508/487-9133** • gay/ straight • apts • private beach • kitchens • lesbian-owned/ run • $75-175 ($950-1995/ week in summer)

Beachfront Realty 151 Commercial St **508/487-1397** • vacation rentals

Beaconlight Guest House 12 Winthrop St **508/487-9603, 800/696-9603** • popular • mostly gay men • award-winning • hot tub • fireplaces • sundecks • smokefree • parking • gay-owned/ run • $55-225

▲ **Benchmark Inn & Central** 6-8 Dyer St **508/487-7440, 888/487-7440** • lesbians/ gay men • hot tub • sauna • fireplace • harbor views • swimming • in heart of Provincetown • smokefree • gay-owned/ run • $95-395

Best Inn **508/487-1711, 800/422-4224** • gay-friendly • swimming • pets ok • also restaurant & lounge • wheelchair access • $69-179

Boatslip Beach Club 161 Commercial St (at Atlantic) **508/487-1669, 800/451-7547** • popular • mostly gay men • resort • swimming • seasonal • also several bars • popular T-dance • gay-owned/ run • $165-225

▲ **The Bradford Carver House** 70 Bradford St **508/487-4966, 800/826-9083** • lesbians/ gay men • restored mid-19th-century home • centrally located • gay-owned/ run • $39-169

Bradford Gardens Inn 178 Bradford St **508/487-1616, 800/432-2334** • mostly women • 1820s Colonial & cottages • full brkfst • gardens • lesbian-owned/ run • $78-250

Bradford House & Motel 41 Bradford St **508/487-0173** • gay-friendly • wheelchair access • women-owned/ run • $65-750

Brass Key Guesthouse 67 Bradford St (at Carver) **508/487-9005, 800/842-9858** • popular • lesbians/ gay men • hot tub • swimming • smokefree • wheelchair access • gay-owned/ run • $225-425

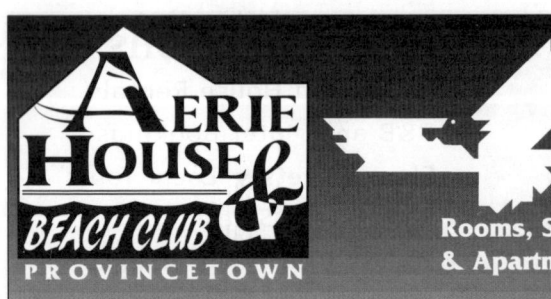

AERIE HOUSE & BEACH CLUB
PROVINCETOWN

Rooms, Suites & Apartments

Some of the best views in Provincetown from either our Guesthouse perched above Miller Hill or our bay front Beach Club.

Private Beach · Hot Tub · Gym · Bicycles Fireplaces
Sun Deck · Parking · Video Library
Airport/Pier pick-up · Open Year-round

184 Bradford Street, Provincetown, MA 02657
800.487.1197 · Email: aerieptown@cs.com

www.aeriehouse.com

PROVINCETOWN...
and the world

TRAVEL • ACCOMMODATIONS • SHOW TICKETS

THE GAY & LESBIAN COMMUNITY UNLIKE ANYWHERE ELSE.

"Swimming" Courtesy of Ruth West of the Charles-Baltivik Gallery, Provincetown

PROVINCETOWN RESERVATIONS SYSTEM®

A FREE SERVICE TO YOU.

When you think of PRS, think of a First Class women's travel agency that can take you anywhere in the world.

1 800 648-0364
ptownres@ptownres.com

www.ptownres.com

Massachusetts • USA

[Reply] [Forward] **[Delete]**

Date: Wed, Nov 7, 2001 12:09:11
From: Girl-on-the-Go
To: Editor@Damron.com
Subject: Provincetown

> Who would have thought that a little New England whaling village at the very tip of Cape Cod would be the country's largest gay and lesbian resort? But Provincetown is just that.

> The season in Provincetown runs according to a time-honored schedule of who does what, when and where. According to one regular, the typical lesbian itinerary goes as follows:

> Arrival: Rent a bike and explore the town's LGBT shops and bookstores. (Nobody drives in Provincetown.) Pick up lunch at a deli on the way to Herring Cove. At the beach, head left to find the women. At the beach: Take off your top, if you like. Just keep an eye out for the cops, who'll give you a ticket if they catch you bare-breasted. And a word to the wise: If you're heading toward the sand dunes for a tryst, don't forget your socks. The hot, white sand can burn your feet (Youch!).

> 3pm: Bike back to your room for a shower, then head to the afternoon T-dance at **Boatslip Beach Club** on Commercial Street. Drink and dance till dinnertime, then take a relaxing few hours for your meal.

> After dinner: Check out the bars; women have their choice between **Vixen, Chaser's,** and **Venus** at **Pied Piper** on the weekends. If you're not into the bar scene or all the sun and surf has tired you out, you can always go shopping. Most stores stay open till 11pm during the summer. When the bars close, grab a slice of pizza and an espresso milkshake at **Spiritus**, and cruise the streets until they're empty—sometimes not till 4 or 5am.

> Before you leave, treat yourself to the excitement of a whale-watching cruise. There are several cruise lines, and **Portuguese Princess Whale Watch** is women-owned.

> But if you really want a whale of a good time, pencil in **Provincetown's Women's Week** in October. The **Women Innkeepers of Provincetown** will be sponsoring an opening party, a community dinner, a golf tournament and fun run, a prom, lots of entertainment...and more. Don't forget to call your favorite guesthouse early—really early—to make your reservations!

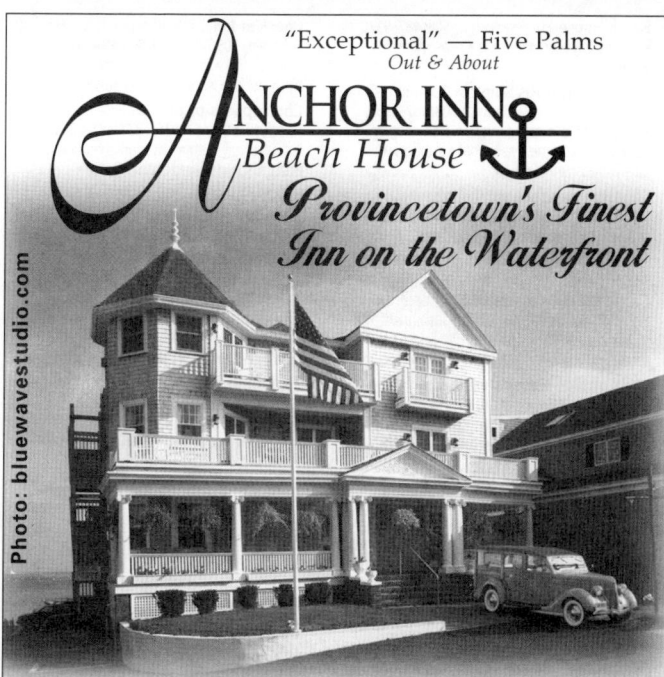

"Exceptional" — Five Palms
Out & About

Anchor Inn Beach House
Provincetown's Finest Inn on the Waterfront

Photo: bluewavestudio.com

*O*ur guestrooms offer private bath, individually-controlled heating and air conditioning, twin-line telephone with voicemail & dataport, TV/VCR, wet bar with sink and refrigerator and luxury bath amenities including robes and hairdryer. Many guestrooms feature deluxe showers, whirlpool baths and/or fireplaces. Sixteen rooms have private balconies overlooking the harbor. A complimentary continental breakfast buffet is served each morning.

175 Commercial St., Provincetown, MA 02657
1.800.858.2657
508.487.0432   Fax: 508.487.6280
Email: ankrinn@capecod.net
Web Site: www.anchorinnbeachhouse.com

Massachusetts • USA

Burch House 116 Bradford St **508/487-9170** • mostly gay men • studios • seasonal • $50-120

The Captain & His Ship 164 Commercial St (btwn Winthrop & Central) **508/487-1850, 800/400-2278** • gay/straight • 19th-century sea captain's home • seasonal • sundeck • gay-owned/run • $65-185

Captain Lysander's Inn 96 Commercial St (at Mechanic) **508/487-2253** • gay-friendly • sundeck w/ harbor view • some shared baths • also apt & cottage • women-owned/run • $55-250

Carpe Diem Guesthouse 12 Johnson St **508/487-4242, 800/487-0132** • lesbians/gay men • also cottage • full German brkfst • hot tub • smokefree • gay-owned/run • $65-250

The Carriage House Guesthouse 7 Central St **508/487-8855, 800/309-0248** • gay/straight • 1700s guesthouse w/ luxurious modern rooms • hot tub • courtyard • gay-owned/run • $100-225

Check'er Inn 25 Winthrop St (btwn Bradford & Brown) **508/487-9029, 800/894-9029** • women only • apts w/ private entrances • hot tub • decks • lesbian-owned/run • $125-200

Christopher's by the Bay 8 Johnson St (at Bradford) **508/487-9263, 877/487-9263** • lesbians/gay men • Victorian guesthouse • full brkfst • some shared baths • patio • smokefree • $50-170

The Clarendon House 118 Bradford St (btwn Ryder & Alden) **508/487-1645, 800/669-8229** • gay/straight • also cottage • hot tub • roof deck • pets ok • gay-owned/run • $60-170

The Commons Guesthouse & Bistro 386 Commercial St (at Pearl) **508/487-7800, 800/487-0784** • gay/straight • deck w/ full bar • also restaurant • gay-owned/run • $119-175

Crown & Anchor 247 Commercial St **508/487-1430** • lesbians/gay men • swimming • also bars • cabaret • $150-350

Provincetown

WHERE THE GIRLS ARE: In this small resort town, you can't miss 'em! At the beach, the girls gather on the left side at Herring Cove.

LGBT PRIDE: May.

ANNUAL EVENTS: June - Golden Threads 802/848-8002. Gathering for lesbians over 50 & their admirers, at the Provincetown Inn. PO Box 60475, Northampton, MA 01060-0475.
August - Provincetown Carnival 800/637-8696.
October - Women's Week 800/637-8696. It's very popular, so make your reservations early!
Fantasia Fair - for TS/TVs & their admirers.
December - Holly Folly.

CITY INFO: Chamber of Commerce 508/487-3424.

ATTRACTIONS: The beach.
Galleries.
Heritage Museum 508/487-7098.
Herring Cove Beach.
Pilgrim Monument.
Provincetown Museum 508/487-1310.
Whale watching.

BEST VIEW: People-watching from an outdoor cafe or on the beach.

WEATHER: New England weather is unpredictable. Be prepared for rain, snow, or extreme heat! Otherwise, the weather during the season consists of warm days and cooler nights.

TRANSIT: Mercedes Cab 508/487-3333.
Provincetown Taxi 508/487-8294.
Ferry Bay State Spray & Provincetown Steamship Co. (from Commonwealth Pier in Boston, during summer) 617/723-7800.

Provincetown • Massachusetts

The BRADFORD-CARVER House

OPEN YEAR ROUND
Your home away from home, where there are no strangers–
only friends you haven't met!

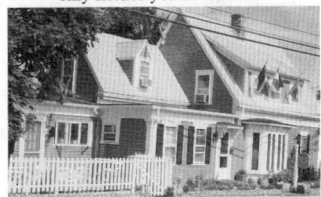

Experience our warm hospitality & cozy accommodations with
a convenient central location

"Highly Recommended" *–Out & About Magazine*

Private Baths • King & Queen Beds • Color Cable TV/VCR • A/C
Refrigerators • Room Phones • Continental Breakfast • Parking
Large Videocassette Library • Patio • Common Room • Fireplaces

508 • 487-4966   800 • 826-9083
70 Bradford Street, Provincetown, MA 02657
www.capecod.net/bradfordcarver   email: bradcarver@capecod.net

---

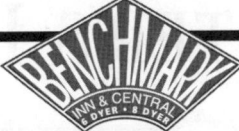

BENCHMARK INN Top-notch comfort and style. Fireplaces, whirlpool baths, wet bars, private balconied entrances, and stunning harborviews.
"Outstanding" 5 Palms & Editor's Choice Award, Out & About

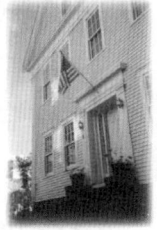

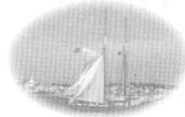

BENCHMARK CENTRAL New for 2001. Seven sunlit, contemporary accommodations, accented by a soaring atrium, heated pool, spa & sauna room and every amenity.

Benchmark. Total luxury is yours.

6 & 8 DYER STREET • PROVINCETOWN • MA 02657
508-487-7440 • TOLL FREE 1-888-487-7440
www.benchmarkinn.com

Massachusetts • USA

Crowne Pointe Historic Inn 82 Bradford St **508/487-6767, 877/276-9631** • lesbians/gay men • 1800s mansion • full brkfst • hot tub • wheelchair access • gay-owned/run • $185-425

▲ **Dexter's Inn** 6 Conwell St (at Railroad) **508/487-1911, 888/521-1999** • lesbians/gay men • B&B • smokefree • sundeck • gay-owned/run • $50-125

The Dunes Motel & Apartments **508/487-1956, 800/475-1833** • lesbians/gay men • rooms & apts • seasonal • decks • $39-175

▲ **Elephant Walk Inn** 156 Bradford St (at Conwell) **508/487-2543 OR 954/730-0664 (NOV-APRIL), 800/889-9255** • popular • mostly gay men • in the heart of Provincetown • smokefree • sundeck • parking • seasonal • gay-owned/run • $56-142

▲ **Fairbanks Inn** 90 Bradford St **508/487-0386, 800/324-7265** • popular • lesbians/gay men • kids ok • smokefree • lesbian-owned/run • $65-275

▲ **Gabriel's Apartments & Guest Rooms** 104 Bradford St **508/487-3232, 800/969-2643** • popular • lesbians/gay men • full brkfst • hot tub • nudity • smokefree • gym • sundecks • workshop center • gay-owned/run • $75-225

Gifford House Inn & Dance Club 11 Carver St **508/487-0688, 800/434-0130** • lesbians/gay men • seasonal • also several bars • also '11 Carver' restaurant • dinner only • seafood • gay-owned/run • $48-239

Gracie House 152 Bradford St (at Conwell) **508/487-4808** • lesbians/gay men • historic, restored Queen Anne • seasonal • smokefree • lesbian-owned/run • $75-105

Grand View Inn 4 Conant St **508/487-9193, 888/268-9169** • lesbians/gay men • decks • gay-owned/run • $45-140

The Gull Walk Inn 300-A Commercial St **508/487-9027** • women only • central location • shared baths • seasonal • sundeck • garden • lesbian-owned/run • $29-89

Halle's 14 W Vine St (at Tremont) **508/487-6310** • mostly women • cottage & apts • sundeck • smokefree • lesbian-owned/run • $100-150

Harbor Lights Guest Apartments 163 Bradford St (at Law St) **508/487-8246** • gay/straight • studio & 1-brm apt • smokefree • parking • lesbian-owned/run • $800-1,250/week in-season, $95/night off-season)

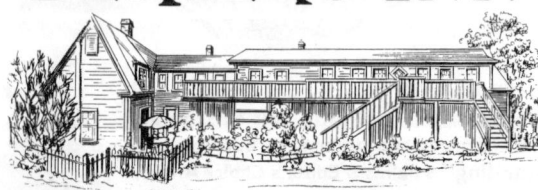

DEXTER'S INN

A Traditional Cape Cod Guest House
Private Baths — Sundeck — Parking — TVs
In-Room Phones — Continental Breakfast
Central Location — Airport Pickup — A/C
OPEN YEAR ROUND

6 Conwell Street, Provincetown, MA 02657
508-487-1911 Toll-free 888-521-1999
e-mail — dextersinn@aol.com
www.ptowndextersinn.com

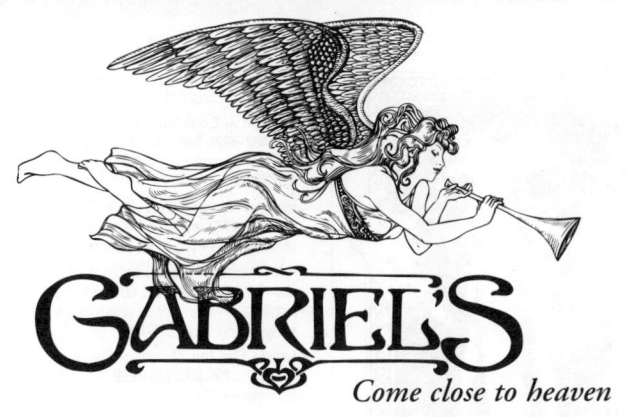

Come close to heaven

APARTMENTS & GUEST ROOMS
FINE ACCOMMODATIONS SINCE 1979

Always Open & In the Heart of Provincetown
One block from the Beach

Breakfast • Fireplaces • Hot Tubs • Steam Room • Sauna
Massage • In-Room Phones & Refrigerators • All Private
Baths • Gardens • Sundecks • Air Conditioned
Color Cable TV • VCRs • Private Parking • Bicycles
Bar-b-que • Exercise Equipment • Internet Access
Companion Animals Welcome • Smoke Free

www.gabriels.com

(800) 9MY-ANGEL

104 Bradford Street (508) 487•3232
Provincetown, MA FAX (508) 487•1605
02657-1440 gabriels@provincetown.com

Massachusetts • USA

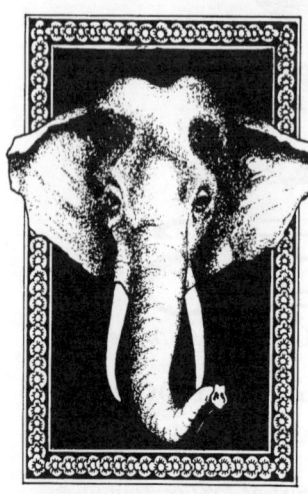

ELEPHANT WALK INN

Spacious, elegant, affordable rooms in the heart of Provincetown.

Private baths, color tv's, vcr's, phones, refrigerators, A/C, sun deck.

Parking. Continental breakfast.

156 Bradford Street
Provincetown, MA 02657
(508) 487-2543

elephant@capecod.net
www.elephantwalkinn.com
Reservations: (800) 889-WALK

Heritage House 7 Center St **508/487-3692** • popular • lesbians/ gay men • shared baths • lesbian-owned/ run • $70-110

The Inn at Cook Street 7 Cook St **508/487-3894, 888/266-5655** • gay-friendly • intimate & quiet • smokefree • gay-owned/ run • $125-160

Ireland House 18 Pearl St (at Arch) **508/487-7132** • lesbians/ gay men • 1820s B&B • garden • gay-owned/ run • $75-130

John Randall House 140 Bradford St (at Standish) **508/487-3533, 800/573-6700** • lesbians/ gay men • open year-round • kids ok • gay-owned/ run • $55-150

Land's End Inn 22 Commercial St **508/487-0706, 800/276-7088** • gay-friendly • smokefree • $87-285

Lotus Guest House 296 Commercial St (at Standish) **508/487-4644, 888/508-4644** • lesbians/ gay men • seasonal • decks • garden • teens ok • gay-owned/ run • $70-130

Mayflower Apartments & Cottages 6 Bangs St (at Commercial St) **508/487-1916** • gay-friendly • kitchens • $140+

Moffett House 296-A Commercial St **508/487-6615, 800/990-8865** • seasonal • mostly gay men • women very welcome • levi/ leather-friendly • gay-owned/ run • $55-110

The Oxford 8 Cottage St **508/487-9103, 888/456-9103** • lesbians/ gay men • recently renovated 1850 Revival • smokefree • parking • gay-owned/ run • $95-295

Pilgrim Colony Inn 670 Shore Rd Rte 6-A, North Truro **508/487-1100** • gay/ straight • private beach • seasonal • gay-owned/ run • $69-99 • cottages $475-1050/ week

▲ **Pilgrim House Inn** 336 Commercial St **508/487-6424** • mostly women • seasonal • also 'Café Crudité' restaurant • 'Vixen' bar/ dance club • wheelchair access • $79-109

The Prince Albert Guest House 166 Commercial St **508/487-0859, 800/992-0859** • mostly gay men • Victorian • smokefree • gay-owned/ run • $85-175

Provincetown Inn 1 Commercial St (at Rotary) **508/487-9500, 800/942-5388** • gay/ straight • swimming • private beach • poolside bar & grill • theater • wheelchair access • $54-194

Ravenwood Guest House 462 Commercial St (at Cook) **508/487-3203** • lesbians/ gay men • 1830 Greek Revival • also apts & cottage • patio • private beach • lesbian-owned/ run • $99-145

Provincetown • Massachusetts

Sandbars Motel
On Private Beach One Mile Outside Provincetown

Immaculate Beachfront Efficiencies

Cable TV • Parking
Air Conditioning
Major Credit Cards Accepted
Double Occupancy
Woman Owned
and Operated
No Pets

**Box 533
Provincetown
MA 02657
(508) 487-1290**

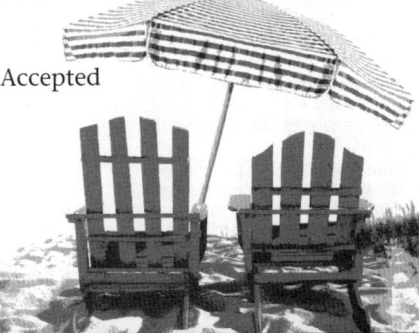

www.sandbarsmotel.com

THE
FAIRBANKS INN
Historic Accommodations

"Exceptional,
Exquisite, ... Unbeatable
Charm and Warmth."
Five Palms & Editors Choice Award — Out & About

"One of the outstanding reasons to
visit New England."
—*Yankee Magazine*

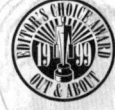

"One of the top places to stay in town."
— *Frommer's '99*

90 Bradford Street, Provincetown
1-800-324-7265   508-487-0386
www.fairbanksinn.com

Massachusetts • USA

Red Inn 15 Commercial St (at Point) **508/487-0050** • lesbians/ gay men • elegant waterfront lodging & dining • gay-owned/ run • $75-225

Revere Guesthouse 14 Court St (btwn Commercial & Bradford) **508/487-2292, 800/487-2292** • lesbians/ gay men • restored 1820s captain's home • also apt • smokefree • $70-165

Romeo's Holiday 97 Bradford St (btwn Gosnold & Masonic) **508/487-6636, 877/MY-ROMEO** • lesbians/ gay men • hot tub • nudity • gay-owned/ run • $78-158

Roomers 8 Carver St (at Commercial St) **508/487-3532** • seasonal • mostly gay men • Greek Revival guesthouse • gay-owned/ run • $100-185

Rose Acre 5 Center St (at Commercial) **508/487-2347** • women only • also apts & cottage • decks • gardens • parking • always open • women-owned/ run • $75-160

Rose & Crown Guest House 158 Commercial St **508/487-3332** • gay/ straight • Victorian antiques • lavish gardens • some shared baths • lesbian-owned • $40-140 • also cottage • $125-225

▲ **Sandbars Motel** 570 Shore Rd, Beach Pt, North Truro **508/487-1290** • mostly women • oceanfront rooms • kitchens • seasonal • private beach • woman-owned/ run • $134-179

Sandpiper Beach House 165 Commercial St **508/487-1928, 800/354-8628** • popular • gay/ straight • Victorian • swimming • sundeck • private beach • smokefree • gay-owned/ run • $115-275

Shamrock Motel, Cottages & Apartments 49 Bradford St (at Central) **508/487-1133, 888/554-7474** • gay/ straight • hot tub • swimming • wheelchair access • gay-owned/ run • $139+

Shiremax Inn 5 Tremont St (btwn Franklin & School) **508/487-1233, 888/744-7362** • lesbians/ gay men • 1900s guesthouse • seasonal • pets ok • gay-owned/ run • $60-105 & $850 (apt)

▲ **Snug Cottage** 178 Bradford St **508/487-1616, 800/432-2334** • gay/ straight • boutique B&B • gay-owned/ run • $85-165

▲ **Somerset House** 378 Commercial St (at Pearl) **508/487-0383, 800/575-1850** • popular • lesbians/ gay men • Victorian mansion • gay-owned/ run • $75-205

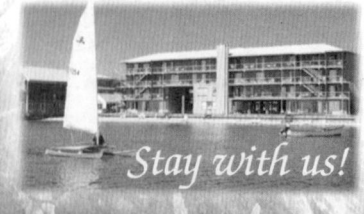

Surfside Beach Club & Surfside Inn

Newly Renovated, Luxurious, Oceanfront Guestrooms

Walking distance to P-Town Shops, Restaurants & Marina. Private Beach & Free Guest Parking.

Stay with us!

Provincetown, MA
543 Commercial St.

(800)421-1726
www.surfsideinn.cc

Provincetown • Massachusetts

A Provincetown classic, beautifully restored.

SNUG COTTAGE
FINE ACCOMMODATIONS

formerly

Bradford Gardens Inn

An historic early 19th century bed and breakfast with eight luxurious rooms, featuring wood-burning fireplaces and private baths.
Early morning coffee, sumptuous continental breakfast buffet, and complimentary afternoon refreshments.

178 Bradford Street Provincetown 800 432 2334
www.snugcottage.com   email: snugcottage@usa.net

Massachusetts • USA

somerset house (accommodations)

GET SERVICED

Provincetown's year-round service oriented guest house

378 Commercial Street
Provincetown, MA 02657
800.575.1850/reservations
www.somersethouseinn.com
getserviced@somersethouseinn.com

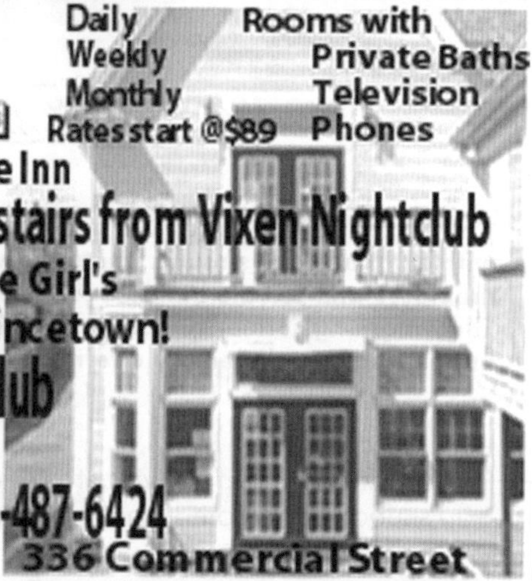

PILGRIM HOUSE INN
VIXEN NIGHTCLUB

Daily
Weekly
Monthly
Rates start @ $89

Rooms with
Private Baths
Television
Phones

Pilgrim House Inn
Located upstairs from Vixen Nightclub
Where the Girl's Play in Provincetown!
Vixen Nightclub
Features
Top DJ's
Dances
Parties
Entertainment

508-487-6424
336 Commercial Street
Provincetown, Ma 02657
www.provincetown.com/vixen

Provincetown • Massachusetts

The Stationmaster's House 27 Center St 508/487-1329 • women only • 1800s guesthouse w/ railroad motif • shared bath • smokefree • lesbian-owned/ run • $75/ night w/ 3-night minimum (10% off if you arrive on motorcycle)

Sunset Inn 142 Bradford St (at Center) 508/487-9810, 800/965-1801 • lesbians/ gay men • some shared baths • seasonal • clothing-optional sundeck • gay-owned/ run • $59-135

▲ **Surfside Inn** 543 Commercial (at Kendall Ln) 508/487-1726, 800/421-1726 • gay/ straight • waterfront motel • lots of amenities • private beach • swimming • kids/ pets ok • gay-owned/ run • $129-189

Three Peaks Guest House 210 Bradford St (at Howland) 508/487-1717, 800/286-1715 • lesbians/ gay men • transgender-friendly • 1870s Victorian • sundeck • smokefree • gay-owned/ run • $110-145

Truro Vineyards Rte 6–A, North Truro 508/487-6200 • gay-friendly • seasonal • inn w/ wine tasting & store • patio • women-owned/ run • $79-129

▲ **The Tucker Inn** 12 Center St 508/487-0381, 800/477-1867 • lesbians/ gay men • 1870s guesthouse • also cottage (rented weekly) • smokefree • lesbian-owned/ run • $99-160

Victoria House 5 Standish St 508/487-4455 • lesbians/ gay men • gay-owned/ run • $35-140

Watermark Inn 603 Commercial St 508/487-0165 • gay-friendly • suites w/ kitchens • beachside • kids ok • smokefree • $80-106/ night off-season, $990-2060/ week in summer

Watership Inn 7 Winthrop St 508/487-0094, 800/330-9413 • popular • mostly gay men • sundeck • gay-owned/ run • $40-215

Westwinds Condominium 28 Commercial St (at Point) 508/487-1841 • lesbians/ gay men • apts & cottages • seasonal • swimming • private beach • gay-owned/ run • $160-275

▲ **White Wind Inn** 174 Commercial St (at Winthrop) 508/487-1526 • popular • lesbians/ gay men • 1800s Victorian • gay-owned/ run • $75-225

Windamar House 568 Commercial St (at Conway) 508/487-0599 • mostly women • 1840s sea captain's home • also apts • lesbian-owned/ run • $60-135

The Tucker Inn

Charming, historic B&B on a quiet side street in the heart of town.

A Romantic Country Inn by the Sea
"this place is a real find."
— Fodors Gay Guide to the USA

800.477.1867
508.487.0381
12 Center Street
Provincetown

Email: info@theTuckerInn.com
Website: www.TheTuckerInn.com

Massachusetts • USA

Windsor Court 15 Cottage St **508/487-2620** • lesbians/ gay men • suites w/ kitchens • hot tub • swimming • gay-owned/ run • $65-150/ night, $1,100-1,700/ week

▲ **Women Innkeepers of Provincetown** PO Box 573, 02657

Bars

The Antro 258 Commercial St **508/487-8800** • 8pm-1am (clsd Nov-April) • mostly gay men • dancing/DJ • cabaret • live shows • call for events • also restaurant • wheelchair access

The Boatslip Beach Club 161 Commercial St (at Central) **508/487-1669, 800/451-7547** • seasonal • popular • lesbians/ gay men • resort • T-dance 3:30pm daily during season • young crowd • special events • swimming • also restaurant • cont'l/ seafood • some veggie • $10-25

Chaser's 293 Commercial St (at Standish) **508/487-7200** • 4pm-1am • mostly women • neighborhood bar • dancing/DJ • live shows • karaoke

Governor Bradford 312 Commercial St (at Standish) **508/487-2781** • 11am-1am • gay-friendly • 'drag karaoke' • also restaurant

The Jungle Cabaret 135 Bradford St (above 'Tropical Joe's' restaurant) **508/487-9941** • open May-Sept • lesbians/ gay men • cabaret shows at 7pm, 8:30pm & 10pm • dinner theater pkgs • gay-owned/ run

The Pied 193-A Commercial St **508/487-1527** • noon-1am • popular • mostly gay men • dancing/DJ • 'After Tea T-Dance' 6:30pm-9:30pm • food served • live shows • women-owned/ run

Rooster Bar 247 Commercial St (in the 'Crown & Anchor') **508/487-1430** • 6pm-1am • lesbians/ gay men • neighborhood bar • dancing/DJ • live shows • videos • also 'Lobby Bar' from 11am

Steve's Alibi 291 Commercial St **508/487-2890** • 11am-1am • popular • gay/ straight • neighborhood bar • drag shows Wed-Mon • local favorite

▲ **Vixen** 336 Commercial St (at Pilgrim House Inn) **508/487-6424** • 4pm-1am, from 11am Fri-Sat, from noon Sun • mostly women • dancing/DJ • live entertainment

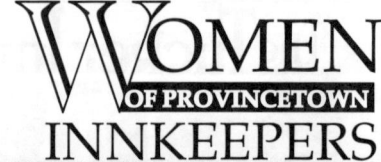

WOMEN INNKEEPERS OF PROVINCETOWN
B&B's ♦ Apartments ♦ Cottages

- **Gabriel's** 800-969-2643
- **Halle's** 508-487-6310
- **Heritage House** 508-487-3692
- **Rose Acre** 508-487-2347
- **Windamar House** 508-487-0599
- **Check'er Inn Resort** 508-487-9029
- **Gracie House** 508-487-4808
- **Kensington Gardens** 888-220-2700
- **The Fairbanks Inn** 800-324-7265

DON'T MISS WOMEN'S WEEK! OCTOBER 14-20, 2002

♦ **womeninnkeepers.com**

P.O. Box 573 ♦ Provincetown ♦ MA 02657

Provincetown • Massachusetts

NIGHTCLUBS

Club Antro 258 Commercial St (at 'The Antro') **508/487-8800** • after 11pm • popular • mostly gay men • dancing/DJ • theme nights • circuit crowd on Sat • wheelchair access

Club Purgatory 9-11 Carver St (at Bradford St) **508/487-8442** • 9pm-1am • mostly gay men • dancing/DJ • levi/leather • theme nights • popular Sun for 'Bound'

Crown & Anchor Ballroom in the 'Crown & Anchor' accommodations **508/487-1430** • 10:30pm-1am (seasonal) • popular • lesbians/gay men • check locally for women's night • dancing/DJ • young crowd

CAFES

No Ordinary Joe 148-A Commercial St **508/487-6656** • 7:30am-11pm • great coffee w/ a view

Post Office Cafe Cabaret 303 Commercial St (upstairs) **508/487-3892** • 8am-midnight (brkfst till 3pm), call for off-season hours • lesbians/ gay men • some veggie

RESTAURANTS

Bayside Betsy's 177 Commercial St **508/487-0120** • brkfst, lunch & dinner on waterfront • also 'Mixers Cocktails' 11:30am-1am • wheelchair access

Bubala's by the Bay 183-185 Commercial **508/487-0773** • 8am-11pm, bar till 1am • popular • seasonal • patio

Café Blasé 328 Commercial St **508/487-9465** • brkfst, lunch & dinner • patio • full bar

Café Crudité 336 Commercial St #6 (upstairs) **508/487-6237** • seasonal • lunch & dinner • vegetarian, vegan & macrobiotic • $7-12

Chester 404 Commercial St **508/487-8200** • dinner from 6pm • popular

Ciro & Sal's 4 Kiley Ct (btwn Bangs St & Lovett's Ct) **508/487-6444** • dinner from 5:30pm • Italian • also bar

Clem & Ursie's 89 Shank Painter Rd **508/487-2333** • 11am-8pm • outdoor dining • cuisine theme nights • affordable • also fish market, deli & grocery

Front Street Restaurant 230 Commercial St **508/487-9715** • 6pm-10:30pm, bar till 1am • lesbians/ gay men • bistro • seasonal

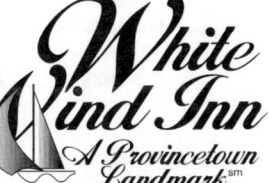

"Highly Recommended"—
Out & About Travel

White Wind Inn
A Provincetown Landmark℠

Well appointed
accommodations,
a "great room" with
fireplace and grand piano,
ideal location, and the best
porch in town…
The place to see and be seen!

174 Commercial Street
1-888-449-WIND • 508-487-1526
email: info@whitewindinn.com
http://www.whitewindinn.com

Massachusetts • USA

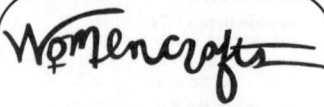

**376 Commercial St.
Provincetown, MA 02657
508 487-2501**

Here's a little bit about us.
Womencrafts is lesbian owned
and operated, and we are well into
our 3rd decade of celebrating women!

We represent over
50 women artists and artisans
from across the United States,
and offer a beautiful selection of
fine jewelry,
hand-thrown pottery,
porcelain,
sculpture,
photographs,
and
artwork.

In addition,
we carry over 700 lesbian and feminist
book titles, both fiction and non-fiction,
and a varied selection
of women's music and videos.

When you are visiting
Provincetown,
please stop in.

**Or look for us at
www.womencrafts.com**

Gallerani's 133 Commercial St **508/487-4433** • dinner • popular • lesbians/ gay men • Italian • pizza • some veggie • beer/ wine • $20-30

Grand Central 5 Masonic St **508/487-7599** • seasonal • popular • dinner • int'l/ seafood • full bar • $15-20

Lobster Pot 321 Commercial St (harborside) **508/487-0842** • noon-10pm • seafood • some veggie • wheelchair access • $15-20

Martin House 157 Commercial St **508/487-1327** • 6pm-close, clsd Wed • outdoor dining • $11-19

The Mews Restaurant & Cafe 429 Commercial St (btwn Lovett's & Kiley) **508/487-1500** • dinner • lunch wknds • popular • cont'l • some veggie • 'Cafe Mews' upstairs • wheelchair access • $15-30

Napi's Restaurant 7 Freeman St **508/487-1145, 800/571-6274** • dinner • lunch Oct-April • int'l/ seafood • plenty veggie • wheelchair access • $15-25

Pucci's Harborside 539 Commercial St **508/487-1964** • seasonal • popular • lunch & dinner • some veggie • full bar • great Bloody Marys • on the water • wheelchair access • $10-20

Sal's Place 99 Commercial St **508/487-1279** • popular • seasonal • seafood/ Italian • publisher's choice: cheese & butter pasta • deck • on the water

Spiritus Pizza 190 Commercial St **508/487-2808** • noon-2am • popular • great espresso shakes & late-night hangout for a slice

Tropical Joe's 135 Bradford St (at Standish) **508/487-9941** • seasonal • 10am-4pm & 6pm-close • Island cuisine • beach lunches to go • outdoor dining • also bar • gay-owned/ run

Entertainment & Recreation

Art's Dune Tours 9 Washington Ave 02657 **508/487-1950, 800/894-1951** • day trips, sunset tours, and charters through historic sand dunes and National Seashore Park • kids ok • $12-15

Off the Coast Kayak 3 Freeman St **508/487-2692, 877/785-2925** • rentals & guided tours for P-town, Truro & Wellfleet • gay-owned/ run

Portuguese Princess Whale Watch 70 Shank Painter Rd (at MacMillan Wharf) **508/487-2651, 800/442-3188** • day & evening cruises • women's event cruises • wheelchair access • women-owned/ run

Ptown Bikes 42 Bradford **508/487-8735** • 9am-7pm • rentals • gay-owned/ run

Waltham • Massachusetts

Spaghetti Strip • nude beach • 1.5 miles south of Race Point Beach

BOOKSTORES

Now, Voyager 357 Commercial St **508/487-0848** • 10am-11pm • 11am-5pm off-season • lgbt

Provincetown Bookshop 246 Commercial St **508/487-0964** • 10am-11pm (till 5pm off-season)

RETAIL SHOPS

Don't Panic 192 Commercial St **508/487-1280** • seasonal • 10am-10pm • lgbt gifts • T-shirts

GayMartUSA 176 Commercial St **508/487-7517** • 10am-close • clothes & gifts

Pride's 182 Commercial St **508/487-1127** • 10am-11pm (in summer), call for off-season hours • lgbt gifts • T-shirts • books

Recovering Hearts 2–4 Standish St **508/487-4875** • 10am-11pm (in summer), call for off-season hours • recovery • lgbt & new age books • wheelchair access

▲ **Womencrafts** 376 Commercial St **508/487-2501** • 10am-11pm, call for off-season hours

PUBLICATIONS

In Newsweekly 617/426-8246 • New England's lgbt newspaper

Provincetown Banner 508/487-7400 • newspaper

Provincetown Magazine 508/487-1000 • seasonal • Provincetown's oldest weekly magazine

GYMS & HEALTH CLUBS

Mussel Beach 35 Bradford St (btwn Montello & Conant) **508/487-0001** • 6am-9pm • lesbians/ gay men

Provincetown Gym 82 Shank Painter Rd (at Winthrop) **508/487-2776** • 6am-8pm • lesbians/ gay men • daily, weekly & monthly rates

EROTICA

Wild Hearts 244 Commercial St **508/487-8933** • 11am-11pm (in summer), noon-5pm, till 11pm wknds (off-season) • toys for women

Quincy

see also Boston

RETAIL SHOPS

Body Xtremes 414 Hancock St, North Quincy **617/471-5836** • body piercing & jewelry • also 'The Xtreme' tattoo parlor across the street, 617/ 984-0956

Randolph

BARS

Randolph Country Club 44 Mazeo Dr/ Rte 139 **781/961-2414** • 2pm-2am, from 10am summer • popular • lesbians/ gay men • dancing/DJ • food served • live shows • karaoke • videos • volleyball court • swimming • wheelchair access

Somerville

see Boston

Springfield

INFO LINES & SERVICES

Gay/ Lesbian Info Service 413/731-5403

BARS

Auntie Em's Lounge 278 Worthington Ave (at Stearns Sq) **413/858-8800** • 4pm-2am • lesbians/ gay men • live music Fri • drag shows Sat

David's 395–405 Dwight St **413/734-0566** • 8pm-2am Th-Sun • mostly gay men • dancing/DJ • live shows • wheelchair access

Just Friends/ Cellblock 23 Hampden St (at Main) **413/781-5878** • 11am-2am • lesbians/ gay men • dancing/DJ Wed-Sun • live shows • videos • wheelchair access • also 'Cellblock' from 10pm • mostly gay men • leather

Pub 382 Dwight (at Taylor) **413/734-8123** • noon-2am • lesbians/ gay men • neighborhood bar • dancing/DJ wknds • live shows • also 'Quarry' from 9pm Th-Sat • mostly gay men • leather • wheelchair access

Waltham

BOOKSTORES

Synchronicity Transgender Bookstore 14 Felton St (at Moody) **781/899-2212** • 11am-4pm, clsd wknds • over 100 TG titles

Ware

ACCOMMODATIONS

The Wildwood Inn 121 Church St **413/967-7798, 800/860-8098** • gay/ straight • 1880s Victorian B&B • full brkfst • some shared baths • smokefree • kids ok • wheelchair access • $50-90

Watertown

see Boston

Williamstown

ACCOMMODATIONS

River Bend Farm B&B 643 Simonds Rd **413/458-3121** • gay-friendly • restored 1770s home • shared baths • seasonal • kids ok • $90

RESTAURANTS

Mezze Bistro & Bar 84 Water St (at Latham St) **413/458-0123** • 5:30pm-1am • gay-friendly • Mediterranean • plenty veggie • full bar • summer theater crowd

Worcester

INFO LINES & SERVICES

AA Gay/ Lesbian 1 Freeland St **508/752-9000** • 7pm Sat

WOBBLES (West of Boston Lesbians) **508/478-0242** • social group • covers eastern MA

BARS

MB Lounge 40 Grafton St (at Franklin) **508/799-4521** • 3pm-2am • mostly gay men • neighborhood bar • wheelchair access

NIGHTCLUBS

A-MEN 90 Commercial St **508/754-7742** • 9pm-2am, clsd Mon • popular • mostly gay men • dancing/DJ • karaoke Tue • live shows • 3 floors • wheelchair access

ENTERTAINMENT & RECREATION

Face the Music WCUW 91.3 FM **508/753-2284 (REQUEST LINE)** • 8pm Th • lesbian/ feminist music

SPIRITUAL GROUPS

Morning Star MCC 624 South Bridge Rd (at the Ramada Inn), Auburn **508/949-7939** • 10am Sun • wheelchair access

GYMS & HEALTH CLUBS

Midtown Athletic Club 22 Front St, 2nd flr (in Midtown Mall) **508/798-9703** • gay-friendly

MICHIGAN

Statewide

PUBLICATIONS

Between the Lines **248/615-7003, 888/615-7003** • lgbt weekly

Cruise Magazine **248/545-9040** • gay entertainment listings

Ann Arbor

INFO LINES & SERVICES

Lesbian/ Gay AA **734/482-5700**

The Office of LGBT Affairs 3200 Michigan Union **734/763-4186** • 9am-7pm Tue & Th • student services • events open to all

BARS

\'aut\ Bar 315 Braun Ct (at Catherine) **734/994-3677** • 4pm-2am, from 10am Sun (brunch) • popular • lesbians/ gay men • 2 flrs • also restaurant • American/ Mexican • some veggie • patio • wheelchair access • $5-8

Crowbar 309 S Main St **734/668-0111** • 8pm-2am, clsd Mon-Tue • lesbians/ gay men • DJ Fri-Sat

NIGHTCLUBS

Club Fabulous **734/763-4186** • lesbians/ gay men • occasional dances during school • young crowd

The Nectarine 516 E Liberty **734/994-5436** • 9pm-2am Tue & Fri only • lesbians/ gay men • dancing/DJ • videos • young crowd • 18+

RESTAURANTS

Cafe 303 303 Detroit St (at Catherine) **734/665-0700** • 11am-10pm, till midnight Fri-Sat • plenty veggie • full bar • patio • wheelchair access • $10-15

Dominick's 812 Monroe St (at Tappan Ave) **734/662-5414** • 10am-10pm • Italian • full bar • wheelchair access

The Earle 121 W Washington (at Ashley) **734/994-0211** • 6pm-10pm, till midnight Fri-Sat, clsd Sun (summer) • cont'l • some veggie • beer/ wine • wheelchair access • $15-25

ENTERTAINMENT & RECREATION

The Ark 316 S Main St (btwn William & Liberty) **734/761-1451** • gay-friendly • concert house • women's music shows

BOOKSTORES

Common Language 215 S 4th Ave (at Liberty) **734/663-0036** • open daily • lgbt • wheelchair access

Detroit • Michigan

Crazy Wisdom Books 114 S Main (btwn Huron & Washington) **734/665-2757** • 10am-10pm, till 11pm Wed-Sat, 11am-7pm Sun • holistic & metaphysical

Nicola's Books 2607 Plymouth Rd (at Nixon, in Traver Village Mall) **734/662-6150** • 9am-10pm • lgbt section • also at 2513 Jackson Rd in Westgate Mall, 734/662-4110

Atwood

Accommodations

Wunderschönes 12410 Antrim Dr, Ellsworth **231/599-2847** • lesbians/ gay men • red cedar log home • full brkfst • smokefree • gay-owned/ run • $75-90

Battle Creek

Nightclubs

Partners 910 North Ave (at Morgan) **616/964-7276** • 6pm-2am • lesbians/ gay men • dancing/DJ • karaoke • wheelchair access

Spiritual Groups

Sign of the Covenant MCC 35 S Cass St (at Jackson) **616/965-8004** • 10:30am Sun

Erotica

Eastown Capri 686 W Michigan (at Grand) **616/964-3070**

Bellaire

Accommodations

Bellaire B&B 212 Park St (at Antrim) **231/533-6077, 800/545-0780** • gay/ straight • stately 1879 home • full brkfst • gay-owned/ run • $70-100

Big Bay

Accommodations

Big Bay Depot Motel **906/345-9350** • gay-friendly • overlooking Lake Independence • kids/ pets ok • smokefree rooms available • $55

Coldwater

Erotica

The Lion's Den Adult Bookstore 570 Jonesville Rd (exit 16, off I-69) **517/278-9577** • 24hrs

Detroit

Info Lines & Services

Affirmations Lesbian/ Gay Community Center 195 W 9–Mile Rd (at Woodward), Ferndale **248/398-7105** • 9am-9pm, till 5pm Sat, 1pm-9pm Sun

Helpline **248/398-4297, 800/398-4297** • 4pm-9pm, till midnight Fri-Sat

Accommodations

The Antheneum Suite Hotel 1000 Brush St (at Lafayette) **313/962-2323, 800/772-2323** • gay-friendly • luxury hotel • restaurant & lounge • gym • wheelchair access

Millner Hotel 1538 Centre St **313/963-3950, 800/521-0592** • gay-friendly • downtown

Shorecrest Motor Inn 1316 E Jefferson Ave **313/568-3000** • gay-friendly • downtown • restaurant • wheelchair access

Bars

Club Gold Coast 2971 E 7–Mile Rd (at Conant) **313/366-6135** • 7pm-2am • popular • mostly gay men • dancing/DJ • live shows • wheelchair access

Gigi's 16920 W Warren (at Clayburn, enter rear) **313/584-6525** • noon-2am, from 2pm wknds • mostly gay men • dancing/DJ • transgender-friendly • male dancers Mon & Fri • drag shows Wed & Sat • gay-owned/ run

The Other Side 16801 Plymouth (at Southfield) **313/836-2324** • noon-2am • lesbians/ gay men • neighborhood bar • food served • karaoke Tue • wheelchair access

Stingers Lounge 19404 Sherwood (at 7–Mile) **313/892-1765** • 6pm-5am, from 8pm wknds • lesbians/ gay men • neighborhood bar • karaoke Wed-Th • grill menu • gay-owned/ run

Sugarbakers 3800 E 8–Mile Rd (at Ryan Ave) **313/892-5203** • 6pm-2am • mostly women • sports bar & grill

The Temple 344 W 9-Mile Rd (2 blks W of Woodward), Ferndale **248/414-7400** • 5pm-2am, clsd Mon • gay/ straight • dancing/DJ • 2 flrs • more gay Wed & Fri • also restaurant • patio • wheelchair access

Nightclubs

Backstreet 415 E Congress (next to St Andrews Hall) **248/358-9844** • 9pm-4am Sat • popular • mostly gay men • dancing/DJ • 5 levels • young crowd • wheelchair access • cover charge

Bleu 1540 Woodward Ave (1 1/2 blks S of Comerica Park) **313/222-1900** • 9pm Wed only • mostly gay men • dancing/ DJ • live shows

Michigan • USA

Club 450 450 S Merriman (btwn Michigan & Cherry Hill), Westland **734/727-0000** • 8pm-2am Th-Sun • lesbians/ gay men • dancing/ DJ • 18+

Cobalt 22061 Woodward Ave, Ferndale **248/591-0106** • 9pm-2am, clsd Mon-Tue • mostly gay men • women's night Sun • popular • live shows • dancing/DJ • wheelchair access • gay-owned/ run

Diamond Jim's Saloon 19650 Warren (E of Evergreen) **313/336-8680** • 6pm-2am • lesbians/ gay men • neighborhood bar • dancing/ DJ • country/ western • food served • dance lessons

One-X 2575 Michigan Ave (at 17th) **313/964-0580** • 10pm-2am, clsd Tue • mostly gay men • dancing/DJ • multiracial • 18+ • young crowd • wheelchair access

The Rainbow Room 6640 E 8-Mile Rd (at Mound) **313/891-1020** • 7pm-2am Wed-Sat, from 5pm Sun • lesbians/ gay men • dancing/DJ • live shows

Stiletto's 1641 Middlebelt Rd (at Michigan Ave), Inkster **734/729-8980** • 8pm-2am, clsd Mon • mostly women • dancing/DJ • strippers

Temple 2906 Cass Ave (btwn Charlotte & Temple) **313/832-2822** • noon-2am • mostly gay men • dancing/DJ • mostly African-American • popular wknds • wheelchair access

Times Square 1431 Times Square (at Grand River Ave) **313/961-0232** • 10pm-close Fri-Sat only • gay/ straight • dancing/ DJ • cover charge

Zippers 6221 E Davison **313/892-8120** • 9pm-2am Th-Sat • popular • lesbians/ gay men • dancing/DJ • more women Sat • mostly African-American • live shows • wheelchair access

Cafes

Avalon Bakery 422 W Willis (at Cass) **313/832-0008** • 6am-6pm, clsd Sun-Mon • lesbian-owned/ run

Restaurants

Como's 22812 Woodward (at 9-Mile), Ferndale **248/548-5005** • 11am-2am, till 3:30am Fri-Sat, from 2pm wknds • Italian • full bar • wheelchair access

Detroit

WHERE THE GIRLS ARE: At the bars on 8-Mile Road between I-75 and Van Dyke Ave., with the boys in Highland Park or Dearborn, or shopping in Royal Oak.

LGBT PRIDE: May/June. 248/547-5878 (Just for Us).

ANNUAL EVENTS: January- Michigan Lesbian & Gay Film Festival 248/547-5878.
August - Michigan Womyn's Music Festival 231/757-4766 or 616/898-3707. One of the biggest annual gatherings of lesbians on the continent, in Walhalla.

CITY INFO: 313/202-1800 or 800/338-7648, web: www.visitdetroit.com.

ATTRACTIONS: Belle Isle Park.
Detroit Institute of Arts 313/833-7900.
Greektown.
Montreux Detroit Jazz Festival.
Motown Historical Museum 313/875-2264.
Museum of African-American History 313/494-5800.
Renaissance Center 313/568-8000.

BEST VIEW: From the top of the 73-story Westin Hotel at the Renaissance Center.

WEATHER: Be prepared for hot, humid summers and cold, dry winters.

TRANSIT: Checker Cab 313/963-7000.
Shuttle 734/283-4800.
DOT bus service) 313/933-1300.
Detroit People Mover 313/962-7245.

Detroit • Michigan

La Dolce Vita 17546 Woodward Ave (at McNichols) **313/865-0331** • dinner, Sun brunch, clsd Mon-Tue • lesbians/ gay men • Italian • plenty veggie • full bar • patio • wheelchair access • $7-16

Pronto 608 S Washington (at 6th St), Royal Oak **248/544-7900** • 11am-10pm, till midnight Fri-Sat, from 9am wknds • plenty veggie • videos

Rhinoceros 265 Riopelle (off Jefferson) **313/259-2208** • 5pm-2am • jazz club • full bar • $15-25

Sweet Lorraines 29101 Greenfield Rd (at 12-Mile), Southfield **248/559-5985** • 11am-10pm, till midnight Fri-Sat • modern American • wheelchair access

Twingo's 4710 Cass Ave **313/832-3832** • 11am-11pm, till 2am Th-Sat, till 8pm Sun • gay/ straight • nouvelle French • full bar • live jazz Fri-Sat • gay-owned/ run

Vivio's 2460 Market St (btwn Gratiot & Russell) **313/393-1711** • lunch & dinner, clsd Sun • Italian • full bar • $6-11

ENTERTAINMENT & RECREATION

Detroit Women's Coffeehouse 4605 Cass Ave (at 1st Unitarian Church) **313/833-9107** • 2nd Sat, except in August • food served • live music • cover charge

---

[Reply] [Forward] [Delete]

```
Date: Thu, Dec 27, 2001 10:14:22
From: Girl-on-the-Go
To: Editor@Damron.com
Subject: Detroit
```

> Known for its cars and stars, 'Motown' is the home of General Motors and was the starting point for many living legends, including Aretha Franklin, Diana Ross & the Supremes, the Temptations, Stevie Wonder, Anita Baker, and Madonna.

> Detroit is also rich in African-American culture. Be sure to check out the Museum of African-American History, multicultural gallery Your Heritage House, the Motown Museum...and the lesbian/gay club **Zippers**. And just across the river in Canada—via the underground Detroit/Windsor Tunnel—is the North American Black Historical Museum in Windsor, Ontario.

> You might want to start your stay with a visit to the **Affirmations Lesbian/Gay Community Center,** the LGBT bookstore **Just 4 Us,** or **A Woman's Prerogative,** the women's bookstore. Later, check out **Sugarbakers,** a women's sports bar, or dance the night away at **Stiletto's**.

> Downtown, discover the impressive Renaissance Center. This office and retail complex that dominates the city skyline houses shopping, restaurants, a 73-story hotel, even an indoor lake! Before moving on to explore the districts of Greektown, Bricktown, or Rivertown, take a spin around the Civic Center district on the Detroit People Mover, an elevated transit system that carries travelers in automated, weatherproof cars.

Michigan • USA

BOOKSTORES

A Woman's Prerogative Bookstore 175 W 9–Mile Rd (at Woodward), Ferndale 248/545-5703 • noon-7pm, till 9pm Th, till 5pm Sat & till 4pm Sun • lesbian • wheelchair access

Chosen Books 120 W 4th St (btwn Main St & Woodward), Royal Oak 248/543-5758 • noon-10pm • lgbt • wheelchair access

Just 4 Us 211 W 9–Mile Rd (at Woodward), Ferndale 248/547-5878 • noon-8pm, clsd Sun • also espresso bar

RETAIL SHOPS

The Dressing Room 42310 Hayes, Clinton Township 810/286-0412 • 1pm-8pm, noon-5pm Sat, clsd Sun • cross-dressing boutique • larger sizes • accessories • transformations

PUBLICATIONS

Between the Lines 248/615-7003, 888/615-7003 • statewide lgbt weekly

Cruise Magazine 248/545-9040 • statewide gay entertainment lisitings

Metra 248/543-3500 • covers IN, IL, MI, OH, PA, WI & Ontario, Canada

Out Post 313/702-0272 • bi-weekly newspaper for metro Detroit

SPIRITUAL GROUPS

Dignity Detroit Marygrove College Campus, on W McNichols, E of Wyoming (in Liberal Arts Bldg) 313/278-4786 • 6pm Sun

Divine Peace MCC 23839 John R (at 9-Mile, at 'Metro Club'), Hazel Park 248/544-8335 • 10am Sun

MCC of Detroit 2441 Pinecrest (at Presbyterian Church), Ferndale 248/399-7741 • 10am & 7pm Sun

EROTICA

Noir Leather 124 W 4th (at Center), Royal Oak 248/541-3979 • wheelchair access

Escanaba

NIGHTCLUBS

Club Xpress 904 Ludington St (at 10th) 906/789-0140 • 8pm-2am, from 6pm Fri-Sat, clsd Sun-Tue • lesbians/ gay men • dancing/DJ • wheelchair access

Flint

BARS

Club MI 2402 N Franklin St (at Davison) 810/234-9481 • 1pm-2am • popular • lesbians/gay men • dancing/ DJ • live shows • multiracial clientele

Pachyderm Pub G–1408 E Hemphill Rd (btwn I–475 & Saginaw St), Burton 810/744-4960 • 3pm-2am • lesbians/gay men • neighborhood bar & restaurant • videos • professional crowd • multiracial clientele • transgender-friendly • gay-owned/ run

State Bar 2510 S Dort Hwy 810/767-7050 • 3pm-2am, from 1pm wknds • popular • lesbians/gay men • dancing/DJ • karaoke • wheelchair access

NIGHTCLUBS

Club Quorum 3212 N Saginaw St (at McClellan) 810/789-7940 • 10:30pm-3am Fri only • lesbians/gay men • dancing/DJ • drag shows • multiracial clientele

Club Triangle 2101 S Dort (at Lippincott) 810/767-7550 • 7pm-2am, clsd Mon • popular • lesbians/gay men • more women Wed • dancing/DJ • 18+

North Star 617 S Dort Hwy (at Court) 810/235-2752 • 5pm-2am Wed-Sun • lesbians/gay men • more women Th-Fri • dancing/DJ • live shows

CAFES

The Good Beans Cafe 328 N Grand Traverse (at 1st Ave) 810/237-4663 • 7:30am-6pm, clsd wknds • espresso & pastries • live entertainment • gay-owned/ run • wheelchair access

SPIRITUAL GROUPS

Redeemer MCC of Flint 1665 N Chevrolet Ave (at Welch) 810/238-6700 • 11am Sun • wheelchair access

Glen Arbor

ACCOMMODATIONS

Duneswood at Sleeping Bear Dunes Nat'l Lakeshore 231/334-3346 • women only • also 'Marge & Joanne's B&B' • $50-85

Grand Rapids

INFO LINES & SERVICES

Lesbian/ Gay Network 907 Cherry SE (at Eastern) 616/458-3511 • 10am-6pm Mon-Fri • lounge • library

BARS

The Apartment 33 Sheldon NE (at Library) 616/451-0815 • noon-2am, from 2pm Sun • mostly gay men • neighborhood bar • sandwiches served • wheelchair access

The Carousel 76 S Division St (at Oakes) 616/454-4499 • 2pm-2am, from 4pm wknds • mostly gay men • dancing/DJ • wheelchair access

Lansing • Michigan

Diversions 10 Fountain St NW (at Division) **616/451-3800** • 8pm-2am, from 8pm wknds • popular • lesbians/ gay men • dancing/DJ • live shows • videos • wheelchair access

CAFES

Discussions 6 Jefferson SE (at Fulton) **616/456-5060** • 10am-midnight, till 4am Fri-Sat, 2pm-midnight Sun • live shows • karaoke • soup & sandwiches • gay-owned/ run • wheelchair access

RESTAURANTS

Brandywine 1345 Lake Drive SE (in East town) **616/774-8641** • lunch & dinner

Cherie Inn 969 Cherry St (at Lake Dr) **616/458-0588** • 7am-3pm, clsd Mon • some veggie • wheelchair access • $4-6

Gaia Cafe 208 Diamond Ave SE (at Lake) **616/454-6233** • 8am-8pm, till 3pm wknds, clsd Mon • vegetarian

BOOKSTORES

Sons & Daughters 962 Cherry SE (at Diamond) **616/459-8877** • noon-midnight • lgbt bookstore & coffeehouse

SPIRITUAL GROUPS

Reconciliation MCC 300 Graceland NE (at Lafayette) **616/364-7633** • 10am Sun

Higgins Lake

ACCOMMODATIONS

Kozy KC 517/821-9620 • lesbians/ gay men • private rental cabin • teens/ pets ok • lesbian-owned/ run • $100/ night, $450/ week

Honor

ACCOMMODATIONS

Labrys Wilderness Resort 231/882-5994 • women only • cabins • lesbian-owned/ run • $45-75

Houghton Lake

ACCOMMODATIONS

Val Halla Motel & Resort 9869 West Houghton Lake Dr **517/422-5137** • gay/ straight • swimming • nr fishing, boating & skiing • campsites & RV hookups • gay-owned/ run • $45-58

Ironwood

ACCOMMODATIONS

Anton-Walsh House 202 Copper St (at US Hwy 51), Hurley, WI **715/561-2065, 715/561-9977** • gay-friendly • historic B&B • full brkfst • nr skiing & Lake Superior • $59-109

Jackson

NIGHTCLUBS

Capitol Club 128 W Michigan Ave (at Mechanic) **517/782-1482** • 9pm-2am Th-Sat • lesbians/ gay men • dancing/DJ • karaoke • also cafe 11am-7pm, till 9pm Th-Sat • gay-owned/ run

Kalamazoo

INFO LINES & SERVICES

Women's Resource Center 616/387-2995 • call for info

BARS

Tradewinds 562 Portage St (at Walnut) **616/383-1814** • 4pm-2am • lesbians/ gay men • neighborhood bar • dancing/DJ • theme nights

NIGHTCLUBS

Brother's Bar 209 Stockbridge (btwn Portage & Burdick) **616/345-1960** • 2pm-2am • lesbians/ gay men • dancing/DJ • live shows • karaoke • private club • patio • wheelchair access

The Zoo 906 Portage St (at Vine) **616/385-9191** • 2pm-2am • mostly gay men • dancing/DJ • 18+

RETAIL SHOPS

Family Wear 305 E Stockbridge **616/381-9928** • noon-7pm, clsd Sun-Mon • gay/ straight • gift shop w/ pride items • also lgbt periodicals & coffee shop

SPIRITUAL GROUPS

Phoenix Community Church 394 S Drake (at Sky Ridge Church) **616/381-3222** • 6pm Sun • wheelchair access

EROTICA

Triangle World 551 Portage Rd (at Walnut) **616/373-4005** • lgbt books • leather • gifts • wheelchair access

Lansing

INFO LINES & SERVICES

AA Gay/ Lesbian East Lansing **517/321-8781** • call for mtg schedule

Michigan • USA

Lansing Lesbian/ Gay Hotline 517/332-3200 • 7pm-10pm, 2pm-5pm Sun, clsd Sat

Accommodations

Leaven Retreat Center & Guesthouse Lyons **517/855-2277** • lesbians/ gay men • some events women only • spiritual retreat center • also guesthouse available for individual use • $30-60

Bars

Club 505 505 E Shiawassee (at Cedar) **517/374-6312** • 6pm-2am, clsd Mon • mostly women • neighborhood bar • dancing/DJ

Esquire 1250 Turner (at Clinton) **517/487-5338** • noon-2am • lesbians/ gay men • neighborhood bar • karaoke

Nightclubs

Paradise 224 S Washington Sq **517/484-2399** • 9pm-2am • popular • mostly gay men • dancing/DJ • live shows • young crowd

Spiral 1247 Center St (at Clinton) **517/371-3221** • 8pm-2am, clsd Mon • mostly gay men • dancing/DJ • theme nights • videos • 18+

Bookstores

Community News Center 418 Frandor Shopping Center **517/351-7562** • 9am-9pm, till 7pm Sun • wheelchair access

Spiritual Groups

Dignity 327 MAC (at St John's Parish), East Lansing **517/351-7341** • 8pm 1st Tue

Marquette

Bookstores

Sweet Violets 413 N 3rd St (btwn Michigan & Arch) **906/228-3307** • 10am-6pm, clsd Sun • feminist

Midland

Accommodations

Jay's B&B 4429 Bay City Rd (at Waldo Rd) **517/496-2498** • gay-friendly • full brkfst • deck • shared baths • smokefree • $60

Munising

Accommodations

Homestead B&B 713 Prospect St **906/387-2542** • gay-friendly • some shared baths • wheelchair access • $65-90

Muskegon

Accommodations

Cybele's Twin Lake **231/828-5666** • gay/ straight • drumming retreats • women-owned/ run

Owendale

Accommodations

Windover Resort 3596 Blakely Rd **517/375-2586** • women only • campsites • swimming • $25/yr membership fee • $15-20 camping fee

Pontiac

Nightclubs

Club Flamingo 352 Oakland Ave (at Montcalm) **248/253-0430** • 4pm-2am, from 2pm Sat • lesbians/ gay men • dancing/DJ • live shows • wheelchair access

Port Huron

Bars

Headwinds 515 Wall St (at Military) **810/987-5732** • 11am-2am, from noon Sat, from 6pm Sun • gay-friendly • DJ Fri-Sat • also full kitchen

Nightclubs

Seekers 3301 24th St (btwn Oak & Little) **810/985-9349** • 7pm-2am, from 4pm Fri-Sat, from 2pm Sun • lesbians/ gay men • dancing/DJ • live shows

Saginaw

Nightclubs

Bambi's 1742 E Genessee (at Holland) **517/752-9179** • 7pm-2am, clsd Mon-Wed • lesbians/ gay men • dancing/DJ • live shows

Saugatuck

Accommodations

Campit Campground 616/543-4335, **877/226-7481** • lesbians/ gay men • campsites • RV hookups • seasonal • pets ok • gay-owned/ run • $12-40

Deerpath Lodge 877/DEER-PATH, **616/857-DEER** • women only • on 45 secluded acres • full brkfst • hot tub • heated pool • kayaks • 2-night minimum stay

Douglas House B&B 41 Spring St, Douglas **616/857-1119, 313/922-4220** • gay/ straight • nr gay beach • gay-owned/ run • $100-140

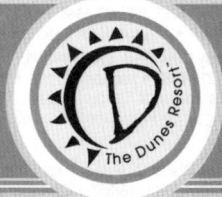

Located on the shores of Lake Michigan is the artist city of Saugatuck... and home to the Midwest's Largest Gay & Lesbian hotel and entertainment

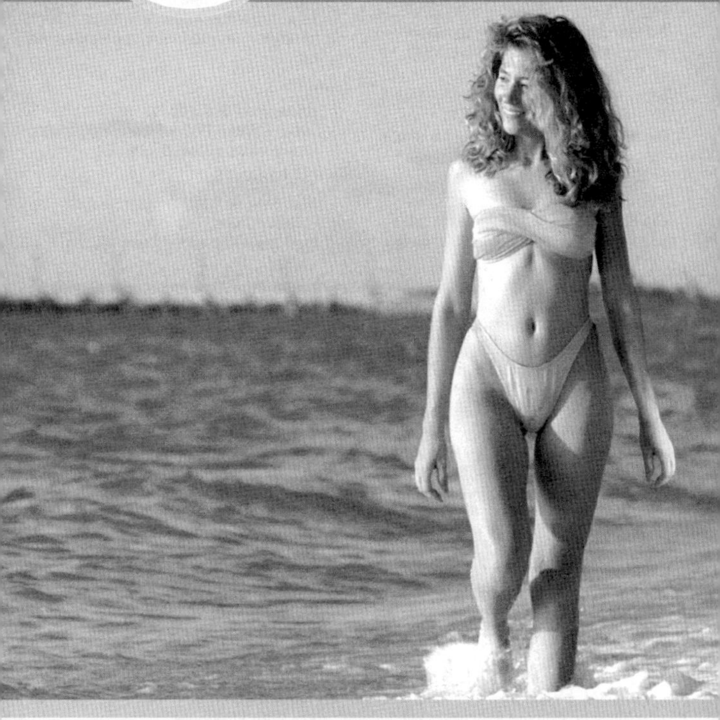

TheDunesResort™

333 Blue Star Hwy. Saugatuck, MI • 616.857.1401

Visit DunesResort.com for a complete list of events and for updates on all the DJ's and fun events all year long!
Open 7 days a week - 12 months a year.

Michigan • USA

Driftwood Cottages 2731 Lakeshore Dr, Fennville **616/857-2586** • mostly women • short drive to Saugatuck • kitchenettes • kids ok • lesbian-owned/ run • $75-200

▲ **The Dunes Resort** 333 Blue Star Hwy, Douglas **616/857-1401** • lesbians/ gay men • motel & cottages • transgender-friendly • swimming • food served • women's wknds in April, June & Oct • dancing/DJ • live shows • kids/ pets ok • wheelchair access • gay-owned/ run • $50-180

Hillby Thatch Cottages 71st St, Glenn **847/864-3553** • gay-friendly • cottages • kitchens • fireplaces • women-owned/ run • $250-350/ wknd

Kirby House 294 W Center (at Blue Star Hwy) **616/857-2904, 800/521-6473** • gay-friendly • Queen Anne Victorian • full brkfst • swimming • smokefree • gay-owned/ run • $100-160

The Lighthouse Motel Douglas **616/857-2271** • gay-straight • swimming • wheelchair access • kids ok • lesbian-owned/ run • $75-125

Moore's Creek Inn 820 Holland St (at Lucy) **616/857-2411, 800/838-5864** • gay/ straight • old-fashioned farmhouse • full brkfst • smokefree • gay-owned/ run • $75-85

The Newnham SunCatcher Inn 131 Griffith (at Mason) **616/857-4249** • gay-friendly • full brkfst • swimming • lesbian-owned/ run • $75-120

The Pines Motel 56 Blue Star Highway (at Center St), Douglas **616/857-5211** • gay/ straight • gay-owned • $55-155

The Spruce Cutter's Cottage 6670 126th Ave (at Blue Star Hwy & M-89), Fennville **616/543-4285, 800/493-5888** • gay/ straight • full brkfst • gay-owned/ run • $80-155

Sturdy Girls B&B 616/543-4335, 877/226-7481 • lesbians/ gay men • full access to Campit Campground amenities (see listing above) • gay-owned/ run • $50-105

BARS

Dunes Disco 333 Blue Star Hwy (at the 'Dunes Resort') **616/857-1401** • 9am-2am • lesbians/ gay men • dancing/DJ • transgender-friendly • 3 bars • cabaret • patio • gay-owned/ run

CAFES

Uncommon Grounds 127 Hoffman (at Water) **616/857-3333** • 7:30am-9:30pm, open later on wknds • coffee & juice bar

RESTAURANTS

Blue Frog To Go in the 'Dunes Resort' **616/857-5711** • 11am-7pm, till 9pm Fri-Sat (open May-Oct only) • lesbians/ gay men • take-out only

Loaf & Mug 236 Culver St (at Butler) **616/857-2974** • 8am-3pm, clsd Tue • some veggie • beer/ wine

Pumpernickel's 202 Butler St (at Mason) **616/857-1196** • seasonal • 8am-3pm (clsd Wed in winter) • sandwiches & fresh breads • some veggie • $5-10

Restaurant Toulouse 248 Culver St (at Griffith) **616/857-1561** • dinner only • country French • some veggie • full bar • wheelchair access • $10-20

Saugatuck

ANNUAL EVENTS: May - Tulip Time Festival, Holland 616/396-4221. June - Waterfront Film Festival 616/857-8351, web: www.waterfrontfilm.com.

CITY INFO: Saugatuck-Douglas Convention & Visitors Bureau 616/857-1701, web: www.saugatuck.com.

ATTRACTIONS: Galleries. Red Barn Playhouse. Saugatuck Dunes State Park.

TRANSIT: Saugatuck Douglas Car Service 616/857-7181. Interurban bus service 616/857-1418.

Ely • Minnesota

RETAIL SHOPS

Hoopdee Scootee 133 Mason (at Butler) **616/857-4141** • 10am-9pm, till 6pm Sun (till 5pm in winter) • clothing • gifts

Sault Ste-Marie

BOOKSTORES

Open Mind Books 223 Ashmun St (at Ridge) **906/635-9008** • 11am-5pm, clsd Sun-Mon • progressive

South Haven

ACCOMMODATIONS

Yelton Manor B&B 140 North Shore Dr (at Dyckman) **616/637-5220** • gay/straight • full brkfst • jacuzzi • smokefree • wheelchair access • $100-260

St Clair

ACCOMMODATIONS

William Hopkins Manor 613 N Riverside Ave **810/329-0188** • gay-friendly • full brkfst • $80-100

St Ignace

ACCOMMODATIONS

Budget Host Inn & Suites 700 N State St **906/643-9666, 800/872-7057** • gay-friendly • swimming • facing harbor of Lake Huron & across from ferries to Mackinac Island • $65-145

Traverse City

ACCOMMODATIONS

Neahtawanta Inn 1308 Neahtawanta Rd **231/223-7315** • gay-friendly • swimming • sauna • wheelchair access • $85-140

NIGHTCLUBS

Side Traxx Nite Club 520 Franklin **231/935-1666** • 6pm-2am • lesbians/gay men • dancing/DJ • wheelchair access

CAFES

Ray's Coffee House 129 E Front St (btwn Cass & Union) **231/929-1006** • 7am-7pm, till 10pm Th-Sat (late hours in summer only) • wheelchair access

BOOKSTORES

The Bookie Joint 120 S Union St (btwn State & Front) **231/946-8862** • 10am-6pm, 11am-5pm Sat, clsd Sun • pride gifts • used books

Union Pier

ACCOMMODATIONS

Blue Fish Guest House & Cottage 16070 Lake Shore Rd **616/469-2907**

Fire Fly Resort 15657 Lakeshore Rd **616/469-0245** • gay/straight • 1 & 2-bdrm units • kitchens • smokefree • $90-135 • also weekly/monthly rates

Ypsilanti

SPIRITUAL GROUPS

Tree of Life MCC 218 N Adams St (at 1st Congregational Church) **734/485-3922** • 6pm Sun & 6pm Wed

EROTICA

The Magazine Rack 515 W Cross **734/482-6944**

MINNESOTA

Duluth

see also Superior, Wisconsin

INFO LINES & SERVICES

Aurora: A Northern Lesbian Center 32 E 1st St #104 (at 1st Ave) **218/722-4903** • discussion groups & socials • library

ACCOMMODATIONS

Stanford Inn B&B 1415 E Superior St **218/724-3044** • gay-friendly • full brkfst • gay-owned/run • $55-115

BOOKSTORES

At Sara's Table 723 S Lake Ave (over Aerial Bridge) **218/723-8569** • 9am-6pm, clsd Tue in winter • also cafe • wheelchair access • women-owned/run

Edina

CAFES

Edina Grind 3940 W 50th St (Wof France Ave, in the Edina 5-0 Mall) **952/928-9004** • 7am-5:30pm, clsd Sun • brkfst & lunch

Ely

ACCOMMODATIONS

Log Cabin Hideaways 1321 N Hwy 21 **218/365-6045** • gay-friendly • remote wilderness cabins • no running water/electricity • smokefree • $340-895

Minnesota • USA

Grand Marais

ACCOMMODATIONS

Old Shore Beach B&B 1434 Old Shore Rd **218/387–9707, 888/387–9707** • gay/ straight • on Lake Superior • full brkfst • sauna • woman-owned/ run • $115-145

Snuggle Inn B&B 8 Seventh Ave W (at Hwy 61) **218/387–2847, 800/823–3174** • gay-friendly • full brkfst • gay-owned/ run • $85-95

Hastings

ACCOMMODATIONS

Thorwood & Rosewood Inns 315 Pine St (at 4th) **651/437–3297, 888/846–7966** • gay-friendly • circa 1880 mansion • full brkfst • $97-277

Hill City

ACCOMMODATIONS

Northwoods Retreat 33804 Mt Ash Dr **218/697–8119** • lesbians/ gay men • cabin w/ 700 ft of lakeshore • all meals included • veggie cuisine • wheelchair access • lesbian-owned/ run

Hinckley

ACCOMMODATIONS

Dakota Lodge B&B 320/384–6052 • gay/ straight • full brkfst • hot tub • wheelchair access • $58-135

Kenyon

ACCOMMODATIONS

Dancing Winds Farm Retreat 6863 County 12 Blvd **507/789-6606** • gay/ straight • B&B on working dairy farm • tentsites • work exchange available • smokefree • lesbian-owned/ run • $75-95

Mankato

INFO LINES & SERVICES

Mankato State U Lesbigay Center **507/389–5131**

CAFES

The Coffee Hag 329 N Riverfront **507/387–5533** • 7:30am-11pm, till midnight Fri, 9am-midnight Sat • veggie menu • live shows • wheelchair access • women-owned/ run • $3-7

Minneapolis/ St Paul

INFO LINES & SERVICES

AA Intergroup 954/922–0880

Chrysalis Women's Center 4432 Chicago Ave S, St Paul **612/871–0118** • 9am-9pm, till 5pm Fri, till 1pm Sat, clsd Sun • many groups • workshops • referrals

District 202 1601 Nicollett Ave (at 16th), Minneapolis **612/871–5559** • 4pm-11pm, till 1am Sat, clsd Tue • resource center for lgbt youth • also cafe

OutFront Minnesota 310 38th St E #204, Minneapolis **612/822–0127, 800/800–0350** • info line w/ 24 hr pre-recorded visitor info

Quatrefoil Library 1619 Dayton Ave, St Paul **651/641–0969** • 7pm-9:30pm, noon-4pm Sat, 1pm-5pm Sun • lgbt library & resource center

U of MN Queer Student Cultural Center 825 Washington Ave S, Suite 104, Minneapolis **612/626–2344** • call for info

ACCOMMODATIONS

Country Guest House 1673 38th St, Somerset, WI **715/247–3520, 888/893–9991** • lesbians/ gay men • secluded romantic getaway • lesbian-owned/ run • $75

Cover Park Manor 15330 58th St N (at Peller), Stillwater **651/430–9292, 877/430–9292** • gay-friendly • full brkfst • in-room jacuzzi & fireplace • wheelchair access • $95-179

Garden Gate B&B 925 Goodrich Ave (at Milton), St Paul **612/227–8430, 800/967–2703** • gay-friendly • 1907 Victorian • massage available • kids ok • $55-75

Nan's B&B 2304 Fremont Ave S (at 22nd), Minneapolis **612/377–5118** • gay-friendly • 1895 Victorian family home • full brkfst • shared bath • $60-70

Regal Minneapolis Hotel 1313 Nicollet Mall (btwn W Grant & 13th St), Minneapolis **612/332–6000, 800/522–8856** • gay-friendly • food served • swimming • wheelchair access • $89-299

BARS

19 Bar 19 W 15th St (at La Salle), Minneapolis **612/871–5553** • 3pm-1am, from 1pm Sat-Sun • mostly gay men • neighborhood bar • beer/ wine • wheelchair access

Bev's Wine Bar 250 3rd Ave N (at Washington Ave), Minneapolis **612/337–0102** • 4:30pm-1am, from 6pm Sat, clsd Sun-Mon • gay-friendly • light food menu • patio

Minneapolis/ St Paul • Minnesota

Boom 401 E Hennepin Ave (at 4th), Minneapolis **612/378-3188** • 4pm-1am, clsd Mon • mostly gay men • videos • also 'Oddfellows' restaurant • dinner nightly • gay-owned/ run

Brass Rail 422 Hennepin Ave (at 4th), Minneapolis **612/333-3016** • noon-1am, from 11am Sun • popular • mostly gay men • live shows • videos • wheelchair access

Bryant Lake Bowl 1810 W Lake St (at corner of Bryant), Minneapolis **612/825-3737** • 8am-1am • gay-friendly • alternative • also theater • restaurant ($5-9) • bowling alley • wheelchair access

Over the Rainbow 719 N Dale St (at Minnehaha), St Paul **651/487-5070** • 3pm-1am, from noon wknds • lesbians/ gay men • dancing/DJ • live shows • karaoke • food served • gay-owned/ run

The Saloon 830 Hennepin Ave (at 9th), Minneapolis **612/332-0835** • 8am-1am, till 3am Fri-Sun, from 10am Sun • popular • lesbians/ gay men • dancing/DJ • food served after 5pm • karaoke • also 'The Tank' leather bar Wed & Sun • wheelchair access • gay-owned/ run

The Town House 1415 University Ave (at Elbert), St Paul **651/646-7087** • 3pm-1am, from noon wknds • popular • lesbians/ gay men • dancing/DJ • theme nights • also 'Blanche's Cabaret' piano bar from 8pm Tue-Sat

Trikkx 490 N Robert St (at 9th St), St Paul **651/224-0703** • 4pm-1am, noon-2am wknds • mostly gay men • dancing/DJ • Latin 3rd Wed • male dancers Fri-Sat • also restaurant • wheelchair access

Nightclubs

Club Metro 733 Pierce Butler Rte (at Minnehaha), St Paul **651/489-0002** • 4pm-1am, 3pm-3am Fri-Sat, from 2pm Sun • popular • lesbians/ gay men • dancing/DJ • patio • transgender-friendly • live shows • food served • karaoke • wheelchair access • $5-15

Gay 90s 408 Hennepin Ave (at 4th), Minneapolis **612/333-7755** • 8am-1am (dinner nightly 5pm-9pm) • popular • mostly gay men • 8-bar complex • dancing/DJ • multiracial clientele • drag king shows Sun • karaoke • wheelchair access

---

Minneapolis/St Paul

LGBT Pride: July. 952/996-9250.

Annual Events: September - Gay Night at Knott's Camp Snoopy in Mall of America.

City Info: 800/445-7412, web: www.minneapolis.org.

Attractions: Mall of America (the largest mall in the US w/indoor theme park) 952/883-8800. Minneapolis Institute of Arts 612/870-3131. Museum of Questionable Medical Devices 612/379-4046. Walker Art Center/Minneapolis Sculpture Garden 612/375-7622. Frederick R Weisman Art Museum 612/625-9494.

Best View: Observation deck of the 32nd story of Foshay Tower (closed in winter).

Weather: Winters are harsh. If driving, carry extra blankets and supplies. The average temperature is 19°, and it can easily drop well below 0°, and then there's the wind chill! Summer temperatures are usually in the upper-80°s to mid-90°s and HUMID.

Transit: Town Taxi (Minn) 612/331-8294. Yellow Cab (St Paul) 651/222-4433. Airport Express 612/827-7777. MTC 612/349-7000.

Minnesota • USA

Reply **Forward** **Delete**

Date: Wed, Dec 19, 2001 12:01:07
From: Girl-on-the-Go
To: Editor@Damron.com
Subject: Minneapolis & St Paul

> If you're searching for a liberal oasis in the heartland of America, if you love Siberian winters, and if you crave a diverse, intensely political lesbian community, you'll fit right into the Twin Cities of Minneapolis and St. Paul.

> Located on the banks of the Mississippi River, these cities share the Minnesota Twins, 936 lakes, 513 parks, and a history of Native American and Northern European settlements. If you want more than glimpses into the various cultures of Minnesota, visit the Minneapolis American Indian Center or the American Swedish Institute.

> Of course, you'll probably have more fun checking out the lesbian cultural scene. The place to go to find out about the latest poetry reading, play, or concert is the **Amazon Bookstore** in Minneapolis. To find social groups for women of color, call **Outfront MN.**

> Or stop by the **Minnesota Women's Press** bookstore and library in St. Paul. Then go cafe-hopping in Minneapolis at the women-owned **Cafe Wyrd** or **Ruby's Cafe.** For a night on the town, you won't find any full-time women's bars, but **Club Metro** and **The Saloon** are popular on weekends. And the **Gay 90s** complex has drag king shows on Sundays.

> Whatever you do, don't stay indoors the whole time. In the summer, boating, fishing, sunbathing, water-skiing, walking, jogging, and bicycling are all popular. In winter, you can enjoy snowmobiling, ice hockey, cross-country skiing, or snuggling by a fire. For women's outdoor adventures, try **Adventures in Good Company** (877/439-4042).

Ground Zero/ The Front 15 NE 4th St (at Hennepin), Minneapolis **612/378-5115, 612/857-1012** • 9pm-1am, clsd Sun-Tue • popular • gay/ straight • more gay Th & Sat • 'Bondage a Go Go' Th • 'Creation' Sat • dancing/ DJ • live shows • wheelchair access • also 'The Front'.from 8pm

Minneapolis/ St Paul • Minnesota

Lucy's 601 N Western Ave (at Thomas Ave), St Paul **651/228-9959** • 3pm-1am, from noon wknds • lesbians/ gay men • dancing/DJ • karaoke • country/ western Th • live shows • gay-owned/ run

Margarita Bella 1032 3rd Ave NE (at Central), Minneapolis **612/331-7955** • 9pm-1am • gay/ straight • more gay Wed • mostly Latino/a clientele • dancing/ DJ • also restaurant 11am-9pm

CAFES

Anodyne at 43rd 4301 Nicollet Ave (at 43rd), Minneapolis **612/824-4300** • 6:30am-10pm, from 7am Sat, from 8am Sun, till midnight wknds • wheelchair access

Cafe Wyrd 1600 W Lake St (at Irving), Minneapolis **612/827-5710** • 7am-1am • lesbians/ gay men • plenty veggie • women-owned/ run • $3-6

Cahoots 1562 Selby Ave (at Snelling), St Paul **651/644-6778** • 7am-9:30pm, 7:30am-11pm wknds • coffee bar

Moose & Sadie's 212 3rd Ave N (at 2nd St), Minneapolis **612/371-0464** • 7:30am-11pm, till 1:30am wknds, 9am-10pm Sun • warehouse district cafe

Ruby's Cafe 1614 Harmon Pl (at Loring Park), Minneapolis **612/338-2089** • 7am-2pm, from 10am Th-Sat, from 8am Sun • popular • lesbians/ gay men • outdoor seating • women-owned/ run

Uncommon Grounds 2809 Hennepin Ave (at 28th Ave), Minneapolis **612/872-4811** • 10am-1am • gay/ straight • outdoor seating

The Urban Bean 3255 Bryant Ave S (at 33rd), Minneapolis **612/824-6611** • 7am-11pm • live entertainment • patio

Vera's Cafe 2901 Lyndale Ave S (at 29th St W), Minneapolis **612/822-3871** • 7am-1am • cozy coffeehouse w/ baked goods & light meals

RESTAURANTS

Al's Breakfast 413 14th Ave SE (at 4th), Minneapolis **612/331-9991** • 6am-1pm, from 9am Sun • popular • great hash

Bobino Cafe & Wine Bar 222 E Hennepin Ave, Minneapolis **612/623-3301** • lunch wkdays, dinner nightly • classic bistro

Campiello 1320 W Lake St (at Hennepin), Minneapolis **612/825-2222** • dinner & Sun brunch • Italian

D'Amico Cucina 100 N 6th St (btwn 1st & 2nd Aves), Minneapolis **612/338-2401** • dinner nightly • à la carte • full bar • live music • $60-70 per person

Goodfellows 40 S 7th (at Hennepin), Minneapolis **612/332-4800** • lunch & dinner, clsd Sun • full bar • upscale American

King & I Thai 1346 LaSalle Ave (at W Grant) **612/332-6928** • 11am-1am, from 5pm Sat, clsd Sun • full bar • plenty veggie • courtyard

La Covina Café 1570 Selby Ave (at Snelling), St Paul **651/645-5288** • lunch & dinner • Mexican • wheelchair access • $6-10

Murray's 26 S 6th St (at Hennepin), Minneapolis **612/339-0909** • lunch Mon-Fri, dinner nightly • steak & potatoes • $21+

Palomino Euro Bistro 825 Hennepin Ave (at 9th St), Minneapolis **612/339-3800** • 11am-1am, 5pm-12:30am Sun • Italian/ Mediterranean

Rudolph's Bar-B-Que 1933 Lyndale (at Franklin), Minneapolis **612/871-8969** • 11am-midnight • full bar • wheelchair access

ENTERTAINMENT & RECREATION

32nd St Beach E side of Lake Calhoun (33rd & Calhoun Blvd), Minneapolis • gay beach

Fresh Fruit KFAI 90.3 FM, Minneapolis **612/341-0980** • 7:30pm-8:30pm Th • gay radio program • also a variety of lgbt programs 9pm-midnight Sun

Vulva Riot 2822 Lyndale Ave S (at 28th), Minneapolis **612/375-7657** • 7pm 1st Sat • women's art & performance • transgender-friendly • smokefree/ alcohol-free space

BOOKSTORES

A Brother's Touch 2327 Hennepin Ave (at 24th), Minneapolis **612/377-6279** • 11am-7pm, till 6pm Sat, noon-5pm Sun • lgbt • wheelchair access

Amazon Bookstore Co-operative 4432 Chicago Ave S, Minneapolis **612/821-9630** • 8am-9pm, from 9am Sat, from 10am Sun, till 6pm wknds • feminist bookstore since 1970 • also gifts, music & art • open mic Fri • cafe • wheelchair access • women-owned/ run • no relation to Seattle's amazon.com

Magus Books, Ltd 1316 SE 4th St (at 13th/ 14th), Minneapolis **612/379-7669, 800/996-2387** • 10am-9pm, till 6pm wknds, from noon Sun • alternative spirituality books • also mail order

RETAIL SHOPS

The Rainbow Road 109 W Grant (at LaSalle), Minneapolis **612/872-8448** • 10am-10pm • lgbt retail & video • wheelchair access

Minnesota/ Mississippi • USA

PUBLICATIONS

Lavender Magazine 612/871-2237, 877/515-9969 • lgbt newsmagazine

Minnesota Women's Press 771 Raymond Ave, St Paul 651/646-3968 • 9am-6pm, till 3pm Sat, clsd Sun • bi-weekly newspaper • also bookshop & library

SPIRITUAL GROUPS

Dignity Twin Cities 22 Orlin Ave (at Prospect Park United Methodist), Minneapolis 612/827-3103 • 7:30pm 2nd & 4th Fri

Lutherans Concerned 100 N Oxford, St Paul 651/224-3371, 612/866-8941 • 7:30pm 3rd Fri • wheelchair access

MCC All God's Children 3100 Park Ave S (at 31st St), Minneapolis 612/824-2673 • 10am Sun & 7pm Wed • wheelchair access

Shir Tikvah 5000 Girard Ave (at Minnehaha Pkwy), Minneapolis 612/822-1440 • 10:30am 1st Sat, then 8pm every Fri • lgbt Jewish congregation • wheelchair access

GYMS & HEALTH CLUBS

Body Quest 245 Aldrich Ave N (at Glenwood), Minneapolis 612/377-7222 • lesbians/ gay men

EROTICA

Fantasy House 709 W Lake (at Lyndale), Minneapolis 612/824-2459 • adult gifts • wheelchair access

Fit 2 A T Leather 733 Pierce Butler Route (in 'Club Metro'), St Paul 651/487-0513 • Th-Sat eves

Triangle @ SexWorld 241 2nd Ave N, 3rd Fl (at Washington), Minneapolis 612/317-1086 • 24hrs

Moorhead

see also Fargo, North Dakota

NIGHTCLUBS

The I-Beam 1021 Center Ave 218/233-7700 • 7pm-1am • lesbians/ gay men • dancing/DJ • videos • food served • wheelchair access

CAFES

Atomic Coffee 15 4th St S (at Main) 218/299-6161 • 7am-11pm, from 9am Sat, from 10am Sun • also gallery • gay-owned/ run

Rochester

INFO LINES & SERVICES

Gay/ Lesbian Community Service 507/281-3265 • 5pm-7pm Mon & Wed

Rushford

ACCOMMODATIONS

Windswept Inn 207 N Mill St 507/864-2545 • gay-friendly • $30-43

Two Harbors

ACCOMMODATIONS

Grand Superior Lodge 2826 Hwy 61 E (near Gooseberry Falls State Park) 218/834-3796, 800/627-9565 • gay-friendly • log cabins on the north shore of Lake Superior • wheelchair ramps available • restaurant • $99-189

Wolverton

RESTAURANTS

District 31 Victoria's 101 First St 218/995-2000 • 5:30pm-9:30pm, clsd Sun • cont'l • beer/ wine • reservations required • $17-40

MISSISSIPPI

Statewide

PUBLICATIONS

▲ **Southern Voice** 404/876-1819 • weekly lgbt newspaper for AL, FL (panhandle), GA, LA, MS, TN w/ resource listings

Biloxi

ACCOMMODATIONS

Lofty Oaks Inn 17288 Hwy 67 228/392-6722, 800/280-4361 • gay-friendly • full brkfst • hot tub • swimming • kids/ pets ok • woman-owned/ run • $99-125

BARS

Joey's on the Beach 1708 Beach Blvd/ Hwy 90 228/435-5639 • 9pm-close, from 6pm Sun, clsd Mon-Tue • lesbians/ gay men • dancing/DJ • live shows • 18+

NIGHTCLUBS

Barcode 153 Veterans Ave 228/388-0092 • 3pm-7am, 24hrs wknds • lesbians/ gay men • dancing/DJ • live shows • karaoke

EROTICA

Satellite News 1632 Pass Rd 228/432-8229 • clsd Sun

Holly Springs

ACCOMMODATIONS

Somerset Cottage 135 W Gholson Ave **662/252-4513** • gay/ straight • smokefree • hot tub • 45 mins to Graceland • woman-owned/ run • $65

Jackson

INFO LINES & SERVICES

Gay/ Lesbian Community Info Line **601/346-4379** • 24hrs • switchboard for many organizations, including youth group

Lambda AA 4872 N State St (at Unitarian Church) **601/346-4379** • 7pm Mon & Wed, 6pm Sat

BARS

Jack's Construction Site (JC's) 425 N Mart Plaza **601/362-3108** • 5pm-close • mostly gay men • more women Wed & Fri • neighborhood bar • beer/ wine • BYOB

NIGHTCLUBS

Club City Lights 200 N Mill St **601/353-0059** • 10pm-close Fri-Sat • lesbians/ gay men • dancing/DJ • mostly African-American • live shows • beer/ wine • BYOB

Jack & Jill's 3911 Northview Dr (at Meadowbrook) **601/982-5225** • 9pm-close Fri-Sat • lesbians/ gay men • dancing/DJ • live shows • beer/ wine • BYOB • wheelchair access

SPIRITUAL GROUPS

Safe Harbor Family Church 4074 Northview Dr **601/923-2728** • 6pm Sun • non-denominational • social events • support groups

Meridian

BARS

Crossroads/ Ollie Mae's exit 142 N I-59 (before Meridian), Enterprise **601/655-8415** • 6pm-1am • lesbians/ gay men • popular • East Mississippi's largest gay complex • 4 bars • dancing/DJ • food served • live shows • wheelchair access

Natchez

ACCOMMODATIONS

Guest House Historic Inn 201 N Pearl St **601/442-1054** • gay/ straight • smokefree • wheelchair access • gay-owned/ run • $94-125

BARS

Under the Hill Saloon 33 Silver St **601/446-8023** • 8am-close • gay-friendly • neighborhood bar • live music

Ovett

ACCOMMODATIONS

Camp Sister Spirit **601/344-1411** • mostly women • 120 acres of camping & RV sites • cabins • smokefree • lesbian-owned/ run • clean & sober space • $10-20 sliding scale includes kitchen use

Tupelo

NIGHTCLUBS

Rumors 637 Hwy 145 (10 miles S of Tupelo), Shannon **662/767-9500, 662/891-0761** • 8pm-1am Th-Sun • gay/ straight • dancing/DJ • live shows • wheelchair access

MISSOURI

Ava

ACCOMMODATIONS

Cactus Canyon Campground 16 miles E of Ava on Hwy 14 (N 1 mile on County 223) **417/683-9199** • mostly gay men • camping & RV • hot tub • nudity • kids/ pets ok • gay-owned/ run • $60-75

Branson

see **Springfield & Eureka Springs, Arkansas**

Cape Girardeau

NIGHTCLUBS

Independence Place 5 S Henderson St (at Independence) **573/334-2939** • 8:30pm-1:30am, from 7pm Fri-Sat, clsd Sun • lesbians/ gay men • dancing/DJ • transgender-friendly • live shows Wed & Sat

SPIRITUAL GROUPS

MCC of Southeast Missouri 519 Broadway **573/335-5106** • 11am Sun

Columbia

INFO LINES & SERVICES

Women's Center 229 Brady Commons UMC **573/882-6621**

Missouri • USA

Bars

SoCo Club 128 E Nifong Blvd #E (at Providence Rd) **573/499-9483** • 6:30pm-1:30am, clsd Sun-Mon • gay/ straight • dancing/DJ • alternative • food served • karaoke • live shows • patio • wheelchair access

Nightclubs

The Rage 6870 E Mexico Gravel Rd (in Lake of the Woods area) **573/474-9086** • 6:30pm-1:30am, till 2am Fri, 9pm-3am Sat, clsd Sun-Wed • lesbians/ gay men • dancing/DJ • karaoke • 18+ • BYOB • lakeside patio

Cafes

Ernie's Cafe 1005 E Walnut (at 10th) **573/874-7804** • 6:30am-3pm

Spiritual Groups

Christ the King Agape Church 515 Hickman Ave **573/443-5316** • 1pm Sun & 7pm Wed

Erotica

Eclectics 1122-A Wilkes Blvd **573/443-0873**

Jefferson City

Accommodations

Jefferson Inn B&B 801 W High St **573/635-7196** • gay-friendly • full brkfst • kids ok • $65-105

Joplin

Bars

Ree's 716 Main St (at 7th) **417/627-9035** • 4pm-1:30am, clsd Sun • lesbians/ gay men • dancing/DJ • karaoke • wheelchair access

Spiritual Groups

United Family Fellowship 531 Kentucky Ave (at 7th) **417/782-6647** • 7pm Sun & Th

Kansas City

Info Lines & Services

Gay/ Lesbian Community Center 1615 W 39th St (2nd flr of 'Supreme Bean' coffeehouse) **816/374-5945** • 7pm-9pm Fri • call for other events

Gay/ Lesbian Hotline **816/753-0700** • 10am-6pm

Live & Let Live AA 5201 Baltimore **816/531-9668** • noon & 6pm daily, 7pm Sat

Passages 3801 Wyandotte (at MCC) **816/691-8740** • Sun 7pm-8:30pm • lgbt youth group

Accommodations

B&B in KC 9215 Slater, Overland Park, KS **913/648-5457** • mostly women • full brkfst • smokefree • lesbian-owned/ run • $30-55

LaFontaine Inn 4320 Oak St **816/753-4434, 888/832-6000**

Kansas City

LGBT Pride: June. 816/420-0100, web: www.prideproductions.org.

City Info: Convention & Visitors Bureau 816/691-3800.

Attractions: Historic 18th & Vine District (includes Kansas City Jazz Museum & the Negro Leagues Baseball Museum).
Nelson-Atkins Museum of Art 816/561-4000.
Thomas Hart Benton Home & Studio 816/931-5722.
Harry S Truman Nat'l Historical Site (in Independence, MO) 816/254-2720.

Transit: Yellow Cab 816/471-5000.
KCI Shuttle 800/243-6383.
Metro 816/221-0660.

Kansas City • Missouri

Southmoreland on the Plaza 116 E 46th St **816/531-7979** • gay-friendly • 1913 B&B • full brkfst • hot tub • sundeck • smokefree • $125-215

Su Casa B&B 9004 E 92nd St **816/965-5647, 866/632-2136** • gay-friendly • Southwest style home • full brkfst wknds • kids/dogs/horses ok • jacuzzi • swimming • smokefree • woman-owned/run • $50-160

BARS

Balanca's 1007 Grand Ave (at 11th) **816/221-9220** • 4pm-1:30am, clsd Sun • lesbians/gay men • neighborhood bar

Dixie Belle Complexx 1915 Main St (at 20th) **816/471-1575** • 11am-3am • popular • 5 bars • mostly gay men • dancing/DJ • food served • also leather shop & bar • wheelchair access

Missie B's 805 W 39th St (at SW Trafficway) **816/561-0625** • 6am-3am, clsd Sun • mostly gay men • neighborhood bar • dancing/DJ • transgender-friendly • live shows • karaoke

The Other Side 3611 Broadway (at 36th/Valentine) **816/931-0501** • 4:30pm-1:30am, clsd Sun • mostly gay men • piano bar wknds • videos • wheelchair access

Ree's of KC 1321 Grand (at Truman) **816/421-1288** • 1:30pm-1:30am • lesbians/gay men • transgender-friendly • neighborhood bar • dancing/DJ • karaoke • live shows • gay-owned

Sidekicks 3707 Main St (at 37th) **816/931-1430** • 2pm-3am, clsd Sun • lesbians/gay men • dancing/DJ • country/western • live shows • wheelchair access

Soakie's 1308 Main St (at 13th) **816/221-6060** • 9am-1:30am, till 3am Fri-Sat, from 11am Sun • lesbians/gay men • dancing/DJ • multiracial • food served • live shows • wheelchair access

Tootsie's 1822 Main (at 18th) **816/471-7704** • noon-3am wknds, clsd Mon • popular • mostly women • dancing/DJ • live shows • wheelchair access • grill menu • some veggie

Wetherbee's 2510 NE Vivian Rd (at Antioch) **816/454-2455** • 6pm-3am • mostly women • dancing/DJ • food served • karaoke • live shows • wheelchair access

NIGHTCLUBS

Club Cabaret 5024 Main St (at 51st) **816/753-6504** • 6pm-3am, from 3pm Sun, clsd Mon-Tue • popular • mostly gay men • dancing/DJ • food served • live shows • young crowd • wheelchair access

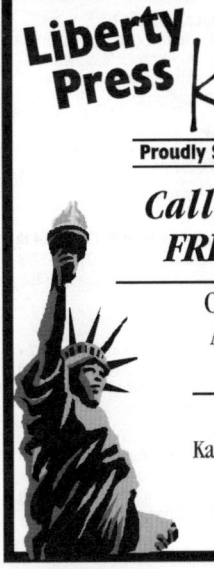

Liberty Press

Kansas City

Proudly Serving the KC Lesbian and Gay Community

Call or click for your FREE Sample issue

Community Events • Cultural Arts
Award-Winning News & Features
Resource Directory

1509 Westport Road • Suite 203B
Kansas City, MO 64111 • fax: 816-931-1420
816-931-3060
www.libertypress.net

Missouri • USA

Club Evos 47 Central Ave (at James), KS **913/321-6100, 816/753-0700** • 9pm-2am • lesbians/ gay men • dancing/ DJ • live shows • 18+ • also restaurant from 10am

The Hurricane 4048 Broadway (at Westport Rd) **816/753-0884** • 3pm-3am • gay-friendly • dancing/DJ • live bands

XO 3954 Central (btwn Westport & Broadway) **816/753-0112** • 9pm-3am, gay Th only • gay/ straight • dancing/DJ • karaoke

Cafes

Broadway Cafe 4106 Broadway Blvd (at Westport) **816/531-2432** • 7am-midnight, from 8:30am wknds

Muddy's 1719 W 39th St (at Bell) **816/756-1997** • 7am-midnight, 8am-6pm Sun • beer/ wine • wheelchair access

Planet Cafe 3535 Broadway Blvd (at 35th) **816/561-7287** • 7am-11pm, till midnight Fri-Sat, from 10am wknds • popular • live music • gay-owned/ run

Restaurants

Classic Cup Cafe 301 W 47th St (at Central) **816/753-1840** • 7am-10pm • wheelchair access

The Corner Restaurant 4059 Broadway (at Main) **816/931-6630** • 7am-3pm daily & 5pm-8pm Mon-Fri • wheelchair access

Metropolis 303 Westport Rd (at Central) **816/753-1550** • dinner only, clsd Sun-Mon • popular • lesbians/ gay men • contemporary American • wheelchair access • $12-25

Otto's Malt Shop 3903 Wyoming (at 39th) **816/756-1010** • 11am-10pm, till midnight wknds • burgers • malts

Sharp's 63rd St Grill 128 W 63rd St **816/333-4355** • 7am-10pm, till 11pm Fri-Sat, from 8am Sat, from 9am Sun • beer/ wine • wheelchair access • women-owned/ run

Strouds 1014 E 85th St (btwn Troost & Holmes) **816/333-2132** • 4pm-10pm, lunch Fri-Sun • fried chicken • $9-20

Entertainment & Recreation

Unicorn Theatre 3820 Main **816/531-3033** • contemporary American theater

Retail Shops

Larry's Gifts & Cards 205 Westport Rd (btwn Main & Broadway) **816/753-4757** • 10am-7pm, till 6:30pm Sat, till 5pm Sun • lgbt

Lion's Den 7719 Wornall **816/523-5070** • tattoos & piercing

Publications

CN Magazine 816/561-2679

EXP 816/753-4242, 877/397-6244 • bi-monthly gay magazine for MO, IL & KS

▲ **The Liberty Press Kansas City** 816/931-3060 • lgbt newspaper serving Kansas City

Spiritual Groups

Spirit of Hope MCC 3801 Wyandotte **816/931-0750** • 10:15am Sun

Erotica

Erotic City 8401 E Truman Rd (at I-435) **816/252-3370** • 24hrs

Hollywood at Home 9063 Metcalf (at 91st), Overland Park, KS **913/649-9666**

Noel

Accommodations

Sycamore Landing 417/475-6460, 800/475-6460 • open May-Sept • gay-friendly • campsites & RV hook ups • canoe rental • kids/pets ok • wheelchair access

Overland

Erotica

Priscilla's 10210 Page Ave (E of Ashby) **314/423-8422**

Poplar Bluff

Nightclubs

Realities Dance Club 67 Hwy S **573/686-0740** • 7pm-1:30pm, 6pm-midnight Sun, clsd Mon-Tue • lesbians/ gay men • dancing/DJ • live shows wknds • lesbian-owned/ run • unconfirmed

Springfield

Info Lines & Services

AA Gay/ Lesbian 680 S Florence **417/823-7125** • 6pm Sat

Gay & Lesbian Community Center of the Ozarks 518 E Commercial St **417/869-3978** • 6pm-10pm Fri-Sun • youth group 3pm Tue • wheelchair access

Bars

The Edge 424 N Boonville **417/831-4700** • 4pm-1:30am, clsd Sun • lesbians/ gay men • dancing/DJ • karaoke • wheelchair access • lesbian-owned/ run

Martha's Vineyard 217-221 W Olive St **417/864-4572, 417/831-6144** • 4pm-1:30am, till midnight Sun, clsd Mon • lesbians/ gay men • neighborhood bar • dancing/DJ • drag shows • 18+ • also martini lounge • patio • wheelchair access

St Louis • Missouri

NIGHTCLUBS

Bar One 1109 E Commercial (at National Ave) **417/865-4570** • 4pm-1:30am • lesbians/ gay men • dancing/DJ • live shows • 18+ • wheelchair access • gay-owned/ run

BOOKSTORES

Renaissance Books & Gifts 1337 E Montclair (at Fremont) **417/883-5161** • 10am-7pm, noon-5pm Sun • women's/ alternative • wheelchair access

RETAIL SHOPS

Springfield Coffee Co 215 W Olive St **417/865-3335** • 7:30am-6pm, 10am-3pm Sat, clsd Sun • pastries • gourmet gifts • gay-owned/ run

EROTICA

Priscilla's 1918 S Glenstone (at Sunshine) **417/881-8444**

St Louis

INFO LINES & SERVICES

Gay/ Lesbian Hotline 314/367-0084 • 6pm-10pm, clsd Sun

PACT (People of All Colors Together) 600 N Euclid Ave (at Trinity Church) 314/995-4683 • mtgs 7pm 2nd Wed

St Louis Gender Foundation 314/367-4128 • transgender info

Steps Alano Club 1935-A Park Ave 314/436-1858 • lgbt 12-step mtgs • call for mtg schedule

ACCOMMODATIONS

2049 Sidney 2049 Sidney St (at McNair) **314/772-2049, 866/772-2049** • gay/ straight • full brkfst • jacuzzi • gay-owned/ run • $75-150

A St Louis Guesthouse 1032-38 Allen Ave (at Menard) **314/773-1016** • mostly gay men • located in historic Soulard district • hot tub (nudity permitted) • smokefree • $75-110

Brewers House B&B 1829 Lami St (at Lemp) **314/771-1542, 888/767-4665** • lesbians/ gay men • 1860s home • jacuzzi • kids ok • gay-owned/ run • $70-75

Lafayette House B&B 2156 Lafayette Ave (at Jefferson) **314/772-4429, 800/641-8965** • gay-friendly • Queen Anne Victorian • full brkfst • hot tub • kids/ pets ok • lesbian-owned/ run • $75-150

MotherSource Travels 187 W 19th St, Alton, IL **314/973-1890, 618/462-4051** • mostly women • reservation service • lesbian-owned/ run

Napoleon's Retreat B&B 1815 Lafayette Ave (at Mississippi) **314/772-6979, 800/700-9980** • gay/ straight • restored 1880s townhouse • full brkfst • smokefree • gay-owned/ run • $85-125

Two Boys Inn B&B 2712 S Compton Ave (at Magnolia) **314/773-6700** • lesbians/ gay men • full brkfst • gay-owned/ run

BARS

Alibi's 3016 Arsenal (at Minnesota) **314/ 772-8989** • 11am-3am • mostly gay men • transgender-friendly • live shows • also dinner & Sun brunch • patio • wheelchair access

Clementine's 2001 Menard (at Allen) **314/664-7869** • 10am-1:30am, from 8:30am Sat, 11am-midnight Sun • popular • mostly gay men • leather • food served • patio • wheelchair access

Club Escapades 113 W Main St, Belleville, IL **618/222-9597** • 5pm-2am • lesbians/ gay men • dancing/DJ • karaoke • live shows

The Drake Bar 3502 Papin St (at Theresa, 1 blk NE of Grand & Chouteau) **314/865-1400** • 4pm-1:30am, clsd Sun • lesbians/ gay men • piano bar • live shows • patio • wheelchair access

Eagle in Exile 17 S Vandeventer (at Forest Park Pkwy) **314/652-0171** • 6pm-1:30am, clsd Sun • mostly gay men • neighborhood bar

Grey Fox Pub/ Spanky's Restaurant 3501 S Spring (at Potomac) **314/772-2150** • 11am-1:30am, from 9am Sat, clsd Sun • lesbians/ gay men • neighborhood bar • transgender-friendly • food served • live shows • patio

Inside Out 3145 W Chain of Rocks Rd, Granite City, IL **618/797-0700** • 8pm-2am, till 3am Sat, from 2pm Sun, clsd Mon-Wed • popular • lesbians/ gay men • food served • live shows • videos • outdoor complex

Knightz Too 4112-14 Manchester Ave **314/ 531-5850** • 4pm-1:30am, clsd Mon • lesbians/ gay men • neighborhood bar • video bar • food served • karaoke Wed-Th • live shows

Loading Zone 16 S Euclid (at Forest Park Pkwy) **314/361-4119** • 2pm-1:30am, clsd Sun • popular • lesbians/ gay men • videos • wheelchair access

Nero Bianco 6 S Sarah (btwn Laclede & Forest Park) **314/531-4123** • 4pm-1am, clsd Sun • mostly gay men • dancing/DJ • mostly African-American • jazz Fri • wheelchair access

Novak's Bar & Grill 4146 Manchester **314/531-3699** • 4pm-1:30am • lesbians/ gay men • live entertainment • karaoke • drag shows • patio • wheelchair access

Missouri • USA

Rainbow's End 4060 Chouteau (at Manchester) 314/652-8790 • 9am-close • lesbians/ gay men • neighborhood bar • food served • drag shows • patio • also leather shop • wheelchair access

Tangerine 1405 Washington Ave (at 14th) 314/621-7335 • 11am-2pm Tue-Fri & 6pm-3am Tue-Sat • gay-friendly • dancing/DJ • live shows • hipster lounge • also restaurant • mostly veggie • $8-12

Nightclubs

Attitudes 4100 Manchester 314/534-3858 • 6pm-3am, clsd Sun-Mon • popular • mostly women • dancing/DJ • food served

The Complex/ Angles 3511 Chouteau (at Grand) 314/772-2645 • 5pm-3am, from 9pm Sun-Tue • popular • lesbians/ gay men • multiple bars • dancing/DJ • live shows • videos • patio • food served • wheelchair access

St Louis

WHERE THE GIRLS ARE: Spread out, but somewhat concentrated in the Central West End near Forest Park. Younger, funkier crowds hang out in the Delmar Loop, west of the city limits, packed with ethnic restaurants.

LGBT PRIDE: June. 314/772-8888

ANNUAL EVENTS: June- Six Flags St Louis Gay Day 636/938-4800.

CITY INFO: 421-1023 or 800/ 888-3861, web: www.explorestlouis.com.

ATTRACTIONS: Anheuser-Busch Brewery.
Argosy Casino 800/336-7568.
Cathedral Basilica of St Louis (world's largest collection of mosaic art).
Dave & Buster's dining & entertainment center 314/209-8015.
Gateway Arch (duh).
Grant's Farm 314/843-1700.
St Louis Art Museum 314/721-0072.
Stone Hill Winery (in Hermann) 800/909-9463.
The extremely quaint town of St. Charles.

BEST VIEW: Where else? Top of the Gateway Arch in the Observation Room.

WEATHER: 100% midwestern. Cold winters—little snow and the temperatures can drop below 0°. Hot, muggy summers raise temperatures back up into the 100°s. Spring and fall bring out the best in Mother Nature.

TRANSIT: County Cab 314/991-5300.
GEM Shuttle 314/427-3311.
The Bi-State Bus System 314/231-2345.

St Louis • Missouri

Faces Complex 130 4th St (at Missouri), East St Louis, IL **618/271-7410** • 3pm-6am • lesbians/ gay men • dancing/DJ • food served • live shows • videos • 18+ wknds • 3 levels • patio

The Galaxy 1227 Washington Ave **314/231-2404** • hours vary • gay-friendly • alternative • fetish night Mon • live music • cover charge

Mabel's Budget Beauty Shop & Chainsaw Repair 602 Belle St (at 6th St), Alton, IL **618/465-8687** • 4pm-1:30am • mostly gay men • dancing/DJ • live shows • wheelchair access

Magnolia's 5 S Vandeventer (at Forest Park Pkwy) **314/652-6500** • 4pm-3am, from 3pm Sun • dinner nightly • popular • mostly gay men • dancing/DJ • country/ western Th • live shows • karaoke • also 'Gateway' Fri-Sun • leather • also full restaurant • wheelchair access

Velvet Lounge 1301 Washington Ave (at 13th Ave) **314/241-8178, 314/241-2997** • 9pm-3am Th-Sun • gay/ straight • dancing/DJ • lounge & house music

CAFES

Classical Coffee 313 Belt Ave (at Waterman) **314/361-1317** • 7am-6pm, till 4pm Wed, from 8am Sat, 9am-2pm Sun

---

Reply **Forward** **Delete**

Date: Fri, Dec 21, 2001 15:21:05
From: Girl-on-the-Go
To: Editor@Damron.com
Subject: St. Louis

> Most visitors come to St. Louis see the famous Gateway Arch, the tallest monument in the U.S. at 630 feet, designed by renowned architect Eero Saarinen.
> After you've ridden the elevator in the Arch and seen the view, come down to earth and take a trip to historic Soulard, the 'French Quarter of St. Louis.' Established in 1779 by Madame and Monsieur Soulard as an open-air market, it's now the place for great food and jazz. And the Market still attracts crowds—LGBT and straight—on the weekends.
> Laclede's Landing is also a popular attraction. While you're down by the Gateway Arch, treat yourself to riverfront dining aboard any of the several riverboat restaurants on the Mississippi. For accommodations, try **MotherSource Travels,** a women's B&B reservations service in nearby Alton, Illinois. Dining and shopping are most fun in the Central West End on Euclid Street between Delmar and Forest Park Boulevards, or in the University City Loop area near Washington University.
> For nightlife, check out **Attitudes,** the loud-and-rowdy dance bar for women, or one of the many mixed establishments, such as **Novak's Bar and Grill.**

Missouri • USA

Coffee Cartel 2 Maryland Plaza (at Euclid) **314/454-0000** • 24hrs • popular

MokaBe's 3606 Arsenal (at S Grand) **314/865-2009** • 11am-1am • from 9am Sun • popular • plenty veggie • occasional shows • wheelchair access

Restaurants

Busch's Grove 9160 Clayton Rd (at Price) **314/993-0011** • lunch & dinner, clsd Sun-Mon • full bar till 1am • $15-25

Cafe Balaban 405 N Euclid Ave (at McPherson) **314/361-8085** • popular • pizza • some veggie • wonderful Sun brunch • full bar • wheelchair access • $10-16

Dressel's 419 N Euclid (at McPherson) **314/361-1060** • great Welsh pub food • full bar • $7-11

Duff's 392 N Euclid Ave (at McPherson) **314/361-0522** • lunch & dinner, clsd Mon • fine dining • some veggie • full bar • wknd brunch • wheelchair access • $13-20

Kirk's Bistro & Bar 512 N Euclid (at Washington) **314/361-1456** • 5pm-10pm, till 11pm Fri-Sat, Sun brunch

Majestic Bar & Restaurant 4900 Laclede (at Euclid) **314/361-2011** • 6am-1:30am • diner fare • $4-7

On Broadway Bistro 5300 N Broadway (at Grand) **314/421-0087** • 11am-3am • full bar • wheelchair access • $4-12

Ted Drewes Frozen Custard 6726 Chippewa (at Jameson) **314/481-2652** • 11am-11pm • seasonal • a St Louis landmark • also 4224 S Grand Blvd, 314/352-7376

Tomatillo Mexican Grill 9641 Olive Blvd (at Warson) **314/991-4995** • 11am-10pm, till midnight wknds

Tony's 410 Market St (at Broadway) **314/231-7007** • dinner only, clsd Sun • Italian fine dining • reservations advised • $8-36

Zinnia 7491 Big Bend Blvd (at Shrewsbury), Webster Groves **314/962-0572** • lunch Tue-Fri & dinner Tue-Sun • California-style bistro • $13-19

Entertainment & Recreation

Anheuser-Busch Brewery Tours/ Grant's Farm **314/577-2626, 314/843-1700** • all-American kitsch: see the Clydesdales in their air-conditioned stables, or visit the Busch family estate that was once the home of Ulysses S Grant

Int'l Bowling Museum & Hall of Fame 111 Stadium Plaza (across from Busch Stadium) **314/231-6340** • 5,000 yrs of bowling history (!) & 4 free frames

Lavender Limelight Radio Show KDHX 88.1FM **314/664-3688** • 7pm Th • lgbt radio show

Wired Women, Inc **314/352-9473** • concerts & events for the women's community

Bookstores

Left Bank Books 399 N Euclid Ave (at McPherson) **314/367-6731** • 10am-10pm, 11am-6pm Sun • feminist & lgbt titles

Planet Proud Books & Gifts 3194 S Grand (at Wyoming) **314/772-4528** • 10am-8pm, till 9pm Fri-Sat, from noon wknds, till 5pm Sun

Retail Shops

Daily Planet News 243 N Euclid Ave (at Maryland) **314/367-1333** • 7am-9pm

Friends & Luvers 3550 Gravois (at Grand) **314/771-9405** • 10am-10pm, noon-7pm Sun • fetish clothes • toys • videos • dating service

Heffalump's 387 N Euclid Ave (at McPherson) **314/361-0544** • 11am-8pm, till 10pm Fri-Sat, noon-5pm Sun • gifts

Publications

EXP **314/367-0397, 877/397-6244** • bi-monthly gay magazine for MO, IL & KS

Vital Voice PO Box 170138 63117 **314/865-3787** • bi-monthly news & feature publication

Women's Yellow Pages of Greater St Louis **314/567-0487**

Spiritual Groups

Agape House 2109 S Spring St (at Russell) **314/664-3588** • 2pm Sun

Dignity St Louis 600 N Euclid (at Trinity Church) **314/997-9897** • 7:30pm Sun

MCC Living Faith 6501 Wydown, Clayton **314/726-2855** • 5pm Sun

MCC of Greater St Louis 5000 Washington Pl (at Kings Hwy) **314/361-3221** • 7pm Wed & 11am Sun

St Louis Gay/ Lesbian Chavurah 77 Maryland Plaza (at Central Reform Cong) **314/324-4936**

Trinity Episcopal Church 600 N Euclid Ave **314/361-4655** • 8am & 10:30am Sun

Erotica

Cheap Trx 3211 S Grand Blvd **314/664-4011** • body piercing • sex supplies

Montana

Billings

Bars

The Loft 2910 2nd Ave N (at 29th) **406/259-9074** • 4:30pm-2am • lesbians/ gay men • dancing/DJ • karaoke

Cafes

Cafe Jones 2712 2nd Ave N **406/259-7676** • 7am-4pm, clsd Sun

Erotica

Big Sky Books 1203 1st Ave N **406/259-0051**

Boulder

Accommodations

Boulder Hot Springs Hotel & Retreat **406/225-4339** • gay-friendly • also B&B • massage • workshops • food served • swimming • nudity allowed in hot springs • smokefree • kids ok • wheelchair access • $45-90

Bozeman

Info Lines & Services

QMSU—LGBT Alliance Strand Union Bldg Rm 273 (at MSU) **406/994-4551** • 7pm Tue

Women's Center 15 Hamilton Hall, MSU **406/994-3836** • some lesbian referrals • open Sept-May

Accommodations

Gallatin Gateway Inn 76405 Gallatin Rd/ Hwy 191 **406/763-4672, 800/676-3522** • gay-friendly • dinner nightly • hot tub • swimming • smokefree rooms available • kids ok • wheelchair access • $70-175

Lehrkind Mansion B&B 719 N Wallace Ave **406/585-6932, 800/992-6932** • gay-friendly • 1897 Queen Anne Victorian • full brkfst • hot tub • smokefree • $78-158

Bars

The Robin Lounge 105 W Main St (at the Baxter Hotel) **406/586-1314** • 4pm-2am • gay-friendly • 'Family Night' from 8pm Tue • karaoke

Cafes

The Leaf & Bean 35 W Main **406/587-1580** • 6:30am-10pm, till 11pm Fri-Sat • desserts • live shows • wheelchair access • women-owned/ run

Restaurants

Spanish Peaks Brewery 14 N Church (at Main) **406/585-2296** • 11:30am-10pm • Italian • some veggie • beer/ wine • wheelchair access • $8-15

Erotica

Ms Kitty's Adult Store 12 N Wilson **406/586-6989**

Butte

Accommodations

Snookums at the Skookum 3541 Harrison Ave **406/494-2153** • gay/ straight • also apts w/ kitchens • kids/ pets ok • $43-50

Bars

Snookums at the Skookum 3541 Harrison Ave **406/533-0919** • 7pm-2am, clsd Mon-Tue • lesbians/ gay men

Restaurants

Matt's Place 2339 Placer (btwn Montana & Rowe) **406/782-8049** • 11:30am-7pm, clsd Sun-Mon • classic soda fountain diner

Pekin Noodle Parlor 117 S Main, 2nd flr **406/782-2217** • 5pm-9pm, clsd Tue • Chinese • some veggie • $3-7

Pork Chop John's 8 W Mercury **406/782-0812** • 10:30am-7:30pm, clsd Sun • $3-5

Uptown Cafe 47 E Broadway **406/723-4735** • lunch & dinner • bistro • full bar • $15-20

Emigrant

Info Lines & Services

Yellowstone Riverview Lodge B&B 186 E River Rd **406/848-2156, 888/848-2550** • gay/ straight • also tipi • minutes from Yellowstone Nat'l Park • full brkfst • swimming • some shared baths • smokefree • gay-owned/ run • $70-110

Great Falls

Restaurants

Black Diamond Bar & Supper Club 64 Castner, Belt **406/277-4118** • 5pm-10pm, clsd Mon • steaks & seafood • 20 miles from Great Falls

Spiritual Groups

MCC Shepherd of the Plains 1501 & 1505 17th Ave SW **406/771-1070** • 11am Sun • call for social activities

Montana • USA

Helena

Info Lines & Services

PRIDE 406/442-9322, 800/610-9322 (in MT) • info • newsletter • political advocacy and education

Rainbow AA 400 S Oakes (at Plymouth Congregational Church) **406/442-9883** • 7pm Sun

Kalispell

Info Lines & Services

Flathead Valley Alliance 406/758-6707 • referrals

Accommodations

Cottonwood Hill Farm Inn 2928 Whitefish Stage Rd **406/756-6404, 800/458-0893** • gay-friendly • renovated farmhouse • full brkfst • smokefree • $80-135

Livingston

Accommodations

The River Inn On The Yellowstone 4950 Hwy 89 S **406/222-2429** • gay-friendly • cabins • full brkfst • smokefree • $95-140

Missoula

Info Lines & Services

Gay/ Lesbian AA 532 University Ave (at Lifeboat) **406/543-0011** • 7pm Mon

Lambda Alliance University Center #209 (at U of MT) **406/243-5922** • 8pm Mon (Sept-May)

Western Montana Gay/ Lesbian Community Center 615 Oak St **406/543-2224** • lgbt resource center • call for hours

Women's Resource Center University Ctr #210, Campus Dr (at U of MT) **406/243-4153** • 10am-3pm Sept-May, clsd wknds • call for summer hrs

Accommodations

Brooks St Motor Inn 3333 Brooks St (at MacDonald) **406/549-5115, 800/538-3260** • gay-friendly • motel • hot tub • smokefree rooms available • kids/ pets ok • wheelchair access • $37-130

Foxglove Cottage B&B 2331 Gilbert Ave **406/543-2927** • gay/ straight • 1800s guesthouse • swimming • sun room • gardens • some shared baths • smokefree • gay-owned/ run • $65-125

Bars

Amvets Club 525 Ryman (at Broadway) **406/543-9174** • noon-2am (more gay after 8pm) • gay-friendly • dancing/DJ

The Oxford 337 N Higgins (at Pine) **406/549-0117** • popular • gay-friendly • 8am-2am • 24hr cafe

Cafes

The Catalyst 111 N Higgins **406/542-1337** • 7am-6pm

The Raven Cafe 130 E Broadway **406/29-8188** • 8am-midnight, from 8am Sat • pool table • lgbt games night 6:30pm 2nd Tue

Restaurants

Montana Club/ Red Baron Casino 2620 Brooks **406/543-3200** • 6:30am-11pm, till midnight wknds, casino open till 2am • full bar • wheelchair access

New Black Dog Cafe 138 W Broadway **406/542-1138** • lunch & dinner, dinner only Sat, clsd Sun • vegetarian & vegan • wheelchair access

Entertainment & Recreation

Gay Outdoors (GO!) **406/543-2224** • gay hiking & rockclimbing expeditions • all levels welcome

Pangaea Expeditions 406/721-7719

Bookstores

Fact & Fiction 220 N Higgins **406/721-2881** • 9am-8pm, 10am-5pm Sat, noon-4pm Sun • many lgbt titles • wheelchair access

University Center Bookstore Campus Dr (at U of MT) **406/243-4921** • 8am-6pm, from 10am Sat, clsd Sun • gender studies section

Spiritual Groups

University Congregation Christian Church 405 University Ave **406/543-6952** • 9am & 10:30am Sun, also 5pm Sat

Erotica

Fantasy for Adults Only 210 E Main St **406/543-7760** • 24hrs Fri-Sat • also 2611 Brooks Ave, 406/543-7510

Ovando

Accommodations

Lake Upsata Guest Ranch **406/793-5890, 800/594-7687** • gay-friendly • cabins • hot tub • seasonal • wildlife programs & outings • outdoor recreation • meals provided • kids ok • $220 per person

Ronan

ACCOMMODATIONS

North Crow Ranch 2360 N Crow Rd 406/676-5169 • seasonal • lesbians/ gay men • cabin • tipis • camping • 80 miles south of Glacier Park • hot tub • nudity • seasonal • lesbian-owned/ run • $15-100

NEBRASKA

Statewide

INFO LINES & SERVICES

Nebraska Travel & Tourism 800/228-4307

Bellevue

ACCOMMODATIONS

Quality Inn & Suites Bellevue 1811 Hillcrest Dr (Hwy 370) 402/292-3800, 800/292-7277 • gay-friendly • kids/ pets ok • swimming • hot tub • wheelchair access • $55-129

Grand Island

INFO LINES & SERVICES

Helpline 308/384-7474 • 24hrs • some gay referrals • crisis calls

ACCOMMODATIONS

Midtown Holiday Inn 2503 S Locust 308/384-1330 • gay-friendly • smokefree rooms available • kids/ pets ok • hot tub • swimming • also 'Images Pink Cadillac Lounge' • wheelchair access • $59-75

Relax Inn 507 W 2nd St 308/384-1000 • gay-friendly • wheelchair access • $35-40

BARS

Desert Rose Saloon 3235 S Locust (at 34th) 308/381-8919 • 7pm-1:30am, clsd Sun-Tue • gay-friendly • wheelchair access

Nathan Detroit's 316 N Pine St 308/384-3655 • 11am-1am • gay-friendly • neighborhood bar • food served • wheelchair access

RESTAURANTS

Tommy's 1325 S Locust 308/381-0440 • 24hrs

GYMS & HEALTH CLUBS

Health Plex Fitness Center 2909 W Hwy 30 308/384-1110 • gay-friendly

EROTICA

Exclusively Yours Shop 214 N Locust 308/381-6984 • adult toys • lingerie

Sweet Dreams Shop 217 W 3rd St 308/381-6349 • lingerie • adult toys

Hastings

INFO LINES & SERVICES

GLB Alliance Health Center, Hastings College (at Turner) 402/461-7372 • call for meeting locations

Kearney

BARS

Captain's Table 110 S 2nd Ave (at Holiday Inn) 308/237-5971 • noon-11pm, later wknds • gay-friendly • restaurant

RETAIL SHOPS

Hastings Store 9 W 39th St 308/234-1130 • 10am-11pm • gay gifts & books

Lincoln

INFO LINES & SERVICES

AA Gay/ Lesbian 2748 'S' St (3rd floor at 'The Meeting Place') 402/438-5214 • 7:30pm Mon

Crisis Center 402/476-2110, 402/475-7273 (24HRS)

Women's Resource Center Nebraska Union Rm 340, UNL 402/472-2597 • lesbian support services • wheelchair access

BARS

Panic 200 S 18th St (at 'N') 402/435-8764 • 4pm-1am, from 1pm wknds • lesbians/ gay men • live shows • karaoke • Internet access • patio • wheelchair access • gay-owned/ run

NIGHTCLUBS

The Q 226 S 9th (btwn 'M' & 'N') 402/475-2269 • 8pm-1am, clsd Mon • lesbians/ gay men • dancing/DJ • live shows • karaoke • 19+ Tue

ENTERTAINMENT & RECREATION

Wimmin's Radio Show KZUM 89.3 FM 402/474-5086 • 12:30pm-3pm Sun • also 'TGI-Femmes' 10am-noon Fri

RETAIL SHOPS

Avant Card 1323 'O' St (btwn 13th & 14th) 402/476-1918 • hours vary • also a location at Gateway Mall (61st & O St) 402/ 476-1918

Omaha

INFO LINES & SERVICES

AA Gay/ Lesbian 851 N 74th (at Presbyterian church) 402/556-1880 • 8:15pm Fri

Nebraska/ Nevada • USA

OPC (Omaha Players Club) 4332 Browne St • S/M education & play group • pansexual mtgs

Rainbow Outreach Center 1719 Leavenworth St **402/341-0330** • 6pm-9pm, noon-6pm Sat, clsd Sun • Fri movie night • 24hr info

Accommodations

Castle Unicorn 57034 Deacon Rd (at Hwy 34 & I-29), Pacific Jct, IA **712/527-5930** • gay/ straight • medieval style B&B • full brkfst • hot tub • sauna • patio • gay-owned/ run

The Cornerstone B&B 140 N 39th St (at Dodge) **402/558-7600** • gay-friendly • 1894 historic mansion • fireplaces • nr downtown • food served • smokefree • commitment ceremonies • $80-110

Howard Johnson Plaza Hotel 4706 S 108th St **402/339-7400** • gay-friendly • kids/ pets ok • swimming • hot tub • $59-84

Bars

Connections 1901 Leavenworth St (at 19th) **402/933-3033** • 3pm-1am • popular • lesbians/ gay men • dancing/DJ • food served • live shows • karaoke • wheelchair access • lesbian-owned/ run

DC's Saloon 610 S 14th St (at Jackson) **402/344-3103** • 3pm-1am, from 2pm wknds • lesbians/ gay men • neighborhood bar • dancing/DJ • country/ western • live shows • wheelchair access

Diamond Bar 712 S 16th St **402/342-9595** • 10am-1am • mostly gay men • neighborhood bar • wheelchair access

Gilligan's Pub 1407 Harney St (at 14th St) **402/449-9147** • 4pm-1am, till 4am Fri-Sat • lesbians/ gay men • neighborhood bar • karaoke • also restaurant • wheelchair access

The Junction 1507 Farnam (at 15th) **402/341-2500** • 4pm-1am • gay-friendly • dancing/DJ • Sun Latin night

Nightclubs

Joy 1516 Jones (at 15th) **402/341-7337** • 4pm-1am, clsd Mon-Wed • lesbians/ gay men • dancing • upscale • live shows • young crowd • gay-owned

The Max 1417 Jackson (at 15th St) **402/346-4110** • 4pm-1am • popular • mostly gay men • 6 bars • dancing/DJ Wed-Sun • live shows Fri & Sun • videos • patio • wheelchair access

Cafes

Stage Right 401 S 16th (at Harney) **402/346-7675** • 7am-11pm, 10am wknds, till 5pm Sun • live shows wknds

Restaurants

Daisy May's 521 S 13th (at Jackson) **402/346-9342** • 11am-9pm, till 10pm Th-Sat, clsd Sun • live shows

Dixie Quick's 105 S 15th (at Dodge) **402/346-3549** • lunch & dinner, Sun brunch, clsd Mon-Tue • Southern

French Cafe 1017 Howard St **402/341-3547** • lunch & dinner, Sun brunch • full bar • $11-22

Entertainment & Recreation

HGRA (Heartland Gay Rodeo Association) **800/561-6918**

River City Mixed Chorus **402/341-7464**

Bookstores

New Realities 1026 Howard St (in the Old Market) **402/342-1863** • 11am-10pm, till 11pm Fri-Sat, till 6pm Sun • progressive • wheelchair access

Retail Shops

Bare Images 4332 Browne St **402/451-7987** • noon-7pm Th-Sat • piercing

Villain's 3629 'Q' St **402/731-0202** • noon-8pm, till 5pm Sun • tattooing • piercing

Spiritual Groups

MCC of Omaha 819 S 22nd St **402/345-2563** • 8:50am & 10:20am Sun • also support groups

Scottsbluff

Restaurants

Pasta Villa 1455 10th St (at "O" St), Gering **308/436-5900** • 11am-8pm, clsd Sun-Mon • lesbian-owned/ run

NEVADA

Lake Tahoe

see also Lake Tahoe, California

Accommodations

Haus Bavaria **775/831-6122, 800/731-6222** • gay-friendly • mountain views • full brkfst • smokefree • kids ok • gay-owned/ run • $99-250

The Mountain Retreat 275 Tramway Dr (at Boulder Ct), Stateline **530/582-5670** • lesbians/ gay men • luxury townhouse • swimming • hot tub • sundeck • also skiing & hiking tours • gay-owned/ run

Nightclubs

Faces 270 Kingsbury Grade, Stateline **775/588-2333** • 5pm-2am, till 4am Fri-Sat • lesbians/ gay men • dancing/DJ

Las Vegas • Nevada

Las Vegas

INFO LINES & SERVICES

Alcoholics Together 2630 State St #233 **702/737-0035** • 12:15pm & 8pm • women-only meeting 6:30pm Fri • lgbt club for 12-step recovery programs • call for directions

Gay/ Lesbian Community Center 912 E Sahara Ave **702/733-9800** • 9am-8pm, clsd wknds

ACCOMMODATIONS

Viva Las Vegas Villas 1205 Las Vegas Blvd **702/384-0771, 800/574-4450** • gay-friendly • campy themed rms • smokefree • onsite disco • also commitment ceremonies • $75-175

BARS

Angles Lounge/ Club Lace 4633 Paradise Rd (at Naples) **702/791-0100** • 3pm-close • lesbians/ gay men • neighborhood bar • videos • also 'Club Lace' from 10:30pm Wed-Sat • dancing/ DJ • more women Fri • wheelchair access

Backdoor Lounge 1415 E Charleston (nr Maryland Pkwy) **702/385-2018** • 24hrs • mostly gay men • neighborhood bar • dancing/DJ • live shows • patio • swimming • Latin night Fri • wheelchair access

Backstreet 5012 S Arville Rd (at Tropicana) **702/876-1844** • popular • lesbians/ gay men • dancing/DJ Wed-Sun • country/ western • wheelchair access

Las Vegas

LGBT PRIDE: May. 702/225-3389 (SNAPI Hotline), web: www.vegaspride.com.

ANNUAL EVENTS: March - NGRA (Nat'l Gay Rodeo Assn) Bighorn Rodeo 888/643-6472, web: members.aol.com/ngra99.

CITY INFO: Convention & Visitors Authority 702/892-0711.

ATTRACTIONS: Bellagio Art Gallery 702/693-7111.
Guinness World Records Museum 702/792-3766.
Hoover Dam.
Imperial Palace Auto Collection 702/731-3311.
King Tut Museum (at the Luxor) 702/262-4000.
La Cage at the Riveria 702/794-9433.
Las Vegas Art Museum 702/360-8000.
Liberace Museum 702/798-5595.
Museum of Natural History 702/384-3466.
StarTrek: The Experience.

BEST VIEW: Top of the Stratosphere. Or hurtling through the loops of the rollercoaster atop the New York New York Hotel. (Note: Do not ride immediately after the buffet.)

TRANSIT: Western Cab 702/382-7100.
Yellow Cab 702/873-2000.
Various resorts have their own shuttle service.
CAT (Citizens Area Transit) 702/228-7433.

Nevada • USA

Badlands Saloon 953 E Sahara #22 (in Commercial Ctr) 702/792-9262 • 24hrs • mostly gay men • neighborhood bar • dancing/DJ • country/western • wheelchair access • gay-owned/run

The Buffalo 4640 Paradise Rd (at Naples) 702/733-8355 • 24hrs • popular • mostly gay men • leather • videos • wheelchair access

Flex 4371 W Charleston (at Arville) 702/385-3539 • 24hrs • lesbians/gay men • dancing/DJ • live shows • karaoke

Freezone 610 E Naples 702/794-2300 • 24hrs • lesbians/gay men • women's night Tue • Latin Wed • neighborhood bar • dancing/DJ • transgender-friendly • live shows • karaoke • young crowd • also restaurant • gay-owned/run

Goodtimes 1775 E Tropicana (at Spencer, in Liberace Plaza) 702/736-9494 • 24hrs • mostly gay men • more women Mon & Wed • neighborhood bar • dancing/DJ Fri, Sat & Mon 10pm-4am • karaoke • wheelchair access

Keys 1000 E Sahara Ave 702/731-2200 • 10am-4am • lesbians/gay men • piano bar • also restaurant • live shows • gay-owned/run

The Las Vegas Eagle 3430 E Tropicana (at Pecos) 702/458-8662 • 24hrs • mostly gay men • leather • DJ Wed, Fri & Sat • also 'The Annex' bar 8pm-4am Wed & Fri

Las Vegas Lounge 900 E Karen Ave 702/737-9350 • 24hrs • neighborhood bar • mostly transgender • live shows • also 2 restaurants • gay-owned/run

Phoenix 40 N Nellis 702/438-3050 • 24hrs • lesbians/gay men

NIGHTCLUBS

The Bird Cage 207 N 3rd (at Ogden) 702/598-2030 • 9pm-5am • lesbians/gay men • dancing/DJ • transgender-friendly • live shows • also restaurant & juice bar • wheelchair access

The Gipsy 4605 S Paradise Rd (at Naples) 702/731-1919 • 10pm-close • popular • mostly gay men • dancing/DJ • Latin night Mon • live shows • videos • young crowd

House of Blues 3950 Las Vegas Blvd S (at Hacienda Ave in 'Madalay Bay') 702/632-7600 • gay-friendly • dancing/DJ • also restaurant • live shows • cover charge • more gay from 11pm Sun & Th

CAFES

Cool Beans 900 E Karen Ave #H108 702/693-6327 • 7am-midnight, from 11am Sun • sandwiches & desserts • plenty veggie • Internet access • women's night Fri • wheelchair access • gay-owned/run

Espresso Roma Cafe 4440 S Maryland Pkwy 702/369-1540 • 7am-midnight, from 8am wknds • open mic Sun-Mon • live music

Mermaid Cafe 2910 Lake East Dr (off Canyon Gate) 702/240-6002 • open till 11pm, till midnight Fri-Sat • beer/wine • live entertainment

RESTAURANTS

Coyote Cafe 3799 S Las Vegas Blvd (in 'MGM Grand') 702/891-7349, 888/757-2572 • 8:30am-11pm • the original Santa Fe chef • wheelchair access • $8-18

Mama Jo's 3655 S Durango 702/869-8099 • lunch & dinner • Italian

The Raw Truth 3620 E Flamingo 702/450-9007 • 9am-9pm, 11am-6pm Sun • organic vegan • juice bar • $4-8

Sushi Boy Desu 4632 S Maryland Pkwy #12 702/736-8234 • 11am-10pm

ENTERTAINMENT & RECREATION

Crystal Palace Skating Rink 4680 Boulder Hwy 702/458-7107 • 8:30pm-11pm 3rd Mon • lgbt skate

Cupid's Wedding Chapel 827 Las Vegas Blvd 702/598-4444, 800/543-2933 • commitment ceremonies • "Have the Vegas wedding you've always dreamed of!"

The Forum Shops at Caesars 3570 Las Vegas Blvd S (in 'Caesars Palace') • you saw it in 'Showgirls' & many other movies, now come shop for yourself

King Tutankhamun's Tomb & Museum 3900 Las Vegas Blvd S (in the 'Luxor Las Vegas') 702/262-4555 • exact replica of the tomb when Howard Carter opened it in 1922

La Cage 2901 Las Vegas Blvd (at the Riviera) 702/794-9433 • the biggest drag show in town • Frank Marino & friends impersonate the divas, from Joan Rivers to Tina Turner

Las Vegas Gay & Lesbian Chorus 702/594-3393

Liberace Museum 1775 E Tropicana Ave 702/798-5595 • this is one queen's closet you have to look into—especially if you love your pianos, clothes & cars covered w/ diamonds

The Volcano at The Mirage 3400 Las Vegas Blvd S • see the gimmick that inspired the rest of the showstoppers along the Strip—erupts every few minutes after dark

BOOKSTORES

Borders 2323 S Decatur (at Sahara) 702/258-0999 • 9am-11pm, till 9pm Sun • lgbt section • cafe • wheelchair access

Reno • Nevada

Get Booked 4640 Paradise #15 (at Naples) **702/737-7780** • 10am-midnight, till 2am Fri-Sat • lgbt

Retail Shops

Sin City 1013 Charleston (at Main) **702/387-6969** • piercing & tattoo studio

Publications

Las Vegas Bugle 702/369-6260 • lgbt newspaper

Lesbian Voice 702/650-0636 • monthly magazine

Out Las Vegas 702/650-0636 • monthly lgbt entertainment newspaper

Spiritual Groups

Christ Church Episcopal 2000 S Maryland Pkwy (at E St Louis) **702/735-7655** • 8am, 10:30am & 6pm Sun, 10am & 6pm Wed

Dignity Las Vegas 1420 E Harmon Ave (in upstairs chapel at First Church) **702/593-5395** • 5:30pm Sat • call for location

MCC of Las Vegas 1140 Almond Tree Ln #302 (in the East Wing) **702/369-4380** • 10am Sun & 6pm Wed

Valley Outreach Synagogue 2020 W Horizon Ridge Pkwy **702/436-4900** • 7:45pm 1st Fri • gay-friendly

Erotica

Bare Essentials Fantasy Fashions 4029 W Sahara Ave (nr Valley View Blvd) **702/247-4711** • exotic/ intimate apparel • toys • gay-owned/ run

Pal Joey's 3084 S Highland #C **702/734-7589** • fetishwear • also tattoos & piercing

Price Video 700 E Naples Dr #102 (at Swenson) **702/734-1342**

Rancho Adult Entertainment Center 4820 N Rancho #D (at Bone Mtn) **702/645-6104** • 24hrs

Video West 5785 W Tropicana (at Jones) **702/248-7055** • gay-owned/ run

Laughlin

see Bullhead City, Arizona

Reno

Info Lines & Services

A Rainbow Place 33 St Lawrence Ave (at Tahoe) **775/789-1780, 800/627-1168(24HRS)** • call for hours • northern NV's lgbt center • movie night Wed • library • mtgs • resources • newsletter • also crisis line: 800/ 856-1162

Accommodations

Holiday Inn & Diamonds Casino 1000 E 6th St (at Wells Ave) **775/786-5151, 800/648-4877** • gay-friendly • swimming • kids/ pets ok • wheelchair access • $59-139

Bars

1099 Club 1099 S Virginia St (at Vassar) **775/329-1099** • 24hrs • popular • lesbians/ gay men • neighborhood bar • live shows • videos • patio • wheelchair access

Carl's Pub 3310 S Virginia St (at Moana) **775/829-8886** • 11am-3am • lesbians/ gay men • neighborhood bar • dancing/DJ • patio

Five Star Saloon 132 West St (at 1st) **775/329-2878** • 24hrs • mostly gay men • neighborhood bar • dancing/DJ • food served • wheelchair access

The Patio 600 W 5th St (btwn Washington & Ralston) **775/323-6565** • 11am-2am • lesbians/ gay men • more women Fri • neighborhood bar

The Quest 210 W Commercial Row (at West) **775/333-2808** • noon-5am, 24hrs wknds • mostly gay men • dancing/DJ • transgender-friendly • live shows

Nightclubs

Visions 340 Kietzke Ln (btwn Glendale & Mill) **775/786-5455** • noon-6am • popular • mostly gay men • dancing/DJ • food served • young crowd • patio • also 'Glitter Palace' gift shop Wed-Sun

Cafes

Sassy's Cafe & Deli 195 N Edison (at Mill) **775/856-3501** • 7:30am-4pm, clsd Sat, call for special coffee hour events Sun • women-owned/ run

Bookstores

Borders 4995 S Virginia St **775/448-9999** • 9am-11pm • lgbt section

Sundance Books 1155 W 4th St (at Keystone) **775/786-1188** • 9am-9pm, 10am-6pm wknds

Publications

Reno Informer 775/747-8833, 877/387-3385 • northern Nevada's lgbt newspaper

Spiritual Groups

MCC of the Sierras 3405 Gulling Rd (at Temple Sinai') **775/829-8602** • 5pm Sun

Erotica

The Chocolate Walrus 160 E Grove **775/825-2267** • clsd Sun • popular

Nevada/ New Hampshire • USA

Fantasy Faire 1298 S Virginia (at Arroyo) 775/323-6969 • leather • fetishwear

Suzie's 195 Kietzke Ln (at E 2nd St) 775/786-8557 • 24hrs

NEW HAMPSHIRE

Statewide

INFO LINES & SERVICES

Rainbow Resources 603/224-1686 • active social & support groups • referrals • covers NH & VT • also some info for ME & northern MA

Travel & Tourism Office 603/271-2666, 800/386-4664

PUBLICATIONS

In Newsweekly 617/426-8246 • New England's lgbt newspaper

Bath

ACCOMMODATIONS

Hibbard House 603/747-3947, 888/338-3947 • gay/ straight • 1822 inn • full brkfst • some shared baths • hot tub • nudity • smokefree • camping available • $40-130

Bridgewater

ACCOMMODATIONS

The Inn on Newfound Lake 1030 Mayhew Trpk Rte 3-A 603/744-9111, 800/745-7990 • gay/ straight • swimming • also restaurant • full bar • gay-owned/ run • $65-225

Dover

INFO LINES & SERVICES

LGBT Helpline 141 Central Ave (at Quaker Mtg House) 603/743-4292, 603/742-4470 • 7pm Sun, support group

ACCOMMODATIONS

Payne's Hill B&B 141 Henry Law Ave 603/742-4139 • women-only • restored 1800s private home • music room • smokefree • lesbian-owned/ run • $80

Durham

INFO LINES & SERVICES

The UNH Alliance 603/862-4522 • 7pm Mon

ACCOMMODATIONS

Three Chimneys Inn 17 Newmarket Rd (at Rte 4) 603/868-7800, 888/399-9777 • gay-friendly • elegant 1649 house on Oyster River nr Portsmouth • food served • jacuzzi • smokefree • wheelchair access • $119-189

Fitzwilliam

ACCOMMODATIONS

Hannah Davis House 603/585-3344 • gay/ straight • historic 1820 Federal bldg • full brkfst • kids ok • smokefree • $70-140

Keene

ACCOMMODATIONS

The Post and Beam B&B 18 Centre St, Sullivan 603/847-3330, 888/376-6262 • gay/ straight • 1797 Colonial farmstead • full brkfst • hot tub • patio • kids 7+/ pets ok • smokefree • wheelchair access • lesbian-owned/ run • $70-125

Manchester

BARS

313 313-B Lincoln St (at Valley) 603/628-6813 • 2pm-1am, from noon wknds • lesbians/ gay men • women's night Mon • country/ western Wed • dancing/DJ • food served • karaoke • live shows • videos • wheelchair access

The Breezeway 14 Pearl St 603/621-9111 • 4pm-close • lesbians/ gay men • popular • neighborhood bar • dancing/DJ • karaoke • gay-owned/ run

Front Runner/ Manchester Civic Club 22 Fir St (at Elm St) 603/623-6477 • 5pm-1:30am, from 3pm Sun • lesbians/ gay men • dancing/DJ Th-Fri • transgender-friendly • live shows • private club

Sporters 361 Pine St (at Hanover) 603/668-9014 • 5pm-1am, mostly gay men • neighborhood bar • food served wknds

North Conway

ACCOMMODATIONS

The Inn at Crystal Lake Route 153 Eaton Center, Conway/ Eaton 603/447-2120, 800/343-7336 • gay/ straight • full brkfst • kids over 8yrs ok • gay-owned • $79-199

Portsmouth

BOOKSTORES

Artistic Amazon Bookstore 28 Chapel St (btwn Daniels & State) 603/422-0702, 877/422-0702 • call for hours • lgbt

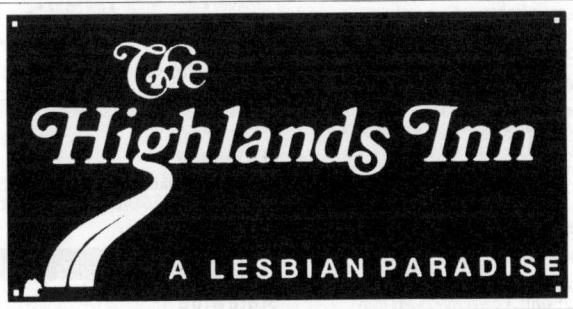

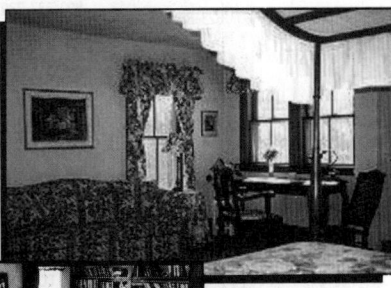

Secluded, romantic mountain hideaway on 100 scenic acres, centrally located between Boston, Montreal & the Maine coast. Close to Provincetown.

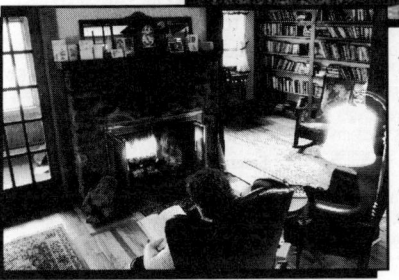

Experience the warm hospitality of a New England country inn YOUR way... a lesbian paradise!

**PO BOX 118WT
VALLEY VIEW LANE
BETHLEHEM, NEW HAMPSHIRE 03574
603 • 869 • 3978
1-877-LES-B-INN (537-2466)
vacation@highlandsinn-nh.com
www.highlandsinn-nh.com**

See Our Listing Under New Hampshire

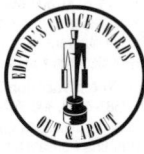

New Hampshire/ New Jersey • USA

EROTICA

Spaulding Book & Video 80 Spaulding Tpke **603/430-9760** • gay-owned/ run

Suncook

ACCOMMODATIONS

White Rabbit Inn 62 Main St, Allenstown **603/485-9494** • gay/ straight • full brkfst • personalized meals offered by chef/ host • swimming • hot tub • also bar • kids/ pets ok • $75-130

White Mtns

ACCOMMODATIONS

Bungay Jar B&B & Cottage **603/823-7775, 800/421-0701** • gay-friendly • renovated farmhouse • full brkfst • sauna • smokefree • kids/ pets ok in cottage • wheelchair access • $105-225

Foxglove, A Country Inn **603/823-8840, 888/343-2220** • gay-friendly • 1898 country estate • full brkfst • smokefree • $85-165/ two people

▲ **Highlands Inn** Bethlehem **603/869-3978, 877/LES-B-INN (537-2466)** • a lesbian paradise • women only • full brkfst • ignore 'no vacancy' sign • hot tub • swimming • kids/ pets ok • 100 mtn acres • special event wknds • wheelchair access • lesbian-owned/ run • $75-125 • see color ad on page 3

The Horse & Hound Inn 205 Wells Rd, Franconia **603/823-5501, 800/450-5501** • clsd April & Nov • gay-friendly • 1830s farmhouse • full brkfst • kids/ pets ok • also restaurant • gay-owned/ run • $86-101

The Inn at Bowman Rte 2, Randolph **603/466-5006, 888/919-8500** • gay/ straight • country inn gracing the White Mtns w/ charm & comfort • swimming • hot tub • smokefree • gay-owned/ run • $79-179

Mulburn Inn at Bethlehem 2370 Main St/ Rte 302, Bethlehem **603/869-3389, 800/457-9440** • gay/ straight • Victorian B&B • full brkfst • hot tub • smokefree • women-owned/ run • $80-155

The Notchland Inn Rte 302, Hart's Location **603/374-6131, 800/866-6131** • gay/ straight • 1860s granite mansion on 400 acres • full brkfst • other meals available • smokefree • gay-owned/ run • $175-285

Top Notch Vacation Rentals Rte 302, Glen **603/383-4133, 800/762-6636** • gay-friendly • 1- to 5-bdrm condos, cottages & chalets • swimming • private wooded areas • mtn views • $75-450

Wildcat Inn & Tavern Rte 16A, Jackson Village **603/383-4245, 800/228-4245** • gay-friendly • also cottage • full brkfst • 2 restaurants • $109-350

Will's Inn Rte 302, Glen **603/383-6757, 800/233-6780** • gay-friendly • traditional New England motor inn • 2-bdrm cottages available • swimming • smokefree • kids ok • $49-199

RESTAURANTS

Polly's Pancake Parlor Rte 117 (exit 38 off 93 N), Sugar Hill **603/823-5575** • 7am-3pm, clsd winters

NEW JERSEY

Statewide

INFO LINES & SERVICES

New Jersey Division of Travel & Tourism **800/537-7397**

ENTERTAINMENT & RECREATION

Out & About **201/843-1749** • lesbian hiking & outdoors adventures • call for events

Asbury Park

BARS

Anybodys 108 St James Pl (at Cookman Ave) **732/774-0123** • 3pm-2am • mostly gay men • neighborhood bar • leather • multiracial clientele • transgender-friendly • live entertainment • 18+ • gay-owned/ run

NIGHTCLUBS

Paradise 101 Asbury Ave (at Ocean Ave) **732/988-6663** • 4pm-2am • lesbians/ gay men • dancing/DJ • 2 dance flrs • live shows • piano bar • tiki/pool bar in summer

RESTAURANTS

Emeralds & Pearls 535 Bangs Ave **732/774-3522** • 4pm-9pm, till 11pm Th-Sat, clsd Sun • also gift shop

SPIRITUAL GROUPS

Trinity Episcopal Church 503 Asbury Ave (at Grand Ave) **732/775-5084** • 8am & 10am Sun • call for Integrity mtg info

Atlantic City

BARS

Brass Rail Bar & Grill at 'Surfside Resort Hotel' **609/348-0192** • 24hrs • popular • lesbians/ gay men • neighborhood bar • karaoke • live shows • food served • gay-owned/ run

Jersey City • New Jersey

Reflections 130 South Carolina Ave (at Pacific) **609/348-1115** • 5pm-4am • lesbians/gay men • neighborhood bar • videos

Nightclubs

Studio Six Video Dance Club upstairs at 'Brass Rail' **609/348-3310** • 10pm-close • popular • lesbians/gay men • dancing/DJ • live shows • videos

Restaurants

Mama Mott's 151 S New York Ave (at Pacific) **609/345-8218** • dinner nightly • Italian & seafood • wheelchair access

White House Sub Shop 2301 Arctic Ave (at Mississippi) **609/345-1564** • 10am-10pm, till 11pm Fri-Sat, from 11am Sun

Bloomingdale

Entertainment & Recreation

Gal-a-vanting **973/838-5318** • sponsors women's parties • call for details

Boonton

Nightclubs

Connexions 202 Myrtle Ave (off Washington) **973/263-4000** • 11:30am-2am, from 4pm wknds • lesbians/gay men • dancing/DJ • country/western Tue • food served • drag shows • karaoke Mon

Camden

see also Philadelphia, Pennsylvania

Entertainment & Recreation

The Walt Whitman House 328 Mickle Blvd (btwn S 3rd & S 4th Sts) **856/964-5383** • the last home of America's great & controversial poet

Cape May

Accommodations

The Virginia Hotel 25 Jackson St (btwn Beach Dr & Carpenter's Ln) **609/884-5700, 800/732-4236** • gay-friendly • also 'The Ebbitt Room' restaurant • seafood/cont'l • $80-345

Cafes

Brad's Beachfront Cafe 314 Beach Dr (at Jackson) **609/898-6050** • 7am-10pm in summer

Cherry Hill

see also Philadelphia, Pennsylvania

Spiritual Groups

Unitarian Universalist Church 401 N Kings Hwy (btwn Chapel & Church) **856/667-3618** • 10:15am Sun

East Rutherford

Nightclubs

Topaz 225 Paterson Ave **973/815-1122** • open Wed-Sun • lesbians/gay men • dancing/DJ • karaoke • live shows

Edison

Spiritual Groups

New Jersey's Lesbian & Gay Havurah **732/650-1010**

Egg Harbor City

Bars

Red Moon Saloon 5027 White Horse Pike **609/965-4755** • 6pm-3am • gay/straight • neighborhood bar • also restaurant

Florence

Erotica

Florence Book Store Rte 130 S (4 miles S of Rte 206) **609/499-9853**

Hoboken

Nightclubs

Excalibur 2001 1000 Jefferson St (at 10th St) **201/795-1023** • 9pm-3am Fri-Sat only • popular • lesbians/gay men • dancing/DJ • live shows • wheelchair access

Maxwell's 1039 Washington St **201/656-9632** • popular • gay-friendly • alternative • live music venue

Jersey City

Nightclubs

Saturdaze at Club Albert's 360 Marin Blvd **973/497-0246 (Mikey), 973/420-5077 (Nita)** • 10:30pm-3am • mostly women • dancing/DJ • hip-hop/R&B • cover charge from midnight

Spiritual Groups

Christ United Methodist Church Tonnele Ave & JFK Blvd **201/332-8996** • also support groups

New Jersey • USA

Lambertville

see also New Hope, Pennsylvania

ACCOMMODATIONS

York Street House B&B 42 York St **609/397-3007** • gay-friendly • full brkfst • smokefree • lesbian-owned/run • $125-185

EROTICA

Joy's Books 103 Springbrook Ave (nr Bridge St) **609/397-2907**

Madison

BOOKSTORES

Pandora Book Peddlers 9 Waverly Pl (at Main) **973/822-8388** • 10am-6pm, noon-5pm Mon, till 8pm Th, clsd Sun • feminist bookstore & book club

Maplewood

SPIRITUAL GROUPS

Dignity Metro New Jersey 550 Ridgewood Rd (at St George's Episcopal Church) **973/857-4040** • 4pm 3rd Sun

Montclair

BOOKSTORES

Cohen's 635 Bloomfield Ave (at Valley) **973/744-2399** • 7am-8pm, clsd Sun

EROTICA

Dressing for Pleasure 590 Valley Rd **973/746-5466** • clsd Mon • lingerie • latex • leather

Morristown

INFO LINES & SERVICES

Gay Activist Alliance in Morris County 21 Normandy Hts Rd (at Unitarian Fellowship) **973/285-1595** • info line 7:30pm-10:30pm • also women's network

New Brunswick

INFO LINES & SERVICES

Pride Center of New Jersey 211 Livingston Ave (at Comstock) **732/846-2232** • info line • meeting space for various groups • call for info

BARS

The Den 700 Hamilton St (at Douglas), Somerset **732/545-7329** • 5pm-2am Tue-Wed, from 8pm Th-Sun, clsd Mon • popular • mostly gay men • dancing/DJ Fri-Sat • country/western Fri • multiracial • live shows • videos • wheelchair access

RESTAURANTS

The Frog and the Peach 29 Dennis St (at Hiram Sq) **732/846-3216** • lunch Mon-Fri, dinner nightly • full bar • wheelchair access • $40-60

Stage Left 5 Livingston Ave (at George) **732/828-4444** • popular • lesbians/gay men • some veggie • full bar • patio • wheelchair access • expensive

SPIRITUAL GROUPS

Emanuel Lutheran Church New & Kirkpatrick **732/545-2673** • 10:30am Sun • wheelchair access

MCC of Christ the Liberator 416 Victoria Ave (at Circle Playhouse), Piscataway **732/846-8227** • 10:45am Sun

Newark

BARS

Murphy's Tavern 59 Edison Pl (btwn Broad & Mulberry) **973/622-9176** • 8pm-2am • lesbians/gay men • neighborhood bar • dancing/DJ Th-Sat • mostly African-American

SPIRITUAL GROUPS

Liberation in Truth Unity Fellowship Church 608 Broad St (in Trinity & St Phillip's Cathedral) **973/621-2100** • 3:30pm Sun

Plainfield

ACCOMMODATIONS

▲ **The Pillars** 922 Central Ave (at 9th St) **908/753-0922, 888/PILLARS (745-5277)** • gay/straight • Georgian/Victorian mansion • full brkfst • smokefree • infants & kids over 12 ok • dogs ok (call first) • gay-owned/run • $99-125

Rahway

CAFES

Eat to the Beat Coffeehouse 1465 Irving St (at E Cherry) **732/381-0505** • 11am-10pm, till midnight Fri-Sat • plenty veggie • live shows

Red Bank

BOOKSTORES

Earth Spirit 16 W Front St (at Broad) **732/842-3855** • 10am-6pm, till 8pm Fri, noon-5pm Sun • new age center & bookstore • lgbt sections

River Edge

Nightclubs

Feathers 77 Kinder Kamack Rd (at Grand) **201/342-6410** • 9pm-2am, till 3am Sat • popular • mostly gay men • dancing/DJ • karaoke • live shows • videos • young crowd • wheelchair access

Rosemont

Restaurants

The Cafe 88 Kingwood-Stockton Rd **609/397-4097** • 8am-3pm, from 9am wknds, dinner 5pm-9pm Wed-Sun, clsd Mon • BYOB

Sayreville

Bars

Sauvage 1 Victory Bridge Plaza (off Rt 9 & 35) **732/727-6619** • 7pm-3am, from 4pm Sun • women only • neighborhood bar • live shows • food served

Nightclubs

Colosseum 7090 Rte 9 N (at Rte 35 N) **732/316-0670** • 9pm-3am, clsd Mon • lesbians/gay men • dancing/DJ • salsa Sat • 18+ • live shows • drag Tue • women's party 3rd Sun

Restaurants

Cagney's Pub & Restaurant 3276 Washington Rd **732/525-5586** • 3pm-2am • also bar • karaoke • dancing/DJ

Sergeantsville

see New Hope, Pennsylvania

Stockton

Accommodations

Woolverton Inn 6 Woolverton Rd **609/397-0802, 888/264-6648** • gay-friendly • full brkfst • jacuzzi • wheelchair access • $100-295

Trenton

Bars

Buddies Pub 677 S Broad St (at Madison) **609/989-8566** • 5pm-2am, from 6pm wknds • lesbians/gay men • neighborhood bar • dancing/DJ wknds

Restaurants

Center House 499 Center St (at Cass) **609/599-9558** • 11am-midnight, till 11pm Fri-Sat, from 5pm Sat, clsd Sun-Mon • also bar

---

The Pillars B&B
Located in the Gay Capital of New Jersey

A restored Victorian Mansion on a secluded acre of trees and wildflowers, in the Van Wyck Brooks Historic District, offering the G/L/B/T guest an experierience of gracious hospitality. Breakfasts feature Swedish home baking or cook your own vegetarian meals. Afternoon and evening wine or other beverages. Private baths, terry robes, and many other amenities for your comfort and convenience. Easy access to NYC, Jersey Shore, Women's bars, major interstate highways. Ideal for the business traveller. Member IGLTA. Call for rates. Reservations required.

922 Central Ave. Plainfield, New Jersey 07060
(800) 888-Pillars • (908)753-0922
Website: http://www.pillars2.com
Email: pillars2@juno.com

New Jersey/ New Mexico • USA

Westville

see also Philadelphia, Pennsylvania

NIGHTCLUBS

Outer Limits 1102 Rte 130 **856/845-1010** • 9pm-2am Wed & Fri-Sat only • lesbians/ gay men • dancing/DJ

NEW MEXICO

Statewide

PUBLICATIONS

Out! Magazine **505/243-2540** • lgbt newsmagazine

Alamogordo

ACCOMMODATIONS

Best Western Desert Aire Motor Inn 1021 S White Sands Blvd **505/437-2110** • gay-friendly • swimming • wheelchair access • $68+

Albuquerque

includes Bernalillo, Corrales, Placitas & Rio Rancho

INFO LINES & SERVICES

AA Gay/ Lesbian 505/266-1900 (AA#) • call for times/ locations • smokefree mtgs • wheelchair access

Alternative Erotic Lifestyles 505/345-6484 • pansexual S/M group

Common Bond Info Line 505/891-3647 • 24hrs • covers lgbt community

New Mexico Outdoors 505/822-1093 • active lgbt outdoors group

Transgender Community Group 505/265-7655 • 7:30pm Fri mtg & social hr • call for info

UNM Women's Resource Center 1160 Mesa Vista Hall, NV **505/277-3716** • 8am-5pm, clsd wknds • resource library w/ computers for students & public • some lesbian outreach • wheelchair access

YIT (Youth In Transition) 4320 Central Ave SE (at Washington) **505/265-7690** • drop-in center for homeless youth 14-24 yrs • very gay-friendly

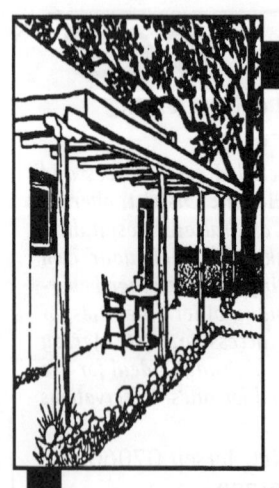
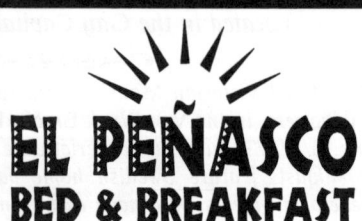

Accommodations

Brittania & W E Mauger Estate B&B 701 Roma Ave NW (at 7th) **505/242-8755, 800/719-9189** • gay-friendly • intimate 1897 Queen Anne residence • full brkfst • smokefree • $79-179

Casa de Alegria B&B 5 Alegria Ln (at Old Church Rd), Corrales **505/890-0176, 888/320-3456** • gay/straight • full brkfst • hot tub • wheelchair access • lesbian-owned/run • $89-109

▲ **El Peñasco** **505/771-8909, 888/576-2726** • mostly women • historic adobe guest house (sleeps 1-4) • full brkfst • btwn Albuquerque & Santa Fe • hot tub under the stars • kids ok • smokefree • lesbian-owned/run • $80-100

▲ **Golden Guesthouses** 2645 Decker NW **505/344-9205, 888/513-GOLD** • lesbians/gay men • individual & shared units

Hacienda Antigua B&B 6708 Tierra Dr NW (close to corner of 2nd & Osuna) **505/345-5399, 800/201-2986** • gay/straight • full brkfst • hot tub • swimming • smokefree • kids/pets ok • gay-owned/run • $109-219

La Hacienda Grande 21 Baros Ln (off Camino del Pueblo), Bernalillo **505/867-1887, 800/353-1887** • gay-friendly • 250 year old historic adobe home btwn Santa Fe & Albuquerque • food served • smokefree • $109-139

Mountain View **505/296-7277** • mostly women • full brkfst wknds • hot tub • smokefree • kids ok • wheelchair access • lesbian-owned/run • $40-65

Nuevo Dia 11110 San Rafael Ave NE (at Browning) **505/856-7910** • gay-friendly • guesthouse • full brkfst • hot tub • kids/pets ok • $60-180

Taracotta 3118 Rio Grande Blvd NW (at Candelaria) **505/344-9443** • gay/straight • hot tub • smokefree • small dogs ok • private patio • gay-owned/run • $70-85

W J Marsh House 301 Edith SE (nr Central & Broadway) **505/247-1001, 888/956-2774** • gay-friendly • full brkfst • shared bath • teens ok • women-owned/run • $50-150

Wyndham Albuquerque Hotel 2910 Yale Blvd SE (at Gibson) **505/843-7000, 800/227-1117** • gay-friendly • 4-star hotel • swimming • also 'Rojo Bar & Grill' • $159

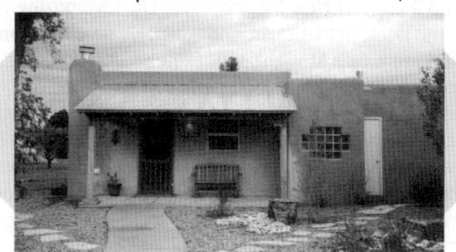

Golden Guesthouses

peaceful southwestern charm
safe • private • romantic

Albuquerque, New Mexico
1.888.513.GOLD or 1.505.344.9205
email: GoldenGH@aol.com
http://www.goldenguesthouses.com

New Mexico • USA

Reply **Forward** **Delete**

```
Date: Fri, Nov 30, 2001 16:25:33
From: Girl-on-the-Go
To: Editor@Damron.com
Subject: Albuquerque
```

> We're going to let you in on a little secret: New Mexico is the overlooked gem of the Southwest. Arizona likes to take the lion's share of the credit for the Southwest style as it basks in its endless sun and endless supply of seniors and new agers. Nevada cashes in on the image too, but goes for the glitz with its desert filled with more casinos that cacti. Colorado likes to brag about how it's God's little green heaven when not under several feet of fresh powder. Even Texas likes to horn in with its vibrant Tejano music and arts. But it's New Mexico, with its fermentation of 300 years of Native American, Spanish, and Anglo cultures, that is the true heart and soul of the Southwest.

> Sprawling in the shadow of Sandia Peak, New Mexico's largest city and cultural center is Albuquerque. The city's history can be glimpsed in its adobe constructions, cowboy decor, and proliferation of arts and crafts. And just outside of Albuquerque lies a more ancient piece of New Mexico's history: Petroglyph National Monument, covered with rock carvings created by the indigenous people of the area.

> During the day, stop in at the LGBT **Sisters & Brothers Bookstore** and pick up a copy of New Mexico's own **Out! Magazine** for the scoop on the latest activities around town. Or, give the **Common Bond Info Line** a call. At night, visit **Renea's,** Albuquerque's lesbian bar. Afterward, turn in for a good night's sleep at one of Albuquerque's lesbian-owned inns: **El Peñasco** and **Mountain View.**

> For something a bit different to do, take to the air for a spectacular view with woman-owned **Hugs 'n Hot Air Ballooning.** Albuquerque is a haven for those who enjoy the out-of-doors. Mountain bikers, especially, will love the scenery and endless terrain.

Albuquerque • New Mexico

BARS

Albuquerque Mining Co (AMC) 7209 Central Ave NE (at Louisiana) **505/255-4022** • 3pm-2am, till midnight Sun • popular • mostly gay men • dancing/DJ • live shows • wheelchair access • also 'Pit Bar' • mostly gay men • leather

Albuquerque Social Club 4021 Central Ave NE (enter rear) **505/255-0887** • noon-midnight, till 2am Fri-Sat • popular • lesbians/ gay men • dancing/DJ • private club

Foxes Lounge 8521 Central Ave NE (btwn Wisconsin & Wyoming) **505/255-3060** • 10am-2am, noon-midnight Sun • mostly gay men • dancing/DJ • live shows • wheelchair access

The Ranch 8900 Central SE (at Wyoming) **505/275-1616** • 11am-2am, till midnight Sun • mostly gay men • dancing/DJ • country/ western • leather • wheelchair access

Renea's 6132 4th NW (near Osuna) **505/343-1554** • 4pm-midnight, till 2am wknds, clsd Mon • mostly women • neighborhood bar • dancing/ DJ wknds • food served • karaoke Sun

NIGHTCLUBS

Pulse 4100 Central Ave SE (at Montclaire, in Nob Hill) **505/255-3334** • 9pm-2am, clsd Mon-Tue • popular • mostly gay men • dancing/DJ • alternative • 18+ Wed-Th • goth Th • live music Sun • cover charge

RESTAURANTS

Artichoke Café 424 Central Ave **505/243-0200** • lunch Mon-Fri & dinner Mon-Sat • bistro • plenty veggie

Chef du Jour 119 San Pasquale SW (at Central) **505/247-8998** • 11am-2pm Mon-Fri, dinner Fri-Sat only • plenty veggie • wheelchair access • $4-9

Double Rainbow 3416 Central SE (2 blks W of Carlisle) **505/255-6633** • 6am-midnight, till 1am wknds • plenty veggie • wheelchair access • $4-8

Frontier 2400 Central SE (at Cornell) **505/266-0550** • 24hrs • good brkfst burritos

Romano's Macaroni Grill 2100 Louisiana NE (at Winrock Mall) **505/881-3400** • lunch & dinner • Italian

Albuquerque

ENTERTAINMENT: New Mexico Gay Rodeo Association www.nmgra.com.

LGBT PRIDE: June. 505/856-0871.

ANNUAL EVENTS: September - Albuquerque AIDS Walk 505/938-7100, email: aidswalk@aol.com. October - Kodak Int'l Hot Air Balloon Fiesta 505/828-2887 or 888/422-7277, web: www.balloonfiesta.com.

CITY INFO: 800/733-6396, web: www.newmexico.com. Albuquerque Lesbian & Gay Chamber of Commerce 505/243-6767.

ATTRACTIONS: Albuquerque Museum 505/243-7255. Indian Pueblo Cultural Center 505/843-7270 or 800/766-4405 (outside NM). New Mexico Museum of Natural History 505/841-2802. Old Town. Rattlesnake Museum 505/242-6569. Wildlife West Nature Park & Chuckwagon 505/281-7655.

BEST VIEW: Sandia Peak Tram (505/856-7325) at sunset.

WEATHER: Sunny and temperate. Warm days and cool nights in summer, with average temperatures from 65° to 95°. Winter is cooler, from 28° to 57°.

New Mexico • USA

Sadie's Cocinita 6230 4th St NW (nr Osuna) **505/345-5339** • 11am-10pm, till 9pm Sun • popular • New Mexican

Entertainment & Recreation

Hugs & Hot Air Ballooning 12272 N Hwy 14, Cedar Crest **505/450-8692** • gay-friendly • scenic balloon rides • woman-owned/run

Women in Movement in New Mexico (WIMIN) 505/899-3627 • production company for the Southwest's premiere women's music & art festival

Bookstores

Bird Song 139 Harvard SE (nr Central) **505/268-7204** • 11am-7pm • used • lgbt section

Page One 11018 Montgomery NE **505/294-2026, 800/521-4122** • 7am-11pm

Sisters & Brothers Bookstore 4011 Silver Ave SE (btwn Morningside & Montclair) **505/266-7317, 800/687-3480 (ORDERS ONLY)** • 10:30am-7pm, till 6pm Sun, clsd Mon • lgbt

Retail Shops

In Crowd 3106 Central SE (at Richmond) **505/268-3750** • 10am-6pm, noon-4pm Sun • local & folk art • clothing • accessories • wheelchair access • gay-owned/run

Publications

Out! Magazine 505/243-2540 • lgbt newsmagazine

Spiritual Groups

Dignity New Mexico 1815 Los Lomas (at University) **505/896-1095** • 7pm 1st Sun

Emmanuel MCC 341 Dallas NE (at Copper) **505/268-0599** • 9am & 11am Sun

First Unitarian Church 3701 Carlisle NE (at Comanche) **505/884-1801** • 10am Sun

Jewish Lesbian/Gay Alliance 505/242-7508 • monthly Sabbath dinners • call for more info

MCC of Albuquerque 1103 Texas NE (near Lomas) **505/268-5252** • 10am Sun

Gyms & Health Clubs

Betty's Bath & Day Spa 1865 Candelaria NW **505/341-3456** • full service spa w/ separate women-only hot tub • men's night Th

Erotica

Castle Superstore 5110 Central Ave SE (at San Mateo) **505/262-2266**

Video Maxxx 810 Comanche NE (at I-25) **505/341-4000** • leather • novelties • books

Chimayo

Accommodations

Casa Escondida B&B 505/351-4805, 800/643-7201 • gay-friendly • full brkfst • hot tub • smokefree • kids/pets ok • women-owned/run • $80-140

Cloudcroft

Accommodations

Good Life Inn B&B 164 Karr Canyon Rd (At Hwy 82) **505/682-5433, 866/543-3466** • gay-friendly • luxurious suites • full brkfst • hot tub • teens ok • lesbian-owned/run • $100-155

Retail Shops

Off The Beaten Path 100 Glorieta Ave (at 1st) **505/682-7284** • 9am-6pm • eclectic gifts • original artwork • wheelchair access

Farmington

Accommodations

Microtel Inn & Suites 1901 E Broadway **505/325-3700** • gay-friendly • kids/pets ok • wheelchair access • $39-99

Las Cruces

Info Lines & Services

AA Gay/Lesbian 505/527-1803

Matrix PO Box 992, Mesilla 88046 • local inquiries • newsletter

Retail Shops

Spirit Winds Gifts & Cafe 2260 S Locust St **505/521-0222** • 7am-9pm, till 9:30pm Fri-Sat, 9:30am-6pm Sun • live music wknds

Spiritual Groups

Holy Family Anglican Church 1701 E Missouri (at Lutheran church) **505/521-1490** • 5:30pm Sun • inclusive Anglican community

Holy Family Parish 1701 E Missouri (at Lutheran Church) **505/522-7119** • 5:30pm Sun • inclusive Evangelical Anglican Church

Unitarian Universalist of Las Cruces 2000 S Solano (at corner of Wofford) **505/522-7281** • 9am & 11am Sun

Madrid

Accommodations

Madrid Lodging 14 Opera House Rd **505/471-3450** • gay-friendly • suite • hot tub • smokefree • $75-85

Santa Fe • New Mexico

BARS

Mineshaft Tavern 2846 State Hwy 14 505/473-0743 • noon-10pm, till 2am wknds • gay-friendly • live shows • also restaurant • some veggie

CAFES

Java Junction 2855 State Hwy 14 505/438-2772 • 8am-7pm • also B&B • $59-69

Santa Fe

INFO LINES & SERVICES

AA Gay/ Lesbian 505/982-8932

ACCOMMODATIONS

Alexander's Inn 529 E Palace Ave (at Delgado) 505/986-1431, 888/321-5123 • gay/ straight • hot tub • kids/ pets ok • gay-owned/ run • $85-175

▲ **Arius Compound** 505/982-8859, 800/735-8453 • gay-friendly • 4 adobe casitas • kitchens • hot tub • patio • fireplace • $90-180

El Farolito B&B 514 Galisteo St (at Paseo de Peralta) 505/988-1631, 888/634-8782 • gay/ straight • adobe compound w/ romantic, private casitas • kids ok • smokefree • gay-owned/ run • $100-210

Four Kachinas Inn 512 Webber St 505/982-2550, 888/634-8782 • gay-friendly • courtyard • kids ok • smokefree • wheelchair access • gay-owned/ run • $90-165

Hacienda Nicholas 320 E Marcy St 505/992-8385, 888/284-3170 • gay/ straight • adobe home • full brkfst • kids/ pets ok • smokefree • wheelchair access • gay-owned/ run • $95-160

Heart Seed B&B Retreat & Spa 505/471-7026 • gay-friendly • located on Turquoise Trail (25 miles S of Santa Fe) • full brkfst • hot tub • smokefree • sundeck • also day spa • kids ok • lesbian-owned/ run • $85-129

▲ **Inn of the Turquoise Bear B&B** 342 E Buena Vista St 505/983-0798, 800/396-4104 • lesbians/ gay men • B&B in historic Witter Bynner estate • smokefree • some shared baths • gay-owned/ run • $95-310

La Tienda Inn & Duran House 445-447 W San Francisco St 505/989-8259, 800/889-7611 • gay-friendly • adobe compound • smokefree • wheelchair access • $100-185

Leadfeather 3888 State Rd 14 (at Hwy 42) 505/438-3131 • gay/ straight • B&B on scenic Turquoise Trail • kids & pets ok • gay-owned • $79-125

ARIUS COMPOUND
SANTA FE VACATION RENTALS ON CANYON ROAD

Classic Adobe Casitas tucked amidst secret gardens and fruit trees, patios and fountain. All with tile floors, corner fireplaces, 1 or 2 bedrooms, fully equipped kitchens. Outdoor cedar hot tub. Ideally located in Santa Fe's historic East Side, walk to restaurants, museums, galleries & the Plaza. Nightly & weekly rates in your own small adobe house.

Old World Charm at Affordable Rates

800-735-8453 • 505-982-8859
WWW.ARIUSCOMPOUND.COM
po box 1111, santa fe, nm 87504 • info@ariuscompound.com

New Mexico • USA

The Madeleine Inn 106 Faithway St 505/982-3465, 888/877-7622 • gay/ straight • Queen Anne Victorian • full brkfst • hot tub • kids/ pets ok • smokefree • gay-owned/ run • $80-175

Marriott Residence Inn 1698 Galisteo St (at St Michaels) 505/988-7300, 800/331-3131 • gay-friendly • hot tub • swimming • kids/ pets ok • wheelchair access • $79-199

Open Sky B&B 134 Turquoise Trail Ct 505/471-3475, 800/244-3475 • gay-friendly • great views • smokefree • jacuzzi • kids/ pets ok (call first) • wheelchair access • lesbian-owned/ run • $70-140

Our Haven Santa Fe 828/669-7580 • gay/ straight • adobe guesthouse • private gardens • nr attractions • lesbian-owned/ run

Saltamontes Retreat—Grasshopper Hill off I—25 (1/2 hr NE of Santa Fe), East Pecos 505/757-2528, 877/Pecos2U • gay/ straight • 3 guestrooms in private home • 2-night minimum stay • communal kitchen • hot tub • smokefree • lesbian-owned/ run • $52-85

Tano Road Casita 15 Tano Pt Ln 505/989-7802, 505/989-7803 • gay/ straight • studio guesthouse • $90

▲ **The Triangle Inn—Santa Fe** 14 Arroyo Cuyamunge (12 miles N of Santa Fe) 505/455-3375 • lesbians/ gay men • secluded rustic adobe compound • hot tub • smokefree casitas available • kids/ pets ok • wheelchair access • lesbian-owned/ run • $65-160

Villas de Santa Fe 400 Griffin St 505/988-3000, 800/869-6790 • gay/ straight • villa-style suites • swimming • hot tub • gym • courtyard • $130-190

The Water Street Inn 427 W Water St 505/984-1193, 800/646-6752 • gay-friendly • historic adobe inn • jacuzzi • smokefree • kids/ pets ok • wheelchair access • $125-215

Nightclubs

Paramount 331 Sandoval (at Montezuma) 505/982-8999 • 5pm-close • popular • gay/ straight • dancing/DJ • theme nights • live bands some nights • also 'Bar B' lounge

Cafes

Aztec Street Cafe 317 Aztec 505/983-9464 • 7:30am-9pm, till 2pm Mon • gay-friendly • gay night weekly, call for info

Restaurants

Anasazi Restaurant 113 Washington Ave (at Palace) 505/988-3236 • brkfst, lunch & dinner • wheelchair access

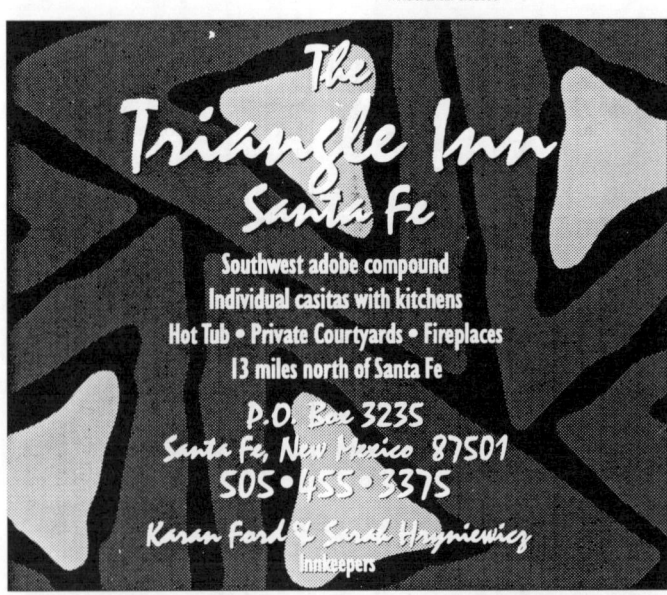

The Triangle Inn Santa Fe

Southwest adobe compound
Individual casitas with kitchens
Hot Tub • Private Courtyards • Fireplaces
13 miles north of Santa Fe

P.O. Box 3235
Santa Fe, New Mexico 87501
505 • 455 • 3375

Karan Ford & Sarah Hryniewicz
Innkeepers

Santa Fe • New Mexico

Cafe Pasqual's 121 Don Gaspar (at Water St) **505/983-9340** • 7am-10:30pm • popular • Southwestern • some veggie • beer/ wine • $7-27

Cowgirl Hall of Fame 319 S Guadalupe (btwn Aztec & Guadalupe) **505/982-2565** • 11am-2am, from 8:30am wknds, till midnight Sun • Southwest cuisine • veggie

Dave's Not Here 1115 Hickock St (at Cortez) **505/983-7060** • 11am-9pm, clsd Sun • New Mexican • some veggie • beer/ wine • women-owned/ run

Geronimo's 724 Canyon Rd (at Camino del Monte Sol) **505/982-1500** • lunch daily, dinner Tue-Sun • eclectic gourmet • full bar 11am-11pm

Paul's 72 Marcy St (at Lincoln & Washington) **505/982-8738** • lunch Mon-Sat, dinner nightly • modern int'l • some veggie • beer/ wine • wheelchair access • $14-19

Santacafe 231 Washington Ave **505/984-1788** • lunch & dinner • New American • some veggie • full bar • wheelchair access • $19-29

Tecolote Cafe 1203 Cerrillos Rd (at Baca) **505/988-1362** • 7am-2pm, clsd Mon • popular • great brkfst • some veggie • wheelchair access • $5-8

Vanessie of Santa Fe 434 W San Francisco (at Guadalupe) **505/982-9966** • 5:30pm-10:30pm (bar till 1am) • popular • lesbians/ gay men • steak house • piano bar

ENTERTAINMENT & RECREATION

One Railroad Circus **505/989-5798** • summer only • women's circus • check local listings for info

Ten Thousand Waves 3451 Hyde Park Rd (3 miles out of town) **505/992-5025** • Japanese health spa & lodging • sit under the stars & look out at the mtns • clothing optional in all tubs • kids ok • call for more info

BOOKSTORES

Downtown Subscription 376 Garcia St (at Acequia Madre) **505/983-3085** • 7am-7pm • newsstand • coffee shop

RETAIL SHOPS

The Ark 133 Romero St (at Agua Fria) **505/988-3709** • 9:30m-7pm, 10am-6pm Sat, 11am-5pm Sun • spiritual

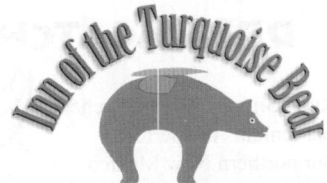

Inn of the Turquoise Bear

gay headquarters for visitors to santa fe, new mexico
an historic bed and breakfast on the Witter Bynner Estate

- ◆ Walk to Plaza, museums, galleries, restaurants & gay nightlife
- ◆ Close to opera, theater, skiing, hiking, biking, tours of pueblos & archaeological sites
- ◆ 11 rooms, private baths & entrances
- ◆ Secluded gardens & patios
- ◆ TV/VCRs
- ◆ Southwest Decor
- ◆ Expanded continental breakfasts & sunset refreshments

www.turquoisebear.net
342 E. Buena Vista Street • Santa Fe, NM 87501-4423 • 800.396.4104
505.983.0798 • FAX 505.988.4225 • IGLTA • email: bluebear@newmexico.com

New Mexico/ New York • USA

Taos

ACCOMMODATIONS

Adobe & Stars B&B 584 State Hwy 150 (at Valdez Rim Rd) 505/776-2776, 800/211-7076 • gay/ straight • luxurious pueblo • full brkfst • nr skiing & Nat'l Forest • fireplaces • smokefree • patios • wheelchair access • woman-owned/ run • $70-220

Brooks Street Inn 505/758-1489, 800/758-1489 • gay-friendly • full brkfst • smokefree • kids 10+ ok • $80-135

Dobson House 475 Tune Dr, El Prado 505/776-5738 • gay-friendly • luxury suites north of Taos • full brkfst • smokefree • $110-130

▲ **The Dreamcatcher B&B** 416 La Lomita (Valverde) 505/758-0613, 888/758-0613 • gay-friendly • nr Taos Plaza • full brkfst • hot tub • smokefree • wheelchair access • $89-119

Orinda B&B 461 Valverde St (on Valverde Park) 505/758-8581, 800/847-1837 • gay/ straight • full brkfst • $80-145

San Geronimo Lodge 1101 Witt Rd (at Kit Carson) 505/751-3776, 800/894-4119 • popular • gay/ straight • full brkfst • swimming • hot tub • massage available • kids/ pets ok • smokefree • wheelchair access • $95-150

NEW YORK

Adirondack Mtns

ACCOMMODATIONS

Country Road Lodge B&B 115 Hickory Hill Rd, Warrensburg 518/623-2207 • gay-friendly • secluded riverside retreat at the end of a country road • full brkfst • smokefree • $58-72

The Doctor's Inn 518/891-3464, 888/518-3464 • gay-friendly • full brkfst • some shared baths • kids/ pets ok (call first) • $65-95

King Hendrick Motel 1602 State Rte 9, Lake George 518/792-0418, 877/242-8762 • gay-friendly • swimming • kids ok • cabins available • wheelchair access • $50-105

Albany

see Capital District

Annandale-on-Hudson

INFO LINES & SERVICES

Bard BiGALA (Bisexual/ Gay/ Lesbian Alliance) Bard College 845/758-6822 (GENERAL SWITCHBOARD), 845/758-7454 (DEAN OF STUDENTS) • active during school year

---

P.O. Box 2069
Taos, NM 87871

DREAMCATCHER

Formerly 'The Ruby Slipper' Dreamcatcher Bed and Breakfast remains the perfect homebase for your northern New Mexico vacation. Owner/innkeepers, Bob and Jill Purtee, have been receiving rave reviews from guests, both repeat and new. Let them help make your Taos visit a relaxing and enjoyable experience that will keep you returning to Taos again and again!

Our 1940's adobe home sits nestled in a quiet, wooded area just a ten-minute walk from Historic Taos Plaza. Relax in our hammocks, snuggle up with a book by the fire or unwind beneath the stars in our hot tub. All 7 of our rooms feature a private exterior entrance, private bath, wood burning or gas log fireplaces, in room coffee maker, refrigerator, ceiling fan, radio/cassette player, hair dryers and comfortable robes.

Toll free (888)758-0613   Email dream@taosnm.com

Buffalo • New York

Beacon

Restaurants

Quinn's Restaurant 330 Main St
845/831-8065 • 5am-2pm, great bread

Berne

Accommodations

Willow Lane Farm 1192 Bradt Hollow Rd
518/872-1189 • gay/ straight • guest house •
hiking • retreats • commitment ceremonies •
25 miles W of Albany

Binghamton

Info Lines & Services

AA Gay/ Lesbian 438 Chenango St (at
United Methodist Church) **607/722-5983** •
7pm Sat

Rainbow Pride Union B2 BU Union
Basement **607/777-2202** • 8pm Mon

Women's Center & Event Line
607/724-3462 • call for events • publish
Celebrating Voices feminist quarterly

Accommodations

Serenity Farms 607/656-4659 • gay/
straight • B&B • camping on 100 secluded
acres • full brkfst • swimming • pets ok • gay-
owned/ run

Bars

Squiggy's 34 Chenango St (at Court)
607/722-2299 • 5pm-1am, till 3am Fri-Sat,
from 8pm Sun • lesbians/ gay men •
neighborhood bar • dancing/DJ Fri-Sat

Nightclubs

Prism 201 State St (at Hawley) **607/772-0710**
• 3pm-close • mostly gay men • dancing/DJ •
live shows • multiracial clientele • gay-owned/
run

Cafes

Lost Dog Cafe 222 Water St **607/771-6063** •
11am-11pm,10am -4pm Sun (clsd Sun July-
Labor Day) • popular • some veggie •
beer/wine • live shows • wheelchair access

Restaurants

The Whole in the Wall 43 S Washington St
607/722-5138 • 11:30am-9pm, clsd Sun-Mon

Entertainment & Recreation

Rainbow Dreams 607/723-4091 • lgbt
chorus

Publications

Amethyst 607/771-4994

Lavender Life 607/771-1986

Spiritual Groups

Affirmation (United Methodist) 83 Main St
(enter in back through parking lot)
607/723-4091 • 7pm Sun

Unitarian Universalist 183 Riverside
607/729-1641 • 10am Sun

Brewster

Bars

Chetti's Road House 182 Route 22
845/279-7844 • from 2pm • lesbians/ gay
men • neighborhood bar • live shows •
karaoke • food served

Buffalo

Info Lines & Services

Gay/ Lesbian Youth Services 190 Franklin
St (across from the Convention Ctr)
716/855-0221 • 6pm-9pm, clsd Wed & wknds

LGB Alliance 362 Student Union, SUNY-
Buffalo, Amherst **716/645-3063**

Accommodations

Arlington Park Inn 168 College St (at
Arlington Park) **716/885- 7585** • gay/ straight
• Victorian B&B • full brkfst • some shared
baths • smokefree • kids ok • lesbian-owned/
run • $70-90

Bars

Buddies 31 Johnson Park (at S Elmwood)
716/855-1313 • 1pm-4am, from noon wknds
• lesbians/ gay men • dancing/DJ Th-Sat • live
shows • wheelchair access

Cathode Ray 26 Allen St (at N Pearl)
716/884-3615 • 1pm-4am • mostly gay men •
neighborhood bar • videos • wheelchair access

Compton's After Dark 1239 Niagara St
(btwn Ferry & Lafayette) **716/885-3275** • call
for hrs • gay/ straight • dancing/DJ • live music
• karaoke Tue • in historic pre-1812 bldg

Fugazi 503 Franklin St (nr Allen St) **716/
881-3588** • 5pm-2am, from 8pm wknds, clsd
Mon • gay-friendly • intimate cocktail lounge

Lavender Door 32 Tonawanda St (at
Dearborn) **716/874-1220** • 6pm-4am, from
4pm Fri, from 7:30pm Sat, clsd Sun-Tue •
mostly women • neighborhood bar • live
music • karaoke • wheelchair access

Mickey's Saloon 44 Allen St (at Franklin)
716/881-2530 • 10am-2am • mostly gay men
• neighborhood bar • dancing/DJ • leather •
live shows • lunch served Mon-Fri • Latin
night Th

New York • USA

Secrets 20 Allen St (at Pearl) **716/886-9323** • 3pm-2am, till 3am Fri-Sat, from noon Sun • lesbians/ gay men • neighborhood bar • dancing/DJ • karaoke • piano bar • live shows • patio

Nightclubs

Club Marcella 622 Main St **716/847-6850** • 9pm-4am, from 4pm Fri, clsd Mon-Tue • lesbians/ gay men • dancing/DJ • 19+ Th • drag shows • wheelchair access

Bookstores

Talking Leaves 3158 Main St (btwn Winspear & Hertel Aves) **716/837-8554** • 10am-6pm, till 8pm Wed-Th, clsd Sun

Spiritual Groups

Dignity **716/833-8995** • call for events

Erotica

Village Books & News 3104 Delaware Ave (at Sheridan), Kenmore **716/877-5027** • 24hrs

Canton

Info Lines & Services

PRISM 3 1/2 E Main St (at Unitarian Universalist Church) **315/265-2422** • support group 1st & 3rd Fri

Capital District

includes Albany, Schenectady & Troy

Info Lines & Services

Gay AA at Community Center, Albany **518/462-6138** • 7:30pm Sun • lesbian AA 7:30pm Tue

Gay Youth Support Group at Community Center, Albany **518/462-6138** • 7:30pm Th & Fri

Lesbian/ Gay Community Center 332 Hudson Ave, Albany **518/462-6138** • 7pm-10pm, till 11pm Fri-Sat, 2pm-10pm Sun • 24hr directory • also cafe

TGIC (Transgenderist Independence Club) Albany **518/436-4513** • 8pm-10pm Th • call for location • also publish newsletter

Women's Building 79 Central Ave, Albany **518/465-1597** • community center

Accommodations

The State House 393 State St, Albany **518/427-6063** • gay/ straight • 1800s townhouse • smokefree • gay-owned/ run • $135-215

Bars

Blythewood 50 N Jay St (off Union), Schenectady **518/382-9755** • 9pm-4am, from 4pm Sun • mostly gay men • neighborhood bar • wheelchair access

Cafe Hollywood 275 Lark St (at Hamilton), Albany **518/472-9043** • 3pm-4am • gay-friendly • neighborhood bar • videos

Oh Bar 304 Lark St (at Madison), Albany **518/463-9004** • 2pm-4am • mostly gay men • neighborhood bar • multiracial • videos • wheelchair access

Power Company 238 Washington Ave (btwn Henry Johnson & Lark), Albany **518/465-2556** • 2pm-2am, till 4am wknds • lesbians/ gay men • dancing/DJ Wed-Sat • wheelchair access

Waterworks Pub 76 Central Ave (btwn Lexington & Northern), Albany **518/465-9079** • 11am-4am • popular • mostly gay men • women's night Th • dancing/DJ wknds • garden bar • wheelchair access

Restaurants

Cafe Lulu 288 Lark St (at Madison), Albany **518/436-5660** • 11am-midnight, till 1am Fri-Sat • Mediterranean • plenty veggie • beer/ wine • $5-9

Debbie's Kitchen 290 Lark St, Albany **518/463-3829** • 10am-9pm, 11am-6pm Sat, clsd Sun • sandwiches • salads • $3-5

Eagle Cafe 184 Washington Ave, Albany **518/449-5210** • lesbians/ gay men • 6:30am-2:30pm, clsd wknds • American • gay-owned/ run • $4-6

El Loco Mexican Cafe 465 Madison Ave (btwn Lark & Willett), Albany **518/436-1855** • 11:30am-10pm, clsd Mon • healthy Tex-Mex • some veggie • full bar

Mother Earth 217 Western Ave (at Quail), Albany **518/434-0944** • 11am-11pm • vegetarian • BYOB • wheelchair access • $3-6

Yono's 64 Colvin (at Armory Center), Albany **518/436-7747** • 5:30pm-10pm, clsd Sun-Tue • Indonesian/ cont'l • some veggie • full bar • live jazz Fri

Entertainment & Recreation

Face the Music WRPI 91.5 FM, Albany **518/276-6248** • 4pm-6pm Sun • feminist radio

Homo Radio WRPI 91.5 FM, Albany **518/276-6248** • noon-2pm Sun

Two Rivers **518/449-0758** • LGBT outdoor club

Cooperstown • New York

RETAIL SHOPS

Romeo's Gifts 199 Lark St (at Madison), Albany **518/434-4014** • 11am-9pm, noon-5pm Sun

PUBLICATIONS

Community 518/462-6138 x37 • monthly newsjournal

SPIRITUAL GROUPS

Congregation Berith Shalom 167 3rd St, Troy **518/272-8872** • 7:30 Fri

First United Presbyterian Church State & Willett Sts, Albany **518/449-7332** • 8:30am & 10:30am Sun • also 10am Sun in Troy • 1915 5th Ave, 518/272-2771

Grace & Holy Innocents Episcopal Church 498 Clinton Ave (at Robbins St), Albany **518/465-1112** • 9am Sun

MCC of Albany 275 State St (btwn Dove & Swan, at Emmanuel Baptist Church), Albany **518/785-7941** • 1pm Sun • wheelchair access

GYMS & HEALTH CLUBS

Fitness for Her 333 Delaware Ave, Delmar **518/478-0237** • 4:30am-9pm, 8:30am-9pm wknds • women-only • child care available • wheelchair access • lesbian-owned/ run

EROTICA

Savage Gifts & Leather 88 Central Ave (at Lexington), Albany **518/434-2324** • clsd Sun

Catskill Mtns

INFO LINES & SERVICES

Wise Woman Center 845/246-8081 • women only • workshops • correspondence courses • newsletter

ACCOMMODATIONS

Bradstan Country Hotel 1561 Rte 17-B/ White Lake **845/583-4114** • gay-friendly • also cottages • piano bar & cabaret • 6pm-1am Fri-Sat • $85-165

Inn at Stone Ridge Rte 209, Stone Ridge **845/687-0736** • gay-friendly • 1700s mansion • full brkfst • also fine dining • full bar • patio

Palenville House B&B 3292 Rte 23A, Palenville **518/678-5649, 877/689-5101** • gay/ straight • Victorian guesthouse • full brkfst • hot tub • some shared baths • smokefree • gay-owned/ run • $60-125

Point Lookout Mountain Inn The Mohican Trail, Rte 23, East Windham **518/734-3381** • gay/ straight • nr Ski Windham & Hunter Mtn • hot tub • smokefree • kids/ pets ok • wheelchair access • gay-owned/ run • $60-155 • also 'Bella Vista Restaurant' • $11-18 • also 'Rainbow Cafe & Cliffside Deck'

River Run B&B Fleischmanns **845/254-4884** • gay/ straight • Queen Anne Victorian • full brkfst • gay-owned/ run • $70-120

Salamander Hill Guesthouse 56 Church St, Long Eddy **845/887-1968** • gay/ straight • shared baths • hot tub • nudity permitted • camping available • $40-150

The Wild Rose Inn 66 Rock City Rd, Woodstock **914/679-8783** • gay-friendly • luxurious Victorian B&B • kids ok • smokefree • lesbian-owned/ run • $100-200

The Woodstock Inn on the Millstream 38 Tannery Brook Rd, Woodstock **845/679-8211, 800/697-8211** • gay-friendly • swimming hole • wheelchair access • $99-129

RESTAURANTS

Catskill Rose 5355 Rte 212, Mt Tremper **845/688-7100** • 5pm-close Th-Sun • some veggie • full bar • patio • $13-17

ENTERTAINMENT & RECREATION

Frog Hollow Farm Old Post Rd, Esopus **845/384-6424** • riding school

Solstice Farm Stable Stanfordville **845/868-1413** • riding school & camp

BOOKSTORES

Golden Notebook 29 Tinker St, Woodstock **845/679-8000** • 10:30am-7pm, till 6pm Sun (till 9pm summers) • lgbt section • wheelchair access

Cobleskill

ACCOMMODATIONS

Lavender Hill B&B HCR 1 Box 133, Warnerville **518/254-0351** • women-only • 1800s Colonial Revival on 15 acres • full brkfst • hot tub • some shared baths • lesbian-owned/ run • $85-125

Cooperstown

see Sharon Springs

New York • USA

Corning

ACCOMMODATIONS

Rufus Tanner House B&B 60 Sagetown Rd, Pine City **607/732-0213** • gay/ straight • full brkfst • jacuzzi • smokefree • wheelchair access • $70-130

Cortland

BOOKSTORES

Mandolin Winds Bookstore 33 Main St (at Central) **607/758-7460** • 10am-5pm, till 7pm Th, till 4pm Sat, clsd Sun • lgbt section

Croton-on-Hudson

ACCOMMODATIONS

Alexander Hamilton House 49 Van Wyck St **914/271-6737** • gay-friendly • full brkfst • swimming • smokefree • kids ok • woman-owned/ run • $120-300

Elmira

NIGHTCLUBS

ANGLES Ultimate Dance Club 511-513 Railroad Ave (btwn Clinton & 3rd) **607/737-7676** • 5pm-1am, till 3am Fri-Sat • popular • lesbians/ gay men • dancing/DJ • live shows • game room • 18+ • also restaurant • gay-owned/ run

SPIRITUAL GROUPS

Ray of Hope Church **800/367-1463, 315/471-6618** • 10:30am Sat, call for location

Fire Island

see also Long Island

INFO LINES & SERVICES

AA Gay/ Lesbian **631/669-1124** • call for info

ACCOMMODATIONS

Black Sheep in Exile B&B 71 Bay Walk E, Fire Island Pines **631/597-6565** • mostly gay men • full brkfst • pets ok • gourmet dinner available • smokefree • $65-120

Boatel The Pines **631/597-6500** • mostly gay men • swimming • also restaurant • wheelchair access

Bob Howard Realtor The Pines **631/597-9400, 212/819-9400** • great source for rentals

Dune Point Guesthouse **631/597-6261** • lesbians/ gay men • hot tub • kids/ pets ok • wheelchair access • gay-owned/ run • $150+

GroveHotel Dock Walk, Cherry Grove **631/597-6600** • mostly gay men • swimming • nudity • smokefree room available • wheelchair access • gay-owned/ run • $40-400

Holly House Holly Walk nr Bayview Walk, Cherry Grove **631/597-6911** • lesbians/ gay men • seasonal • shared baths • smokefree • $40-150

Pines Place **631/597-6162** • mostly gay men • guesthouse offers rooms in 2 locations • swimming • some shared baths • $150-325

BARS

Cherry's 158 Bayview Walk, Cherry Grove **631/597-6820** • seasonal • noon-4am • popular • lesbians/ gay men • piano bar • live shows • also restaurant • patio

The Island Club & Grille 36 Fire Island Blvd, The Pines **631/597-6001** • seasonal • 6pm-4am, from 4pm wknds • grille open 6pm-11pm, clsd Wed • mostly gay men • dancing/DJ • also piano bar • $15-28 (grille)

NIGHTCLUBS

Grove Hotel (formerly the 'Ice Palace') Cherry Grove **631/597-6600** • hours vary • popular • lesbians/ gay men • dancing/DJ • live shows • young crowd • wheelchair access

The Pavilion Fire Island Blvd, The Pines **631/597-6131** • seasonal • noon-8am • lesbians/ gay men • popular • dancing/DJ • also 'Yacht Club' restaurant • wheelchair access

RESTAURANTS

Cherry Grove Pizza Dock Walk (under the 'Grove Hotel'), Cherry Grove **631/597-6766** • 11am-11pm

Michael's Dock Walk, Cherry Grove **631/597-6555** • seasonal • 7am-midnight • upscale diner fare

Rachel's at the Grove Lewis Walk, Cherry Grove **631/597-4174** • lesbians/ gay men • brkfst, lunch & dinner • outdoor seating • ocean views • also bar

Top of the Bay Dock Walk at Bay Walk, Cherry Grove **631/597-6699** • seasonal • 7pm-midnight • popular • lesbians/ gay men • $18-23

ENTERTAINMENT & RECREATION

Invasion of the Pines the Pines dock (July 4th wknd) • come & enjoy the annual fun as boatloads of drag queens from Cherry Grove arrive to terrorize the posh Pines

Livingston Manor • New York

Geneva

Accommodations

Belhurst Castle State Rte 14 S (near Snell Rd) **315/781-0201** • gay-friendly • also restaurant • $70-315

Glens Falls

Bars

Seventy South Street Pub 70 South St **518/798-9809** • noon-4am • gay/ straight • dancing/DJ • karaoke

Highland

see also Poughkeepsie, New Paltz

Accommodations

Inn at Applewood 120 North Rd **845/691-2516** • gay/ straight • full brkfst • also restaurant • lesbian-owned/ run • $95

Nightclubs

Prime Time Rte 9 W **845/691-8550** • 9:30pm-4am Fri-Sun only • mostly gay men • theme parties/ male strippers Fri • dancing/DJ Sat • X-rated bingo Sun (AIDS benefit) • 18+

Restaurants

The Would Restaurant 120 North Rd (off Rte 9 W) **845/691-9883** • lunch Mon-Fri & dinner nightly, clsd Sun • some veggie • full bar • patio • $16-22 • lesbian-owned/ run

Hudson

Accommodations

Hudson City B&B 326 Allen St (at Rte 9-G/ 3rd St) **518/822-8044** • gay/ straight • 18th-century Victorian in antique district • some shared baths • full brkfst • hot tub • kids/small pets ok • gay-owned/ run • $99-169

St Charles Hotel 16-18 Park Pl **518/822-9900** • gay-friendly • kids/ pets ok • also 2 restaurants • $79-109

Ithaca

Info Lines & Services

AA Gay/ Lesbian First Baptist Church (at Dewitt Park) **607/273-1541** • 6pm Sun

Women's Community Building 100 W Seneca (at Cayuga) **607/272-1247** • 9am-5pm, evenings & wknds by appt

Accommodations

Frog Haven Women's B&B 578 W King Rd (at Rte 96B S) **607/272-3238** • women-only • in contemporary log-sided home • pond • smokefree • lesbian-owned/ run • $65-85

Bars

Common Ground 1230 Danby Rd/ Rte 96-B (at Comfort) **607/273-1505** • 4pm-1:30am • popular • lesbians/ gay men • dancing/DJ • multiracial • live music Fri • young crowd • also restaurant Wed & Fri-Sun • some veggie • wheelchair access • $5-8

Cafes

Harvest Deli 171 E State St (in Ithaca Commons), Center Ithaca **607/272-1961** • 7am-6pm, from 9am Sat, clsd Sun • veggie deli • lesbian-owned/ run

Restaurants

ABC Cafe 308 Stewart Ave (at Buffalo) **607/277-4770** • lunch & dinner, wknd brunch, clsd Mon • beer/ wine • vegetarian • $6-8

Entertainment & Recreation

Out Loud Chorus 800/367-1463

Bookstores

Borealis Bookstore 111 N Aurora St (at State) **607/272-7752** • 10am-9pm, 11am-5pm Sun • independent alternative • lgbt section • wheelchair access

Jamestown

Bars

Rascals 701 N Main St/ Rte 60 (at 7th) **716/484-3220** • 3pm-2am • lesbians/ gay men • dancing/DJ Fri-Sun

Kingston

Restaurants

Armadillo Bar & Grill 97 Abeel St **845/339-1550** • lunch & dinner • some veggie • full bar • patio

Livingston Manor

Accommodations

Magical Land of Oz B&B 753 Shandelee Rd **845/439-3418** • gay/ straight • each room has Oz character theme • shared baths • hot tub • kids ok • gay-owned/ run • $75-85

New York • USA

Long Island

Long Island is divided into 2 geographical areas:
Long Island—Nassau County
Long Island—Suffolk County
see also Fire Island

Long Island—Nassau County

INFO LINES & SERVICES

Gay/Lesbian Switchboard of Long Island (GLSB of LI) 631/242-4669 • seasonal • 7pm-11pm only

Pride for Youth Coffeehouse 2050 Bellmore Ave, Bellmore **516/679-9000** • 7:30pm-11:30pm Fri • ages 13-20 • live music

BARS

Auntie M's 3546 Merrick Rd (at Blockbuster Shopping Plaza), Seaford **516/679-8820** • 5pm-4am, from 3pm Sun • lesbians/gay men • neighborhood bar • live shows wknds

RESTAURANTS

Rattlesnake Jones 153 Merrick Ave (off Sunrise), Merrick **516/378-7177** • dinner, clsd Mon • women-owned/run

SPIRITUAL GROUPS

Dignity Nassau at Church of the Advent, Westbury **516/781-6225** • 8pm 2nd Sat

Long Island—Suffolk County

INFO LINES & SERVICES

EEGO (East End Gay Organization) 631/324-3699 • social events

Gay/Lesbian Switchboard of Long Island (GLSB of LI) 516/737-1615 • 7pm-10pm only

ACCOMMODATIONS

132 North Main 132 N Main, East Hampton **516/324-2246** • mostly gay men • seasonal • mini-resort • swimming • smokefree • wheelchair access • $125-225

Centennial House of East Hampton 13 Woods Ln, East Hampton **516/324-9414** • gay/straight • full brkfst • smokefree • swimming • also 3-bdrm cottage • gay-owned/run • kids/dogs ok • $250-425

Cozy Cabins Motel 631/537-1160 • lesbians/gay men • seasonal • hot tub • sundeck • kids/pets ok • gay-owned/run • $99-150

EconoLodge—MacArthur Airport 3055 Rte 454, Ronkonkoma **631/588-6800, 800/553-2666** • gay-friendly • budget motel • smokefree rooms available • wheelchair access

EconoLodge—Smithtown/Hauppauge 755 Rte 347, Smithtown **631/724-9000, 800/553-2666** • gay-friendly • $84-114

House on Newtown B&B 172 Newtown Ln (at McGuirk St), East Hampton **631/324-1858** • gay/straight • lovely turn-of-the-century home • smokefree

Summit Motor Inn 501 E Main St (at Brentwood Rd), Bay Shore **631/666-6000, 800/869-6363** • gay-friendly • $79-119

Sunset Beach 35 Shore Rd, Shelter Island **631/749-2001** • gay-friendly • seasonal • food served • $175-395

BARS

Club 608 608 Sunrise Hwy (at Belmont Ave), West Babylon **631/661-9580** • 2pm-4am • lesbians/gay men

Forever Green 841 N Broome Ave, Lindenhurst **631/226-8280** • 8pm-4am, from 5pm Fri, from 7pm Sun • mostly women • neighborhood bar • dancing/DJ • live shows • karaoke • lesbian-owned/run

NIGHTCLUBS

Bunkhouse 192 N Main St/Montauk Hwy (at Foster Ave), Sayville **631/567-2865** • 7pm-4am • popular • mostly gay men • dancing/DJ • karaoke Mon • live shows • wheelchair access • gay-owned/run

Nocturnal 54 Montauk Hwy, Southampton • Sat only • mostly gay men • dancing/DJ

Want More?

Subscribe to our online travel guide:
www.damron.com

More listings. More destinations (like Australia, South Africa & Asia). More up-to-the-minute info.

NYC—Overview • New York

Shi 121 Woodfield Rd, West Hempstead **516/486-9516** • 8pm-4am, clsd Mon • popular • mostly women • dancing/DJ Fri • live shows Sat • wheelchair access

The Swamp 378 Montauk Hwy (at Eastgate Rd), East Hampton **631/537-3332** • 6pm-4am, clsd Tue-Wed in winter • call for winter hours • mostly gay men • dancing/DJ • young crowd • also 'Annex' restaurant • cont'l/ seafood • wheelchair access • $16-20

Thunders 1017 E Jericho Tpke, Huntington Station **631/423-5241** • 9pm-4am, clsd Mon • popular • lesbians/ gay men • dancing/DJ • piano bar Tue-Fri • live shows • 18+ wknds • huge outdoor area • gay-owned/ run

Restaurants

Babette's 66 Newtown Ln, East Hampton **631/329-5377** • brkfst, lunch & dinner • healthy • plenty veggie • woman-owned/ run

Entertainment & Recreation

Fowler Beach Southampton

Spiritual Groups

Unitarian Universalist Fellowship 109 Browns Rd, Huntington **631/427-9547** • 9:30am & 11:15am Sun

Mahopac

Info Lines & Services

Putnam/ N Westchester Women's Resource Ctr 2 Mahopac Plaza **845/628-9284** • drop-in hrs 10am-4pm Mon-Fri

Mt Morris

Bars

Fred's Tavern 36 Main St (at State) **716/658-3267** • noon-2am • gay/ straight • neighborhood bar

New Paltz

Accommodations

Ujjala's B&B 2 Forest Glen **845/255-6360** • gay-friendly • full brkfst • body therapy • sweat lodges • kids/ pets ok • woman-owned/ run • $80-125

Restaurants

Locust Tree Inn 215 Huguenot St (behind conference ctr) **845/255-7888** • lunch & dinner, clsd Mon • cont'l • full bar • patio • $14-20

Northern Spy Cafe Rte 213, High Falls **845/687-7298** • dinner nightly & Sun brunch, clsd Wed • plenty veggie • full bar • wheelchair access • $11-18

New York City

New York City is divided into 8 geographical areas:
NYC—Overview
NYC—Soho, Greenwich & Chelsea
NYC—Midtown
NYC—Uptown
NYC—Brooklyn
NYC—Queens
NYC—Bronx
NYC—Staten Island

NYC—Overview

Info Lines & Services

AA Gay/ Lesbian Intergroup at Lesbian/ Gay Community Ctr **212/647-1680** • call for mtg schedule

African Ancestral Lesbians United for Societal Change at Lesbian/ Gay Community Ctr **212/620-7310, 212/529-8021** • 8pm Th

Asian Pacific Alliance of NY 718/966-4010, 718/699-5922 • call for info

Bisexual Gay/ Lesbian Transgender Youth of NY at Lesbian/ Gay Community Ctr **212/620-7310** • 3:30pm Sat

Bisexual Network 212/459-4784 • info on variety of social & political groups

Bisexual Women's Group at Lesbian/ Gay Community Ctr **212/620-7310** • 6:30pm Wed

Butch/ Femme Society at Lesbian/ Gay Community Ctr **212/388-2736** • 6:30pm 3rd Wed

Eulenspiegel Society 24 Bond St (btwn Lafayette & the Bowery) **212/388-7022** • 7:30pm Tue-Wed • $8 for non-members • pansexual S/M group • newsletter

FLAB (Fat is a Lesbian Issue) at Lesbian/ Gay Community Ctr **201/843-4629** • fat-positive discussion group & dinner • allies welcome

Gay/ Lesbian Switchboard of New York Project 212/989-0999 • 4pm-midnight Mon-Fri, noon-5pm Sat

Hetrick-Martin Institute 2 Astor Pl **212/674-2400, 212/674-8695 (TTY)** • extensive services for lgbt youth

Identity House 39 W 14th St #205 (btwn 5th & 6th Aves) **212/243-8181** • walk-in 6pm-9pm Mon, Tue & Fri & 1pm-4pm wknds • peer-counseling • info & referrals

New York • USA

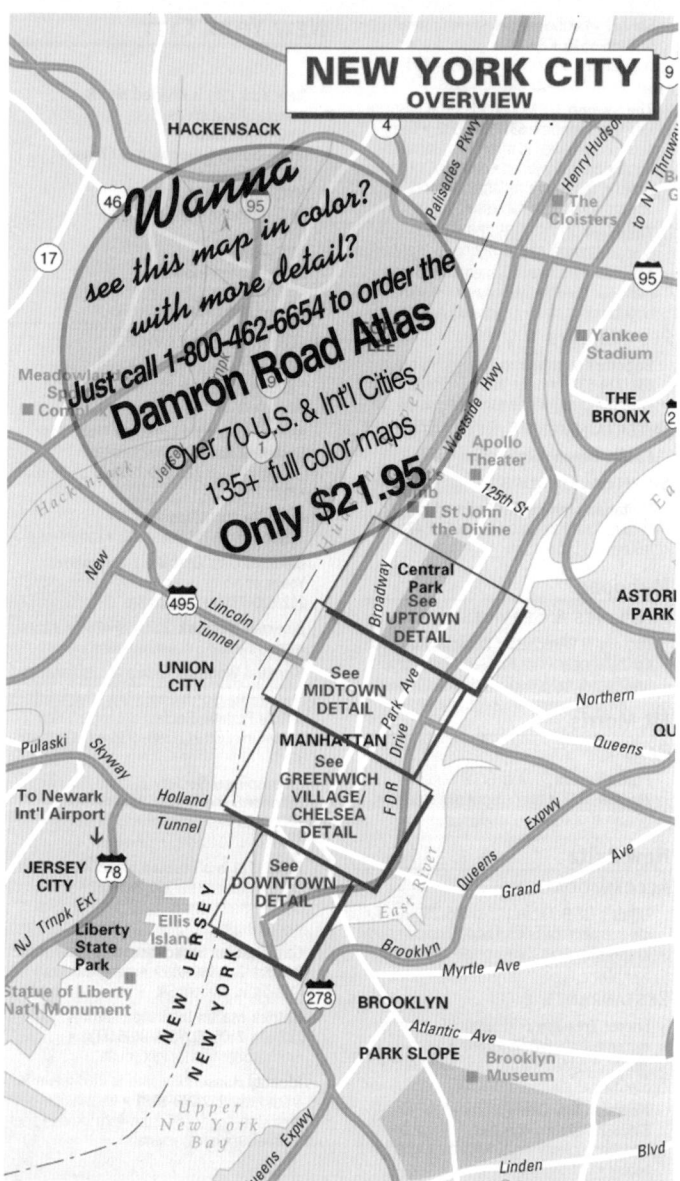

NYC—Overview • New York

Just Couples at Lesbian/Gay Community Ctr 212/252-3154 • 3:30pm 1st Sun

Las Buenas Amigas at Lesbian/Gay Community Ctr **718/596-0342 EXT 44** • 2pm 1st Sun • Latina lesbian group

Lesbian/Gay Community Services Center 208 W 13th **212/620-7310** • 9am-11pm • popular • many group meetings & resources • also cafe • wheelchair access

Lesbian Herstory Archives 718/768-3953 • exists to gather & preserve records of lesbian lives & activities • located in Park Slope, Brooklyn • wheelchair access

NY CyberQueers at Lesbian/Gay Community Ctr **718/522-6553** • 6pm 3rd Th (not in summer) • lgbt 'computer pros'

SAGE: Senior Action in a Gay Environment at Lesbian/Gay Community Ctr **212/741-2247** • call for events

New York City

WHERE THE GIRLS ARE: Upwardly mobile literary types hang in the West Village, hipster dykes cruise the East Village, upper-crusty Lesbians have cocktails in Midtown, and working-class dykes live in Brooklyn.

LGBT PRIDE: Last Sunday in June. 212/807-7433, web: www.nycpride.org.
Bronx Pride - June. 718/670-3396.
Brooklyn Pride - June. 718/670-3337.

ANNUAL EVENTS: March - Saint-at-Large Black Party.
May - AIDS Walk-a-thon 212/807-9255.
June - New York Int'l Gay/Lesbian Film Festival 212/254-7228.
September - Wigstock 212/439-5139. Outrageous wig/drag/performance festival in Tompkins Square Park in the East Village.
New York Lesbian/Gay Experimental Film/Video Fest 212/571-4242.

CITY INFO: 212/397-8222, web: nycvisit.com.

ATTRACTIONS: Broadway.
Carnegie Hall 212/903-9600.
Central Park.
Ellis Island.
Empire State Building 212/736-3100.
Greenwich Village.
Guggenheim Museum 212/423-3600.
Lincoln Center 212/546-2656.
Metropolitan Museum of Art.
Museum of Modern Art 212/708-9400.
Radio City Music Hall 212/247-4777.
Rockefeller Center.
Statue of Liberty.
Times Square.
United Nations.
Wall Street.
World Trade Center 212/435-4170.

BEST VIEW: Coming over any of the bridges into New York, the Empire State Building, or the World Trade Center.

WEATHER: A spectrum of extremes with pleasant moments thrown in. Spring and fall are the best times to visit.

TRANSIT: Wave an arm on any streetcorner for a taxi.
Public transit MTA 718/330-1234.

New York • USA

Reply **Forward** **Delete**

Date: Thu, Nov 9, 2001 12:26:42
From: Girl-on-the-Go
To: Editor@Damron.com
Subject: New York City

> In the flm *Mondo New York*, demi-monde denizen Joey Arias put it best: 'New York is the clit of the world!'

> Get ready for the most stimulating trip of your life! You've come to *the* city of world-famous tourist attractions: from the skyscrapers to the subway, New York is like no other place. Whether you pride yourself on your cultural sophistication, or lack thereof, you're going to find endless entertainment. There are plays, musicals, operas, museums and gallery shows, performance art, street theater, and street life...and that's just for starters.

> To get the most out of your visit, do your homework before you come. Call for a calendar of events at the **Lesbian/Gay Community Services Center,** which houses meeting spaces for every conceivable group of LGBT+ people.

> New York's performance art is a must-see for any student of modern culture. The best bets for intelligent, cutting edge shows by women and queers are **WOW (Women's One World) Cafe** and **PS 122,** where lesbian artist Holly Hughes got her start. For 'two-fers'— half-price tickets to Broadway and off-Broadway shows available the day of the show—stop by the TKTS booth on 47th St. at Broadway. For the latest reviews and hot off-off-Broadway theaters, check the queer-friendly *Village Voice* newspaper.

> Of course, you can stimulate a lot more than your cultural sensibilities in New York. Gourmands cans experience oral orgasms ranging from a delicate quiver to a blinding throb every day. For instance, before that Broadway show, head to one of the many restaurants along 46th St. at 9th Ave. When in Brooklyn, brunch along 7th Ave.; you'll find plenty of LGBT company on a Sunday morning.

> Shopping, too, affords shivers of delight. Check out the fabulous thrift shops and the designer boutiques. Cruise Midtown on Madison Ave., E. 57th St., or 5th Ave. in the 50s, at Trump Tower or another major shopping mall, and touch clothing more expensive than your last car. Other recommended districts for blowing cash on hipster fashions and accessories include St. Mark's Place in the Village (8th St. between 1st and 2nd Aves.); Broadway from 8th to Canal St.; and

any major intersection in Soho and the East Village.

> To titillate your mind, peruse the shelves at **Creative Visions, Bluestockings,** or **Oscar Wilde Memorial Bookshop**, or make an appointment to stop by the **Lesbian Herstory Archives** in Brooklyn. If you're in the mood for love, visit **Eve's Garden,** New York's women's erotic boutique; men are only allowed in if accompanied by a woman.

> You could spend days at the big art museums in Uptown near Central Park, but budget some time for the galleries in SoHo (south of Houston—pronounced How-ston, not like the city in Texas—between Broadway and 6th Ave.). You can pick up a gallery map in the area.

> For musical entertainment, make your pilgrimage to the Kitchen, legendary site of experimental and freestyle jazz, or CBGB's, legendary home of noisy music (the Ramones started American punk here in 1974).

> Nightlife...we know you've been holding your breath! Run, don't walk to the **Clit Club**; Friday nights at the Flamingo are the sexiest, hottest dyke nights in town. **Crazy Nanny's** really happens seven days a week, and several other women's bars are nearby. **Shescape** produces women's club nights at various locations, so call for their latest events. (New York is also home to plenty of one-nighters, so be sure to pick up a copy of **HX** for up-to-the-minute club happenings.) You can get your groove on at one of the nightly events produced by Girlz Party (888/784-8535, www.girlzparty.com), and no one should miss the Drag King scene in this gender-bending city.

> If this isn't enough excitement, experience the City in June when New York hosts numerous LGBT Pride-related cultural events, from their week-long Film Festival to the Pride March itself.

> One last bit of advice: there's more to New York City than Manhattan. Brooklyn has long been home to lesbians escaping the extortionist rents of Manhattan. To taste dyke life in this borough, stop by **Rising Cafe**. If you'll be out on Long Island, stop by one of the two women's bars: **Forever Green** and **Shi**.

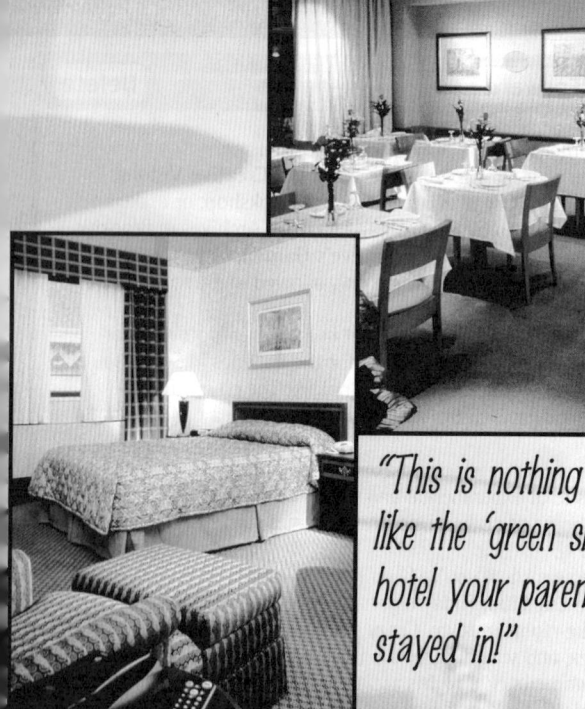

"This is nothing like the 'green sign' hotel your parents stayed in!"

- **The easiest business decision on Wall Street.**
- **The most technologically advanced rooms among any business hotel.**
- **Your closest commute to Wall Street.**
- **Location, Location, Location.**

Holiday Inn®
Wall Street District

**15 Gold Street • New York, NY 10023
tel: 212.232.7700 • fax: 212.425.7800
Reservations: 212.232.7800**

SALGA (South Asian Lesbian/ Gay Association) at Lesbian/ Gay Community Ctr **212/358-5132** • 3:30pm 2nd Sat

Sirens Motorcycle Club at Lesbian/ Gay Community Ctr **212/749-6177** • 8pm 3rd Tue

Support Group for Single Lesbians at Lesbian/ Gay Community Ctr **212/620-7310** • 6pm Fri

Twenty Something at Lesbian/ Gay Community Ctr **212/971-4756** • 8pm 1st & 3rd Tue • social alternative for lgbts in late teens to 30s

Nightclubs

Sea Tea leaves from Pier 40 **212/675-4357** • seasonal sailing T-dance • mostly gay men • buffet • live shows

Entertainment & Recreation

Before Stonewall 212/439-1090 • lesbian/ gay history tour

Dyke TV (Free Speech TV) 212/989-8310 • TV show produced by lesbians for lesbians' • also do public screenings every other month

Think It's Not When It Is 718/949-5162 • theater company promoting positive lgbt images

Townhouse Tours 212/539-2683 • tours of New York's gay history

Publications

Empire 212/352-3535 • stylish glossy for gay New York

HX Magazine 212/352-3535 • complete weekly guide to gay New York at night

LGNY (Lesbian & Gay New York) 212/691-1100 • lgbt newspaper

Manhattan Spirit 212/268-0454 • weekly community newspaper

New York Blade News 242 W 30th St, 4th flr **212/268-2701** • weekly lgbt newspaper

Next 212/627-0165 • party paper

Spiritual Groups

Buddhist Lesbians/ Gays: Maitri Dorje at Lesbian/ Gay Community Ctr **212/619-4099** • 6pm 2nd Tue

Church of St Luke in the Fields (Episcopal) 487 Hudson St (at Christopher) **212/924-0562** • call for mtg times

Congregation Beth Simchat Torah 296 9th Ave (at 28th St) **212/929-9498** • 8:30pm Fri • lgbt synagogue • wheelchair access • also 57 Bethune St location • call for other mtg times

Dignity 218 W 11th St (at Waverly Pl, at St John's) **212/627-6488** • 7:30pm Sun • also 8pm Sat at the Center

Integrity NYC 212/691-7181

MCC of New York 446 W 36th St (btwn 9th & 10th) **212/629-7440** • 10am & 7pm Sun

Society of Friends (Quakers) Earl Hall (Columbia University, at 116th & Broadway) **212/777-8866** • 11am Sun

NYC—Soho, Greenwich & Chelsea

Accommodations

Abingdon Guesthouse 13 8th Ave (at W 12th St) **212/243-5384** • gay/ straight • quiet, mature clientele • smokefree • wheelchair access • $157-222

Chelsea Inn 46 W 17th St (btwn 5th & 6th Aves) **212/645-8989, 800/640-6469** • gay-friendly •European-style inn • $99-259

Chelsea Pines Inn 317 W 14th St (btwn 8th & 9th Aves) **212/929-1023** • lesbians/ gay men • some shared baths • gay-owned/ run • $99-149

The Chelsea Savoy Hotel 204 W 23rd St (at 7th Ave) **212/929-9353** • gay/ straight • wheelchair access • kids ok • $99-195

East Village B&B 244 E 7th St **212/260-1865** • women only • in the heart of the Village • smokefree • lesbian-owned • $65-95

The Gramercy Park Hotel 2 Lexington Ave (at E 21st St) **212/475-4320, 800/221-4083** • gay-friendly • aging hotel across from Gramercy Park • $175-260

Holiday Inn 138 Lafayette St (btwn Canal & Howard, in Chinatown) **212/966-8898** • gay-friendly

Hotel Washington Square 103 Waverly Pl (at MacDougal St) **212/777-9515, 800/222-0418** • gay-friendly • renovated 100-yr-old hotel • 'C3' restaurant 7:30am-10:30pm • $120-220

Incentra Village House 32 8th Ave (at W 12th St) **212/206-0007** • lesbians/ gay men • smokefree • gay-owned/ run • $99-179

Soho Grand Hotel 310 W Broadway (at Canal St) **212/965-3000, 800/965-3000** • gay-friendly • big, glossy, over-the-top hotel • wheelchair access • $374-529

Southern Comforts 323/850-5623, 800/889-7359 • gay/ straight • handsome condo in the heart of the Village • wheelchair access • gay-owned/ run • $185-375

New York • USA

Bars

Bar d'O 29 Bedford St (at Downing St) **212/627-1580** • 7:30pm-3am • gay-friendly • live shows • women's night Mon

Barracuda 275 W 22nd St (at 8th Ave) **212/645-8613** • 4pm-4am • popular • mostly gay men • live DJs • drag shows

Blu 161 W 23rd St (at 7th Ave) **212/633-6113** • 4pm-4am • mostly gay men • DJ Tue-Sun • Internet access

The Boiler Room 86 E 4th St (at 2nd Ave) **212/254-7536** • 4pm-4am • popular • mostly gay men • neighborhood bar

Boots & Saddle 76 Christopher St (at 7th Ave S) **212/929-9684** • 8am-4am, noon-4pm Sun • mostly gay men • neighborhood bar

The Cock 188 Ave 'A' (at 12th St) **212/946-1871** • 10:30pm-4am • mostly gay men • a 'sleazy rock 'n roll bar' • live DJs • strippers • karaoke

Crazy Nanny's 21 7th Ave S (at Leroy) **212/929-8356, 212/366-6312 (EVENT LINE)** • 4pm-4am • mostly women • dancing/DJ from 9pm Th-Sat • transgender-friendly • live shows • karaoke Th • videos

Cubbyhole 281 W 12th St (at 4th St) **212/243-9041** • 4pm-3am, from 2pm wknds • mostly women • neighborhood bar

The Dugout 185 Christopher St (at Weehawken St) **212/242-9113** • 4pm-2am, from 1pm Sun • mostly gay men • neighborhood bar • sports bar • wheelchair access

g 223 W 19th St (at 7th Ave) **212/929-1085** • 4pm-4am • popular • mostly gay men • lounge • live DJs • juice bar

hell 59 Gansevoort St (at Washington) **212/727-1666** • 7pm-4am, from 5pm Fri • lesbians/gay men • swanky lounge • DJ Tue-Th & Sun

Henrietta Hudson 438 Hudson (at Morton) **212/924-3347** • 4pm-4am, from 1pm wknds • mostly women • neighborhood bar • wheelchair access

Marie's Crisis 59 Grove St (at 7th Ave) **212/243-9323** • 4pm-4am • lesbians/gay men • piano bar from 9:30pm, from 5pm Fri-Sun

Meow Mix 269 E Houston St (at Suffolk) **212/254-0688** • 7pm-4am • popular • mostly women • dancing/DJ • live music/shows

The Monster 80 Grove St (at W 4th St, Sheridan Sq) **212/924-3558** • 4pm-4am, from 2pm wknds • popular • mostly gay men • dancing/DJ • piano bar & cabaret • 'Sabor Latino' Mon • disco Tue • wheelchair access

Phoenix 447 E 13th St (at Ave A) **212/477-9979** • 4pm-4am • lesbians/gay men • neighborhood bar • patio

Rubyfruit Bar & Grill 531 Hudson St (at Charles St) **212/929-3343** • 3pm-2am, till 4am Fri-Sat • mostly women • full menu 5pm-11pm, till midnight Fri-Sat • $13-25

Starlight Bar & Lounge 167 Ave 'A' (at 11th St) **212/475-2172** • 9pm-3am, clsd Mon-Wed • lesbians/gay men • more women Sun for 'Starlette' • live DJs • live shows

Stonewall Inn 53 Christopher St (at 7th Ave) **212/463-0950** • 2:30pm-4am • mostly gay men • dancing/DJ

Wonder Bar 505 E 6th St (at Ave 'A') **212/777-9105** • 6pm-4am • popular • lesbians/gay men • trendy cocktail lounge w/ DJ • videos • wheelchair access

Nightclubs

13 Bar & Lounge 35 E 13th St (at University Pl) **212/979-6677** • 10pm-4am • lounge from 5pm • gay-friendly • dancing/DJ • more gay Th

Big Apple Ranch 39 W 19th St, 5th flr (btwn 5th & 6th, at 'Dance Manhattan') **212/358-5752** • 8pm-1am Sat only • lesbians/gay men • dancing/DJ • country/western • two-step lessons • beer only • cover charge

Body & Soul at Vinyl 6 Hubert St (at Hudson) **212/330-9169** • 3pm Sun • gay/straight • happy classic house dancing • a New York must (bring ear-plugs!) • multiracial • also 'Shelter' • 11pm Sat • alcohol-free dance party • cover charge

Clit Club 219 2nd Ave (at 13th St, at the Flamingo) **212/533-2860** • 10pm-4am Fri only • popular • mostly women • dancing/DJ • multiracial • live shows • wheelchair access

Flamingo East 219 2nd Ave (at 13th St) **212/533-2860** • mostly women for 'Clit Club' Fri • popular • dancing/DJ • multiracial

Fourplay 28 W 20th St (btwn 5th & 6th Aves, at Lava) **212/627-7867** • Mon only • mostly women • boys welcome

Legendary Buddha Bar Party 28 7th Ave (at Leroy, at 'Neva Lounge') **888/784-8538** • 9pm Sun only • mostly women • dancing/DJ • multiracial • live shows

Limelight 660 6th Ave (at W 20th St) **212/807-9109** • 10pm-4am Wed-Sun, afterhours Fri-Sat • popular • gay-friendly • gay night Sun (more men Sun at 'Drama!') • dancing/DJ • cover charge

NYC—Soho, Greenwich & Chelsea • New York

LoverGirl NYC 28 E 23rd St (btwn Broadway & Park, at 'True') 212/631-1000, 212/726-8302 • 10pm-4:30am Sat • mostly women • dancing/DJ • multiracial • live shows • cover charge

Nowbar 22 7th Ave S (at Leroy St) 212/802-9502 • 10pm Th-Sat • mostly gay men • transgender-friendly • drag shows • cover charge

Pyramid 101 Ave 'A' (at 7th St) 212/462-9077 • gay-friendly • 10pm-4am • more gay Fri at '1984', New Wave party

Roxy 515 W 18th St (at 10th Ave) 212/645-5156 • 11pm-4am Fri-Sat (rollerdisco from 7pm Wed) • popular • gay/ straight • gay Sat • dancing/DJ • alternative • live shows • cover charge

Shescape 212/686-5665 • women only • dance parties held at various locations throughout NYC area

Squeeze Box 511 Greenwich St (at Spring St, at 'Don Hill's') 212/334-1390 • 10pm last Fri • gay/ straight • dancing/DJ • alternative • rock bands & punk drag queens • cover charge

Cafes

Big Cup 228 8th Ave (at 22nd St) 212/206-0059 • 7am-2am • popular • gay boy central

Caffe Raffaella 134 7th Ave S (at Charles St) 212/929-7247 • 11am-2am • armchair cafe

Restaurants

7A 109 Ave 'A' (at 7th St) 212/673-6583 • 24hrs • popular • American • $9-15

Around the Clock 8 3rd Ave (at 9th St) 212/598-0402 • 24hrs

Benny's Burritos 93 Ave 'A' (at 6th St) 212/254-2054 • 11:30am-midnight • cheap & huge • also 113 Greenwich (at Jane), 212/727-0584

Blue Ribbon 97 Sullivan St (at Spring St) 212/274-0404 • 4pm-4am • clsd Mon • chef hangout • wheelchair access

Brunetta's 190 1st Ave (btwn 11th & 12th Sts) 212/228-4030 • popular • lesbians/gay men • Italian • some veggie • patio • $8-10

Chelsea Bistro & Bar 358 W 23rd St (at 9th Ave) 212/727-2026 • 5pm-11pm • trendy French • full bar

The Cloister Cafe 238 E 9th St (at 2nd Ave) 212/777-9128 • 11am-midnight • garden dining

Cola's 148 8th Ave (at 17th St) 212/633-8020 • 4:30pm-11pm • popular • Italian • some veggie • $8-12

East of Eighth 254 W 23rd St (at 8th) 212/352-0075 • lunch, dinner till midnight, till 2am wknds

Eighteenth & Eighth 159 8th Ave 212/242-5000 • boys, boys, boys

Empire Diner 210 10th Ave (at 22nd St) 212/243-2736 • 24hrs

First 87 1st Ave (at 6th St) 212/674-3823 • 6pm-2am, till 3am Fri Sat, 11am-1am Sun • cont'l • hip crowd

Flamingo East 219 2nd Ave (at 13th St) 212/533-2860 • also bar w/ dancing & 'offbeat rec room'

Florent 69 Gansevoort St (at Washington) 212/989-5779 • 9am-5am, 24hrs Fri-Sat • popular • French diner • $10-15

Food Bar 149 8th Ave (at 17th St) 212/243-2020 • Mediterranean • $10+

Garage 99 7th Ave S (at Grove St) 212/645-0600 • plenty veggie • live jazz

Global 33 99 2nd Ave (at 5th Ave) 212/477-8427 • 5pm-midnight • int'l tapas • full bar • $8-15

La Nouvelle Justine 101 E 2nd St 212/673-8908 • dominants & slaves serve it up in this SM-themed restaurant

LaVagna 545 E 5th St (btwn 'A' & 'B') 212/979-1005 • Italian • some veggie • $12-15

Life Cafe 343 E 10th St (at Ave 'B') 212/477-8791 • 11am-1am, till 3am Fri-Sat • vegetarian artist hangout

Lips 2 Bank St (at Greenwich) 212/675-7710 • 6pm-midnight, till 3am Sat, 'Disco Fever Brunch' noon-6pm Sun • 'the Hard Rock Cafe of drag' • Italian/American served by queens

Lucky Cheng's 24 1st Ave (at 2nd St) 212/473-0516 • 5pm-midnight • popular • Asian/fusion • full bar • drag shows • karaoke

Mary's Restaurant 42 Bedford St (at 7th Ave S) 212/741-3387 • 6pm-midnight, brunch Sun (except summers)

Miracle Grill 112 1st Ave (at 6th St) 212/254-2353 • garden dining

Restivo 209 7th Ave (at 22nd St) 212/366-4133 • noon-midnight • Italian • intimate ambiance • gay-owned/ run

Sacred Chow 522 Hudson St (at W 10th St) 212/337-0863 • 7:30am-11pm • gourmet vegan • wheelchair access

Sazerac House Bar & Grill 533 Hudson (at Charles) 212/989-0313 • noon-11pm • Cajun • full bar • $8-20

New York • USA

Stingy Lulu's 129 St Marks Pl (at Ave 'A') **212/674-3545** • 11am-4am • funky American diner • popular brunch • drag queen servers

Trattoria Pesce Pasta 262 Bleecker St (at 6th Ave) **212/645-2993** • noon-midnight

The Viceroy 160 8th Ave (at 18th St) **212/633-8484** • noon-midnight • popular • fusion • full bar

Entertainment & Recreation

DrédKing Drag King/ Gender-Illusionist **212/946-4475** • one of the best known Drag Kings since 1995 • call for performance dates/details

Leslie-Lohman Gay Art Foundation Gallery 127-B Prince St, lower level **212/673-7007** • 1pm-6pm, clsd Sun-Mon

PS 122 150 1st Ave (at E 9th St) **212/477-5288, 212/477-5029** • it's rough, it's raw, it's real New York performance art

Wessel & O'Connor 242 W 26th St (btwn 7th & 8th Aves) **212/242-8811** • open Tue-Sun in winter, Mon-Fri in summer • gay photography gallery

WOW Cafe Cabaret 59 E 4th St, 4th fl (btwn 2nd Ave & Bowery) **212/777-4280** • open Th-Sat • women's theater

Bookstores

Bleecker Street Books 350 Bleecker St (at W 10th St) **212/675-2084** • 10:30am-11:30pm

Bluestockings Women's Bookstore 172 Allen St (btwn Stanton & Rivington) **212/777-6028** • noon-8pm, from 2pm Sun • live music & performances • also cafe

▲ **Creative Visions Books** 548 Hudson St (btwn Perry & Charles) **212/645-7573, 800/997-9899** • noon-10pm, till 11pm Fri-Sat • lgbt

Oscar Wilde Memorial Bookshop 15 Christopher St (at 7th Ave) **212/255-8097** • 11am-8pm, noon-7pm Sun • lgbt

Soho Books 351 W Broadway (at Grant) **212/226-3395** • 10am-midnight

Retail Shops

DeMask 135 W 22nd St (btwn 6th & 7th Aves) **212/352-2850** • 11am-7pm • European fetish fashion

DV8 211 W 20th St (at 7th Ave) **212/337-9744** • noon-8pm, till 7pm Sat, clsd Sun-Mon • gay-owned/ run

Flight 001 96 Greenwich (btwn Jane & 12th) **212/691-1001** • noon-8pm, clsd Sun • travel gear

---

CREATIVE VISIONS

New York's Lesbian Home for books, videos, dvds, unique gifts and so much more!

Open 7 days 12-10pm
548 Hudson Street
New York, NY 10014
212 645-7573 • (800) 997-9899
www.creativevisionbooks.com

Rainbows & Triangles 192 8th Ave (at 19th St) **212/627-2166** • 11am-9pm, till 10pm Fri-Sat • lgbt

Gyms & Health Clubs

19th St Health & Fitness 22 W 19th St (btwn 5th & 6th) **212/929-6789** • lesbians/ gay men • day passes available

David Barton Gym 552 6th Ave (btwn 15th & 16th) **212/727-0004** • lesbians/ gay men • day passes available

New York Sports Club 128 8th Ave (btwn 16th & 17th) **212/627-0065** • popular • mostly gay men • day passes available

Sex Clubs

Throb **718/788-5122** • 8pm-1am 1st Th only • women-only play party • call for location

Erotica

Pleasure Chest 156 7th Ave S (at Charles) **212/242-2158**

Toys in Babeland 94 Rivington (btwn Orchard & Ludlow) **212/375-1701** • noon-10pm, till 8pm Sun

NYC—Downtown

Accommodations

▲ **Holiday Inn Wall Street District** 15 Gold St **212/232-7700, 800/465-4329** • gay/ straight • all suites & rooms have 'virtual offices' • also 'Platinum Cafe' • wheelchair access • $229+ • see ad page 346

Nightclubs

After Work Wednesdays 330 W38th St (btwn 8th & 9th Aves) **888/784-8538** • 6pm-2am Wed • mostly women • multiracial • networking & karaoke 6pm-10pm • free buffet • dancing/DJ from 10pm

NYC—Midtown

Accommodations

Gershwin Hotel 7 E 27th St (at 5th Ave) **212/545-8000** • gay-friendly • artsy, seedy hotel w/ model's floor dorms & rooms • also bar & cafe • jazz room • art gallery

Habitat Hotel 130 E 57th St (at Lexington) **212/753-8841, 800/255-0482** • gay-friendly, upscale budget hotel

Holiday Inn Martinique on Broadway 49 W 32nd St (btwn Broadway & 5th) **212/736-3800, 888/694-6543** • gay/ straight • restaurant

The Hotel Metro 45 W 35th St (at 5th Ave) **212/947-2500, 800/356-3870** • gay-friendly • slick art deco hotel • 1 blk from Empire State Bldg • $150+

Ivy Terrace **516/662-6862** • private studio rental • terrace • women-owned/ run • $150-225

Park Central Hotel 870 7th Ave (at 56th St) **212/247-8000, 800/346-1359** • gay-friendly • also restaurant • wheelchair access • $179+

Travel Inn 515 W 42nd St (at 10th Ave) **212/695-7171, 800/869-4630** • gay-friendly • swimming • $125-200

Bars

BS New York 405 3rd Ave (at 29th St) **212/684-8376** • 3pm-4am • mostly gay men • neighborhood bar • videos • theme nights

Cleo's Saloon 656 9th Ave (at 46th St) **212/307-1503** • 8am-4am, from noon Sun • mostly gay men • neighborhood bar

Danny's Skylight Room 346 W 46th St (at 9th Ave) **212/265-8133** • 4pm-midnight, brunch 11:30am-3pm Wed & wknds • gay-friendly • piano bar from 6pm • cabaret • cover + 2 drink minimum

Don't Tell Mama 343 W 46th St (at 9th Ave) **212/757-0788** • 4pm-4am • popular • gay-friendly • young crowd • piano bar & cabaret • cover + 2 drink minimum • call for shows

Dusk 147 W 24th St (btwn 6th & 7th) **212/924-4490** • 6pm-close, clsd Sun • gay/ straight

Hannah's Lava Lounge 923 8th Ave (at 55th St) **212/974-9087** • noon-4am • lesbians/ gay men • art exhibits

Julie's 305 E 53rd St, 2nd Fl (btwn 2nd & 3rd Ave) **212/688-1294** • 5pm-4am • mostly women • professional crowd • DJ Wed-Sun • piano bar • theme nights

Oscar Wilde 221 E 58th St (at 2nd Ave) **212/486-7309** • 4pm-4am • mostly gay men • professional crowd

Regents 317 E 53rd St (at 2nd Ave) **212/593-3091** • 5pm-4am • mostly gay men • also restaurant • plenty veggie • $7-17

The Web 40 E 58th St (at Madison) **212/308-1546** • 4pm-3am • mostly gay men • dancing/DJ • Asian-American clientele • live shows • theme nights • karaoke Sun

Nightclubs

Escuelita 301 W 39th St (at 8th Ave) **212/631-0588** • 10pm-4am • mostly gay men • mostly women for 'Spicy Fridays' • dancing/ DJ • Latino/a clientele

Female Fridaze 133 W 33rd St (btwn 6th & 7th, at 'Club Midtown 133') **888/784-8538** • 10pm Fri only • mostly women • dancing/DJ • multiracial

New York • USA

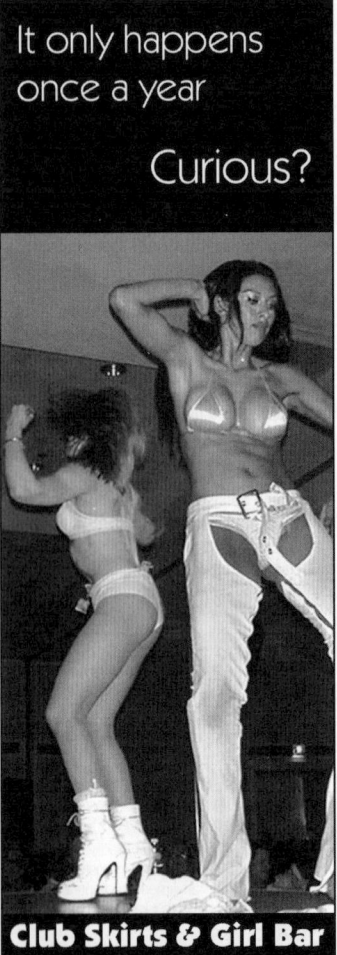

Club Skirts & Girl Bar
Dinah Shore Weekend
March 28-31, 2002
1-800-44-DINAH

Her/ She Bar 301 W 39th St (at 8th Ave, at 'Escuelita') **212/631–1093** • 10pm-4am Fri • mostly women • dancing/DJ • cover charge

CAFES

Cafe Un Deux Trois 123 W 44th St (at Broadway) **212/354–4148** • noon-midnight • popular • bistro • $12-24

RESTAURANTS

Bar Nine 807 9th Ave (at W 53rd St) **212/399–9336** • 5pm-4am

Comfort Diner 216 E 45th St (at 3rd Ave) **212/867–4555** • 7am-10pm • reasonable '50s diner

Mangia e Bevi 800 9th Ave (at W 53rd St) **212/956–3976** • noon-midnight • Italian

Martino's 230 E 58th St (btwn 2nd & 3rd Ave) **212/751–0029** • dinner, Sun brunch • Italian • popular w/ local lesbians • nr 'Julie's' bar

Revolution 611 9th Ave (at 43rd St) **212/489–8451** • 5pm-midnight • trendy video dining • bar till 3am

Rice & Beans 744 9th Ave (at 50th St) **212/265–4444** • 11am-10pm • Latin/ Brazilian • plenty veggie

Scopa 27 E 28th St (at Madison) **212/686–8787** • publisher's choice • great Italian deli from 8am, lunch & dinner daily in the main dining room, full bar

Townhouse Restaurant 206 E 58th St (at 3rd Ave) **212/826–6241** • lunch & dinner, Sun brunch (open late wknds) • popular • lesbians/ gay men • $10-23

EROTICA

Come Again 353 E 53rd St (at 2nd Ave) **212/308–9394** • clsd Sun • woman-owned erotica store

Eve's Garden 119 W 57th St #1201 (btwn 6th & 7th) **212/757–8651** • 11am-7pm, clsd Sun • women's sexuality boutique

NYC—Uptown

ACCOMMODATIONS

333 West 88th Associates 333 W 88th St (at Riverside Dr) **212/724–9818, 800/724–9888** • gay-friendly • apts & B&B rooms • kitchens • fireplaces • gay-owned/ run • $494-1011/ week

BARS

Brandy's Piano Bar 235 E 84th St (at 2nd Ave) **212/650–1944** • 4pm-4am • mostly gay men

Bridge Bar 309 E 60th St (at 2nd Ave) **212/223–9104** • 4pm-4am • mostly gay men

NYC—Bronx • New York

Nightclubs

Intimate Collaborations 2611 Frederick Douglas Blvd/ 8th Ave (at 139th St) **212/894-3724 x 1285** • 7pm-close Th • mostly women • dancing/ DJ • 18+ • multiracial clientele • food served • wheelchair access • lesbian run

Restaurants

Carnegie Delicatessen 854 7th Ave (nr 55th St) **212/757-2245** • 7am-4am • one of NYC's most famous delis

NYC—Brooklyn

Info Lines & Services

Audre Lorde Project 85 S Oxford St **718/596-0342, 718/596-0016** • 10am-6pm, till 9pm Tue-Th, 1:30pm-9pm Sat, clsd Sun • lgbt center for people of color • events • resources • HIV services • library

Brooklyn Pride **718/670-3337** • host events • also publish newsletter

Bars

The Abbey 536 Driggs Ave (btwn N 7th & 8th), Williamsburg **718/599-4400** • from 4pm • gay/ straight • more gay Sun night • neighborhood bar • dancing/DJ

Bar 4 444 7th Ave (at 15th St, in Park Slope) **718/832-9800** • 6pm-4am • gay/ straight • neighborhood bar • DJ Sat • live music & performances

Excelsior 390 5th Ave (btwn 6th & 7th), Brooklyn **718/832-1599** • 6pm-4am, from 2pm wknds • lesbians/ gay men • more women Th • patio

Ginger's Bar 363 5th Ave (btwn 5th & 6th Sts, in Park Slope) **718/788-0924** • 6pm-4am, from 2pm wknds • lesbians/ gay men • more women Th • neighborhood bar • DJ Sat

Rising Cafe 186 5th Ave (at Sackett) **718/789-6340** • 5pm-midnight, from 1pm Fri, from 10am-2am wknds • live music • performances • poetry

Nightclubs

Club Ovations 860 Atlantic Ave (btwn Vanderbilt & Clinton), Brooklyn **888/784-8538** • Sat only • mostly women • dancing/ DJ • multiracial clientele

Spectrum 802 64th St (at 8th Ave) **718/238-8213** • 9:30pm-4am Th-Sat • lesbians/ gay men • dancing/DJ • live shows • karaoke Fri

Cafes

Halcyon 227 Smith (at Butler), Carroll Gardens **718/260-9299** • noon-midnight • beer/ wine • also antiques & record store

Restaurants

200 Fifth 200 5th Ave (btwn Union & Sackett) **718/638-0023, 718/638-2925** • 4pm-close • eclectic • full bar • live shows

Aunt Suzie 247 5th Ave (at Garfield Pl) **718/788-2868** • dinner only • Italian

Johnny Mack's 1114 8th Ave (btwn 11th & 12th) **718/832-7961** • 4pm-11pm, till 1am Fri-Sat, Sun brunch noon-3:30pm

Max & Moritz 426-A 7th Ave (btwn 14th & 15th) **718/499-5557** • 5:30pm-close, wknd brunch • French/ American

Santa Fe Grill 62 7th Ave (at Lincoln) **718/636-0279** • 5:30pm-close • also bar

Sweet Mama's 168 7th Ave (nr 1st St), Brooklyn **718/768-8766** • dinner only

Entertainment & Recreation

Sing Out! Brooklyn **718/769-1421** • concerts & special events

Spiritual Groups

Brooklyn Heights Synagogue 131 Remsen St (btwn Henry & Clinton) **718/522-2070** • 6:30pm Fri

First Unitarian Church of Brooklyn 48 Monroe Pl (btwn Pierpont & Clark) **718/624-5466** • 11am Sun

NYC—Queens

Info Lines & Services

Q-GLU (Queens Gay/ Lesbians, Inc) **718/205-6605** • 1st Tue

Bars

Albatross 36-19 24th Ave (at 37th), Astoria **718/274-9164** • 6pm-close • mostly women • neighborhood bar • lesbian-owned/ run

Nightclubs

Atlantis 2010 76-19 Roosevelt Ave (at 77th St), Jackson Hts **718/457-3939** • 10pm-4am Fri-Sun only • lesbians/ gay men • dancing/DJ • mostly Latina/o • live shows

Krash 34-48 Steinway St, Astoria **718/937-2400** • open Mon & Th-Sat • lesbians/ gay men • more women Sat • dancing/DJ Fri-Sat • multiracial

NYC—Bronx

Nightclubs

Negra's Way 1306 Union Port Rd (at Westchester Ave) **718/822-9274** • 9pm-4am Wed only

Damron Women's Traveller 2002

New York • USA

The Warehouse 141 E 140th St (btwn Grand Concourse & Walton) **718/992-5974** • 11pm-close Fri-Sat • mostly gay men • dancing/DJ • cover charge

NYC—Staten Island

INFO LINES & SERVICES

Lambda Associates of Staten Island **718/876-8786**

Niagara Falls

see also Buffalo, New York & Niagara Falls, Ontario, Canada

Nyack

BARS

Coven Cafe 162 Main St **845/358-9829** • 5pm-1am, noon-3am Fri-Sat, Sun brunch, clsd Mon • gay-friendly • women's night Tue • T-dance 4pm Sun in summer • also restaurant • cont'l w/ Southern accent • wheelchair access • $8-20

NIGHTCLUBS

Barz 327 Rte 9 W **845/353-4444** • 8pm-4am, from 3pm Sun • lesbians/ gay men • dancing/DJ • wheelchair access

Orange County

NIGHTCLUBS

Zippers 658 Rte 211 E (exit 120, off Rte 17), Middletown **845/692-9093** • 9pm-4am Fri-Sat only • lesbians/ gay men • dancing/DJ • patio • 18+ • wheelchair access

RESTAURANTS

Folderol II 795 Rte 284, Westtown **845/726-3822** • 5pm-close, clsd Mon-Tue • French/ farmhouse • some veggie • piano Sat • wheelchair access • gay-owned/ run • $13-23

EROTICA

Exotic Gifts & Videos 658 Rte 211 E (exit 120, off Rte 17), Middletown **845/692-6664**

Ossining

SPIRITUAL GROUPS

Trinity Episcopal Church 7 S Highland/ Rte 9 **914/941-0806** • 7:30am & 10am Sun

Oswego

INFO LINES & SERVICES

SUNY Oswego Women's Center 243 Hewitt Union, 2nd flr **315/341-2967**

Plattsburgh

BARS

Backstreet 30 Marion St (btwn Clinton & Court) **518/563-8211** • 6pm-2am • lesbians/ gay men • dancing/DJ • 2nd Sat women's dance • special events • 18+ • live shows • transgender-friendly • wheelchair access • gay-owned/ run

Port Chester

see also Greenwich & Stamford, Connecticut

BARS

Sandy's Old Homestead 325 N Main St (at Wilkins) **914/939-0758** • noon-4am • gay-friendly • food served • monthly women's parties w/ go-go girls • wheelchair access

Poughkeepsie

INFO LINES & SERVICES

Poughkeepsie GALA (Gay/ Lesbian Association) 20 Carrol St (at Christ Episcopal Church) **845/431-6756** • 7:30pm Tue • call for events

BARS

Congress 411 Main St (off Academy) **845/486-9068** • 3pm-4am, from 8pm Sun • lesbians/ gay men • neighborhood bar • wheelchair access

Rochester

INFO LINES & SERVICES

AA Gay/ Lesbian 244 Alexander St (at Genesee Hospital) **716/232-6720 (AA#)**

Coalition for Lesbian Visibility 315/ **568-9364** • 2nd Sat socials • call for details

Gay Alliance of the Genesee Valley (GAGV) 179 Atlantic Ave (at Elton) **716/244-8640** • 1pm-9pm Mon-Th, 1pm-6pm Fri, clsd wknds • community ctr • also info line

Latino Mission 1350 University Ave (btwn Culver & Winton, at AIDS Rochester) • 7pm 2nd & 4th Th

Transgender Organization at GAGV Ctr • 6:30pm 3rd Wed & 2pm last Sat

BARS

Anthony's 522 522 E Main St (at Scio) **716/325-2060** • noon-2am • lesbians/ gay men • neighborhood bar • karaoke

Sharon Springs • New York

Avenue Pub 522 Monroe Ave (at Goodman) 716/244-4960 • 4pm-2am • popular • mostly gay men • neighborhood bar • dancing/DJ • patio

Enigma 113 State St (at Andrews) 716/262-2650 • 11am-2am • lesbians/ gay men • neighborhood bar

Muther's 40 S Union St (at Gardiner Park) 716/325-6216 • 2am-2pm Mon-Th, till 3am Fri-Sun • popular • lesbians/gay men • dancing/DJ • live shows Sun • gay-owned/ run

RJ's Pub 140 Alexander St 716/256-1000 • 3pm-2am • mostly gay men • neighborhood bar • also restaurant • dancing/DJ • gay-owned/ run

Tara Lounge 153 Liberty Pole Wy (at Andrews) 716/232-4719 • noon-2am • popular • lesbians/ gay men • neighborhood bar • piano bar Fri-Sat • older crowd

NIGHTCLUBS

GQ 444 Central Ave 716/546-7270, 716/234-4807 • 5pm-2am Th-Fri, 10pm-3am Sat-Sun, clsd Mon-Wed • lesbians/gay men • dancing/DJ • also country/ western line dancing • live shows • 18+

CAFES

Little Theatre Cafe 240 East Ave 716/258-0412 • 5:30pm-10pm, from noon wknds, till midnight Fri-Sat • popular • beer/ wine • soups • salads • live jazz Fri-Sat • wheelchair access • $5-10

RESTAURANTS

Edibles 704 University Ave (at Oxford) 716/271-4910 • clsd Sun • lunch & dinner • also bar & lounge

Slice of Life Cafe 742 South Ave (at Caroline) 716/271-8010 • 11:30am-8pm, 10am-2pm Sun, clsd Mon-Wed • vegetarian • women-owned/ run

Triphammer Grill 60 Browns Race (btwn Platt & Commercial) 716/262-2700 • lunch Mon-Fri, dinner nightly, clsd Sun • patio • full bar • $10-22

RETAIL SHOPS

Outlandish 274 N Goodman St (in the Village Gate) 716/760-8383 • 11am-11pm, noon-5pm Sun • videos • pride items • books • toys • gay-owned/ run

The Pride Connection 728 South Ave (1 blk from Gregory) 716/242-7840 • 10am-9pm, noon-6pm Sun • lgbt gifts & books

PUBLICATIONS

Empty Closet 716/244-9030 • lgbt newspaper • resource listings

SPIRITUAL GROUPS

Dignity/ Integrity 17 S Fitzhugh St (at Broad, in Church of St Luke & St Simon Cyrene...look for the pink steeple) 716/234-5092 • 5pm Sun

Open Arms MCC 175 Norris Dr (off Culver Rd, nr Cobbs Hill Park) 716/271-8478 • 10:30am & 6:30pm Sun • wheelchair access

Saratoga Springs

ACCOMMODATIONS

Saratoga B&B 434 Church St 518/584-0920, 800/584-0920 • gay-friendly • 1850 farmhouse • full brkfst • fireplaces • smokefree • lesbian-owned/ run • $85-225

BOOKSTORES

Nahani 482 Broadway 518/587-4322 • 10am-7pm, noon-5pm Sun • wheelchair access

Schenectady

see Capital District

Seneca Falls

ACCOMMODATIONS

Guion House 32 Cayuga St 315/568-8129, 800/631-8919 • gay-friendly • 1870s brick mansion • full brkfst • some shared baths • smokefree • woman-owned/ run • $69-85

Sharon Springs

ACCOMMODATIONS

American Hotel Main St/ Rte 10 518/284-2105 • gay/ straight • also restaurant & bar • kids ok • wheelchair access • gay-owned/ run • $120+

Brimstonia Cottage 149 Main St (on Rte 10) 518/284-2839 • gay-friendly • cottage suites w/ kitchens • smokefree • $80-110

Edgefield 518/284-3339 • gay/ straight • full brkfst • smokefree • well-appointed English Country house • gay-owned/ run • $110-165

New Yorker Guest House Center St 518/284-2093 • gay-friendly • seasonal • full brkfst wknds • kids 7+ ok • smokefree • woman-owned/ run • $65-135

The TurnAround Spa 201 Washington St 518/284-2271, 212/628-9008 • lesbians/ gay men • small hotel & health spa • full brkfst • hot tub • food served • smokefree • kids ok • clsd Nov-May • gay-owned/ run • $45-75

New York • USA

RETAIL SHOPS

The Finishing Touch 123 Main St (Rte 10) **518/284-2884** • 9am-4pm, clsd Mon • gallery & gift shop

Syracuse

INFO LINES & SERVICES

AA Gay/ Lesbian 315/463-5011 (AA#) • call for mtg schedule

Pride Community Center 745 N Salina St **315/426-1650** • 6pm-9pm Tue-Fri, noon-6pm Sat • hrs vary, call first

SAGE Upstate 620 W Genessee (1st Presbyterian Church) **315/478-1923** • mtg & potluck 2nd Sun for lgbt folks 40+ & friends

Women's Information Center 601 Allen St **315/478-4636** • 10am-4pm, clsd wknds • also Lesbian Social Group & Lesbian Discussion Group • wheelchair access

BARS

My Bar 205 N West St (at W Genessee) **315/471-9279** • 10am-2am, till 4am Fri-Sat, from noon Sun • lesbians/ gay men • neighborhood bar • food served • live entertainment • women-owned/ run

Rain Lounge 218 N Franklin St (at Herald Pl) **315/474-3401** • 3pm-2am • mostly gay men • neighborhood bar • professional • multiracial • transgender-friendly • gay-owned/ run

The Starlight Room 400 S Clinton St **315/471-9059** • 8am-2am • mostly gay men • neighborhood bar • wheelchair access

NIGHTCLUBS

Trexx 319 N Clinton St (exit 18 off Rte 81) **315/474-6408** • 8pm-2am, till 4am Fri-Sat, T-dance from 4pm Sun, clsd Mon-Tue • mostly gay men • dancing/DJ • drag shows Sun • videos • 18+ • wheelchair access

CAFES

Happy Endings 317 S Clinton St (at W Fayette) **315/475-1853** • 10am-midnight, from 1pm wknds • lunch & coffee • live shows • wheelchair access

RESTAURANTS

Tu Tu Venue 731 James St (enter on Willow St) **315/475-8888** • 5pm-11pm, clsd Sun-Mon, bar open later wknds • popular • lesbians/ gay men • women-owned/ run • $12-15

BOOKSTORES

My Sisters' Words 304 N McBride St (at James) **315/428-0227** • 10am-6pm, till 8pm Fri, open Sun in winter • women's • community bulletin board

SPIRITUAL GROUPS

Ray of Hope Church 315/471-6618 • 6pm Sun

Tivoli

RESTAURANTS

Cafe Pongo 69 Broadway **845/757-4403** • lunch Th-Fri, dinner Tue-Sun, brunch wknds, clsd Mon • 'everything made from scratch' • full bar • live shows • wheelchair access

Troy

see Capital District

Utica

NIGHTCLUBS

That Place 216 Bleecker St (at Genessee) **315/724-1446** • 8pm-2am, from 4pm Fri • popular • mostly gay men • dancing/DJ • leather • young crowd • wheelchair access

CAFES

Crystal Mountain Coffee House & Witch Shoppe 241 Genessee St **315/732-4120** • 6pm-11pm, till midnight Fri, from noon Sat, clsd Sun-Mon • 'coffee, tea, tarot' • light menu w/ desserts • gay-owned/ run

White Plains

INFO LINES & SERVICES

Lesbian Line 914/949-3203 • 6pm-10pm

The Loft 180 E Post Rd (lower level) **914/948-4922** • lgbt community ctr • open evenings & wknds • also newsletter

Woodstock

see Catskill Mtns

Asheville • North Carolina

NORTH CAROLINA

Statewide

PUBLICATIONS

▲ **The Front Page** 919/829-0181 • lgbt newspaper for the Carolinas

Arden

EROTICA

Southeastern Fantasy & Video 2317 Henderson Rd **828/684-2821** • toys

Asheville

includes Black Mountain

INFO LINES & SERVICES

CLOSER (Community Liaison for Support, Education & Reform) 828/277-7815

Lambda AA All Souls Church, Biltmore Village **828/254-8539 (AA#)** • 8pm Fri

ACCOMMODATIONS

The 1900 Inn on Montford 296 Montford Ave **828/254-9569, 800/254-9569** • gay-friendly • popular • English cottage • full brkfst • $155-275

▲ **27 Blake Street** 27 Blake St **828/252-7390** • women only • romantic room w/ private entrance in Victorian home • gardens • Southern hopsitality • smokefree • $70

Acorn Cottage B&B 25 St Dunstans Cir **828/253-0609, 800/699-0609** • gay/ straight • 1925 granite home • full brkfst • smokefree • woman-owned/ run • $75-110

The Bird's Nest B&B 41 Oak Park Rd **828/252-2381** • lesbians/ gay men • comfortable, secluded & quiet B&B • located on the 2nd flr of a turn-of-the-century home • kids ok • lesbian-owned/ run • $85

Bodhi Tree House 395 Lakey Gap Acres, Black Mountain **828/669-3889** • mostly women • transgender-friendly • guesthouse • fireplace • 5 decks • nr hiking trails • smokefree • lesbian-owned/ run • $55-200

Brook Haven Weaverville **828/649-0619** • gay/ straight • cabin on trout stream • 15 mins from Asheville • smokefree • woman-owned/ run • $70-100

▲ **Camp Pleiades** **828/688-9201, 888/324-3110** • open Memorial Day thru mid-October • women-only • mtn retreat • cabins & camping • all meals included • some shared baths • swimming • smokefree • lesbian-owned/ run • $45-88

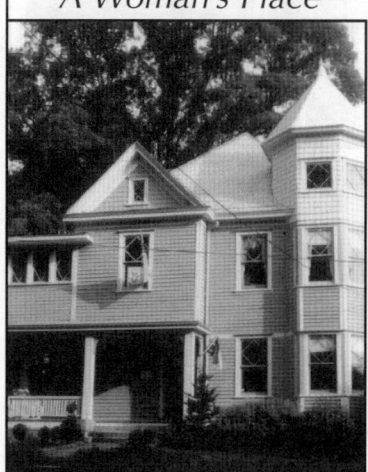

27 Blake Street
"A Woman's Place"

A beautiful Victorian home, charmingly landscaped and located in the Historic Montford District just a few blocks from downtown Asheville, NC & I-240.

Give yourself or that special someone a memorable experience in your romantic room with your own *private entrance*.

Enjoy a visit to **27 Blake Street**, convenient to all that makes Asheville a fun, diverse "Land of the Sky."

Call: 828-252-7390
27 Blake Street
Asheville, NC 28801
email: puckberry@aol.com

North Carolina • USA

Asheville

ANNUAL EVENTS: July - NC International Folk Festival (world cultural heritage celebration) 828/452-2997 or 877/365-5872, web: www.folkmoot.com.

CITY INFO: 828/258-6101, web: www.ashevillechamber.org.

ATTRACTIONS: Biltmore Estate 800/543-2961.
Blue Ridge Parkway.
North Carolina Arboretum 828/665-2492.

WEATHER: Gorgeous: temperate summers and mild winters, with a beautiful spring and fall.

TRANSIT: New Bluebird Taxi 828/258-8331.
Sky Shuttle 828/253-0006.
Asheville Transit System 828/252-8785.

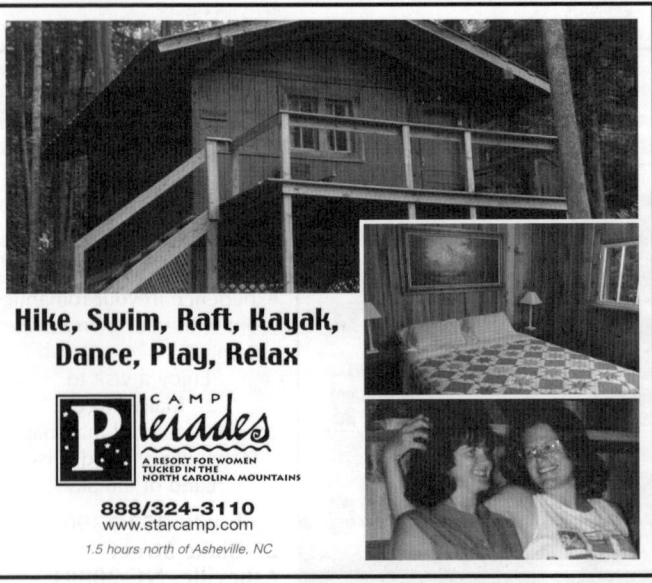

Hike, Swim, Raft, Kayak, Dance, Play, Relax

CAMP Pleiades
A RESORT FOR WOMEN TUCKED IN THE NORTH CAROLINA MOUNTAINS

888/324-3110
www.starcamp.com

1.5 hours north of Asheville, NC

Asheville • North Carolina

Compassionate Expressions Mtn Inn 207 Robinson Cove Rd, Leicester **828/683-6633** • mostly women • 'rooms w/ a view' of Blue Ridge Mtns • 2 RV hookups • on 40 acres • women-owned/run

Cottage at Woodhaven 828/299-8757 • lesbians/gay men • cottage rental • deck • fireplace • smokefree • lesbian-owned/run • $75

Emy's Nook 828/281-4122 • women only • gracious older house north of downtown Asheville • lesbian-owned/run • $55-60

The Hawk & Ivy B&B 133 N Fork Rd, Barnardsville 28709 **828/626-3486, 888/395-7254** • gay/straight • full brkfst • smokefree • kids ok • wheelchair access • $90-125

Mountain Laurel B&B 139 Lee Dotson Rd, Fairview **828/628-9903** • lesbians/gay men • 25 miles from Asheville • full brkfst • smokefree • lesbian-owned/run • $90-110

Our Haven In the Mountains Black Mountain **828/669-7580** • women only • secluded cottage • hiking trails • waterfalls • lesbian-owned/run • $60

Our Haven 828/669-7580 • mostly lesbians • private guest cottage • scenic view • nr downtown • lesbian-owned/run • $75

▲ **Owl's Nest Inn at Engadine** 2630 Smokey Park Hwy (off I-40 at exit 37), Candler **828/665-8325, 800/665-8868** • gay/straight • 1880s Victorian • full brkfst • fireplace • lesbian-owned/run • $120-195

River Watch & Raven Crest 4736 Sharon Rd, Ste W-125, Charlotte **704/643-1211** • gay/straight • mtn cabins nr Asheville • smokefree • shared baths • kids/pets ok • gay-owned/run • $120-170

WhiteGate Inn & Cottage 173 E Chestnut St **828/253-2553, 800/485-3045** • popular • gay/straight • full-service B&B • 3-course brkfst • gay-owned/run • $145-185

BARS

O'Henry's 59 Haywood St (nr Civic Center) **828/254-1891** • 1pm-2am, from noon wknds • lesbians/gay men • neighborhood bar • dancing/DJ • live shows • private club

Tressa's 28 Broadway **828/254-7072** • 4pm-2am, from 7pm Sat, clsd Sun • gay/straight • jazz/cigar bar • live entertainment

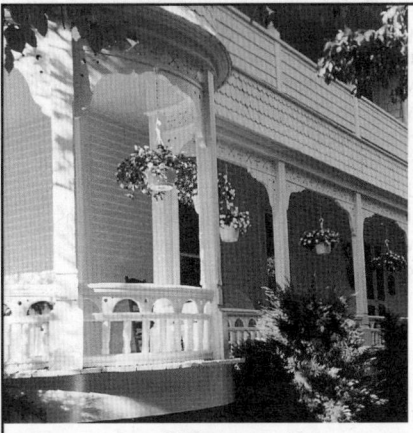

Elegant 1885 Victorian inn nestled in the mountains just outside Asheville

- Full breakfast
- Private baths
- Fireplaces
- Whirlpool suite
- Evening wine and cheese
- Mountain views

OWL'S NEST INN AT ENGADINE
2630 Smokey Park Hwy, Candler, NC 28715
(828) 665-8325   800-665-8868
www.engadineinn.com

North Carolina • USA

Reply **Forward** **Delete**

Date: Fri, Nov 16, 2001 10:31:23
From: Ottersen@yahoo.com
To: Editor@Damron.com
Subject: Asheville

> Magical. This word tends to appear in any discussion of Asheville. Maybe it's the ancient blue mountains on every horizon, or the alchemy of mixing artists, new agers, and an amazing lesbian population with mountain folk and Bible Belters, in one small Southern city. Whatever the reason, Asheville lives up to her magical reputation.

> Downtown you will find a lively, walkable city center brimming with galleries, eclectic shops, and coffee houses. **Malaprop's Bookstore & Cafe** is a hub of womyn's community. Of particular note is 'Cafe of our Own,' a women's poetry reading held every third Saturday at Malaprop's and hosted by an inspiring lesbian poet. Malaprop's' bulletin boards and free alternative newspapers are invaluable in finding things to see and do. **Community Connections,** the LGBT monthly, contains a community calendar.

> While you're downtown, catch a film at the 'Fine Arts Theater,' stop by **Rainbow's End** books & gifts for rainbow stickers and videos, and wander the galleries. At night, sample cool jazz at **Tressa's.** Weekends, dance late-nite at **Scandals.** You'll see lesbians everywhere—after all, Asheville is rumored to have one of the largest per capita populations of lesbians in the country. You can get a preview from Asheville's lesbian website: www.a-SHEville.com.

> Downtown is just a part of what this area has to offer. Check out 'New Morning Gallery' and 'Blue' goldsmiths, both in Biltmore Village. Hop on the Blue Ridge Parkway and you'll find mountains, overlooks, and waterfalls, with great hiking and whitewater to tantalize outdoor types. Explore it all!

Blowing Rock • North Carolina

NIGHTCLUBS

The Hairspray Cafe 38 N French Broad Ave (at Patton Ave) **828/258-2027** • 8pm-3am • lesbians/ gay men • dancing/DJ • live shows • karaoke

Scandals 11 Grove St (at Patton) **828/252-2838** • 10pm-3am Fri-Sat only • lesbians/ gay men • 3 bars • dancing/DJ • live shows • videos • 18+ • private club • wheelchair access

CAFES

Beanstreets Coffee 3 Broadway **828/255-8180** • 7:30am-6pm, till 10pm Wed, till 12:30am Th-Sat, 9am-4am Sun

Laurey's 67 Biltmore Ave **828/252-1500** • 10am-6pm, till 4pm Sat, clsd Sun • popular • bright cafe w/ delicious salads & cookies • also dinners to go • lesbian-owned/ run • wheelchair access

RESTAURANTS

Grove Street Cafe on Hayward 57 Hayward St **828/255-0010** • 6pm-1am Wed-Sun, Sun brunch • T-dance & bbq 2pm-8pm Sun in summer • steaks/ seafood • some veggie • also John Henry's Bar • patio • $10-15

Laughing Seed Cafe 40 Wall St (at Hayword) **828/252-3445** • 11:30am-9pm, till 10pm Fri-Sat, Sun brunch, clsd Tue • vegetarian/ vegan • beer/ wine • patio • wheelchair access • $4-9

ENTERTAINMENT & RECREATION

Tantrum Watersports **828/254-2756** • custom excursions on Lake James • watersports instruction • camping trips • lesbian-owned/ run

BOOKSTORES

Downtown Books & News 67 N Lexington Ave (btwn Walnut & Hiawassee) **828/253-8654** • 8am-6pm • used books & new magazines • lgbt section

Malaprop's Bookstore & Cafe 55 Haywood St (at Walnut) **828/254-6734, 800/441-9829** • 9am-9pm, till 11pm Fri-Sat, till 6pm Sun • readings • performances • women's poetry reading 8pm 3rd Sat

Rainbow's End 10 N Spruce St **828/285-0005** • 10am-5pm, till 6pm Fri-Sat, 2pm-4pm Sun • lgbt • also gifts & video rentals • lesbian-owned/ run

Reader's Corner 31 Montford Ave **828/285-8805** • 11am-7pm, 10am-6pm Sat, from 1pm Sun • used books

RETAIL SHOPS

The Goddess Store 382 Montford Ave **828/258-3102** • noon-6pm Th-Sat only • lesbian/ feminist gifts • divination tools • Wiccan items • call for class schedules • wheelchair access • woman-owned/ run

Jewels That Dance: Jewelry Design 63 Haywood St **828/254-5088** • 10am-6pm, clsd Sun • gay-owned/ run

PUBLICATIONS

Community Connections **828/251-2449** • monthly lgbt magazine

SPIRITUAL GROUPS

The Cathedral of All Souls Biltmore Village **828/274-2681** • 8am, 9am & 11:15am Sun, noon & 5:45pm Wed • wheelchair access

MCC of Asheville 420 Swannanoa Rd **828/296-0062** • 6:30pm Sun • wheelchair access

St Joan of Arc Catholic Church 919 Haywood Rd (at Mitchell Ave) **828/252-3151** • 5pm & 7pm Sat, 8:30am & 11:30am Sun

Unitarian Universalist Church of Asheville 1 Edwin Pl (at Charlotte) **828/254-6001** • 9:30am & 11:15am Sun (10am Sun summers) • wheelchair access

EROTICA

Bedtyme Stories 2334 Hendersonville Rd, Arden **828/684-8250**

Atlantic Beach

ACCOMMODATIONS

Royal Pavilion Resort 125 Salter Path Rd **252/726-5188, 800/533-3700** • gay-friendly • oceanfront hotel • hot tub • gym • swimming • also restaurant & bar

Blowing Rock

ACCOMMODATIONS

Stone Pillar B&B 144 Pine St **828/295-4141, 800/962-9955** • gay/ straight • historic 1920s house • full brkfst • wheelchair access • gay-owned/ run • $65-110

StoneRidge **828/963-2525, 877/963-2525** • gay-friendly • seasonal mtn lodge • some shared baths • pets ok • gay-owned/ run • $75-80

North Carolina • USA

Cashiers

ACCOMMODATIONS

Jane's Aerie Cottage 828/743-9002 • mostly women • cottage in great mtn location • $95/night, $450/week

Chapel Hill

see Raleigh/Durham/Chapel Hill

Charlotte

INFO LINES & SERVICES

AA Gay/Lesbian 3200 Park Rd (at St Luke's Lutheran Church) **704/332-4387 (AA#)** • 8pm Fri

Gay/Lesbian Switchboard **704/535-6277** • 6:30pm-10:30pm Sun-Th

ACCOMMODATIONS

Chez Arlaine B&B 425 Pecan Ave (at 7th) **704/643-1211** • gay/straight • elegant 1920 house • full brkfst • smokefree • lesbian-owned/run • $90-150

The Morehead Inn 1122 E Morehead St **704/376-3357, 888/667-3432** • gay-friendly • antique-filled suites in historic neighborhood • full brkfst • kids ok • wheelchair access • gay-owned/run • $120-190

Vanlandingham Estate 2010 The Plaza **704/334-8909, 888/524-2020** • gay-friendly • Bungalow-style estate • full brkfst • smokefree • wheelchair access • gay-owned/run • $135-185

BARS

Brass Rail 3707 Wilkinson Blvd (at Morehead) **704/399-8413** • 5pm-2:30am, from 3pm Sun • popular • mostly gay men • neighborhood bar • leather • private club • wheelchair access

Central Station 2131 Central Ave (at The Plaza) **704/377-0906** • 5pm-2am • lesbians/gay men • neighborhood bar • multiracial • private club

Hartigan's Irish Pub 601 S Cedar St **704/347-1841** • 11am-10pm, till 2am wknds, from 5pm Sun • gay/straight • neighborhood bar • food served • popular lesbian hangout • gay-owned/run

Have a Nice Day Cafe 314 N College St (btwn 6th & 7th) **704/373-2233** • 9pm-2am, from 8pm Sat • gay-friendly • dancing/DJ • 18+

Liaisons 316 Rensselaer Ave (at South Blvd) **704/376-1617** • 5pm-1am • popular • lesbians/gay men • neighborhood bar • also restaurant Wed-Sun • videos • private club • women-owned/run

NIGHTCLUBS

Club Myxx 3110 S Tryon St **704/525-5001** • 10pm-4am Sat & 9pm-close Sun • lesbians/gay men • dancing/DJ • mostly African-American • live shows • private club

Genesis 605 W 5th St (at N Graham) **704/358-0322** • Fri-Sat nights • mostly gay men • dancing/DJ

Mythos 300 N College St (at 6th) **704/375-8765, 704/559-5959 (INFO LINE)** • 10pm-3am, till 4am wknds, 11pm-4am Sun, clsd Mon • popular • gay-friendly • more gay Th & Sun • dancing/DJ • alternative • live shows • 18+ • private club • wheelchair access

---

Charlotte

LGBT PRIDE: May. Web: www.charlottepride.com.

CITY INFO: Convention & Visitors Bureau 704/334-2282 or 800/231-4636, web: charlottecvb.org.

ATTRACTIONS: Discovery Place 704/372-0471 (for tickets). Mint Museum of Art 704/337-2000.

TRANSIT: Yellow Cab 704/332-6161. S&S Airport Shuttle 704/534-4131. Charlotte Transit 704/336-7433.

Fayetteville • North Carolina

Salamandra 300 E Morehead **704/559-4141** • 9pm-3am Fri-Sat • gay-friendly • Latin dance club • patio • 18+ Wed • dress code • cover charge

Scorpios 2301 Freedom Dr **704/373-9124** • 9pm-3:30am, clsd Mon • popular • lesbians/ gay men • dancing/DJ • multiracial • Latin night Fri • karaoke • videos • 18+ • private club • also 'Diva's' show bar & 'Queen City Saloon' (country/western) • wheelchair access

Cafes

Caribou Coffee 1531 East Blvd (nr Scott) **704/334-3570** • 6am-11pm, till midnight Fri-Sat

Tic Toc Coffeeshop 512 N Tryon St (btwn 8th & 9th) **704/375-5750** • 7am-3pm, clsd wknds • plenty veggie

Restaurants

300 East 300 East Blvd (at Cleveland) **704/332-6507** • 11:30am-10pm, till 11pm Tue-Th, till midnight Fri-Sat • New American • some veggie • full bar • $8-18

Alexander Michaels 401 W 9th St (at Pine) **704/332-6789** • lunch & dinner, clsd Sun • pub fare • full bar

Cafe Dada 1220 Thomas St (at Pecan) **704/373-0001** • 11am-midnight, till 2am Fri-Sat • Southwestern wraps • full bar • plenty veggie

Cosmos Cafe 300 N College (at 6th) **704/372-3553** • 11am-2am, from 5pm wknds • gay-friendly • new world cuisine • tapas • jazz brunch 11am-3pm Sun • $4-20 • also 'Thirsty Camel' cigar/martini lounge • also 'Microcosm' art gallery

Fat City 3127 N Davidson St (at 35th) **704/343-0240** • noon-2am, from 2pm Sun

Lupie's Cafe 2718 Monroe Rd (nr 5th St) **704/374-1232** • 11am-11pm, from noon Sat, clsd Sun • homestyle cookin' • some veggie

Bookstores

Paper Skyscraper 330 East Blvd (at Euclid Ave) **704/333-7130** • 10am-7pm, till 6pm Sat, noon-5pm Sun • books • funky gifts • wheelchair access

White Rabbit Books & Things 834 Central Ave (at 7th) **704/377-4067** • 11am-9pm, 1pm-6pm Sun • lgbt • also magazines, T-shirts & gifts

Retail Shops

Urban Evolution 1329 East Blvd (at Scott) **704/332-8644** • 10am-9pm, 1pm-6pm Sun • clothing & more

Publications

▲ **The Front Page** **919/829-0181** • lgbt newspaper for the Carolinas

Q Notes **704/531-9988** • biweekly lgbt newspaper for the Carolinas

Spiritual Groups

MCC Charlotte 1825 Eastway Dr (btwn Windham Pl & Shamrock Dr) **704/563-5810** • 10:45am & 6:30pm Sun

Unitarian Universalist of Charlotte 234 N Sharon Amity Rd (at Hardwick) **704/366-8623** • 9:30am & 11:15am Sun (10:30am in summer)

Gyms & Health Clubs

Charlotte 24-Hour Fitness Center 3900 E Independence Blvd **704/537-9060** • gay-friendly

Erotica

Carolina Video Source 8829 E Harris Blvd **704/566-9993**

Columbia

Accommodations

The River House B&B 202 Bridge St (at Hwy 64) **252/796-1855** • gay/straight • shared baths • kids ok • commitment ceremonies • woman-owned/run • $65

Duck

Accommodations

Advice 5¢, a B&B 111 Scarborough Ln **252/255-1050, 800/238-4235** • gay-friendly • welcoming seaside cottage in village of Duck on North Carolina's outer banks • women-owned/run • $115-185

Durham

see Raleigh/Durham/Chapel Hill

Fayetteville

Nightclubs

Circles Nightclub 2869 Owen Dr **910/221-1001** • 8pm-4am, clsd Mon • lesbians/gay men • transgender-friendly • dancing/DJ • live shows • 18+ • private club • wheelchair access • gay-owned/run

Club Spektrum 107 Swain St (at Bragg Blvd) **910/868-4279** • 8pm-3am, clsd Mon • lesbians/gay men • dancing/DJ • live shows • multiracial • patio

North Carolina • USA

Studio 315 315 Hay St **910/486-9315** • 9pm-2am Wed-Sat • mostly gay men • dancing/DJ • alternative • drag shows & strippers • goth Fri • private club • wheelchair access

SPIRITUAL GROUPS

Emmaus MCC 1705 St Augustine Ave **910/678-8813** • 6pm Sun & 7pm Wed

EROTICA

Fort Video & News 4431 Bragg Blvd (nr 401 overpass) **910/868-9905** • 24hrs

Priscilla's 3800 Sycamore Dairy Rd (at Bragg Blvd) **910/860-1776**

Franklin

ACCOMMODATIONS

Phoenix Nest **850/421-1984** • lesbians/ gay men • mtn cabin • sleeps 4 • seasonal • kids ok • smokefree • wheelchair acces • lesbian-owned • $85

Rainbow Acres **828/369-5162** • women only • rental home • smokefree • fireplace • some shared baths • great views • $750/ week

Greensboro

INFO LINES & SERVICES

Gay/ Lesbian Hotline **336/855-8558** • 7pm-10pm

Live & Let Live AA 415 N Edgeworth **336/854-4278** • 8pm Tue

ACCOMMODATIONS

Biltmore Greensboro Hotel 111 W Washington (at Elm St) **336/272-3474, 800/332-0303** • gay-friendly • fully restored historic hotel • gay-owned/ run • $75-125

NIGHTCLUBS

The Palms 413 N Eugene St (at Smith) **336/272-6307** • 9pm-2:30am • mostly gay men • dancing/DJ • live shows • private club

Sky Bar 221 S Elm St **336/275-1006** • 9:30pm-2:30am • popular • lesbians/ gay men • dancing/DJ • alternative • call for events

Warehouse 29 1011 Arnold St **336/333-9333** • 9:30pm-3:30am Fri-Sat only • also open 3pm-3am Sun summers • mostly gay men • dancing/DJ • live shows Fri • videos • patio bar • volleyball court (games Sun) • private club

BOOKSTORES

White Rabbit Books & Things 1833 Spring Garden St (at Chapman) **336/272-7604** • 10am-9pm, 1pm-7pm Sun • lgbt

PUBLICATIONS

Shout! PO Box 21201, Roanoke, VA 24018 **540/529-6363** • entertainment • personals

SPIRITUAL GROUPS

St Mary's MCC 504 Edwardia Dr (nr W Market) **336/297-4054** • 6pm Sun

EROTICA

Treasure Box Video & News 1205 E Bessemer **336/373-9849**

Greenville

NIGHTCLUBS

Paddock Club 1008-B Dickinson Ave **252/758-0990** • 9pm-2:30am, clsd Mon-Tue • mostly gay men • more women Fri • dancing/DJ • alternative • live shows • 18+ • private club • wheelchair access

SPIRITUAL GROUPS

Unitarian Universalist Congregation 131 Oakmont Dr (at Charles) **252/355-6658** • 10:30am Sun

Hickory

NIGHTCLUBS

Club Cabaret 101 N Center St (at 1st Ave) **828/322-8103** • 9pm-2am, clsd Sun-Tue • lesbians/ gay men • dancing/DJ • live shows • private club • wheelchair access

SPIRITUAL GROUPS

MCC Hickory 109 11th Ave NW (at Unitarian Church) **828/310-9788** • 11am Sun

Hot Springs

ACCOMMODATIONS

The Duckett House Inn **828/622-7621** • gay/ straight • Victorian farmhouse • full brkfst • shared baths • smokefree • creek swimming • also vegetarian restaurant (reservations required) • gay-owned/ run • $80-125

Jacksonville

EROTICA

Priscilla's 113-A Western Blvd **910/355-0765**

New Bern

ACCOMMODATIONS

Harmony House Inn 215 Pollock St **252/636-3810, 800/636-3113** • gay-friendly • 1850 Greek Revival • full brkfst • kids ok • smokefree • $99-150

Raleigh/Durham/Chapel Hill

Info Lines & Services

Center for LGBT Life at Duke University 919/684-6607 • 9am-5pm Mon-Fri

Gay/ Lesbian Helpline of Wake County 919/821-0055 • 6:30pm-9:30pm Sun-Th

Orange County Women's Center 210 Henderson, Chapel Hill **919/968-4610** • 9am-7:30pm, till 2pm Fri, clsd wknds • wheelchair access

Queer Network for Change at UNC, Chapel Hill **919/962-4401** • student group • call for events

Steps, Traditions & Promises AA 80 Watts St (at Watts Baptist Church), Durham **919/286-9499 (AA#)** • 8pm Fri

Accommodations

Joan's Place 919/942-5621 • gay/ straight • 2 guest rooms w/ shared bath • smokefree • infants/ pets ok • wheelchair access • lesbian-owned/ run • $65-75

Fickle Creek Farm 4122 Buckhorn Rd (at Chestnut Ridge Rd) **919/304-6287** • gay/ straight • passive solar B&B • full brkfst • jacuzzi • some shared baths • kids ok • gay-owned/ run • $65-85

Mineral Springs Inn 718 S Mineral Springs Rd (nr Hwy 70), Durham **919/596-2162** • mostly gay men • full brkfst • jacuzzi • swimming • nudity • smokefree • $69

Morehead Manor B&B 914 Vickers Ave (at Morehead), Durham **919/687-4366, 888/437-6333** • gay/ straight • splendidly decorated Colonial home • full brkfst • teens ok • smokefree • woman-owned/ run • $120-450

The Oakwood Inn B&B 411 N Bloodworth St (at Oakwood), Raleigh **919/832-9712, 800/267-9712** • gay-friendly • Victorian in the heart of Raleigh • full brkfst • $85-140

Bars

Backdoor 4801 Leigh Dr (at Green Rd), Raleigh **919/872-6818** • 9pm-2:30am Sat only • mostly women • dancing/DJ • 18+ • private club

Chambers 19 W Hargett St (at Salisbury), Raleigh **919/834-1938** • 5:30pm-11pm, till midnight wknds, clsd Sun • gay/ straight • also restaurant • dinner • 'retro American' • live entertainment • 'Family' night Th

---

Raleigh/Durham/Chapel Hill

LGBT Pride: September.

City Info: 919/834-5900 or 800/849-8499, web: www.raleighcvb.org.

Attractions: Duke University, Durham.
Exploris (interactive global learning center), Raleigh 919/834-4040.
NC Museum of Art, Raleigh 919/839-6262.
NC Museum of Life & Science, Durham 919/220-5429.
Oakwood Historic District, Raleigh.
University of North Carolina, Chapel Hill.

Transit: Bus (Capital Area Transit) 919/828-7228.
Triangle Transit Authority 919/549-9999.

The FRONT PAGE

Serving the Carolina's Gay & Lesbian Communities for Over **20 Years.**

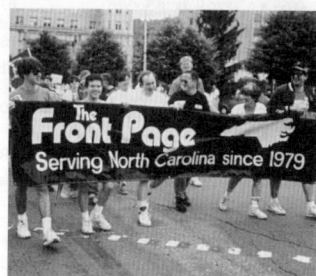

Local, National and World News • Opinion AIDS/HIV Coverage • Features • Cartoons Film, Music & Book Reviews • Calendar Community Resources via our Website Horoscope • Ms. Behavior • Classifieds

To send news, letters, or Calendar Items and for advertising information:
P.O. Box 27928 • Raleigh, NC 27611
(919) 829-0181 • Fax (919) 829-0830
E-mail: frntpage@aol.com

**Check out our website:
FrontPageNews.com**

Available Free across the Carolinas and by Subscription.

Biweekly - 26 issues per year
$30 – Bulk Rate • $52 – First Class Rate
$2 – Sample copy

Raleigh/Durham/Chapel Hill • North Carolina

NIGHTCLUBS

The Capital Corral (CC) 313 W Hargett St (at Harrington), Raleigh **919/755-9599** • 8pm-close, from 6pm Sun • mostly gay men • dancing/DJ • more multiracial Th • live shows • 18+ • also piano bar • private club • wheelchair access

Insomnia 306 W Franklin St (at 'Gotham' nightclub), Chapel Hill **919/967-2852** • 10pm-3am Fri • lesbians/ gay men • dancing/DJ • 18+

Legends 330 W Hargett St (at Harrington), Raleigh **919/831-8888** • 9pm-close • lesbians/ gay men • dancing/DJ • live shows • young crowd • private club • patio • wheelchair access

Power Company 315 W Main St (at Ramseur, enter rear), Durham **919/683-1151** • 11pm-close 2nd & 4th Fri • lesbians/ gay men • dancing/DJ • mostly African-American • free buffet • male & female dancers • 18+ • wheelchair access • $8-10 cover

Visions 711 Rigsbee Ave, Durham **919/688-3002** • call for hrs • mostly women • dancing/DJ • live music • karaoke • deck • volleyball court • private club • wheelchair access

RESTAURANTS

The Artist's Escape 137 E Franklin St, Chapel Hill **919/960-3717** • noon-2am, from 5pm wknds • lesbians/ gay men • also bar

Crooks Corner 610 Franklin St (at Merritt Mill Rd), Chapel Hill **919/929-7643** • 5:30pm-10:30pm Mon-Sat, brunch 10:30am-2pm Sun • Southern • some veggie • full bar • patio • wheelchair access • $6-17

Elmo's Diner 776 9th St (in the Carr Mill Mall), Chapel Hill **919/929-2909** • 6:30am-10pm, till 11pm wknds • some veggie

Irregardless Cafe 901 W Morgan St (at Hillsborough), Raleigh **919/833-8898** • lunch Mon-Fri, dinner Mon-Sat, Sun brunch • plenty veggie • $9-15

Magnolia Grill 1002 9th St (at Knox), Durham **919/286-3609** • 6pm-9:30pm, clsd Sun-Mon • upscale Southern • full bar • wheelchair access • $14-21

Rathskeller 2412 Hillsborough St (at Chamberlain), Raleigh **919/821-5342** • 11:30am-10pm, till 11pm Wed-Sat, from noon Sun • comfort food • plenty veggie • also bar • wheelchair access • $4-16

Vertigo Diner 426 S McDowell St (at Cabarrus), Raleigh **919/832-4477** • lunch Tue-Fri, dinner Wed-Sat, Sun brunch • full bar till 2am • retro chic

Weathervane Cafe Eastgate Shopping Ctr, Chapel Hill **919/929-9466** • 10am-9pm, till 10pm Fri-Sat, till 6pm Sun • plenty veggie • full bar • great brunch • patio • wheelchair access • $8-15

BOOKSTORES

Internationalist Books 405 W Franklin St (at Columbia), Chapel Hill **919/942-1740** • 11am-8pm, noon-6pm Sun, from 2pm Mon • progressive/ alternative • readings & events

Quail Ridge Books 3522 Wade Ave (at Ridgewood Ctr), Raleigh **919/828-1588, 800/672-6789** • 9am-9pm, lgbt section

Reader's Corner 3201 Hillsborough St (at Rosemary), Raleigh **919/828-7024** • 10am-8pm, noon-6pm wknds • used books

Regulator Bookshop 720 9th St (btwn Hillsborough & Perry), Durham **919/286-2700** • 9am-9pm, till 6pm Sun • also cafe

White Rabbit Books & Things 309 W Martin St (btwn Dawson & Harrington), Raleigh **919/856-1429** • 11am-9pm, till 7pm Sat, 1pm-6pm Sun • lgbt • gifts • wheelchair access

RETAIL SHOPS

Innovations 517 Hillsborough St (at Glenwood), Raleigh **919/833-4833** • 11am-7pm, from 1pm Sun, clsd Mon • leather • fetishwear • piercings

PUBLICATIONS

▲ **The Front Page** **919/829-0181** • lgbt newspaper for the Carolinas

Hotspots Magazine **304/782-3358** • serving the Carolinas

SPIRITUAL GROUPS

Community Church (Unitarian Universalist) 106 Purefoy Rd (at Mason Farm Rd), Chapel Hill **919/942-2050** • 9am & 11am Sun

Imani MCC of Durham 4907 Garrett Rd (at Eno River Unitarian Church), Durham **919/403-6881** • 3pm Sun

St John's MCC 805 Glenwood Ave, Raleigh **919/834-2611** • 11am & 7:15pm Sun

Unitarian Universalist Fellowship 3313 Wade Ave (at Dixie Tr), Raleigh **919/781-7635** • 9:30am & 11:15am Sun

EROTICA

Castle Video & News 1210 Capitol Blvd, Raleigh **919/836-9189** • 24hrs

North Carolina • USA

Salisbury

ACCOMMODATIONS

Renaissance Lodge 704/647-0919 • women only • B&B • swimming • outdoor recreation • kids ok • $170-600/week

Spruce Pine

ACCOMMODATIONS

The Lemon Tree Inn 872 Greenwood Rd 828/765-6161 • gay/straight • gay-owned/run

Spruce Ridge

ACCOMMODATIONS

Shepherd's Ridge 828/765-7809 • open March-Nov • mostly women • cottage in the woods • sleeps 2-4 • smokefree • $60/night, $300/week • woman-owned/run

Statesville

ACCOMMODATIONS

Madelyn's in the Grove 1836 W Memorial Hwy, Union Grove 704/539-4151, 800/948-4473 • gay/straight • B&B • full brkfst • 'murder mystery' wknds • $75-145

Wilmington

ACCOMMODATIONS

Blue Heaven B&B 517 Orange St 910/772-9929, 800/338-1748 • gay-friendly • 1800s historic home • full brkfst • smokefree • $85-125

Coastline Inn 503 Nutt St 910/763-2800, 800/617-7732 • gay/straight • kids/small pets ok • smokefree • wheelchair access • gay-owned/run • $69-169

Fifteenth St B&B 111 N 15th St 910/763-2136, 877/506-3974 • gay-friendly • 1921 Colonial • full brkfst • kids/pets ok • smokefree • $95-179

Hidden Treasure Beach 113 S 4th Ave (at 'K' Ave), Kure Beach 910/458-3216 • gay/straight • 3 private units w/ kitchens • swimming • smokefree • $55-105

Ocean Princess Inn 824 Ft Fischer Blvd S, South Kure Beach 910/458-6712, 800/762-4863 • gay/straight • full brkfst • swimming • hot tub • smokefree • wheelchair access • gay-owned/run • $99-159

Rosehill Inn B&B 114 S 3rd St (at Dock St) 910/815-0250, 800/815-0250 • gay-friendly • full brkfst • jacuzzi • smokefree • $149-225

The Taylor House Inn 14 N 7th St 910/763-7581, 800/382-9982 • gay/straight • romantic 1905 house • full brkfst • smokefree • kids ok • $110-225

BARS

Mickey Ratz 115-117 S Front St (at Church Alley) 910/251-1289 • 5pm-2:30am, clsd Mon • lesbians/gay men • dancing/DJ • live shows • private club

SPIRITUAL GROUPS

St Jude's MCC 507 Castle St (at 5th) 910/762-5833 • 9:30am, 11am & 6pm Sun

Wilson

SPIRITUAL GROUPS

GLAD (Gay & Lesbian Affirming Disciples) Alliance 252/291-7370

Winston-Salem

INFO LINES & SERVICES

Gay/Lesbian Hotline 336/855-8558 • 7pm-10pm

BARS

Satellite 701 N Trade St (at 7th) 336/722-8877 • 5pm-2:30am • lesbians/gay men • more women Tue • dancing/DJ • drag shows Fri-Sun • karaoke Wed • Latin night Sat

NIGHTCLUBS

1001 1001 Burke St 336/761-0048 • 4pm-close, from 8pm Fri-Sat, clsd Mon-Tue • lesbians/gay men • dancing/DJ • live music • karaoke • private club

Club Enchanted 2915 Starlight Dr (at Lexington Rd), Winston 336/771-0980 • 9pm-3am Wed-Sat • lesbians/gay men • dancing/DJ • karaoke • live shows • patio • gay-owned/run

Club Odyssey 4019-A Country Club Rd 336/774-1077 • 9pm-3am, clsd Mon • popular • lesbians/gay men • dancing/DJ • live shows • 18+

SPIRITUAL GROUPS

Holy Trinity Church 2873 Robinhood Rd 336/725-5355 • 10:30am & 6:30pm Sun, 7pm Wed

MCC of Winston-Salem 2315 Huff St 336/784-8009 • 11am & 6pm Sun

NORTH DAKOTA

Fargo

INFO LINES & SERVICES

Hotline 701/235-7335 • 24hrs • general info hotline • some lgbt resources

Pride Collective and Community Center 116 12th St S (at Main Ave), Moorhead, MN **218/287-8034** • noon-5pm Sat • referrals • support • social groups

NIGHTCLUBS

I-Beam 1021 Center Ave (at 11th), Moorhead, MN **218/233-7700** • 5pm-1am, clsd Sun • lesbians/ gay men • dancing/DJ

RESTAURANTS

Fargo's Fryn' Pan 301 E Main St (at 4th) **701/293-9952** • 24hrs • popular • wheelchair access

Luigi's Restaurant & Bar 1501 42nd St S **701/241-4200** • 11am-close • gay/ straight

RETAIL SHOPS

Zandbroz Variety 420 Broadway **701/239-4729** • 9am-9pm, noon-5pm Sun • books & gifts

SPIRITUAL GROUPS

St Mark's Lutheran 701/235-5591

EROTICA

Adult Books & Cinema X 417 N Pacific Ave **701/232-9768** • 24hrs

Grand Forks

INFO LINES & SERVICES

The 10% Society 701/777-3269, 701/777-4321 • 8pm Mon • educational/ social group

EROTICA

Plain Brown Wrapper 102 S 3rd St (at Kittson) **701/772-9021** • 24hrs

Minot

EROTICA

Risque's 1514 S Broadway 701/838-2837

OHIO

Statewide

INFO LINES & SERVICES

Ohio Division of Travel & Tourism 800/282-5393

PUBLICATIONS

Exposé Magazine 800/699-6131 • covers Cleveland, Akron, Canton, Warren, Youngstown & Lorain

Gay People's Chronicle 216/631-8646, 800/426-5947 • Ohio's largest weekly lgbt newspaper w/ extensive listings

Hotspots Magazine 304/782-3358 • serving all of Ohio

Akron

INFO LINES & SERVICES

AA Intergroup 330/253-8181 (AA#) • call for times & locations

Akron Pride Center 71 N Adams St (off E Market St) **330/253-2220** • 2pm-6pm, till 8pm Tue & Th, from noon Sat, 1pm-5pm Sun

BARS

Adams Street Bar 77 N Adams St **330/434-9794** • 4:30pm-2:30am, from 9pm Sun • popular • mostly gay men • piano bar Wed • dancing/DJ Fri-Sat • also 'Pecs' w/ drag shows & strippers

Cocktails 1009 S Main St **330/376-2625** • 4:30pm-2:30am • mostly gay men • videos • drag shows Tue • hip-hop Tue & Sat

Lydia's 1348 S Arlington St (in Arlington Plaza) **330/773-3001** • 5pm-2:30am, from 8pm Mon, from 6pm Tue, clsd Wed • mostly women • neighborhood bar • live entertainment wknds

The Roseto Club 627 S Arlington St **330/724-4228** • 6pm-2:30am, till 1am Mon-Tue • mostly women • dancing/DJ • wheelchair access

The Speakeasy 41 Stanton Ave (at Main) **330/434-7788** • 5pm-2:30am, from 10pm Sun • mostly gay men • dancing/DJ • male strippers

Tear-Ez 360 S Main (nr Exchange St) **330/376-0011** • 11am-2:30am, from noon Sun • mostly gay men • neighborhood bar • live shows • wheelchair access

NIGHTCLUBS

Babylon 820 W Market St (btwn Portage Pass & Rhodes Ave) **330/252-9000** • 4pm-2:30am • mostly gay men • dancing/DJ • live shows • videos • wheelchair access • gay-owned/ run

Interbelt 70 N Howard St (nr Perkins & Main) **330/253-5700** • 9:30pm-2:30am, from 2pm Sun, clsd Tue • lesbians/ gay men • dancing/DJ • live shows • videos • patio

Ohio • USA

Cafes

Angel Falls Coffee Company 792 W Market St (btwn S Highland & Grand) **330/376-5282**
• lunch & desserts • patio • wheelchair access • gay-owned/run

Restaurants

Bruegger's Bagels 1682 W Market St **330/869-9393** • 6am-7pm, 7am-4pm Sun

The Sandwich Board 1667 W Market St (at Hawkins) **330/867-5442** • 11am-8pm, clsd Sun • plenty veggie

Spiritual Groups

Cascade Community Church 1196 Inman St **330/773-5298** • 2pm Sun

New Hope Temple 1190 Inman St **330/724-8575** • 10am Sun & 7pm Wed

Athens

Accommodations

Susan B Anthony Women's Land Trust PO Box 5853, 45701 **740/448-6424** • women only • cabins & camping • summer workshops • swimming • lesbian-owned/run

Brunswick

see also Akron & Cleveland

Restaurants

Pizza Marcello 67-A Pearl Rd (nr Boston Rd) **330/225-1211** • 4pm-10:30pm, till 11:30pm Fri-Sat, from 1pm wknds • Italian

Canton

Nightclubs

540 Eagle 540 Walnut Ave NE (at 6th) **330/456-8622** • 9pm-2:30am, 10pm-close Sun • mostly gay men • dancing/DJ • neighborhood bar • leather

Boardwalk 1227 W Tuscarawas **330/453-8000** • 5pm-2:30am • mostly gay men • dancing/DJ Th-Sat • 18+ wknds • wheelchair access

Diamonds Nightclub 2360 Mahoning Rd (at Superior) **330/452-8098** • 5pm-2:30am, clsd Sun-Tue • mostly women • dancing/DJ Sat • wheelchair access

Erotica

Market Street News 440 Market St (at 5th) **330/453-1275**

Tower Bookstore 219 12th St NE (nr Walnut) **330/455-1254**

Cincinnati

Info Lines & Services

AA Gay/Lesbian 320 Resor Ave (in St John's Unitarian Church), Clifton **513/351-0422 (AA#)** • 8pm Mon, Wed & Fri • call about wknd mtgs

Cincinnati Youth Group 513/684-8405, **800/347-8336 (OH ONLY)** • 24hr info

Gay/Lesbian Community Center of Greater Cincinnati 4119 Hamilton Ave (nr Blue Rock) **513/591-0200** • 6pm-9pm, noon-4pm Sat, clsd Sun

Gay/Lesbian Community Switchboard **513/591-0222**

Ohio Lesbian Archives The Women's Building, 4039 Hamilton Ave, Room 304 (above 'Crazy Ladies Books') **513/541-1917** • call for appt

PACT (People of All Colors Together) **513/395-7728** • multiracial & multicultural social/support group • call for events

Women Helping Women 216 E 9th St **513/872-9259, 513/977-5545 (TTY)** • 24hr hotline • crisis center • support groups • lesbian referrals

Accommodations

Cincinnatian Hotel 601 Vine St (nr 8th) **513/381-3000, 800/942-9000** • gay-friendly • restaurant & lounge

The Vernon Manor Hotel 400 Oak St **513/281-3300, 800/543-3999** • gay-friendly • restaurants • gym

Bars

Bullfishes 4023 Hamilton Ave (at Blue Rock) **513/541-9220** • 7pm-close, from 5pm Sun • mostly women • neighborhood bar • dancing/DJ • live entertainment

Golden Lion 340 Ludlow (at Telford), Clifton **513/281-4179** • 4pm-2:30am • mostly gay men • neighborhood bar • dancing/DJ • live shows

Junkers Tavern 4156 Langland (at Pullan) **513/541-5470** • 7:30am-1am • gay-friendly • neighborhood bar

Milton's 301 Milton St (at Sycamore) **513/784-9938** • 4pm-2:30am • gay-friendly • neighborhood bar

Plum St Pipeline 241 W Court (at Plum) **513/241-5678** • 4pm-2:30am • popular • mostly gay men • neighborhood bar • dancing/DJ wknds on 3rd flr • live shows

The Serpent 4042 Hamilton Ave (at Blue Rock) **513/681-6969** • 7pm-2:30am, clsd Mon, dress code Fri-Sat • mostly gay men

Cincinnati • Ohio

Shirley's 2401 Vine St **513/721–8483** • 8pm-2:30am, from 4pm Sun, clsd Mon • mostly women • neighborhood bar • dancing/DJ • wheelchair access

Shooters 927 Race St (at Court) **513/381–9900** • 4pm-2:30am • mostly gay men • dancing/DJ • country/ western • dance lessons 8pm Th • more women Th • karaoke Wed

Simon Says 428 Walnut (at 5th) **513/381–7577** • 11am-2:30am, from 1pm Sun • popular • mostly gay men • professional • neighborhood bar • wheelchair access

Spurs 1119 Race St **513/621–2668** • 4pm-2:30am • popular • mostly gay men • leather • also 'Acme Leather & Toy Co' • wheelchair access

The Subway 609 Walnut St (at 6th) **513/421–1294** • 6am-2:30am, from noon Sun • mostly gay men • neighborhood bar • dancing/DJ • live shows • food served

Nightclubs

The Dock 603 W Pete Rose Wy (nr Central) **513/241–5623** • 5pm-2:30am, till 4am wknds (from 8pm winter), clsd Mon • popular • lesbians/ gay men • dancing/DJ • karaoke • live shows • 19+ • volleyball court • wheelchair access

DV8 1120 Walnut St **513/723–0700** • 10am-3am Th & 11am-4am Fri-Sat • gay-friendly • dancing/DJ • alternative

Jacobs on the Avenue 4029 Hamilton Ave (at Blue Rock) **513/591–2100** • 5pm-2:30am, from 7pm Sat-Mon, till 1am Sun-Mon • mostly gay men • dancing/DJ • karaoke • live shows

Oscar's 700 Pete Rose Way **513/421–3007** • wknds only • gay/ straight • more gay Sun

Warehouse 1313 Vine St (2 blks N of Central Pkwy) **513/684–9313** • 10pm-2:30am Wed, till 4am Fri-Sat • gay-friendly • dancing/DJ • alternative • food served • 18+ • patio

Cafes

Kaldi's Cafe & Books 1204 Main St (at 12th) **513/241–3070** • 9am-1am, 10am-2am Fri-Sat, 10am-midnight Sun • plenty veggie • full bar • live shows • wheelchair access

Restaurants

Boca 4034 Hamilton Ave (btwn Knowlton St & Broadway) **513/542–2022** • lunch & dinner, clsd Mon • nouvelle int'l • full bar • patio • $12-18

Carol's on Main 825 Main St (btwn 8th & 9th) **513/651–2667** • 11am-1am, till 2:30am Th-Sat, from 4pm wknds • popular • bistro • wheelchair access • gay-owned/ run • $6-9

The Diner on Sycamore 1203 Sycamore (at 12th) **513/721–1212** • 11am-midnight, till 1am Fri-Sat • great meatloaf • full bar • wheelchair access • $7-17

Mullane's Parkside Café 723 Race St (btwn 7th & Garfield) **513/381–1331** • 11:30am-11pm, till midnight Fri-Sat, from 5pm Sat, clsd Sun • eclectic • plenty veggie • beer/ wine • wheelchair access • $7-14

Cincinnati

LGBT Pride: September. 513/591-0200 (GLCC #).

City Info: 513/621-2142 or 800/344-3445 (in OH), web: www.cincyusa.com.

Attractions: The Beach waterpark (in Mason) 513/398-2040. Carew Tower 513/241-3888. Cincinnati Art Museum 513/721-5204.
Fountain Square.
Krohn Conservatory 513/421-4086. Museum Center at Union Terminal 513/287-7000.

Best View: Mt. Adams & Eden Park.

Transit: Yellow Cab 513/241-2100. Queen City Metro 513/621-4455.

Ohio • USA

ENTERTAINMENT & RECREATION
Alternating Currents WAIF 88.3 FM **513/333-9243, 513/961-8900** • 3pm Sat • lgbt public affairs radio program • also 'Everywomon' 1pm Sat

BOOKSTORES
Crazy Ladies Bookstore 4039 Hamilton Ave (at Blue Rock) **513/541-4198** • 11am-8pm, till 6pm Sat, noon-4pm Sun • popular • women's

RETAIL SHOPS
Pink Pyramid 907 Race St (btwn 9th & Court) **513/621-7465** • 11am-10:30pm, till midnight Fri-Sat, 1pm-8pm Sun • pride items

SPIRITUAL GROUPS
Dignity 3960 Winding Wy (nr Xavier Univ, at Friends Mtg House) **513/557-2111** • 7:30pm 1st & 3rd Sat

New Spirit MCC 5501 Hamilton Ave (at Belmont, in Grace Episcopal Church) **513/681-9090** • 7pm Sun

EROTICA
Pyramid Leather Crypt & Art Gallery 4040 Hamilton **513/591-1700** • fetish clothing • toys

Cleveland

INFO LINES & SERVICES
AA Gay/ Lesbian 7801 Detroit Ave (at St Augustine Manor) **216/241-7387** • 8:30pm Fri

BlackOut **216/462-0257, 888/825-5226** • nonprofit org for 'Cleveland's African American Same Gender Loving (SGL) community' • sponsors popular 'BlackOut Weekend'

Cleveland Lesbian/ Gay Community Center 6600 Detroit Ave **216/651-5428** • noon-10pm, 6pm-9pm Sun • wheelchair access

GLOWS (Gay/ Lesbian Older Wiser Seniors) **440/331-6302** • 7:30pm 2nd Tue

Women's Center of Greater Cleveland 6209 Storer Ave **216/651-1450, 216/651-4357 (HELPLINE)** • 9am-5pm, clsd wknds

ACCOMMODATIONS
Clifford House 1810 W 28th St (at Jay) **216/589-9432, 216/589-0121** • gay/ straight • 1868 historic brick home • nr downtown • fireplaces • smokefree • gay-owned/ run • $85-125

Edgewater Estates 9803 Lake Ave **216/961-1764** • gay/ straight • English Tudor on Lake Erie • full brkfst • pets ok • patio • women-owned/ run • $95-150

Grandmother's Haven 3560 W 45th St (at Fulton) **216/631-1231** • lesbians/ gay men • 2-bdrm suite • kids ok • $60-120

Cleveland

WHERE THE GIRLS ARE: Dancing downtown near Public Square, hanging out on State Rd below the intersection of Pearl and Broadview/ Memphis.

LGBT PRIDE: June. 216/371-0214, web: www.clevelandpride.org

CITY INFO: 216/621-4110, web: www.travelcleveland.com.

ATTRACTIONS: Cleveland Metroparks Zoo 216/661-6500.
Cleveland Museum of Art 216/421-7340.
Coventry Road district.
Cuyahoga Valley National Recreation Area.
The Flats.
Rock and Roll Hall of Fame 216/781-7625.

TRANSIT: Yellow Cab 216/623-1500.
AmeriCab 216/881-1111.
Regional Transit Authority (RTA) 216/621-9500.
Lolly the Trolley 216/771-4484.

Cleveland • Ohio

Greystone B&B 10405 Lake Ave (at W 104th St) **216/939-0405** • gay/straight • gay-owned/run • $85-95 • weekly rates available

BARS

A Man's World 2909 Detroit Ave (at 29th St) **216/574-2203** • noon-2:30am • lesbians/gay men • dancing/DJ wknds • patio

Deco 11213 Detroit Ave **216/221-8576** • 3pm-2:30am • mostly gay men • neighborhood bar • dancing/DJ • live shows

The Hawk 11217 Detroit Ave (at 112th St) **216/521-5443** • 10am-2:30am, from noon Sun • lesbians/gay men • neighborhood bar • wheelchair access

Hi & Dry Inn 2207 W 11th St (at Fairfield) **216/621-6166** • 11:30am-2am, clsd Sun • gay-friendly • jazz club • also restaurant • plenty veggie • patio • $10-15

Locker Room 2032 W 25th St (at Lorain & 24th) **216/781-9191** • 4pm-2:30am • mostly gay men • neighborhood bar • dancing/DJ • wheelchair access

MJ's Place 11633 Lorain Ave (at W 117th St) **216/476-1970** • 4pm-2:30am, clsd Sun • popular • lesbians/gay men • neighborhood bar • professional crowd • piano bar Mon • karaoke • live shows • women very welcome at 'the gay Cheers'

Muggs 3194 W 25th St (nr Clark) **216/398-7012** • 11am-2:30am, from 9:30am wknds • gay-friendly • neighborhood bar

The Nickel/Five Cent Decision 4365 State Rd (Rte 94, at Montclair) **216/661-1314** • 6pm-2:30am • mostly women • neighborhood bar • dancing/DJ • food served Th

Paradise Inn 4488 State Rd (Rte 94, at Rte 480) **216/741-9819** • 11am-close, till 1am wknds • mostly women • neighborhood bar

Scarlet Rose's Lounge 2071 Broadview Rd (at Roanoke) **216/351-7511** • noon-2am • gay-friendly • neighborhood bar

Twist 11633 Clifton (at 117th St) **216/221-2333** • 9am-2:30am, from noon Sun • popular • lesbians/gay men • dancing/DJ • professional crowd

---

[Reply] [Forward] **[Delete]**

```
Date: Fri, Dec 28, 2001 14:21:22
From: Girl-on-the-Go
To: Editor@Damron.com
Subject: Cleveland
```

> Cleveland has made quite a comeback, since the recession and several economic facelifts of the '90s. Actually, only some districts, like the Flats, have had a beauty makeover. Other districts never lost their funky charm in this city that's home both to the Rock 'N Roll Hall of Fame and the Cleveland Symphony Orchestra.

> Speaking of funky, flash back to the '60s with a trip down Coventry Road. University Circle is rumored to be another hangout of the avant garde, as is Murray Hill, known for its many galleries. While you're at it, make time for some serious art appreciation in the galleries of the world-famous Cleveland Museum of Art.

> To touch base with the lesbian community, pick up a copy of the **Gay People's Chronicle** and find out more about the ever-changing bar/coffeehouse scene. For a wholesome meal, try the women-run **Inn on Coventry.** After dinner, head out to dance at the **Rec Room.** For a more laid-back atmosphere, check out **Paradise Inn** or the **Five Cent Decision** (known to locals as the **Nickel**).

Ohio • USA

Victory's 13603 Madison Ave (at W 85th St) **216/228-5777** • 7pm-2:30am, from 5pm Fri, clsd Sun • lesbians/ gay men • neighborhood bar • dancing/DJ • wheelchair access

Nightclubs

Aunt Charley's The Cage 9506 Detroit Ave (at W 95th) **216/651-0727** • 8pm-2:30am • popular • mostly gay men • dancing/DJ • transgender-friendly • live shows • karaoke

Club Atlantis 620 Frankfort **216/621-6900** • 9pm-2:30am, 10pm-4am Sat, clsd Mon-Tue • gay/ straight • fetish Fri • more gay Sat • dancing/DJ • alternative • multiracial • videos • wheelchair access

The Rec Room 15320 Brookpark Rd **216/433-1669** • 6pm-1am • mostly women • dancing/DJ • food served • wheelchair access • women-owned/ run

Cafes

Johnny Mango 3120 Bridge Ave (btwn Fulton & W 32nd) **216/575-1919** • 11am-10pm, till 11pm Fri-Sat, from 9am wknds • healthy world food • juice bar • also full bar • wheelchair access

Lonesome Dove Cafe 3093 Mayfield Rd (at Lee) **216/397-9100** • 7am-6pm, till 5pm Sat, clsd Sun • some veggie • beer/ wine • $5-7

Restaurants

Cafe Tandoor 2096 S Taylor Rd (at Cedar), Cleveland Hts **216/371-8500, 216/371-8569** • lunch & dinner • Indian • plenty veggie

Club Isabella 2025 University Hospital Rd (at Euclid Ave) **216/229-1177** • lunch Mon-Fri & dinner nightly, clsd Sun • Italian • full bar • live jazz nightly • $15-25

Harmony Bar & Grille 3359 Fulton **216/398-5052** • lunch & dinner, clsd Mon (also clsd Sun summers) • live shows

Hecks 2927 Bridge Ave (at W 30th) **216/861-5464** • lunch & dinner • popular • gourmet burgers • wheelchair access • $10-20

The Inn on Coventry 2785 Euclid Heights Blvd (at Coventry), Cleveland Hts **216/371-1811** • 7am-9pm, from 8:30am Sat, 9am-3pm Sun, 8am-3pm Mon • popular Bloody Marys • some veggie • full bar • wheelchair access • women-owned/ run • $5-20

Entertainment & Recreation

Rock & Roll Hall of Fame 1 Key Plaza **216/781-ROCK** • even if you don't like rock, be sure to stop by & check out IM Pei's architectural gift to Cleveland

Bookstores

Bookstore on W 25th St 1921 W 25th St (at Lorain) **216/566-8897** • 10am-6pm, noon-5pm Sun • lgbt section

Borders Bookshop & Espresso Bar 2101 Richmond Rd (at Cedar, in LaPlace Mall), Beachwood **216/292-2660** • 9am-11pm, till 9pm Sun

Retail Shops

Bank News 4025 Clark Ave (at W 41st St) **216/281-8777** • 10:30am-8:30pm, clsd Sun

Body Language 3291 W 115th St (at Lorain Ave) **216/251-3330, 888/429-7733** • 11am-10pm, till 6pm Sun • 'an educational store for adults in alternative lifestyles'

Body Work Productions 2710 Detroit Ave (at W 28th) **216/623-0744** • 1pm-8pm • piercing

City Dweller 12005 Detroit Ave, Lakewood **216/226-7106** • 10am-9pm • gifts & home decorations • gay-owned/ run

The Clifton Web 11512 Clifton Blvd (at W 117th) **216/961-1120** • 11am-8pm, from 10am Sat, till 5pm Sun • cards & gifts

Diverse Universe 12011 Detroit Ave (at Hopkins), Lakewood **216/221-4297** • 10am-9pm, noon-6pm Sun • lgbt • books • videos • clothing • pride gifts • wheelchair access • gay-owned/ run

Publications

Exposé Magazine **800/699-6131** • covers Cleveland, Akron, Canton, Warren, Youngstown & Lorain

Gay People's Chronicle **216/631-8646, 800/426-5947** • Ohio's largest weekly lgbt newspaper w/ extensive listings

Hotspots Magazine **304/782-3358** • serving all of Ohio

Spiritual Groups

Chevrei Tikva 2728 Lankershire Rd (at the Unitarian Ctr), Cleveland Hts **216/932-5551** • 8pm 1st & 3rd Fri • lgbt synagogue

Integrity NE Ohio Shaker Hts **216/939-0405** • 5pm 3rd Sat • call for directions

More Light Presbyterians 2780 Noble Rd, Cleveland Hts **216/932-1458** • 5:30pm 2nd Sat • potluck & mtg

Erotica

Laws Leather Shop 1112 Clifton Blvd **216/961-0544** • hours vary, clsd Mon-Tue

Columbus • Ohio

Columbus

INFO LINES & SERVICES

AA Gay/ Lesbian 614/253-8501 • call for mtg schedule

Dragon Leather Club 614/258-7100 • pansexual leather group

GLB Alliance 1739 N High St, Rm 464 (on Ohio State U campus) **614/292-6200** • student group • call for info

Sisters of Lavender 93 W Weisheimer Rd (at Unitarian Church) **614/675-1175** • 7:30pm Th • lesbian social/ support group

Stonewall Columbus Community Center/ Hotline 1160 N High St **614/299-7764** • 10am-7pm, till 5pm Fri, clsd wknds • wheelchair access

WOW (Women's Outreach for Women) 1950–H N 4th St **614/291-3639** • 9am-5pm, mtgs 5pm-8pm • women's recovery center • wheelchair access

ACCOMMODATIONS

Columbus B&B 763 S 3rd St **614/444-8888** • gay-friendly • in historic district • kids ok • gay-owned/ run • $65-75

Courtyard by Marriott 35 W Spring St (at Front St) **614/228-3200, 800/321-2211** • gay-friendly • wknd discounts • wheelchair access • $89-170

The Gardener's House 556 Frebis Ave (at Ann St) **614/444-5445** • mostly gay men • smokefree • gay-owned/ run • $58-108

[Reply] [Forward] **[Delete]**

```
Date: Sat, Dec 29, 2001 15:16:03
From: Girl-on-the-Go
To: Editor@Damron.com
Subject: Columbus
```

> The center of lesbian life in Columbus is Clintonville (affectionately known as 'Clitville'), just north of the OSU campus. While you're in the neighborhood, stop by the popular dyke hangout **Summit Station**. Don't leave before picking up a copy of one of the several newspapers and magazines that cover Columbus and central Ohio.

> Besides Clintonville, there is the Short North—the stretch of High Street just north of Downtown. This funky, artsy neighborhood hosts a Gallery Hop the first Saturday of every month. After the shops start closing around 10pm (or later), check out **Blazer's Pub**, or try the Short North Pole for fantastic ice cream concoctions. If you need to refuel, try the **Coffee Table**; we hear it's as popular with local dykes as with the cruisin' gay boys.

> Sports dykes, check out Berliner Park, any season, to watch women's softball, volleyball, or basketball leagues. Even the non-athletic head to the **Far Side** or **Slammers** afterward to celebrate the thrill of victory.

> The best time of all to be in Columbus is during the Gay Pride March that always falls the same weekend in June as ComFest. This is the community festival at Goodale Park in Victorian Village which hosts a wide variety of merchants, food, information, and music.

Ohio • USA

Springwood Hocking Hills Cabins 28560 Blackjack Rd (Rte 664), Logan **740/385-2042** • lesbians/ gay men • secluded cabins on the water • fireplace • hot tub • hiking trails • smokefree • pets ok • lesbian-owned/ run • $100-130

Summit Lodge Resort & Guesthouse 740/385-3521 • popular • gay-friendly • clothing-optional resort • 45 miles to Columbus • camping available • hot tub • swimming • also restaurant • $50-110

BARS

Blazer's Pub 1205 N High St (at 5th) **614/299-1800** • 4pm-2:30am, 3pm-9pm Sun • mostly women • neighborhood bar

Club Diversity 124 E Main (btwn 3rd & 4th Sts) **614/224-4050** • 5pm-2am, from 6pm Fri-Sat, clsd Sun-Mon • lesbians/ gay men • piano bar • patio • also coffeehouse

Downtown Connection 1126 N High St (at 4th Ave) **614/299-4880** • 5pm-2am, from 3pm wknds • mostly gay men • sports bar

The Far Side 1662 W Mound St (at Reed) **614/276-5817** • 5pm-1am, till 2:30am Fri-Sat, from 6pm Sun • mostly women • neighborhood bar • food served • live bands wknds

Garrett's Saloon 1071 Parsons Ave (at Stewart) **614/449-2351** • 11am-2:30am • mostly gay men • neighborhood bar • country/ western during day • Top 40 at night • karaoke Mon

Havana Video Lounge 862 N High (at 1st Ave) **614/421-9697** • 5pm-2:30am • popular • lesbians/ gay men • neighborhood bar • videos • male strippers Sun

Kelly's 73 E Gay St (at 3rd St) **614/221-8463** • 5pm-2:30am • lesbians/ gay men • wheelchair access

Remo's 1409 S High St (at Jenkins) **614/443-4224** • 11am-2:30am, clsd Sun • lesbians/ gay men • neighborhood bar • live shows • karaoke

Slammers Pizza Pub 202 E Long St (at 5th St) **614/469-7526** • 11am-2:30am, from 2:30pm wknds • lesbians/ gay men • wheelchair access

The South Bend Tavern 126 E Moler St (at 4th St) **614/444-3386** • noon-2:30am • mostly gay men • neighborhood bar • wheelchair access

Summit Station 2210 Summit St (btwn Alden & Oakland) **614/261-9634** • 4pm-2:30am • mostly women • neighborhood bar • karaoke • live shows

Columbus

WHERE THE GIRLS ARE: Downtown with the boys, north near the University area, or somewhere in-between.

LGBT PRIDE: June. 614/299-7764 (Stonewall #).

ANNUAL EVENTS: June - Pagan Spirit Gathering in Athens campground, 1.5 hrs south of Columbus 608/924-2216 (Wisconsin office). September - Ohio Lesbian Festival 614/267-3953.

CITY INFO: 614/221-2489, web: www.ohiotourism.com.

ATTRACTIONS: Columbus Museum of Modern Art 614/221-6801. Columbus Zoo 614/645-3550. German Village district. Wexner Center for the Arts 614/292-0330.

WEATHER: Truly midwestern. Winters are cold, summers are hot.

TRANSIT: Yellow Cab 614/444-4444. Northway Taxicab 614/299-4118, 614/299-1191. Independent 614/235-5551. Airport Express Shuttle 614/476-3004. Central Ohio Transit Authority (COTA) 614/228-1776.

Columbus • Ohio

Union Station Video Cafe 630 N High St (at Goodale) **614/228-3740** • 11am-2am • popular • lesbians/ gay men • video bar • professional crowd • food served • plenty veggie • Internet access • wheelchair access • $6-10

Nightclubs

Axis 775 N High St (at Hubbard) **614/291-4008** • 10pm-2:30am • popular • mostly gay men • dancing/DJ • 18+ • Varsity Night Th w/ dancers • wheelchair access • gay-owned/ run

Club Utopia 115 Parsons Ave (at Franklin) **614/470-2272** • 2pm-2:30am, from noon Sun • lesbians/ gay men • dancing/DJ • food served • live shows • country/ western Wed • wheelchair access

Tradewinds II 117 E Chestnut (at 3rd St) **614/461-4110** • 4pm-2:30am, clsd Mon • mostly gay men • 3 bars • dancing/DJ • leather • videos • also restaurant • wheelchair access

Wall Street 144 N Wall St (at Long) **614/464-2800** • 8pm-2:30am, from 9pm Wed, clsd Mon-Tue • popular • lesbians/ gay men • dancing/DJ • country/ western • live shows • young crowd • wheelchair access

Cafes

The Coffee Table 731 N High St (at Buttles) **614/297-1177** • 7:30am-midnight, till 1am wknds, 8am-10pm Sun • lesbians/ gay men

Cup-O-Joe Cafe 627 3rd St (at Sycamore) **614/221-1563** • 6:30am-11pm, till midnight Fri-Sat, from 7:30am Sun

Restaurants

Chinese Village 2124 Lane St (at High) **614/297-7979** • 11am-10pm

Fresno's 782 N High St (at Buttles Ave) **614/298-0031** • 11am-11pm, from 4pm Sat, clsd Sun • popular

L'Antibes 772 N High St #106 (at Warren) **614/291-1666** • 5pm-close, clsd Sun-Mon • French • full bar • wheelchair access • gay-owned/ run • $21-29

Lemon Grass 641 N High (N of Goodale St) **614/224-1414** • lunch & dinner, from 3pm Sat, clsd Sun • popular • Pacific Rim Asian cuisine • reservations advised

Nacho Mama's 5277 US Hwy 23 **740/548-5655**

No Attitude Bar & Grill 53 Parsons Ave (at Oak) **614/464-3663** • 11am-2pm & 5pm-10pm, clsd wknds • popular • some veggie • full bar • gay-owned/ run

Out on Main 122 E Main (btwn 3rd & 4th) **614/224-9510** • 5pm-10pm, till 11pm Fri-Sat, brunch 11am-2:30pm Sun • popular • lesbians/ gay men • upscale casual dining • piano wknds • full bar till 2:30am • wheelchair access

Entertainment & Recreation

The Reality Theatre 736 N Pearl St (btwn Lincoln & Warren) **614/294-7541** • lgbt plays & new releases • call for show dates

Bookstores

The Book Loft of German Village 631 S 3rd St (at Sycamore) **614/464-1774** • 10am-11pm, till midnight Fri-Sat • lgbt section

The Shadow Realm 3347 N High St (1 blk S of N Broadway) **614/262-1175** • metaphysical & occult bookstore • readings, workshops & classes • sponsors the annual 'Witch's Ball' in Oct • wheelchair access

Retail Shops

ACME Art Company 1129 N High St (at 4th Ave) **614/299-4003** • alternative art space • call for hours

Creative-A-Tee 874 N High St **614/297-8844** • noon-7pm, till 5pm Sat, clsd Sun-Mon• gay pride T-shirts • silkscreening

Hausfrau Haven 769 S 3rd St (at Columbus) **614/443-3680** • 10am-6:30pm, till 5pm Sun • greeting cards • wine • gifts

KRT (Kukula's Rainbow Tribe) 636 N High St (at Russell) **614/228-8337** • noon-9pm, till midnight Fri-Sat, till 6pm Sun • lgbt gifts • tanning salon

Metro Video 848 N High St (at Hubbard) **614/291-7962** • 11am-midnight, from noon Sun • lgbt videos • large selection

Pierceology 872 N High St (S of 1st) **614/297-4743** • noon-9pm, till 10pm Fri-Sat, 1pm-7pm Sun • body piercing studio

Wallich Gallery 745 N High St (btwn Buttles & Hubbard) **614/291-2787** • 11am-7pm, till 5pm Sat, clsd Sun-Mon • jewelry • gifts

Publications

Hotspots Magazine 304/782-3358 • serving all of Ohio

Outlook 614/268-8525, 866/452-6397 • lgbt newspaper • good resource pages

Spotlight Magazine 614/805-5664 • bi-weekly lgbt paper for Central Ohio

The Stonewall Journal 614/299-7764

Ohio • USA

SPIRITUAL GROUPS

Dignity Greater Columbus 444 E Broad St (at First Congregational Church UCC, side entrance) **614/447-6546** • Roman Catholic Mass 6pm 2nd & 4th Sun

Lutherans Concerned 1555 S James Rd **614/447-7018** • 1pm 1st Sun

New Creation MCC 787 E Broad St (at St Paul's Episcopal Church) **614/224-0314** • 10:30am Sun, 7pm Wed

Spirit of the Rivers 588 S 3rd St (at German Village Mtg House) **614/470-0816** • 10am Sun • ecumenical service

St Paul's Episcopal Church 787 E Broad St (at I-71 intersection) **614/221-1703** • 5pm Sun • wheelchair access

EROTICA

Bexley Video 3839 April Ln (at Courtright) **614/235-2341**

Garden 1186 N High St (at 5th Ave) **614/294-2869** • adult toys

IMRU 235 N Lazelle (at Hickory, above the 'Eagle') **614/228-9660** • leather, pride & fetish store

Dayton

INFO LINES & SERVICES

AA Gay/Lesbian 20 W 1st St (off Main, at Christ Episcopal Church) **937/222-2211** • 8pm Sat

Dayton Lesbian/Gay Hotline **937/274-1776** • 24hr hotline, 7pm-11pm (volunteer staff)

Youth Quest **937/640-3333** • 7pm Wed • lgbt youth group (22 & under)

BARS

City Cafe 121 N Ludlow St (in Talbot Tower Bldg) **937/223-1417** • 5pm-2:30am • mostly gay men • DJ Mon & Th-Sat • karaoke • live shows • wheelchair access

Club Diva 6303 Rip Rap Rd (off I-75, Little York exit) **937/235-9511** • 7pm-close, clsd Sun-Mon • mostly women • volleyball court • patio • gay-owned/run

Lady Hawk Social Club 2600 Valley **937/233-5879** • 7pm-2:30am, clsd Tue • mostly women • karaoke Th & Sun

Reflections 629 S Main St (at Patterson) **937/223-1595** • 3pm-2:30am, from 1pm Fri-Sun • lesbians/gay men • dancing/DJ • multiracial • karaoke Th • live shows

Right Corner 105 E 3rd St (at Jefferson) **937/228-1285** • noon-2:30am • mostly gay men • neighborhood bar • wheelchair access

Stage Door 44 N Jefferson (at 2nd) **937/223-7418** • noon-2:30am, from 2pm Wed & wknds • mostly gay men • leather • wheelchair access

NIGHTCLUBS

1470 West 34 N Jefferson St (btwn 2nd & 3rd) **937/461-1470** • 9pm-2:30am, till 4am Th & Sat, clsd Mon-Wed • popular • lesbians/gay men • dancing/DJ • live shows • videos • wheelchair access

The Asylum 605 S Patterson Blvd **937/228-8828** • 9pm-close, clsd Sun-Mon • gay-friendly • dancing/DJ • alternative • 18+

Jessie's Celebrity Showbar 850 N Main St (off I-75) **937/461-2582** • 9pm-2:30am, till 4am Fri-Sat • popular • mostly gay men • dancing/DJ • karaoke Th • strippers Fri-Sat • wheelchair access

CAFES

Gloria Jean's Coffee Bean 2727 Fairfield Commons (in mall), Beavercreek **937/426-1672** • 9:30am-9pm, noon-6pm Sun • gay-owned/run

RESTAURANTS

Cold Beer & Cheeseburgers 33 S Jefferson St **937/222-2337** • 11am-11pm, noon-8pm Sun • grill • full bar • wheelchair access

The Spaghetti Warehouse 36 W 5th St (at Ludlow) **937/461-3913** • 11:30am-10pm, till 11pm Fri-Sat • more gay Mon w/ 'Friends of the Italian Opera'

BOOKSTORES

Books & Co 350 E Stroop Rd (at Farhills) **937/298-6540** • 9am-11pm, till 8pm Sun

RETAIL SHOPS

Q Gift Shop 1904 N Main St (at Ridge Ave) **937/274-4400** • noon-7pm, till 5pm Sun • lgbt gifts

SPIRITUAL GROUPS

Community Gospel Church 546 Xenia Ave (at Steele Ave) **937/252-8855** • adult Sun School 10am Sun, worship service 11am • wheelchair access

Eternal Joy MCC 2382 Kennedy Ave (at Highridge) **937/254-2087** • 10:30am & 6pm Sun

Toledo • Ohio

Findlay

ACCOMMODATIONS

Zelkova Country Manor 2348 S CR 19 (off 224), Tiffin **419/447-4043** • gay/ straight • full brkfst • smokefree • kids ok • $75-150

Kent

INFO LINES & SERVICES

Kent LGB Union KSU **330/672-2068**

CAFES

The Zephyr Cafe 106 W Main St **330/678-4848** • 8am-9pm, till 7pm Sun, till 8pm Mon • vegetarian • live shows • wheelchair access • $3-7

Lima

NIGHTCLUBS

Somewhere 804 W North St **419/227-7288** • 6pm-2:30am, from 8pm wknds • lesbians/ gay men • dancing/DJ Fri-Sat • live shows

Logan

ACCOMMODATIONS

Glenlaurel—A Scottish Country Inn & Cottages 14940 Mt Olive Rd (off State Rte I-80), Rockbridge **740/385-4070, 800/809-7378** • gay/ straight • on 133 acres • full brkfst & dinner • hot tub • smokefree • wheelchair access • $119-289

Lorain

BARS

The Serpent 2223 Broadway (btwn 22nd & 23rd) **440/246-9002** • 8pm-2:30am, clsd Mon • lesbians/ gay men • neighborhood bar • dancing/DJ • live shows • patio • wheelchair access

Mentor

INFO LINES & SERVICES

Gay/ Lesbian Info Line 440/974-8909 • 7pm-9pm Wed, 24hr recorded info • lgbt info & referrals for Ashtabula, Geauga & Lake Counties

Monroe

BARS

Old St Saloon 13 Old St **513/539-9183** • 8pm-2:30am, clsd Sun-Tue • lesbians/ gay men • drag shows Fri-Sat • female strippers 1st Wed • male strippers 1st Th

Oberlin

RETAIL SHOPS

Stitch by Stitch 31 S Main St **440/774-4544** • noon-6pm, till 5pm Sat, clsd Sun-Mon • many lgbt items

Oxford

INFO LINES & SERVICES

Miami University GLB Alliance 513/529-3823 • meets 8:30pm Th

Sandusky

ACCOMMODATIONS

2-Twelve Guesthouse 212 Decatur St **419/625-8292** • lesbians/ gay men • 1890s house • kids/ pets ok

NIGHTCLUBS

Xcentricities 306 W Water St **419/624-8118** • 8pm-2:30am • lesbians/ gay men • dancing/DJ • karaoke • live shows • patio

BOOKSTORES

City News 139 Columbus Ave (btwn Market & Water) **419/626-1265** • 8am-5:30pm, clsd Sun

Springfield

NIGHTCLUBS

Chances 1912-14 Edwards Ave **937/324-0383** • 8:30pm-2:30am, clsd Tue • gay-friendly • dancing/DJ • live shows • patio

Steubenville

NIGHTCLUBS

Club 2000 122 N 6th St (at Market) **740/284-1291** • 8pm-2:30am, clsd Sun-Mon • lesbians/ gay men • dancing/DJ • live shows

Toledo

INFO LINES & SERVICES

AA Gay/ Lesbian 2272 Collingwood Blvd (at St Mark's Episcopal Church) **419/472-8242** • 8pm Wed & Sun

Pro Toledo Info Line 419/472-2364 • 7pm-11pm

BARS

Blu Jean Cafe 3606 Sylvania Ave (nr Monroe) **419/474-0690** • 4pm-2:30am, clsd Sun • popular • lesbians/ gay men • more women Th-Sat • transgender-friendly • karaoke Th • also restaurant • wheelchair access

Ohio/ Oklahoma • USA

Hooterville Station 119 N Erie St (btwn Jeff & Monroe) **419/241-9050** • 5:30pm-2:30am • mostly gay men • dancing/DJ • leather • karaoke • patio

Rip Cord 115 N Erie (btwn Jefferson & Monroe) **419/243-3412** • 1pm-2:30am • mostly gay men • leather • live shows

Nightclubs

Bretz 2012 Adams St **419/243-1900** • 4pm-2:30am, till 4am Fri-Sat, clsd Mon-Tue • lesbians/ gay men • dancing/DJ • live shows • videos • 18+ • wheelchair access

Caesar's Show Bar 725 Jefferson **419/241-5140** • 8pm-2:30am, clsd Mon-Th • lesbians/ gay men • dancing/DJ • live shows • wheelchair access

Cafes

Sufficient Grounds 3160 Markway (at Cricket West Mall) **419/537-1988** • 7:30am-11pm, till midnight Fri-Sat, from 8am Sun • popular • live shows • wheelchair access • also 420 Madison, 419/243-5282

Bookstores

People Called Women 3153 W Central Ave (in Cricket West Ctr) **419/535-6455** • 11am-7pm, noon-5pm Sun, clsd Mon • multicultural • feminist

Thackeray's 3301 W Central Ave (at Secor, in Westgate Shopping Center) **419/537-9259** • 9am-9pm, 10am-6pm Sun • wheelchair access

Retail Shops

Rainy Day Creations 452 W Delaware Ave (at Collingwood Blvd) **419/242-4992, 866/242-4992** • noon-6pm, clsd Sun-Wed • rainbow novelties • cards & gifts • lesbian-owned/ run

Spiritual Groups

Eagle's Wing Christian Church 1483 W Sylvania (btwn Jackman Rd & Lewis Ave) **419/476-8197** • 10am Sun

MCC Good Samaritan 720 W Delaware (in Old W End) **419/244-2124** • 10am Sun

Warren

Bars

The Queen of Hearts 132-136 Pine St (btwn Market & Franklin) **330/395-1100** • 3pm-2:30am, from 4pm Sun • lesbians/ gay men • neighborhood bar • dancing/DJ • live shows • karaoke Wed • patio • also 'Queen's Dungeon' levi/ leather bar Fri-Sat downstairs

Nightclubs

The Alley 441 E Market St (enter rear) **330/394-9483** • 4pm-2:30am, from 2pm Fri-Sun • lesbians/ gay men • dancing/DJ • live shows • wheelchair access

Wooster

Accommodations

Kimbilio Farm 6047 TR 501, Big Prairie **330/378-2481** • women only • log house & cabins • full brkfst • swimming • 45 mins from Akron • shared baths • kids/ pets ok (cabin only) • wheelchair access (cabin only) • lesbian-owned/ run • $60

Yellow Springs

Restaurants

Winds Cafe & Bakery 215 Xenia Ave **937/767-1144** • lunch & dinner, Sun brunch, clsd Mon • plenty veggie • full bar • wheelchair access • women-owned/ run • $15-20

Bookstores

Epic Bookshop 232 Xenia Ave **937/767-7997** • noon-6pm, 1pm-5pm Sun, clsd Mon

Youngstown

Bars

Club Blue Note 2810 Market (at Hilda) **330/782-3694** • 4pm-2:30am • lesbians/ gay men • dancing/DJ • food served • patio • wheelchair access

The Mixx 21 W Hilda (off Market) **330/782-6991** • 4pm-2:30am • lesbians/ gay men • neighborhood bar • dancing/DJ Th-Sun • karaoke Wed • live shows Sun • wheelchair access

OKLAHOMA

Statewide

Publications

Gayly Oklahoman **405/528-0800** • lgbt newspaper

El Reno

Accommodations

The Good Life RV Resort Exit 108 I-40 (1/4 mile S) **405/884-2994, 405/893-2345** • gay-friendly • 32 acres • 100 campsites & 100 RV hookups • pond w/ pedal boats • swimming • kids ok • gay-owned/ run • $10-17 (full hookup)

Oklahoma City • Oklahoma

Enid

Erotica

Priscilla's 4810-A W Garriott (at Garland) **580/233-5511** • toys • lingerie • books • videos

Lawton

Bars

Triangles 8–1/2 NW 2nd St (enter rear) **580/351-0620** • 9pm-2am, till 1am Sun, clsd Mon-Tue • lesbians/ gay men • neighborhood bar • dancing/DJ • live shows • karaoke

Bookstores

Ingrid's Books 1124 NW Cache Rd **580/353-1488** • 10am-10pm, clsd Sun • new & used books • magazines • also adult novelties

Spiritual Groups

Great Plains MCC 1415 SW Wisconsin **580/357-7899** • 5pm Sun

Lexington

Accommodations

Blue Sky Ranch 14001 Banner **405/872-2583** • mostly women • cabin • camping • 2 RV hookups • swimming • pets ok • wheelchair access • lesbian-owned/ run • $100-125

Norman

see also Oklahoma City

Info Lines & Services

OU GLB Alliance 405/325-4452

Bookstores

Borders Books 300 Norman Ctr **405/573-4907** • lgbt section

Retail Shops

Mystic Forest Treasures 323 White St (Campus Corner) **405/447-5111** • 11am-6pm, clsd Sun • pride gifts • music • metaphysical supplies • lesbian-owned

Oklahoma City

Info Lines & Services

AA Live & Let Live 3405 N Villa **405/947-3834** (CLUB#), **405/525-2437** • call for mtg schedule

COTA (Central OK Transgendered Associations) PO Box 90354, 73146 **405/260-0192** • 6pm 2nd Sat • support group • call for directions

The Center 2135 NW 39th St **405/524-6000, 405/525-2437** • 11am-7pm Mon-Th, till midnight Fri, clsd wknds • wheelchair access

Herland Sister Resources 2312 NW 39th St **405/521-9696** • 1pm-5pm wknds • women's resource center w/ books, crafts & lending library • also sponsors monthly events • wheelchair access

Young Gay/ Lesbian Alliance 4400 N Lincoln Blvd (Red Rock Mental Health Ctr) **405/524-6000, 405/524-6500** • support group & more for lgbt youth • 6:30pm-8pm Tue • also 7pm Th & Fri at 'The Center'

Oklahoma City

LGBT Pride: June. 405/525-2437 (The Center #).

Annual Events: May - Herland Spring Retreat 405/521-9696. Music, workshops.
September - Herland Fall Retreat.

City Info: 405/297-8912, web: www.okccvb.org.

Attractions: Historic Paseo Arts District.
Myriad Gardens' Crystal Bridge 405/297-3995.
National Cowboy Hall of Fame 405/478-2250.
National Softball Hall of Fame 405/424-5266.
Omniplex 405/602-6664.
Will Rogers Park.

Transit: Yellow Cab 405/232-6161.
Airport Express 405/681-3311.
Metro Transit 405/235-7433.

Oklahoma • USA

Accommodations

America's Crossroads B&B 405/495-1111 • reservation service for private homes • gay-owned/ run • $35-50

▲ **Habana Inn** 2200 NW 39th Expwy (at Youngs) 405/528-2221, 800/988-2221 (RESERVATIONS ONLY) • popular • lesbians/ gay men • resort • swimming • also 3 clubs • piano bar • restaurant • gift shop • wheelchair access • $35-108

Tommy's Ranch 13700 S Sooner Rd, Edmond 405/216-8669 • gay/ straight • 20 mins from OK City • cabins • full brkfst • camping • swimming • horseback riding • massage therapy • wheelchair access • gay-owned/ run • $50-70

Bars

▲ **The Finishline** at 'Habana Inn' 405/525-2900 • noon-2am • lesbians/ gay men • dancing/DJ • country/ western • lessons 7pm Tue-Wed • poolside bar • wheelchair access

Hi-Lo Club 1221 NW 50th St (btwn Western & Classen) 405/843-1722 • noon-2am • lesbians/ gay men • neighborhood bar • live bands weekly

KA's 2024 NW 11th (at Pennsylvania) 405/525-3734 • 3pm-2am • mostly women • neighborhood bar • dancing/DJ • beer bar • live entertainment monthly • wheelchair access

▲ **The Ledo** at 'Habana Inn' 405/525-0730 • 4pm-close • lesbians/ gay men • cabaret & lounge • piano bar • food served • karaoke Th-Fri • drag shows Sat • wheelchair access

Partners 2805 NW 36th St (at May Ave) 405/942-2199 • 5pm-close, from 6pm Fri, from 7pm Sat, clsd Mon-Tue • popular • mostly women • neighborhood bar • patio • dancing/DJ • live shows • wheelchair access

Sisters 2120 NW 39th St (at Youngs) 405/521-9533 • 8pm-close Th-Sat, from 2pm Sun • mostly women • dancing/DJ • live shows Fri • gay-owned/ run

Tramps 2201 NW 39th St (at Barnes) 405/521-9888 • noon-2am, from 10am wknds • popular • mostly gay men • dancing/DJ • drag shows • wheelchair access

Nightclubs

Angles 2117 NW 39th St (at Pennsylvania) 405/524-3431 • 9pm-2am, clsd Mon-Wed • popular • lesbians/ gay men • dancing/DJ • live shows • wheelchair access

▲ **The Copa** at 'Habana Inn' 405/525-0730 • 9pm-2am, clsd Mon • lesbians/ gay men • dancing/DJ • live shows • wheelchair access • cover charge Sun

Wreck Room 2127 NW 39th St (at Pennsylvania) 405/525-7610 • 10pm-close Th-Sat • popular • lesbians/ gay men • dancing/DJ • live shows • young crowd • 18+ after 1am • juice bar

Cafes

Grateful Bean Cafe & Soda Fountain 1039 Walker 405/236-3503 • 11am-5pm, clsd wknds • plenty veggie • 'Seattle-style' espresso

Restaurants

Bricktown Brewery Restaurant 1 N Oklahoma (at Sheridan) 405/232-2739 • 11am-10pm, till 2am Fri-Sat • live bands Fri-Sat

▲ **Gusher's Bar & Grill** at 'Habana Inn' 405/528-2221 x411 • 11am-10:30pm, from 9am wknds, till 3:30am Fri-Sat for after-hours brkfst • wheelchair access

Painted Desert 3700 N Shartel (at NW 36th St) 405/524-5925 • 11am-2:30am • pizza • sandwiches • full bar

Terra Luna Grille 7408 N Western (at 73rd) 405/879-0009 • lunch & dinner

Retail Shops

23rd St Body Piercing 411 NW 23rd St (at N Hudson) 405/524-6824

Ziggyz 4005 N Pennsylvania (at I-240) 405/521-9999 • novelty gifts • smokeshop • also 3426 SW 29th, 405/682-2299

Publications

Gayly Oklahoman 405/528-0800 • lgbt newspaper

The Herland Voice 405/521-9696 • newsletter

Spiritual Groups

Cathedral of Hope OKC 600 NW 13th St (at First Unitarian Church) 405/232-4673 • 6:30pm Sun

Epworth United Methodist Church 1901 N Douglas 405/525-2346 • 10:45am Sun

Oklahoma City Religious Society of Friends (Quakers) 312 SE 25th St 405/631-4174, 405/632-7574 • 7pm most Sundays

Open Arms UCC 1212 N Hudson 405/272-9555 • 10:45am Sun

Erotica

Christie's Toy Box 3126 N May Ave (at 30th) 405/946-4438 • also 1039 S Meridian, 405/948-3333

OKLAHOMA CITY'S HABANA INN

The Southwest's Largest All Gay Resort

175 Guest Rooms ★ Two Swimming Pools
Poolside Rooms ★ Suites ★ Cable TV

Park Once And Party All Night!
Located In The Habana Inn Complex

THE COPA

OKC's Hottest Dance Club
Newly Redecorated

- Tuesday Amatuer Strip-Off
- Wednesday Kitty's Comedy Capers
- Thursday Open Talent Dong Show
- Friday HOT - HOT Male Dancers
- Saturday HOT - HOT Male Dancers
- Sunday The COPA Show

Open 9pm - 2am   Closed Mondays

Finishline

OKC's Only Country Dance Floor
OPEN 7 days a week

COUNTRY MUSIC & DANCING
POOL BAR during season

Darts **Noon - 2am** Pool

GUSHER'S Bar & Grill

Finest Prime Rib in OKC

OPEN
Mon - Fri 11am
Sat & Sun 9am

SERVING UNTIL
Sun - Thurs 10:30pm
Fri & Sat 3:30am

The Ledo Cabaret & Lounge

Open 4pm Daily

| Karaoke Every Thursday & Friday from 9pm Join the Fun Sing Along! | OKC'S Only Piano Bar Best Martini's in Town | ShowBiz Saturday's 10:00pm OKC's Top Female Impersonators with host Ginger Lamar |

2200 NW 39th Expressway, Oklahoma City, OK 73112
Call for rates and information
(405) 528-2221   Reservations only: 1-800-988-2221
Website: www.habanainn.com

Oklahoma • USA

Jungle Red at 'Habana Inn' **405/524-5733** • 1pm-close, from noon wknds • novelties • leather • gifts • wheelchair access

Priscilla's 615 E Memorial **405/755-8600**

Randi's Playthings 4711 S Pennsylvania (at 44th) **405/681-0308** • adult toys • lingerie • some plus sizes

Tulsa

INFO LINES & SERVICES

BLGTA at TU 2839 E 8th St (Canterbury Center, U of Tulsa) **918/583-9780 (UNITED MINISTRIES CTR #)** • 6:30pm Sun

Gay/ Lesbian AA 2545 S Yale Ave (at Community of Hope) **918/747-6300** • 7:30pm Tue & 6:30pm Sat

The Tulsa LGBT Community Center 2114 S Memorial **918/743-4297** • touchtone info • center open 6pm-10pm, noon-9pm Sat • lesbian movie night 7pm Fri • wheelchair access

BARS

Bamboo Lounge 7204 E Pine **918/832-1269** • noon-2am • oldest gay bar in OK • mostly gay men • neighborhood bar • dancing/DJ • live shows • patio • wheelchair access

CW's 1737 S Memorial (at 21st St) **918/610-5323** • 4pm-2am • lesbians/ gay men • neighborhood bar • dancing/DJ • country/ western • leather • wheelchair access

New Age Renegade/ The Rainbow Room 1649 S Main St (at 17th) **918/585-3405** • 2pm-2am • popular • lesbians/ gay men • neighborhood bar • live shows • karaoke • patio

Schatzi's Pub/ Grill 2619 S Memorial **918/280-1316** • 11am-2am, from 2pm wknds • mostly women • dancing/DJ Fri-Sat • food served

TNT's 2114 S Memorial **918/660-0856** • 4pm-2am • popular • mostly women • neighborhood bar • dancing/DJ

The Yellow Brick Road 2630 E 15th **918/293-0304** • 4pm-2am • mostly gay men • neighborhood bar • dancing • karaoke • male strippers Fri • wheelchair access

NIGHTCLUBS

Silver Star Saloon 1565 S Sheridan **918/834-4234** • 9pm-2am Wed-Sun • mostly gay men • dancing/DJ • live shows • wheelchair access

CAFES

Java Dave's 1326 E 15th St (at Lincoln Plaza) **918/592-3317** • 6:30am-9pm, from 7am Sat, from 8am Sun

RESTAURANTS

St Michael's Alley 3324 E 31st (in Ranch Acres) **918/745-9998** • lunch & dinner

Wild Fork 1820 Utica Sq **918/742-0712** • 7am-10pm, clsd Sun • full bar • wheelchair access • women-owned/ run • $10-20

ENTERTAINMENT & RECREATION

Gilcrease Museum 1400 Gilcrease Museum Rd **918/596-2787** • one of the best collections of Native American & cowboy art in the US

Philbrook Museum of Art 2727 S Rockford Rd (1 blk E of Peoria, at end of 27th St) **918/749-7941** • clsd Mon • Italian villa built in the '20s oil boom complete w/ kitschy lighted dance flr, now museum • the gardens are a must in spring & summer

RETAIL SHOPS

Body Piercing by Nicole 2727 E 15th St (btwn Harvard & Lewis) **918/712-1122** • 11am-9pm, noon-6pm Sun

The Pride Store 2114 S Memorial (in LGBT Community Center) **918/743-4297** • 6pm-9pm, from noon Sat • lgbt cards • gifts • shirts • some books • wheelchair access

PUBLICATIONS

Tulsa Family News 918/583-1248 • monthly lgbt newspaper

SPIRITUAL GROUPS

MCC United of Tulsa 1623 N Maplewood **918/838-1715** • 11am Sun

EROTICA

Priscilla's 11344 E 11th (at Garnett) **918/423-8422** • toys • lingerie • books • videos • 3 other locations: 5634 W Skelly Rd (at 56th), 918/446-6336 • 2333 E 71st, 918/499-1661 • 7925 E 41st (at Memorial), 918/627-4884

Astoria • Oregon

OREGON

Statewide

INFO LINES & SERVICES

Gay Resource Connection/ Oregon AIDS Hotline 503/223-2437, 800/777-2437 (PACIFIC NW ONLY) • 9am-6pm, noon-6pm Sat

Oregon Tourism Commission 800/547-7842 • call for free catalog

PUBLICATIONS

Just Out 503/236-1252 • lgbt newspaper w/ extensive resource directory

Ashland

INFO LINES & SERVICES

The Abdill-Ellis Community Center 281 4th St (at the Fouth Street Studio) 541/488-6990 • 9:30am-6pm, clsd Sun • mtgs • events • also pride store

Gay/ Lesbian AA 175 N Main St upstairs (at Methodist Church) 541/482-3647 • 7pm Mon

Womansource 541/482-7416, 541/482-2026 • lesbian/ feminist group • sponsors cultural activities like 1st Fri Dance & annual Fall Gathering (wheelchair access) • also publishes 'Community News'

Women's Resource Center 1250 Siskiyou Blvd 541/552-6216 • hours vary • library • mtg space • gallery

ACCOMMODATIONS

The Arden Forest Inn 261 W Hersey St 541/488-1496, 800/460-3912 • gay/ straight • full brkfst • smokefree • swimming • kids 10+ ok • wheelchair access • gay-owned/ run • $85-150

Country Willows Inn 1313 Clay St 541/488-1590, 800/945-5697 • gay-friendly • full brkfst • swimming • jacuzzi • smokefree • teens ok • wheelchair access • gay-owned/ run • $110-225

Dandelion Garden Cottage 541/488-4463 • women only • peaceful retreat • kids ok • smokefree • lesbian-owned/ run • $55

Lithia Springs Inn 2165 W Jackson Rd 541/482-7128, 800/482-7128 • gay/ straight • full brkfst • natural hot-springs-fed whirlpools in rooms • smokefree • teens ok • $110-250

Neil Creek House B&B 341 Mowetza Dr 541/482-6443, 800/460-7860 • gay-friendly • full brkfst • swimming • smokefree • teens ok • $85-190

Pedigrift House B&B 407 Scenic Dr 541/482-1888, 800/262-4073 • gay-friendly • restored 1888 Queen Anne Victorian • full brkfst • patio • smokefree • $100-130

Rogues Inn Apartments 541/488-5162, 800/276-4837 • gay-friendly • apts • smokefree • kids ok • pets ok w/ deposit • $95+

CAFES

Ashland Bakery/ Cafe 38 E Main 541/482-2117 • 8am-8pm, till 3pm Mon-Tue • plenty veggie • wheelchair access • $6-10

Renaissance Chocolates 342 Lithia Way (at 2nd) 541/488-8344 • 8am-6pm, 10am-4pm Sat, clsd Sun

RESTAURANTS

The Black Sheep 51 N Main St (on the Plaza) 541/482-6414 • lunch & dinner • full bar till 1am • eclectic pub fare

Geppetto's 345 E Main 541/482-1138 • 8am-midnight • Italian • full bar • wheelchair access • $8-13

Greenleaf Restaurant 49 N Main St (on The Plaza) 541/482-2808 • 8am-9pm • Mediterranean/ Italian • creekside dining • beer/ wine

BOOKSTORES

Bloomsbury Books 290 E Main St (btwn 1st & 2nd) 541/488-0029 • 8am-10pm, 9am-9pm Sat, 10am-9pm Sun

RETAIL SHOPS

Travel Essentials 264-A E Main St 541/482-7383 • 10am-5:30pm, 11am-4pm Sun • luggage • guidebooks • maps • travel accessories • clothing

PUBLICATIONS

Prizm 281 4th St 541/488-6990 • lgbt monthly newspaper for southern OR

Astoria

INFO LINES & SERVICES

North Coast Pride Network Gay/ Lesbian Resource Center 10 6th St #209 503/338-0161 • 5:30pm-7:30pm Mon

ACCOMMODATIONS

Rosebriar Hotel 636 14th St 503/325-7427, 800/487-0224 • gay-friendly • upscale classic hotel • full brkfst • kids ok • wheelchair access • $59-165

Oregon • USA

Beaverton

Restaurants

Swagat Indian Cuisine 4325 SW 109th Ave **503/626-3000** • lunch & dinner • beer/wine

Bend

Info Lines & Services

Beyond the Closet **541/317-8966** • social/support • newsletter

Out & About **541/388-2395** • lgbt info

Cafes

Royal Blend 1075 NW Newport **541/383-0873** • 6:30am-6pm

Sweet Baby Jane's 945 NW Bond St **541/385-5931** • 8am-10pm, till 2:30am wknds • also bar • live entertainment

Blue River

Accommodations

River's Edge Inn 91241 Blue River Rd **541/822-3258, 800/250-1812** • gay/straight • Victorian B&B • 40 miles east of Eugene • full brkfst • smokefree • gay-owned/run • $85-125

Corvallis

Info Lines & Services

After 8 Club 101 NW 23rd **541/752-8157** • 7pm 2nd Tue • lgbt educational & support group

Rainbow Continuum **541/737-6360** • 7pm Mon at Women's Ctr Sept-May

Bookstores

Book Bin 228 SW 3rd (btwn Madison & Jefferson) **541/752-0040** • 9am-9pm, till midnight Fri-Sat, noon-5pm Sun

Grass Roots Bookstore 227 SW 2nd St (btwn Jefferson & Madison) **541/754-7668** • 9am-7pm, till 9pm Fri, till 5:30pm Sat, 11am-5pm Sun • music section • espresso bar • wheelchair access

Eugene

Info Lines & Services

Gay/Lesbian AA 1414 Kincaid (at Koinonia Ctr) **541/342-4113** • 7pm Wed

LGBT Alliance **541/346-3360** • 9am-5pm • various drop-in groups • wheelchair access

TLC (The Lesbian Connection) 2360 Fillmore **541/683-2793** • active lesbian social group

Women's Center University of Oregon (in EMU Bldg, #3) **541/346-4095, 541/346-3327** • 8am-5pm Mon-Fri • some lesbian outreach

Bars

Neighbor's 1417 Villard St (at Franklin) **541/338-0334** • 8am-2:30am, from 11am Sun • lesbians/gay men • neighborhood bar • dancing/DJ • karaoke • live shows • also restaurant

Restaurants

Glenwood Cafe 1340 Alder St (at 13th St) **541/687-0355** • 7am-10pm

Keystone Cafe 395 W 5th (at Lawrence) **541/342-2075** • 7am-3pm • popular brkfst • plenty veggie

Entertainment & Recreation

Soromundi **541/684-6767** • lesbian chorus of Eugene

Bookstores

Hungry Head Bookstore 1212 Willamette (at 13th) **541/485-0888** • 10:30am-6pm, clsd Sun • progressive/alternative titles • some lgbt titles

▲ **Mother Kali's Books** 720 E 13th Ave (at Hilyard) **541/343-4864** • 9:30am-6pm, clsd Sun • lgbt, feminist, multiracial, kids, new & used • events & resources • women's community calendar • wheelchair access

Retail Shops

High Priestess Piercing 675 Lincoln St (at 7th St) **541/342-6585** • noon-8pm, 11am-10pm Wed-Sat • piercing studio

Ruby Chasm 152 W 5th Ave #4 (btwn Olive & Charnelton) **541/344-4074** • 10am-6pm, noon-5pm Sun • goddess gifts • books • wheelchair access

Erotica

Exclusively Adult 1166 S 'A' St (at 10th St), Springfield **541/726-6969** • 24hrs

Gaston

Accommodations

Art Springs 40789 SW Hummingbird Ln **503/985-9549** • women only • B&B, cabin & camping on 12 acres of women's land • hot tub • smokefree • chem-free • also retreats • lesbian-owned/run • $15-75

Medford • Oregon

Grants Pass

ACCOMMODATIONS

WomanShare 541/862-2807 • women only • country retreat ctr • cabins • shared kitchen • bathhouse • hot tub • special events • girls/pets ok • smokefree • lesbian-owned/run • $15-35 (sliding scale)

CAFES

Sunshine Natural Foods Cafe 128 SW 'H' (at 5th St) 541/474-5044 • 9am-6pm, till 4pm Sat, 11am-4pm Sun • vegetarian • also market

SPIRITUAL GROUPS

Unitarian Universalist Fellowship 229 W 'G' St (at 4th St) 541/476-5600 • 10:30am Sun Sept-June

Jacksonville

ACCOMMODATIONS

The Touvelle House 455 N Oregon St (at E St) 541/899-8938, 800/846-8422 • gay-friendly • full brkfst • swimming • $110-185

Lincoln City

RESTAURANTS

Road's End Dory Cove 75819 Logan Rd (at 59th St) 541/994-5180 • 11:30am-8pm, till 9pm Fri-Sat, noon-8pm Sun • steak & seafood

Surf Tides 2945 NW Jetty Ave 541/994-3877 • 8am-10pm, lounge open later wknds • $12-18

McMinneville

ACCOMMODATIONS

Middle Creek Run 25400 Harmony Rd, Sheridan 503/843-7606, 800/843-7606 • gay/straight • Victorian B&B • full brkfst • hot tub • swimming • some shared baths • smokefree • gay-owned/run • $100-115

Medford

ACCOMMODATIONS

The Bybee House B&B 4491 Jackson Hwy, Central Point 541/773-3026 • gay-friendly • smokefree • $125

Mother Kali's Books
Celebrating Women's Lives in all our Diversities

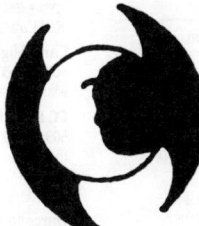

SPECIAL ORDERS

CARDS

NEW BOOKS

VIDEO RENTALS

MUSIC

USED BOOKS

LOCAL REFERRALS
IN STORE EVENTS

720 E. 13th Ave. (at Hilyard)   (541) 343-4864

www.motherkalis.com
email: Kali@EFN.Org

Free parking in basement   WCA

Oregon • USA

Nightclubs

Ground Zero 123 S Front St **541/779-4827** • 8pm-2am • gay-friendly • more gay Th at 'Alternative Night'

Restaurants

Cadillac Cafe 207 W 8th St (at Holly) **541/857-9411** • 10:30am-2pm Mon-Fri

Mac's Rock & Rod Diner 1150 E Barnett Rd (E of Exit 27) **541/608-7625** • 6am-10pm, till 11pm wknds • more gay Th eves

Retail Shops

McGee on Main 406 E Main St (at Riverside) **541/770-5591** • 10am-5:30pm, clsd Sun • women's clothing

Spiritual Groups

Medford First Christian Church 1900 Crater Lake Ave (at Brookhurst) **541/772-8030** • 10am Sun

Erotica

Castle Megastore 1113 Progress Wy (at Bittle) **541/608-9540**

Newport

Accommodations

Cliff House B&B **541/563-2506** • gay-friendly • oceanfront • full brkfst • hot tub • smokefree • $110-225

Restaurants

Mo's Annex 657 SW Bay Blvd **541/265-7512** • great chowder

Portland

see also Vancouver, Washington

Info Lines & Services

50+ Portland **503/281-4424, 503/331-0415** • 3rd Sat • social group for lesbians 50+

Asian/ Pacific Islander LGBT Info Hotline **503/299-0120** • educational/ social/ support group

Lesbian Community Project 1001 E Burnside **503/233-3913** • multicultural political & social events

Live & Let Live Club 2940-A SE Belmont St **503/238-6091** • 12-step mtgs • call for schedule

Love Makes a Family **503/228-3892** • many groups • call for locations

Northwest Gender Alliance **503/646-2802** • 3rd Tue & 2nd Sat • transgender support group • newsletter

Portland Bisexual Alliance **503/775-9717** • support & social group w/ weekly events

Accommodations

The Clyde Hotel 1022 SW Stark St (at 10th) **503/224-8000** • lesbians/ gay men • some shared baths • kids/ small pets ok • gay-owned/ run • $59-140

Fifth Avenue Suites Hotel 506 SW Washington (at 5th Ave) **503/222-0001, 800/711-2971** • gay-friendly • restaurant • gym • $79+

Hotel Vintage Plaza 422 SW Broadway **503/228-1212, 800/263-2305** • popular • gay-friendly • upscale hotel • restaurant & lounge • wheelchair access • $109-399

MacMaster House 1041 SW Vista Ave (at Park Pl) **503/223-7362, 800/774-9523** • gay-friendly • historic mansion nr the Rose Gardens • smokefree • $85-130

The Mark Spencer Hotel 409 SW Eleventh Ave (nr Stark) **503/224-3293, 800/548-3934** • gay-friendly • kids/ pets ok • $89-149

Sullivan's Gulch B&B 1744 NE Clackamas St (at 17th) **503/331-1104** • lesbians/ gay men • decks • gay-owned/ run • pets ok • $70-85

Bars

Bar of the Gods 4801 SE Hawthorne (at 48th Ave) **503/232-2037** • 5pm-2:30am • gay/ straight • neighborhood bar • beer/ wine • wheelchair access

Boxxes 1035 SW Stark (at SW 11th Ave) **503/226-4171** • 11:30am-2:30am, from 3pm wknds • popular • mostly gay men • karaoke • videos • wheelchair access • also 'Brig' from 9pm • lesbians/ gay men • dancing/DJ • also 'Red Cap Garage' restaurant • noon-2:30am

Candlelight Room 2032 SW 5th (at Lincoln) **503/222-3378** • 10am-2:30am, from 11am wknds • gay-friendly • live shows • food served

CC Slaughter's 219 NW Davis (at 3rd) **503/248-9135** • 11am-2:30am • popular • mostly gay men • dancing/DJ • country/ western Wed & Fri • karaoke • videos • food served till 5am Sat

Darcelle XV 208 NW 3rd Ave (at NW Davis St) **503/222-5338** • 5pm-11pm, 6pm-2am Sat, clsd Sun-Tue • gay/ straight • live shows • food served • wheelchair access

Eagle PDX 1300 W Burnside (at 13th Ave) **503/241-0105** • 4pm-2:30am • mostly gay men • leather • videos

Portland • Oregon

The Egyptian Club 3701 SE Division (at SE 37th Ave) **503/236-8689** • 11:30am-2:30am, from 4pm wknds, Sun brunch • popular • mostly women • dancing/DJ & karaoke Th-Sat • strippers Tue • food served • $5-12 • wheelchair access • lesbian-owned/run

Fox & Hound 217 NW 2nd Ave (btwn Everett & Davis) **503/243-5530** • 9:30am-2am, from 8:30am wknds • mostly gay men • poker bar • karaoke • also restaurant • brunch Sun • wheelchair access

The Frontline 1135 SW Washington (at 12th) **503/243-2181** • 11am-midnight, bar till 2:30am Fri-Sat, restaurant till 5am • mostly gay men • neighborhood bar

Gail's Dirty Duck Tavern 439 NW 3rd (at Glisan) **503/224-8446** • 3pm-1:30am, from noon wknds • mostly gay men • neighborhood bar • leather • older crowd • wheelchair access

Hobo's 120 NW 3rd Ave (btwn Davis & Couch) **503/224-3285** • 4pm-2:30am • gay/straight • piano bar • also restaurant • some veggie • wheelchair access • $5-20

Silverado 1217 SW Stark St (btwn SW 11th & 12th Aves) **503/224-4493** • 9am-2:30am • popular • mostly gay men • dancing/DJ • live shows • karaoke • also restaurant • wheelchair access

Starky's 2913 SE Stark St (at SE 29th Ave) **503/230-7980** • 11am-2am • popular • lesbians/gay men • neighborhood bar • also restaurant • some veggie • patio • wheelchair access • $10-20

Tiger Bar 317 NW Broadway (btwn Everett & Flanders) **503/222-7297** • 5pm-2:30am • open for lunch Tue-Fri • popular • gay-friendly • wheelchair access

NIGHTCLUBS

Embers 110 NW Broadway (at NW Couch St) **503/222-3082** • 11:30am-2:30am • popular • mostly gay men • dancing/DJ • live shows • also restaurant • wheelchair access

Panorama 341 SW 10th Ave (at Stark) **503/221-7262** • 9pm-4am Fri-Sat only • popular • gay-friendly • dancing/DJ • beer/wine • wheelchair access

Portland

WHERE THE GIRLS ARE: Try along SE Hawthorne & Belmont streets where some of the women's businesses are, or the NW section, 21st & 23rd Ave, for the more upscale lesbians.

LGBT PRIDE: June. 503/295-9788.

ANNUAL EVENTS: June - The Gathering. Annual pagan camp in the Oregon Woods.
August - Annual Women's Softball 503/233-3913 (LCP #).
September - Northwest Women's Music Celebration.
Portland LGBT Film Festival 503/242-0818, web: www.sensoryperceptions.org.

CITY INFO: 503/222-2223 or 877/678-5263.
Oregon Tourism Commission 800/547-7842, web: www.pova.com.

ATTRACTIONS: Microbreweries.
Mt Hood Festival of Jazz.
Old Town.
Pioneer Courthouse Square.
Rose Festival.
Washington Park.

BEST VIEW: International Rose Test Gardens at Washington Park.

WEATHER: The wet and sometimes chilly winter rains give Portland its lush landscape that bursts into beautiful colors in the spring and fall. Summer brings sunnier days. (Temperatures can be in the 50°s one day and the 90°s the next.)

TRANSIT: Radio Cab 503/227-1212.
Raz 503/684-3322.
Tri-Met System 503/238-7433.

Oregon • USA

CAFES

Bread & Ink Cafe 3610 SE Hawthorne Blvd (at 36th) **503/239-4756** • 7am-9pm, till 10pm Fri-Sat, from 9am Sun (clsd btwn lunch & dinner) • popular • beer/wine • wheelchair access

Cafe Lena 2239 SE Hawthorne Blvd (at SE 23rd) **503/238-7087** • 8am-9:30pm, till 3pm Sun, clsd Mon • popular • live shows • wheelchair access

Cup & Saucer Cafe 3566 SE Hawthorne Blvd (btwn 34th & 36th) **503/236-6001** • 7am-9pm • popular • full menu • smokefree

Marco's Cafe & Espresso Bar 7910 SW 35th (at Multnomah Blvd), Multnomah **503/245-0199** • 7am-9:30pm, from 8am wknds, till 2pm Sun

The Pied Cow 3244 SE Belmont **503/230-4866** • 4pm-midnight, till 1am wknds • funky Victorian • great desserts • patio

---

[**Reply**] [**Forward**]   [**Delete**]

Date: Sat, Dec 15, 2001 09:45:12
From: Girl-on-the-Go
To: Editor@Damron.com
Subject: Portland

> Sprawling along the Columbia River at the foot of Mount Hood, you'll find this city that's home to rainy days, roses, and an active women's community. If you're searching for the proof that Portland is a lesbian-friendly city, look no further than the Portland Building. Atop the roof you'll find a statue of Portlandia, a city landmark and an amazon icon.

> Nearby you can explore the Mount St. Helens National Volcanic Monument or the 5,000 acres of Macleay Park. And if you love jazz, head for the hills: the Mount Hood Festival of Jazz brings the best of the jazz world to town every August.

> Lesbian life here focuses on the outdoors and cocooning at home with small groups of friends. To get in touch, pick up a recent copy of the statewide newspaper **Just Out,** call the **Lesbian Community Project,** or contact **Sisterspirit,** a women's spirituality resource.

> The **Egyptian Club** is the heart of women's nightlife in Portland. For a nourishing meal, visit **Old Wives Tales,** or savor the java and art at the smokefree **Cup & Saucer Cafe.** On weekends, you can enjoy live music at the lesbian-owned **Touchstone Coffee House.**

> Culturally minded visitors won't want to miss **In Other Words,** the only women's bookstore in town. They carry music along with a large selection of women's literature. **Powell's** is a new/used bookstore that's both legendary and huge, and we've heard that its LGBT section is a good meeting place on weekend nights—there's even a little cafe. **It's My Pleasure** serves up erotica for women, and **In Her Image Gallery** shows women's art.

Portland • Oregon

Saucebox 214 SW Broadway (at Stark) **503/241-3393** • 11:30am-1:30pm & 6pm-10pm, clsd Sun-Mon • lesbians/ gay men • pan-Asian • plenty veggie • full bar • wheelchair access

Touchstone Coffee House 7631 NE Glisan St **503/262-7613** • 7am-9pm, till 10pm Th-Fri, 8am-10pm Sat, till 3pm Sun • live music wknds • lesbian-owned/ run

RESTAURANTS

The Adobe Rose 1634 SE Bybee Blvd (at Milwaukee) **503/235-9114** • 11:30am-2pm, also 5pm-9pm Fri-Sat, clsd Sun-Mon • New Mexican • some veggie • beer/ wine • $5-7

Assaggio 7742 SE 13th (at Lambert) **503/232-6151** • 5pm-9:30pm, clsd Sun-Mon • Italian • plenty veggie • wine bar

Bastas Trattoria 410 NW 21st (at Flanders) **503/274-1572** • lunch Mon-Fri & dinner nightly • northern Italian • some veggie • full bar till 1am • $7-12

Bijou Cafe 132 SW 3rd Ave (at Pine St) **503/222-3187** • 7am-2pm, from 8am wknds, also 6pm-10pm Tue-Sat • popular • plenty veggie • $4-7

Brasserie Montmartre 626 SW Park (at Alder) **503/224-5552** • lunch & dinner, Sun brunch • bistro • live jazz • full bar

Daydream Cafe 1740 SE Hawthorne (at 17th) **503/233-4244** • 7am-7:30pm, till 5pm wknds • popular • gay-owned/ run

Delta 4607 SE Woodstock **503/771-3101** • 5pm-10pm, from noon wknds • Southern • plenty veggie • wheelchair access

Dot's Cafe 2521 SE Clinton **503/235-0203** • lunch & dinner till 2am • popular • full bar • eclectic American • plenty veggie

Esparza's Tex-Mex Cafe 2725 SE Ankeny St (at 28th) **503/234-7909** • 11:30am-10pm, clsd Sun-Mon • popular

Fish Grotto 1035 SW Stark (at SW 11th Ave, at 'Boxxes') **503/226-4171** • 5pm-close, clsd Mon • popular • some veggie • full bar • $8-24

Hobo's 120 NW 3rd Ave (btwn Davis & Couch) **503/224-3285** • 4pm-2:30am • popular • live shows • wheelchair access

Majas Taqueria 1000 SW Morrison **503/226-1946** • 11am-9:30pm

Montage 301 SE Morrison **503/234-1324** • lunch & dinner till 2am • popular • Louisiana-style cookin' • full bar • wheelchair access

Nicholas' 318 SE Grand **503/235-5123** • 10am-9pm, noon-8pm Sun • Middle Eastern

Old Wives Tales 1300 E Burnside St (at 13th) **503/238-0470** • 8am-9pm, till 10pm Fri-Sat • multi-ethnic vegetarian • beer/ wine • wheelchair access

The Original Pancake House 8600 SW Barbur Blvd **503/246-9007** • 7am-3pm, clsd Mon-Tue • great brkfst

Paradox Cafe 3439 SE Belmont **503/232-7508** • 8am-9pm, till 10pm Fri-Sat • popular • healthy vegetarian diner grub • killer Reuben

Pizzacato 505 NW 23rd (at Glisan) **503/242-0023** • 11:30am-10pm, till 11pm Fri-Sat • popular • plenty veggie • beer/ wine

The Roxy 1121 SW Stark St **503/223-9160** • 24hrs, clsd Mon • popular • lesbians/ gay men • American • wheelchair access

Starky's 2913 SE Stark St **503/230-7980** • 11am-2pm & 5:30pm-9:30pm, from 9:30am Sun • also full bar till 2:30am • lesbians/ gay men

Vista Spring Cafe 2440 SW Vista (at Spring) **503/222-2811** • 11am-10pm, from noon wknds, till 9pm Sun • pasta & pizza • beer/ wine

Wildwood 1221 NW 21st Ave (at Overton) **503/248-9663** • 11am-9pm (reservations advised) • popular • full bar

ENTERTAINMENT & RECREATION

Sauvie's Island Beach 25 miles NW (off US 30) • follow Reeder Rd to the Collins beach area, park at the farthest end of the road, then follow path to beach

BOOKSTORES

Countermedia 927 SW Oak (btwn 9th & 10th) **503/226-8141** • 11am-7pm, noon-6pm Sun • alternative comics • vintage gay books/ periodicals

In Other Words 3734 SE Hawthorne Blvd (at 37th) **503/232-6003** • 10am-9pm, 11am-6pm Sun • women's books • music • resource center • wheelchair access

Laughing Horse Bookstore 3652 SE Division (at 37th) **503/236-2893** • 11am-7pm, clsd Sun • alternative/ progressive • wheelchair access

Looking Glass Bookstore 318 SW Taylor (btwn 3rd & 4th) **503/227-4760** • 9am-6pm, from 10am Sat, clsd Sun • general • some lgbt titles

Powell's Books 1005 W Burnside St (at 10th) **503/228-4651, 800/878-7323** • 9am-11pm • largest new & used bookstore in the world • cafe • wheelchair access

Oregon • USA

Reading Frenzy 921 SW Oak St **503/274-1449** • 11am-7pm, noon-6pm wknds • zines • comics • lgbt selection • wheelchair access

Twenty-Third Ave Books 1015 NW 23rd Ave (at Lovejoy) **503/224-5097** • 9:30am-9pm, from 10am Sat, 11am-7pm Sun • general • lgbt section • wheelchair access

Retail Shops

In Her Image Gallery 3208 SE Hawthorne (at 32nd) **503/231-3726** • 11am-6pm, 10am-5pm wknds, clsd Mon-Tue • wheelchair access

It's My Pleasure 3106 NE 64th Ave (at Sandy Blvd) **503/280-8080** • books • erotica • toys • gifts • workshops • call for hours

The Jellybean 721 SW 10th Ave (at Morrison) **503/222-5888** • 10am-6pm, noon-5pm Sun • cards • T-shirts • gifts • wheelchair access

Presents of Mind 3633 SE Hawthorne (at 37th Ave) **503/230-7740** • 10am-7pm • jewelry • cards • unique toys • wheelchair access

Publications

Just Out **503/236-1252** • lgbt newspaper w/ extensive resource directory

Spiritual Groups

Congregation Neveh Shalom 2900 SW Peaceful Ln (at Beaverton/Hillsdale Hwy) **503/246-8831** • 8:15pm Fri & 9am Sat • conservative synagogue w/ lgbt outreach • call for directions

MCC Portland 2400 NE Broadway (at 24th Ave) **503/281-8868** • 9am & 11am Sun • wheelchair access

Sisterspirit 3430 SE Belmont #102 **503/736-3297** • celebration of women sharing spirituality • also 12-step pagan group • wheelchair access

St Stephen's Episcopal Church 1432 SW 13th Ave (at Clay) **503/223-6424** • 7:45am & 10am Sun, 12:10pm Wed

Gyms & Health Clubs

Inner City Hot Tubs 2927 NE Everett St (btwn 29th & 30th) **503/238-1065** • 10am-11pm, from 1pm Sun • gay-friendly • wellness center • reservations required

Nelson Nautilus Plus 614 SW 11th Ave (at Alder) **503/222-2639** • gay-friendly

Erotica

The Crimson Phoenix 1876 SW 5th Ave (btwn Harrison & Hall) **503/228-0129** • clsd Sun • 'sexuality bookstore for lovers' • wheelchair access

Fantasy for Adults 3137 NE Sandy Blvd (nr NE 39th) **503/239-6969** • 24hrs

Spartacus Leathers 302 SW 12th Ave (at Burnside) **503/224-2604**

Roseburg

Info Lines & Services

Gay/ Lesbian Switchboard **541/672-4126** • 24hrs • also newsletter

Accommodations

Owl Farm **541/679-4655** • women only • women's land open to visitors • camping sites available

Salem

Accommodations

Brightridge Farm B&B 18575 SW Brightridge Rd, Sheridan **503/843-5230** • gay-friendly • in the rural heart of Oregon wine country • full brkfst • $105-115

Nightclubs

300 Club 300 Liberty St SE (at Trade St) **503/365-9721** • 5pm-2am • gay/straight • women's night Th • dancing/DJ • live shows • also 'Right Side Showbar' • cabaret Fri • food served • wheelchair access

Restaurants

Off Center Cafe 1741 Center St NE (at 17th) **503/363-9245** • brkfst & lunch daily, dinner Th-Sat • some veggie • wheelchair access

Bookstores

Rosebud & Fish 524 State St (at High) **503/399-9960** • 10am-7pm, noon-5pm Sun • alternative bookstore

Publications

Community News **503/363-0006** • monthly

Spiritual Groups

Sweet Spirit MCC 4774 Lilac Ln NE (at American Legion) **503/315-7923** • 11am Sun

Unitarian Universalist Congregation of Salem 5090 Center St NE **503/364-0932** • 10:30am Sun

Sunriver

Accommodations

DiamondStone Guest Lodge & Gallery 16693 Sprague Loop, La Pine **541/536-6263, 800/600-6263** • gay-friendly • Western hotel-style B&B • full brkfst • hot tub • kids ok • pets ok (extra fee) • smokefree • $80-120

East Stroudsburg • Pennsylvania

Tiller

ACCOMMODATIONS

Kalles Family RV Ranch 233 Jackson Creek Rd **541/825-3271** • lesbians/ gay men • camping sites • RV hookups • btwn Medford & Roseburg • kids/ pets ok • lesbian-owned/ run • $10 (incl electric)

Yachats

ACCOMMODATIONS

Morning Star*—A Bed & Breakfast 95668 Hwy 101 S **541/547-4412** • gay/ straight • oceanfront • full brkfst • hot tub • kids/ pets ok • smokefree • $100-200

Ocean Odyssey 541/547-3637, 800/800-1915 • gay-friendly • coastal vacation rental homes in Yachats & Waldport • women-owned/ run • $85-225

The Oregon House 94288 Hwy 101 **541/547-3329** • gay-friendly • ocean views • patio • massage • smokefree • wheelchair access • $55-160

See Vue Motel 95590 Hwy 101 **541/547-3227** • gay-friendly • kids/ pets ok • wheelchair access • lesbian-owned • $42-75

PENNSYLVANIA

Adamstown

ACCOMMODATIONS

The Barnyard Inn 2145 Old Lancaster Pike, Reinholds **717/484-1111, 888/738-6624** • gay-friendly • full brkfst • 150-yr-old restored German school house • petting zoo • kids ok • $80-155

Allentown

see also Bethlehem

BARS

Candida's 247 N 12th St (at Chew) **610/ 434-3071** • 2pm-2am • lesbians/ gay men • neighborhood bar • food served • karaoke

Moose Lounge/ Stonewall 28–30 N 10th St (at Hamilton) **610/432-0706** • 7pm-2am, clsd Mon • popular • lesbians/ gay men • dancing/ DJ • live shows • food served • karaoke

EROTICA

Adult World 80 S West End Blvd/ Rte 309, Quakerstown **215/538-1522**

Altoona

NIGHTCLUBS

Escapade 2523 Union Ave, Rte 36 **814/946-8195** • 8pm-2am • lesbians/ gay men • dancing/ DJ • gay-owned/ run

Rumors 1413 11th Ave (enter rear) **814/941-0803** • 9pm-2am, clsd Sun-Mon • lesbians/ gay men • dancing/ DJ • patio • gay-owned/ run

RESTAURANTS

Michael's Cafe 1413 11th Ave (enter rear) **814/941-0803** • 7am-2pm • brkfst & lunch • gay-owned/ run

Bethlehem

INFO LINES & SERVICES

Kindred Spirits 610/868-0248 • lesbian social/ support group

NIGHTCLUBS

Diamonz 1913 W Broad St (at Pennsylvania Ave) **610/865-1028** • 4pm-2am, from 3pm wknds • mostly women • dancing/ DJ • live shows • also restaurant (clsd Tue) • fine dining • some veggie • wheelchair access

SPIRITUAL GROUPS

MCC of the Lehigh Valley 424 Center St (at Unitarian Church) **610/954-7775** • 5:50pm Sun

Bridgeport

NIGHTCLUBS

The Lark 302 Dekalb St/ Rte 202 N **610/275-8136** • 8pm-2am, from 4pm Sun (dinner served) • lesbians/ gay men • dancing/ DJ • live shows

Bristol

EROTICA

Bristol News World 576 Bristol Pike/ Rte 13 N **215/785-4770** • 24hrs

East Stroudsburg

BARS

Secrets Business Rte 209 **570/420-8716** • 5pm-2am • mostly gay men • dancing • swimming • food served • game room • theme nights • also motel • gay-owned/ run

Pennsylvania • USA

Erie

ACCOMMODATIONS

The Castle Guest House 231 W 21st St **814/461-8770** • lesbians/gay men • smokefree • $45-55

NIGHTCLUBS

The Village Supper Club 133 W 18th St (at Peach) **814/452-0125** • 9pm-2am • lesbians/gay men • dancing/DJ • live shows • karaoke • wheelchair access

The Zone 1711 State St (at 17th) **814/459-1711** • 4pm-2am, clsd Sun • lesbians/gay men • dancing/DJ

CAFES

Aroma's Coffeehouse 2164 W 8th St **814/456-5282** • 7am-11pm, 9am-1am Sat, till 4pm Sun • light fare • smokefree

Cup-A-Ccinos Coffeehouse 18 N Park Row (nr Erie County Courthouse) **814/456-1151** • 7:30am-10pm, till midnight Th-Sat, from 9am Sat, till 8pm Sun • live shows • wheelchair access

RESTAURANTS

Matthew's Trattoria 153 E 13th St (at Lovell Place) **814/459-6458** • lunch & dinner, clsd Mon • live music

Pie in the Sky Cafe 463 W 8th St (at Walnut) **814/459-8638** • 7:30am-2pm, dinner from 5pm Fri-Sat, clsd Sun • BYOB • wheelchair access

PUBLICATIONS

Gay People's Chronicle 216/631-8646, 800/426-5947 • Ohio's largest weekly lgbt newspaper w/ extensive listings

SPIRITUAL GROUPS

Temple Anshe Hesed 930 Liberty St 814/454-2426 • 8pm Fri

Unitarian Universalist Congregation of Erie 7180 New Perry Hwy **814/864-9300** • 10:30am Sun

Gettysburg

ACCOMMODATIONS

Maplecrest Farm 749 Dicks Dam Rd, New Oxford **717/624-3339** • gay/straight • swimming • gay-owned/run • $125-325

The Old Barn 1 Main Trail, Carroll Valley **717/642-5711, 800/640-2276** • gay/straight • b&b in historic Civil War landmark • swimming • wheelchair access • gay-owned/run • $80-130

Greensburg

NIGHTCLUBS

RK's Safari Lounge 108 W Pittsburgh St (at Pennsylvania Ave) **724/837-6614** • 9pm-2am, clsd Sun • popular • mostly gay men • dancing/DJ • patio • wheelchair access

Harrisburg

INFO LINES & SERVICES

Gay/Lesbian Switchboard 717/234-0328 • 6pm-9pm Mon-Fri (volunteers permitting)

BARS

704 Strawberry 704 N 3rd St **717/234-4228** • 2pm-2am • popular • mostly gay men • neighborhood bar • videos • young crowd • wheelchair access

Want More?

Subscribe to our online travel guide:
www.damron.com

More listings. More destinations (like Australia, South Africa & Asia). More up-to-the-minute info. Check with Damron before you leave, or from the road with your laptop!

New Hope • Pennsylvania

The Brownstone Lounge 412 Forster St (btwn 3rd & 6th) **717/234-7009** • 11am-2am, 1pm-2am Sun • lesbians/ gay men • food served • wheelchair access

Neptune's Lounge/ Paper Moon 268 North St (at 3rd) **717/233-3078, 717/233-0581** • 4pm-2am • popular • lesbians/ gay men • neighborhood bar • dancing/ DJ • young crowd • dinner 6pm-10pm, Sun brunch

The Pink Lizard 891 Eisenhower Blvd (near exit 19) **717/939-1123** • 7pm-2am, clsd Sun-Tue • lesbians/ gay men • transgender-friendly • dancing/DJ • food served • live shows • videos • women-owned/ run

Nightclubs

Stallions 706 N 3rd St (enter rear) **717/232-3060** • 7pm-2am • popular • mostly gay men • dancing/DJ • karaoke • young crowd • wheelchair access

Restaurants

Colonnade 300 N 2nd St (at Pine) **717/234-8740** • 7am-8:30pm, clsd Sun • seafood • full bar • wheelchair access • $8-15

Spiritual Groups

MCC of the Spirit 2973 Jefferson St (nr Uptown Shopping Plaza) **717/236-7387** • 10:30am & 7pm Sun

Johnstown

Nightclubs

Lucille's 520 Washington St (nr Central Park) **814/539-4448** • 6pm-2am, clsd Sun • lesbians/ gay men • dancing/DJ • live shows

Kutztown

Accommodations

Grim's Manor B&B 10 Kern Rd **610/683-7089** • lesbians/ gay men • 200 yr old stone farmhouse on 5 acres • full brkfst • smokefree • gay-owned/ run • $65-70

Lancaster

Accommodations

The Noble House B&B 113 W Market St, Marietta **717/426-4389, 888/277-6426** • gay/ straight • full brkfst • smokefree • $99-145

Bars

Tally Ho 201 W Orange (at Water) **717/299-0661** • 6pm-2am, from 8pm Sun • popular • lesbians/ gay men • dancing/DJ • young crowd

Nightclubs

Sundown Lounge 429 N Mulberry St (at James) **717/392-2737** • 8pm-2am, from 3pm Fri-Sat, clsd Sun • mostly women • dancing/DJ

Restaurants

Loft above 'Tally Ho' bar **717/299-0661** • lunch Mon-Fri, dinner Mon-Sat • French • $15-25

Bookstores

Borders Bookshop 940 Plaza Blvd (at Harrisburg Pike) **717/293-8022** • 9am-11pm, till 9pm Sun • lgbt section

Spiritual Groups

MCC Vision of Hope 130 E Main St, Mountville **717/285-9070** • 10:30am & 7pm Sun

Manheim

Bars

Cellar Bar 168 S Main St (below 'Dad's Bar & Grill') **717/665-1960** • 8pm-2am Th-Sat • lesbians/ gay men • restaurant upstairs

Monroeville

Erotica

Monroeville News 2735 Stroschein Rd (off Rte 22) **412/372-5477** • 24hrs

Montgomeryville

Erotica

Adult World Book Store Rtes 202 & 309 **215/362-9560**

Mt Pleasant

Bars

Yuppie's 241 E Main St **724/547-0430** • 9pm-2am, from 8pm Fri-Sat, 8pm-1am Sun • lesbians/ gay men • neighborhood bar • food served

New Hope

see also Lambertville & Sergeantsville, New Jersey

Info Lines & Services

AA Gay/ Lesbian 215/923-7900 (AA#)

Accommodations

Best Western New Hope Inn 6426 Lower York Rd/ Rte 202 **215/862-5221, 800/467-3202** • gay-friendly • swimming • also restaurant & lounge • kids/ pets ok • wheelchair access • $89-149

Pennsylvania • USA

Cordials B&B 143 Old York Rd (at Sugan Rd) **215/862-3919, 877/219-1009** • lesbians/gay men • hot tub • wheelchair access • gay-owned/run • $85-130

The Fox & Hound B&B 246 West Bridge St **215/862-5082, 800/862-5082** • gay-friendly • 1850s stone manor • gay-owned/run • $75+

The Lexington House 6171 Upper York Rd **215/794-0811** • gay/straight • 1749 country home • swimming • smokefree • gay-owned/run • $120-200

The New Hope Motel 400 W Bridge St/Rte 179 **215/862-2800** • gay/straight • patios • lounge • swimming • $59-119

Silver Maple Organic Farm & B&B 483 Sergeantsville Rd (Rte 523), Sergeantsville, NJ **908/237-2192** • gay/straight • 200-yr-old farmhouse • full brkfst • hot tub • swimming • smokefree • kids/pets ok • wheelchair access • gay-owned/run • $75-145

The Wishing Well Guesthouse 144 Old York Rd **215/862-8819** • gay/straight • B&B • smokefree • kids/pets ok • gay-owned/run • $80-135

York Street House B&B 42 York St, Lambertville, NJ **609/397-3007** • gay-friendly • 1909 Manor house • smokefree • lesbian-owned/run • $95-169

BARS

The Raven Bar & Restaurant 385 West Bridge St **215/862-2081** • 11am-2am • lesbians/gay men • also motel • swimming • $81-108

NIGHTCLUBS

The Cartwheel 437 Old York Rd/US 202 **215/862-0880** • 5pm-2am • popular • lesbians/gay men • dancing/DJ • live shows • piano bar • also restaurant • wheelchair access • $6-18

RESTAURANTS

Havana 105 S Main St **215/862-9897** • 11am-midnight, bar till 2am • some veggie • live shows • $9-16

Karla's 5 W Mechanic St **215/862-2612** • lunch & dinner, late night brkfst Fri-Sat • Mediterranean • some veggie • full bar • $15-25

Mother's 34 N Main St **215/862-5270** • 11am-9pm, clsd Mon • some veggie • $10-20

Nouveau Country Diner 463 Old York Rd/Rte 202 **215/862-5575** • 7am-10pm • full bar • wheelchair access • $7-12

Odette's South River Rd **215/862-3000** • 11am-10pm, piano bar & cabaret till 1am • some veggie • wheelchair access • $15-25

The Raven 385 West Bridge St **215/862-2081** • noon-3pm & 6pm-10pm • popular • mostly gay men • cont'l • $16-21 • also motel • swimming

Wildflowers 8 W Mechanic St **215/862-2241** • (seasonal) noon-10pm, till 11pm Fri-Sat • some veggie • BYOB • outdoor dining • $8-15

RETAIL SHOPS

Bucks County Video & CD Exchange 415–C York Rd **215/862-0919** • 10am-10pm • gay-themed & adult videos • gay-owned/run

EROTICA

Grownups 4 E Mechanic St (at Main) **215/862-9304** • gay-owned/run

Le Chateau Exotique 31-A W Mechanic St **215/862-3810** • fetishwear

New Kensington

BARS

Zebra Lounge 910 Constitution Blvd (at 9th) **724/339-0298** • 4pm-2am, from 1pm Sat, clsd Sun • lesbians/gay men • dancing/DJ

New Milford

ACCOMMODATIONS

Oneida Camp & Lodge **570/465-7011** • mostly gay men • oldest gay-owned/operated campground dedicated to the lgbt community • swimming • nudity • seasonal

Philadelphia

INFO LINES & SERVICES

AA Gay/Lesbian **215/923-7900** • call for mtg schedule

Penn Women's Center 3643 Locust Walk **215/898-8611**

Philadelphia Convention & Visitors Bureau 16th St & JFK Blvd **215/636-4400, 800/225-5745**

Sisterspace of the Delaware Valley **215/546-4890** • sponsors 'Sisterspace Weekend' & other events • newsletter

William Way LGBT Community Center 1315 Spruce St (at Juniper) **215/732-2220** • noon-10pm Mon-Th, till 7pm Sat, till 8pm Sun

Women in Transition Hotline **215/751-1111** • 24hr crisis line

ACCOMMODATIONS

▲ **The Alexander Inn** Spruce (at 12th) **215/923-3535, 877/253-9466** • gay/straight • gym • gay-owned/run • $99-159

Philadelphia • Pennsylvania

Antique Row B&B 341 S 12th St (at Pine) **215/592-7821** • gay-friendly • 1820s townhouse in heart of gay community • full brkfst • $65-100

Doubletree Hotel 237 S Broad St (at Locust) **215/893-1600, 800/222-8733** • gay-friendly

Embassy Suites Center City 1776 Ben Franklin Pkwy (at 18th) **215/561-1776, 800/362-2779** • gay-friendly • $109-209

Gaskill House 312 Gaskill St (btwn Lombard & South St) **215/413-0669** • gay/ straight • on Society Hill • full brkfst • kids/pets ok • smokefree • gay-owned/ run • $145-200

Glen Isle Farm 30 miles out of town, in Downingtown **610/269-9100, 800/269-1730** • gay-friendly • full brkfst • smokefree • older kids ok (call first) • $60-75

Latham Hotel 135 S 17th St (at Walnut) **215/563-7474, 800/528-4261** • gay-friendly

Rittenhouse Hotel 210 W Rittenhouse Sq (at 19th) **215/546-9000, 800/635-1042** • gay-friendly • food served • $195+

Rodeway Inn 1208 Walnut St (btwn 12th & 13th) **215/546-7000, 800/887-1776** • gay-friendly • kids ok • $99-145

Spring Garden Manor 2025 Spring Garden St (at 20th) **215/567-2484** • gay/ straight • full brkfst • located in city center nr museums • gay-owned/ run • $119-149

Bars

Key West 207–209 S Juniper (btwn Walnut & Locust) **215/545-1578** • 4pm-2am, from 2pm Sun • lesbians/ gay men • neighborhood bar • dancing/DJ • live shows • piano bar • wheelchair access

The Khyber 56 S 2nd St (btwn Market & Chestnut) **215/238-5888** • gay-friendly • live shows • also restaurant (lunch only)

Love Lounge 232 South St (btwn 2nd & 3rd) **215/922-0499** • 10pm-close wknds only • call first • gay/ straight

Tavern on Camac 243 S Camac St (at Spruce) **215/545-0900** • noon-2am • lesbians/ gay men • dancing/DJ wknds • piano bar • food served • karaoke

Tyz 1418 Rodman St (nr 15th & Richmond) **215/546-4195** • 11pm-3am • mostly gay men • dancing/DJ wknds

Valanni 1229 Spruce St **215/790-9494** • gay/ straight • also restaurant

The Westbury 261 S 13th (at Spruce) **215/546-5170** • 10am-2am, dinner till 10pm, till 11pm wknds • mostly gay men • neighborhood bar • wheelchair access

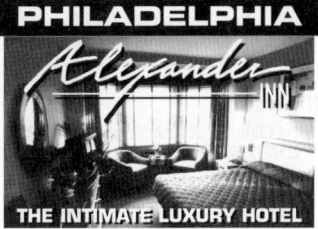

PHILADELPHIA
Alexander INN
THE INTIMATE LUXURY HOTEL

European Charm and amenities in a most convenient Center City location — in the midst of Convention Center, Avenue of the Arts, Independence Hall, Antique Row, major museums, shopping, nightlife and fine restaurants.

American Comfort in a historic building restored with 48 elegant guest rooms, each featuring luxurious bath with fluffy towels, DirecTV with 4 complimentary movie channels, phones with modem port. Continental Breakfast Buffet with fresh baked goods. 24-hour Fitness Center.

Rooms from $99.00 DBL
Spruce at Twelfth Street, Philadelphia, PA

Toll Free: (877) ALEX-INN
(215) 923-3535   Fax: (215) 923-1004   www.alexanderinn.com

IGLTA

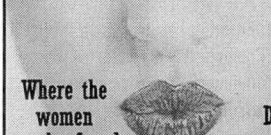

SISTERS

Your nights will come to LIFE!

Where the women can be found

7 Days a week

**1320 Chancellor St.
Philadelphia, Pa
215.735.0735**
www.sistersnightclub.com

Pennsylvania • USA

Woody's 202 S 13th St (at Walnut) **215/545-1893** • 11am-2am • popular • mostly gay men • dancing/DJ • country/western • dance lessons • food served • young crowd • 18+ Wed • cover charge some nights • wheelchair access

Nightclubs

2-4 Club 1221 St James St (off 13th & Locust) **215/735-5772** • 1am-3am Mon-Tue, from midnight Wed & Sun, from 10pm Fri-Sat • mostly gay men • dancing/DJ • private club • cover charge

Bike Stop 204-206 S Quince St (at St James) **215/627-1662, 800/859-8480** • 4pm-2am, from 2pm wknds • popular • mostly gay men • 4 flrs • dancing/DJ • leather (very leather-women-friendly) • live bands Sun

Fluid 613 S 4th St (at South) **215/629-3686** • 10pm-2am • gay-friendly • more gay wknds • dancing/DJ • drag shows • theme nights • cover charge

Gasoline Eighth St (at Callowhill St) **215/925-1900** • 9pm-2am Fri-Sat, from 10pm Sun • gay/ straight • dancing/ DJ

Palmer Social Club 601 Spring Garden St (at 6th) **215/925-5000** • 11pm-3am, from 1am Mon-Tue, from midnight Th, clsd Wed • gay-friendly • dancing/DJ • 3 flrs • private club

Proto Lounge 125 S 2nd St (at Chestnut) **215/351-9026** • 8pm-close Th-Sat • gay/straight • dancing/DJ • live shows

Shampoo 417 N 8th St (at Willow) **215/922-7500** • 9pm-2am, clsd Tue-Wed • gay-friendly • more gay Fri • dancing/DJ • alternative

▲ **Sisters** 1320 Chancellor St (at Juniper) **215/735-0735** • 5pm-2am • mostly women • dancing/DJ • live shows • karaoke • also restaurant • dinner Wed-Sun • wheelchair access

Cafes

10th Street Pour House 262 S 10th St (at Spruce) **215/922-5626** • 7:30am-3pm, from 8:30am wknds

Cheap Art Cafe 260 S 12th St (btwn Locust & Spruce) **215/735-6650** • 24hrs • popular

Millennium Coffee 212 S 12th St (btwn Locust & Walnut) **215/731-9798** • open till midnight

Stellar Coffee 1101 Spruce St (at 11th) **215/625-7923** • 6:30am-9pm

Restaurants

The Adobe Cafe 4550 Mitchell St (at Greenleaf), Roxborough **215/483-3947** • lunch & dinner, till 11pm Fri-Sat

---

[Reply] [Forward]   [Delete]

Date: Sun, Nov 11, 2001 11:23:46
From: Girl-on-the-Go
To: Editor@Damron.com
Subject: Philadelphia

> Though it's packed with sites of rich historical value, don't miss out on Philadelphia's multicultural present. To get a feel for this city, browse the Reading Terminal Market, a quaint old farmer's market preserved within the new Convention Center. Here, smalltime grocers and farmers of many cultures sell their fresh food.

A vital element in many of these cultures is the growing lesbian community. To connect with the scene, call the **William Way LGBT Community Center**, or check out **Sisters**, a women's dance bar. And don't even think of leaving town before you visit **Giovanni's Room**, Philadelphia's legendary LGBT bookstore. Here you can pick up the latest lesbian bestseller, the love of your life, or copies of the **Philadelphia Gay News** and **Swirl**.

Philadelphia • Pennsylvania

Astral Plane 1708 Lombard St (btwn 17th & 18th) **215/546-6230** • lunch & dinner • some veggie • full bar • $10-20

Circa 1518 Walnut St (btwn 15th & 16th) **215/545-6800** • lunch, dinner, Sun brunch • wheelchair access

The Continental 138 Market St (at 2nd) **215/923-6069** • dinner nightly • wknd brunch • also bar

Frangelica 200 S 12th St (at Walnut) **215/731-9930** • lunch Mon-Fri, dinner nightly

Harmony Vegetarian 135 N 9th St (at Cherry) **215/627-4520** • 11am-10pm, till midnight Fri-Sat

The Inn Philadelphia 251 S Camac St (btwn Locust & Spruce) **215/732-2339** • 5pm-10pm, Sun brunch, clsd Mon • some veggie • full bar

Judy's Cafe 627 S 3rd St (at Bainbridge) **215/928-1968** • 5:30pm-midnight, Sun brunch from 10:30am • full bar • women-owned/run • $9-17

Katie Quinn's Cafe Rte 202 (in Buckingham Green Shopping Ctr) **215/794-8661** • 9am-5pm, clsd Sun • old-fashioned soda fountain

L2 2201 South St (at 22nd) **215/732-7878** • dinner nightly • also bar • live entertainment

Latimer's Deli 255 S 15th St (at Latimer) **215/545-9244** • 9am-9pm, till 11pm Fri • Jewish deli

Liberties 705 N 2nd St (at Fairmount) **215/238-0660** • lunch & dinner, Sun brunch • full bar • $10-16

My Thai 2200 South St (at 22nd) **215/985-1878** • 5pm-10pm, till 11pm Fri-Sat

Palladium/ Gold Standard 3601 Locust Walk (at 36th) **215/387-3463** • lunch & dinner, bar till 12:30am • wheelchair access

Philadelphia

WHERE THE GIRLS ARE: Partying downtown near 12th St., south of Market.

LGBT PRIDE: June. 215/875-9288.

ANNUAL EVENTS: April/May - PrideFest America Philadelphia 215/732-3378, web: www.pridefest.org. Weekend of lgbt film, performances, literature, sports, seminars, parties & more. June - Womongathering 856/694-2037. Women's spirituality fest.

CITY INFO: 215/636-1666.

ATTRACTIONS: Academy of Natural Sciences 215/299-1000.
African American Museum 215/574-0380.
Betsy Ross House 215/686-1252.
Independence Hall.
Liberty Bell Pavilion.
National Museum Of American Jewish History 215/923-3811.
Norman Rockwell Museum 215/922-4345.
Philadelphia Museum of Art 215/763-8100.
Rodin Museum 215/763-8100.

BEST VIEW: Top of Center Square, 16th & Market.

WEATHER: Winter temperatures hover in the 20°s. Summers are humid with temperatures in the 80°s and 90°s.

TRANSIT: Quaker City Cab 215/728-8000.
Transit Authority (SEPTA) 215/580-7800.

Pennsylvania • USA

Roosevelt's Pub 2222 Walnut (at 23rd) **215/636-9722** • lunch & dinner • some veggie • full bar • $5-12

Shing Kee 52 N 9th St **215/829-8983** • lunch & dinner • BYOB • gay-owned/run

Striped Bass 1500 Walnut St (at 15th) **215/732-4444** • lunch, dinner & Sun brunch • upscale dining

Swanky Bubbles 10 S Front St (at Market) **215/928-1200** • dinner nightly • also bar

Waldorf Cafe 20th & Lombard Sts **215/985-1836** • dinner, clsd Mon • some veggie • full bar • wheelchair access • $12-18

White Dog Cafe 3420 Sansom St (at Walnut) **215/386-9224** • lunch & dinner • full bar • $7-18

ENTERTAINMENT & RECREATION

Amazon Country WXPN-FM 88.5 **215/898-6677** • 9pm Sun • lesbian radio

'Q Zine' WXPN-FM 88.5 **215/898-6677** • 10pm Sun • lgbt radio

The Walt Whitman House 328 Mickle Blvd (btwn S 3rd & S 4th Sts), Camden, NJ **856/964-5383** • the last home of America's great & controversial poet, just across the Delaware River

BOOKSTORES

Afterwords 218 S 12th St (btwn Locust & Walnut) **215/735-2393** • 11am-10pm

Giovanni's Room 345 S 12th St (at Pine) **215/923-2960** • call for hours, open daily • popular • lgbt bookstore

Ring of Fire Books 236 Haverford Ave (at Narbeth), Narbeth **610/617-3442** • used

RETAIL SHOPS

Infinite Body Piercing 626 S 4th St (at South) **215/923-7335**

PUBLICATIONS

Greater Philadelphia Women's Yellow Pages **610/446-4747**

PGN (Philadelphia Gay News) **215/625-8501** • lgbt newspaper w/ extensive listings

Swirl Magazine **215/625-8501** • nightlife guide

SPIRITUAL GROUPS

Beth Ahavah 8 Letitia St (btwn Market & Chestnut) **215/923-2003** • 8pm 1st, 3rd & 5th Fri

Christ Episcopal Church 2nd above Market (at Church) **215/922-1695** • 9am & 11am Sun

Dignity 330 S 13th St (btwn Spruce & Pine) **215/546-2093** • 7pm Sun

Integrity 1904 Walnut St (at the church) **215/382-0794** • 7pm 1st & 3rd Wed • pastoral counseling available

MCC 1315 Spruce St, 3rd flr (at William Way GLBT Center) **215/735-6223** • 11am & 7pm Sun (except summer)

Old First Reformed Church (United Church of Christ) 4th & Race Sts **215/922-4566** • 11am

GYMS & HEALTH CLUBS

12th St Gym 204 S 12th St (btwn Locust & Walnut) **215/985-4092** • 5:30am-11pm • gay-friendly

EROTICA

Condom Kingdom 437 South St (at 5th) **215/829-1668** • safer sex materials • toys

Fetishes Boutique 704 S 5th St (at Bainbridge) **215/829-4986, 877/2-CORSET**

The Pleasure Chest 2039 Walnut (btwn 20th & 21st) **215/561-7480** • clsd Sun-Mon

Pittsburgh

INFO LINES & SERVICES

AA Gay/ Lesbian **412/471-7472**

FACT (Friends of all Colors Together) **412/441-4441**

Gay/ Lesbian Community Center 5808 Forward Ave (at Murray, 2nd flr) **412/422-0114** • 6:30pm-9:30pm, 3pm-6pm Sat, clsd Sun

ACCOMMODATIONS

Camp Davis 311 Red Brush Rd, Boyers **724/637-2402** • May thru 2nd wknd in Oct • cabins & campsites • lesbians/ gay men • adults 21+ only • call for events • 1 hr from Pittsburgh

The Inn on the Mexican War Streets (at Bogg's Mansion) 604 W North Ave **412/231-6544** • lesbians/ gay men • located on the historic & gay-friendly North Side • also restaurant • gay-owned/ run • $79-129

The Priory 614 Pressley (nr Cedar Ave) **412/231-3338** • gay-friendly • 24-rm Victorian • kids ok • $68-175

The Waterford 3337 Brownsville Rd **412/881-1111** • gay-friendly • $90-165

BARS

Brewery Tavern 3315 Liberty Ave (at Herron Ave) **412/681-7991** • 10am-2am, from noon Sun • gay-friendly

Pittsburgh • Pennsylvania

Images 965 Liberty Ave (at 10th St) **412/391-9990** • 2pm-2am, from 7pm Sat, from 9pm Sun • mostly gay men • karaoke Mon & Th • videos

Liberty Avenue Saloon 941 Liberty Ave (at Smithfield) **412/338-1533** • 11am-2am, from 5pm Sat-Sun • lesbians/ gay men • neighborhood bar • drag shows • also restaurant

New York, New York 5801 Ellsworth Ave (at Maryland) **412/661-5600** • 4pm-2am, from 2pm Sun • popular • lesbians/ gay men • also restaurant • some veggie • $9-15

Pittsburgh Eagle 1740 Eckert St (nr Beaver) **412/766-7222** • 9pm-2am, clsd Sun-Tue • popular • mostly gay men • dancing/DJ • leather • wheelchair access

Real Luck Cafe 1519 Penn Ave (at 16th) **412/566-8988** • 3pm-2am • lesbians/ gay men • neighborhood bar • food served • cafe menu • some veggie • wheelchair access

Senator's 401 Hastings St (at Reynolds) **412/362-1600** • 4pm-2am, clsd Sun • lesbians/ gay men • also restaurant

Sidekicks 931 Liberty Ave (at Smithfield) **412/642-4435** • 5pm-midnight, clsd Sun • lesbians/ gay men • piano bar • also restaurant

Nightclubs

CJ Deighan's 2506 W Liberty Ave, Brookline **412/561-4044** • 8pm-2am, clsd Sun-Mon • mostly women • dancing/DJ • live shows • food served • wheelchair access

Donny's Place 1226 Herron Ave (at Liberty) **412/682-9869** • 4pm-2am, from 3pm Sun • popular • lesbians/ gay men • dancing/DJ • live shows • food served • leather bar downstairs

House of Tilden 941 Liberty Ave, 2nd flr (at Smithfield) **412/391-0804** • 10pm-3am • lesbians/ gay men • dancing/DJ • private club

M 1600 Smallman St **412/261-4512** • 8pm-2am Wed-Sun • lesbian/ gay night Th w/ 'Babylon' • popular • gay-friendly • dancing/DJ • alternative • live shows • food served • wheelchair access

---

Pittsburgh

LGBT Pride: June. 412/422-0114 (GLCC #).

City Info: 412/281-7711 or 800/359-0758, web: www.pittsburgh-cvb.org.

Attractions: Andy Warhol Museum 412/237-8300.
Carnegie Museums of Pittsburgh 412/622-3131.
Fallingwater (in Mill Run) 724/329-8501.
Frick Art & Historical Center 412/371-0600.
Golden Triangle district.
National Aviary 412/323-7235.
Phipps Conservatory 412/622-6914.
Rachel Carson Homestead (in Springdale) 724/274-5459.
Station Square.

Transit: Yellow Cab 412/665-8100.
Airline Transportation Co. 412/321-4990.
Port Authority Transit (PAT) 412/442-2000.

Pennsylvania • USA

Pegasus Lounge 818 Liberty Ave (at 9th) **412/281-2131** • 9pm-2am, clsd Sun-Mon • popular • mostly gay men • dancing/DJ • drag shows • young crowd

Restaurants

Rosebud 1650 Smallman St **412/261-2221** • dinner nightly, clsd Mon • live music • wheelchair access • $8-15

Tuscany Cafe 1501 E Carson St (15th) **412/488-4475** • 7am-2am, from 8am wknds • full bar

Entertainment & Recreation

Andy Warhol Museum 117 Sandusky St (at General Robinson) **412/237-8300** • clsd Mon-Tue • is it soup or is it art—see for yourself

Bookstores

The Bookstall 3604 5th Ave (at Meyran) **412/683-2644** • 9:30am-5pm, till 4:30pm Sat, clsd Sun

St Elmo's Books & Music 2208 E Carson St (at 22nd St) **412/431-9100** • 10am-9pm • progressive

Retail Shops

A Pleasant Present 2301 Murray Ave (at Nicholson) **412/421-7104** • 10am-7pm, till 8:30pm Th, till 6pm Fri, clsd Sun-Mon • wheelchair access

Joe's Closet 945 Liberty Ave (at Smithfield) **412/201-9001** • 11am-8pm, till midnight Fri, 1pm-midnight Sat, clsd Sun

Slacker 1321 E Carson St (btwn 13th & 14th) **412/381-3911** • 11am-9pm, till 11pm Fri-Sat, noon-6pm Sun • magazines • clothing • leather • piercing • wheelchair access

Publications

Hotspots Magazine 304/782-3358 • free monthly lgbt guide to bars, clubs & the scene in Pittsburgh

Out 412/243-3350 • lgbt newspaper

Spiritual Groups

First Unitarian Church 605 Moorewood Ave (at Ellsworth) **412/621-8008** • 11am Sun (10am summers)

MCC of Pittsburgh 4836 Ellsworth Ave (at Devonshire, at Friends Mtg House) **412/683-2994** • 7pm Sun

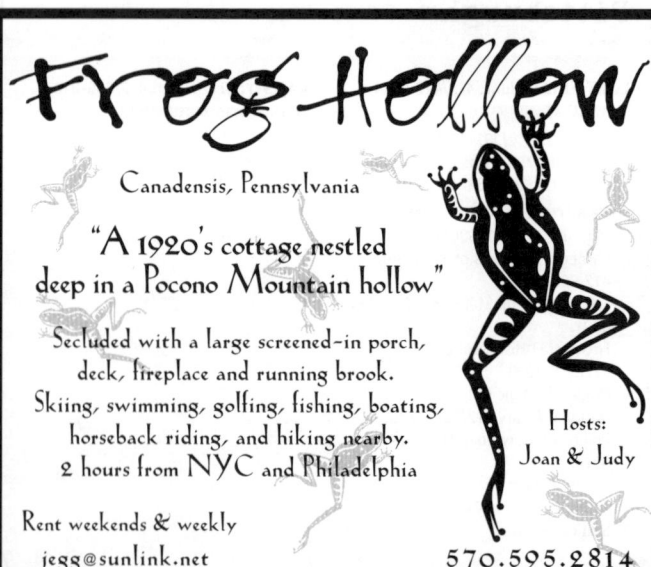

Reading • Pennsylvania

Erotica

Boulevard Videos & Magazines 346 Blvd of the Allies (at Smithfield) **412/261-9119** • 24hrs • leather • toys

Golden Triangle News 816 Liberty Ave (at 9th) **412/765-3790** • 24hrs

Poconos

Accommodations

The Arrowheart Inn 3021 Valley View Dr (at Fox Gap Rd), Bangor **610/588-0241, 888/546-6001 x9435** • gay-friendly • B&B • full brkfst • hot tub • nr skiing, hiking, biking, river • kids ok • gay-owned/run • $75-125

▲ **Blueberry Ridge 570/629-5036** • women only • full brkfst • hot tub • smokefree • holiday packages • lesbian-owned/run • $55-80

▲ **Frog Hollow 570/595-2814** • lesbians/gay men • secluded 1920s cottage • deck • fireplace • kids/pets ok • lesbian-owned/run • $100-150

Milanville House B&B Kellow Rd (River Rd), Milanville **717/729-8236, 800/820-5111** • gay/straight • restored 19th-century inn 5 mins from Delaware River • full brkfst • gay-owned/run • $45-110

Rainbow Mountain Resort 570/223-8484 • popular • lesbians/gay men • atop Pocono Mtn on 26 acres • transgender-friendly • swimming • also bar • dancing/DJ • karaoke • live shows • gay-owned/run

▲ **Stoney Ridge 570/629-5036** • lesbians/gay men • secluded log home • kitchen • kids/pets ok • lesbian-owned/run • $250/wknd, $550/week

Quakertown

Restaurants

The Brick Tavern Inn 2460 Old Bethlehem Pike (at Brick Tavern Rd) **215/538-0865** • full bar

Reading

Bars

Nostalgia 1101 N 9th St (at Robinson) **610/372-5557** • 10am-midnight, till 2am Fri-Sat • mostly women • neighborhood bar

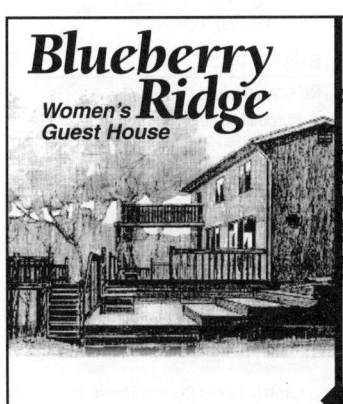

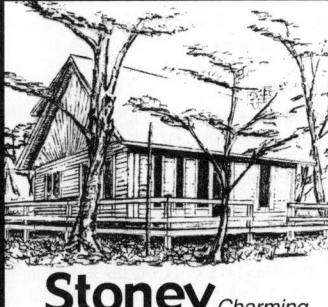

Two beautiful, secluded homes to choose from nestled in the Pocono Mountains. Both are completely furnished with all the modern conveniences and located to nearby skiing. Open year round.

Reservations & Info: Pat or Greta **(570) 629-5036**

Pennsylvania/ Rhode Island • USA

Red Star 11 S 10th St (at Penn) **610/375-4116** • 6pm-2am, clsd Mon-Tue • popular • mostly gay men • dancing/DJ • leather • live shows

Nightclubs

Scarab 724 Franklin (at Lemon) **610/375-7878** • 9pm-2am, clsd Sun • popular • lesbians/ gay men • dancing/DJ • young crowd

State College

Info Lines & Services

GLBT Switchboard 814/237-1950 • 6pm-9pm most evenings • info • referrals and resources

Women's Resource Center 140 W Nittany Ave (at Frasier) **814/234-5050 (24HR HOTLINE), 814/234-5222** • 9am-7pm, clsd wknds

Bars

Chumley's 108 W College **814/238-4446** • 5pm-2am, from 6pm Sun • popular • lesbians/ gay men • wheelchair access

Nightclubs

Players 112 W College Ave **814/234-1031** • 9pm-2am, clsd Mon & Wed • gay/ straight • more gay Sun • dancing/DJ • young crowd

Wilkes-Barre

Info Lines & Services

Coming Home (AA) 97 S Franklin Blvd (at Presbyterian Church) • noon Th

Nightclubs

Twist Fox Ridge Plaza **570/825-7300** • 8pm-2am, from 6pm Sun • popular • mostly gay men • dancing/DJ • patio • also restaurant • wheelchair access

Williamsport

Bars

Peachie's 144 E 4th St **570/326-3611** • 3pm-2am, clsd Sun • lesbians/gay men • dancing/DJ wknds • food served • wheelchair access

Nightclubs

Manhattan's 761 W 4th St (at Camel St) **570/320-0230** • 7pm-2am, clsd Sun • popular • gay/ straight • dancing/DJ • live shows

York

Info Lines & Services

Lesbian Alliance of South Central PA 717/848-9142

York Area Gay Info 717/846-2560

Bars

14 Karat 659 W Market • lesbians/ gay men

Nightclubs

Altland's Ranch 8505 Orchard Rd, Spring Grove **717/225-4479** • 8pm-2am Fri-Sat only • mostly gay men • dancing/DJ • country/ western Fri

The Velvet Rope 36-38 W 11th St **717/812-1474** • 3pm-2am Wed-Sun • lesbians/ gay men • women's night Wed • dancing/ DJ • food served

Erotica

Cupid's Connection Adult Boutique 244 N George St (at North) **717/846-5029** • 9pm-2am, noon-midnight Sun

Rhode Island

Statewide

Publications

In Newsweekly 617/426-8246 • New England's lgbt newspaper

Options 401/781-1193 • extensive resource listings

Spiritual Groups

RI & SE Mass Gay Jewish Group 508/992-7927 • call for info

Bristol

Restaurants

Hotpoint Restaurant 31 State St (in Bristol Harbor area) **401/254-7474** • from 5pm, clsd Mon • American Bistro • $10-25

Newport

Info Lines & Services

Sobriety First 135 Pelham St (at Channing Memorial Church) **401/438-8860** • 8pm Fri

Accommodations

Brinley Victorian Inn 23 Brinley St **401/849-7645, 800/999-8523** • gay-friendly • smokefree • $89-229

Captain James Preston House 378 Spring St (at Pope) **401/847-7077** • gay-friendly • elegant Victorian B&B • smokefree • $80-195

Hydrangea House Inn 16 Bellevue Ave **401/846-4435, 800/945-4667** • popular • gay/ straight • full brkfst • nr beach • gay-owned/ run • $145-280

Providence • Rhode Island

The Melville House Inn 39 Clarke St
401/847-0640, 800/711-7184 • popular • gay/
straight • full brkfst • smokefree • gay-owned/
run • $110-175

The Prospect Hill Guest House 32
Prospect Hill St **401/847-7405** • gay/straight
• smokefree • gay-owned/run • $115-205

RESTAURANTS

Restaurant Bouchard 505 Thames St
401/846-0123 • dinner, clsd Tue • $16-26

Whitehorse Tavern 26 Marlborough (at
Farewell) **401/849-3600** • upscale dining •
$30+

Pawtucket

INFO LINES & SERVICES

Gay & Lesbian AA 71 Park Place (at
Congregational church) **401/438-8860** •
7:30pm Tue

Providence

INFO LINES & SERVICES

Enforcers RI • lgbt leather/ SM & fetish
activities & fundraising • meetings 3rd Sat

Gay/ Lesbian Helpline of Rhode Island
401/751-3322 • 7pm-10pm Mon, Wed & Fri

GLBT Alliance **401/863-3062** • student
group at Brown

Sarah Doyle Women's Center 185 Meeting
St (Brown University) **401/863-2189** •
referrals • also lesbian collective group

Sisters in Sobriety 25 Pomona (at
Pemberton, at St Peter & Andrew Church)
401/438-8860 • 7pm Sat

BARS

Deville's 42 Blundell St (off Thurbers & Eddy)
401/751-7166 • 7pm-1am, till 2am Fri-Sat,
clsd Mon-Tue • popular • mostly women •
neighborhood bar • dancing/DJ Th-Sat •
wheelchair access

The Providence Eagle 200 Union St (at
Weybosset) **401/421-1447** • 3pm-1am, from
noon wknds, till 2am Fri-Sat • mostly gay men
• leather • wheelchair access

Union Street Station 69 Union St (at
Washington) **401/331-2291** • noon-1am, till
2am Fri-Sat • mostly gay men • dancing/DJ •
live shows • wheelchair access

Wheels 125 Washington (at Mathewson)
401/272-6950 • noon-1am, till 2am Fri-Sat •
lesbians/ gay men • dancing/DJ wknds •
karaoke • videos • wheelchair access

NIGHTCLUBS

Bar One 1 Throop Alley (off S Main St)
401/621-7112 • gay/ straight • gay on Sun •
dancing/DJ • 18+ • call for events

Gerardo's 1 Franklin Sq (btwn Allens &
Eddy) **401/274-5560** • 8pm-1am, till 2am Fri-
Sat • gay/ straight • dancing/DJ • live shows •
karaoke • theme parties • wheelchair access

Mirabar 35 Richmond St (at Weybosset)
401/331-6761 • 3pm-1am, till 2am Fri-Sat •
mostly gay men • dancing/DJ • karaoke Mon •
live shows • wheelchair access

Pulse 86 Crary St (at Plain) **401/272-2133** •
9pm-close, from 6pm Sun, clsd Mon-Tue •
lesbians/ gay men • dancing/DJ • live shows •
karaoke Sun • 18+ Wed-Th • cover charge

CAFES

The Castro 77 Ives (at Wickenden) **401/421-
1144** • 7am-11pm, from 8am Sun, till
midnight Fri-Sat • pizza • salads • sandwiches

Providence

LGBT PRIDE: June. 401/467-2130.

CITY INFO: 401/274-1636 (in RI) or
800/233-1636, web:
www.providencecvb.com.

ATTRACTIONS: Newport.
RISD Museum 401/454-6500, web:
www.risd.edu.
Waterfire (on Providence River
every 3rd Sat).

TRANSIT: Yellow Cab 401/941-1122.
RIPTA Bus Service 401/781-9400.

Rhode Island/ South Carolina • USA

Coffee Cafe 257 S Main St (at Power) **401/421-0787** • 7am-5pm, 8am-4pm Sat, clsd Sun • patio • gay-owned/ run

Restaurants

Al Forno 577 S Main St **401/273-9760** • dinner only, clsd Sun-Mon • popular • Little Rhody's best dining experience • $13-24

Camille's 71 Bradford St (at Atwell's Ave) **401/751-4812** • lunch & dinner, dinner only Sat • full bar

Down City Diner 151 Weybosset St **401/331-9217** • lunch & dinner • popular Sun brunch (very gay) • full bar • wheelchair access

Julian's 318 Broadway (at Vinton) **401/861-1770** • 9am-2pm Wed-Sun & 6pm-10pm Wed-Sat, clsd Mon-Tue

Rue de l'Espoir 99 Hope St (at John) **401/751-8890** • lunch & dinner, clsd Mon • popular • full bar • women-owned/ run • $12-20

Trent 748 Hope St **401/861-5363** • 11:30am-9pm, clsd Sun-Mon • BYOB

Viola's 58 DePasquale Plaza (on Federal Hill) **401/861-5766** • lunch Wed-Sun, dinner Wed-Mon • patio

Bookstores

Books on the Square 471 Angell St (at Wayland) **401/331-9097** • 9am-9pm, till 10pm Fri-Sat, 10am-6pm Sun • some lgbt

Retail Shops

Esta's on Thayer St 257 Thayer St (across from Avon cinema) **401/831-2651** • videos • pride items • Tarot readings

Publications

In Newsweekly 617/426-8246 • New England's lgbt newspaper

Metroline 860/233-8334 • regional newspaper & entertainment guide, covers CT, RI & MA

Options 401/781-1193 • extensive resource listings

Spiritual Groups

Bell St Chapel (Unitarian) 5 Bell St **401/273-5678** • 10am Sun

Morning Star MCC 624 Southbridge St (at Ramada Inn), Auburn, MA **508/892-4320** • 10am Sun

St Peter's & Andrew's Episcopal Church 25 Pomona Ave **401/272-9649** • 8am & 10am Sun, 7pm Wed (healing service)

Smithfield

Bars

The Loft 325 Farnum Pike **401/231-3320** • noon-1am, from 10am wknds and summers • lesbians/ gay men • dancing/DJ • swimming • wheelchair access

Warwick

Cafes

Side Street Cafe & Deli 79 Soule St **401/738-7979** • 8:30am-3pm, clsd wknds

Bookstores

Barnes & Noble 1441 Bald Hill Rd/ Rte 2 **401/828-7900** • 9am-11pm, 11am-7pm Sun • lgbt section

Westerly

Accommodations

The Villa 190 Shore Rd **401/596-1054, 800/722-9240** • gay-friendly • nr beach • hot tub • swimming • smokefree • $85-245

Restaurants

Mary's Rte 1 & Post Rd (off I-A) **401/322-0444** • 5pm-close, from 3pm Sun, clsd Mon • Italian

Woonsocket

Bars

Kings & Queens 285 Front St (at Vernon) **401/762-9538** • 7pm-1am, till 2am wknds • lesbians/ gay men • neighborhood bar • dancing/DJ Fri-Sat • karaoke

SOUTH CAROLINA

Statewide

Publications

▲ **The Front Page** 919/829-0181 • lgbt newspaper for the Carolinas

Aiken

see also Augusta, Georgia

Nightclubs

Marlboro Station 141 Marlboro St **803/644-6485** • 8pm-5am, till 3am Sat, clsd Mon-Tue • lesbians/ gay men • dancing/DJ • live shows • 18+

Columbia • South Carolina

Anderson

Nightclubs

The Cove II Lounge & Club 818 Hwy 28 Bypass S (1/2 mi N of Wal-Mart) **864/224-9050** • 8pm-2am, from 6pm Sun, clsd Mon-Tue • lesbians/ gay men • dancing/DJ • live shows • private club • patio • wheelchair access

Charleston

Info Lines & Services

Acceptance Group (Gay AA) St Stephen's Episcopal on Anson St (btwn Society & George) **843/762-2433, 843/723-9633 (AA#)** • 8pm Tue & 6:30pm Sat

LGLA (Lowcountry Gay/ Lesbian Alliance) Infoline 843/720-8088

Accommodations

1854 B&B 34 Montagu St **843/723-4789** • lesbians/ gay men • private home in historic district • kids/ small pets ok • gay-owned/ run • $95-115

65 Radcliffe Street 65 Radcliffe St **843/577-6183** • lesbians/ gay men • 1880 home • kids/ pets ok • smokefree • $75

A B&B @ 4 Unity Alley 4 Unity Alley **843/577-6660** • gay/ straight • full brkfst • smokefree • parking inside • $125-245

Blue Heron Inn 122 E Arctic Ave (btwn 2nd & Ashley), Folly Beach **843/588-3343, 877/488-3343** • gay-friendly • 1-bdrm villas w/ ocean view • smokefree • woman-owned/ run • $500-750/ week

Calhoun House 273 Calhoun St (Ashley Ave) **843/722-7341** • lesbians/ gay men • comfortable lodging in historic district • gay-owned/ run • $90-145

Charleston Beach B&B 118 W Arctic, Folly Beach 29439 **843/588-9443** • lesbians/ gay men • nr beach • full brkfst • swimming • nudity • 8-person hot tub • wheelchair access • gay-owned/ run • $45-100

Bars

Downtown 346 King St (at Calhoun St) **843/722-4799** • 4pm-3am • mostly gay men • neighborhood bar • dancing/ DJ • live shows • karaoke • videos • private club

Patrick's Pub 1377 Ashley River Rd/ Hwy 61 **843/571-3435** • 4pm-2am, till 1am Mon & Tue • lesbians/ gay men • neighborhood bar • transgender-friendly • DJ Fri-Sat • karaoke Th • live shows & music • wheelchair access

Nightclubs

Deja Vu II 4628 Spruill Ave **843/554-5959** • 5pm-3am, clsd Sun-Mon, from 8pm Fri-Sat • mostly women • dancing/DJ • live shows • karaoke • food served • private club • wheelchair access • lesbian-owned/ run

Cafes

Bear E Patch 801 Folly Rd **843/762-6555** • 7am-8pm, 9am-3pm Sun • patio • wheelchair access

Restaurants

Blossom Cafe 171 E Bay St **843/722-9200** • 11:30am-11pm, till midnight wknds

Cafe Suzanne 4 Center St **843/588-2101** • 5:30pm-9:30pm, Sun brunch, clsd Mon-Tue • live jazz • $10-15

Mickey's 137 Market St (at King St) **843/723-7121** • 7am-3pm, till 4pm Fri-Sat • popular

St Johns Island Cafe 3140 Maybank Hwy, St Johns Island **843/559-9090** • brkfst, lunch & dinner • popular • Southern homecooking • beer/ wine • $6-15

Vickery's of Beaufain Street 15 Beaufain St (at St Philip) **843/577-5300** • 11:30am-2am • popular • Cuban influence • some veggie • full bar • $6-15

Entertainment & Recreation

Historic Charleston Foundation 108 Meeting St **843/723-1623** • call for info on city walking tours

Spoleto Festival USA 843/722-2764 • 2-week avant-garde art festival in late May–early June

Publications

▲ **The Front Page** 919/829-0181 • lgbt newspaper for the Carolinas

The Loop 843/571-6942 • Charleston's gay newspaper

Q Notes 704/531-9988 • biweekly lgbt newspaper for the Carolinas

Spiritual Groups

MCC Charleston 7860 Dorchester Rd, North Charleston **843/760-6114** • 9:30am & 11am Sun • wheelchair access

Columbia

Info Lines & Services

AA Gay/ Lesbian 5220 Clemson Rd (in the house behind St Martin's Church) **803/254-5301(AA#)** • noon Mon-Fri

South Carolina • USA

South Carolina Pride Center 1108 Woodrow St **803/771-7713** • 24hr message, live 2pm-10pm Sat

Accommodations

Lord Camden Inn 1502 Broad St, Camden **803/713-9050, 800/737-9971** • gay/ straight • 1832 mansion • full brkfst • 35 mins east of Columbia • swimming • kids/ pets ok • smokefree • $75-110

Bars

Capital Club 1002 Gervais St **803/256-6464** • 5pm-2am • mostly gay men • neighborhood bar • professional crowd • private club • wheelchair access

Nightclubs

Candy Shop 1903 Two Notch Rd • Fri-Sat only • mostly gay men • dancing/DJ • mostly African-American • private club • unconfirmed

Metropolis/OZ 1800 Blanding St (at Barnwell) **803/799-8727** • 9pm-4am, 7pm-2am Sun, clsd Mon-Th • lesbians/ gay men • dancing/DJ • live shows • private club • also Oz cocktail/ video lounge • 9pm-close daily

Restaurants

Alley Cafe 911 Lady St **803/771-2778** • dinner Tue-Sat • full bar • $4-9

Bookstores

Intermezzo 2015 Devine St **803/799-2276** • 10am-11pm, till midnight Th-Sat • lgbt section • wheelchair access

Retail Shops

Moxie 631-C Harden St **803/929-0644** • 11am-6pm, clsd Sun-Mon • lgbt gifts • cards • books

Spiritual Groups

MCC Columbia 1111 Belleview (at Main St) **803/256-2154** • 11am Sun • women's group 7pm Wed

Florence

Bars

Rascal's Deli & Lounge 526 S Irby St **843/665-2555** • 5pm-2am, from 9pm-close Fri-Sat, from 5pm Sun • lesbians/ gay men • dancing/DJ • live shows • patio • private club • wheelchair access

Greenville

Accommodations

Walnut Lane Inn 110 Ridge Rd (at Groce Rd), Lyman **864/949-7230** • gay-friendly • B&B • kids ok • gay-owned/ run • $85-115

Nightclubs

The Castle 8-B Legrand Blvd **864/235-9949** • 9:30pm-4am, till 3am Sun, clsd Mon-Wed • popular • lesbians/ gay men • dancing/DJ • drag shows • videos • food served • young crowd • private club • wheelchair access

New Attitude 706 W Washington St **864/233-1387** • 10pm-close Sat-Sun only • popular • lesbians/ gay men • dancing/DJ • mostly African-American

Bookstores

Out of Bounds 219-E W Antrim Dr **864/239-0106** • 11am-7pm, from noon Sat, clsd Sun-Mon • cards • gifts • magazines

Spiritual Groups

MCC 314 Lloyd St (at Duncan) **864/233-0919** • 11am Sun, 6pm 4th Sun

Hilton Head

Bars

Bar Eleven 11 Heritage Plaza (at Pope Ave) **843/842-9195** • 8pm-2am • mostly gay men • neighborhood bar • live shows • videos • wheelchair access • gay-owned/ run

Myrtle Beach

Accommodations

Teakwood Inn 7201 N Ocean Blvd (at 72nd Ave) **843/449-6700, 800/868-0046** • gay/ straight • hotel • swimming • hot tub • gay-owned/ run • wheelchair access • $44-160

Bars

Time Out 520 8th Ave N (at Oak) **843/448-1180** • 5pm-close, till 2am Sat • popular • mostly gay men • neighborhood bar • dancing/DJ • karaoke Tue & Sun • live shows • patio bar • private club • wheelchair access

Nightclubs

Club Paradox 515 9th Ave N (btwn Kings Hwy & Broadway) **843/916-0999** • 4pm-close, from 9pm Fri-Sat • mostly gay men • show bar w/ dancing/DJ

Rainbow House 815 N Kings Hwy **843/626-7298** • 11:30am-5am, 12:30pm-2am wknds • lesbians/ gay men • dancing/DJ • full restaurant • karaoke • live shows • patio • wheelchair access

Rock Hill

Bars

Hideaway 405 Baskins Rd **803/328-6630** • 8pm-close Th-Sat • lesbians/ gay men • neighborhood bar • private club

Spartanburg

Nightclubs

The Cove Lounge & Club 9112 Greenville Hwy **864/576-2683** • 8pm-2am, from 6pm Sun • lesbians/ gay men • dancing/DJ • live shows • private club • patio • wheelchair access

SOUTH DAKOTA

Statewide

Info Lines & Services

South Dakota Dept of Tourism 800/952-3625 (IN-STATE ONLY), 800/732-5682 (OUT-OF-STATE ONLY)

Aberdeen

Bars

Baby Boomers 208 S Main St **605/226-2140** • 1pm-2am, clsd Sun • gay-friendly • more gay late

Batesland

Accommodations

Wakpamni B&B (on the Pine Ridge Indian Reservation) **605/288-1800** • gay-friendly • unique rooms & tipis • full brkfst • dinner available • hot tub • gift shop • on Indian reservation • $60-100

Hot Springs

Entertainment & Recreation

Springs Bath House 146 N Garden St **605/745-4424, 888/817-1972** • 10am-9pm (seasonal) • gay-friendly • 1880s bathhouse w/ hot mineral water soaking pools (indoor & outdoor) • massage ctr • day-spa services

Rapid City

Info Lines & Services

Gay/ Lesbian Talk Line 605/394-8080 • 6pm-10pm, clsd Sun

United Live & Let Live AA 605/381-1325 • 8pm Fri • call for info

Nightclubs

TW's 702 Box Elder Rd W (I-90 E exit 63), Box Elder **605/923-2153** • 5pm-2am, clsd Sun • lesbians/ gay men • dancing/ DJ • karaoke • live shows • country/ western • leather • volleyball • bbq pit • also camping & RV hookups • gay-owned/ run

Spiritual Groups

MCC of the Black Hills 605/721-0640 • 11am Sun, call for info

Erotica

Heritage Bookstore 912 Main St **605/394-9877**

Salem

Accommodations

Camp America 25495 US 81 **605/425-9085** • gay-friendly • 35 miles west of Sioux Falls • camping • RV hookups • kids/ pets ok • lesbian-owned/ run • $12-20

Sioux Falls

Info Lines & Services

Rainbow Wildbunch AA 400 N Western **605/332-4017** • 7pm Sat

The Sioux Empire Gay & Lesbian Coalition 605/333-0603 • info line, monthly mtgs & socials

Nightclubs

Touchez 323 S Phillips Ave (enter rear) **605/335-9874** • 8pm-2am, from 5pm Fri, clsd Sun • popular • lesbians/ gay men • dancing/DJ • food served • karaoke • also 'Downstairs Bar' from 10pm Sat

Spiritual Groups

The Church of St Matthew the Martyr 500 S Main Ave **605/332-3966** • 5:30pm Sun

Erotica

Studio One Book Store 311 N Dakota Ave (btwn 6th & 7th) **605/332-9316** • 24hrs

Spearfish

Cafes

The Bay Leaf Cafe 126 1/2 W Hudson St **605/642-5462** • lunch & dinner • plenty veggie • espresso bar

Tennessee

Statewide

Publications

▲ **Southern Voice** 404/876–1819 • weekly lgbt newspaper for AL, FL (panhandle), GA, LA, MS, TN w/ resource listings

Bristol

Accommodations

Penshurst Cottage 529 Sharp's Creek Rd 423/878-3242 • women only • newly renovated cabin in the Cherokee Nat'l Forest • full brkfst • creek, paths & birds • kids/pets ok • lesbian-owned/run • $50-150

Chattanooga

Bars

Chuck's II 27-1/2 W Main (at Market) 423/265-5405 • 6pm-1am, till 3am Fri-Sat • lesbians/gay men • neighborhood bar • dancing/DJ • karaoke • leather night Sat • patio

Nightclubs

Alan Gold's 1100 McCallie Ave (at Central) 423/629-8080 • 4:30pm-3am • popular • lesbians/gay men • dancing/DJ • drag shows Tue-Sun • food served • young crowd • wheelchair access

Images 6005 Lee Hwy 423/855-8210 • 5pm-3am • lesbians/gay men • dancing/DJ • drag shows • also restaurant • wheelchair access

Tool Box 1401 E 23rd St 423/697-9400 • 3pm-3am • popular • mostly gay men • country/western • dancing/DJ • karaoke • live shows • full restaurant • wheelchair access

Spiritual Groups

MCC of Chattanooga 1601 Foust St 423/629-2737 • 6pm Sun

Clarksville

Bars

The Rail Complex 116 Public Sq (btwn Main & Franklin) 931/503-0238 • 5pm-1:30am, till 3am wknds • gay/straight • dancing/DJ • live shows

Gatlinburg

Accommodations

Stonecreek Cabins 423/429-0400 • lesbians/gay men • 14-acre paradise in Smoky Mtns • hot tub • lesbian-owned/run • $125-150

Haley

Restaurants

Our House 1059 Haley Rd **931/389-6616**, 800/876-6616 • clsd Sun-Mon • popular • fine dining • some veggie • by reservation only • BYOB • wheelchair access

Jackson

Bars

The Other Side 3883 Hwy 45 N (at Ashport) 901/668-3749 • 5pm-midnight, till 3am Fri-Sat, from 7pm Fri-Sun • lesbians/gay men • karaoke • live shows

Johnson City

Accommodations

Safehaven Farm 336 Stanley Hollow Rd, Roan Mountain 423/725-4262 • gay-friendly • cabins • creekside privacy • fireplace & wraparound porch • kids/pets ok • $80-90

Bars

Try-Angles 123 E Springbrook Dr 423/915-0015 • 7pm-2am, till 3am Th-Sat, clsd Mon • lesbians/gay men • neighborhood bar • dancing/DJ • drag shows Fri-Sat

Nightclubs

New Beginnings 2910 N Bristol Hwy 423/282-4446 • 9pm-3am, from 8pm Fri-Sat, clsd Mon • popular • mostly gay men • dancing/DJ • live shows • also restaurant • wheelchair access

Retail Shops

Spikes Gift Shop 2910 N Bristol Hwy (inside 'New Beginnings') 423/753-0072 • 10pm-3am Wed, Fri-Sat only • pride gifts

Spiritual Groups

MCC of the Tri-Cities Coast Valley Unitarian Church 423/283-7554 • 7pm Sun

Knoxville

Info Lines & Services

AA Gay/Lesbian 607 Market St (at Fairbanks Roasting Room) 865/522-9667 • 7:30pm Wed

Gay/Lesbian Helpline 865/531-2539 (MCC#) • 7am-11pm

Lesbian Social Group 865/479-0775 • meet Wed 8pm at Rainbow Club • call for other events

Memphis • Tennessee

NIGHTCLUBS

Carousel II 1501 White Ave (on U Tenn campus, behind the law library) **865/522-6966** • 9pm-3am • popular • lesbians/gay men • dancing/DJ • live shows • also restaurant till 4am

Electric Ballroom 1213 Western Ave **865/525-6724** • 9pm-3am, from 6pm Fri-Sat, clsd Mon • mostly gay men • dancing/DJ • karaoke • live shows • food served • 18+ • wheelchair access

Rainbow Club 131 S Central (at Western) **865/522-6610** • 5pm-3am • lesbians/gay men • more women Wed • dancing/DJ • food served • karaoke • live shows • wheelchair access

CAFES

Java Coffee House 5115 Homberg Dr **865/558-9100** • 9am-11pm, till midnight Fri-Sat

RESTAURANTS

Adrian's Cafe 10133 Kingston Pike, Ste 104 (at Center Park Dr) **865/693-6888** • 11am-6pm, clsd Sun • eclectic • plenty veggie

SPIRITUAL GROUPS

MCC Knoxville 1059 Tranquilo (off Nubbins Ridge, look for unmarked driveway to church) **865/531-2539** • 11am & 6pm Sun

Memphis

INFO LINES & SERVICES

Memphis Area Gay Youth 901/335-6249 • peer support group for lgbt youth 13-21

Memphis Lambda Center (AA) 1488 Madison **901/276-7379** • mtg place for 12-Step groups • call for times

ACCOMMODATIONS

French Quarter Suites 2144 Madison **901/728-4000, 800/843-0353** • gay-friendly • also 'Bourbon St Cafe'

Talbot Heirs Guesthouse 99 S 2nd St (btwn Union & Peabody Pl) **901/527-9772, 800/955-3956** • gay-friendly • suites w/ kitchens • funky decor • smokefree • kids ok • $150-250

BARS

Crossroads 1278 Jefferson (at Claybrook) **901/276-8078** • noon-3am • lesbians/gay men • neighborhood bar • drag shows Th-Sat • beer & set-ups only • country/western Wed • also 'Crossroads II' at 111 N Claybrook

The Jungle 1474 Madison (at McNeil) **901/278-4313** • 2pm-3am, from noon Sat • mostly gay men • neighborhood bar • leather • food served • beer & set-ups only

Lorenz 1528 Madison Ave (at Avalon) **901/274-8272** • 11am-midnight, from 9:30am Sun • lesbians/gay men • dancing/DJ • country/western • live shows • patio, 'Aftershock' 9pm-11am

Madison Flame 1588 Madison (at Avalon) **901/278-9839** • 7pm-3am Wed, Fri-Sat only • lesbians/gay men • more women Sat • neighborhood bar • dancing/DJ

Memphis

WHERE THE GIRLS ARE: On Madison Ave., of course, just east of US-240.

CITY INFO: 901/543-5333, web: www.memphistravel.com.

ATTRACTIONS: Beale Street.
Graceland 800/238-2000.
Mud Island.
Nat'l Civil Rights Museum 901/521-9699.
Overton Square.
Sun Studio 901/521-0664.

BEST VIEW: A cruise on any of the boats that ply the river.

WEATHER: Suth'n. H-O-T and humid in the summer, cold (30°s-40°s) in the winter, and a relatively nice (but still humid) spring and fall.

TRANSIT: Yellow Cab 901/526-2121.
MATA 901/274-6282.

Tennessee • USA

The Metro 1349 Autumn St (at Cleveland) **901/274-8010** • 6pm-3am • lesbians/gay men • dancing/DJ • karaoke Tue • disco Wed • drag shows wknds • T-dance 3pm Sun • food served • patio • wheelchair access

One More 2117 Peabody Ave (at Cooper) **901/278-6673** • 11am-3am, from noon Sun • gay-friendly • neighborhood bar • multiracial • food served • patio

Nightclubs

Amnesia 2866 Poplar (nr Walnut Grove) **901/454-1366** • 8pm-3am, clsd Mon-Wed • popular • lesbians/gay men • dancing/DJ • drag shows • patio • swimming • also dinner nightly • wheelchair access • cover charge

Backstreet 2018 Court Ave (at Morrison) **901/276-5522** • 8pm-3am, till 6am wknds, clsd Tue-Th • lesbians/gay men • dancing/DJ • wheelchair access • beer & set-ups only

N-cognito 338 S Front (at Vance) **901/523-0599** • 10pm-3:30am Th-Fri, till 5am Sat, 4pm-midnight Sun • lesbians/gay men • dancing/DJ • African-American • live shows • theme nights

Cafes

Buns on the Run 2150 Elzey Ave (at Cooper) **901/278-2867** • 7am-2pm, till 1:30pm Sat, clsd Sun

Java Cabana 2170 Young Ave (at Cooper) **901/272-7210** • 11am-10pm, till midnight Fri, noon-midnight Sun • also art gallery

Otherlands Coffee Bar 641 S Cooper **901/278-4994** • 7am-8pm

P&H Cafe 1532 Madison (at Adeline) **901/726-0906** • 11am-3am, from 5pm Sat, clsd Sun • beer/wine • wheelchair access

Restaurants

Automatic Slim's Tonga Club 83 S 2nd St (at Union) **901/525-7948** • lunch & dinner Mon-Fri, dinner till 11pm Fri-Sat, clsd Sun • Caribbean & Southwestern • plenty veggie • full bar • wheelchair access

Cafe Society 212 N Evergreen Ave (btwn McLean & Belvedere) **901/722-2177** • lunch & dinner, till 10pm Fri-Sat • full bar • wheelchair access

Lilly's 903 S Cooper (at Oliver) **901/276-9300** • 11am-9pm, till 10pm Fri-Sat, noon-6pm Sun • popular • pan-Asian • dim sum

Melange 948 S Cooper (at Young) **901/276-0002** • dinner till 10:30pm, bar till 3am

Saigon Le 51 N Cleveland **901/276-5326** • 11am-9pm, clsd Sun • Chinese/Vietnamese/Thai

---

[Reply] [Forward]   [Delete]

```
Date: Sat, Dec 22, 2001 15:38:12
From: Girl-on-the-Go
To: Editor@Damron.com
Subject: Memphis
```

> Many people around the world know Memphis as the city of two musical phenomena—the blues and the King. The blues were born when W.C. Handy immortalized 'Beale Street', and, as for the King, Elvis lived and died here. From everywhere on earth, people come to visit his home and pay their respects at Graceland (800/238-2000). There are a number of mixed bars & clubs, like the popular **Amnesia** and **Madison Flame,** which are often patronized by women. For the complete rundown of local groups and events, check out the latest editions of **Family & Friends** and **Triangle Journal News.**

Nashville • Tennessee

ENTERTAINMENT & RECREATION

Aphrodite • women's performance group

Center for Southern Folklore 119 S Main St (at Peabody Pl) **901/525-3655** • 11am-7pm, till 11pm Th-Sat • live music • gallery • cyber cafe • food served

Graceland PO Box 16508 38186 **901/332-3322, 800/238-2000** • no visit to Memphis would be complete without a trip to see The King

Studio on the Square Overton Square (behind Paulette's) **901/681-2020 (HOTLINE), 901/725-7151** • alternative cinema • also cafe • beer/ wine

BOOKSTORES

Davis Kidd Booksellers 397 Perkins Rd Ext (at Poplar & Walnut Grove) **901/683-9801** • 9am-10pm, 10am-8pm Sun • general • some lgbt titles • also cafe

RETAIL SHOPS

Inz & Outz 553 S Cooper **901/728-6535** • 10am-6pm, from 1pm Sun • pride items • books • gifts • wheelchair access

PUBLICATIONS

Family & Friends 901/682-2669 • lgbt newsmagazine

Triangle Journal News 901/454-1411 • lgbt newspaper • extensive resource listings

SPIRITUAL GROUPS

First Congregational Church 246 S Watkins **901/278-6786** • 9am & 10:30am Sun, 6pm Wed

Holy Trinity Community Church 3430 Summer Ave **901/320-9376** • 11am Sun

Integrity 102 N Second St (at Calvary Episcopal Church) **901/525-6602** • 6:30pm 3rd Tue

Safe Harbor MCC 1488 Madison (at Lambda Center) **901/458-0501** • 10:30am

EROTICA

Cherokee Books 2947 Lamar **901/744-7494** • 24hrs

Nashville

INFO LINES & SERVICES

AA Gay/ Lesbian 3700 Woodmont (at St Andrews church) **615/831-1050** • 7:30pm Th

The Center for GLBT Life in Nashville 703 Berry Rd **615/297-0008** • daily mtgs & events • call for info

ACCOMMODATIONS

Comfort Suites of Brentwood 622 E Church St, Brentwood **615/277-4000** • gay-friendly

---

Nashville

WHERE THE GIRLS ARE: Just north of I-65/40 along 2nd Ave. S. or Hermitage Ave.

LGBT PRIDE: September.

CITY INFO: 615/259-4730, web: www.nashvillecvb.com.

ATTRACTIONS: Country Music Hall of Fame 615/416-2001.
Grand Ole Opry & Opryland USA 615/889-6611.
Jack Daniel Distillery 615/327-1551.
The Parthenon 615/862-8431.
Ryman Auditorium 615/254-1445.
Tennessee Antebellum Trail 931/486-9055.

BEST VIEW: Try a walking tour of the city.

WEATHER: See Memphis.

TRANSIT: Yellow Cab 615/256-0101.
Music City Taxi 615/889-0038.
Gray Line Airport Shuttle 615/275-1180.
MTA 615/862-5950.

Tennessee • USA

IDA 904 Vickers Hollow Rd, Dowelltown **615/597-4409** • lesbians/ gay men • rural queer arts community • 1 hr southeast of Nashville • camping available May-Sept (no RV hookups) • veggie meals included • kids ok • smokefree • gay-owned/ run • $10+

Rainbow Falls Resort 6251 Marrowbone Lake Rd, Joelton **615/876-9194, 877/545-2433** • lesbians/ gay men • chalets, cabins & campsites • swimming • hot tub • restaurant • private lake • gay-owned/ run • clsd Tue - Wed • $15-150

Savage House 165 8th Ave N (btwn Church & Commerce) **615/244-2229** • gay/ straight • 1840s Victorian townhouse • full brkfst • also 'Gas Lite Lounge' • gay-owned/ run • $65-95

Bars

The Cabaret: Episode 2 833 Murfreesboro Rd **615/367-1995** • 8pm-3am, clsd Mon • lesbians/ gay men • dancing/ DJ • live shows

Chez Collette 300 Hermitage Ave (at Lea) **615/256-9134** • 6pm-3am, clsd Mon-Tue • mostly women • neighborhood bar • dancing/ DJ • karaoke • live shows • women-owned/ run

The Gas Lite Lounge 167-1/2 8th Ave N (btwn Church & Commerce) **615/254-1278** • 4:30pm-1am, till 3am Fri-Sat, from 3pm wknds • lesbians/ gay men • piano bar • also restaurant

TC's Triangle 1401 4th Ave S (btwn Lafayette & Chestnut) **615/242-8131** • 1pm-3am, from noon wknds • lesbians/ gay men • neighborhood bar • also restaurant • wheelchair access

---

Date: Sat, Dec 22, 2001 11:25:39
From: Girl-on-the-Go
To: Editor@Damron.com
Subject: Nashville

> There's only one 'Country Music Capital of the World,' and that's Nashville. And there's no better place on earth to enjoy country and western music than at the Grand Ole Opry (615/889-6611). Be sure to plan ahead and get a performance schedule.
> Many of the greats of country music have homes in Nashville, and there are plenty of bus tours to show you exactly where your favorite stars live. The Country Music Hall of Fame and Museum (615/416-2001) is also a favorite stop for diehard fans.
> After you've sat still listening to great music so long you can't stand it, get up and dance. Nashville has one women's bar—**Chez Collette**—and several mixed bars, such as **TC's Triangle.** Keep your star-gazing eyes open while you're cloggin' away on the floor; you never know who you might see! For more sedate activities, check out the latest issue of **Query** or **Xenogeny,** which you can pick up at the **Center for GLBT Life** or at **Outloud Books.**
> If you're driving east, you'll pass through Knoxville—a small city with a quaint old town section and the main University of Tennessee. Call the **Lesbian Social Group** or the **Gay/ Lesbian Helpline** about local events.

Amarillo • Texas

NIGHTCLUBS

The Chute Complex 2535 Franklin Rd (at Wedgewood) **615/297-4571** • 5pm-3am • 6 bars • popular • mostly gay men • dancing/DJ • country/western • leather • karaoke • live shows • also 'Silver Stirrup' restaurant/piano bar • wheelchair access

Connection Complex 901 Cowan St (at Jefferson) **615/742-1166** • 8pm-3am, clsd Mon • popular • lesbians/ gay men • dancing/ DJ • country/ western • live shows • videos • gift shop • also restaurant from 8pm Wed-Sun • some veggie • wheelchair access • $5-15

RESTAURANTS

Calypso Cafe 2305 Elliston Pl **615/321-3878** • 11am-9pm • Caribbean

International Market 2010 Belmont Blvd (atInternational) **615/297-4453** • lunch & dinner • Thai/ Chinese • plenty veggie

The Mad Platter 1239 6th Ave N (at Monroe) **615/242-2563** • lunch Tue-Sat, dinner by reservation only, clsd Mon • Californian • some veggie • wheelchair access • $20-30

Radio Cafe 1313 Woodland St (at 14th) **615/262-1766** • 11am-close Mon-Fri, from 8am wknds

Towne House Tea Room 165 8th Ave N (btwn Church & Commerce) **615/254-1277** • brkfst & lunch Mon-Fri, clsd wknds • buffet • $5-7

World's End 1713 Church St (at 17th & 18th) **615/329-3480** • 4pm-1am, clsd Mon • lesbians/ gay men • American • full bar • $8-15

BOOKSTORES

Davis-Kidd Booksellers 4007 Hillsboro Rd (at Abbot-Martin) **615/385-2645** • 9am-10pm, till 11pm Fri-Sat, 10am-7pm Sun • lgbt section

Outloud Books & Gifts 1709 Church St (at 18th Ave) **615/340-0034** • 11am-9pm, till 10pm Fri-Sat, noon -6pm Sun • lgbt

PUBLICATIONS

Query **615/259-4135** • lgbt newspaper

Xenogeny/ Southern X-posure **615/831-1806** • lgbt newspaper & bar guide

SPIRITUAL GROUPS

MCC 4425 Ashland City Hwy (at Briley Pkwy) **615/259-9636** • 10am & 7pm Sun

Stonewall Mission Church 419 Woodland St (at St Ann's Episcopal Church, Howe Hall) **615/269-3480** • 6pm Sun

Newport

ACCOMMODATIONS

Christopher Place, An Intimate Resort 1500 Pinnacles Wy **423/623-6555, 800/595-9441** • gay/ straight • full brkfst • swimming • smokefree • wheelchair access • gay-owned/ run • $150-300

Pigeon Forge

ENTERTAINMENT & RECREATION

Dollywood 1020 Dollywood Ln **865/428-9488** • Dolly Parton's 'wholesome Smoky Mountain theme park' • 35 miles southeast of Knoxville

TEXAS

Statewide

INFO LINES & SERVICES

Texas Tourist Division **512/462-9191, 800/888-8TEX**

PUBLICATIONS

Texas Ourve **915/566-0894** • monthly lgbt newsmagazine for Texas, southern New Mexico & Ciudad Juárez, Mexico

Texas Triangle **214/946-0401, 877/903-8407** • lgbt weekly newspaper w/ arts calendar & resource list

Abilene

SPIRITUAL GROUPS

Exodus MCC 1933 S 27th **915/692-9830** • 10:45am Sun

Amarillo

BARS

212 Club 212 W 6th St (at Taylor) **806/372-7997** • 2pm-2am • lesbians/ gay men • neighborhood bar • dancing/DJ • wheelchair access

Bubba's 323 W 10th Ave (at Van Buren) **806/342-4119** • 2pm-2am • lesbians/ gay men • DJ Th & Sat • karaoke Fri • patio • wheelchair acces

Sassy's 309 W 6th St **806/374-3029** • 3pm-2am • mostly women • dancing/DJ Wed-Sat • karaoke Wed

Whiskers 1219 W 10th Ave **806/371-8482** • 6pm-2am • lesbians/ gay men • neighborhood bar

Texas • USA

NIGHTCLUBS

Open Mind 519 E 10th St (at Buchanan) **806/374-2435** • 4pm-2am, from 8pm Sun-Tue • gay/ straight • dancing/DJ • live shows • wheelchair access

RESTAURANTS

Italian Delight 2710 W 10th Ave (at Georgia) **806/372-5444** • lunch & dinner, clsd Sun • some veggie • beer/ wine • wheelchair access • $5-10

SPIRITUAL GROUPS

Amarillo Unitarian Universalist Fellowship 4901 Cornell (at 49th) **806/355-9351** • 10am Sun, 11am in winter

MCC of Amarillo 2123 S Polk St (at 22nd St) **806/372-4557** • 10:30am Sun

Soul Journers 4600 S Virginia **806/355-4566** • 11:15am Sun, bible study 10:30am Sun

EROTICA

Boulevard Book Store & Video 601 N Eastern (at Eastern) **806/379-9002** • 24hrs

Studio One 9000 Triangle Dr **806/372-0648** • 24hrs

Arlington

see also Fort Worth

INFO LINES & SERVICES

Tarrant County Lesbian/ Gay Alliance **817/877-5544** • info line

Women's Fellowship 609 Truman (at Trinity MCC) **817/265-5454** • monthly social/ support group • seasonal

NIGHTCLUBS

Arlington 651 1851 W Division (at Fielder) **817/275-9651** • 4pm-2am • mostly gay men • dancing/DJ • live shows • karaoke Tue • 18+ on Tue, Fri, & Sat • wheelchair access

SPIRITUAL GROUPS

Trinity MCC 609 Truman St (at Sandford) **817/265-5454** • 10:45am Sun • call for other events

Austin

INFO LINES & SERVICES

ALLGO (Austin Latino/a Lesbian/ Gay Organization) 1715 E 6th St #112 **512/472-2001** • events • groups

Bisexual Network of Austin **512/370-9573** • social/ support group • call for events

Lambda AA (Live and Let Live) 2700 W Anderson Ln #412 (in the Village Shopping Ctr) **512/453-1441** • 8pm nightly & 1pm Sun

Out Youth 909 E 49 1/2 St (btwn I-35 & Airport Blvd) **512/419-1233** • services & support groups for lgbt youth 12-19 yrs • drop-in open 4:30pm-8:30pm Tue-Th & Sun

ACCOMMODATIONS

1888 Miller Crockett House 112 Academy Dr (at Congress Ave) **512/441-1600, 888/441-1641** • gay-friendly • New Orleans style estate • full brkfst • nr outdoor recreation • kids/ pets ok • wheelchair access • woman-owned • $109-169

Carrington's Bluff 1900 David St (at W 22nd St) **512/479-0638, 800/871-8908** • gay-friendly • full brkfst • wheelchair access • $79-109

Days Inn North 820 E Anderson Ln (Hwy 183) **512/835-4311, 800/DAYSINN** • gay-friendly • swimming • kids/ pets ok • wheelchair access • $45-89

Driskill Hotel 604 Brazos St (at 6th) **512/474-5911, 800/252-9367** • gay-friendly • food served • wheelchair access • $175-275 (even if you don't stay in this landmark hotel, be sure to check out the lobby)

Governor's Inn 611 W 22nd St (at Rio Grande) **512/477-0711, 800/871-8908** • gay-friendly • neo-classical Victorian • full brkfst • $59-109

Hotel San Jose 1316 S Congress Ave **512/444-7322, 800/574-8897** • gay/ straight • small boutique hotel • swimming • kids/ dogs ok • wheelchair access • $69-175

Lazy Oak Inn 211 W Live Oak (btwn S 1st & Congress) **512/447-8873, 877/947-8873** • gay-friendly • 1911 plantation-style farmhouse • full brkfst • hot tub • $80-150

Omni Hotel 700 San Jacinto (at 8th) **512/476-3700, 800/843-6664** • gay-friendly • rooftop pool • health club • wheelchair access

Park Lane Guest House 221 Park Ln (at Drake) **512/447-7460, 800/492-8827** • lesbians/ gay men • swimming • also cottage • wheelchair access • lesbian-owned/ run • $85-149

Summit House B&B 1204 Summit St (at Lupine) **512/445-5304** • lesbians/ gay men • reservations required • full brkfst • swimming • smokefree • pets ok • gay-owned/ run • $69-110 (barter for gardeners)

Austin • Texas

[Reply] [Forward] **[Delete]**

Date: Tue, Nov 27, 2001 10:41:26
From: Girl-on-the-Go
To: Editor@Damron.com
Subject: Austin

> Austin is a cultural oasis in the fiery heart of Texas. A refreshing bastion of left-wing, non-confrontational radicalism and the home of the South By Southwest (SXSW) music festival, this most collegiate of cities seems to belong anywhere but the Lone Star State. But it does. In fact, Austin is actually the state capital and the seat of the Texas legislature.

> When harried urbanites in Dallas and Houston want a quick getaway, many head to the natural beauty of the Texas Hill Country. Just outside of the capital city, local boys and girls entertain themselves in the naturally cool (68° year-round) waters of Barton Springs. And Hippie Hollow, site of the LGBT First and Last Splash Festivals, has long been a favorite of the clothing-optional crowd.

> In town, entertainment centers around the Mardi Gras atmosphere of 6th Street downtown, where live and recorded music offerings run the gamut from hardcore punk to tear-jerkin' country & western. Most of the bars are mixed, female and male, straight and gay. But if you want a rousin' good time at a women's bar, then check out **Gaby & Mo's**.

> The popular bookstore, **Book Woman,** is a great resource for connecting with like-minded women of every hue. The store regularly schedules seminars, book signings, and discussion groups; check in for details on all the women's events around town. Austin Women's Rugby Club matches are also popular, as are spring and summer softball and volleyball leagues. Try Fans of Women's Sports for the latest schedules and contacts.

> Austin's LGBT newsweekly, the **Texas Triangle,** is the best source for checking out all the current goings-on.

Texas • USA

BARS

'Bout Time 9601 N IH-35 (at Rundberg) 512/832-5339 • 2pm-2am • popular • lesbians/gay men • neighborhood bar • transgender-friendly • drag shows • volleyball court • wheelchair access

The Boyz Cellar 213 W 4th (at Colorado) 512/479-8482 • 6pm-2am, till 4am Fri-Sat, clsd Mon-Tue • mostly gay men • dancing/DJ

Casino El Camino 516 E 6th St (at Red River) 512/469-9330 • 4pm-2am • gay-friendly • neighborhood bar • psychedelic punk jazz lounge • great burgers

The Forum 408 Congress Ave (at 4th) 512/476-2900 • 2pm-2am, afterhours Th-Sat, clsd Sun (seasonal) • popular • mostly gay men • more women Mon • dancing/DJ • live shows • patio

Gaby & Mo's 1809 Manor Rd (at Chicon) 512/457-9027 • 7am-midnight, from 9am wknds, Sun brunch • mostly womyn • neighborhood bar • multiracial • 18+ • beer/wine • also cafe • plenty veggie • live shows • wheelchair access • lesbian-owned/run

Rainbow Cattle Company 305 W 5th St (btwn Guadalupe & Lavaca) 512/472-5288 • 2pm-2am • lesbians/gay men • dancing/DJ • country/western

Splash Video Bar 406 Brazos St (at 4th) 512/477-6969 • 3pm-2am Mon-Fri, from 2pm wknds • mostly gay men • patio

NIGHTCLUBS

1920's Club 918 Congress Ave (at E 11th St) 512/479-7979 • 5pm-midnight, till 2am wknds, from 6pm Sun • jazz club • food served

Dick's Dejà Disco 113 San Jacinto Blvd (btwn 1st & 2nd) 512/457-8010 • 2pm-2am, from noon wknds • mostly gay men • dancing/DJ • patio

Austin

WHERE THE GIRLS ARE: Downtown along Red River St., or 4th/5th St. near Lavaca, or at the music clubs and cafes downtown and around the University.

ANNUAL EVENTS: May & Labor Day - Splash Days. Weekend of parties in clothing-optional Hippie Hollow. August/September - Austin G/L Int'l Film Festival 512/302-9889.

CITY INFO: Texas Tourist Division 800/888-8839.
Greater Austin Chamber of Commerce 512-478-9383.

ATTRACTIONS: Aqua Festival.
Elisabet Ney Museum 512/458-2255.
George Washington Carver Museum 512/472-4809.
Hamilton Pool.
Laguna Gloria Art Museum 512/458-8191.
McKinney Falls State Park.
Mount Bonnell.
Museo del Barrio de Austin.
Zilker Park/Barton Springs.

BEST VIEW: State Capitol.

WEATHER: Summers are real scorchers (high 90°s—low 100°s) and last forever. Spring, fall and winter are welcome reliefs.

TRANSIT: Yellow-Checker 512/472-1111.
Various hotels have their own shuttles.
Capital Metro 512/474-1200.

Beaumont • Texas

Cafes

High Life Cafe 407 E 7th St (btwn Trinity & Neches) **512/474-5338** • 9am-midnight, till 1am Fri-Sat • bistro fare

Joe's Bakery & Coffeeshop 2305 E 7th St **512/472-0017** • 7am-3pm, clsd Mon • Tex-Mex

Little City Espresso Bar & Cafe 916 Congress Ave (at E 11th St) **512/476-2489** • 7am-midnight, from 9am Sat, till 10pm Sun • popular gay hangout

Restaurants

Castle Hill Cafe 1101 W 5th St (at Baylor) **512/476-0728** • lunch & dinner, clsd Sun • $11-16

City Grill 401 Sabine St **512/479-0817** • dinner nightly from 5pm • beer/wine • gay-owned/run • $12-15

Eastside Cafe 2113 Manor Rd (at Coleto, by bright yellow gas station) **512/476-5858** • lunch & dinner • some veggie • beer/wine • wheelchair access • $8-15

El Sol y La Luna 1224 S Congress Ave (at Academy) **512/444-7770** • 7am-3am, till 10pm Wed-Sat • great brkfst • live music Fri-Sat • wheelchair access • lesbian-owned/run

Fonda San Miguel 2330 W North Loop **512/459-4121** • dinner only, popular Sun brunch • Mexican • full bar • gay-owned/run • $13-20

Jo's Coffee Shop 1300 S Congress Ave **512/444-3800** • 7am-7pm • lesbian-owned/run

Katz's 618 W 6th St (at Rio Grande) **512/472-2037** • 24hrs • NY-style deli • full bar • wheelchair access • $8-15

Romeo's 1500 Barton Springs Rd (nr Lamar) **512/476-1090** • 11am-10pm, till 11pm Fri-Sat • Italian • some veggie • beer/wine • wheelchair access • $10-14

Suzi's Chinese Kitchen 1152 S Lamar (at Treadwell) **512/441-8400** • lunch & dinner, clsd Sun

Threadgill's 6416 N Lamar (at Koenig) **512/451-5440** • 11am-10pm, till 9pm Sun • great chicken-fried steak

West Lynn Cafe 1110 W Lynn (at W 12th St) **512/482-0950** • vegetarian • beer/wine • $5-10

Entertainment & Recreation

Barton Springs Barton Springs Rd • natural swimming hole

Bat Colony Congress Ave Bridge (at Barton Springs Dr) • everything's bigger in Texas—including the colony of bats that flies out from under this bridge every evening March-Oct

Historic Austin Tours 201 E 2nd St (in the Visitor Information Center) **512/478-0098, 800/926-2282 x4577** • free guided & self-guided tours of the Capitol, Congress Ave & 6th St, Texas State Cemetery, Hyde Park

Bookstores

Book Woman 918 W 12th St (at Lamar) **512/472-2785** • 10am-9pm, noon-6pm Sun • cards • jewelry • music • wheelchair access • women-owned/run

Lobo 3204-A Guadalupe (btwn 32nd & 33rd) **512/454-5406** • 10am-10pm, till 11pm Fri-Sat • lgbt • wheelchair access

Retail Shops

Celebration! 108 W 43rd (at Speedway) **512/453-6207** • 10am-6:30pm, clsd Sun • eclectic gift shop • women-owned/run

Publications

Texas Triangle 611 W 6th St **512/476-0576, 877/903-8407** • lgbt weekly newspaper w/ arts calendar & statewide resource list

Spiritual Groups

First Unitarian Universalist Church 4700 Grover Ave (at 49th) **512/452-6168** • 9:30am & 11:15am Sun • wheelchair access

MCC Austin 8601 S First St (at Slaughter Ln) **512/291-8601** • 9am, 11am Sun

Erotica

Forbidden Fruit 512 Neches (btwn 5th & 6th) **512/478-8358**

Beaumont

Info Lines & Services

Lambda AA 1385 Calder Ave **409/866-6165** • 8pm Wed & Sat

Nightclubs

Copa 304 Orleans St (at Liberty) **409/832-4206** • 9pm-2am, till 3am Fri-Sat • popular • lesbians/gay men • dancing/DJ • live shows • wheelchair access

Crockett Street Station 497 Crockett St (at Park) **409/833-3989** • 5pm-2am, from 4pm Sun • lesbians/gay men • dancing/DJ Sat

Restaurants

Carlo's 2570 Calder (btwn 9th & 10th) **409/833-0108** • 11am-10pm, till 11pm Fri-Sat, clsd Sun • Italian/Greek • live shows • full bar

Texas • USA

SPIRITUAL GROUPS

Spindletop Unitarian Church 1575 Spindletop Rd (off Martin Luther King Pkwy) **409/833-6883** • 10:25am Sun

College Station

INFO LINES & SERVICES

Gayline Texas A&M GLB Student Services **979/847-0321**

Lambda AA Bryan **979/361-7976 (AA#)** • call for mtg schedule

Corpus Christi

INFO LINES & SERVICES

Lambda AA 1315 Craig (at MCC Corpus Christi) **361/882-8255** • 8pm Tue

ACCOMMODATIONS

Anthony's By The Sea 732 S Pearl St, Rockport **361/729-6100, 800/460-2557** • gay/ straight • quiet retreat • full brkfst • swimming • hot tub • wheelchair access • gay-owned/ run • $80-100

The Belles by the Sea **361/749-5221** • gay/ straight • Euro-style inn on dunes of Mustang Island & Port Aransas • swimming • $89-135

Christy Estates Suites 3942 Holly St (at Weber) **361/854-1091, 800/678-4836** • gay-friendly • hot tubs & spas • swimming • smokefree rooms available • wheelchair access • $79-199

BARS

The Closet 511 Carroll Ln (at Hilldale) **361/ 857-8380** • 6pm-2am • lesbians/ gay men • neighborhood bar

The Hidden Door 802 S Staples St (at Coleman) **361/882-5002** • 3pm-2am, from noon wknds • lesbians/ gay men • neighborhood bar • wheelchair access

Mingles 512 S Staples (at Mary) **361/884-8022** • 9pm-2am, from 7pm Sun, clsd Mon-Tue • mostly women • dancing/DJ • drag shows Fri (more men)

The Rose 213 S Staples **361/881-8181** • 6pm-2am, from 3pm Sun • mostly women • neighborhood bar

NIGHTCLUBS

Liquid 208 N Water **361/888-8767** • 9pm-4am Wed-Sun • gay/ straight • dancing/DJ • live shows • 18+ • patio

SPIRITUAL GROUPS

MCC of Corpus Christi 1315 Craig St (at 11th St nr Morgan & Staples) **361/882-8255** • 11am Sun • wheelchair access

Dallas

see also Fort Worth

INFO LINES & SERVICES

Crossdressers/ TV Helpline **214/367-8500**

John Thomas Gay/ Lesbian Community Center 2701 Reagan St (at Brown) **214/528-9254** • 9am-9pm, till 5pm wknds, from noon Sun • wheelchair access

Lambda AA 2438 Butler #106 **214/267-0222** • call for mtg schedule

Lesbianas Latinas de Dallas **214/890-6976** • social/ support group • meets 4th Sun at Cathedral of Hope MCC

NAL (Nat'l Leather Assoc)—Dallas at Community Ctr **214/521-5342** • 7pm 1st Tue • pansexual educational/ support group for BDSM & fetish lifestyle

OutYouth at Community Ctr **214/521-5342 x688** • 7:30pm Th • social/ support group for lgbt youth up to 22 yrs

ACCOMMODATIONS

The Courtyard on the Trail 8045 Forest Trail (at White Rock Trail) **214/553-9700, 800/484-6260 x0465** • gay/ straight • full brkfst • swimming • smokefree • gay-owned/ run • $105-155

Holiday Inn Select Dallas Central 10650 N Central Expwy (at Meadow) **214/373-6000, 888/477-STAY** • gay/ straight • swimming • $59-149

Melrose Hotel 3015 Oak Lawn Ave (at Cedar Springs) **214/521-5151, 800/635-7673** • gay-friendly • full brkfst • swimming • smokefree rooms available • also piano bar & lounge • also 4-star restaurant • wheelchair access • $155-290

BARS

After Dark 4026 Cedar Springs (at Throckmorton) **214/219-1099** • 4pm-2am • lesbians/ gay men • piano & jazz bar • wheelchair access

Buddies II 4025 Maple Ave (at Throckmorton) **214/526-0887** • 11am-2am, from noon Sun, clsd Mon • mostly women • dancing/DJ • country/ western wknds • live shows • volleyball court

Dallas • Texas

Dewayne's Oasis 5334 Lemmon Ave (at Hudnall) **214/528-6234** • 11am-2am • mostly gay men • neighborhood bar • dancing/DJ • food seved • karaoke • live shows

The Fraternity House 2525 Wycliff (at Dallas Tollway) **214/252-9071** • noon-2am • mostly gay men • show bar • male dancers Fri-Sat • karaoke Sun • also game room • wheelchair access

Hideaway Club 4144 Buena Vista (at Fitzhugh) **214/559-2966** • 8am-2am, from noon Sun • lesbians/ gay men • professional crowd • piano bar • patio

JR's Bar & Grill 3923 Cedar Springs Rd (at Throckmorton) **214/559-0650** • 11am-2am • popular • mostly gay men • grill till 4pm • wheelchair access

Moby Dick 4011 Cedar Springs Rd (btwn Douglas & Throckmorton) **214/520-6629** • noon-2am • lesbians/ gay men • videos • wheelchair access

Side 2 Bar 2615 Oak Lawn Ave (btwn Fairmount & Brown) **214/528-2026** • 8am-2am, from noon Sun • mostly gay men • neighborhood bar • wheelchair access

The Studio 3851 Cedar Springs Rd (at Reagan) **214/521-7079** • 9am-2am, from noon Sun • lesbians/ gay men • neighborhood bar • live shows

Sue Ellen's 3903 Cedar Springs Rd (at Reagan) **214/559-0650** • 3pm-2am, from noon wknds • popular • mostly women • dancing/DJ • live shows/ bands • 'Sue Ellen's Variety Show' Th • bbq/ volleyball Sun • patio • wheelchair access

Twisted Lemmon Club 5006 Lemmon Ave **214/219-5006** • 2pm-2am • mostly gay men • neighborhood bar

Upstaged 1802-A Greenville Ave **214/827-7070** • 5pm-2am, clsd Mon-Tue • gay-friendly • stand-up comedy & improv after 8pm • cover charge

NIGHTCLUBS

Bamboleo's 5027 Lemmon Ave **214/520-1124** • 9pm-2am, clsd Mon-Wed • lesbians/ gay men • dancing/DJ • mostly Latina/o clientele • wheelchair access

Club NV 3100 Main St. #208 (at Indiana & Malcolm X) **214/742-2708** • 9pm-2am, from 8pm Sun • mostly women • dancing/DJ • professional crowd • mostly African-American • Sun bbq (BYO-bbq-ables) • 23+

One 3025 Main (in Deep Ellum) **214/741-1111** • 10pm-4am, clsd Sun-Wed • gay/ straight • more gay Fri • dancing/DJ • alternative house

Round-Up Saloon 3912-14 Cedar Springs Rd (at Throckmorton) **214/522-9611** • 3pm-2am, from noon wknds • popular • mostly gay men • dancing/DJ • country/ western • lessons Tue & Th • wheelchair access

Village Station 3911 Cedar Springs Rd **214/559-0650** • 9pm-3am, from 5pm Sun • popular • mostly gay men • dancing/DJ • T-dance Sun • also 'Rose Room' cabaret

CAFES

Dream Cafe 2800 Routh St (in the 'Quadrangle') **214/954-0486** • 7am-10pm, till 11pm Fri-Sat, till 3pm Mon-Tue • plenty veggie • wheelchair access

RESTAURANTS

Ali Baba Cafe 1905 Greenville Ave (nr Ross) **214/823-8235** • lunch & dinner, clsd Sun-Mon • Middle Eastern

Black-Eyed Pea 3857 Cedar Springs Rd (at Reagan) **214/521-4580** • 11am-10pm • Southern homecookin' • some veggie • wheelchair access • $5-10

Blue Mesa Grill 5100 Beltline Rd (at Tollway), Addison **972/934-0165** • 11am-10pm • great fajitas • full bar

The Bronx Restaurant & Bar 3835 Cedar Springs Rd (at Oak Lawn) **214/521-5821** • lunch & dinner, Sun brunch, clsd Mon • some veggie • wheelchair access • gay-owned/ run • $8-15

Cremona Bistro & Cafe 3136 Routh St (at Cedar Springs) **214/871-1115** • 5pm-10pm Mon-Th • Italian • full bar

Fresh Start Market & Deli 4108 Oak Lawn (nr Avondale) **214/528-5535** • 7am-7pm, 9am-6pm Sat, noon-6pm Sun • organic • plenty veggie • wheelchair access • gay-owned/ run

Hunky's 4000 Cedar Springs Rd (at Throckmorton) **214/522-1212** • 11am-10pm, till 11pm Fri-Sat, from noon Sun • popular • beer/ wine • patio • wheelchair access • gay-owned/ run

Mansion on Turtle Creek 2821 Turtle Creek Blvd (at Gillespie) **214/526-2121** • lunch, dinner, Sun brunch • Southwestern • $26-48

Monica Aca y Alla 2914 Main St (at Malcolm X) **214/748-7140** • popular • clsd Mon • Tex-Mex • full bar • live shows Fri-Sat • transgender-friendly • wheelchair access

Sushi on McKinney 4500 McKinney Ave (at Armstrong) **214/521-0969** • lunch & dinner, till 11pm Fri-Sat • full bar • wheelchair access

Thai Soon Coit & Beltline **972/234-6111** • lunch & dinner, till midnight Fri-Sat

Texas • USA

Reply **Forward** **Delete**

```
Date: Mon, Nov 26, 2001 12:26:42
From: Girl-on-the-Go
To: Editor@Damron.com
Subject: Dallas
```

> Despite Dallas's conservative reputation as the buckle of the Bible Belt, this city has mellowed a great deal since the economic meltdown of the late 1980s. Two openly gay men have been elected to the City Council and sexual orientation is included in the city's anti-discrimination policy.

> Dallas is a relatively young city, but wealthy residents have created a legacy of art museums, historical sites, and entertainment districts that will keep you busy. The Arts District in downtown is home to the Dallas Museum of Art (DMA) and a fabulous collection of modern masters, pre-Columbian artifacts, and the Reeves Collection of Impressionist art and decorative pieces. The 6th Floor Museum, on the site where Oswald allegedly perched while assassinating JFK, is a fascinating exploration of the facts and conspiracy theories. Old City Park recreates a pioneer village with original dwellings, period reenactments, and exhibits. The West End, home of Planet Hollywood, the West End Marketplace, and the Dallas World Aquarium, offers a concentration of shops, restaurants, and diversions in one spot.

> East of downtown is Deep Ellum, one of Dallas's earliest African-American communities ('ellum' is the way early residents pronounced Elm). Today it's live music central, with a variety of clubs offering a host of local and national bands, seven nights a week. Just about anything goes here, as long as it's left of center. Every segment of the population is represented in an ever-growing collection of offbeat bars, restaurants, shops, and tattoo parlors.

> Further east is Fair Park, site of the State Fair of Texas every fall. Any time of the year you can enjoy a wonderful day here touring the African-American Museum, the Science Place and its IMAX theater, and the Dallas Aquarium and Horticulture Center. The surrounding neighborhood is the current habitué of choice for artists, with studios, showrooms, and gathering places along State and Parry Streets.

> The lesbian and gay community of Dallas is thriving, concentrated in Oak Lawn, just north of downtown. Most of the businesses along the Cedar Springs Strip (Cedar Springs Road between Douglas and Oak Lawn Avenue) are gay-owned, and all are LGBT-friendly. Same-

Dallas • Texas

[Reply] [Forward] **[Delete]**

sex couples populate the sidewalks and restaurant tables day and night. Parking can be next to impossible on weekend nights, though, and take care if you decide to park on darkened side streets.

> The local women's community is less visible than the gay men's, but you will find two full-time women's bars—**Buddies II** and **Sue Ellen's**—and one women's nightclub—**Club NV**—and several active women's organizations. Want just the facts, ma'am? Then call the **John Thomas Gay/Lesbian Community Center**. Dallas's churches and sports groups are also popular meeting places for singles. Lesbian couples are concentrated in the suburb of Oak Cliff or in Casa Linda, near White Rock Lake.

Dallas

WHERE THE GIRLS ARE: Oak Lawn in central Dallas is the gay and lesbian stomping grounds, mostly on Cedar Springs Ave.

LGBT PRIDE: September. Web: www.dallaspride.org.

CITY INFO: 214/571-1000, web: www.dallascvb.com.

ATTRACTIONS: Dallas Arboretum & Botanical Garden 214/327-8263.
Dallas Museum of Art 214/922-1200.
Dallas Theatre Center/ Frank Lloyd Wright.
Texas State Fair & State Fair Park 214/565-9931.

BEST VIEW: Hyatt Regency Tower.

WEATHER: Can be unpredictable. Hot summers (90°s—100°s) with possible severe rain storms. Winter temperatures hover in the 20°s through 40°s range.

TRANSIT: Yellow Cab 214/426-6262. Dallas Area Rapid Transit (DART) 214/979-1111.

Texas • USA

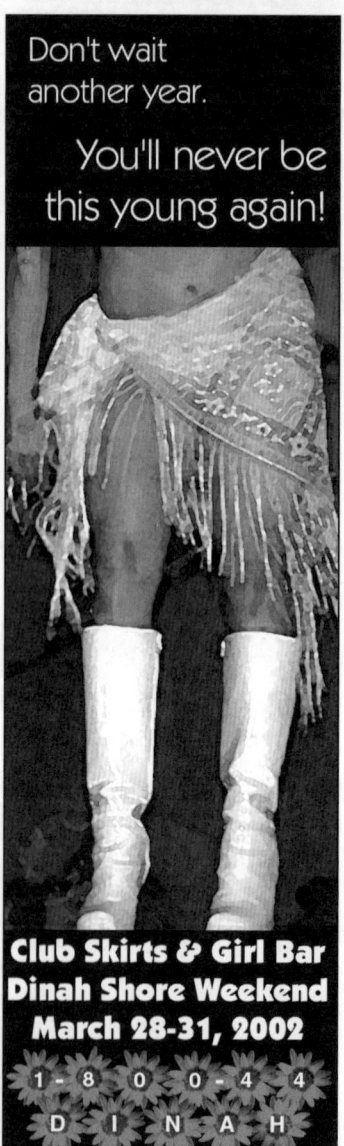

Club Skirts & Girl Bar Dinah Shore Weekend
March 28-31, 2002
1-800-44-DINAH

Vitto's 316 W 7th St (at Bishop) **214/946-1212** • lunch & dinner, till 11pm Fri-Sat • Italian • beer/wine • wheelchair access • gay-owned/run

Ziziki's 4514 Travis St, #122 (in Travis Walk) **214/521-2233** • 11am-11pm, till midnight Fri-Sat, Sun brunch • Greek • full bar • wheelchair access

ENTERTAINMENT & RECREATION

Conspiracy Museum 110 S Market (in the Katy Bldg) **214/741-3040** • 9am-5pm, 10am-7pm wknds • dedicated to infamous US assassinations since 1835 & their cover-ups

Lambda Weekly KNON 89.3 FM **214/823-8930** • 8pm-10pm • lgbt radio show for northern TX

The Women's Chorus of Dallas (TWCD) 3630 Harry Hines Blvd (at Sammons Ctm for the Arts) **214/520-7828** • several subscription concerts throughout year & 'beaucoup CDs'

BOOKSTORES

Crossroads Market Bookstore/ Cafe 3930 Cedar Springs Rd (at Throckmorton) **214/521-8919** • 9am-11pm • lgbt • wheelchair access

RETAIL SHOPS

An Occasional Piece 3922 Cedar Springs Rd (at Throckmorton) **214/520-0868** • gifts • cards • collectibles

Off the Street 4001-B Cedar Springs (at Throckmorton) **214/521-9051** • 10am-9pm, noon-6pm Sun • lgbt gifts

Tapelenders 3946 Cedar Springs Rd (at Throckmorton) **214/528-6344** • 9am-midnight, from 11am Sun • lgbt gifts • video rental • gay-owned/run

PUBLICATIONS

Dallas Voice **214/754-8710** • lgbt newspaper w/ extensive resource listings

SPIRITUAL GROUPS

Cathedral of Hope 5910 Cedar Springs Rd (at Inwood) **214/351-1901** • 8:30am, 10am, 11:30am Sun, 6:30pm Wed • wheelchair access

Dignity Dallas 4523 Cedar Springs Rd (at Bethany Presbyterian Church) **214/521-5342 x1732** • 6pm Sun • wheelchair access

First Unitarian Church of Dallas 4015 Normandy (at Preston) **214/528-3990** • 9am & 11:15am Sun (10am Sun summers)

Honesty Texas (Baptist) 5910 Cedar Springs (Cathedral of Hope MCC) **214/521-5342 x466** • 7:30pm 1st Tue

Fort Worth • Texas

St Thomas the Apostle Episcopal Church 6525 Inwood Rd (at Mockingbird Ln) **214/352-0410** • 8am, 10am, & 5:30pm Sun

White Rock Community Church 9353 Garland Rd **214/320-0043** • 10:45am Sun

GYMS & HEALTH CLUBS

Centrum Sports Club 3102 Oak Lawn (at Cedar Springs) **214/522-4100** • gay-friendly • swimming • $15 day pass

EROTICA

Alternatives 1720 W Mockingbird Ln (at Hawes) **214/630-7071**

Leather by Boots—Dallas 2525 Wycliff #124 (at Maple) **214/528-3865**

Shades of Grey Leather 3930-A Cedar Springs Rd (at Throckmorton) **214/521-4739** • wheelchair access

Denison

BARS

Good Time Lounge 2520 Hwy 91 N **903/463-9944** • 7pm-2am • lesbians/ gay men • private club

Denton

NIGHTCLUBS

Bedo's 1215 E University Dr **940/566-9910** • 8pm-midnight, from 6pm Fri, till 1am Sat, from 5pm Sun • lesbians/ gay men • dancing/DJ • live shows • private club • wheelchair access • women-owned/ run • unconfirmed

CAFES

Cupboard Natural Foods 200 W Congress St (at Elm) **940/387-5386** • 9am-9pm, 11am-6pm Sun • health food store & cafe

SPIRITUAL GROUPS

Harvest MCC 2011 Carpenter Ln (in Corinth) **940/321-2332** • 11am Sun, 7pm Wed

El Paso

see also Ciudad Juárez, Mexico

INFO LINES & SERVICES

GLBT Community Center 216 S Ochoa **915/562-4297** • 24hr hotline • crisis help & info • also 'Generation Q' pride store • also 'The Cafe,' open 6pm-3am Fri-Sat, till midnight Th & Sun

Lambda Line 915/562-4297 • 24 hr hotline, crisis help & info

Youth OUTreach 216 S Ochoa **915/562-4297** • services for youth under 21 • support groups • activites

BARS

Briar Patch 508 N Stanton (at Missouri) **915/577-9555** • noon-2am • lesbians/ gay men • neighborhood bar • patio

Chiquita's Bar 602 Magoffin (at Ochoa) **915/351-0095** • 2pm-2am • lesbians/ gay men • neighborhood bar • mostly Latina/o clientele • wheelchair access

J&R's Lounge 408 East St **915/591-6077** • 5pm-2am • mostly women • neighborhood bar • dancing/DJ wknds • mostly Latina

The Whatever Lounge 701 E Paisano St (at Ochoa) **915/533-0215** • 2pm-2am • mostly gay men • dancing/DJ • mostly Latino/a • wheelchair access

NIGHTCLUBS

The New Old Plantation 301 S Ochoa St (at Paisano) **915/533-6055** • 9pm-2am, till 4am Fri-Sat, clsd Mon-Wed • popular • lesbians/ gay men • dancing/DJ • live shows Sun • videos • wheelchair access • also 'Generation Q II' pride store upstairs

San Antonio Mining Co 800 E San Antonio Ave (at Ochoa) **915/533-9516** • 3pm-2am • popular • lesbians/ gay men • dancing/DJ • live shows • videos • patio • wheelchair access

CAFES

Ol' Gay Cafe 216 S Ochoa • 3pm-8pm, till midnight Th & Sun, till 3am Fri-Sat

RESTAURANTS

The Little Diner 7209 7th St, Canutillo **915/877-2176** • 11am-8pm • true Texas fare

SPIRITUAL GROUPS

MCC of El Paso 9828 Montana, Ste R (in Plaza del Sol) **915/591-4155** • 10:30am Sun

Fort Worth

see also Dallas

INFO LINES & SERVICES

Tarrant County Lesbian/ Gay Alliance **817/877-5544** • info line • newsletter

ACCOMMODATIONS

YesterYears 804 S Alamo St (at Akard), Weatherford **817/596-9316** • gay/ straight • modernized 1898 home • full brkfst • women-owned/ run • $70-135

BARS

The Corral Club & Patio Bar 621 Hemphill St (at Pennsylvania) **817/335-0196** • 11am-2am, from noon Sun • mostly gay men • live shows wknds • patio • wheelchair access

Texas • USA

Crossroads 515 S Jennings Ave
817/332-0071 • 11am-2am, from noon Sun • mostly gay men • neighborhood bar

Nightclubs

651 Club Fort Worth 651 S Jennings Ave (at Pennsylvania) **817/332-0745** • 4pm-2am • mostly gay men • more women wknds • dancing/DJ • country/western • wheelchair access

Cafes

Paris Coffee Shop 704 W Magnolia (at Hemphill) **817/335-2041** • 6am-2:30pm, till 11am Sat, clsd Sun

Publications

Alliance News 817/877-5544

Spiritual Groups

Agape MCC 4615 California Pkwy (take the Anglin exit off I-20) **817/535-5002** • 10:30am Sun, 7pm Wed • wheelchair access

First Jefferson Unitarian Universalist 1959 Sandy Ln (at Meadowbrook Dr) **817/451-1505** • 11am Sun • lgbt group 7pm 1st Th • wheelchair access

Fredericksburg

Accommodations

Town Creek B&B 304 N Edison (at W Travis) **830/997-6848** • gay/straight • full brkfst • $110-190

Galveston

Accommodations

Cottage by the Beach 810 Ave 'L' (at Seawall & 8th) **409/770-9332** • gay-friendly • patio • pets ok • gay-owned/run • $90-250

Hollywood at Galveston 3028 Seawall Blvd **409/750-8900, 888/899-0899** • gay-friendly • guesthouse • swimming • gay-owned/run

Paradise Guesthouse & Resort 2317 Ave 'P' **409/762-6677, 877/919-6677** • lesbians/gay men • swimming • 1 blk from beach • Bloody Marys w/ brkfst • smokefree • wheelchair access • gay-owned/run

Rainbow Reflections B&B 409/763-2450 • women only • 1/2 blk from beach & many restaurants • friendly home atmosphere • hot tub • smokefree • lesbian-owned/run • $55

Bars

Boulevard Saloon 3102 Seawall Blvd (at 31st) **409/750-8571** • 4pm-2am, from 2pm Fri-Sun • lesbians/gay men • on the beach • karaoke Th • cabaret wknds • gay-owned/run

Purgatory 2515 Mechanic St (at 25th) **409/770-9389** • noon-2am • lesbians/gay men • dancing/DJ • patio

Robert's Lafitte 2501 'Q' Ave (at 25th St) **409/765-9092** • 8am-2am, from noon Sun • mostly gay men • drag shows wknds • patio • wheelchair access

Nightclubs

Evolution 2214 Ships Mechanic Rd (at 23rd) **409/763-4212** • 8pm-2am, till 4am Fri-Sat • popular • lesbians/gay men • dancing/DJ Th-Sun • videos

Granbury

Accommodations

Pearl Street Inn B&B 319 W Pearl St **817/579-7465, 888/732-7578** • gay-friendly • full brkfst • hot tub • $79-119

Groesbeck

Accommodations

Rainbow Ranch Campground Rte 2, Box 165 **254/729-5847, 888/875-7596** • lesbians/gay men • open all year • located on Lake Limestone • campsites & RV hookups • women-owned/run • $10/person

Gun Barrel City

Accommodations

Triple 'B' Cottages 903/451-5105 • gay/straight • 78 miles from Dallas on Cedar Creek Lake • motor homes & travel trailers welcome • kids/pets ok • gay-owned/run • $75-145

Bars

Friends 410 S Gun Barrel/Hwy 198 **903/887-2061** • 4pm-midnight, till 1am Sat, from 3pm wknds • lesbians/gay men • neighborhood bar • food served • patio • wheelchair access

Houston

Info Lines & Services

BiNet Houston 1201-C Westheimer (at 'Oscar's Creamery') **713/467-4380 (PRIVATE HOME)** • 7:30pm Wed • bisexual social/support group

Gay/Lesbian Switchboard 713/529-3211 • 7pm-10pm

Houston Area Women's Center/Hotline 1010 Waugh Dr (at W Dallas) **713/528-2121** • 8am-9pm, 8:30am-4pm Sat, clsd Sun • wheelchair access

Houston • Texas

Houston Lesbian/ Gay Community Center 803 Hawthorne **713/524-3818** • 6pm-9pm, noon-4pm Sat, clsd Sun

Lambda AA Center 1201 W Clay (btwn Montrose & Waugh) **713/521-1243** • noon-midnight, from 8pm Sat • wheelchair access

LOAFF (Lesbians Over Age Fifty) 2700 Albany (at Hollyfield Center) **713/869-1482** • 2pm 3rd Sun

ACCOMMODATIONS

Angel Arbor B&B Inn 848 Heights Blvd (at 9th) **713/868-4654, 800/722-8788** • gay-friendly • full brkfst • smokefree • nr downtown • $95-125

The Lovett Inn 501 Lovett Blvd, Montrose (at Whitney) **713/522-5224, 800/779-5224** • popular • gay/straight • historic home of former Houston mayor & Federal Court judge • hot tub • swimming • gay-owned/run • $75-175

[Reply] [Forward]   [Delete]

```
Date: Sun, Nov 25, 2001 12:45:11
From: Girl-on-the-Go
To: Editor@Damron.com
Subject: Houston
```

> With mild winters and blazing summers, Houston is the hottest lesbian spot in the Southwest. From the Astrodome to San Jacinto, Houston welcomes sports fans, historians, and shoppers. This thriving urban center even has bars bigger than your hometown where you can dance the night away.

> First things first, get yourself copies of the **Houston Voice** and **OutSmart**. You can find them at Houston's LGBT bookstores **Crossroads Market** and **Lobo.** Stay and enjoy their hip coffee bars and periodicals.

> Later, grab a bite. Good eats and beautiful women can be found all over the cruisy Montrose (where lesbians are said to shop and party) and Heights neighborhoods. Try the elegant **Baba Yega's** or saddle up to a plate of Southern comfort food at the **Black-Eyed Pea**. Relax after your meal with a cup of coffee at—where else—**Java Java**. While you're in the neighborhood, take some time to admire the mansions of the Montrose and the elegant Victorian homes of the Heights. Then head over to Houston's hotspot for women, **Club Rainbow**, featuring two levels of dancing and go-go girls!

> If you want to get even more up-close-and-personal with the Gulf of Mexico, head out to Galveston Island Beach, about a one-hour drive south. While you're there, plunge into the nightlife at **Evolution,** a popular LGBT club.

> After you've seen and done all that Houston has to offer, collapse in your jacuzzi suite at the historic **Lovett Inn.**

Texas • USA

Patrician B&B Inn 1200 Southmore Blvd (at San Jacinto) **713/523-1114, 800/553-5797** • gay-friendly • 1919 three-story mansion • full brkfst • $95-145

BARS

Chances 1100 Westheimer (at Waugh) **713/523-7217** • 2pm-2am, from noon wknds • lesbians/ gay men • dancing/DJ • live shows • wheelchair access

Cousins 817 Fairview (at Converse) **713/528-9204** • 11am-2am, from noon Sun • lesbians/ gay men • neighborhood bar • live shows

Decades 1205 Richmond (btwn Mandel & Montrose) **713/521-2224** • 11am-2am, from noon Sun • lesbians/ gay men • neighborhood bar • women-owned/ run

Guava Lamp 2159 Portsmouth (btwn Shepherd & Greenbriar, in Shepherd Plaza) **713/524-3359** • 4pm-2am • mostly gay men • swanky lounge w/ martinis & more • karaoke Wed & Sun • drag shows Sat • wheelchair access

JR's 808 Pacific (at Grant) **713/521-2519** • noon-2am • popular • mostly gay men • more women Sun • live shows • videos • patio • wheelchair access

Meteor 2306 Genesee (at Fairview) **713/521-0123** • 4pm-2am • mostly gay men • cocktail lounge and cruise bar • professional crowd

Michael's Outpost 1419 Richmond (at Mandell) **713/520-8446** • 11am-2am, from noon Sun • mostly gay men • neighborhood bar

The New Barn 1100 Westheimer (at Waugh) **713/521-9533** • 2pm-2am, from noon wknds • lesbians/ gay men • dancing/DJ • country/ western

Rainbow Room 527 Barren Springs Dr (at Ella Blvd) **281/872-0215** • noon-2am • mostly women • dancing/DJ wknds

NIGHTCLUBS

Charlie's 1100 Westheimer (at Montrose) **713/522-4065** • 7pm-2am Wed-Sat • lesbians/ gay men • dancing/ DJ • wheelchair access

Houston

WHERE THE GIRLS ARE: Strolling the Montrose district near the intersection of Montrose and Westheimer or out on Buffalo Speedway at the Plaza.

LGBT PRIDE: June. 713/529-6979.

ANNUAL EVENTS: May/June - Gay & Lesbian Film Festival, web: www.hglff.org.

CITY INFO: 713/227-3100.

ATTRACTIONS: Astroworld 713/799-1234.
Contemporary Arts Museum 713/284-8250.
The Galleria.
Menil Museum 713/525-9400.
Museum of Fine Arts 713/639-7300.
Rothko Chapel 713/524-9839.

BEST VIEW: Spindletop, the revolving cocktail lounge on top of the Hyatt Regency.

WEATHER: Humid all year round—you're not that far from the Gulf. Mild winters, although there are a few days when the temperatures drop into the 30°s. Winter also brings occasional rainy days. Summers are very hot.

TRANSIT: Yellow Cab 713/236-1111.
Metropolitan Transit Authority 713/635-4000.

Houston • Texas

Club Nsomnia 202 Tuam Ave (at Helena St) 713/522-6100 • 2am-5am Wed-Th & Sun, till 6am Fri-Sat • mostly gay men • dancing/DJ • BYOB

Club Rainbow 1417-B Westheimer 713/522-5166 • 8pm-2am, clsd Mon-Tue • mostly women • dancing/DJ • live shows • 2 levels

Incognito 2524 McKinney (at Live Oak) 713/237-9431 • 9pm-2am, from 6pm Sun, clsd Tue-Th • lesbians/ gay men • mostly African-American • live shows

Inergy 5750 Chimney Rock (at Glenmont) 713/666-7310 • 8pm-2am, clsd Mon-Tue • popular • lesbians/gay men • dancing/DJ • mostly Latina/o • dancers wknds

Numbers 300 Westheimer (at Taft) 713/526-6551 • gay-friendly • dancing/DJ • live music venue • young crowd

Pacific Street 710 Pacific St (at Crocker) 713/523-0213 • 9pm-2am, from 7pm Fri & Sun • popular • mostly gay men • dancing/DJ • leather • live shows • videos • patio • wheelchair access

Rascals 1318 Westheimer (at Commonwealth) 713/942-2582 • 10pm-2am, clsd Mon-Wed • lesbians/gay men • dancing/DJ • mostly African-American • live shows • 18+

Rich's 2401 San Jacinto (at McIlhenny) 713/759-9606 • 9pm-2am, from 7pm Sun, clsd Mon-Wed • popular • mostly gay men • dancing/DJ • alternative • 18+ • live shows

Cafes

Diedrich Coffee 4005 Montrose (btwn Richmond & W Alabama) 713/526-1319 • 6am-midnight

Java Java Cafe 911 W 11th (at Shepherd) 713/880-5282 • open till midnight Fri-Sat • popular

Restaurants

Baba Yega's 2607 Grant (at Pacific) 713/522-0042 • 11am-10pm, till 11pm Fri-Sat • popular • full bar • patio • wheelchair access

Barnaby's Cafe 604 Fairview (at Stanford) 713/522-0106 • 11am-10pm, till 11pm Fri-Sat, clsd Mon • popular • beer/ wine • wheelchair access • also 1701 S Shepard, 713/520-5131

Black-Eyed Pea 2048 W Grey (at Shepherd) 713/523-0200 • 11am-10pm • popular • Southern • wheelchair access • $5-10

Brasil 2604 Dunlavy (at Westheimer) 713/528-1993 • 9am-2am • bistro • plenty veggie • beer/ wine

Cafe Annie 1728 Post Oak Blvd (at San Felipe) 713/840-1111 • lunch Mon-Fri, dinner Mon-Sat, clsd Sun

Captain Benny's Half Shell 8506 S Main 713/666-5469 • lunch & dinner, clsd Sun • beer/ wine

Chapultepec 813 Richmond (btwn Montrose & Main) 713/522-2365 • 24hrs • Mexican • some veggie • beer/ wine • $8-15

Fox Diner 2815 S Shepherd Dr 713/523-5369 • lunch & dinner Mon-Fri, dinner Sat, brunch Sun • gourmet salads • steak • fish • beer/ wine • smokefree • gay-owned/ run

House of Pies 3112 Kirby (at Richmond/ Alabama) 713/528-3816 • 24hrs • popular • wheelchair access • $5-10

Magnolia Bar & Grill 6000 Richmond Ave (at Fountain) 713/781-6207 • Cajun • full bar • wheelchair access

Ming's Cafe 2703 Montrose (at Westheimer) 713/529-7888 • 11am-10pm • Chinese

Mo Mong 1201 Westheimer #B (at Montrose) 713/524-5664 • 11am-11pm, till midnight Fri-Sat • Vietnamese • full bar

Ninfa's 2704 Navigation 713/228-1175 • 11am-10pm • popular • Mexican • some veggie • full bar • $7-12

Ninos 2817 W Dallas (btwn Montrose & Waugh) 713/522-5120 • lunch Mon-Fri, dinner Mon-Sat, clsd Sun • Italian • some veggie • full bar • $10-20

Pot Pie Pizzeria 2207 Richmond 713/528-4350 • 11am-11pm, till 10pm Sun • some veggie • beer/ wine • gay-owned/ run

Spanish Flower 4701 N Main (at Airline) 713/869-1706 • 24hrs, till 10pm Tue • Mexican • beer/ wine

Entertainment & Recreation

'After Hours' KPFT 90.1 FM 713/526-4000 • midnight-3am Sat • lgbt radio • also 'Lesbian/ Gay Voices' 8pm Mon

Bookstores

Crossroads Market Bookstore/ Cafe 1111 Westheimer (at Yoakum) 713/942-0147 • 7am-midnight • lgbt • wheelchair access

Lobo—Houston 3939 Montrose Blvd (at Alabama) 713/522-5156 • 9am-midnight • lgbt books • videos • also cafe • wheelchair access

Texas • USA

Retail Shops

Basic Brothers 1232 Westheimer (at Commonwealth) **713/522-1626** • 10am-9pm, noon-6pm Sun • lgbt gifts • clothes • wheelchair access

Lucia's Garden 2942 Virginia (at W Alabama) **713/523-6494** • 10am-6pm, till 7pm Tue & Th, clsd Sun • spiritual herb center

Publications

Houston Voice 713/529-8490, 800/729-8490 • lgbt newspaper

OutSmart 713/520-7237 • free monthly lgbt newsmagazine

Spiritual Groups

Dignity Houston 1307 Yale #H **713/880-2872** • 7:30pm Sat

Maranatha Fellowship MCC 1311 Holman (at Central Congregational Church) **713/528-6756** • 6:30pm Sun

Mishpachat Alizim 713/748-7079 • 8pm 2nd Fri • Jewish worship & social/ support group

Resurrection MCC 2025 W 11th St **713/861-9149** • 9am & 11am Sun, 7pm Wed

Gyms & Health Clubs

Fitness Exchange 4040 Milam **713/524-9932** • gay-friendly

YMCA Downtown 1600 Louisiana St (at Pease) **713/659-8501** • gay-friendly • swimming

Erotica

BJ's 24 Hour News 6314 Gulf Fwy **713/649-9241** • 24hrs

Diners News 240 Westheimer (at Mason) **713/522-9679** • 24hrs

Eros 1207 1207 Spencer Hwy (at Allen Genoa) **713/944-6010** • gay-owned/ run

Leather Forever 604 Westheimer **713/526-6940**

Killeen

Nightclubs

Krosover 1509 E Veterans Memorial Blvd, Harker Heights **254/680-5239** • 9pm-2am Th-Sun, clsd Tue • lesbians/ gay men • dancing/DJ • live shows • dress code

Laredo

Nightclubs

Discovery 2019 Farragut **956/722-9032** • 7pm-2am, clsd Mon-Tue • lesbians/ gay men • dancing/DJ • mostly Latina/o • live shows • beer/ wine

Longview

Bars

The Competition Lounge 2920 Estes (nr Hwy 20) **903/753-6855** • 5pm-2am • mostly gay men • neighborhood bar

Decisions 2103 E Marshall (2 blks E of Eastman Rd) **903/757-4884** • 5pm-2am • lesbians/ gay men • dancing/DJ Fri-Sun • live shows Fri & Sun • wheelchair access

Spiritual Groups

MCC Longview (Church With A Vision) 420 E Cotton St **903/753-1501** • 11am Sun • wheelchair access

Lubbock

Info Lines & Services

AA Lambda 4501 University Ave (at MCC) **806/828-3316** • 8pm Tue & Fri

Bars

Rue 52 2401 Main St (at Ave 'X') **806/744-4222** • 8pm-2am • lesbians/ gay men • dancing/DJ • live shows • wheelchair access • cover charge

Nightclubs

Club Luxor 2211 4th St (at 'V') **806/744-3744** • 9pm-close Th-Sat • gay/ straight • dancing/DJ

Spiritual Groups

MCC 4501 University Ave (at 45th) **806/792-5562** • 11am & 6pm Sun, 7:30pm Wed • wheelchair access

Odessa/Midland

Nightclubs

Fictxions 409 N Hancock **915/580-5449** • 9:30pm-2am, clsd Mon • lesbians/ gay men • dancing/DJ • live shows • wheelchair access

Miss Lillie's Nitespot 8401 Andrews Hwy **915/366-6799** • 8pm-2am, clsd Mon • lesbians/ gay men • dancing/DJ • live shows • videos • wheelchair access

Spiritual Groups

God's Rainbow Promises Fellowship 2608 W Front Ave, Midland **915/570-5624** • 10:30am Sun

San Antonio • Texas

EROTICA

B&L Adult Bookstore 5890 W Univ Blvd (at Mercury) **915/381-6855** • clsd Sun

Rio Grande Valley

ACCOMMODATIONS

La Mirada Country Estates 8901 W Business Hwy 83 (at Tamm Ln), Harlingen **956/428-1966** • gay-friendly • swimming • hot tub • club house • also camping & RV hookups • gay-owned/run

BARS

Dolce Vita 424 W Van Buren (at 'D' St), Harlingen **956/428-4349** • 8pm-2am, clsd Sun-Wed • lesbians/gay men • dancing/DJ • mostly Latina/o • live shows

PBD's 2908 Ware Rd (at Daffodil), McAllen **956/682-8019** • 7pm-2am • mostly gay men • dancing/DJ Th-Sat • live shows • wheelchair access

San Antonio

INFO LINES & SERVICES

Gay/Lesbian Community Center 3126 N St Mary's (at Hwy 281) **210/732-4300** • 1pm-8pm, till 6pm Sun • counseling • social activities • wheelchair access

The Happy Foundation 411 Bonham (next to the Alamo) **210/227-6451** • lgbt archives

Lambda Club AA 923 E Mistletoe **210/732-4300** • call for times

LISA Line (Lesbian Information San Antonio) 210/828-5472

Transgendered Community Circle of SA at G/L Community Ctr **210/732-4300** (CTR #) • 7pm Mon • support group for TG, TS, TV & intersexed

ACCOMMODATIONS

Adams House B&B 231 Adams St (at S Alamo) **210/224-4791, 800/666-4810** • gay-friendly • full brkfst • also carriage house • $99-169

Arbor House Inn & Suites 540 S St Mary's St (btwn S Alamo & S St Mary's) **210/472-2005, 888/272-6700** • gay/straight • kids/pets ok • gay-owned/run • $95-195

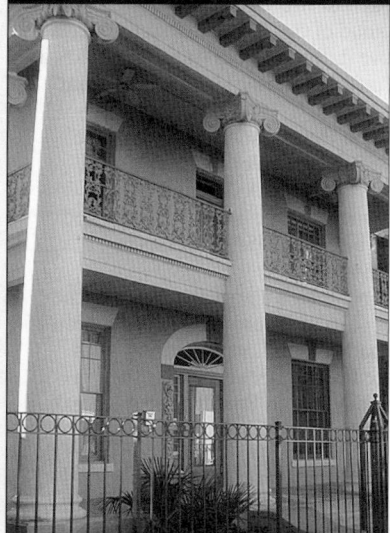

VOTED MOST ROMANTIC AND BEST B&B IN SAN ANTONIO*

The Painted Lady Inn

Luxurious suites and guestrooms. Two with jacuzzi tubs, three with fireplaces. Six blocks from the River Walk and the Alamo. Walk to major convention hotels and convention center. Rates from $80, includes breakfast delivered to your room.

210-220-1092
INFO@THEPAINTEDLADYINN.COM

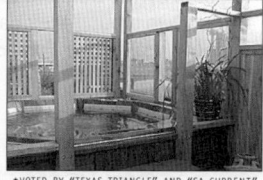

*VOTED BY "TEXAS TRIANGLE" AND "SA CURRENT"

Texas • USA

Desert Hearts Cowgirl Club 10101 Hwy 173 N, Bandera **830/796-7446** • women only • 2-bdrm cabin on 30-acre ranch • dinner served • kitchen • swimming • horseback riding • smokefree • lesbian-owned/ run • $250/ two nights

The Garden Cottage **210/828-7815** • gay-friendly • private cottage • swimming • smokefree • woman-owned/ run • $60-80/ night (ask about weekly rates)

▲ **The Painted Lady Inn on Broadway** 620 Broadway (at 6th) **210/220-1092** • popular • lesbians/ gay men • full brkfst • private art deco suites • kids/ pets ok • rooftop deck & spa • $80-200

Villager Lodge 1126 E Elmira (at Wilmington) **210/222-9463, 800/584-0800** • gay-friendly • $34

BARS

2015 Place 2015 San Pedro (at Woodlawn) **210/733-3365** • 4pm-2am, from 2pm wknds • mostly gay men • neighborhood bar • patio

The Annex 330 San Pedro Ave (at Euclid) **210/223-6957** • 4pm-2am • mostly gay men • neighborhood bar • patio • wheelchair access

Cobalt Club 2022 McCullough **210/734-2244** • 4pm-2am, from 2pm wknds • lesbians/ gay men • neighborhood bar • live shows • wheelchair access

---

Reply **Forward** **Delete**

Date: Wed, Nov 28, 2001 09:22:21
From: Girl-on-the-Go
To: Editor@Damron.com
Subject: San Antonio

> Although its moment of glory was more than 150 years ago, the Alamo has become a mythological symbol that still greatly influences San Antonians of today. Here at this mission, a handful of Texans—including Davy Crockett and Jim Bowie—kept a Mexican army of thousands at bay for almost two weeks.

> San Antonians are fiercely proud of this heritage, and maintain a rough-n-ready attitude to prove it. This is just as true of the dykes in San Antonio as anyone else. You'll find most of them at **Petticoat Junction,** the local women's bar.

> Though there's no gay ghetto in this spread-out city, there are some lesbian-friendly businesses clustered along various streets, including the 5000 blocks of S. Flores and McCullough, the 1400-1900 blocks of N. Main, and scattered along Broadway and San Pedro. But get the real 411 by calling **LISA,** the **Lesbian Information Line,** at 210/828-5472.

> For more traditional sightseeing, there's always the Alamo or the River Walk. The architecture in old San Antonio is quaint and beautiful—stop by the **Bonham Exchange** for an eyeful and stay for a twirl or two around their dance floor. Better yet, try out the view from the deck of the **Painted Lady Inn on Broadway** bed & breakfast.

San Antonio • Texas

Copa SA 119 El Mio (at San Pedro) 210/342-2276 • 4pm-2am • mostly gay men • neighborhood bar • dancing/DJ wknds • also large game room • wheelchair access

The Hideout 5307 McCullough (nr Basse) 210/828-4222 • 4pm-2am • lesbians/ gay men • neighborhood bar • patio • wheelchair access

Petticoat Junction 1818 N Main (at Dewey) 210/737-2344 • 7pm-2am • mostly women • dancing/DJ • live shows • patio • wheelchair access

Silver Dollar Saloon 1418 N Main Ave (at Laurel) 210/227-2623 • 2pm-2am • mostly gay men • dancing/DJ • country/ western • live shows • theme nights • karaoke • 2-story patio bar • wheelchair access

Nightclubs

The Bonham Exchange 411 Bonham St (at 3rd/ Houston) 210/271-3811 • 4pm-2am, from 8pm wknds, till 4am Fri-Sat • popular • lesbians/ gay men • dancing/DJ • videos • 18+ • gay-owned/ run

El Torro 3000 N St Mary's (at Rte 281) 210/732-3150 • gay/ straight, more gay Fri (call for theme nights) • dancing/DJ • multiracial • live shows

The Saint 1430 N Main (at Evergreen) 210/225-7330 • 9pm-2am, till 4am Sat • lesbians/ gay men • dancing/DJ • alternative • live shows • 18+

Sparks 8011 Webbles St (at Walzem) 210/653-9941 • 3pm-2am • mostly gay men • dancing/DJ • live shows • videos

Cafes

Candlelight Coffeehouse 3011 N St Mary's (at Rte 281) 210/738-0099 • 4pm-midnight, till 1am wknds, clsd Mon

Restaurants

Giovanni's Pizza & Italian Restaurant 913 S Brazos (at Guadalupe) 210/212-6626 • 10am-8pm, clsd wknds • some veggie • $7-12

Madhatter's Tea 3606 Ave 'B' (at Mulberry) 210/821-6555 • 7am-10pm, from 9am wknds, till 3pm Sun • BYOB • patio • wheelchair access

Retail Shops

Backbone Body Mods 4741 Fredericksburg Rd (off Loop 10) 210/349-6637 • 1pm-8pm, till 10pm Fri-Sat • piercing

Dark Fire Gallery 7126 Eckert Rd, Ste 8 210/682-3500 • 2pm-7pm Wed or by appt • pride, BDSM & fetish items

FleshWorks/ Skins & Needles 110 Jefferson (at Houston) 210/472-0313 • 1pm-8pm, from noon wknds, till 6pm Sun, clsd Mon

Minx 1621 N Main Ave #2 (behind San Antonio College) 210/225-2639 • 1pm-7pm, clsd Sun-Wed • piercing studio

---

San Antonio

WHERE THE GIRLS ARE: Coupled up in the suburbs or carousing downtown.

LGBT PRIDE: June. 210/732-4300 (Center).

ANNUAL EVENTS: Late April - Fiesta San Antonio.

CITY INFO: 210/270-8748, 800/447-3372, web: www.sanantoniocvb.com.

ATTRACTIONS: The Alamo 210/225-1391.
Hemisfair Park.
El Mercado.
Plaza de Armas.
River Walk.
San Antonio Museum of Art 210/978-8100.

BEST VIEW: From the deck of The Inn on Broadway.

WEATHER: 60°s-90°s in the summer, 40°s-60°s in the winter.

TRANSIT: Yellow Cab 210/226-4242. Via Info 210/362-2020.

Texas/ Utah • USA

On Main 2514 N Main (btwn Woodlawn & Mistletoe) **210/737–2323** • 10am-6pm, till 5pm Sat, clsd Sun • gifts • cards • T-shirts

Zebra'z 1608 N Main **210/472–2800, 800/788–4729** • 11am-9pm • lgbt dept store

Publications

WomanSpace **210/828-5472** • monthly newsletter

Spiritual Groups

Dignity St Anne's St & Ashby Pl (at St Anne's Convent) **210/433–1222** • 5pm Sun

MCC of San Antonio 611 E Myrtle (btwn McCullough & N St Mary's) **210/472–3597** • 10:30am Sun

River City Living MCC 202 Holland St (nr McCullough & Hildebrand) **210/822–1121** • 11am Sun

Erotica

Apollo News 2376 Austin Hwy (at Walzem) **210/653–3538** • 24hrs

Shelbyville

Accommodations

English Bay Marina on Toledo Bend (1 1/2 mi W of marker 3184) **409/368–2554** • gay/ straight • cafe, motel, cabins & RV hookups • full brkfst • in very remote area overlooking Toledo Bend Lake • kids/ pets ok • wheelchair accessible • lesbian-owned/ run • $35-50

South Padre Island

Accommodations

New Upper Deck Hotel & Bar 120 E Atol (at Padre Blvd) **956/761–5953** • mostly gay men • swimming • nudity • bar open from 2pm, from 5pm off-season (Oct-April) • wheelchair access • $55-120

Temple

Bars

Leon Valley Social Club 1602 S 1st St (at Ave 'P') **254/778–9494** • 6pm-2am, clsd Mon-Tue • lesbians/ gay men • neighborhood bar • 6pm-2am, clsd Mon-Tue • patio

Tyler

Nightclubs

Outlaws Hwy 110 (4 miles S of Loop 323) **903/509–2248** • gay-friendly • more gay Wed • dancing/DJ • 18+

Spiritual Groups

St Gabriel's Community Church 13904 Country Rd 193 **903/581–6923** • 10:30am Sun • newsletter • wheelchair access

Waco

Info Lines & Services

Gay/ Lesbian Alliance of Central Texas **254/715–6501** • info • newsletter • events

Nightclubs

David's 507 Jefferson (at N 5th St) **254/753–9189** • 9pm-2am, open later Fri-Sat • lesbians/ gay men • dancing/DJ • live shows • wheelchair access

Spiritual Groups

Central Texas MCC From the Heart 1601 Clay Ave (at 16th) **254/752–5331** • 11am Sun

Unitarian Universalist Fellowship of Waco 4209 N 27th St **254/754–0599** • 10:45am Sun

Unity Church of the Living Christ 400 S 1st, Hewitt **254/666–9102** • 11am Sun

Wichita Falls

Bars

Rascals 408 N Scott (at Lincoln) **940/723–1629** • 3pm-2am • lesbians/ gay men • neighborhood bar • BYOB • patio

Spiritual Groups

MCC 1407 26th St (at Holliday) **940/322–4100** • 11am Sun & 7pm Wed

Wimberley

Accommodations

Bella Vista 2121 Hilltop **512/847–6425** • lesbians/ gay men • swimming • smokefree • wheelchair access • gay-owned/ run • $95-125

UTAH

Boulder

Accommodations

Eagle Star Ranch 330 E Boulder Pines Rd **435/335–7438** • gay-friendly • working 350-acre ranch • full brkfst • hot tub • kids/ pets ok • smokefree • lesbian-owned/ run • $75-100

Salt Lake City • Utah

Capitol Reef

ACCOMMODATIONS

Capitol Reef Inn & Cafe 360 W Main St, Torrey **435/425-3271** • gay-friendly • seasonal • hot tub • gift shop • $44-57 • also restaurant • plenty veggie • beer/wine

Sky Ridge B&B Inn **435/425-3222** • gay-friendly • full brkfst • hot tubs • nr Capitol Reef Nat'l Park • smokefree • woman-owned/run • $107-158

Escalante

ACCOMMODATIONS

Rainbow Country B&B **435/826-4567, 800/252-8824** • gay-friendly • full brkfst • hot tub • smokefree • kids/pets ok • $45-65

Logan

INFO LINES & SERVICES

Utah State University Pride Alliance Taggart Student Center, Rm 335 **435/797-5694** • call for meeting time Sept-May

Moab

ACCOMMODATIONS

Los Vados Canyon House **801/971-3325** • gay/straight • retreat house in a red rock canyon • swimming • gay-owned/run • $200-225

Mayor's House B&B 505 East Rosetree Ln (at 400 E) **435/259-3019, 888/791-2345** • gay-friendly • full brkfst • swimming • 2 hot tubs • kids ok • smokefree • gay-owned/run • $90-150

Mt Peale Resort / Country Inn Hwy 46, milepost 14, La Sal **435/686-2284, 888/687-3253** • gay-friendly • popular • hot tub • hiking • food served • lesbian-owned/run • $70-150

Monument Valley

ACCOMMODATIONS

Pioneer House **435/672-2446, 888/637-2582** • gay-friendly • full brkfst • also guided tours • $56-70

Ogden

BARS

Attractions Club 2510 Washington Blvd (in Ben Lomond Suite Hotel, 11th flr) **801/778-0031** • 3pm-1:30am • lesbians/gay men • dancing/DJ Fri-Sat • snacks served Mon-Fri • full dinners wknds • karaoke • occasional drag shows • private club

Brass Rail 103 27th St (at Wall) **801/399-1543** • 5:30pm-1am, 3pm-2am Fri-Sat, 2pm-midnight Sun • popular • lesbians/gay men • women's night Fri • dancing/DJ Th-Sat • live shows • appetizers served • private club

SPIRITUAL GROUPS

Glory to God MCC 210 W 22nd St **801/394-0204** • 10:30am Sun

Unitarian Universalist Society of Ogden 2261 Adams Ave (YCC) **801/394-3338** • 10:30am Sun

Park City

ACCOMMODATIONS

The 1904 Imperial Hotel 221 Main St **435/649-1904, 800/669-8824** • gay-friendly • full brkfst • hot tub • kids ok • $80-220

The Old Miners Lodge—A B&B Inn **435/645-8068, 800/648-8068** • gay-friendly • full brkfst • hot tub • smokefree • kids ok • $70-270

Resort Property Management **800/243-2932**

Salt Lake City

INFO LINES & SERVICES

AA Gay/Lesbian 361 N 300 W (at GL Community Center) **801/539-8800** • call for info

Aardvark Lesbigay Helpline **801/533-0928** • info • support

Gay/Lesbian Community Center of Utah 361 N 300 W **801/539-8800, 888/874-2743** • info • resource center • mtgs • coffee shop • programs • much more

U of U Women's Resource Center **801/581-8030** • info • lesbian support group

ACCOMMODATIONS

Anton Boxrud B&B 57 S 600 E (at S Temple) **801/363-8035, 800/524-5511** • gay-friendly • full brkfst • hot tub • some shared baths • kids ok • $69-140

Hotel Monaco Salt Lake City 15 W 200 S **801/595-0000, 877/294-9710** • gay-friendly • restaurant & bar • gym • kids/pets ok • wheelchair access • $125-189

Maple Grove B&B 539 E 3rd Ave **801/322-5372** • gay-friendly • hot tub • shared baths • smokefree • gay-owned/run • $75+

Parrish Place 720 E Ashton Ave **801/832-0970, 888/832-0869** • gay/straight • Victorian mansion • hot tub • smokefree • gay-owned/run • $89-120

Utah • USA

Peery Hotel 110 W 300 S **801/521-4300, 800/331-0073** • popular • gay-friendly • full brkfst • kids ok • also 2 restaurants • full bar • wheelchair access • $88-150

Saltair B&B/ Alpine Cottages 164 S 900 E **801/533-8184, 800/733-8184** • popular • gay-friendly • full brkfst • hot tub • also cottages from 1870s • smokefree • $55-229

Bars

Paper Moon 3424 S State St **801/466-8517** • 3pm-1am • mostly women • dancing/DJ • karaoke Tue • country/ western Th • live music • private club • food served • wheelchair access

Radio City 147 S State St (btwn 1st & 2nd) **801/532-9327** • 11am-1am • mostly gay men • beer only • wheelchair access

The Trapp 102 S 600 W (at 1st St S) **801/531-8727** • 11am-1am • lesbians/ gay men • dancing/DJ • country/ western • food Sun • private club • wheelchair access

Nightclubs

Bricks Tavern 579 W 200 S (at 600 W) **801/328-0255** • 9:30pm-2am, clsd Sun-Mon • popular • gay/ straight • more gay Th-Fri • dancing/DJ • karaoke • 18+ • patio • private club

Club Axis 100 S 500 W (at 100 S) **801/519-2947** • 9:30pm-close • popular • gay/ straight • more women Wed • more gay Fri • dancing/DJ • live shows • 18+ • private club

Club Manhattan 5 E 400 S **801/364-7651** • lunch & dinner • live jazz • more gay after 11pm Th

Cafes

Coffee Garden 898 E 900 S **801/355-3425** • 6:30am-11pm, till midnight wknds • wheelchair access

Cup of Joe 353 W 200 S (btwn 300 & 400 W) **801/363-8322** • 7am-midnight • Internet access

Restaurants

Baci Trattoria 134 W Pierport Ave **801/328-1333** • lunch & dinner, lunch only Sat, clsd Sun • some veggie • full bar • wheelchair access • $6-25

Lambs Restaurant 169 S Main St **801/364-7166** • 7am-9pm, till 8pm Sat, clsd Sun • wheelchair access

Market St Grill 48 W Market St **801/322-4668** • lunch & dinner, Sun brunch • seafood & steak • full bar • wheelchair access • $15-30

Rio Grande Cafe 270 S Rio Grande **801/364-3302** • lunch & dinner • popular • Mexican • some veggie • full bar • $4-8

Santa Fe 2100 Emigration Canyon **801/582-5888** • dinner, Sun brunch • some veggie • $10-12

Entertainment & Recreation

Concerning Gays & Lesbians KRCL 90.9 FM **801/363-1818** • 12:30pm-1pm Wed

Lambda Hiking Club 700 E 200 S (in MacFrugal's parkling lot) **801/532-8447** • 10am 1st & 3rd Sat

Bookstores

Golden Braid Books 151 S 500 E **801/322-1162, 801/322-0404 (CAFE)** • 10am-9pm, till 10pm Fri-Sat, till 6pm Sun • general • also 'Oasis Cafe' 7am-9:30pm Mon-Fri • gay/ straight

Retail Shops

Cahoots 878 E 900 S (at 900 E) **801/538-0606** • 10am-8pm, noon-5pm Sun • unique gift shop • wheelchair access • gay-owned/ run

Gypsy Moon Emporium 1011 E 900 S **801/521-9100** • hours vary, clsd Sun • metaphysical

---

Salt Lake City

LGBT Pride: June. 801/461-5002, web: www.utahpride.org

Annual Events: Winterfest Utah Gay ski weekend (call Center).

City Info: 801/521-2868, web: www.saltlake.org.

Attractions: Great Salt Lake. Temple Square. Trolley Square.

Transit: Yellow Cab 801/521-2100. Utah Transit Authority (UTA) 801/287-4636.

Bridgewater Corners • Vermont

PUBLICATIONS

The Pillar of the Gay/Lesbian Community 801/265-0066 • lgbt newspaper

SPIRITUAL GROUPS

Restoration Church (Mormon) 2900 S State #205 **801/359-1151** • 1pm Sun • call for midweek schedule

Sacred Light of Christ MCC 823 S 600 E **801/595-0052** • 11am Sun

South Valley Unitarian Universalist Society 6876 S Highland Dr **801/944-9723** • 10:30am Sun

EROTICA

All For Love 3072 S Main St (at 33rd St S) **801/487-8358** • clsd Sun • leather/SM boutique • wheelchair access

Blue Boutique 2106 S 1100 E (at 2100 S) **801/485-2072** • also piercing

Mischievous 559 S 300 W (at 6th St S) **801/530-3100** • clsd Sun

Video One 484 S 900 W **801/524-9883** • also cult & art films

Zion Nat'l Park

ACCOMMODATIONS

Red Rock Inn 998 Zion Park Blvd, Springdale **435/772-3139** • gay/straight • cottages w/ canyon views • full brkfst • hot tub • 1 mile to Zion Nat'l Park • smokefree • wheelchair access • lesbian-owned/run • $79-135

VERMONT

Statewide

INFO LINES & SERVICES

Rainbow Resources 603/224-1686 • active social & support groups • referrals • covers VT & NH • also some info for ME & northern MA

ENTERTAINMENT & RECREATION

The Vermont Rainbow Connection 802/442-8868 • TV show by & for VT's lgbt community • channels & times vary

PUBLICATIONS

In Newsweekly 617/426-8246 • New England's lgbt newspaper

Out in the Mountains (OITM) PO Box 1078, Richmond 05477-1078 • monthly newspaper covering Vermont & beyond

Andover

ACCOMMODATIONS

The Inn At High View 753 E Hill Rd **802/875-2724** • gay/straight • full brkfst • swimming • smokefree • gay-owned/run • $125-175

Arlington

RESTAURANTS

Arlington Inn Rte 7-A **802/375-6532, 800/443-9442** • dinner from 5:30pm, clsd Sun-Mon • cont'l

Belmont

ACCOMMODATIONS

Alice's Place 802/259-2596 • gay-friendly • full brkfst • women-owned/run

Bennington

ACCOMMODATIONS

Country Cousin B&B 802/375-6985, 800/479-6985 • lesbians/gay men • 1824 farmhouse • full brkfst • hot tub • smokefree • gay-owned/run • $90-100

Brattleboro

BARS

Rainbow Cattle Company 940 Rte 5 (btwn exits 3 & 4, off I-91), Dummerston **802/254-9830** • 8pm-2am, clsd Mon-Tue • lesbians/gay men • dancing/DJ • drag shows • wheelchair access

RESTAURANTS

Common Ground 25 Elliott St (at Main) **802/257-0855** • lunch and dinner, Sun brunch, clsd Mon & Wed • plenty veggie • local seafood • beer/wine • $6-13

Peter Haven's 32 Elliott St (at Main) **802/257-3333** • 6pm-10pm, clsd Sun-Mon • cont'l

BOOKSTORES

Everyone's Books 25 Elliott St **802/254-8160** • 9:30am-6pm, till 8pm Fri, from 10am Sat, 11am-5pm Sun • wheelchair access

Bridgewater Corners

RESTAURANTS

Blanche & Bill's Pancake House US Rte 4 **802/422-3816** • 7am-2pm Wed-Sun • great flapjacks & maple syrup

Vermont • USA

Burlington

Info Lines & Services

Outright Vermont 802/865-9677, 800/452-2428 (in VT) • support/ education for lgbt youth • also hotline

R.U.1.2? 802/860-RU12 (7812) • social events • support group • coffeehouse nights • also planning community ctr

Univ of VT GLBT Alliance 802/656-0699 • 7pm Mon

Vermont Gay Social Alternatives • social events • newsletter

Accommodations

Allyn House B&B 57 Main St, Essex Junction 802/878-9408 • gay/ straight • 1890s Victorian • full brkfst • swimming • smokefree • gay-owned/ run • $75-95

The Black Bear Inn 4010 Bolton Access Rd, Bolton Valley 802/434-2126, 800/395-6335 • gay/ straight • full brkfst • hot tub • swimming • smokefree • wheelchair access • gay-owned/ run • $79-185

Hartwell House B&B 170 Ferguson Ave 802/658-9242, 888/658-9242 • gay-friendly • swimming • shared bath • woman-owned/ run • $45-65

Bars

135 Pearl 135 Pearl St 802/863-2343 • 7:30pm-2am, from 5pm Fri-Sat • lesbians/ gay men • dancing/DJ • smokefree dance flr wknds • karaoke Wed • monthly women's dance

Restaurants

Daily Planet 15 Center St (at College) 802/862-9647 • 11:30am-10:30pm, dinner only summers • plenty veggie • full bar till 1am • $6-15

Loretta's 44 Park St (nr 5 Corners), Essex Junction 802/879-7777 • lunch Tue-Fri, dinner Tue-Sat • Italian • plenty veggie

Parima Thai 185 Pearl St 802/864-7917 • 5pm-9pm, till 10pm Fri-Sat • courtyard garden

Silver Palace 1216 Williston Rd 802/864-0125 • lunch & dinner • Chinese • some veggie • full bar • $10-15

Retail Shops

Peace & Justice Store 21 Church St (at Pearl) 802/863-8326 • 10am-6pm, till 8pm Fri-Sat, noon-5pm Sun • pride store

Spiritual Groups

Burlington UU Circle 152 Pearl (at First Unitarian Universalist) 802/655-4378 • eclectic Pagan group • monthly rituals on Sun closest to full moon at 6pm

Dignity Vermont 802/655-6706

First Unitarian Universalist Society 152 Pearl St (at top of Church St) 802/862-5630 • 'Interweave' (LGBT Group) • 12:30pm 2nd Sun

Chester

Accommodations

Chester House Inn 266 Main St 802/875-2205, 888/875-2205 • gay/ straight • full brkfst • smokefree • kids ok • wheelchair access • gay-owned/ run • $89-169 • also restaurant • beer/ wine

The Stone Hearth Inn 698 Rte 11 W 802/875-2525, 888/617-3656 • gay/ straight • historic 1810 country inn • full brkfst • hot tub • tavern • kids ok • gay-owned/ run • $79-139

Killington

Accommodations

The Salt Ash Inn 4758 Rte 100A (at Rt 100) 802/672-3748, 800/625-8274 • gay/ straight • 1830s country inn • full brkfst • hot tub • swimming • food served • pub • nr skiing • kids/ small pets ok • wheelchair access • gay-owned/ run • $85-200

Lyndonville

Restaurants

Miss Lyndonville Diner Rte 5 802/626-9890 • 6am-8pm

Manchester

Cafes

The Black Swan Rte 7-A S 802/362-3807 • dinner from 5:30pm, clsd Tue-Wed • cont'l/ game • wheelchair access

Little Rooster Cafe Rte 7-A, Manchester Center 802/362-3496 • 7am-2:30pm, clsd Wed (winters)

Restaurants

Bistro Henry Rtes 11 & 30, Manchester Village 802/362-4982 • dinner only, clsd Mon • also bar • reservations

Chanticleer Rte 7-A N, Manchester Center 802/362-1616 • clsd Mon-Tue

Richford • Vermont

BOOKSTORES

Northshire Bookstore 4869 Main St, Manchester Center **802/362-2200** • 10am-9pm, till 7pm Sun-Th (seasonal)

Marlboro

ACCOMMODATIONS

▲ **Colonel Williams Inn** Rte 9 (at Staver Rd) **802/257-1093, 877/765-6639** • gay-friendly • full brkfst • also restaurant • jacuzzi • kids/pets ok • wheelchair access • $125-175

RESTAURANTS

Skyline Restaurant Rte 9, Hogback Mountain **802/464-5535** • 7:30am-3pm, dinner Fri-Sun, clsd Tue-Th (winters) • wheelchair access

Montgomery Center

ACCOMMODATIONS

Phineas Swann B&B **802/326-4306** • gay/straight • Gingerbread Victorian • full brkfst • smokefree • gay-owned/run • $85-165

Montpelier

INFO LINES & SERVICES

Women of the Woods **802/229-0109** • lesbian social group

RESTAURANTS

Julio's 54 State **802/229-9348** • lunch & dinner till midnight, from 4pm Sun • Mexican

Sarducci's 3 Main St **802/223-0229** • 11:30am-9:30pm, till 10pm Fri-Sat, from 4:30pm Sun • Italian • some veggie • full bar • wheelchair access • $8-15

Wayside Restaurant Rte 302 **802/223-6611** • 6:30am-9:30pm • wheelchair access

RETAIL SHOPS

Phoenix Rising 34 State St **802/229-0522** • 10am-5:30pm, till 6pm Fri, from 11am wknds, till 3pm Sun • metaphysical • jewelry • gifts • pride items • lesbian-owned/run

Richford

PUBLICATIONS

Golden Threads PO Box1688, Demorest, GA **706/776-3959** • for lesbians 50+ & their friends

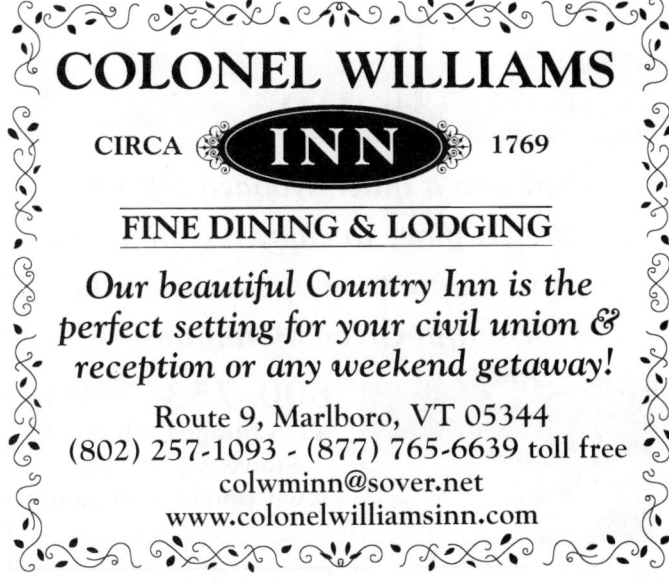

Vermont • USA

Richmond

ACCOMMODATIONS

The Spa 961 Hinesburg-Richmond Rd (at Huntington Rd) **802/434–3846** • overnight women-only health spa • swimming • exercise room

Rutland

ACCOMMODATIONS

Cortina Inn & Resort Rte 4, Killington **802/773–3333, 800/451–6108** • gay-friendly • hot tub • also tavern • food served • wheelchair access

Lilac Inn 53 Park St, Brandon **802/247–5463, 800/221–0720** • full brkfst • $120–260

Maplewood Inn Rte 22-A S, Fair Haven **802/265–8039, 800/253–7729** • gay-friendly • romantic, historic-register 1843 Greek Revival • beautiful antiques • $80-140

St Albans

RESTAURANTS

Jeff's Maine Seafood 65 N Main St **802/524–6135** • lunch Mon-Sat, dinner Tue-Sat

St Johnsbury

INFO LINES & SERVICES

Umbrella Women's Center 1 Prospect Ave **802/748–8645** • 8am-4:30pm Mon-Fri • lesbian support & resources

ACCOMMODATIONS

Greenhope Farm B&B 802/533–7772 • mostly women • full brkfst (vegetarian) • horseback-riding, camping, skiing & hiking on 140 private acres • smokefree • kids ok • call for free brochure • lesbian-owned/ run • $65-125

▲ **Highlands Inn** Bethlehem, NH **603/869–3978, 877/LES–B–INN (537–2466)** • a lesbian paradise • women only • ignore 'no vacancy' sign • hot tub • swimming • 100 mountain acres • special event wknds • wheelchair access • $75-125

Stowe

ACCOMMODATIONS

Buccaneer Country Lodge 3214 Mountain Rd **802/253–4772, 800/543–1293** • gay/ straight • full brkfst • hot tub • swimming • smokefree • $55-250

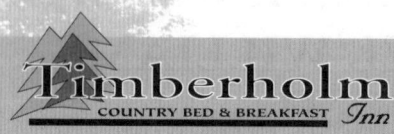
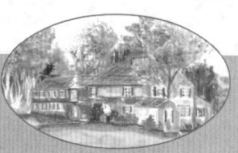
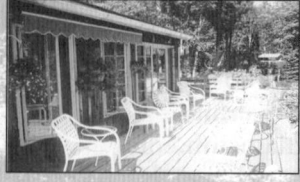

Tucked into a quiet, wooded hillside... the perfect place to enjoy a civil union or a romantic Stowe getaway in the beautiful Green Mountains.

800-753-7603
452 Cottage Club Road
Stowe, VT 05672
www.timberholm.com

Gay-Owned and Operated

Fitch Hill Inn 802/888-3834, 800/639-2903 • gay/straight • full brkfst • hot tub • older kids ok • $89-199

Gardner's Inn 150 Upper Sky Acres Dr **802/253-8464** • gay-friendly • luxury apt rental • hot tub • smokefree • $150-200

Honeywood Inn 4583 Mountain Rd **802/253-4846, 800/821-7891** • gay/straight • full brkfst • jacuzzi • swimming • $89-229

Northern Lights Lodge 4441 Mountain Rd **802/253-8541, 800/448-4554** • gay-friendly • full brkfst • hot tub • swimming • sauna • kids/pets ok • gay-owned/run • $58-148

▲ **Timberholm Inn** 452 Cottage Club Rd **802/253-7603, 800/753-7603** • gay/straight • B&B • full brkfst • hot tub • gay-owned/run

Winding Brook, A Classic Mountain Lodge 199 Edson Hill Rd **802/253-7354, 800/426-6697** • gay/straight • smokefree • full brkfst • kids ok • gay-owned/run • $65-195 + 12% service charge

Waterbury

ACCOMMODATIONS

Grünberg Haus B&B & Cabins 94 Pine St, Rte 100 S **802/244-7726, 800/800-7760** • gay/straight • Austrian chalet • full brkfst • hot tub • sauna • fireplace • smokefree • kids/pets ok • $59-145

Moose Meadow Lodge 607 Crossett Hill **802/244-5378** • gay-friendly • log home on 86-acre wooded estate • full brkfst • hot tub • gay-owned • $105-125

Williston

INFO LINES & SERVICES

Both Sides Now PO Box 50 05495 **802/879-1147 (PRIVATE HOME)** • bisexual group

Woodstock

ACCOMMODATIONS

The Ardmore Inn 23 Pleasant St **802/457-3887, 800/497-9652** • gay-friendly • 1880s Greek revival • full brkfst • jacuzzi • smokefree • $110-175

Rosewood Inn **802/457-4485, 203/829-1499** • gay-friendly • full brkfst • smokefree • kids ok • $70-125

VIRGINIA

Statewide

INFO LINES & SERVICES

Virginia Division of Tourism 800/847-4882

Virginians for Justice 804/643-4816 • lgbt organization

PUBLICATIONS

Shout! 540/529-6363 • entertainment & personals for the Virginias & Carolinas

The Virginia GayZette 804/355-7939 (RICHMOND #), 757/622-3701 (ROANOKE #) • statewide lgbt newspaper

Alexandria

see also Washington, District of Columbia

SPIRITUAL GROUPS

Church of the Resurrection (Episcopal) 2280 N Beauregard St **703/998-0888** • 8am & 10am Sun, 10am Wed

Mt Vernon Unitarian Church 1909 Windmill Ln (off Fort Hunt Rd) **703/765-5950** • 9am & 11am Sun (10am summer)

Arlington

see also Washington, District of Columbia

INFO LINES & SERVICES

Arlington Gay/Lesbian Alliance 703/522-7660 • monthly mtgs • call for schedule

ACCOMMODATIONS

Best Western Arlington Hotel 2480 S Glebe Rd (at 24th St) **703/979-4400, 800/486-6228** • gay-friendly • restaurant & lounge • swimming • wheelchair access • $60+

CAFES

Java Shack 2507 N Franklin Rd (at Wilson Blvd & N Barton) **703/527-9556** • 7am-10pm, from 8am wknds • lesbians/gay men

The Mouse Trap 2336 Wilson Blvd (at N Adams) **703/294-4008** • 10am-9pm, till 10pm Sat, noon-8pm Sun • Internet cafe & lounge • gay-owned/run

PUBLICATIONS

Woman's Monthly 202/965-5399 • articles • calendar of community/arts events for greater DC/Baltimore area

SPIRITUAL GROUPS

Clarendon Presbyterian Church 1305 N Jackson St **703/527-9513** • 10am Sun

Virginia • USA

DELOACH ANTIQUES

(434) 979-7209
410 EAST JEFFERSON STREET
1211 WEST MAIN STREET
CHARLOTTESVILLE, VA 22903

THE INN AT COURT SQUARE

ELEGANT ACCOMMODATIONS
LUNCH WITH PATIO SEATING
PRIVATE PARTIES
www.innatcourtsquare.com
(866) 466-2877 • (434) 295-2800
410 EAST JEFFERSON STREET
CHARLOTTESVILLE, VA 22902

THE EIGHTEEN SEVENTEEN

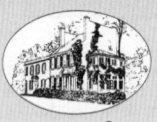

HISTORIC BED & BREAKFAST
• AFTERNOON TEA
• PRIVATE PARTIES

www.1817inn.com

(800) 730-7443 • (434) 979-7353
1211 WEST MAIN STREET
CHARLOTTESVILLE, VA 22903

Ashland

CAFES

Coffee Talk Cafe 10396 Leadbetter Rd **804/550-0887** • 7am-5pm, 7:30am-2pm Sat, clsd Sun • pasta

Cape Charles

see also Norfolk & Virginia Beach

ACCOMMODATIONS

Cape Charles House B&B 645 Tazewell Ave (at Fig) **757/331-4960** • gay-friendly • 1912 Colonial Revival home filled w/ antiques • smokefree • $85-120

Sea Gate B&B 9 Tazewell Ave **757/331-2206** • gay-friendly • full brkfst • afternoon tea • nr beach on quiet, tree-lined street • gay-owned/ run • $80-90

Sterling House B&B 9 Randolph Ave (at Bay Ave) **757/331-2483** • gay/ straight • 1913 beach bungalow • full brkfst • hot tub • teens ok • gay-owned/ run • $95-125

Wilson-Lee House B&B 403 Tazewell Ave **757/331-1954** • gay/ straight • full brkfst • smokefree • gay-owned/ run • $85-120

Charlottesville

INFO LINES & SERVICES

Gay AA at Church House, Thomas Jefferson Unitarian Church, Rugby Rd **804/293-8227** • call for times

LGBT Helpline **804/982-2773** • active during school yr

Women's Center 14th & University, UVA **804/982-2361** • 8:30am-5pm, clsd wknds

ACCOMMODATIONS

1817 Historic B&B 1211 W Main St (at 12 1/2 St) **804/979-7353, 800/730-7443** • gay-friendly • also antique shop & cafe • kids ok • 5 miles to Monticello • smokefree • $99-259

Campout **804/783-6001** • women only • 100-acre rustic campground • smokefree • wheelchair access • women-owned/ run • $10 membership fee

▲ **The Inn at Court Square** 410 E Jefferson St **804/295-2800, 866/466-2877** • gay/ straight • restored house w/ period antiques • jacuzzi • lunch served Mon-Fri • kids ok • smokefree • women-owned/ run • $149-259

Norfolk • Virginia

The Mark Addy B&B 56 Rodes Farm Dr, Nellysford **804/361-1101, 800/278-2154** • gay/ straight • full brkfst • dinner available • swimming • tennis • hot tub • smokefree • wheelchair access • gay-owned/ run • $90-145

Nightclubs

Club 216 216 W Water St (enter rear, nr South St) **804/296-8783** • 10pm-5am Fri-Sat, some Sun events • popular • lesbians/ gay men • dancing/DJ • live shows • private club • wheelchair access

Restaurants

Bistro 151 Valley Green Center, Nellysford **804/361-1463** • lunch & dinner, clsd Mon • full bar till midnight, till 2am wknds

Eastern Standard/ Escafe in West End downtown mall (next to the Omni Hotel) **804/295-8668** • 5:30pm-10pm Wed-Sat • gay/ straight • Asian/ American fusion • some veggie • also 'Escafe' downstairs • 5:30pm-midnight, till 2am Th-Sat, from 4:30pm Sun, clsd Mon • bistro • full bar • music Th & Sun • gay-owned/ run

Spiritual Groups

MCC 717 Rugby Rd (at Thomas Jefferson Memorial Church) **804/979-5206** • 6pm Sun

Christiansburg

Accommodations

River's Edge 6208 Little Camp Rd, Riner **540/381-4147, 888/786-9254** • gay-friendly • full brkfst • dinner served • smokefree • $150-165

Fairfax

Spiritual Groups

MCC of Northern VA 10383 Democracy Ln **703/691-0930** • 11am Sun

Fredericksburg

Restaurants

Merrimans 715 Caroline St (btwn Charlotte & Hanover) **540/371-7723** • lunch & dinner, lounge till 2am • popular • lesbians/ gay men • fresh natural homemade cuisine • plenty veggie • full bar • dancing/DJ • wheelchair access • $7-22

Hampton

see Newport News

Harrisonburg

Cafes

Artful Dodger Coffeehouse 47 W Court Sq **540/432-1179** • 8am-11pm, from noon Sun • wheelchair access

Luray

Accommodations

Piney Hill B&B 1048 Piney Hill Rd (at Mill Creek Crossroads) **540/778-5261** • gay/ straight • 1750s farmhouse in Shenandoah Valley • gay-owned/ run

Lynchburg

Info Lines & Services

Gay/ Lesbian Helpline 804/847-5242 • live 7pm-10pm Mon, Tue & Fri • info for central & southwest VA

Newport News

see also **Norfolk & Virginia Beach**

Bars

Corner Pocket 3516 Washington Ave **757/247-6366** • 4pm-2am • lesbians/ gay men • neighborhood bar • food served till midnight • wheelchair access

Erotica

Mr D's Leather & Novelties 9902-A Warwick Blvd (at Randolph Rd) **757/599-4070**

Norfolk

see also **Virginia Beach**

Accommodations

Hawthorn Hotel & Suites 245 Granby St (at Tazwell St) **757/623-6200** • gay-friendly • full brkfst • kids ok • wheelchair access • $109-170

Bars

The Garage 731 Granby St (at Brambleton) **757/623-0303** • 8am-2am, from noon Sun • popular • mostly gay men • neighborhood bar • food served • wheelchair access • $3-9

Hershee Bar 6117 Sewells Pt Rd (at Norview) **757/853-9842** • 4pm-2am, from noon wknds • mostly women • dancing/DJ • live shows Fri • karaoke Sun • food served • some veggie • Sun buffet • $2-7 • wheelchair access • woman-owned/ run

Nutty Buddy's 143 E Little Creek Rd **757/588-6474** • 4pm-2am • popular • mostly gay men • dancing/DJ • live shows • also restaurant • some veggie • wheelchair access

Virginia • USA

The Wave 4107 Colley Ave (at 41st St) **757/440-5911** • 4pm-2am, from 5pm Sat, clsd Tue & Th • lesbians/ gay men • dancing/DJ • live shows • also restaurant • lunch & dinner • $3-12 • wheelchair access

Cafes

Oasis Cafe 142 W York St #101A (in York Center bldg) **757/627-6161** • 7:30am-5pm Mon-Fri • gay-owned/ run

Restaurants

Charlie's Cafe 1800 Granby St (at 18th) **757/625-0824** • 7am-3pm • some veggie • beer/ wine • $3-7

Uncle Louie's 132 E Little Creek Rd (at Granby) **757/480-1225** • 8am-11pm, till midnight Fri-Sat, till 10pm Sun • Jewish fine dining • also bar & deli • karaoke • wheelchair access

Bookstores

Lambda Rising 9229 Granby St (at Tidewater) **757/480-6969** • 10am-10pm • lgbt • wheelchair access

Phoenix Rising East 619B Colonial Ave (at Olney) **757/622-3701** • noon-9pm, till 7pm Sun • lgbt

Publications

Shout! **540/529-6363** • entertainment & personals for the Virginias & Carolinas

Spiritual Groups

New Life MCC 4035 E Ocean Ave **757/362-3056** • 10:30am Sun

Erotica

Leather & Lace 149 E Little Creek Rd (at Granby) **757/583-4334** • clsd Sun

Petersburg

Accommodations

Walker House B&B 3280 S Crater Rd (at Wagner) **804/861-5822** • gay-friendly • antebellum farmhouse • full brkfst • smokefree • kids ok • gay-owned/ run • $95-115

Richmond

Info Lines & Services

AA Gay/ Lesbian **804/355-1212** • call for mtg schedule

Richmond Lesbian Feminist PO Box 7216 23221-0216 **804/796-9988** • community entertainment & educational group

---

Norfolk

LGBT Pride: June. 757/456-1972, web: www.hamptonroadspride.com.

City Info: 800/368-3097, web: www.vgnet.com.

Attractions: Busch Gardens (in Williamsburg) 757/253-3350.
The Chrysler Museum of Art 757/664-6200.
Douglas Macarthur Memorial 757/441-2965.
Hermitage Foundation Museum 757/423-2052.
Historic Williamsburg.
Norfolk Naval Base 757/444-7955.
St Paul's Episcopal Church 757/627-4353.
Waterside Festival Marketplace.

Transit: Yellow Cab 757/622-3232.
Norfolk Airport Shuttle 757/857-1231.
Hampton Roads Transit 757/222-6000.

Roanoke • Virginia

Richmond Organization for Sexual Minority Youth (ROSMY) 804/353-2077 • 3pm-8pm Mon & Wed

ACCOMMODATIONS

Bellmont Manor B&B Inn 6600 Belmont Rd, Chesterfield 804/745-0106, 800/809-9041 x69 • gay/ straight • full brkfst • other meals available • smokefree • wheelchair access • gay-owned/ run • $75-125

The High Street Inn 405 High St (at Cross St), Petersburg 804/733-0505, 888/733-0505 • gay-friendly • Victorian mansion • full brkfst • kids ok • $90-125

BARS

Babe's of Carytown 3166 W Cary St (at Auburn) 804/355-9330 • 11am-1am, till 2am Th-Sat, from 8pm Sat, 9am-3pm Sun • mostly women • dancing/DJ • live music • food served • homecooking • some veggie • wheelchair access • women-owned/ run

Broadway Cafe & Bar 414 E Main St (btwn 4th & 5th) 804/643-9667 • 5pm-2am, from 6pm Sun • mostly gay men • neighborhood bar • food served • beer/ wine only • wheelchair access

Casablanca Lounge & Restaurant 6 E Grace St (btwn 1st & Foushee Sts) 804/648-2040 • 11am-2am, from 3pm Sat • mostly gay men • neighborhood bar • karaoke • videos • food served • Sun brunch • some veggie • wheelchair access

Cheers 3156 West Cary St 804/355-5527 • 11am-2am, from 4pm Sun • neighborhood bar • food served • gay-owned

Godfrey's 308 E Grace St 804/648-3957 • 5pm-2am, lunch daily, clsd Mon-Tue, drag brunch Sun • lesbians/ gay men • also restaurant • dancing/DJ • country/ western Tue • karaoke • live shows

NIGHTCLUBS

Club Colours 536 N Harrison St (at Broad) 804/353-9776 • 9pm-4am Sat • lesbians/ gay men • more women until 11:30pm • dancing/DJ • multiracial • food served • live shows • wheelchair access

Club Fahrenheit 119 N 18th St 804/783-2608 • 9pm-2am Th-Sat • lesbians/ gay men • dancing/DJ • live shows • also restaurant

Fielden's 2033 W Broad St 804/359-1963 • midnight-close, clsd Mon-Wed • popular • mostly gay men • dancing/DJ • live shows • BYOB • private club • wheelchair access

RESTAURANTS

The Village 410 N Harrison 804/353-8204 • 8:30am-11:30pm, bar till 2am • American • plenty veggie

BOOKSTORES

Carytown Books 2930 W Cary St (at Sheppard) 804/359-4831 • 10am-7pm, till 5pm Sun • lgbt section • wheelchair access

Phoenix Rising 19 N Belmont Ave 804/355-7939, 800/719-1690 • 11am-7pm • lgbt • wheelchair access

PUBLICATIONS

Shout! 540/529-6363 • entertainment & personals for the Virginias & Carolinas

The Virginia GayZette 804/355-7939 (RICHMOND #), 757/622-3701 (ROANOKE #) • statewide lgbt newspaper

SPIRITUAL GROUPS

Gentle Shepherd 518 W Grace St (at Belvedere) 804/355-1377 • 11am Sun

MCC Richmond 2501 Park Ave (at Davis) 804/353-9477 • 10:45am Sun

Roanoke

BARS

Backstreet Cafe 356 Salem Ave (off Jefferson) 540/345-1542 • 7pm-2am, till midnight Sun • lesbians/ gay men • neighborhood bar • food served

NIGHTCLUBS

The Park 615 Salem Ave 540/342-0946 • 9pm-close Fri-Sun • popular • lesbians/ gay men • dancing/DJ • live shows Sun • videos • young crowd • wheelchair access

BOOKSTORES

Out Word Connections 129 Salem Ave 540/985-6886 • noon-8pm • lgbt

PUBLICATIONS

Blue Ridge Lambda Press 540/381-6478 • covers western VA

Shout! 540/529-6363 • entertainment & personals for the Virginias & Carolinas

SPIRITUAL GROUPS

MCC of the Blue Ridge 101 Kirk Ave #A 540/344-4444 • 11am & 6pm Sun, 7pm Wed

Unitarian Universalist Church 2015 Grandin Rd SW 540/342-8888 • 11am Sun (10am summers)

Virginia • USA

Lavender Sea B&B

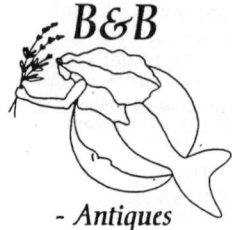

- Antiques
- Art
- Abloom

Lavender Sea B&B is a unique lodging experience a few paces from historic Williamsburg, VA. Lavender has long been used as a soothing herb. In that spirit, we strive to offer a refuge in the comforting hues found in nature. Part ocean, part garden, we have one antique and art filled room with a private bath for an overnight stay or a relaxing weekend.

507 Capitol Landing Rd.
Williamsburg, VA
23185
Lavenderseabandb@aol.com
www.lavenderseabandb.com
757-345-0198

Shenandoah Valley

INFO LINES & SERVICES

SVGLA (Shenandoah Valley Gay/ Lesbian Assoc) 540/574-4636 • 24hr touchtone info • weekly mtgs • also dances & potlucks

ACCOMMODATIONS

The Ruby Rose Inn 275 Chapel Rd Stanley **540/778-4680** • gay/straight • 1890 Victorian w/ cottages • full brkfst • jacuzzi • smokefree • kids ok • women-owned/ run • $115-145

Ruffner House 440 Ruffner House Ln (at Hwy 340 & 211), Luray **540/743-7855, 888/969-7855** • gay/ straight • 1700s home • full brkfst • smokefree • $90-150

The White House 275 Chapel Rd, Stanley 22851 **540/778-4680, 800/211-9885** • gay/ straight • 1890 Victorian w/ cottages • full brkfst • jacuzzi • smokefree • kids ok • women-owned/ run • $115-145

Virginia Beach

see also Norfolk

BARS

Klub Ambush 475 S Lynnhaven Rd (at Lynnhaven Pkwy) **757/498-4301** • 5pm-2am, from 3pm Sun • mostly gay men • neighborhood bar • dancing/DJ • food served • live shows • karaoke

In Between 5266 Princess Anne Rd (bwtn Witchduck Rd & Newton Rd) **757/490-9498** • 4pm-2am, from 11am Sun • lesbians/ gay men • male dancers Mon, Wed & Fri • also restaurant • gay-owned/ run

Rainbow Cactus 3472 Holland Rd (at Diana Lee) **757/368-0441** • 6pm-2am, clsd Mon • mostly gay men • dancing/DJ • country/ western • food served • karaoke Tue • wheelchair access

PUBLICATIONS

Lambda Directory 757/486-3546

EROTICA

Oceana Video & News 1301 Oceana Blvd **757/428-1498** • also lingerie, toys

Williamsburg

ACCOMMODATIONS

▲ **Lavender Sea B&B** 507 Capitol Landing Rd (at Washington St) **757/345-0198** • mostly women • 1938 home & haven for arts • kids ok • lesbian-owned/ run • $75-95

Washington

Bellevue

see also Seattle

Spiritual Groups

East Shore Unitarian Church 12700 SE 32nd St (1 1/2 blks from Richards Rd) **425/747-3780** • 9am & 11am Sun (10am summers) • wheelchair access

Bellingham

Info Lines & Services

LGBT Alliance Western Washington University **360/650-6120** • social/ political group Sept-May

Bars

Rumours 1119 Railroad Ave (at Chestnut) **360/671-1849** • 4pm-2am • lesbians/ gay men • dancing/DJ Wed-Sun • multiracial • also restaurant

Cafes

Tony's Coffee 1101 Harris Ave (at 11th), Fairhaven **360/738-4710** • 7am-9pm, till 10pm wknds • plenty veggie • patio • wheelchair access

Restaurants

Skylark's Hidden Cafe 1308-B 11th St (at McKenzie) **360/715-3642** • 7am-9pm, till 10pm Fri-Sat • great soups • beer/ wine • outdoor seating

Bookstores

Village Books 1210 11th St (at Harris) **360/671-2626** • 9am-10pm, from 10am Sun • new & used

Retail Shops

Kalamalka Studio 2518 Meridian **360/733-3832** • 11am-7pm, clsd Sun-Mon • tattoos • piercings

Erotica

Great Northern Bookstore 1308 Railroad Ave (at Holly) **360/733-1650**

Bremerton

Info Lines & Services

AA Gay/ Lesbian 700 Callahan Dr (at St Paul Episcopal) **360/475-0775** • 7:30pm Tue

Out Kitsap 360/337-6150 • weekly social events

Bars

Brewski's 2810 Kitsap Wy (enter off Wycuff St) **360/479-9100** • 11am-2am • gay-friendly • neighborhood bar • food served • wheelchair access

Chelan

Accommodations

Whaley Mansion 415 3rd St **509/682-5735, 800/729-2408** • gay-friendly • full brkfst • smokefree • woman-owned/ run • $85-135

Enumclaw

Accommodations

Corner of the Sky 41007 292nd Ave SE **360/825-3090** • women only • open June-Oct • gardens • hiking • 45 mins to Seattle • smokefree • lesbian-owned/ run • $65-70

Everett

Info Lines & Services

AA Gay/ Lesbian 2624 Rockefeller **425/252-2525** • 7pm Sun

Nightclubs

Everett Underground 1212 California St (at Grand Ave) **425/339-0807** • 4pm-2am, from 3pm Fri-Sun • lesbians/ gay men • dancing/DJ • multiracial • karaoke Wed • live shows Th • food served • wheelchair access

Glacier

Accommodations

Mt Baker B&B 9447 Mt Baker Hwy **360/599-2299** • gay-friendly • modern chalet • full brkfst • hot tub • kids ok • some shared baths • $75-95

Kent

Accommodations

Madrigal Inn B&B 14421 SE 232nd St **253/638-6566** • gay/ straight • full brkfst • $65-115

Bars

Trax Bar & Grill 226 1st Ave S (btwn Titus & Gowe) **253/854-8729** • noon-2am • lesbians/ gay men • dancing/DJ wknds • karaoke Wed

Bookstores

New Woman Books 213 W Meeker (at 3rd Ave W) **253/854-4311** • 10am-5:30pm, clsd Sun-Mon • also 'Wild Woman Gallery'

Washington • USA

EROTICA

The Voyeur 604 Central Ave S **253/850-8428**
• videos • toys • clothing

La Conner

ACCOMMODATIONS

The Wild Iris 121 Maple Ave **360/466-1400**
• gay-friendly • inn • smokefree • full brkfst •
restaurant with dinner on wknds only • teens
ok • wheelchair access • $95-180

Long Beach Peninsula

ACCOMMODATIONS

Anthony's Home Court 1310 Pacific Hwy N,
Long Beach **360/642-2802, 888/787-2754** •
gay/ straight • cabins & RV hookups • gay-
owned/ run • $50-135

**The Historic Sou'wester Lodge, Cabins &
RV Park** Beach Access Rd/ 38th Place,
Seaview **360/642-2542** • gay-friendly •
inexpensive suites • cabins w/ kitchens •
vintage trailers • RV hook-ups • pets ok •
smokefree • $39-129

Shakti Cove Cottages **360/665-4000** •
lesbians/ gay men • cabins on the peninsula •
pets ok • lesbian-owned/ run • $65-110

Lynnwood

RETAIL SHOPS

Lynnwood Tattoo 15315 Hwy 99, #7 (at
153rd) **425/742-8467** • noon-10pm, till
midnight Fri-Sat

Mt Vernon

ACCOMMODATIONS

The White Swan Guesthouse 15872 Moore
Rd **360/445-6805** • gay-friendly • farmhouse
B&B • also cottage • smokefree • kids ok •
$75-150

RESTAURANTS

Deli Next Door 210 S 1st St (at Memorial
Hwy) **360/336-3886** • 9am-8pm, till 6pm Sun
• healthy American • plenty veggie •
wheelchair access • $4-7

BOOKSTORES

Scott's Bookstore 121 Freeway Dr
360/336-6181 • 9am-8pm, till 5pm Sun, till
6pm Mon

Olympia

INFO LINES & SERVICES

Free at Last AA 11th & Washington (at
United Church) **360/352-7344** • 7pm Mon

Queer Alliance Evergreen State College
360/866-6000 x6544 • social/ support group •
call for mtg times

ACCOMMODATIONS

Oyster Bay 2830 Bloomfield Rd, Shelton
360/427-7643 • lesbians/ gay men • private
decks • smokefree • $85-140

BARS

Hannah's 123 5th Ave W **360/357-9890** •
11am-midnight, 7am-2am Fri-Sat, 7am-
midnight Sun • gay/ straight • neighborhood
bar

NIGHTCLUBS

Thekla 425 Franklin St **360/352-1855** • 8pm-
2am • popular • gay Th & Sun only •
dancing/DJ • food served • karaoke • patio •
wheelchair access

CAFES

Darby's Cafe 211 SE 5th Ave (at
Washington) **360/357-6229** • 7am-3pm, 8am-
2pm wknds, clsd Mon • lesbians/ gay men

Otto's 111 Washington St NE **360/352-8640**
• 6am-7pm • espresso & freshly baked bagels

RESTAURANTS

Saigon Rendez-Vous 117 5th Ave SW
360/352-1989 • lunch & dinner • Vietnamese
• plenty veggie

Urban Onion 116 Legion Wy SE (at Capitol)
360/943-9242 • 7am-10pm, till 11pm wknds
• plenty veggie • wheelchair access

RETAIL SHOPS

Dumpster Values 117 Washington St NE
360/705-3772 • 11am-8pm, noon-5pm Sun •
new & used clothing • zines • records • toys •
women-owned/ run

EROTICA

Desire Video 3126 Pacific Ave SE ((off I-5 at
exit 107)) **360/352-0820** • 24 hrs • videos •
toys • extensive lgbt section

Pasco

NIGHTCLUBS

Out & About 327 W Lewis **509/543-3796,
877/388-3796** • 7pm-2am, clsd Mon-Tue •
lesbians/ gay men • dancing/DJ Fri-Sat •
karaoke Th • live shows • also restaurant •
wheelchair access

Seattle • Washington

Port Townsend

ACCOMMODATIONS

Bearheart Inn B&B 1290 Gardiner Beach Rd (at Hwy 101 & Diamond Pt Rd), Sequim 360/797-7500, 888/206-0899 • gay/ straight • full brkfst • kids ok • lesbian-owned/ run • $60-75

The James House 1238 Washington St 800/385-1238 • gay-friendly • Victorian B&B • full brkfst • smokefree • $120-225

Ravenscroft Inn 533 Quincy St (at Clay St) 360/385-2784, 800/782-2691 • gay-friendly • seaport inn w/ views of Puget Sound • gourmet brkfst • hot tub • smokefree • $85-190

Sunset Marine Resort 40 Buzzard Ridge Rd, Sequim 360/681-4166 • gay-friendly • waterfront cabins • smokefree • kids ok • lesbian-owned/ run • $75-155

Pullman

INFO LINES & SERVICES

Washington State U GLBA Program 509/335-6388

San Juan Islands

ACCOMMODATIONS

Blue Rose B&B 1811 9th St, Anacortes 360/293-5175, 877/293-3285 • gay-friendly • private home • full brkfst • nr waterfront • $95-110

Lopez Farm Cottages & Tent Camping 555 Fisherman Bay Rd, Lopez Island 360/468-3555, 800/440-3556 • gay/ straight • on 30-acre farm • hot tub • smokefree • also camping • $28-150

Spring Bay Inn on Orcas Island 360/376-5531 • gay/ straight • full brkfst • kayak tour included in price • $220-260

The Whidbey Inn 106 1st St, Langley 360/221-7115, 888/313-2070 • gay-friendly • full brkfst • located on bluff over Saratoga Passage Waterway & Mtns • smokefree • $85-160

Seattle

INFO LINES & SERVICES

Capitol Hill Alano 1222 E Pine St, 2nd flr (at 13th) 206/587-2838 (AA#), 206/322-9590 (CLUB) • 12-step mtgs daily

Counseling Service for Sexual Minorities 112 Broadway Ave E 206/323-0220 • 8am-5pm Mon-Fri

FTM Outreach Phoneline 1812 E Madison St #106 (Ingersoll Gender Center) 206/329-6651 • live one-on-one info/ support for FTMs

Lambert House 1818 15th Ave (at Denny) 206/322-2515 • 4pm-10pm, till midnight Fri-Sat, clsd Sun • drop-in center for sexual minority youth

Lesbian Resource Center 2214 S Jackson St (at 23rd St) 206/322-DYKE (3953) • drop-in noon-7pm Tue-Fri, & till 5pm Sat

Seattle Bisexual Women's Network PO Box 30645, Greenwood Sta, 98103-0645 206/517-7767 • active social/ support organization • also newsletter

ACCOMMODATIONS

Ace Hotel 2423 1st Ave (at Wall St) 206/448-4721 • gay/ straight • modern & stylish • some shared baths • kids/ pets ok • gay-owned/ run • $65-175

Alexis Hotel 1007 1st Ave (at Madison) 206/624-4844, 800/426-7033 • gay-friendly • luxury hotel w/ Aveda spa • whheelchair access • $240-825

Amaranth Inn 1451 S Main St (at 16th) 206/322-5574, 800 /720-7161 • gay/ straight • 1890s mansion • full brkfst • smokefree • $85-145

Artist's Studio Loft B&B 16529 91st Ave SW, Vashon Island 206/463-2583 • gay-friendly • hot tub • smokefree • $95-160

Bacon Mansion 959 Broadway E (at E Prospect) 206/329-1864, 800/240-1864 • gay/ straight • Edwardian-style Tudor • wheelchair access • $94-164

Chambered Nautilus B&B 5005 22nd Ave NE (at N 50th St) 206/522-2536, 800/545-8459 • gay-friendly • colonial home • full brkfst • sundecks • $94-129

Gaslight Inn 1727 15th Ave (at E Howell St) 206/325-3654 • popular • gay/ straight • swimming • smokefree • also 'Howell St Suites' next door • gay-owned/ run • $88-188

Gypsy Arms B&B 3628 Palatine Ave N 206/547-8194 • gay/ straight • Victorian inn w/ full dungeon • leather • hot tub • smokefree • gay-owned/ run • $85-100

Hawthorn Inn & Suites 2224 8th Ave (at Blanchard) 206/624-6820, 800/437-4867 • gay-friendly • hotel • full brkfst • smokefree • kids/ pets ok • wheelchair access • $79-169

Hill House B&B 1113 E John St (at 12th Ave) 206/720-7161, 800/720-7161 • gay-friendly • full brkfst • smokefree • $75-155

Washington • USA

Hotel Vintage Park 1100 5th Ave (at Spring) **206/624-8000, 800/853-3914** • gay-friendly • ultra luxe sleep in Seattle • also restaurant • $205-525

▲ **Landes House B&B** 712 11th Ave E (at Aloha) **206/329-8781, 888/329-8781** • lesbians/gay men • two 1906 houses joined by deck • hot tub • gay-owned/run • $70-120

MarQueen Hotel 600 Queen Anne Ave N (btwn Roy & Mercer) **206/282-7407, 888/445-3076** • gay/straight • $125-325

Pioneer Square Hotel 77 Yesler Wy (at 1st St) **206/340-1234, 800/800-5514** • gay-friendly • gym • restaurant & saloon • wheelchair access • $99-249

Salisbury House B&B 750 16th Ave E (at Roy) **206/328-8682** • gay-friendly • full brkfst • jacuzzi • smokefree • women-owned/run • $95-149

The Shafer-Baillie Mansion 907 14th Ave E (at Aloha) **206/322-4654, 800/922-4654** • gay-friendly • some shared baths • smokefree • $95-145

Wild Lily Ranch B&B 360/793-2103 • popular • lesbians/gay men • cabins on Skykomish River • authentic Sioux tipis • 1 hr from Seattle • hot tub • swimming • camping available • smokefree • gay-owned/run • $75+

BARS

The Bad Juju Lounge 1518 11th Ave (at Pike) **206/709-9951** • 3pm-2am • gay/straight • dancing/DJ • food served • 'Estrogen Lounge' for women Mon

The Baltic Room 1207 Pine St (at Melrose) **206/625-4444** • 5pm-2am, clsd Mon • gay/straight • piano bar

CC Attle's 1501 E Madison (at 15th Ave) **206/726-0565** • 6am-2am • popular • mostly gay men • neighborhood bar • videos

Changes 2103 N 45th St (at Meridian) **206/545-8363** • noon-2am • mostly gay men • neighborhood bar • food served • karaoke • videos • wheelchair access

The Cuff 1533 13th Ave (at Pine) **206/323-1525** • 11am-2am • popular • mostly gay men • dancing/DJ • leather • uniform bar • 4 bar areas • also restaurant • wheelchair access

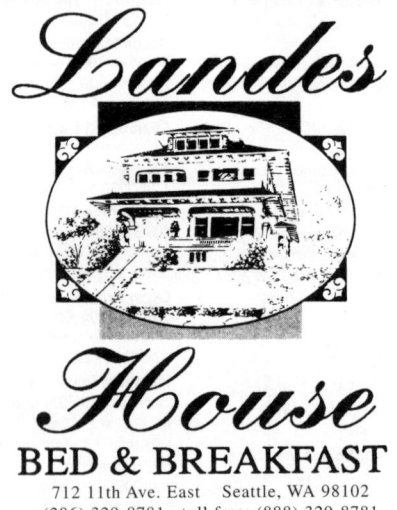

Landes House
BED & BREAKFAST
712 11th Ave. East   Seattle, WA 98102
(206) 329-8781   toll free: (888) 329-8781
www.landeshouse.com

Seattle • Washington

Double Header 407 2nd Ave (at Washington) **206/464-9918** • 10am-midnight, till 2am wknds • mostly gay men • neighborhood bar • 'one of the oldest gay bars in the US'

Elite Tavern 622 Broadway Ave (at Roy) **206/324-4470** • 10am-2am • lesbians/ gay men • neighborhood bar • beer/ wine only • wheelchair access

Hana's Restaurant & Lounge 1914 8th Ave (at Stewart) **206/340-1591** • noon-2am • mostly gay men • dancing/DJ • Korean food 11am-6pm • wheelchair access

Manray 514 E Pine (at Belmont) **206/568-0750** • 4pm-2am • mostly gay men • dancing/DJ • food served • Sun brunch

R Place 619 E Pine (at Boylston) **206/322-8828** • 2pm-2am • mostly gay men • neighborhood bar • food served • karaoke • videos • 3 stories • wheelchair access

Rendezvous 2320 2nd Ave (at Battery) **206/441-5823** • 6am-2am • gay-friendly • neighborhood bar • live bands Th-Sat

The Seattle Eagle 314 E Pike St (at Bellevue) **206/621-7591** • 2pm-2am • mostly gay men • leather • rock 'n' roll • patio • wheelchair access

Thumpers 1500 E Madison St (at 15th) **206/328-3800** • 11am-2am • popular • mostly gay men • videos • full restaurant • more women in dining room • $7-15 • wheelchair access • gay-owned/ run

Timberline Tavern 2015 Boren Ave (nr Fairview & Denny) **206/883-0242** • 6pm-2am, from 4pm Sun, clsd Mon • lesbians/ gay men • dancing/DJ • country/ western • dance lessons Tue-Wed • disco T-dance Sun • beer/ wine only

Watertown 106 1st Ave N (at Denny) **206/284-5003** • 4pm-2am, from 8pm Sat, till 3am wknds • gay-friendly • dancing/DJ Th-Sat

Wildrose Tavern & Restaurant 1021 E Pike St (at 11th) **206/324-9210** • 3pm-midnight, from noon Th-Fri, till 1am Tue-Th, till 2am Fri-Sat • mostly women • neighborhood bar • dancing/DJ • karaoke • live shows • wheelchair access

Seattle

WHERE THE GIRLS ARE: Living in the Capitol Hill District, south of Lake Union, and working in the Broadway Market, Pike Place Market, or somewhere in between.

ENTERTAINMENT: Team Seattle 206/322-7769, a 35-team gay network.

LGBT PRIDE: Last Sunday in June. 206/324-0405.

ANNUAL EVENTS: September - AIDSwalk 206/329-6923. Power Surge, biannual women's SM conference 206/233-8429. October - Seattle Gay & Lesbian Film Festival 206/323-4274.

CITY INFO: 206/461-5800, web: www.seattle.com.

ATTRACTIONS: International District.
Pike Place Market.
Pioneer Square.
Seattle Art Museum 206/654-3100.
Space Needle 206/443-9800.
Woodland Park Zoo 206/684-4800.

BEST VIEW: Top of the Space Needle, but check out the World's Fair Monorail too.

WEATHER: Winter's average temperature is 50° while summer temperatures can climb up into the 90°s. Be prepared for rain at any time during the year.

TRANSIT: Farwest 206/622-1717.
Gray Top Cab 206/622-4800.
Airport Shuttle Express 206/622-1424.
Metropolitan Transit 206/553-3000.

Washington • USA

Reply **Forward** **Delete**

Date: Sun, Dec 16, 2001 14:46:56
From: Girl-on-the-Go
To: Editor@Damron.com
Subject: Seattle

> Seattle's lush natural beauty—breathtaking views of Puget Sound and the Cascade Mountains—is actually more incredible than most let on.

> You can see for yourself from the deck of the Space Needle. This Seattle landmark is located in the Seattle Center, a complex that includes an opera house, the Arena Coliseum, the Experience Music Project, and the Pacific Science Center. If the line isn't too long, take the Monorail from downtown. (Be sure to sit on the right-hand side and keep your face pressed to the window. This scenic ride is almost over before it begins.) Another landmark is the quaint/touristy Pike Place Market (where all those commercials that feature mounds of fish are filmed).

> For the perfect day trip, ferry over to the Olympic Peninsula and enjoy the fresh wilderness, or cruise by 'Dykiki', a waterfront park on Lake Washington. Or sign up for an adventure with the LGBT outdoor group **Out Ventures** (who are also active in the spring and fall).

If you enjoy island life, ferry over to the San Juan Islands for a relaxing stay at one of the lesbian-friendly guesthouses. Or head up north to Vancouver, British Columbia, Seattle's beautiful Canadian cousin.

> But Seattle is more than just another pretty place. It has a small-town friendliness that you won't always find in a big West Coast city, as well as an international reputation for sophisticated cafe culture and cyber-cool.

> Speaking of java, if you like yours strong, stop in at **Espresso Vivace** on Denny. Or visit **2 Gals Juice & Java.**

> For shopping, the Broadway Market in queer Capitol Hill is a multicultural shopping center. The **Pink Zone** lesbian-owned body art shop is here, and we're told the girl-watching is best from the Market's espresso bar. If you're not a caffeine junkie, check out the

Seattle • Washington

Gravity Bar at the Market, where you can get almost any fruit or vegetable in liquid, shake, or sandwich form. And while you're in Capitol Hill, don't forget to stop by the dyke-owned **Toys in Babeland** for all your sex toy and erotica needs.

> **Beyond the Closet** is the local LGBT bookstore where you can get a copy of the **Seattle Gay News**. Seattle's main women's bar is the **Wildrose Tavern**. For dancing, head to the alterna-queer **Re-bar** on Saturdays. Country gals can line-dance at **Timberline**.

Nightclubs

Ego 916 E Pike (at Broadway) **206/709-2227** • 10pm-4am Wed-Fri, till 4am Sat, from 7pm Sun • gay/ straight • more women Wed • dancing/DJ

Jazz Alley 2033 6th Ave (at Lenora) **206/441-9729** • gay-friendly • call for events & reservations • live music • cover charge • also restaurant

Neighbours Restaurant & Dance Club 1509 Broadway (at E Pike, enter in alley) **206/324-5358** • 3pm-2am, till 4am Fri-Sat • popular • lesbians/ gay men • dancing/DJ • 2 flrs • young crowd • wheelchair access

Re-bar 1114 Howell (at Boren Ave) **206/233-9873** • open till 2am • popular • gay/ straight • women's night Sat • dancing/DJ Th-Sun • cabaret/ theater

Showbox 1426 1st Ave (at Pike) **206/628-3151** • gay-friendly • dancing/DJ • live music • 'Zoot Suit Sundays' w/ swing lessons • cover charge

The Vogue 1516 11th Ave (at Pine) **206/324-5778** • 9pm-2am • gay-friendly • dancing/DJ • alternative • live shows • theme nights

Cafes

2 Galz Java & Juice 102 15th Ave E (at Denny) **206/789-2233** • open early • cafe & bakery • call for events • also Ballard location: 5905 15th Ave NW • lesbian-owned/ run

Espresso Vivace 901 E Denny Wy #100 **206/860-5869** • 6:30am-11pm • popular • very cute girls

Restaurants

Addis Cafe 61224 E Jefferson (at 12th) **206/325-7805** • 8am-10pm • popular • Ethiopian • $3-7

Al Boccalino 1 Yesler Wy (at Alaskan) **206/622-7688** • lunch Mon-Fri, dinner nightly • classy southern Italian

Broadway New American Grill 314 Broadway E (at E Harrison) **206/328-7000** • 9am-1:30am, from 8am wknds • popular • full bar

Cafe Septieme 214 Broadway Ave E (at Thomas & John) **206/860-8858** • 9am-midnight • popular • lesbians/ gay men • also bar

Campagne 86 Pine St (at 1st) **206/728-2800** • 5:30pm-10pm • French • reservations advised • also 'Cafe Campagne' • brkfst, lunch & dinner

Washington • USA

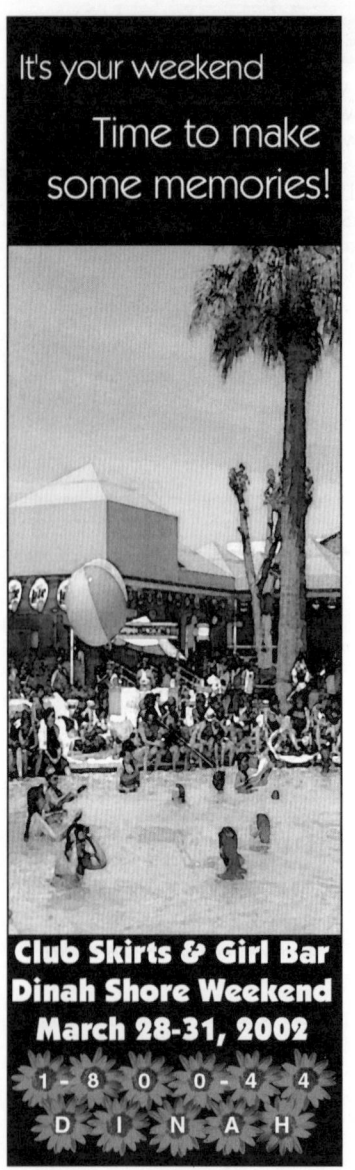

Dahlia Lounge 1904 4th Ave (at Virginia) **206/682-4142** • lunch & dinner • some veggie • full bar • $9-20

Frontier Restaurant & Bar 2203 1st Ave (at Blanchard) **206/441-3377** • 10am-2am • best cheap food in town • full bar • wheelchair access

Giorgina's Pizza 131 15th Ave E (at John) **206/329-8118** • 11am-10pm, from 5pm wknds

Gravity Bar 415 Broadway E (at Harrison) **206/325-7186** • 10am-10pm, till 11pm Fri-Sat • vegetarian • juice bar • wheelchair access

Kokeb 9261 12th Ave **206/322-0485** • 5pm-10pm, till 11pm Fri-Sat, clsd Sun • Ethiopian • some veggie • beer/ wine • $5-10

Mae's Phinney Ridge Cafe 6410 Phinney Ridge N (at 65th) **206/782-1222** • 7am-3pm • popular • brkfst menu • some veggie • wheelchair access

Mama's Mexican Kitchen 2234 2nd Ave (in Belltown) **206/728-6262** • lunch & dinner • cheap & funky

Queen City Grill 2201 1st Ave (at Blanchard) **206/443-0975** • noon-11pm, from 5pm wknds • popular • fresh seafood • some veggie • wheelchair access

Rosebud Restaurant & Bar 719 E Pike St (at Harvard Ave) **206/323-6636** • lunch Mon-Fri, dinner nightly, wknd brunch

Sunlight Cafe 6403 Roosevelt Wy NE (at 64th) **206/522-9060** • 7am-9:30pm • vegetarian • beer/ wine • wheelchair access • $3-9

Szmania's 3321 W McGraw St (in Magnolia Bluff) **206/284-7305** • lunch Tue-Fri, dinner Tue-Sun, clsd Mon

Wild Ginger Asian Restaurant & Satay Bar 1400 Western Ave (at Union) **206/623-4450** • lunch Mon-Sat, dinner nightly • popular • bar till 1am

Entertainment & Recreation

Gay Bingo 15th & E Union (at Temple De Hirsch Sinai) **206/323-0069, 206/328-8979** • monthly, run by the Chicken Soup Brigade

Harvard Exit 807 E Roy St **206/323-8986** • rep film theater

House of Dames Productions **206/720-5252, 206/720-1729** • women's theater group

Northwest Lesbian & Gay History Museum Project **206/903-9517** • exhibits & free newsletter

Out Ventures **206/720-1000** • outdoor fun for Puget Sound's lgbt community

Spokane • Washington

Pro Homo Voci • gay/ straight musical theater troupe

Tacky Tourist Clubs 206/679-3960 • fabulous social events

BOOKSTORES

Bailey/ Coy Books 414 Broadway Ave E (at Harrison) 206/323-8842 • 10am-10pm, till 11pm Fri-Sat • wheelchair access

Beyond the Closet Bookstore 518 E Pike St (at Belmont) 206/322-4609, 800/238-8518 • 10am-10pm • lgbt

Edge of the Circle 701 E Pike (at Boylston) 206/726-1999 • noon-9pm • alternative spirituality store

Fremont Place Book Company 621 N 35th (at Fremont Ave N) 206/547-5970 • 10am-8pm, till 9pm Wed-Sat, till 6:30pm Sun

Left Bank Books 92 Pike St (at 1st Ave) 206/622-0195 • 10am-7pm, noon-6pm Sun • worker-owned collective • new & used books • lgbt section

Pistil Books & News 1013 E Pike St (at 11th) 206/325-5401 • 10am-10pm, till 8pm Sun • new & used lgbt books

RETAIL SHOPS

Archie McPhee 2428 NW Market (in Ballard) 206/297-0240 • 9am-7pm, 10am-6pm Sun • weird & wonderful toys & trinkets • also mail order

Broadway Market 401 E Broadway (at Harrison & Republican) • popular mall full of funky, queer & hip stores

Metropolis 7220 Greenwood Ave N (at 73rd) 206/782-7002 • 10am-8pm • cards & gifts

The Pink Zone 211 Broadway (at John) 206/325-0050 • 10am-10pm • tattoos & piercings • also pride items

Sunshine Thrift Shops 1718 12th Ave (at Pike/ Broadway) 206/324-9774 • 10am-6:30pm • nonprofit for AIDS organizations • call for details • wheelchair access

Venus 1015 E Pike St (btwn 12th & Broadway) 206/322-5539 • noon-7pm, clsd Sun-Mon • plus-size consignment clothing, leather & corsets • transgender-friendly • lesbian-owned/ run

PUBLICATIONS

Pride Magazine 773/769-6328 • also publish Seattle Pink Pages

Seattle Gay Standard 206/322-9027 • weekly lgbt newspaper

SGN (Seattle Gay News) 206/324-4297, 206/322-7188 • weekly lgbt newspaper

The Stranger 206/323-7101 • queer-positive alternative weekly

SPIRITUAL GROUPS

Congregation Tikvah Chadashah 20th Ave E & E Prospect (at Prospect Cong Church) 206/329-2590 • 8:15pm 2nd & 4th Fri • lgbt Shabbat services

Dignity Seattle 723 18th Ave E (at St Joseph's Church on Capitol Hill) 206/325-7314 • 7:30pm Sun • Catholic

Grace Gospel Chapel 2052 64th St NW (at 22nd Ave N), Ballard 206/784-8495 • 11am Sun, 7pm Wed

Integrity Puget Sound 1245 10th Ave E (at Chapel of St Mark's) 206/525-4668 • 7pm Sun • Episcopal

MCC 300 3rd Ave W (at Western, in the Mountaineers Club) 206/325-2421 • 11am Sun

GYMS & HEALTH CLUBS

Hothouse Spa & Sauna 1019 E Pike St #HH (at 11th, 2 blks E of Broadway) 206/568-3240 • noon-midnight, clsd Tue • women only • baths • hot tub • massage

World Gym 825 Pike St (at 8th Ave) 206/583-0640 • gay-friendly

EROTICA

The Crypt 1113 10th Ave E (at Denny) 206/325-3882

Fantasy Unlimited 2027 Westlake Ave (at 7th) 206/682-0167 • 24hrs

Onyx Leather 1605 12th Ave #8 206/328-1965 • by appt only

Toys in Babeland 707 E Pike (btwn Harvard & Boylston) 206/328-2914 • 11am-10pm, noon-8pm Sun • wheelchair access • lesbian-owned/ run

Spokane

INFO LINES & SERVICES

AA Gay/ Lesbian 224 S Howard (upstairs) 509/624-1442 • 6:30pm Mon

Lesbian/ Gay Community Services Hotline 509/489-2266 • 24hrs

Odyssey 509/325-3637, 509/324-1547 • lgbt youth support & services • drop-in 4:30pm-9:30pm Tue & Th-Fri

Rainbow Regional Community Center 206 1/2 E Wellesley Ave (at Division) 509/458-2741 • drop-in resouce center • support groups • events

Washington • USA

ACCOMMODATIONS

Sun Flower Cottage 4114 N Wall St **509/326-7707** • lesbians/ gay men • 1911 bungalow • full brkfst • some shared baths • smokefree • gay-owned/ run • $45-55

BARS

Pumps II 211 N Division (at Main) **509/747-8940** • 3pm-2am, from noon wknds • lesbians/ gay men • dancing/DJ Fri-Sat • live shows Wed • karaoke Tue-Th • food served • wheelchair access

Rumors 415 415 W Sprague (at Washington) **509/838-6947** • noon-2am • lesbians/ gay men • dancing/ DJ Fri-Sat

NIGHTCLUBS

Dempsey's Brass Rail 909 W 1st St (btwn Lincoln & Monroe) **509/747-5362** • 3pm-2am, till 4am Fri-Sat • popular • lesbians/ gay men • dancing/DJ Th-Sat • drag shows Fri-Sat • cabaret Sun • also restaurant • wheelchair access • $5-12

RESTAURANTS

Cafe 5-Ten 2727 Mt Vernon (at 29th Ave) **509/533-0064** • lunch & dinner Mon-Sat • neighborhood bistro

Mizuna 214 N Howard **509/747-2004** • lunch Mon-Fri, dinner Tue-Sat • seaonal menu • plenty veggie • also wine bar

The Top Notch Cafe 825 N Monroe **509/327-7988** • 8am-2pm • homecookin'

BOOKSTORES

Auntie's Bookstore & Cafe 402 W Main St (at Washington) **509/838-0206** • 9am-9pm, till 10pm Fri, 11am-6pm Sun • wheelchair access

RETAIL SHOPS

Hat Over Heels 206 1/2 E Wellesley Ave (at Division) **509/489-1914** • 1pm-6pm Wed-Fri, 10am-6pm Sat, 1pm-5pm Sun, clsd Mon-Tue • pride gifts • T-shirts • jewelry • video rentals • run by Rainbow Ctr (nonprofit) • transgender-friendly • gay-owned/ run

PUBLICATIONS

Stonewall News Northwest **509/456-8011** • monthly lgbt newspaper for Spokane & NW

SPIRITUAL GROUPS

Emmanuel MCC 307 W 4th Ave (btwn Washington & Bernard) **509/838-0085** • 10:30am Sun

EROTICA

Castle Superstore 11324 E Sprague (btwn Gillis & Bowdish) **509/893-1180**

Suquamish

INFO LINES & SERVICES

Kitsap Lesbian/ Gay AA 18732 Division Ave NE (at Geneva) **360/475-0775** • 7:30pm Sun

Tacoma

INFO LINES & SERVICES

AA Gay/ Lesbian 209 S 'J' St (at the church, enter on alley) **253/474-8897** • 7:30pm Fri

Oasis **253/534-3204** • 4pm Th-Sat • lgbt youth group 14-24yrs

Rainbow Center 1501 Pacific Ave #310D **253/383-2318** • 8am-6pm Mon-Fri, drop-in hrs 1pm-7pm Tue • community center • call for meetings & events

Tacoma Lesbian Concern **253/752-6724** • social events • resource list • newsletter

ACCOMMODATIONS

Chinaberry Hill 302 Tacoma Ave N **253/272-1282** • gay-friendly • 1889 Victorian inn • also cottage • very romantic • full brkfst • jacuzzis • kids ok • smokefree • $120-195

Commencement Bay B&B 3312 N Union Ave **253/752-8175, 800/406-4088** • mostly women • full brkfst • hot tub • bi-owned/ run • $110-140

Sheraton Tacoma Hotel 1320 Broadway Plaza (at S 15th) **253/572-3200, 800/325-3535** • gay-friendly • restaurants & bars • wheelchair access • $99-199

BARS

Airport Tavern 5406 S Tacoma Wy **253/475-9730** • 2pm-2am • lesbians/ gay men • neighborhood bar • beer/ wine only

NIGHTCLUBS

Club Silverstone 739 1/2 St Helens Ave **253/404-0273** • 11am-2am • lesbians/ gay men • dancing/DJ • karaoke • live shows • also restaurant

Destiny's 754 Pacific Ave **253/627-0987** • 9:30pm-2am • lesbians/ gay men • dancing/DJ • live shows • also restaurant

SPIRITUAL GROUPS

New Heart MCC 2150 S Cushman **253/272-2382** • 11am Sun & 7pm Wed

EROTICA

Castle Superstore 6015 Tacoma Mall Blvd **253/471-0391**

Vancouver

see also Portland, Oregon

Charleston • West Virginia

Bars

North Bank Tavern 106 W 6th St/ Main **360/695-3862** • noon-1am, till 2am Fri-Sat, noon-midnight Sun • lesbians/ gay men • beer/ wine only • food served • wheelchair access

Spiritual Groups

MCC of the Gentle Shepherd 2200 Broadway, Suites E&F **360/695-1480** • 10am Sun, 7pm Wed • wheelchair access

Wenatchee

Cafes

The Cellar Café 249 N Mission St (at 5th) **509/662-1722** • 9am-5pm, 10am-4pm Sat, clsd Sun • some veggie • beer/ wine • patio • lesbian-owned/ run • $5-9

Whidbey Island

Accommodations

Whid-Wood Inn **360/679-7472** • gay-friendly • near historic Coupeville • gay-owned

Winthrop

Accommodations

Chewuch Inn 223 White Ave **509/996-3107, 800/747-3107** • gay-friendly • inn & cabins • E of N Cascades Mtns • hot tub • kids ok • smokefree • $60-125

WEST VIRGINIA

Statewide

Info Lines & Services

West Virginia Tourism Division **800/225-5982**

Publications

Hotspots Magazine **304/782-3358** • free monthly lgbt guide to bars, clubs & the scene in WV

Beckley

Erotica

Blue Moon Video 3427 Robert C Byrd Dr (at New River Dr) **304/255-1200**

Bluefield

Bars

Miss Helen's Shamrock Lounge 326 Princeton Ave **304/431-7002** • 9pm-2am Wed, Fri-Sat only • lesbians/ gay men • dancing/DJ • live shows • gay-owned/ run

Nightclubs

The Zodiac Club 714 Raleigh St • mostly gay men • dancing/DJ • live shows

Charleston

Info Lines & Services

AA Gay/ Lesbian 501 Elizabeth St (at Asbury United Methodist Church) **304/343-5330, 304/342-7811** • 8pm Th

COGLES (Community Oriented Gay/ Lesbian Events/ Services) **304/345-0491** • local info & resources

West Virginia Lesbian/ Gay Coalition **304/343-7305** • recording of bars & resources

Bars

The Tap Room 1022 Quarrier St (enter rear) **304/342-9563** • 5pm-close • mostly gay men • neighborhood bar • leather night 1st Sat • private club

Nightclubs

Broadway 210 Broad St (at Lee) **304/343-2162** • 3:30pm-3am, from 1pm wknds • gay/ straight • dancing/DJ • live shows • private club

Grand Palace 617 Brook St (nr Lee; take Broad St exit, off I-64) **304/342-9532** • noon-3am, till 2:30am Sun • lesbians/ gay men • dancing/DJ • drag shows • private club

Trax 504 W Washington (at Maryland) **304/345-8931** • 4pm-3am, till 2:30am Sat • gay/ straight • dancing/DJ Wed-Sun • live shows • drag Th

Entertainment & Recreation

Living AIDS Memorial Garden 1620 Washington St E (at Sidney Ave) **304/346-0246**

Publications

About PO Box 2624 25329

Graffiti 1425 Lee St **304/342-4412** • alternative entertainment guide • mostly non-gay

Hotspots Magazine **304/782-3358** • free monthly lgbt guide to bars, clubs & the scene in WV

Shout! **540/529-6363** • entertainment & personals for the Virginias & Carolinas

Spiritual Groups

Appalachian MCC 520 Kanawha Blvd W (in Unitarian Bldg) **304/343-5330** • 6pm Sun

West Virginia • USA

Huntington

BARS

The Driftwood-Beehive Lounge 1121 7th Ave **304/696-9858** • 5pm-3am • lesbians/gay men • dancing/DJ • karaoke • live shows • videos • young crowd • wheelchair access

Polo Club 733 7th Ave (enter rear) **304/522-3146** • 5pm-1am • mostly gay men • dancing/DJ Th-Sun • live shows • private club • wheelchair access

The Stonewall 820 7th Ave (enter rear) **304/523-1069** • 6pm-3:30am • popular • lesbians/gay men • dancing/DJ • karaoke • live shows • wheelchair access

RESTAURANTS

Calamity Cafe 1555 3rd Ave **304/525-4171** • 11am-10pm, till 3am wknds • live shows • Southern/Western • plenty veggie • full bar • wheelchair access • $10-15

EROTICA

House of Video 1109 4th Ave (at 11th) **304/525-2194**

Lewisburg

ACCOMMODATIONS

Lee Street Inn B&B 200 N Lee St **304/647-5599, 888/228-7000** • gay-friendly • grand 1876 house • jacuzzi • garden • teens ok • gay-owned/run • $65-120

SPIRITUAL GROUPS

Greenbrier Spiritual Community **304/392-5103** • non-denominational group • call for info

Lost River

ACCOMMODATIONS

The Guesthouse Settlers Valley Wy **304/897-5707** • lesbians/gay men • full brkfst • swimming • hot tub • gym • smokefree • $116-140

Martinsburg

EROTICA

Variety Books & Video 244 N Queen St (at Race) **304/263-4334** • 24hrs

Morgantown

BARS

Purple Rain 3117 University Ave **304/598-0919** • 6pm-3am • gay/straight • neighborhood bar • food served till 10pm • karaoke

NIGHTCLUBS

Vice Versa 335 High St (enter rear) **304/292-2010** • 8pm-3am Th-Sun • lesbians/gay men • dancing/DJ • live shows • private club • wheelchair access

Parkersburg

BARS

Genders Video Bar 316 5th St **304/485-2929** • 9pm-close • lesbians/gay men • dancing/DJ • karaoke • live shows

Shepherdstown

INFO LINES & SERVICES

Lambda Panhandlers PO Box 1961, 25443 • 'serving lgbt communities of eastern WV panhandle & nearby VA, MD, PA & DC'

BOOKSTORES

On the Wings of Dreams PO Box 1433 25443-1433 **304/876-0244** • metaphysical

Upper Tract

ACCOMMODATIONS

Wildernest Inn **304/257-9076** • gay-friendly • April-Dec • full brkfst • hot tub • gym • smokefree • $85-105

Vienna

BARS

True Colors 102 12th St (at Grand Central) **304/295-8783** • 7pm-3am, clsd Mon-Tue • lesbians/gay men • dancing/DJ • live shows • 18+ • private club

Weston

ACCOMMODATIONS

FriendSheep Farm **304/462-7075** • mostly women • secluded farm retreat • cottages • B&B • campsites • smokefree • work/stay available • horses • women-owned/run • $75-95

Wheeling

CAFES

Cafe Le News 1200 Market St **304/232-7170** • 7am-7pm • coffee shop & newsstand

EROTICA

Market St News 1437 Market St (at 14th St) **304/232-2414** • 24hrs

Green Bay • Wisconsin

WISCONSIN

Statewide

INFO LINES & SERVICES

Wisconsin Department of Tourism Madison **800/432-8747**

PUBLICATIONS

IN Step 414/278-7840 • lgbt newspaper

Appleton

BARS

Rascals Bar & Grill 702 E Wisconsin Ave (at Meade) **920/954-9262** • 4pm-2am, from noon Sun • lesbians/ gay men • more women Fri • food served • patio

SPIRITUAL GROUPS

Angels of Hope MCC 815 N Richmond St **920/991-0128** • 5pm Sun

EROTICA

Eldorado's 2545 S Memorial Dr (at Hwys 47 & 441) **920/830-0042**

Clinton

ACCOMMODATIONS

Carvers Rock B&B 11044 E Creek Rd **608/676-2219** • gay/ straight • full brkfst • smokefree • wheelchair access • gay-owned/ run • $85 • 2-bdrm suite available ($100)

Cumberland

ACCOMMODATIONS

Wild Iris Shores 2741 11th St **715/822-8594** • log cabins on 38 wooded acres • kids ok • wheelchair accessible • woman-owned/ run • $85-110

Eagle River

ACCOMMODATIONS

The Edgewater Hotel & Resort 5054 Hwy 70 W **715/479-4011, 888/334-3987** • gay/ straight • also waterfront cottages • gay-owned/ run • $39-69 room • $270-868 cottage

Eau Claire

ACCOMMODATIONS

Back of the Moon S3625 County Rd N, Augusta **715/286-2409** • women only • B&B retreat • smokefree • $35-40

BARS

Wolfe's Den 302 E Madison **715/832-9237** • 6pm-2:30am • mostly gay men • neighborhood bar

NIGHTCLUBS

CJ's Great Escape 304 Eau Claire St (at Barstow) **715/838-9494** • 6pm-2am, till 2:30am Fri-Sat, clsd Sun • lesbians/ gay men • dancing/DJ • videos • live shows

Scooters 411 Galloway (at Farwell) **715/835-9959** • 5pm-2am, from 3pm wknds • lesbians/ gay men • dancing/DJ • live shows • wheelchair access

Geneva Lakes

ACCOMMODATIONS

Allyn Mansion Inn 511 E Walworth Ave (btwn 5th & 6th), Delavan **262/728-9090** • gay/ straight • full brkfst • smokefree • gay-owned/ run • $75-150

Eleven Gables Inn on the Lake 493 Wrigley Dr, Lake Geneva **262/248-8393, 800/362-0395** • gay-friendly • full brkfst wknds • smokefree • kids/ pets ok • wheelchair access • $89-285

Green Bay

INFO LINES & SERVICES

Gay AA 920/494-9904 • call for mtg schedule

BARS

Brandy's II/ Boogie Nights 1126 Main St (nr Webster Ave) **920/437-3917** • 1pm-2am • lesbians/ gay men • neighborhood bar • dancing/DJ Wed-Sun • wheelchair access

Napalese Lounge 1351 Cedar St **920/432-9646** • 11am-2am, till 2:30am Fri-Sat • mostly gay men • neighborhood bar • DJ Fri-Sat • food served • live shows monthly • wheelchair access

Sass 840 S Broadway **920/437-7277** • 6pm-2am, from noon Sun (winters) • lesbians/ gay men • dancing/DJ wknds

ENTERTAINMENT & RECREATION

Historic West Theater 405 W Walnut **920/435-1057** • films • full bar • dancing wknds • food served

PUBLICATIONS

Quest 920/433-0611, 800/578-3785

SPIRITUAL GROUPS

Angels of Hope MCC 3607 Libal St **920/432-0830** • 11am Sun

Wisconsin • USA

Hayward

Accommodations

The Lake House 5793 Division, Stone Lake **715/865–6803** • gay-friendly • full brkfst • swimming • smokefree • kids ok by arrangement • wheelchair access • lesbian-owned/ run •$65-85

Hazelhurst

Bars

Willow Haven Resort/ Supper Club 4877 Haven Dr (at Willow Dam Rd) **715/453–3807** • 5pm-10om • gay-friendly • also cabin rentals

Kenosha

see also Racine

Bars

Capers Illusions 6305 120th Ave (on E frontage road of 94) **262/857–3744** • 8pm-2am • lesbians/ gay men • dancing/DJ • live shows

Clubhouse Filling Station 6325 120th Ave (on E frontage road of 94) **262/857–3744** • 7pm-2am, from noon Sun • lesbians/ gay men • dancing/DJ • live shows • food served • also antique shop wknds & by appt

Nightclubs

Club 94 9001 120th Ave (off I-94) **262/857–9958** • 7pm-2am, from 3pm Sun, clsd Mon • popular • lesbians/ gay men • dancing/DJ • live shows • videos

Cafes

Becca's Cafe 4015 80th St **262/694–7160** • 7am-10pm • lesbian-owned

La Crosse

Info Lines & Services

Gay/ Lesbian Support Group 126 N 17th St **608/784–7600** • 7:30pm Sun

Accommodations

Chela's Forest Camping Retreat Gay Mills **608/735–4829** • women only • pets ok • lesbian-owned/ run• $25-60

Rainbow Ridge Farms B&B N 5732 Hauser Rd (at County St), Onalaska **608/783–8181** • gay-friendly • restored farmhouse on 35 acres • full brkfst • hot tub • smokefree • $65-95

Trillium B&B 608/625–4492 • gay-friendly • cottage (sleeps 5) • 35 miles from La Crosse • full brkfst • kids ok • smokefree • $60-100

Bars

Cavalier Lounge 144 5th Ave N (at Main) **608/782–9061** • 5pm-close • mostly gay men • dancing/DJ wknds

My Place 3201 South St (at East Ave) **608/788–9073** • 3pm-close • lesbians/ gay men • friendly neighborhood bar • karaoke • games • gay-owned/ run

Players 214 Main **608/784–2353** • 5pm-2am, from 3pm Fri-Sun • popular • lesbians/ gay men • dancing/DJ • shows • wheelchair access • gay-owned/ run

Rainbow's End 417 Jay St (at 4th) **608/782–5105** • 3pm-2am, (from noon during football season) • lesbians/ gay men • neighborhood bar

Bookstores

Pearl Street Books 323 Pearl St **608/782–3424** • 9:30am-8pm, till 9pm Fri, from noon Sun • lgbt section

Retail Shops

Under the Rainbow 122 5th Ave S (at Jay) **608/796–0383** • 10am-5pm, clsd Sun • wheelchair access

Publications

Leaping La Crosse • newsletter

Laona

Accommodations

Laona Hostel 5397 Beech St **715/674–2615** • gay-friendly • dorm-style/ youth hostel rooms • gay-owned/ run • $15

Madison

Info Lines & Services

Campus Women's Center 800 Langdon, 4th flr Memorial Union, UW **608/262–8093** • support programs

LesBiGay Campus Center 800 Langdon, 2nd flr Memorial Union, UW **608/265–3344** • drop-in 10am-5pm • social events • general info

OutReach 600 Williamson St **608/255–8582** • 9am-9pm, noon-3pm Sat, clsd Sun • drop-in center • library • newsletter • AA group meets 6pm Sat

Accommodations

Wild Rose Guest House 1437 CTH W (off I-90), Stoughton **608/877–9942** • gay/straight • full brkfst • 5 acres of nature located btwn Madison & Janesville • smokefree • lesbian-owned/ run • $78

Milwaukee • Wisconsin

BARS

Club 5 5 Applegate Ct (btwn Fish Hatchery Rd & W Beltline Hwy) **608/277-9700, 608/277-8700** • 11am-2am Th-Fri, 4pm-2am Sat-Mon • lesbians/ gay men • dancing/DJ • karaoke • live shows • restaurant • also 'The Foxhole' women's bar & 'Planet Q' video bar

Green Bush 914 Regent St (at Park) **608/257-2874** • 4pm-midnight, clsd Sun • gay-friendly • food served

Rainbow Room 121 W Main (at Fairchild) **608/251-5838** • 10am-2am • lesbians/ gay men • dancing/DJ • live shows • wheelchair access

Ray's Bar & Grill 3054 E Washington (at Milwaukee) **608/241-9335** • 4pm-2am, from 3pm wknds • lesbians/ gay men • neighborhood bar • food served • patio in summer

Shamrock 117 W Main St (at Fairchild) **608/255-5029** • 2pm-2am, Sun brunch from 10am • lesbians/ gay men • also grill

NIGHTCLUBS

Cardinal 418 E Wilson St (at S Franklin) **608/251-0080** • 8pm-2am, clsd Mon • gay-friendly • more gay Tue & early Fri • dancing/DJ • call for events

RESTAURANTS

Fyfe's 1344 E Washington (at Dickinson) **608/251-8700** • lunch Mon-Fri, dinner nightly • popular • some veggie • full bar • $10-25

Monty's Blue Plate Diner 2089 Atwood Ave (at Winnebago) **608/244-8505** • 7am-10pm, till 9pm Sun-Tue, from 7:30am wknds • some veggie • beer/ wine • wheelchair access

Wild Iris 1225 Regent St (at Mills) **608/257-4747** • noon-10pm, from 9am wknds • Italian/ Cajun • some veggie • beer/ wine • $8-12

ENTERTAINMENT & RECREATION

Nothing to Hide cable Ch 4 **608/241-2500** • 2pm-3pm Sun, 9pm-11pm Wed • lgbt TV show

BOOKSTORES

A Room of One's Own Feminist Bookstore & Coffeehouse 307 W Johnson St **608/257-7888** • 8am-8pm, 11am-6pm Sun • wheelchair access

Borders Book Shop 3416 University Ave **608/232-2600** • 9am-11pm, till 9pm Sun • lgbt section • also espresso bar

Mimosa 210 N Henry **608/256-5432** • 11am-6pm, 1pm-5pm Sun • self-help books

RETAIL SHOPS

Piercing Lounge 461 W Gilman (at University) **608/284-0870** • 11am-11pm, till midnight Fri, noon-7pm Sun

PUBLICATIONS

Of a Like Mind **608/226-9998** • women's newsjournal of goddess spirituality

SPIRITUAL GROUPS

Integrity/ Dignity 1001 University Ave (at St Francis Episcopal) **608/836-8886** • 6pm 2nd & 4th Sat

James Reeb Unitarian Universalist Church 2146 E Johnson St (at 4th St) **608/242-8887** • 10am Sun (summers) • 9am & 11am (winter)

EROTICA

A Woman's Touch 600 Williamson (at Gateway Mall) **608/250-1928, 888/621-8880** • 11am-6pm, till 8pm Tue-Th, from noon wknds, till 5pm Sun • wheelchair access

Red Letter News 2528 E Washington (at North) **608/241-9958** • 24hrs

Maiden Rock

ACCOMMODATIONS

Eagle Cove B&B **715/448-4302, 800/467-0279** • gay/ straight • hot tub • smokefree • wheelchair access • gay-owned/ run • $40-100

Milton

ACCOMMODATIONS

Chase on the Hill B&B 11624 State Rd 26 **608/868-6646** • gay/ straight • $45-80

Milwaukee

INFO LINES & SERVICES

AA Galano Club 2408 N Farwell Ave (at North) **414/276-6936** • call after 5pm for mtg schedule

Gay Information & Services **414/444-7331** • 24hr referral service

Gay People's Union Hotline **414/645-0585**

Gay Youth Milwaukee **414/272-8336** • 7pm-11pm Fri-Sat

Gemini Gender Group **414/297-9328** • 2nd Sat • transgender support • call for location

Lesbian Alliance 170 S 2nd St, suite 104 **414/272-9442** • social and educational group • newsletter • visitors welcome

Wisconsin • USA

Milwaukee LGBT Community Center 170 S 2nd St (at Pittsburgh) **414/271-2656** • drop-in Th-Fri eves • movie night every other Sat

SAGE Milwaukee **414/271-0378** • for older lgbts • call after 4pm

Accommodations

The Milwaukee Hilton 509 W Wisconsin Ave (at 5th St) **414/271-7250, 800/445-8667** • gay-friendly • food service • swimming

Park East Hotel 916 E State St (at Marshall) **414/276-8800, 800/328-7275** • gay-friendly • smokefree • also restaurant • some veggie • wheelchair access

Bars

1100 Club 1100 S 1st St (at E Washington) **414/647-9950** • 7am-2am • mostly gay men • food served

Club 219 219 S 2nd St (btwn Florida & Pittsburgh) **414/276-2711** • 7pm-2am, from 4pm wknds • lesbians/ gay men • dancing/DJ • multiracial • live shows

▲ **Dish** 235 S 2nd St (at Oregon) **414/273-3474** • 8pm-close, clsd Mon-Tue • popular • gay/straight • dancing/DJ • alternative music • wheelchair access

---

[Reply] [Forward] **[Delete]**

```
Date: Thu, Dec 20, 2001 15:20:47
From: Girl-on-the-Go
To: Editor@Damron.com
Subject: Milwaukee
```

> Milwaukee holds a place of honor in the collective dyke cultural memory as the home of TV's *Laverne & Shirley,* a cute couple if we ever saw one. (You didn't really think that big 'L' on Laverne's chest was a monogram, did you?)

> You'll find plenty of breweries in this historically German-American city...and plenty of lesbians, too. Milwaukee has three (count em', three!) women's bars: **Kathy's Nut Hut, Fannie's/The Club,** and **Station 2. Club 219** is a mixed lesbian/gay bar with dancing, shows, and a multiracial clientele. **OutWords** is the LGBT bookstore, and it's got an espresso bar to boot.

> Just an hour and a half west of Milwaukee is Madison—home of the University of Wisconsin, and, from what we hear, a hotbed of academic and cultural feminism. So if you live to make passes at girls who wear glasses—and who wouldn't—then you'll love Madison. Call the **Campus Women's Center,** the **LesBiGay Campus Center,** or **OutReach** for current women's events. Better still, stop by the feminist bookstore **A Room of One's Own** for a cup of coffee and a good look around. Later, take your face out of that new book and get over to the Foxhole (at **Club 5**), the local women's bar.

Milwaukee • Wisconsin

Fannie's/ The Club 200 E Washington St **414/649-9003** • 7pm-2am, clsd Sun-Wed • mostly women • neighborhood bar • dancing/DJ Fri-Sat • wheelchair access

Henry's Pub & Grill 2523 E Belleview Pl (at Downer) **414/332-9690** • 3pm-2am • gay/ straight • full menu • wheelchair access

In Between 625 S 2nd St (at Bruce) **414/273-2693** • 5pm-2am, from 3pm wknds • lesbians/ gay men • neighborhood bar • wheelchair access

Kathy's Nut Hut 1500 W Scott (at 15th St) **414/647-2673** • 2pm-2am, from noon Fri-Sun • mostly women • neighborhood bar

M&M Club 124 N Water St (at Erie) **414/347-1962** • 11am-2am, from 10:30am Sun • mostly gay men • live shows • food served • some veggie • wheelchair access

The Nomad 1401 E Brady St (at Warren) **414/224-8111** • 1pm-2am, from noon wknds • gay-friendly

▲ **Redroom** 1875 N Humboldt (at North) **414/224-7666** • gay/ straight • appetizers • coffee bar • wheelchair access

South Water Street Dock 354 E National (at Water St) **414/225-9676** • 5pm-2am, from 3pm wknds • mostly gay men • neighborhood bar • wheelchair access

Station 2 1534 W Grant (at 15th Pl) **414/383-5755** • 6pm-2am, from 3pm Sun, clsd Mon-Tue • mostly women • neighborhood bar

Switch 124 W National Ave (at 1st) **414/220-4340** • 5pm-2am, from 2pm wknds, lesbians/ gay men • neighborhood bar • patio

Taylor's Bar 795 N Jefferson St (at Wells) **414/271-2855** • 4pm-2am, from 5pm wknds • gay/ straight • patio • wheelchair access • gay-owned/ run

Woody's 1579 S 2nd St (at Lapham St) **414/672-0806** • 4pm-2am, from 2pm wknds • lesbians/ gay men • neighborhood bar

NIGHTCLUBS

Club Boom 625 S 2nd **414/277-5040** • 8pm-2am Tue-Sun • lesbians/ gay men • dancing/DJ • videos

Fluid Lounge 819 S 2nd St (at National) **414/645-8330** • 5pm-2am • lesbians/ gay men • mostly African American • live jazz/DJ

DISH

Wisconsin's most popular mixed nightclub

Superstar DJs, dancing, outdoor patio

8pm-close, call ahead for events
235 South 2nd St (at Oregon)

414/273-DISH • www.clubdish.com

---

stop by **Redroom**, our new lounge & coffee bar!
girls • boys • cocktails • appetizers
1875 N Humboldt (at North) • 414/224-ROOM

Wisconsin • USA

La Cage (Dance, Dance, Dance) 801 S 2nd St (at National) **414/383-8330** • 9pm-2am • popular • mostly gay men • more women wknds • dancing/DJ • live shows • videos • food served • young crowd • wheelchair access

Cafes

Alterra Coffee Roasters 2211 N Prospect Ave (at North) **414/273-3753** • 7am-10pm, 8am-11pm Fri-Sat, 8am-9pm Sun

Fuel Cafe 818 E Center St **414/374-3835** • 7am-midnight, from 9am wknds • infamous for their stong coffee

Wild Thyme Cafe 231 E Buffalo (btwn Water & Broadway) **414/276-3144** • lunch till 3pm

Restaurants

Cafe Vecchio Mondo 1137 N Old World Third St (at Juneau) **414/273-5700** • lunch & dinner • full bar

Coquette Cafe 316 N Milwaukee St (btwn Buffalo & St Paul) **414/291-2655** • lunch Mon-Fri, dinner Mon-Sat, clsd Sun

The Knick 1030 E Juneau Ave (at Waverly) **414/272-0011** • 11am-midnight, from 9am wknds • popular • some veggie • full bar • wheelchair access

La Perla 734 S 5th St (at National) **414/645-9888** • 11am-10:30pm, till 11:30pm Fri-Sat, 10am-10pm Sun • Mexican

Sanford Restaurant 1547 N Jackson St **414/276-9608** • dinner only, clsd Sun • elegant Milwaukee Euro-style • $20-25

Entertainment & Recreation

Boerner Botanical Gardens 5879 S 92nd St (in Whitnall Park), Hales Corners **414/529-1870** • 8am-dusk • 40-acre garden & arboretum, garden clsd in winter

Mitchell Park Domes 524 S Layton Blvd (at Pierce) **414/649-9830** • 9am-5pm • botanical gardens

Bookstores

OutWords 2710 N Murray (at Park) **414/963-9089** • 11am-10pm, 11am-6pm Sun • lgbt • wheelchair access

Peoples' Books 2122 E Locust St (at Maryland) **414/962-0575** • 11am-7pm, till 6pm Sat, clsd Sun

Schwartz Bookstore 2559 N Downer Ave **414/332-1181** • 9am-10pm, till 11pm Fri-Sat, till 9pm Sun

---

Milwaukee

Where the Girls Are: In East Milwaukee south of downtown, spread out from Lake Michigan to S Layton Blvd.

LGBT Pride: June. 414/645-3378, web: www.pridefestmilwaukee.com

Annual Events: September - AIDS Walk.

City Info: 414/273-7222 or 800/231-0903.

Attractions: Annunciation Greek Orthodox Church.
Breweries.
Grand Avenue.
Mitchell Park Horticultural Conservatory.
Pabst Theatre 414/286-3665.
Summerfest.

Best View: 41st story of Firstar Center. Call 414/765-5733 to arrange a visit to the top floor observatory.

Weather: Summer temperatures can get up into 90°s. Spring and fall are pleasantly moderate but too short. Winter brings snow, cold temperatures, and even colder wind chills.

Transit: Yellow Cab 414/271-6630. Milwaukee Transit 414/344-6711.

Stevens Point • Wisconsin

RETAIL SHOPS

Adambomb Gallery 524 S 2nd St (at Bruce) 414/276-2662 • 11am-9pm, till 6pm Sat, clsd Sun-Mon • tattoo studio

Designing Men 1200 S 1st St (at Scott) 414/389-1200 • noon-7pm, till 9pm Fri-Sat, till 6pm Sun

Miss Groove 1225 E Brady (btwn Arlington & Franklin) 414/298-9185 • 11am-6pm, noon-4pm Sun, clsd Mon • accessories & gifts • gay-owned/run

Out of Solitude 918 E Brady (at Astor) 414/223-3101 • 11am-6pm, till 4pm Sun, clsd Sun • jewelry & gifts • gay-owned/run

Yellow Jacket 2225 N Humboldt Ave (at North Ave) 414/372-4744 • noon-7pm, till 5pm Sun, clsd Mon in summer • vintage clothes

You Should Be Dancing 6421 W North Ave 414/258-2705 • 11am-7pm, noon-6pm Sat, clsd Sun • lingerie • drag • shoes

PUBLICATIONS

IN Step 414/278-7840 • lgbt newspaper

Quest 800/578-3785, 920/433-0611 • good bar list

SPIRITUAL GROUPS

Dignity 76th & Wright St (at St Pius X Church) 414/873-9591 • 6pm 2nd Sun • call for more info

First Unitarian Society 1342 N Astor (at Ogden) 414/273-5257 • 9:15am & 11:15 Sun

Lutherans Concerned 414/372-9663 • call for info

Milwaukee MCC 1239 W Mineral (btwn 12th & 13th) 414/383-1100 • 11am Sun & 7pm Th

St James Episcopal Church 833 W Wisconsin Ave 414/271-1340 • 10:30am Sun

EROTICA

Booked Solid 7035 W Greenfield Ave (at 70th), West Allis 414/774-7210

Popular News 225 N Water St (at Buffalo) 414/278-0636 • toys • videos

Norwalk

ACCOMMODATIONS

Daughters of the Earth 18134 Index Ave 608/269-5301 • women only • women's land • camping • retreat space

Oshkosh

see also Appleton

EROTICA

Pure Pleasure 1212 Oshkosh Ave (off Hwy 21) 920/235-9727

Portage

EROTICA

Naughty But Nice Hwy 33, at exit 106 (off I-90) 608/742-8060

Racine

ACCOMMODATIONS

Lochnaiar Inn 1121 Lake Ave (at 11th St) 262/633-3300 • gay-friendly • English Tudor on Lake Michigan • full brkfst wknds • non-smoking rooms available • wheelchair access • $80-175

BARS

What About Me? 600 6th St (at Villa) 262/632-0171 • 6pm-2am, from 3pm Tue & Fri, clsd Mon • lesbians/gay men • neighborhood bar

NIGHTCLUBS

JoDee's International 2139 Racine St/S Hwy 32 (at 22nd) 262/634-9804 • 7pm-close • lesbians/gay men • dancing/DJ • live shows • courtyard • park in rear

Rhinelander

ACCOMMODATIONS

Musky Bay Resort 3850 Limberlost Rd (at County Hwy 'C') 715/369-0677 • gay-friendly • cabins on the Moens Chain of Lakes • kids ok • lesbian-owned/run • $ 70-95/night, $500-625/week

Sheboygan

BARS

The Blue Lite 1029 N 8th St (off Rte 143) 920/457-1636 • 7pm-2am, from 3pm Sun • lesbians/gay men • neighborhood bar • dancing/DJ Fri-Sat

Stevens Point

INFO LINES & SERVICES

Women's Resource Center 1209 Fremont (University of Wisconsin Nelson Hall) 715/346-4242 x4851 • 10am-4pm, clsd wknds • some lesbian outreach

EROTICA

Eldorado's 3219 Church St (at Business 51 S) 715/343-9877

Wisconsin • USA

Sturgeon Bay

Accommodations

Blacksmith Inn B&B 8152 Hwy 57, Baileys Harbor **920/839-9222, 800/769-8619** • gay-friendly • smokefree • wheelchair access • $165-195

The Chadwick Inn 25 N 8th Ave **920/743-2771** • gay-friendly • 1890 Queen Anne • smokefree • lesbian-owned/ run • $105-125

▲ **The Chanticleer Guest House** 4072 Cherry Rd **920/746-0334** • gay-friendly • on 70 acres • swimming • hot tub • smokefree • wheelchair access • gay-owned/ run • $120-210

Superior

Bars

Jook Joint 820 Tower Ave (at Winter) **715/392-5373** • 1pm-2am, till 2:30am Fri • lesbians/ gay men • neighborhood bar • wheelchair access

JT's Bar & Grill 1506 N 3rd St (at Blaknik Bridge) **715/394-2580** • 3pm-2am, from 1pm wknds • popular • lesbians/ gay men • dancing/DJ • patio • wheelchair access

The Main Club 1217 Tower Ave (at 12th) **715/392-1756** • 3pm-2am, till 2:30am Fri-Sat • popular • mostly gay men • dancing/DJ • country/ western • leather • Internet access • wheelchair access

Molly & Oscar's 405 Tower Ave **715/394-7423** • 5pm-2am, till 2:30am Fri-Sat • gay-friendly • neighborhood bar

Wascott

Accommodations

Wilderness Way **715/466-2635** • women only • resort property • cabins • camping • RV sites • swimming • camping $14 • cottages $58-92

Wausau

Nightclubs

Oz 320 Washington **715/842-3225** • 7pm-2am, from 5pm Sun • mostly gay men • dancing/DJ • videos • wheelchair access

---

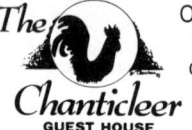

The Chanticleer GUEST HOUSE

Our quaint B&B is situated on 70 private acres, perfect for a romantic Door County getaway! Relax in your own private whirlpool as a crackling fire burns nearby.

• **MIDWEEK SPECIALS!** •

All 8 Suites Include:
Fireplace • Double Whirlpool • Private Bath
Private Balconies
Entertainment Center
Breakfast delivered to your room

Also 2 Luxury Cabins with Full Kitchens, Cathedral Ceilings, Whirlpools & Fireplaces. Heated Pool & Hiking Trails on Premises Cross Country Skiing & Snowshoeing right from your door.

Gay Owned & Operated
Call BRYON or DARRIN at **(920)746-0334**

www.chanticleerguesthouse.com
4072 Cherry Road (Hwy HH) Sturgeon Bay, WI 54235

WYOMING

Casper

CAFES

Coffee Shamanthe 232 E 2nd St (at Durbin) **307/234–1599** • 8am-6pm, 10am-6pm Sat, clsd Sun • also bookstore

J-Dub's Java'd House 319 W Yellowstone (at Ash St) **307/234–1145** • 2pm-11pm, till midnight Th-Sat, clsd Sun • gay-owned/run

Cheyenne

INFO LINES & SERVICES

United Gays and Lesbians of Wyoming **307/778–7645** • 9am-6:00pm Mon-Wed & Fri-Sat• info • referrals • also newsletter • weekly support groups

ENTERTAINMENT & RECREATION

Hart Center Coffeehouse 1611 Morrie Ave (nr Lincoln Wy) **307/635–5262** • Th eve only • call for info

EROTICA

Cupid's 511 W 17th (at Thomes) **307/635–3837**

Etna

RETAIL SHOPS

Blue Fox Studio & Gallery 107452 Hwy 89 **307/883–3310** • open 7 days • hours vary • pottery & jewelry studio • local travel info

Jackson

ACCOMMODATIONS

Bar H Ranch 208/354–2906, 888/216–6025 • lesbians/gay men • seasonal • also women-only horseback-riding trips in Grand Tetons (see 'Bar H Ranch' under Tour Operators section) • lesbian-owned/run • $125/night, $775/week

Fish Creek Lodging 208/652–7566 • lesbians/gay men • rental log cabin nr Yellowstone Nat'l Park & Jackson Hole • women-owned/run • $140/night, $780/week

Grove Creek Lodge 774 S 450 W (at Cedron Rd), Victor, ID **208/787–9110** • mostly women • luxury cabins • hot tub • kids/pets ok • wheelchair access • lesbian-owned/run • $189-239

Nowlin Creek Inn PO Box 2766, Jackson Hole 83001 **307/733–0882** • gay-friendly • B&B • log cabin • full brkfst • hot tub • $105-350

Spring Creek Ranch 1800 Spirit Dance Rd **307/733–8833, 800/443–6139** • popular • gay-friendly • food served • swimming • smokefree rooms available • wheelchair access • $150-250

Riverton

RESTAURANTS

Country Cove 301 E Main (at First) **307/856–9813** • 7am-3pm, clsd Sun • plenty veggie • wheelchair access • women-owned/run • $3-7

Want More?

Subscribe to our online travel guide:
www.damron.com

More listings. More destinations (like Australia, South Africa & Asia). More up-to-the-minute info. Check with Damron before you leave, or from the road with your laptop!

Alberta • CANADA

ALBERTA

Calgary

INFO LINES & SERVICES

Front Runners AA 1315 7th St SW (at Wesley United Church, enter on 14th Ave) **403/777-1212** • 8:30pm Tue, Th & Sat

Gay/ Lesbian Centre & Info Line 223 12th Ave SW #206 **403/234-8973** • 7pm-10pm • many groups

Illusions Transgender Club of Alberta **403/265-7789** • bi-monthly meeting • social/ support group

Xtensions **403/777-9499, 877/882-2011 (IN CANADA ONLY)** • provincewide lgbt info line

ACCOMMODATIONS

11th Street Lodging **403/209-0111** • gay/ straight • kids 10+ ok • 'no shoe' policy inside • smokefree • gay-owned/ run • Can$40-139

Calgary Westways Guest House 216 25th Ave SW **403/229-1758** • gay/ straight • full brkfst • hot tub • smokefree • pets ok • gay-owned/ run • Can$55-160

The Foxwood B&B 1725 12th St SW **403/244-6693** • lesbians/ gay men • smokefree • spa • some shared baths • gay-owned/ run • Can$67-150

Westpoint Executive B&B 101 Westpoint Gardens SW (at Old Banff Coach Rd SW) **403/248-5668** • gay-friendly • some shared baths • gay-owned/ run • Can$75-95

BARS

The Backlot 209 10th Ave SW (at 1st St SW) **403/265-5211** • 2pm-2am, from 4pm winters • mostly gay men • martini lounge • patio • wheelchair access

Detour 318 17th Ave SW **403/244-8537** • 10pm-3am • mostly gay men • neighborhood bar • dancing/DJ • drag show Sun

Midnight Cafe/ Bar 840 14th Ave SW (at Best Western Hotel) **403/229-9322** • 7am-2am, from 9am Sat, 11am-midnight Sun • gay-friendly • food served • patio • wheelchair access

Money Pennies 1742 10th Ave SW (nr 14th St) **403/263-7411** • 11am-2am, till midnight Sun-Wed • lesbians/ gay men • neighborhood bar • food served • patio • wheelchair access

Rooks Bar & Eatery 820 11th Ave SW **403/277-1922** • 11am-3am, till midnight Sun, from 4pm Mon-Tue • mostly women • dancing/DJ • food served • brunch 11am-3pm Sun

NIGHTCLUBS

The Warehouse 731 10th Ave SW (alley entrance) **403/264-0535** • 8pm-3am Fri-Sat only • gay-friendly • dancing/DJ • young crowd • private club • guests welcome

CAFES

Cafe Beano 1613 9th St SW (at 17th Ave) **403/229-1232** • 6am-midnight, from 7am wknds • some veggie • wheelchair access

Grabbajabba 1610 10th St SW (btwn 16th & 17th Ave) **403/244-7750** • 7am-11pm, from 8am Sun • lesbians/ gay men • some veggie • patio • wheelchair access • $3-7

RESTAURANTS

Melrose Cafe 730 17th Ave SW (at 7th St) **403/228-3566** • 11am-midnight, from 10am wknds • full bar till 2am • patio

Thai Sa-On 351 10th Ave SW (at 4th) **403/264-3526** • lunch & dinner • Thai

Victoria's 306 17th Ave SW **403/244-9991** • lunch, dinner, wknd brunch • homecooking • some veggie • full bar • wheelchair access • $6-10

Wicked Wedge Pizza 618 17th Ave SW (at 6th St) **403/228-1024** • open late

BOOKSTORES

A Woman's Place 1404 Centre St S (at 14th Ave) **403/263-5256** • 10am-5:30pm, clsd Sun • women's bookstore • large lgbt section • wheelchair access

Books 'n Books 738-A 17th Ave SW (at 7th St) **403/228-3337** • 10am-6pm, till 8pm Fri, from noon Sun • lgbt section • wheelchair access

Daily Globe News Shop 1004 17th Ave SW **403/244-2060** • 9am-11pm • periodicals

With the Times 2203 4th St SW (at 22nd Ave) **403/244-8020** • 9am-11pm

RETAIL SHOPS

Rainbow Pride Resource Centre 822 11th Ave SW #L-100 **403/266-5685** • noon-10pm, noon-6pm Sun • pride items & info • gay-owned/ run

PUBLICATIONS

Outlooks **403/228-1157, 888/228-1157** • lgbt magazine

Perceptions **306/244-1930** • covers the Canadian prairies

SPIRITUAL GROUPS

Integrity Calgary 1121 14th Ave SW (at St Stephen's Church) **403/701-5699** • 7:30pm 2nd • transdenominational Christian fellowship

Rocky Mtn House • Alberta

Erotica

Adult Depot 3505 32 St NE **403/264-7399** • clsd Sun • also 626 58 Ave SE, 403/258-2777

B&D Emporium 426 8th Ave SE **403/265-7789** • clsd Sun • drag/ fetish items

Tad's Bookstore 1421 9th Ave SE **403/237-8237** • wheelchair access

Edmonton

Info Lines & Services

AA Gay/ Lesbian 12530 110th Ave (at Unitarian church, Green Rm) **780/424-5900** • 8pm Fri

Gay/ Lesbian Community Centre 10612 124th St #103 **780/488-3234** • 1:30pm-5:30pm & 7pm-10pm, clsd wknds • also youth group 7pm Sat

Gay/ Lesbian Info Line 780/488-3234 • 24hr recorded info & event listing

Womonspace 780/482-1794 • dances & other events

Xtensions 877/882-2011 (in Canada only) • provincewide lgbt info line

Accommodations

Labyrinth Lake Lodge Site 2, Box 3, RR 1, Millet T0C 1Z0 **780/878-3301** • gay/ straight • lodge on private lake • hot tubs • kids/ pets ok • Can$150-200

Northern Lights B&B 8216 151st St **780/483-1572** • lesbians/ gay men • full brkfst • swimming • gay-owned/ run • Can$60-70

Bars

Boots 'N Saddles/ Garage Burger Bar 10242 106th St (at 103rd Ave) **780/423-5014** • 3pm-2am • cafe 11am-8pm, till 10pm Fri • mostly gay men • dancing/DJ • live shows • private club • wheelchair access

Buddy's Pub 11725-B Jasper **780/488-6636** • 3pm-3am • lesbians/ gay men • neighborhood bar • karaoke • live shows

The Roost 10345 104th St **780/426-3150** • 8pm-3am • lesbians/ gay men • dancing/DJ • live shows • private club

Secrets Bar & Grill 10249 107th St **780/990-1818** • 4pm-3am • lesbians/ gay men • neighborhood bar • dancing/DJ • also restaurant • karaoke Tue • music/ sports Th • wheelchair access

Cafes

Urban Grind 10124 124th St **780/451-1039** • 7am-2am, from 10am Sat, from 11am Sun • soup & sandwiches • beer/ wine

Restaurants

Cafe de Ville 10137 124th St (side entrance) **780/488-9188** • 11:30am-10pm, till 11pm Th, till midnight Fri-Sat, Sun brunch • cont'l

Divine's 9712 111th St (at 97th Ave) **780/482-6402** • 11am-10pm, till 11pm wknds • full bar

Entertainment & Recreation

Gaywire CJSR FM 88.5 **780/492-5244** • 6pm-7pm Th • lgbt radio

Bookstores

Audrey's Books 10702 Jasper Ave (at 107th) **780/423-3487** • 9am-9pm, 9:30am-5:30pm Sat, noon-5pm Sun • large lgbt section • wheelchair access

The Front Page 10356 Jasper Ave (at 104th St) **780/426-1206** • 9am-8pm, clsd Sun • periodicals

Greenwood's Bookshoppe 10355 82nd Ave (at 104th St) **780/439-2005** • 9am-9pm, till 5:30pm Sat, noon-5pm Sun

Orlando Books 10123 Whyte Ave **780/432-7633** • 10am-6pm, till 9pm Fri, noon-5pm Sun • women's • lgbt section • wheelchair access

Retail Shops

Divine Decadence 10441 82nd Ave (at 105th) **780/439-2977** • hip fashions • accessories

Publications

Times .10 10121 124th St **780/415-5616**

Spiritual Groups

Lambda Christian Church 11148 84th Ave (at Garneau United Church) **780/474-0753** • 7pm Sun

Lethbridge

Info Lines & Services

GALA/LA (Gay/ Lesbian Alliance of Lethbridge and Area) **403/329-4666** • peer support line 7pm-10pm Mon & Wed • coffee night Tue • dance last Sat • movie nights • also youth group

Rocky Mtn House

Accommodations

Country Cabin B&B 403/845-4834 • gay-friendly • cabin • hot tub • swimming • kids/ pets ok • $75

British Columbia • CANADA

BRITISH COLUMBIA

Birken

ACCOMMODATIONS

Birkenhead Resort Portage Rd **604/452–3255** • gay-friendly • cabins • campsites • hot tub • swimming • pets ok • also restaurant • lesbian-owned/run • Can$80-100

Courtenay

INFO LINES & SERVICES

Women's Resource Centre 780 Grant, unit 103 (btwn 6th & Cumberland) **250/338–1133, 250/334–9251** • 10am-4pm, clsd Fri-Sun

Cranbrook

INFO LINES & SERVICES

Cranbrook Women's Resource Centre 32 13th Ave S **250/426–2912** • 9am-4pm Mon-Th, clsd wknds

Fairmont Hot Springs

ACCOMMODATIONS

McMillan Chalet B&B 5021 Fairmont Close **250/345–9553, 800/856–9551** • gay-friendly • full brkfst • located in mtns nr skiing & hiking • some shared baths • smokefree • kids ok • Can$65-95

Fort Nelson

INFO LINES & SERVICES

Women's Resource Centre 5004 52nd Ave W **250/774–3069** • 1pm-6pm Mon-Tue & Th, till 4pm Wed, 2pm-5pm Fri, clsd wknds • call for appts

Golden

INFO LINES & SERVICES

Golden Women's Resource Centre 419C N 9th Ave **250/344–5317** • 10am-5pm, till 4pm Fri, clsd wknds

Gulf Islands

INFO LINES & SERVICES

Gays & Lesbians of Salt Spring Island (GLOSSI) 250/537–7773 • social events • newsletter • support • info line

ACCOMMODATIONS

Bellhouse Inn 29 Farmhouse Rd **250/539–5667, 800/970–7464** • gay-friendly • full brkfst • smokefree • Can$85-195

The Blue Ewe B&B, Private Cabin 1207 Beddis Rd, Salt Spring Island **250/537–9344** • lesbians/gay men • full brkfst • hot tub w/ ocean view • nudity ok • gay-owned/run • Can$69-150

Clare's Cottage 425 Fulford Ganges Rd, Salt Spring Island **250/537–5912, 877/537–5912** • lesbians/gay men • rental house & cottage • kids/pets ok • lesbian-owned/run • Can$59-135

Eden Guesthouse 127 Orchard Rd, Salt Spring Island **250/653–9962, 800/774–4591** • lesbians/gay men • also cottage • full brkfst • hot tub • nudity • gay-owned/run • Can$59-109

Hawthorne House 6436 Porlier Pass Rd, Galiano Island **250/539–5815** • gay/straight • rental home • sleeps 10 • smokefree • wheelchair access • lesbian-owned/run • Can$125-200

Madrona Bay Hideaway 122 Madrona Rd (at Churchill Rd), Salt Spring Island **250/537–2227** • lesbians/gay men • suite • hot tub • pond & gardens • kids/pets ok • lesbian-owned/run • $68-95

The Rex Galiano Island **250/539–2365** • mostly gay men • designer log home on 5 acres • full brkfst • deck w/ hot tub • nudity ok

Summerhill Guesthouse 209 Chu–An Dr, Salt Spring Island **250/537–2727** • lesbians/gay men • on the water • full brkfst • gay-owned/run • Can$100-140

Tutu's B&B 3198 Jemima Rd, Denman Island **250/335–0546, 877/560–8888** • gay-friendly • lakefront • private dock • swimming • Can$40-60

Wheatley's Country Home 2154 Sturdies Bay Rd, Galiano Island **250/539–5980, 877/537–5912** • lesbians/gay men • rental house & cottage • kids/pets ok • smokefree • lesbian-owned/run • Can$59-135

BARS

Moby's Pub 124 Upper Ganges, Salt Spring Island **250/537–5559** • 10am-midnight, 11am-1am Fri-Sun • gay-friendly • neighborhood bar • food served

Kelowna

INFO LINES & SERVICES

Kelowna Women's Resource Centre 347 Leon #107 **250/762–2355** • 9am-4pm Mon-Th

Okanagan Rainbow Coalition 991 Richter St **250/860–8555** • info line Mon-Fri eves • support groups • social events • dances

Qualicum Beach • British Columbia

CAFES

Bean Scene 274 Bernard Ave **250/763-1814** • 7am-10pm, till 11pm Fri-Sat • patio • gay coffee night 7pm Mon • wheelchair access

RESTAURANTS

Greek House 3159 Woodsdale Rd **250/766-0090** • 11am-10pm, from 4pm wknds • cont'l • $7-17

Ladysmith

ACCOMMODATIONS

Stonewall Guest House 4171 Stonewall Dr **250/245-3346** • gay-friendly • hot tub • full brkfst • lesbian-owned/ run • $85-150

Nanaimo

ACCOMMODATIONS

Dorchester Hotel 70 Church St **250/754-6835, 800/661-2449** • gay-friendly • $90-160

Howard Johnson Hotel & Suites Nanaimo 1 Terminal Ave (at Comox St), Nanaimo **250/753-2241, 800/663-7322** • gay-friendly • swimming • kids ok • restaurant & pub • Can$69-109

RESTAURANTS

Flo's Diner 187 Commercial St **250/753-2148** • 8am-8pm, till 3am Fri-Sat, from 9am wknds, till 3pm Sun • beer/ wine • gay-owned/ run

Nelson

INFO LINES & SERVICES

Nelson Women's Centre 420 Mill St (at Ward) **250/352-9916** • noon-4pm Tue-Fri • occasional wknd events

ACCOMMODATIONS

Dragonfly Inn 1016 Hall Mines Rd **250/354-1128** • gay/ straight • full brkfst • shared baths • hot tub • kids/pets ok • smokefree • lesbian-owned/ run • Can$65-85

Penticton

ACCOMMODATIONS

Bear's Den B&B **250/497-6721** • gay/ straight • full brkfst • hot tub • smokefree • great views • wheelchair access • gay-owned/ run • Can$85-135

Port Renfrew

ACCOMMODATIONS

Wild Women Retreat **250/388-0754** • 3-bdrm rental home • steps from the ocean on the west coast of Vancouver Island • kids/dogs ok • lesbian-owned/ run • Can$50-70

Powell River

ACCOMMODATIONS

Beacon B&B 3750 Marine Ave **604/485-5563, 877/485-5563** • gay-friendly • full brkfst • hot tub • massage • smokefree • wheelchair access • Can$85-135

Prince George

INFO LINES & SERVICES

GALA North **250/562-6253** • 24hr recorded info • social group • call for drop-in hours & location

ACCOMMODATIONS

Hawthorne B&B 829 PG Pulp Mill Rd **250/563-8299** • gay-friendly • full brkfst • hot tub • smokefree • gay-owned/ run • Can$60-70

CAFES

The Isle Pierre Pie Co 409 George St **250/564-1300** • 9am-5:30pm Mon-Wed, till 10pm Fri-Sat

RESTAURANTS

Pete's Cuisine 1645 3rd Ave **250/564-6391** • 8:30am-2pm & 5pm-10pm • cont'l • full bar • gay-owned/ run

EROTICA

XXXtreme Adult 1412 Patricia Blvd **250/614-1411** • 24hrs • videos • magazines • toys • lingerie

Prince Rupert

INFO LINES & SERVICES

Prince Rupert Gay Info Line **250/627-8900**

Qualicum Beach

ACCOMMODATIONS

Bahari B&B 5101 Island Hwy W **250/752-9278, 877/752-9278** • gay-friendly • full brkfst • hot tub • apt rental • smokefree • kids ok • Can$125-250

British Columbia • CANADA

Quesnel

INFO LINES & SERVICES

Women's Resource Centre 690 Mclean St **250/992-8472** • 9am-4pm, clsd wknds

Tofino

ACCOMMODATIONS

Alder View Suite/ B&B 1108 Abraham Dr **250/725-4427** • gay-friendly • also cottage & cabin • hot tub • kids/ pets ok • gay-owned/ run • Can$60-120

Beachwood 1368 Chesterman Beach Rd **250/725-4250** • private house • steps to the beach • gay-friendly • gay-owned/ run • $110-165

BriMar B&B 1375 Thornberg Crescent **250/725-3410, 800/714-9373** • gay/ straight • on the beach • full brkfst • teens ok • Can$85-165

Lone Cone Guest Suites 170 2nd St **250/725-3394** • gay-friendly • pets ok • $50-105

West Wind 1321 Pacific Rim **250/725-2224** • lesbians/ gay men • 5 mins from beach • hot tub • nudity permitted • gym • sundecks • smokefree • gay-owned/ run • Can$95-195

The WindRider Retreat for Women 231 Main St **250/725-3240** • women only • waterfront & sunset views • shared bath • kids ok • drug- & alcohol-free • $25-60

RESTAURANTS

Blue Heron 634 Campbell St **250/725-4266** • 7am-2am & 5pm-9pm • full bar • wheelchair access

Vancouver

INFO LINES & SERVICES

AA Gay/ Lesbian 604/434-3933, 604/434-2553 (TDD)

The Greater Vancouver Pride Line 604/684-6869 • 7pm-10pm • info & support

Vancouver Gay/ Lesbian Centre 1170 Bute St (btwn Davie & Pendrell Sts) **604/684-5307, 800/566-1170** • 9am-7pm • also 'Out on the Shelves' lgbt lending library • workshops • youth groups • legal clinic

ACCOMMODATIONS

The Albion Guest House 592 W 19th Ave (at Ash) **604/873-2287, 877/717-2287** • gay-friendly • full brkfst • hot tub • kids ok • smokefree • Can$85-155

Apricot Cat Guest House 628 Union St (4 blks E of Main) **604/215-9898** • gay-friendly • restored 1898 character home • kids/pets ok • women-owned/ run • $45-70

Aubusson House B&B 1470 Town Ho End, Gabriola Island **250/247-9952** • mostly women • luxurious • full brkfst • hot tub • gardens • smokefree • women-owned/ run • wheelchair access • $65

Barclay House B&B 1351 Barclay St (at Jervis) **604/605-1351, 800/971-1351** • gay/ straight • restored Victorian • full brkfst • gay-owned/ run • $79-155

Barefoot Moon Guesthouse 1620 Adanac St (at Commercial Dr) **604/251-9774** • lesbians/gay men • healthy full brkfst • smokefree • woman-owned/ run • $45-135

The Buchan Hotel 1906 Haro St (btwn Denman & Gilford) **604/685-5354, 800/668-6654** • gay-friendly • some shared baths • kids ok • Can$45-135

The Chelsea Cottage B&B 2143 W 46th Ave (at West Blvd) **604/266-2681** • gay-friendly • full brkfst • hot tub • smokefree • Can$95-150

Colibri B&B 1101 Thurlow St (at Pendrell) **604/689-5100, 877/312-6600** • lesbians/ gay men • deck • gay-owned/ run • Can$55-160

Columbia Cottage 205 W 14th Ave (at Manitoba) **604/874-5327** • gay-friendly • 1920s Tudor • full brkfst • smokefree • kids ok • Can$95-135 (winter rates lower)

Downtown Accommodations/ Furnished Suites 1415 W Georgia St (at Broughton) **604/454-8179, 877/454-8179** • gay-friendly • condos • swimming • Can$1,110-3,500/ month

Dufferin Hotel 900 Seymour St (at Smithe) **604/683-4251, 877/683-5522** • gay/ straight • food served • kids ok • $70-100 • also 3 bars • mostly men • karaoke • live shows

▲ **Hawks Ave B&B** 734 Hawks Ave **604/253-0989, 604/728-9441** • women only • townhouse • full brkfst • smokefree • nr downtown • $85-95

Heather Cottage 5425 Trafalgar St (btwn 38th & 39th) **604/261-1442** • gay-friendly • full brkfst • hot tub • Can$85-135

Hotel Dakota/ Comfort Inn 654 Nelson St (at Granville) **604/605-4333, 888/605-5333** • gay-friendly • hip boutique-style hotel in the heart of entertainment district • also restaurant & bar • gay-owned/ run • Can$69-169 • ask for IGLTA Pride rate (10% off)

The Johnson Heritage House B&B 2278 W 34th Ave (at Vine) **604/266-4175** • gay-friendly • full brkfst • smokefree • Can$75-180

Vancouver • British Columbia

The Langtry 968 Nicola, Ste 1 **604/687-7798** • gay/straight • b&b apts in West End • full brkfst • smokefree • gay-owned/run • Can$129-195

Les n' Bo's Escape for Womyn **604/886-4227** • women only • cottage rental • 40-min ferry ride from Vancouver • sauna • steps to beach • kids/pets ok • $90

The Manor Guest House 345 W 13th Ave (at Alberta) **604/876-8494** • gay-friendly • full brkfst • hot tub • some shared baths • also apt available • smokefree • $65-130

Nelson House B&B 977 Broughton St (btwn Nelson & Barclay) **604/684-9793** • lesbians/gay men • Edwardian mansion • full brkfst • jacuzzi in suite • sundeck • gay-owned/run • Can$58-178

'O Canada' House 1114 Barclay St (at Thurlow) **604/688-0555, 877/688-1114** • gay/straight • restored 1897 Victorian home • full brkfst • gay-owned/run • Can$150-225

Penny Farthing Inn 2855 W 6th Ave (at MacDonald) **604/739-9002** • gay-friendly • 1912 heritage house in Kitsilano • full brkfst • smokefree • Can$95-170

Penny's 810 Commercial Dr (at Venables) **604/254-2229** • gay-friendly • antique filled b&b • kitchens • smokefree • kids/pets ok • $50-65

Pillow & Porridge Guest Suites 2859 Manitoba St (btwn 12th & 13th Aves) **604/879-8977** • gay-friendly • apts w/ private entrances • kitchens • fireplaces • kids ok • wheelchair access • women-owned/run • Can$85-270

River Run Cottages 4551 River Rd W, Ladner **604/946-7778** • gay-friendly • on the Fraser River • full brkfst • wheelchair access • Can$120-210

Royal Hotel 1025 Granville St **604/685-5335, 877/685-5337** • gay/straight • also 'Royal Pub' bar • gay-owned/run • Can$59-139

Rural Roots B&B 4939 Ross Rd, Mt Lehman **604/856-2380** • lesbians/gay men • 1 hr from Vancouver • full brkfst • nudity ok at hot tub • smokefree • wheelchair access • gay-owned/run • $65-95

Sunshine Hills B&B 11200 Bond Blvd, North Delta **604/596-6496** • gay-friendly • full brkfst • shared bath • smokefree • Can$60-70

Treehouse B&B 2490 W 49th Ave (btwn Larch & Balsam) **604/266-2962** • gay-friendly • full brkfst • jacuzzi • Can$105-175

Hawks Avenue
Bed & Breakfast for Women

734 HAWKS AVENUE, VANCOUVER, BC,
CANADA V6A 3J3 (604) 253-0989 / CEL 728-9441

Heritage townhouse, quiet, comfortable accommodation
10 min. to downtown, theatres, shops & restaurants,
Gastown, Chinatown, delicious breakfast, street parking,
close to public transportation.

Reasonable Seasonal Rates. Non-smokers preferred

For reservations and more information

please call Louise
(604) 253-0989 / cel 728-9441
No credit cards accepted

British Columbia • CANADA

The West End Guest House 1362 Haro St (at Broughton) **604/681–2889** • gay/ straight • 1906 historic Victorian • full brkfst • gay-owned/ run • $105-235

BARS

The Fountainhead Pub 1025 Davie St **604/687-2222** • 11am-midnight, till 1am Fri-Sat • mostly gay men • neighborhood bar • patio

Global Beat 1249 Howe St **604/689-2444** • 4pm-2am • lesbian/ gay men • restaurant & lounge • beer/ wine • gay-owned/ run

The Lotus Hotel 455 Abbott St **604/685-7777** • 3 bars • 'Lotus Sound Lounge' • gay/straight dancing/DJ • young crowd • clsd Sun • 'Milk' • lesbians/ gay men • lounge • drag shows • live music • DJs • 'Honey' • lesbians/ gay men • dancing/DJ • light food served • women's night 8pm Sat at Milk & Honey • cover charge

The Oasis 1240 Thurlow **604/685-1724** • 3:30pm-Midnight, till 1am Th-Sat • mostly gay men • martini bar • piano bar • food served

The Royal Pub 1025 Granville St (at 'Royal Hotel') **604/685-5335** • noon-midnight • mostly gay men • neighborhood bar • drag shows Mon • gay bingo Tue • popular Fri happy hour

Vancouver

WHERE THE GIRLS ARE: In the West End, between Stanley Park and Gastown, or exploring the beautiful scenery elsewhere.

ENTERTAINMENT: Wreck Beach (great gay beach).

LGBT PRIDE: August. 604/687-0955.

ANNUAL EVENTS: January - New Year's Day Polar Bear Swim.
May - Vancouver International Marathon 604/872-2928.
June - Dragon Boat Festival 604/688-2382.
Du Maurier Jazz Festival Vancouver 604/872-5200.
Stonewall Festival in the Park 604/684-6869.
July - Folk Music Festival 604/602-9798.
September/October - International Film Festival 604/685-0260, web: www.viff.org.
November - Vancouver Lesbian Week 604/669-9110.

CITY INFO: 604/683-2000, web: www.tourism-vancouver.org. Vancouver Travel Info Center 604/683-2000.

ATTRACTIONS: Capilano Suspension Bridge.
Chinatown.
Gastown.
Science World 604/443-7440.
Stanley Park.
Van Dusen Botanical Gardens 604/878-9274.

BEST VIEW: Biking in Stanley Park, or on a ferry between peninsulas and islands. Atop one of the surrounding mountains.

WEATHER: It's cold and wet in the winter (32-45°F), but it's absolutely gorgeous in the summer (52-75°F)!

TRANSIT: Yellow Cab 604/681-1111.
Vancouver Airporter 604/946-8866.
BC Transit 604/521-0400.
A Visitors' Map of all bus lines is available through the tourist office.

Vancouver • British Columbia

Reply **Forward** **Delete**

Date: Mon, Dec 17, 2001 15:18:21
From: Girl-on-the-Go
To: Editor@Damron.com
Subject: Vancouver

> Just three hours north of Seattle is Vancouver, one of the most beautiful cities in the world. Much of its charm and attraction lie in natural scenery and outdoor activities. Great skiing is close by, and snow bunnies might want to schedule their trip to Vancouver around **Altitude,** Whistler's annual LGBT ski week.

> Be sure to visit Stanley Park, the largest city park in North America. There you can see the Aquarium, the Zoo, and famous Native American totem poles. Also worth a visit is the historic Gastown district: a lively area of boutiques, antique shops, and a vast array of restaurants. Once you've seen these sites, it's time to appreciate the beauty of the women of Vancouver. And, like everything in Vancouver, they are beautiful.

> Dyke dancing machines should check out the women's nights at the city's many mixed bars. On Fridays there's **Flygirl** at 7 Alexander, and the place to be on Saturdays is **Milk & Honey** at the Lotus. If you love a good laugh, you should check out one of the **Laff Riot Girls'** weekly shows.

> For bookstores, try **Women in Print** or the famous LGBT bookstore, **Little Sister's.** At either one, you can pick up a copy of **Xtra! West,** British Columbia's splashy LGBT paper. And don't forget to check out **Womyn's Ware** for all your erotica needs.

> Vegetarians will fare well at **Naam** or **Dish,** the only vegetarian fast-food place we know of. Vancouver has tons of lesbian-friendly services, so inquire at the **Vancouver Gay/Lesbian Centre** to find the perfect activity. If you're plugged in, log on to **www.bcgrrls.com** to discover one-off parties and other events.

British Columbia • CANADA

Nightclubs

Chameleon Lounge 801 W Georgia **604/669-0806** • 9pm-close • gay/ straight • dancing/DJ • live shows • more gay Sun

Flygirl 7 Alexander St (at 'Club 7') **604/688-9378 x 2154** • 9pm-2am Fri • mostly women • dancing/DJ • cover charge • call hotline for other events

Moulin Rouge 860 Denman (btwn Haro & Robson) **604/669-9933** • 8pm-2am, till midnight Sun • gay Wed only • cover charge

Ms T's Cabaret 339 W Pender St **604/682-8096** • 8pm-2am • lesbians/ gay men • dancing/DJ • transgender-friendly • karaoke

The Odyssey 1251 Howe St (at Davie) **604/689-5256** • 9pm-2am • popular • mostly gay men • dancing/DJ • drag shows Wed • young crowd

Sublime 816 Granville • 1am-6am Fri-Sat

Cafes

Delany's 1105 Denman St **604/662-3344** • 6am-11pm • coffee shop

Melriches Coffeehoue 1244 Davie St **604/689-5282** • 7am-11pm

Moonbeans 1262 Davie **604/632-0032** • 7am-11pm, till midnight Fri-Sat • popular • lesbians/ gay men • patio

Restaurants

Cafe S'il Vous Plaît 500 Robson St (at Richards) **604/688-7216** • lunch & dinner till 9pm, till 11pm Sat, clsd Sun

Chianti's 1850 W 4th St (at Burrard) **604/738-8411** • lunch & dinner

Cincin 1154 Robson (off Bute) **604/688-7338** • lunch & dinner only wknds • Italian/ Mediterranean • full bar

Delilah's 1789 Comox St (at Denman) **604/687-3424** • 5:30pm-11pm • some veggie • full bar • wheelchair access • $21-33

The Dish 1068 Davie St **604/689-0208** • 7am-9pm, 9am-9pm Sun • lowfat vegetarian fast food • gay-owned/ run

Elbow Room Café 560 Davie St (at Seymour) **604/685-3628** • 8am-4pm, till 5pm wknds • great brkfst

Hamburger Mary's 1202 Davie St (at Bute) **604/687-1293** • 7am-3am, till 4am Fri-Sat, till 2pm Sun • some veggie • full bar

Henry's Landing 2607 Ware St (at S Fraser Wy) **604/854-3679** • lunch & dinner • full bar

India Gate 616 Robson St (at Granville) **604/684-4617** • lunch & dinner

Luxy Bistro 1235 Davie St (btwn Bute & Jervis) **604/669-5899** • 11am-10pm, till 11pm wknds • some veggie • full bar • wheelchair access • $9-17

Mario's 33555 S Fraser Wy (at Kent Ave) **604/852-6919** • lunch & dinner • Italian

Martini's 151 W Broadway (btwn Cambie & Main) **604/873-0021** • 11am-2am, 3pm-3am Sat, till 1am Sun • great pizza • full bar • $7-14

Milestone's 1145 Robson St (at Thurlow) **604/682-4477** • lunch & dinner • full bar • $4-12

Naam 2724 W 4th St (at MacDonald) **604/738-7151, 604/738-7180** • 24hrs • vegetarian • wheelchair access • $3-10

Riley Cafe 1661 Granville St (at Beech) **604/684-3666** • 11:30am-10pm, from 10:30am wknds • BBQ • some veggie • full bar • wheelchair access • $5-12

Entertainment & Recreation

Laff Riot Girls • stand-up comedienne group • 9pm Th at Gastown Comedy Store • 19 Water St, 604/682-1727 • doors at 7:30pm • also restaurant • also 9pm Sat at Zesty's Restaurant • 920 Commercial Dr, 604/255-0470 • doors at 7pm • cover charge • part of profits goes to community groups

Lotus Land Tours 1251 Cardero St, Ste 2005 **604/684-4922, 800/528-3531** • day paddle trips • whale-watching trips • no experience necessary (price includes pick-up & meal)

Rockwood Adventures 1330 Fulton Ave, West Vancouver **604/926-7705** • rain forest walks for all levels w/ free hotel pick-up

Sunset Beach right in the West End

Bookstores

Little Sister's 1238 Davie St (btwn Bute & Jervis) **604/669-1753, 800/567-1662 (IN CANADA ONLY)** • 10am-11pm • popular • lgbt • wheelchair access • please support this great store in their on-going legal battle against Canadian Customs by buying a book today

Spartacus Books 311 W Hastings (at Hamilton) **604/688-6138** • 10am-8:30pm, 11am-7pm Sat, noon-7pm Sun • progressive

Women in Print 3566 W 4th Ave (at Dunbar/ Collingwood) **604/732-4128** • 10am-6pm, noon-5pm Sun • women's • wheelchair access • women-owned/ run

Retail Shops

Mack's Leathers 1043 Granville (at Nelson) **604/688-6225** • 11am-7pm, till 8pm Th-Fri • also body piercing

Victoria • British Columbia

Next Body Piercing 1068 Granville St (at Nelson) 604/684-6398 • noon-6pm • also tattooing

State of Mind 1100 Davie St (at Thurlow) 604/682-7116 • 9am-8pm • designer queer clothes

PUBLICATIONS

Rainbow Choices Directory 416/762-1320, 888/241-3569 (CANADA ONLY) • lgbt entertainment & business directory for Canada

Xtra! West 604/684-9696 • lgbt newspaper

SPIRITUAL GROUPS

Christ Alive! MCC 1155 Thurlow 604/739-7959 • 7:15pm Sun

Dignity/ Integrity 604/432-1230 • call for info

EROTICA

Love's Touch 1069 Davie St 604/681-7024

Womyn's Ware 896 Commercial Dr (at Denables, in East End) 604/254-2543, 888/WYM-WARE (ORDERS ONLY) • noon-6pm, till 7pm Th-Fri, till 5pm Sun • toys • fetishwear • lesbian-owned/ run

Vernon

INFO LINES & SERVICES

NOGLO (North Okanagan Gay/ Lesbian Org) 250/542-4838 • social/ support group

ACCOMMODATIONS

Rainbow's End 8282 Jackpine Rd 250/542-4842 • lesbians/ gay men • full brkfst • hot tub • some shared baths • pets ok • wheelchair access • gay-owned/ run • $35-45

Victoria

INFO LINES & SERVICES

Gay/ Lesbian AA 250/383-7744 • 8pm Sun & Tue • call for locations

LGB Alliance 250/472-4393 • student group

Women's Creative Network 250/382-7768 • women's private social club • mtgs • dances • events • visitors most welcome • also 'G-spot' club • call for hrs

ACCOMMODATIONS

Arts and Antiques B&B 58 Government St (at Battery) 250/386-0410, 877/438-7799 • gay/ straight • Victorian home • full brkfst • 1 blk to ocean & park • smokefree • gay-owned/ run • Can$95-125

The Back Hills Guest House for Women 4470 Leefield Rd 250/478-9648 • women only • 30 mins from Victoria in the Metchosin Hills • full brkfst • smokefree • girls 10+ ok • lesbian-owned/ run • Can$50-60

The Fairmont Empress 721 Government St 250/384-8111, 800/441-1414 • gay-friendly • Victoria landmark • 4 restaurants & lounges • swimming • fitness center • full-service spa • famous afternoon tea • kids/ small pets ok • wheelchair access • $209+

Garden Oaks PO Box 5713 Sta B V8R 6S8 250/388-7791, 250/812-3891 • gay/ straight • make your own full brkfst • smokefree • gay-owned/ run • $85-328

Howard Johnson Hotel & Suites Victoria 4670 Elk Lake Dr 250/704-4656, 866/300-4656 • gay-friendly • swimming • hot tub • kids ok • restaurant & lounge • wheelchair access • Can$89-149

Ifanwen B&B 44 Simcoe St 250/384-3717 • lesbians/ gay men • full brkfst • gardens • sundeck • gay-owned/ run • $55-70

Oak Bay Guest House 1052 Newport Ave 250/598-3812, 800/575-3812 • gay-friendly • 1912 Tudor-style house • full brkfst • nr beaches • kids 10+ ok • Can$75-180

BARS

BJ's Lounge 642 Johnson (enter on Broad St) 250/388-0505 • noon-2am, till midnight Sun • lesbians/ gay men • dancing/DJ • karaoke • live shows • videos • wheelchair access

NIGHTCLUBS

G Spot 250/382-7768 • women's private social club • visitors most welcome • call for hrs & location

Hush 1325 Government St (in basement) 250/385-0566 • 9pm-2am, till midnight Sun, clsd Mon-Tue • gay/ straight • dancing/DJ • drag shows Sun

RESTAURANTS

Rosie's Diner 615 Johnson St 250/381-2277 • 8am-8pm • 50's & 60's music and videos • wheelchair access • gay-owned/ run

Santiago's Cafe 660 Oswego St 250/388-7376 • 10am-10pm, from 7am summers • tapas bar • patio • gay-owned/ run

BOOKSTORES

Bleeding Rose Books & Multimedia 102-764 Yates St (on alley btwn Yates & Johnson) 250/385-3099 • 10am-7pm, clsd Sun • new & used books • video rentals • community bulletin board • pride gifts • lesbian-owned/ run

British Columbia/ Manitoba • CANADA

Bolen Books 1644 Hillside Ave #111 (in shopping ctr) **250/595-4232** • 8:30am-10pm • lgbt section

Retail Shops

Side Show 560 Johnson St, #43 (in Market Square) USA **250/920-7469** • 11am-6pm, noon-5pm Sun • fetish wear

Publications

Lavender Rhinoceros **250/385-3099** • Victoria's lgbt magazine

National Publications

Rainbow RV vice 627–340 Island Hwy **250/514-1002** • RV club for the gay camping enthusiast

Erotica

Kiss & Tell 531 Herald St **250/380-6995** • gay-owned/ run

Whistler

Accommodations

The AnneRose Inn 3016 St Anton Way **604/938-9868** • gay/ straight • Japanese-themed b&b • gourmet full brkfst • hot tub • kids 10+ ok • pets ok in summer • smokefree • gay-owned/ run • Can$110-225

Coast Whistler Hotel 4005 Blackcomb Wy **604/932-2522, 800/663-5644** • gay-friendly • full-service resort hotel • full bar & restaurant • hot tub • swimming • wheelchair access • $105-199

Cafes

Death By Chocolate at base of the Gondola **604/938-1323** • fancy desserts like 'Joseph's Technicolour Dreamcake'

Restaurants

Boston Pizza 2011 Innsbruck Dr **604/932-7070** • 11am-11pm, till midnight wknds • full bar

La Rua 4557 Blackcomb Blvd **604/932-5011** • 6pm-close • Italian/ cont'l

Monks Grill base of Blackcomb **604/932-9677** • 11:30am-10pm • grill menu • full bar

MANITOBA

Brandon

Info Lines & Services

GLOBE (Gays/ Lesbians of Brandon & Elsewhere) **204/727-4297** • 7pm-9pm 3rd Fri • socials & coffeehouses

LGBT Youth Group 731B Princess Ave **204/727-0417** • for youth under 25

Winnipeg

Info Lines & Services

Rainbow Resource Centre 1-222 Osborne St S **204/284-5208, 888/399-0005** • 1pm-4:30pm Wed-Fri, 7:30pm-10pm Mon-Fri, clsd Sun • also infoline • many social/ support groups

Women's Centre at U of Winnipeg **204/786-9788** • drop-in resource center during school year • lending library

Women's Resource Centre 1088 Pembina Hwy **204/477-1123** • 9am-noon, 1pm-4pm Mon-Fri, clsd wknds

Accommodations

Masson's B&B 181 Masson St **204/237-9230** • gay/ straight • full brkfst • hot tub • shared baths • gay-owned/ run • $40-55

Winged Ox Guest House 82 Spence St **204/783-7408** • lesbians/ gay men • full brkfst • smokefree • shared baths • gay-owned/ run • Can$35-50

Bars

Club 200 190 Garry St (at St Mary Ave) **204/943-6045** • 4pm-2am, till 10pm Sun • lesbians/ gay men • dancing/DJ • live shows • wheelchair access • dinner served • some veggie • $7-11

Nightclubs

Gio's 272 Sherbrook St (nr Portage) **204/786-1236** • 8pm-2am, 7pm-1am Th, till 3am Fri-Sat, clsd Sun • lesbians/ gay men • dancing/DJ • live shows • private club

Happenings 274 Sherbrook St (upstairs) **204/774-3576** • 9pm-2am, till 4am Sat, clsd Sun • lesbians/ gay men • dancing/DJ • Karaoke Mon • live shows • private club

Ms Purdy's Women's Club 226 Main St **204/989-2344** • 8pm-2am, till midnight Tue-Th, clsd Sun-Mon • women only • men welcome Fri-Sat • dancing/DJ • live shows • private club • wheelchair access • lesbian-owned/ run

Restaurants

Step'N Out 283 Bannatyne Ave (at King St) **204/956-7837** • lunch & dinner, clsd Sun • fresh dynamic entrees • wheelchair access

Times Change Blues Cafe 234 Main **204/957-0982** • 8pm-2am • some veggie • live shows • under $6

Village Grill & Eatery 102 Sherbrook St **204/783-7011** • 9am-9pm, till 11pm Fri-Sat • full bar

Stevenville • Newfoundland

BOOKSTORES

Dominion News 262 Portage Ave **204/942-6563** • 8am-9pm • some gay periodicals

McNally Robinson 1120 Grant Ave #4000 (in the mall) **204/453-2644** • 9am-10pm, till 11pm Fri, noon-6pm Sun • some gay titles • wheelchair access

PUBLICATIONS

Perceptions **306/244-1930** • covers the Canadian prairies

Swerve **204/942-4599** • lgbt newspaper

SPIRITUAL GROUPS

Dignity **204/287-8583** • 7:30pm 2nd Fri • call for location

EROTICA

Discreet Boutique 340 Donald (at Ellice) **204/947-1307** • also 'Discreet Video' next door

NEW BRUNSWICK

Fredericton

ACCOMMODATIONS

Hatfield Heritage Inn 370 Main St (at Queen), Hartland **506/375-8000, 877/637-8200** • gay/straight • 1870s antique-filled home • kids ok • gay-owned/run • Can$65-125

NIGHTCLUBS

G Spot 377 King St, 3rd flr (above 'Corleone Pizza') **506/455-7768** • 8pm-2am, clsd Mon-Tue • lesbians/gay men • dancing/DJ

Moncton

NIGHTCLUBS

Triangles 234 St George St (at Archibald) **506/857-8779** • 7pm-2am, from 8pm wknds, clsd Mon • lesbians/gay men • dancing/DJ • karaoke Th

Saint John

ACCOMMODATIONS

Mahogany Manor 220 Germain St, E2L 2G4 **506/636-8000, 800/796-7755** • gay/straight • full brkfst • smokefree • kids ok • wheelchair access • gay-owned/run • Can$85-95

NIGHTCLUBS

Bogarts 9 Sydney St (off King Sq) **506/652-2004** • 8pm-2am, clsd Mon-Tue • lesbians/gay men • dancing/DJ

St Leonard

ACCOMMODATIONS

L'Auberge du Haut St-Jean 760 Rue Principale **506/423-9229, 888/423-9229** • gay/straight • large 1904 home in Acadian community • shared baths • kids ok • smokefree • gay-owned/run • Can$50-60

NEWFOUNDLAND

Corner Brook

INFO LINES & SERVICES

Corner Brook Women's Resource Centre **709/639-8522**

St John's

INFO LINES & SERVICES

Gay/Lesbian Info Line **709/753-4297** • 7pm-10pm Th

Women's Centre 83 Military Rd **709/753-0220** • 9:30am-5pm, clsd wknds

ACCOMMODATIONS

Banberry House 116 Military Rd (at Rawlins Cross) **709/579-8006, 877/579-8226** • gay/straight • full brkfst • kids/small pets ok • smokefree • gay-owned/run • $69-99

Bluestone Inn 34 Queen's Rd (at Water St) **709/754-7544, 877/754-9876** • gay-friendly • full brkfst • jacuzzi • gay-owned/run • Can$79-149

BARS

Schroders Piano Bar 10 Bates Hill (off Queens Rd) **709/753-0807** • 4:30pm-1am, till 2am Fri-Sat, till midnight Sun • gay-friendly • also 'Zapata's' restaurant downstairs • Mexican • some veggie

NIGHTCLUBS

Zone 216 216 Water St **709/754-2492** • 9pm-2am, till 4:30am Fri-Sat, clsd Sun-Wed • lesbians/gay men • dancing/DJ

BOOKSTORES

Bennington Gate Bookstore 8-10 Rowan St, Churchill Sq (lower level, Terrace on the Square) **709/576-6600** • 10am-6pm, till 9pm Th-Fri, noon-5pm Sun • lgbt section

Stevenville

INFO LINES & SERVICES

Bay St George Women's Centre 54 St Clare Ave **709/643-4444**

Nova Scotia

Annapolis Royal

ACCOMMODATIONS

King George Inn 902/532-5286, 888/799-5464 • lesbians/ gay men • full brkfst • jacuzzi • smokefree • seasonal • Can$89-299

Bear River

ACCOMMODATIONS

Lovett Lodge Inn 1820 Main St 902/467-3917, 800/565-0000 (CANADA ONLY) • seasonal • gay-friendly • full brkfst • swimming • smokefree • kids ok • gay-owned/ run • $40-66

Chéticamp

ACCOMMODATIONS

Seashell Housekeeping Units 125 Chéticamp Island Rd 902/224-1563, 902/224-3569 (SUMMER) • gay-friendly • housekeeping units on the ocean • seasonal • kids/ pets ok • smokefree • lesbian-owned/ run • Can$45-85

Guysborough

ACCOMMODATIONS

Barrens at Bay Coastal Cottages 6870 Hwy 16 (at Halfway Cove) 902/358-2157 • gay/ straight • jacuzzi • kids/pets ok • wheelchair access • gay-owned/ run • Can$175-210

Halifax

ACCOMMODATIONS

Bob's Guest House 2715 Windsor St (btwn North & Almond) 902/454-4374, 877/890-4060 • gay/ straight • full brkfst • hot tub • Can$75-150

Centretown Guest House 2016 Oxford St (at Quinpool Rd) 902/422-2380 • mostly gay men • hot tub • smokefree/ scentfree • some shared baths • French spoken • gay-owned/ run • Can$89-119

Forevergreen House B&B 18 Garden Rd (at Hwy 214), Belman 902/883-4445 • gay-friendly • full brkfst • smokefree • women-owned/ run • $55-75

Fresh Start B&B 2720 Gottingen St (at Black) 902/453-6616, 888/453-6616 • gay-friendly • full brkfst • some shared baths • kids/ pets ok • women-owned/ run • Can$60-100

The Old Fisher House B&B 204 Paddys Head Rd, RR 1, Indian Harbour 902/823-2228 • gay/ straight • shared baths • kids ok • lesbian-owned/ run • Can$75-95

BARS

The Eagle Pub & Eatery 1567 Grafton St 902/425-1889 • noon-2am, full menu till 5pm • lesbians/ gay men • food served • full menu till 5pm

Reflections Cabaret 5184 Sackville St (at Barrington) 902/422-2957 • 4pm-3:30am • lesbians/ gay men • dancing/DJ • live shows • wheelchair access

CAFES

The Daily Grind 5686 Spring Garden Rd (nr South Park) 902/429-6397 • 7am-10pm, from 8am wknds • also newsstand

RESTAURANTS

Le Bistro 1333 South Park (nr Spring Garden Rd) 902/423-8428 • 11:30am-10pm, till 11pm Fri-Sat • some veggie • full bar • wheelchair access • $7-16

Satisfaction Feast 1581 Grafton St (off Blower St) 902/422-3540 • 11am-9pm, from 4pm Sun • vegetarian • patio • $5-12

Soho 1582 Granville St (at Sackville) 902/423-3049 • 11:30am-10pm, clsd Sun • cont'l • $6-14

Sweet Basil 1866 Upper Water St (nr Duke) 902/425-2133 • 11:30am-10pm • full bar

ENTERTAINMENT & RECREATION

Queer News CKDU 97.5 FM 902/494-6479 • 12:05pm Fri

BOOKSTORES

Atlantic News 5560 Morris St (at Queen) 902/429-5468 • 8am-10pm • periodicals

Entitlement Book Sellers Lord Nelson Arcade (on Spring Garden Rd) 902/420-0565 • 9:30am-7:15pm, till 6pm Sat & Mon, from noon Sun

Frog Hollow Books 5640 Spring Garden Rd, 2nd flr (at Dresden Row) 902/429-3318 • 9:30am-6pm Mon-Wed, till 9pm Th-Fri, noon-5pm Sun

Schooner Used Books 5378 Inglis St (at Victoria Rd) 902/423-8419 • 9:30am-6pm, till 9pm Fri, till 5:30pm Sat, clsd Sun • large selection of women's titles

Smithbooks 5201 Duke St (in Scotia Sq) 902/423-6438 • 9:30am-6pm, till 9pm Th-Fri

Trident Booksellers & Cafe 1256 Hollis St (at Morris St) 902/423-7100 • 8:30am-5pm, from noon Sun

Grand Valley • Ontario

Retail Shops

Venus Envy 1598 Barrington St **902/422-0004** • 11am-6pm, till 8pm Wed-Fri, from 1pm Sun • 'a store for women and the people who love them' • books • sex toys • alternative health products

Publications

Wayves 902/889-2288

Spiritual Groups

Safe Harbour MCC 5500 Inglis St (church) **902/453-9249** • 7:30pm Sun

Yarmouth

Accommodations

Charles C Richards House Historic B&B 17 Collins St **902/742-0042** • gay/ straight • brick mansion • full brkfst • some shared baths • gay-owned/ run • Can$115-160

Murray Manor B&B 225 Main St (at Forest St) **902/742-9625, 877/742-9629** • gay-friendly • heritage home w/ lovely gardens & greenhouse • full brkfst • shared baths • kids ok • one all-natural-fiber, environmentally friendly room available • $65-75

ONTARIO

Provincewide

Publications

fab 416/925-5221 • Ontario's gay scene magazine

Barrie

Accommodations

Babes in the Woods 1 Monica Ct, RR4, Coldwater **705/835-0278** • women only • b&b nr skiing • full brkfst • lesbian-owned/ run • Can$70

Belleville

Accommodations

Nightingale's Therapeutic Spa & Rehabilitation 305 Main St, Box 352, Bloomfield **613/393-5335** • mostly women • suite • full brkfst • hot tub • swimming • smokefree • lesbian-owned/ run • $Can95-125

Brighton

Accommodations

Apple Manor 96 Main St, Box 11 **613/475-0351** • gay-friendly • 150-year-old Victorian • full brkfst • shared baths • swimming • smokefree • $55-75

Butler Creek Country Inn 613/475-1248 • gay-friendly • full brkfst • kids ok • Can$70-90

Bookstores

Lighthouse Books 17 Prince Edward St **613/475-1269** • 9:30am-5:30pm, till 7pm Fri, clsd Sun (also clsd Mon in winter)

Cambridge

Accommodations

Blairview B&B 519/621-9335 • gay-friendly • award-winning antique filled home • full brkfst • woman-owned/ run • Can$90-120

Bars

Robin's Nest 26 Hobson St (in Farmers Bldg, Galt St entrance) **519/621-2688** • seasonal • mostly women • country/ western

Dutton

Accommodations

Victorian Court B&B 235 Main St **519/762-2244** • lesbians/ gay men • restored Victorian • smokefree • $60-90

Gananoque

Accommodations

Boathouse Country Inn & Heritage Boat Tours 17–19 Front St, 1000 Islands, Rockport **613/659-2348, 800/584-2592** • gay/ straight • full brkfst • smokefree • wheelchair access • $75-150

Rockport Village House Rental 11 Front St, 1000 Islands (at 1000 Islands Pkwy), Rockport **613/659-3845** • gay-friendly • riverside home • seasonal • smokefree • kids/ pets ok • women-owned/ run • Can$575-825/ week

Trinity House Inn 90 Stone St S, 1000 Islands **613/382-8383, 800/265-4871 (ON ONLY)** • gay-friendly • historic country inn • fine dining • smokefree • kids ok in suites • sailing charters • gay-owned/ run • Can$100-200

Grand Valley

Accommodations

Rainbow Ridge Hwy 9 (at Trafalgar Rd) **519/928-3262** • lesbians/ gay men • trailers & tents • swimming

Ontario • CANADA

Guelph

INFO LINES & SERVICES
Out Line 519/836-4550 • volunteer hrs vary

ACCOMMODATIONS
Dr WF Savage House B&B 45 Colborne St, Elora 519/846-5325 • lesbians/ gay men • full brkfst • wheelchair access • gay-owned/ run • Can$60-90

BOOKSTORES
Bookshelf Cafe 41 Quebec St 519/821-3311 • 9am-10pm, 10:30am-9pm Sun (bar noon-1am) • also cinema & restaurant • some veggie • $5-10

Hamilton

ACCOMMODATIONS
The Cedars Tent & Trailer Park 1039 5th Concession W Rd, Waterdown 905/659-3655 • lesbians/gay men • private campground • swimming • also bar • dancing/DJ • wknd restaurant • some veggie

BARS
Bombay Club 121 Hughson St N (at Canon) 905/540-8008 • noon-2am • lesbians/ gay men • neighborhood bar • dancing/DJ • karaoke • also 'Frathouse' dance club from 10:30pm Th-Sat

Windsor Bar & Grill 31 John St N (at King William) 905/308-9939 • 11am-2am • lesbians/gay men • dancing/DJ • live shows

BOOKSTORES
Gomorrah's 233 Locke St S (nr Charlton) 905/526-1074, 888/338-8278 • 11am-6pm, till 8pm Fri, noon-4pm Sun • books • magazines • videos • pride gifts • jewelry • toys

Kingston

INFO LINES & SERVICES
LGBT Phoneline & Directory 613/531-8981, 877/9-KLGBTA (IN ON ONLY) • 7pm-9pm, clsd Fri-Sun

ACCOMMODATIONS
Westend B&B 872 Winchester Ln (btwn Princess & Gardiner's Rd) 613/389-7652, 866/866-0466 • mostly gay men • full brkfst • gay-owned/ run • Can$45-85

NIGHTCLUBS
Club 477 477 Princess St (at University) 613/547-2923 • 11am-2am, till 9am Fri-Sat • popular • lesbians/gay men • dancing/DJ • alternative • karaoke Tue

Kitchener

NIGHTCLUBS
Club Renaissance 24 Charles St W 519/570-2406, 877/635-2352 • 9pm-3am, clsd Mon-Tue • lesbians/gay men • dancing/DJ • food served • live shows

London

INFO LINES & SERVICES
AA Gay/ Lesbian 649 Colborne (at 'Halo Club') 519/433-3762 • 7pm Mon & Wed • Al-Anon 7pm Th

Halo Club (Gay/ Lesbian Community Centre) 649 Colborne St 519/433-3762 • also monthly newsletter

BARS
The Apartment 189 Dundas St (at Colbourne St) 519/679-1255 • 8:30am-2am, from 2pm Sat • gay/ straight • dancing/DJ • karaoke • live shows • wheelchair access

NIGHTCLUBS
Club H2O 194 Dundas St (enter on Queens) 519/850-9922 • 5pm-close Wed-Sun • lesbians/gay men • dancing/ DJ • live shows

RESTAURANTS
Blackfriars Cafe 46 Blackfriars (2 blks S of Oxford) 519/667-4930 • lunch & dinner, Sun brunch • popular • lesbians/gay men • plenty veggie • full bar • $6-30

The Green Tomato 172 King St (at Richmond) 519/660-1170 • 11am-11pm, till 10pm Sun • full bar

Marla Jane's 460 King St (at Maitland) 519/858-8669 • lunch & dinner, dinner only wknds • French/ Cajun cuisine • gay-owned/ run

Murano 394 Waterloo St (at Dundas) 519/434-7565 • dinner only, clsd Sun • northern Italian • gay-owned/ run

Veranda 546 Dundas St (at William St) 519/434-6790 • lunch & dinner, clsd Sun-Mon • gay-owned/ run

BOOKSTORES
Mystic Book Shop 612 Dundas St (at Adelaide) 519/673-5440 • 11am-6pm, clsd Sun • spiritual

SPIRITUAL GROUPS
Holy Fellowship MCC 717 Dundas St (at Cross-Cultural Learning Center) 519/645-0744 • 10:30am Sun

Ottawa • Ontario

Maberly

ACCOMMODATIONS

Stonegarden Retreat 2236 Old Brooke Rd USA **613/268-2828** • gay-friendly • peaceful country location • full brkfst • jacuzzi • kids ok • lesbian-owned • Can$100-125

Maynooth

ACCOMMODATIONS

Wildewood Guesthouse 613/338-3134 • lesbians/ gay men • brkfst & dinner included • hot tub • smokefree • wheelchair access • gay-owned/ run • Can$150+

Meaford

ACCOMMODATIONS

The Cedars on Georgian Bay (Lake Huron) **519/538-3974** • women only • full brkfst • hot tub • nr skiing & beaches • lesbian-owned/ run • Can$68-75

Niagara Falls

see also Niagara Falls & Buffalo, New York, USA

ACCOMMODATIONS

Acute B&B 127 Mary St (at Hwy 55/ Mississauga St), Niagara-on-the-Lake **905/468-1328, 888/208-2340** • gay-friendly • 1843 home • full brkfst • garden • courtesy bicycles • smokefree • $80

Bampfield Hall B&B 4761 Zimmerman Ave **905/352-8522, 877/353-8522** • gay-friendly • historic Gothic home nr Niagara Falls • full brkfst • kids ok • gay-owned/ run •Can$65-150

Fairbanks House 4965 River Rd **905/371-3716** • gay/ straight • 1877 restored Victorian • full brkfst • fireplaces • kids ok • smokefree • lesbian-owned/ run • $85-160

Niagara Inn B&B 4300 Simcoe St (at River Rd) **905/353-8522, 877/353-8522** • gay-friendly • restored Victorian nr Niagara Falls • full brkfst • kids ok • gay-owned/ run • $50-105

Rivervine 15526 Niagara River Pkwy, Niagara-on-the-Lake **905/468-5550** • gay/ straight • B&B-private home • full brkfst • swimming • small pets ok • gay-owned • Can$105-130

The Saltbox 223 Gate St (at Queen St), Niagara-on-the-Lake **905/468-5423** • gay-friendly • full brkfst • charming 1820s downtown home • smokefree • shared baths • teens ok • Can$60

Niagara-on-the-Lake

ACCOMMODATIONS

The Pride of Niagara B&B 279 Nassau St, Box 485 (at Johnson) **905/468-8181, 877/586-1212** • gay/ straight • swimming • smokefree • gay-owned • Can$125+

North Bay

INFO LINES & SERVICES

LGBT North Bay Area 705/495-4545 • 7pm-9pm Mon • social/ support group • coffee night 7pm-10pm Tue at 'Jaeger Meisters' at 455 Main St East • newsletter

Oshawa

NIGHTCLUBS

Club 717 717 Wilson Rd S #7 **905/434-4297** • 9pm-1am Th, till 3am Fri-Sat, 7pm-midnight Sun, clsd Mon-Wed • mostly gay men • dancing • also referral service

Ottawa

see also Hull, Province of Québec

INFO LINES & SERVICES

237-XTRA 613/237-9872 • touch-tone lgbt info

Gayline/ Télégai 613/238-1717 • 7pm-10pm • bilingual helpline

Pink Triangle Services 71 Bank St (above McD's) **613/563-4818** • 1pm-5pm Mon & Wed • many groups & services

Women's Place 755 Somerset St W **613/231-5144** • 9am-4pm, clsd wknds • drop-in center

ACCOMMODATIONS

Ambiance B&B 330 Nepean St **613/563-0421** • gay-friendly • full brkfst • some shared baths • kids ok • $65-90

Inn on Somerset 282 Somerset St W (at Elgin) **613/236-9309, 800/658-3564** • gay-friendly • Victorian • full brkfst • some shared baths • kids ok • smokefree • Can$70-120

BARS

Centretown Pub 340 Somerset St W (at Bank) **613/594-0233** • 2pm-2am • lesbians/ gay men • dancing/DJ • videos • leather bar upstairs • 'Silhouette Lounge' piano bar downstairs Th-Sat

Club Polo Pub 65 Bank St (2nd floor, at Sparks) **613/235-5995** • 11am-2am • mostly gay men • neighborhood bar • dancing/DJ • food served • free Internet access • free pool • rooftop patio in summer

Ontario • CANADA

The Lookout 41 York, 2nd flr **613/789-1624**
• noon-2am • lesbians/ gay men • food served
• balcony • wheelchair access

Market Station Bar & Bistro 15 George St
(downstairs) **613/562-3540** • 3pm-2am, from
2pm Wed-Fri, from noon wknds • gay/ straight
• dancing/DJ • patio • also 'The Well' Th-Sat
downstairs

VIP 313-315 Bank St **613/594-8287** • 11am-
2am • lesbians/ gay men • neighborhood bar

Nightclubs

Circus 21 Jacques-Cartier **613/224-4056** •
Mon only • mostly gay men • dancing/DJ •
patio

Icon 366 Lisgar St (at Bank) **613/235-4005** •
8pm-3am, clsd Mon-Tue • popular • lesbians/
gay men • martini lounge • dancing/DJ from
4pm Wed-Fri • karaoke • drag shows • videos

Zaphod Beeblebrox 27 York **613/562-1010**
• 4pm-2am • gay/ straight • neighborhood bar
• dancing/DJ • live music

Cafes

AE Micro Internet Cafe 288 Bank St (at
Somerset) **613/230-9000** • 9:30am-11pm, till
midnight Wed-Sat, 11am-10pm wknds • light
menu

Restaurants

Alfonsetti's 5830 Hazeldern, Stittsville
613/831-3008 • noon-11pm, from 5pm Sat,
clsd Sun • Italian • plenty veggie • $12-22

Fairouz 343 Somerset St W (btwn Bank &
O'Connor) **613/233-1536** • lunch & dinner,
dinner only wknds • Lebanese

Manfred's 2280 Carling Ave **613/829-5715** •
lunch & dinner, dinner only on wknds • cont'l •
some veggie • full bar • $10-16

Rock Bottom Grill 307 Dalhousie St (at
Clarence) **613/562-1414** • lunch Tue-Fri,
dinner nightly, Sun brunch, clsd Mon •
lesbians/ gay men

Bookstores

After Stonewall 370 Bank St (nr Gilmour)
613/567-2221 • 10am-6pm, till 9pm Fri, till
5:30pm Sat, noon-5pm Sun • lgbt

Mags & Fags 254 Elgin St (btwn Somerset
& Cooper) **613/233-9651** • till 10pm • gay
magazines

mother tongue books/ femmes de parole
1067 Bank St (at Sunnyside Ave)
613/730-2346, 800/366-0514 (Canada only) •
10am-6pm, till 8pm Fri (clsd Sun summer)

Octopus Books 116 3rd Ave (at Bank)
613/233-2589 • 10am-6pm, noon-5pm Sun •
progressive

Retail Shops

One in Ten 216 Bank St (at Nepean) **613/
563-0110, 888/563-0110** • noon-midnight, till
9pm wknds • pride gifts • T-shirts • videos • toys

Venus Envy 110 Parent Ave **613/789-4646** •
11am-6pm, till 8pm Wed-Fri, from 1pm Sun •
'a store for women and the people who love
them' • books • sex toys • alternative health
products

Wilde's 367 Bank St **613/234-5512** • noon-
8pm, till 5pm Sun • pride items, toys, videos &
more • wheelchair access

Publications

Capital Xtra! **613/237-7133** • lgbt newspaper

Rainbow Choices Directory **416/762-1320,
888/241-3569 (Canada only)** • lgbt
entertainment & business directory for Canada

Spiritual Groups

Dignity Ottawa Dignité 386 Bank St
613/746-7279

Peterborough

Info Lines & Services

Rainbow **705/876-1845, 877/554-4210
(Canada only)** • phoneline from 10pm • many
social events

Erotica

Forbidden Pleasures 91 George St N
705/742-3800

Picton

Accommodations

Hadden-Holme B&B 79 W Mary St **613/
476-7555** • gay-friendly • 1883 Victorian • full
brkfst • smokefree • gay-owned/ run • Can$75-85

Puslinch

Accommodations

Cedarbrook Farm B&B 812 8th Conc Rd W,
RR 3 **905/659-1566** • gay/ straight • full brkfst
• smokefree • lesbian-owned/ run • $75-115

Simcoe

Accommodations

The Point Tent & Trailer Resort 918
Charlotteville Rd #2, RR 1, Vittoria
519/426-7275 • mostly gay men • nudity
permitted • swimming • leather • 'tent &
trailer resort' on 50 acres • Can$15-50

Toronto • Ontario

Stratford

ACCOMMODATIONS

A Hundred Church Street 100 Church St **519/272-8845** • gay/ straight • full brkfst • hot tub • some shared baths • smokefree • kids 10+ ok • gay-owned/ run • Can$70-98

Burnside Guest Home 139 William St **519/271-7076** • gay-friendly • on Lake Victoria • full brkfst • jacuzzi • smokefree • gay-owned/ run • $50-85

The Maples of Stratford 220 Church St **519/273-0810** • gay-friendly • smokefree • some shared baths • woman-owned • $55-95

RESTAURANTS

Down the Street 30 Ontario St **519/273-5886** • 11am-midnight, bar till 2am • int'l • full bar • $15-20

Old English Parlour 101 Wellington St (at St Patrick) **519/271-2772** • 11:30am-midnight, Sun-Mon till 8pm • some veggie • wheelchair access • $10-16

Sudbury

ACCOMMODATIONS

Rainbow Guest House 43 Lorne St **705/688-0561** • lesbians/ gay men • some shared baths • gay-owned/ run • Can$30-40

Thunder Bay

INFO LINES & SERVICES

Northern Women's Centre 184 Camelot St (at Water) **807/345-7802** • 9:30am-5pm, clsd Fri-Sun

ACCOMMODATIONS

Pine Brook Lodge B&B **807/683-6114** • gay-friendly • full brkfst • plenty veggie • some shared baths • jacuzzi • sauna • kids/ pets ok • wheelchair access • $55-150

BOOKSTORES

Northern Women's Bookstore/ Choices Cafe 65 Court St S (at Wilson) **807/344-7979** • 11am-6pm, clsd Sun-Mon • cafe open 10am-7pm, till 4pm Sat, clsd Sun-Mon • wheelchair access

Rainbow Books 264 Bay St (at Court St) **807/345-6272** • 11am-10pm, noon-6pm Sun

Toronto

INFO LINES & SERVICES

519 Church St Community Centre 519 Church St (on Cawthra Park) **416/392-6874** • 9am-10pm, 11am-5pm wknds • location for numerous events • also cafe • wheelchair access

925-XTRA **416/925-9872** • touch-tone lgbt visitors' info

AA Gay/ Lesbian **416/487-5591** • call for mtg schedule

Canadian Lesbian/ Gay Archives 56 Temperance St #201 **416/777-2755** • 7:30pm-10pm Tue-Th & by appt

LGBT Youth Line **416/962-9688, 800/268-9688 (CANADA ONLY)** • 4pm-9:30pm, clsd Sun

Toronto Area Gay/ Lesbian Phone Line **416/964-6600** • 7pm-10pm Mon-Fri • counseling

Toronto Convention & Visitors Association **800/363-1990**

Transsexual Transition Support Group at 519 Center **416/925-9872 x2121** • 7pm-10pm 2nd & 4th Fri • for all members of the gender community & their significant others

Two-Spirited People of the First Nations 43 Elm St **416/944-9300** • lgbt Native group

Women's Centre 563 Spadina Ave #100 (at U of Toronto) **416/978-8201** • pro-lesbian center • 10am-3pm M-Th

ACCOMMODATIONS

213 Carlton Street - Toronto Townhouse **416/323-8898, 877/500-0466** • gay/ straight • upscale townhouse • full brkfst • some shared baths • wheelchair access • gay-owned/ run • Can$69-149

Allenby B&B 223 Strathmore Blvd (nr Danforth & Greenwood) **416/461-7095** • gay-friendly • smokefree • shared bath • Can$55-65

Amazing Space B&B 246 Sherbourne St (at Dundas) **416/968-2323, 800/205-3694** • lesbians/ gay men • also 'Immaculate Reception' on Cawthra Park • Can$85-110

Amblecote B&B 109 Walmer Rd (at Bernard) **416/927-1713** • gay-friendly • smokefree • Can$65-125

Banting House B&B 73 Homewood Ave (at Wellesley) **416/924-1458** • lesbians/ gay men • Edwardian home • $60-100

Ontario • CANADA

Reply **Forward** **Delete**

```
Date: Sun, Dec 30, 2001 14:51:53
From: Girl-on-the-Go
To: Editor@Damron.com
Subject: Toronto
```

> Toronto is more than just the capital city of Ontario, eh! It's the cultural and financial center of English-speaking Canada. And though it's not far from Buffalo, New York, and Niagara Falls, Toronto has a European ambiance, fostered by its eclectic architecture and peaceful diversity of cultures, that makes it a great vacation getaway.

> Restaurants and shops from Asia, India, Europe, and many other points on the globe attract natives and tourists alike to the exotic Kensington Market. And just around the corner from Kensington, you'll find a bargain hunter's bonanza: two blocks of vintage clothing stores.

> If your idea of high fashion doesn't include hand-me-downs, you can do some serious window-shopping in the upscale boutiques lining the quaint streets of the Bloor-Yorkville area. And, of course, there's something for everyone in the enormous Eaton Centre mall.

> For intrepid shoppers, Toronto has a lot to offer. **Out in the Street** carries LGBT accessories. **Good For Her** is a women's erotica shop. **Secrets from Your Sister** offers women's lingerie in "realistic sizes" (what a concept!). And the **Omega Centre** is the place for metaphysical literature and supplies.

> Toronto is home to Canada's largest LGBT community, and it shows. You'll see lesbians and gay men everywhere, but the heart of the community is the Church and Wellesley area. Stop in at the **519 Community Centre** to check the bulletin boards, then grab a cup of joe at **Second Cup.** Pick up some "made-to-order" natural body care products at **Planet Earth,** browse the magazines at **This Ain't the Rosedale Library,** then have some lunch. In the warmer months, the patios at **Zelda's** and **Wilde Oscars** are bustling. Over on Yonge Street, pay a visit to the LGBT **Glad Day Bookshop.** At the top of the stairs you'll find the latest issues of **Xtra!** (the LGBT weekly), **Siren** (Toronto's lesbian newsmagazine), and **fab** (Ontario's scene magazine), along with piles of flyers and ideas of things to do. In the evening, have a drink at **Tango,** a women's bar, or **Slack Alice,** a mixed bar popular with women.

> You'll also find sisters in Old Cabbagetown, a funky neighborhood that's home to families, queers, and a mix of cultures. (West Coasters

take note: It's also home to the strongest coffee in town—Jet Fuel.) While you're here, grab a pint and a bite to eat at the **House On Parliament.** Or stop in at nearby **Queen's Head Pub,** an English-style dark-wood pub and restaurant with a friendly atmosphere (also said the be the oldest LGBT bar in Toronto). Later in the evening you'll find the girls at **Pope Joan,** either grooving on the dance floor, lounging downstairs, or chatting on the patio.

> If it's more dancing you want, join the boys at **5ive** and, on Saturdays, at **Fly.** You can dance into the wee hours at Fly, catch a few hours' sleep, and then come back for a great buffet brunch when they transform the pounding club into a restaurant at 11am. And if you love salsa, don't miss Fridays and Saturdays at **El Convento Rico** in Little Italy. On Sundays, you'll find the girls getting down to great music at the small but hip **Ciao Edie.** For the latest queer hotspot or one-off party, check out the listings in Klublife magazine, found at bars and clubwear boutiques.

> If you're an outdoorsy type, you'll be glad to find that Toronto is rather green for such a large city. Don't miss Toronto Islands Park, the string of islands off the Waterfront area, dedicated to recreation. Take a ferry over and rent a bike. In addition to miles of bike paths, the islands feature an amusement park, picnic areas, sports field, boat rentals, and beaches (Hanlan's Beach is the gay beach).

> Toronto is also well-known for its repertory film scene, so try not to miss the Lesbian/Gay Film Fest in late May or early June, or the Film Festival of Festivals in September. In April, Toronto has two weeks of leather pride events, topped off by the Ms. & Mr. Leather Toronto contests. And Toronto Pride in June is said to be one of the largest gatherings of lesbians and gay men on the continent.

Ontario • CANADA

Cawthra Park B&B 10 Monteith St (nr Church & Wellesley) 416/351-1503, 877/580-5015 • gay/ straight • Victorian townhouse • some shared baths • garden • deck • gay-owned/ run • Can$70-110

Cawthra Square B&B—Great Inns of Toronto 416/966-3074, 800/259-5474 • lesbians/ gay men • some shared baths • fireplaces • smokefree • gay-owned/ run • Can$58-250

Dundonald House 35 Dundonald St, M4Y 1K3 416/961-9888, 800/260-7227 • mostly gay men • full brkfst • hot tub • sauna • gym • bicycles • smokefree • gay-owned/ run • Can$55-130

Executive Apartments 416/918-8467 • gay/ straight • full kitchens • $95-295 • 3-day minimum stay

Toronto

WHERE THE GIRLS ARE: In 'The Ghetto'—south of Bloor St., between Yonge and Parliament. The Cabbagetown area (Parliament St.) is more laid-back, while the intersection of Church & Wellesley is queer ground zero.

LGBT PRIDE: June/July. 416/927-7433, web: www.torontopride.com.

ANNUAL EVENTS: May - International Gay & Lesbian Comedy and Music Festival, web: members.aol.com/werefunny.
Inside Out: Lesbian & Gay Film and Video Festival 416/977-6847, web: insideout.on.ca.
June - duMaurier Downtown Jazz Festival 416/928-2033, web: www.tojazz.com.
International Dragon Boat Race Festival 416/364-0046.
July - Caribana Caribbean festival 416/969-3110.
September - International Film Festival 416/968-3456, web: www.bell.ca/filmfest.

CITY INFO: 800/363-1990, web: www.tourism-toronto.com.

ATTRACTIONS: Art Gallery of Ontario 416/979-6648.
Bata Shoe Museum.
CN Tower 416/868-6937, www.cntower.ca.
Dr Flea's International Flea Market 416/745-3532.
Gardiner Museum of Ceramic Art, 416-586-8080.
Harbourfront Centre 416/973-3000, www.harbourfront.on.ca.
Hockey Hall of Fame 416/360-7735.
Kensington Market.
Ontario Place 416/314-9900.
Royal Ontario Museum 416/586-8000, www.rom.on.ca.
SkyDome 416/341-2300.
Underground City.

BEST VIEW: The top of one of the world's tallest buildings, of course: the CN Tower. Or try a sightseeing air tour or a three-masted sailing ship tour.

WEATHER: Summers are hot (upper 80°s—90°s) and humid. Spring is gorgeous. Fall brings cool, crisp days. Winters are cold and snowy, just as you'd imagined they would be in Canada!

TRANSIT: Co-op Taxi 416/504-2667.
Grey Coach 416/393-7911.
TTC 416/393-4636, www.city.toronto.on.ca/ttc.

Toronto • Ontario

House on McGill 110 McGill St (at Church & Carlton) **416/351-1503, 877/580-5015** • gay/ straight • Victorian townhouse • shared baths • garden w/ deck • smokefree • Can$50-90

Huntley House 65 Huntley St (at Bloor) **416/923-6950** • gay-friendly • 1871 historic house • full brkfst • smokefree • Can$95-135

Immaculate Reception B&B 34 Monteith St (at Church) **416/925-4202, 800/335-9190** • lesbians/ gay men • 1880s row house • full brkfst • gay-owned/ run • Can$90-125

The Mansion 46 Dundonald St (at Church) **416/963-8385** • gay/ straight • elegant Victorian • Can$60-80

Pimblett's Rest B&B 242 Gerrard St E **416/929-9525, 416/921-6898** • Victorian • gay/ straight • hot tub • theme rooms • gay-owned/ run • Can$75-95

Toronto B&B Box 269, 253 College St **416/588-8800 OR 905/ 403-9399** • gay-friendly • reservation service • Can$70-150

Toronto Downtown B&B 572 Ontario St (at Dundas) **416/921-3533, 877/950-6200** • gay/ straight • luxurious • full brkfst • kids ok • in gay village • smokefree • gay-owned/ run • $99-199

Victoria's Mansion Inn & Guest House 68 Gloucester St **416/921-4625** • gay-friendly • converted mansion • kids/ small pets ok • Can$65-120

'With Friends' B&B 12 Monteith St (at Church & Wellesley) **416/925-2798** • gay/ straight • restored 1877 terrace house • overlooks Cawthra Square Park • deck • Can$70-125

BARS

Bar 501 501 Church (at Wellesley) **416/944-3272** • 11am-2am • lesbians/ gay men • neighborhood bar • live shows • infamous 'Window Show' Sun

Carrington's 618 Yonge, upstairs (at St Joseph) **416/944-0559** • 11am-2am • mostly gay men • sports bar

Ciao Edie 489 College St (at Markham) **416/927-7774** • 8pm-2am • gay/ straight • 'Here Kitty Kitty' womens' night Sun • oh-so-nice cocktail lounge w/ DJ • food served

Crews/ Tango 508 Church **416/972-1662** • noon-3am • mostly gay men • neighborhood bar • deck overlooking Church St • also 'Tango' from 8pm Tue-Sat • mostly women • popular Sat • dancing/DJ • live shows

The Hair of the Dog 425 Church St **416/964-2708** • 11:30am-2am • lesbians/ gay men • neighborhood pub & restaurant • patio

The House On Parliament Pub 456 Parliament St **416/925-4074** • gay/ straight • neighborhood bar • food served • patio

The Lounge 940 Danforth Ave (E of Donlands, above Replay Sports Bar) **416/469-5002** • wknds only • lesbians/ gay men • karaoke • gay-friendly sports bar downstairs

Midtown 552 College St (W of Euclid) **416/920-4533** • 5pm-2am, from 3pm Fri, from 1pm wknds • lesbians/ gay men • neighborhood pool bar

Pegasus Billiard Lounge 489-B Church St (at Wellesley, upstairs) **416/927-8832** • 11am-2am • lesbians/ gay men • neighborhood bar

Queen's Head Pub (aka Pimblett's Pub) 263 Gerrard St E (btwn Seaton & Parliament) **416/929-9525** • 4pm-3am • gay/ straight • friendly neighborhood pub • also restaurant • food served 5:30pm-11pm • patio • gay-owned/ run • wheelchair access

Red Spot Lounge & Bar 459 Church St (at Carlton) **416/967-7768** • 4pm-2am • lesbians/ gay men • lounge • food served • karaoke • live shows • comedy to drag

Slack Alice 562 Church St (at Wellesley) **416/969-8742** • 4pm-2am, from 11am wknds • popular • lesbians/ gay men • also restaurant

Survivors 1 Nelson St W (at Hwy 10/ Queen St, across from the bus station) **905/453-2116** • 7pm-2am, from 4pm Sun, clsd Mon-Tue • lesbians/ gay men • women's night Th • neighborhood bar • dancing/DJ • food served

Trax V 529 Yonge St (at Maitland) **416/963-5196** • 11am-2am • popular • mostly gay men • piano bar • drag shows nightly • bingo • wheelchair access

Woody's/ Sailor 465–467 Church (at Maitland) **416/972-0887** • noon-2am • popular • mostly gay men • neighborhood bar • food served • brunch from 10am wknds • wheelchair access

Zipperz 72 Carlton St (at Church) **416/921-0066** • noon-3am • mostly gay men • dancing/DJ • drag shows • piano bar • patio

NIGHTCLUBS

5ive 5 St Joseph St (at Yonge) **416/964-8685** • 10pm-2am, clsd Mon • also 'Life Lounge,' open from 5pm • popular • mostly gay men • dancing/DJ • food served • cover charge

Ontario • CANADA

El Convento Rico 750 College St (at Crawford) **416/588-7800** • 8pm-4am Fri-Sat only • popular • lesbians/ gay men • dancing/DJ • Latin/ salsa music • multiracial • transgender-friendly • drag shows at 1am • cover charge

Fluid 217 Richmond St W **416/593-6116** • 10pm-4am, clsd Mon • gay/ straight • more gay wknds • dancing/DJ • dress code • wheelchair access • cover charge

Fly 6–8 Gloucester St (at Yonge) **416/410-5426** • 9pm-close Sat only • popular • mostly gay men • dancing/DJ • cover charge

Kitty Kitty Bang Bang 19 Balmuto St (nr Yonge & Bloor, at Manhattan Club) **416/920-9119 (CLUB)** • women only • 9pm-2am 3rd Fri only • dancing/DJ • multiracial clientele

Manhattan Club 19 Balmuto St (nr Yonge & Bloor) **416/920-9119** • queer night Sat

Pope Joan 547 Parliament (at Winchester) **416/925-6662, 416/925-9990** • 7pm-close, clsd Sun-Wed • mostly women • popular Fri • dancing/DJ • live shows Th • seasonal beach, pool & patio • food served • some veggie • brunch from noon summer wknds • women-owned/ run

Tallulah's Cabaret 12 Alexander St (at 'Buddies in Bad Times' theater) **416/975-8555** Fri-Sat only • mostly gay men • 'Sissy Saturdays' are popular

Whiskey Saigon 250 Richmond W (at Duncan) **416/593-4646** • 9pm-3am Fri-Sun gay-friendly • dancing/DJ • live shows • rooftop patio • cover charge • dress code

CAFES

Cafe Diplomatico 594 College (at Clinton, in Little Italy) **416/534-4637** • 8am-2am • popular • patio

The Joy of Java 884 Queen St E **416/465-8855** • 8am-11pm • live jazz Sat • patio

The Second Cup 548 Church St (at Wellesley) **416/964-2457** • 24hrs (except Mon-Wed) • popular • coffee & desserts

Sweet City Bakery 24 Wellesley St W (at Yonge) **416/962-0358** • 6:30am-5:30pm, 8am-4pm Sat, clsd Sun

RESTAURANTS

Allen's Restaurant 143 Danforth Ave (at Broadview) **416/463-3086** • lunch & dinner • great scotch selection • Irish music/ dancing • patio • Can$15

Avalon 270 Adelaide St W (at John) **416/979-9918** • dinner nightly, lunch Th only, clsd Sun • intimate dining • Can$26-38

Babylon 553 Church St **416/923-2626** • 3pm-2am • also martini bar

Bistro 422 422 College St **416/963-9416** • 4pm-2am

Byzantium 499 Church St (S of Wellesley) **416/922-3859** • 5:30pm-11pm • mostly gay men • chic • Continental/ global • also martini bar till 2am • patio

Cafe Jambalaya 501 Yonge St (at Alexander, in Little Italy) **416/922-5262** • 11:30am-10pm, clsd Sun • Cajun, Caribbean & vegetarian • patio

Cafe Volo 587 Yonge St (at Dundonald) **416/928-0008** • 11am-11pm • Italian • some veggie

Ethiopian House 4 Irwin Ave (2 blks N of Wellesley, off Yonge) **416/923-5438** • noon-1am • plenty veggie

Fly 6–8 Gloucester St (at Yonge) **416/410-5426** • clsd Mon • fantastic buffet brunch Sun

Golden Thai 105 Church St (at Richmond) **416/868-6668** • 11:30am-10:30pm, from 5pm wknds

The Gypsy Co-Op 817 Queen St W (W of Bathurst) **416/703-5069** • noon-3am, 6pm-2am Mon, clsd Sun • women's night Wed • also bar • eclectic & kitschy • resident spiritualists

Hughie's Burgers, Fries & Pies 777 Bay St (at College) **416/977-2242** • 11:30am-11pm • Sun brunch • full bar • patio

Il Fornello 1560 Yonge St (1 blk N of St Clair) **416/920-7347** • 11:30am-10:30pm, no lunch Sat • Italian • plenty veggie • also 214 King W (at Simcoe), 416/977-2855 • also 576 Danforth Ave (at Carlaw), 416/466-2931

La Hacienda 640 Queen St W (nr Bathurst) **416/703-3377** • lunch & dinner • Mexican • sleazy, loud & fun

The Living Well Restaurant & Bar 692 Yonge St (at Isabella) **416/922-6770** • 11:30am-1am, till 1:30am Fri-Sat • lesbians/ gay men • plenty veggie • $8-12 • also upstairs bar • open 6pm-2am • live DJ • drag shows • 80s Sat • 'Dirty Bingo' Mon • patio

Mary's Bar & Grill 399 Church St (at Carlton) **416/598-4544** • 11am-11pm, till midnight Fri-Sat • burgers, salads, pasta • full bar • gay-owned/ run

Oasis 294 College St (at Spadina) **416/975-0845** • 5pm-2am • eclectic tapas • also bar • live shows

Toronto • Ontario

PJ Mellon's 489 Church St (at Wellesley) **416/966-3241** • 11:30am-11pm • some veggie • wine bar • wheelchair access • $7-12

Rashnaa 307 Wellesley St E (at Parliament) **416/929-2099** • 11:30am-11:30pm, buffet lunch till 3pm • inexpensive & good South Indian/Sri Lankan • plenty veggie/vegan • full bar

Rivoli Cafe 332 Queen St W (at Spadina) **416/597-0794** • 10am-11:30pm • bar till 1am • some veggie

Solo on Yonge 605 Yonge St **416/920-0607** • creative seafood & pasta dishes • int'l wine list • reservations recommended wknds

Splendido 88 Harbord St (at Spadina) **416/929-7788** • 5pm-11pm, clsd Sun • great decor & gnocchi • full bar • wheelchair access • Can$45+

The Superior Restaurant 253 Yonge St (across from Eaton Ctr) **416/214-0416** • 11:30am-midnight • oysters • full bar • wheelchair access

Tantra 634 Church St (at Isabella) **416/926-0313** • lunch & dinner • also bar & lounge • patio

Trattoria Al Forno 459 Church St (at Carlton) **416/944-8852** • lunch Mon-Fri & dinner nightly • full bar

The Village Rainbow 477 Church St (at Maitland) **416/961-0616** • 7am-midnight, till 1am Th-Sat, from 8am Sun • full bar • big patio

Wilde Oscars 518 Church St (at Maitland) **416/921-8142** • 11am-2am • lesbians/gay men • Mediterranean • huge patio • also lounge (clsd summer) upstairs

Zelda's 542 Church St **416/922-2526** • 11am-2am • popular • lesbians/gay men • full drag service Sat • all-you-can-eat brunch wknds • full bar • big patio

Zelda's Satellite Lounge 76 Wellesley St E **416/922-4221** • lesbians/gay men • cafe & bar

ZiZi Trattoria 456 Bloor St W (E of Bathurst) **416/533-5117** • 5pm-close

ENTERTAINMENT & RECREATION

AIDS Memorial in Cawthra Park

Buddies in Bad Times Theatre 12 Alexander St **416/975-8555** • lgbt theater • also bar

Gay/Lesbian History Walking Tour **416/515-7155** • 2 hour tour • meets at 519 Church St Community Centre

Get Out of Town **416/994-1699** • day trips w/ in 2 hrs of Toronto: outdoor activities, winery tours, beaches, theater

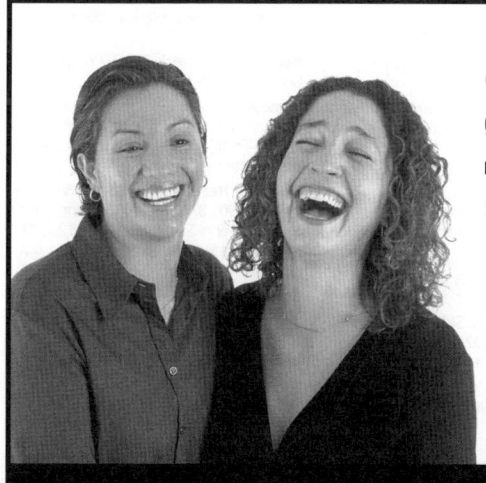

Canada's **gay & lesbian** media group
1-800-268-XTRA

Ontario • CANADA

Iris: Toronto Women's Chorus 416/463-0017

BOOKSTORES

A Different Booklist 746 Bathurst St (at Bloor) **416/538-0889** • 10am-6pm, till 7pm Th-Fri, clsd Sun • multicultural titles & authors

Glad Day Bookshop 598–A Yonge St (at Wellesley) **416/961-4161, 877/783-3725** • 10am-7pm, till 9pm Th-Fri, from noon Sun • popular • great selection of lgbt books, mags & videos

The Omega Centre 29 Yorkville Ave (btwn Yonge & Bay) **416/975-9086, 888/663-6377 (IN CANADA)** • 10am-9pm, till 6pm Sat, 11am-5pm Sun • metaphysical

This Ain't The Rosedale Library 483 Church St (at Wellesley) **416/929-9912** • 10am-10pm, till 11pm Fri-Sat, 1pm-9pm Sun • lgbt books & magazines

Toronto Women's Bookstore 73 Harbord St (at Spadina) **416/922-8744, 800/861-8233** • 10:30am-6pm, till 8pm Th-Fri, 10:30am-6pm Sat, noon-5pm Sun

Wonderworks 79-A Harbord St (at Spadina) **416/323-3131** • 10:30am-6pm • books & gifts

RETAIL SHOPS

Out in the Street 551 Church St **416/967-2759, 800/263-5747** • 10am-8pm, from 11am Sun • lgbt accessories

Passage Body Piercing 473 Church St **416/929-7330** • noon-7pm, clsd Sun-Mon • also tattoos & scarification

Planet Earth 473 Church St **416/929-2007, 877/503-7374 (MAIL-ORDER)** • 10am-6pm • all-natural body care products

Secrets From Your Sister... 476 Bloor St W **416/538-1234** • 11am-6pm, till 7pm Th-Sat, from noon Sun • 'beautiful lingerie in realistic sizes for the modern woman' • wheelchair access

Stargazer Studios 460 Parliament St #1 **416/928-3579** • body piercing by appt only

Take a Walk On the Wild Side 161 Gerrard St E (at Jarvis) **416/921-6112** • 10am-7pm, till 11pm Sat, noon-4pm Sun • transgender-friendly • drag emporium

Vixon 620 Yonge St **416/960-6464** • 11am-8pm • clubwear

PUBLICATIONS

The Pink Pages **416/972-7418** • annual lgbt directory

Rainbow Choices Directory **416/762-1320, 888/241-3569 (CANADA ONLY)** • lgbt entertainment & business directory for Canada

Siren **416/778-9027** • lesbian newsmagazine

▲ **Xtra!** **416/925-6665** • lgbt newspaper

SPIRITUAL GROUPS

Christos MCC 427 Bloor St W (at Spadina in Trinity St Paul's Church) **416/925-7924** • 7pm Sun

Congregation Keshet Shalom **416/925-9872 x2073, 416/925-1408**

Dignite 11 Earl St (at Sherbourne, Our Lady of Lourdes Church) **416/925-9872 x2011, 416/925-9872 x2011** • 7pm 4th Sat, upstairs in Loyola Hall

Integrity Toronto at Bloor & Avenue Rd (at Church of the Redeemer) **416/925-9872 x2050, 416/323-0389** • 7:30pm 3rd Mon

MCC Toronto 115 Simpson Ave (at Howland Rd) **416/406-6228** • 9am & 11am Sun • wheelchair access

GYMS & HEALTH CLUBS

The Bloor Valley Club 555 Sherbourne St (at Bloor) **416/961-4695** • gay-friendly • squash & fitness club • swimming

EROTICA

Aslan Leather 135 Tecumseth St, Unit 4 (rear) **416/306-0462** • by appt only • fine bondage gear

Body Exotic Lingerie 357–1/2 Yonge St (at Gould) **416/597-3953**

Come As You Are 701 Queen St W (at Bathurst) **416/504-7934** • 11am-7pm, till 9pm Th-Fri, till 6pm Sat, noon-5pm Sun • co-op owned sex store

Good For Her 175 Harbord St (nr Bathurst) **416/588-0900, 877/588-0900** • 11am-7pm, till 8pm Fri, till 6pm Sat, women-only till 2pm Th & noon-5pm Sun • women's sexuality products • wheelchair access

North Bound Leather 586 Yonge **416/972-1037** • toys & clothing • wheelchair access

Priape 465 Church St (at Wellesley, above Woody's) **416/586-9914, 800/461-6969** • clubwear • leather • books • toys & more

Seduction 577 Yonge St **416/966-6969**

Waterloo

CAFES

Grabbajabba 80 King St **519/886-9590** • 7:30am-9:30pm

Cornwall • Prince Edward Island

RESTAURANTS

Ethel's Lounge 114 King St S (at Spring) **519/725-2361** • 11am-2am • full bar • patio

Whitby

NIGHTCLUBS

Diva's 110 Dundas St W (at Brock) **905/666-2093** • 9pm-3am, clsd Mon-Wed • lesbians/ gay men • dancing/DJ • karaoke • live shows

Windsor

see also Detroit, Michigan

INFO LINES & SERVICES

Gay/ Lesbian AA 1440 Windsor Ave (at Canadian Mental Health Association) **519/973-7671** • 7pm Th

LGBT Phone Line **519/973-7671 (24HR INFO)** • 7pm-9pm Tue & Th

BARS

Club Happy Tap Tavern 1056 Wyandotte St E (at Langlois) **519/256-8998** • 2pm-2am, from 4pm Sun • mostly gay men • more women Tue • dancing/DJ • nude dancers

Club Paradox 800 Wellington Ave **519/258-6731** • 8pm-2am, till 5am wknds, clsd Mon • lesbians/ gay men • dancing/DJ

The Honest Lawyer 300 Ouellete Ave **519/977-0599** • 11am-2am, from 4pm Sun • gay-friendly • food served

NIGHTCLUBS

The Complex 634 Chilver Rd (at Wyandotte East) **519/252-1774** • 1pm-close • lesbians/ gay men • dancing/DJ from 10pm Fri-Sat • food served • drag shows • video bar • karaoke Sun • gay-owned/ run

ENTERTAINMENT & RECREATION

Queer Radio **519/253-4232** • 9pm Mon • CJAM 91.5 FM

SPIRITUAL GROUPS

MCC Windsor 1680 Dougall Ave (at Tecumseh) **519/258-1471** • 1:30pm Sun

Woodstock

ACCOMMODATIONS

Nunn's Hollow Guest Suites 21 Delatre St (Dundas St) **519/539-9780** • mostly gay men • full brkfst

PRINCE EDWARD ISLAND

Alabany

ACCOMMODATIONS

Evening Primrose 114 Lord's Pond Rd, Albany **902/437-3134** • 40 mins from Charlottetown • B&B, cottage, and studio • full brkfst • nr outdoor recreation • smokefree • kids/ pets ok • cottage & studio wheelchair accessible • Can$55/ night, $600/ week

Charlettetown

INFO LINES & SERVICES

Abegweit Rainbow Collective PO Box 1765, Charlottetown C1A 7N4 **902/894-5776, 877/380-5776** • 24hr info line, staffed 7pm-10pm Tue & Th

Charlottetown

INFO LINES & SERVICES

Women's Network PEI 902/368-5040

ACCOMMODATIONS

Charlottetown Hotel 75 Kent St (at Pownall) **902/894-7371** • gay-friendly • swimming • also restaurant • cont'l/ seafood • lounge clsd Sun • wheelchair access • $10-25

Rainbow Lodge 07519 Trans Canada Hwy, Vernon Bridge, C0A 2E0 **902/651-2202, 800/268-7005** • lesbians/ gay men • full brkfst • 15 mins outside of town • smokefree • gay-owned/ run • Can$80

BARS

Baba's Lounge 81 University Ave **902/892-7377** • noon-2am, from 5pm Sun • gay-friendly • live bands • also 'Cedars' restaurant • Canadian/ Lebanese • some veggie

BOOKSTORES

Book Mark 172 Queen St (in mall) **902/566-4888** • 8:30am-9pm, 9am-5:30pm wknds • will order lesbian titles

EROTICA

Afternoon Delight 218 University Ave, Charlotte **902/892-3469, 877/424-5469** • woman-owned/ run

Cornwall

ACCOMMODATIONS

Rainbow Inn P.E.I 4992 Rte 19A **902/675-2393** • renovated farm house • nr outdoor recreation • full brkfst • kids/ pets ok • lesbian-owned • Can$75

PEI/ Province of Québec • CANADA

Souris

Accommodations

Johnson Shore Inn RR #3 Rte16 **902/687–1340, 877/510–9669** • gay/ straight • country inn on 50 acres • full brkfst • wheelchair access • lesbian-owned/ run • Can$195-250

Summerside

Info Lines & Services

East Prince Women's Info Centre 75 Central St **902/436–9856** • 9am-4pm Mon-Fri

Province of Québec

Provincewide

Info Lines & Services

Gay Line/ Gai Ecoute 888/505–1010 • 7pm-11pm

Chicoutimi

see also Jonquière

Bars

Bistro des Anges 332 rue du Havre **418/698–4829** • 11am-3am • lesbians/ gay men • neighborhood bar • food served

Drummondville

Accommodations

Motel Alouette 1975 boul Mercure **819/478-4166** • gay-friendly • $55–95

Bars

Nuance 336 rue Lindsay, 2nd flr **819/471–4252** • 4pm-close, clsd Mon-Tue • lesbians/ gay men • neighborhood bar

Granby

Accommodations

Le Campagnard B&B 146 Denison Ouest J2G 4C8 **450/770–1424** • gay-friendly • in a quiet village • bikes available • also camping • smokefree • Can$45-70

Hull

see also Ottawa, Ontario

Bars

Le Pub de Promenade 175 Promenade de Portage **819/771–8810** • 11am-2am • popular • lesbians/ gay men • neighborhood bar • dancing/DJ

Joliette

Accommodations

L'Oasis des Pins 381 boul Brassard, St-Paul-de-Joliette **450/754–3819** • lesbians/ gay men • swimming • camping April-Sept • restaurant open year-round

Jonquière

see also Chicoutimi

Bars

Bar le Stool 2732 boul du Saguenay **418/548–0168** • 9pm-3am Th-Sat, from 2pm Sun, clsd Mon-Wed • lesbians/ gay men • dancing/DJ

Laurentides (Laurentian Mtns)

Accommodations

B&B du Mont Sauvage 2340 chemin du Mont Sauvage, Ste-Adèle **450/229–7821** • gay-friendly • swimming

Sainte-Adèle 1694 chemin Pierre-Peladeau, Ste-Adèle **450/228-3140, 888/825–4273 (in Québec only)** • lesbians/ gay men • superb ancestral home • nr slopes • swimming • Can$65-70

Le Septentrion B&B 901 chemin St-Adolphe, Morin-Heights **450/226–2665** • lesbians/ gay men • Victorian • full brkfst • swimming • jacuzzi • smokefree • gay-owned/ run • Can$100-150

Nightclubs

Différent 257 St-Georges (Autoroute 15, take exit 'sortie 43'), St-Jérôme **450/569–8769** • 9pm-3am, clsd Mon-Tue • lesbians/ gay men • dancing/DJ

Magog

see also Sherbrooke

Accommodations

Au Gîte du Cerf Argenté 2984 chemin Georgeville (off Rte 10) **819/847–4264, 514/521–2712** • lesbians/ gay men • B&B in century-old farmhouse • 4 beaches nearby • kids/ pets ok • Can$92-148

Cafes

Café Croute Magogue 299 Principale Ouest **819/847–3925** • 8am-9pm • gay/ straight • café-bar

Montréal • Province of Québec

Montréal

INFO LINES & SERVICES

AA Gay/ Lesbian 514/376-9230, 514/276-8527 • call for mtg times & locations (in French or English)

Gay/ Lesbian Community Centre of Montréal 2075 rue Plessis, local 110 (at Ontario) 514/528-8424 • 9am-noon & 1pm-4pm, clsd wknds

Gay Line/ Gai Ecoute 514/866-5090 (ENGLISH), 514/866-0103 (FRENCH) • 7pm-11pm

Women's Centre of Montréal 3585 St-Urbain 514/842-1066, 514/842-4780 • 9am-5pm Mon-Fri • wheelchair access

ACCOMMODATIONS

Angelica Blue B&B 1213 Ste-Elisabeth (at Ste-Catherine) 514/844-5048, 800/878-5048 • gay/ straight • theme rms • full brkfst • some shared baths • lesbian-owned/ run • Can$65+

Au Stade B&B PO Box 60542 H1V 3T8 514/254-1250 x1 • lesbians/ gay men

Auberge de la Fontaine 1301 rue Rachel Est (at Chambord) 514/597-0166, 800/597-0597 • gay-friendly • kids ok • wheelchair access • Can$119-234

▲ **Aux Chambres au Village** 850 de la Gauchetière Est (at St-Hubert) 514/844-6941 • gay/ straight • B&B • shared baths • gay-owned/ run • Can$55-75

Le Chasseur B&B 1567 rue St-André (at Maisonneuve) 514/521-2238, 800/451-2238 • mostly gay men • 1920s European townhouse • summer terrace • Can$49-150

Chateau Cherrier 550 rue Cherrier (at St-Hubert) 514/844-0055, 800/816-0055 • lesbians/ gay men • seasonal • full gourmet brkfst • $65-85

Chez Roger Bontemps 1441 Wolfe (at Ste-Catherine) 514/598-9587, 888/634-9090 • gay/ straight • B&B in two 1873 homes • also furnished apts • Can$55-240

Crowne Plaza Metro Centre 505 rue Sherbrooke Est (at Berri) 514/842-8581, 800/561-4644 • gay-friendly • breathtaking views of Montréal • full brkfst • swimming • hot tub • restaurant • bar • wheelchair access • $159-270

La Douillette 7235 rue de Lorimier (at Jean Talon) 514/376-2183 • women only • full brkfst • homey & cozy • lesbian-owned/ run • Can$40-60

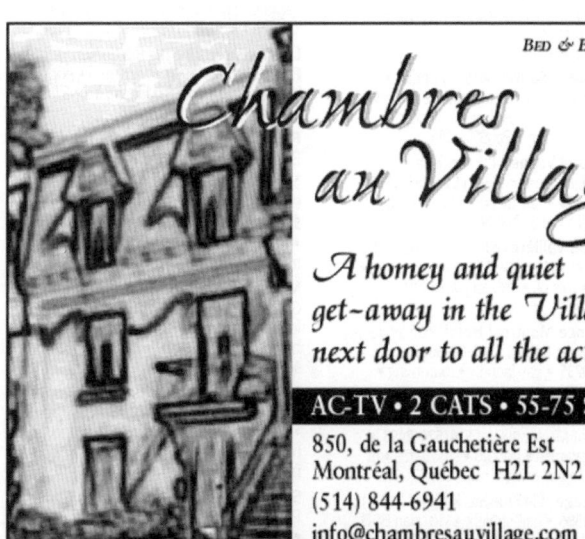

BED & BREAKFAST

Chambres au Village

A homey and quiet get-away in the Village, next door to all the action!

AC-TV • 2 CATS • 55-75 $CAN

850, de la Gauchetière Est
Montréal, Québec H2L 2N2
(514) 844-6941
info@chambresauvillage.com

HAVE A LOOK! www.chambresauvillage.com

Province of Québec • CANADA

Ginger Bread House 1628 St-Christophe (at Maisonneuve) **514/597-2804** • lesbians/ gay men • full brkfst • shared bath • smokefree • gay-owned/ run • Can$40-65

Hébergement Touristique du Plateau Mont-Royal 1131 rue Rachel Est **514/527-2394, 800/597-0597** • gay-friendly • reservation service

Home Suite Hom **514/523-4642, 800/429-4983** • lesbians/ gay men • home exchange

Hotel du Fort 1390 rue du Fort (at Ste-Catherine) **514/938-8333, 800/565-6333** • gay/ straight • wheelchair access • Can$115-350

Hotel Kent 1216 rue St-Hubert (at Ste-Catherine) **514/845-9835** • gay-friendly • Can$30-65

Hotel Lord Berri 1199 rue Berri (at Ste-Catherine) **514/845-9236, 888/363-0363** • gay-friendly • smokefree rms available • also restaurant • Italian/cont'l • $99-159

Hotel Manoir des Alpes 1245 rue St-André (at Ste-Catherine) **514/845-9803, 800/465-2929** • gay-friendly • Can$55-75

Hotel Pierre 169 Sherbrooke Est (btwn St-Denis & St-Laurent) **514/288-8519, 877/288-8577** • gay-friendly • kitchen • Can$65-125

Hotel Visitel Network 1617 rue St-Hubert (at Maisonneuve) **514/529-0990** • hotel & reservation service

Lindsey's B&B 3974 av Laval (nr Duluth) **514/843-4869, 888/655-8655** • popular • women only • charming townhouse nr Square St-Louis & rue Prince Arthur • full brkfst • lesbian-owned/ run • Can$55-115

Loews Hotel Vogue 1425 rue de la Montagne (nr Ste-Catherine) **514/285-5555, 800/465-6654** • gay-friendly • full-service 5-star hotel • Can$179-439

Le Pension Vallières 6562 de Lorimier St (at Beaubien) **514/729-9552** • women only • full brkfst • cats ok • lesbian-owned/ run • Can$52-75

Renaissance Montreal Hotel 3625 av du Parc (at Prince Arthur) **514/288-6666, 800/363-0735** • gay-friendly • swimming • Can$135-199

Le Roy d'Carreau Guest House 1637 rue Amherst (at Maisonneuve) **514/524-2493** • lesbians/ gay men • hot tub • smokefree • in Gay Village • gay-owned/ run • Can$75-175

Ruta Bagage 1345 rue Ste-Rose (at Panêt) **514/598-1586** • gay/ straight • Victorian B&B • full brkfst • shared baths • Can$65-95

Le Traversin 4124 rue St-Hubert, H2L 4A8 **514/597-1546** • full brkfst • some shared baths • hot tub • smokefree • Can$100-150

Turquoise B&B 1576 rue Alexandre de Sève (at Maisonneuve) **514/523-9943, 877/707-1576** • mostly gay men • Victorian B&B • shared baths • gay-owned/ run • Can$50-90

BARS

Cabaret L'Entre Peau 1115 Ste-Catherine Est (below 'Le Campus' at Amherst) **514/525-7566** • 1pm-3am • popular • lesbians/ gay men • drag shows • wheelchair access

Le Campus 1111 rue Ste-Catherine Est, 2nd flr (at Amherst) **514/526-3616** • 3pm-3am • mostly gay men • nude dancers • couples shows Th-Sun • ladies night some Sun nights 9pm-3am (call first)

Citibar 1603 Ontario Est (at Champlain) **514/525-4251** • 11am-3am • gay/ straight • neighborhood bar

Club Bolo 960 rue Amherst (at Viger) **514/849-4777** • 8pm-1am Fri, 9pm-2am Sat • lesbians/ gay men • dancing/DJ • country/ western • T-dance from 4pm Sun • private club • cover charge

Club Date 1218 rue Ste-Catherine Est (at Beaudry) **514/521-1242** • 8am-3am • lesbians/ gay men • neighborhood bar • karaoke • singers

Le Drugstore 1366 rue Ste-Catherine Est (at Panêt) **514/524-1960** • 9am-3am • popular • lesbians/ gay men • 8-bar complex • 3 flrs • food served

Foufounes Electriques 87 Ste-Catherine Est (at St-Laurent) **514/844-5539** • 3pm-3am • gay-friendly • dancing/DJ • live bands • patio

Fun Spot 1151 rue Ontario Est (at Wolfe) **514/522-0416** • 11am-3am • mostly gay men • neighborhood bar • dancing/DJ • transgender-friendly • karaoke • drag shows

Météor 1661 rue Ste-Catherine Est (at Champlain) **514/523-1481** • 11am-3am • lesbians/ gay men • dancing/DJ • '60s themed bar • ballroom dancing • karaoke • food served • 40+ crowd

La Relaxe 1309 Ste-Catherine Est, 2nd flr **514/523-0578** • noon-3am • mostly gay men • neighborhood bar • open to the street • as the name implies, a good place to relax & people-watch

Sisters 1333 rue Ste-Catherine Est, 2nd flr (at Panêt) **514/522-4717** • 6pm-3am Th-Sat only • popular • women-only • men welcome on Tue • dancing/DJ • live shows • upstairs from 'Le Saloon Café'

Montréal • Province of Québec

[Reply] [Forward] **[Delete]**

Date: Fri, Nov 2, 2001 15:08:22
From: Girl-on-the-Go
To: Editor@Damron.com
Subject: Montréal

> Montréal is the world's second-largest French-speaking city. As you take in the architecture and arts, the fashion and the food, the style and sophistication of Canada's most cosmopolitan city, you will catch glimpses of the world's largest French-speaking city, Paris.

> But, make no mistake; while it does have strong historical and cultural ties to Paris (it too has a Latin Quarter), Montréal is no 'Paris-lite.'

> Montréal is home to many museums, like the Musée d'art contemporain de Montréal and the Montréal Museum of Fine Arts. Theater, dance, and music companies as well as a celebrated symphony orchestra thrive in this historic city. There is also a wealth of Old World architecture in the streets of Old Montréal and around Mont Royal.

> Then there are the various symbols and events that mark Montréal as its own force in the contemporary world, like the World Film Festival (every August) and the Palais des Congrès and Montréal World Trade Center.

> But, clichéd as it may sound, what makes Montréal such a beautiful city to visit is its people. And they are beautiful.

> Just take a walk through the Plateau Mont-Royal neighborhood and stroll through St-Louis Square to the rue Prince-Arthur. You'll not only see an interesting mix of tourists and Quebeçois but you'll also pass several of the women's guesthouses, including **Lindsey's.**

> Or, better yet, head over to the Village, Montréal's gay community. Though, at first glance, it's a thriving Boy's Town, you'll see plenty of sisters in the bars and shops and stores along Ste-Catherine, especially in the excellent LGBT bookstore **L'Androgyne.** When you tire of the testosterone, take off for **Sisters,** Montréal's women's bar. We also hear there are plenty of women to be found on the second floor of **Le Drugstore.** And the **Unity Club** is said to be popular with women on Friday nights. Check the latest issue of **Fugues** for the latest in one-off parties.

> Just remember that the people of Montréal are proud of their French heritage and language. Most signs will be in French—sometimes with an English translation, sometimes not. So brush up on your French, or at least learn some of the polite basics: s'il vous plaît (please), merci (thank you), pardon (excuse me), and the all-important question, Parlez-vous anglais? (Do you speak English?).

Province of Québec • CANADA

Le St-Sulpice 1680 rue St-Denis (at Ontario) 514/844-9458 • 11:30am-3am • popular cafe-bar • gay/straight • dancing/DJ

Unity Pub 1171 Ste-Catherine Est (below 'Unity Club') 514/523-4429 • lesbians/gay men • neighborhood bar • terrace

West Side 1071 Beaver Hall (at Belmont) 514/866-4963 • 4pm-3am, from 7pm wknds • mostly gay men • nude dancers • ladies night Wed & Sat

NIGHTCLUBS

Club Mississippi 1584 rue Ste-Catherine Est (at 'Hotel Bourbon') 514/521-1419 • lesbians/gay men • dancing/DJ • transgender-friendly • live shows

Club Studio 54 8080 boul Taschereau, Brossard 450/463-4553 • Fri-Sat only • gay-friendly • dancing/DJ • cover charge • unconfirmed

Disco Cleo/ Chez Cleopatra 1230 boul St-Laurent (at Ste-Catherine) 514/871-8065 • 8pm-3am • mostly gay men • dancing/DJ • transgender-friendly • drag shows

Exotica 417 rue St-Pierre (in Old Montreal) 514/281-1773 • 10pm-3am Th-Sun • mostly gay men • dancing/DJ • mostly Latino/a

Les Libertins 5938 rue St-Hubert 514/271-6799 • 8pm-3am, clsd Mon • women only • dancing/DJ

Red Light 195 rue Notre-Dame de Fatima, Laval 450/967-3057 • wknds only • popular • gay-friendly • after-hours club

Sky Club 1474 rue Ste-Catherine Est 514/529-6969 • 10pm-3am • popular • lesbians/gay men • 'Sky Pub' on 1st flr • disco upstairs • T-dance Sun from 4pm • also 'Sky Jack' (leather bar) • also the 'Suite' (drag shows)

Montreal

WHERE THE GIRLS ARE: In the popular Plateau Mont-Royal neighborhood or in the bohemian area on Ste-Catherine est.

ENTERTAINMENT: Info Gay Events Hotline 514/252-4429.

LGBT PRIDE: July/August. 514/285-4011.

ANNUAL EVENTS: June - Festival International de Jazz de Montréal 514/871-1881, www.montrealjazzfest.com.
August - Montréal World Film Festival 514/848-9933.
October - Black & Blue Party 514/875-7026. AIDS benefit dance & circuit party.

CITY INFO: 514/844-5400, web: www.tourism-montreal.org.

ATTRACTIONS: Bonsecours Market 514/872-7730.
Latin Quarter.
Montréal Botanical Garden & Insectarium 514/872-1400.
Montréal Museum of Fine Arts 514/285-2000.
Old Montréal & Old Port.
Olympic Park.
Underground City.

BEST VIEW: From a caleche ride (horse-drawn carriage), from the top of the Montréal Tower, or from the patio of the old hunting lodge atop Mont Royal.

WEATHER: It's north of New England so winters are for real. Beautiful spring and fall colors. Summers get hot and humid.

TRANSIT: Diamond Cab 514/273-6331.
Montréal Urban Transit 514/280-5100.

Montréal • Province of Québec

Sona 1439 rue Bleury (at Place des Arts, across from the Imperial Cinema) **514/282-1000** • wknds only • gay/ straight • after-hours club • cover charge

Stéréo 858 rue Ste-Catherine Est **514/282-3307** • after-hours • lesbians/ gay men • inquire locally

Unity Club 1400 rue Montcalm (above 'Unity Pub') **514/523-4429** • open Th-Sun • popular • lesbians/ gay men • women's night Fri • dancing/DJ • 4 flrs & great rooftoop terrace • T-dance Sun • live shows • young crowd

CAFES

Café Titanic 445 St-Pierre (in Old Montréal) **514/849-0894** • 7am-5pm, clsd wknds • popular • salad & soup

The Second Cup 1351 Ste-Catherine Est **514/285-4468** • smokefree coffee shop

RESTAURANTS

L' Ambiance (Salon de thé) 1874 Notre-Dame Ouest (at des Seigneurs) **514/939-2609** • 11am-4pm Mon-Fri • dinner for large groups only • by reservation

L' Anecdote I 801 rue Rachel Est (at St-Hubert) **514/526-7967** • 8am-10pm • lesbians/ gay men • burgers • plenty veggie • also 3751 av des Pins (at St-Urbain) • 514/282-0972 • more women at this location

Après le Jour 901 rue Rachel Est (at St-Andre) **514/527-4141** • dinner only, from 4pm Sun • lesbians/ gay men • Italian/ French • seafood

Aubergell.com 1641 rue Amherst **514/597-0878** • 7am-10pm, from 5pm wknds • bistro • full bar

Bacci 4205 rue St-Denis (at Rachel) **514/844-3929** • 11am-3am • full bar

Bato Thai 1310 rue Ste-Catherine Est **514/524-6705** • lunch & dinner • lesbians/ gay men • beer/ wine • Can$6-14

Bazou 2004 Hôtel de Ville (at Ontario) **514/982-0853** • 5pm-11pm • Californian

La Campagnola 1229 rue de la Montagne (at Ste-Catherine) **514/866-3234** • 11am-1am • popular • Italian • great eggplant! • some veggie • beer/ wine • Can$12-20

Chablis 1639 rue St-Hubert (at Maisonneuve) **514/523-0053** • 11am-11pm, from 5pm wknds • Spanish/ French • some veggie • full bar • terrace • Can$6-18

Le Christopher 1800 rue Ste-Catherine Est (at Papineau) **514/527-5666** • 11am-10pm, till 11pm Th-Fri, from 9am wknds • trendy • Can$15-30

Chuchai 4088 rue St-Denis (at Rachel) **514/843-4194** • lunch & dinner • veggie-only Thai • full bar • Can$7-13

Commensal 1720 St-Denis **514/845-2627** • open till 10pm • vegetarian

Da Salossi 3441 St-Denis (at Sherbrooke) **514/843-8995** • lunch & dinner, dinner only Sat, lunch only Mon • Italian • some veggie • beer/ wine • wheelchair access

L' Exception 1200 rue St-Hubert (at Réné-Lévesque) **514/282-1282** • burgers & sandwiches • plenty veggie • terrace

L' Express 3927 rue St-Denis (at Duluth) **514/845-5333** • 8am-2am, 1pm-10pm Sun • popular • French bistro • full bar • great pâté • Can$11-20

La Paryse 302 rue Ontario Est (nr Sanguinet) **514/842-2040** • 11am-11pm (from 2pm in July) • lesbians/ gay men • 50s-style diner • lesbian-owned/ run • Can$8-10

Piccolo Diavolo 1336 rue Ste-Catherine Est (at Panêt) **514/526-1336** • 5pm-2am, lunch Tue & Fri • popular • Italian • Can$11-22

Le Planète 1451 rue Ste-Catherine Est **514/528-6953** • lunch & dinner, brunch only Sun • global cuisine • young crowd • beer/ wine • Can$10-12

Le Queen 1329 rue Ste-Catherine Est (at Panêt) **514/526-6011** • noon-midnight • live shows Sat

Le Saloon Café 1333 rue Ste-Catherine Est (at Panêt) **514/522-1333** • 11am-midnight, till 2am Fri-Sat • popular • int'l • big dishes & even bigger drinks • Can$6-11 • 'Sisters' upstairs

Thai Grill 5101 boul St-Laurent **514/270-5566**

ENTERTAINMENT & RECREATION

Ça Roule 27 rue de la Commune Est **514/866-0633** • in case you want to join all the other beautiful & buffed ones inline skating up & down Ste-Catherine

Cinéma du Parc 3575 Parc (btwn Milton & Prince Arthur) **514/281-1900** • repertory film theater

Prince Arthur Est at boul St-Laurent, not far from Sherbrooke Métro station • closed-off street w/ many outdoor restaurants & cafés • touristy but oh-so-European

BOOKSTORES

L' Androgyne 1436 Amherst (at Ste-Catherine) **514/842-4765** • 9am-6pm, till 9pm Th-Fri, 10am-5pm Sun • popular • lgbt bookstore w/ English & French titles • wheelchair access

Province of Québec • CANADA

RETAIL SHOPS

Priape 1311 Ste-Catherine Est (at Visitation) **514/521-8451** • 10am-9pm, noon-9pm Sun • clubwear • leather • books • toys & more

Screaming Eagle 1424 boul St-Laurent **514/849-2843** • leather shop

PUBLICATIONS

Fugues 514/848-1854 • glossy lgbt bar/entertainment guide

Rainbow Choices Directory 416/762-1320, 888/241-3569 (CANADA ONLY) • lgbt entertainment & business directory for Canada

GYMS & HEALTH CLUBS

Body Tech 1010 Ste-Catherine Est (at Amherst) **514/849-7000**

Physotech 1657 rue Amherst (nr Maisonneuve) **514/527-7587** • lesbians/ gay men

EROTICA

Il Bolero 6842-46 St-Hubert (btwn St-Zotique & Bélanger) **514/270-6065** • fetish & clubwear emporium • ask about monthly fetish party

North Hatley

see Sherbrooke

Québec

INFO LINES & SERVICES

Relais d'espérance 1001 av 14ème (at av 10ème) **418/522-3301** • infoline (in French) • also lgbt center & coffeehouse

ACCOMMODATIONS

727 Guest House 727 rue d'Aiguillon (btwn St-Augustin & Côte Ste-Geneviève) **418/648-6766, 800/652-6766** • lesbians/ gay men

Apts & Studios Ste-Angèle 30 rue Ste-Angèle **418/648-1000** • gay-friendly • studios, 1 & 2-bdrm apts • kids ok • women-owned/ run • Can$400-900/ week

L' Auberge du Quartier 170 Grande Allée Ouest (at av Cartier) **418/525-9726, 800/782-9441 (IN QUÉBEC ONLY)** • gay-friendly • buffet brkfst • kids ok • smokefree • Can$60-120

Le Coureur des Bois Guest House 15 rue Ste-Ursule (at St-Jean, in Old Québec) **418/692-1117, 800/269-6414** • lesbians/ gay men • also apts • shared baths • gay-owned/ run • Can$44-100

Le Gîte de la Jeunesse 772 côte Ste-Geneviève (nr St-Jean) **418/648-9497** • gay-friendly • kids ok • Can$30-50

Hôtel Dominion 1912 126 rue St-Pierre **418/692-2224, 888/833-5253** • gay-friendly • boutique hotel in city's 1st skyscraper • Can$199-270

Quebec

LGBT PRIDE: September. 418/836-6066.

ANNUAL EVENTS: January/February - Carnaval (Winter Celebration) 418/626-3716, web: www.carnaval.qc.ca.
March - Ski Out.
July - Summer Festival.

CITY INFO: 800/363-7777, web: www.tourisme.gouv.qc.ca.

ATTRACTIONS: Change of Guards at the Citadel.
Château Frontenac 418/692-3861.
Grand Allée.
Hôtel du Parlement.
Notre-Dame-de-Québec Basilica.
Old Québec.
Quartier du Petit-Champlain.

TRANSIT: Taxi Québec 418/525-8123.
Autobus La Quebecoise 888/872-5525, web: www.autobus.qc.ca.
CTCUQ (bus service) 418/627-2511.

Sherbrooke • Province of Québec

Loews Le Concorde 1225 cour du Général-De Montcalm **418/647-2222, 800/463-5256** • gay-friendly • 4-star hotel • located on Grand Allée • revolving restaurant • swimming • Can$120-300

La Lucarne Enchantée 225 chemin Royal, St-Jean-De-L'Ile d'Orléans **418/829-3792** • gay-friendly • full brkfst • animals on premises • nr beach • swimming • lesbian-owned/ run • Can$65-70

BARS

L' Amour Sorcier 789 côte Ste-Geneviève (at St-Jean) **418/523-3395** • 2pm-3am • popular • lesbians/ gay men • neighborhood bar • food served • videos • terrace

Bar 321 321 de la Couronne (at La Salle) **418/525-5107** • 8am-3am • mostly gay men • transgender-friendly

Bar 889 889 côte Ste-Geneviève **418/524-5000** • 8am-3am • lesbians/ gay men • neighborhood bar • live shows • patio

Bar L' Eveil 670 rue Bouvier #118 **418/628-0610** • 3pm-close, from 8pm Sat, clsd Mon-Wed • mostly women • neighborhood bar • patio

Paradisio Café-Bar 161 rue St-Jean (at Turnbull) **418/522-6014** • 2pm-midnight, clsd Mon • mostly women • neighborhood bar

Pub La Malette 698 rue D'Aiguillon **418/523-8279** • 3pm-3am • lesbians/ gay men

Taverne Le Drague 815 rue St-Augustin (at St-Joachim) **418/649-7212** • 8am-3am • popular • mostly gay men • neighborhood bar • dancing/DJ Fri-Sun • food served • drag shows • beer/ wine • terrace • wheelchair access

NIGHTCLUBS

Hangar du Vieux Port 84 Dalhousie • 2nd & 4th Sat only • mostly gay men • unconfirmed

RESTAURANTS

Le Commensal 860 rue St-Jean **418/647-3733** • 11am-10pm • vegetarian/ vegan • Can$5-12

Le Hobbit 700 rue St-Jean (at Ste-Geneviève) **418/647-2677** • 8am-close • some veggie • Can$9-11

La Playa 780 rue St-Jean (at St-Augustin) **418/522-3989** • lunch Th-Fri, dinner nightly • 'West Coast cuisine' • martini bar • heated terrace • gay-owned/ run

Poisson d'Avril 115 rue St-André (at St-Paul) **418/692-1010** • lunch & dinner • French for 'April Fools'

Restaurant Diana 849 rue St-Jean (at St-Augustine) **418/524-5794** • 8am-1am, till 2am Fri-Sat • popular • Italian & Greek

Zorba Grec 854 rue St-Jean (near Dufferin) **418/525-5509** • 24hrs • Canadian, Greek & Italian • BYOB • wheelchair access

ENTERTAINMENT & RECREATION

Le Château Frontenac 1 rue des Carrières **418/692-3861, 800/441-1414** • this hotel disguised as a castle remains the symbol of Québec—even if you can't afford the princess' ransom to stay the night, you can come & enjoy the view from outside

Ice Hotel **418/661-4522, 877/505-0423** • sometimes getting put on ice isn't a bad thing—check this gay-friendly hotel out before it melts away, 9 km E of Québec City in Montmorency Falls Park • Jan-March only

RETAIL SHOPS

FinFinaud 847 rue St-Jean **418/648-9526** • 11am-close • club & fetish clothes

EROTICA

Importation André Dubois 46 côte de la Montagne (at Frontenac Castle) **418/692-0264** • transgender-friendly • wheelchair access

Rimouski

INFO LINES & SERVICES

Maison des Femmes de Rimouski 16 Evèche (at rue Cathédral) **418/723-0333** • 9am-noon & 3pm-6pm, clsd wknds • women's resource center

ACCOMMODATIONS

Gîte aux Trois Pains 3 rue des Pins, CP 127, Baie-des-Sables **418/772-6047, 877/210-2910** • gay-friendly • 1880 renovated home • full brkfst • shared baths • dinner on request • gay-owned/ run • Can$50

Rouyn-Noranda

BARS

Station D 82 Perreault Ouest **819/797-8696** • 3pm-3am, till 11pm Tue-Wed • lesbians/ gay men • dancing/DJ • drag shows • karaoke

Sherbrooke

ACCOMMODATIONS

The Abenaki Lodge 4030 chemin Magog, CP628, North Hatley **819/842-4455** • gay/ straight • full brkfst • on the lake • nr skiing • Can$130-145

Auberge La Raveaudiere B&B 11 Hatley Ctr, North Hatley **819/842-2554** • gay/ straight • 19th-c country inn • full brkfst • 1/2 hr from Montreal • gay-owned/ run • Can$120-155

Province of Québec • CANADA

NIGHTCLUBS

Complex 17-13 13-15-17 Bowen Sud (at rue King) **819/569-5580** • 11am-3am • lesbians/gay men • dancing/DJ • pub & dance club • strippers Fri-Sun • lesbian bar downstairs

RESTAURANTS

Café Bla-Bla 2 rue Wellington S (at King) **819/565-1366** • 11am-12:30am, till 2am wknds • full bar

St-Adèle

ACCOMMODATIONS

Auberge de la Gare B&B 1694 chemin Pierre Peladeau **450/228-3140** • gay/ straight • Can$60-65 (for 2)

St-Didace

ACCOMMODATIONS

La Barcarolle 480 Principale **450/835-3154** • gay-friendly • 100-yr-old home in quaint village • pets ok • swimming • bikes available • gay-owned/ run • Can$40-60

St-Donat

ACCOMMODATIONS

Havre du Parc Auberge 2788 Rte 125 N **819/424-7686** • gay/ straight • quiet lakeside inn for nature lovers • full brkfst • kids ok • gay-owned/ run • Can$115-130

St-Hyacinthe

BARS

Bistrot Mondor 1400 Cascades Ouest **450/773-1695** • 8am-3am • mostly women • neighborhood bar

La Main Gauche 470 rue Mondor **450/774-5556** • 3pm-3am • lesbians/gay men • dancing/DJ • live shows

Ste-Catherine-de-Hatley

ACCOMMODATIONS

L' Auberge Ste-Catherine-de-Hatley 2 rue Grand **819/868-1212** • gay-friendly • also bar & restaurant • terrace • kids ok • Can$32-48

Trois Rivières

ACCOMMODATIONS

Le Gîte du Huard 42 rue St-Louis **819/375-8771** • gay-friendly • Can$45-60

BARS

La Station 1198 rue Champflour **819/376-0481** • 3pm-3am • lesbians/gay men • dancing/DJ • food served • karaoke

Verdun

INFO LINES & SERVICES

Centre des Femmes de Verdun 4255 rue Wellington **514/767-0384** • clsd wknds • general women's center • limited lesbian info

Want More?

Subscribe to our online travel guide:
www.damron.com

More listings. More destinations (like Australia, South Africa & Asia). More up-to-the-minute info. Check with Damron before you leave, or from the road with your laptop!

Saskatchewan

Ravenscrag

Accommodations

Spring Valley Guest Ranch 306/295–4124
• popular • gay-friendly • 1913 character home • cabin & tipis • full brkfst • kids/ pets ok • also restaurant • country-style • gay-owned/ run • Can$40-60

Regina

Info Lines & Services

The Gay & Lesbian Community of Regina 2070 Broad St (at Victoria) **306/569-1995, 306/522-7343** • 7pm-1am Mon-Wed, 6pm-2am Th-Sun • lesbians/ gay men • also a bar

Pink Triangle Community Services 2070 Broad St **306/525-6046** • 5pm-10pm

Regina Women's Community Centre 1933 8th Ave #250 (at Hamilton St) **306/522-2777** • 9am-4:30pm, clsd wknds

Accommodations

Two Spirit PO Box 33084, S4T 7X2 **866/737-2200** • 160-acre ranch • guest rooms, bunkhouse & tent camping • lesbian-owned • $10-70

Nightclubs

The Outside 2070 Broad St (at Victoria) **306/569-1995, 306/522-7343** • Th-Sat only • lesbians/ gay men • dancing/DJ • 'Homo-Depot' gay store inside 7pm-10pm

Entertainment & Recreation

Oscar Wilde & Company 2232 Retallack St **306/352-2919** • gay theater troupe

Bookstores

Buzzword Books 2926B 13th Ave **306/522-6562** • 11am-6pm, clsd Sun • some gay titles

Publications

Sensible Shoes News 306/522-7343 • celebrating the diversity of Saskatchewan's lesbian, bisexual & transgendered women's community

Spiritual Groups

Dignity Regina Dignité 1351 Elphinstone St **306/569-3666** • 6:30pm 3rd Sun

Saskatoon

Info Lines & Services

Circle of Choice Gay/ Lesbian AA 10th St & Broadway (at Grace Westminster United Church) **306/665-5626** • 8pm Wed

Gay/ Lesbian Line & Drop-In 203-220 3rd Ave S (at Gay/ Lesbian Health Services) **306/665-1224, 800/358-1833** • noon-10pm, till 6pm Sat, clsd Sun • library • many social/ support groups

Accommodations

Brighton House 1308 5th Ave N **306/664-3278** • gay-friendly • full brkfst • hot tub • smokefree • kids ok (family rate available) • lesbian-owned/ run • $50-70 + tax

Nightclubs

Diva's 220 3rd Ave S #110 (alley entrance) **306/665-0100** • 8pm-2am, clsd Sun • lesbians/ gay men • dancing/DJ • private club

Bookstores

Spiritworks 1814 Lorne Ave (at Taylor) **306/653-7966** • 10am-6pm, till 9pm Th, noon-5pm Sun • spiritual & women's

Retail Shops

Out of the Closet 203-220 3rd Ave S, 3rd flr **306/665-1224** • boutique run by the 'Gay/ Lesbian Line' • lgbt gifts

The Trading Post 226 2nd Ave S **306/653-1769** • 10am-5:30pm • clothing

Publications

Perceptions 306/244-1930 • covers the Canadian prairies

Yukon

Whitehorse

Info Lines & Services

Gay/ Lesbian Alliance of the Yukon Territory PO Box 5604 Y1A 5H4 **867/667-7857** • events • newsletter

Victoria Faulkner Women's Centre 503 Hanson **867/667-2693** • drop in centre • 11am-3pm, clsd wknds

Accommodations

Inn on the Lake Lot 76 McClintock Pl, Marsh Lake **867/660-5253** • gay-friendly • luxury lakefront log inn • Canada Select rated 4.5 stars • smokefree • Can$98-125

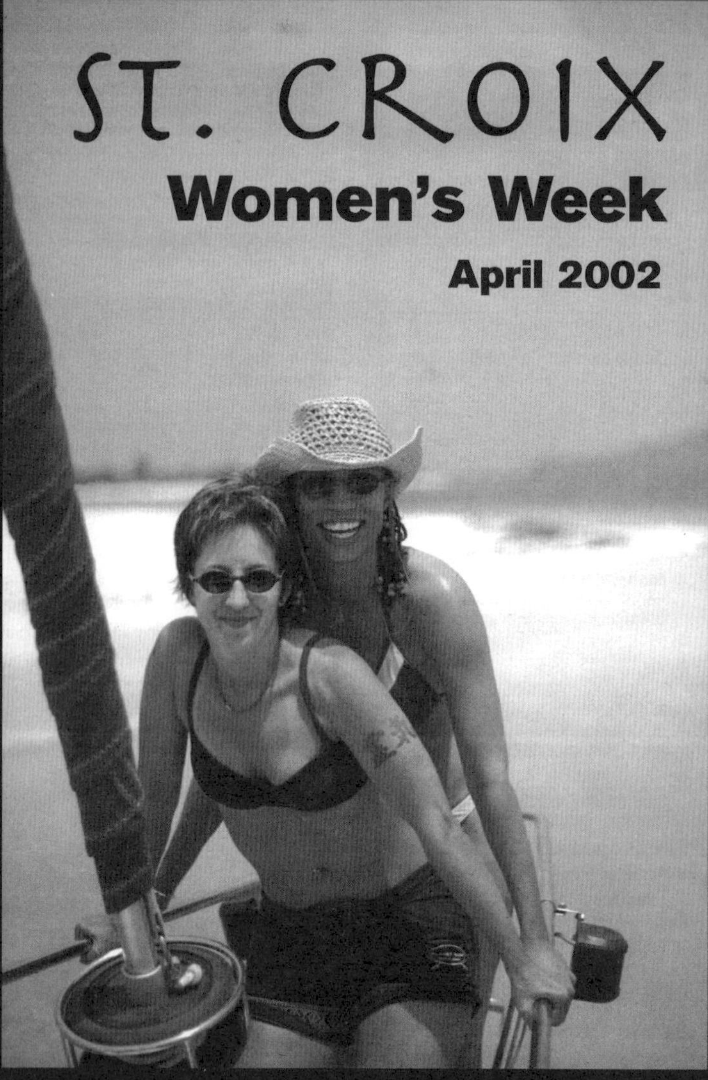

ST. CROIX
Women's Week
April 2002

SPONSORED BY

7ᵀᴴ ANNUAL WOMEN WEEK SPACE IS LIMITED

VISIT OUR WEBSITE AT **www.curvemag.com**

CALL NOW FOR DETAILS **(800) 998-5565**

Santo Domingo • Dominican Republic

BAHAMAS

Eleuthera

ACCOMMODATIONS

Cigatoo Resort Governor's Harbour **242/332-3060** • gay-friendly • resort • on hill overlooking the Atlantic Ocean • swimming • $165-252

Nassau

INFO LINES & SERVICES

BGLAD (Bahamian Gays & Lesbians Against Discrimination) 242/327-1249 • support/ advocacy group • hotline 9am-midnight daily

Hope TEA 242/328-1816 (HOTLINE) • lgbt support group • hotline staffed 8pm-10pm Mon (lesbians), Tue (TV/TS) & Wed-Th (gay men)

BARS

Club Waterloo E Bay St (1/2 mile E of Paradise Island Bridge) **242/393-7324** • 11:30am-4am • gay-friendly • indoor/ outdoor complex w/ 5 bars • dancing/DJ • live music • restaurant • swimming

The Drop-Off Pub Bay St (at East St, downstairs, across from 'Planet Hollywood') **242/322-3444** • 11am-6am • gay-friendly • dancing/DJ from 10pm • also restaurant • lunch & dinner • English & Bahamian pub fare

Pams/ The Car Parlor Greater Chippingham **242/326-5085** • lesbians/ gay men • neighborhood bar • also restaurant • dinner & late-night snacks

NIGHTCLUBS

Endangered Species West Bay St (in Cable Beach Shopping Center, no sign) **242/327-0127** • 11pm-close Fri-Sun • lesbians/ gay men • dancing/DJ • drag shows • 18+ • lesbian-owned

RESTAURANTS

Café Paradiso Bay St, btwn Elizabeth & Victoria Aves (3 blks E of Rawson Sq) **242/356-5282** • brkfst & lunch, clsd Sun • beer/ wine • sometimes becomes a disco on Sat nights, call for more info

BARBADOS

Bridgetown

RESTAURANTS

The Waterfront Cafe The Careenage **246/427-0093** • trendy • also bar • outdoor seating (not surprisingly, on the waterfront)

Christchurch

ACCOMMODATIONS

Roman Beach Apartments Enterprise-on-Sea Road (6 miles from Bridgetown), Oistinstown **246/428-7635** • gay-friendly • apt-hotel on beach • kitchens • $40-60

St James

ACCOMMODATIONS

Hogarth House Holders Hill, West Coast Barbados **246/432-6402** • gay-friendly • nr golf & beach • jacuzzi

DOMINICAN REPUBLIC

Boca Chica

ACCOMMODATIONS

Residencial El Candil Calle el Candil #2 (at 20 de Deciembre) **809/523-4252** • gay-friendly • apts • 5 mins from beach • swimming • gay-owned/ run • $45-55

Puerto Plata

ACCOMMODATIONS

Apt-Hotel Barlovento Calle Cadiz, Costambar **809/970-7075** • gay-friendly • studios & apts • nr beach • hot tub • swimming • also Restaurant Le Pierre • steak/ seafood • full bar • wheelchair access • US$40-70

Santo Domingo

ACCOMMODATIONS

Aida Hotel Calle El Conde 464 **809/685-7692** • gay-friendly • nr gay bars • US$24

El Duque de Wellington Hotel Av Independencia #304 **809/682-4525** • gay-friendly • located in the Colonial City • gay-owned/ run

Renaissance Jaragua Hotel & Casino 367 George Washington Ave **809/221-2222, 800/468-3571** • gay-friendly • 14-acre resort • tropical gardens, lagoon & waterfalls • US$140-220

BARS

Atlantis Disco 555 Ave George Washington (at Malecon) **809/685-2011** • mostly gay men • dancing/DJ • live shows • popular late nights

Le Pousse Calle 19 de Marzo 10, Zona Colonial (nr harbor) • 10pm-2am, clsd Mon-Wed • popular • lesbians/ gay men • dancing/DJ

Llego Jose Reyes 10, Zona Colonial **809/689-8250** • mostly gay men • piano bar • strippers

The Phoenix Calle Polvorin 10, Zona Colonial **809/689-7572** • 7pm-1am • mostly gay men • friendly neighborhood bar

Dutch/ French West Indies/ Jamaica • CARIBBEAN

RESTAURANTS

Café Coco 53 Padre Billini (in Colonial Zone) **809/687-9624** • noon-10pm • English • full bar • live shows

DUTCH WEST INDIES/ARUBA

Aruba

BARS

Café the Paddock 94 LG Smith Blvd #13, Oranjestad **297/83-23-34** • 10am-2am • gay-friendly • neighborhood bar • food served

The Cellar Klipstraat 2, Oranjestad • 3pm-5am • popular • gay-friendly • neighborhood bar • also 'TMF' late-night dance bar upstairs

Don't Tell Your Mama La Cabana Resort & Casino (in the Tropicana showroom), Oranjestad **297/87-90-00, 800/835-7193** • gay-friendly • drag shows

Jimmy's Place Waterweg & Middenweg, Oranjestad **297/82-25-50** • 4pm-2am • popular • gay-friendly • neighborhood bar • dancing/ DJ • food served

RESTAURANTS

Green House 29 Palm Beach, Palm Beach Aruba **297/86-52-41** • lunch & dinner • vegetarian • US$14

ENTERTAINMENT & RECREATION

Sonesta Island European (topless) side, Oranjestad

FRENCH WEST INDIES

St Barthelemy

ACCOMMODATIONS

Hotel Normandie **590/27-61-66** • gay-friendly

Hotel St-Barth Isle De France Plage des Flamands **508/528-7727, 800/421-3396** • gay-friendly • ultra-luxe hotel • $300-800

St Barth's Beach Hotel Grand Cul de Sac **590/27-60-70** • gay-friendly • swimming

Village St-Jean **596/ 27-61-39, 800/633-7411** • gay-friendly • hotel & cottages • swimming • US$95-160 (rms), US$130-490 (cottages)

ENTERTAINMENT & RECREATION

Anse Gouverneur St Jean Beach • nudity

Anse Grande Saline Beach • nudity • gay section on the right side of Saline

L'Orient Beach • gay beach

St Martin

ACCOMMODATIONS

Holland House 43 Front St, Philipsburg **599/ 52-25-72** • gay-friendly • on the beach • $79-195

Meridien L'Habitation Anse Marcel **590/87-67-00, 800/543-4300** • gay-friendly • beachfront resort • swimming • $260-550

Orient Beach Mont Vernon 1 **590/87-31-10, 800/818-5992** • gay-friendly • studios • 1 & 2-bdrm villas • steps from St Martin's most beautiful clothing-optional beach • $95-250

NIGHTCLUBS

Pink Mango at Laguna Beach Hotel, Nettle Bay (look for the rainbow flag, ring to enter) **590/87-59-99** • 10pm-3am • popular • lesbians/ gay men • dancing/DJ

RESTAURANTS

Cheri's Cafe Maho Reef **599/54-53-361** • 11am-1:30am, clsd Tue • popular • full bar • wheelchair access

Le Pressoir 30 Blvd de Grand Case **590/87-76-62** • $18-20

Rainbow 176 Blvd de Grand Case (at W end of beach) **590/87-55-80** • lunch & dinner • French/ int'l • $23-27

Wajang Doll 167 Front St, Philipsburg **599/ 54-22-687** • lunch daily, dinner only Mon & Sat • Indonesian • gay-owned/ run • US$12-25

ENTERTAINMENT & RECREATION

Cupecoy Beach • gay beach

JAMAICA

Montego Bay

ACCOMMODATIONS

Half Moon Golf, Tennis & Beach Club **876/953-2211, 800/626-0592** • gay-friendly • upscale resort • $240-1190

Moun Tambrin Retreat in the mtns 28 miles from Montego Bay **876/918-4486** • gay/ straight • art deco house furnished & built from tropical woods • formerly owned by Alex Haley • food served • swimming • $210/ person (all incl'd)

Negril

ACCOMMODATIONS

Tingalaya's B&B West End Rd, Negril, Westmoreland **414/924-4269** • gay-friendly • rustic thatched cottages • private beach & gardens • swimming • nudity • $65-85

San Juan • Puerto Rico

Port Antonio

ACCOMMODATIONS

Hotel Mocking Bird Hill 876/993-7267 • gay/ straight • eco-friendly inn • fresh local food served • swimming • massage • kids ok • wheelchair access • lesbian-owned/ run • $125-230

PUERTO RICO

Note: For those w/ rusty or no Spanish, 'carretera' means 'highway.' 'Calle' means 'street.'

Aguada

ACCOMMODATIONS

San Max 787/868-2931 • lesbians/ gay men • guesthouse/ studio apt on the beach • $30/ day • weekly rentals • 3-day minimum stay

BARS

Johnny's Bar Carretera 115 • gay-friendly • inquire at 'San Max' accommodations for directions

Aguadilla

BARS

The Factory Club C Belt 703 Punto Borinquen Shopping Ctr (at Base Ramey) **787/890-1530** • 9pm-close Th-Sun • dancing/DJ • live shows

Bayamón

BARS

Gilligan's Pub Av Betances D-18, **Hnas?** Davila (nr Pepin Ct) **787/786-5065** • 8:30am-4am Fri-Sat, till 1:30am Th • lesbians/ gay men • dancing/DJ • live shows • private club

Coamo

ACCOMMODATIONS

Parador Baños de Coamo end of Rte 546 **787/825-2186, 787/825-2239** • gay-friendly • resort • mineral baths • also restaurant • full bar • kids ok • public baths • $75-85

Fajardo

ACCOMMODATIONS

Villas Margarita 787/889-2098 • lesbians/ gay men • tree house villa • private veranda • swimming • $750/ week

Isabela

NIGHTCLUBS

Ricomar Club 8 Calle Paz, Carretera 459, Barrio Jobos (across from Brendy Pizza) • 8:30pm-close, from 10pm Sun, clsd Mon-Th • lesbians/ gay men • dancing/DJ • live shows

San German

BARS

Norman's Bar Ctra 318, Barrio Maresúa • 6pm-1am • lesbians/ gay men • neighborhood bar • dancing/DJ • salsa & merengue

San Juan

INFO LINES & SERVICES

GEMA Hotline 787/723-4538 • lesbian alternative to the bar scene • en español

Madres Lesbianas 787/764-9639 • lesbian mothers group

ACCOMMODATIONS

At Wind Chimes Inn 53 Taft St, Condado 800/946-3244 • gay-friendly • restored Spanish Villa • 1 blk from Condado beach • $65-140

Atlantic Beach Hotel Calle Vendig 1, Condado (off Av Ashford) **787/721-6900, 888/611-6900** • popular • lesbians/ gay men • swimming • rooftop deck w/ hot tub • some shared baths • restaurant • $70-150

Casa del Caribe Guest House Calle Caribe 57, Condado **787/722-7139** • gay-friendly • $35-50

Condado Inn Av Condado 6 (at Av Ashford) **787/724-7145** • lesbians/ gay men • nr beach • also bar

El San Juan Hotel & Casino Av Isla Verde 6063 (at Baldorioty de Castro), Isla Verde **787/791-1000, 800/468-2818** • gay-friendly • great Asian restaurant & cigar bar • swimming

Embassy Guest House Calle Seaview 1126, Condaso (off Calle Vendig) **787/725-8284, 787/724-7440** • gay/ straight • across street from beach • swimming • also bar & grill • $45-145

Hotel El Convento Calle Cristo 100, Old San Juan (btwn Caleta de las Monjas & Calle Sol) **787/723-9020, 800/468-2779** • popular • gay-friendly • 17th-c former Carmelite convent • swimming • 'plunge' jacuzzi • $190-300

Hotel Iberia Av Wilson 1464, Condado (btwn Avs de Diego & Washington) **787/722-5380, 787/723-0200** • gay/ straight • European-style hotel • also restaurant & bar 'La Fonda de Cervantes' • lunch & dinner daily • Spanish/ int'l cuisine • gay-owned/ run • $88-132

Puerto Rico • CARIBBEAN

L' Habitation Beach Guesthouse Calle Italia 1957, Ocean Park (nr Santa Ana) **787/727-2499** • lesbians/ gay men • on the beach • also restaurant & bar • gay-owned/ run • $55-91

Marriott Resort & Casino Av Ashford 1309 (at Av Condado) **787/722-7000, 800/223-6388** • gay-friendly • food served • swimming • $190-280

Numero Uno on the Beach Calle Santa Ana 1, Ocean Park (nr Calle Italia) **787/726-5010, 787/727-9687** • gay/ straight • swimming • also full bar & grill • Caribbean • brkfst, lunch & dinner • wheelchair access • $65-185

BARS

Atlantic Beach Bar Calle Vendig 1 (at Atlantic Beach Hotel') **787/721-6900** • 11am-1am • lesbians/ gay men • live shows • T-dance Sun w/ strippers & show • food served

Baccheus Calle Parque 609, Local LM-9, Santurce • Th-Sun • mostly women • neighborhood bar

Bebo's Playa Piñones, Isla Verde • noon-close Wed-Sun • lesbians/ gay men • beachfront neighborhood bar • dancing/DJ • strippers Wed • drag shows Sun • fun crowd

Café Bohemio Calle Cristo 100, Old San Juan (in 'Gran Hotel El Convento') **787/723-9200** • 11am-2am • gay-friendly • professional crowd • popular Tue • also restaurant • Puerto Rican/ int'l • food served till 11pm

Cups Calle San Mateo 1708, Santurce (btwn Calles Barbe & San Jorge) **787/268-3570, 787/268-5640** • 7pm-close, clsd Mon-Tue • mostly women

Junior's Calle Condado 602, Santurce (btwn Calle Benito Alonso & Av Ponce de León) Puerto Rico **787/723-9477** • 5:30pm-6:30am • lesbians/ gay men • neighborhood bar • drag & strip shows • local crowd

Nuestro Ambiente Av Ponce de León 1412, Santurce (across from Central High School) **787/724-9093** • 8pm-close • mostly women • live music wknds

Panache Oceanfront Bar Calle Seaview 1127 (off Calle Vendig at Embassy guest house) **787/724-7440** • seasonal • dinner only, clsd Tue • 'California' French

Paraiso del Mar Carretera 187, Piñones, Isla Verde • 2pm-close Fri-Sun • lesbians/ gay men • fun beachfront neighborhood bar • dancing/DJ • live shows Sun • women-owned/ run

San Juan

LGBT PRIDE: June. 787/261-2590.

ANNUAL EVENTS: February - Ponce Carnival.
June - Casals Festival 787/728-5744.
October - Bomba y Plena (African-Caribbean music festival).

CITY INFO: 800/223-6530.

ATTRACTIONS: Condado Beach.
La Fortaleza.
Historic Old San Juan.
El Morro Fortress & Fort San Cristobal 787/729-6960.
Pablo Casals Museum 787/723-9185.
Quincentennial Plaza.
San José Church.
San Juan Museum of Art & History 787/724-1875.

BEST VIEW: From El Morro or alternatively, one of the harbor cruises that depart from Pier 2 in Old San Juan.

WEATHER: Tropical sunshine year-round, with temperatures that average in the mid-80°s from November to May. Expect more rain on the northern coast.

TRANSIT: Metro Bus 787/763-4141.

San Juan • Puerto Rico

Rivera Hermanos Calle San Sebastián 157, Old San Juan **787/724-5828** • 10am-7pm • gay-friendly • liquor shop & bar

Tia Maria's Av Jose de Diego 326, Stop 22, Santurce (at Ponce de León) **787/724-4011** • 10am-midnight, till 1am Th-Sun • popular • lesbians/ gay men • liquor shop & bar

Nightclubs

Bachelor Av Condado 112, Santurce (behind Egypto) • 10pm-close, clsd Mon-Tue • mostly gay men • dancing/DJ • drag & strip shows • theme nights • rooftop garden • unconfirmed

Concepts (The Downtown Club) Av Chardón 9 (in 'Le Chateau'), Hato Rey **787/763-7432** • Sun only • lesbians/ gay men • dancing/DJ • popular drag shows

Eros Av Ponce de León 1257, Santurce (btwn Calles Villamil & Labra) **787/722-1131** • 10pm-5am, from 9pm Sun, clsd Mon-Tue • popular • lesbians/gay men • dancing/DJ • live shows • theme nights • gay-owned/ run

Laguna Club Calle Barranquitas 53, Condado (btwn Calle Mayagüez & Av Ashford) • 11pm-late • popular • mostly gay men • dancing/DJ • live shows

Paraiso Av Eleanor Roosevelt (across from TeleVideo), Hato Rey • open wknds • lesbians/gay men

Cafes

Café Berlin Calle San Francisco 407, Plaza Colón, Old San Juan (btwn Calles Norzagary & O'Donnel) **787/722-5205** • 9am-11pm • popular • espresso bar • plenty veggie

Restaurants

Al Dente Calle Recinto S, Old San Juan **787/723-7303** • lunch & dinner • Italian • $10-16

La Bombonera Calle San Francisco 259, Old San Juan **787/722-0658** • 7:30am-8pm • popular • come for the strong coffee & pastries • since 1903!

Café Amadeus Calle San Sebastián 104, Old San Juan (btwn Calles San José & del Cristo) **787/722-8635** • lunch & dinner • popular • nouvelle Puerto Rican/ cont'l • also bar • noon-midnight Tue-Sat • gay-owned/ run

Dragonfly S Fortaleza St (across from Parrot Club) **787/977-3886** • lunch & dinner • Latin/ Asian fusion

Fussion Calle Fortaleza 317, Old San Juan **787/721-7997** • lunch & dinner, Sun brunch • French/ Latin • also bar

The Gallery Cafe Calle Fortaleza 305, Old San Juan **787/725-8676** • 11am-3pm Mon-Fri & 5:30pm-close Tue-Sat • also swanky & hip 'Gallery Lounge' upstairs • live music & DJs

Golden Unicorn Calle Laurel 2415 **787/728-4066** • 11am-11pm • Chinese • $6-26

The Parrot Club Calle Fortaleza 363, Old San Juan (btwn Plaza Colón & Callejón de la Capilla) **787/725-7370** • lunch & dinner • chic Nuevo Latino bistro & bar • live music Tue, Th & Sat • $20+

Sam's Patio Calle San Sebastián 102, Old San Juan **787/723-1149** • lunch & dinner • Mexican • $9-22

Transylvania Restaurant Recinto Sur 317, Old San Juan **787/977-2328** • 11am-2pm Tue-Sat & 5pm-11pm nightly • Romanian • also bar • art gallery • live music

Villa Appia Av Ashford 1350, Condado **787/725-8711** • 11am-11pm • Italian • $8-15

Entertainment & Recreation

Animation Cruises **787/725-3500** • gay cruises Th eves • lesbians/ gay men • dancing/DJ • full bar • call for reservations

Condado Bicycle Av Ashford 1106 **787/722-6288, 888/721-0066**

Bookstores

The Book Store Calle San José 255, Old San Juan (btwn Calles Tetuán & Fortaleza) **787/724-1815** • 9am-7pm • Spanish & English titles • lgbt section • also cafe

Scriptum Av Ashford 1129-B, Condado (at Calle Vendig) **787/724-1123** • Spanish & English titles • lgbt section • also newspapers & magazines • cafe

Publications

Puerto Rico Breeze **787/724-3411** • lgbt newspaper

Gyms & Health Clubs

Muscle Factory Av Ashford 1302, Condado (btwn Avs Cervantes & Caribe) **787/721-0717** • 6am-10pm • gay/ straight

Erotica

Condom World Calle San Francisco 353, Old San Juan (btwn Calles O'Donnel & Tamarindo) **787/722-5348** • condoms, toys, videos & more • 13 locations in Puerto Rico

Pleasure Paradise Av Roosevelt 1367 (in Plazoleta Julio Garriga) **787/706-0855**

Puerto Rico/Trinidad & Tobago/Virgin Islands • CARIBBEAN

Vieques Island

ACCOMMODATIONS

Inn on the Blue Horizon 787/741-3318 • gay-friendly • country inn & cottages • beach access • restaurant • $170-300

Rainbow Realty HC-01 Box 6307 787/741-4312 • gay/ straight • 20 fully-equipped properties available • most w/ views • some on the water • lesbian-owned/ run • $450-2,400

RESTAURANTS

Cafe Blu 787/741-3318

TRINIDAD & TOBAGO

Tobago

ACCOMMODATIONS

Grafton Beach Resort 868/639-0191 • gay-friendly • food served • swimming • $140-250

Kariwak Village Crown Point, Scarborough 868/639-8442, 868/639-8545 • gay-friendly • 1-rm cabañas • swimming • outdoor jacuzzi with waterfall • holistic activites • restaurant • $80-125

RESTAURANTS

Rouselles Bacolet St, Scarborough 868/639-4738 • West Indian/ int'l • $12-15

Trinidad

BARS

Pelican Pub 2-4 Coblentz Ave (next to the Hilton), Port of Spain 868/624-7486 • gay/ straight

Pier One Chaguanas 868/634-4472 • popular • gay-friendly

VIRGIN ISLANDS

St Croix

ACCOMMODATIONS

▲ **Cormorant Beach Club & Hotel** 4126 La Grande Princesse, Christiansted 340/778-8920, 800/548-4460 • popular • lesbians/ gay men • beachfront resort • food served • swimming • gay-owned/ run • $180-230

King Christian Hotel 59 Kings Wharf, Christiansted 340/773-6330, 800/524-2012 • gay-friendly • swimming • also restaurant • $85-150

Sand Castle on the Beach 127 Smithfield, Frederiksted 340/772-1205, 800/524-2018 • gay-friendly • hotel • swimming • kitchens • wheelchair access • $115-250+tax

Pink Fancy Hotel 27 Prince St, Christiansted 340/773-8460, 800/524-2045 • gay-friendly • swimming • cont'l brkfst • $75-120

Richards & Ayre Associates Frederiksted 340/772-0420 • gay-friendly • upscale vacation rentals

Seaview Farm Inn 180 Two Brothers, Frederiksted 340/772-5367, 800/792-5060 • gay-friendly • suites w/ kitchenettes • also restaurant • $65-160

BARS

The Last Hurrah 57 King St, Frederiksted • mostly gay men • neighborhood bar • dancing

RESTAURANTS

Le St-Tropez 227 King St (at Pier 69), Frederiksted 340/772-3000 • French cuisine • full bar • $15-24

Villa Madeleine Teague Bay 340/778-7377, 340/773-8141 • Italian/ cont'l • $20-25

St John

ACCOMMODATIONS

Gallows Point Suite Resort Cruz Bay 340/776-6434, 800/323-7229 • gay-friendly • beachfront resort • all suites • swimming • kitchens • also restaurant • full bar • wheelchair access • $160-365

Maho Bay Camps & Harmony Studios VI National Park 340/776-6226, 800/392-9004 • gay-friendly • rustic cottages & studios • environmentally aware resort • $70-195

Sago Palms Estate 2B, Denis Bay 340/776-6384, 340/776-6876 • gay-friendly • private homes • $980-$1680/ week for two

St John Inn 340/693-8688, 800/666-7688 • gay-friendly • kids ok • swimming • smokefree • $79-195

RESTAURANTS

Asolare Rte 20, Cruz Bay 340/779-4747 • Asian/ French fusion • $22-32

Le Château de Bordeaux Centerline Rd, Jct 10 340/776-6611 • 5:30pm-8:30pm • great view • $20-36

ENTERTAINMENT & RECREATION

Solomon Bay • nude beach • 20-min hike on Salomon Beach Trail

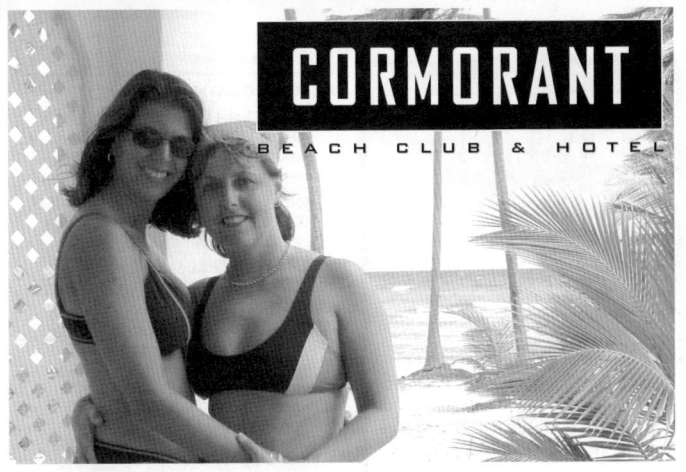

CORMORANT
BEACH CLUB & HOTEL

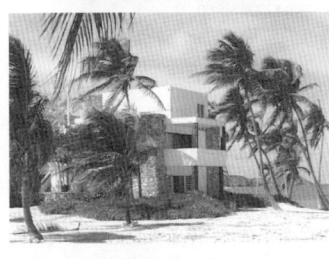

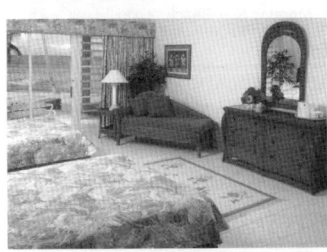

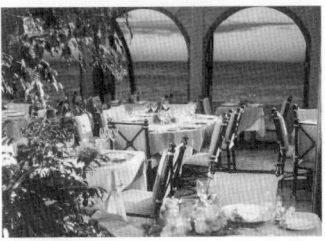

Situated on the north shore of St. Croix (the Gay & Lesbian friendly Caribbean), The Cormorant Beach Club is the *only gay owned and operated* hotel on St. Croix and perhaps in the entire Caribbean. Our oceanfront rooms and suites are spread over six acres of palm-studded white sand beach, where you'll enjoy romantic seaside dining, a lively open-air bar, attentive staff, large pool, tennis courts, great beach snorkeling and *lots* of relaxation.

The Cormorant isn't a scene, but it *is* scenic. Clothing isn't optional at our pool, but then *your* lover already knows what *you* look like. Our rooms do not have a kitchenette, but then the Cormorant has one of the best restaurants on the island and the only one, where you can hold hands, kiss or do a Cher imitation. *OCEANFRONT ROOMS START AT $110 SINGLE AND $130 DOUBLE PER NIGHT.*

800.548.4460
www.CormorantBeachClub.com

CARIBBEAN/ MEXICO

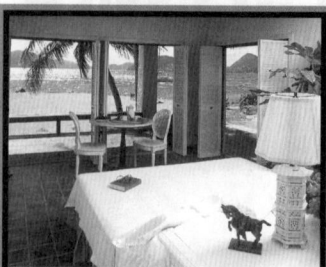

Fort Recovery Villas
Tortola, British Virgin Islands

Luxury 3-4 bedroom house on beach from $515/nt (6 pers).
1 and 2 bedroom beachfront villas from $145/nt (2 pers).

Deluxe Package for Two
7 Nights / 8 Days

Includes: 1 bedroom Beachfront Villa with Tax/Service Charge, Week Jeep Rental, Daily Cont'l Breakfast, 3 Dinners/Guest, Boat Trip (half day), Massage (half hour/guest), Yoga Sunset Class on Dock, Pedicure, Swimming Pool, Beach Towels, Lounge Chairs, AC, Cable TV, Housekeeping Service.

$1,843/couple (4/15–12/17)
$2,628/couple (12/18–4/14)

(284) 495-4354
Fx: (284) 495-4036
(800) 367-8455
(please wait for ring)

www.fortrecovery.com

St Thomas

ACCOMMODATIONS

Danish Chalet Guest House 340/774-5764, 800/635-1531 • gay-friendly • overlooking harbor • spa • deck • limited wheelchair access • $68-99

Hotel 1829 Government Hill 340/776-1829, 800/524-2002 • gay-friendly • swimming • also full bar & restaurant • $75-275

The Inn at Blackbeard's Castle 340/776-1234, 800/344-5771 • gay/ straight • also restaurant

Pavilions & Pools Hotel 6400 Estate Smith Bay 340/775-6110, 800/524-2001 • gay-friendly • 1-bdrm villas each w/ own private swimming pool • $180-275

BARS

Cabana Lounge at Blackbeard's Castle Hotel • Tue-Sun • popular • lesbians/ gay men • food served

NIGHTCLUBS

R&R Back St (at Baker Square) • 10pm-close Fri-Sat only • lesbians/ gay men • also Lemon Grass Cafe

RESTAURANTS

Lulu's 340/774-6800 • Tue-Sat 6pm-9:30pm, bar open till 11pm • popular • creative New World cuisine • full bar • live jazz wknds in season • $15-23

ENTERTAINMENT & RECREATION

Morning Star Beach • popular gay beach

Tortola

ACCOMMODATIONS

▲ **Fort Recovery Villa Estate** 284/495-4354, 800/367-8455 • gay-friendly • grand home on beach & private beachfront villas • swimming • kids ok • wheelchair access • women-owned/ run • $145-260 or house $480-710

MEXICO

Please Note: Mexican cities are often divided into districts or Colonias which we abbreviate as Col. Please use these when giving addresses for directions.

Acapulco

ACCOMMODATIONS

Casa Condesa Bella Vista 125 52-7/484.16.16 • mostly gay men • full brkfst • nr beach • US$75-150

Cancún • Mexico

Fiesta Americana Condesa Av Costera Miguel Alemán 1200 **52-7/484.23.55, 800/223-2332 (US#)** • popular • gay-friendly • deluxe hotel above the gay beach • swimming • 4-star dining • US$135-155

Hotel Acapulco Tortuga Av Costera Miguel Alemán 132 **52-7/484.88.89, 800/832-7491** • gay-friendly • across from the gay beach

Las Brisas **52-7/469.69.00, 888/559-4329 (US#)** • popular • gay-friendly • luxury resort • private pools • US$240+

Quinta Encanto Privada Roca Sola 108, Col Club Deportivo (off Costera Blvd) **52-7/484.65.08, 310/657-1945 (US#)** • gay-friendly • small house rental • sleeps up to 4 • swimming • US$175+

Sunscape Acapulco Calle Caracol 70, Fracc Amiento Farallón **52-7/484.37.07** • gay-friendly • swimming • food served • US$59-125

Nightclubs

Princess Calle Juan de la Cosa 12 (across from the Hotel Continental) **52-7/484.76.01** • after-hours • gay-friendly • popular • dancing/DJ

Relax Calle Lomas de Mar 4 (Zona Dorada) **52-7/484.04.21** • 10pm-late, clsd Mon-Wed • popular • lesbians/ gay men • dancing/DJ • drag & strip shows wknds • young crowd

Tequila's Le Club Calzada A, Urdaneta 29 (near the Zocalo) **52-7/485.86.23** • 10:30pm-close • popular • gay/ straight • drag shows

Restaurants

Los Amigos near the Zocalo • inexpensive American

Beto's Beach Restaurant Av Costera Miguel Alemán 99 (at Condesa Beach) **52-7/484.04.73** • 11am-midnight • lesbians/ gay men • full bar • palapas • also 'Mangos' next door, 52-74/84.47.62 • upscale

El Cabrito Restaurante Avenida Costera M Aleman 1480 (near Convention Center) **52-7/484.77.11**

Café Tres Amigos Calle La Paz 10 (behind the Hotel Alameda) • cheap, local hangout

Carlos' & Charlie's Costera Miguel Aleman #112 **52-74/84.00.39** • lunch and dinner • entertainment • int'l

Coyuca 22 Av Coyuca 22 **52-7/482.34.68, 52-7/483.50.30** • dress code • great views

La Jardin des Artistes Yanez Pinzon 11 **52-7/484.83.44** • French

Kookaburra Carretera Escénica (at Marina Las Brisas) **52-74/46.60.20** • popular • int'l • US$20-25

La Tortuga Calle Lomas del Mar 5–A **52-7/484.69.85** • 10am-2am • full bar • good Mexican, seafood • patio • gay-owned/ run

Primo's Costera Miguel Aleman 149 **52-7/486.63.19** • Italian

La Rebanadota on the Zocalo • pizza • gay-owned/ run

Su Casa/ La Margarita Av Anahuac 110 **52-7/484.43.50** • traditional cuisine • great views

Suntory de Acapulco Costera Miguel Aleman **52-7/484.87.66** • Japanese

Aguascalientes

Nightclubs

Mandiles Av Lopez Mateos 730 W (btwn Agucate & Chabacano) **52-49/15.32.81** • lesbians/ gay men • dancing/DJ

Restaurants

Restaurant Mitla Calle Madero 220

Cabo San Lucas

Accommodations

Chile Pepper Inn 16 de Septiembre y Abasolo **52-1/143-8611, 143-8612 or 143-8613** • gay/ straight • smokefree • kids/ pets ok • wheelchair access • US$47-99 • also weekly rates

Hotel Hacienda Beach Resort Playa el Medano **52-114/3.01.22, 800/733-2226 (US#)** • gay-friendly • upscale • US$145-350

Bars

The Rainbow Bar & Grill Marina Cabo Plaza #39-E **52-114/3.14.55** • popular • lesbians/ gay men • dancing/DJ • patio

Restaurants

Casa Rafael's Playa el Medano **52-114/3.07.39** • 7pm-10pm • elegant • US$19-42

Mi Casa Av Cabo San Lucas **52-114/3.19.33** • great chicken mole • US$8-16

Cancún

see also Cozumel & Playa del Carmen

Accommodations

Camino Real Paseo Kukulcán **52-98/48.70.00, 800/722-6466 (US#)** • gay-friendly • swimming • 2 beaches • 3 restaurants

Casa Cancún **212/598-0469 (US#)** • mostly women • rental home on the beach • 20 mins south of Cancún • smokefree • lesbian-owned/ run • US$60-80

MEXICO

Playa Del Sol Av Yaxchilan 31 52-98/84.36.90 • gay-friendly • US$65-95

Rosa's House Calle Barracuda 14 SM 3 (nr Bonampak & Uxmal) 52-98/87.82.96 • gay/ straight • B&B w/ 2 suites • swimming • kitchens • gay-owned/ run • US$85-110

Villa Catarina Calle Privada (btwn 12th & 14th), Playa del Carmen 52-98/73.20.98 • gay-friendly • US$40-75

Zona Hotelera (The Hotel Zone) Blvd Kukulcán • Cancún's answer to the Las Vegas Strip: resorts ranging from the Sheraton Cancún's Mayan pyramids to small boutique hotels

BARS

Picante Bar Av Tulum 20, Centro (E of Av Uxmal, next to Plaza Galeriás) 52-98/45.55.87 • 9am-5am, clsd Mon • popular • mostly gay men • dancing/DJ • young crowd

NIGHTCLUBS

Karamba Av Tulum 9 altos, 2nd fl 52-98/84.00.32 • 10pm-7am, clsd Mon • popular • lesbians/ gay men • dancing/DJ • drag shows Wed & Sun

RESTAURANTS

Avenida Tulum • take a stroll & take your pick

ENTERTAINMENT & RECREATION

Chichén Itza • the must-see Mayan ruin 125 miles from Cancún

Playa Delfines in the Hotel Zone (next to Hilton's beach) • gay beach

Celaya

BARS

Los Caballos Hidalgo 220 (Centro) • Fri-Sat only • mostly gay men • dancing/DJ • live shows • cover charge

Ciudad Juárez

see also El Paso, Texas, USA

ACCOMMODATIONS

Hotel de Luxe Av S Lerdo de Tejada 300 S, Col Monumental 52-16/15.02.02 • gay-friendly • restaurant & bar • inexpensive

BARS

Club La Escondida Calle Ignacio de la Peña 366 W • gay/ straight • neighborhood bar

RESTAURANTS

El Coyote Invalido Av Lerdo S (next to the 'Plaza Continental') • 24hrs

Taco Cabaña Av Lerdo S (next to the 'Plaza Continental') • cheap, popular late-night

Cozumel

see also Cancún & Playa del Carmen

ACCOMMODATIONS

Sol Cabañas del Caribe beachfront 52-98/72.00.61, 800/336-3542 (US#) • gay-friendly • food served • US$86-195

Cruz de Loreto

ACCOMMODATIONS

Hotelito Desconocido 52-32/22.25.26, 800/851-1143 • gay/ straight • eco-resort on the beach • swimming • sauna • $400-500/ dbl (includes meals & airport transfers)

Cuernavaca

ACCOMMODATIONS

Nido de Amor 52-73/18.06.31 • gay-friendly • suites in private home

BARS

La Cortesana Comonfort 6-B 52-73/18.77.68 • dancing/DJ

RESTAURANTS

La India Bonita Calle Dwight Morrow 52-73/18.69.67 • clsd Mon • in historic home of former US ambassador & father-in-law of Charles Lindbergh

ENTERTAINMENT & RECREATION

Diego Rivera Murals Plaza de Museo (in Cuauhnáhuac Regional Museum)

Durango

BARS

Eduardos 20 de Noviembre W 805 • lesbians/ gay men

Ensenada

BARS

La Ola Verde Calle 2a #459 (btwn Av Castelo & Calle Miramar, Zona Roja) • 9pm-2am Th-Sun only • popular late • lesbians/ gay men • live music • small dance floor

NIGHTCLUBS

Club Ibis at Blvd Costero & Av Sangines • 9pm-2am Th-Sun • mostly gay men • dancing/DJ • drag shows • cover charge

Coyote Club Blvd Costero #1000 (nr Corona Hotel) • Wed-Sun • dancing/DJ • cover charge

RESTAURANTS

Casamar Blvd Lázaro Cárdenas 987, Centro (at Blvd Costero) 52-68/74.04.17 • popular

Guadalajara

ACCOMMODATIONS

Hacienda Aldama Aldama 22 (off Main Crta), Ajijic **52-3/766.09.44** • gay/ straight • 3 rms in private home • full brkfst • smokefree • wheelchair access • gay-owned/ run • US$40-75

Hotel Calinda Roma Av Juárez 170 (Sector Juárez) **52-3/614.86.50** • gay-friendly • also rooftop restaurant

BARS

Gerardo Av de la Paz 2529 (Sector Juárez) **52-3/616.12.07** • 9pm-2am, till 4am wknds • popular • upscale • mostly gay men • food served • live music Th & Sun • patio

Maskara's Calle Maestranza 238 (at Prisciliano Sánchez) **52-3/614.81.03** • 8am-2am • lesbians/ gay men • neighborhood bar • colorful atmosphere • live music • food served

NIGHTCLUBS

Candilejas Av Niños Héroes 961 (next to the Hotel Carlton) **52-3/614.55.12** • 8pm-4am, clsd Mon • gay/ straight • dancing/DJ • lavish drag shows • cover charge

The Louvre Madero 676 (at Federalismo) **52-3/826-8530** • clsd Mon-Tue • mostly gay men • dancing/DJ • live shows • cover charge

Monica's Disco Bar Av Álvaro Obregón 1713 (btwn Calles 68 & 70, Sector Libertad; no sign, look for canopy under a big palm tree) **52-3/643.95.44** • 10pm-5am, clsd Mon-Tue • popular after midnight • mostly gay men • dancing/DJ • drag/ strip shows wknds • young crowd • cover charge • take a taxi to & from

SOS Club Av La Paz 1413 (Sector Hidalgo) **52-3/826.41.79** • 9pm-3am, clsd Mon-Tue • lesbians/ gay men • popular lesbian hangout • dancing/DJ • drag shows wknds • patio • cover charge

RESTAURANTS

El Paraíso at 'Angel's' club **52-3/615.25.25** • clsd Sun-Mon

Sanborn's Av Juárez 305 (at Av 16 de Septiembre)

Sanborn's Vallarta Av Vallarta 1600, downtown Juárez District

Guanajuato

ACCOMMODATIONS

Castillo Santa Cecilia Camino a La Valenciana **52-47/32.04.77** • popular • gay-friendly • excellent food

Hotel Museo Posada Sante Fe downtown **52-47/32.00.84** • gay-friendly

RESTAURANTS

La Mancha Galarza 7 (at Pocitos & San Roque Sq) **52-47/32.46.33** • 8am-midnight • also bar

Hacienda San Miguel

ACCOMMODATIONS

Villa Las Anclas Av 5a Sur #325 (btwn 3rd & 5th Sts), Cozumel **52-9/872-5476** • gay-friendly • B&B • 1 blk from main plaza • $60-80

Irapuato

BARS

Blanco y Negro Av Ejército National 890 **52-462/4.23.81** • Th-Sun only • gay-friendly • dancing/DJ

Jalapa

NIGHTCLUBS

D K Ché at Calles Zaragoza & Prolongación (take road to Banderilla, 2 blks south of the hwy, at the town border, on a rough dirt road) • 10pm-close Fri-Sat • popular • lesbians/ gay men • dancing/DJ • drag shows • cover charge

La Mansión take a cab toward Banderilla (20 mins NW of town, turn right at sign for El Paraíso Campestre & go past RR tracks) • 9pm-4am Fri-Sat only • lesbians/ gay men • dancing/DJ • live shows • cover charge

La Paz

ACCOMMODATIONS

La Casa Mexicana Inn Calle Bravo 106 (btwn Madero & Mutualismo) **52-112/5.27.48** • open Nov-June • gay-friendly • smokefree • woman-owned • $60-85

Hotel Mediterrane Allende 36 (at malecón) **52-112/5.11.95** • lesbians/ gay men • food served 7am-11pm • sun terrace • gay-owned/ run • US$50-80

BARS

¡No Que No! Sonora & Topete • lesbians/ gay men • dancing/DJ

León

NIGHTCLUBS

La Bizantina 20 de Eñero 204, Centro (off Pedro Moreno) **52-47/13.44.85** • Fri-Sun only • mostly gay men • dancing/DJ • live shows

MEXICO

Manzanillo

ACCOMMODATIONS

Las Hadas Santiago Peninsula **52–33/31.01.01** • gay-friendly • great resort & location • US$180-400

Mexico's Villa Montaña Adventure Outpost 46 Los Angeles Locos, La Manzanilla **206/932-7012** • gay-friendly • 2-bdrm hilltop villa • ocean views • $79-120

San Luis Av de la Republica (nr Zaragoza & Lopez Mateos)

BARS

OK Independencia 42 (Centro) • Th-Sun only • mostly gay men • dancing/DJ • drag shows • cover charge

Mazatlán

ACCOMMODATIONS

Hotel Los Sábalos Rodolfo T Loaiza #190 (Zona Dorada) **52–69/83.53.33, 800/528-8760 (US#)** • gay-friendly • upscale resort • swimming • beach • health club • also popular 'Joe's Oyster Bar'

BARS

Pepe Toro Av de las Garzas 18, Zona Dorada (1 blk W of Av Camarón Sábalo) **52–69/14,41.76** • 9pm-4am, clsd Mon-Wed • popular • mostly gay men • dancing/DJ • drag/ strip shows

CAFES

Panama Restaurant Pasteleria at Avs de las Garzas & Camarón Sábalo • lesbians/ gay men

RESTAURANTS

Roca Mar Av del Mar (at Calle Isla de Lobos, Zona Costera) **52–69/81.60.08** • till 2am • popular • seafood • full bar • lesbian-owned

Señor Frogs Av del Mar, Zona Costera **52–69/82.19.25, 52–69/82.11.10** • upscale • seafood • full bar • dancing/DJ

Mérida

ACCOMMODATIONS

Gran Hotel Calle 60 #496 **52–99/24.77.30** • gay-friendly • historic turn-of-the-century hotel • courtyard w/ balconies • also restaurant

BARS

Kumbala Calle 16 # 519 (btwn 64 and 66)

Los Panchos Calle 59 (btwn 65 & 67) **52–99/23.09.42** • popular • gay/ straight • dancing/ DJ • also restaurant

NIGHTCLUBS

El Establo 482-A Calle 60 (btwn Calles 60 & 62) • popular • gay/straight • dancing/ DJ • young crowd

Kabuki's Av Jacinto Canek 381 (ext of Calle 59-A, W of Calle 124, along the Corralón) • lesbians/ gay men • dancing/DJ • drag/ strip shows • cover charge • location has changed frequently—follow the crowd

RESTAURANTS

La Bella Época Calle 60 #447 (upstairs in the Hotel del Parque) **52–99/28.19.28** • 4pm-1am • Yucatécan cuisine • try to get one of the balcony tables

Mexicali

BARS

Cantine Tare at Calle Uxmal & Av Jalisco, Pueblo Nuevo (across the Rio Nuevo from downtown) • 9pm-4am, clsd Mon • mostly gay men • neighborhood bar • drag shows

Cinco Estrellas corner of Av Jalisco & Calle 3 (next door to 'Cantine Tare') • call for hrs • popular • mostly women • neighborhood bar

Galerie 232 Av Zuazua 232 (in Zona Centro) **52–65/543.01.61** • dancing/DJ • videos

El Rey de Copas Av Baja California (at Av Tuxtla Gutierrez, Pueblo Nuevo) • open till 3am • mostly women • neighborhood bar

El Taurino Av Juan de Zuazua 480 (nr Morelos) • open late, clsd Mon • popular • mostly gay men • dancing/DJ

Mexico City

Note: Mexico City is divided into 'Zonas' (ie, Zona Rosa) & 'Colonias' (abbreviated here as Col). Remember to use these when giving addresses to taxi drivers.

INFO LINES & SERVICES

Canal Amigo Av Lázaro Cárdenas 228, #102, Col Obrera **52–5/588.19.93** • social club for lesbians & gay men • women only Tue • call for events

Centro Cultural de la Diversidad Sexual Colima 267, Col Roma **52–5/514.25.65**

Gay/ Lesbian AA Av Chapultepec 465-202, Col Juárez (Metro Sevilla) • 8pm Mon-Fri, 7pm Sat

ACCOMMODATIONS

Aristos Paseo de la Reforma 276 **52–5/211.01.12, 800/527-4786 (US#)** • gay-friendly • swimming • gym • 2 restaurants

Mexico City • Mexico

Hotel Casa Blanca Lafragua 7 **52–5/705.13.00, 800/448–8355 (US#)** • gay-friendly • swimming • food served • US$105-150

Hotel Del Ángel Calle Río Lerma 154, Col Cuauhtémoc (at Calle Río Tiber) **52–5/533.10.32, 800/010-2300** • gay-friendly • swimming • rooftop restaurant & bar • inexpensive

Hotel Geneve Calle Londres 130 (Zona Rosa) **52–5/211.00.71** • gay-friendly • 3-story colonial style hotel • no AC • moderately priced • also restaurant

Hotel Krystal Rosa Liverpool 155 **52–5/228.99.28, 800/231–9860 (US#)** • gay-friendly • upscale • 2 restaurants • nightclub • swimming

Hotel Michelangelo Calle Rio Amazonas 78 **52–5/566.98.77** • gay-friendly • kitchen • US$40

Marco Polo Amberes 27 (Zona Rosa) **52–5/511.18.39, 800/223–0888 (US#)** • gay-friendly • upscale hotel

Westin Galeria Plaza Hamburgo 195, Col Juárez (Zona Rosa) **52–5/230.17.17** • gay-friendly • swimming • 2 restaurants • disco

BARS

Enigma Calle Morelia 111, Col Roma (4 blks from Metro Niño Héroes, Zona Rosa) **52–5/207.73.67** • 9pm-3:30am, 6pm-2am Sun, clsd Mon • lesbians/ gay men • dancing/DJ • shows for women Th • live shows • cover charge

NIGHTCLUBS

Amazona's Insurgentes Sur 226 **52–5/525.18.36** • Wed-Sat • mostly lesbians • live shows

El Ansia Calle Algéciras 26, Col Insurgentes Mixcoac (in Centro Armand) **52–5/611.61.18** • 9:30pm-3am Th-Sat • mostly gay men • dancing/DJ • live shows

Anyway/ Exacto/ The Doors Calle Monterrey 47, Col Roma (Zona Rosa) **52–5/533.16.91** • 9pm-4am • popular • lesbians/ gay men • 3 flrs • 'The Doors', 1st flr, is women's bar • 'Exacto', 2nd flr, is mixed • 'Anyway', 3rd flr, is men's bar • food served • live shows • cover charge

Bongoo Insurgentes Centro 96 • mostly gay men • go-go dancers • cover charge

Mexico City

LGBT PRIDE: June/July. 52–5/574.30.12.

CITY INFO: México City Tourist Assistance 52–5/250.01.23. Mexican Tourism 800-44-MEXICO (US#).

ATTRACTIONS: Ballet Folklorico. Frida Kahlo House 52–5/554.59.99. Metropolitan Cathedral. Museo Diego Rivera. Museo Dolores Olmedo (largest collection of Kahlo's works) 52–5/555.16.42. Museum of Anthropology 52–5/553.63.86. Museum of Modern Art 52–5/553.62.33. Shrine to Our Lady of Guadalupe. Tamayo Museum of Contemporary Art 52–5/286.58.89. Teotihuacan Pyramids.

WEATHER: Temperate and dry most of the year, with most of the annual rainfall coming in May-Oct. When the smog gets unbearable, head for a museum or other indoor activity.

TRANSIT: 52–5/516.60.20, 52–5/519.76.90. Don't hail a taxi on the street. It costs more to call an official taxi, but it's worth it. Mexico City has an excellent Metro (subway) system.

MEXICO

Butterflies Calle Izazaga 9 (at Av Lazaro Cárdenas S, Centro Historico) **52-5/761.13.51, 52-5/761.18.81** • 9pm-3am, till 4:30am Fri-Sat, clsd Mon • popular • lesbians/ gay men • dancing/DJ • 2 flrs • lavish drag shows Fri-Sat • cover charge

Caztzi Calle Carlos Arellano 4, Ciudad Satélite (E of Periférico, on S side of Plaza Satélite) **52-5/393.66.91** • 10pm-6am Th-Sat • lesbians/ gay men • dancing/DJ • drag/ strip shows • cover charge

Paradisso Calle Querétaro 217, Col Roma (btwn Calles Monterrey & Medellín) **52-5/574.38.22, 52-5/574.37.43** • 9pm-4am Wed-Sat, 8pm-3am Sun • mostly gay men • dancing/DJ • drag & strip shows • cover charge

Penelope Calle Antonio Caso 60 (at Insurgentes N) **52-5/566.14.72, 52-5/566.69.92** • 10:30pm-close Th-Sat • lesbians/ gay men • dancing/DJ • live shows • cover charge

RESTAURANTS

El Almacén Av Florencia 37-A, Zona Rosa (above 'El Taller') **52-5/207.69.56** • open late • lesbians/ gay men • Mediterranean • full bar • popular happy hour • videos

Before Anything Oaxaca 37 • also cafe & bar • entertainment • videos

El Deco Chilpancingo N 46 **52-5/574.55.10** • also bar and art gallery

Fonda San Ángel Plaza San Jacinto 3, Col San Ángel (across from Bazar San Ángel) **52-5/550.19.42** • popular after 7pm Fri-Sat • classic Mexican dishes

El Hábito Madrid 13 (Coyocán District) **52-5/552.44.81** • avante-garde theater & bar

Maria Bonita Cuernavaca 68 (btwn Juan Escutia and Montes de Oca) **52-5/553.04.03** • full bar

Meson d'Miss Calle Tlacotalpan 18 **52-5/564.53.28** • 1pm-11pm, till 6pm Sun, clsd Mon • lesbians/ gay men • Mexican & int'l

Sanborn's Madera 4 (in Casade los Azulejos) **52-5/512.98.20** • brkfst, lunch & dinner • superstore

La Taberna Griega Av Insurgentes S 1381 (at Calle Algéciras) **52-5/611.69.58** • 1:30pm-midnight, till 6pm Sun-Mon • Greek & int'l • 'gay day' Wed • live music wknds

Vips Hamburgo Calle Hamburgo 126 (Zona Rosa) • American-style • also at Paseo de la Reforma & Florencia, nr Independence Angel Statue • popular after-hours

ENTERTAINMENT & RECREATION

Frida Kahlo House Calle Londres 247 (Coyoacán) **52-5/554-5999** • originial furniture, letters & Frida's dresses

The Great Temple Museum Calle Seminario 8 (Zocalo) **52-5/542.49.43** • 9am-5pm, clsd Mon • artifacts from the central Aztec temple at Tenochtitlán

Museo de Arte Carillo Gil Av Revolución 1608 (San Angel) **52-5/550.62.60, 52-5/550.39.83** • 10am-6pm, clsd Mon • contemporary art

Museo de Arte Moderno Paseo de la Reforma (at Gandhi, Chapultepec Forest) **52-5/553.62.33, 52-5/211.87.29** • 10am-6pm, clsd Mon

National Museum of Anthropology Paseo de la Reforma (at Gandhi) **52-5/553.63.86, 52-5/553.63.81** • 9am-7pm, clsd Mon

BOOKSTORES

Las Sirenas Av de la Paz 57 (San Angel) **52-5/500.93.86** • women's

PUBLICATIONS

Ser Gay **52-5/534.38.04** • covers all Mexico nightlife, limited resources

Monterrey

ACCOMMODATIONS

Hotel Rio Calle Padre Mier 194 N (at Garibaldi, Centro) **52-8/345.15.16, 800/432-2520 (US#)** • gay-friendly • nr Zona Rosa • swimming • also restaurant

BARS

Charao's at Calles Isaac Garza E & Zaragoza W (Centro) • 10pm-6am, clsd Sun • lesbians/ gay men • dancing/DJ • strippers • popular after-hours • cover charge

NIGHTCLUBS

Arcanos Calle Ruperto Martínez 845 (at Calle Cuauhtémoc) • open Wed-Sat • lesbians/ gay men • dancing/DJ • drag shows Sat • video bar downstairs • cover charge

Morelia

ACCOMMODATIONS

Casa Camelinas B&B **52-43/14.09.63, 415/661-5745 (US#)** • gay-friendly • mostly women • 3 1/2 hours from Mexico City

NIGHTCLUBS

Con la Rojas Aldama 343 (Centro) **52-43/12.15.78** • 11pm-2am, clsd Sun-Wed • mostly gay men • upscale • dancing/DJ • cover charge

Puerto Vallarta • Mexico

¡No Que No! Periférico República 7551, Col Sindurio **52-43/11.14.25** • 10pm-3am, clsd Mon • mostly gay men • dancing/DJ • live shows

Restaurants

La Capila Ignacio Zaragoza 90 (at Posada de la Soledad Hotel) **52-43/12.18.18** • in charming old hotel in converted convent

Fonda de las Mercedes Calle Leon Guzmán 47 **52-43/12.61.13, 52-43/13.32.22** • popular • inside beautiful colonial home

Oaxaca

Accommodations

El Camino Real Oaxaca Calle 5 de Mayo 300 **52-951/6.06.11, 800/722-6466 (US RESERVATIONS)** • popular • gay-friendly • 5-star hotel in restored 16th-century convent • frescoes & courtyards abound • restaurant • swimming • US$195-315

Los Helechos Posada Guerrero 1029-B **52-9/514.00.57** • gay/ straight • small guesthouse located in historical center of town • full brkfst

Mission de los Angeles Hotel Calzada Porfirio Díaz 102 **52-951/5.15.00 OR 5.10.00, 800/221-6509 (US#)** • gay-friendly • resort w/ bungalows • restaurant & dance clubs • swimming • tennis courts • US$104-180

Bars

Bar Jardin Portal de Flores 10 (on the zócalo) **52-951/6.20.92** • 7:30am-1am • gay/ straight • sidewalk cafe • more gay as day goes by • also restaurant

Nightclubs

Disco Snob Calzada Niños Héroes de Chupultepec (1 blk west of bus station) • gay from 10pm Wed only • dancing/DJ

Restaurants

El Asador Vasco Portal de Flores 11 (above 'Bar Jardin') **52-951/4.47.55** • popular • great views • authentic Oaxacan cuisine (can you say ¡mole!)

Orizaba

Nightclubs

Sky Drink Madero N 1280 • clsd Sun-Tue • mostly gay men • dancing/DJ • drag/ strip shows Sat • cover charge

Pátzcuaro

Accommodations

Hotel Posada San Rafael Plaza Vasco de Quiroga **52-45/42.07.70** • gay-friendly

Playa del Carmen

see also Cancún & Cozumel

Accommodations

Aventura Mexicana Resort Av 10 (at Calle 22) **954/462-6035 (US#), 52-987/3.18.76** • gay-friendly • swimming • jacuzzi • nudity permitted • 15 mins to gay nude beach • also restaurant & bar • US$44-85

Pension San Juan 5a Av 165 (btwn Calles 6 & 8 N) **52-987/3.06.47** • gay-friendly motel • smokefree • kids ok

Poza Rica

Nightclubs

El 42 Plaza 18 de Marzo (Centro) • Fri-Sat only • gay-friendly • dancing/DJ • live shows • cover charge

Puebla

Bars

La Cigarra Calle 5 W 538 (at Calle 7, Centro) • 5pm-3am • popular • mostly gay men • beer bar

Nightclubs

Cherri's Prolongacíon 11, Col Mayorazgo (at Zapotecas) **52-22/28.89.37** • Fri-Sat only • gay-friendly • dancing/DJ • drag shows • cover charge

Garrotos 22 Orient E 602 (close to Blvd 5 de Mayo, Xenenetla) **52-22/42.42.32** • Fri-Sat only • gay-friendly • dancing/DJ • cover charge

Keops Disco Calle 14 N 101 (at Calle 5 de Mayo), Cholula **52-22/47.03.68** • 10pm-3am Th-Sun • popular • lesbians/ gay men • dancing/DJ • drag/ strip shows Fri-Sat • videos • young crowd

Puerto Vallarta

Accommodations

BeachCondoInPV.com 156 Amapas St #401-402 **415/282-8924** • gay/ straight • on gay beach • jacuzzi • swimming • kids ok • wheelchair access • $50-195

Blue Chairs Beach Resort Malecon and Almendro #4 (on Playa Los Muertos), Puerto Vallarta, Jalisco **229/336-9979** • lesbians/ gay men • right on the beach • $98-170

Bugambilia Blanca Carretera Barra de Navidad #602, Col Emiliano Zapata (Off Hwy 200) **52-322/2.11.52** • gay/ straight • 4 levels • suites • also 2- & 3-bdrm apts • full brkfst • 6-min walk to gay beach • gay-owned/ run • US$100-250

MEXICO

Casa Boana Torre Malibu Calle Amapas 325 52-322/2.00.99, 52-322/2.66.95 • popular • lesbians/ gay men • condo-hotel • bay views • food served • swimming • poolside bar

Casa de los Arcos 52-322/2.59.90, 800/424-3434 x277 (US#) • lesbians/ gay men • private villa • sleeps 8 • swimming • terrace w/ amazing view of Bandera Bay

Casa dos Comales Calle Aldama 274 52-322/3.20.42, 888/881-1822 (US#) • gay-friendly • guesthouse & apts nr Old Town • swimming • US$50-125

Casa Fantasía 203 Pino Suarez, Col Emiliano Zapata (nr the Rio Quale) 52-322/3.24.44 • mostly gay men • B&B made up of 3 traditional haciendas • full brkfst • terrace • swimming • gay-owned/ run • US$80-120

Casa Palapa B&B Paseo de Las Conchas Chinas #107, Colonia Conchas Chinas CP, Jalisco 1-888/872-7620, 52-322/15561 • mostly gay men • swimming • ocean-views • full brkfst • gay-owned/ run • $175-195

Casa Ventana 135 Calle Hortencias, Penthouse 649/376-6230 • gay-friendly • luxury condo • sleeps 6 • swimming • gay-owned/ run • US$1,400-3,150/ week

Discovery Vallarta 52-322/2.69.18 • gay accommodations reservation service

Doin' It Right Travel 619/297-3642 (US#), 800/936-3646 (US#) • Puerto Vallarta gay travel specialist • also publishes newsletter 'PV-PS' ('Puerto Vallarta Purple Sheets')

Paco Paco Descanso del Sol Hotel Pino Suárez #583, Zona Romantica 52-322/3.02.77, 52-322/2.52.29 • popular • lesbians/ gay men • apts, casitas & tents • swimming • rooftop bar w/ incredible sunset views • gay-owned/ run • US$40-110

Paco's Hidden Paradise 30 mins S of Puerto Vallarta 52-322/3.02.77, 52-322/2.18.99 • lesbians/ gay men • secluded beach resort accessible only by boat • condos & tents • bar • restaurant • gay-owned/ run • $50-85

Paco's Olas Altas B&B Olas Altas #463 52-322/3.02.77, 52-322/2.18.99 • lesbians/ gay men • full brkfst • private sundeck • jacuzzi • also bar • gay-owned/ run • $40-50

Quinta Maria Cortez 132 Calle Sagitario, Playa Conchas Chinas 801/536-5850 (US#), 888/640-8100 (US#) • gay/ straight • 'Mexaterranian Villa' w/ sunny terraces & spectacular ocean views • swimming • $100-235

Villa Felíz 52-322/2.07.98, 800/424-3434 x277 (US#) • lesbians/ gay men • in Old Town • full brkfst • swimming • great views • US$60-95

Villas David B&B Calle Galeana 348 (at Calle Miramar) 724/573-4693 (US#), 52-322/3.03.15 (MX #) • mostly gay men • swimming • rooftop jacuzzi & pool • nude sunbathing • balconies • gay-owned/ run • US$53-140

BARS

Apaches Olas Altas 439 (at Rodriguez) 52-322/2.52.35 • 5pm-2am, till 1am Sun-Mon • gay/ straight • classy martini bar • tapas • lesbian-owned/ run

Aria Pino Suárez 210 (at Madero) 52-322/2.57.32 • 8pm-2am • popular • gay/ straight • piano bar

Los Balcones Calle Juárez 182, 2nd flr (at Calle Libertad) 52-322/2.46.71 • 9pm-3am, till 4am wknds • popular • mostly gay men • dancing/DJ • T-dance 6pm-11pm Sun

Blue Chairs (Tito's) S Los Muertos Beach • mostly gay men • food served

Boana's Bar Calle Amapas 325 (at 'Casa Boana Torre Malibu') 52-322/2.00.99 • 1pm-7pm • gay/ straight • poolside bar • seasonal

La Bola Calle Pilitas 174 (at 'Vallarta Cora' hotel) 52-322/3.28.15 • 3pm-10pm • popular poolside bar • mostly gay men • mtg spot after Amadeus day cruises

Kit Kat Bar Pulpito 120 (next door to 'Chiles' restaurant) 52-322/3.00.93 • 5pm-1:30am • popular • lesbians/ gay men • swanky New York-style cocktail lounge • drag shows 11:30pm some nights • also restaurant (pricey but fun) • gay-owned/ run

Paco's Olas Altas Olas Altas 465 (at Emiliano Zapata) 52-322/3.43.47 • noon-8pm, clsd Mon • lesbians/ gay men • rooftop bar • jacuzzi

Paco's Sunset Bar Calle Pino Suárez 583 (on rooftop of 'Paco Paco Descanso del Sol') 52-322/3.20.77 • noon-10pm • popular • lesbians/ gay men • the spot to watch the sun set • swimming • restaurant • gay-owned/ run

NIGHTCLUBS

Anthropology Calle Morelos 101, Plaza Río (at Rodriguez) 52-322/2.63.92 • noon-4am • lesbians/ gay men • 3 levels: intimate rooftop bar, game bar, basement disco • drag shows • strippers • young crowd

The Cactus Club Ignacio Vallarta 399 52-322/2.60.37 • gay-friendly • gay Wed

Club Paco Paco Calle Ignacio Vallarta 278 (at Carranza) 52-322/2.18.99 • 3pm-6am • popular • lesbians/ gay men • cantina on 2nd flr • disco downstairs from 10pm • also rooftop terrace w/ live piano • cover charge • gay-owned/ run

Puerto Vallarta • Mexico

Paco's Ranch Calle Carranza 239 (walk thru 'Club Paco Paco' to back of dance flr) 52-322/3.05.37 • 8pm-6am • popular • mostly gay men • dancing/DJ • leather • country/western • packed for nightly strip shows • videos • cover charge • gay-owned/run

CAFES

A Page in the Sun Olas Altas 299 52-322/2.36.08 • 8am-10pm • popular • coffee shop & English bookstore

Este Cafe Libertad 336, Centro (around corner from flea market) 52-322/2.42.61 • 8am-10pm, clsd Sun • popular • espresso & juice bar • desserts • ice cream • gay-owned/run

The Net House Calle Ignacio Vallarta 232 52-322/2.69.53 • 7am-2am • popular • cybercafe • organic coffee & baked goods • gay-owned/run

Señor Book Cafe Olas Altas 490 52-322/2.03.24 • 8am-11:30pm • cafe & new/used English bookstore

Vallarta 179 Ignacio Vallarta 179 52-322/2.61.42 • 8am-1am • cybercafe • gay-owned/run

RESTAURANTS

Adobe Café Calle Basilio Badillo 252 (at Ignacio Vallarta) 52-322/2.67.20, 52-322/3.19.25 • 6pm-11pm, clsd Tue (& Aug-Sept) • popular • Southwestern flair • full bar • gay-owned/run • $10

Bombo's Corona 327, Centro (at Matamoros) 52-322/2.51.64 • 4pm-midnight • upscale French • great views of Bandera Bay • reservations req'd • gay-owned/run

Café des Artistes Calle Guadalupe Sánchez 740 (at Leona Vicario) 52-322/2.32.28, 52-322/2.32.30 • popular • upscale French w/ a Mexican twist • reservations required • expensive

Chez Elena Matamoros 520, Centro 52-322/2.01.61 • 6pm-11pm • seasonal • garden restaurant • Mexican/int'l • some veggie • also rooftop bar • woman-owned/run

¡Chiles! Pulpito 122 (at Olas Altas) 52-322/3.03.73 • 11am-6pm, clsd Sun, seasonal (clsd July-Sept) • popular • roasted chicken • sandwiches • hamburgers • large patio • gay-owned/run

Green Chairs (Looney Tunes) S Los Muertos Beach (at 'Looney Tunes' restaurant) • mostly gay men • bar also

Le Bistro Jazz Café Isla Rio Cuale 16–A (on the island, at the East Bridge) 52-322/2.02.83 • 9am-midnight, clsd Sun • popular • PV's classiest • gay-owned/run

Memo's Casa de los Hotcakes Calle Basilio Badillo 289 52-322/2.62.72 • 8am-2pm • popular • long lines for cheap & good brkfsts • indoor patio • Mexican cooking classes offered in evening

Red Cabbage Calle Rio Ribera 206-A (at Basilio Badillo) 52-322/3.04.11 • Mexican • on Rio Cuale w/ great kitschy decor • lesbian-owned/run

Rosie's Cafe 31 de Octubre 149 (nr McDonalds, 2 blks from Malecón) 52-322/2.44.77 • 6pm-11pm • good homecooked American fare for the homesick

Trio's Guerrero 264 52-322/2.21.96 • 6pm-midnight, clsd Sun • Mediterranean/Mexican • patio • live music • reservations advised

Vegetariano Iturbide 270 52-322/2.30.73 • buffet-style

ENTERTAINMENT & RECREATION

Amadeus Tours meet at Vallarta Cora Hotel 52-322/3.28.15 • 10:45am-5pm Mon & Th • party for 20 on catamaran • includes snorkeling, lunch & stop at secluded beach • also a sunset cruise 5pm Wed, meet at Muertos Pier • US$60

Boana Tours Calle Amapas 325 (at Casa Boana Torre Malibu) 52-322/2.00.99 • boat cruises (Mon, Wed & Sat) • horseback tours (Wed) • bbq & tour of traditional hat factory

Diana's Cruise the Bay Tour meet at los Muertos pier 52-322/2.15.10 • 10:30am-6pm Fri • lesbians/gay men • cruise on 33-ft trimaran • limited to 20 people • snorkeling equipment • food served • open bar • US$55 • contact Diana for information on her other tours

Playa Los Muertos S of Rio Cuale (southern end by green chairs at 'Looney Tunes') • popular • the gay beach

RETAIL SHOPS

La Rosa de Cristal Insurgentes 272 (at Cardenas) 52-322/2.56.98 • 10am-8pm • local handicrafts & beautiful blown-glass items • gay-owned/run

La Tienda Rodolfo Gomez 122 52-322/2.15.35 • 10am-2pm & 4pm-8pm • furniture & home accessories • also Basilio Badillo 276 location, 52-322/3.06.92 • gay-owned/run

Safari Accents Olas Altas 224 52-322/3.26.60 • 10am-11pm • pricey but beautiful home furnishings • gay-owned/run

MEXICO

Querétaro

BARS

Villa Jardín/ Bar Oz Blvd Bernardo Quintana 556, Col Arboledas (across from Cinemark) **52-42/24.13.96** • Sat only • mostly gay men • dancing/DJ • cover charge

NIGHTCLUBS

La Creación Monte Sinai 113, Col Vista Hermosa (before 'Disco Qui') **52-42/13.51.90** • Fri-Sat • gay-friendly • dancing/DJ • cover charge

La Iguana Av Universidad 308 (at Hotel Maria Teresa) • 9pm-2am Fri-Sat • gay-friendly • dancing/DJ • strippers

San Jose del Cabo

ACCOMMODATIONS

Palmilla Apdo Postal 52, 23400 **714/935-2000 (US#), 800/637-2226 (US#)** • gay-friendly • upscale resort w/ golf course • swimming

San Luis Potosí

BARS

Sheik Prolongación Zacatecas 347 **52-481/2.74.57, 52-481/4.49.85** • 10pm-3am Fri-Sat • mostly gay men • dancing/DJ • drag shows Fri • strippers Sat • cover charge

San Miguel de Allende

ACCOMMODATIONS

Casa de Sierra Nevada Calle Hospicio 35 **52-415/2.04.15, 800/223-6510 (US#)** • gay-friendly • suites • horseback riding on premises • also spa • swimming • fireplaces • patios

Casa Schuck Garita 3 **52-415/2.06.57** • gay-friendly • B&B • full brkfst • swimming • $98-150

BARS

La Lola Calle Ancha de San Antonio 31 (across from the Instituto Allende) **52-415/2.40.50** • 1pm-2am, clsd Mon • gay/ straight • young crowd • also restaurant • gay-owned/ run

NIGHTCLUBS

Cien (100) Ángeles Tinajitas 24, Col San Antonio (across from Hotel Real de Minas) • 9pm-3am Fri-Sat • mostly gay men • dancing/DJ • live shows • cover charge

Tijuana

INFO LINES & SERVICES

Gay/ Lesbian Community Center Calle 1 #7648 (Zona Centro) **52-66/80.99.63**

Gay/ Lesbian Info Line **52-66/88.02.67, 52-66/85.91.63**

ACCOMMODATIONS

Playas de Rosarito 179 via de la Olas, Rosarito Beach, Baja California (at Ave Benito) **52-66/13.16.45** • gay/ straight • 20 mins south of Tijuana • safe & serene • shared baths • 1 blk to beach • gay-owned/ run • $40-65

BARS

Cladira's Madero (btwn Galeano & Hidlago) • 1pm-1am • mostly lesbians • food served

Emilio's Cafeteria Musical Calle 3/ Puerto #1810, Ste 11 (in entry to 'Parking América' complex) **52-66/88.02.67** • 8pm-4am • lesbians/ gay men • live music • beer/ wine bar • also cafe • open 8am-6pm • many local lgbt groups meet here

Noa Noa Av 'D'/ Miguel F Martínez 678 (at Calle 1) **52-66/81.79.01** • 5pm-3am, till 4am Fri, till 5am Sat • popular • lesbians/ gay men • dancing/DJ • drag shows • young crowd

Planet G Av Revolución 1328 (btwn 9th & 10th) • 4pm-close, from 2pm wknds, clsd Mon-Tue • mostly gay men • video bar

NIGHTCLUBS

Los Equipales Calle 7/ Galeana #8236 (at Av Revolución, opposite Jai Alai Palace) **52-66/88.30.06** • 9pm-3am, clsd Mon-Tue • popular • lesbians/ gay men • dancing/DJ • live shows • young crowd

Exstasis Larroque 213 (in Plaza Viva Tijuana, next to the border) **52-66/82.83.39** • 8pm-late, from 6pm Sun, clsd Mon-Wed • popular • mostly gay men • women's night Th • dancing/DJ • strippers • cover charge

Mike's Disco Av Revolución 1220 (at Calle 6A) **52-66/85.35.34** • 8pm-5am, till 3am Th, clsd Wed • popular • lesbians/ gay men • dancing/DJ • drag shows • videos

Terraza 9 Calle 6/ Flores Magón #8150 (at Av Revolución) **52-66/85.35.34** • 5pm-2am, till 5am Fri-Sat, clsd Mon • lesbians/ gay men • dancing/DJ • drag/ strip shows • cover charge

RESTAURANTS

The Boy'z Plaza Santa Cecilia (Zona Centro) • 7am-11pm

Vittorio's Av Revolución 1687 (at 9th) **52-66/85.17.29** • pizza & pasta

PUBLICATIONS

Bandera Gay **52-66/80.99.63**

Frontera Gay **52-66/88.02.67** • monthly lgbt newspaper

Toluca

Bars

Vip's Toluca Paseo Tollocán & Blvd Isidoro Fabela • lesbians/ gay men

Tuxtla Gutierrez

Bars

Sandy's Bar Calle 9 S & 8 N (inside 'Via Fontana') • gay-friendly • transgender-friendly

Veracruz

Accommodations

Hotel Imperial Portales de Miguel Lerdo de Tejada 153 (N side of the Plaza de Armas) **52-29/32.12.04** • gay-friendly • food served • expensive

Hotel Villa del Mar Blvd Miguel Ávila Camacho 2707, Col Zaragoza (across street from Playa del Mar beach) **52-29/31.15.90** • gay-friendly • hotel w/ separate motel & bungalows • moderate price

Nightclubs

Deeper Calle Icazo 1005 (btwn Avs Victoria & Revillagigedo N) **52-29/35.02.65** • 9pm-4am Th-Sun • popular • mostly gay men • dancing/DJ • cover charge

Shooters Calle 3 #1221 (btwn Enriquez & Alcocer) • popular • lesbians/ gay men • dancing/DJ • drag/ strip shows • warehouse club in a residential neighborhood • 10-min cab ride from downtown

Vieu Carre Av Independencia N 19-A (at Calle Padilla, Centro) **52-29/15.14.20** • 10pm-close Th-Sun • popular • mostly gay men • huge club • dancing/DJ • drag shows

Entertainment & Recreation

San Juan de Ulua Fortress • 9am-4:30pm, clsd Mon • impressive early colonial-era fortress

Veracruz Aquarium Blvd Avila (at Xicolencat) **52-29/32.79.84** • 10am-7pm • one of the largest & best in the world • don't miss it!

Villahermosa

Accommodations

Hotel Don Carlos Av Madero 418, Centro **52-93/12.24.99** • gay-friendly • food served

Hyatt Villahermosa Av Juarez 106, Col Linda Vista (across from Tomas Garrido Park) **52-93/15.12.34, 800/233-1234 (US#)** • gay-friendly

Zacatecas

Info Lines & Services

Closet Sor Juana 52-492/3.76.78 • women's group • call for info

Accommodations

Quinta Real Zacatecas Av Rayon 434, Col Centro **52-492/2.91.04, 800/457-4000 (US#)** • gay-friendly • full-service 5-star hotel

Nightclubs

Escándalo Feria Zacatecan, Terraza 4 **52-492/4.14.76** • 9pm-3am Fri-Sat • lesbians/ gay men • dancing/DJ • live shows

Cafes

Café Acropolis Av Hidalgo

Zihuatanejo

Restaurants

Paul's Benito Juarez #23 **755/4.65.28** • also 'El Mascarero Piano Bar' from 9pm

Splash at Calles Ejido & Vincente Guerrero **52-753/4.08.80** • noon-midnight • popular • lesbians/ gay men • also bar

Nightclubs

Tequila Town Cuauhtehoc 3 (off Malecon) • gay-friendly • more gay after 11pm • karoake

Costa Rica

Alajuela

see also San José

Bars

Marguiss (250 meters S of Almacénes Llobet, on 2nd flr) **506/443-5310** • 6pm-close, clsd Mon • popular • lesbians/ gay men • neighborhood bar • live shows last Sun

Arenal

Accommodations

Arenal Lodge 506/228-3189 • gay-friendly • volcano views • US$69-123

Entertainment & Recreation

The Arenal Volcano • hourly eruptions

Tabocon Hot Springs La Fortuna **506/222-1072** • 10am-10pm • US$14

Costa Rica • CENTRAL AMERICA

Guanacaste

ACCOMMODATIONS

Villa Decary Nuevo Arenal, 5717 Tilaran **506/383-3012** • former coffee farm on 7 acres overlooking Lake Arenal • gay-friendly • gay-owned/run • US$69-119

Manuel Antonio, Quepos

ACCOMMODATIONS

Big Ruby's La Plantacion Apdo 94-6350 **506/777-1332** OR **506/ 777-1115, 800/477-7829 (US#)** • mostly gay men • women welcome • infinity pool • shuttle service to gay beach • full brkfst • also 'Madres' restaurant • gay-owned/run • US$90-320

Casa Lydia Luxury Oceanview Villa 407/ 228-6654, 407/897-3638 • gay/straight • luxury 3-story villa • swimming • kids ok • smokefree • $275-500/night, $2,000-3,200/week

Casa Paraiso 213/330-0231 • gay/straight • full brkfst • kids ok • wheelchair access • gay-owned/run • $64-79

Géminis del Pacifico 773/472-7127 • gay/straight • luxurious modern vacation home • jacuzzi • swimming • nr beaches & bars • kids ok • gay-owned/run • $2,000-3,000/week

Hotel Casa Blanca & The Miranon Center 506/777-0253, 506/777-1790 • gay/straight • also spiritual retreat • short hike to gay beach • swimming • gay-owned/run • US$50-180, ask about retreat

Hotel Villa Roca 506/777-1349 • mostly gay men • great ocean views • nr beaches • swimming • gay-owned/run • US$40-90

Makanda by the Sea 506/777-0442 • gay-friendly • private oasis • swimming • US$110-250

El Parador 506/777-1437, 800/451-4398 **(US#)** • gay-friendly • large resort w/ mini golf course & health club • swimming • also gourmet restaurant

El Parque 506/777-0096, 888/498-9177 • gay-friendly • hillside condos • ocean views • waterfall swimming pool • restaurant • US$66-207

Si Como No 506/777-0777, 800/237-8207 **(US#)** • popular • gay-friendly • swimming • US$140-250

Villas Nicolas 506/777-0481 • gay-friendly • oceanview rental suites • swimming • US$65-180

BARS

Cockatoo Bar across from Escuela d'Amore Spanish-language school (nr Manuel Antonio Park) • 4pm-close • lesbians/gay men

Kamuk Pub at Katuk Hotel (downtown) 506/ 777-0379 • till 4am • gay-friendly • live shows

Mar y Sombra on Playa Espadilla • gay-friendly • local flavor • dancing/DJ (Nov-April) • also full restaurant

Vela Bar 1st Beach (at Vela Bar Hotel) 506/777-0413 • 7am-10:30pm • gay-friendly • also restaurant

NIGHTCLUBS

Arco Iris behind iron bridge at the waterfront 506/777-0449 • 7pm-close • gay-friendly • more gay late night & wknds • dancing/DJ • live shows wknds

RESTAURANTS

El Barba Roja 506/777-0331 • popular • great sunset location

El Gran Escape 506/777-0395 • clsd Tue • Tex-Mex • full bar

Karola's top of hill right in front of Cafe Milagro 506/777-1557 • 11am-11pm • lunch & dinner w/ a view • some veggie • full bar • gay-owned/run

Madres at 'La Plantacion Big Ruby's' 506/ 777-1332 • 8am-9pm • bar till 10pm • Int'l

The Plinio at the 'Hotel Plinio' 506/777-0055 • Italian • full bar • some veggie

Playa Jaco

ACCOMMODATIONS

Hotel Poseidon Calle del Bohio (30 meters W of Jaco Centro) 506/643-1642 • gay-friendly • 50 meters to beach • also bar & restaurant

Puntarenas

BARS

Capitan Moreno Paseo de Los Turistas 506/661-0810 • gay-friendly

San José

INFO LINES & SERVICES

Uno @ Diez Calle 1 (btwn Avdas 9 & 11) 506/258-4561 • 9am-10pm • lgbt tourist info center • Internet access • cafeteria

ACCOMMODATIONS

Barcel Amon 800/575-1253 • gay-friendly • modern hotel • quiet location • food served • $100

Tamarindo • Costa Rica

Cariari Hotel & Country Club 800/227-4474 • gay-friendly • luxury resort w/ great golfing • swimming • US$115

Colours Resort El Triangulo Noroeste, Blvd Rohrmoser (200 m before end of blvd) 506/232-3504, 877/932-6652 (US#) • popular • mostly gay men • premier full-service accommodations w/ tours & reservation services throughout Costa Rica • swimming • also bar & restaurant • events • $49-119

Don Carlos B&B 506/221-6707 • popular • gay-friendly • US$50-70

Hotel Kekoldi Avda 9 (Calle 3 Bis, Barrio Amón) 506/223-3244 • gay-friendly

Joluva Guesthouse Barrio Amón 506/223-7961, 800/298-2418 (US#) • lesbians/ gay men • $25-50

Las Banderas B&B (200 meters S of Hotel Tara, San Antonio de Escazu) 506/288-1405, 506/381-5768 • mostly gay men • intimate & homey • US$40-70

BARS

Buenas Vibraciones Avda 14 (btwn Calles 7 & 9, in front of parking for 'Más x Menos,' Paseo de los Estudiantes) 506/223-4573 • 6pm-close • mostly women • neighborhood bar

Cantábrico Avda 6 (btwn Calles Central & 2) 506/233-5797 • gay-friendly

Puchos Calle 11 (btwn Avdas 8 & 10, knock to enter) 506/256-1147 • 6pm-2:30am • lesbians/ gay men • strippers Mon, Wed & Fri • also restaurant

La Tertulia 100 meters E & 150 meters N of Iglesia de San Pedro, San Pedro 506/225-0250 • clsd Sun • mostly women • neighborhood bar • food served

NIGHTCLUBS

La Avispa 834 Calle 1 (pink house btwn Avdas 8 & 10) 506/223-5354 • 7pm-2:30am, clsd Mon & Th • lesbians/ gay men • mostly women last Wed • popular T-dance Sun • dancing/DJ

Déjà Vú Calle 2 (btwn Avdas 14 & 16) 506/223-3758 • 8pm-close, from 9pm Fri-Sat, clsd Mon-Th • popular • lesbians/ gay men • dancing/DJ • 2 dance flrs • live shows • also 'Sinners' lounge Fri-Sat only • take a taxi

Los Cucha Avda 6 (btwn Calles Central & 1, 75 meters E of Farmacia Jara—no sign; look for big, black wooden doors & enter) 506/233-4310F • 7pm-close, clsd Mon-Tue • mostly gay men • dancing/DJ • live shows • transgender-friendly

CAFES

Café de Teatro National National Theatre 506/223-4488 • lunch

RESTAURANTS

Anochecer 2 km from Centro Aserri on Carretera A Tarbaca (nr 'Colours') 506/230-5152 • 11am-midnight • full bar • authentic 'Tico' dinners • scenic view

El Bochinche Calle 11 (btwn Avdas 10 & 12, Paseo de los Etudiantes), San Pedro 506/221-0500 • 7pm-2am Wed-Sun • Mexican • also video bar

Café Mundo Avda 9 & Calle 15 (200 meters E of parking lot for INS, Barrio Amón) 506/222-6190 • Italian • garden seating • also cafe-bar

La Cocina de Leña in El Pueblo complex 506/255-1360 • popular • 5 mins from downtown • Costa Rican • US$12

La Piazetta Paseo Colón • Italian • US$18

Vishnu Vegetarian Restaurant Avda 1 (btwn Calles 3 & 1) • popular

PUBLICATIONS

Gayness Apdo Postal 1581-1002, Paseo Estudiantes 506/280-4832, 506/225-9824 • monthly lgbt newsmagazine • also map w/ listings (en español w/ some English)

Gente 10 Apdo Postal 1910-2100, Sector Guadalupe 506/280-8886 • bimonthly lgbt magazine • also map w/ listings (en español w/ some English)

EROTICA

Tabú 75 meters W of 'Banco Popular', San Pedro 506/283-7320 • also locations in Escazú & Real Cariari

XXX Adult World Calle 2 (btwn Avenida 3 & 5) 506/221-7165

Tamarindo

ACCOMMODATIONS

Hotel Sueño del Mar Playa Langosa 011-506/653-0284 • gay-friendly • private hacienda on the beach • full brkfst • swimming • $105-160

Austria • EUROPE

AUSTRIA

Vienna

INFO LINES & SERVICES

Gay & Lesbian AA 43-1/799.55.77 • 7pm Sat • call for location

Rosa-Lila-Tip Linke Wienzeile 102 (nr Hofmühlgasse, U4-Pilgramgasse) 43-1/586.81.50 • Austrian lgbt switchboard • staffed 5pm-8pm Tue-Th • also mtg place for various groups • also cafe-bar

ACCOMMODATIONS

Arcotel Wimberger Neubaugürtel 34-36 (at Goldschlagstr) 43-1/521.65.0 • gay-friendly • centrally located 4-star hotel • restaurant & bar on premises • also fitness club • AS2,000-2,600

Hotel Urania Obere Weißgerberstr 7 (U-Schwedenplatz) 43-1/713.17.11 • gay-friendly • centrally located • pizzeria & bar on premises • wheelchair access • AS430-890

Pension Wild Lange Gasse 10 (off Lerchenfelder Str) 43-1/406.51.74 • mostly gay men • rooms & apts • also restaurant • AS490+

BARS

Bip Opernring 6 43-1/512.84.60 • 9am-3am, from 2pm Sun • gay/straight • food served

Brot & Rosen Ratschkygasse 48/2-4 43-1/967.08.06 • 6pm-midnight • lesbians/gay men • cafe-bar • special events include monthly 'Frauenfest'

Café Berg Berggasse 8 (at Wasagasse, U2-Schottentor) 43-1/319.57.20 • 10am-1am • popular • lesbians/gay men • cafe-bar • young crowd

Cafe Reimann Schönbrunner Str 285 43-1/813.57.67 • 7am-2am, till 4am Fri-Sat, from 8am Sun, clsd Mon • lesbians/gay men • food served • cabaret nights

Café Savoy Linke Wienzeile 36 (at Köstlergasse) 43-1/586.73.48 • 5pm-2am, from 9am Sat, clsd Sun • popular • lesbians/gay men • upscale cafe-bar

Café Stein Währinger Str 6-8 (nr U-Schottentor) 43-1/319.72.41 • 7am-1am, from 9am Sun • gay-friendly • cafe-bar • Internet access • terrace

---

Vienna

LGBT PRIDE: June.

ANNUAL EVENTS: May - Life Ball (AIDS benefit), web: www.lifeball.at. Summer - Vienna Festival 43-1/589.22.0.

CITY INFO: 43-1/211.14.0, web: www.vienna-tourism.at. In US, call 212/944-6880 or 310/477-3332.

ATTRACTIONS:
Art Nouveau buildings.
Belvedere Palace/Austrian Gallery 43-1/795.57.261.
Sigmund Freud Museum 43-1/319.1596.
House of Music 43-1/51.648.51.
Imperial Palace 43-1/533.75.70.
Jewish Museum 43-1/535.0431.
Museum of Fine Arts 43-1/525.24.0.
Schönbrunn Palace 43-1/811.13.
St Stephen's Cathedral 43-1/515.52.3526.
State Opera House 43-1/514.44.2613.
Vienna Boys' Choir 43-1/216.39.42.

BEST VIEW: Overlooking the city from the top of the Giant Ferris Wheel.

WEATHER: Mild, rainy summers and chilly winters. September is a good time to visit.

TRANSIT: Vienna Airport Lines. Vienna has an excellent public transit system. Consider purchasing a Vienna Card for 72 hours of unlimited travel by subway, bus, and tram, plus discounts on airport shuttle, at museums, and at many shops and restaurants. 43-1/211.14.0.

Vienna • Austria

Café-Bar Robi Schönbrunner Str 10
43-1/586.35.18 • 10am-2am, from 5pm wknds
• gay/ straight • food served

Frauencafé Lange Gasse 11 **43-1/406.37.54**
• 5pm-2am (sometimes clsd Sun-Mon) •
mostly women • cafe-bar

Frauenzentrum Beisl Währingerstr 59 **43-1/402.87.54** • mostly women • food served

Peter's Operncafé Hartauer Riemergasse 9
(at Singer) **43-1/512.89.81** • 6pm-2am, clsd
Sun • gay/ straight • food served • terrace

Sonderbar Marc Aurel Str 7 **43-1/969.05.11**
• 6pm-2am, Fri-Sat till 4am • lesbians and gay
men • dancing/DJ • young crowd

Das Versteck Grünangergasse 10, downstairs
(at Nikolaigasse, U1-Stephansplatz)
43-1/513.40.53 • 6pm-midnight, till 4am Fri-
Sat, clsd Sun • gay/ straight • young crowd

NIGHTCLUBS

Arriba Gumpendorferstr 9 (off Getreidemarkt)
• 10pm-close Fri only • mostly women •
dancing/DJ

Club Jedermann Westbanstr 14
43-1/524.29.29 • open late, clsd Sun-Mon •
lesbians/ gay men • dancing/DJ • also billiards
lounge • also restaurant

Heaven Gay Night at U4 Schönbrunner Str
222 (at Meidlinger, U4-Meidlinger Hauptstr)
43-1/815.83.07 • 11pm-5am Th only • popular
• mostly gay men • dancing/DJ • transgender-
friendly • live shows • wheelchair access

Liquid Rotgasse 9 **43-1/535.99.956** • 11pm-
close Fri only • mostly gay men • dancing/DJ •
live shows

Resis.Danse Novarragasse 40 (at Hosi Gay &
Lesbian Center) • 9pm-midnight Fri only

Stanek Gay Dance Grashofgasse 1a
43-1/513.42.92 • 10pm 1st Fri • lesbians/ gay
men • ballroom dancing • cover charge

Why Not? Tiefer Graben 22 (at Wipplinger, U-
Schottentor) **43-1/925.30.24** • 10pm-close Fri-
Sat • mostly gay men • dancing/DJ • live
shows • videos

CAFES

Santo Spirito Kumpfgasse 7 (U-Stefansplatz)
43-1/512.99.98 • 6pm-2am, 11am-3am Fri-Sat
• Mediterranean/ vegetarian • also bar •
terrace • wheelchair access

Smart Cafe Kostlergasse 9 **43-1/585.71.65** •
4pm-2am, Fri-Sat till midnight, clsd Sun • gay/
straight • fetish cafe

RESTAURANTS

Café-Restaurant Willendorf Linke Wienzeile
102 (nr Hofmuhlgasse, U4-Pilgramgasse)
43-1/587.17.89 • 6pm-2am, from 10am wknds,
food served till midnight • lesbians/ gay men •
plenty veggie • full bar • terrace

The Living Room Franzensgasse 18 (at
Grüngasse, U4-Kettenbrückengasse)
43-1/585.37.07 • 6pm-3:30am, bar open till
2am • mostly gay men • Viennese

Margaritaville Bartensteingasse 3 (U-
Lerchenfelder Str) **43-1/405.47.86** • 6pm-
2am, food served till midnight • Tex-Mex • full
bar • terrace

Motto Schönbrunner Str 30 **43-1/587.06.72** •
6pm-4am • popular • gay/ straight • trendy •
also bar • terrace

nice rice Mariahilfer Str 45/49 **43-1/586.28.39**
• 9am-midnight • vegetarian

Orlando Mollardgasse 3 (U-Pilgramgasse)
43-1/967.35.50 • 6pm-2am (food served till
midnight) • popular • lesbians/ gay men • also
bar • terrace • lesbian-owned/ run

ENTERTAINMENT & RECREATION

Kunsthistorisches Museum Maria-
Theresien-Platz **43-1/525.24.401** • 10am-6pm,
till 11pm Th • not to be missed • works from
Ancient Egypt to the Renaissance to the Klimts

BOOKSTORES

American Discount Rechte Wienzeile 5 (at
Paniglgasse) **43-1/587.57.72** • 9:30am-6:30pm,
9am-5pm Sat, clsd Sun • int'l magazines & books
• also Neubaugasse 39 location, 43-1/523.37.07 •
also Donaustadt Str 1 location, 43-1/203.95.18

Frauenzimmer Lange Gasse 11 **43-1/522.48.92** • 9am-6pm, till 1pm Sat, clsd Sun •
women's

Löwenherz Berggasse 8 (next to 'Cafe Berg',
enter on Wasagasse, U2-Schottentor)
43-1/317.29.82 • 10am-7pm, till 5pm Sat, clsd
Sun • lgbt • large selection of English titles

PUBLICATIONS

Bussi **43-1/505.07.42** • free city mag w/ event
& club listings

g **43-1/961.98.38** • lgbt magazine

Vienna Gay Guide **43-1/789.97.37** • city-
map & guide

EROTICA

Art-X Percostr 3 **43-1/258.04.44,
43-2622/88.555** • 10am-8pm, till 5pm Sat,
clsd Sun • leather, latex, rubber • toys • music
• videos • magazines

MarG Hamburgerstr 20
43-1-0699/1051-9337 • sex shop for women

England • EUROPE

ENGLAND

LONDON

London is divided into 6 regions:
London—Overview
London—Central
London—West
London—North
London—East
London—South

London—Overview

INFO LINES & SERVICES

Audre Lorde Clinic 44-020/7377-7312, 44-020/8846-1576/ 7 • Wed & Fri • lesbian health clinic • call for appt & location

Black Lesbian/ Gay Centre 5/5A Westminster Bridge Rd, Rm 113 **44-020/7620-3885** • 11:30am-5:30pm Tue & Th

Freedom Cab Company 44-020/7734-1313 • gay and lesbian taxi service

London Bisexual Women's Group • meets 7pm-9pm Th at 'Vespa Lounge'

London Holiday Accommodation Bureau 44-020/8800-5908 • apts & rooms in central London • £30+

London Lesbian/ Gay Switchboard 44-020/7837-7324 • 24hrs

London Lesbian Line 44-020/7251-6911 • 2pm-10pm Mon & Fri, 7pm-10pm Tue & Th

The London Women's Centre The Wheel, Wild Court (Holborn) **44-020/7831-6946** • also cafe, theater & gym • call for events

Outlinks LGBT Youth Project 44-020/7378-8732 • drop-in 4pm-7pm Tue • call for more info

ENTERTAINMENT & RECREATION

Gay Sweatshop Limited 44-020/7242-1168 • gay theater troupe

PUBLICATIONS

Attitude 44-020/7308-5090

Diva 44-020/7482-2576 • glorious glossy lesbian magazine

Gay Times 44-020/7482-2576, 44-020/7267-0021 • gay glossy

The Pink Paper 44-020/7296-6000 • free lgbt newspaper

Time Out 44-020/7813-3000 • weekly city scene guide w/ gay section

SPIRITUAL GROUPS

Jewish Gay/ Lesbian Group 44-020/8922-5214

MCC London Camden Trinity URC, Buck St, Kentish Town Rd **44-020/8304-2374** • 7pm Sun • also MCC Brixton, 44-020/8678-0200 • also MCC Mile End, 44-020/7538-8376

London—Central

London—Central includes Soho, Covent Garden, Bloomsbury, Mayfair, Westminster, Pimlico & Belgravia

ACCOMMODATIONS

Central London Guestrooms & Apts Tottenham Court Rd (at Charing Cross Rd) **44-020/7497-7000** • lesbians/ gay men • guesthouse & apartment • smokefree • gay-owned/ run • 3-night minimum stay • £75-200

Manors & Co 1 Baker St **44-020/7486-5982, 800/454-4385** • gay-friendly • luxury apts

Noel Coward Hotel 111 Ebury St (off Eccleston St, Belgravia) **44-020/7730-2094, 44-020/7730-9005** • gay-friendly • swimming • some shared baths • US$103-120

Waverley House Hotel 130-134 Southampton Row (Bloomsbury) **44-020/7833-3691, 44-020/7833-2579** • gay-friendly • full brkfst • £79-220

BARS

Note: 'Pub hours' usually means 11am-11pm Mon-Sat and noon-3pm & 7pm-10:30pm Sun

The Admiral Duncan 54 Old Compton St (Soho) **44-020/7437-5300** • pub hours • popular • lesbians/ gay men • neighborhood bar • transgender-friendly

Bar Aquda 13–14 Maiden Ln (btwn Bedford & Southampton, Covent Garden) **44-020/7577-9891** • popular • lesbians/ gay men • cafe-bar

The Box 32–34 Monmouth St, Seven Dials (nr Shaftesbury Ave, Covent Garden) **44-020/7240-5828** • 6pm-3am, 3pm-midnight Sun • popular • lesbians/ gay men • dancing/DJ • cafe-bar • videos • wheelchair access

The Candy Bar 23–24 Bateman St (at Greek, in Soho) **44-020/7437-1977** • 5pm-1am, till 3am Wed-Fri, 3pm-3am Sat, till midnight Sun • popular • women-only (men welcome as guests) • 2 flrs • dancing/DJ • live shows • theme nights • call for events • food served • outdoor seating

London—Central • England

Reply **Forward** **Delete**

Date: Tue, Jan 1, 2002 15:12:09
From: Girl-on-the-Go
To: Editor@Damron.com
Subject: London

> London is well known for its history, fine museums, and fog, but this world-class city offers much, much more. Over 7 million people, representing hundreds of cultures, languages, and religions, call London home. And the city has been going through yet another growth spurt in recent years: Haute cuisine and funky fusion restaurants abound. Cutting-edge buildings dot the skyline. And cell phones are omnipresent.

> Don't worry, though, you can still get bangers and mash. This sprawling city can easily accommodate change. As a matter of fact, when you start navigating around (recommendably via the Underground) you'll see that London is really a collection of smaller towns and neighborhoods, each with a distinct feel. Of these, you'll find more lesbians and gay men in Soho and Earl's Court.

> Like London itself, the women's scene is varied and vast. Take a break from sightseeing to visit **Silver Moon Women's Bookstore,** or **Gay's the Word,** and pick up a copy of **Diva**—London's slick lesbian magazine. To check in on what's happening, visit the **London Women's Centre**—which also houses a gym, theater, and cafe! For more suggestions on how to experience it all, call the **London Lesbian Line.** Or check out **www.gingerbeer.co.uk,** a stylish online guide to the local lesbo scene.

> In the evening, start out at one of London's trendy cafe-bars, like **Aquda, Freedom, Kudos,** or the **Box.** For a meal with less of a bar atmosphere, get a table at **Therapy,** popular with local women.

> London has three (!) full-time women's bars—**Candy Bar, Glass Bar,** and the **Vespa Lounge**—and a vast array of women's nights at various mixed bars and clubs. Check with one of the resources above, and look for flyers.

> If you like dancing well into the morning hours, and mixing it up with the boys, check out one of London's popular clubs like **G.A.Y., Heaven, DTPM,** or late-night weekends at **Turnmills.** For a comprehensive listing of mixed clubs in and around London, pick up a copy of the **Pink Paper** or the scene guide **Time Out.**

> For something a bit different, check out the **Drill Hall Theatre & Bar:** an alternative theater, bar, and vegetarian restaurant; Mondays are women-only, and Thursdays are smokefree.

England • EUROPE

Compton's of Soho 53 Old Compton St **44-020/7479-7961** • noon-11pm, 7pm-10:30pm Sun • popular • mostly gay men • leather • food served • wheelchair access

Drill Hall Theater & Bar 16 Chenies St (btwn Alfred Pl & Ridgmount, Bloomsbury) **44-020/7637-8270, 44-020/7631-5107** • 5pm-11pm • gay/straight • women-only Mon • 200-seat theater • workshops • also bar • 6pm-11pm, clsd Sun • smokefree Th • also vegetarian restaurant • 10:30am-8:30pm, noon-4:30pm Sun • wheelchair access

The Edge 11 Soho Sq **44-020/7439-1313** • midnight-late, noon-10:30pm Sun • popular • 4 flrs • cafe-bar • dancing/DJ • live music • outdoor seating • wheelchair access

The Escape 10 Brewer St (nr Regent St) **44-020/7734-2626** • 11am-3am, noon-11:30pm Sun • popular • mostly gay men • dancing/DJ • 'bar with a nightclub feel in the evenings'

Glass Bar West Lodge, 190 Euston Rd **44-020/7387-6184** • 5:30pm-close, from 7:30pm Mon, from 6:30pm Sat, clsd Sun • women only • 2 flrs • theme nights • events • private club • £1 day membership

King's Arms 23 Poland St (Soho) **44-020/7734-5907** • pub hours • lesbians/gay men • neighborhood bar • karaoke • food served

Ku Bar 75 Charing Cross Rd (at Shaftesbury, Soho) **44-020/7437-4303** • pub hours • lesbians/gay men • trendy cafe-bar

London

LGBT PRIDE: July. www.pridelondon.org.

ANNUAL EVENTS: March/April - Lesbian & Gay Film Festival 44-020/7928-3232, web: www.bfi.org.uk.
May - Soho Pink Weekend.
Mr Gay UK Contest.
June - Mardi Gras 44-020/7494-2225.
August - Summer Rites 44-020/7737-2629.
October - Stonewall Equality Show 44-020/7336-8860. Huge charity concert.

CITY INFO: 44-020/7824-8844, web: www.LondonTown.com.

ATTRACTIONS: British Museum 44-020/7323-8000.
Buckingham Palace 44-020/7839-1377.
Globe Theatre 44-020/7401-9919.
Kensington Palace 44-020/7937-9561.
Madame Tussaud's 44-020/7935-6861.
National Gallery 44-020/7839-3321.
Oscar Wilde's house (34 Tite Street).
St Paul's Cathedral 44-020/7236-4128.
Tate Gallery 44-020/7887-8000.
Tower of London 44-020/7680-9004.
Westminster Abbey 44-020/7222-5152.

BEST VIEW: From Tower Bridge (Tower Hill Tube).

WEATHER: London is warmer and less rainy than you may have heard. Summer temperatures reach the 70°s and the average annual rainfall is about half of that of Atlanta, GA or Hartford, CT.

TRANSIT: Freedom Cars 44-020/7734-1313.
Ladycabs 44-020/7254-3501.
London Travel Information (Tube & buses) 44-020/7222-1234, 24hr info.

London—Central • England

Kudos 10 Adelaide St (off the Strand) 44-020/7379-4573 • pub hours • lesbians/ gay men • professional crowd • trendy cafe-bar • wheelchair access • gay-owned/ run

Loose 30 Dean St (at 'Sunset Strip') • 9pm-1am Tue only • strippers/dancers perform for women-only audience

Matrix 125 Cleveland St 44-020/7637-5352 • 5pm-11pm Mon-Fri, clsd wknds • mostly gay men • dancing/DJ • food served

The Retro Bar 2 George Ct (off the Strand) 44-020/7839-4012 • pub hours • lesbians/ gay men • neighborhood bar • dancing/DJ • karaoke

Rupert Street Cafe-Bar 50 Rupert St (off Brewer) 44-020/7734-5614 • pub hours • lesbians/gay men • wheelchair access

Vespa Lounge Centre Point House, St Giles High St (upstairs, across the way from 'First Out') 44-020/7836-8956 • 6pm-11pm, till 10:30pm Sun • women-only (men welcome as guests) • theme nights • comedy last Sun (cover charge) • private club

The Village Soho 81 Wardour St (at Old Compton) 44-020/7434-2124, 44-020/7436-2468 • pub hours • mostly gay men • trendy • young crowd • cafe menu till 5pm • wheelchair access

West Central 29-30 Lisle St (behind Leicester Sq cinemas) 44-020/7479-7981 • pub hours • lesbians/ gay men • dancing/DJ • transgender-friendly • drag shows • basement bar open 10:30pm-3am Fri

Wow Bar • parties for women, including '100% babe' & '4 u girl' • check local media for venue/ dates

The Yard 57 Rupert St (off Brewer) 44-020/7437-2652 • pub hours • lesbians/ gay men • queer comedy night Wed upstairs at 'Screamers' • young crowd • food served till 5pm • wheelchair access • US$5-10

NIGHTCLUBS

Atelier 18 W Central St (at 'The End') 44-020/7419-9199 • 9pm-3:30am Th • trendy • mostly gay men • dancing/DJ • cover charge

Factor 25 at 'Rock', Hungerford House (Victoria Embankment) • 7pm-late Sun only • mostly gay men • dancing/DJ • cover charge

G.A.Y. 157 Charing Cross Rd (at Oxford St, in London Astoria theatre complex) 44-020/7434-9592, 44-020/7734-6963 • 10:30pm-late Mon & Th-Sat • popular • mostly gay men • dancing/DJ • live shows • young crowd • retro Mon • cover charge

Heaven The Arches (off Villiers St) 44-020/7930-2020, 00 44 20/7930-8306 • popular • the mother of all London gay clubs • call for hours/ events • mostly gay men • dancing/DJ • 'Popcorn' Mon • 'Fruit Machine' Wed

Home 1 Leicester Sq 44-0900/102-0107 (INFO LINE) • open Th-Sat, gay Sun from 4pm • gay-friendly • huge club on 7 flrs • dancing/DJ • live shows • cover charge

The Limelight at 'The Sound Club,' Swiss Centre (Leicester Square) 44-020/7437-4303, 44-020/7434-0572 • 6pm-midnight Sun only • popular T-dance • lesbians/ gay men • dancing/DJ

Off the Hook 143 Charing Cross Rd (at 'Velvet Underground') 44-020/0973-628585 • 10pm-3am Mon • popular • mostly gay men • diverse crowd & funky music

The Tube 5-6 Falconberg Court (off Charing Cross, behind the 'Astoria') 44-020/7287-3726 • 10:30pm-3:30am, till 5am Fri-Sat • mostly gay men • dancing/DJ • live shows • theme nights • 'Mama Mia' (60s/ 70s/ 80s) Wed • 'Babe' Fri • 'Wig Out' Sat

CAFES

First Out 52 St Giles High St (btwn Charing Cross & Shaftesbury) 44-020/7240-8042 • 10am-11pm, 11am-10:30pm Sun • lesbians/ gay men • cont'l • full bar • smokefree upstairs • women-only Fri at 'Girl Friday'

Freedom Cafe-Bar 60-66 Wardour St (off Old Compton St) 44-020/7734-0071 • 9am-11pm, till 10:30pm Sun • trendy scene cafe • young crowd • US$6-11 • also downstairs bar • open till 2am Mon-Sat • live shows

Old Compton Cafe 34 Old Compton St 44-020/7439-3309 • 24hrs • popular • lesbians/ gay men • sandwiches & salads • all-day brkfst • terrace • US$3-7

RESTAURANTS

Balans 60 Old Compton St 44-020/7437-5212 • 8am-5am, till 6am Fri-Sat, till 2am Sun • all-day/ night brunch • popular • cafe-bar • transgender-friendly • live shows • wheelchair access • US$10-22

Food for Thought 31 Neal St, downstairs (Covent Garden) 44-020/7836-0239, 44-020/7836-9072 • noon-8pm • vegetarian • US$5-10

The Gay Hussar 2 Greek St (on Soho Sq) 44-020/7437-0973 • lunch & dinner, clsd Sun • Hungarian • wheelchair access • US$28-41

Mildred's 58 Greek St (off Shaftesbury) 44-020/7494-1634 • noon-11pm, clsd Sun • plenty veggie & vegan

England • EUROPE

Steph's 39 Dean St **44-020/7734-5976** • noon-3pm Mon-Fri & 5:30pm-11:30pm Mon-Sat, clsd Sun • English • US$12-26

The Stockpot 18 Old Compton St **44-020/7287-1066** • 11:30am-11:30pm • cheap!

Therapy 10-11 Lancashire Ct (off New Bond St) **44-020/7499-5554** • noon-4pm & 7pm-10:30pm, clsd Sun • lesbians/gay men • contemporary • plenty veggie/vegan • full bar • woman-owned/run

Wagamama Noodle Bar 10a Lexington St **44-020/7292-0990, 44-020/7631-3140** • noon-11pm, 12:30pm-10pm Sun • Japanese • smokefree • £5-10 • also locations in Bloomsbury & Covent Garden

Entertainment & Recreation

Gay Film Night at Prince Charles Cinema (Leicester Pl) **44-020/7437-8181** • every Mon • discount tickets available at 'Ku Bar'

Laughing Cows/ Hersterics at Vespa Lounge, under Centre Point House (St Giles Circus) **44-020/7836-8956** • 8pm-11pm Sun • lesbian comedy club

SOHO Gay and Lesbian Walk 56 Old Compton St **44-020/7437-6063**

Bookstores

Gay's the Word 66 Marchmont St (nr Russell Sq) **44-020/7278-7654** • 10am-6:30pm, 2pm-6pm Sun • lgbt • new & used books • magazines

Silver Moon Women's Bookshop 64-68 Charing Cross Rd **44-020/7836-7906** • lesbian/feminist • wheelchair access

Retail Shops

American Retro 35 Old Compton St **44-020/7734-3477** • 10:15am-7pm, clsd Sun • clothing & gifts

Metal Morphosis 10-11 Moor St (at Old Compton St) **44-020/7434-4554** • piercing studio, body jewelry

Prowler 3-7 Brewer St (behind 'Village Soho' bar) **44-020/7734-4031** • popular • large gay department store

Gyms & Health Clubs

Covent Garden Health Spa 29 Endell St **44-020/7836-2236** • sauna • steam • solarium • jacuzzi • holistic services • also bar

Erotica

RoB London 24-25 Wells St (nr Berwick St) **44-020/7735-7893** • leather/fetish shop • wheelchair access

London — West

London—West includes Earl's Court, Kensington, Chelsea & Bayswater

Accommodations

Bailey's Hotel 140 Gloucester Rd (at Old Brompton Rd, Kensington) **44-020/7373-6000** • gay-friendly 4-star hotel • located in the heart of Kensington • £120-250 • also 'Olives' restaurant & bar • Mediterranean

Comfort Inn Kensington 22-32 W Cromwell Rd (Earl's Court) **44-020/7373-3300** • gay-friendly • food served • also bar • £95-140

George Hotel 58-60 Cartwright Gardens (N of Russell Sq) **44-020/7387-8777** • gay-friendly • full brkfst • some shared baths • £50-100

Prince William Hotel 42-44 Gloucester Ter (Windsor) **44-020/7724-7414** • gay/straight • centrally located townhouse • some shared baths • US$78-129

Redcliffe Hotel 268 Fulham Rd (Chelsea) **44-020/7823-3494** • lesbians/gay men • also restaurant & bar • US$103-120

Reeves Hotel 48 Shepherd's Bush Green (Hammersmith) **44-020/8740-1158** • women only

Bars

The George Music Bar 114 Twickenham Rd **44-020/8560-1456** • 5pm-11pm, from noon Sat, noon-10:30pm Sun • 'George Cabaret' every Fri-Sat & every other Sun

The Penny Farthing 135 King St (Hammersmith) **44-020/8600-0941, 44-020/8748-7045** • noon-midnight, till 10:30pm Sun • popular • lesbians/gay men • neighborhood bar • food served • cabaret • wheelchair access

Richmond Arms 20 The Square (at Princess) **44-020/8940-2118** • pub hrs • mostly gay men • dancing/DJ • professional crowd • live shows

The Rocket 10-13 Churchfield Rd (Acton) **44-020/8992-1545** • 6pm-11pm, from noon wknds, till 10:30pm Sun • lesbians/gay men • dancing/DJ • cabaret bar downstairs • men's cruise bar upstairs

Restaurants

Balans West 239 Old Brompton Rd **44-020/7244-8388** • 8am-1am • lesbians/gay men • English • £7-15

Phoenicia 11-13 Abingdon Rd **44-020/7937-0120** • Lebanese/Mediterranean • £7-15

Wilde About Oscar at the 'Philbeach Hotel'
44-020/7835-1858, 44-020/7373-1244 •
7pm-11pm • lesbians/ gay men • eclectic/
French • reservations required • wheelchair
access • garden • US$15-22

Willi's at the 'Prince William Hotel'
44-020/7724-7414 • English

GYMS & HEALTH CLUBS

Soho Athletic Club 254 Earls Ct Rd
44-020/7370-1402 • gay-friendly • also
Camden Town location • 193 Camden High St,
44-020/7482-4524

London—North

London—North includes Paddington,
Regents Park, Camden, St Pancras &
Islington

ACCOMMODATIONS

Rainbowstay Guest House 14 Thornhill
Bridge Wharf (Islington) **44-020/7713-5287** •
lesbians/ gay men • gay-owned/ run

BARS

Bar Fusion 45 Essex Rd (at Queen's Head
St, Islington) **44-020/7688-2882** • 1pm-
midnight • lesbians/ gay men • trendy cafe-bar

Blush 8 Cazenove Rd (Stoke Newington)
44-020/7923-9202 • 5pm-midnight, brunch
from noon wknds, clsd Mon • lesbians/ gay
men • women only from 8pm Fri • friendly
cafe-bar • beer garden • all-day brkfst • salads
• live music Sun

Due South 35 Stoke Newington High St (at
Arcola St, Stoke Newington)
44-020/7249-7543 • 5pm-midnight, from
noon wknds • lesbians/ gay men • women-
only Th • neighborhood bar • karaoke • salsa
lessons Mon • also restaurant

Duke of Wellington 119 Balls Pond Rd
(Islington) **44-020/7254-4338** • noon-
midnight, till 11:30pm Sun • lesbians/ gay men
• neighborhood bar

The Flag 29 Crouch Hill **44-020/7272-4748**
• lesbians/ gay men • friendly neighborhood
pub

King William IV 77 Hampstead High St
(Hampstead) **44-020/7435-5747** • pub hours
• lesbians/ gay men • neighborhood bar •
transgender-friendly • drag shows • food
served • wheelchair access

The Oak Bar 79 Green Lanes **44-020/
7354-2791** • 5pm-midnight, till 2am Fri-Sat,
from 1pm wknds • lesbians/ gay men •
dancing/DJ & cabaret wknds • food served •
women-only Fri at 'Hoochy Koochy' • women-
only last Sat at 'Liberté' • 'Hoppa' for Cypriots,
Greeks, Turks & friends 3rd Sat • women-owned

NIGHTCLUBS

Club Kali 1 Dartmouth Park Hill (at 'The
Dome') **44-020/7272-8153 (DOME #)** • 10pm-
3am 1st & 3rd Fri • popular • lesbians/ gay men
• dancing/DJ • South Asian music • cover charge

Fiction at The Cross Bagleys Yard (Kings
Cross) **44-020/7251-8778** • 10:30pm-late Fri •
lesbians/ gay men • dancing/DJ • see-and-be-
seen • cover charge

The Liquid Lounge 257 Pentonville Rd
(Kings Cross) **44-020/7837-3218** • lesbians/
gay men • dancing/DJ • theme nights • 'Miss-
Shapes' indie/ alternative women's night
5:30pm-3am Sat • cover charge

Popstarz at 'Scala,' 275 Pentonville Rd
(Kings Cross) **44-020/7833-9988** • popular •
10pm-5am Fri • lesbians/ gay men • dancing/DJ
• Britpop & indie music • cover charge

BOOKSTORES

Compendium 234 Camden High St
(Camden Town) **44-020/7485-8944** • lgbt

EROTICA

Sh! Women's Erotic Emporium 39 Coronet
St (off Old St & Pitfield St, Shoreditch)
44-020/7613-5458 • 11:30am-6:30pm, till
8pm Th, clsd Sun • also mail order

Zipper Store 283 Camden High St (Camden
Town) **44-020/7284-0537, 44-020/7267-0021
(MAIL ORDER)** • fetishwear • books • videos •
sex toys • also mail order

London—East

London—East includes City, Tower,
Clerkenwell & Shoreditch

BARS

The Coronet 119 The Grove (Stratford)
44-020/8522-0811 • 3pm-midnight, till 2am
Fri-Sat, clsd Sun • lesbians/ gay men •
dancing/DJ wknds • cabaret nights • karaoke

The Joiner's Arms 116-118 Hackney Rd (nr
Shoreditch) **44-020/7739-9654** • 6pm-2am,
noon-10:30pm Sun, lesbians/ gay men •
neighborhood bar • live shows • after-hrs party
Sun night (dancing/DJ)

England • EUROPE

The Old Ship 17 Barnes St (in Stepney) **44-020/7790-4082** • 6pm-11pm, from 7:30pm Sat, 1:30pm-10:30pm Sun • lesbians/ gay men • neighborhood bar • drag shows • wheelchair access

Royal Oak 73 Columbia Rd (Bethnal Green, in the flower market) **44-020/7739-8204** • 11am-late, from 8am Sun • popular • lesbians/ gay men • neighborhood bar • transgender-friendly • food served

The Spiral 138 Shoreditch High St (across from Shoreditch Church) **44-020/7613-1351** • 10pm-2am, 9pm-4am Fri-Sat, till 3:30am Sun, clsd Mon-Tue • lesbians/ gay men • neighborhood bar • dancing/DJ • 'Trash Disco' Th • karaoke Fri • cabaret Sat • piano bar Sun

NIGHTCLUBS

Benjy's 2000 562-A Mile End Rd **44-020/ 8980-6427** • 9pm-1am Sun only • popular • lesbians/ gay men • dancing/DJ • young crowd

Club Travestie Extraordinaire at 'Stepneys,' 373 Commercial Rd (enter on Aylward St, off Jubilee St, Stepney) **44-020/8788-4154** • TV/TS night 9pm-2am 2nd & 4th Sat • lesbians/ gay men • dancing/DJ • drag shows • wheelchair access

DTPM 77a Charterhouse St, Smithfield Mkt (at 'Fabric') **44-020/7251-8778 (INFO LINE)** • 8pm-late Sun • popular • lesbians/ gay men • dancing/DJ • huge, stylish techno club • young crowd • cover charge

Turnmills 63B Clerkenwell Rd (Clerkenwell) **44-020/7250-3409** • after hours • mostly gay men • dancing/DJ • private club • cover charge • 'Trade' 4am-1pm Sun & 'Habit' 10pm-7am Sun are very popular

Way Out Club 9 Crosswall (at 'Charlie's') **44-020/8363-0948** • 9pm-4am Sat only • transsexuals & their friends • dancing/DJ • live shows • private club • cover charge

EROTICA

Expectations 75 Great Eastern St (Shoreditch) **44-020/7739-0292** • 11am-7pm, till 8pm Sat, noon-5pm Sun • leather/ rubber store • also mail order

London—South

London—South includes Southwark, Lambeth, Kennington, Vauxhall, Battersea, Lewisham & Greenwich

BARS

Buzz Bar 136 Battersea High St **44-020/7207-3895** • lesbians/ gay men • bar & restaurant • food served noon-8pm

Centre Stage 118 Lower Rd (Rotherhithe) **44-020/7394-9766** • 7pm-midnight • mostly gay men • neighborhood bar • quiz night Tue • piano bar Wed • 'Trash Disco' (dancing/DJ) Th till 1am • 'Fresh' (dancing/DJ) Fri till 2am • 'Showtime' Sat till 2am • lunch served 3pm-7pm Sun

Fridge Bar 22 Town Hall Parade (Brixton Hill) **44-020/7326-5100** • 10am-11pm, till 2am Th, till 4am Fri-Sat, clsd Sun • popular • gay/ straight • dancing/DJ • also The Fridge Club next door

The Gloucester 1 King William Walk (btwn Greenwich Pk & Footway Tunnel, Greenwich) **44-020/8858-2666** • pub hours • mostly gay men • neighborhood bar • food served • live shows • wheelchair access

Kazbar 50 Clapham High St (Clapham) **44-020/7622-0070** • 4pm-midnight, from noon Sat, till 11:30pm Sun • mostly gay men • transgender-friendly • cafe-bar

The Little Apple 98 Kennington Ln **44-020/7735-2039** • noon-midnight, till 11pm Sun • lesbians/ gay men • dancing/DJ • transgender-friendly • food served • terrace • wheelchair access

The Queen's Arms 63 Court Hill Rd (Lewisham) **44-020/8318-7305** • noon-11pm • lesbians/ gay men • neighborhood bar • dancing/DJ Fri • upscale cabaret bar • beer garden • wheelchair access

The Roebuck 25 Rennell St (off Lewisham High St) **44-020/8852-1705** • 11am-midnight, till 1am Th-Sat, till 11pm Sun • lesbians/ gay men • neighborhood bar • dancing/DJ • karaoke • live shows • also restaurant

The Two Brewers 114 Clapham High St (Clapham) **44-020/7498-4971, 44-020/7622-3621** • 6pm-1am, noon-3am Fri-Sat, lunch noon-6pm Sun • lesbians/ gay men • dancing/DJ • cabaret

NIGHTCLUBS

Crash Arch 66, Goding St **44-020/7278-0995** • 10:30pm-late Sat • popular • mostly gay men • dancing/DJ • cover charge

Duckie 373 Kennington Ln (Vauxhall), SE11 **44-020/7582-0833** • 9pm-2am every Sat • popular • 70's & 80's music

Royal Vauxhall Tavern 372 Kennington Ln (Vauxhall) **44-020/7582-0833** • 8pm-1am, till 2am Sat, noon-midnight Sun • mostly gay men • neighborhood bar • dancing/DJ • transgender-friendly • drag shows • wheelchair access

Paris—01 • France

CAFES

Surf.Net Cafe 13 Deptford Church St (at Deptford Broadway) **44-020/8488-1200** • 11am-9pm, till 7pm Sat, clsd Sun • cybercafe

RESTAURANTS

Fileric 12 Queenstown Rd **44-020/7720-4844** • French

Il Pinguino 62 Brixton Rd **44-020/7735-3822** • Italian

ENTERTAINMENT & RECREATION

Oval Theatre Cafe Bar 52-54 Kennington Oval **44-020/7582-7680** • 6pm-8pm, till 11pm Th-Sun, clsd Wed • call to inquire about current theatre and art • food served

RETAIL SHOPS

London Piercing Clinic 13 Portland Rd (S Norwood) **44-020/8656-7180** • 11am-7pm, 2pm-6pm Sun

GYMS & HEALTH CLUBS

Paris Gymnasium Arch 73, Goding St (behind 'Vauxhall Tavern,' Vauxhall) **44-020/7735-8989** • mostly gay men • £6.50 day pass

FRANCE

PARIS

Note: M°=Métro station

Paris is divided by arrondissements (city districts); 01=1st arrondissement, 02=2nd arrondissement, etc

Paris—Overview

Note: When phoning Paris from the US, dial the country code + the city code + the local phone number

INFO LINES & SERVICES

Centre gai et lesbien 3 rue Keller (M°Bastille) **33-1/43.57.21.47** • drop-in 2pm-8pm, till 7pm Sun • women 8pm Fri • call for other events/ groups • also wine bar

Ecoute Gaie **33-1/44.93.01.02** • helpline staffed 6pm-10pm Mon-Fri & 6pm-8pm Sat

Gay AA 9 passage St-Paul (M°St-Paul) **33-1/43.25.75.00 (24HR INFO), 33-1/48.06.43.68** • 8:30pm Fri

La Maison des Femmes 163 rue de Charenton **33-1/43.43.41.13, 33-1/46.28.54.94** • lesbian archives & library • open to public 7pm-9:30pm Tue & by appt • also cafe

Les Maudites Femelles ('Damned Females') **33-6/62.05.93.96** • SM/ fetish events for women

ACCOMMODATIONS

A Parisian Home **33-1/47.03.02.25** • furnished apts in Paris

Insightful Travelers **617/859-0720 (US#)** • gay-friendly • short-term apt rentals • 5-day minimum stay • daily & monthly rates

Marais & Left Bank Historic Rentals 25 rue des Rosiers (at rue des Ecouffes) **800/537-5408 (US#)** • gay-friendly • 1-bdrm apts • full kitchen • US$600-900/ week

Paris Séjour Réservation **312/587-7707 (US#), 800/582-7274** • gay-friendly • short-term apt rentals

RentParis.com 27 rue Rossini, Vitry sur Seine **415/255-8270 (US#)** • lesbians/ gay men • fully furnished studios & apts • gay-owned/ run

PUBLICATIONS

Double Face **33-1/48.04.58.00** • lifestyle magazine, event/ party listings, free at venues around Paris

e.m@le **33-1/53.35.98.54** • weekly magazine w/ events & club listings • free at venues around Paris

Housewife **33-1/40.26.60.31** • monthly satirical club scene 'zine for lesbians • published by 'Pulp' nightclub • free at venues around Marais • also sell such can't-live-without items as Lesbian Powder ("great for office parties!")

Lesbia **33-1/43.48.89.54** • monthly glossy magazine

Têtu **33-1/56.80.20.80** • stylish & intelligent lgbt monthly (en français)

SPIRITUAL GROUPS

Beit Haverim et Haverot **33-1/44.84.08.54, 33-1/40.40.00.71** • 8pm Wed & last Th at CGL • lgbt Jewish social group

David & Jonathan 92 bis, rue de Picpus (12) **33-1/43.42.09.49** • 6:30pm-8:30pm Fri • interdenominational lgbt Christian group

Paris—01

ACCOMMODATIONS

Agora 7 rue de la Cossonnerie (at rue St-Denis, M°Châtelet) **33-1/42.33.46.02, 33-1/42.33.80.90** • gay-friendly hotel • 540FF+

Castille 37 rue Cambon **33-1/44.58.44.58, 800/448-8355 (US#)** • gay-friendly • ultra-luxe hotel • wheelchair access • 2100-3600FF

France • EUROPE

Hôtel Louvre Richelieu 51 rue de Richelieu (M°Palais-Royal) **33-1/42.97.46.20** • gay-friendly • gay-owned/ run • 345FF+

The Ritz 15 place Vendôme (M°Tuileries) **33-1/43.16.30.70, 800/223-6800 (US#)** • gay-friendly • ultra-luxe hotel • 2,450-4,150FF

BARS

Le Banana Café 13–15 rue de la Ferronnerie (nr rue St-Denis, M°Châtelet) **33-1/42.33.35.31** • 4pm-dawn • trendy • lesbians/ gay men • dancing/DJ • tropical decor • theme nights • Latina/o night Sun • live shows • young crowd • wheelchair access • terrace

Le Cap Horn 37 rue des Lombards (M°Châtelet) **33-1/40.28.03.08** • noon-2am • lesbians/ gay men • cafe-bar • dancing/DJ • naval decor

Le Tropic Café 66 rue des Lombards (M°Châtelet) **33-1/40.13.92.62** • noon-5am • lesbians/ gay men • transgender-friendly • kitschy, fun bar • tapas served • terrace • young crowd • wheelchair access

Le Vagabond 14 rue Thérèse (at av de l'Opera, M°Pyramides) **33-1/42.96.27.23** • 6pm-close, clsd Mon • oldest gay bar & restaurant in Paris

RESTAURANTS

L' Amazonial 3 rue Ste-Opporture (at rue Ferronnerie, M°Châtelet) **33-1/42.33.53.13** • noon-3pm & 7pm-1am • brunch wknds • lesbians/ gay men • Brazilian/ int'l • bingo Mon-Tue • cabaret Th • drag shows Sat • heated terrace • wheelchair access • 85-129FF

Paris

LGBT PRIDE: June. 33-1/47.70.01.50, web: www.gaypride.fr.
Lesbian Pride (June). 33-1/40.37.79.87, web: www.multimania.com/fiertelesbienne.

ANNUAL EVENTS: July 13 - Bastille Ball.
December - Paris Gay & Lesbian Film Festival.

CITY INFO: 33-1/49.52.53.54, 127 av des Champs-Elysées (8e), web: www.paris.org.

ATTRACTIONS: Arc de Triomphe 33-1/43.80.31.31.
Notre Dame Cathedral 33-1/42.34.56.10.
Eiffel Tower 33-1/44.11.23.45.
Louvre 33-1/40.20.51.51.
Musée d'Orsay 33-1/40.49.48.14.
Picasso Museum 33-1/42.71.25.21.
Rodin Musuem 33-1/44.18.61.10.
Sacre-Coeur Basilica 33-1/53.41.89.00.
Sainte-Chapelle 33-1/53.73.78.41.

BEST VIEW: Eiffel Tower (of course!) and Sacre Coeur.

WEATHER: Paris really is beautiful in the springtime. Chilly in the winter, the temperatures reach the 70°s during the summer.

TRANSIT: Alpha Taxi 33-1/45.85.85.85.
Taxi Bleu 33-1/49.36.10.10.
Taxi-Radio Étoile 33-1/42.70.41.41.
RATP (bus and Métro) 33-8/44.68.20.20 (in French), 33-8/36.68.41.14 (in English), web: www.ratp.fr.

Au Diable des Lombards 64 rue des Lombards (at rue St-Denis, M°Châtelet) **33-1/42.33.81.84** • 10am-1am • brunch daily • American • full bar • terrace • 65-120FF

Au Petit Bonheur 9 rue St-Germain-d'Auxerrois (M°Châtelet) **33-1/42.21.17.12** • noon-2pm Tue-Fri & 7pm-1am Tue-Sun, clsd Mon • lesbians/ gay men • traditional French • live shows • 65-115FF

Au Rendez-Vous des Camionneurs 72 quai des Orfèvres (M°Pont Neuf) **33-1/43.54.88.74** • noon-2:30pm & 7pm-11:30pm, noon-11:30pm Sun • mostly gay men • traditional French bistro • 88-200FF

Chez Max 47 rue St-Honoré (M°Châtelet) **33-1/45.08.80.13** • noon-2pm Mon-Fri & 7:30pm-midnight Mon-Sat, clsd Sun • clsd Aug • North African • 65-150FF

Le Comptoir 14 rue Vauvilliers (M°Châtelet) **33-1/40.26.26.66** • noon-2am, till 4am Fri-Sat • popular • int'l • also bar

Le Gut 64 rue J-J-Rousseau (M°Châtelet) **33-1/42.36.14.90** • 8am-7pm, clsd Sun • French bistro • also bar

La Poule au Pot 9 rue Vauvilliers (M°Les Halles) **33-1/42.36.32.96** • 7pm-5am, clsd Mon • clsd Aug • bistro • traditional French • 160-250FF

ENTERTAINMENT & RECREATION

Les Halles • underground sports/ entertainment complex w/ museums, theater, shops, clubs, cafes & more

GYMS & HEALTH CLUBS

Gymnase Club 147b rue St–Honoré (M°Louvre) **33-1/40.20.03.03** • gay-friendly • day passes available • many locations throughout the city

Paris—02

BARS

La Champmeslé 4 rue Chabanais (at rue des Petits Champs, M°Pyramides) **33-1/42.96.85.20** • 5pm-late, clsd Sun • popular • mostly women • cabaret Th • theme nights • wheelchair access • a lesbian landmark, in business for over 20 years

NIGHTCLUBS

Le Pulp 25 bd Poissonnière (M°Grands-Blvds) **33-1/40.26.01.93** • 11pm-close, clsd Sun-Mon • popular • mostly women • men welcome as guests • dancing/DJ • theme nights • cover charge Fri-Sat

Le Scorp 25 bd Poissonnière (M°Grands-Blvds) **33-1/40.26.01.50, 33-1/40.26.28.30** • midnight-7am • mostly gay men • dancing/DJ • shows Sun-Tue • disco Wed • young crowd • cover charge Fri-Sat

CAFES

Lezard Café 41 rue Tiquetonne (M°Etienne-Marcel) **33-1/42.33.22.73** • noon-4pm & 7pm-midnight • tarts (no, not that sort!) • 60-100FF • also bar • open 9am-2am • terrace

RESTAURANTS

Aux Trois Petits Cochons 31 rue Tiquetonne (at rue St-Denis, M°Etienne-Marcel) **33-1/42.33.39.69** • 8pm-midnight • lesbians/ gay men • gourmet French made w/ fresh seasonal produce • menu changes daily • reservations recommended • gay-owned/ run • 135-159FF

Le Dénicheur 4 rue Tiquetonne (M°Etienne-Marcel) **33-1/42.21.31.01** • noon-midnight, from 7pm Mon • seafood • 35-85FF

L' Homosapiens 29 rue Tiquetonne (M°Etienne-Marcel) **33-1/40.26.94.85** • noon-2:30pm & 7:30pm-11:30pm, 8pm-midnight Sat, clsd Sun • French • 50-85FF

Le Loup Blanc 42 rue Tiquetonne (M°Etienne-Marcel) **33-1/40.13.08.35** • 7:30pm-midnight, till 1am Sat, also brunch 11am-4:30pm Sun • popular • lesbians/ gay men • French/int'l • 80-120FF

Matinée-Soirée 5 rue Marie Stuart (M°Etienne-Marcel) **33-1/42.21.18.00** • noon-2:30pm & 7pm-10:30pm, clsd Sun • clsd Aug • French • terrace • 78-200FF

Le Monde à l'envers 35 rue Tiquetonne (M°Etienne-Marcel) **33-1/40.26.13.91** • noon-2pm Tue-Fri & 8pm-midnight Tue-Sun • traditional French • 78-135FF

ENTERTAINMENT & RECREATION

Cour et Jardin 2 impasse St-Denis **33-1/39.75.19.08** • amateur lgbt theater group • performances 7pm Th & 5pm Sun

BOOKSTORES

Le Kiosque des Amis 29 bd des Italiens (M°Opéra) **33-1/42.65.00.94** • 10am-10pm • lgbt • French & int'l magazines

Paris—03

ACCOMMODATIONS

Hôtel de Saintonge 16 rue de Saintonge (off rue du Perche btwn rue Charlot & rue Vieille du Temple, M°Filles-du-Calvaire) **33-1/42.77.91.13** • gay-friendly • 560-790FF

France • EUROPE

Reply **Forward** **Delete**

Date: Wed, Jan 2, 2002 15:22:47
From: Girl-on-the-Go
To: Editor@Damron.com
Subject: Paris

> It's hard not to wax poetic about Paris. The most romantic city in the world, Paris has all the characteristics of a capricious lover. Beautiful and witty, dignified and grand, flirtatious and coy—Paris's admirers will tell you she's worthy of lifelong devotion. It's not surprising, then, that so many artists and thinkers have made Paris their home. Whether it's the museums, the couture, the cafes, the history, the churches, or the people...Paris seduces at every turn.*

> During the day, enjoy the incredible sights of Paris. After you've had your fill of famed landmarks, artworks, and boulevards, drop out of the tourist circuit and find out for yourself why they call it 'Gay Paree.' Of course, for Parisians, nowhere is as *très gai* as the Marais district (most of the Marais's listings can be found with those in the 4th arrondissement).

> To get the latest editions of Paris LGBT magazines and to scope out the latest in one-off parties and hot club nights of the moment, drop in at **Les Mots à la Bouche, Pause Lecture,** or **Le Kiosque des Amis.** Or pay a visit to the **Centre gai et lesbien** on rue Keller. To find out about lesbian-specific activities and events, drop in at the women's bookstore **La Librairie des Femmes.**

> At night, Paris truly is 'The City of Lights.' Don't even dare turn in for bed until you've made the most of this city's incredible nightlife.

> There is a dizzying array of women's bars and clubs in Paris. For pre-dinner cocktails, stop by **L'Unity Bar** in Les Halles; **La Champmeslé** (a 'lesbian landmark' located near the Palais Royal and the Bibliothéque Nationale); **L'Alcantara** (in the heart of the Marais); **L'Utopia** (near the Centre Pompidou); or **Les Scandaleuses,** located in the heart of the Marais. You'll also find plenty of hip urban dykes at one of the trendy, mixed cafe-bars like **L'Open.**

> Then head for a lesbian-friendly restaurant; once again, there are choices! There are many lesbo-popular eateries in the

Montparnasse/Grenelle area, including **L'Accent, Au Feu Follet, Le Boudoir, L'Hemis,** and **L'Imprevu** (whose clientele is said to be 'exclusively *lesbienne*').

After dinner, groove till dawn at one of the (you guessed it!—there are several) women's nightclubs.... **Pulp** is popular and open late. If your *français* is halfway decent, pick up a copy of the club 'zine **Housewife** to find out what theme nights are coming up. (Look in cafes, bars, and clubs for the latest issue. Even if you don't speak a word of French, you'll get a kick out of the clever collages and retro ads.) **La Rive-Gauche** is open on Friday and Saturday nights only. Of course, there are also various one-nighters (see above) and plenty of mixed clubs (like the aptly named **Queen**).

*(Paris's streets, however, confuse if you don't understand there's a method to her madness. The city spirals out from the Louvre and Jardin des Tuileries in a string of districts called arrondissements. We've divided our listings according to arrondissements, using the following notation: 01=1st, 02=2nd, 03=3rd, etc. So, before you go, you might want to look over your maps and get a general idea of what falls in which district. Once you're there, you can get around using a combination of Métro stops and district names and numbers. *Bonne chance*—good luck!)

France • EUROPE

Bars

Le Duplex 25 rue Michel-le-Comte (at rue Beaubourg, M°Rambuteau) **33–1/42.72.80.86** • 8pm-2am • lesbians/ gay men • neighborhood bar • bohemian types • live shows • Internet access

Ladies Room 10 rue aux Ours (at 'Le Dépôt') **33–1/44.54.96.96** • 11pm-dawn Wed only • women only • dancing/DJ • cover charge

L' Unity Bar 176–178 rue St-Martin (nr rue Réaumur, M°Rambuteau) **33–1/42.72.70.59** • 4pm-2am • mostly gay men • men welcome as guests • neighborhood bar • young crowd

L' Utopia 15 rue Michel-le-Comte (M°Rambuteau) **33–1/42.71.63.43** • 5pm-2am, clsd Sun • clsd 8/1-8/15 • mostly women • men welcome as guests • neighborhood bar • live shows • theme nights • dancing/DJ Sat • Internet access • wheelchair access

Nightclubs

Les Bains 7 rue du Bourg-l'Abbé (at bd de Sébastopol, M°Etienne-Marcel) **33–1/48.87.01.80** • midnight-close • gay-friendly • gay Sun & Mon • dancing/DJ • cover charge

Le Tango 13 rue au Maire (M°Arts-et-Métiers) **33–1/42.72.17.78** • 8pm-2am Th, 10:30pm-5am Fri-Sat • clsd Aug • lesbians/ gay men • dancing/DJ • waltz, tango • live shows • T-dance 6pm-2am Sun • cover charge

Restaurants

Au Marais Gourmand 26 rue Charlot (M°Republique) **33–1/48.87.63.08** • lunch & dinner, clsd Sun • French • 68-112FF

Les Epicuriens du Marais 19 rue Commines (M°Filles-du-Calvaire) **33–1/40.27.00.83** • noon-3pm & 7pm-midnight, till 1:30am wknds • traditional French • 69-149FF

La Fontaine Gourmande 11 rue Charlot **33–1/42.78.42.40** • noon-2pm Tue-Fri & 7:30pm-close Tue-Sun, clsd Mon • French • woman-owned/ run • 150FF

La Madame sans gène 19 rue de Picardie (M°Filles-du-Calvaire) **33–1/42.71.31.71** • noon-2:30pm daily & 7:30pm-11:30pm Mon-Fri • clsd Aug • mostly gay men • inexpensive traditional French • live shows • theme nights • 59-115FF

Les Saveurs de Temps 3 rue Bernard de Clairvaux (M°Rambuteau) **33–1/48.87.78.68** • 11:30am-3pm Mon-Fri & 7pm-midnight nightly • Mediterranean • theme parties

Les Trois Axes 157 rue St-Martin (M°Rambuteau) **33–1/42.74.68.34** • lunch Mon-Fri, dinner Mon-Sat, clsd Sun • homestyle French • great desserts • 78FF

Le Valet de Carreau 2 rue du Petit Thouars (M°République) **33–1/42.72.72.60** • noon-2:30pm Mon-Fri, 8pm-10:30pm Mon-Sat, clsd Sun • creative cuisine • terrace • 75-180FF

Entertainment & Recreation

Musée Picasso 5 rue de Thorigny (in the Hôtel Salé, M°St-Paul) **33–1/42.71.25.21** • 9:30am-6pm, clsd Tue • wheelchair access

Erotica

Rexx 42 rue de Poitou (at rue Charlot, M°St-Sébastien-Froissard) **33–1/42.77.58.57, 33–1/42.77.36.22** • clsd Sun • new, custom & secondhand leather & S/M accessories

Paris—04

Accommodations

Hôtel Beaubourg 11 rue Simon le Franc (btwn rue Beaubourg & rue du Temple, M°Hôtel-de-Ville) **33–1/42.74.34.24** • gay/ straight • US$71-94

Hôtel de la Bretonnerie 22 rue Ste-Croix-de-la-Bretonnerie (M°Hôtel-de-Ville) **33–1/48.87.77.63** • gay-friendly • clsd Aug • 17th-century hotel w/ Louis XIII decor • US$96-156

Hôtel du Vieux Marais 8 rue du Plâtre (M°Hôtel-de-Ville) **33–1/42.78.47.22** • gay-friendly • centrally located • $100

Libertel Grand Turenne 6 rue de Turenne (at rue St-Antoine, M°St-Paul) **33–1/42.78.43.25, 800/637-2873 (US#)** • gay-friendly • 918-989FF

Bars

AccesSoir Café 41 rue des Blancs-Manteaux (M°Rambuteau) **33–1/42.72.12.89** • 6pm-2am • mostly gay men • live shows • theme nights • food served • 59FF

Akhenaton Café 12 rue de Plâtre (btwn rue du Temple & rue des Archives, M°Hôtel-de-Ville) **33–1/48.87.51.04** • 5pm-2am • lesbians/ gay men • neighborhood cafe-bar

L' Alcantara 18 rue du Roi de Sicile (M°Hôtel-de-Ville) **33–1/42.74.45.00** • 5pm-2am • mostly women • friendly cafe-bar

Amnésia Café 42 rue Vieille du Temple (at rue des Blancs-Manteaux, M°Hôtel-de-Ville) **33–1/42.72.16.94, 33–1/42.72.02.59** • 10:30am-2am • popular • lesbians/ gay men • food served • brunch daily 70FF

Le Bar du Palmier 16 rue des Lombards (at bd de Sébastopol, M°Châtelet) **33-1/42.78.53.53** • 5pm-5am • lesbians/gay men • food served • terrace

Le Mixer Bar 23 rue Ste-Croix-de-la-Bretonnerie (at rue des Archives, M°Hôtel-de-Ville) **33-1/48.87.55.44** • 5pm-2am • popular • lesbians/gay men • dancing/DJ • 3-flr techno/ house bar • theme nights • young crowd

Monkey's Café 30 rue du Roi-de-Sicile (M°St-Paul) **33-1/42.74.45.00** • noon-2am • lesbians/gay men • food served • Italian

Okawa 40 rue Vieille du Temple (at rue Ste-Croix-de-la-Bretonnerie, M°Hôtel-de-Ville) **33-1/48.04.36.09** • 9am-2am • gay/straight • trendy cafe-bar in 12th/13th century caves • theme nights • cabaret • piano bar Tue-Wed • young crowd • restaurant from 7pm • 85-160FF

L' Open 17 rue des Archives (at rue Ste-Croix-de-la-Bretonnerie, M°Hôtel-de-Ville) **33-1/42.72.26.18** • 10am-2am, Sun brunch • popular • lesbians/gay men • sidewalk cafe-bar • also L'Open Coffee Shop • 15 rue des Archives, 33-1/48.87.80.25 • salads & sandwiches

Les Scandaleuses 8 rue des Ecouffes (btwn rue de Rivoli & rues des Rosiers, M°St-Paul) **33-1/48.87.39.26** • 6pm-2am • mostly women • live shows • videos

Le Sun Café 35 rue Ste-Croix-de-la-Bretonnerie (at rue du Temple, M°Hôtel-de-Ville) **33-1/40.29.44.40** • 8am-2am • mostly gay men • bar upstairs • tanning salon downstairs • food served • theme nights • DJs

Cafes

Café Beaubourg 100 rue St-Martin (M°Rambuteau) **33-1/48.87.63.96** • next to Centre Pompidou • chic cafe-bar • large terrace

Le Coffe-Shop 3 rue Ste-Croix-de-la-Bretonnerie (at rue Vieille du Temple, M°Hôtel-de-Ville) **33-1/42.74.24.21** • noon-2am • lesbians/gay men • full bar • 35-50FF

Restaurants

A 2 Pas du Dos 101 rue Vieille-du-Temple (at rue des Quatre Fils, M°Hôtel-de-Ville) **33-1/42.77.10.52** • noon-2:30pm Tue-Fri & 8pm-11:30pm Tue-Sat, clsd Sun-Mon • popular • lesbians/gay men • 79-200FF

L' Alivi 27 rue du Roi-de-Sicile (M°Hôtel-de-Ville) **33-1/48.87.90.20** • noon-2pm & 7pm-11pm • Corsican fare • 122-230FF

Amadéo 19 rue François-Miron (M°St-Paul) **33-1/48.87.01.02** • lunch Tue-Fri, dinner Mon-Sat, clsd Sun • creative gourmet • 75-185FF

Au Tibourg 29 rue du Bourg-Tibourg (M°Hôtel-de-Ville) **33-1/42.74.45.25** • noon-2pm & 7pm-11pm • French • quiet & romantic setting • 115-200FF

L' Auberge de la Reine Blanche 30 rue St-Louis-en-l'Ile (nr Rue des 2 Ponts, M°Pont-Marie) **33-1/46.33.07.87** • lunch & dinner, dinner only Th, clsd Wed • homestyle French • 89-250FF

Le Bucheron 9 rue du Roi-de-Sicile (M°St-Paul) **33-1/48.87.71.31** • lunch Mon-Sat & dinner nightly • gay/straight • Italian • 58-110FF • also bar

La Canaille 4 rue Crillon (M°Quai-de-la-Rapée) **33-1/42.78.09.71** • lunch Mon-Fri, dinner Mon-Sat, clsd Sun • lesbians/gay men • bistro fare • full bar • 61-150FF

Cat'Man 12 rue du Temple (M°Hôtel-de-Ville) **33-1/42.74.43.32** • 11am-11pm, clsd Mon • salads • crepes • terrace • 60FF

Le Chant des Voyelles 4 rue des Lombards (M°Châtelet) **33-1/42.77.77.07** • 11:30am-3pm & 6:30pm-midnight (open all day in summer) • lesbians/gay men • traditional French • terrace • 68-120FF

Le Croc' Man 6 rue Geoffroy l'Angevin (M°Rambuteau) **33-1/42.77.60.02** • 7pm-close, clsd Tue • mostly gay men • 69-120FF

Le Divin 41 rue Ste-Croix-de-la-Bretonnerie (at rue du Temple, M°Hôtel-de-Ville) **33-1/42.77.10.20** • noon-2pm Tue-Sat & 7:30pm-11:30pm Tue-Sun, clsd Mon • traditional & Provençal cuisine • wheelchair access • 89-170FF

Le Dos de la Baleine 40 rue des Blancs-Manteaux (M°Rambuteau) **33-1/42.72.38.98** • noon-3pm Tue-Fri & 8pm-11pm Tue-Sun, clsd Mon • clsd Aug • gourmet seafood • reservations recommended • 79-145FF

Eclache & Cie 10 rue St-Merri (M°Hôtel-de-Ville) **33-1/42.74.62.62** • lunch & dinner, brunch wknds • bistro fare • terrace • 100-150FF

L' Églantine 9 rue de la Verrerie (M°Hôtel-de-Ville) **33-1/48.04.75.58** • 11:30am-2pm Tue-Sat & 7:30pm-11pm Tue-Sun, clsd Mon • French • 73-200FF

Equinox 33–35 rue des Rosiers (M°St-Paul) **33-1/42.71.92.41** • 11:30am-3:30pm & 7pm-midnight, clsd Mon • Québeçois/French • full bar • piano bar • shows Th-Fri • 69-170FF

Le Flyer 94 rue St-Martin (M°Hôtel-de-Ville) **33-1/48.04.78.75** • noon-2:30pm & 7pm-2am, clsd Mon • in 14th-c caves w/ 50s decor • 50-132FF

France • EUROPE

Le Fond de Cour 3 rue Ste-Croix-de-la-Bretonnerie (in back courtyard, M°Hôtel-de-Ville) **33–1/42.74.71.52** • noon-3:30pm & 8pm-11:30pm, brunch till 4:30pm Sun • gourmet French • terrace • wheelchair access • reservations recommended • 160-210FF

Le Gai Moulin 4 rue St-Merri (at the du Temple, M°Hôtel-de-Ville) **33–1/48.87.47.59** • noon-midnight • lesbians/ gay men • French/ int'l • 59-100FF

Le Krokodil 20 rue de la Reynie (at bd Sébastopol, M°Châtelet) **33–1/48.87.55.67** • noon-2am, Sun brunch • popular • gay men • traditional French • also bar • live DJ • shows Mon-Wed • terrace • 165FF

Les Mauvais Garçons 4 rue des Mauvais Garçons (M°Hôtel-de-Ville) **33–1/42.72.74.97**

O'2F 4 rue du Roi-de-Sicile (M°St-Paul) **33–1/42.72.75.75** • 7:30pm-12:30am, clsd Mon • gay/ straight • homestyle French • live entertainment • 78-128FF

Le Petit Picard 42 rue Ste-Croix-de-la-Bretonnerie (M°Hôtel-de-Ville) **33–1/42.78.54.03** • noon-1:45pm Tue-Fri & 7:30pm-11:30pm Tue-Sun, clsd Mon • lesbians/ gay men • reservations recommended • 85FF+

La Petite Chaumière 41 rue des Blancs-Manteaux (M°Rambuteau) **33–1/42.72.13.90** • 7:30pm-11:30pm • French • menu changes daily • 89-129FF

Un Piano dans la Cuisine 20 rue de la Verrerie (M°Hôtel-de-Ville) **33–1/42.72.23.81** • 8:30pm-midnight • drag shows Tue-Sun • 199FF

Piccolo Teatro 6 rue des Ecouffes **33–1/42.72.17.79** • noon-3pm & 7pm-11pm, clsd Mon • vegetarian • 90-115FF

Les Piétons 8 rue des Lombards (M°Châtelet) **33–1/48.87.82.87** • 11am-9pm, brunch noon-6pm Sun • gay/ straight • Spanish/ tapas • 45-100FF • also bar • open till 2am • dancing/DJ from 8pm Wed

Plateau 26 26 rue des Lombards (M°Châtelet) **33–1/48.87.10.75** • 7pm-2am, till 3:30am wknds • theater-cafe • piano bar • karaoke from 11:30pm Sat • 85-155FF

Le Rude 23 rue du Temple (at rue Ste-Croix-de-la-Bretonnerie, M°Hôtel-de-Ville) **33–1/42.74.05.15** • noon-2am • mostly gay men • French/ American • also bar • wheelchair access • 79-160FF

BOOKSTORES

Les Mots à la Bouche 6 rue Ste-Croix-de-la-Bretonnerie (nr rue du Vieille du Temple, M°Hôtel-de-Ville) **33–1/42.78.88.30** • 11am-11pm, 2pm-8pm Sun • lgbt • English titles

Pause Lecture 61 rue de Quincampoix (at rue Rambuteau) **33–1/44.61.95.05** • 11am-midnight, from 1pm Sun • lgbt

RETAIL SHOPS

7H10 22 rue des Ecouffes (nr rue des Rosiers) **33–1/42.71.77.10** • jewelry • gifts • antiques • lesbian-owned/ run

Abraxas 9 rue St-Merri **33–1/48.04.33.55** • noon-9pm, from 3pm Sun • tattoos • piercing • large selection of body jewelry

EROTICA

Phylea 61 rue Quincampoix (M°Rambuteau) **33–1/42.76.01.80** • clsd Sun • vinyl, leather, rubber, corsets, S/M accessories • original creations

Paris—05

ACCOMMODATIONS

Hôtel des Nations 54 rue Monge (nr rue des Écoles, M°Pl-Monge) **33–1/43.26.45.24** • gay-friendly • small hotel in the Latin Quarter • pets ok • US$79-104

La Vie en Rose Quai de la Tournelle **33–1/43.54.03.46, 888/866-4730 (US#)** • gay-friendly • luxury vessel on the Seine • full brkfst • smokefree • deck w/ garden • US$2000 • 3-night minimum stay

CAFES

Clickside 14 rue Domat (off rue Dante, M°St-Michel) **33–1/56.81.03.00** • 10am-midnight, 1pm-11pm wknds • cybercafe

RESTAURANTS

Restaurant le Petit Prince de Paris 12 rue de Lanneau (M°Maubert-Mutualité) **33–1/43.54.77.26** • 7:30pm-midnight • popular • French • 82-118FF

ENTERTAINMENT & RECREATION

Open-Air Sculpture Museum **33–1/42.71.25.21** • along the Seine btwn the Jardin des Plantes & the Institut du Monde Arabe

Paris—06

ACCOMMODATIONS

L' Hôtel 13 rue des Beaux-Arts (btwn rue Bonaparte & rue de Seine, M°St-Germain-des-Prés) **33-1/44.41.99.00** • gay-friendly • eccentric hotel where Oscar Wilde died • US$190-560

NIGHTCLUBS

La Rive-Gauche 1 rue du Sabot (M°St-Sulpice) **33-1/42.22.51.70** • 11pm-dawn Fri-Sat only • mostly women • dancing/DJ • cover charge

BOOKSTORES

Les Amazones 68 rue Bonaparte **33-1/40.46.08.37** • specializes in antique, lesbian & feminist books

La Librairie des Femmes 74 rue de Seine **33-1/42.22.60.74** • 11am-7pm, clsd Sun • women's

The Village Voice 6 rue Princesse (M°Mabillon) **33-1/46.33.36.47** • 10am-8pm, from 2pm Sun-Mon, till 7pm Sun • English-language bookshop

Paris—07

ACCOMMODATIONS

Hôtel Muguet 11 rue Chevert (nr av de Tourville, nr the Eiffel Tower) **33-1/47.05.05.93** • gay-friendly • recently renovated • US$82+

Paris—08

ACCOMMODATIONS

Crillon 10 place de la Concorde **33-1/44.71.15.01, 800/888-4747 (US#)** • gay-friendly • ultra-luxe hotel • restaurant • 3600FF+

BARS

Le Day-Off 10 rue de l'Isly (M°Gare-St-Lazare) **33-1/45.22.87.90** • noon-3am Mon-Fri only • gay/ straight • cocktail bar • food served • woman-owned • 74-128FF

NIGHTCLUBS

Le Queen 102 av des Champs-Élysées (btwn rue Washington & rue de Berri, M°Georges-V) **33-1/42.89.31.32** • 11:30pm-dawn • popular • mostly gay men • dancing/DJ • theme nights • drag shows • young crowd • selective door • cover charge

RESTAURANTS

Le Petit Yvan 1 bis, rue Jean-Mermoz (M°F-D-Roosevelt) **33-1/42.89.49.65** • noon-2:30pm Mon-Fri & 8pm-midnight Mon-Sat, clsd Sun • traditional French • 148-200FF

Paris—09

ACCOMMODATIONS

The Grand 2 rue Scribe **33-1/40.07.32.32, 800/327-0200 (US#)** • gay-friendly • ultra-luxe art deco hotel

NIGHTCLUBS

Folies Pigalle 11 place Pigalle (M°Pigalle) **33-1/48.78.55.25, 33-1/42.80.12.03 (BBB INFO LINE)** • midnight-dawn Tue-Sat • gay/ straight • dancing/DJ • more gay at popular 'Black, Blanc, Beur' T-dance 6pm-midnight Sun • 'Escualita' from midnight Sun • transgender-friendly • multiracial • cover charge

RESTAURANTS

Le 48 Condorcet 48 rue Condorcet (M°Anvers) **33-1/45.26.98.19** • noon-2pm Mon-Fri & 7pm-midnight Mon-Sat, clsd Sun • clsd Aug • French • 58-180FF

Les Colonnes de Madeleine 6 rue de Sèze (M°Madeleine) **33-1/42.42.60.55** • noon-3pm & 7pm-midnight, clsd Sun • French bistro • 80-120FF • also bar 7pm-4am

Gilles et Gabriel 24 rue Rodier (M°Cadet) **33-1/45.26.86.26** • noon-2:30pm Mon-Fri & 7pm-10:30pm Mon-Sat, clsd Sun • clsd Aug • 45-99FF

Paris—10

ACCOMMODATIONS

Hôtel Moderne du Temple 3 rue d'Aix **33-1/42.08.09.04** • gay/ straight • economy-class hotel • some shared baths • kids ok • gay-owned/ run • 140-250FF

BARS

Le Coming-Out 20 rue Beaurepaire (M°République) **33-1/42.01.01.77** • 5pm-2am • lesbians/ gay men • neighborhood bar • food served • terrace

RESTAURANTS

Le Châlet Maya 5 rue des Petits Hôtels (M°Gare de l'Est) **33-1/47.70.52.78** • 11:30am-2:30pm Mon-Fri & 6:30pm-midnight Mon-Sat, clsd Sun • lesbians/ gay men • French • 60FF-165FF

L' Insensé 10 rue Marie-et-Louise (M°Goncourt) **33-1/42.01.25.26** • noon-2:30pm & 8pm-11pm, till midnight Fri-Sat, clsd Sun • homestyle French • 59-95FF

France • EUROPE

Paris—11

ACCOMMODATIONS

Hôtel Beaumarchais 3 rue Oberkampf (btwn bd Beaumarchais & bd Voltaire, M°Filles-du-Calvaire) **33–1/53.36.86.86** • gay/ straight • beautiful hotel • US$81-89

Hôtel Mondia 22 rue du Grand-Prieuré (M°République) **33–1/47.00.93.44** • gay-friendly • 320-450FF

Libertel Croix-de-Malté 5 rue de Malté (M°Oberkampf) **33–1/48.05.09.36, 800/ 949–7562 (US#)** • gay-friendly • 570-636FF

BARS

L' Arambar 7 rue de la Folie-Méricourt (M°St-Ambroise) **33–1/48.05.57.79** • noon-2am • lesbians/ gay men • neighborhood bar • art exhibits • theme nights

Interface 34 rue Keller (M°Bastille) **33–1/47.00.67.15** • 3pm-2am • lesbians/ gay men • live shows

Le K 20 rue Keller (M°Bastille) **33–1/53.36.03.96** • 5pm-2am, clsd Mon • lesbians/ gay men • also restaurant • 8pm-11:30pm • Provençal • 100FF

NIGHTCLUBS

Le Gibus Club 18 rue du Faubourg-du-Temple (M°République) **33–1/47.00.78.88** • midnight-close, clsd Mon-Tue • gay-friendly • gay Th & Sat • dancing/DJ • also piano bar • live music Sat • cover charge

RESTAURANTS

Le Temps Au Temps 13 rue Paul Bert (M°Faidherbe-Chaligny) **33–1/43.79.63.40** • 8pm-11pm, clsd Sun • lesbians/ gay men • French bistro • 130FF

Le Sofa 21 rue St-Sabin (M°Bastille) **33–1/43.14.07.46** • 6pm-midnight, till 2am Th-Sat, clsd Sun-Mon • also bar • 100-150FF

Terranova 45 rue de Montreuil (M°Faidherbe-Chaligny) **33–1/43.67.82.83** • noon-2:30pm Mon-Fri & 7pm-11pm nightly, clsd Sun • clsd Aug • Italian • pizza • 92-120FF

BOOKSTORES

Le Funambule 48 rue Jean-Pierre Timbaud (M°Parmentier) **33–1/48.06.74.94** • 2pm-7pm Tue-Sat & by appt • fine art/ photography books • lgbt section

Livralire 145 rue de Charonne **33–1/43.73.33.22** • 11am-8pm, clsd Sun-Mon • lgbt section

EROTICA

Démonia 10 Cité Joly (M°Pere-Lachaise) **33–1/43.14.82.70** • clsd Sun • BDSM shop • lingerie • videos • toys

Paris—12

RESTAURANTS

Bella Tavola 161 ave Daumesnil (M°Daumesnil) **33–1/44.74.07.06** • 11:30am-11:30pm

Caviar & Co 5 rue de Reuilly (M°Faidherbe-Chaligny) **33–1/43.56.13.98** • noon-2pm Tue-Fri & 7:30pm-midnight Tue-Sat, clsd Sun-Mon • clsd Aug • lesbians/ gay men • foies gras & caviar • 79-129FF

Paris—13

RESTAURANTS

L' ArtiShow 27 rue de la Colonie (M°Corvisart) **33–1/45.88.30.98** • lunch Mon-Fri & dinner Tue-Sat, clsd Sun • French/ Thai • cabaret Sat • 72-145FF

Au Pet de Lapin 2 rue Dunois (M°Massena) **33–1/45.86.58.21** • noon-2pm & 8pm-10:30pm, clsd Sun-Mon • clsd Aug • foies gras & seafood • 69-150FF

ENTERTAINMENT & RECREATION

Bibliotheque Marguerite Durand 79 rue Nationale **33–1/45.70.80.30** • 2pm-6pm, clsd Sun-Mon • unique collection of books by & about women

Paris—14

RESTAURANTS

Au Feu Follet 5 rue Raymond Losserand (M°Gaîté) **33–1/43.22.65.72** • 7:30pm-close, clsd Sun • mostly women • southeast French • 85-150FF

Le Petit Léo 7 rue Léopold-Robert (M°Raspail) **33–1/43.20.76.55** • noon-2pm Mon-Fri & 7pm-11:30pm nightly • hearty French • 65-200FF

La Route du Château 36 rue Raymond Losserand (M°Gaîté) **33–1/43.20.09.59** • noon-2pm Tue-Sat & 7:30pm-10pm Mon-Sat, clsd Sun • clsd Aug • lesbians/ gay men • French • 86-200FF

ENTERTAINMENT & RECREATION

Catacombes 1 place Denfert Rochereau **33–1/43.22.47.63** • a ghoulish yet intriguing tourist destination, these burial tunnels were the headquarters of the Résistance during World War II

Paris—15

Restaurants

L' Accent 93 rue de Javel (M°Charles-Michel) **33-1/45.79.20.26** • 8pm-12:30am, clsd Sun • mostly women • pizzeria • 70-150FF

Le Boudoir 22 rue Frémicourt (M°La-Motte-Picquet) **33-1/40.59.82.28** • noon-2:30pm Tue-Fri & 5:30pm-1am Tue-Sun, clsd Mon • mostly women • French • 98FF+ • also bar • 5:30pm-1am

L' Hémis 21 rue Mademoiselle (M°Commerce) **33-1/48.56.80.32** • lunch Tue-Fri & dinner Tue-Sat, clsd Sun-Mon • mostly women • French • reservations req'd • 73-110FF • also bar • live shows

L' Imprevu 7 rue de Cadix **33-1/40.45.09.81** • 11:30am-3pm & 6pm-2am • lesbians • good fondue & raclette • also bar • woman-owned/run

Paris—17

Restaurants

L' Insolence 66 rue Legendre (M°Rome) **33-1/42.29.57.96** • noon-2:15pm & 7:30pm-11pm, clsd Sun • clsd Aug • small terrace • 70-140FF

Macis et Muscade 110 rue Legendre (M°Rome) **33-1/42.26.62.26** • lunch & dinner • cuisine infused w/ essential oils • 130-180FF

Paris—20

Entertainment & Recreation

Père Lachaise Cemetery bd de Ménilmontant (M°Père-Lachaise) • perhaps the world's most famous resting place, where lie such notables as Chopin, Gertrude Stein, Oscar Wilde, Sarah Bernhardt, Isadora Duncan, Edith Piaf & Jim Morrison

GERMANY

BERLIN

Berlin is divided into 5 regions:
Berlin—Overview
Berlin—Kreuzberg
Berlin—Prenzlauer Berg–Mitte
Berlin—Schöneberg-Tiergarten
Berlin—Outer

Berlin—Overview

Info Lines & Services

Compania Anklamer Str 18 (in Mitte) **49-30/44.35.87.04** • noon-5pm Mon-Fri • services & tours for lesbians • no sex

Enjoy B&B Motzstr 5 (at M-O-M) **49-30/215.16.66** • lesbians/ gay men • accommodation referral service • DM50+

Gay AA for English Speakers at M-O-M **49-30/216.80.08** • 5pm Tue, also Gay AA 8pm Th

Lesbenberatung (Lesbian Advice) Kulmer Str 20a (in Kreuzberg) **49-30/215.20.00** • switchboard & center • staffed 4pm-7pm Mon, Tue & Th & 1pm-5pm Fri • various mtgs • youth line 4pm-5pm Wed

Mann-O-Meter Motzstr 5 (at Nollendorfplatz) **49-30/216.80.08** • open 5pm-10pm, from 4pm wknds • gay switchboard & center • also cafe • also B&B referral service

Sonntags Club Griefenhagener Str 28 (S/U-Schönhauser Allee) **49-30/449.75.90, 49-30/442.37.02 (TRANSGENDER LINE)** • info line 10am-6pm daily • lgbt info • counseling • mtgs • also cafe-bar • 5pm-midnight Fri-Sun • lesbians/ gay men • transgender-friendly • live shows • videos • regular parties

Spinnboden Lesbian Archive Anklamer Str 38 (in Mitte) **49-30/448.58.48** • 2pm-7pm Wed & Fri and by appt

Nightclubs

MegaDyke Productions • popular parties & events for lesbians, including 'Subterra' & 'Gravity' at SchwuZ & biannual mega 'Lesben Planet' parties • check local publications for more details

Entertainment & Recreation

Schwules (Gay) Museum Mehringdamm 61 (at Gneisenaustr, U-Mehringdamm) **49-30/693.11.72** • 2pm-6pm, till 7pm Sat • exhibits, archives & library

Germany • EUROPE

PUBLICATIONS

BlattGold 49–30/215.66.28 • monthly entertainment guide for women (in German)

Siegessäule 49–30/23.55.39-0, 49–30/23.55.39–32 • free monthly lgbt city magazine (in German)

SPIRITUAL GROUPS

Yachad—Lesbigay Jewish Association 49–30/624.87.65 • brunch 1st Sun at Melitta Sundström • contact M-O-M for more info

Berlin—Kreuzberg

ACCOMMODATIONS

Transit Hagelberger Str 53–54 (U-Mehringdamm) 49–30/789.04.70 • gay-friendly • also bar • DM35-105

BARS

Bierhimmel Oranienstr 183 (U-Kottbusser Tor) 49–30/615.31.22 • 3pm-3am • gay/straight • young crowd

BKA Cabaret Mehringdamm 32–34 (at Gneisenaustr, U-Mehringdamm) 49–30/251.01.12 • gay/straight • shows 8pm Wed-Sun • dancing/DJ from 11pm Fri-Sat • wheelchair access • cover charge

Roses Oranienstr 187 (at Kottbusser Tor) 49–30/615.65.70 • 10pm-close • popular • lesbians/gay men • transgender-friendly • young crowd

NIGHTCLUBS

SchwuZ (SchwulenZentrum) Mehringdamm 61 (at Fuggerstr, beneath the 'Schwules Museum', U-Mehringdamm) 49–30/69.50.78.92 • 11pm Sat • popular • mostly gay men • dancing/DJ • live shows • young crowd • cover charge • theme nights include 'Club 69' (retro) 1st Fri • 'Subterra' (more women) 2nd Fri • 'Rock Nacht' 4th Fri • 'Gravity' (more women) 5th Fri • standards, Latin & soul

SO 36 Oranienstr 190 (at Kottbusser Tor) 49–30/61.40.13.06, 49–30/61.40.13.07 • popular • lesbians/gay men • dancing/DJ • transgender-friendly • live shows • videos • young crowd • wheelchair access • theme nights include 'Café Fatal' (ballroom dancing) 7pm-1am Sun • 'Electric Ballroom' 11pm-close Mon • 'Hungrige Herzen' 11pm-close Wed • 'Gayhane' (Turkish night) 11pm 4th Sat

CAFES

Melitta Sundström Mehringdamm 61 (at Gneisenaustr, U-Mehringdamm) 49–30/692.44.14 • 10am-8pm, till 4pm Sat, clsd Sun • lesbians/gay men • terrace • wheelchair access • also lgbt bookstore

Schoko-Café Mariannenstr 6 (at Kottbusser Tor) 49–30/615.15.61, 49–30/694.10.77 • 5pm-close • women only • community center • also cafe & bar • dancing/DJ • live music • also 'Hamam' steam bath

RESTAURANTS

Abendmahl Muskauer Str 9 (U-Görlitzer Bahnhof) 49–30/612.51.70 • 6pm-11:30pm • vegetarian & seafood • also bar (open till 1am) • terrace • wheelchair access

Locus Marheinekeplatz 4 49–30/691.56.37 • 10am-2am • popular • lesbians/gay men • Mexican • full bar • lesbian-owned/run

BOOKSTORES

Chronika Buchhandlung Kreuzberg Bergmannstr 26 (at Marheinekeplatz) 49–30/693.42.69 • 10am-7pm, till 3pm Sat • many lesbian titles

EROTICA

Playstixx Waldemarstr 24 49–30/61.65.95.00 • toys • also sex counseling

Sexclusivitäten Fürbringer Str 2 49–30/693.66.66 • lesbian sex shop • toys • leather • videos • also escort service

Berlin—Prenzlauer Berg-Mitte

ACCOMMODATIONS

Schall & Rauch Pension Gleimstr 23 (at Schönhauser Allee) 49–30/443.39.70, 49–30/448.07.70 • lesbians/gay men • also bar & restaurant

BARS

Bar 808 Oranienburger Str 42–43 (at Auguststr) 49–30/28.04.67.28 • 5pm-3am, from noon wknds • lesbians/gay men • cocktail lounge • DJ Th & Sat • food served • brunch 11am-4pm Sun

Cafe Amsterdam Gleimstr 24 (at Schönhauser Allee) 49–30/44.00.94.54, 49–30/231.67.96 • 9am-3am, till 5am Fri-Sat • cafe-bar • gay/straight • transgender-friendly • young crowd • terrace • wheelchair access

Café Senefelder Schönhauser Allee 173 (at Senefelder Platz) 49–30/449.66.05 • 6pm-3am, 8pm-5am Fri-Sat • lesbians/gay men • dancing/DJ Fri-Sat • food served • lesbian-owned/run

Flax Chodowieckistr 41 (off Greifswalder Str) 49–30/44.04.69.88, 49–30/441.98.56 • 3pm-3am, till 4am Sat • lesbians/gay men • also restaurant • brunch 10am-5pm Sun • DM11

Berlin—Prenzlauer Berg-Mitte • Germany

[Reply] [Forward] **[Delete]**

Date: Sun, Jan 6, 2002 16:01:32
From: Girl-on-the-Go
To: Editor@Damron.com
Subject: Berlin

> In the past century, Berlin has seen just about everything: the outrageous art and cabaret of the Weimar era; the ravages of world war; ideological standoffs that physically divided families, lovers, and the city itself; and a largely peaceful revolution that brought Germany and the world together. Through it all, the Berliners have retained their own brand of cheeky humor—*Berliner Schnauze*, it's called—and a fierce loyalty to their city. While Berlin's museums and monuments are world-class, the city's real charm is in its cafes and counter-cultural milieu.

> You may find the women's scene in Berlin more political than in other places, but as a result you'll find a lot of support for women's culture and arts here, too. Berlin has two major women's community/social centers: The **Schoko-Café** in Kreuzberg is a community center with a bar, cafe, and steam bath! And **Begine,** located in Schöneberg, is a women's cafe, bar, and cultural center.

> After stopping in at one of the women's centers, grab a bite to eat and do some people-watching at **Café Berio.** If you're a girl who just wants to have fun, visit **Sexclusivitäten** for women's erotica.

> Later, check out one of the women's bars—**Pour Elle,** a fixture in the lesbian scene, or the women's cafe-bar **Furiosa. SO 36, Die Busche,** and **SchwuZ** are popular mixed clubs; call for upcoming theme nights and women's nights. Pick up a copy of the local LGBT newsmagazine **Siegessäule** or the women's entertainment mag **BlattGold** (both in German) for the latest hot spots. Or give **MegaDyke Productions** a call—these women organize not-to-be-missed monthly parties and other events.

> After your night of dancing, wind down in Kreuzberg at **Roses,** a popular late-night spot.

> If the club scene is not your scene, you might enjoy spending some time at **Cafe Seidenfaden** (in Mitte)—a chem- and alcohol-free women's cafe. Check their info board for more ideas of things to do.

Germany • EUROPE

Image Jägerstr 67 (U-Französische Str) **49-30/20.45.25.80** • 9am-close, from 2pm Sat, from 11am Sun • lesbians/gay men • cafe-bar • all-you-can-eat brunch buffet till 4:30pm Sun • terrace • wheelchair access

Jim's Eberswalder Str 37 (at Fr-Ludwig-Jahn-Sportpark) **49-30/440.63.79** • 8am-close, from noon Sun • lesbians/gay men • neighborhood bar • also restaurant

Na und Prenzlauer Allee 193 (at Dimitroffstr, S-Prenzlauer Allee) **49-30/442.89.78** • 24hrs • gay/straight • neighborhood bar • food served • terrace

Oh-Ase Rathausstr 5 (at Alexanderplatz, in Rathaus passage) **49-30/242.30.30** • noon-2am, from 3pm wknds • mostly gay men • cafe-bar • terrace • tropical theme

Romeo Greifenhagener Str 16 (S/U-Schönhauser Allee) **49-30/447.67.89** • 11pm-8am • gay-friendly • cafe-bar

Shambala Greifenhagener Str 12 (S/U-Schönhauser Allee) **49-30/447.62.26** • 6pm-3am • gay/straight • neighborhood cafe-bar • women only from 9pm Mon

Berlin

LGBT Pride: 3rd or 4th Saturday in June. 49-30/21.68.08 (M-O-M).

Annual Events: January - Tuntenball. Drag ball.
February - Berlinale: Berlin Int'l Film Festival.
July - Love Parade, web: www.prehm.com/kudamm/LoveParade.
October - Jazz Fest Berlin.
Lesbian Film Festival.
November - Queer Film Festival 49-30/861.45.32.

City Info: Europa Center 49-30/62.60.31. Budapester Str 2. Berlin Hotline 49-30/25.00.25.

Attractions: Bauhaus Design Museum 49-30/254.00.20.
Brandenburg Gate.
Charlottenburg Palace 49-30/32.09.11.
Egyptian Museum 49-30/20.90.55.55.
Homo Memorial (at Nollendorfplatz station).
Kaiser Wilhelm Memorial Church.
Käthe-Kollwitz Museum 49-30/882.52.10.
Museuminsel (Museum Island).
New National Gallery 49-30/266.26.51.
Reichstag.

Weather: Berlin is on the same parallel as Newfoundland, so if you're visiting in the winter, prepare for snow and bitter cold. Summer is balmy while spring and fall are beautiful, if sometimes rainy.

Transit: Taxifunk Berlin 49-30/44.33.22.
Express-Bus X9 from Tegel Airport to central Berlin.
U-Bahn (subway) 49-30/194.49.
S-Bahn (elevated train).
Bus 49-30/301.80.28.

Sonderbar Käthe-Niederkirchner-Str 34 (nr 'Märchenbrunnen') **49-30/425.84.94** • 8pm-8am • lesbians/ gay men • food served • terrace • young crowd • also art gallery

Stiller Don Erich-Weinert-Str 67 (at Schönhauser Allee) **49-30/445.59.57** • 7pm-close • popular • lesbians/ gay men • neighborhood bar • leather • food served

NIGHTCLUBS

Ackerkeller Ackerstr 12 (Hinterhaus, enter at Ackerstr 13, U-Rosenthaler Platz) **49-30/280.72.26** • 9pm-close Tue & 10pm-close Fri-Sat • popular • mostly gay men • dancing/DJ • young crowd

GMF at WMF Ziegelstr 22 (S-Oranienburger Str) **49-30/215.23.83, 49-30/21.47.41.00** • popular T-dance 9pm-3am Sun • mostly gay men • dancing/DJ • transgender-friendly • live shows • gay-owned/ run • cover charge

CAFES

Cafe Seidenfaden Dircksenstr 47 (U-Alexanderplatz) **49-30/283.27.83** • 11am-9pm, from 1pm Sun, clsd Sat • women only • drug- & alcohol-free cafe • info board

Kapelle Zionskirchplatz 22–24 (U-Rosenthaler Platz) **49-30/449.22.62** • 10am-3am • food served till midnight • gay/ straight • young crowd • also cocktail bar from 8pm

November Husemannstr 15 (at Sredzkistr) **49-30/442.84.25** • 10am-2am • lesbians/ gay men • cafe-bar • terrace • brkfst buffet wknds

oxon magenta Griefenhagener Str 48 (S/U-Schönhauser Allee) **49-30/44.73.64.82** • 10am-close • vegetarian & seafood • terrace

RESTAURANTS

Schall & Rauch Wirtshaus Gleimstr 23 (at Schönhauser Allee) **49-30/443.39.70, 49-30/448.07.70** • 10am-close • lesbians/ gay men

Thüringer Stuben Stargarder Str 28 (at Dunckerstr, S/U-Schönhauser Allee) **49-30/44.63.33.91** • 4pm-1am, from noon wknds • full bar

EROTICA

Black Style Seelower Str 5 (S/U-Schönhauser Allee) **49-30/44.68.85.95** • clsd Sun • latex & rubber wear • also mail order

Berlin—Schöneberg-Tiergarten

ACCOMMODATIONS

Arco Hotel Geisbergstr 30 (at Ansbacherstr, U-Wittenbergplatz) **49-30/235.14.80** • gay/ straight • centrally located • wheelchair access • gay-owned/ run • US$67-94

Berlin Gay B&B Perleberger Str 7 (at Stephan Str) **49-30/81.85.19.88** • lesbians/ gay men • hot tub • shared bath • seasonal • smokefree • kids/ pets ok • gay-owned/ run • US$20

Hotel California Kurfürstendamm 35 (at Knesebeckstr, U-Uhlandstr) **49-30/88.01.20** • gay-friendly • non-smoking floor • DM194–355

Hotel Hansablick Flotowstr 6 (at Bachstr, off Str des 17 Juni) **49-30/390.48.00** • gay-friendly • full brkfst • kids/ pets ok

Hotel Sachsenhof Motzstr 7 (at Nollendorfplatz) **49-30/216.20.74** • gay/ straight • centrally located • DM57-156

Pension Niebuhr Niebuhrstr 74 (at Savigny-platz) **49-30/324.95.95, 49-30/324.95.96** • gay/ straight • some shared baths • DM95-170

BARS

Chez Nous Marburger Str 14 (at Tauentzien-str, U-Wittenbergplatz) **49-30/213.18.10** • gay/ straight • famous drag revue • shows 8:30pm & 11pm nightly • pricey 1-drink minimum

Fledermaus Joachimsthaler Str 14–19 (U-Kurfürstendamm) **49-30/292.11.36** • noon-4am, till 6am Fri-Sat • mostly gay men • neighborhood bar

Heile Welt Motzstr 5 **49-30/21.91.75.07** • 6pm-close • lesbians/ gay men • food served

Kleist Casino Kleiststr 35 (U-Wittenberg-platz) **49-30/23.62.19.76** • 9pm-close, clsd Mon-Tue • mostly gay men • dancing/DJ from 10pm Fri-Sat • live shows • terrace

Kumpelnest 3000 Lützowstr 23 (at Pots-damer Str, U-Kurfürstenstr) **49-30/261.69.18** • 5pm-5am, till 8am Fri-Sat • popular wknds • gay-friendly • cocktail bar • dancing/DJ • transgender-friendly • young crowd

Memory's Fuggerstr 37 (U-Wittenbergplatz) **49-30/213.52.71** • 4pm-close • gay/ straight • cafe-bar • terrace

Pour Elle Kalckreuthstr 10 (at Nollendorfplatz) **49-30/218.75.33** • 7pm-2am, from 9pm Fri-Sat, clsd Tue • women only • dancing/DJ • terrace • young crowd • Germany's oldest lesbian bar • men welcome as guests Mon & Wed

Pussy-Cat Kalckreuthstr 7 (at Nollendorfplatz) **49-30/213.35.86** • 6pm-6am, clsd Sun • lesbians/gay men • dancing/DJ • transgender-friendly • live shows • food served • terrace

Vagabund Knesebeckstr 77 (at Uhlandstr) **49-30/881.15.06** • 5pm-late • mostly gay men • some dancing • professional crowd • terrace

Germany • EUROPE

Cafes

Begine Potsdamer Str 139 (at Bülowstr) **49-30/215.43.25, 49-30/215.14.14** • 5pm-1am, noon-midnight, clsd Sun • women only • full bar • also cultural center • dancing/DJ Sat

The Berlin Connection Cafe & Bistro Martin-Luther-Str 19 (at Motzstr, U-Nollendorfplatz) **49-30/213.11.16** • 2pm-2am • popular • mostly gay men • also bar • terrace

Café Berio Maaßenstr 7 (at Winterfeldtstr, U-Nollendorfplatz) **49-30/216.19.46** • 8am-11:30pm • popular • int'l • brkfst all day • bar till 1am • seasonal terrace • wheelchair access

Café PositHiv Alvenslebenstr 26 (at Potsdamer Str, U-Bülowstr) **49-30/216.86.54** • 3pm-close, from 1pm Th, from 6pm Sat, clsd Mon • for HIV+ & HIV- men and women

Café Savigny Grolmanstr 53-54 (at Savignyplatz) **49-30/312.81.95** • 9am-1am • artsy crowd • full bar • terrace

Windows Martin-Luther-Str 22 (at Motzstr, U-Wittenbergplatz) **49-30/214.23.94** • 2pm-4am, from 11am Sun • lesbians/ gay men • full bar • terrace

Restaurants

Arc Fasanenstr 81-A (at Kantstr, in S-Bahn arches, Charlottenburg, S/U-Zoologischer Garten) **49-30/313.26.25** • 8am-2am, from 10am wknds • lesbians/ gay men • int'l cuisine • wheelchair access • US$11-18 • also bar

Doi Suthep Emdener Str 1 (at Turmstr) **49-30/396.50.32** • noon-midnight • Thai

Berlin—Outer

Accommodations

Artemisia Women's Hotel Brandenburgischestr 18 (at Konstanzerstr) **49-30/873.89.05, 49-30/869.93.20** • the only hotel for women in Berlin • a real bargain • quiet rooms • bar • sundeck w/ an impressive view • some shared baths • US$94-122

Charlottenburger Hof Stuttgarter Platz 14 (at Wilmersdorfer Str) **49-30/32.90.70** • gay-friendly • centrally located • also 'Cafe Voltaire' • open 24hrs • also bar • US$67-100

Hotel Kronprinz Berlin Kronprinzendamm 1 (at Kurfürstendamm, in Halensee) **49-30/89.60.30** • gay-friendly • kids ok • DM195-380

Bars

Café Grünberg Kopernikusstr 23 (in Friedrichshain) **49-30/29.66.85.07** • 4pm-midnight, from 2pm wknds • lesbians/ gay men • cafe-bar • young crowd

Furiosa Habelschwerdter Allee 45 (nr Freie Universität) • mostly women • cafe-bar

Lützower Lampe Witzlebenstr 38 (U-Kaiserdamm, in Charlottenburg) **49-30/321.20.97** • 10:30pm-close • mostly gay men • some dancing • cabaret & piano bar • drag shows • wheelchair access

Nightclubs

Die Busche Mühlenstr 11-12 (at Kurfürstenstr, in Friedrichshain, S/U-Warschauer Str) **49-30/296.08.00** • 9:30pm-5am Wed & Sun, 10pm-6am Fri-Sat • popular • lesbians/ gay men • dancing/DJ • live shows • terrace • cover charge • also 'Kleine (Little) Busche' at Warschauer Platz 18

Cafes

Virtuality Cafe Joachimstaler Str 41 (S5-Charlottenberg) **49-30/88.67.96.30** • 10am-close • cybercafe • not gay

Restaurants

Cafe Rix Karl-Marx-Str 141 (in Neükolln) **49-30/686.90.20** • 10am-5pm • Mediterranean • plenty veggie • also bar • open till 1am

Jung Stuttgarter Platz 21 (in Charlottenburg) **49-30/32.70.24.46** • 9am-4pm • terrace

Gyms & Health Clubs

Apollo Fitness Haupstr 150 (U-Kleistpark) **49-30/784.82.03** • 10am-10pm, 1pm-6pm wknds • mostly gay men • also Borodinstr 16 location, 49-30/927.42.31 • gay-friendly

Swiss Training Albinostr 36-42 (nr Tempelhof Airport) **49-30/754.15.91** • gay-friendly • also Prenzlauer Berg location • Immanuelkirchstr 14, 44.35.83.44

Rome • Italy

ITALY

Rome

INFO LINES & SERVICES

Arci-Gay Caravaggio Via Orvinio 2 **39–06/8638.51.12** • helpline staffed 4pm-8pm Mon-Fri • mtgs Sun

Arci-Lesbica Roma Via dei Monti di Pietralata 16 (Metro Tiburtina) **39–06/418.03.69** • helpline • also weekly get-togethers & other special events for women

Circolo Mario Mieli Via Corinto 5 (at Via Efeso, Metro San Paolo) **39–06/541.39.85** • 10am-6pm Mon-Fri • switchboard, mtgs & discussion groups • hosts women-only club night 8:30pm-11pm Wed

Coordinamento Lesbiche Italiano Via San Francesco di Sales 1/a **39–06/686.42.01** • lesbian cultural center & archives • also publish newsletter

ACCOMMODATIONS

Campo dei Fiore Via del Biscione 6 **39–06/6880.6865, 39–06/687.48.86** • gay-friendly • some shared baths • US$78-156

Center Hotel Via Achille Grandi 7 (Metro Manzoni) **39–06/7047.49.67, 39–06/7030.0059** • gay-friendly • wheelchair access

Domus International 39–06/6889.2918 • lesbians/gay men • short-term apt rentals in the heart of Rome

Hotel Eden Via Ludovisi 49 **39–06/478.121, 800/848-2412 (US#)** • gay-friendly • restaurant & rooftop bar • wheelchair access • US$290+

Hotel Scotthouse Via Gioberti 30 **39–06/446.53.79** • gay-friendly • L100,000-220,000

Locanda Cairoli Club House Hotel Piazza Benedetto Cairoli 2 **39–06/6880.9278** • gay-friendly • charming hotel in center of Rome

Scalinata di Spagna Piazza Trinità di Monti 17 (Metro Piazza di Spagna) **39–06/6994.0896, 39–06/679.30.06** • gay-friendly • roof garden • US$169-250

BARS

L' Angelo Azzuro Via Cardinal Merry del Val 13 (in Trastevere, Tram 8) **39–06/580.04.72** • 11pm-late Fri-Sun only • lesbians/gay men • women only Fri • dancing/DJ • transgender-friendly • cover charge

Cum Via del Capellari 36 (at Campo Dei Fiori) **39–06/767.07.66** • 10pm-2am, clsd Mon • mostly gay men • neighborhood bar • dancing/DJ • live shows • bears • leather • multiracial clientele • wheelchair access • gay-owned/run

Garbo Vicolo di Santa Margherita 1a (in Trastevere, Tram 8) **39–06/5832.0782, 39–06/581.67.00** • 10pm-3am • lesbians/gay men • cocktail bar • food served

Shelter Via dei Vascellari 35 (in Trastevere, Tram 8) **39–06/588.0862** • 9pm-3am • lesbians/gay men • transgender-friendly • cocktail bar • food served • live shows • private club

NIGHTCLUBS

L' Alibi Via di Monte Testaccio 39–44 (Metro Piramide) **39–06/574.34.48** • 11pm-4am, clsd Mon-Tue • popular • lesbians/gay men • dancing/DJ • live shows • rooftop garden in summer • young crowd

Frutta e Verdura Via Placido Zurla 66/70 (Metro Vittorio) **39–06/904.60.31** • 8pm-midnight, later Fri-Sat, clsd Mon • lesbians/gay men • dancing/DJ • full restaurant

Jam Via del Cardello 13a **39–06/6994.2419** • Wed only • mostly gay men • dancing/DJ • music bar

Jolie Couer Via Sirte 5 (Viale Eritrea) **39–06/8621.5827** • 10pm-5am Sat • women only • dancing/DJ • karaoke • videos • cover charge

Muccassassina Via di Portonaccio 212 (at 'The Qube') **39–06/541.39.85** • 10:30pm-5am Fri only • popular • lesbians/gay men • dancing/DJ • live shows • cover charge

Stomp Night Via Tagliamento 9 (at Piper) **03–47/778.56.89** • Sat only, 11pm-5am • gay/straight • dancing/DJ

CAFES

TreviNet Pl@ce Internet Point Via in Arcione 103 (btwn Trevi Fountain & Via del Traforo) **39–06/699.22320** • 10:30am-10:30pm, from 3pm Sun • Internet cafe • 20% discount for lesbians/gays • free calls to USA • digital cameras • posters • lesbian-owned/run

RESTAURANTS

Asinocotto Ristorante Via dei Vascellari 48 (in Travestere, Tram 8) **39–06/589.89.85, 212/858-5771 (US RESERVATIONS FAX LINE)** • dinner, clsd Mon • creative gourmet Mediterranean • reservations req'd • gay-owned/run

Da Nerone Via delle Terme di Tito 96 **39–06/481.79.52** • clsd Sun • full bar • US$15

Le Suselustre Via San Francesco di Sales 1/a **39–06/686.42.01** • women-only • also bar

Taverna del Campo Via del Pellegrino 163 **39–06/6880.95.54** • lunch and dinner • Italian • plenty veggie • also Campo dei Fiori 16, 39–06/687.44.02

Italy • EUROPE

BOOKSTORES

La Libreria Babele Via dei Banchi Vecchi 116 **39-06/687.66.28** • 9:30am-7:30pm, clsd Sun • lgbt • some English titles

Queer Via del Boschetto 25 (at Via Nazionale) **39-06/474.06.91** • 9:30am-7:30pm, from 2:30pm Mon, clsd Sun • lgbt • videos • pride items • T-shirts • cards • more

Rinascita Via delle Botteghe Oscure 1 **39-06/679.71.36, 39-06/679.74.60** • large lgbt section

PUBLICATIONS

Aut 39-06/541.39.85 • monthly magazine w/ news & event listings • free around Rome

EROTICA

La Bancarella di Andy Capp Piazza Alessandria 2 (nr Porta Pia, Metro Repubblica) **39-06/853.03.71** • erotic comics & lgbt magazines

Europa 92 Via Vitelleschi 38–40 (nr Piazza Risorgimento) **39-06/687.12.10** • clsd Sun • clothing • magazines • books • videos

Rome

WHERE THE GIRLS ARE: Discussing politics at a cafe, or dancing at one of the one-nighters that make up lesbian nightlife in Rome. Visit the Coordinamento Lesbiche Italiano center, the bulletin board at the Libreria Babele, or the Circolo Mario Mieli center for the latest events.

LGBT PRIDE: June/July.

ANNUAL EVENTS: May - Maratona Gay/Lesbian Festival.

CITY INFO: APT (Tourism Office) 39-06/4889.9253.
Enjoy Rome 39-6/445.18.43, web: www.enjoyrome.com. Via Marghera 8a.

ATTRACTIONS: Baths of Caracalla 39-06/575.86.26.
Campo dei Fiori.
Capitoline Museums 39-06/6710.3069.
Colosseum 39-06/700.42.61.
Galleria Borghese 39-06/32.81.01.
Pantheon 39-06/6830.0230.
Roman Forum 39-06/699.01.10.
Spanish Steps.
St. Peter's.
Trevi Fountain.
The Vatican and Vatican Museums (includes National Etruscan Museum, Sistine Chapel, and Raphael Rooms) 39-06/698.33.33.

WEATHER: Late summer is hot & humid. Winter is mild but rainy. The best times to visit Rome are late spring and early fall.

TRANSIT: Taxi stands are located in several popular piazzas. Only hire official yellow or white taxis. You can also call 3570 for pick-up service.
ATAC 39-06/4695.2252.

Netherlands

Amsterdam

Amsterdam is divided into 5 regions:
Amsterdam—Overview
Amsterdam—Centre
Amsterdam—Jordaan
Amsterdam—Rembrandtplein
Amsterdam—Outer

Amsterdam—Overview

Info Lines & Services

COC Amsterdam Rozenstr 14 (in the Jordaan) **31-20/626.30.87** • 1pm-6pm, clsd Sun-Tue • queer center • also cafe, theater & disco • popular women's dance every Sat

Gay/ Lesbian Switchboard **31-20/623.65.65, 31-20/422.65.65 (TTY)** • 10am-10pm • English spoken

Homodok/ Lesbian Archives Amsterdam Nieuwportkade 2a **31-20/606.07.12** • lgbt info center & archives • open 10am-5pm Mon-Fri

Het Vrouwenhuis Nieuwe Herengracht 95 **31-20/625.20.66** • women's center & library • Internet access • bar at night

Wild Side 31-71/512.86.32 • women's SM support group • mtgs, events & play parties

Entertainment & Recreation

The Anne Frank House Prinsengracht 263 (in the Jordaan) **31-20/556.71.00, 31-20/626.45.33** • the final hiding place of Amsterdam's most famous resident

Homomonument Westermarkt (in the Jordaan) • moving sculptural tribute to lesbians & gays killed by Nazis

The van Gogh Museum Paulus Potterstr 7 (on the Museumplein) **31-20/570.52.52** • a must-see museum dedicated to this Dutch master painter

Publications

Gay News 31-20/679.15.56 • bilingual paper • extensive listings

Gay & Night 31-20/420.42.04 • free monthly bilingual entertainment paper w/ club listings

Shark 31-20/420.6775 • bi-weekly queer-oriented alternative culture guide & calendar (in English)

Amsterdam—Centre

Accommodations

Clemens Hotel 39 Raadhuisstraat (at Herengracht) **31-20/624.60.89** • gay-friendly • small hotel in Amsterdam's center • some shared baths • woman-owned/ run • Dfl75-350

Golden Tulip Grand Hotel Krasnapolsky Dam 9 **31-20/554.91.11** • gay-friendly • full-service hotel • in the city center opposite Royal Palace • business center • 5 restaurants

Holiday Inn Crowne Plaza Amsterdam City Centre NZ Voorburgwal 5 **31-20/620.05.00, 800/465-4329 (US#)** • gay-friendly • swimming

Hotel Brian Singel 69 **31-20/624.46.61** • gay-friendly • bargain rooms

Hotel New York Herengracht 13 (at Brouwersgracht) **31-20/624.30.66** • lesbians/ gay men • also bar & coffee shop • US$105-132

Maes B&B Herenstr 26 **31-20/427.51.65** • lesbians/ gay men • smokefree • NLG175-250

Tulip Inn Spuistr 288-292 **31-20/420.45.45, 800/344-1212 (US#)** • gay-friendly • NLG330

Bars

Getto Warmoesstr 51 **31-20/421.51.51** • 4pm-1am, from 7pm Tue, 1pm-midnight Sun • popular • lesbians/ gay men • live DJs • drag-queen bingo Th • also restaurant till 11pm • Sun brunch • eclectic cuisine • US$10-14

Vrankrijk Spuistr 216 • gay/ straight • rowdy squat bar • alternative • more gay Mon

Restaurants

Camp Cafe Kerkstr 45 (at Leidsestr) **31-20/622.15.06** • 3pm-1am, till 3am Fri-Sat • popular • lesbians/ gay men • cont'l • kitchen open till 11:30pm • full bar • terrace • gay-owned/ run • US$10-14

Gerard Geldersekade 23 **31-20/638.43.38** • 5:30pm-11pm, clsd Tue • French

Hemelse Modder Oude Waal 9 **31-20/624.32.03** • 6pm-10pm, clsd Mon • French/ int'l • wheelchair access • US$24-30

La Strada NZ Voorburgwal 93 **31-20/625.02.76** • 4pm-1am, till 2am wknds • popular • food served till 10pm • Mediterranean • plenty veggie • full bar • terrace • lesbian-owned/ run • US$14-17

No 7 & 9 Warmoesstr 7 **31-20/624.51.73** • 8am-11pm • full bar • gay-owned

Oibibio Prins Hendrikkade 20-21 **31-20/553.93.28** • 10:30am-10pm • vegetarian • wheelchair access

Netherlands • EUROPE

Pygma-lion Nieuwe Spiegelstr 5a (in Spiegelhof Arcade) **31-20/420.70.22** • 11am-10pm, till 3pm Mon, clsd Sun • South African • gay-owned/ run • US$13-19

't Sluisje Torensteeg 1 **31-20/624.08.13** • 6pm-close, clsd Mon-Tue • popular steakhouse • lesbians/ gay men • transgender-friendly • full bar (open later) • drag shows nightly • US$13-20

Song Kwae Kloveniersburgwal 14a (nr Nieuwmarkt & Chinatown) **31-20/624.25.68** • 1pm-10:30pm • Thai • full bar • terrace • Dfl25-35

Tom Yam Staalstr 22 **31-20/622.95.33** • 6pm-10:30pm, clsd Sun-Mon • eclectic/ Thai • terrace • wheelchair access • gay-owned

Walem Keizersgracht 449 **31-20/625.35.44** • 10am-10:30pm • int'l • inexpensive • local crowd • patio • wheelchair access • lesbian-owned

BOOKSTORES

The American Book Center Kalverstr 185 (at Heiligeweg) **31-20/625.55.37** • 10am-8pm, till 10pm Th, 11am-6pm Sun • books & magazines in English imported from US & UK • large lgbt section • wheelchair access

Boekhandel Vrolijk Gay & Lesbian Bookshop Paleisstr 135 (nr Dam Sq) **31-20/623.51.42** • 10am-6pm, from 1pm Mon, till 9pm Th, till 5pm Sat, clsd Sun • lgbt books, videos & gadgets • also mail order

RETAIL SHOPS

Conscious Dreams Kokopelli Warmoesstr 12 **31-20/421.70.00** • 11am-10pm • 'smart warehouse'

Magic Mushroom Spuistr 249 **31-20/427.57.65** • 11am-7pm, till 8pm Fri-Sat • 'smartshop': magic mushrooms & more

Amsterdam

ENTERTAINMENT: MacBike (31-20/620.09.85) rents bikes & has created a self-guided tour-by-map of Amsterdam's gay points of interest.

LGBT PRIDE: August. 31-20/623.65.65, web: www.amsterdampride.nl.

ANNUAL EVENTS: April 30 - Queen's Birthday.
May 4-5 - Memorial Day & Liberation Day.
June - Holland Festival.
July - Zomerfestijn. International performing arts festival.
August - Heart's Day. Drag festival.
October - Leather Pride 31-20/422.37.37, web: www.leatherpride.nl.

CITY INFO: VVV 900/400.40.40, web: www.visitholland.com. Visit their office directly opposite Centraal Station.

ATTRACTIONS: Anne Frank House 31-20/556.71.00.
Homomonument.
Jewish Historical Museum 31-20/626.99.45.
Rembrandt House 31-20/520.04.00.
Rijksmuseum 31-20/674.70.47.
Royal Palace 31-20/620.40.60.
Stedelijk Museum of Modern Art 31-20/573.27.37.
Vincent van Gogh Museum 31-20/570.52.00.

WEATHER: Temperatures hover around freezing in the winter and rise to the mid-60°s in the summer. Rain is possible year-round.

TRANSIT: 31-20/677.77.77. Can also be found at taxi stands on the main squares. KLM Bus. GVB 33-6/92.92 or visit their office across from the Centraal Station. Trams, buses, and subway.

Amsterdam—Rembrandtplein • Netherlands

Erotica

DeMask Zeedijk 64 **31-20/620.56.03** • clsd Sun • fetish fashion

Female & Partners Spuistr 100 **31-20/620.91.52** • fashions & toys for women

Amsterdam—Jordaan

Accommodations

Barangay B&B 31-0-62/504-5432 • lesbians/ gay men • 1777 townhouse • nr tourist attractions • full brkfst • smokefree • gay-owned/ run

Freeland Hotel Marnixstr 386 **31-20/622.75.11, 31-20/627.75.78** • gay-friendly • full brkfst

Hotel Pulitzer Prinsengracht 315–331 **31-20/523.52.35, 800/325-3535 (US#)** • gay-friendly • occupies 24 17th-century buildings on 2 of Amsterdam's most picturesque canals • Dfl720-895

Rembrandt Residence Hotel Herengracht 255 **31-20/622.17.27** • gay/ straight • non-smoking rooms available • NLG350+

Bars

Saarein Elandsstr 119 **31-20/623.49.01** • 8pm-1am, till 2am Fri-Sat, clsd Mon • lesbians/ gay men • cafe-bar

Nightclubs

COC Rozenstr 14 **31-20/623.40.79, 31-20/626.30.87** • 10pm-5am Fri • lesbians/ gay men • dancing/DJ • women only 10pm-4am Sat • multiculti disco 8pm-2am Sun • HIV+ 8pm-12:30am Th • call for many other parties/ events • cover charge

Mazzo Rozengracht 114 (nr Westermarkt) **31-20/626.75.00** • 11pm-4am, till 5am Fri-Sat, clsd Mon-Tue • gay-friendly • dancing/DJ • young, raver crowd • cover charge

de Trut **31-20/612.35.24** • 11pm-4am Sun only • lesbians/ gay men • hip underground dance party • alternative • young crowd

Cafes

Café 't Smalle Egelantiersgracht 12 **31-20/623.96.17** • 10am-1pm • brown cafe • full bar • outdoor seating

Tops Prinsengracht 480 • smoking Internet cafe

't Wonder Huidenstr 13 (at Bijbelsmuseum) **31-20/639.10.32** • 2pm-midnight, clsd Mon • smoking coffee shop

Restaurants

Bojo Lange Leidsedwarsstr 49–51 (nr Leidseplein) **31-20/622.74.34** • noon-close Th-Sun • popular • Indonesian

De Bolhoed Prinsengracht 60 (at Tuinstr) **31-20/626.18.03** • noon-10pm • vegetarian/ vegan • US$8-13

Burger's Patio 2e Tuindwarsstr 12 **31-20/623.68.54** • Italian • plenty veggie

Granada Leidsekruisstr 13 **31-20/625.10.73** • 5pm-close, clsd Tue • Spanish • tapas • also bar • live music wknds

't Swarte Schaep Korte Leidsedwarsstr 24 (nr Leidseplein) **31-20/622.30.21** • noon-11pm • French • US$22-31

De Vliegende Schotel Nieuwe Leliestr 162 **31-20/625.20.41** • 5pm-11pm • vegetarian

Entertainment & Recreation

De Looier Antiques Market Elandsgracht 109 **31-20/624.90.38**

Bookstores

Vrouwenindruk Westermarkt 5 **31-20/624.50.03** • antiquarian & secondhand books by & about women • also lgbt

Xantippe Unlimited Prinsengracht 290 **31-20/623.58.54, 31-20/679.96.09** • women's bookstore • lesbian section • English titles • lesbian-owned

Retail Shops

Clubwear House Herengracht 265 (nr Dam Sq) **31-20/622.87.66** • noon-6pm, till 8pm Th, clsd Sun-Mon • clothing • club tickets & flyers

Erotica

Black Body Lijnbaansgracht 292 (across from Rijksmuseum) **31-20/626.25.53** • clsd Sun • rubber clothing specialists • leather • toys • wheelchair access

Amsterdam—Rembrandtplein

Accommodations

Doelen Hotel Nieuwe Doelenstr 24 **31-20/554.06.00, 31-20/554.07.77** • gay-friendly • grand hotel on the River Amstel • NLG351-531

Golden Tulip Schiller Rembrandtplein 26–36 **31-20/554.07.00** • gay-friendly • art deco style • recently renovated • NLG421+

Hotel Monopole Amstel 60 **31-20/624.62.71** • gay-friendly • centrally located • Dfl165-225 • also 'Cafe Rouge', 31-20/624.64.51 • open 4pm-1am, till 3am Fri-Sat • mostly gay men

Netherlands • EUROPE

Reply **Forward** **Delete**

Date: Fri, Jan 4, 2002 16:58:12
From: Girl-on-the-Go
To: Editor@Damron.com
Subject: Amsterdam

> The day that Amsterdam is known as the *Lesbian* and Gay Capital of Europe, there will be a lot of 'loud and proud' women-loving-women walking around. Until then, you're really going to have to search hard to find them.

> For the sad truth is that most Dutch dykes hold back more than just water. Still, we encourage you to keep the faith—not all Dutch girls are as straightlaced as they seem.

> In fact, just looking back over three centuries of dyke drama, there's reason to believe it's only a matter of time before the riot grrrls take Amsterdam. Way back in 1792, the jealous, murderous Bartha Schuurman was hung from the gallows back for knifing her girlfriend's lover to death. In the 1970s, lesbian activists—in between scrawling pro-dyke graffiti—did manage to squat a few places and start some women's collectives. In fact, many of the women's establishments enjoyed today—ranging from bars to bookshops—emerged directly as a result of that era when Dutch dykes did indeed get mad and get rad.

> Until the spirit of those good ol' days returns, lesbian visitors can enjoy a pleasant time—if you can stand the ubiquitous cloud of smoke—at most of the gay establishments. And one thing they definitely can share with those naughty Dutch boys is Amsterdam's largely tolerant atmosphere that allows same-sex couples to walk the quaint canals and winding streets hand-in-hand.

> While you're out and about, experience a little of Amsterdam's touted counter-culture for yourself...stop in at one of the famous brown cafes. Or take a tour of the Heineken brewery.

> To find out what queer events are going on about town, or just to take a break from sight-seeing, stop by the **COC** center/cafe. Or head over to the women's bookstore **Xantippe,** the LGBT bookstore **Vrolijk,** or the **American Book Center,** to pick up some flyers, the local newspaper **Gay News, Gay & Night** scene guide, and a copy of the bi-weekly entertainment guide **Shark.**

> Have a meal at one of the lesbian-friendly restaurants in town. Try **La Strada, Sarah's Grannies, Walem,** or **'t Sluisje** (if you like your steak served by drag queens).

Amsterdam—Rembrandtplein • Netherlands

> At night, hang out with the lipstick femmes and cute baby dykes at **Vive la Vie**. Later, hit the dancefloor at the lesbian dance club **You II**. Don't miss the weekly women-only party at the **COC** nightclub on Saturdays.
>
> There are a number of popular mixed bars, including the hip **Getto** and **Mix Cafe**. The big gay clubs are **iT** and **Exit**.
>
> If you're looking for a different kind of 'culture,' don't miss the incredible masterworks this city's museums have to offer. (There is even an entire museum dedicated to van Gogh.) One very Amsterdam-esque way to see them is to take the 'Museum Boat' along the canal from museum to museum. The fare entitles you to discounted admissions.

Hotel Orlando Prinsengracht 1099 (at Amstel River) **31-20/638.69.15** • gay-friendly • beautifully restored 17th-c canalhouse • US$76-118

ITC Hotel Prinsengracht 1051 (at Utrechtsestr) **31-20/623.02.30** • mostly gay men • 18th-c canal house • great location • also bar & lounge • Dfl160-175

Jolly Hotel Carlton Vijzelstr 4 **31-20/622.22.66** • gay-friendly • overlooking the famous flower market & Munt Tower • NLG405

Waterfront Hotel Singel 458 **31-20/421.66.21, 31-20/623.97.75** • gay-friendly • Dfl145+

BARS

April Reguliersdwarsstr 37 (at Rembrandtplein) **31-20/625.95.72** • 2pm-1am, till 3am Fri-Sat • popular happy hour • mostly gay men • videos

Entre-Nous Halvemaansteeg 14 (at Rembrandtplein) **31-20/623.17.00** • 8pm-3am, till 4am Fri-Sat • lesbians/ gay men • neighborhood bar

Havana Reguliersdwarsstr 17–19 **31-20/620.67.88** • 4pm-1am, till 3am Fri-Sat, from 2pm wknds • mostly gay men • more women Fri • cafe-bar • dancing/DJ wknds

Mix Cafe Amstel 50 **31-20/622.52.02** • popular • 8pm-3am, till 4am Fri-Sat • lesbians/ gay men

Vive la Vie Amstelstr 7 (at Rembrandtplein) **31-20/624.01.14** • 3pm-1am, till 3am Fri-Sat • mostly women

NIGHTCLUBS

The Back Door Amstelstr 32 **31-6/214.318.61** • Fri & Sun only • T-dance 6pm-close Sun • mostly gay men • dancing/DJ • cover charge

Exit Reguliersdwarsstr 42 **31-20/625.87.88** • 11pm-4am, till 5am Fri-Sat • popular • mostly gay men • dancing/DJ • 4 flrs • cover charge

iT Amstelstr 24 **31-20/625.01.11** • 11pm-4am Th-Sun, open later Fri-Sat • popular • gay/ straight • more gay Th & Sat • dancing/DJ • private club • cover charge

You II Amstel 178 (at Wagenstraat) **31-20/420.43.11** • 10pm-4am, till 5am Fri-Sat, 4pm-1am Sun, clsd Mon-Wed • mostly women • dancing/DJ

CAFES

Downtown Reguliersdwarsstr 31 **31-20/622.99.58** • 10am-8pm • popular • mostly gay men • terrace open in summer

Netherlands • EUROPE

Global Chillage Kerkstr 51 **31–20/777.97.77** • 11am-midnight, till 1am Fri-Sat • smoking coffee shop • publisher's choice

The Other Side Reguliersdwarsstr 6 **31–20/421.10.14** • 10am-1am • mostly gay men • smoking coffee shop • gay-owned/run

Restaurants

Dia de Sol Reguliersdwarsstr 23 **31–20/623.42.59** • open till midnight • tapas/Mediterranean

Garlic Queen Reguliersdwarsstr 27 **31–20/422.64.26** • 6pm-close, clsd Tue • even the desserts are made with garlic!

Golden Temple Utrechtsestr 126 **31–20/626.85.60** • 5pm-10pm, noon-3pm Tue & Sat • Indian-influenced vegetarian & vegan • smokefree • Dfl21.50+

Kort Amstelveld 12 **31–20/626.11.99** • 10am-10pm, till 11pm Fri-Sat, clsd Tue • French/Mediterranean • terrace • US$9-19

Malvesijn Prinsengracht 598 **31–20/638.08.99** • 10am-midnight • food served till 10pm • lesbians/gay men • Dutch • also bar • terrace overlooking the canal • US$10-17

Le Monde Rembrandtplein 6 **31–20/626.99.22** • 8am-11pm, brkfst till 4pm (open 4pm-10pm Mon-Fri in winter) • lesbians/gay men • Dutch • plenty veggie • terrace dining • gay-owned/run

Rose's Cantina Reguliersdwarsstr 38–40 (nr Rembrandtplein) **31–20/625.97.97** • 5pm-11pm • popular • Mexican • full bar • US$13-22

Sarah's Grannies Kerkstr 176 **31–20/624.01.45** • 10am-5pm, clsd Sun-Mon • mostly women • terrace

Saturnino Reguliersdwarsstr 5 **31–20/639.01.02** • noon-midnight • Italian • full bar

't Schooiertje Lijnbaansgracht 190 (at Looier Antiques Market) **31–20/638.40.35** • 9am-9pm, clsd Fri • full bar

Shizen Kerkstr 108 **31–20/622.86.27** • lunch & dinner, clsd Mon • macrobiotic Japanese

Entertainment & Recreation

Bridge-Sociëteit de Looier Lijnbaansgracht 185 **31–20/627.93.80** • gay prize bridge 7:30pm Wed

Retail Shops

Conscious Dreams Kerkstr 93 **31–20/626.69.07** • 11am-7pm, till 8pm Th-Sat, noon-5pm Sun • 'psychedelicatessen' • Internet access • fl10/hour

Amsterdam—Outer

Accommodations

Aadam Wilhelmina Hotel Koninginneweg 169 **31–20/662.54.67** • gay-friendly • charming • recently renovated • Dfl65-395

Chico's Guesthouse St Willibrordusstr 77 **31–20/675.42.41** • gay-friendly • Dfl40-140

Hotel Sander Jacob Obrechtstr 69 **31–20/662.75.74** • gay-friendly • also 24hr bar & coffee lounge • Dfl185+

Hotel Sander Jacob Obrechtstr 69 **31–20/662.75.74** • gay-friendly • also 24hr bar & coffee lounge • Dfl185+

Johanna's B&B Van Hogendorpplein 62 **31–20/684.85.96** • women only • smokefree

Liliane's Home Sarphatistr 119 **31–20/627.40.06** • women only • full brkfst • shared bath • smokefree • also apt • US$68-137

Prinsen Hotel Vondelstr 36-38 (nr Leidseplein) **31–20/616.23.23** • gay-friendly • $80-150

Quentin Hotel Leidsekade 89 (at Lijnbaansgracht) **31–20/626.21.87** • gay-friendly • some shared baths • US$58-97

Toro Hotel Koningslaan 64 (next to Vondelpark) **31–20/673.72.23** • gay-friendly • refurbished mansion • NLG275

Nightclubs

De Brug NZ Kolk 25 (at 'Akhnaton') • 9pm-2am 1st Sat • for lesbians & bisexual women 35 & older • ballroom dancing till 11pm • disco from 11pm

Melkweg Lijnbaansgracht 234 **31–20/624.84.92** • gay/ straight • popular music venue • more women 3rd Sun for 'Planet Pussy' • smoking cafe

Restaurants

De Vrolijke Abrikoos Weteringschans 76 **31–20/624.46.72** • 5pm-11:30pm • eclectic organic cuisine • plenty veggie • patio

De Waaghals Frans Halsstr 29 **31–20/679.96.09** • 5pm-11pm int'l vegetarian

Gyms & Health Clubs

Eastern Bath House Zaanstr 88 **31–20/681.48.18** • women-only Turkish sauna

Fenomeen Eerste Schinkelstraat 14 (nr Vondelpark) **31–20/671.67.80** • women-only Mon • Turkish bath • sauna • snacks

Barcelona • Spain

SPAIN

Barcelona

INFO LINES & SERVICES

Casal Lambda Verdaguer y Calle 10 (Metro Drassanes) **34/933.195.550** • 5pm-9pm, till 11pm Sat, clsd Sun • community ctr • cafe • archives • library • also publish magazine

Colectivo Gay de Barcelona (CGB) 34/93.318.16.66 • staffed 7pm-9pm Mon-Fri • also publish 'Info Gai'

Coordinadora Gai Lesbiana Finlandia 45, E–08014 **34/93.298.00.29, 34/902.120.140** • nat'l gay group

Telefono Rosa 34/900/601.601 (IN SPAIN), 34/934.863.171 • 6pm-10pm Mon-Fri

ACCOMMODATIONS

California Hotel Rauric 14 (at Fernando, Metro Liceu) **34/93.317.77.66** • gay/ straight • 6.000-10.000 ptas

Catalonia Albinoni Avenida Portal de L'Angel 17 **34/93.318.41.41** • gay-friendly • 3-star hotel

Catalonia Barcelona Plaza Plaza d'Espanya 6–8 (across from Montjuïc Castle) **34/93.426.26.00** • gay-friendly • swimming • jacuzzi • also restaurant & piano bar • 15.700ptas+

Gran Hotel Catalonia Balmes 142–146 **34/93.415.90.90** • gay-friendly • 4-star hotel • food served • wheelchair access

Hotel Albeniz Aragó 591–593 **34/93.265.26.26** • gay-friendly • food served • wheelchair access • 13.500ptas+

Hotel Duques de Bergara Bergara 11 **34/93.301.51.51** • gay-friendly • 4-star hotel in the heart of old Barcelona • food served • 22.900ptas+

Hotel Mikado Paseo de Bonanova 58 **34/93.211.41.66** • gay-friendly • 3-star hotel in a beautiful residential area • food served • 14.200ptas+

Barcelona

LGBT PRIDE: June.

ANNUAL EVENTS: February - Carnival.
July - Grec Summer Festival 34/933.017.775, web: www.grecbcn.com.
August - Festa Major de Gràcia (huge street party).
October/November - Gay/Lesbian Film Festival, 34/93.412.72.72 (Casal Lambda).

CITY INFO: 34/933.689.730 (outside Spain), 34/906.30.1282 (in Spain), web: www.barcelonaturisme.com.

ATTRACTIONS: Barcelona Museum of Contemporary Art 34/93.412.08.10.
Barri Gotic.
Catedral de Barcelona 34/93.315.15.54.
Fundació Joan Miró 34/93.329.19.08.
Museu Picasso 34/93.319.63.10.
National Museum of Catalan Art 34/93.622.03.60.
Parc Güell.
La Sagrada Familia 34/93.207.30.31.

WEATHER: Barcelona boasts a mild Mediterranean climate, with summer temperatures in the 70°s-80°s, and 40°s-50°s in winter. Rain is possible year-round, with July being the driest month.

TRANSIT: 34/932.235.151.
Aerobus to Plaza de Cataluña 34/934.156.020.34/010.

Spain • EUROPE

Reply **Forward** **Delete**

Date: Tue, Jan 8, 2002 15:26:01
From: Girl-on-the-Go
To: Editor@Damron.com
Subject: Barcelona

> An enormous open-air museum to its patron artist Gaudí, Barcelona is by turns handsome, quaint, sleek, wry, and hip. Gaudí's Dr. Seuss–like art nouveau apartment buildings are scattered throughout the city, and you can't miss his massive still-under-construction cathedral—La Sagrada Familia—or the amusing Park Güell overlooking the city.

> As all the guidebooks will tell you, the Barri Gotic is both the tourists' quarter and a crowded maze of ancient Gothic towers, narrow alleys, plazas, and cathedrals bisected by a wide pedestrian mall known as Las Ramblas.

> The Ramblas is the main artery of the quarter, and most days you can't walk more than a few feet without bumping into street hawkers, cartoonists, jugglers, clowns, live statues, and buskers of all sorts—in between the omnipresent bright red ¡Hola! bookstands, knots of tourists, and sidewalk cafes. Unlike many tourist areas, the Ramblas is also frequented by locals strolling for evening and weekend entertainment.

> A few blocks away, Raurich Street (*carrer* in Catalan, the local tongue of Barcelona; or *calle* in Spanish, pronounced 'kí-yay') meanders past most of the gay bars and bookstores in the Barri Gotic. But the heart of gay Barcelona is in L'Eixample, the most recently redeveloped part of town, with wide streets and sidewalks and plush middle-class businesses. You'll find well-dressed lesbians here among the chic gay boys at expensive dance clubs like **Satanassa,** whose life-size mirror-encrusted statue of a fat-and-happy goddess deserves some adoration.

> Urban dykes may feel more at home in the less glossy Gracia (remember to pronounce all c's appearing in the middle of a word like a short 'th') neighborhood, home to a mix of queers, families of color, punks, and other misfits—most of whom still go to the Barri Gotic for excitement.

> During the day, visit the **Casal Lambda,** a community center and cafe that also publishes a local LGBT magazine. Or drop by one of the two LGBT bookstores in town: **Cómplices** and **Antinous.**

> For casual hanging out, there's **La Illa**, a tiny, friendly dyke bar,

Barcelona • Spain

[**Reply**] [**Forward**]   [**Delete**]

Bahía, a laid-back lesbian bar with good music, or the **Café de la Calle,** which is actually a bar-cum-community center that opens at 6pm but doesn't start filling up till 10pm. If you wander around its mazes, you'll find a narrow hallway in the back crammed with gay papers, flyers, free disco tickets, and all the current information you need.

> The current hotspot for women is **Aire,** a trendy cafe-bar. If you feel like dancing, you can get down with the girls at **La Rosa.**

> Of course, the most exciting women's nights happen monthly or so. Look for flyers advertising events for *dones* ('women' in Catalan), or ask the friendly bartenders, many of whom will answer you in English if your accent gives you away.

Hotel Roma Av de Roma 31 34/93.410.66.33 • gay-friendly • 4-star hotel next to the Sants train station • food served • 13.500ptas+

Regencia Colon Hotel Sagristans 13–17 (in the Barri Gotic, Metro Jaume I) 34/93.318.98.58, 800/223-1356 • gay-friendly • some shared baths • swimming • 13.500-20.500 ptas + tax

BARS

Aire/ Sala Diana Enrique Granados 48/ Valencia 236 34/93.451.84.62 • 10pm-3am, clsd Mon • mostly women • cafe-bar • young crowd

Bahía Séneca 12 (Metro Diagonal) • 7pm-3am, after-hrs wknds • mostly women • dancing/DJ • food served

Café de la Calle Vic 11 (Metro Gracia) 34/93.218.38.63 • 6pm-3am • lesbians/ gay men • food served • young crowd

Dietrich Consell de Cent 255 (btwn Muntaner & Aribau, Metro Universitat) 34/93.451.77.07 • 6pm-3am • popular • lesbians/ gay men • dancing/DJ • upscale • theater-cafe • drag shows

Este Bar Consell de Cent 257 (Metro Universitat) 34/93.323.64.06 • 10pm-3am • popular late • lesbians/ gay men • young crowd

Imagine Mariano Cubí 4 • mostly women • dancing/DJ

Medusa Café Casanova 75 (Metro Gran Vía) 34/93.454.53.63 • 4:30pm-2:30am • lesbians/ gay men • dancing/DJ • food served • drag shows

Members Séneca 3 34/93.237.12.04 • 8pm-3am • lesbians/ gay men

Padam Padam Rauric 9 34/93.302.50.62 • 7pm-3am, clsd Sun • lesbians/ gay men • also cafe

Punto BCN Muntaner 63–65 (enter on Consejo de Ciento Yragón, Metro Universitat) 34/93.453.61.23 • 6pm-2:30am, till 3am wknds • popular • mostly gay men • upscale cafe-bar • wheelchair access

La Rosa Brusi 39 (btwn Augusta & San Elias, Metro Plaza Molina) 34/93.414.61.66 • 8pm-3am Th-Sun • mostly women • dancing/DJ • live shows

Theseo Comte Borrell 119 (Metro Urgell) 34/93.453.87.96 • 8:30am-2:30am, clsd Sun • gay/ straight • young crowd • also restaurant • wheelchair access

NIGHTCLUBS

Arena Balmes 32 (at Diputació, Metro Universitat) 34/93.487.83.42 • 12:30am-5am, clsd Mon except in Aug • popular • mostly gay men • dancing/DJ • food served • live shows Wed • videos • young crowd • cover charge

Spain • EUROPE

Arena Classic Diputación 233 (at Balmes, Metro Universitat) **34/93.487.83.42** • 12:30am-6am Th-Sat only • popular • mostly gay men • dancing/DJ • live shows • videos • theme nights • young crowd • cover charge

Arena VIP Gran Vía 593 (Metro Universitat) **34/93.487.83.42** • 1am-6am Fri-Sat only • popular • mostly gay men • dancing/DJ • live shows • videos • young crowd • cover charge

Glamour Moià 1 • midnight-5am • mostly gay men • dancing/DJ • live shows

Metro Sepúlveda 185 (Metro Universitat) **34/93.323.52.27** • midnight-5am • popular • mostly gay men • dancing/DJ • leather • drag shows • videos • young crowd • T-dance 7pm-10:30pm Sun • also cafe • cover charge

Salvation Ronda San Pere 19–21 (at Plaza Urquinaona) **34/93.318.06.86** • midnight-close Wed-Sat • mostly gay men • dancing/DJ • drag shows • strippers • videos • food served • young crowd • cover charge

Tatu Cai Celi 7 (Metro Plaza d'Espanya) **34/93.425.33.50** • 10pm-4am, from 7pm Sun • mostly gay men • dancing/DJ • transgender-friendly • drag shows • patio • cover charge

Cafes

Alternativ Villarroel 71 **34/658.86.50.60** • 8pm-2:30am Tue-Sat, 6pm-midnight Sun • alternative late-night cafe w/ electronic music

G Café Muntaner 24 (Metro Universitat) **34/93.451.65.36** • 8:30am-10pm, 10am-2am Fri-Sun • lesbians/ gay men • funky decor • cafe by day • bar by night

Restaurants

Café Miranda Casanova 30 (btwn Gran Vía & Sepúlveda, Metro Gran Vía) **34/93.453.52.49** • 9pm-1am • popular • lesbians/ gay men • int'l/ Mediterranean • full bar • campy decor • drag shows

Castro Casanova 85 (Metro Urgell) **34/93.323.67.84** • 1pm-4pm & 9pm-11:30pm, clsd Sun • mostly gay men • Mediterranean • full bar • leather • live shows • 1.200-3.000 ptas

Comme-Bio Gran Via Corts Catalanes 603 **34/93.301.03.76** • vegetarian

Cosmopolita Muntaner 6 **34/93.453.00.75** • lunch Mon-Fri, dinner Tue-Sun • int'l • 1.190-3.500 ptas

La Diva Diputació 172 (Metro Universitat) **34/93.454.63.98** • lunch & dinner, clsd Mon • lesbians/ gay men • transgender-friendly • creative Mediterranean • fabulous drag cabaret • 1.275-3.000 ptas

Eterna Casanova 42 (Metro Universitat) **34/93.453.17.86** • lunch & dinner • lesbians/ gay men • nightly shows • 975+ ptas

Little Italy Rec 30 (nr Plaza del Born) **34/93.319.79.73** • 1:30pm-4pm & 9pm-midnight

La Mossegada Diputació 214 **34/93.454.72.75** • 8pm-1am • lesbians/ gay men • live shows

Sal i Pebre Diputacio 214 **34/93.454.72.75** • 9am-midnight, clsd Sun • tapas • sandwiches • 950 ptas

La Singular Calle Francisco Giner 50 **34/93.237.50.98** • 1pm-midnight, till 1:30am Fri-Sat, clsd Wed • mostly women • Spanish/ tapas • women-owned/ run

La Veronica Avinyo 30 **34/93.412.11.22** • lunch & dinner, clsd Mon-Tue • pizza • terrace • 1.200 ptas

Bookstores

Antinous Josep Anselm Clavé 6 (btwn Las Ramblas & Ample, Metro Drassanes) **34/93.301.90.70** • 10:30am-2pm & 4:30pm-9pm • lgbt • books • gifts • also cafe • wheelchair access

Cómplices Cervantes 2 (at Avinyó, Metro Liceu) **34/93.412.72.83** • 10:30am-8:30pm, from noon Sat, clsd Sun • lgbt • Spanish & English titles

Retail Shops

Ovlas Portaferrissa 25, Tienda 34 (in Galerias Grand Hall) **34/93.412.12.52** • clothing • also restaurant • Italian • DJ & shows Sat

Publications

Info Gai **34/93.318.16.66** • free bi-monthly newspaper in Catalan

Spiritual Groups

EXODE **34/93.301.31.37** • Christian lesbian & gay men's group

Gay Christians of Catalunya PO Box 854, 08080 **34/93.398.16.84, 34/93.301.31.37**

Erotica

Condonería Plaza Sant Josep Oriol 7 (Metro Liceu) **34/93.302.77.21** • clsd Sun

Erotic Museum of Barcelona Ramblas 3 **34/93.318.98.65** • 10am-midnight

Zeus Gay Shop Riera Alta 20 (Metro Sant Antoni) **34/93.442.97.95** • clsd Sun • ask for 'MENsual' gay map

Madrid • Spain

Madrid

INFO LINES & SERVICES

COGAM (Colectivo de Lesbianas y Gays de Madrid) Fuencarral 37 (Metro Tribunal) 34/91.522.45.17 • lgbt center • groups • library • also cafe-bar

Feministas Lesbianas de Madrid Barquillo 44 34/91.319.36.89 • lesbian-feminist group

Fundación Triangulo Eloy Gonzalo 25 34/91.593.05.40

Gai Inform 34/91.523.00.70 • 5pm-9pm • helpline

ACCOMMODATIONS

Gay Hostal Puerta del Sol Plaza Puerta del Sol 14, 4° (at Calle de Alcalá, Metro Sol) 34/91.522.51.26 • mostly gay men • centrally located • gay-owned/run • 4.000-6.000 ptas

Hostal Hispano Hortaleza 38, 3° izq (at Perez Galdos, Metro Chueca) 34/91.531.48.71 • mostly gay men • 4.200-5.500 ptas

Hostal Oporto Calle Zorilla 9, 1st flr (Metro Sol) 34/91.429.78.56 • gay-friendly • 10-min walk to gay scene • some shared baths • 3.000-5.500 ptas

Hostal Sonsoles Fuencarral 18, 2° dcha (Metro Chueca) 34/91.532.75.23, 34/91.532.75.22 • mostly gay men

Hotel A Gaudí Gran Vía 9 (at Alcalá) 34/91.531.22.22 • 4-star hotel • 21.900+ ptas

Mónaco Hotel Residencia Barbieri 5 34/91.522.46.30 • gay-friendly

Suecia Hotel Marqués de Casa Riera 4 34/91.531.69.00, 800/448-8355 • gay-friendly

The Westin Palace Plaza de Las Cortes, 7 34/91.360.77.77, 800/325-3589 • gay-friendly • grand hotel w/ prices to match

BARS

A Diario Zurita 39 (Metro Lavapiés) 34/91.530.27.80 • 7:30pm-close • lesbians/ gay men • DJ wknds

Ambient San Mateo 21 (Metro Tribunal) • 9pm-3am, clsd Mon • mostly women • neighborhood bar • pizza served • info board

La Bohemia Plaza de Chueca 10 (Metro Chueca) • 8pm-close, from 9pm wknds • mostly women • neighborhood cafe-bar

El Candil Hernán Cortés 21 (Metro Chueca) 34/91.522.71.48 • 8pm-2am • gay/ straight • transgender-friendly • drag shows Fri-Sat

Chueca's Friends Plaza de Chueca 9 • mostly women • seasonal terrace

---

Madrid

LGBT PRIDE: June.

ANNUAL EVENTS: October/ November - International Gay & Lesbian Film Festival, web: www.fundaciontriangulo.es.

CITY INFO: 34/91.541.23.25. Information Turistica 34/91.366.54.77.

ATTRACTIONS: Museo del Prado 34/91.420.28.36.
Museo Thyssen-Bornemisza 34/91.369.01.51.
Queen Sofía Nat'l Art Center (home of Picasso's 'Guernica') 34/91.467.50.62.
Royal Palace 34/91.542.00.59.

BEST VIEW: From the funicular in the Parque des Atracciones.

WEATHER: Winter temps average in the 40°s (and maybe even a little snow!). Summer days in Madrid are hot, with highs well into the 80°s.

TRANSIT: Metro 34/91.552.59.09.

Spain • EUROPE

[Reply] [Forward] [Delete]

Date: Wed, Jan 9, 2002 11:27:21
From: Girl-on-the-Go
To: Editor@Damron.com
Subject: Madrid

> The sprawling capital of Spain, Madrid is both grandiose and intimate, more gifted in spirit and street life than in tourist spots. Of course, even if museums aren't your thing, you shouldn't miss Picasso's *Guernica* in the Sophia Reina Museum, or Hieronymus Bosch's phantasmagoric paintings in the Prado museum. And definitely poke your head into one of the 'Museo del Jamon' sandwich shops festooned with hanging hamhocks—it's a truly Madrileño experience.

> But the quintessential Madrileño activity—some would argue the quintessential Spanish activity—is *la marcha*, the full night of barhopping that most Spaniards apparently engage in many nights a week. What is not clear, is which—*la marcha* or the three-hour lunchtime siesta—came first, but now they are inextricably intertwined.

> After a modest dinner around 10pm—or perhaps just some *cañas* (half-bottles of beer) and *tapas* (hearty snackfood you're guaranteed with almost any alcohol purchase after 6pm)—it's off to another bar several blocks away for another single drink...then a 10 to 15-minute brisk walk to yet another bar for another single drink.

> The combination of friendly company, mild alcohol, plentiful snacks, and exercise is what keeps the evening going until at least 2 or 3am. Don't be surprised to find yourself in the middle of a crowded street or plaza at 4 or 5 in the morning!

> Generally the cafe-bars serving snacks close around midnight, and then it's on to a bar—which won't have wine, but may have *calamocho*, a *marcha*-fueling drink of wine mixed with cola. After 3am you'll have to find a nightclub, which may charge a cover, at least on Fridays and Saturdays, but the cover usually includes a drink ticket.

> The lesbo stronghold of the city is Embajadores, southeast of the Center. Here you'll find the gay-friendly film house and the mixed artsy gay bar **La Lupe** (in honor of the performer-icon of the same name, sort of a Latina version of Judy Garland). Not far is the lesbian dance bar **Medea,** which packs 'em in on Thursdays with free entrance.

> You'll also find plenty of sisters in the gay barrio of Chueca. After browsing the shelves at the LGBT **Berkana Bookstore,** visit the girls at **La Bohemia, Chueca's Friends,** or **Olivia 51.** Or get your groove on at **Truco.** For more nightlife ideas, pick up a copy of the free paper **Shangay Express.** Whatever you do, don't forget to take your siesta!

Madrid • Spain

The Fame Pérez Galdós 1 (at Fuencarral, Metro Chueca) **34/91.532.12.86** • 5pm-2am, till 3am Sat • lesbians/ gay men • transgender-friendly • dancing/DJ • live shows wknds • food served • young crowd

Freedom Infantas 12 (Metro Gran Vía) **34/91.523.45.38** • 10:30pm-3:30am, clsd Mon • lesbians/ gay men • DJs wknds

Lucas San Lucas 11 (Metro Chueca) • 8:30pm-3:30am • lesbians/ gay men • dancing/DJ • drag shows • young crowd

La Lupe Torrecilla del Leal 12 (Metro Antón Martín) **34/91.527.50.19** • 5pm-2am, till 3:30am Fri-Sat, from 1pm Sun • popular • lesbians/ gay men • neighborhood bar • bohemian crowd • live shows • also cafe

Medea Cabeza 33 (Metro Antón Martín) • 11pm-7am, till 10am Fri-Sat • popular wknds • women only • men welcome as guests • dancing/DJ • young crowd • cover charge

El Mojito Olmo 6 (Metro Antón Martin) **34/91.539.46.17** • 9pm-2:30am, till 3:30am Fri-Sat • lesbians/ gay men • cocktail bar

El Moskito Torrecilla del Leal 13 (Metro Antón Martín) • 8pm-3am • lesbians/ gay men • dancing/DJ

Olivia 51 San Bartolomé 6 (btwn Figueroa & San Marcos) • 8pm-close Wed-Sat • mostly women • dance bar • live shows • food served

Priscilla San Bartolomé 12 (Metro Gran Vía) • 10pm-6am, till 8am Fri-Sat • gay/ straight • trendy dance bar

Ras Barbieri 7 (btwn San Marcos & Infantas, Metro Chueca) **34/91.522.43.17** • 10pm-4am, clsd Sun • popular • gay/ straight • 'Arabian Nights' theme • live shows • young crowd

Regine's Terraza Paseo de la Castellana 56 (nr Plaza Emilo Castelar) **34/91.559.28.75** • 9pm-close • lesbians/ gay men • terrace bar • young crowd

Sutileza Plaza de Chueca 6 • lesbians/ gay men • seasonal terrace

Truco Gravina 10 (at Plaza de Chueca) **34/91.532.89.21** • 8pm-close, from 9pm Fri-Sat • popular • mostly women • dance bar • great parties • seasonal terrace

Why Not? San Bartolomé 7 (Metro Gran Vía) **34/91.523.05.81** • 10pm-6am, till 8am Fri-Sat • popular • mostly gay men • fun dance bar • cover charge

Nightclubs

Coppelia Plaza de los Mostenses 11 (at Gran Vía) • midnight-6am Fri-Sat • lesbians/ gay men • dancing/DJ • Internet lounge • video game room • cover charge

Escape Gravina 13 (at Plaza de Chueca) • 11pm-4:30am Th & 1am-7am Fri-Sat • lesbians/ gay men • dancing/DJ • drag shows

Goa After Club Mesoneros Romanos 13 (at 'Flamingo Club,' Metro Callao) **34/91.531.48.27** • 6am-close wknds • also 'Cream' (popular) midnight Th • gay/ straight • dancing/DJ • cover charge

Griffin's Villalar 8 (Metro Banco) **34/91.576.07.25** • midnight-5am • mostly gay men • dancing/DJ • live shows • theme nights

Heaven Veneras 2 (at Plaza Santo Domingo, Metro Callao) **34/91.548.20.22** • midnight-6am, from 8pm wknds • mostly gay men • transgender-friendly • 3 flrs • dancing/DJ • live shows • videos • young crowd • cover charge

Ohm Plaza del Callao 4 (at 'Bash,' Metro Callao) • midnight-close Fri-Sat • popular • mostly gay men • dancing/DJ

Pasapoga Gran Vía 37 (Metro Callao) **34/91.547.57.11** • Fri-Sat only • mostly gay men • dancing/DJ

Rick's Clavel 8 (at Infantas, Metro Gran Vía, ring to enter) **34/91.531.91.86** • 11pm-5am • mostly gay men • dancing/DJ • young crowd • trendy

The Room Arlabán 7 (Metro Sevilla) • 1am-6am Fri-Sat • gay/ straight • dancing/DJ • live shows

Sachas Plaza de Chueca 1 (Metro Chueca) • 8pm-5am Th-Sun, bar open 8pm-3am nightly • lesbians/ gay men • dancing/DJ • drag shows

Shangay Tea Dance Gran Vía 37 (at Sala Pasapoga, Metro Gran Vía) **34/91.531.48.27** • 9pm-2am Sun • popular • lesbians/ gay men • dancing/DJ • live shows • young crowd • cover charge

Tábata Vergara 12 (next to Teatro Real, Metro Opera) **34/91.547.97.35** • 10:30pm-late Wed-Sat • lesbians/ gay men • dancing/DJ • young crowd • cover charge

Week-end Plaza del Callao 4 (at 'Bash,' Metro Callao) • midnight-6am Sun • popular • lesbians/ gay men • dancing/DJ • alternative

Cafes

Cafe Acuarela Gravina 10 (Metro Chueca) **34/91.532.87.35, 34/91.570.69.07** • 3pm-2am, till 4am Fri-Sat • lesbians/ gay men • bohemian cafe-bar • cocktails

Spain • EUROPE

Café la Troje Pelayo 26 (at Figueroa, Metro Chueca) • 4pm-2am, till 3am Wed • lesbians/ gay men • full bar

Ciber Espacio Cafe Pelayo 42 (Metro Chueca) 34/91.308.14.62 • noon-2am • Internet cafe • also bar

Color Augusto Figueroa 11 (Metro Chueca) 34/91.522.48.20 • brkfst, lunch & dinner • mostly gay men • tapas • desserts • full bar

Corazón Negro Colmenares 5 • full bar

El Jardin Infantas 9 34/91.523.12.18 • lesbians/gay men

Mama Inés Hortaleza 22 (Metro Chueca) 34/91.523.23.33 • 9am-2am, 10am-3am Fri-Sat • sandwiches • pies

La Sastrería Hortaleza 74 (at Gravina, Metro Chueca) 34/91.532.07.71 • 10am-2am, till 3am Fri-Sat, from 11am wknds • lesbians/gay men • trendy cafe-bar

Star's Marqués de Valdeiglesias 5 (at Infantas, Metro Banco) 34/91.522.27.12 • 9am-2am, till 4am Th-Fri, 8pm-4am Sat, clsd Sun • mostly gay men • cafe-bar • dancing/DJ Th-Sat • 1.400-1.900 ptas

Urania's Cafe Fuencarral 37 (at COGAM ctr, Metro Tribunal) 34/91.522.45.17 • 5pm-midnight, till 1am Fri-Sat • lesbians/gay men • cafe-bar

RESTAURANTS

El 26 de Libertad Libertad 26 34/91.522.25.22 • lunch & dinner, clsd Sun • also bar • 1.200-2.500 ptas

A Brasileira Pelayo 49 (Metro Chueca) 34/91.308.36.25 • lunch & dinner • Brazilian • US$15

Abaco Jovellanos 6 34/91.420.11.64 • dinner Mon-Sat, clsd Sun • elegant • 2.000+ ptas

Al Natural Zorrilla 11 (Metro Sevilla) 34/91.369.47.09 • lunch & dinner • vegetarian • 1.350+ ptas

El Armario San Bartolomé 7 (btwn Figueroa & San Marcos, Metro Chueca) 34/91.532.83.77 • lunch & dinner • lesbians/ gay men • Mediterranean • 1.250-2.700 ptas

Artemisa Ventura de la Vega 4 (at Zorrilla) 34/91.429.50.92 • lesbians/gay men • vegetarian • also Tres Cruces 4 location, 34/91.521.87.21

Café del Mercado Fuencarral 49 34/91.531.68.77 • popular • full bar • terrace

Café Miranda Barquillo 29 (downstairs) 34/91.521.29.46 • 9pm-close • lesbians/gay men • kitschy decor • drag shows

Cañeiro Fernán González 4 34/91.575.51.87 • lesbians/gay men • Galician

Casa Santa Cruz Bolsa 12 34/91.521.86.23 • Spanish • $40

Casa Vallejo San Lorenzo 9 34/91.308.61.58 • creative homestyle • 1.800-2.800 ptas

El Castro de San Francisco Hernán Cortés 19 (Metro Chueca) 34/91.531.27.40, 34/63.628.52.32 • 11am-1:30am, clsd Sun • lesbians/gay men • upscale cafe-bar & restaurant

Chez Pomme Pelayo 4 (Metro Chueca) 34/91.532.16.46 • 1:30pm-4pm & 9pm-midnight • int'l/ vegetarian • 975+ ptas

El Convento Canario Valverde 6 (downstairs) 34/91.532.01.88 • noon-4pm & 8pm-midnight, till 1am Fri-Sat • Canarian cuisine

Cornucopia Flora 1 (at Plaza Descalzas Reales, Metro Opera) 34/91.547.64.65 • 1:30pm-4pm Tue-Fri & 8:30pm-midnight Tue-Sun, clsd Mon • lesbians/gay men • European/American • knock to enter

La Dame Noire Pérez Galdós 3 (Metro Gran Vía) 34/91.531.04.76 • 9pm-2am, clsd Mon • creative French • 2.300 ptas

Divina La Cocina Colmenares 13 (at San Marcos, Metro Chueca) 34/91.531.37.65 • 1:30pm-4pm Mon-Sat & 9pm-close Tue-Sat • lesbians/gay men • elegant & trendy • 1.500-3.000 ptas

La Dolce Vita Cardenal Cisneros 58 (Metro Quevedo) 34/91.445.04.36 • 1:30pm-4pm & 9pm-midnight • Italian • full bar

Ecocentro Esquilache 4 (at Pablo Iglesias, Metro Rios Rosas) 34/91.553.55.02 • open till midnight • natural foods • also shop • herbalist • school

Los Girasoles Hortaleza 106 34/91.308.44.94 • clsd Sun • creative Spanish • tapas • 1.300+ ptas

Gula Gula Infante 5 34/91.420.29.19 • lunch & dinner, clsd Mon • popular • lesbians/gay men • buffet/ salad bar • full bar • live shows • 1.500-2.000 ptas • also Gran Vía 1 location, 34/91.522.87.64

Hudson Hortaleza 37 (Metro Gran Vía) 34/91.532.33.46 • 11:30am-3am, clsd Mon • mostly gay men • American • pizza • also bar

Lombok Augusto Figueroa 32 34/91.531.35.66 • lunch & dinner • int'l • 1.500 ptas

Mexico 1800 Estrella 5 34/91.523.14.35

El Modelo Cansado Vergara 7 (Metro Ópera) 34/91.547.14.18 • 1pm-5pm & 8pm-1am • 1.100-3.300 ptas

Momo Augusto Figueroa 41 (Metro Chueca) **34/91.532.71.62** • 1pm-4pm & 9pm-midnight • creative vegetarian • smokefree! • 1.200-1.700 ptas

Restaurante Rochí Pelayo 19 **34/91.521.83.10** • lunch & dinner • Spanish

El Restaurante Vegetariano Marqués de Santa Ana 34 (Metro Noviciado) **34/91.532.09.27** • 1:30pm-4pm & 9pm-11:30pm, clsd Mon • vegetarian • full bar

El Rincón de Pelayo Pelayo 19 (Metro Chueca) **34/91.521.84.07** • lunch & dinner • lesbians/ gay men • 1.100-1.600ptas

Sarrasín Libertad 8 (Metro Chueca) **34/91.532.73.48** • 1pm-4pm & 9pm-midnight, clsd Sun • popular • wheelchair access • 1.275-1.850 ptas

Yerbabuena Barbieri 15 (Metro Chueca) **34/91.521.00.23** • lunch & dinner • Basque • tapas & full menu • 1.200+ ptas

BOOKSTORES

A Different Life Pelayo 30 (Metro Chueca) **34/91.532.96.52** • 11am-2pm & 5pm-10pm, till midnight Sat, clsd Sun • lgbt • books • magazines • music • videos • sex shop downstairs

Berkana Bookstore Gravina 11 (Metro Chueca) **34/91.532.13.93** • 10:30am-2pm & 5pm-8:30pm, noon-2pm & 5:30pm-8pm Sat, clsd Sun • lgbt • Spanish & English titles • ask for free gay map of Madrid • wheelchair access

RETAIL SHOPS

XXX San Marcos 8 (Metro Chueca) **34/91.522.17.70** • clsd Sun • men's underwear • also Barquillo 41 location, 34/91.30.38.60 • women's underwear

PUBLICATIONS

Entiendes? Apdo 18165, 28080 Madrid • bimonthly gay info & culture magazine

Shangay Express 34/91.308.11.03, 34/91.308.66.23 • free biweekly gay paper

Zero 34–91/701.00.89 • stylish & intelligent lgbt monthly (en español)

SPIRITUAL GROUPS

Cohesión Apdo de Correos 51057, 28080 **34/93.955.41.81** • lgbt Christians

EROTICA

California Valverde 20 (at Gran Vía)

Condoms & Co Colón 3

Sitges

ACCOMMODATIONS

Apartments Bonaventura San Buenaventura 7 **34/93.894.97.62** • gay-friendly • studio apts • 6.500-13.500 ptas

Hostal Madison Sant Bartomeu 9 **34/93.894.61.47** • gay-friendly • 4.500-8.500 ptas

Hotel Calípolis Paseo Maritimo **34/93.894.15.00** • gay-friendly • upscale hotel • US$100-150

Hotel Montserrat Espalter 27 **34/93.894.03.00** • popular • gay/ straight

Hotel Renaixença Isla de Cuba 7 **34/93.894.83.75** • gay-friendly • full brkfst • some shared baths

Hotel Romàntic Sant Isidre 33 **34/93.894.83.75** • popular • gay/ straight • 19th-c villa • full brkfst • some shared baths • seasonal • kids/ pets ok • full bar • US$50-100

Madison Bahía Hotel Parellades 31–33 **34/93.894.00.12** • popular • gay-friendly • 5.500-9.500 ptas

Mirador Apartments San Gaudencio 32–34 **34/93.894.24.12** • gay-friendly • studio apts • US$60-110

San Sebastian Playa Port Alegre 53 **34/93.894.86.76** • gay-friendly • swimming • US$70-125

Sitges Holiday Apts Francisco Gum 25, 08870 **34-93/894–1333** • gay-friendly • centrally located 1-brdm apts • nr beach • pets ok • US$230-460/ week

El Xalet Isla de Cuba 35 **34/93.894.55.79** • gay-friendly • food served

BARS

Bourbon's Sant Bonaventura 13 **34/93.894.33.47** • 10:30pm-3:30am (Sat only off-season) • popular • mostly gay men • dancing/DJ • videos • young crowd

El Candil Carreta 9 **34/93.894.73.86** • seasonal • 10pm-3am, till 3:30am Fri-Sat • popular • mostly gay men • dancing/DJ • food served from 7pm • videos • clsd Oct-Jan

The Edge Isla de Cuba 9 **34/93.811.02.57** • 7pm-3am • lesbians/ gay men • dancing/DJ • live shows

Mediterraneo Sant Bonaventura 6 **34/93.894.33.47** • 10pm-3:30am • popular • mostly gay men • dance bar • patio • young crowd

Spain • EUROPE

Parrot's Pub Plaza Industria 2 (at Primero de Mayo) **34/93.894.78.81** • seasonal, 5pm-3am, from 3pm wknds • lesbians/ gay men • seasonal • leather • live shows • patio

Phillip's Port Alegre 10 (at San Sebastian Beach) **34/93.894.97.43** • 10:30am-3am • gay/ straight • food served • terrace • seasonal

Pym's Sant Bonaventura 37 **34/92.971.06.24** • 8pm-3am • lesbians/ gay men • dancing/DJ

Nightclubs

The Organic Club Bonaire 15 **34/93.894.22.30** • 1:30pm-6am • Wed only off-season • mostly gay men • transgender-friendly • dancing/DJ • strippers Wed

Trailer Angel Vidal 36 • midnight-5am • seasonal • popular • mostly gay men • dancing/DJ • young crowd

Restaurants

La Borda San Buenaventura 5 **34/93.811.20.02** • 1pm-4pm & 6pm-midnight

Can Pagès Sant Pere 24–26 **34/93.894.11.95** • 1pm-4pm & 8pm-midnight, clsd Mon • lesbians/ gay men

Casa Hidalgo San Pablo 12 **34/93.894.38.95** • Galician • seafood • wheelchair access • US$30+

Chez Jeanette Sant Pau 23 **/93.894.00.48** • 1pm-4pm & 7pm-11:30pm • clsd Nov-Dec

Flamboyant Pau Barrabeitg 16 **34/93.894.58.11** • 8pm-11:30pm • mostly gay men • int'l • full bar • terrace dining • seasonal

Ma Maison Bonaire 28 **34/93.894.60.54** • 8:30pm-1am, also 1:30pm-3:30pm wknds • popular • lesbians/ gay men • French • full bar • terrace • clsd Nov

Malu Sant Pau 34 **34/93.894.77.13**

Sucré-Salé Sant Pau 39 **34/93.894.23.02** • 1:30pm-3:30pm & 8:30pm-12:30am, clsd Tue • lesbians/ gay men • crepes • salads

El Trull Mossèn Felix Clará 3 (off Major) **34/93.894.47.05** • 7:30pm-close • popular • lesbians/ gay men • French

Sitges

ENTERTAINMENT: Platjes del Mort ("Beach of the Dead") is the gay beach.

ANNUAL EVENTS: February/March - Carnival, web: www.sitges.com/carnival.
July/August - Women's Week 34/93.811.1627.
August - Festa Major.
October - International Film Festival, web: www.sitges.com/cinema.

CITY INFO: 34/93.811.76.30.

ATTRACTIONS: Museu Cau Ferrat 34/93.894.03.64.

TRANSIT: 34/93.490.02.02.

Camping & RV Spots 570

2002 Tours & Tour Operators

Cruises 577
Luxury Tours 577
Great Outdoors Adventures 578
Spiritual/Health Vacations 583
Thematic Tours 584
Custom Tours 586
Various Tour Operators 586

2002 Calendar

Lesbian/Gay Events 587
Women's Festivals & Gatherings 597
Film Festivals 601
Leather & Fetish Events 604
Conferences & Retreats 605
Spiritual Gatherings 606
Breast Cancer Benefits 608
Kids' Stuff 611

Mail Order 612
Updates 616

ALABAMA • USA — Camping & RV Spots

USA

ALABAMA

Geneva

Spring Creek Campground 163 Campground Rd (at Hwy 52 & Country Rd 4) **334/684-3891** • mostly gay men • cabins • also tent & RV sites • swimming • nudity permitted • theme wknds w/ DJ • gay-owned/ run • $15-60

ALASKA

Fairbanks

Billie's Backpackers Hostel 2895 Mack Rd **907/457-2034** • gay-friendly • hostel & campsites • kids ok • food served • women-owned/ run • $18

ARIZONA

Prescott

Edge of the Sky Tipi&B HC 31, Box 398 86303 **520/899-8733** • mostly women • rustic mtn lodge • full brkfst • hot tub • tipi & campsites • lesbian-owned/ run • $10 (camping) • call for lodge pkgs

Surprise

RVing Women Inc PO Box 1960 85378-1960 **888/557-8464 (55R-VING)**, **623/975-2250** • women's RV club

Tucson

Adobeland Campground 12150 W Calle Seneca **520/883-6471** • women only • tents & cabins • lesbian-owned/ run • $3

ARKANSAS

Eureka Springs

Greenwood Hollow Ridge B&B **501/253-5283** • exclusively lgbt • on 5 quiet acres • some shared baths • kitchens • pets ok • RV hookups • wheelchair access • gay-owned • $75

CALIFORNIA

Clear Lake

Edgewater Resort 6420 Soda Bay Rd (at Hohape Rd), Kelseyville **707/279-0208, 800/396-6224** • gay-owned, straight-friendly • cabin • camping & RV hookups • lake access & pool • theme wknds • boat facilities • pets ok • $25-250

Garberville

Giant Redwoods RV & Camp **707/943-3198** • gay-friendly • campsites • RV • located off the Avenue of the Giants on the Eel River • shared baths • kids/ pets ok • $19(tent)-27

Pescadero

Costanoa 2001 Rossi Rd **650/879-1100, 800/738-7477** • gay/ straight • also tent bungalows & cabins • 1 hr south of San Francisco • $70-205

Placerville

Rancho Cicada Retreat 209/245-4841 • mostly gay men • secluded riverside retreat in the Sierra foothills w/2-person tents & cabin • swimming • nudity • gay-owned/ run • $100-200 (lower during week)

Russian River

Faerie Ring Campground 16747 Armstrong Woods Rd, Guerneville **707/869-2746** • gay-friendly • on 14 acres • RV spaces • nr outdoor recreation • pets ok • lesbian-owned/ run • $20-25

Fife's Resort 16467 River Rd (at Brookside Ln), Guerneville **707/869-9500, 800/734-3371** • lesbians/ gay men • cabins • campsites • swimming • also restaurant • some veggie • full bar • gym • wheelchair access • $50-215

Schoolhouse Canyon Park 12600 River Rd (at Oddfellows Park Rd), Guerneville **707/869-2311** • gay-friendly • open May-Sept • campsites • RV • private beach • kids/ pets ok • $25

The Willows 15905 River Rd (at Hwy 116), Guerneville **707/869-2824, 800/953-2828** • lesbians/ gay men • old-fashioned country lodge & campground • smokefree • $79-139

Sacramento

Verona Village River Resort 6985 Garden Hwy, Nicolaus **530/656-1320** • lesbians/ gay men • RV space $15 • trailers for rent • full bar • restaurant • store • marina

Ukiah

Orr Hot Springs 13201 Orr Springs Rd **707/462-6277** • gay-friendly • mineral hot springs • hostel-style cabins, private cottages & campsites • clothing optional • kids ok • guests must bring all own food • $40-168 per person

Camping & RV Spots

COLORADO

Fort Collins

Never Summer Nordic 970/482-9411 • lesbians/ gay men • camping in yurts (Mongolian round houses) • $55-105

Trinidad

High Desert Decadence PO Box 44, Aguilar 81020 **719/680-0418** • lesbians/ gay men • B&B • camping & 2 RV hookups • on 400 acres • hot tub • kids/ pets ok • lesbian-owned/ run • $45-100

FLORIDA

Dade City

Sawmill Camping Resort 352/5830664 • popular • mostly gay men • theme wknds • RV • cabins • tent spots • swimming • nudity • gay-owned/ run

Miami

Something Special 7762 NW 14th Ct (private home) **305/696-8826** • women only • rental apt & tent space • also vegetarian restaurant

West Palm Beach

The Whimsy 561/686-1354 • camping/ RV space & apt • wheelchair access

GEORGIA

Athens

The River's Edge 2311 Pulliam Mill Rd, Dewy Rose **706/213-8081** • mostly gay men • cabins • camping • RV • swimming • nudity • wheelchair access

Dahlonega

Swiftwaters Womanspace 706/864-3229, 888/808-5021 • women only • on river • full brkfst • hot tub • seasonal • dogs ok • women-owned/ run • $40-50 (cabins)/ $10 (camping)

HAWAII

Hawaii (Big Island)

Kalani Oceanside Eco-Resort & Adventures 808/965-7828, **800/800-6886** • gay/ straight • coastal retreat & spa • on 113 acres • full brkfst • swimming • food served • wheelchair access • gay-owned/ run • $60-240 • $20-25 camping

ILLINOIS

Du Quoin

The Pit 7403 Persimmon Rd **618/542-9470** • lesbians/ gay men • primitive camping • 18+ • nudity • swimming • wheelchair access • gay-owned/ run

IOWA

Des Moines

Racoon River Resort 515/279-7312, 515/996-2829 • lesbians/ gay men • rustic lodge • camping & RV • hot tub • nudity • wheelchair access • $15-50

MAINE

Sebago Lake

Bear Mountain Village 207/583-6980 (SUMMER), 207/782-2275 (WINTER) • gay/ straight • on lake • hiking • boat rentals • women's camping area • cabins $50+ • campsites $10-25

Tenants Harbor

Blueberry Cove Camp Harts Neck Road 207/372-6353, 617/876-2897 • gay-friendly • cabins • campsites

MICHIGAN

Houghton Lake

Val Halla Motel & Resort 9869 West Houghton Lake Dr **517/422-5137** • gay/ straight • swimming • campsites & RV hookups • gay-owned/ run • $45-58

Owendale

Windover Resort 3596 Blakely Rd **517/375-2586** • women only • swimming • $25/yr membership • $15-20 camping

Saugatuck

Campit Campground 616/543-4335, 877/226-7481 • lesbians/ gay men • campsites • RV hookups • seasonal • pets ok • gay-owned/ run • $12-40

MINNESOTA

Kenyon

Dancing Winds Farm Retreat 6863 County 12 Blvd **507/789-6606** • gay/ straight • B&B on working dairy farm • tentsites • work exchange available • smokefree • lesbian-owned/ run • $75-95

Mississippi • USA — Camping & RV Spots

MISSISSIPPI

Ovett

Camp Sister Spirit 601/344-1411 • mostly women • 120 acres of camping & RV sites • cabins • lesbian-owned/ run • clean & sober • $10-20 sliding scale

MISSOURI

Ava

Cactus Canyon Campground 16 miles E of Ava on Hwy 14 (N 1 mile on County 223) **417/683-9199** • mostly gay men • camping & RV • hot tub • nudity • kids/ pets ok • gay-owned/ run • $60-75

Noel

Sycamore Landing 417/475-6460, 800/475-6460 • open May-Sept • gay-friendly • campsites & RV hookups • canoe rental • kids/ pets ok • wheelchair access

MONTANA

Ronan

North Crow Ranch 2360 N Crow Rd **406/676-5169** • seasonal • lesbians/ gay men • cabin • tipis • camping • 80 miles south of Glacier Park • hot tub • nudity • seasonal • lesbian-owned/ run • $15-100

NEW HAMPSHIRE

Bath

Hibbard House 603/747-3947, **888/338-3947** • gay/ straight • 1822 inn • full brkfst • some shared baths • hot tub • nudity • smokefree • camping available • $40-130

NEW YORK

Binghamton

Serenity Farms 607/656-4659 • gay/ straight • B&B • camping on 100 secluded acres • full brkfst • swimming • pets ok • gay-owned/ run

Catskill Mtns

Solstice Farm Stable Stanfordville **845/868-1413** • riding school & camp

NORTH CAROLINA

Asheville

▲ **Camp Pleiades** 828/688-9201, **888/324-3110** • open Memorial Day thru mid-October • women-only • mtn retreat • cabins & camping • all meals included • some shared baths • swimming • smokefree • lesbian-owned/ run • $45-88

Compassionate Expressions Mtn Inn 207 Robinson Cove Rd, Leicester **828/683-6633** • mostly women • 'rooms w/ a view' of Blue Ridge Mtns • 2 RV hookups • on 40 acres • women-owned/ run

OHIO

Athens

Susan B Anthony Women's Land Trust PO Box 5853 45701 **740/448-6424** • women only • cabins & camping • summer workshops • swimming • lesbian-owned/ run

Columbus

Summit Lodge Resort & Guesthouse **740/385-3521** • popular • gay-friendly • clothing-optional resort • 45 miles to Columbus • camping available • hot tub • swimming • also restaurant • $50-110

OKLAHOMA

El Reno

The Good Life RV Resort Exit 108 I-40 (1/4 mile S) **405/884-2994, 405/893-2345** • gay-friendly • 32 acres • 100 campsites & 100 RV hookups • pond w/ pedal boats • swimming • kids ok • gay-owned/ run • $10-17 (full hookup)

Lexington

Blue Sky Ranch 14001 Banner **405/872-2583** • mostly women • cabin • camping • 2 RV hookups • swimming • pets ok • wheelchair access • lesbian-owned/ run • $100-125

Oklahoma City

Tommy's Ranch 13700 S Sooner Rd, Edmond **405/216-8669** • gay/ straight • 20 mins from OK City • cabins • full brkfst • camping • swimming • horseback riding • massage therapy • wheelchair access • gay-owned/ run • $50-70

OREGON

Gaston

Art Springs 40789 SW Hummingbird Ln 503/985-9549 • women only • B&B, cabin & camping on 12 acres of women's land • hot tub • smokefree • chem-free • also retreats • lesbian-owned/ run • $15-75

Grants Pass

WomanShare 541/862-2807 • women only • country retreat ctr • cabins • shared kitchen • bathhouse • hot tub • special events • girls/ pets ok • smokefree • lesbian-owned/ run • $15-35 (sliding scale)

Roseburg

Owl Farm 541/679-4655 • women only • women's land open to visitors • campsites available

Tiller

Kalles Family RV Ranch 233 Jackson Creek Rd 541/825-3271 • lesbians/ gay men • campsites • RV hookups • btwn Medford & Roseburg • kids/ pets ok • lesbian-owned/ run • $10 (incl electric)

PENNSYLVANIA

New Milford

Oneida Camp & Lodge 570/465-7011 • mostly gay men • oldest gay-owned/ operated campground dedicated to the lgbt community • swimming • nudity • seasonal

Pittsburgh

Camp Davis 311 Red Brush Rd, Boyers 724/637-2402 • May thru 2nd wknd in Oct • cabins & campsites • lesbians/ gay men • adults 21+ only • call for events • 1 hr from Pittsburgh

SOUTH DAKOTA

Batesland

Wakpamni B&B (on the Pine Ridge Indian Reservation) 605/288-1800 • gay-friendly • unique rooms & tipis • full brkfst • dinner available • hot tub • gift shop • on Indian reservation • $60-100

Rapid City

TW's 702 Box Elder Rd W (I-90 E exit 63), Box Elder 605/923-2153 camping & RV hookups • also bar • volleyball • bbq pit • gay-owned/ run

Salem

Camp America 25495 US 81 605/425-9085 • gay-friendly • 35 miles west of Sioux Falls • camping • RV hookups • kids/ pets ok • lesbian-owned/ run • $12-20

TENNESSEE

Nashville

IDA 904 Vickers Hollow Rd, Dowelltown 615/597-4409 • lesbians/ gay men • rural queer arts community • 1 hr SE of Nashville • camping available May-Sept (no RV hookups) • veggie meals included • kids ok • smokefree • gay-owned/ run • $10+

Rainbow Falls Resort 6251 Marrowbone Lake Rd, Joelton 615/876-9194, 877/545-2433 • lesbians/ gay men • chalets, cabins & campsites • swimming • hot tub • restaurant • private lake • gay-owned/ run • clsd Tue-Wed • $15-150

TEXAS

Groesbeck

Rainbow Ranch Campground Rte 2, Box 165 254/729-5847, 888/875-7596 • lesbians/ gay men • open all year • located on Lake Limestone • campsites & RV hookups • women-owned/ run • $10/ person

Gun Barrel City

Triple 'B' Cottages 903/451-5105 • gay/ straight • 78 miles from Dallas on Cedar Creek Lake • motor homes & travel trailers welcome • kids/ pets ok • gay-owned/ run • $75-145

Rio Grande Valley

La Mirada Country Estates 8901 W Business Hwy 83 (at Tamm Ln), Harlingen 956/428-1966 • gay-friendly • swimming • hot tub • clubhouse • also camping & RV hookups • gay-owned/ run

Texas • USA — Camping & RV Spots

Shelbyville

English Bay Marina on Toledo Bend (1 1/2 mi W of marker 3184) **409/368-2554** • gay/ straight • cafe, motel, cabins & RV hookups • full brkfst • in very remote area overlooking Toledo Bend Lake • kids/ pets ok • wheelchair access • lesbian-owned/ run • $35-50

VERMONT

St Johnsbury

Greenhope Farm B&B 802/533-7772 • mostly women • full brkfst (vegetarian) • horseback-riding, camping, skiing & hiking on 140 private acres • smokefree • kids ok • call for free brochure • lesbian-owned/ run • $65-125

VIRGINIA

Charlottesville

Campout 804/783-6001 • women only • 100-acre rustic campground • smokefree • wheelchair access • women-owned/ run • $10 membership fee

WASHINGTON

Long Beach Peninsula

Anthony's Home Court 1310 Pacific Hwy N, Long Beach **360/642-2802, 888/787-2754** • gay/ straight • cabins & RV hookups • gay-owned/ run • $50-135

The Historic Sou'wester Lodge, Cabins & RV Park Beach Access Rd/ 38th Place, Seaview **360/642-2542** • gay-friendly • inexpensive suites • cabins w/ kitchens • vintage trailers • RV hookups • pets ok • smokefree • $39-129

San Juan Islands

Lopez Farm Cottages & Tent Camping 555 Fisherman Bay Rd, Lopez Island **360/468-3555, 800/440-3556** • gay/ straight • on 30-acre farm • hot tub • smokefree • also camping • $28-150

Seattle

Wild Lily Ranch B&B 360/793-2103 • popular • lesbians/ gay men • cabins on Skykomish River • authentic Sioux tipis • 1 hr from Seattle • hot tub • swimming • camping available • smokefree • gay-owned/ run • $75+

WEST VIRGINIA

Weston

FriendSheep Farm 304/462-7075 • mostly women • secluded farm retreat • cottages • B&B • campsites • smokefree • work/ stay available • horses • women-owned/ run • $75-95

WISCONSIN

La Crosse

Chela's Forest Camping Retreat Gay Mills **608/735-4829** • women only • pets ok • lesbian-owned/ run • $25-60

Norwalk

Daughters of the Earth 18134 Index Ave **608/269-5301** • women only • women's land • camping • retreat space

Wascott

Wilderness Way 715/466-2635 • women only • resort property • cabins • camping • RV sites • swimming • camping $14 • cottages $58-92

CANADA

BRITISH COLUMBIA

Birken

Birkenhead Resort Portage Rd **604/452-3255** • gay-friendly • cabins • campsites • hot tub • swimming • pets ok • also restaurant • lesbian-owned/ run • Can$80-100

Victoria

Rainbow RV 250/514-1002 • RV club for the gay camping enthusiast

ONTARIO

Grand Valley

Rainbow Ridge Hwy 9 (at Trafalgar Rd) **519/928-3262** • lesbians/ gay men • trailers & tents • swimming

Hamilton

The Cedars Tent & Trailer Park 1039 5th Concession W Rd, Waterdown **905/659-3655** • lesbians/ gay men • private campground • swimming • also bar • dancing/DJ • restaurant wknds

Camping & RV Spots

Simcoe

The Point Tent & Trailer Resort 918 Charlotteville Rd #2, RR 1, Vittoria **519/426-7275** • mostly gay men • nudity permitted • swimming • leather • 'tent & trailer resort' on 50 acres • Can$15-50

PROVINCE OF QUÉBEC

Granby

Le Campagnard B&B 146 Denison Ouest J2G 4C8 **450/770-1424** • gay-friendly • in a quiet village • bikes available • also camping • smokefree • Can$45-70

Joliette

L'Oasis des Pins 381 boul Brassard, St-Paul-de-Joliette **450/754-3819** • lesbians/ gay men • swimming • camping April-Sept • restaurant open year-round

SASKATCHEWAN

Ravenscrag

Spring Valley Guest Ranch **306/295-4124** • popular • gay-friendly • 1913 character home • cabin & tipis • full brkfst • kids/ pets ok • also restaurant • country-style • gay-owned/ run • Can$40-60

Regina

Two Spirit PO Box 33084, S4T 7X2 **866/737-2200** • 160-acre ranch • guest rooms, bunkhouse, and tent camping • lesbian-owned • $10-70

CARIBBEAN

VIRGIN ISLANDS

St John

Maho Bay Camps & Harmony Studios VI National Park **340/776-6226, 800/392-9004** • gay-friendly • rustic cottages & studios • environmentally aware resort • $70-195

MEXICO

Puerto Vallarta

Paco Paco Descanso del Sol Hotel Pino Suárez #583, Zona Romantica **52-322/3.02.77, 52-322/2.52.29** • popular • lesbians/ gay men • apts, casitas & tents • swimming • rooftop bar w/ incredible sunset views • gay-owned/ run • US$40-110

Paco's Hidden Paradise 30 mins S of Puerto Vallarta **52-322/3.02.77, 52-322/2.18.99** • lesbians/ gay men • secluded beach resort accessible only by boat • condos & tents • bar • restaurant • gay-owned/ run • $50-85

EUROPE

IRELAND

Cork

Amazonia Coast Rd, Fountainstown, Myrtleville, County Cork **353-21/831115** • women only • beautiful rural location overlooking beach & rocky coastline • private wood cabin • camping

NETHERLANDS

Bourtange

Boerderij 'La Cagnotte' 1e Pallertweg **31-59/935-4274** • lgbt campground • also 2 cabins

SPAIN

Figueres

Hostal Androl y Camping Pous Crta Nacional II A, km 8.5 **34/97.267.54.96** • gay/ straight • hotel & campsites • also bar & restaurant • gay-owned/ run

Mallorca

Valle de la Luna Can Alfonso 2, Puerto Soller **34/97.163.28.21** • women-only • cottages & campsites • swimming • some shared baths • kitchens • 3-day minimum stay • 3.800-6.900 ptas

Queveda

Posada La Fontana Queveda, Cantabria **34/94.289.59.20** • gay/ straight • b&b • campsites • hot tub • kids/ pets ok • also dinner & full bar • wheelchair access • lesbian-owned/ run

Sitges

La Roca Cami cal Antoniet **34/93.894.00.43** • popular • gay-friendly • campsites

Travel TWO for ONE!

Our World Magazine
in print

Get a **FREE 1 year (10 issue) subscription**
for a friend or loved one when you order your own subscription
at the regular low price of **ONLY $35!!!**

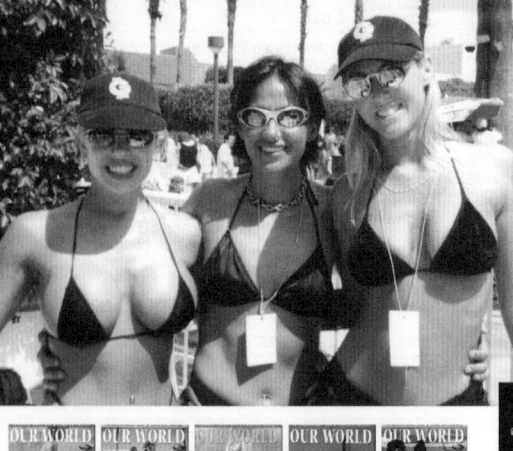

Your window on the world of gay and lesbian travel for over 11 years ...you'll visit the latest hotspots, join adventure seekers touring the globe, sail aboard the world's best cruise ships and charter yachts, and discover accommodations to suit every taste ...with glossy color photography, in-depth unbiased reporting, resource listings and advertising from your favorite travel suppliers.

LOOK for the ALL-NEW
"Our World in a Download"
subscription (the complete magazine downloaded to your computer each month from our website). Starting with the **June '00 Issue**, available **May 20th**. Read at your leisure... no waiting for the mailman... and at *only US$12* for all ten issues *It's a steal!*

www.ourworldmag.com

Phone: (904) 441-5367
Fax: (904) 441-5604

E-mail: subscribe@ourworldmag.com
Website: www.ourworldmag.com

Or write down both U.S. mailing addresses, noting which one is the gift with your personal greeting, and send with your payment to:

**OUR WORLD - TWO For ONE Offer,
1104 North Nova Road, Suite 251,
Daytona Beach, FL 32117**

Offer valid only if both mailing addresses are within U.S.A. First issue mails in 2–6 weeks in plain envelope. Refunds only apply to unshipped issues of a pre-paid subscription. Free subscription does not qualify for refund. Outside USA, single 1 year (10 issue) airmail subscription rates: Canada – US$45; All Others – US$60. 2 for 1 offer not available outside USA

CRUISES

Women Only

▲ **Olivia Cruises** 510/655-0364, 800/631-6277 4400 Market St, Oakland, CA 94608 • exclusive cruise & resort vacations • Bahamas, Caribbean, Alaska, Mexico, Scandinavia & Greece • see ad in front section • **IGLTA** member • *www.olivia.com*

Professional Marine Services 256/574-2137, 256/572-1989, 888/847-6580 PO Box 1628, Scottsboro, AL 35768 • sightseeing & commitment ceremonies on Lake Guntersville & the Tennessee River • *www.mackinac.com/services/ProMarine.html*

Gay/Lesbian

Bounty International 954/760-4730, 888/760-4730 PO Box 21516, Fort Lauderdale, FL 33335 • gay & lesbian yacht charter company • worldwide • *www.bountyintl.com*

Ocean Voyager 212/921-9047, 800/435-2531 1501 Broadway #506, New York City, NY 10036 • hosted gay groups on mainstream upscale cruise ships • **IGLTA** member • *www.oceanvoyager.com*

Port Yacht Charters 516/883-0998, 800/213-0465 9 Belleview Ave, Port Washington, NY 11050 • custom charters worldwide, specializing in the Caribbean • commitment ceremonies • gourmet cuisine • *www.portyachtcharters.com*

Raffles Sailing 954/522-5865, 800/825-3632 PO Box 7500, Fort Lauderdale, FL 33338 • sailing in the Caribbean with gay captain & crew • *www.journeysbysea.com*

Rainbow Charters 808/396-5995, 808/396-5995 939 Kawaiki Pl, Honolulu, HI 96825 • gay & lesbian weddings • custom sailing cruises • whale watching • snorkeling

▲ **RSVP** 612/729-1113, 800/328-7787 2800 University Ave SE, Minneapolis, MN 55414 • cruises & all-gay/ lesbian resorts in the Caribbean, Mexico & Alaska • see ad in front section • **IGLTA** member • *www.rsvp.net*

Sailing Affairs 917/453-6425 PO Box 468, Jersey City, NJ 07303 • sailboat charters, day trips, sunset sails & sailing vacations • based in NY Harbor • **IGLTA** member

Straight/Gay

Amazon Tours & Cruises 305/227-2266, 800/423-2791 275 Fontainebleau Blvd #173, Miami, FL 33172 • weekly cruises, including upper Amazon • **IGLTA** member • *www.amazontours.net*

Whelk Women 941/964-2027 PO Box 1006-D, Boca Grande, FL 33921 • custom boat tours • accommodation arrangements

Whitney Yacht Charters 941/966-9767, 800/223-1426 3214 Casey Key Rd, Nokomis, FL 34275 • yacht charters in the Caribbean, Mediterranean & New England states • **IGLTA** member • *www.whitneyyachtchaters.com*

LUXURY TOURS

Gay/Lesbian

DavidTours 949/723-0699, 888/723-0699 310 Dahlia Pl, Ste A, Corona del Mar, CA 92625-2821 • luxury tours to Europe, South Africa, Morocco, Peru, Tanzania, Kenya, Iceland, India & more • long-weekend getaways • **IGLTA** member • *www.DavidTours.com*

GREAT OUTDOORS ADVENTURES

Women Only

Adventure Associates 206/932-8352, 888/532-8352 PO Box 16304, Seattle, WA 98116 • stateside and int'l outdoor adventures • cruises, treks, safaris & more • call for complete schedule • **IGLTA** member • *www.adventureassociates.net*

Adventures for Women 973/644-3592 15 Victoria Ln, Morristown, NJ 07960 • hiking & kayaking NJ, the Adirondacks & beyond • *www.adventuresforwomen.org*

Adventures in Good Company 651/998-0120, 877/439-4042 5506 Trading Post Tr S, Afton, MN 55001 • outdoor & adventure travel for women of all ages & abilities • call for complete catalog • *www.goodadventure.com*

Alaska Women of the Wilderness Foundation PO Box 773556, Eagle River, AK 99577 • wilderness & spiritual empowerment programs for women & girls • *www.whirlingrainbow.org*

Arctic Ladies 907/783-1954 PO Box 308, Girdwood, AK 99587 • adventure packages in Alaska & Canada, Peru, Egypt, New Zealand & more • *www.arcticladies.com*

Atlantis Yacht Charters 415/332-0800 Schoonmaker Pt Marina, 85 Liberty Ship Way #110-A, Sausalito, CA 94965 • sailing classes for all levels • *www.yachtcharter.com*

Bar H Ranch 208/354-2906, 888/216-6025 PO Box 297, Driggs, ID 83422 • guesthouse & summer horseback trips in Grand Tetons • near Jackson Hole, WY • *www.tetontrailrides.com*

Bushwise Women 64-3/332-4952 PO Box 28010, Christchurch 2, New Zealand • multi-day & multi-sport wilderness & cultural trips in New Zealand, South Pacific & Europe • also a B&B • *www.bushwise.co.nz*

Call of the Wild Wilderness Trips 510/849-9292, 888/378-1978 (OUTSIDE CA) 2519 Cedar St, Berkeley, CA 94708 • hiking, kayaking, backpacking & wilderness trips for all levels in Western US & Mexico • longest-running adventure travel company for women • *www.callwild.com*

Cloud Canyon Backpacking 805/692-9615 PO Box 41359, Santa Barbara, CA 93140-1359 • seasonal wilderness backpacking in Utah & the Sierra Nevadas • *www.cloudcanyon.com*

Earth Island Expeditions 802/425-4710 201 Ten Stones Cir, Charlotte, VT 05445 • wilderness trips for women with a spiritual focus • herbal medicine workshops & retreats • also co-ed trips • *www.earthislandexpeditions.org*

Equinox Wilderness Expeditions 907/274-9087, 877/615-9087 618 W 14th Ave, Anchorage, AK 99501 • wilderness trips in Alaska & the Southwest US by raft, canoe, sea kayak & backpack • *www.equinoxexpeditions.com*

Gaia Adventures 604/875-0066 875 E 31st Ave, Vancouver, BC V5V 2X2, Canada • outdoor adventures for women • hiking, rock climbing & more • ecotourism • *www.gaiaadventures.com*

Grand Canyon Field Institute 520/638-2485 PO Box 399, Grand Canyon, AZ 86023 • women's backpacking classes in the Grand Canyon • also co-ed trips • *www.grandcanyon.org/fieldinstitute*

Herizen Sailing for Women, Inc 250/741-1753 36 Cutlass Lookout, Nanaimo, BC V9R 6R1, Canada • women-only sailing retreats • *www.island.net/~herizen/*

It's Our Nature 727/441-2599, 888/535-7448 929 Bay Esplanade, Clearwater, FL 33767 • kayak & hike the Tampa Bay area of Florida • co-ed trips available • *www.itsournature.com*

LunaTours 406/222-9631, 877/404-6476 200 Mountain Brook Rd, Livingston, MT 59047 • fully supported road bike tours in Montana, Northern California, Hawaii & more • custom fundraising tours • *www.lunatours.com*

Mangrove Mistress 305/745-8886 Murray Marine, 5710 US 1, Key West, FL 33040 • snorkeling • nature exploring • sunset cruises • ceremonies • *www.keywest.com*

Mariah Wilderness Expeditions 510/233-2303, 800/462-7424 PO Box 70248, Point Richmond, CA 94807 • unique vacations for women on roads less traveled • multi-sport adventures • unique cultural & eco-explorations • *www.mariahwe.com*

2002 TOURS — GREAT OUTDOORS ADVENTURES

National Women's Sailing Association 800/566-6972 16731 McGregor Blvd, Fort Myers, FL 33908 • sailing seminars & workshops • *www.sailnet.com/nwsa*

Nurture Through Nature 207/787-2379 RR2 Box 550-F, Naples, ME 04055 • holistic outdoor adventure retreats for women & girls • *nurturethroughnature.tripod.com*

OceanWomyn Kayaking 206/325-3970 620 11th Ave E, Seattle, WA 98102 • guided sea kayaking adventures

Octopus Reef Dive Training & Tours 808/875-0183 Maui, HI • experienced guides teach SCUBA diving in Maui • all levels • *www.OctopusReef.com*

Pacific Yachting & Sailing 831/462-6835 OR 423-7245 790 Mariner Park Way, Santa Cruz, CA 95062 • international & local yachting vacations for lesbians • also sailing instruction • *www.pacificsail.com*

Pangaea Expeditions 406/721-7719, 888/721-7719 PO Box 5753, Missoula, MT 59806 • river rafting in Montana • co-ed trips also available • call for complete calendar • *www.bigsky.net/pangaea*

Prairie Women Adventures & Retreat 316/753-3465 RR 1 Box 24, Matfield Green, KS 66862 • working ranch where guests help out • specialty weekends • call or write for details • *www.guestranches.com/homestead*

Raven Retreat 207/546-2456, 800/841-4586 PO Box 12, Millbridge, ME 04658 • hiking, biking, kayaking & yoga in Maine's coastal mountain wilderness

Sea Sense 860/444-1404, 800/332-1404 PO Box 1961, St Petersburg, FL 33731 • women's sailing & powerboating school • worldwide custom sailing courses • *www.seasenseboating.com*

Sheri Griffith River Expeditions 435/259-8229, 800/332-2439 PO Box 1324, Moab, UT 84532 • women-only river journeys on Colorado & Green Rivers • fitness trips • women writers workshop • *www.griffithexp.com*

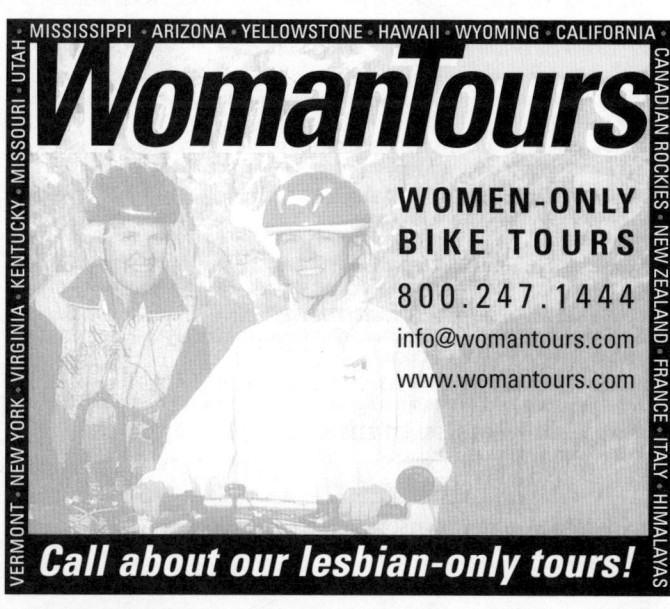

Great Outdoors Adventures — 2002 Tours

Silver Waters Sailing 315/594-1906 PO Box 202, Wolcott, NY 14590 • sailing instruction on Lake Ontario • also day trips • www.silverwaters.com

Sisters of the Earth Adventures, Inc 616/695-1201 1583 E Galien-Buchanan Rd, Buchanan, MI 49107 • backpacking & canoe trips in Michigan

South American Expeditions 818/352-8289, 800/884-7474 9921 Cabanas Ave, Tujunga, CA 91042 • hiking, fishing, camping & more in Peru & South American • co-ed trips available • www.southamericaexp.com

South Sea Mermaid Tours Ltd 64-3/540-3934 PO Box 268, Motueka, New Zealand • tours for spirited women • group discounts • www.southseamermaids.co.nz

Tethys Offshore Sailing for Women 206/789-5118, 877/379-3880 4020 Leary Way NW, #823, Seattle, WA 98107 • join Capt Nancy Erley for a segment in her circumnavigation of the world • www.tethysoffshore.com

Walking Women 44 0/1926 313321 22 Duke St, Leamington Spa, Warwicks CV32 4TR, England • walking holidays in the Lake District, Scotland, Italy & more • some lesbian-only trips • all levels • www.walkingwomen.com/lesbians.htm

WanderWomen 64 9/360 7330 PO Box 68-058, Newton, Auckland, New Zealand • sea kayaking, multi-activity wknds, adventure treks & more • all levels welcome • co-ed trips, too • www.wanderwomen.co.nz

Wild Women Expeditions 705/866-1260, 888/993-1222 PO Box 145, Stn B, Sudbury, ON P3E 4N5, Canada • Canada's outdoor adventure company for women • wilderness canoe trips in Ontario's near-North • x-country skiing & dogsledding in winter • getaways at 200-acre waterfront property • www.wildwomenexp.com

Wild Women Snowboard Camps 212/651-5385, 877/SHE-RIPS 3341 Love Cir, Nashville, TN 37212 • 3-day instructional vacation for women of all levels • www.wildwomencamps.com

Winter Moon Summer Sun 218/848-2442 3388 Petrell, Brimson, MN 55602 • dogsledding trips in winter • kayaking Lake Superior in summer • rustic accommodations with meals provided

▲ **Woman Tours** 208/354-2652, 800/247-1444 PO Box 746, Driggs, ID 83422 • bicycle tours for women • call for complete calendar • www.womantours.com

Womanship 410/267-6661, 800/342-9295 137 Conduit St, Annapolis, MD 21401 • live-aboard learning cruises for women • sail & 'see' adventures offered around the world • www.womanship.com

Women in Motion 760/757-5912, 888/469-6636 PO Box 4533, Oceanside, CA 92052 • active vacations for women, with women, by women • www.gowomen.org

Women in the Wilderness 651/227-2284 566 Ottawa Ave, St Paul, MN 55107 • adventure travel in the Arctic, the Amazon, and beyond • wilderness skills & retreats in Minnesota & Wisconsin

Women On A Roll 310/578-8888 PO Box 5112, Santa Monica, CA 90409-5112 • travel, sporting, cultural & social club for women • wide range of events & trips • www.womenonaroll.com

Women Sail Alaska 907/463-3372, 888/272-4525 245 Irwin St, Juneau, AK 99801 • experience the pristine beauty of southeast Alaska with lesbian guides • groups of 4 or less on a private yacht • www.alaska.net/~sailak

Women's Flyfishing® 907/274-7113 PO Box 243963, Anchorage, AK 99524 • women-only fly-fishing schools & guided trips in different locations around Alaska • www.halcyon.com/wffn/

Women's Wilderness Ways 501/677-2235 PO Box 112, St Paul, AR 72760 • ancient life skills • nature-awareness school

Mostly Women

Earthwise Journeys 503/736-3364 PO Box 16177, Portland, OR 97292 • research & promote responsible travel companies

Kennebec Tidewater Charters 207/737-4695 13 Church St, Richmond, ME 04357 • fly-fishing & light tackle fishing trips on Maine's coast & inland waters • scenic tours • all levels welcome • *www.kennebectidewater.com*

Mountain Trek Fitness Retreat & Health Spa 250/229-5636, 800/661-5161 Box 1352, Ainsworth Hot Springs, BC V0G 1A0, Canada • a vacation for the mind & body • comprehensive health programs • *www.hiking.com*

Venus Charters 305/292-9403 PO Box 4394, Key West, FL 33041 • snorkeling • light tackle fishing • dolphin watching

Gay/Lesbian

Alaska Fantastic Fishing Charters 800/478-7777 PO Box 2807, Homer, AK 99603 • deluxe cabin cruiser for big-game fishing (halibut) • *www.alaskafantasticfishing.com*

Alyson Adventures 617/542-1177, 800/825-9766 PO Box 180179, Boston, MA 02118 • active adventure vacations • **IGLTA** member • *www.alysonadventures.com*

Big Daddy Scuba Tours 808/922-2600, 888/922-3483 Honolulu • diving trips in Hawaii • *www.takemediving.com*

Off The Coast Kayak 508/487-2692, 877/785-2925 Whaler's Wharf, Provincetown • rentals & guided tours for P-town & Truro • *www.offthecoastkayak.com*

OutWest Adventures 406/446-1533, 800/743-0458 PO Box 2050, Red Lodge, MT 59068 • specializing in active outdoor vacations worldwide • **IGLTA** member • *www.outwestadventures.com*

Rainbow Adventures, Inc 808/965-9011 PO Box 983, Pahoa, HI 96778 • intimate group tours for kayaking, camping & snorkeling around ancient, sacred sites • moonlit hikes • also B&B • *alohafun.com*

Undersea Expeditions 858/270-2900, 800/669-0310 PO Box 9455, Pacific Beach, CA 92169 • warm-water diving & scuba trips worldwide • **IGLTA** member • *www.underseax.com*

Straight/Gay

10,000 Waves 406/549-6670, 800/537-8315 PO Box 7924, Missoula, MT 59807 • white-water rafting & kayaking • *www.10000-waves.com*

Adventure Photo Tours 702/889-8687, 888/363-8687 3111 S Valley View Blvd #X-106, Las Vegas, NV 89102 • off-road sightseeing tours • *www.adventurephototours.com*

Ahwahnee Whitewater 209/533-1401, 800/359-9790 PO Box 1161, Columbia, CA 95310 • women-only, co-ed & charter rafting • **IGLTA** member • *www.ahwahnee.com*

Alpenglow Adventure Tours 530/582-5670, 888/325-7456 PO Box 6961, Stateline, NV 89449 • outdoor adventure at Lake Tahoe & the Sierras • small groups • *www.tahoetours.com*

Amphibious Horizons 410/267-8742, 888/458-8786 600 Quiet Waters Park Rd, Annapolis, MD 21403 • lesbian-owned sea kayaking & adventure travel in the Chesapeake Bay Region • all levels • *www.amphibioushorizons.com*

Blue Moon Explorations 360/856-5622 4658 Blank Rd, Sedro-Woolley, WA 98284 • sea kayaking & ski trips in Pacific Northwest & Hawaii • women-only & co-ed trips • *www.home.cio.net/bluemoon*

Bluff Expeditions 435/672-2446, 888/637-2582 PO Box 219, Bluff, UT 84512 • guided back-country archaeological tours by foot, bike, skis, or van • *www.pioneerhouseinn.com*

Fool's Gold Excursions 307/883-3783 PO Box 112, Freedom, WY 83120 • natural history explorations & day hikes in the mountains of Wyoming • lesbian-owned/ run • *www.foolsgoldwyoming.com*

Great Canadian Ecoventures 867/920-7110, 800/667-9453 PO Box 2481, Yellowknife, NT X1A 2P8, Canada • wildlife photography tours • *www.thelon.com*

Greentracks 970/884-6107, 800/9-MONKEY 10 Town Plaza, Ste 231, Durango, CO 81301 • Amazon expeditions • *www.greentracks.com*

GREAT OUTDOORS ADVENTURES — 2002 TOURS

Keane Bush Tours 61 2/9545 4955 PO Box 823, Sutherland, NSW 1499, Australia • unique natural experiences in Sydney's non-tourist locations • also a women-only tour of Aboriginal sacred sites • *www.bushtours.com.au*

Lotus Land Tours 604/684-4922, 800/528-3531 1251 Cardero St, Ste 2005, Vancouver, BC V6G 2H9, Canada • guided 1/2-day sea-kayak adventure & salmon bbq for novices • includes hotel pick-up • *www.lotuslandtours.com*

McKinley Air Service 907/733-1765, 800/564-1765 PO Box 544, Talkeetna, AK 99676 • '2 babes & a bird' • women-owned flight-seeing company at Mt McKinley, AK • *alaska.net/~mckair/*

Mountain Madness 206/937-8389, 800/328-5925 4218 SW Alaska, Ste 206, Seattle, WA 98116 • climbs in US & abroad • *www.mountainmadness.com*

Natural Habitat Adventures 303/449-3711, 800/543-8917 2945 Center Green Ct, Ste H, Boulder, CO 80301 • up-close encounters worldwide with wildlife in their natural habitats • *www.nathab.com*

Open Eye Tours 808/572-3483 PO Box 324, Makawao, HI 96768 • customized land tours of Maui • visit places seldom seen • *www.openeyetours.com*

Outland Adventures 206/932-7012 PO Box 16343, Seattle, WA 98116 • ecologically sensitive cultural tours with snorkeling & biking in Central America, Canada, Alaska & Washington State • *www.outlandadventures.natureavenue.com*

▲ **Paddling South & Saddling South** 707/942-4550, 800/398-6200 PO Box 827, Calistoga, CA 94515 • horseback, mountain biking & sea kayak trips in Baja • call for complete calendar • *www.tourbaja.com*

Passage to Utah 801/519-2400, 800/677-0553 113 South 900 East, Salt Lake City, UT 84102 • custom trips in the West • hiking, horseback riding & river riding • *www.passagetoutah.com*

Planet Explorer 250/656-5181, 877/732-5238 PO Box 8659, Victoria, BC V8W 3S2, Canada • worldwide adventure travel • *www.PlanetExplorer.ca*

PADDLING SOUTH

ADVENTURES IN
BAJA!

✿ Sea Kayak ✿ Sail ✿
✿ Mountain Bike ✿ Hike ✿
✿ Mule Pack ✿

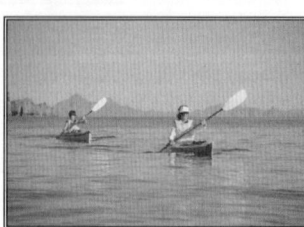

Sea of Cortez & Sierra de la Giganta

- ✿ **All Women & Coed Trips**
- ✿ **All Skill Levels Welcome**
- ✿ **20 Years offering great guided adventures**
- ✿ **800 398-6200**

**U.S. Contact: Paddling South
P.O. Box 827
Calistoga, CA 94515
Email: info@tourbaja.com
www.tourbaja.com**

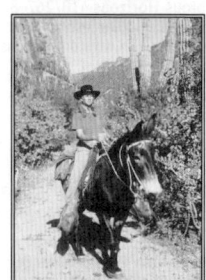

Trudi Angell, owner, on a favorite mule, Josefina

Puffin Family Charters 907/278-3346, 800/978-3346 PO Box 90743, Anchorage, AK 99509 • www.puffincharters.com

Rockwood Adventures 604/926-7705, 888/236-6606 1330 Fulton Ave, West Vancouver, BC V7T 1N8, Canada • rain forest walks for all levels with free hotel pick-up • www.cool.mb.ca/rockwood

Sea Safaris Sailing 800/497-2508 3630 County Line Rd, Lakeland, FL 33811 • sailing from St Petersburg • some women-only charter sail trips & cruises to the Keys

Sila Sojourns 867/633-8453 Box 31258, Whitehorse, YK Y1A 5P7, Canada • wilderness & creative journeys • workshops • custom rafting, sea kayaking & camping trips • www.silasojourns.com

Snow Lion Expeditions 801/355-6555, 800/525-8735 350 South 400 East #G-2, Salt Lake City, UT 84111 • tours, treks & active vacations in the Himalayas, Tibet, SE Asia, China & more • gay and mixed tours available • www.snowlion.com

SNV International 604/683-5101, 800/263-1600 Ste 402, 1045 Howe St, Vancouver, BC V6Z 2A9, Canada • hiking & helicopter-hiking trips in northern & western Canada • www.snvintl.com

Voyager North Outfitters 218/365-3251, 800/848-5530 1829 E Sheridan, Ely, MN 55731 • canoe outfitting & trips • www.vnorth.com

Water Sport People 305/296-4546 1430 Thompson, Key West, FL 33040 • snorkeling, scuba-diving instruction & group charters

West Virginia Whitewater Tours 800/989-7238 PO Box 30, Fayetteville, WV 25840 • rafting in the mtns of WV • day & overnight trips available • members.aol.com/rj927/main.htm

Whitewater Connection 530/622-6446, 800/336-7238 PO Box 270, Coloma, CA 95613 • whitewater rafting adventures • www.whitewaterconnection.com

Wildlife Safari 925/376-5595, 800/221-8118 346 Rheem Blvd #107, Moraga, CA 94556 • photographic safaris • eastern & southern Africa, Egypt, Mauritius & Seychelles Islands • **IGLTA** member • www.wildlife-safari.com

SPIRITUAL/HEALTH VACATIONS

Women Only

Her Wild Song 207/721-9005 PO Box 515, Brunswick, ME 04011 • contemplative wilderness journeys for women • www.herwildsong.org

Sacred Journeys for Women 707/526-7888, 888/779-6696 PO Box 8007, Roseland Station, CA 95407 • mystical adventures in England & Ireland, Crete & Hawaii • www.sacredjourneys.com

Sounds & Furies 604/253-7189, 604/253-7195 PO Box 21510, 1850 Commercial Dr, Vancouver, BC V5N 4A0, Canada • spiritual events for women • www.soundsandfuries.com

Tropical Tune-ups 808/883-3419, 800/587-0405 PO Box 4488, Waikoloa, HI 96738 • women's wellness retreats on the island of Hawaii • www.tropicaltuneups.com

Venus Adventures 207/773-9235 PO Box 7616, Portland, ME 04112 • Goddess tours for women to sacred sites in England & Ireland

Wilderness Rites 415/457-3691 20 Spring Grove Ave, San Rafael, CA 94901 • vision quests for women • www.wildernessrites.com

Mostly Women

Hawk, I'm Your Sister 505/984-2268 PO Box 9109-WT, Santa Fe, NM 87504 • women's wilderness canoe trips & writing retreats in the Americas, Norway & New Zealand • www.womansplace.com

Gay/Lesbian

Spirit Journeys 828/258-8880, 800/490-3684 PO Box 3046, Asheville, NC 28802 • spiritual retreats, workshops & adventure trips • www.spiritjouneys.com

THEMATIC TOURS

Tellardians 705/789-8596 GB, RR 4, Huntsville, ON P1H 2J6, Canada • guided spiritual retreats with rustic camping • into Algonquin Park & beyond

THEMATIC TOURS

Women Only

Canyon Calling 520/282-0916, 800/664-8922 200 Carol Canyon Dr, Sedona, AZ 86336 • enriching, fun-filled vacations in the Tetons, Maine, Southwest canyons, Greece, Hawaii, Switzerland, New Zealand & more for women over 30 • www.canyoncalling.com

Club Skirts 888/5-SKIRTS 584 Castro St #878, San Francisco, CA 94114 • Club Skirts/Girl Bar Dinah Shore Women's Weekend parties • Dinah Shore hotline: 888-44-DINAH • Club Skirts Labor Day in Monterey • Club Skirts Puerto Vallarta Women's Week • Club Skirts Windjammer Caribbean Cruise • www.clubskirts.com

In the Company of Women 407/331-3466 PO Box 522344, Longwood, FL 32752 • affordable gatherings & special getaway events for women • www.companyofwomen.com

International Women's Studies Institute 650/654-6346 PO Box 1067, Palo Alto, CA 94302 • travel-study programs • cross-cultural • school credit available • www.iwsi.org

Robin Tyler Tours 818/893-4075 15842 Chase St, North Hills, CA 91343 • www.robintylertours.com

RVing Women 623/975-2250, 888/557-8464 PO Box 1960, Surprise, AZ 85378 • RV club for women • call for events • www.RVingWomen.com

Tours of Exploration 604/886-7300, 800/690-7887 PO Box 48225, Vancouver, BC V7X 1N8, Canada • eco-cultural journeys to Ecuador for women • www.toursexplore.com

Towanda Women 828/253-4826 (IN US), 64-3/313-2342 (IN NZ) 2 Scott St, Rangiora, New Zealand • women's motorcycle tours in New Zealand • www.towanda.org

Women's Motorcyclist Foundation 716/768-6054 7 Lent Ave, LeRoy, NY 14482 • works to improve the sport of motorcycling • also raises money for breast cancer • www.ponyexpressrides.org

Mostly Women

Lost Coast Llama Caravans 77321 Usal Rd, Whitehorn, CA 95489 • women-led pack trips

Gay/Lesbian

Adventure Tours 207/885-9889, 888/206-6523 PO Box 6538, Scarborough, ME 04070-6538 • custom individual & group packages to Costa Rica, Montreal & Quebec City • **IGLTA** member • www.gayadventuretours.com

African Outing 27-21/671-4028 5 Alcyone Rd, Claremont, Capetown 7700, South Africa • gay/lesbian safaris & more • tours customized to your needs • **IGLTA** member • www.afouting.com

African Safari Dundee 27-11/82-411-4046 31 Ballyclare Drive, Johannesburg, Gauteng 2021, South Africa • customized gay/ lesbian safari trips • www.africasafaridundee.com

Aloha Lambda Weddings 808/922-5176, 800/982-5176 PO Box 159005, Honolulu, HI 96830 • all-inclusive wedding ceremonies in Hawaii • www.global-aloha.com/gayweddings

Arco Iris Gay Mexico Travel Experts 619/297-0897, 800/765-4370 1286 University Ave, #154, San Diego, CA 92103 • gay Mexico experts • www.arcoiristours.com

ATG Transportation 415/587-1053 4192 Mission St #3, San Francisco, CA 95122 • gay-owned van touring company • pre-planned or custom trips in Northern California • www.sfvantours.com

Bali Rainbow Leisure 62-361/757-008 Jl Legian Kaja 486, 80361 Bali, Indonesia • exclusively gay & lesbian tours in Bali • www.bali-rainbow.com

Brazil Fiesta Tours 415/986-1134, 800/200-0582 323 Geary St #701, San Francisco, CA 94102 • tours to Brazil & Central & South America • **IGLTA** member • www.brazilfiesta.com

2002 Tours — Thematic Tours

Cruisin' the Castro 415/550-8110 375 Lexington St, San Francisco, CA 94110 • guided walking tour of the Castro, includes brunch • **IGLTA** member • *www.webcastro.com/castrotour/*

Cyber Travel 30-1/771-4249 86 Evrou, 11527 Athens, Greece • specializing in gay Greece • *gay.gr/gaytourism*

Doin' It Right In Puerto Vallarta 619/297-3642, 800/936-3646 1010 University Ave #C113-741, San Diego, CA 92103 • your gay Puerto Vallarta specialist • **IGLTA** member • *www.DoinItRight.com*

GALA Ecuador 593-9/807-887 Cordero, Quito, Ecuador • discover the natural wonders of Ecuador • hike, scuba dive, bike & more • *www.galasouthamerica.com*

Going Your Way Tours 860/447-1845 OR 447-9180, 800/283-8408 109 Dayton Rd #A, Waterford, CT 06385 • small group tours & custom individual travel worldwide • tours for foodies & wine lovers • *www.goingyourwaytours.com*

Good Time Gay Productions 305/864-9431, 888/429-3527 485 South Shore Dr, Miami Beach, FL 33141 • specializing in gay Florida • custom packages worldwide • **IGLTA** member • *www.goodtimegaytravel.com*

MexGay Vacations 213/413-7884, 866/639-4299 350 N Glendale Blvd, Los Angeles, CA 90026 • specializing in gay travel to Mexico • *www.mexgay.com*

Mistral Tours 33 490/438 690 4 Rue Pissantour, 13150 Boulbon, France • sightseeing, hiking, biking in Provence, France • also French language courses

National Gay Pilots Association 301/941-1066 5530 Wisconsin Ave #1210, Chevy Chase, MD 20815 • several annual gatherings • call for more info • *www.ngpa.org*

Pacific Ocean Holidays 808/923-2400, 800/735-6600 Honolulu, HI • Hawaii vacation packages • **IGLTA** member • *gayhawaii.com/guide*

Pro Musica Tours 800/916-0312 48 Eighth Ave #127, New York, NY 10014 • gay-only or mixed • performing arts/cultural tours • gay-owned/run • *www.promusicatours.com*

Touristic Service Center 34 952/43 70 67 Centro Comercial Churriana, Oficina 2, Crta C-344, 29140 Malaga, Spain • gay/ lesbian dream vacations in Spain • *www.andalusienreisen.com*

Venture Out 415/626-5678, 888/431-6789 575 Pierce St #604, San Francisco, CA 94117 • cultural & soft adventure travel in 8 different countries • *www.venture-out.com*

Victorian Home Walks 415/252-9485 2226 15th St, San Francisco, CA 94114 • historical walking tour of San Francisco's Victorian homes • **IGLTA** member • *www.victorianwalk.com*

Way To Go Costa Rica 919/782-1900, 800/835-1223 2801 Blue Ridge Rd, Raleigh, NC 27607 • personalized itineraries • **IGLTA** member • *www.waytogocostarica.com*

Straight/Gay

Alaska Railroad Scenic Tours 907/265-2494, 800/544-0552 PO Box 107500, Anchorage, AK 99510-7500 • *www.akrr.com*

Asian Pacific Adventures 818/886-5190, 800/825-1680 9010 Reseda Blvd #227, Northridge, CA 91324-5872 • custom tours to Asia, India, Nepal & more • call for complete schedule • *www.asianpacificadventures.com*

Carol Nashe Group 617/437-9757 566 Commonwealth Ave #601, Boston, MA 02215 • golf trips to Ireland • some women-only trips • *www.golfonthego.com*

Earth Walks 505/988-4157 PO Box 8534, Santa Fe, NM 87504 • custom, guided tours of American Southwest & Mexico • *members.aol.com/earthwalks/health.html*

Ecotour Expeditions, Inc 401/423-3377, 800/688-1822 PO Box 128, Jamestown, RI 02835-1822 • small group boat tours of the Amazon & more • call for color catalog • *www.naturetours.com*

Escape Cruises 305/296-4608 Key West Bight Marina, Key West, FL • 3-hr reef trip & sunset cruise on 'SS Sunshine'

THEMATIC TOURS

Heritage Tours 212/206–8400, 800/378–4555 216 W 18th St #1001, New York, NY 10011 • custom trips to Turkey, Spain, South Africa & Morocco • www.heritagetoursonline.com

Holbrook Travel 352/377–7111, 800/451–7111 3540 NW 13th St, Gainesville, FL 32609 • natural history tours in Central America, South America & Africa • small groups • www.holbrooktravel.com

Kenny Tours, Ltd 410/548–2200, 800/648–1492 5530 Abbey Ln, Salisbury, MD 21801-2323 • trips to Ireland & Britain • **IGLTA** member • www.kenny-tours.com

Lima Tours 51-1/424–5110 Belen 1040, Lima 1, Peru • customized, gay-friendly tours to Peru • www.limatours.com.pe

New England Vacation Tours 802/464–2076, 800/742–7669 PO Box 560, West Dover, VT 05356 • gay/lesbian tours (including fall foliage) conducted by a mainstream tour operator • www.sover.net/~nevt

Pacha Tours 800/722–4288 1560 Broadway #316, New York, NY 10036 • trips to Turkey • **IGLTA** member • www.pachatours.com

Ski Connections/ France Vacations 310/337–9956, 800/754–1888 9841 Airport Blvd #1102, Los Angeles, CA 90045 • **IGLTA** member • www.passport2europe.com

Skunk Train California Western 707/459–5248 299 E Commercial St, Willits, CA • scenic train trips in Northern California • www.skunktrain.com

Stockler Expeditions 954/472–7163, 800/591–2955 10266 NW 4th Ct, Plantation, FL 33324 • trips to Bolivia, Brazil, Costa Rica & more

CUSTOM TOURS

Gay/Lesbian

Maxes 2721/782–6979 PO Box 37546, Valyland 7978, Capetown, South Africa • gay travel arrangements in Southern Africa • www.maxes.co.za

VARIOUS TOURS

Women Only

International Association for Women's Accommodation 011–031/331–5497 Polygonstr 5, CH-3014 Bern, Switzerland • organization arranging overnight accommodations for travelling women on the basis of reciprocity • $25 membership

Silke's Travel for Women 61-2/8347–2000 PO Box 1099, Darlinghurst, NSW 2010, Australia • www.silkes.com.au

Gay/Lesbian

All About Destinations 602/331–8943, 800/375–2703 Phoenix, AZ • **IGLTA** member • www.aadintl.com

Footprints 416/962–8111, 888/962–6211 23 College St, Toronto, ON M5G 2B3, Canada • adventures in Vietnam, Thailand, Nepal, Tibet, South America & more • **IGLTA** member • www.footprintstravel.com

Friends of Dorothy Travel 415/864–1600 1177 California St #B, San Francisco, CA 94108 • luxury gay & lesbian adventures • individual & group arrangements • **IGLTA** member • www.fodtravel.com

Out & About Travel 800/842–4753 161 Federal Street, Providence, RI 02903 • tours, cruises, commitment ceremonies & more • www.outandabouttravel.com

Postcard Destinations 814/539–4999, 800/484–3250 **EX** 2621 188 Crystal St, Johnstown, PA 15906 • www.postcarddestinations.com

Events

January 2002

19-26: Aspen Gay Ski Week — *Aspen, CO*
gay/lesbian • 2000+ attendees ☎970/925-9249, 800/367-8290 ✉ c/o Aspen Gay/Lesbian Community Fund, PO Box 3143, Aspen, CO 81612 Email: aspengay@rof.net Web: www.gayskiweek.com

24-27: Women's Ski Camp — *Jackson Hole, WY*
4 days of skiing & parties on the slopes • women only ☎307/739-2663, 800/450-0477 ✉ c/o Women's Ski Camp, PO Box 290, Teton Village, WY 83025 Email: skischool@jacksonhole.com Web: www.jacksonhole.com

February 2002

1-3: Girlz 'n the Snow — *Copper Mountain, CO*
benefit for National Center for Lesbian Rights • women only ☎303/433-9234 Email: girlznsnow@aol.com Web: www.girlznthesnow.com

12: Mardi Gras — *New Orleans, LA*
North America's rowdiest block party • mixed gay/straight ☎504/566-5011, 800/672-6124 ✉ c/o New Orleans Convention & Visitors Bureau, 1520 Sugarbowl Dr, New Orleans, LA 70112 Web: www.neworleanscvb.com

TBA: Whistler Gay Ski Week: Altitude 2002 — *Whistler, BC*
annual gay/lesbian ski week • parties for boys and girls! • popular destination 75 miles N of Vancouver • gay/lesbian ☎604/899-6209, 888/258-4883 ✉ c/o Out On The Slopes Productions, 101-1184 Denman St #190, Vancouver, BC, Canada V6G 2M9 Email: altitude@outontheslopes.com Web: www.outontheslopes.com

March 2002

on-going: Women on Top Theatre Festival — *Boston, MA*
ground-breaking theater from local female artists • takes place during Women's History Month • mostly women • $16-35 ☎781/643-6916 Email: ccarr-kelly@undergroundrailwaytheater.org Web: www.undergroundrailwaytheater.org

3-10: Winterfest — *Lake Tahoe, NV*
nightly entertainment, performers & skiing at 4 world-class ski resorts • 1000 attendees ☎877/777-4950 ✉ c/o Nevada Gay/Lesbian Visitor & Convention Bureau, PO Box 2215, Carson City, NV 89702 Email: nglvcb@aol.com Web: www.LakeTahoeWinterfest.com

25-31: Nabisco Golf Championship — *Palm Springs, CA*
see Club Skirts under Tour Operators for party & accomodation info • mostly women ☎760/324-4546 ✉ c/o Nabisco Championship, 2 Racquet Club Dr, Rancho Mirage, CA 92270 Email: borsont@nabisco.com Web: www.nabiscochampionship.com

28-31: Dinah Shore Women's Weekend — *Palm Springs, CA*
huge gathering of lesbians for mega dance parties, huge pool parties, comedy, national recording artists & yes, some golf watching • women only ☎888/44-DINAH ✉ c/o Club Skirts & Girl Bar, 584 Castro St, San Francisco, CA 94114 Email: info@clubskirts.com Web: www.clubskirts.com

31: Desert AIDS Walk — *Palm Springs, CA*
benefits Desert AIDS Project • gay/lesbian ☎760/325-4402 ✉ c/o Desert AIDS Project, PO Box 2890, Palm Springs, CA 92263 Email: kkatz@desertaidsproject.org Web: www.desertaidsproject.org

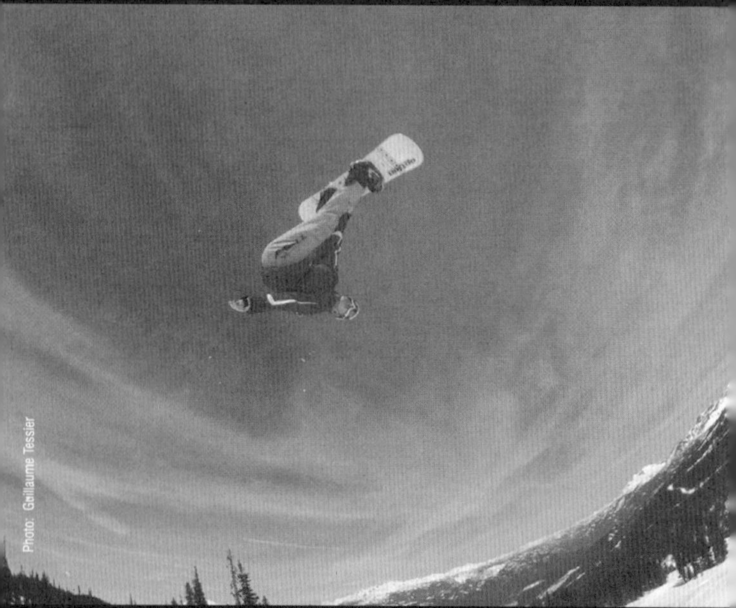

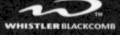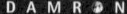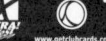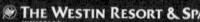

2002 Calendar — Events

April 2002

5-7: Rainbow Ski Weekend — *Mammoth Mountain, CA*
3 days of fun on the slopes in Northern California • complete packages available • book early • gay/lesbian ☎619/435-0996 ✉ c/o Rainbow Ski Weekend, PO Box 182170, Coronado, CA 92178-2170 EMAIL: Leftie69@aol.com WEB: www.rainbowski.com

13: Boybutante Ball — *Athens, GA*
gay/lesbian • 1000+ attendees ☎706/227-3543 ✉ c/o Boybutante AIDS Foundation, Inc, PO Box 6013, Athens, GA 30604-6013 EMAIL: missthing@boybutante.org WEB: www.boybutante.org

25-28: Philadelphia Black Gay Pride — *Philadelphia, PA*
a weekend of social & cultural activities • films, BBQ, spoken word, parties & more • gay/lesbian ☎215/496-0330 ✉ c/o Philadelphia Black Pride, Inc, 1201 Chestnut St, 5th Fl, Philadelphia, PA 19107 EMAIL: colours@coloursinc.com WEB: www.phillyblackpride.com

29-May 5: PrideFest America — *Philadelphia, PA*
national conference on lesbian & gay culture • film, performances, literature, sports, seminars, parties & more • gay/lesbian ☎215/732-3378, 800/990-3378 ✉ c/o Pridefest America, 200 S Broad St #600, Philadelphia, PA 19102 EMAIL: info@pridefestamerica.com WEB: www.pridefestamerica.com

30: Queensday — *Amsterdam, Netherlands*
huge street festival to celebrate what was originally the birthday of the Queen Mother • gay/lesbian

TBA: Russian River Women's Wknd — *Guerneville, CA*
this tiny town is packed with dykes for a fun weekend of parties • 2 hrs north of San Francisco • mostly women ☎707/869-3533, 800/253-8800

May 2002

1-4: We're Funny That Way — *Toronto, ON*
comedians from around the world perform at Canada's International Gay/Lesbian Comedy Festival • gay/lesbian ☎416/699-1974 ✉ c/o WFTW Productions, 2060 Queen St E #45, Toronto, ON, Canada M4E 1C9 EMAIL: funnythat@aol.com WEB: members.aol.com/werefunny

13: Art for AIDS/ Art for Change — *Pittsburgh, PA*
huge party benefitting AIDS charities • gay/lesbian ☎412/441-9786 ✉ c/o Persad Center, 5150 Penn Ave, Pittsburgh, PA 15224

20: Minnesota AIDS Walk — *Minneapolis, MN*
enjoy a walk through Minnehaha Park & raise money for local AIDS organizations • mixed gay/straight • 12,000 attendees ☎ 612/373-2411 ✉ Gus Presents, 1459 18th St PMB#141, San Francisco, CA 94107 EMAIL: development1@mnaidsproject.org WEB: www.mnaidsproject.org

24: Gay/ Lesbian Night at Great America — *Santa Clara, CA*
join 10,000 men & women for a special night at Northern California's favorite amusement park • live performances • dancing till 3am ☎ 415/646-0890 ✉ Gus Presents, 1459 18th St PMB#141, San Francisco, CA 94107 EMAIL: gus@guspresents.com WEB: www.guspresents.com

23-26: Annual Tournament of the Int'l Gay Bowling Organization — *Fort Lauderdale, FL*
✉ c/o IGBO, PO Box 312, Westerville, OH 43086 EMAIL: igbo2001@aol.com WEB: www.igbo.org

23-27: Pensacola Memorial Day Weekend — *Pensacola, FL*
many parties on beaches & in bars • gay/lesbian • 35,000+ attendees ☎850/438-0333 EMAIL: DeltaDyke1@aol.com

24-June 9: Spoleto Festival — *Charleston, SC*
one of the continent's premier avant-garde cultural festivals • mixed gay/straight ☎843/722-2764 ✉ c/o Spoleto Festival USA, PO Box 157, Charleston, SC 29402-0157 WEB: www.spoletousa.org

EVENTS — 2002 CALENDAR

25-27: **Club Curve Women's Weekend** — *Pensacola, FL*
☎800/998-5565, 415/863-6538 EMAIL: curvemag@aol.com WEB: www.curvemag.com

Memorial Day Wknd: **Black Lesbian/ Gay Pride Weekend** — *Washington, DC*
gay/lesbian ☎202/667-8188 ✉ c/o BLGPD, PO Box 77071, Washington, DC 20013 EMAIL: dcblkpride@aol.com WEB: www.dcblackpride.org

30-June 15: **SNAP! Fest** — *Omaha, NE*
local theater festival • mixed gay/straight ☎402/342-9053 ✉ c/o SNAP! Productions, PO Box 8464, Omaha, NE 68105 EMAIL: info@snapproductions.com WEB: www.snapproductions.com

TBA: **AIDS Walk New York** — *New York City, NY*
AIDS benefit • mixed gay/straight ☎212/807-9255 ✉ c/o Gay Men's Health Crisis, PO Box 10, Old Chelsea Stn, New York, NY 10113-0010 EMAIL: info@gmhc.org WEB: www.gmhc.org

TBA: **AIDS Walk St Louis** — *St Louis, MO*
☎314/367-7273 ✉ c/o AIDS Foundation of St Louis, 5615 Pershing Ave #11, St Louis, MO 63112 EMAIL: aidstl@earthlink.net WEB: www.aidstl.org

TBA: **Splash: Houston Black Gay Pride** — *Houston, TX*
gay/lesbian ☎713/237-9431 ✉ c/o Houston Splash, PO Box 35431, Houston, TX EMAIL: info@houstonsplash.com WEB: www.houstonsplash.com

TBA: **Wigswood** — *Atlanta, GA*
annual festival of peace, love & wigs • street party fundraiser • wig watchers welcome • 1000+ attendees ☎404/874-6782 ✉ c/o Act Up Atlanta, 828 W Peachtree St NW, Ste 206-A, Atlanta, GA 30308-1146 EMAIL: actupatl@mindspring.com

June 2002

on-going: **LGBT Pride** — *Everywhere, USA*
celebrate yourself & attend one – or many – of the hundreds of Gay Pride parades & festivities happening in cities around the continent EMAIL: info@interpride.org WEB: www.interpride.org

on-going: **Music in the Mountains** — *Nevada City, CA*
summer music festival • mixed gay/straight ☎530/265-6124, 800/218-2188 ✉ c/o Music in the Mountains, PO Box 1451, Nevada City, CA 95959 EMAIL: mim@musicinthemountains.org WEB: www.musicinthemountains.org

June thru July: **National Queer Arts Festival** — *San Francisco, CA*
performances & exhibitions in the San Francisco Bay Area highlighting artists from around the country • gay/lesbian ☎415/552-7709, 415/552-7200 ✉ c/o National Queer Arts Festival, PMB 451, 584 Castro St, San Francisco, CA 94114 EMAIL: nqaf@aol.com WEB: www.QueerCulturalCenter.org

1-3: **Gay Days Orlando** — *Orlando, FL*
including Gay Day at Disney & Islands of Adventure • 4 days of parties & fun for boys & girls alike! • gay/lesbian ☎407/896-8431 ✉ c/o GayDays, Inc, 1011 Virginia Dr #101, Orlando, FL 32803 EMAIL: info@gaydays.com WEB: gaydays.com

2: **AIDS Walk & 5K Run Boston** — *Boston, MA*
mixed gay/straight • 12,000 attendees ☎617/424-WALK ✉ c/o AIDS Action Committee, 131 Clarendon St, Boston, MA 02116 EMAIL: walkinfo@aac.org WEB: www.aidswalkboston.org

2-8: **California AIDS Ride 9** — *San Francisco, CA*
AIDS benefit bike ride from San Francisco to LA • mixed gay/straight ☎800/825-1000 ✉ c/o Pallotta TeamWorks, 2709 Media Center Drive, Building 1, Los Angeles, CA 90065 EMAIL: info@bethepeople.com WEB: www.bethepeople.com

7-9: **PrideFest** — *Milwaukee, WI*
celebrate lgbt pride at Henry W Maier Festival Park • gay/lesbian ☎414/645-3378 ✉ c/o PrideFest, PO Box 511763, Milwaukee, WI 53203-0301 EMAIL: pridemilw@aol.com WEB: www.pridefestmilwaukee.com

13-16: **Washington DC AIDS Ride** — *Washington, DC*
AIDS benefit bike ride from North Carolina to Washington, DC • mixed gay/straight
☎800/825-1000 ✉ c/o Pallotta TeamWorks, 2709 Media Center Drive, Building 1, Los Angeles, CA 90065 EMAIL: info@bethepeople.com WEB: www.bethepeople.com

14-16: **Black Lesbian/ Gay Pride** — *Oakland, CA*
celebrate with a weekend of conferences, awards ceremonies & parties • gay/lesbian
☎510/268-0646 ✉ c/o People in Pride, 484 Lakepark Ave #1, Oakland, CA 94610 WEB: www.bglt.org

20: **Pearl Day at Six Flags** — *Atlanta, GA*
unofficial gay celebration at Six Flags amusement park • show your support with a string of Commemorative Pearls • proceeds go to local charities • gay/lesbian
☎404/885-6800 EXT 232, 404/872-3975 EMAIL: info@pearlday.com WEB: www.pearlday.com

22: **San Francisco Dyke March** — *San Francisco, CA*
join thousands of dykes of all shapes, colors & sizes for music, marching & more through the streets of the Mission & the Castro ☎415/241-8882 EMAIL: grafix@sirius.com WEB: www.fireworx.org/dykemarch.html

22-23: **San Francisco LGBT Pride Parade/ Celebration** — *San Francisco, CA*
gay/lesbian ☎415/864-3733 ✉ c/o SFLGBTPCC, 1390 Market St #903, San Francisco, CA 94102 EMAIL: sfpride@aol.com WEB: www.sfpride.org

27-July 1: **Gay Pride Week** — *Mexico City, Mexico*
5 days of parties & more • gay/lesbian ☎619/297-6419, 800/765-4370 EMAIL: arcoiris7@aol.com WEB: www.mexcity.8m.com

28-July 4: **At the Beach Weekend** — *Los Angeles, CA*
celebrate a weekend of Black gay pride in Malibu • gay/lesbian ☎323/293-4282 ✉ c/o ATB, 3765 Motor Ave #126, Los Angeles, CA 90034 EMAIL: atbla@aol.com WEB: www.atbla.com

28-July 4: **Independence 2002:**
Celebrate the African-American Lesbigaytrans Community — *Chicago, IL*
a weekend of parties, seminars & more • gay/lesbian ☎773/731-8665 ✉ c/o Chicago Black Pride, Inc, 7836 S Kingston Ave, Chicago, IL 60649 EMAIL: chicagobp@aol.com WEB: www.chicagoblackpride.org

TBA: **Baltimore Black Gay Pride** — *Baltimore, MD*
gay/lesbian

TBA: **Black Gay Pride** — *Memphis, TN*
gay/lesbian ☎901/521-6922 WEB: www.chocolatecityusa.com/hotspots/events.htm

TBA: **Gay Day at Six Flags** — *Jackson, NJ*
unofficial Gay Day at this popular amusement park • wear red to show your support • gay/lesbian

TBA: **Juneteenth Jamboree of New Plays** — *Louisville, KY*
annual theater festival • new works about the African-American experience • many with gay themes • mixed gay/straight ☎502/636-4200 ✉ c/o Juneteenth Legacy Theatre, 316 W Main St, Louisville, KY 40202 EMAIL: juneteenthfest@aol.com

TBA: **Tampa Jamz** — *Tampa, FL*
celebrate African-American gay pride in sunny Tampa • gay/lesbian
WEB: www.clikque.com

TBA: **Unofficial Gay Day at Cedar Point** — *Sandusky, OH*
wear red to show your support on the unofficial Gay Day at this popular amusement park • mixed gay/straight EMAIL: info@lgcsc.org

July 2002

3-7: **Country Western Dance Annual Convention** — *Norfolk, VA*
check website for other events during the year • gay/lesbian • 500-600 attendees
☎954/463-4563 ✉ c/o IAGLCWDC, 5534 Edmondson Pike, PMB 107, Nashville, TN 37211 EMAIL: info@iaglcwdc.org WEB: www.iaglcwdc.org

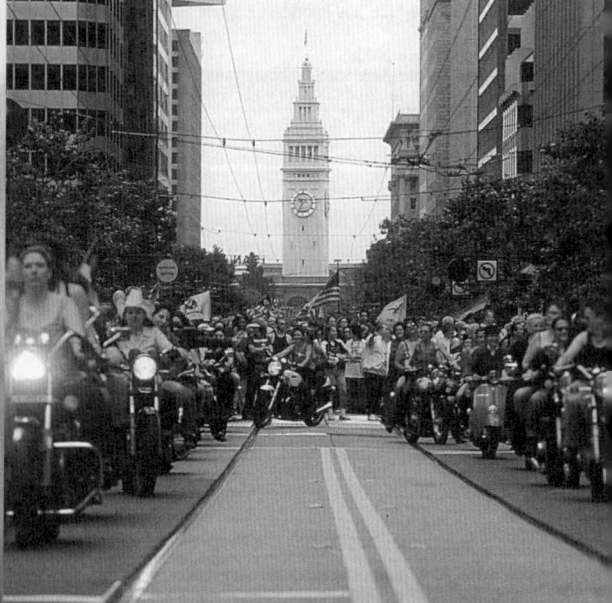

2002 CALENDAR — EVENTS

22-27: Heartland AIDS Ride *Minneapolis, MN*
bike from Minneapolis to Chicago • proceeds donated to AIDS charities • mixed gay/straight ☎800/825-1000 ✉ c/o Pallotta TeamWorks, 2709 Media Center Drive, Building 1, Los Angeles, CA 90065 EMAIL: info@bethepeople.com WEB: www.bethepeople.com

27: Girl Party *San Diego, CA*
mostly women • 1000 attendees • $25-35 ☎619/220-2137 ✉ c/o Powerhouse Productions, 7140 Engineer Rd, San Diego, CA 92111 EMAIL: info@powerhouse-productions.com WEB: www.powerhouse-productions.com

TBA: AIDS Walk San Francisco *San Francisco, CA*
mixed gay/straight • 27,000+ attendees ☎415/392-9255 ✉ c/o Miller Zeichik & Assoc, PO Box 193920, San Francisco, CA 94119-3920 EMAIL: aidswalksf@yahoo.com WEB: www.aidswalk.net

TBA: Crape Myrtle Festival *Raleigh-Durham, Chapel Hill, NC*
weeklong festival to raise money for AIDS & lgbt concerns • movies • tournaments • raffle • gala Saturday • mixed gay/straight • 1500 attendees ☎919/832-2103 ✉ c/o Crape Myrtle Festival, Inc, PO Box 10043, Raleigh, NC 27605 EMAIL: crapemyrtleorg@hotmail.com WEB: www.crapemyrtlefest.org

TBA: EuroPride 2002 *TBA*
parties, politics, performance & more • there is something for everyone at this massive celebration of gay pride • gay/lesbian EMAIL: info@pride.at WEB: www.interpride.org

TBA: Hotter Than July Weekend *Detroit, MI*
celebrate African-American gay pride in the Motor City • gay/lesbian ✉ c/o Hotter Than July, PO Box 3025, Detroit, MI 48231

August 2002

3-4: Minnesota AIDS Trek *St Paul, MN*
annual 150-mile bike ride to fight AIDS • mixed gay/straight ☎651/917-3504 ✉ 499 Lynhurst Ave W, St Paul, MN 55104 EMAIL: info@aids-trek.org WEB: www.aids-trek.org

16-18: Aspen Summerfest *Aspen, CO*
comedy • BBQ • music • hiking, softball & more • gay/lesbian • 350+ attendees ☎970/925-9249, 970/925-4123 ✉ c/o Aspen Gay/Lesbian Community Fund, PO Box 3143, Aspen, CO 81612 EMAIL: aspengay@rof.net WEB: www.gayskiweek.com

19-25: Camp Camp *Kezar Falls, ME*
summer camp for lgbt adults • sports, pottery, theater, yoga & more • $825 ☎888/924-8380 ✉ c/o Camp Camp, 91 Jamaica St, Boston, MA 02130 EMAIL: info@campcamp.com WEB: www.campcamp.com

28-Sept 1: Pallotta TeamWorks AIDS Vaccine Ride *Montréal, QC*
ride from Montréal to Maine to raise money for the AIDS vaccine • mixed gay/straight ☎800/825-1000 ✉ c/o Pallotta TeamWorks, 2709 Media Center Drive, Building 1, Los Angeles, CA 90065 EMAIL: info@bethepeople.com WEB: www.bethepeople.com

31-Sept 1: Festival of Babes *San Francisco, CA*
annual soccer tournament for women 'in comfortable shoes' • women only ☎510/428-1489, 510/848-4684 EMAIL: fobsoccer@email.com WEB: members.xoom.com/fobsoccer

TBA: Black Gay Pride *New York City, NY*
gay/lesbian ☎212/613-0097 ✉ c/o Black Pride NYC Inc, PO BOX 20399, London Terrace Station, New York City, NY 10011-0004 EMAIL: blackpridenyc@hotmail.com WEB: www.blackpridenyc.com

TBA: Black Gay Pride *Cleveland, OH*
gay/lesbian WEB: www.chocolatecityusa.com/hotspots/events.htm

TBA: Black Gay Pride *Minneapolis/St Paul, MN*
gay/lesbian WEB: www.chocolatecityusa.com/hotspots/events.htm

EVENTS — 2002 CALENDAR

TBA: Black Out 2001 — *Cleveland, OH*
Ohio's oldest & largest event celebrating African American gay/lesbian culture • gay/lesbian ☎216/462-0257, 888/825-5226 ✉ c/o Black Out, PO Box 14553, Cleveland, OH 44114 EMAIL: shakaspr94@aol.com WEB: www.chocolatecityusa.com/hotspots/events.htm

TBA: Black Pride — *Jacksonville, FL*
celebrate African American gay/lesbian culture • gay/lesbian ✉ 440 Brody Cove Tr, Jacksonville, FL EMAIL: cldima@aol.com

TBA: Brooklyn Black Pride — *Brooklyn, NY*
gay/lesbian ☎718/346-3589 ✉ c/o Brooklyn NY Pride, 780 Dumont Ave, Brooklyn, NY 11207 EMAIL: umeno07@aol.com

TBA: National Gay Softball World Series — *Portland, OR*
gay/lesbian ☎412/362-1247 ✉ c/o NAGAAA, 1014 King Ave, Pittsburgh, PA 15206 EMAIL: ndyke@bigfoot.com WEB: www.nagaaa.com

TBA: Northalsted Market Days — *Chicago, IL*
a good ol' summer block party on Main St of Boys' Town, USA • gay/lesbian ☎773/883-0500 ✉ c/o Chicago Area Gay & Lesbian Chamber of Commerce, 3713 North Halsted, Chicago, IL 61613

TBA: Rendezvous 2002 — *Cheyenne, WY*
5-day camping festival to celebrate gay pride • gay/lesbian • 400+ attendees ☎307/778-7645 ✉ c/o United Gay/Lesbians of Wyoming, PO Box 6837, Cheyenne, WY 82001 EMAIL: info@uglw.org WEB: www.uglw.org

September 2002

1: Wigstock — *New York City, NY*
outrageous wig/drag/performance festival on Pier 54 in the West Village • gay/lesbian ☎212/439-5139 ✉ c/o DBK Events, 20 W 20th St, 2nd fl, New York City, NY 10011 EMAIL: dbkevents@hotmail.com WEB: www.wigstock.nu

1-3: In the Life Weekend — *Atlanta, GA*
celebrate Black Pride over Labor Day weekend in Atlanta • gay/lesbian ☎404/872-6410 ✉ c/o In The Life, 828 W Peachtree St #207, Atlanta, GA 30308 EMAIL: inthelife@mindspring.com WEB: www.inthelifeatl.com

6-8: Club Skirts Monterey Bay Women's Wknd — *Monterey, CA*
3 huge dance parties • pool party with live girl bands • live comedy night • book early! • mostly women ☎888/5-SKIRTS ✉ c/o Club Skirts, 584 Castro St, San Francisco, CA 94114 EMAIL: info@clubskirts.com WEB: www.clubskirts.com

14: New York to the Hamptons Challenge — *Long Island, NY*
100-mile bike ride to benefit local AIDS organizations • gay/lesbian ☎631/479-0010 ✉ c/o LINCS, PO Box 4169, Huntington Stn, NY 11743 EMAIL: info@bikechallenge.com WEB: www.BikeChallenge.com

15: Gay/Lesbian Day at Waterworld — *Concord, CA*
20 acres of wet'n'wild waterslide fun • all-park exclusive • lots of soaking wet boys & girls! • music & dancing ☎415/646-0890 ✉ c/o Gus Presents, 1459 18th St PMB#141, San Francisco, CA 94107 EMAIL: gus@guspresents.com WEB: www.guspresents.com

22-29: European Gay Summer Week — *Otranto, Italy*
6 days at Club Med • sailing, golf, cycling & more • disco & evening entertainment • gay/lesbian ☎44-0207/701-7040 ✉ c/o Alternative Holidays Ltd, PO Box 16393, London, UK, United Kingdom SE1 4NU EMAIL: info@alternative-holidays.com WEB: www.alternative-holidays.com

TBA: AIDS Walk Denver — *Denver, CO*
☎303/837-0166 ✉ c/o Colorado AIDS Project, PO Box 18529, Denver, CO 80218-0529 EMAIL: cap@coloaids.org WEB: www.capwalk.org

TBA: AIDS Walk Seattle — *Seattle, WA*
mixed gay/straight • 7000+ attendees ☎206/329-6923 ✉ c/o Lifelong AIDS Alliance, 127 Broadway E #200, Seattle, WA 98102 EMAIL: webmaster@lifelongaidsalliance.org WEB: www.lifelongaidsalliance.org

TBA: **AIDS Walk Toronto** — Toronto, ON
walk in Toronto & cities across Canada to raise money to fight AIDS • gay/lesbian ☎416/340-2437 ✉ c/o **AIDS Committee of Toronto**, 399 Church St, Toronto, ON, Canada M5B 2J6 EMAIL: ask@actoronto.org WEB: www.actoronto.org

TBA: **Gay Day at Paramount Kings Island** — Cincinnati, OH
gay/lesbian ☎513/591-0200 ✉ c/o **Gay & Lesbian Community Center**, 4119 Hamilton Ave, Cincinnati, OH 45223 EMAIL: mail@glbtcentercincinnati.com WEB: www.glbtcentercincinnati.com

TBA: **Gay Night at Magic Mountain** — Los Angeles, CA
gay/lesbian ☎805/222-7788 ✉ c/o **Odyssey Adventures**, PO Box 221477, Newhall, CA 91322 EMAIL: odsyadv@pacbell.net WEB: www.odysseyadventures.com

TBA: **Great Alberta Campout** — Red Deer, AB
3 days of friendly camping fun • meet & greet Friday • pancake breakfast Saturday • games, dances, more • presented by Gay & Lesbian Assoc of Central Alberta • gay/lesbian ☎403/309-7733 ✉ c/o **GALACA**, Box 1078, Red Deer, AB, Canada T4N 6S5 EMAIL: glcce@compusmart.ab.ca

TBA: **Ladyfest East** — New York City, NY
event produced by and for women, to showcase & encourage the creative work of women • performance, readings, visual arts, bands & more! • dance parties • mixed gay/straight • $30-55 ☎360/252-2086 EMAIL: info@ladyfesteast.org WEB: www.ladyfesteast.org

TBA: **Northeast AIDS Ride** — Boston, MA
AIDS benefit bike ride from Boston to New York • mixed gay/straight ☎800/825-1000 ✉ c/o **Pallotta TeamWorks**, 2709 Media Center Drive, Building 1, Los Angeles, CA 90065 EMAIL: info@bethepeople.com WEB: www.bethepeople.com

TBA: **Russian River Women's Wknd** — Guerneville, CA
this tiny town is packed with dykes for a fun weekend of parties • 2 hrs north of San Francisco • mostly women ☎707/869-3533, 800/253-8800

TBA: **Wild Women's Weekend** — Clearlake, CA
parties • BBQ • tournaments • not for the mild mannered! • women only • $25+ • camping/RV ☎707/279-0208, 800/396-6224 ✉ c/o **Edgewater Resort**, 6420 Soda Bay Rd, Kelseyville, CA 95451 WEB: www.edgewaterresort.net

October 2002

on-going: **October is Breast Cancer Awareness Month** — Cross-country, USA
check local listings for fund-raising events in your area to fight breast cancer

5-7: **Black Lesbian/ Gay Pride** — San Francisco, CA
celebrate with a weekend of conferences, awards ceremonies & parties • gay/lesbian ☎510/268-0646 ✉ c/o **People in Pride**, 484 Lakepark Ave #1, Oakland, CA 94610 WEB: www.bglt.org

6: **Castro Street Fair** — San Francisco, CA
arts & community groups street fair • co-founded by Harvey Milk ☎415/467-3354

11: **National Coming Out Day** — Everytown, USA
check local listings for events in your area ☎202/628-4160, 800/866-6263 ✉ c/o **National Coming Out Project**, 919 18th St, #800, Washington, DC 20006 EMAIL: ncop@hrc.org WEB: www.hrc.org

13: **AIDS Walk** — Long Island, NY
gay/lesbian ☎631/385-2451 ✉ c/o **LIAAC**, PO Box 2859, Huntington Stn, NY 11746 EMAIL: info@aidswalkli.org WEB: www.AIDSwalkLongIsland.org

14-20: **Provincetown Women's Week** — Provincetown, MA
very popular – make your reservations early! • mostly women ✉ c/o **Women Innkeepers of Provincetown**, PO Box 573, Provincetown, MA 02657 EMAIL: wip@provincetown.com WEB: www.womeninnkeepers.com

Events — 2002 Calendar

19-26: Puerto Vallarta Vacation for Women — *Puerto Vallarta, Mexico*
weeklong vacation at a beautiful, private resort • entertainment, optional excursions, all food & drink included • women only ☎888/575-4787 ✉ c/o Club Skirts, 584 Castro St, San Francisco, CA 94114 EMAIL: info@clubskirts.com WEB: www.clubskirts.com

20: AIDS Walk Philly — *Philadelphia, PA*
gay/lesbian ☎215/731-9255 ✉ c/o AIDSFUND, 1227 Locust St, Philadelphia, PA EMAIL: aidsfund@aidsfundphilly.org WEB: www.aidsfundphilly.org

25-Nov 9: Gay Games 2002 — *Sydney, Australia*
2 weeks of sports, cultural events, conferences & workshops in Sydney • gay/lesbian ☎61-2/9235-7000 EMAIL: admin@sydney2002.org.au WEB: www.sydney2002.org.au

26-Nov 2: Annual Black Lesbian/ Gay Cruise — *departs from San Juan*
sail to St Thomas, Tortola, Dominica, Martinique, Barbados & St Kitts • gay/lesbian ☎415/922-2916, 888/922-2916 EMAIL: bgc@songmaster1.com WEB: www.songmaster1.com

TBA: AIDS Walk Atlanta — *Atlanta, GA*
mixed gay/straight • 10,000+ attendees ☎404/870-7700 ✉ c/o MZA Events, Inc, 1438 W Peachtree St NW #100, Atlanta, GA 30309 EMAIL: aidswalkat@mzainc.com WEB: www.aidswalk.net

TBA: AIDS Walk LA — *Los Angeles, CA*
annual AIDS fundraiser at Paramount Pictures • mixed gay/straight ☎213/201-9255 ✉ c/o AIDS Walk LA, 3550 Wilshire Blvd #890, Los Angeles, CA 90010 EMAIL: aidswalkLA@aol.com WEB: www.aidswalk.net

TBA: Black Gay Pride — *Dallas, TX*
gay/lesbian ☎972/283-1047 ✉ c/o Underground Station, PO Box 224571, Dallas, TX 75222 WEB: www.chocolatecityusa.com/hotspots/events.htm

TBA: Pink Ball Classic — *Dallas, TX*
fundraising golf tournament • mostly women ☎214/521-5342 x 886 x 4 ✉ c/o DSGA, PO Box 190869, Dallas, TX 75219 EMAIL: DSGADallas@yahoo.com

November 2002

24-30: Club Skirts Windjammer Caribbean Cruise — *departs from Grenada*
cruise the Spice Islands on a 200-ft-tallship • island tours, snorkeling, celestial navigation • join us for an adventure! • mostly women ☎888/5-SKIRTS ✉ c/o Club Skirts, 584 Castro St, San Francisco, CA 94114 EMAIL: info@clubskirts.com WEB: www.clubskirts.com

TBA: Divas in the Desert: Black Gay Pride Weekend — *Phoenix, AZ*
mostly men ✉ c/o FinWill Productions, 5713 W Zoe Ella Wy, Glendale, AZ 85306

December 2002

27-Dec 2: White Party Week — *Miami, FL*
six days of festivities capped by the annual 'White Party at Vizcaya' • benefitting Care Resource • gay/lesbian • $100+ ☎305/667-9296 ✉ c/o CARE Resource, 1320 S Dixie Hwy, #485, Coral Gables, FL 33146 EMAIL: caidsdevel@aol.com WEB: www.whiteparty.net

31: Mummer's Strut — *Philadelphia, PA*
big New Year's Eve party • followed by New Year's Day Parade • mixed gay/straight • $40-50 ☎215/732-3378 EMAIL: parade@mummers.com WEB: mummers.com

TBA: Holly Folly — *Provincetown, MA*
gay & lesbian holiday celebration • fabulous parties • holiday concert • open houses ☎888/887-8696 WEB: www.hollyfolly.com

June 2004

TBA: 2004 Nora Games — *Montréal, QC*
first annual North American games for gays & lesbians • gay/lesbian ☎514/528-5581

Women's Festivals & Gatherings

March 2002

18-April 1: Southern Womyn's Festival — *on the St Mary's River, southeast GA*
join womyn of the Southeast for music, camping, comedy, workshops & more! • women only • 1000 attendees ☎904/**259-1456** ⌨ c/o SWF, c/o Docuspace, PO Box 262, Macclenny, FL 32063 EMAIL: gaywomyn@aol.com WEB: www.gaywomyn.org/festival

29-31: Gulf Coast Womyn's Festival at Camp SisterSpirit — *Ovett, MS*
a celebration of womyn's land in the South! • 2 1/2 hours from New Orleans, LA • entertainment & politics • camping available • mostly women ☎601/**344-1411** ⌨ c/o Camp SisterSpirit, PO Box 12, Ovett, MS 39464 EMAIL: sisterspir@aol.com

TBA: Texas Lesbian Conference — *Austin, TX*
workshops, lectures, films & more • host city rotates between Dallas, Austin, Houston & San Antonio • women only ☎214/**521-5342 x468** EMAIL: TLCSanAntonio@aol.com WEB: hometown.aol.com/tlcsanantonio/myhomepage/

April 2002

5-7: Friends Fest Music Festival — *Dripping Springs, TX*
women only • also in Sept, open to all ☎512/**894-0567** ⌨ c/o Recreation Plantation Campground, 3650 Pursley Rd, Dripping Springs, TX 78620
WEB: www.womensfestival.com/friendsfest/

TBA: Herland Spring Retreat — *Oklahoma City, OK*
music, workshops, campfire events & potluck • boys under 10 only • $15-60 sliding scale registration • mostly women ☎405/**521-9696** ⌨ c/o Herland, 2312 NW 39th, Oklahoma City, OK 73112 EMAIL: herland@mailroom.com WEB: www.herlandsisters.org

TBA: Women's Week St Croix — *St Croix, VI*
relax at the beautiful Cormorant Beach Club • women only ☎800/**998-5565**, 415/**863-6538** EMAIL: advertising@curvemag.com WEB: www.curvemag.com

May 2002

13-20: Midwest Wimmin's Festival — *Lake of the Ozarks State Park, MO*
enjoy fun & sun at the Lake • women only ☎573/**443-6935** ⌨ c/o Missouri Ozark Lesbian Community, 1009 Coats St, Columbia, MO 65201
EMAIL: midwestwimmin@hotmail.com WEB: www.angelfire.com/mo2/MidwestWimmin

24-26: Wiminfest — *Albuquerque, NM*
music, comedy, art, recreation & dances • mostly women ☎800/**499-5688**, 505/**899-3627** ⌨ c/o Women in Movement in New Mexico (WIMINM), PO Box 80204, Albuquerque, NM 87198 EMAIL: wiminfest@hotmail.com WEB: www.wiminfest.org

Memorial Weekend: Women Outdoors National Gathering — *Peterborough, NH*
camping • hiking • workshops • women only • 110+ attendees • $120-220
☎860/**563-3522** ⌨ c/o Women Outdoors, Inc, 55 Talbot Ave, Medford, MA 02155
EMAIL: info@women-outdoors.org WEB: www.women-outdoors.org

31-June 2: Hopland Women's Festival — *Hopland, CA*
women only ☎707/**523-9593 VOICE MAIL** ⌨ c/o HWF, 4381 25th St, San Francisco, CA 94114 EMAIL: hopland@aol.com WEB: www.hoplandwomensfestival.com

TBA: Desert Hearts Women's Festival — *Bandera, TX*
weekend of music, camping, games & more on a private ranch • women only • $75 ☎830/**796-7446** ⌨ 10101 Hwy 173 N, Bandera, TX 78003 EMAIL: cowgirlj@aol.com WEB: members.aol.com/cowgirlj/

Women's Festivals & Gatherings — 2002 Calendar

June 2002

6-9: Womongathering — *Pocono Mtns, PA*
women's spirituality fest • women only • 300+ attendees • $265 ☎856/**694-2037**, 301/**598-9035** (TTY) ✉ c/o Womongathering, PO Box 559, Franklinville, NJ 08322 EMAIL: womongathr@aol.com WEB: www.womongathering.com

7-9: Southern Ontario Womyn's Drum Camp — *Grand Bend, ON*
all levels welcome • on Lake Huron • women only • 120 attendees • Can$200-300 ☎519/**435-0861** ✉ c/o JT Productions, 1090 Kipps Ln #112, London, ON, Canada N0M 1P0 EMAIL: jtprod@yahoo.com WEB: www.jtproductions.lweb.net

15: Tri-State Womonfest — *Dry Ridge, KY*
spend the day sharing music, food, crafts, workshops & fun • women only ☎606/**442-5993**, 513/**236-4428** ✉ c/o Womonfest, PO Box 983, Covington, KY 41012 EMAIL: womonfest@hotmail.com

20-23: Golden Threads Celebration — *Provincetown, MA*
annual gathering of older lesbians • no age exclusion! • women only ☎802/**848-8002** ✉ c/o Golden Threads, PSC 485 Box 200, FPO, AP 96321 EMAIL: goldentred@aol.com WEB: members.aol.com/goldentred/

TBA: National Women's Music Festival — *Muncie, IN*
mostly women ☎317/**927-9355** ✉ c/o NWMF, PO Box 1427, Indianapolis, IN 46206 EMAIL: wia@wiaonline.org WEB: wiaonline.org

July 2002

4th wknd: Alaska Women's Music Festival — *Fairbanks, AK*
music, comedy, sports & camping • women only • 500 attendees ☎907/**456-2471**, 907/**322-7950** ✉ PO Box 80164, Fairbanks, AK 99708 EMAIL: denabug@gci.net WEB: www.geocities.com/akwomensfest

19-21: LandFest — *Holmes County, OH*
camping • workshops • music & more • women only • 100+ attendees ☎216/**459-1950**, 330/**378-2481** ✉ c/o Egg Moon Farm & Kimbilio Farm, 1340 Orchard Hts Dr, Mayfield, OH 44124 EMAIL: landfest2001@gurlmail.com WEB: egg_moon.tripod.com

20-22: Women's Voices Festival — *Plantagenet, ON*
camping, comedy & music in a lovely country setting • women only • 1200 attendees ☎613/**850-0996** ✉ c/o Women's Voice Festival, 53 Rosebery Ave, Ottawa, ON K1S 1W1 EMAIL: hotline@womensvoices.on.ca WEB: www.womensvoices.on.ca

TBA: Women's Motorcycle Ride In — *Catskill Mtns, NY*
scenic rides • bike show • mixed gay/straight ☎845/**657-6227**, 845/**657-6227** ✉ c/o Women for Safe Riding, PO Box 146, West Shokan, NY 12494 EMAIL: womenride@aol.com WEB: www.womenride.com

August 2002

13-18: Michigan Womyn's Music Festival — *near Hart, MI*
40 theater, music & dance performances • workshops, film festival & craft fair • ASL interpreting & differently-abled resources • child care • women only • 5000-8000 attend ☎231/**757-4766** ✉ c/o WWTMC, PO Box 22, Walhalla, MI 49458 WEB: www.michfest.com

TBA: Women Celebrating Our Diversity — *Luisa, VA*
usually last wknd in Aug • camping, music & more • mostly women ☎540/**894-5126** ✉ c/o Twin Oaks Community, 138 Twin Oaks Rd, Luisa, VA 23093 EMAIL: gathering@twinoaks.org WEB: www.twinoaks.org

September 2002

2: Midwest Womyn's Autumnfest — *Dekalb, IL*
one-day outdoor festival the Sunday of Labor Day Weekend • music, crafts, workshops & more • women only ☎815/**748-5359** ✉ c/o Athena Productions, 217 S 2nd St #193, Dekalb, IL 60115 EMAIL: mwautumn@aol.com WEB: www.mwautumnfest.com

2002 Calendar — Women's Festivals & Gatherings

6-8: Sisterspace Wknd — *MD*
sliding scale • women only ☎215/546-4890 • c/o Sisterspace of the Delaware Valley, 1315 Spruce St, Philadelphia, PA 19107 EMAIL: sistrgen@sisterspace.org WEB: www.sisterspace.org

6-8: The Fall Gathering — *Ashland, OR*
annual women's camp near Oregon mountain lake • vegetarian & vegan meals provided • workshops • crafts • entertainment • women only • 150+ attendees • $65-95 ☎541/773-2928, 541/488-1907 • c/o Womansource, PO Box 335, Ashland, OR 97520

7: Ohio Lesbian Festival — *Columbus, OH*
women only • 3000 attendees ☎614/267-3953 • c/o Lesbian Business Assoc, PO Box 82086, Colombus, OH 43202 EMAIL: info@OhioLBA.org WEB: www.ohiolba.org

13-15: Femm Fest — *Lava Hot Springs, ID*
camping on the Portneuf River • workshops • entertainment • women only ☎208/776-5800 • c/o Aura Soma Lava, PO Box 129, Lava Hot Springs, ID 83246 EMAIL: aurasomalava@aol.com WEB: www.aurasomalava.com

13-16: Wyld Womyn's Weekend — *Maui, HI*
concerts • games • workshops • craft fair • open talent night • women only ☎808/573-3011 • c/o On Top Productions, PO Box 1185, Kula, HI 96790 EMAIL: ontoppro@hotmail.com WEB: wyldwomyn.org

TBA: Herland Fall Retreat — *Oklahoma City, OK*
music, workshops, campfire events & potluck • boys under 10 only • $15-60 sliding scale registration • mostly women ☎405/521-9696 • c/o Herland, 2312 NW 39th, Oklahoma City, OK 73112 EMAIL: herland@mailroom.com WEB: www.herlandsisters.org

TBA: Houston Women's Festival — *Houston, TX*
women from Houston & surrounding areas gather to enjoy music, art & culture • produced by the Athena Art Project ☎713/861-3316 • c/o Houston Women's Festival, PO Box 70102, Houston, TX 77270 EMAIL: hwfestival@earthlink.com WEB: www.hwfestival.org

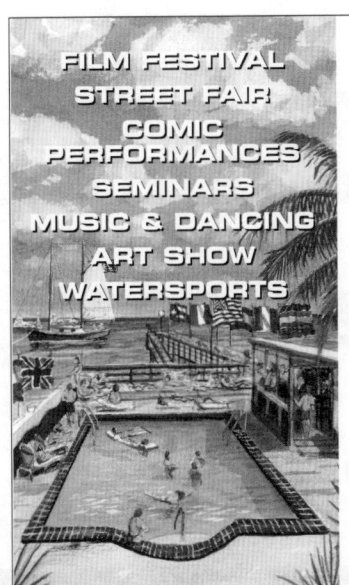

FILM FESTIVAL
STREET FAIR
COMIC
PERFORMANCES
SEMINARS
MUSIC & DANCING
ART SHOW
WATERSPORTS

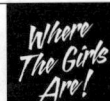

Where The Girls Are!

KEY WEST • SEPT 3-9

womenfest
WWW.WOMENFEST.NET

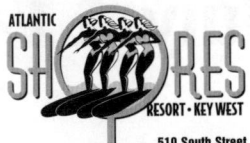

ATLANTIC SHORES RESORT • KEY WEST
510 South Street
Key West, FL 33040

www.atlanticshoresresort.com
U.S. TOLL FREE 877-292-9665

THE FLORIDA KEYS & KEY WEST
Come as you are

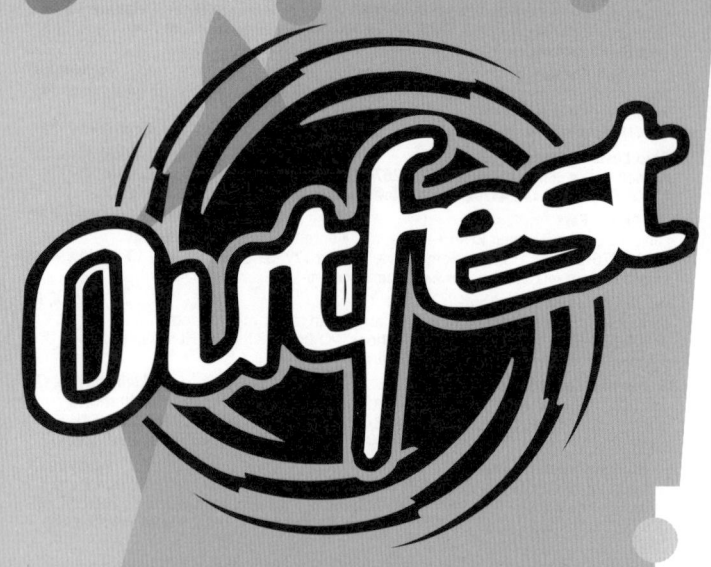

THE 20TH LOS ANGELES GAY AND LESBIAN FILM FESTIVAL

July 11-22, 2002

www.outfest.org

TBA: **Iowa Women's Music Festival** *Iowa City, IA*
  mostly women ☎319/**335-1486** ✉ c/o Prairie Voices Productions, PO Box 3411, Iowa City, IA 52244 Email: iwmfest@prairievoices.net Web: www.prairievoices.net

TBA: **Northwest Women's Music Celebration** *Portland, OR*
  participatory event for musicians, songwriters & singers, NOT performance-oriented • mostly women ✉ PO Box 66842, Portland, OR 97290

TBA: **WomenFest** *Key West, FL*
  concerts, dances, theater, fair, film festival, seminars & more • mostly women ☎305/**296-2491**, 800/**526-3559** ✉ 201 Coppitt Rd #106A, Key West, FL 33040 Email: info@atlanticshoresresort.com Web: www.womenfest.net

October 2002

11-13: **Desert Hearts Women's Festival** *Bandera, TX*
  weekend of music, camping, games & more on a private ranch • women only • $75 ☎830/**796-7446** ✉ 10101 Hwy 173 N, Bandera, TX 78003 Email: cowgirlj@aol.com Web: members.aol.com/cowgirlj/

TBA: **SISTAHfest** *Malibu, CA*
  join other lesbians of African heritage for a weekend of activites that will nourish your mind, body & spirit • women only ☎323/**960-5051** ✉ c/o ULOAH (United Lesbians of African Heritage), 1626 N Wilcox Ave #190, Los Angeles, CA 90028 Email: uloah@aol.com Web: www.uloah.com

November 2002

TBA: **Women Living Large** *West Coast*
  fat women & their female allies • contact Judy Freespirit for exact date • women only ✉ c/o NAAFA Feminist Caucus, PO Box 29614, Oakland, CA 94614 Email: womenlivinglarge@aol.com Web: www.womenlivinglarge.homestead.com

Film Festivals

January 2002

24-31: **Women in Cinema Festival** *Seattle, WA*
  mixed gay/straight ☎206/**464-5830** ✉ c/o Cinema Seattle, 911 Pine St, 6th Fl, Seattle, WA 98101 Email: info@seattlefilm.com Web: www.seattlefilm.com

25-27: **Moondance International Film Festival** *Boulder, CO*
  mixed gay/straight ✉ c/o Moondance Film Festival, PO Box 3348, Boulder, CO 80307 Email: MoondanceFF@aol.com Web: www.moondancefilmfestival.com

March 2002

TBA: **Women in the Director's Chair Int'l Film Festival** *Chicago, IL*
  largest & longest-running women's film festival • get your tickets early for 'dyke night'! • mostly women ☎773/**907-0610** ✉ c/o WIDC, 941 W Lawrence #500, Chicago, IL 60640 Email: widc@widc.org Web: www.widc.org

April 2002

25-May 5: **Miami Gay & Lesbian Film Festival** *Miami, FL*
  ☎305/**534-9924** ✉ 1521 Alton Rd #147, Miami Beach, FL 33139 Email: festivalinfo@the-beach.net Web: www.miamigaylesbianfilm.com

Film Festivals — 2002 Calendar

May 2002

16-26: Inside Out — *Toronto, ON*
annual lesbian & gay fim fest ☎416/**977–6847**, 416/**925–XTRA EXT 2229** ✉ c/o Inside Out, 401 Richmond St W #219, Toronto, ON, Canada M5V 3A8 EMAIL: inside@insideout.on.ca WEB: www.insideout.on.ca

31-June 8: Connecticut Gay/ Lesbian Film Festival — *Hartford, CT*
gay/lesbian ☎860/**586–1136**, 860/**232–3402** ✉ c/o Alternatives, Inc, PO Box 231192, Hartford, CT 06123 EMAIL: glff@yahoo.com WEB: www.CTGLFF.org

TBA: Boston Gay/ Lesbian Film/ Video Festival — *Boston, MA*
☎617/**369–3300** ✉ c/o Museum of Fine Arts, 465 Huntington Ave, Boston, MA 02115 WEB: www.mfa.org/film

TBA: Honolulu Gay/ Lesbian Film Festival — *Honolulu, HI*
☎808/**941–0424 EXT 18** ✉ c/o Honolulu Gay & Lesbian Cultural Foundation, 1877 Kalakaua Ave, Honolulu, HI 96815 EMAIL: info@hglcf.org WEB: www.hglcf.org

TBA: London Lesbian Film Festival — *London, ON*
mostly women ☎519/**680–9956** ✉ c/o London Lesbian Film Fest, PO Box 46014, 956 Dundas St E, London, ON, Canada N5W 3A1 EMAIL: ybacitygrrl@usa.net

June 2002

6-16: New York Lesbian & Gay Film Festival — *New York City, NY*
weeklong fest in early June ☎212/**254–7228** ✉ c/o The New Festival, 47 Great Jones St, 6th flr, New York, NY 10012 EMAIL: info@newfestival.org WEB: www.newfestival.org

20-30: San Francisco Int'l Lesbian/ Gay Film Festival — *San Francisco, CA*
get your tickets early for a slew of films about us • gay/lesbian • 53,000+ attendees ☎415/**703–8650** ✉ c/o Frameline, 346 9th St, San Francisco, CA 94103 EMAIL: info@frameline.org WEB: www.frameline.org

TBA: Reeling 2001: Chicago Lesbian/ Gay Int'l Film Fest — *Chicago, IL*
☎773/**293–1447** ✉ c/o Chicago Filmmakers, 5243 N Clark St, 2nd flr, Chicago, IL 60640 EMAIL: reeling@chicagofilmmakers.org WEB: www.chicagofilmmakers.org

July 2002

11-22: Outfest — *Los Angeles, CA*
Los Angeles' lesbian/gay film & video festival in mid-July ☎/**960–9200** ✉ c/o Outfest, 1125 N McCadden Pl #235, L.A, CA 90038 EMAIL: outfest@outfest.org WEB: www.outfest.org

11-22: Philadelphia Gay/ Lesbian Film Festival — *Philadelphia, PA*
☎215/**733–0608**, 800/**333–8521 EXT 1** ✉ c/o TLA Video, 234 Market St, Philadelphia, PA 19106 EMAIL: rmurray@tlavideo.com WEB: www.phillyfests.com/piglff

August 2002

8-11: North Carolina Gay/ Lesbian Film Festival — *Durham, NC*
☎919/**560–3040 EXT 226** ✉ c/o Carolina Theatre, 309 W Morgan St, Durham, NC 27701 EMAIL: steve@carolinatheatre.org WEB: www.carolinatheatre.org

8-18: Vancouver Queer Film & Video Festival — *Vancouver, BC*
gay/lesbian ☎604/**844–1615** ✉ c/o Out on Screen, 405-207 West Hastings St, Vancouver, BC, Canada V6B 1H7 EMAIL: general@outonscreen.com WEB: www.outonscreen.com

23-Sept 5: Austin Gay/ Lesbian International Film Festival — *Austin, TX*
☎512/**302–9889** ✉ c/o AGLIFF, 1216 E 51st St, Austin, TX 78723 EMAIL: kino@agliff.org WEB: www.agliff.org

September 2002

19-29: Interntional Film & Video Festival — *Montreal, QC*
gay/lesbian ☎514/**285–4467** ✉ c/o Image + Nation, 4067 boul St Laurent #404, Montréal, QC H2W 1Y7 EMAIL: info@image-nation.org WEB: www.image-nation.org

2002 Calendar — Film Festivals

TBA: **Making Scenes** — *Ottawa, ON*
Ottawa's lesbian/gay film festival • also production workshops ☎613/**566-2113** ⌨ c/o Making Scenes c/o Arts Court, 2 Daly Ave, Ottawa, ON, Canada K1N 6E2 Email: scenes@fox.nstn.ca Web: fox.nstn.ca/~scenes

TBA: **St Louis Int'l Lesbian/ Gay Film Festival** — *St Louis, MO*
☎314/**997-9846** ⌨ c/o SLILAG, PMB 388, 6614 Clayton Rd, St Louis, MO 63117 Email: slilagff@aol.com Web: www.slilagfilmfestival.org

October 2002

3-13: **Tampa Int'l Gay/ Lesbian Film Festival** — *Tampa Bay, FL*
☎727/**865-9004** ⌨ c/o Tampa Bay Arts, 3000 34th St S #B-204, St Petersburg, FL 33711 Email: TPABayArts@aol.com Web: www.tampabayarts.com

10-20: **Reel Affirmations Film Festival DC** — *Washington, DC*
lesbian/gay films ☎202/**986-1119** ⌨ c/o One In Ten, PO Box 73528, Washington, DC 20056 Email: info@reelaffirmations.org Web: www.reelaffirmations.org

16-20: **St John's International Women's Film & Video Festival** — *St John's, NF*
mixed gay/straight • 2500 attendees ☎709/**754-3141** ⌨ PO Box 984, St John's, NF, Canada A1C 6C2 Email: filmfest@thezone.net Web: www.womensfilmfestival.com

TBA: **International Gay/ Lesbian Film Festival** — *Pittsburgh, PA*
gay/lesbian ☎412/**232-3277** ⌨ c/o PILGFF, PO Box 81237, Pittsburgh, PA 15217 Email: pilgff@aol.com Web: www.pilgff.org

TBA: **Out on Film** — *Atlanta, GA*
gay/ lesbian film festival ☎404/**352-4225** ⌨ c/o IMAGE Film & Video Center, 75 Bennett St NW, Ste N-1, Atlanta, GA 30309 Email: afvf@imagefv.org Web: www.outonfilm.com

TBA: **Portland LGBT Film Festival** — *Portland, OR*
gay/lesbian ☎503/**242-0818** ⌨ c/o Sensory Perceptions, 818 SW 3rd #1224, Portland, OR 97204 Email: info@sensoryperceptions.org Web: www.sensoryperceptions.org

TBA: **Seattle Lesbian/ Gay Film Festival** — *Seattle, WA*
gay/lesbian ☎206/**323-4274** ⌨ c/o Three Dollar Bill Cinema, 1122 E Pike St #1313, Seattle, WA 98122 Email: filmfest@seattlequeerfilm.com Web: www.seattlequeerfilm.com

November 2002

9-11: **Fresno Reel Pride** — *Fresno, CA*
annual lesbian & gay film festival in central California ☎559/**488-6562** ⌨ PO Box 4647, Fresno, CA 93744 Email: reelpride@aol.com Web: www.reelpride.com

14-18: **Seeing Queerly** — *Denver, CO*
Mountain State's annual lesbian/gay film festival ☎303/**733-7743** EXT 15 ⌨ c/o The Center, PO Box 9798, Denver, CO 80209 Email: cntrevents@aol.com

TBA: **Mix: New York Lesbian/ Gay Experimental Film/ Video Fest** — *New York City, NY*
film, videos, installations & media performances • write for info ☎212/**571-4242** ⌨ 29 John St PMB 132, New York, NY 10038 Email: info@mixnyc.org Web: www.mixnyc.org

TBA: **Out on Film** — *Palm Springs, CA*
come out for a weekend of gay films, film makers & parties ☎760/**770-2042**

December 2002

1: **Blowing Bubbles** — *Italy*
international film & video contest promoting AIDS prevention & education • gay/lesbian ☎0039-051/**644-6824** ⌨ c/o Il Cassero- Gay & Lesbian Centre, PO Box 691, 40100 Bologna, Italy Email: blowingbubbles@cassero.it Web: www.cassero.it/blowingbubbles

TBA: **Sonoma County Lesbian/ Gay Film Festival** — *Santa Rosa, CA*
gay/lesbian ☎530/**272-1106** Email: harmonynetwork@juno.com

LEATHER

January 2002

18-21: Mid-Atlantic Leather Weekend *Washington, DC*
gay/lesbian ☎202/**388-1010** c/o Centaur MC, PO Box 34193, Washington, DC 20043
EMAIL: centaurmc@dcpride.org WEB: www.centaurmc.org

February 2002

8-10: Portland Uniform Weekend *Portland, OR*
gay/lesbian ☎503/**228-6935** c/o In Uniform Magazine, PO Box 3226, Portland, OR 97208 EMAIL: uniformmag@aol.com WEB: www.inuniform.net

TBA: Pantheon of Leather *New Orleans, LA*
annual SM community service awards • mixed gay/straight • 5306 Romaine, Hollywood, CA 90029 EMAIL: tljandcuir@aol.com WEB: www.TheLeatherJournal.com/pantheon

April 2002

5-7: Rubbout Rubber Weekend *Vancouver, BC*
annual • mostly men • 60-100 attend ☎604/**253-1258** PO Box 2253, Vancouver, BC, Canada V6B 3W2 EMAIL: nrthwnd@rocketmail.com WEB: rubbout.iwarp.com

12-14: Leather Leadership Conference *Los Angeles, CA*
join us to develop & strengthen problem-solving & camaraderie in the leather community • gay/lesbian c/o LLC, PO Box 4494, Woodbridge, VA 22194-4494 EMAIL: llcsix@hotmail.com WEB: www.leatherleadership.org

June 2002

6-9: Southeast Leatherfest *Atlanta, GA*
gay/lesbian ☎800/**279-1106 x01** c/o Southeast Leatherfest, PO Box 78974, Atlanta, GA 30357 EMAIL: nstipe@emory.edu WEB: www.seleatherfest.com

16: Folsom Street East *New York City, NY*
New York City's answer to the famous San Francisco fetish street fair • gay/lesbian ☎212/**727-9878** c/o GMSMA, 332 Bleecker St #D-23, New York City, NY 10014 EMAIL: info@gmsma.org WEB: www.gmsma.org/gmsma.html

July 2002

4-8: Living in Leather *Dallas, TX*
national conference for the leather, SM & fetish communities • gay/lesbian • 600 attendees • $150-300 c/o National Leather Association: International, 4038 Cedars Springs #961, Dallas, TX 75219 EMAIL: information@livinginleather.org WEB: www.livinginleather.org

27-29: Thunder in the Mountains *Denver, CO*
weekend of pansexual leather events & seminars in the Rocky Mountains • Mr & Ms Rocky Mountain Leather contest • gay/lesbian • 600+ attendees ☎303/**698-1207** c/o Thunder Mountain Leather, 258 Acoma St, Denver 80223-1339 EMAIL: MrLthrCO@aol.com WEB: www.thunderinthemountains.com

TBA: International Ms Bootblack Contest *San Jose, CA*
during International Ms Leather weekend • mostly women ☎402/**451-7987** c/o Bare Images, 4332 Browne St, Omaha, NE 68111 EMAIL: bareimages@aol.com WEB: www.IMsL.org

TBA: International Ms Leather Contest *San Jose, CA*
contest • workshops • parties • mixed gay/straight ☎402/**451-7987** c/o Bare Images, 4332 Browne St, Omaha, NE 68111 EMAIL: bareimages@aol.com WEB: www.IMsL.org

September 2002

29: Folsom Street Fair — *San Francisco, CA*
huge SM/leather street fair, topping a week of kinky events • gay/lesbian • thousands of local & visiting kinky men & women attendees ☎415/**861-3247** ✉ c/o SMMILE, 584 Castro, PMB 553, San Francisco, CA 94114 EMAIL: smmile@folsomstreetfair.com WEB: www.folsomstreetfair.com

TBA: Power Surge — *Seattle, WA*
biannual leatherwomen's SM conference • women only ☎206/**233-8429** ✉ c/o Seattle Madness, Broadway Stn, PO Box 23352, Seattle, WA 98102

October 2002

25-27: Women at Amsterdam Leather Pride — *Amsterdam, Netherlands*
annual international women's SM conference • women only ☎31-71/**512-8632** ✉ c/o WALP, PO Box 842, 2300 AV Leiden, Netherlands EMAIL: walp@dds.nl WEB: www.dds.nl/~walp

TBA: Central Valley Leatherfest — *Fresno, CA*
gay/lesbian ☎559/**252-7583** ✉ c/o Knights of Malta, Yosemite Chapter, PO Box 4162, Fresno, CA 93744

TBA: Santa Clara County Leather Weekend — *San Jose, CA*
3 days of leather celebration in the South Bay • gay/lesbian ☎408/**293-2429** ✉ c/o Billy DeFrank L/G Community Ctr, 938 The Alameda, San Jose, CA 95126 EMAIL: sccla@sccleather.org WEB: www.SCCLeather.org

CONFERENCES & RETREATS

April 2002

5-6: National Lesbian & Gay MBA Conference — *Chicago, IL*
discussions of sexual orientation in the workplace by MBA students & representatives from big-name companies • gay/lesbian • 300+ attendees WEB: www.gaybiz.org

May 2002

TBA: Lambda Literary Awards — *New York, NY*
the 'Lammies' are the Oscars of lgbt writing & publishing • gay/lesbian ☎202/**682-0952** ✉ c/o Lambda Literary Foundation, PO Box 73910, Washington, DC 20056 EMAIL: LLF@lambdalit.org WEB: www.lambdalit.org

June 2002

30-July 7: Dyke Art Retreat Encampment (DARE) — *Roseburg, OR*
exciting week of group & individual art projects • vegetarian meals • send SASE for info • women only ☎541/**679-4655** ✉ c/o DARE, 6018 Coos Bay Wagon Rd, Roseburg, OR 97470

TBA: Healing Works: Nat'l Conference on Lesbians & Cancer — *Washington, DC*
sponsored by the Mautner Project for Lesbians w/ Cancer ☎202/**332-5536** ✉ c/o Mautner Project, 1707 'L' St NW, #500, Washington, DC 20036 EMAIL: mautner@mautnerproject.org WEB: www.mautnerproject.org

July 2002

TBA: Black Gay/ Lesbian Conference — *Detroit, MI*
gay/lesbian ☎510/**302-0930** ✉ c/o Nat'l Black Gay/Lesbian Leadership Forum, 1714 Franklin St #100-140, Oakland, CA 94612 EMAIL: natblkforum@aol.com

Conferences & Retreats — 2002 Calendar

September 2002

TBA: **National Lesbian/ Gay Journalists Association Convention** — *Philadelphia, PA*
workshops • keynote speakers • entertainment • gay/lesbian ☎202/**588-9888** ✉ c/o NLGJA, 1420 'K' St NW #910, Washington, DC 20006 EMAIL: info@nlgja.org WEB: www.nlgja.org

October 2002

10-14: **National Latino/a Lesbian/Gay Conference** — *Miami, FL*
come together to empower the Latina/o LGBT community ☎202/**408-5380** ✉ c/o LLEGO, 1420 'K' St NW #200, Washington, DC 20005 EMAIL: encuentro@llego.org WEB: www.llego.org

TBA: **National LGBT Writers' Conference** — *New Orleans, LA*
gay/lesbian ☎202/**682-0952** ✉ c/o Lambda Literary Foundation, PO Box 73910, Washington, DC 20056 EMAIL: llf@lambdalit.org WEB: www.lambdalit.org

November 2002

TBA: **Creating Change Conference** — *TBA, USA*
for lbgt people & queers into social activism • gay/lesbian • 2000+ attend
☎202/**332-6483** x3329 ✉ c/o National Gay/Lesbian Task Force, 1700 Kalorama Rd NW, Washington, DC 20009 EMAIL: delliot@ngltf.org WEB: www.ngltf.org

April 2003

TBA: **National Black Lesbian Conference** — *TBA*
speakers, workshops, community forums, banquets, dances, and more • women only
☎510/**482-1671** ✉ c/o ZUNA Institute, 6114 LaSalle Ave #527, Oakland, CA 94611
EMAIL: info@zunainstitute.org WEB: www.zunainstitute.org

July 2003

TBA: **RAD Conference: Rainbow Alliance of the Deaf** — *Orlando, FL*
workshops • conferences • keynote speakers • social events • come celebrate deaf culture & identity EMAIL: secretary@rad.org WEB: www.rad.org

SPIRITUAL

February 2002

8-10: **Our Story Too: LGBT Christians Reclaim the Bible** — *Lyons, MI*
take a fresh look at the Bible in an affirming setting • women only ☎517/**855-2277** ✉ c/o Leaven, PO Box 23233, Lansing, MI 48909 EMAIL: leavencenter@leaven.org WEB: www.leaven.org

15-18: **Pantheocon** — *San Jose, CA*
pagan convention • mixed gay/straight ☎510/**653-3244** ✉ c/o Ancient Ways, 4075 Telegraph Ave, Oakland, CA 94609 EMAIL: store@ancientways.com WEB: www.ancientways.com

April 2002

TBA: **Moonsisters Drum Camp** — *San Francisco, CA*
women only • 150 attendees • $215 ☎510/**547-8386** ✉ c/o Moonsisters Drum Camp, PO Box 20918, Oakland, CA 94620 EMAIL: moonsistah@aol.com

May 2002

TBA: **A Gathering of Priestesses** — *Southwestern WI*
women's spirituality conference • women only ☎608/**226-9998** ✉ c/o Reformed Congregation of the Goddess, PO Box 6530, Madison, WI 53716 EMAIL: rcgi@itis.com WEB: www.goddesswomen.com

2002 Calendar — Spiritual

TBA: Ancient Ways Festival — *Harbin Hot Springs, CA*
annual 4-day mixed gender/orientation spring festival in May or June • pan-pagan rituals, workshops & music w/ lesbian/gay campsite • mixed gay/straight ☎510/**653-3244** ✉ c/o **Ancient Ways**, 4075 Telegraph Ave, Oakland, CA 94609 EMAIL: store@ancientways.com WEB: www.ancientways.com

June 2002

TBA: Pagan Spirit Gathering — *near Athens, OH*
summer solstice celebration • primitive camping • workshops • rituals • advance registration required • mixed gay/straight ☎608/**924-2216** ✉ c/o **Circle Sanctuary**, PO Box 219, Mt Horeb, WI 53572 EMAIL: circle@mhtc.net WEB: www.circlesanctuary.org/psg

July 2002

TBA: BC Witchcamp — *near Vancouver, BC*
weeklong Wiccan intensive • mixed gay/straight ☎604/**253-7189**, 604/**253-7195** ✉ c/o **Sounds & Furies**, PO Box 21510, 1850 Commercial Dr, Vancouver, BC, Canada V5N 4A0 EMAIL: path@lynx.bc.ca WEB: www.soundsandfuries.com

TBA: Sappho's Sisters — *Saco Bay, ME*
lesbian & bisexual women can focus on their own growth in a safe, nurturing community • workshops • group activities • Unitarian Universalist • women only ☎207/**284-8612** EMAIL: bubolz@valley.net WEB: users.massed.net/~muffitt/ssist/

August 2002

TBA: Elderflower Womenspirit Festival — *Mendocino, CA*
in the Mendocino Woodlands • earth-centered spirituality retreat • reasonably priced, volunteer-run • women only ☎415/**263-5719**, 510/**869-3828** ✉ PO Box 72079, Oakland, CA 94612 EMAIL: elderflower@onemain.com WEB: www.elderflower.org

September 2002

12-15: International Goddess Festival — *La Honda, CA*
bi-annual celebration of goddess culture & Beltane • workshops, rituals, dances, music • women only ☎510/**444-7724** ✉ c/o **Women's Spirituality Forum**, PO Box 11363, Oakland, CA 94611 EMAIL: Silverzb@aol.com WEB: www.zbudapest.com

TBA: Moonsisters Drum Camp — *San Francisco, CA*
women only • 100 attendees • $75 ☎510/**547-8386** ✉ c/o **Moonsisters Drum Camp**, PO Box 20918, Oakland, CA 94620 EMAIL: moonsistah@aol.com

TBA: Sappho Lesbian Witchcamp — *near Vancouver, BC*
weeklong gathering • women only • 35-40 attendees ☎604/**253-7189**, /**253-7195** ✉ c/o **Sounds & Furies**, PO Box 21510, 1850 Commercial Dr, Vancouver, BC, Canada V5N 4A0 EMAIL: path@lynx.bc.ca WEB: www.soundsandfuries.com

November 2002

1-3: Real Witches Ball — *Columbus, OH*
weekend pagan celebration of Samhain • mixed gay/straight ☎614/**421-7557** ✉ c/o **Salem West**, 1209 N High St, Columbus, OH 43201 EMAIL: ajdrew@neopagan.com WEB: www.neopagan.com

Breast Cancer Benefits

January 2002

on-going throughout the year: **Race for the Cure** *Cross-country, USA*
5K & 1-mile run/fitness walks in cities around the country to fight breast cancer • call for local city dates • organized & funded by Susan G Komen Breast Cancer Foundation volunteers • mostly women ☎888/**603–7223** ✉ c/o Susan G Komen Breast Cancer Foundation: Race for the Cure, 5005 LBJ Fwy #370, Dallas, TX 75244 EMAIL: raceforthecure@komen.org WEB: www.raceforthecure.com

on-going throughout the year: **Walk for Hope Against Breast Cancer** *Cross-country, USA*
walk to raise money to fight breast cancer • proceeds benefit City of Hope National Medical Center & Beckman Research Institute • events in cities across the country • call for dates in your city • mostly women ☎800/**266–7920** ✉ c/o City of Hope, 208 W 8th St, Los Angeles, CA 90014 WEB: walk.coh.org

April 2002

12-14: **Avon's Breast Cancer 3-Day Walk** *San Diego, CA*
walk from Laguna Beach to Del Mar to raise money to fight breast cancer • mostly women ☎800/**825–1000** ✉ c/o Pallotta TeamWorks, 2709 Media Center Drive, Building 1, Los Angeles, CA 90065 EMAIL: info@bethepeople.com WEB: www.bethepeople.com

19-21: **Avon's Breast Cancer 3-Day Walk** *Boca Raton to Miami, FL*
raise money to fight breast cancer • mostly women ☎800/**825–1000** ✉ c/o Pallotta TeamWorks, 2709 Media Center Drive, Building 1, Los Angeles, CA 90065 EMAIL: info@bethepeople.com WEB: www.bethepeople.com

26-28: **Avon's Breast Cancer 3-Day Walk** *Fort Worth to Dallas, TX*
raise money to fight breast cancer • mostly women ☎800/**825–1000** ✉ c/o Pallotta TeamWorks, 2709 Media Center Drive, Building 1, Los Angeles, CA 90065 EMAIL: info@bethepeople.com WEB: www.bethepeople.com

TBA: **Boarding for Breast Cancer: Snowboard & Music Festival** *Lake Tahoe, CA*
annual fundraiser, featuring live music & pro exihibitions • mixed gay/straight ☎877/**814–B4BC** ✉ PO Box 20657, Seattle, WA 98102 EMAIL: email@b4bc.org WEB: www.b4bc.org

May 2002

3-5: **Avon's Breast Cancer 3-Day Walk** *Baltimore, MD to Washington, DC*
raise money to fight breast cancer • mostly women ☎800/**825–1000** ✉ c/o Pallotta TeamWorks, 2709 Media Center Drive, Building 1, Los Angeles, CA 90065 EMAIL: info@bethepeople.com WEB: www.bethepeople.com

17-19: **Avon's Breast Cancer 3-Day Walk** *Fitchburg to Boston, MA*
raise money to fight breast cancer • mostly women ☎800/**825–1000** ✉ c/o Pallotta TeamWorks, 2709 Media Center Drive, Building 1, Los Angeles, CA 90065 EMAIL: info@bethepeople.com WEB: www.bethepeople.com

31-June 2: **Avon's Breast Cancer 3-Day Walk** *Ann Arbor to Detroit, MI*
raise money to fight breast cancer • mostly women ☎800/**825–1000** ✉ c/o Pallotta TeamWorks, 2709 Media Center Drive, Building 1, Los Angeles, CA 90065 EMAIL: info@bethepeople.com WEB: www.bethepeople.com

June 2002

14-16: **Avon's Breast Cancer 3-Day Walk** *Chicago, IL*
walk from Kenosha, WI to Chicago to raise money to fight breast cancer • mostly women ☎800/**825–1000**, 773/**525–2960** ✉ c/o Pallotta TeamWorks, 2709 Media Center Drive Building 1, Los Angeles, CA 90065 EMAIL: info@bethepeople.com WEB: www.bethepeople.com

2002 CALENDAR — BREAST CANCER BENEFITS

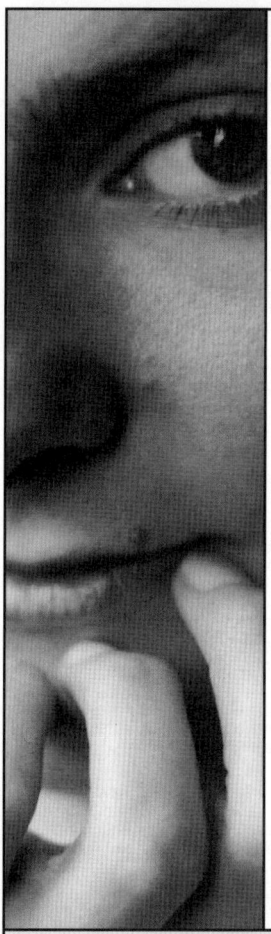

We BELIEVE people LIVING with life-threatening illnesses NEED more than TRIPS to the hospital

Destination Foundation grants dream trips to people in the San Francisco Bay Area gay community who are living with life-threatening illnesses such as AIDS and breast cancer. We know that dream trips can simply be alternative medicine to heal the body and spirit.

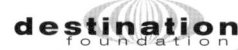

giving the world can make all the difference

To learn more or to make a donation:

Destination Foundation, Inc.
584 Castro Street #114
San Francisco, CA 94114
(415) 970-3333
www.destinationfoundation.org

BREAST CANCER BENEFITS — 2002 CALENDAR

July 2002

12-14: **Avon's Breast Cancer 3-Day Walk** — *San Jose to San Francisco, CA*
raise money to fight breast cancer • mostly women ☎800/**825-1000** ✉ c/o Pallotta TeamWorks, 2709 Media Center Drive, Building 1, Los Angeles, CA 90065 EMAIL: info@bethepeople.com WEB: www.bethepeople.com

August 2002

2-4: **Avon's Breast Cancer 3-Day Walk** — *Fort Collins to Boulder, CO*
raise money to fight breast cancer • mostly women ☎800/**825-1000** ✉ c/o Pallotta TeamWorks, 2709 Media Center Drive, Building 1, Los Angeles, CA 90065 EMAIL: info@bethepeople.com WEB: www.bethepeople.com

9-11: **Avon's Breast Cancer 3-Day Walk** — *Seattle, WA*
walk from Enumclaw to Seattle to raise money to fight breast cancer • mostly women ☎800/**825-1000** ✉ c/o Pallotta TeamWorks, 2709 Media Center Drive, Building 1, Los Angeles, CA 90065 EMAIL: info@bethepeople.com WEB: www.bethepeople.com

TBA: **'Fore Women & A Few Good Men' Golf Tournament** — *Boston, MA*
tournament to raise money for breast cancer research • terrific prizes! • mixed gay/straight • 100+ attendees ☎617/**437-9757**, 888/**562-2874** ✉ c/o Carol Nashe Group, 566 Commonwealth Ave, Boston, MA 02215 EMAIL: nashe@priority1.net WEB: www.golfonthego.com

September 2002

TBA: **America's Breast Cancer Ride** — *San Diego, CA to Jacksonville, FL*
42-day bicycle ride across the southern USA • San Diego, CA to Jacksonville, FL • mostly women ☎760/**630-9880** ✉ c/o Women in Motion, PO Box 4533, Oceanside, CA 92052-4533 EMAIL: eventsrus@aol.com WEB: abcride.org

October 2002

on-going: **October is Breast Cancer Awareness Month** — *Cross-country, USA*
check local listings for fund-raising events in your area to fight breast cancer

4-6: **Avon's Breast Cancer 3-Day Walk** — *Atlanta, GA*
walk from Lake Lanier to Atlanta to raise money to fight breast cancer • mostly women ☎800/**825-1000**, 877/**257-5553** ✉ c/o Pallotta TeamWorks, 2709 Media Center Drive Building 1, Los Angeles, CA 90065 EMAIL: info@bethepeople.com WEB: www.bethepeople.com

11-13: **Avon's Breast Cancer 3-Day Walk** — *New York City, NY*
walk from Bear Mtn to Manhattan to raise money to fight breast cancer • mostly women ☎800/**825-1000** ✉ c/o Pallotta TeamWorks, 2709 Media Center Drive, Building 1, Los Angeles, CA 90065 EMAIL: info@bethepeople.com WEB: www.bethepeople.com

18-20: **Avon's Breast Cancer 3-Day Walk** — *Los Angeles, CA*
walk from Santa Barbara to Malibu to raise money to fight breast cancer • mostly women ☎800/**825-1000** ✉ c/o Pallotta TeamWorks, 2709 Media Center Drive, Building 1, Los Angeles, CA 90065 EMAIL: info@bethepeople.com WEB: www.bethepeople.com

on-going throughout the year: **Race for the Cure** — *Cross-country, USA*
5K & 1-mile run/fitness walks in cities around the country to fight breast cancer • call for local city dates • organized & funded by Susan G Komen Breast Cancer Foundation volunteers • mostly women ☎888/**603-7223** ✉ c/o Susan G Komen Breast Cancer Foundation: Race for the Cure, 5005 LBJ Fwy #370, Dallas, TX 75244 EMAIL: raceforthecure@komen.org WEB: www.raceforthecure.com

Kids' stuff

June 2002

on-going thru the summer: **Prairie Youth Adventures** *Matfield Green, KS*
weeklong summer sessions focusing on horseback skills & historic prairie activities • camp takes place on the women-run Homestead Ranch • separate camps for boys & girls • youth ages 10-14 ☎316/**753-3465** ✉ c/o **Homestead Ranch**, RR 1 Box 24, Matfield Green, KS 66862 EMAIL: jprairie@wheatstate.com WEB: www.guestranches.com/homestead

July 2002

13-20: **Camp Lavender Hill** *Sierra Nevada, CA*
one-week summer camp for kids with lgbt parents • swimming • hiking • theater & more • kids 7-17 ☎707/**544-8150** ✉ c/o **Camp Lavender Hill**, PO Box 11275, Santa Rosa, CA 95406

14-20: **Family Week** *Saugatuck, MI*
join hundreds of GLBT parents & their children for a week of BBQs, boat rides, campfires, sandcastle competitions & more • gay/lesbian ☎619/**296-0199** ✉ c/o **Family Pride Coalition**, PO Box 34337, San Diego, CA 92163 EMAIL: pride@familypride.org WEB: www.familypride.org

August 2002

4-11: **Family Week** *Provincetown, MA*
join hundreds of GLBT parents & their children for a week of clam bakes, BBQs, boat rides, campfires, sandcastle competitions & more • gay/lesbian ☎619/**296-0199** ✉ c/o **Family Pride Coalition**, PO Box 34337, San Diego, CA 92163 EMAIL: pride@familypride.org WEB: www.familypride.org

TBA: **Camp for Children of LGBT Parents** *Halifax, NS*
fun-filled weekend where kids & parents are valued and respected ☎902/**462-8079** ✉ c/o **Pride Family Camping Association**, Site 6-C, Box 21, RR 1, Waverly, NS, Canada B0N 2S0 EMAIL: familypride@hotmail.com

TBA: **Mountain Meadow Summer Camp** *Southern New Jersey*
camp for kids with lgbt parents & their allies • sliding scale fee • girls & boys age 9-17 ☎215/**772-1107** ✉ c/o **Mountain Meadow Country Experience**, 1315 Spruce St #407, Philadelphia, PA 19107 EMAIL: inquiries@mountainmeadow.org WEB: www.mountainmeadow.org

September 2002

TBA: **Keshet Camp: Jewish Family Camp** *Yosemite, CA*
a rainbow camp for lgbt families & their friends • sports, music, arts & crafts & more • gay/lesbian ☎415/**543-2267** ✉ c/o **Camp Tawonga**, 121 Steuart St, San Francisco, CA 94105 EMAIL: info@tawonga.org WEB: www.tawonga.org

BOOKS & MAGAZINES Womens' Mail Order

All the Books YOU Want to Read

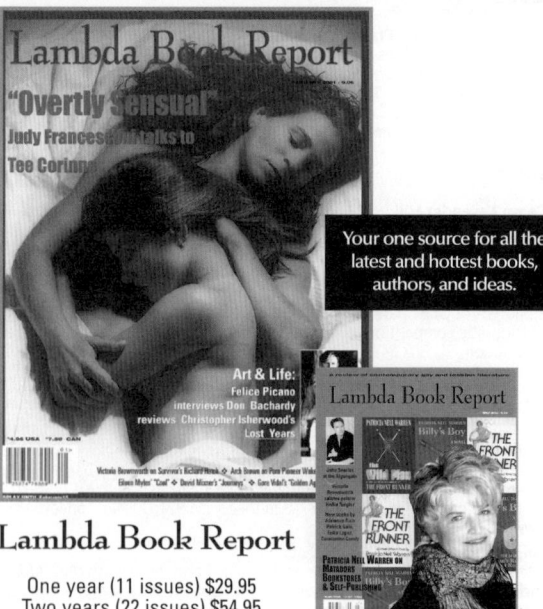

Lambda Book Report

One year (11 issues) $29.95
Two years (22 issues) $54.95

Save now: both magazines for only $40/year!
Save even more: $75/for two years

Subscribe!
☐ **1 YEAR $29.95 (45% off)** Canada/Mexico $46.95 (U.S.) Foreign $58.95 (U.S.)
☐ **2 YEARS $54.95 (50% off)** Canada/Mexico $83.95 (U.S.) International $107.95 (U.S. curency only)

Name
Address
City_____ State/ZIP
Card #/Exp_____ Amt Paid (US only) $
Signature
Phone
☐ **check** (payable to the Lambda Literary Foundation) ☐ **money order** ☐ **Visa** ☐ **MC** ☐ **Discover** ☐ **Amex**

Send to LLF/Damron 2002 Subs, PO Box 73910, Washington, DC 20056-3910
Subscribe On Line: www.lambdalit.org

Women's Mail Order — Clothing

Books & Magazines

A Different Light Bookstores books • calendars • videos EMAIL: adl@adlbooks.com WEB: www.adlbooks.com

Brigit Books ☎727/502-5642 lesbian & feminist titles EMAIL: brigit@tampabay.rr.com WEB: www.brigitbooks.com

▲ **Lambda Book Report** ☎202/682-0952 nat'l review of latest lgbt literature EMAIL: llf@lambdalit.com WEB: www.lambdalit.org

Lammas women's books • music • jewelry WEB: www.abebooks.com/home/lammasbooks

▲ **Lesbian Health News, Inc** ☎614/481-7656 see ad below ✉ PO Box 12121, Columbus, OH 43212 EMAIL: lhnews@aol.com

Magus Books ☎612/379-7669 spirituality titles ✉ 1316 SE 4th St, Minneapolis, MN 55414 EMAIL: store@magusbooks.com WEB: www.magusbooks.com

Naiad Press, Inc. ☎850/539-5965, 800/533-1973 lesbian books & videos ✉ PO Box 10543, Tallahassee, FL 32302 EMAIL: charitybarnes@naiadpress.com WEB: www.naiadpress.com

Spinsters Ink ☎303/761-5552, 800/301-6860 **(ORDERS ONLY)** feminist fiction & nonfiction ✉ Po Box 22005, Denver, CO 802220 WEB: www.spinsters-ink.com

Thunder Road Books ☎201/863-3931, 888/846-3773 lesbian mail order • books • CDs ✉ PO Box 354, Union, NJ 07083 EMAIL: thunderrd@thunderroadbooks.com WEB: www.thunderroadbooks.com

Womansline Books ☎519/672-8480 ✉ Box 24092, London, ON N6H 5C4 Canada EMAIL: contact@womansline.com WEB: www.womansline.com

Women in the Wilderness ☎651/227-2284 books for outdoorswomen & armchair adventurers ✉ 566 Ottawa Ave, St Paul, MN 55107

Women's Press ☎416/929-2774 lesbian/ feminist book publisher • catalog available WEB: www.womenspress.ca

Clothing

Girl World Sports ☎713/290-9969 T-shirts ✉ 10606 Hempstead Rd #114, Houston, TX 77092

GLADrags ☎888/452-3748 tasteful casualwear for the community • catalog

Mystic Women & Mystic Kids ☎617/718-1622, 877/241-5676 clothing & accessories for lgbt families ✉ 35 Adrian St, Somerville, MA 02143 EMAIL: info@mysticwomen.com WEB: www.mysticwomen.com

---

Lesbian Health News, Inc.

A National Bi-Monthly Publication spanning all aspects of lesbian health, including personal and professional narratives, research and analysis.

P.O. Box 12121 Columbus, OH 43212
614-481-7656 LHNews@aol.com
Send $2.00 for a sample copy

JEWELRY — Womens' Mail Order

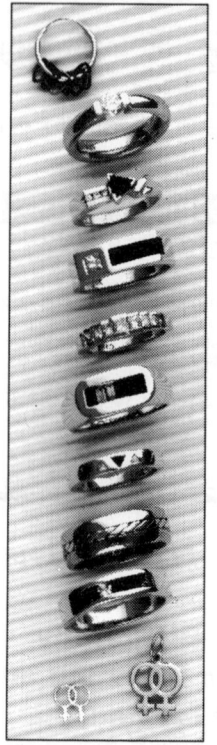

Jewelry by Poncé
Serving our community since 1983

UNCONDITIONAL 30-DAY GUARANTEE
Specializing in: Commitment Rings • Custom Designs • White & Yellow 14K & 18K Leather Pride • Exotic Body Jewelry • Pendants • Earrings • Watches • Inlay Stone Rings (onyx, lapis) • Chains • Bracelets • Silver

for info/free brochure call:
1-800-969-RING
Visit our store in Laguna Beach, CA or our Web site at www.jewelrybyponce.com
WHOLESALE INQUIRIES WELCOME

Strip T's ☎603/755-2926 feminist T-shirts • catalog ✉ PO Box 605, Farmington, NH 03835 EMAIL: piro@worldpath.net WEB: www.stephaniepiro.com

www.girlfiend.com ☎323/791-2207 hip dyke tees and accessories ✉ 264 S LaCienega Blvd #744, Beverly Hills, CA 90211 EMAIL: sales@girlfiend.com WEB: www.girlfiend.com

JEWELRY

▲ **Jewelry by Poncé** ☎949/497-4154, 800/969-7464 specializing in commitment rings • free brochure ✉ 668 N Coast Hwy #331, Laguna Beach, CA 92651 EMAIL: jewelry@jewelrybyponce.com WEB: www.jewelrybyponce.com

Lizzie Brown/Pleiades ☎413/245-6552 woman-identified jewelry ✉ PO Box 389, Brimfield, MA 01010

VARIETY

Amazon, Incorporated ☎828/251-9603 musical instruments • gifts & more ✉ 599 N Louisiana Ave #8, Asheville, NC 28806 EMAIL: sales@villageoftheamazons.com WEB: www.villageoftheamazons.com

Avena Botanicals ☎207/594-0694 organically grown herbal products for women • catalog ✉ 219 Mill St, Rockport, ME 04856 EMAIL: avena@avenaherbs.com WEB: www.avenaherbs.com

Femail Creations ☎800/996-9223 catalog for, by & about womyn WEB: www.femailcreations.com

Griffin Woods ☎707/824-6939 specializing in cedar boxes, chests & cabinets ✉ 2061 Pleasant Hill Rd, Sebastopol, CA 95472 EMAIL: grifwoods@aol.com

Key West Aloe ☎800/445-2563 ✉ 524 Front St, Key West, FL 33040 WEB: www.keywestaloe.com

LadySlipper, Inc. ☎800/634-6044 women's music • videos ✉ 3205 Hillsboro Rd, Durham, NC 27705 EMAIL: info@ladyslipper.org WEB: www.ladyslipper.org

Snake & Snake Productions ☎919/401-9591 goddess • crone • astrology items ✉ 3037 Dixon Rd, Durham, NC 27707 WEB: www.snakeandsnake.com

The Shenis ☎214/616-5454 the penis with a 'she' • no more squatting to pee • $19.99 +s/h ✉ 5521 Greenville Ave #104-433, Dallas, TX 75206 EMAIL: kiki@shenis.com WEB: www.shenis.com

Women's Mail Order — EROTICA

We're Everywhere ☎773/404-0590, 800/772-6411 noon-9pm, 11am-8pm wknds ✉ 3434 N Halsted St, Chicago, IL 60657 WEB: www.wereeverywhere.com

Wildfire Glass ☎419/836-2294 womyn-owned glass studio • catalog ✉ PO Box 12, Millbury, OH 43447 EMAIL: glassgrrls@hotmail.com

Women Fly Inc ☎800/304-9342 T-shirts • caps • coffee mugs • free catalog ✉ Po Box 246, Greensboro, MD 21639 EMAIL: womenfly@friend.ly.net WEB: www.womenfly.com

EROTICA

Eve's Garden ☎212/757-8651, 800/848-3837 sex toys • books • videos • all from the first sexuality boutique created by women for women • send $3 for catalog ✉ 119 W 57th St # 420, New York, NY 10019 EMAIL: admin@evesgarden.com WEB: www.evesgarden.com

▲ **Good Vibrations** ☎415/974-8990, 800/289-8423 lesbian-made erotica • sex toys • books • videos • send $2 for catalog ✉ 1210 Valencia St, San Francisco, CA 94110 EMAIL: goodvibe@well.com WEB: www.goodvibes.com

Greedy Dyke Productions ☎505/890-1376 women-crafted sex toys ✉ 2400 Rio Grande NW #1-110, Albuquerque, NM 87104 EMAIL: misskell@nmia.com WEB: www.nmia.com/~misskell/gdprod.html

Lashes by Sarah ☎510/638-3564 high quality hand-crafted leather floggers ✉ PO Box 5245, Oakland, CA 94605 EMAIL: lashes@sirius.com WEB: www.sirius.com/~topgrrl/sarah.htm

Pitiful Boot Licker hand-crafted leather goods ✉ PO Box 62, Patagonia, AZ 85624 EMAIL: pblicker@abcs.com WEB: www.abcs.com/pblicker

Pleasure Chest ☎800/753-4536 for all your erotic needs • catalog WEB: www.thepleasurechest.com

Pleasure Place ☎800/386-2386 erotic gifts • toys • catalog WEB: www.pleasureplace.com

SIR Video dyke porn is back! WEB: www.sirvideo.com

Wolfe Video ☎408/268-6782, 800/438-9653 video productions by lesbians ✉ PO Box 64, New Almaden, CA 95042 WEB: www.wolfevideo.com

Xandria Collection ☎800/242-2823 sexual products from around the world • send $4 for catalog ✉ PO Box 319005, San Francisco, CA 94131 EMAIL: info@xandria.com WEB: www.xandria.com

---

Where do **you** go to learn about sex?

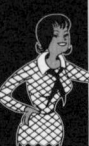

Good Vibrations

Whether you're traveling around the world or around the corner, Good Vibrations has everything you need for your next sexual adventure!

- vibrators
- dildos
- harnesses
- lube
- books
- videos
- bondage gear
- safe sex supplies
- honest sex info
- friendly staff
- women-owned & operated

Good Vibrations
Making your pleasure our business since 1977

1-800-BUY-VIBE
goodvibes.com

UPDATE

Hey! Don't Forget...

Do you know of a new business we should list? Or a business that's closed since publication? Found out some new information about a listing we already have? We reward the best letters (those packed with new info we haven't already found) with a **FREE COPY** of next year's edition—***Please let us know!***

Business Name _____

Type of Business/Clientele _____

Street Address _____

City/State/Zip _____

★Phone/Fax _____

Email/Web _____

Description _____

Please suggest a **lesbian/gay-oriented activity or attraction** we should list under **ENTERTAINMENT & RECREATION** in your favorite city (for example, theater, music, skate/bowl, or tourist attraction):

City/State _____

Attraction _____

★Phone/Fax _____

Description _____

My Name _____

Address _____

City/State/Zip _____

Daytime Phone/Email _____

We will only contact you discreetly, if we need to verify or clarify information.
☐ *Check this box if you do not wish to be added to our mailing list.*

Please Mail to:	Damron Updates — Attn. Editor PO Box 422458 San Francisco, CA 94142-2458 USA
or e-mail:	**Updates@Damron.com**
or fax:	**(415) 703-9049**